WIRELE
COMMUNICATIONS

PRINCIPLES AND PRACTICE

SECOND EDITION

Theodore S. Rappaport

WIRELESS COMMUNICATIONS

PRINCIPLES AND PRACTICE

SECOND EDITION

Theodore S. Rappaport

Prentice-Hall of India Private Limited
New Delhi-110001
2005

This Indian Reprint—Rs. 325.00
(Original U.S. Edition—Rs. 4499.00)

WIRELESS COMMUNICATIONS—Principles and Practice, 2nd Ed.
by Theodore S. Rappaport

ISBN-81-203-2381-5

Published by Asoke K. Ghosh, Prentice-Hall of India Private Limited, M-97, Connaught Circus, New Delhi-110001 and Printed by Meenakshi Art Printers, Delhi-110006.

The Lord has blessed me
with a wonderful family
to whom this book is dedicated.

To my wife Brenda Marie,
and to our children
Matthew, Natalie, and Jennifer

Contents

Preface

The second edition of this text has been written to initiate the newcomer to wireless personal communications, one of the fastest growing fields in the engineering world. Technical concepts which are at the core of design, implementation, research, and invention of wireless communication systems are presented in an order that is conducive to understanding general concepts, as well as those specific to current and evolving wireless communication systems and standards. This text is based upon my experiences as an educator, researcher, technical trainer, and consultant, and continues to be modeled from an academic course first developed for electrical engineering students in 1990, when there were fewer than five million cellular subscribers worldwide. As we begin the 21st century, more than 600 million people, about 10% of the world's population, pay a monthly subscription for wireless telephone service, and this figure will approach 50% by the end of the first decade of the 21st century.

This text continues to evolve, and has been modified and updated since its first edition, making it a useful book for practicing engineers, as well as for researchers, graduate students, and undergraduate students. The text has been prepared to provide fundamental treatment about many practical and theoretical concepts that form the basis of wireless communications, and has been designed for easy but thorough treatment of vital material that all wireless practitioners must be comfortable with. I have tried to emphasize the technical concepts with worked example problems, and numerous, carefully crafted homework problems at the end of each chapter that are based on real-world industry issues. The second edition contains dozens of new homework problems and examples, as well as up-to-the minute technical details of the many emerging wireless standards throughout the world, making this book particularly useful for industry short-courses or state-of-the-art academic classroom use.

References to journal articles are used liberally throughout this text to enable the interested reader to delve into additional reading that is always required to master any field. To support newcomers to the wireless field, and at the request of the Institute of Electrical and Electronics Engineers (IEEE), I have also prepared a low-cost two volume compendium of many of the original journal articles that first taught the fundamentals that are now used throughout the wireless industry—this compendium series is a useful, but not required, supplement to this text. Whether you intend to use this book for individual study, or for classroom use, or for use as a handbook, this text has been written as a complete, self-contained teaching and reference book. The numerous examples and problems found throughout the text have been provided to help the reader solidify the material.

This book has been designed for the student or practicing engineer who is already familiar with technical concepts such as probability, communication theory, and basic electromagnetics. However, like the wireless communications industry itself, this book combines material from many different technical disciplines, so it is unlikely that any one person will have had introductory courses for all of the topics covered. To accommodate a wide range of backgrounds, important concepts throughout the text are developed from first principles, so that readers learn the foundations of wireless communications. This approach makes it possible to use this book as a handbook or as a useful teaching tool in a classroom setting.

The material and chapter sequence in this text have been adapted from an entry-level graduate course which I first taught in 1991 at the Virginia Polytechnic Institute and State University. Chapter 1 demonstrates the historic evolution of the wireless communications industry, and the evolution of wireless systems from first generation analog to second generation (2G) digital systems. Chapter 1 also documents the rapid early growth of cellular radio throughout the world and provides a state of the industry in the mid 1990s. Chapter 2 provides an overview of the major modern wireless communication systems of the 21st century, such as third generation (3G), Wireless Local Area Networks (WLANs), Local Multipoint Distribution Services (LMDS), and Bluetooth. Chapter 2 causes the reader to see how wireless networks are beginning to penetrate our daily lives for data and multimedia applications, as well as voice service. Chapter 3 covers fundamental cellular radio concepts such as frequency reuse and handoff, which are at the core of providing wireless communication service to subscribers on the move using limited radio spectrum. Chapter 3 also demonstrates the principal of trunking efficiency, and how trunking and interference issues between mobiles and base stations combine to affect the overall capacity of cellular systems. Chapter 4 presents radio propagation path loss, link-budgets, and log-normal shadowing, and describes different ways to model and predict the large-scale effects of radio propagation in many operating environments. Chapter 5 covers small-scale propagation effects such as fading, time delay spread, and Doppler spread, and describes how to measure and model the impact that signal bandwidth and motion have on the instantaneous received signal through the multipath channel. Radio wave propagation has historically been the most difficult problem to analyze and design for, since unlike a wired communication system which has a constant, stationary transmission channel (i.e., a wired path), radio channels are random and undergo shadowing and multipath fading, particularly when one of the terminals is in motion. New material in Chapter 5 also teaches a fundamental and new way of modeling spatial-temporal channels, which is vital for the development of *smart antennas* and position location systems.

Chapter 6 provides extensive coverage of the most common analog and digital modulation techniques used in wireless communications and demonstrates tradeoffs that must be made in selecting a modulation method. Issues such as receiver complexity, modulation and demodulation implementation, bit error rate analysis for fading channels, and spectral occupancy are presented. Channel coding, adaptive equalization, and antenna diversity concepts are presented in Chapter 7. In portable radio systems where people communicate while walking or driving, these methods may be used individually or in tandem to improve the quality (that is, reduce the bit error rate) of digital mobile radio communications in the presence of fading and noise.

Chapter 8 provides an introduction to speech coding. In the past decade, there has been remarkable progress in decreasing the needed data rate of high quality digitized speech, which enables wireless system designers to match end-user services to network architectures. Principles which have driven the development of adaptive pulse code modulation and linear predictive coding techniques are presented, and how these techniques are used to evaluate speech quality in existing and proposed cellular, cordless, and personal communication systems are discussed. Chapter 9 introduces time, frequency, and code division multiple access, as well as more recent multiple access techniques such as packet reservation and space division multiple access. Chapter 9 also describes how each access method can accommodate a large number of mobile users and demonstrates how multiple access impacts capacity and the network infrastructure of a cellular system. Chapter 10 describes networking considerations for wide area wireless communication systems, and presents practical networking approaches that are in use or have been proposed for future wireless systems. Chapter 11 unites all of the material from the first nine chapters by describing and comparing the major existing second generation (2G) cellular, cordless, and personal communication systems throughout the world. The tradeoffs made in the design and implementation of wireless personal communications systems are illuminated in this final chapter. The compilation of the major wireless standards makes Chapter 11 particularly useful as a single source of information for a wide range of wireless systems that are commercially deployed today.

Appendices which cover trunking theory, noise figure, noise calculations, and the Gaussian approximation for spread spectrum code division systems provide details for those interested in solving many practical wireless communications problems. The appendices also include hundreds of mathematical formulas and identities for general engineering work. I have attempted to place numerous useful items in the appendices, so that this text may be easily used by students or practicing engineers to solve a wide range of problems that may be outside the scope of the immediate text.

For industry use, Chapters 1–5, 9, and 11 will benefit working engineers in the cellular/PCS system design and radio frequency (RF) deployment, operations, and maintenance areas. Chapters 1, 2, 6–8, and 11 are tailored for modem designers and digital signal processing (DSP) engineers new to wireless. Chapters 1, 2, 10, and 11 should have broad appeal to network operators and managers, business and legal professionals, as well as working engineers.

To use this text at the undergraduate level, the instructor may wish to concentrate on Chapters 1–6, or Chapters 1–5, and 9, leaving the other chapters for treatment in a second semester undergraduate course or a graduate level course. Alternatively, traditional undergraduate courses on communications or network theory may find in Chapters 1, 2, 3, 4, 6, 8, 9, and 10 useful material that can be inserted easily into the standard curriculum. In using this text at the graduate level, I have been successful in covering most of the material in Chapters 1–6 and 10 during a standard half-year semester and Chapters 7–11 in a follow-on graduate course. In Chapters 2, 10, and 11, I have attempted to cover important but rarely compiled information on practical network implementations and worldwide standards.

Without the help and ingenuity of several former graduate students, this text could not have been written. I am pleased to acknowledge the help and encouragement of Rias Muhamed, Varun Kapoor, Kevin Saldanha, and Anil Doradla—students I met in class while teaching an early version of the course *Cellular Radio and Personal Communications*, as well as my friend and former doctoral student, Greg Durgin. Kevin Saldanha also provided camera-ready copy for the first edition of this text (which turned out to be no small task!). The assistance of these students in compiling and editing materials for several chapters of this text was invaluable, and they were a source of constant encouragement throughout the project. Others who offered helpful suggestions, and whose research efforts are reflected in portions of this text, include Scott Seidel, Joe Liberti, Dwayne Hawbaker, Marty Feuerstein, Yingie Li, Ken Blackard, Victor Fung, Weifang Huang, Prabhakar Koushik, Orlando Landron, Francis Dominique, Greg Bump, and Bert Thoma. Zhigang Rong, Jeff Laster, Michael Buehrer, Keith Brafford, and Sandip Sandhu also provided useful suggestions and helpful reviews of early drafts. For the second edition, I also express my sincere gratitude to Hao Xu, Roger Skidmore, Paulo Cardieri, Greg Durgin, Kristen Funk, Ben Henty, Neal Patwari, and Aurelia Scharnhorst who have helped me greatly in preparing added material.

This text benefits greatly from practical input provided by several industry reviewers. Roman Zaputowycz of Bell Atlantic Mobile Systems, Mike Bamburak of McCaw Communications, David McKay of Ortel, Jihad Hermes of PrimeCo, Robert Rowe of Ariel Communications, William Gardner of Qualcomm, John Snapp of AT&T Wireless, and Jim Durcan of Comcast Cellular provided extremely valuable input as to what materials were most important, and how they could best be presented for students and practicing engineers. Marty Feuerstein of Metawave and Mike Lord of Cellular One provided comprehensive reviews which have greatly improved the manuscript. Larry Sakayama of Agilent Technologies, Professor Philip DiPiazza of Florida Institute of Technology, and Jeff Stosser of Triplecom, Inc. provided valuable reviews of the new material in the second edition. The technical staff at Wireless Valley Communications, Inc. also provided feedback and practical suggestions during the development of this text.

From the academic perspective, a number of faculty in the wireless communications field provided useful suggestions which I readily incorporated. These reviewers include Prof. J. Keith Townsend of North Carolina State University, Prof. William H. Tranter of Virginia Tech, and Prof. Thomas Robertazzi of State University of New York. Professors Jeffrey Reed and Brian Woerner of Virginia Tech also provided excellent recommendations from a teaching perspective. I am grateful for the invaluable contributions from all of these individuals. Also, I wish to thank the numerous faculty, students, and practicing engineers from around the world, who continue to provide me with valuable feedback and suggestions, and who are using this book in their classrooms, short courses, and everyday work life.

I am pleased to acknowledge the support of the National Science Foundation, the Defense Advanced Research Projects Agency, and the many sponsors and friends who have supported my research and educational activities in wireless communications since 1988. It is from the excellent faculty at Purdue University, particularly my advisor, the late Clare D. McGillem, that I formally learned about communications and how to build a research program. I consider myself fortunate to have been one of the many graduate students who was stimulated to pursue a dual career in engineering and education upon graduation from Purdue.

Finally, it is a pleasure to acknowledge my family and students, as well as Bernard Goodwin of Prentice Hall, who commissioned this work and helped me bring this text to you.

Theodore S. Rappaport

CHAPTER 1

Introduction to Wireless Communication Systems

The ability to communicate with people on the move has evolved remarkably since Guglielmo Marconi first demonstrated radio's ability to provide continuous contact with ships sailing the English channel. That was in 1897, and since then new wireless communications methods and services have been enthusiastically adopted by people throughout the world. Particularly during the past ten years, the mobile radio communications industry has grown by orders of magnitude, fueled by digital and RF circuit fabrication improvements, new large-scale circuit integration, and other miniaturization technologies which make portable radio equipment smaller, cheaper, and more reliable. Digital switching techniques have facilitated the large scale deployment of affordable, easy-to-use radio communication networks. These trends will continue at an even greater pace during the next decade.

1.1 Evolution of Mobile Radio Communications

A brief history of the evolution of mobile communications throughout the world is useful in order to appreciate the enormous impact that cellular radio and *Personal Communication Services* (PCS) will have on all of us over the next several decades. It is also useful for a newcomer to the cellular radio field to understand the tremendous impact that government regulatory agencies and service competitors wield in the evolution of new wireless systems, services, and technologies. While it is not the intent of this text to deal with the techno-political aspects of cellular radio and personal communications, techno-politics are a fundamental driver in the evolution of new technology and services, since radio spectrum usage is controlled by governments, not by service providers, equipment manufacturers, entrepreneurs, or researchers. Progressive involvement in technology development is vital for a government if it hopes to keep its own country competitive in the rapidly changing field of wireless personal communications.

Wireless communications is enjoying its fastest growth period in history, due to enabling technologies which permit widespread deployment. Historically, growth in the mobile communications field has come slowly, and has been coupled closely to technological improvements. The ability to provide wireless communications to an entire population was not even conceived until Bell Laboratories developed the cellular concept in the 1960s and 1970s [Nob62], [Mac79], [You79]. With the development of highly reliable, miniature, solid-state radio frequency hardware in the 1970s, the wireless communications era was born. The recent exponential growth in cellular radio and personal communication systems throughout the world is directly attributable to new technologies of the 1970s, which are mature today. The future growth of consumer-based mobile and portable communication systems will be tied more closely to radio spectrum allocations and regulatory decisions which affect or support new or extended services, as well as to consumer needs and technology advances in the signal processing, access, and network areas.

The following market penetration data show how wireless communications in the consumer sector has grown in popularity. Figure 1.1 illustrates how mobile telephony has penetrated our daily lives compared with other popular inventions of the 20th century. Figure 1.1 is a bit misleading since the curve labeled "mobile telephone" does not include nontelephone mobile radio applications, such as paging, amateur radio, dispatch, citizens band (CB), public service, cordless phones, or terrestrial microwave radio systems. In fact, in 1990, licensed noncellular radio systems in the U.S. had over 12 million users, more than twice the U.S. cellular user population at that time [FCC91]. With the phenomenal growth of wireless subscribers in the late 1990s, combined with Nextel's novel business approach of purchasing private mobile radio licenses for bundling as a nationwide commercial cellular service, today's subscriber base for cellular and *Personal Communication Services* (PCS) far outnumbers all noncellular licensed users. Figure 1.1 shows that the first 35 years of mobile telephony saw little market penetration due to high cost and the technological challenges involved, but how, in the past decade, wireless communications has been accepted by consumers at rates comparable to television and the video cassette recorder.

By 1934, 194 municipal police radio systems and 58 state police stations had adopted amplitude modulation (AM) mobile communication systems for public safety in the U.S. It was estimated that 5,000 radios were installed in mobiles in the mid 1930s, and vehicle ignition noise was a major problem for these early mobile users [Nob62]. In 1935, Edwin Armstrong demonstrated frequency modulation (FM) for the first time, and since the late 1930s, FM has been the primary modulation technique used for mobile communication systems throughout the world. World War II accelerated the improvements of the world's manufacturing and miniaturization capabilities, and these capabilities were put to use in large one-way and two-way consumer radio and television systems following the war. The number of U.S. mobile users climbed from several thousand in 1940 to 86,000 by 1948, 695,000 by 1958, and about 1.4 million users in 1962 [Nob62]. The vast majority of mobile users in the 1960s were not connected to the *public switched telephone network* (PSTN), and thus were not able to directly dial telephone numbers from their vehicles. With the boom in CB radio and cordless appliances such as garage door

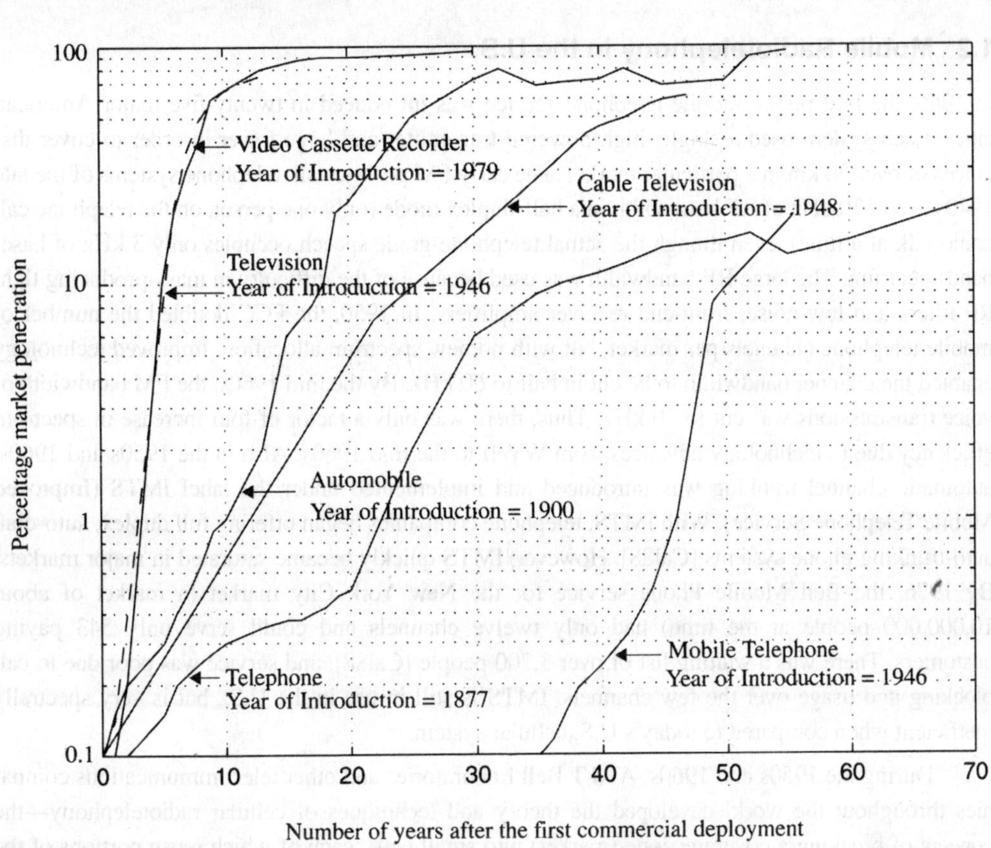

Figure 1.1 The growth of mobile telephony as compared with other popular inventions of the 20th century.

openers and telephones, the number of users of mobile and portable radio in 1995 was about 100 million, or 37% of the U.S. population. Research in 1991 estimated between 25 and 40 million cordless telephones were in use in the U.S. [Rap91c], and this number is estimated to be over 100 million as of late 2001. The number of worldwide cellular telephone users grew from 25,000 in 1984 to about 25 million in 1993 [Kuc91], [Goo91], [ITU94], and since then subscription-based wireless services have been experiencing customer growth rates well in excess of 50% per year. As shown in Chapter 2, the worldwide subscriber base of cellular and PCS subscribers is approximately 630 million as of late 2001, compared with approximately 1 billion wired telephone lines. In the first few years of the 21st century, it is clear there will be an equal number of wireless and conventional wireline customers throughout the world! At the beginning of the 21st century, over 1% of the worldwide wireless subscriber population had already abandoned wired telephone service for home use, and had begun to rely solely on their cellular service provider for telephone access. Consumers are expected to increasingly use wireless service as their sole telephone access method in the years to come.

1.2 Mobile Radiotelephony in the U.S.

In 1946, the first public mobile telephone service was introduced in twenty-five major American cities. Each system used a single, high-powered transmitter and large tower in order to cover distances of over 50 km in a particular market. The early FM push-to-talk telephone systems of the late 1940s used 120 kHz of RF bandwidth in a half-duplex mode (only one person on the telephone call could talk at a time), even though the actual telephone-grade speech occupies only 3 kHz of baseband spectrum. The large RF bandwidth was used because of the difficulty in mass-producing tight RF filters and low-noise, front-end receiver amplifiers. In 1950, the FCC doubled the number of mobile telephone channels per market, but with no new spectrum allocation. Improved technology enabled the channel bandwidth to be cut in half to 60 kHz. By the mid 1960s, the FM bandwidth of voice transmissions was cut to 30 kHz. Thus, there was only a factor of four increase in spectrum efficiency due to technology advances from WWII to the mid 1960s. Also in the 1950s and 1960s, automatic channel trunking was introduced and implemented under the label IMTS (Improved Mobile Telephone Service). With IMTS, telephone companies began offering full duplex, auto-dial, auto-trunking phone systems [Cal88]. However, IMTS quickly became saturated in major markets. By 1976, the Bell Mobile Phone service for the New York City market (a market of about 10,000,000 people at the time) had only twelve channels and could serve only 543 paying customers. There was a waiting list of over 3,700 people [Cal88], and service was poor due to call blocking and usage over the few channels. IMTS is still in use in the U.S., but is very spectrally inefficient when compared to today's U.S. cellular system.

During the 1950s and 1960s, AT&T Bell Laboratories and other telecommunications companies throughout the world developed the theory and techniques of cellular radiotelephony—the concept of breaking a coverage zone (market) into small cells, each of which reuse portions of the spectrum to increase spectrum usage at the expense of greater system infrastructure [Mac79]. The basic idea of cellular radio spectrum allocation is similar to that used by the FCC when it allocates television stations or radio stations with different channels in a region of the country, and then reallocates those same channels to different stations in a completely different part of the country. Channels are only reused when there is sufficient distance between the transmitters to prevent interference. However, cellular telephony relies on reusing the same channels within the same market or service area. AT&T proposed the concept of a cellular mobile system to the FCC in 1968, although technology was not available to implement cellular telephony until the late 1970s. In 1983, the FCC finally allocated 666 duplex channels (40 MHz of spectrum in the 800 MHz band, each channel having a one-way bandwidth of 30 kHz for a total spectrum occupancy of 60 kHz for each duplex channel) for the U.S. Advanced Mobile Phone System (AMPS) [You79]. According to FCC rules, each city (called a market) was only allowed to have two cellular radio system providers, thus providing a *duopoly* within each market which would assure some level of competition. As described in Chapters 3 and 11, the radio channels were split equally between the two carriers. AMPS was the first U.S. cellular telephone system, and was deployed in late 1983 by Ameritech in Chicago, IL [Bou91]. In 1989, the FCC granted an additional 166 channels (10 MHz) to U.S. cellular service providers to accommodate the rapid growth and demand. Figure 1.2 illustrates the spectrum

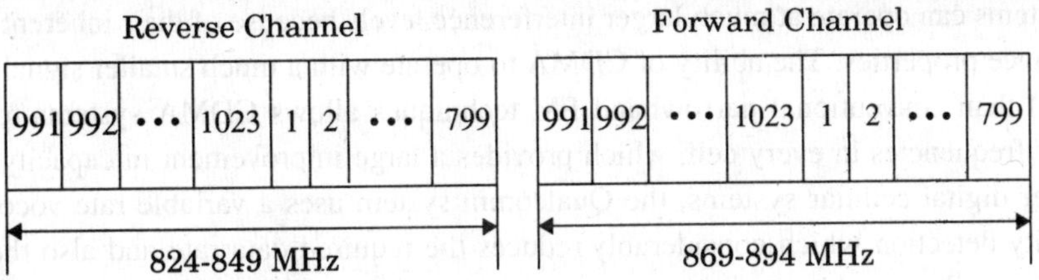

	Channel Number	Center Frequency (MHz)
Reverse Channel	$1 \le N \le 799$	$0.030N + 825.0$
	$991 \le N \le 1023$	$0.030(N - 1023) + 825.0$
Forward Channel	$1 \le N \le 799$	$0.030N + 870.0$
	$991 \le N \le 1023$	$0.030(N - 1023) + 870.0$

(Channels 800–990 are unused)

Figure 1.2 Frequency spectrum allocation for the U.S. cellular radio service. Identically labeled channels in the two bands form a forward and reverse channel pair used for duplex communication between the base station and mobile. Note that the forward and reverse channels in each pair are separated by 45 MHz.

currently allocated for U.S. cellular telephone use. Cellular radio systems operate in an interference-limited environment and rely on judicious frequency reuse plans (which are a function of the market-specific propagation characteristics) and frequency division multiple access (FDMA) to maximize capacity. These concepts will be covered in detail in subsequent chapters of this text.

In late 1991, the first US Digital Cellular (USDC) system hardware was installed in major U.S. cities. The USDC standard (Electronic Industry Association Interim Standard IS-54 and later IS-136) allowed cellular operators to replace gracefully some single-user analog channels with digital channels which support three users in the same 30 kHz bandwidth [EIA90]. In this way, U.S. carriers gradually phased out AMPS as more users accepted digital phones. As discussed in Chapters 9 and 11, the capacity improvement offered by USDC is three times that of AMPS, because digital modulation ($\pi/4$ differential quadrature phase shift keying), speech coding, and time division multiple access (TDMA) are used in place of analog FM and FDMA. Given the rate of digital signal processing advancements, speech coding technology will increase the capacity to six users per channel in the same 30 kHz bandwidth within a few years, although Chapter 2 demonstrates how IS-136 will eventually be replaced by wideband CDMA technology.

A cellular system based on code division multiple access (CDMA) was developed by Qualcomm, Inc. and standardized by the Telecommunications Industry Association (TIA) as an Interim Standard (IS-95). This system supports a variable number of users in 1.25 MHz wide channels using direct sequence spread spectrum. While the analog AMPS system requires that the signal be at least 18 dB above the co-channel interference to provide acceptable call quality,

CDMA systems can operate at much larger interference levels because of their inherent interference resistance properties. The ability of CDMA to operate with a much smaller signal-to-noise ratio (SNR) than conventional narrowband FM techniques allows CDMA systems to use the same set of frequencies in every cell, which provides a large improvement in capacity [Gil91]. Unlike other digital cellular systems, the Qualcomm system uses a variable rate vocoder with voice activity detection which considerably reduces the required data rate and also the battery drain by the mobile transmitter.

In the early 1990s, a new specialized mobile radio service (SMR) was developed to compete with U.S. cellular radio carriers. By purchasing small groups of radio system licenses from a large number of independent private radio service providers throughout the country, Nextel and Motorola formed an extended SMR (E-SMR) network in the 800 MHz band that provides capacity and services similar to cellular. Using Motorola's integrated radio system (MIRS), SMR integrates voice dispatch, cellular phone service, messaging, and data transmission capabilities on the same network [Fil95]. In 1995, Motorola replaced MIRS with the *integrated digital enhanced network* (iDen).

Personal Communication Service (PCS) licenses in the 1800/1900 MHz band were auctioned by the U.S. Government to wireless providers in early 1995, and these have spawned new wireless services that complement, as well as compete with, cellular and SMR. One of the stipulations of the PCS license was that a majority of the coverage area be operational before the year 2000. Each PCS licensee was able to "build-out" each market well in advance of this deadline. As many as five PCS licenses are allocated for each major U.S. city (see end of Chapter 11).

1.3 Mobile Radio Systems Around the World

Many mobile radio standards have been developed for wireless systems throughout the world, and more standards are likely to emerge. Tables 1.1 through 1.3 list the most common paging, cordless, cellular, and personal communications standards used in North America, Europe, and Japan. The differences between the basic types of wireless systems are described in Section 1.4, and are covered in detail in Chapter 11.

The world's most common paging standard is the Post Office Code Standard Advisory Group (POCSAG) [CCI86], [San82]. POCSAG was developed by the British Post Office in the late 1970s and supports binary frequency shift keying (FSK) signaling at 512 bps, 1200 bps, and 2400 bps. New paging systems, such as FLEX, ReFLEX, and ERMES, provide up to 6400 bps transmissions by using 4-level modulation and are currently being deployed throughout the world.

The CT2 and *Digital European Cordless Telephone* (DECT) standards developed in Europe are the two most popular cordless telephone standards throughout Europe and Asia. The CT2 system makes use of microcells which cover small distances, usually less than 100 m, using base stations with antennas mounted on street lights or on sides of buildings. The CT2 system uses battery efficient frequency shift keying along with a 32 kbps adaptive differential pulse code modulation (ADPCM) speech coder for high quality voice transmission. Handoffs between base stations are not supported in CT2, as it is intended to provide short range access to the PSTN. The DECT system accommodates data and voice transmissions for office and business

Table 1.1 Major Mobile Radio Standards in North America

Standard	Type	Year of Introduction	Multiple Access	Frequency Band	Modulation	Channel Bandwidth
AMPS	Cellular	1983	FDMA	824-894 MHz	FM	30 kHz
NAMPS	Cellular	1992	FDMA	824-894 MHz	FM	10 kHz
USDC	Cellular	1991	TDMA	824-894 MHz	π/4-DQPSK	30 kHz
CDPD	Cellular	1993	FH/ Packet	824-894 MHz	GMSK	30 kHz
IS-95	Cellular/ PCS	1993	CDMA	824-894 MHz 1.8-2.0 GHz	QPSK/ BPSK	1.25 MHz
GSC	Paging	1970s	Simplex	Several	FSK	12.5 kHz
POCSAG	Paging	1970s	Simplex	Several	FSK	12.5 kHz
FLEX	Paging	1993	Simplex	Several	4-FSK	15 kHz
DCS-1900 (GSM)	PCS	1994	TDMA	1.85-1.99 GHz	GMSK	200 kHz
PACS	Cordless/ PCS	1994	TDMA/ FDMA	1.85-1.99 GHz	π/4-DQPSK	300 kHz
MIRS	SMR/PCS	1994	TDMA	Several	16-QAM	25 kHz
iDen	SMR/PCS	1995	TDMA	Several	16-QAM	25 kHz

users. In the U.S., the PACS standard, developed by Bellcore and Motorola, is likely to be used inside office buildings as a wireless voice and data telephone system or radio local loop. The Personal Handyphone System (PHS) standard supports indoor and local loop applications in Japan. Local loop concepts are explained in Chapter 10.

The world's first cellular system was implemented by the Nippon Telephone and Telegraph company (NTT) in Japan. The system, deployed in 1979, uses 600 FM duplex channels (25 kHz for each one-way link) in the 800 MHz band. In Europe, the Nordic Mobile Telephone system

Table 1.2 Major Mobile Radio Standards in Europe

Standard	Type	Year of Introduction	Multiple Access	Frequency Band	Modulation	Channel Bandwidth
ETACS	Cellular	1985	FDMA	900 MHz	FM	25 kHz
NMT-450	Cellular	1981	FDMA	450-470 MHz	FM	25 kHz
NMT-900	Cellular	1986	FDMA	890-960 MHz	FM	12.5 kHz
GSM	Cellular /PCS	1990	TDMA	890-960 MHz	GMSK	200 kHz
C-450	Cellular	1985	FDMA	450-465 MHz	FM	20 kHz/ 10 kHz
ERMES	Paging	1993	FDMA	Several	4-FSK	25 kHz
CT2	Cordless	1989	FDMA	864-868 MHz	GFSK	100 kHz
DECT	Cordless	1993	TDMA	1880-1900 MHz	GFSK	1.728 MHz
DCS-1800	Cordless /PCS	1993	TDMA	1710-1880 MHz	GMSK	200 kHz

Table 1.3 Major Mobile Radio Standards in Japan

Standard	Type	Year of Introduction	Multiple Access	Frequency Band	Modulation	Channel Bandwidth
JTACS	Cellular	1988	FDMA	860-925 MHz	FM	25 kHz
PDC	Cellular	1993	TDMA	810-1501 MHz	$\pi/4$-DQPSK	25 kHz
NTT	Cellular	1979	FDMA	400/800 MHz	FM	25 kHz
NTACS	Cellular	1993	FDMA	843-925 MHz	FM	12.5 kHz
NTT	Paging	1979	FDMA	280 MHz	FSK	12.5 kHz
NEC	Paging	1979	FDMA	Several	FSK	10 kHz
PHS	Cordless	1993	TDMA	1895-1907 MHz	$\pi/4$-DQPSK	300 kHz

(NMT 450) was developed in 1981 for the 450 MHz band and uses 25 kHz channels. The European Total Access Cellular System (ETACS) was deployed in 1985 and is virtually identical to the U.S. AMPS system, except that the smaller bandwidth channels result in a slight degradation of signal-to-noise ratio (SNR) and coverage range. In Germany, a cellular standard called C-450 was introduced in 1985. The first generation European cellular systems are generally incompatible with one another because of the different frequencies and communication protocols used. These systems are now being replaced by the Pan European digital cellular standard GSM (Global System for Mobile) which was first deployed in 1990 in a new 900 MHz band which all of Europe dedicated for cellular telephone service [Mal89]. As discussed in Chapters 2 and 11, the GSM standard has gained worldwide acceptance as the first universal digital cellular system with modern network features extended to each mobile user, and is the leading digital air interface for PCS services above 1800 MHz throughout the world. In Japan, the Pacific Digital Cellular (PDC) standard provides digital cellular coverage using a system similar to North America's USDC.

1.4 Examples of Wireless Communication Systems

Most people are familiar with a number of mobile radio communication systems used in everyday life. Garage door openers, remote controllers for home entertainment equipment, cordless telephones, hand-held walkie-talkies, pagers (also called paging receivers or "beepers"), and cellular telephones are all examples of mobile radio communication systems. However, the cost, complexity, performance, and types of services offered by each of these mobile systems are vastly different.

The term *mobile* has historically been used to classify *any* radio terminal that could be moved during operation. More recently, the term *mobile* is used to describe a radio terminal that is attached to a high speed mobile platform (e.g., a cellular telephone in a fast moving vehicle) whereas the term *portable* describes a radio terminal that can be hand-held and used by someone at walking speed (e.g., a walkie-talkie or cordless telephone inside a home). The term *subscriber* is often used to describe a mobile or portable user because in most mobile communication systems, each user pays a subscription fee to use the system, and each user's communication device is called a *subscriber unit*. In general, the collective group of users in a wireless system are called *users* or *mobiles*, even though many of the users may actually use portable terminals. The mobiles communicate to fixed *base stations* which are connected to a commercial power source and a fixed *backbone network*. Table 1.4 lists definitions of terms used to describe elements of wireless communication systems.

Mobile radio transmission systems may be classified as *simplex, half-duplex* or *full-duplex*. In simplex systems, communication is possible in only one direction. Paging systems, in which messages are received but not acknowledged, are simplex systems. Half-duplex radio systems allow two-way communication, but use the same radio channel for both transmission and reception. This means that at any given time, a user can only transmit or receive information. Constraints like "push-to-talk" and "release-to-listen" are fundamental features of half-duplex systems. Full duplex systems, on the other hand, allow simultaneous radio transmission and reception between a

Table 1.4 Wireless Communications System Definitions

Base Station	A fixed station in a mobile radio system used for radio communication with mobile stations. Base stations are located at the center or on the edge of a coverage region and consist of radio channels and transmitter and receiver antennas mounted on a tower.
Control Channel	Radio channel used for transmission of call setup, call request, call initiation, and other beacon or control purposes.
Forward Channel	Radio channel used for transmission of information from the base station to the mobile.
Full Duplex Systems	Communication systems which allow simultaneous two-way communication. Transmission and reception is typically on two different channels (FDD) although new cordless/PCS systems are using TDD.
Half Duplex Systems	Communication systems which allow two-way communication by using the same radio channel for both transmission and reception. At any given time, the user can only either transmit or receive information.
Handoff	The process of transferring a mobile station from one channel or base station to another.
Mobile Station	A station in the cellular radio service intended for use while in motion at unspecified locations. Mobile stations may be hand-held personal units (portables) or installed in vehicles (mobiles).
Mobile Switching Center	Switching center which coordinates the routing of calls in a large service area. In a cellular radio system, the MSC connects the cellular base stations and the mobiles to the PSTN. An MSC is also called a mobile telephone switching office (MTSO).
Page	A brief message which is broadcast over the entire service area, usually in a simulcast fashion by many base stations at the same time.
Reverse Channel	Radio channel used for transmission of information from the mobile to base station.
Roamer	A mobile station which operates in a service area (market) other than that from which service has been subscribed.
Simplex Systems	Communication systems which provide only one-way communication.
Subscriber	A user who pays subscription charges for using a mobile communications system.
Transceiver	A device capable of simultaneously transmitting and receiving radio signals.

subscriber and a base station, by providing two simultaneous but separate channels (frequency division duplex, or FDD) or adjacent time slots on a single radio channel (time division duplex, or TDD) for communication to and from the user.

Frequency division duplexing (FDD) provides simultaneous radio transmission channels for the subscriber and the base station, so that they both may constantly transmit while simultaneously receiving signals from one another. At the base station, separate transmit and receive antennas are used to accommodate the two separate channels. At the subscriber unit, however, a single antenna is used for both transmission to and reception from the base station, and a device called a *duplexer* is used inside the subscriber unit to enable the same antenna to be used for simultaneous transmission and reception. To facilitate FDD, it is necessary to separate the transmit and receive frequencies by about 5% of the nominal RF frequency, so that the duplexer can provide sufficient isolation while being inexpensively manufactured.

In FDD, a pair of simplex channels with a fixed and known frequency separation is used to define a specific radio channel in the system. The channel used to convey traffic to the mobile user from a base station is called the *forward channel*, while the channel used to carry traffic from the mobile user to a base station is called the *reverse channel*. In the U.S. AMPS standard, the reverse channel has a frequency which is exactly 45 MHz lower than that of the forward channel. Full duplex mobile radio systems provide many of the capabilities of the standard telephone, with the added convenience of mobility. Full duplex and half-duplex systems use *transceivers* for radio communication. FDD is used exclusively in analog mobile radio systems and is described in more detail in Chapter 9.

Time division duplexing (TDD) uses the fact that it is possible to share a single radio channel in time, so that a portion of the time is used to transmit from the base station to the mobile, and the remaining time is used to transmit from the mobile to the base station. If the data transmission rate in the channel is much greater than the end-user's data rate, it is possible to store information bursts and provide the appearance of full duplex operation to a user, even though there are *not* two simultaneous radio transmissions at any instant. TDD is only possible with digital transmission formats and digital modulation, and is very sensitive to timing. It is for this reason that TDD has only recently been used, and only for indoor or small area wireless applications where the physical coverage distances (and thus the radio propagation time delay) are much smaller than the many kilometers used in conventional cellular telephone systems.

1.4.1 Paging Systems

Paging systems are communication systems that send brief messages to a subscriber. Depending on the type of service, the message may be either a numeric message, an alphanumeric message, or a voice message. Paging systems are typically used to notify a subscriber of the need to call a particular telephone number or travel to a known location to receive further instructions. In modern paging systems, news headlines, stock quotations, and faxes may be sent. A message is sent to a paging subscriber via the paging system access number (usually a toll-free telephone number) with a telephone keypad or modem. The issued message is called a *page*. The paging system then transmits the page throughout the service area using base stations which broadcast the page on a radio carrier.

Paging systems vary widely in their complexity and coverage area. While simple paging systems may cover a limited range of 2 to 5 km, or may even be confined to within individual buildings, wide area paging systems can provide worldwide coverage. Though paging receivers are simple and inexpensive, the transmission system required is quite sophisticated. Wide area paging systems consist of a network of telephone lines, many base station transmitters, and large radio towers that simultaneously broadcast a page from each base station (this is called *simulcasting*). Simulcast transmitters may be located within the same service area or in different cities or countries. Paging systems are designed to provide reliable communication to subscribers wherever they are; whether

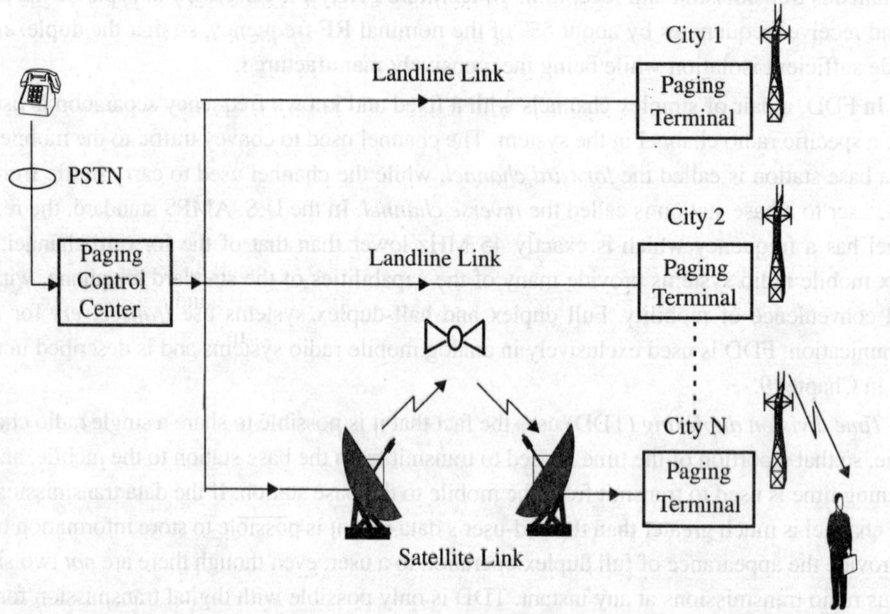

Figure 1.3 A wide area paging system. The paging control center dispatches pages received from the PSTN throughout several cities at the same time.

inside a building, driving on a highway, or flying in an airplane. This necessitates large transmitter powers (on the order of kilowatts) and low data rates (a couple of thousand bits per second) for maximum coverage from each base station. Figure 1.3 shows a diagram of a wide area paging system.

Example 1.1

Paging systems are designed to provide ultra-reliable coverage, even inside buildings. Buildings can attenuate radio signals by 20 or 30 dB, making the choice of base station locations difficult for the paging companies. For this reason, paging transmitters are usually located on tall buildings in the center of a city, and simulcasting is used in conjunction with additional base stations located on the perimeter of the city to flood the entire area. Small RF bandwidths are used to maximize the signal-to-noise ratio at each paging receiver, so low data rates (6400 bps or less) are used.

1.4.2 Cordless Telephone Systems

Cordless telephone systems are full duplex communication systems that use radio to connect a portable handset to a dedicated base station, which is then connected to a dedicated telephone line with a specific telephone number on the public switched telephone network (PSTN). In first generation cordless telephone systems (manufactured in the 1980s), the portable unit communicates

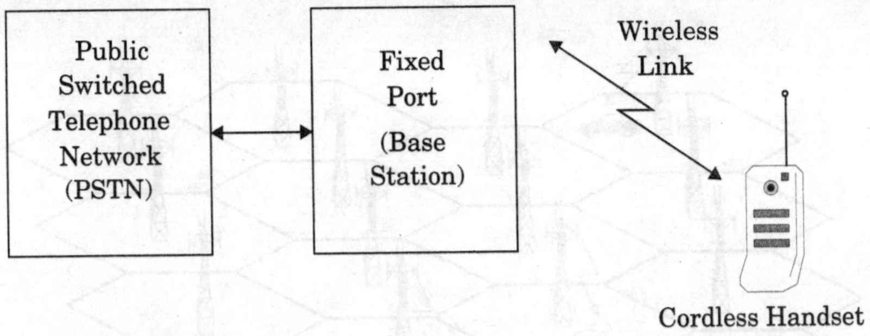

Figure 1.4 A cordless telephone system.

only to the dedicated base unit and only over distances of a few tens of meters. Early cordless telephones operate solely as extension telephones to a transceiver connected to a subscriber line on the PSTN and are primarily for in-home use.

Second generation cordless telephones have recently been introduced which allow subscribers to use their handsets at many outdoor locations within urban centers such as London or Hong Kong. Modern cordless telephones are sometimes combined with paging receivers so that a subscriber may first be paged and then respond to the page using the cordless telephone. Cordless telephone systems provide the user with limited range and mobility, as it is usually not possible to maintain a call if the user travels outside the range of the base station. Typical second generation base stations provide coverage ranges up to a few hundred meters. Figure 1.4 illustrates a cordless telephone system.

1.4.3 Cellular Telephone Systems

A cellular telephone system provides a wireless connection to the PSTN for any user location within the radio range of the system. Cellular systems accommodate a large number of users over a large geographic area, within a limited frequency spectrum. Cellular radio systems provide high quality service that is often comparable to that of the landline telephone systems. High capacity is achieved by limiting the coverage of each base station transmitter to a small geographic area called a *cell* so that the same radio channels may be reused by another base station located some distance away. A sophisticated switching technique called a *handoff* enables a call to proceed uninterrupted when the user moves from one cell to another.

Figure 1.5 shows a basic cellular system which consists of *mobile stations, base stations* and a *mobile switching center* (MSC). The mobile switching center is sometimes called a *mobile telephone switching office* (MTSO), since it is responsible for connecting all mobiles to the PSTN in a cellular system. Each mobile communicates via radio with one of the base stations and may be handed-off to any number of base stations throughout the duration of a call. The mobile station contains a transceiver, an antenna, and control circuitry, and may be mounted in a vehicle or used as a portable hand-held unit. The base stations consist of several transmitters and receivers which simultaneously handle full duplex communications and generally have towers which support several transmitting and receiving antennas. The base station

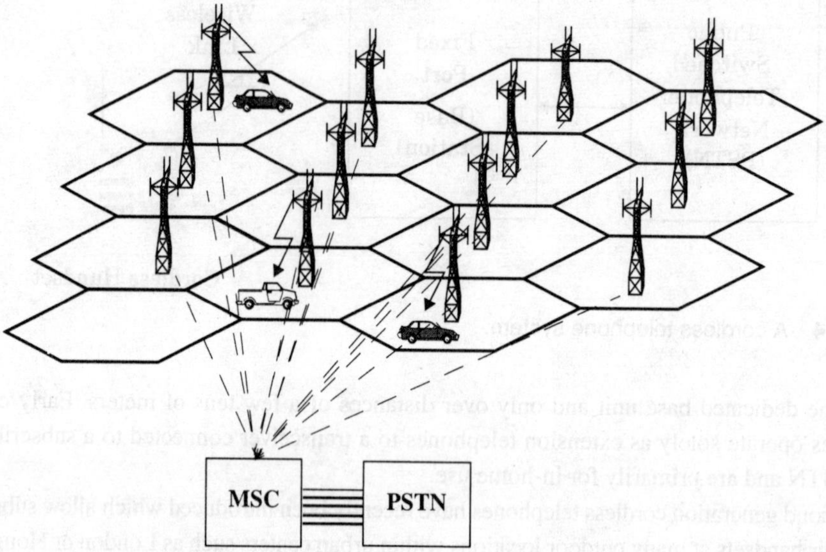

Figure 1.5 A cellular system. The towers represent base stations which provide radio access between mobile users and the mobile switching center (MSC).

serves as a bridge between all mobile users in the cell and connects the simultaneous mobile calls via telephone lines or microwave links to the MSC. The MSC coordinates the activities of all of the base stations and connects the entire cellular system to the PSTN. A typical MSC handles 100,000 cellular subscribers and 5,000 simultaneous conversations at a time, and accommodates all billing and system maintenance functions, as well. In large cities, several MSCs are used by a single carrier.

Communication between the base station and the mobiles is defined by a standard *common air interface* (CAI) that specifies four different channels. The channels used for voice transmission from the base station to mobiles are called *forward voice channels* (FVC), and the channels used for voice transmission from mobiles to the base station are called *reverse voice channels* (RVC). The two channels responsible for initiating mobile calls are the *forward control channels* (FCC) and *reverse control channels* (RCC). Control channels are often called *setup channels* because they are only involved in setting up a call and moving it to an unused voice channel. Control channels transmit and receive data messages that carry call initiation and service requests, and are monitored by mobiles when they do not have a call in progress. Forward control channels also serve as beacons which continually broadcast all of the traffic requests for all mobiles in the system. As described in Chapter 11, supervisory and data messages are sent in a number of ways to facilitate automatic channel changes and handoff instructions for the mobiles before and during a call.

Example 1.2 Cellular systems rely on the frequency reuse concept, which requires that the forward control channels (FCCs) in neighboring cells be different. By defining a relatively small number of FCCs as part of the common air interface, cellular phones can be manufactured by many companies which can rapidly scan all of the possible FCCs to determine the strongest channel at any time. Once finding the strongest signal, the cellular phone receiver stays "camped" to the particular FCC. By broadcasting the same setup data on all FCCs at the same time, the MSC is able to signal all subscribers within the cellular system and can be certain that any mobile will be signaled when it receives a call via the PSTN.

1.4.3.1 How a Cellular Telephone Call is Made

When a cellular phone is turned on, but is not yet engaged in a call, it first scans the group of forward control channels to determine the one with the strongest signal, and then monitors that control channel until the signal drops below a usable level. At this point, it again scans the control channels in search of the strongest base station signal. For each cellular system described in Tables 1.1 through 1.3, the control channels are defined and standardized over the entire geographic area covered and typically make up about 5% of the total number of channels available in the system (the other 95% are dedicated to voice and data traffic for the end-users). Since the control channels are standardized and are identical throughout different markets within the country or continent, every phone scans the same channels while idle. When a telephone call is placed to a mobile user, the MSC dispatches the request to all base stations in the cellular system. The *mobile identification number* (MIN), which is the subscriber's telephone number, is then broadcast as a paging message over all of the forward control channels throughout the cellular system. The mobile receives the paging message sent by the base station which it monitors, and responds by identifying itself over the reverse control channel. The base station relays the acknowledgment sent by the mobile and informs the MSC of the handshake. Then, the MSC instructs the base station to move the call to an unused voice channel within the cell (typically, between ten to sixty voice channels and just one control channel are used in each cell's base station). At this point, the base station signals the mobile to change frequencies to an unused forward and reverse voice channel pair, at which point another data message (called an *alert*) is transmitted over the forward voice channel to instruct the mobile telephone to ring, thereby instructing the mobile user to answer the phone. Figure 1.6 shows the sequence of events involved with connecting a call to a mobile user in a cellular telephone system. All of these events occur within a few seconds and are not noticeable by the user.

Once a call is in progress, the MSC adjusts the transmitted power of the mobile and changes the channel of the mobile unit and base stations in order to maintain call quality as the subscriber moves in and out of range of each base station. This is called a *handoff.* Special control signaling is applied to the voice channels so that the mobile unit may be controlled by the base station and the MSC while a call is in progress.

MSC		Receives call from PSTN. Sends the requested MIN to all base stations.			Verifies that the mobile has a valid MIN, ESN pair.	Requests BS to move mobile to unused voice channel pair.		Connects the mobile with the calling party on the PSTN.
Base Station	FCC		Transmits page (MIN) for specified user.				Transmits data message for mobile to move to specific voice channel.	
	RCC			Receives MIN, ESN, Station Class Mark and passes to MSC.				
	FVC							Begin voice transmission.
	RVC							Begin voice reception.
Mobile	FCC		Receives page and matches the MIN with its own MIN.				Receives data messages to move to specified voice channel.	
	RCC			Acknowledges receipt of MIN and sends ESN and Station Class Mark.				
	FVC							Begin voice reception.
	RVC							Begin voice transmission.

time →

Figure 1.6 Timing diagram illustrating how a call to a mobile user initiated by a landline subscriber is established.

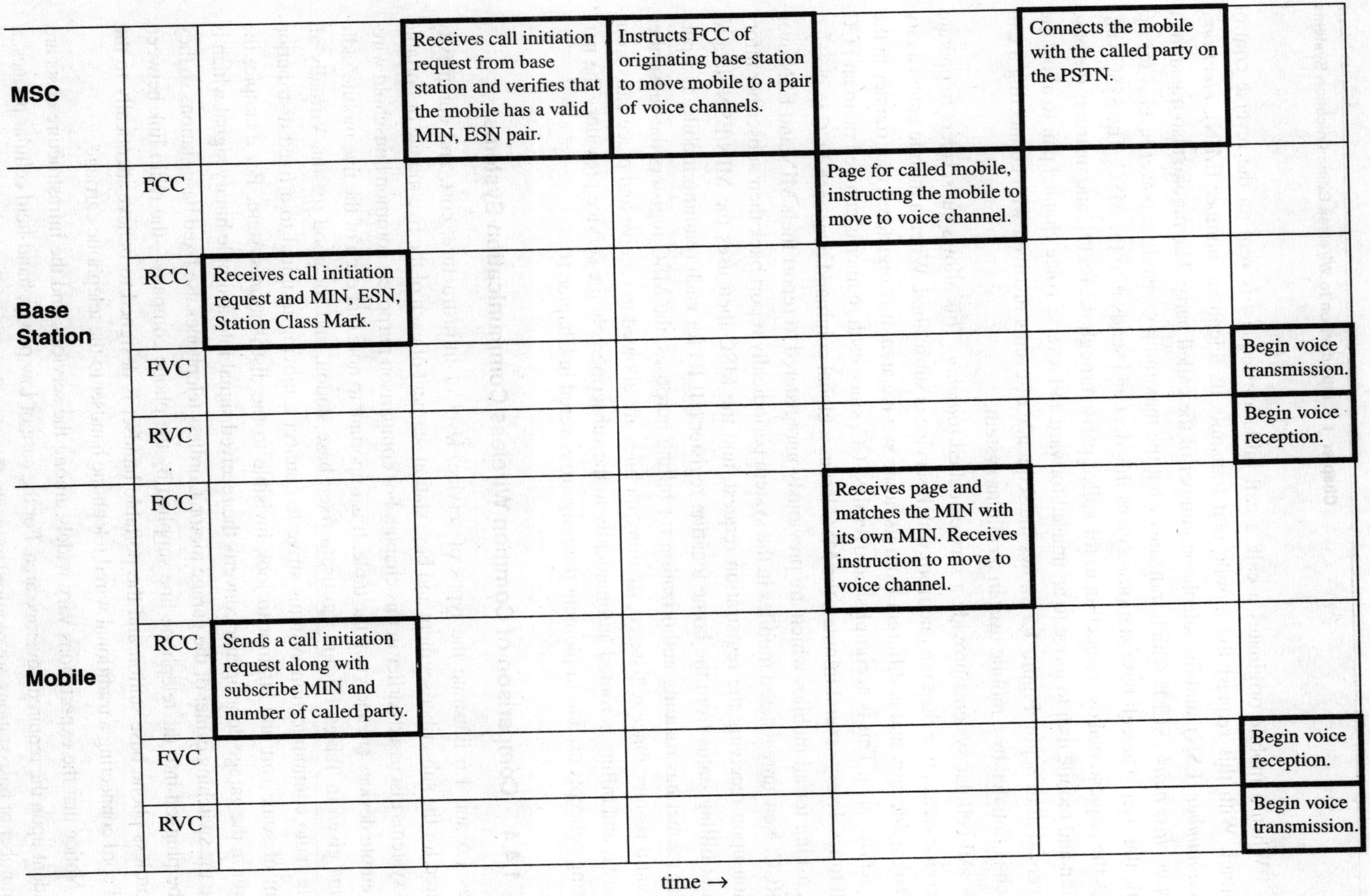

Figure 1.7 Timing diagram illustrating how a call initiated by a mobile is established.

When a mobile originates a call, a call initiation request is sent on the reverse control channel. With this request the mobile unit transmits its telephone number (MIN), *electronic serial number* (ESN), and the telephone number of the called party. The mobile also transmits a *station class mark* (SCM) which indicates what the maximum transmitter power level is for the particular user. The cell base station receives this data and sends it to the MSC. The MSC validates the request, makes connection to the called party through the PSTN, and instructs the base station and mobile user to move to an unused forward and reverse voice channel pair to allow the conversation to begin. Figure 1.7 shows the sequence of events involved with connecting a call which is initiated by a mobile user in a cellular system.

All cellular systems provide a service called *roaming*. This allows subscribers to operate in service areas other than the one from which service is subscribed. When a mobile enters a city or geographic area that is different from its home service area, it is registered as a roamer in the new service area. This is accomplished over the FCC, since each roamer is camped on to an FCC at all times. Every several minutes, the MSC issues a global command over each FCC in the system, asking for all mobiles which are previously unregistered to report their MIN and ESN over the RCC. New unregistered mobiles in the system periodically report back their subscriber information upon receiving the registration request, and the MSC then uses the MIN/ESN data to request billing status from the home location register (HLR) for each roaming mobile. If a particular roamer has roaming authorization for billing purposes, the MSC registers the subscriber as a valid roamer. Once registered, roaming mobiles are allowed to receive and place calls from that area, and billing is routed automatically to the subscriber's home service provider. The networking concepts used to implement roaming are covered in Chapter 10.

1.4.4 Comparison of Common Wireless Communication Systems

Tables 1.5 and 1.6 illustrate the types of service, level of infrastructure, cost, and complexity required for the subscriber segment and base station segment of each of the five mobile or portable radio systems discussed earlier in this chapter. For comparison purposes, common household wireless remote devices are shown in the table. It is important to note that each of the five mobile radio systems given in Tables 1.5 and 1.6 use a fixed base station, and for good reason. Virtually all mobile radio communication systems strive to connect a moving terminal to a fixed distribution system of some sort and attempt to look invisible to the distribution system. For example, the receiver in the garage door opener converts the received signal into a simple binary signal which is sent to the switching center of the garage motor. Cordless telephones use fixed base stations so they may be plugged into the telephone line supplied by the phone company—the radio link between the cordless phone base station and the portable handset is designed to behave identically to the coiled cord connecting a traditional wired telephone handset to the telephone carriage.

Notice that the expectations vary widely among the services, and the infrastructure costs are dependent upon the required coverage area. For the case of low power, hand-held cellular phones, a large number of base stations are required to insure that any phone is in close range to a base station within a city. If base stations were not within close range, a great deal of transmitter power would be

Table 1.5 Comparison of Mobile Communication Systems—Mobile Station

Service	Coverage Range	Required Infra-structure	Complexity	Hardware Cost	Carrier Frequency	Functionality
TV Remote Control	Low	Low	Low	Low	Infrared	Transmitter
Garage Door Opener	Low	Low	Low	Low	< 100 MHz	Transmitter
Paging System	High	High	Low	Low	< 1 GHz	Receiver
Cordless Phone	Low	Low	Moderate	Low	1–3 GHz	Transceiver
Cellular Phone	High	High	High	Moderate	< 2 GHz	Transceiver

Table 1.6 Comparison of Mobile Communication Systems—Base Station

Service	Coverage Range	Required Infra-structure	Complexity	Hardware Cost	Carrier Frequency	Functionality
TV Remote Control	Low	Low	Low	Low	Infrared	Receiver
Garage Door Opener	Low	Low	Low	Low	< 100 MHz	Receiver
Paging System	High	High	High	High	< 1 GHz	Transmitter
Cordless Phone	Low	Low	Low	Moderate	1–3 GHz	Transceiver
Cellular Phone	High	High	High	High	< 2 GHz	Transceiver

required of the phone, thus limiting the battery life and rendering the service useless for hand-held users. Because of the extensive telecommunications infrastructure of copper wires, microwave line-of-sight links, and fiber optic cables—all of which are fixed—it is highly likely that future land-based mobile communication systems will continue to rely on fixed base stations which are connected to some type of fixed distribution system. However, emerging mobile satellite networks will require orbiting base stations.

1.5 Trends in Cellular Radio and Personal Communications

Since 1989, there has been enormous activity throughout the world to develop personal wireless systems that combine the network intelligence of today's PSTN with modern digital signal processing and RF technology. The concept, called Personal Communication Services (PCS), originated in the United Kingdom when three companies were given spectrum in the 1800 MHz range to develop Personal Communication Networks (PCN) throughout Great Britain [Rap91c]. PCN was seen by the U.K. as a means of improving its international competitiveness in the wireless field while developing new wireless systems and services for citizens. Presently, field trials are being conducted throughout the world to determine the suitability of various modulation, multiple-access, and networking techniques for future 3G PCN and PCS systems.

The terms PCN and PCS are often used interchangeably. PCN refers to a wireless networking concept where any user can make or receive calls, no matter where they are, using a light-weight, personalized communicator. PCS refers to new wireless systems that incorporate more network features and are more personalized than existing cellular radio systems, but which do not yet embody all of the concepts of an ideal PCN. Today, cellular and PCS are identical in functionality and differ only in frequency band.

Indoor wireless networking products are rapidly emerging and promise to become a major part of the telecommunications infrastructure within the next decade. As discussed in Chapter 2, an international standards body, IEEE 802.11, is developing standards for wireless access between computers inside buildings. The European Telecommunications Standard Institute (ETSI) is also developing the 20 Mbps HIPERLAN standard for indoor wireless networks. Breakthrough products such as Motorola's 18 GHz Altair WIN (wireless information network) modem, that was not commercialized, and Avaya's (formerly NCR and Lucent) / ORiNOCO waveLAN computer modem have been available as wireless ethernet connections since 1990 [Tuc93] and are beginning to penetrate the business world. As we enter the 21st century, products are emerging that allow users to link their phone with their computer within an office environment, as well as in a public setting, such as an airport or train station.

A worldwide standard, the Future Public Land Mobile Telephone System (FPLMTS)—renamed International Mobile Telecommunication 2000 (IMT-2000) in mid-1995—has been formulated by the International Telecommunications Union (ITU) which is the standards body for the United Nations, with headquarters in Geneva, Switzerland. The technical group TG 8/1 standards task group is within the ITU's Radiocommunications Sector (ITU-R). ITU-R was formerly known as the Consultative Committee for International Radiocommunications (CCIR).

TG 8/1 is considering how worldwide wireless networks should evolve and how worldwide frequency coordination might be implemented to allow subscriber units to work anywhere in the world. FPLMTS (now IMT-2000) is a third generation universal, multi-function, globally compatible digital mobile radio system that will integrate paging, cordless, and cellular systems, as well as low earth orbit (LEO) satellites, into one universal mobile system. A total of 230 MHz in frequency bands 1885 to 2025 MHz and 2110 to 2200 MHz was targeted by the ITU's 1992 World Administrative Radio Conference (WARC). In March 1999, ITU-R agreed to additional spectrum allocations that include the frequency bands 806 to 960 MHz, 1710 to 2200 MHz, and 2520 to 2670 MHz. This additional spectrum allocation was approved in May 2000 at the ITU World Radio Conference (WRC-2000). The types of modulation, speech coding, and multiple access schemes to be used in IMT-2000 were also locked down by the ITU Radio General Assembly in mid-2000. As discussed in Chapter 2, the selected radio interfaces for terrestrial wireless service include expansions of today's GSM and IS-95 CDMA, as well as a new time-code CDMA standard proposed by China.

Worldwide standards are also required for low earth orbit (LEO) satellite communication systems that were developed in the 1990s but which failed commercially at the turn of the century. Due to the very large areas on earth which are illuminated by satellite transmitters, satellite-based cellular systems will never approach the capacities provided by land-based microcellular systems. However, satellite mobile systems were touted as offering tremendous promise for paging, data collection, and emergency communications, as well as for global roaming. In early 1990, the aerospace industry demonstrated the first successful launch of a small satellite on a rocket from a jet aircraft. This launch technique was pioneered by Orbital Sciences Corp. and was more than an order of magnitude less expensive than conventional ground-based launches and allowed rapid deployment, suggesting that a network of LEOs could be rapidly launched for wireless communications around the globe. While several companies, such as Motorola's Iridium, proposed systems and service concepts for worldwide paging, cellular telephone, and emergency navigation and notification in the early 1990s [IEE91], the capital markets have not supported mobile satellite systems in general.

In emerging nations, where existing telephone service is almost nonexistent, fixed cellular telephone systems are being installed at a rapid rate. This is due to the fact that developing nations are finding it is quicker and more affordable to install cellular telephone systems for fixed home use, rather than install wires in neighborhoods which have not yet received telephone connections to the PSTN.

The world is undergoing a major telecommunications revolution that will provide ubiquitous communication access to citizens, wherever they are. The wireless telecommunications industry requires engineers who can design and develop new wireless systems, make meaningful comparisons of competing systems, and understand the engineering trade-offs that must be made in any system. Such understanding can only be achieved by mastering the fundamental technical concepts of wireless personal communications. These concepts are the subject of the remaining chapters of this text.

1.6 Problems

1.1 Write an equation that relates the speed of light, c, to carrier frequency, f, and wavelength, λ.

1.2 If 0 dBm is equal to 1 mW (10^{-3} W) over a 50 Ω load; express 10 W in units of dBm.

1.3 Why do paging systems need to provide low data rates? How does a low data rate lead to better coverage?

1.4 Qualitatively describe how the power supply requirements differ between mobile and portable cellular phones, as well as the difference between pocket pagers and cordless phones. How does coverage range impact battery life in a mobile radio system?

1.5 In simulcasting paging systems, there usually is one dominant signal arriving at the paging receiver. In most, but not all cases, the dominant signal arrives from the transmitter closest to the paging receiver. Explain how the FM capture effect could help reception of the paging receiver. Could the FM capture effect help cellular radio systems? Explain how.

1.6 Where would walkie-talkies fit in Tables 1.5 and 1.6? Carefully describe the similarities and differences between walkie-talkies and cordless telephones. Why would consumers expect a much higher grade of service for a cordless telephone system?

1.7 Between a pager, a cellular phone, and a cordless phone, which device will have the longest battery life between charging? Why?

1.8 Between a pager, a cellular phone, and a cordless phone, which device will have the shortest battery life between charging? Why?

1.9 Assume a 1 Amp-hour battery is used on a cellular telephone (often called a cellular subscriber unit). Also assume that the cellular telephone draws 35 mA in idle mode and 250 mA during a call. How long would the phone work (i.e., what is the battery life) if the user leaves the phone on continually and has one 3-minute call every day? Every 6 hours? Every hour? What is the maximum talk time available on the cellular phone in this example?

1.10 Modern wireless devices, such as 2-way pagers, and GSM phones, have sleep modes which greatly reduce the duty cycle of the power supply. Work Problem 1.9 above, then consider a wireless communicator that has three different battery states (1 mA in idle, 5 mA in wake-up receive mode, and 250 mA in transceiver mode). Consider the effects of different duty cycles and transmit times to see the wide range of battery lifetimes one may expect before recharging. Plot your results of battery lifetime as a function of the duty cycles and durations of the wake-up mode. Hint: 1 Amp-hour describes a battery that can supply 1 Amp of current for a period of one hour. This same battery may supply 100 mA for 10 hours, and so on.

1.11 Assume a CT2 subscriber unit has the same size battery as the phone in Problem 1.9, but the paging receiver draws 5 mA in idle mode and the transceiver draws 80 mA during a call. Recompute the CT2 battery life for the call rates given in Problem 1.9. Recompute the maximum talk time for the CT2 handset.

1.12 Why would one expect the CT2 handset in Problem 1.11 to have a smaller battery drain during transmission than a cellular telephone?

1.13 Why is FM, rather than AM, used in most mobile radio systems today? List as many reasons as you can think of, and justify your responses. Consider issues such as fidelity, power consumption, and noise.

1.14 List the factors that led to the development of (a) the GSM system for Europe, and (b) the U.S. digital cellular system. Compare and contrast the importance for both efforts to (i) maintain compatibility with existing cellular phones; (ii) obtain spectral efficiency; (iii) obtain new radio spectrum.

1.15 Assume that a GSM, an IS-95, and a US Digital Cellular (IS-136) base station transmit the same power over the same distance. Which system will provide the best SNR at a mobile receiver? What is the SNR improvement over the other two systems? Assume a perfect receiver with only thermal noise present in each of the three systems. Review Appendix B to determine how noise figure might impact your answers, and describe the importance of receiver noise figure in actual systems.

1.16 Discuss the similarities and differences between a conventional cellular radio system and a space-based (satellite) cellular radio system. What are the advantages and disadvantages of each system? Which system could support a larger number of users for a given frequency allocation? Why? How would this impact the cost of service for each subscriber?

1.17 There have been a large number of wireless standards proposed throughout the world in the past 18 months. Using the trade literature and the Internet, find three new wireless standards (one each for the paging, PCS, and satellite market sectors), and identify the multiple access technique, continent of operation, frequency band, modulation, and channel bandwidth for each standard. The standards that you identify must be new (i.e., do not appear in Tables 1.1, 1.2, or 1.3). Include a paragraph description of each standard, cite the references you used to learn about it, and describe why the standard was proposed (what niche or competitive advantage does it offer). Challenge: Try to find standards that are not yet popular on your continent.

1.18 Assume that wireless communication standards can be classified as belonging to one of the following four groups:

High power, wide area systems (cellular)
Low power, local area systems (cordless telephone and PCS)
Low data rate, wide area systems (mobile data)
High data rate, local area systems (wireless LANs)

Classify each of the wireless standards described in Tables 1.1–1.3 using these four groups. Justify your answers. Note that some standards may fit into more than one group.

1.19 Discuss the importance of regional and international standards organizations such as ITU-R, ETSI, and WARC. What competitive advantages are there in using different wireless standards in different parts of the world? What disadvantages arise when different standards and different frequencies are used in different parts of the world?

1.20 Based on the proliferation of wireless standards throughout the world, discuss how likely it is for the IMT-2000 vision to eventually be adopted. Provide a detailed explanation, along with probable scenarios of services, spectrum allocations, and cost.

1.21 This assignment demonstrates how rapidly wireless has emerged in the telecommunications field. You will be investigating new services, systems, and technologies for wireless communications that have been proposed in the past couple of years. Using the library, the WWW, industry and consumer web pages, and various trade magazines and journals, learn and describe the present state of technology for these new systems.

To proceed, consider the following categories of wireless communications systems: a) Wireless Local Loop (also called Fixed Wireless Access); b) Broadband Wireless Communications (also known as Local Multipoint Distribution Service—LMDS in the US, LMCS in Canada and Europe); c) Third Generation Wireless Systems (also called "3G"); d) Wireless Local Area Networks (WLANs); e) Satellite/Cellular wireless systems; and f) in-home wireless networks and small office/home office (SOHO) appliance data networks. For each of these six broadband wireless system areas, do the following:

(a) Carefully define each of the six broad categories of wireless systems listed above. Your definitions should provide compelling reasons why such systems have been proposed, what type of user the system is intended to serve, and what are the technical enablers and justifications given for the new systems. That is, why are the new systems emerging, and what are the compelling reasons for them? What are the target markets, applications, and eventual adoption rates being planned for?

(b) To help with (a), it is useful to determine the international or national standards bodies involved with the creation and definition of such systems. Using the library, journals, and the WWW, determine the major standards bodies involved with each of the six systems, on both a national and international level. identify the key organizations and key players who are helping to create a forum or who are providing technical leadership for each of the six systems, on each of the major continents. Describe these organizations and provide references (i.e., web address or citations in the literature) so that others can learn more about these organizations and how they work to forge the standards.

(c) Using the references found in (a) and (b), you can now begin to determine the technical issues and specifications for the emerging wireless systems. Provide detailed technical written descriptions of the various technologies which have been proposed to satisfy the broad system concepts, and provide a list of key technological attributes of each proposal. Note: In many cases, there will be multiple system proposals for each broad system concept. Describe the technical attributes of each of the competing technologies and list, in tabular form similar to Tables 1.1–1.3, how the different parts of the world are approaching these broad system concepts, and what carrier frequencies, data rates, modulation techniques, multiple access techniques, RF bandwidths, and baseband bandwidths are being proposed. Also illustrate unique or interesting technical issues surrounding the various proposals for each system concept.

CHAPTER 2

Modern Wireless Communication Systems

Since the mid 1990s, the cellular communications industry has witnessed explosive growth. Wireless communications networks have become much more pervasive than anyone could have imagined when the cellular concept was first developed in the 1960s and 1970s. As shown in Figure 2.1, the worldwide cellular and personal communication subscriber base surpassed 600 million users in late 2001, and the number of individual subscribers is projected to reach 2 billion (about 30% of the world's population) by the end of 2006! Indeed, most countries throughout the world continue to experience cellular subscription increases of 40% or more per year. The widespread adoption of wireless communications was accelerated in the mid 1990s, when governments throughout the world provided increased competition and new radio spectrum licenses for personal communications services (PCS) in the 1800–2000 MHz frequency bands.

The rapid worldwide growth in cellular telephone subscribers has demonstrated conclusively that wireless communications is a robust, viable voice and data transport mechanism. The widespread success of cellular has led to the development of newer wireless systems and standards for many other types of telecommunication traffic besides mobile voice telephone calls.

For example, next generation cellular networks are being designed to facilitate high speed data communications traffic in addition to voice calls. New standards and technologies are being implemented to allow wireless networks to replace fiber optic or copper lines between fixed points several kilometers apart (*fixed wireless access*). Similarly, wireless networks have been increasingly used as a replacement for wires within homes, buildings, and office settings through the deployment of *wireless local area networks* (WLANs). The evolving *Bluetooth* modem standard promises to replace troublesome appliance communication cords with invisible wireless connections within a person's personal workspace.

Used primarily within buildings, WLANs and Bluetooth use low power levels and generally do not require a license for spectrum use. These license-free networks provide an interesting

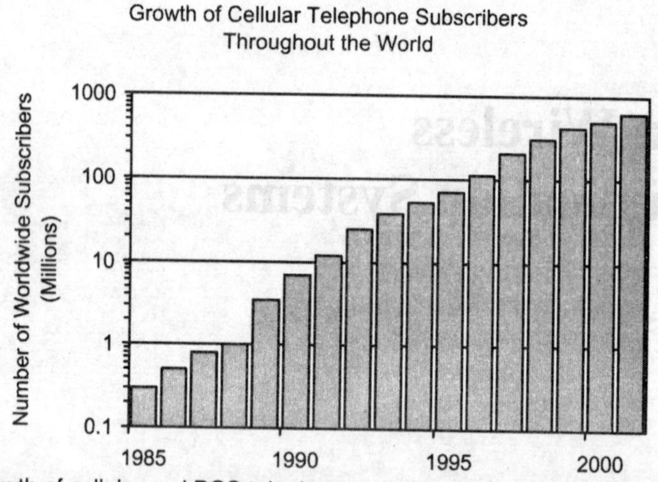

Figure 2.1 Growth of cellular and PCS telephone subscribers throughout the world.

dichotomy in the wireless market, since ad-hoc high data rate networks are being deployed by individuals within buildings without a license, whereas wireless carriers who own the spectrum licenses for mobile cellular telephone service have focused on providing outdoor voice coverage and have been slow to provide reliable in-building coverage and high data rate services to their cellular subscribers. While it is still too early to tell, it appears that the in-building wireless access market may become a huge battleground between licensed and unlicensed services, and this is prompting the architects of today's popular cellular standards to design for high data rate packet-based networking capabilities in the next generation of cellular technology.

This chapter highlights the key developments, technical details, and standards activities of the major modern wireless communications systems throughout the world. First, the state-of-the-art of the most popular cellular and PCS standards is presented, and the many competing evolutionary paths toward third generation (3G) mobile networks are described. Then, standards activities and recent developments in wireless fixed access techniques such as Local Multipoint Distribution Systems (LMDS) are presented. Finally, this chapter focuses on wireless systems and standards such as the worldwide wireless LAN (WLAN) movement and the Bluetooth standard that provide wireless connectivity across campuses to indoor users.

2.1 Second Generation (2G) Cellular Networks

Most of today's ubiquitous cellular networks use what is commonly called *second generation* or *2G* technologies which conform to the second generation cellular standards. Unlike first generation cellular systems that relied exclusively on FDMA/FDD and analog FM, second generation standards use digital modulation formats and TDMA/FDD and CDMA/FDD multiple access techniques.

The most popular second generation standards include three TDMA standards and one CDMA standard: (a) *Global System Mobile (GSM)*, which supports eight time slotted users for each 200 kHz radio channel and has been deployed widely in the cellular and PCS bands by service providers in Europe, Asia, Australia, South America, and some parts of the US (in the PCS spectrum band only) [Gar99]; (b) *Interim Standard 136 (IS-136)*, also known as North American Digital Cellular (NADC) or US Digital Cellular (USDC), which supports three time slotted users for each 30 kHz radio channel and is a popular choice for carriers in North America, South America, and Australia (in both the cellular and PCS bands); (c) *Pacific Digital Cellular (PDC)*, a Japanese TDMA standard that is similar to IS-136 with more than 50 million users; and (d) the popular 2G CDMA standard *Interim Standard 95 Code Division Multiple Access (IS-95)*, also known as *cdmaOne*, which supports up to 64 users that are orthogonally coded and simultaneously transmitted on each 1.25 MHz channel. CDMA is widely deployed by carriers in North America (in both cellular and PCS bands), as well as in Korea, Japan, China, South America, and Australia [Lib99, ch. 1], [Kim00], [Gar00].

The 2G standards mentioned above represent the first set of wireless air interface standards to rely on digital modulation and sophisticated digital signal processing in the handset and the base station. As discussed in Chapter 11, second generation systems were first introduced in the early 1990s, and evolved from the first generation of analog mobile phone systems (e.g., AMPS, ETACS, and JTACS). Today, many wireless service providers use both first generation and second generation equipment in major markets and often provide customers with subscriber units that can support multiple frequency bands and multiple air interface standards. For example, in many countries it is possible to purchase a single tri-mode cellular handset phone that supports CDMA in the cellular and PCS bands in addition to analog first generation technology in the cellular band. Such tri-mode phones are able to automatically sense and adapt to whichever standard is being used in a particular market. Figure 2.2 illustrates how the world subscriber base was divided between the major 1G and 2G technologies as of late 2001. Table 2.1 highlights the key technical specifications of the dominant GSM, CDMA, and IS-136/PDC second generation standards.

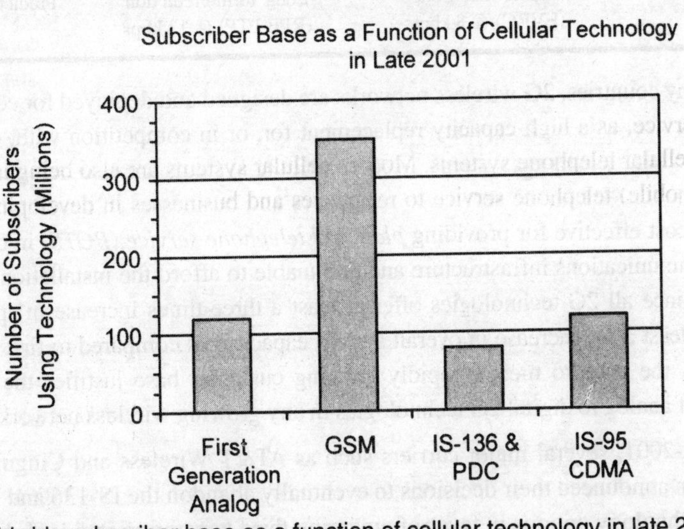

Figure 2.2 Worldwide subscriber base as a function of cellular technology in late 2001.

Table 2.1 Key Specifications of Leading 2G Technologies (adapted from [Lib99])

	cdmaOne, IS-95, ANSI J-STD-008	GSM, DCS-1900, ANSI J-STD-007	NADC, IS-54/IS-136, ANSI J-STD-011, PDC
Uplink Frequencies	824-849 MHz (US Cellular) 1850-1910 MHz (US PCS)	890-915 MHz (Europe) 1850-1910 MHz (US PCS)	800 MHz, 1500 MHz (Japan) 1850-1910 MHz (US PCS)
Downlink Frequencies	869-894 MHz (US Cellular) 1930-1990 MHz (US PCS)	935-960 MHz (Europe) 1930-1990 MHz (US PCS)	869-894 MHz (US Cellular) 1930-1990 MHz (US PCS) 800 MHz, 1500 MHz (Japan)
Duplexing	FDD	FDD	FDD
Multiple Access Technology	CDMA	TDMA	TDMA
Modulation	BPSK with Quadrature Spreading	GMSK with $BT = 0.3$	$\pi/4$ DQPSK
Carrier Separation	1.25 MHz	200 kHz	30 kHz (IS-136) (25 kHz for PDC)
Channel Data Rate	1.2288 Mchips/sec	270.833 kbps	48.6 kbps (IS-136) (42 kbps for PDC)
Voice channels per carrier	64	8	3
Speech Coding	Code Excited Linear Prediction (CELP) @ 13 kbps, Enhanced Variable Rate Codec (EVRC) @ 8 kbps	Residual Pulse Excited Long Term Prediction (RPE-LTP) @ 13 kbps	Vector Sum Excited Linear Predictive Coder (VSELP) @ 7.95 kbps

In many countries, 2G wireless networks are designed and deployed for conventional mobile telephone service, as a high capacity replacement for, or in competition with, existing older first generation cellular telephone systems. Modern cellular systems are also being installed to provide fixed (non-mobile) telephone service to residences and businesses in developing nations—this is particularly cost effective for providing *plain old telephone service (POTS)* in countries that have poor telecommunications infrastructure and are unable to afford the installation of copper wire to all homes. Since all 2G technologies offer at least a three-times increase in spectrum efficiency (and thus at least a 3X increase in overall system capacity) as compared to first generation analog technologies, the need to meet a rapidly growing customer base justifies the gradual, ongoing change out of analog to digital 2G technologies in any growing wireless network.

In mid-2001, several major carriers such as AT&T Wireless and Cingular in the US and NTT in Japan announced their decisions to eventually abandon the IS-136 and PDC standards as long term technology options in favor of emerging third generation standards based on the GSM

TDMA platform. Simultaneously, international wireless carrier Nextel announced its decision to upgrade its iDen air interface standard to support up to five times the number of current users based on a data compression methodology using Internet protocol (IP) packet data. Most other carriers throughout the world had already committed to adopting a 3G standard based on either GSM or CDMA prior to 2001. Decisions like these have set the stage for the inevitability of two universal and competing third generation (3G) cellular mobile radio technologies, one based on the philosophy and backward compatibility of GSM, and the other based on the philosophy and backward compatibility of CDMA.

2.1.1 Evolution to 2.5G Mobile Radio Networks

Since the mid 1990s, the 2G digital standards have been widely deployed by wireless carriers for cellular and PCS, even though these standards were designed before the widespread use of the Internet. Consequently, 2G technologies use circuit-switched data modems that limit data users to a single circuit-switched voice channel. Data transmissions in 2G are thus generally limited to the data throughput rate of an individual user, and this rate is of the same order of magnitude of the data rate of the designated speech coders given in Table 2.1. (As discussed in Chapter 11, each of the 2G standards specify different coding schemes and error protection algorithms for data transmissions versus voice transmissions, but the data throughput rate for computer data is approximately the same as the throughput rate for speech coded voice data in all 2G standards.) From inspection of Table 2.1, it can be seen that all 2G networks, as originally developed, only support single user data rates on the order of 10 kilobits per second, which is too slow for rapid email and Internet browsing applications. Chapter 11 presents the technical specifications of the original GSM, CDMA, and IS-136 standards which originally supported 9.6 kilobits per second transmission rates for data messages.

Even with relatively small user data rates, 2G standards are able to support limited Internet browsing and sophisticated short messaging capabilities using a circuit switched approach. *Short messaging service (SMS)* is a popular feature of GSM, and allows subscribers to send short, real-time messages to other subscribers in the same network by simply dialing a recipient's cell phone number. SMS first became popular in Europe through the dominant network of GSM service providers, and then became popular in Japan through the NTT DoCoMo PDC network. As of late 2001, SMS had not yet become widespread in the USA, since the wireless markets there are fragmented between many different types of technologies and network owners, and SMS presently only works between users of the same network.

In an effort to retrofit the 2G standards for compatibility with increased throughput data rates that are required to support modern Internet applications, new data-centric standards have been developed that can be overlaid upon existing 2G technologies. These new standards represent *2.5G* technology and allow existing 2G equipment to be modified and supplemented with new base station add-ons and subscriber unit software upgrades to support higher data rate transmissions for web browsing, e-mail traffic, mobile commerce (*m-commerce*), and location-based mobile services. The 2.5G technologies also support a popular new web browsing format language, called *Wireless*

Applications Protocol (WAP), that allows standard web pages to be viewed in a compressed format specifically designed for small, portable hand held wireless devices. Numerous other competing web page compression protocols have also been developed recently [Ald00].

It is interesting to note that Japan, one of the world's first countries to adopt commercial cellular telephony in the late 1970s, was the first country to enjoy a successful widespread mobile data service and web browser capability that preceded the introduction of WAP. NTT DoCoMo introduced its own proprietary wireless data service and Internet microbrowser technology, called *I-mode*, on its PDC network in 1998, and is currently distributing its I-mode technology to other wireless carriers throughout the world. I-mode supports games, color graphics, and interactive web page browsing using the modest 2G PDC data transmission rate of 9.6 kilobits per second. As of late 2001, DoCoMo's I-mode was supporting wireless web access for over 25 million Japanese subscribers.

The appropriate 2.5G upgrade path for a particular wireless carrier must match the original 2G technology choice made earlier by the same carrier. For example, a 2.5G upgrade solution designed for GSM must dovetail with the original GSM air interface standard [Gar99], since it would otherwise be incompatible and require wholesale equipment changes at each base station. For this reason, a wide range of 2.5G standards have been developed to allow each of the major 2G technologies (GSM, CDMA, and IS-136) to be upgraded incrementally for faster Internet data rates. Figure 2.3 illustrates the various 2.5G and 3G upgrade paths for the major 2G technologies [Tel01]. Table 2.2 describes the required changes to the network infrastructure (e.g., the base station and the switch) and the subscriber terminals (e.g., the handset) for the various upgrade options for 2.5G and 3G. The technical features of each 2.5G upgrade path are described below.

2.1.2 Evolution for 2.5G TDMA Standards

Three different upgrade paths have been developed for GSM carriers, and two of these solutions also support IS-136. The three TDMA upgrade options include: (a) High Speed Circuit Switched Data (HSCSD); (b) General Packet Radio Service (GPRS); and (c) Enhanced Data Rates for GSM Evolution (EDGE). These options provide significant improvements in Internet access speed over today's GSM and IS-136 technology and support the creation of new Internet-ready cell phones.

2.1.2.1 HSCSD for 2.5G GSM

As the name implies, High Speed Circuit Switched Data is a circuit switched technique that allows a single mobile subscriber to use consecutive user time slots in the GSM standard. That is, instead of limiting each user to only one specific time slot in the GSM TDMA standard, HSCSD allows individual data users to commandeer consecutive time slots in order to obtain higher speed data access on the GSM network. HSCSD relaxes the error control coding algorithms originally specified in the GSM standard for data transmissions and increases the available application data rate to 14,400 bps, as compared to the original 9,600 bps in the GSM specification. By using up to four consecutive time slots, HSCSD is able to provide a raw transmission rate of up to 57.6 kbps to

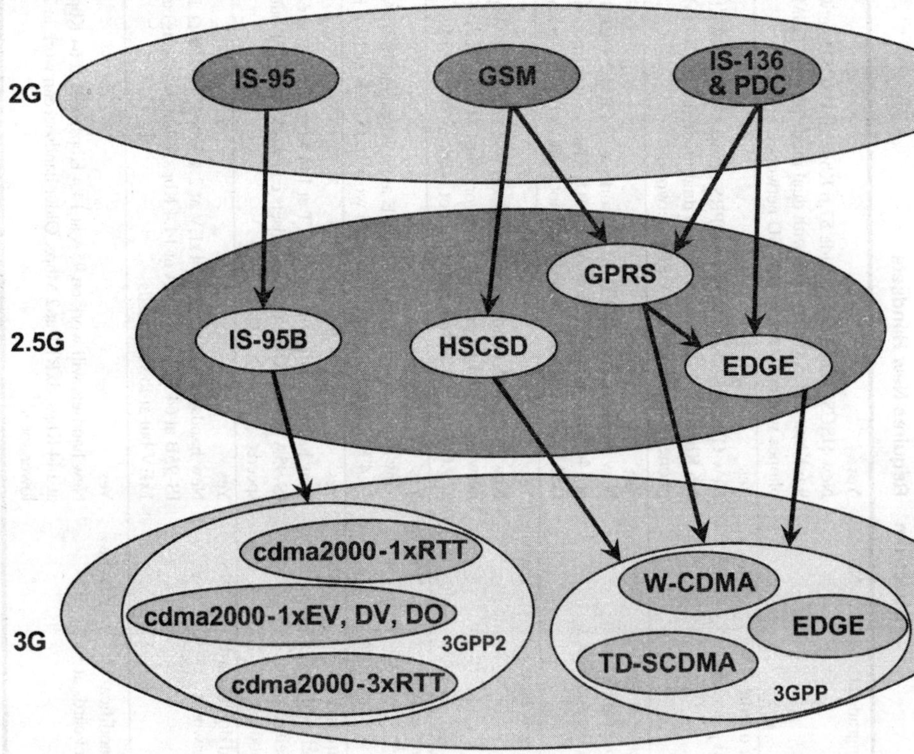

Figure 2.3 Various upgrade paths for 2G technologies.

individual users, and this enhanced data offering can be billed as a premium service by the carrier. HSCSD is ideal for dedicated streaming Internet access or real-time interactive web sessions and simply requires the service provider to implement a software change at existing GSM base stations.

2.1.2.2 GPRS for 2.5G GSM and IS-136

General Packet Radio Service is a packet-based data network, which is well suited for non-real time Internet usage, including the retrieval of email, faxes, and asymmetric web browsing, where the user downloads much more data than it uploads on the Internet. Unlike HSCSD, which dedicates circuit switched channels to specific users, GPRS supports multi-user network sharing of individual radio channels and time slots. Thus, GPRS can support many more users than HSCSD, but in a bursty manner. Similar to the Cellular Digital Packet Data (CDPD) standard developed for the North American AMPS systems in the early 1990s (see Chapter 10), the GPRS standard provides a packet network on dedicated GSM or IS-136 radio channels. GPRS retains the original modulation formats specified in the original 2G TDMA standards, but uses a completely redefined air interface in order to better handle packet data access. GPRS subscriber units are automatically instructed to tune to dedicated GPRS radio channels and particular time slots for "always on" access to the network.

Table 2.2 Current and Emerging 2.5G and 3G Data Communication Standards

Wireless Data Technologies	Channel BW	Duplex	Infrastructure change	Requires New Spectrum	Requires New Handsets
HSCSD	200 KHz	FDD	Requires software upgrade at base station.	No	Yes New HSCSD handsets provide 57.6 Kbps on HSCSD networks, and 9.6 Kbps on GSM networks with dual mode phones. GSM-only phones will not work in HSCSD networks.
GPRS	200 KHz	FDD	Requires new packet overlay including routers and gateways.	No	Yes New GPRS handsets work on GPRS networks at 171.2 Kbps, 9.6 Kbps on GSM networks with dual mode phones. GSM-only phones will not work in GPRS networks.
EDGE	200 KHz	FDD	Requires new transceiver at base station. Also, software upgrades to the base station controller and base station.	No	Yes New handsets work on EDGE networks at 384 Kbps, GPRS networks at 144 Kbps, and GSM networks at 9.6 Kbps with tri-mode phones. GSM and GPRS-only phones will not work in EDGE networks.
W-CDMA	5 MHz	FDD	Requires completely new base stations.	Yes	Yes New W-CDMA handsets will work on W-CDMA at 2 Mbps, EDGE networks at 384 Kbps, GPRS networks at 144 Kbps, GSM networks at 9.6 Kbps. Older handsets will not work in W-CDMA.
IS-95B	1.25 MHz	FDD	Requires new software in base station controller.	No	Yes New handsets will work on IS-95B at 64 Kbps and IS-95A at 14.4 Kbps. CdmaOne phones can work in IS-95B at 14.4 Kbps.
cdma2000 1xRTT	1.25 MHz	FDD	Requires new software in backbone and new channel cards at base station. Also need to build a new packet service node.	No	Yes New handsets will work on 1xRTT at 144 Kbps, IS-95B at 64 Kbps, IS-95A at 14.4 Kbps. Older handsets can work in 1xRTT but at lower speeds.
cdma2000 IxEV (DO and DV)	1.25 MHz	FDD	Requires software and digital card upgrade on 1xRTT networks.	No	Yes New handsets will work on 1xEV at 2.4 Mbps, 1xRTT at 144 Kbps, IS-95B at 64 Kbps, IS-95A at 14.4 Kbps. Older handsets can work in 1xEV but at lower speeds.
cdma2000 3xRTT	3.75 MHz	FDD	Requires backbone modifications and new channel cards at base station.	Maybe	Yes New handsets will work on 95A at 14.4 Kbps, 95B at 64 Kbps, 1xRTT at 144 Kbps, 3xRTT at 2 Mbps. Older handsets can work in 3X but at lower speeds.

When all eight time slots of a GSM radio channel are dedicated to GPRS, an individual user is able to achieve as much as 171.2 kbps (eight time slots multiplied by 21.4 kbps of raw uncoded data throughput). Applications are required to provide their own error correction schemes as part of the carried data payload in GPRS. As is the case for any packet network, the data throughput experienced by an individual GPRS user decreases substantially as more users attempt to use the network or as propagation conditions become poor for particular users. Just as in the case of CDPD, and as described in Table 2.2, implementation of GPRS merely requires the GSM operator to install new routers and Internet gateways at the base station, along with new software that redefines the base station air interface standard for GPRS channels and time slots—no new base station RF hardware is required.

It is worth noting that GPRS was originally designed to provide a packet data access overlay solely for GSM networks, but at the request of North American IS-136 operators (see UWC-136 Air Interface in Table 2.3), GPRS was extended to include both TDMA standards. As of late 2001, GPRS has been installed in markets serving over 100 million subscribers, and is poised to be the most popular near-term packet data solution for 2G TDMA-based technologies. The dedicated peak 21.4 kbps per channel data rate specified by GPRS works well with both GSM and IS-136 and has successfully been implemented.

2.1.2.3 EDGE for 2.5G GSM and IS-136

EDGE, which stands for Enhanced Data rates for GSM (or Global) Evolution is a more advanced upgrade to the GSM standard, and requires the addition of new hardware and software at existing base stations. Interestingly, EDGE was developed from the desire of both GSM and IS-136 operators to have a common technology path for eventual 3G high speed data access, but the initial impetus came from the GSM user community.

EDGE introduces a new digital modulation format, 8-PSK (octal phase shift keying), which is used in addition to GSM's standard GMSK modulation. EDGE allows for nine different (autonomously and rapidly selectable) air interface formats, known as *multiple modulation and coding schemes* (MCS), with varying degrees of error control protection. Each MCS state may use either GMSK (low data rate) or 8-PSK (high data rate) modulation for network access, depending on the instantaneous demands of the network and the operating conditions. Because of the higher data rates and relaxed error control covering in many of the selectable air interface formats, the coverage range is smaller in EDGE than in HSDRC or GPRS. EDGE is sometimes referred to as Enhanced GPRS, or EGPRS [Noe01].

EDGE uses the higher order 8-PSK modulation and a family of MCSs for each GSM radio channel time slot, so that each user connection may adaptively determine the best MCS setting for the particular radio propagation conditions and data access requirements of the user. This adaptive capability to select the "best" air interface is called *incremental redundancy*, whereby packets are transmitted first with maximum error protection and maximum data rate throughput, and then subsequent packets are transmitted with less error protection (usually using punctured convolutional codes) and less throughput, until the link has an unacceptable outage or delay. Rapid feedback between the base station and subscriber unit then restores the previous acceptable air interface state, which is presumably at an acceptable level but with minimum required coding and minimum bandwidth and power drain. Incremental redundancy ensures that the radio link for each user will quickly reach a condition that uses the minimum amount of overhead, thereby providing acceptable link quality for each user while maximizing user capacity on the network.

When EDGE uses 8-PSK modulation without any error protection, and all eight times slots of a GSM radio channel are dedicated to a single user, a raw peak throughput data rate of 547.2 kbps can be provided. In practice, the slotting schemes used in EDGE, when combined with practical network contention issues and error control coding requirements, limits practical raw data rates to about 384 kilobits per second for a single dedicated user on a single GSM channel. By combining the capacity of different radio channels (e.g., using *multicarrier transmissions*), EDGE can provide up to several megabits per second of data throughput to individual data users.

2.1.3 IS-95B for 2.5G CDMA

Unlike the several GSM and IS-136 evolutionary paths to high speed data access, CDMA (often called *cdmaOne*) has a single upgrade path for eventual 3G operation. The interim data solution for CDMA is called IS-95B. Like GPRS, IS-95B is already being deployed worldwide, and provides high speed packet and circuit switched data access on a common CDMA radio channel by dedicating multiple orthogonal user channels (Walsh functions) for specific users and specific purposes. As seen in Chapter 11, each IS-95 CDMA radio channel supports up to 64 different user channels. The original IS-95 throughput rate specification of 9600 bps was not implemented in practice, but was improved to the current rate of 14,400 bps as specified in IS-95A. The 2.5G CDMA solution, IS-95B, supports *medium data rate* (MDR) service by allowing a dedicated user to command up to eight different user Walsh codes simultaneously and in parallel for an instantaneous throughput of 115.2 kbps per user (8 × 14.4 kbps). However, only about 64 kbps of practical throughput is available to a single user in IS-95B due to the slotting techniques of the air interface.

IS-95B also specifies hard handoff procedures that allow subscriber units to search different radio channels in the network without instruction from the switch so that subscriber units can rapidly tune to different base stations to maintain link quality. Prior to IS-95B, the link quality experienced by each subscriber had to be reported back to the switch through the serving base station several hundreds of times per second, and at the appropriate moment, the switch would initiate a soft-handoff between the subscriber and candidate base stations. The new hard handoff capability of IS-95B is more efficient for multiple channel systems now being used in today's more congested CDMA markets [Lib99], [Kim00], [Gar00], [Tie01].

2.2 Third Generation (3G) Wireless Networks

3G systems promise unparalleled wireless access in ways that have never been possible before. Multi-megabit Internet access, communications using Voice over Internet Protocol (VoIP), voice-activated calls, unparalleled network capacity, and ubiquitous "always-on" access are just some of the advantages being touted by 3G developers. Companies developing 3G equipment envision users having the ability to receive live music, conduct interactive web sessions, and have simultaneous voice and data access with multiple parties at the same time using a single mobile handset, whether driving, walking, or standing still in an office setting.

As mentioned in Chapter 1, and described in detail in [Lib99], the International Telecommunications Union (ITU) formulated a plan to implement a global frequency band in the 2000 MHz range that would support a single, ubiquitous wireless communication standard for all countries throughout the world. This plan, called International Mobile Telephone 2000 (IMT-2000), has been successful in helping to cultivate active debate and technical analysis for new high speed mobile telephone solutions when compared to 2G. However, as can be seen in Figures 2.2 and 2.3, the hope for a single worldwide standard has not materialized, as the worldwide user community remains split between two camps: GSM/IS-136/PDC and CDMA.

The eventual 3G evolution for 2G CDMA systems leads to cdma2000. Several variants of CDMA 2000 are currently being developed, but they all are based on the fundamentals of IS-95 and IS-95B technologies. The eventual 3G evolution for GSM, IS-136, and PDC systems leads to Wideband CDMA (W-CDMA), also called Universal Mobile Telecommunications Service (UMTS). W-CDMA is based on the network fundamentals of GSM, as well as the merged versions of GSM and IS-136 through EDGE. It is fair to say that these two major 3G technology camps, cdma2000 and W-CDMA, will remain popular throughout the early part of the 21st century.

Table 2.3 illustrates the primary worldwide proposals that were submitted for IMT-2000 in 1998. Since 1998, many standards proposals have capitulated and joined with either the cdma2000 or UMTS (W-CDMA) camps. Commercial grade 3G equipment is expected to be available in the 2002-2003 time frame. Two good Internet sources for up-to-the-minute 3G developments can be found at GSM World (*www.gsmworld.com*) and the CDMA Developers Group (*www.cdg.org*). The ITU IMT-2000 standards organizations are currently separated into two major organizations reflecting the two 3G camps: 3GPP (3G Partnership Project for Wideband CDMA standards based on backward compatibility with GSM and IS-136/PDC) and 3GPP2 (3G Partnership Project for cdma2000 standards based on backward compatibility with IS-95).

Countries throughout the world are currently determining new radio spectrum bands to accommodate the 3G networks that will likely be deployed in the 2004-2005 time frame. ITU's 2000 World Radio Conference established the 2500–2690 MHz, 1710–1885 MHz, and 806–960 MHZ bands as candidates for 3G. In the US, additional spectrum in the upper UHF television bands near 700 MHz is also being considered for 3G. Given the economic downturn of the telecommunications industry during 2001, many governments throughout the world, including the US, had postponed their 3G auctions and spectrum decisions as of late 2001.

Some European governments, however, auctioned off radio spectrum for 3G well before the telecommunications industry depression of 2001. The sale price of the spectrum was astounding! England's first ever spectrum auction netted $35.5 Billion USD in April 2000 for five nationwide 3G licenses. Germany's 3G auction generated $46 Billion USD later the same year, for four competing nationwide licenses [Buc00, pp. 32-36.].

Table 2.3 Leading IMT-2000 Candidate Standards as of 1998 (adapted from [Lib99])

Air Interface	Mode of Operation	Duplexing Method	Key Features
cdma2000 US TIA TR45.5	Multi-Carrier and Direct Spreading DS-CDMA a $N = 1.2288$ Mcps with $N = 1, 3, 6, 9, 12$	FDD and TDD Modes	• Backward compatibility with IS-95A and IS-95B. Downlink can be implemented using either Multi-Carrier or Direct Spreading. Uplink can support a simultaneous combination of Multi-Carrier or Direct Spreading • Auxiliary carriers to help with downlink channel estimation in forward link beamforming.
UTRA (UMTS Terrestrial Radio Access) ETSI SMG2	DS_CDMA at Rates of $N \times 0.960$ Mcps with $N = 4, 8, 16$	FDD and TDD Modes	• Wideband DS_CDMA System. • Backward compatibility with GSM/DCS-1900. • Up to 2.048 Mbps on Downlink in FDD Mode. • Minimum forward channel bandwidth of 5 MHz. • The collection of proposed standards represented here each exhibit unique features, but support a common set of chip rates, 10 ms frame structure, with 16 slots per frame. • Connection-dedicated pilot bits assist in downlink beamforming.
W-CDMA/NA (Wideband CDMA) North America) USA T1P1-ATIS			
W-CDMA/Japan (Wideband CDMA) Japan ARIB			
CDMA II South Korea TTA			
WIMS/W-CDMA USA TIA TR46.1			
CDMA I South Korea TTA	DS-CDMA at $N \times 0.9216$ Mcps with $N = 1, 4, 16$	FDD and TDD Modes	• Up to 512 kbps per spreading code, code aggregation up to 2.048 Mbps.
UWC-136 (Universal Wireless Communications Consortium) USA TIA TR 45.3	TDMA - Up to 722.2 kbps (Outdoor/Vehicular), Up to 5.2 Mbps (Indoor Office)	FDD (Outdoor/ Vehicular), TDD (Indoor Office)	• Backward compatibility and upgrade path for both IS-136 and GSM. • Fits into existing IS-136 and GSM. • Explicit plans to support adaptive antenna technology.
TD-SCDMA China Academy of Telecommunication Technology (CATT)	DS-CDMA 1.1136 Mcps	TDD	• RF channel bit rate up to 2.227 Mbps. • Use of smart antenna technology is fundamental (but not strictly required) in TD-SCMA.
DECT ETSI Project (EP) DECT	1150-3456 kbps TDMA	TDD	• Enhanced version of 2G DECT technology.

2.2.1 3G W-CDMA (UMTS)

The Universal Mobile Telecommunications System (UMTS) is a visionary air interface standard that has evolved since late 1996 under the auspices of the European Telecommunications Standards Institute (ETSI). European carriers, manufacturers, and government regulators collectively developed the early versions of UMTS as a competitive open air-interface standard for third generation wireless telecommunications.

UMTS was submitted by ETSI to ITU's IMT-2000 body in 1998 for consideration as a world standard. At that time, UMTS was known as UMTS Terrestrial Radio Access (UTRA), as shown in Table 2.3, and was designed to provide a high capacity upgrade path for GSM. Around the turn of the century, several other competing wideband CDMA (W-CDMA) proposals agreed to merge into a single W-CDMA standard, and this resulting W-CDMA standard is now called UMTS.

UMTS, or W-CDMA, assures backward compatibility with the second generation GSM, IS-136, and PDC TDMA technologies, as well as all 2.5G TDMA technologies. The network structure and bit level packaging of GSM data is retained by W-CDMA, with additional capacity and bandwidth provided by a new CDMA air interface. Figure 2.3 illustrates how the various 2G and 2.5G TDMA technologies will evolve into a unified W-CDMA standard. Today, W-CDMA is the primary focus of the 3GPP world standard body, and while ETSI remains the organizational body that coordinates the W-CDMA standards effort, W-CDMA development now involves leading manufacturers, carriers, engineers, and regulators from throughout the world within the 3GPP community. The 3GPP standards body is developing W-CDMA for both wide area mobile cellular coverage (using FDD) as well as indoor cordless type applications (using TDD).

The 3G W-CDMA air interface standard had been designed for "always-on" packet-based wireless service, so that computers, entertainment devices, and telephones may all share the same wireless network and be connected to the Internet, anytime, anywhere. W-CDMA will support packet data rates up to 2.048 Mbps per user (if the user is stationary), thereby allowing high quality data, multimedia, streaming audio, streaming video, and broadcast-type services to consumers. Future versions of W-CDMA will support stationary user data rates in excess of 8 Mbps. W-CDMA provides public and private network features, as well as videoconferencing and *virtual home entertainment* (VHE). W-CDMA designers contemplate that broadcasting, mobile commerce (m-commerce), games, interactive video, and virtual private networking will be possible throughout the world, all from a small portable wireless device.

W-CDMA requires a minimum spectrum allocation of 5 MHz, which is an important distinction from the other 3G standards. Although W-CDMA is designed to provide backward compatibility and interoperability for all GSM, IS-136/PDC, GPRS, and EDGE switching equipment and applications, it is clear that the wider air interface bandwidth of W-CDMA requires a complete change out of the RF equipment at each base station. With W-CDMA, data rates from as low as 8 kbps to as high as 2 Mbps will be carried simultaneously on a single W-CDMA 5 MHz radio channel, and each channel will be able to support between 100 and 350 simultaneous voice calls at once, depending on antenna sectoring, propagation conditions, user velocity, and antenna polarizations. As shown in Table 2.3, W-CDMA employs variable/selectable direct sequence spread spectrum chip rates that can exceed 16 Megachips per second per user. A common rule of thumb is that W-CDMA will provide at least a six times increase in spectral efficiency over GSM when compared on a system wide basis [Buc00].

Because W-CDMA will require expensive new base station equipment, the installation of W-CDMA will likely be slow and gradual throughout the world. Thus, the evolutionary path to 3G will require dual mode or tri-mode cell phones that can automatically switch between the incumbent 2G TDMA technology, EDGE, or W-CDMA service where its available. By 2010, it is likely that W-CDMA will be fully installed, eliminating the need for backward compatibility with GSM/GPRS, IS-136, PDC, and EDGE.

2.2.2 3G cdma2000

The cdma2000 vision provides a seamless and evolutionary high data rate upgrade path for current users of 2G and 2.5G CDMA technology, using a building block approach that centers on the original 2G CDMA channel bandwidth of 1.25 MHz per radio channel. Based upon the original IS-95 and IS-95A (cdmaOne) CDMA standards, as well as the 2.5G IS-95B air interface, the cdma2000 3G standard allows wireless carriers to introduce a family of new high data rate Internet access capabilities in a gradual manner within existing systems, while assuring that such upgrades maintain backward compatibility with existing cdmaOne and IS-95B subscriber equipment. Thus, current CDMA operators may seamlessly and selectively introduce 3G capabilities at each cell without having to change out entire base stations or reallocate spectrum [Tie01], [Gar00], [Kim00].

The cdma2000 standard is being developed under the auspices of working group 45 of the Telecommunications Industry Association (TIA) of the US, and involves the participation of the international technical community through the 3GPP2 working group. The first 3G CDMA air interface, cdma2000 1xRTT, implies that a single 1.25 MHz radio channel is used (e.g. 1X simply implies one times the original cdmaOne channel bandwidth, or, put another way, a multicarrier mode with only one carrier). Within the ITU IMT-2000 body, cdma2000 1xRTT is also known as G3G-MC-CDMA-1X. The initials MC stand for multicarrier, and the initials RTT stand for *Radio Transmission Technology*, language suggested by the IMT-2000 body. For convenience, it is common to omit the MC and RTT designations, and simply refer to the standard as cdma2000 1X.

cdma2000 1X supports an instantaneous data rate of up to 307 kbps for a user in packet mode, and yields typical throughput rates of up to 144 kbps per user, depending on the number of users, the velocity of a user, and the propagation conditions. cdma2000 1X can also support up to twice as many voice users as the 2G CDMA standard, and provides the subscriber unit with up to two times the standby time for longer lasting battery life. As seen in Table 2.3, cdma2000 is being developed for both FDD (mobile radio) and TDD (in-building cordless) applications.

The improvements in cdma2000 1X over 2G and 2.5G CDMA systems are gained through the use of rapidly adaptable baseband signaling rates and chipping rates for each user (provided through incremental redundancy) and multi-level keying within the same gross framework of the original cdmaOne standard. No additional RF equipment is needed to enhance performance—the changes are all made in software or in baseband hardware. As can be seen in Table 2.2, to upgrade from 2G CDMA to cdma2000 1X, a wireless carrier merely needs to purchase new backbone software and new channel cards at the base station, without having to change out RF system components at the base station.

cdma2000 1xEV is an evolutionary advancement for CDMA originally developed by Qualcomm, Inc. as a proprietary *high data rate* (HDR) packet standard to be overlaid upon existing IS-95, IS-95B, and cdma2000 networks. Qualcomm later modified its HDR standard to be compatible with W-CDMA as well, and in August 2001, ITU recognized cdma2000 1xEV as part of IMT-2000. cdma2000 1xEV provides CDMA carriers with the option of installing radio channels with *data only* (cdma2000 1xEV-DO) or with *data and voice* (cdma2000 1xEV-DV). Using cdma2000 1xEV technology, individual 1.25 MHz channels may be installed in CDMA base stations to provide specific high speed packet data access within selected cells. The cdma2000 1xEV-DO option dedicates the radio channel strictly to data users, and supports greater than 2.4 Mbps of instantaneous high-speed packet throughput per user on a particular CDMA channel, although actual user data rates are typically much lower and are highly dependent upon the number of users, the propagation conditions, and vehicle speed. Typical users may experience throughputs on the order of several hundred kilobits per second, which is sufficient to support web browsing, email access, and m-commerce applications. cdma2000 1xEV-DV supports both voice and data users, and can offer usable data rates up to 144 kilobits per second with about twice as many voice channels as IS-95B.

The ultimate 3G solution for CDMA relies upon multicarrier techniques that gang adjacent cdmaOne radio channels together for increased bandwidth. The cdma2000 3xRTT standard uses three adjacent 1.25 MHz radio channels that are used together to provide instantaneous packet data throughput speeds in excess of 2 Mbps per user, although actual throughput depends upon cell loading, vehicle speed, and propagation conditions. Three non-adjacent radio channels may be operated simultaneously and in parallel as individual 1.25 MHz channels (in which case no new RF hardware is required at the base station), or adjacent channels may be combined into a single 3.75 MHz super channel (in which case new RF hardware is required at the base station). With peak user data rates in excess of 2 Mbps, it is clear that cdma2000 3X has a very similar user data rate throughput goal when compared to W-CDMA (UMTS). Advocates of cdma2000 claim their standard gives a wireless service provider a much more seamless and less expensive upgrade path when compared to W-CDMA, since cdma2000 allows the same spectrum, bandwidth, RF equipment, and air interface framework to be used at each base station as the 3G upgrades are introduced over time.

2.2.3 3G TD-SCDMA

In China, GSM is the most popular wireless air interface standard, and the wireless subscriber growth in China is unmatched anywhere in the world. For example, in late 2001 more than eight million cell phone subscribers were added in just one month in China alone! Given the huge potential market for wireless services in China, and China's desire to craft its own wireless vision, The China Academy of Telecommunications Technology (CATT) and Siemens Corporation jointly submitted an IMT-2000 3G standard proposal in 1998, based on Time Division-Synchronous Code Division Multiple Access (TD-SCDMA). This proposal was adopted by ITU as one of the 3G options in late 1999.

TD-SCDMA relies on the existing core GSM infrastructure and allows a 3G network to evolve through the addition of high data rate equipment at each GSM base station. TD-SCDMA combines TDMA and TDD techniques to provide a data-only overlay in an existing GSM network. Up to 384 kbps of packet data is provided to data users in TD-SCDMA [TD-SCDMA Forum]. The radio channels in TD-SCDMA are 1.6 MHz in bandwidth and rely on smart antennas, spatial filtering, and joint detection techniques to yield several times more spectrum efficiency than GSM. A 5 millisecond frame is used in TD-SCDMA, and this frame is subdivided into seven time slots which are flexibly assigned to either a single high data rate user or several slower users. By using TDD, different time slots within a single frame on a single carrier frequency are used to provide both forward channel and reverse channel transmissions. For the case of asynchronous traffic demand, such as when a user downloads a file, the forward link will require more bandwidth than the reverse link, and thus more time slots will be dedicated to providing forward link traffic than for providing reverse link traffic. TD-SCDMA proponents claim that the TDD feature allows this 3G standard to be very easily and inexpensively added to existing GSM systems.

2.3 Wireless Local Loop (WLL) and LMDS

The rapid growth of the Internet has created a concurrent demand for broadband Internet and computer access from businesses and homes throughout the world. Particularly in developing nations where there is inadequate telecommunications backbone infrastructure, there is a tremendous need for inexpensive, reliable, rapidly deployable broadband connectivity that can bring individuals and enterprises into the information age. In fact, as voice over Internet protocols (VoIP) become prevalent, it is quite conceivable that a single broadband Internet connection could someday provide all of the needed telecommunications services, including telephone service, television, radio, fax, and Internet, for a home or business customer.

Fixed wireless equipment is extremely well suited for rapidly deploying a broadband connection in many instances, and this approach is steadily becoming more popular for providing "last mile" broadband local loop access, as well as for emergency or redundant point-to-point or point-to-multipoint private networks.

Unlike mobile cellular telephone systems described earlier in this chapter, fixed wireless communication systems are able to take advantage of the very well-defined, time-invariant nature of the propagation channel between the fixed transmitter and fixed receiver. Furthermore, modern fixed wireless systems are usually assigned microwave or millimeter radio frequencies in the 28 GHz band and higher, which is greater than ten times the carrier frequency of 3G terrestrial cellular telephone networks. At these higher frequencies, the wavelengths are extremely small, which in turn allows very high gain directional antennas to be fabricated in small physical form factors. At higher frequencies, too, more bandwidth can be easily used. As we see in later chapters, high gain antennas have spatial filter properties that can reject multipath signals that arrive from directions other than the desired line-of-sight (LOS), and this in turn supports the transmission of very wide bandwidth signals (on the order of tens or hundreds of megabits per second) without distortion. Also, since the carrier frequencies of these fixed wireless access terminals are so high, the radio channel behaves much like an optical channel—if you can see an antenna, you can successfully communicate to it! Conversely, if you cannot see the antenna, you will be unable to communicate with it. Thus, fixed wireless networks at very high microwave frequencies are only viable where there are no obstructions, such as in a relatively flat suburban or rural setting.

Microwave wireless links can be used to create a wireless local loop (WLL) such as the one shown in Figure 2.4. As we see in Chapter 10, the local loop can be thought of as the "last mile" of the telecommunication network that resides between the central office (CO) and the individual homes and businesses in close proximity to the CO. In most developed countries, copper or fiber optic cable already has been installed to residences and businesses. However, in many developing nations, cable is too expensive or can take months or years to install. Wireless equipment, on the other hand, can usually be deployed in just a couple of hours. An additional benefit of WLL technology is that once the wireless equipment is paid for, there are no additional costs for transport between the CO and the customer premises equipment (CPE), whereas buried cables often must be leased from a service provider or utility company on a monthly basis. It is possible that WLL systems could compete with copper-wire based Digital Subscriber Loop (DSL) technologies that are rapidly proliferating [Sta99].

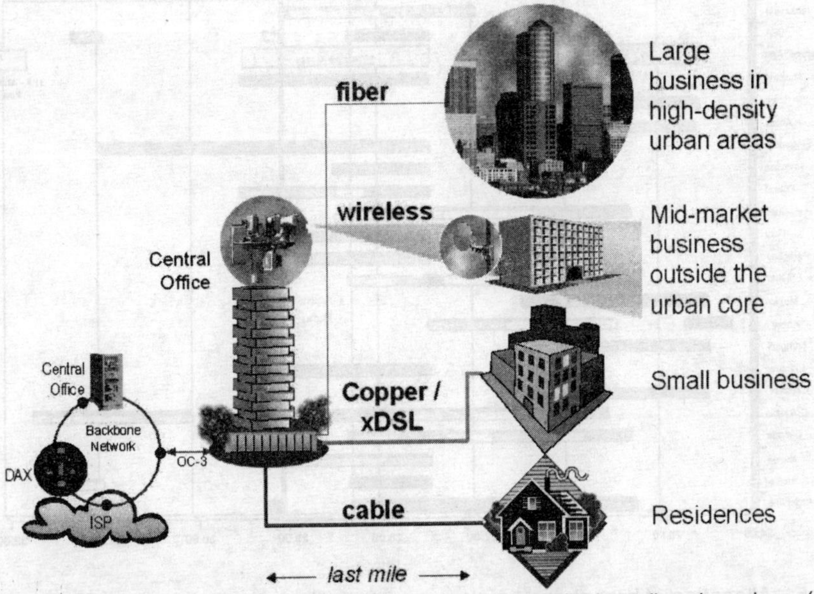

Figure 2.4 Example of the emerging applications and markets for broadband services. (Courtesy of Harris Corporation, ©1999, all rights reserved.)

Governments throughout the world have realized that WLL could greatly improve the efficiency of their citizens while stimulating competition that could lead to improved telecommunications services. A vast array of new services and applications have been proposed and are in the early stages of commercialization. These services include the concept of Local Multipoint Distribution Service (LMDS), which provides broadband telecommunications access in the local exchange [Cor97], [And98], [Xu00].

In 1998, 1300 MHz of unused spectrum in the 27–31 GHz band was auctioned by the US government to support LMDS. Similar auctions have been held in other countries around the world. Figure 2.5 illustrates various spectrum allocations made by countries throughout the world. Note that most LMDS allocations share frequencies with the Teledesic band which was approved by the ITU World Radio Conference for broadband satellite systems. The Teledesic band was originally established for the Motorola Iridium System, whose spectrum was later merged into the Teledesic system. Ironically, as of late 2001, broadband low earth orbit (LEO) satellite services were not yet commercially viable.

To gain a perspective of the enormous amount of bandwidth that is available for fixed wireless services such as LMDS, and how such licenses represent an unprecedented opportunity for wireless carriers, consider Figure 2.6. The figure compares the total spectrum bandwidths of various spectrum offerings for different wireless communication services in the United States from 1983 through 1998. Figure 2.6 also shows the tremendous amount of spectrum in the 59–64 GHz range that is earmarked for unlicensed WLAN use.

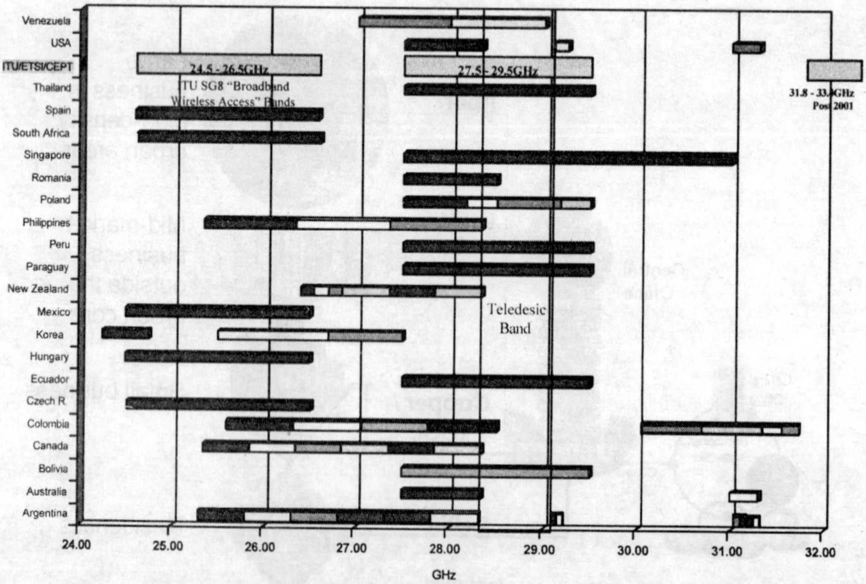

Figure 2.5 Allocation of broadband wireless spectrum throughout the world. (Courtesy of Ray W. Nettleton and reproduced by permission of Formus Communications.)

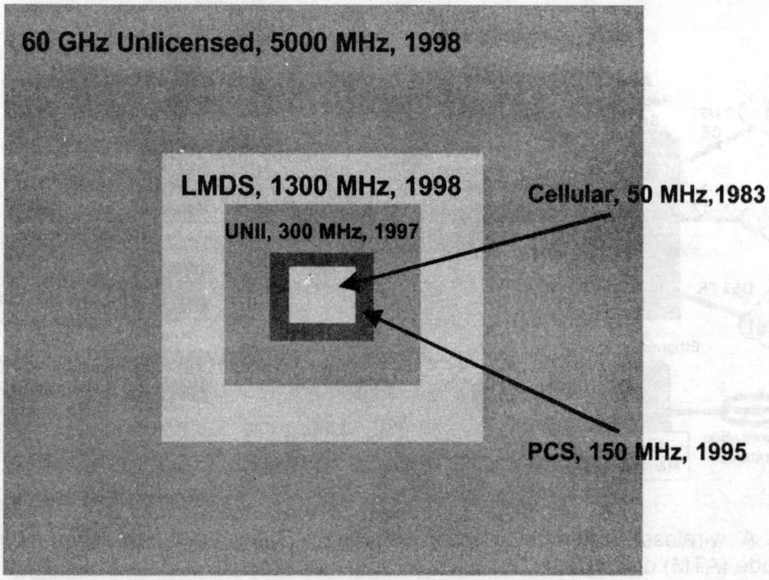

- A voice channel occupies ≈ 10 kHz of spectrum.
- A TV channel occupies ≈ 5 MHz of spectrum.

Figure 2.6 Comparison of spectrum allocations for various US wireless communications services. The areas of the rectangles are proportional to the amount of bandwidth allocated for each service.

The US LMDS band is 27.5–28.35 GHz, 29.1–29.25 GHz, and 31.075–31.225 GHz. The IEEE 802.16 Standards Committee is developing interoperability standards for fixed broadband wireless access. In Europe, a similar standard, HIPERACCESS, is being developed by a standardization committee for Broadband Radio Access Networks (BRAN) for operation in the 40.5–43.5 GHz band; it will use TDMA. Also, HIPERLINK is a very high speed short range interconnection for HIPERLANs and HIPERACCESS, up to 155 Mbps within 150 meters, and is planned to operate in the 17 GHz band in Europe.

In Figure 2.6, each rectangle has an area proportional to the amount of radio spectrum allocated to the specified service. For example, the US cellular service was first issued spectrum in 1983 and currently occupies 50 MHz of total bandwidth. The PCS service occupies 150 MHz of bandwidth, and the unlicensed National Information Infrastructure (UNII) band, discussed in Section 2.4, occupies 300 MHz. LMDS, on the other hand, was allocated a whopping 1300 MHz of bandwidth—enough spectrum to provide over 200 broadcast quality television channels or 65,000 full duplex voice channels! Yet, the revenues generated from the auction of all the US LMDS licenses was a paltry $500 million, compared to the more than $30 billion generated from the PCS auctions held three years earlier! This market difference is due to the fact that LMDS is a brand new type of service, vastly unproven, and dependent upon millimeter wave equipment that is still expensive. Nevertheless, the vast bandwidth capabilities of LMDS for WLL applications

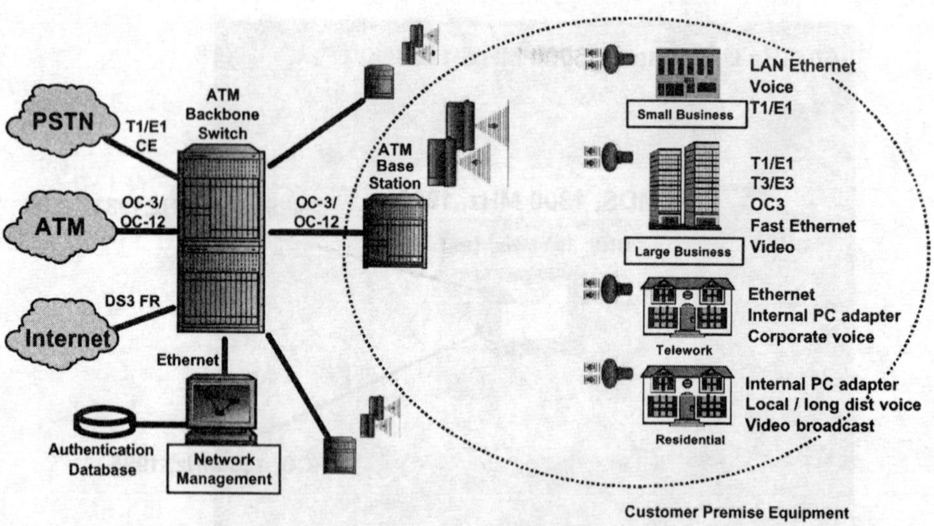

Figure 2.7 A wireless Competitive Local Exchange Carrier (CLEC) using Asynchronous Transfer Mode (ATM) distribution.

will someday prove valuable. The free spectrum available at 60 GHz provides an enormous incentive to reduce the cost of millimeter wave electronics for consumer use.

One of the most promising applications for LMDS is in a local exchange carrier (LEC) network. Figure 2.7 shows a typical network configuration, where the LEC owns a very wide bandwidth asynchronous transfer mode (ATM) or Synchronous Optical Network (SONET) backbone switch, capable of connecting hundreds of megabits per second of traffic with the Internet, the PSTN, or to its own private network. As long as a LOS path exists, LMDS will allow LECs to install wireless equipment on the premises of customers for rapid broadband connectivity without having to lease or install its own cables to the customers.

Unfortunately, finding a line-of-sight path is not the only requirement for maintaining a suitable fixed wireless connection for millimeter wave fixed wireless links. Rain, snow, and hail can create large changes in the channel gain between transmitter and receiver. In [Xu00], an extensive experimental study was conducted on various short-hop fixed wireless links in various weather conditions to determine signal loss and multipath effects due to weather impairments. In [Xu00], a novel design method was found to accurately predict received power and multipath delay for any fixed wireless link in the vicinity of surrounding buildings and in weather. Figure 2.8 from [Xu00] illustrates actual measured received power levels, as a function of precipitation, for a fixed 605 meter wireless hop operating at 38 GHz over several different days. Note that on a clear day, the received signal level is –47 dBm, and during a relatively light 40 mm/hr rain rate, the received signal level drops 4.8 dB to –51.8 dBm. However, when measured during a hail storm, the received signal level drops to –72.7 dBm, a full 25.7 dB loss from clear sky conditions!

Figure 2.9 shows how the instantaneous received power is directly a function of the instantaneous rain rate. Note that over a 41 minute period, the received signal level fluctuates by about

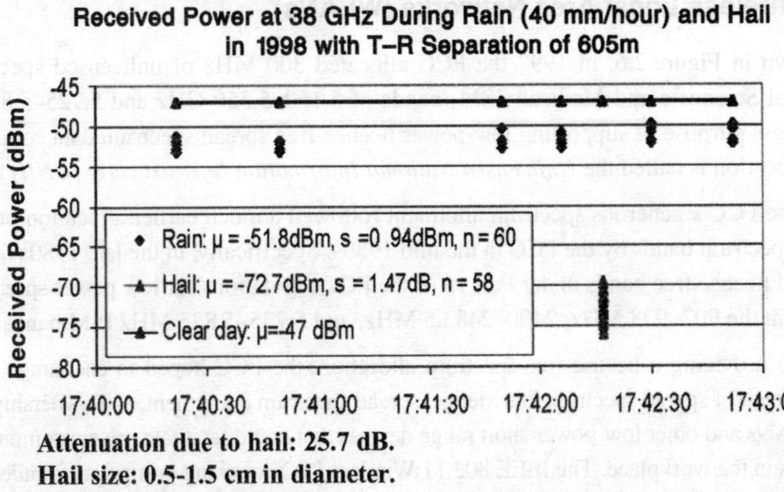

Figure 2.8 Measured received power levels over a 605 m 38 GHz fixed wireless link in clear sky, rain, and hail [from [Xu00], ©IEEE].

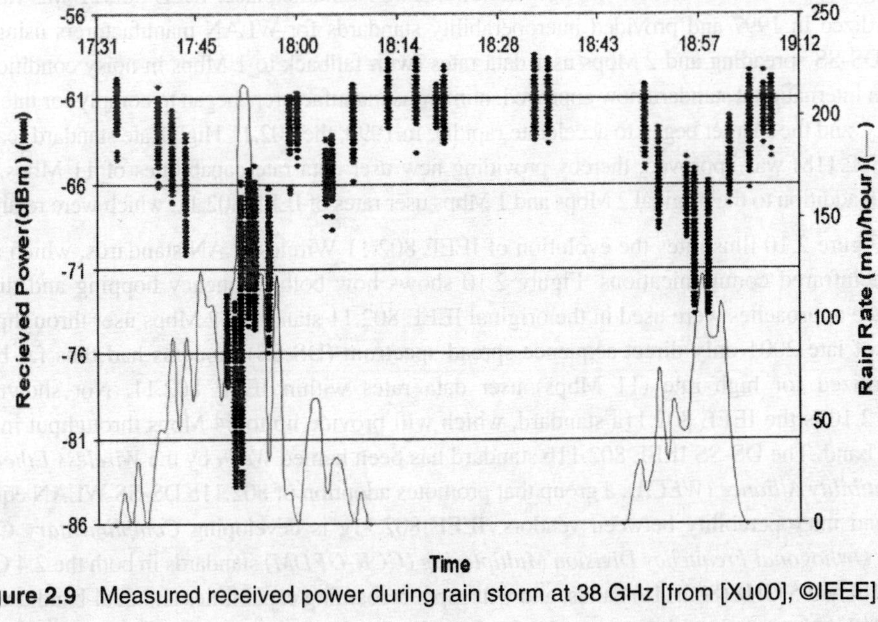

Figure 2.9 Measured received power during rain storm at 38 GHz [from [Xu00], ©IEEE].

27 dB. As shown in Chapters 4 and 5, the attenuation caused by weather effects must be statistically accounted for in the proper design of a fixed wireless network so that an outage probability can be computed based on local rain patterns and rain statistics.

2.4 Wireless Local Area Networks (WLANs)

As shown in Figure 2.6, in 1997 the FCC allocated 300 MHz of unlicensed spectrum in the Industrial Scientific and Medical (ISM) bands of 5.150–5.350 GHz and 5.725–5.825 GHz for the express purpose of supporting low-power license-free spread spectrum data communication. This allocation is called the *Unlicensed National Information Infrastructure (UNII)* band.

The FCC's generous spectrum allotment followed a much earlier allocation of unlicensed spread spectrum bands by the FCC in the mid 1980s. Specifically, in the late 1980s the FCC first provided license free bands under Part 15 of the FCC regulations for low power spread spectrum devices in the 902–928 MHz, 2400–2483.5 MHz, and 5.725–5.825 MHz ISM bands.

By providing a license-free spectrum allocation, the FCC hoped to encourage competitive development of spread spectrum knowledge, spread spectrum equipment, and ownership of individual WLANs and other low-power short range devices that could facilitate private computer communications in the workplace. The IEEE 802.11 Wireless LAN working group was founded in 1987 to begin standardization of spread spectrum WLANs for use in the ISM bands. Despite the unrestricted spectrum allocation and intense industry interest, the WLAN movement did not gain momentum until the late 1990s, when the phenomenal popularity of the Internet combined with widescale acceptance of portable, laptop computers finally caused WLAN to become an important and rapidly growing segment of the modern wireless communications marketplace. IEEE 802.11 was finally standardized in 1997 and provided interoperability standards for WLAN manufacturers using 11 Mcps DS-SS spreading and 2 Mbps user data rates (with fallback to 1 Mbps in noisy conditions). With an international standard now approved, numerous manufacturers began to comply for interoperability, and the market began to accelerate rapidly. In 1999, the 802.11 High Rate standard (called IEEE 802.11b) was approved, thereby providing new user data rate capabilities of 11 Mbps, 5.5 Mbps in addition to the original 2 Mbps and 1 Mbps user rates of IEEE 802.11, which were retained.

Figure 2.10 illustrates the evolution of IEEE 802.11 Wireless LAN standards, which also include infrared communications. Figure 2.10 shows how both frequency hopping and direct sequence approaches were used in the original IEEE 802.11 standard (2 Mbps user throughput), but as of late 2001 only direct sequence spread spectrum (DS-SS) modems had thus far been standardized for high rate (11 Mbps) user data rates within IEEE 802.11. Not shown in Figure 2.10 is the IEEE 802.11a standard, which will provide up to 54 Mbps throughput in the 5 GHz band. The DS-SS IEEE 802.11b standard has been named *Wi-Fi* by the *Wireless Ethernet Compatibility Alliance (WECA)*, a group that promotes adoption of 802.11b DS-SS WLAN equipment and interoperability between vendors. IEEE 802.11g is developing *Complimentary Code Keying Orthogonal Frequency Division Multiplexing (CCK-OFDM)* standards in both the 2.4 GHz (802.11b) and 5 GHz (802.11a) bands, and will support roaming capabilities and dual-band use for public WLAN networks, while supporting backward compatibility with 802.11b technology.

The frequency-hopping spread spectrum (FH-SS) proponents of IEEE 802.11 have formed the HomeRF standard that supports frequency hopping equipment. In 2001, HomeRF developed a 10 Mbps FH-SS standard called HomeRF 2.0. It is worth noting that both DS and FH types of

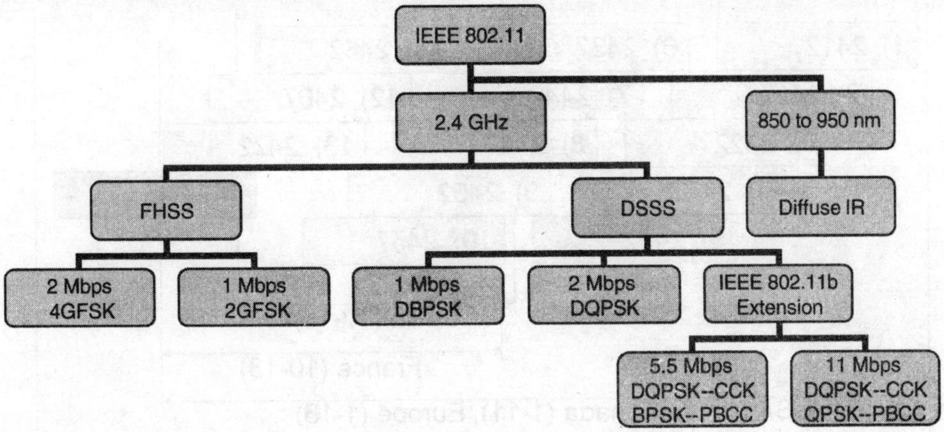

Figure 2.10 Overview of the IEEE 802.11 Wireless LAN standard.

Figure 2.11 Photographs of popular 802.11b WLAN equipment. Access points and a client card are shown on left, and PCMCIA Client card is shown on right. (Courtesy of Cisco Systems, Inc.)

WLANs must operate in the same unlicensed bands that contain cordless phones, baby monitors, Bluetooth devices, and other WLAN users. Both DS and FH vendors claim to have advantages over the other for operation in such radio environments [Are01]. Figure 2.11 shows the popular CISCO Aironet WLAN products in various form factors. Table 2.4 lists international channel allocations for DS and FH WLANs in the 2.4 GHz band.

Figure 2.12 illustrates the unique WLAN channels that are specified in the IEEE 802.11b standard for the 2400–2483.5 MHz band. All WLANs are manufactured to operate on any one of the specified channels and are assigned to a particular channel by the network operator when the WLAN system is first installed. The channelization scheme used by the network installer becomes very important for a high density WLAN installation, since neighboring access points must be separated from one another in frequency to avoid interference and significantly degraded performance. As we show in Chapter 3, *all* wireless systems must be designed with knowledge of

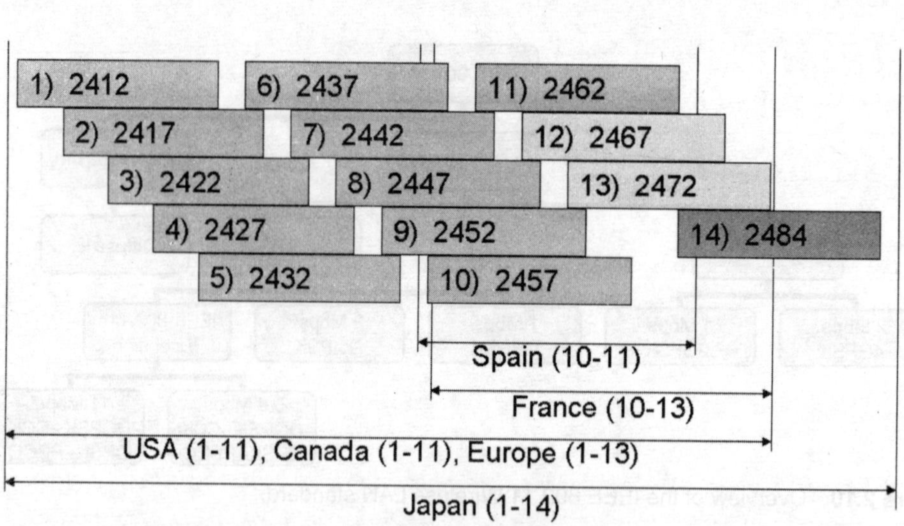

Figure 2.12 2400 MHz channelization scheme for IEEE 802.11b throughout the world.

the interference and propagation environment—prudent WLAN deployment dictates that the placement of transmitters and their frequency assignments be done systematically to minimize impact. Even though WLAN networks are designed to work in an interference-rich environment, and manufacturers may downplay the importance of planning, the fact is that the ability to measure or predict the coverage and interference effects caused by specific placements of access points can provide *orders of magnitude* of improvement in cost and end user data throughputs in a heavily loaded system. Research conducted in [Hen01] showed that the user throughput performance changes radically when access points or clients are located near an interfering transmitter or when frequency planning is not carefully conducted.

Using new computer-aided design (CAD) measurement and prediction software such as *SitePlanner* by Wireless Valley [Wir01], WLAN deployments can be done very rapidly without any trial and error. By loading the blueprint of the building or campus within a computer, propagation modeling techniques can now predict user data throughput based on radio signal strength and interference prediction algorithms [Hen01]. Figure 2.13 illustrates how the proper placements for WLAN access points can be rapidly found before ever setting foot in the building. By using an interactive computer program, the network operator can rapidly provision and plan the channelization scheme, as well as the locations of the access points, before doing an actual network deployment. In fact, email and Internet correspondence can be done to rapidly provision any physical environment. When the deployment is complete, the same CAD environment is able to archive the exact physical locations, cost and maintenance records of the network, and the specific channelization schemes for future use and modification as network growth occurs.

Figure 2.13 shows the result of coverage for an actual WLAN installation made in a large modern lecture hall on a university campus. The design was first conducted blind in less than ten minutes, over the Internet, using a CAD design product. Then, the student used his complete

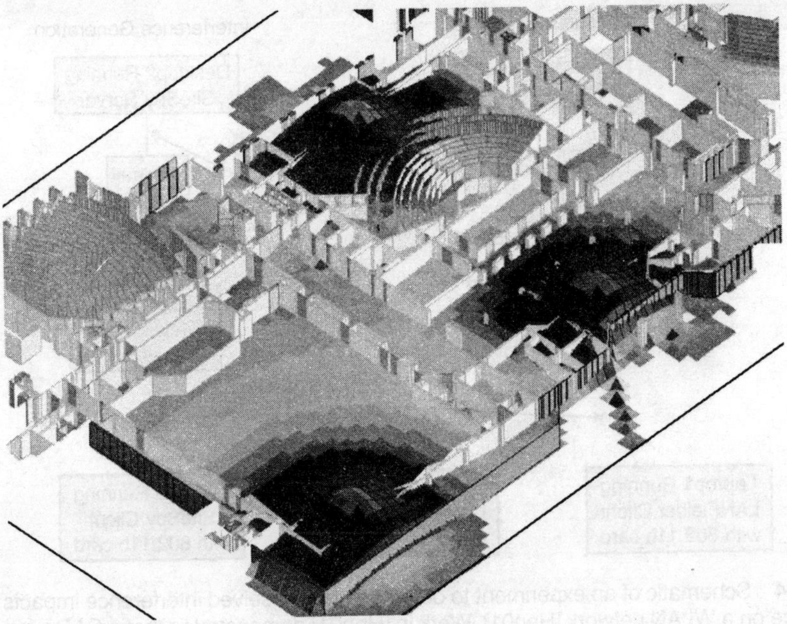

Figure 2.13 A predicted coverage plot for three access points in a modern large lecture hall. (Courtesy of Wireless Valley Communications, Inc., ©2000, all rights reserved.)

strawman design of the WLAN system and visited the building to place the access points, and verified the design by measuring network performance with the CAD product as he walked throughout the building. In under 30 minutes, the student was able to verify his strawman design and had completely measured and archived the true user throughput and delays experienced at specific locations throughout the building (due to both propagation loss and interference) with all access points in operation. During the validation field test, the student was able to keep track of actual field measurements directly on an electronic blueprint while storing all measurements, all predictions, and all system parameters (such as the channelization scheme used and physical location of access points). In [Hen01], the *SitePlanner* design environment was used with WLAN measurement products (*LANFielder* and *SiteSpy*) to enable new and efficient methods for collecting and using in-the-field network measurements for rapid network validation and tuning for optimal WLAN design. As WLANs proliferate and interference levels rise, having a design and archiving environment that can be tuned to measurements will be increasingly important. Figure 2.14 illustrates one of the measurement experiments conducted in [Hen01] in order to model the end user's throughput data as a function of signal strength and interference.

In Europe in the mid 1990s, the *High Performance Radio Local Area Network* (HIPERLAN) standard was developed to provide a similar capability to IEEE 802.11. HIPERLAN was intended to provide individual wireless LANs for computer communications and used the 5.2 GHz and the 17.1 GHz frequency bands. HIPERLAN provides asynchronous user data rates

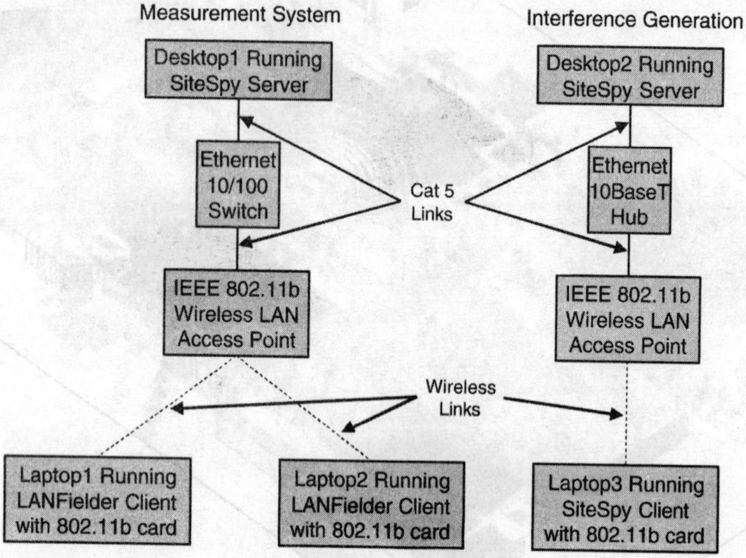

Figure 2.14 Schematic of an experiment to determine how received interference impacts end user performance on a WLAN network [Hen01]. Work in [Hen01] demonstrated that a CAD prediction and measurement environment can be used to accurately and rapidly predict true end user throughput in a multi-node network using blind prediction. Such capabilities will be vital as user densities increase in WLAN networks within buildings or campuses.

of between 1 to 20 Mbps, as well as time bounded messaging at rates of 64 kbps to 2.048 Mbps. HIPERLAN was designed to operate up to vehicle speeds of 35 km/hr, and typically provided 20 Mbps throughput at 50 m range.

Convergence in the WLAN industry appears to be on the horizon, as standard organizations in Europe, North America, and Japan begin to coordinate spectrum allocations and end user data rates. In 1997, Europe's ETSI established a standardization committee for Broadband Radio Access Networks (BRANs). The goal of BRAN is to develop a family of broadband WLAN-type protocols that allow user interoperability, covering both short range (e.g., WLAN) and long range (e.g., fixed wireless) networking. HIPERLAN/2 has emerged as the next generation European WLAN standard and will provide up to 54 Mbps of user data to a variety of networks, including the ATM backbone, IP based networks, and the UMTS core. HIPERLAN/2 is anticipated to operate in the 5 GHz band. Meanwhile, IEEE 802.11a is emerging as North America's next generation WLAN. Like HIPERLAN/2, IEEE 802.11a supports up to 54 Mbps user data rate for integration into backbone ATM, UMTS, and IP networks and will operate in the 5.15–5.35 GHz ISM band. Meanwhile, Japan's Multimedia Mobile Access Communication System (MMAC) has been developing high data rate (25 Mbps) WLAN standards for use in the 5.15–5.35 GHz band.

As wireless data rates increase and worldwide standards begin to converge, new applications for WLANs become evident. Numerous companies have been exploring a public LAN (publan) concept whereby a nationwide Wireless Internet Service Provider (WISP) builds a nationwide infrastructure of WLAN access points in selected hotels, restaurants, airports, or coffee shops, and then charges a monthly subscription fee to users who wish to have always-on Internet access in those select locations. Other recent ideas suggest that WLANs could be used to provide access for the last 100 meters into homes and businesses, in competition with fixed wireless access, and in competition with IMT-2000. Certainly, the price point for WLAN hardware is far below 3G base stations and fixed wireless millimeter wave equipment. However, the WLAN spectrum is unlicensed, and unless judicious frequency planning and radio engineering is employed, careless WLAN deployments in buildings or neighborhoods could become saturated. This again points to the need for WLAN deployment strategies that use knowledge of the interference and propagation conditions, such as shown in Figure 2.13.

It is instructive to investigate how a futuristic WLAN system might work in a typical neighborhood if WLAN access points were mounted on lamp poles along the street. Consider the neighborhood shown in Figure 2.15, where three homes are located in a heavily wooded area. In [Dur98], measurements were conducted in several homes and in different types of foliage using street-mounted lamp-post transmitters in the 5.8 GHz band. Houses were measured for WLAN signal strength, both outside the house (for an externally mounted Customer Premises Equipment (CPE) antenna at roof height and at head height) and inside the house (at head height to represent a cordless phone or portable antenna). Figure 2.16 shows actual measured path loss values for various antenna heights within the house. Note that the street-mounted transmitter is

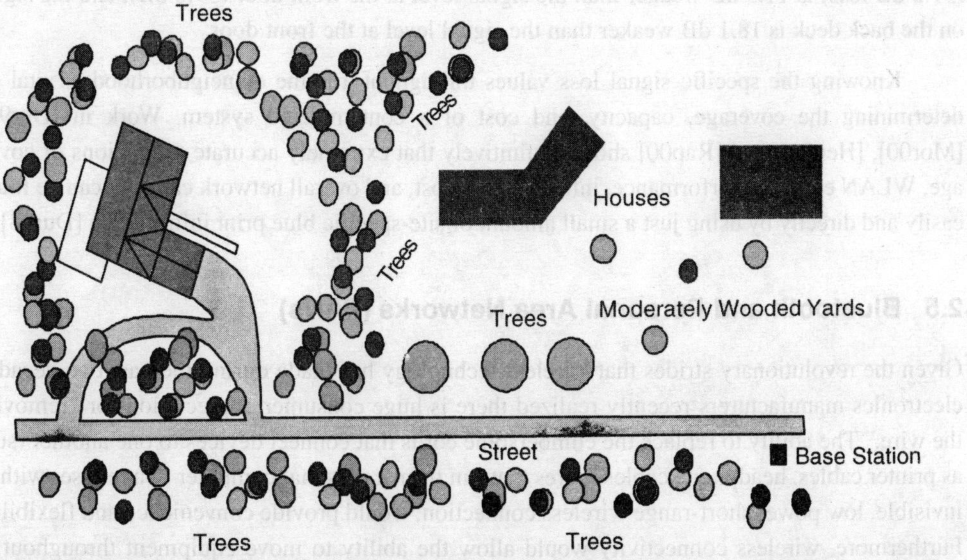

Figure 2.15 A typical neighborhood where high speed license free WLAN service from the street might be contemplated [Dur98b].

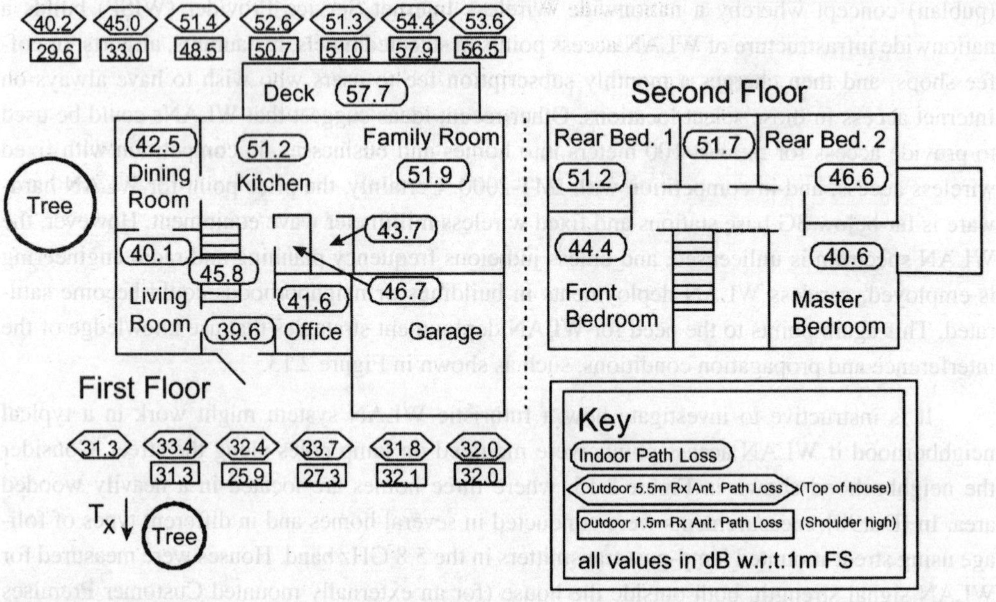

Figure 2.16 Measured values of path loss using a street-mounted lamp-post transmitter at 5.8 GHz, for various types of customer premise antenna [from [Dur98], ©IEEE].

located on the bottom left of Figure 2.16. It can be seen that the signal level in the kitchen (51.2 dB loss) is 11.5 dB weaker than the signal level at the front door (39.6 dB), and the signal on the back deck is 18.1 dB weaker than the signal level at the front door.

Knowing the specific signal loss values throughout a home or neighborhood is vital for determining the coverage, capacity, and cost of a contemplated system. Work in [Dur98], [Mor00], [Hen01], and [Rap00] shows definitively that extremely accurate predictions of coverage, WLAN end-user performance, infrastructure cost, and overall network capacity can be found easily and directly by using just a small amount of site-specific blue print information [Dur98].

2.5 Bluetooth and Personal Area Networks (PANs)

Given the revolutionary strides that wireless technology has made during the past two decades, electronics manufacturers recently realized there is huge consumer appreciation for "removing the wire." The ability to replace the cumbersome cords that connect devices to one another (such as printer cables, headphone cables, wires that run from a personal computer to a mouse) with an invisible, low power short-range wireless connection, would provide convenience and flexibility. Furthermore, wireless connectivity would allow the ability to move equipment throughout an office, and would allow collaborative communication between individuals, their appliances, and their environment.

Table 2.4 IEEE 802.11b Channels for Both DS-SS and FH-SS WLAN Standards

Country	Frequency Range Available	DSSS Channels Available	FHSS Channels Available
United States	2.4 to 2.4835 GHz	1 through 11	2 through 80
Canada	2.4 to 2.4835 GHz	1 through 11	2 through 80
Japan	2.4 to 2.497 GHz	1 through 14	2 through 95
France	2.4465 to 2.4835 GHz	10 through 13	48 through 82
Spain	2.445 to 2.4835 GHz	10 through 11	47 through 73
Remainder of Europe	2.4 to 2.4835	1 through 13	2 through 80

Bluetooth is an open standard that has been embraced by over 1,000 manufacturers of electronic appliances. It provides an ad-hoc approach for enabling various devices to communicate with one another within a nominal 10 meter range. Named after King Harald Bluetooth, the 10th century Viking who united Denmark and Norway, the Bluetooth standard aims to unify the connectivity chores of appliances within the personal workspace of an individual [Rob01].

Bluetooth operates in the 2.4 GHz ISM Band (2400–2483.5 MHz) and uses a frequency hopping TDD scheme for each radio channel. Each Bluetooth radio channel has a 1 MHz bandwidth and hops at a rate of approximately 1600 hops per second. Transmissions are performed in 625 microsecond slots with a single packet transmitted over a single slot. For long data transmissions, particular users may occupy multiple slots using the same transmission frequency, thus slowing the instantaneous hopping rate to below 1600 hops/second. The frequency hopping scheme of each Bluetooth user is determined from a cyclic code of length $2^{27} - 1$, and each user has a channel symbol rate of 1 Mbps using GFSK modulation. The standard has been designed to support operation in very high interference levels and relies on a number of forward error control (FEC) coding and automatic repeat request (ARQ) schemes to support a raw channel bit error rate (BER) of about 10^{-3}.

Different countries have allocated various channels for Bluetooth operation. In the US and most of Europe, the FHSS 2.4 GHz ISM band is available for Bluetooth use (see Table 2.4). A detailed list of states are defined in the Bluetooth standard to support a wide range of applications, appliances, and potential uses of the Personal Area Network. Audio, text, data, and even video is contemplated in the Bluetooth standard [Tra01]. Figure 2.17 provides a depiction of the Bluetooth concept where a gateway to the Internet via IEEE 802.11b is shown as a conceptual possibility.

The IEEE 802.15 standards committee has been formed to provide an international forum for developing Bluetooth and other PANs that interconnect pocket PCs, personal digital assistants (PDAs), cellphones, light projectors, and other appliances [Bra00]. With the rapid proliferation of

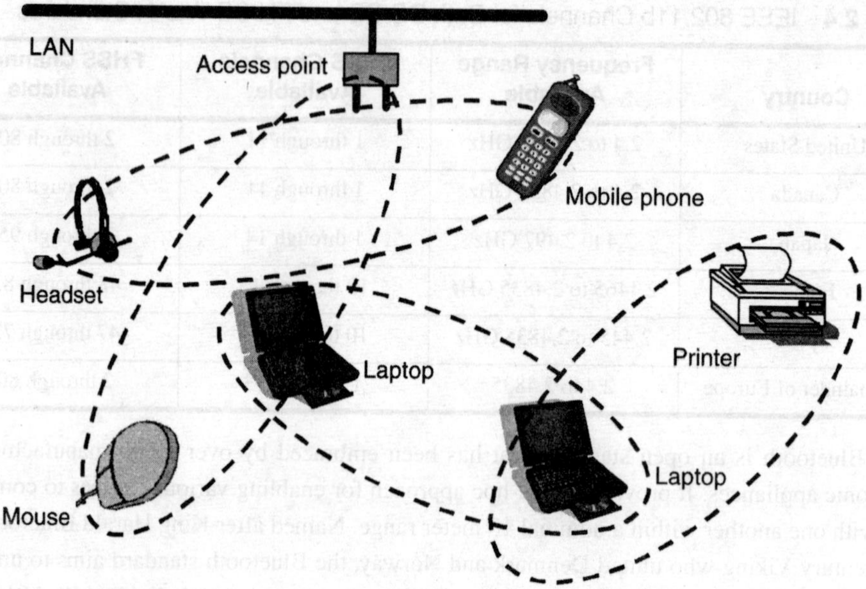

Figure 2.17 Example of a Personal Area Network (PAN) as provided by the Bluetooth standard.

wearable computers, such as PDAs, cellphones, smart cards, and position location devices, PANs may provide the connection to an entire new era of remote retrieval and monitoring of the world around us.

2.6 Summary

This chapter has provided an overview of the modern wireless communication networks that are currently being developed throughout the world. From mobile telephone, to broadband wireless access, to inside buildings and across campuses, it is clear that wireless communications will become a ubiquitous means of transport for information in the 21st century. In this chapter, the convergence of second generation mobile telephone standards into third generation standards was described, and the interim 2.5G data solutions were explained for all major mobile technologies. The current state-of-the-art of broadband millimeter wave systems were presented, along with the vision for wireless LMDS broadband networks as a complement to the existing fiber backbone. Current WLAN developments, and the evolution of WLANs from incompatible low data rate devices to powerful multi-megabit standardized networks were highlighted. Current WLAN standard activities were also presented. Finally, the emergence of Bluetooth, and the concept of a personal area network (PAN) were described. Armed with a high level understanding of the various emerging markets and competing technology choices facing the wireless telecommunication industry, the reader is now ready to study the fundamental technical issues that impact all wireless systems. The remaining chapters of this book provide such fundamental treatment.

2.7 Problems

2.1 In your place of work, how many modern wireless communications networks are available to you? Identify the types of services, the types of technologies, the commercial names of the service providers, and the commercial names of the equipment manufacturers that offer these wireless access capabilities.

2.2 In your home, how many modern wireless communications networks are available to you? Identify the types of services, the types of technologies, the commercial names of the service providers, and the commercial names of the equipment manufacturers that offer these wireless access capabilities.

2.3 Create a table that lists all 2G, 2.5G, and 3G mobile telephone standards. Carefully research the latest sources to determine the following parameters for each standard: a) RF channel BW; b) peak data rate; c) typical data rate; d) responsible standards body; e) maximum number of concurrent users; f) modulation type.

2.4 Conduct research to find out all of the accepted air interface standards for IMT-2000. Briefly describe the technical features and discuss the political and business motivations of each of the groups that proposed the winning standards. What is your favorite IMT-2000 standard? Justify your answer.

2.5 Specify the unlicensed frequency bands and the channel assignment plans that European, Japanese, and North American wireless local area network (WLAN) equipments are allowed to use within the 2 to 6 GHz range. How does international frequency compatibility help the growth of air interface standards in an unlicensed frequency band?

2.6 Why would an entrenched US wireless carrier announce that its long term plan is to abandon its IS-136 North American Digital Cellular standard in favor of a W-CDMA 3rd generation standard with foundations in GSM? Consider the decision in the face of the following business, political, and technical considerations: a) availability of low price equipment from manufacturers; b) compatibility with competing US wireless carriers; c) compatibility with carriers it considers its business allies; d) compatibility with wireless carriers outside of the US; d) access to field-proven equipment that provides off-the-shelf 3G capabilities; e) domain experience by its current engineering staff; f) cost and maintainability of the infrastructure; g) other factors not mentioned above.

2.7 If an IS-136 operator desires to provide competitive high speed Internet access to customers, it must choose to either adopt GPRS, or alternatively it may wish to change out its existing infrastructure to GSM and then use the various options available to GSM operators. Conduct a literature search to determine the current state of GPRS for IS-136 carriers. Given your findings, what is the most sensible option for the IS-136 carrier based on price, availability, and user experience?

2.8 Compare and contrast the various 2.5G technology paths that each of the major 2G standards provide. Which path has the highest Internet access speed? Is this speed true user speed, or peak instantaneous throughput speed? Which technology path is easiest to implement in existing subscriber handsets? Which path would be best suited for real-time network access?

2.9 How would multicarrier transmissions impact an operator's approach to allocating resources to accommodate a growing subscriber database that increasingly desires data connectivity over voice? How would heavy HSCSD usage impact a cellular carrier's strategy in allocating channels in the base stations of a cellular network? How would the rapid adoption of Voice over Internet Protocol (VoIP) impact cellular congestion? Explain.

2.10 Determine the maximum raw instantaneous data rate that can be provided to a single user in EDGE, assuming that a single time slot on a single GSM channel is available.

2.11 Find the maximum raw instantaneous data rate that can be provided using IS-95B if four user channels are dedicated to a single user.

CHAPTER 3

The Cellular Concept—System Design Fundamentals

The design objective of early mobile radio systems was to achieve a large coverage area by using a single, high powered transmitter with an antenna mounted on a tall tower. While this approach achieved very good coverage, it also meant that it was impossible to reuse those same frequencies throughout the system, since any attempts to achieve frequency reuse would result in interference. For example, the Bell mobile system in New York City in the 1970s could only support a maximum of twelve simultaneous calls over a thousand square miles [Cal88]. Faced with the fact that government regulatory agencies could not make spectrum allocations in proportion to the increasing demand for mobile services, it became imperative to restructure the radio telephone system to achieve high capacity with limited radio spectrum while at the same time covering very large areas.

3.1 Introduction

The cellular concept was a major breakthrough in solving the problem of spectral congestion and user capacity. It offered very high capacity in a limited spectrum allocation without any major technological changes. The cellular concept is a system-level idea which calls for replacing a single, high power transmitter (large cell) with many low power transmitters (small cells), each providing coverage to only a small portion of the service area. Each base station is allocated a portion of the total number of channels available to the entire system, and nearby base stations are assigned different groups of channels so that all the available channels are assigned to a relatively small number of neighboring base stations. Neighboring base stations are assigned different groups of channels so that the interference between base stations (and the mobile users under their control) is minimized. By systematically spacing base stations and their channel groups throughout a market, the available channels are distributed throughout the geographic region and may be reused as many times as necessary so long as the interference between co-channel stations is kept below acceptable levels.

As the demand for service increases (i.e., as more channels are needed within a particular market), the number of base stations may be increased (along with a corresponding decrease in transmitter power to avoid added interference), thereby providing additional radio capacity with no additional increase in radio spectrum. This fundamental principle is the foundation for all modern wireless communication systems, since it enables a fixed number of channels to serve an arbitrarily large number of subscribers by reusing the channels throughout the coverage region. Furthermore, the cellular concept allows every piece of subscriber equipment within a country or continent to be manufactured with the same set of channels so that any mobile may be used anywhere within the region.

3.2 Frequency Reuse

Cellular radio systems rely on an intelligent allocation and reuse of channels throughout a coverage region [Oet83]. Each cellular base station is allocated a group of radio channels to be used within a small geographic area called a *cell*. Base stations in adjacent cells are assigned channel groups which contain completely different channels than neighboring cells. The base station antennas are designed to achieve the desired coverage within the particular cell. By limiting the coverage area to within the boundaries of a cell, the same group of channels may be used to cover different cells that are separated from one another by distances large enough to keep interference levels within tolerable limits. The design process of selecting and allocating channel groups for all of the cellular base stations within a system is called *frequency reuse* or *frequency planning* [Mac79].

Figure 3.1 illustrates the concept of cellular frequency reuse, where cells labeled with the same letter use the same group of channels. The frequency reuse plan is overlaid upon a map to indicate where different frequency channels are used. The hexagonal cell shape shown in Figure 3.1 is conceptual and is a simplistic model of the radio coverage for each base station, but it has been universally adopted since the hexagon permits easy and manageable analysis of a cellular system. The actual radio coverage of a cell is known as the *footprint* and is determined from field measurements or propagation prediction models. Although the real footprint is amorphous in nature, a regular cell shape is needed for systematic system design and adaptation for future growth. While it might seem natural to choose a circle to represent the coverage area of a base station, adjacent circles cannot be overlaid upon a map without leaving gaps or creating overlapping regions. Thus, when considering geometric shapes which cover an entire region without overlap and with equal area, there are three sensible choices—a square, an equilateral triangle, and a hexagon. A cell must be designed to serve the weakest mobiles within the footprint, and these are typically located at the edge of the cell. For a given distance between the center of a polygon and its farthest perimeter points, the hexagon has the largest area of the three. Thus, by using the hexagon geometry, the fewest number of cells can cover a geographic region, and the hexagon closely approximates a circular radiation pattern which would occur for an omnidirectional base

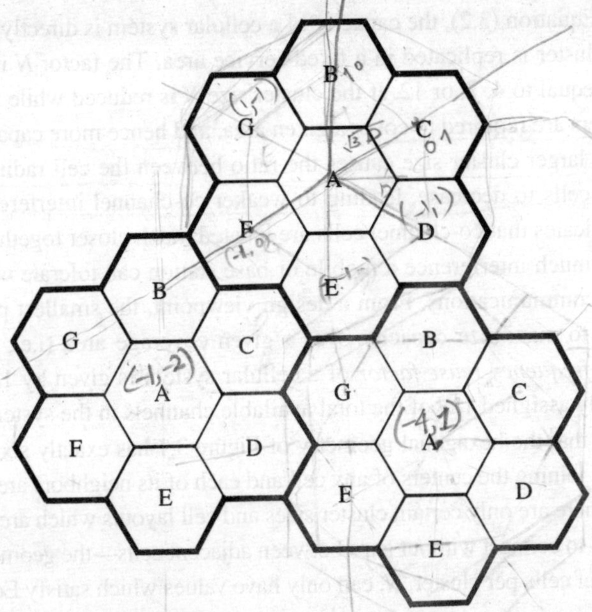

Figure 3.1 Illustration of the cellular frequency reuse concept. Cells with the same letter use the same set of frequencies. A cell cluster is outlined in bold and replicated over the coverage area. In this example, the cluster size, N, is equal to seven, and the frequency reuse factor is 1/7 since each cell contains one-seventh of the total number of available channels.

station antenna and free space propagation. Of course, the actual cellular footprint is determined by the contour in which a given transmitter serves the mobiles successfully.

When using hexagons to model coverage areas, base station transmitters are depicted as either being in the center of the cell (center-excited cells) or on three of the six cell vertices (edge-excited cells). Normally, omnidirectional antennas are used in center-excited cells and sectored directional antennas are used in corner-excited cells. Practical considerations usually do not allow base stations to be placed exactly as they appear in the hexagonal layout. Most system designs permit a base station to be positioned up to one-fourth the cell radius away from the ideal location.

To understand the frequency reuse concept, consider a cellular system which has a total of S duplex channels available for use. If each cell is allocated a group of k channels ($k < S$), and if the S channels are divided among N cells into unique and disjoint channel groups which each have the same number of channels, the total number of available radio channels can be expressed as

$$S = kN \tag{3.1}$$

The N cells which collectively use the complete set of available frequencies is called a *cluster*. If a cluster is replicated M times within the system, the total number of duplex channels, C, can be used as a measure of capacity and is given by

$$C = MkN = MS \tag{3.2}$$

As seen from Equation (3.2), the capacity of a cellular system is directly proportional to the number of times a cluster is replicated in a fixed service area. The factor N is called the *cluster size* and is typically equal to 4, 7, or 12. If the cluster size N is reduced while the cell size is kept constant, more clusters are required to cover a given area, and hence more capacity (a larger value of C) is achieved. A larger cluster size causes the ratio between the cell radius and the distance between co-channel cells to decrease, leading to weaker co-channel interference. Conversely, a small cluster size indicates that co-channel cells are located much closer together. The value for N is a function of how much interference a mobile or base station can tolerate while maintaining a sufficient quality of communications. From a design viewpoint, the smallest possible value of N is desirable in order to maximize capacity over a given coverage area (i.e., to maximize C in Equation (3.2)). The *frequency reuse factor* of a cellular system is given by $1/N$, since each cell within a cluster is only assigned $1/N$ of the total available channels in the system.

Due to the fact that the hexagonal geometry of Figure 3.1 has exactly six equidistant neighbors and that the lines joining the centers of any cell and each of its neighbors are separated by multiples of 60 degrees, there are only certain cluster sizes and cell layouts which are possible [Mac79]. In order to tessellate—to connect without gaps between adjacent cells—the geometry of hexagons is such that the number of cells per cluster, N, can only have values which satisfy Equation (3.3).

$$N = i^2 + ij + j^2 \tag{3.3}$$

where i and j are non-negative integers. To find the nearest co-channel neighbors of a particular cell, one must do the following: (1) move i cells along any chain of hexagons and then (2) turn 60 degrees counter-clockwise and move j cells. This is illustrated in Figure 3.2 for $i = 3$ and $j = 2$ (example, $N = 19$).

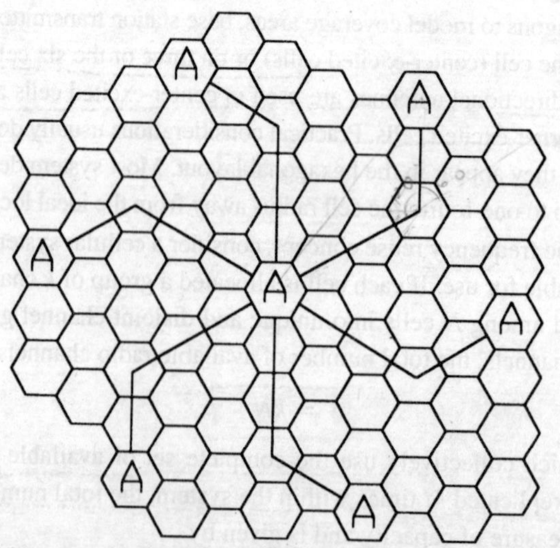

Figure 3.2 Method of locating co-channel cells in a cellular system. In this example, $N = 19$ (i.e., $i = 3$, $j = 2$). (Adapted from [Oet83] © IEEE.)

Example 3.1

If a total of 33 MHz of bandwidth is allocated to a particular FDD cellular telephone system which uses two 25 kHz simplex channels to provide full duplex voice and control channels, compute the number of channels available per cell if a system uses (a) four-cell reuse, (b) seven-cell reuse, and (c) 12-cell reuse. If 1 MHz of the allocated spectrum is dedicated to control channels, determine an equitable distribution of control channels and voice channels in each cell for each of the three systems.

Solution

Given:

Total bandwidth = 33 MHz

Channel bandwidth = 25 kHz $\times$ 2 simplex channels = 50 kHz/duplex channel

Total available channels = 33,000/50 = 660 channels

(a) For $N = 4$,
total number of channels available per cell = 660/4 $\approx$ 165 channels.

(b) For $N = 7$,
total number of channels available per cell = 660/7 $\approx$ 95 channels.

(c) For $N = 12$,
total number of channels available per cell = 660/12 $\approx$ 55 channels.

A 1 MHz spectrum for control channels implies that there are 1000/50 = 20 control channels out of the 660 channels available. To evenly distribute the control and voice channels, simply allocate the same number of voice channels in each cell wherever possible. Here, the 660 channels must be evenly distributed to each cell within the cluster. In practice, only the 640 voice channels would be allocated, since the control channels are allocated separately as 1 per cell.

(a) For $N = 4$, we can have five control channels and 160 voice channels per cell. In practice, however, each cell only needs a single control channel (the control channels have a greater reuse distance than the voice channels). Thus, one control channel and 160 voice channels would be assigned to each cell.

(b) For $N = 7$, four cells with three control channels and 92 voice channels, two cells with three control channels and 90 voice channels, and one cell with two control channels and 92 voice channels could be allocated. In practice, however, each cell would have one control channel, four cells would have 91 voice channels, and three cells would have 92 voice channels.

(c) For $N = 12$, we can have eight cells with two control channels and 53 voice channels, and four cells with one control channel and 54 voice channels each. In an actual system, each cell would have one control channel, eight cells would have 53 voice channels, and four cells would have 54 voice channels.

3.3 Channel Assignment Strategies

For efficient utilization of the radio spectrum, a frequency reuse scheme that is consistent with the objectives of increasing capacity and minimizing interference is required. A variety of channel assignment strategies have been developed to achieve these objectives. Channel assignment strategies can be classified as either *fixed* or *dynamic*. The choice of channel assignment strategy impacts the performance of the system, particularly as to how calls are managed when a mobile user is handed off from one cell to another [Tek91], [LiC93], [Sun94], [Rap93b].

In a fixed channel assignment strategy, each cell is allocated a predetermined set of voice channels. Any call attempt within the cell can only be served by the unused channels in that particular cell. If all the channels in that cell are occupied, the call is *blocked* and the subscriber does not receive service. Several variations of the fixed assignment strategy exist. In one approach, called the *borrowing strategy*, a cell is allowed to borrow channels from a neighboring cell if all of its own channels are already occupied. The mobile switching center (MSC) supervises such borrowing procedures and ensures that the borrowing of a channel does not disrupt or interfere with any of the calls in progress in the donor cell.

In a dynamic channel assignment strategy, voice channels are not allocated to different cells permanently. Instead, each time a call request is made, the serving base station requests a channel from the MSC. The switch then allocates a channel to the requested cell following an algorithm that takes into account the likelihood of future blocking within the cell, the frequency of use of the candidate channel, the reuse distance of the channel, and other cost functions.

Accordingly, the MSC only allocates a given frequency if that frequency is not presently in use in the cell or any other cell which falls within the minimum restricted distance of frequency reuse to avoid co-channel interference. Dynamic channel assignment reduce the likelihood of blocking, which increases the trunking capacity of the system, since all the available channels in a market are accessible to all of the cells. Dynamic channel assignment strategies require the MSC to collect real-time data on channel occupancy, traffic distribution, and *radio signal strength indications* (RSSI) of all channels on a continuous basis. This increases the storage and computational load on the system but provides the advantage of increased channel utilization and decreased probability of a blocked call.

3.4 Handoff Strategies

When a mobile moves into a different cell while a conversation is in progress, the MSC automatically transfers the call to a new channel belonging to the new base station. This handoff operation not only involves identifying a new base station, but also requires that the voice and control signals be allocated to channels associated with the new base station.

Processing handoffs is an important task in any cellular radio system. Many handoff strategies prioritize handoff requests over call initiation requests when allocating unused channels in a cell site. Handoffs must be performed successfully and as infrequently as possible, and be imperceptible to the users. In order to meet these requirements, system designers must specify an optimum signal level at which to initiate a handoff. Once a particular signal level is specified as the minimum usable signal for acceptable voice quality at the base station receiver (normally taken as between –90 dBm and –100 dBm), a slightly stronger signal level is used as a threshold at which a handoff is made. This margin, given by $\Delta = P_{r\ handoff} - P_{r\ minimum\ usable}$, cannot be too large or too small. If Δ is too large, unnecessary handoffs which burden the MSC may occur, and if Δ is too small, there may be insufficient time to complete a handoff before a call is lost due to weak signal conditions. Therefore, Δ is chosen carefully to meet these conflicting requirements. Figure 3.3 illustrates a handoff situation. Figure 3.3(a) demonstrates the case where a handoff is not made and the signal drops below the minimum acceptable level to keep the channel active. This dropped call event can happen when there is an excessive delay by the MSC in assigning a handoff or when the threshold Δ is set too small for the handoff time in the system. Excessive delays may occur during high traffic conditions due to computational loading at the MSC or due to the fact that no channels are available on any of the nearby base stations (thus forcing the MSC to wait until a channel in a nearby cell becomes free).

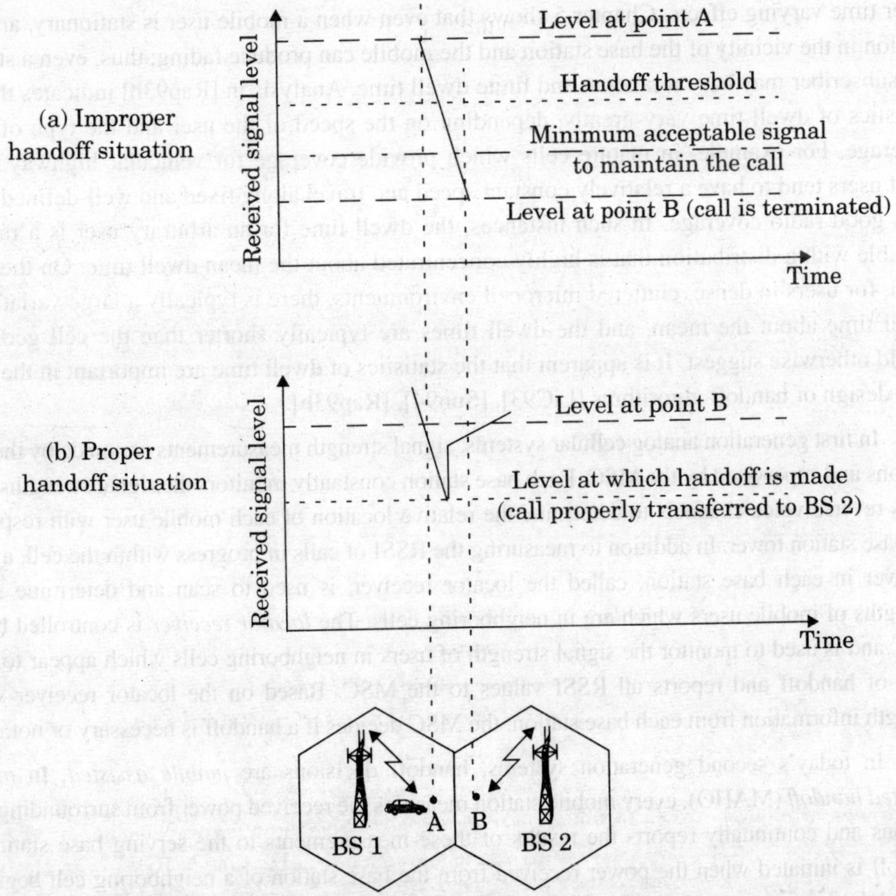

Figure 3.3 Illustration of a handoff scenario at cell boundary.

In deciding when to handoff, it is important to ensure that the drop in the measured signal level is not due to momentary fading and that the mobile is actually moving away from the serving base station. In order to ensure this, the base station monitors the signal level for a certain period of time before a handoff is initiated. This running average measurement of signal strength should be optimized so that unnecessary handoffs are avoided, while ensuring that necessary handoffs are completed before a call is terminated due to poor signal level. The length of time needed to decide if a handoff is necessary depends on the speed at which the vehicle is moving. If the slope of the short-term average received signal level in a given time interval is steep, the handoff should be made quickly. Information about the vehicle speed, which can be useful in handoff decisions, can also be computed from the statistics of the received short-term fading signal at the base station.

The time over which a call may be maintained within a cell, without handoff, is called the *dwell time* [Rap93b]. The dwell time of a particular user is governed by a number of factors, including propagation, interference, distance between the subscriber and the base station, and other time varying effects. Chapter 5 shows that even when a mobile user is stationary, ambient motion in the vicinity of the base station and the mobile can produce fading; thus, even a stationary subscriber may have a random and finite dwell time. Analysis in [Rap93b] indicates that the statistics of dwell time vary greatly, depending on the speed of the user and the type of radio coverage. For example, in mature cells which provide coverage for vehicular highway users, most users tend to have a relatively constant speed and travel along fixed and well-defined paths with good radio coverage. In such instances, the dwell time for an arbitrary user is a random variable with a distribution that is highly concentrated about the mean dwell time. On the other hand, for users in dense, cluttered microcell environments, there is typically a large variation of dwell time about the mean, and the dwell times are typically shorter than the cell geometry would otherwise suggest. It is apparent that the statistics of dwell time are important in the practical design of handoff algorithms [LiC93], [Sun94], [Rap93b].

In first generation analog cellular systems, signal strength measurements are made by the base stations and supervised by the MSC. Each base station constantly monitors the signal strengths of all of its reverse voice channels to determine the relative location of each mobile user with respect to the base station tower. In addition to measuring the RSSI of calls in progress within the cell, a spare receiver in each base station, called the locator receiver, is used to scan and determine signal strengths of mobile users which are in neighboring cells. The *locator receiver* is controlled by the MSC and is used to monitor the signal strength of users in neighboring cells which appear to be in need of handoff and reports all RSSI values to the MSC. Based on the locator receiver signal strength information from each base station, the MSC decides if a handoff is necessary or not.

In today's second generation systems, handoff decisions are *mobile assisted*. In *mobile assisted handoff* (MAHO), every mobile station measures the received power from surrounding base stations and continually reports the results of these measurements to the serving base station. A handoff is initiated when the power received from the base station of a neighboring cell begins to exceed the power received from the current base station by a certain level or for a certain period of time. The MAHO method enables the call to be handed over between base stations at a much faster rate than in first generation analog systems since the handoff measurements are made by each mobile, and the MSC no longer constantly monitors signal strengths. MAHO is particularly suited for microcellular environments where handoffs are more frequent.

During the course of a call, if a mobile moves from one cellular system to a different cellular system controlled by a different MSC, an *intersystem handoff* becomes necessary. An MSC engages in an intersystem handoff when a mobile signal becomes weak in a given cell and the MSC cannot find another cell within its system to which it can transfer the call in progress. There are many issues that must be addressed when implementing an intersystem handoff. For instance, a local call may become a long-distance call as the mobile moves out of its home system and becomes a roamer in a neighboring system. Also, compatibility between the two MSCs must be determined before implementing an intersystem handoff. Chapter 10 demonstrates how intersystem handoffs are implemented in practice.

Different systems have different policies and methods for managing handoff requests. Some systems handle handoff requests in the same way they handle originating calls. In such systems, the probability that a handoff request will not be served by a new base station is equal to the blocking probability of incoming calls. However, from the user's point of view, having a call abruptly terminated while in the middle of a conversation is more annoying than being blocked occasionally on a new call attempt. To improve the quality of service as perceived by the users, various methods have been devised to prioritize handoff requests over call initiation requests when allocating voice channels.

3.4.1 Prioritizing Handoffs

One method for giving priority to handoffs is called the *guard channel concept*, whereby a fraction of the total available channels in a cell is reserved exclusively for handoff requests from ongoing calls which may be handed off into the cell. This method has the disadvantage of reducing the total carried traffic, as fewer channels are allocated to originating calls. Guard channels, however, offer efficient spectrum utilization when dynamic channel assignment strategies, which minimize the number of required guard channels by efficient demand-based allocation, are used.

Queuing of handoff requests is another method to decrease the probability of forced termination of a call due to lack of available channels. There is a tradeoff between the decrease in probability of forced termination and total carried traffic. Queuing of handoffs is possible due to the fact that there is a finite time interval between the time the received signal level drops below the handoff threshold and the time the call is terminated due to insufficient signal level. The delay time and size of the queue is determined from the traffic pattern of the particular service area. It should be noted that queuing does not guarantee a zero probability of forced termination, since large delays will cause the received signal level to drop below the minimum required level to maintain communication and hence lead to forced termination.

3.4.2 Practical Handoff Considerations

In practical cellular systems, several problems arise when attempting to design for a wide range of mobile velocities. High speed vehicles pass through the coverage region of a cell within a matter of seconds, whereas pedestrian users may never need a handoff during a call. Particularly with the addition of microcells to provide capacity, the MSC can quickly become burdened if high speed users are constantly being passed between very small cells. Several schemes have been devised to handle the simultaneous traffic of high speed and low speed users while minimizing the handoff intervention from the MSC. Another practical limitation is the ability to obtain new cell sites.

Although the cellular concept clearly provides additional capacity through the addition of cell sites, in practice it is difficult for cellular service providers to obtain new physical cell site locations in urban areas. Zoning laws, ordinances, and other nontechnical barriers often make it more attractive for a cellular provider to install additional channels and base stations at the same physical location of an existing cell, rather than find new site locations. By using different antenna heights (often on the same building or tower) and different power levels, it is possible to provide "large" and "small" cells which are co-located at a single location. This technique is called the *umbrella cell* approach and is used to provide large area coverage to high speed users while providing small area coverage to users traveling at low speeds. Figure 3.4 illustrates an umbrella cell which is co-located with some smaller microcells. The umbrella cell approach ensures that the number of handoffs is minimized for high speed users and provides additional microcell channels for pedestrian users. The speed of each user may be estimated by the base station or MSC by evaluating how rapidly the short-term average signal strength on the RVC changes over time, or more sophisticated algorithms may be used to evaluate and partition users [LiC93]. If a high speed user in the large umbrella cell is approaching the base station, and its velocity is rapidly decreasing, the base station may decide to hand the user into the co-located microcell, without MSC intervention.

Another practical handoff problem in microcell systems is known as *cell dragging*. Cell dragging results from pedestrian users that provide a very strong signal to the base station. Such a situation occurs in an urban environment when there is a line-of-sight (LOS) radio path between the subscriber and the base station. As the user travels away from the base station at a very slow speed, the average signal strength does not decay rapidly. Even when the user has traveled well beyond the designed range of the cell, the received signal at the base station may be above the handoff threshold, thus a handoff may not be made. This creates a potential interference and traffic management problem, since the user has meanwhile traveled deep within a neighboring cell. To solve the cell dragging problem, handoff thresholds and radio coverage parameters must be adjusted carefully.

In first generation analog cellular systems, the typical time to make a handoff, once the signal level is deemed to be below the handoff threshold, is about 10 seconds. This requires that the value for Δ be on the order of 6 dB to 12 dB. In digital cellular systems such as GSM, the mobile assists with the handoff procedure by determining the best handoff candidates, and the handoff, once the decision is made, typically requires only 1 or 2 seconds. Consequently, Δ is

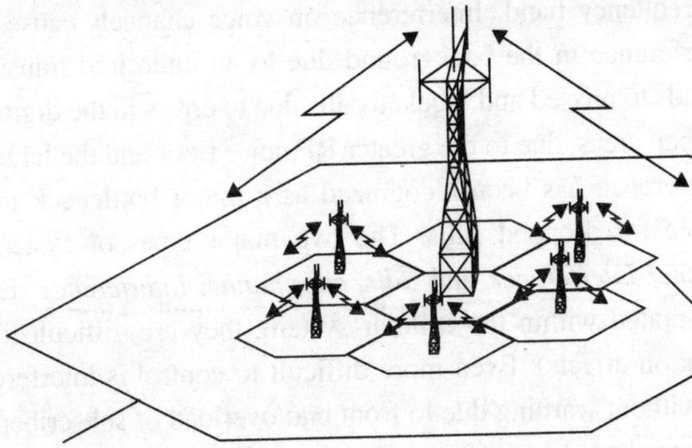

Figure 3.4 The umbrella cell approach.

usually between 0 dB and 6 dB in modern cellular systems. The faster handoff process supports a much greater range of options for handling high speed and low speed users and provides the MSC with substantial time to "rescue" a call that is in need of handoff.

Another feature of newer cellular systems is the ability to make handoff decisions based on a wide range of metrics other than signal strength. The co-channel and adjacent channel interference levels may be measured at the base station or the mobile, and this information may be used with conventional signal strength data to provide a multi-dimensional algorithm for determining when a handoff is needed.

The IS-95 code division multiple access (CDMA) spread spectrum cellular system described in Chapter 11 and in [Lib99], [Kim00], and [Gar99], provides a unique handoff capability that cannot be provided with other wireless systems. Unlike channelized wireless systems that assign different radio channels during a handoff (called a *hard handoff*), spread spectrum mobiles share the same channel in every cell. Thus, the term *handoff* does not mean a physical change in the assigned channel, but rather that a different base station handles the radio communication task. By simultaneously evaluating the received signals from a single subscriber at several neighboring base stations, the MSC may actually decide which version of the user's signal is best at any moment in time. This technique exploits macroscopic space diversity provided by the different physical locations of the base stations and allows the MSC to make a "soft" decision as to which version of the user's signal to pass along to the PSTN at any instance [Pad94]. The ability to select between the instantaneous received signals from a variety of base stations is called *soft handoff*.

3.5 Interference and System Capacity

Interference is the major limiting factor in the performance of cellular radio systems. Sources of interference include another mobile in the same cell, a call in progress in a neighboring cell, other base stations operating in the same frequency band, or any noncellular system which inadvertently leaks energy into the cellular frequency band. Interference on voice channels causes cross talk, where the subscriber hears interference in the background due to an undesired transmission. On control channels, interference leads to missed and blocked calls due to errors in the digital signaling. Interference is more severe in urban areas, due to the greater RF noise floor and the large number of base stations and mobiles. Interference has been recognized as a major bottleneck in increasing capacity and is often responsible for dropped calls. The two major types of system-generated cellular interference are *co-channel interference* and *adjacent channel interference.* Even though interfering signals are often generated within the cellular system, they are difficult to control in practice (due to random propagation effects). Even more difficult to control is interference due to out-of-band users, which arises without warning due to front end overload of subscriber equipment or intermittent intermodulation products. In practice, the transmitters from competing cellular carriers are often a significant source of out-of-band interference, since competitors often locate their base stations in close proximity to one another in order to provide comparable coverage to customers.

3.5.1 Co-channel Interference and System Capacity

Frequency reuse implies that in a given coverage area there are several cells that use the same set of frequencies. These cells are called *co-channel cells*, and the interference between signals from these cells is called *co-channel interference*. Unlike thermal noise which can be overcome by increasing the signal-to-noise ratio (SNR), co-channel interference cannot be combated by simply increasing the carrier power of a transmitter. This is because an increase in carrier transmit power increases the interference to neighboring co-channel cells. To reduce co-channel interference, co-channel cells must be physically separated by a minimum distance to provide sufficient isolation due to propagation.

When the size of each cell is approximately the same and the base stations transmit the same power, the co-channel interference ratio is independent of the transmitted power and becomes a function of the radius of the cell (R) and the distance between centers of the nearest co-channel cells (D). By increasing the ratio of D/R, the spatial separation between co-channel cells relative to the coverage distance of a cell is increased. Thus, interference is reduced from improved isolation of RF energy from the co-channel cell. The parameter Q, called the *co-channel reuse ratio*, is related to the cluster size (see Table 3.1 and Equation (3.3)). For a hexagonal geometry

$$Q = \frac{D}{R} = \sqrt{3N} \tag{3.4}$$

A small value of Q provides larger capacity since the cluster size N is small, whereas a large value of Q improves the transmission quality, due to a smaller level of co-channel interference. A trade-off must be made between these two objectives in actual cellular design.

Table 3.1 Co-channel Reuse Ratio for Some Values of N

	Cluster Size (N)	Co-channel Reuse Ratio (Q)
$i = 1, j = 1$	3	3
$i = 1, j = 2$	7	4.58
$i = 0, j = 3$	9	5.20
$i = 2, j = 2$	12	6

Let i_0 be the number of co-channel interfering cells. Then, the signal-to-interference ratio (S/I or SIR) for a mobile receiver which monitors a forward channel can be expressed as

$$\frac{S}{I} = \frac{S}{\sum_{i=1}^{i_0} I_i} \tag{3.5}$$

where S is the desired signal power from the desired base station and I_i is the interference power caused by the ith interfering co-channel cell base station. If the signal levels of co-channel cells are known, then the S/I ratio for the forward link can be found using Equation (3.5).

Propagation measurements in a mobile radio channel show that the average received signal strength at any point decays as a power law of the distance of separation between a transmitter and receiver. The average received power P_r at a distance d from the transmitting antenna is approximated by

$$P_r = P_0\left(\frac{d}{d_0}\right)^{-n} \tag{3.6}$$

or

$$P_r(\text{dBm}) = P_0(\text{dBm}) - 10n\log\left(\frac{d}{d_0}\right) \tag{3.7}$$

where P_0 is the power received at a close-in reference point in the far field region of the antenna at a small distance d_0 from the transmitting antenna and n is the path loss exponent. Now consider the forward link where the desired signal is the serving base station and where the interference is due to co-channel base stations. If D_i is the distance of the ith interferer from the mobile, the received power at a given mobile due to the ith interfering cell will be proportional to $(D_i)^{-n}$. The path loss exponent typically ranges between two and four in urban cellular systems [Rap92b].

When the transmit power of each base station is equal and the path loss exponent is the same throughout the coverage area, S/I for a mobile can be approximated as

$$\frac{S}{I} = \frac{R^{-n}}{\sum_{i=1}^{i_0} (D_i)^{-n}} \tag{3.8}$$

Considering only the first layer of interfering cells, if all the interfering base stations are equidistant from the desired base station and if this distance is equal to the distance D between cell centers, then Equation (3.8) simplifies to

$$\frac{S}{I} = \frac{(D/R)^n}{i_0} = \frac{(\sqrt{3N})^n}{i_0} \tag{3.9}$$

Equation (3.9) relates S/I to the cluster size N, which in turn determines the overall capacity of the system from Equation (3.2). For example, assume that the six closest cells are close enough to create significant interference and that they are all approximately equidistant from the desired base station. For the U.S. AMPS cellular system which uses FM and 30 kHz channels, subjective tests indicate that sufficient voice quality is provided when S/I is greater than or equal to 18 dB. Using Equation (3.9), it can be shown in order to meet this requirement, the cluster size N should be at least 6.49, assuming a path loss exponent $n = 4$. Thus a minimum cluster size of seven is required to meet an S/I requirement of 18 dB. It should be noted that Equation (3.9) is based on the hexagonal cell geometry where all the interfering cells are equidistant from the base station receiver, and hence provides an optimistic result in many cases. For some frequency reuse plans (e.g., $N = 4$), the closest interfering cells vary widely in their distances from the desired cell.

Using an exact cell geometry layout, it can be shown for a seven-cell cluster, with the mobile unit at the cell boundary, the mobile is a distance $D - R$ from the two nearest co-channel interfering cells and is exactly $D + R/2$, D, $D - R/2$, and $D + R$ from the other interfering cells in the first tier, as shown rigorously in [Lee86]. Using the approximate geometry shown in Figure 3.5, Equation (3.8), and assuming $n = 4$, the signal-to-interference ratio for the worst case can be closely approximated as (an exact expression is worked out by Jacobsmeyer [Jac94])

$$\frac{S}{I} = \frac{R^{-4}}{2(D-R)^{-4} + 2(D+R)^{-4} + 2D^{-4}} \tag{3.10}$$

Equation (3.10) can be rewritten in terms of the co-channel reuse ratio Q, as

$$\frac{S}{I} = \frac{1}{2(Q-1)^{-4} + 2(Q+1)^{-4} + 2Q^{-4}} \tag{3.11}$$

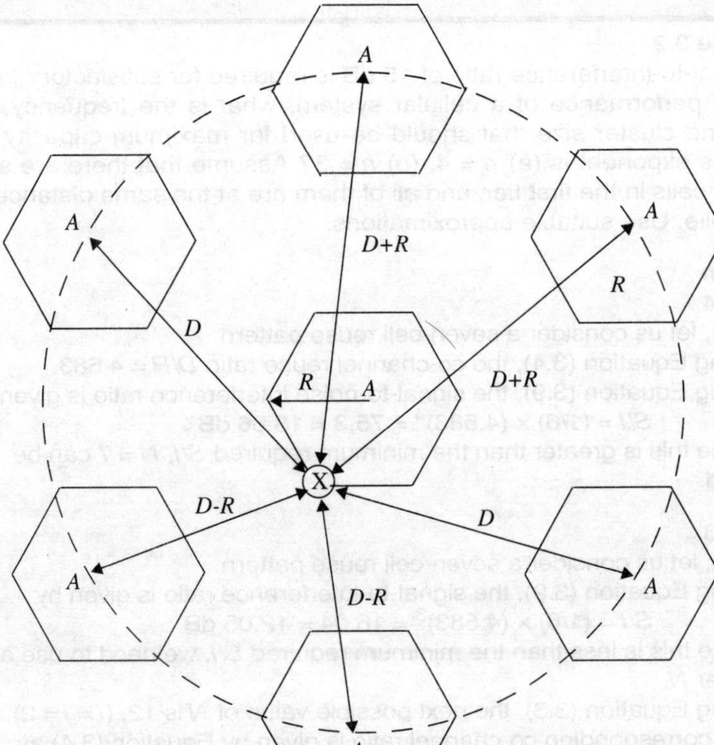

Figure 3.5 Illustration of the first tier of co-channel cells for a cluster size of $N = 7$. An approximation of the exact geometry is shown here, whereas the exact geometry is given in [Lee86]. When the mobile is at the cell boundary (point X), it experiences worst case co-channel interference on the forward channel. The marked distances between the mobile and different co-channel cells are based on approximations made for easy analysis.

For $N = 7$, the co-channel reuse ratio Q is 4.6, and the worst case S/I is approximated as 49.56 (17 dB) using Equation (3.11), whereas an exact solution using Equation (3.8) yields 17.8 dB [Jac94]. Hence for a seven-cell cluster, the S/I ratio is slightly less than 18 dB for the worst case. To design the cellular system for proper performance in the worst case, it would be necessary to increase N to the next largest size, which from Equation (3.3) is found to be 9 (corresponding to $i = 0, j = 3$). This obviously entails a significant decrease in capacity, since 9-cell reuse offers a spectrum utilization of 1/9 within each cell, whereas seven-cell reuse offers a spectrum utilization of 1/7. In practice, a capacity reduction of 7/9 would not be tolerable to accommodate for the worst case situation which rarely occurs. From the above discussion, it is clear that co-channel interference determines link performance, which in turn dictates the frequency reuse plan and the overall capacity of cellular systems.

Example 3.2

If a signal-to-interference ratio of 15 dB is required for satisfactory forward channel performance of a cellular system, what is the frequency reuse factor and cluster size that should be used for maximum capacity if the path loss exponent is (a) $n = 4$, (b) $n = 3$? Assume that there are six co-channel cells in the first tier, and all of them are at the same distance from the mobile. Use suitable approximations.

Solution

(a) $n = 4$

First, let us consider a seven-cell reuse pattern.
Using Equation (3.4), the co-channel reuse ratio $D/R = 4.583$.
Using Equation (3.9), the signal-to-noise interference ratio is given by

$$S/I = (1/6) \times (4.583)^4 = 75.3 = 18.66 \text{ dB}$$

Since this is greater than the minimum required S/I, $N = 7$ can be used.

(b) $n = 3$

First, let us consider a seven-cell reuse pattern.
Using Equation (3.9), the signal-to-interference ratio is given by

$$S/I = (1/6) \times (4.583)^3 = 16.04 = 12.05 \text{ dB}$$

Since this is less than the minimum required S/I, we need to use a larger N.
Using Equation (3.3), the next possible value of N is 12, ($i = j = 2$).
The corresponding co-channel ratio is given by Equation (3.4) as

$$D/R = 6.0$$

Using Equation (3.3), the signal-to-interference ratio is given by

$$S/I = (1/6) \times (6)^3 = 36 = 15.56 \text{ dB}$$

Since this is greater than the minimum required S/I, $N = 12$ is used.

3.5.2 Channel Planning for Wireless Systems

Judiciously assigning the appropriate radio channels to each base station is an important process that is much more difficult in practice than in theory. While Equation (3.9) is a valuable rule of thumb for determining the appropriate frequency reuse ratio (or cluster size) and the appropriate separation between adjacent co-channel cells, the wireless engineer must deal with the real-world difficulties of radio propagation and imperfect coverage regions of each cell. Cellular systems, in practice, seldom obey the homogenous propagation path loss assumption of Equation (3.9).

Generally, the available mobile radio spectrum is divided into channels, which are part of an *air interface* standard that is used throughout a country or continent. These channels generally are made up of control channels (vital for initiating, requesting, or paging a call), and voice channels (dedicated to carrying revenue-generating traffic). Typically, about 5% of the entire mobile spectrum is devoted to control channels, which carry data messages that are very brief and bursty in nature, while the remaining 95% of the spectrum is dedicated to voice channels. Channels may be assigned by the wireless carrier in any manner it chooses, since each market may have its own particular propagation conditions or particular services it wishes to offer and may wish to adopt its own particular frequency reuse scheme that fits its geographic conditions or air interface technology choice. However, in practical systems, the air interface standard ensures a distinction between voice and control channels, and thus control channels are generally not allowed to be used as voice channels, and vice versa. Furthermore, since control channels are vital in the successful launch of any call, the frequency reuse strategy applied to control channels is different and generally more conservative (e.g., is afforded greater S/I protection) than for the voice channels. This can be seen in Example 3.3, where the control channels are allocated using 21-cell reuse, whereas voice channels are assigned using seven-cell reuse. Typically, the control channels are able to handle a great deal of data such that only one control channel is needed within a cell. As described in Section 3.7.2, sectoring is often used to improve the signal-to-interference ratio which may lead to a smaller cluster size, and in such cases, only a single control channel is assigned to an individual sector of a cell.

One of the key features of CDMA systems is that the cluster size is $N = 1$, and frequency planning is not nearly as difficult as for TDMA or first generation cellular systems [Lib99]. Still, however, propagation considerations require most practical CDMA systems to use some sort of limited frequency reuse where propagation conditions are particularly ill-behaved in a particular market. For example, in the vicinity of bodies of water, interfering cells on the same channel as the desired serving cell can create interference overload that exceeds the dynamic range of CDMA power control capabilities, leading to dropped calls. In such instances, the most popular approach is to use what is called *f1/f2 cell planning*, where nearest neighbor cells use radio channels that are different from its closest neighbor in particular locations. Such frequency planning requires CDMA phones to make hard handoffs, just as TDMA and FDMA phones do.

In CDMA, a single 1.25 MHz radio channel carries the simultaneous transmissions of the single control channel with up to 64 simultaneous voice channels. Thus, unlike in 30 kHz IS-136 or 200 kHz GSM TDMA systems, where the coverage region and interference levels are well defined when specific radio channels are in use, the CDMA system instead has a dynamic, time varying coverage region which varies depending on the instantaneous number of users on the CDMA radio channel. This effect, known as a *breathing cell*, requires the wireless engineer to carefully plan the coverage and signal levels for the best and worst cases for serving cells as well as nearest neighbor cells, from both a coverage and interference standpoint. The breathing cell phenomenon can lead to abrupt dropped calls resulting from abrupt coverage changes simply due to an increase in the number of users on a serving CDMA base station. Thus, instead of having to make careful decisions about the channel assignment schemes for each cellular base station, CDMA engineers must instead make difficult decisions about the power levels and thresholds assigned to control channels, voice channels, and how these levels and thresholds should be adjusted for changing traffic intensity. Also, threshold levels for CDMA handoffs, in both the soft handoff case and hard handoff case, must be planned and often measured carefully before turning up service. In fact, the f1/f2 cell planning issue led to the development of TSB-74, which added hard-handoff capabilities between different CDMA radio channels to the original IS-95 CDMA specification described in Chapter 11.

3.5.3 Adjacent Channel Interference

Interference resulting from signals which are adjacent in frequency to the desired signal is called *adjacent channel interference*. Adjacent channel interference results from imperfect receiver filters which allow nearby frequencies to leak into the passband. The problem can be particularly serious if an adjacent channel user is transmitting in very close range to a subscriber's receiver, while the receiver attempts to receive a base station on the desired channel. This is referred to as the *near–far* effect, where a nearby transmitter (which may or may not be of the same type as that used by the cellular system) captures the receiver of the subscriber. Alternatively, the near–far effect occurs when a mobile close to a base station transmits on a channel close to one being used by a weak mobile. The base station may have difficulty in discriminating the desired mobile user from the "bleedover" caused by the close adjacent channel mobile.

Adjacent channel interference can be minimized through careful filtering and channel assignments. Since each cell is given only a fraction of the available channels, a cell need not be assigned channels which are all adjacent in frequency. By keeping the frequency separation between each channel in a given cell as large as possible, the adjacent channel interference may be reduced considerably. Thus instead of assigning channels which form a contiguous band of frequencies within a particular cell, channels are allocated such that the frequency separation between channels in a given cell is maximized. By sequentially assigning successive channels in the frequency band to different cells, many channel allocation schemes are able to separate adjacent channels in a cell by as many as N channel bandwidths, where N is the cluster size. Some channel allocation schemes also prevent a secondary source of adjacent channel interference by avoiding the use of adjacent channels in neighboring cell sites.

If the frequency reuse factor is large (e.g., small N), the separation between adjacent channels at the base station may not be sufficient to keep the adjacent channel interference level within tolerable limits. For example, if a close-in mobile is 20 times as close to the base station as another mobile and has energy spillout of its passband, the signal-to-interference ratio at the base station for the weak mobile (before receiver filtering) is approximately

$$\frac{S}{I} = (20)^{-n} \tag{3.12}$$

For a path loss exponent $n = 4$, this is equal to –52 dB. If the intermediate frequency (IF) filter of the base station receiver has a slope of 20 dB/octave, then an adjacent channel interferer must be displaced by at least six times the passband bandwidth from the center of the receiver frequency passband to achieve 52 dB attenuation. Here, a separation of approximately six channel bandwidths is required for typical filters in order to provide 0 dB SIR from a close-in adjacent channel user. This implies more than six channel separations are needed to bring the adjacent channel interference to an acceptable level. Tight base station filters are needed when close-in and distant users share the same cell. In practice, base station receivers are preceded by a high Q cavity filter in order to reject adjacent channel interference.

Example 3.3

This example illustrates how channels are divided into subsets and allocated to different cells so that adjacent channel interference is minimized. The United States AMPS system initially operated with 666 duplex channels. In 1989, the FCC allocated an additional 10 MHz of spectrum for cellular services, and this allowed 166 new channels to be added to the AMPS system. There are now 832 channels used in AMPS. The forward channel (870.030 MHz) along with the corresponding reverse channel (825.030 MHz) is numbered as channel 1. Similarly, the forward channel 889.98 MHz along with the reverse channel 844.98 MHz is numbered as channel 666 (see Figure 1.2). The extended band has channels numbered as 667 through 799, and 990 through 1023.

In order to encourage competition, the FCC licensed the channels to two competing operators in every service area, and each operator received half of the total channels. The channels used by the two operators are distinguished as *block A* and *block B* channels. Block B is operated by companies which have traditionally provided telephone services (called *wireline operators*), and Block A is operated by companies that have not traditionally provided telephone services (called *nonwireline operators*).

Out of the 416 channels used by each operator, 395 are voice channels and the remaining 21 are control channels. Channels 1 through 312 (voice channels) and channels 313 through 333 (control channels) are block A channels, and channels 355 through 666 (voice channels) and channels 334 through 354 (control channels) are block B channels. Channels 667 through 716 and 991 through 1023 are the extended Block A voice channels, and channels 717 through 799 are extended Block B voice channels.

Each of the 21 control channels are assigned such that one control channel is provided for each bank of trunked voice channels. Thus, control channels are often reused differently, often with more SIR protection, than the traffic generating voice channels. For an AMPS system, a single cell is assigned a single control channel, so that a seven-cell reuse scheme would have seven control channels assigned to seven neighboring cells that form a cluster. Two neighboring clusters would be assigned the remaining 14 control channels. Thus, control channels obey a 21-cell reuse scheme and are assigned over three clusters before being reused, even though the voice channels may be assigned using a seven-cell reuse scheme.

Each of the 395 voice channels are divided into 21 subsets, each containing about 19 channels. In each subset, the closest adjacent channel is 21 channels away. In a seven-cell reuse system, each cell uses three subsets of channels. The three subsets are assigned such that every channel in the cell is assured of being separated from every other channel by at least seven channel spacings. This channel assignment scheme is illustrated in Table 3.2. As seen in Table 3.2, each cell uses channels in the subsets, iA + iB + iC, where i is an integer from 1 to 7. The total number of voice channels in a cell is about 57. The channels listed in the upper half of the chart belong to block A and those in the lower half belong to block B. The shaded set of numbers correspond to the control channels which are standard to all cellular systems in North America.

Table 3.2 AMPS Channel Allocation for A and B Side Carriers

1A	2A	3A	4A	5A	6A	7A	1B	2B	3B	4B	5B	6B	7B	1C	2C	3C	4C	5C	6C	7C	
1	2	3	4	5	6	7	8	9	10	11	12	13	14	15	16	17	18	19	20	21	
22	23	24	25	26	27	28	29	30	31	32	33	34	35	36	37	38	39	40	41	42	
43	44	45	46	47	48	49	50	51	52	53	54	55	56	57	58	59	60	61	62	63	
64	65	66	67	68	69	70	71	72	73	74	75	76	77	78	79	80	81	82	83	84	
85	86	87	88	89	90	91	92	93	94	95	96	97	98	99	100	101	102	103	104	105	
106	107	108	109	110	111	112	113	114	115	116	117	118	119	120	121	122	123	124	125	126	
127	128	129	130	131	132	133	134	135	136	137	138	139	140	141	142	143	144	145	146	147	
148	149	150	151	152	153	154	155	156	157	158	159	160	161	162	163	164	165	166	167	168	
169	170	171	172	173	174	175	176	177	178	179	180	181	182	183	184	185	186	187	188	189	
190	191	192	193	194	195	196	197	198	199	20	201	202	203	204	205	206	207	208	209	210	A
211	212	213	214	215	216	217	218	219	220	221	222	223	224	225	226	227	228	229	230	231	SIDE
232	233	234	235	236	237	238	239	240	241	242	243	244	245	246	247	248	249	250	251	252	
253	254	255	256	257	258	259	260	261	262	263	264	265	266	267	268	269	270	271	272	273	
274	275	276	277	278	279	280	281	282	283	284	285	286	287	288	289	290	291	292	293	294	
295	296	297	298	299	300	301	302	303	304	305	306	307	308	309	310	311	312	-	-	-	
313	314	315	316	317	318	319	320	321	322	323	324	325	326	327	328	329	330	331	332	333	
-	-	-	-	-	-	-	-	-	-	-	-	-	-	-	-	-	-	667	668	669	
670	671	672	673	674	675	676	677	678	679	680	681	682	683	684	685	686	687	688	689	690	
691	692	693	694	695	696	697	698	699	700	701	702	703	704	705	706	707	708	709	710	711	
712	713	714	715	716	-	-	-	-	991	992	993	994	995	996	997	998	999	1000	1001	1002	
1003	1004	1005	1006	1007	1008	1009	1010	1011	1012	1013	1014	1015	1016	1017	1018	1019	1020	1021	1022	1023	
334	335	336	337	338	339	340	341	342	343	344	345	346	347	348	349	350	351	352	353	354	
355	356	357	358	359	360	361	362	363	364	365	366	367	368	369	370	371	372	373	374	375	
376	377	378	379	380	381	382	383	384	385	386	387	388	389	390	391	392	393	394	395	396	
397	398	399	400	401	402	403	404	405	406	407	408	409	410	411	412	413	414	415	416	417	
418	419	420	421	422	423	424	425	426	427	428	429	430	431	432	433	434	435	436	437	438	
439	440	441	442	443	444	445	446	447	448	449	450	451	452	453	454	455	456	457	458	459	
460	461	462	463	464	465	466	467	468	469	470	471	472	473	474	475	476	477	478	479	480	
481	482	483	484	485	486	487	488	489	490	491	492	493	494	495	496	497	498	499	500	501	
502	503	504	505	506	507	508	509	510	511	512	513	514	515	516	517	518	519	520	521	522	
523	524	525	526	527	528	529	530	531	532	533	534	535	536	537	538	539	540	541	542	543	B
544	545	546	547	548	549	550	551	552	553	554	555	556	557	558	559	560	561	562	563	564	SIDE
565	566	567	568	569	570	571	572	573	574	575	576	577	578	579	580	581	582	583	584	585	
586	587	588	589	590	591	592	593	594	595	596	597	598	599	600	601	602	603	604	605	606	
607	608	609	610	611	6612	613	614	615	616	617	618	619	620	621	622	623	624	625	626	627	
628	629	630	631	632	633	634	635	636	637	638	639	640	641	642	643	644	645	646	647	648	
649	650	651	652	653	654	655	656	657	658	659	660	661	662	663	664	665	666	-	-	-	
-	-	-	-	-	717	718	719	720	721	722	723	724	725	726	727	728	729	730	731	732	
733	734	735	736	737	738	739	740	741	742	743	744	745	746	747	748	749	750	751	752	753	
754	755	756	757	758	759	760	761	762	763	764	765	766	767	768	769	770	771	772	773	774	
775	776	777	778	779	780	781	782	783	784	785	786	787	788	789	790	791	792	793	794	795	
796	797	798	799																		

3.5.4 Power Control for Reducing Interference

In practical cellular radio and personal communication systems, the power levels transmitted by every subscriber unit are under constant control by the serving base stations. This is done to ensure that each mobile transmits the smallest power necessary to maintain a good quality link on the reverse channel. Power control not only helps prolong battery life for the subscriber unit, but also dramatically reduces the reverse channel S/I in the system. As shown in Chapters 9 and 11, power control is especially important for emerging CDMA spread spectrum systems that allow every user in every cell to share the same radio channel.

3.6 Trunking and Grade of Service

Cellular radio systems rely on *trunking* to accommodate a large number of users in a limited radio spectrum. The concept of trunking allows a large number of users to share the relatively small number of channels in a cell by providing access to each user, on demand, from a pool of available channels. In a trunked radio system, each user is allocated a channel on a per call basis, and upon termination of the call, the previously occupied channel is immediately returned to the pool of available channels.

Trunking exploits the statistical behavior of users so that a fixed number of channels or circuits may accommodate a large, random user community. The telephone company uses trunking theory to determine the number of telephone circuits that need to be allocated for office buildings with hundreds of telephones, and this same principle is used in designing cellular radio systems. There is a trade-off between the number of available telephone circuits and the likelihood of a particular user finding that no circuits are available during the peak calling time. As the number of phone lines decreases, it becomes more likely that all circuits will be busy for a particular user. In a trunked mobile radio system, when a particular user requests service and all of the radio channels are already in use, the user is blocked, or denied access to the system. In some systems, a queue may be used to hold the requesting users until a channel becomes available.

To design trunked radio systems that can handle a specific capacity at a specific "grade of service," it is essential to understand trunking theory and queuing theory. The fundamentals of trunking theory were developed by Erlang, a Danish mathematician who, in the late 19th century, embarked on the study of how a large population could be accommodated by a limited number of servers [Bou88]. Today, the measure of traffic intensity bears his name. One Erlang represents the amount of traffic intensity carried by a channel that is completely occupied (i.e. one call-hour per hour or one call-minute per minute). For example, a radio channel that is occupied for thirty minutes during an hour carries 0.5 Erlangs of traffic.

The *grade of service (GOS)* is a measure of the ability of a user to access a trunked system during the busiest hour. The busy hour is based upon customer demand at the busiest hour during a week, month, or year. The busy hours for cellular radio systems typically occur during rush hours, between 4 p.m. and 6 p.m. on a Thursday or Friday evening. The grade of service is a benchmark used to define the desired performance of a particular trunked system by specifying a desired likelihood of a user obtaining channel access given a specific number of channels available in the system. It is the wireless designer's job to estimate the maximum required capacity and to allocate the proper number of channels in order to meet the *GOS*. *GOS* is typically given as the likelihood that a call is blocked, or the likelihood of a call experiencing a delay greater than a certain queuing time.

Table 3.3 Definitions of Common Terms Used in Trunking Theory

Set-up Time: The time required to allocate a trunked radio channel to a requesting user.

Blocked Call: Call which cannot be completed at time of request, due to congestion. Also referred to as a *lost call*.

Holding Time: Average duration of a typical call. Denoted by H (in seconds).

Traffic Intensity: Measure of channel time utilization, which is the average channel occupancy measured in Erlangs. This is a dimensionless quantity and may be used to measure the time utilization of single or multiple channels. Denoted by A.

Load: Traffic intensity across the entire trunked radio system, measured in Erlangs.

Grade of Service (GOS): A measure of congestion which is specified as the probability of a call being blocked (for Erlang B), or the probability of a call being delayed beyond a certain amount of time (for Erlang C).

Request Rate: The average number of call requests per unit time. Denoted by λ seconds^{-1}.

A number of definitions listed in Table 3.3 are used in trunking theory to make capacity estimates in trunked systems.

The traffic intensity offered by each user is equal to the call request rate multiplied by the holding time. That is, each user generates a traffic intensity of A_u Erlangs given by

$$A_u = \lambda H \tag{3.13}$$

where H is the average duration of a call and λ is the average number of call requests per unit time for each user. For a system containing U users and an unspecified number of channels, the total offered traffic intensity A, is given as

$$A = UA_u \tag{3.14}$$

Furthermore, in a C channel trunked system, if the traffic is equally distributed among the channels, then the traffic intensity per channel, A_c, is given as

$$A_c = UA_u/C \tag{3.15}$$

Note that the offered traffic is not necessarily the traffic which is *carried* by the trunked system, only that which is *offered* to the trunked system. When the offered traffic exceeds the maximum capacity of the system, the carried traffic becomes limited due to the limited capacity (i.e. limited number of channels). The maximum possible carried traffic is the total number of channels, C, in Erlangs. The AMPS cellular system is designed for a GOS of 2% blocking. This implies that the channel allocations for cell sites are designed so that 2 out of 100 calls will be blocked due to channel occupancy during the busiest hour.

There are two types of trunked systems which are commonly used. The first type offers no queuing for call requests. That is, for every user who requests service, it is assumed there is no setup time and the user is given immediate access to a channel if one is available. If no channels are available, the requesting user is blocked without access and is free to try again later. This type of trunking is called *blocked calls cleared* and assumes that calls arrive as determined by a Poisson distribution. Furthermore, it is assumed that there are an infinite number of users as well as the following: (a) there are memoryless arrivals of requests, implying that all users, including blocked users, may request a channel at any time; (b) the probability of a user occupying a channel is exponentially distributed, so that longer calls are less likely to occur as described by an exponential distribution; and (c) there are a finite number of channels available in the trunking pool. This is known as an M/M/m/m queue, and leads to the derivation of the Erlang B formula (also known as the *blocked calls cleared* formula). The Erlang B formula determines the probability that a call is blocked and is a measure of the GOS for a trunked system which provides no queuing for blocked calls. The Erlang B formula is derived in Appendix A and is given by

$$Pr[blocking] = \frac{\frac{A^C}{C!}}{\sum_{k=0}^{C} \frac{A^k}{k!}} = GOS \tag{3.16}$$

where C is the number of trunked channels offered by a trunked radio system and A is the total offered traffic. While it is possible to model trunked systems with finite users, the resulting expressions are much more complicated than the Erlang B result, and the added complexity is not warranted for typical trunked systems which have users that outnumber available channels by orders of magnitude. Furthermore, the Erlang B formula provides a conservative estimate of the GOS, as the finite user results always predict a smaller likelihood of blocking. The capacity of a trunked radio system where blocked calls are lost is tabulated for various values of GOS and numbers of channels in Table 3.4.

Table 3.4 Capacity of an Erlang B System

Number of Channels C	Capacity (Erlangs) for GOS = 0.01	= 0.005	= 0.002	= 0.001
2	0.153	0.105	0.065	0.046
4	0.869	0.701	0.535	0.439
5	1.36	1.13	0.900	0.762
10	4.46	3.96	3.43	3.09
20	12.0	11.1	10.1	9.41
24	15.3	14.2	13.0	12.2
40	29.0	27.3	25.7	24.5
70	56.1	53.7	51.0	49.2
100	84.1	80.9	77.4	75.2

The second kind of trunked system is one in which a queue is provided to hold calls which are blocked. If a channel is not available immediately, the call request may be delayed until a channel becomes available. This type of trunking is called *Blocked Calls Delayed*, and its measure of GOS is defined as the probability that a call is blocked after waiting a specific length of time in the queue. To find the GOS, it is first necessary to find the likelihood that a call is initially denied access to the system. The likelihood of a call not having immediate access to a channel is determined by the Erlang C formula derived in Appendix A

$$Pr[delay > 0] = \frac{A^C}{A^C + C!\left(1 - \frac{A}{C}\right)\sum_{k=0}^{C-1}\frac{A^k}{k!}} \tag{3.17}$$

If no channels are immediately available the call is delayed, and the probability that the delayed call is forced to wait more than t seconds is given by the probability that a call is delayed, multiplied by the conditional probability that the delay is greater than t seconds. The GOS of a trunked system where blocked calls are delayed is hence given by

$$\begin{aligned} Pr[delay > t] &= Pr[delay > 0]Pr[delay > t | delay > 0] \\ &= Pr[delay > 0]\exp(-(C-A)t/H) \end{aligned} \tag{3.18}$$

The average delay D for all calls in a queued system is given by

$$D = Pr[delay > 0]\frac{H}{C-A} \tag{3.19}$$

where the average delay for those calls which are queued is given by $H/(C-A)$.

The Erlang B and Erlang C formulas are plotted in graphical form in Figures 3.6 and 3.7. These graphs are useful for determining GOS in rapid fashion, although computer simulations are often used to determine transient behaviors experienced by particular users in a mobile system.

To use Figures 3.6 and 3.7, locate the number of channels on the top portion of the graph. Locate the traffic intensity of the system on the bottom portion of the graph. The blocking probability *Pr*[*blocking*] is shown on the abscissa of Figure 3.6, and *Pr*[*delay*] > 0 is shown on the abscissa of Figure 3.7. With two of the parameters specified, it is easy to find the third parameter.

Example 3.4

How many users can be supported for 0.5% blocking probability for the following number of trunked channels in a blocked calls cleared system? (a) 1, (b) 5, (c) 10, (d) 20, (e) 100. Assume each user generates 0.1 Erlangs of traffic.

Solution

From Table 3.4, we can find the total capacity in Erlangs for the 0.5% GOS for different numbers of channels. By using the relation $A = UA_u$, we can obtain the total number of users that can be supported in the system.

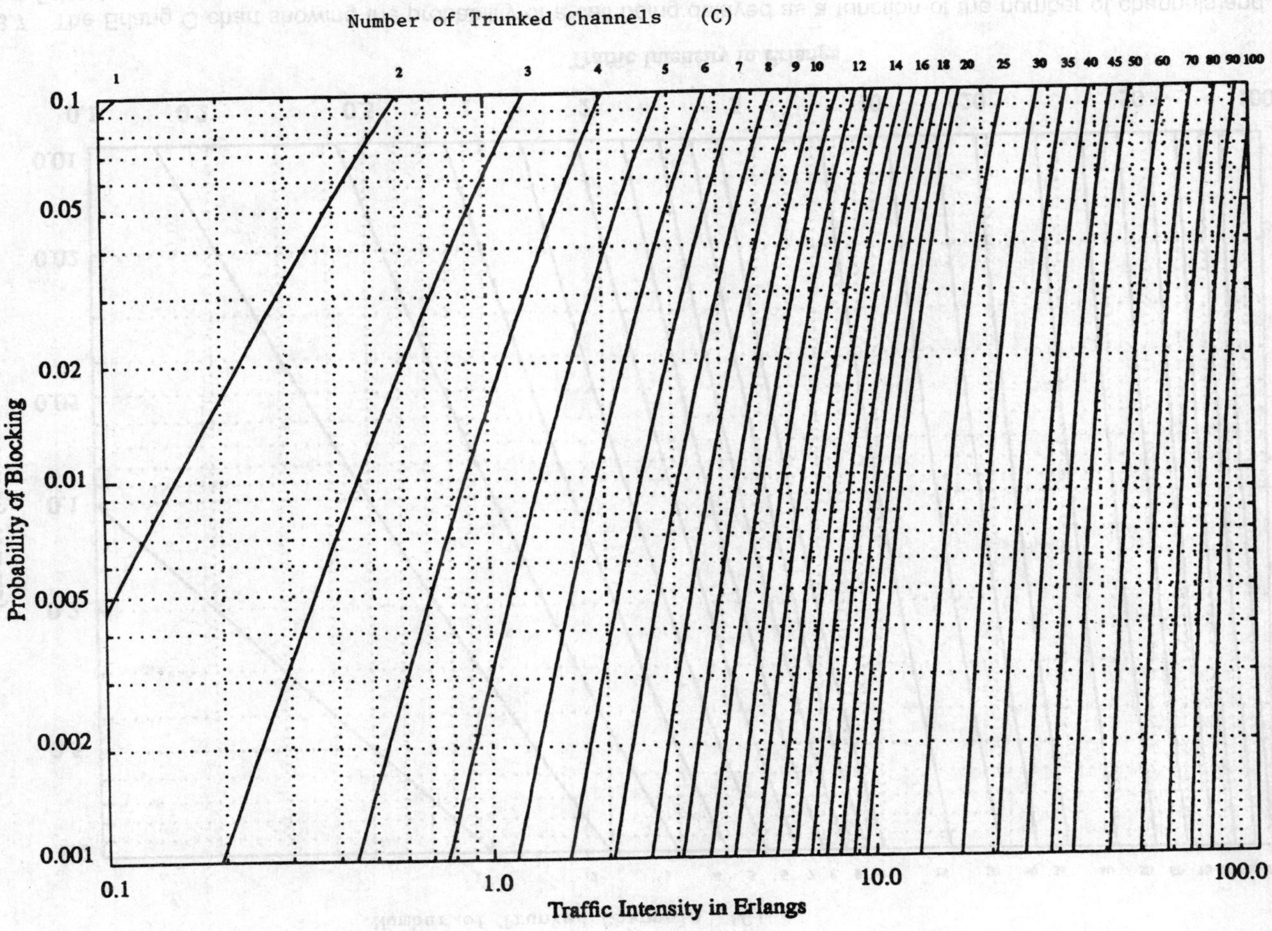

Figure 3.6 The Erlang B chart showing the probability of blocking as functions of the number of channels and traffic intensity in Erlangs.

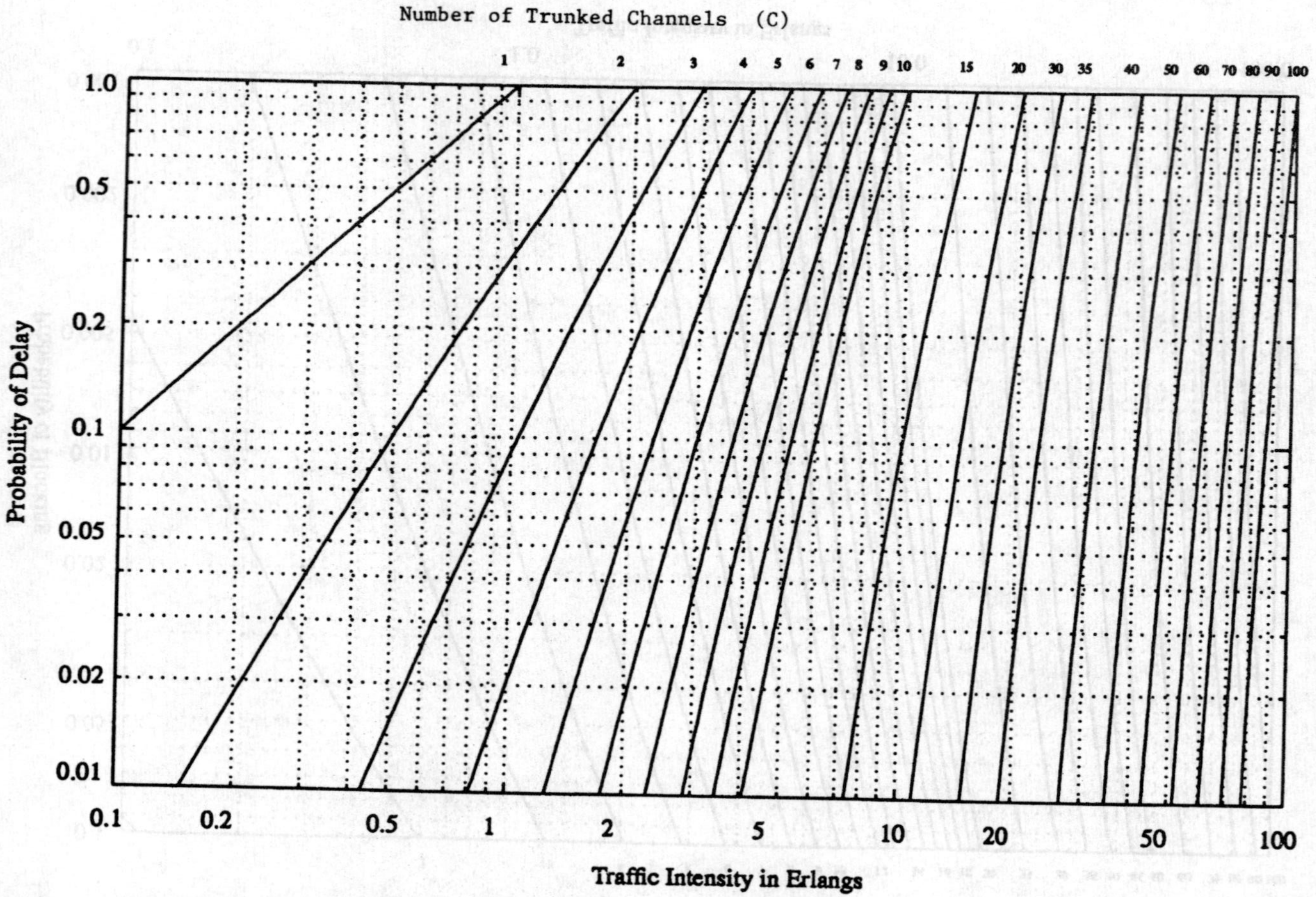

Figure 3.7 The Erlang C chart showing the probability of a call being delayed as a function of the number of channels and traffic intensity in Erlangs.

(a) Given $C = 1$, $A_u = 0.1$, $GOS = 0.005$
From Figure 3.6, we obtain $A = 0.005$.
Therefore, total number of users, $U = A/A_u = 0.005/0.1 = 0.05$ users.
But, actually one user could be supported on one channel. So, $U = 1$.

(b) Given $C = 5$, $A_u = 0.1$, $GOS = 0.005$
From Figure 3.6, we obtain $A = 1.13$.
Therefore, total number of users, $U = A/A_u = 1.13/0.1 \approx 11$ users.

(c) Given $C = 10$, $A_u = 0.1$, $GOS = 0.005$
From Figure 3.6, we obtain $A = 3.96$.
Therefore, total number of users, $U = A/A_u = 3.96/0.1 \approx 39$ users.

(d) Given $C = 20$, $A_u = 0.1$, $GOS = 0.005$
From Figure 3.6, we obtain $A = 11.10$.
Therefore, total number of users, $U = A/A_u = 11.1/0.1 \approx 110$ users.

(e) Given $C = 100$, $A_u = 0.1$, $GOS = 0.005$,
From Figure 3.6, we obtain $A = 80.9$.
Therefore, total number of users, $U = A/A_u = 80.9/0.1 = 809$ users.

Example 3.5

An urban area has a population of two million residents. Three competing trunked mobile networks (systems A, B, and C) provide cellular service in this area. System A has 394 cells with 19 channels each, system B has 98 cells with 57 channels each, and system C has 49 cells, each with 100 channels. Find the number of users that can be supported at 2% blocking if each user averages two calls per hour at an average call duration of three minutes. Assuming that all three trunked systems are operated at maximum capacity, compute the percentage market penetration of each cellular provider.

Solution

System A

Given:
Probability of blocking = 2% = 0.02
Number of channels per cell used in the system, $C = 19$
Traffic intensity per user, $A_u = \lambda H = 2 \times (3/60) = 0.1$ Erlangs

For $GOS = 0.02$ and $C = 19$, from the Erlang B chart, the total carried traffic, A, is obtained as 12 Erlangs.
Therefore, the number of users that can be supported per cell is
$U = A/A_u = 12/0.1 = 120$
Since there are 394 cells, the total number of subscribers that can be supported by System A is equal to $120 \times 394 = 47280$

System B

Given:
Probability of blocking = 2% = 0.02
Number of channels per cell used in the system, $C = 57$
Traffic intensity per user, $A_u = \lambda H = 2 \times (3/60) = 0.1$ Erlangs

For $GOS = 0.02$ and $C = 57$, from the Erlang B chart, the total carried traffic, A, is obtained as 45 Erlangs.

Therefore, the number of users that can be supported per cell is

$U = A/A_u = 45/0.1 = 450$

Since there are 98 cells, the total number of subscribers that can be supported by System B is equal to $450 \times 98 = 44{,}100$

System C

Given:

Probability of blocking = 2% = 0.02

Number of channels per cell used in the system, $C = 100$

Traffic intensity per user, $A_u = \lambda H = 2 \times (3/60) = 0.1$ Erlangs

For $GOS = 0.02$ and $C = 100$, from the Erlang B chart, the total carried traffic, A, is obtained as 88 Erlangs.

Therefore, the number of users that can be supported per cell is

$U = A/A_u = 88/0.1 = 880$

Since there are 49 cells, the total number of subscribers that can be supported by System C is equal to $880 \times 49 = 43{,}120$

Therefore, total number of cellular subscribers that can be supported by these three systems are $47{,}280 + 44{,}100 + 43{,}120 = 134{,}500$ users.

Since there are two million residents in the given urban area and the total number of cellular subscribers in System A is equal to 47280, the percentage market penetration is equal to

$47{,}280/2{,}000{,}000 = 2.36\%$

Similarly, market penetration of System B is equal to

$44{,}100/2{,}000{,}000 = 2.205\%$

and the market penetration of System C is equal to

$43{,}120/2{,}000{,}000 = 2.156\%$

The market penetration of the three systems combined is equal to

$134{,}500/2{,}000{,}000 = 6.725\%$

Example 3.6

A certain city has an area of 1,300 square miles and is covered by a cellular system using a seven-cell reuse pattern. Each cell has a radius of four miles and the city is allocated 40 MHz of spectrum with a full duplex channel bandwidth of 60 kHz. Assume a GOS of 2% for an Erlang B system is specified. If the offered traffic per user is 0.03 Erlangs, compute (a) the number of cells in the service area, (b) the number of channels per cell, (c) traffic intensity of each cell, (d) the maximum carried traffic, (e) the total number of users that can be served for 2% GOS, (f) the number of mobiles per unique channel (where it is understood that channels are reused), and (g) the theoretical maximum number of users that could be served at one time by the system.

Solution

(a) Given:
Total coverage area = 1300 miles, and cell radius = 4 miles
The area of a cell (hexagon) can be shown to be $2.5981R^2$, thus each cell covers $2.5981 \times (4)^2$ 41.57 sq. mi.
Hence, the total number of cells are $N_c = 1300/41.57 = 31$ cells.

(b) The total number of channels per cell (C)
= allocated spectrum /(channel width × frequency reuse factor)
= 40,000,000/(60,000 × 7) = 95 channels/cell

(c) Given:
$C = 95$, and $GOS = 0.02$
From the Erlang B chart, we have
traffic intensity per cell $A = 84$ Erlangs/cell

(d) Maximum carried traffic = number of cells × traffic intensity per cell
= 31 × 84 = 2604 Erlangs.

(e) Given traffic per user = 0.03 Erlangs
Total number of users = Total traffic / traffic per user
= 2604 / 0.03 = 86,800 users.

(f) Number of mobiles per channel = number of users/number of channels
= 86,800 / 666 = 130 mobiles/channel.

(g) The theoretical maximum number of served mobiles is the number of available channels in the system (all channels occupied)
$= C \times N_C = 95 \times 31 = 2945$ users, which is 3.4% of the customer base.

Example 3.7

A hexagonal cell within a four-cell system has a radius of 1.387 km. A total of 60 channels are used within the entire system. If the load per user is 0.029 Erlangs, and $\lambda = 1$ call/hour, compute the following for an Erlang C system that has a 5% probability of a delayed call:

(a) How many users per square kilometer will this system support?
(b) What is the probability that a delayed call will have to wait for more than 10 s?
(c) What is the probability that a call will be delayed for more than 10 seconds?

Solution

Given:
Cell radius, $R = 1.387$ km
Area covered per cell is $2.598 \times (1.387)^2 = 5$ sq km
Number of cells per cluster = 4
Total number of channels = 60
Therefore, number of channels per cell = 60 / 4 = 15 channels.

(a) From Erlang C chart, for 5% probability of delay with $C = 15$, traffic intensity = 9.0 Erlangs.

Therefore, number of users = total traffic intensity / traffic per user
= 9.0/0.029 = 310 users
= 310 users/5 sq km = 62 users/sq km

(b) Given $\lambda = 1$, holding time
$H = A_u/\lambda = 0.029$ hour = 104.4 seconds.
The probability that a delayed call will have to wait longer than 10 s is
$Pr[delay > t | delay] = \exp(-(C - A)t/H)$
$= \exp(-(15 - 9.0)10/104.4) = 56.29\%$

(c) Given $Pr[delay > 0] = 5\% = 0.05$
Probability that a call is delayed more than 10 seconds,
$Pr[delay > 10] = Pr[delay > 0] Pr[delay > t | delay]$
$= 0.05 \times 0.5629 = 2.81\%$

Trunking efficiency is a measure of the number of users which can be offered a particular GOS with a particular configuration of fixed channels. The way in which channels are grouped can substantially alter the number of users handled by a trunked system. For example, from Table 3.4, 10 trunked channels at a GOS of 0.01 can support 4.46 Erlangs of traffic, whereas two groups of five trunked channels can support 2 × 1.36 Erlangs, or 2.72 Erlangs of traffic. Clearly, 10 channels trunked together support 60% more traffic at a specific GOS than do two five channel trunks! It should be clear that the allocation of channels in a trunked radio system has a major impact on overall system capacity.

3.7 Improving Coverage and Capacity in Cellular Systems

As the demand for wireless service increases, the number of channels assigned to a cell eventually becomes insufficient to support the required number of users. At this point, cellular design techniques are needed to provide more channels per unit coverage area. Techniques such as *cell splitting*, *sectoring*, and *coverage zone approaches* are used in practice to expand the capacity of cellular systems. Cell splitting allows an orderly growth of the cellular system. Sectoring uses directional antennas to further control the interference and frequency reuse of channels. The *zone microcell* concept distributes the coverage of a cell and extends the cell boundary to hard-to-reach places. While cell splitting increases the number of base stations in order to increase capacity, sectoring and zone microcells rely on base station antenna placements to improve capacity by reducing co-channel interference. Cell splitting and zone microcell techniques do not suffer the trunking inefficiencies experienced by sectored cells, and enable the base station to oversee all handoff chores related to the microcells, thus reducing the computational load at the MSC. These popular capacity improvement techniques will be explained in detail.

3.7.1 Cell Splitting

Cell splitting is the process of subdividing a congested cell into smaller cells, each with its own base station and a corresponding reduction in antenna height and transmitter power. Cell splitting increases the capacity of a cellular system since it increases the number of times that channels are reused. By defining new cells which have a smaller radius than the original cells and by installing these smaller cells (called *microcells*) between the existing cells, capacity increases due to the additional number of channels per unit area.

Imagine if every cell in Figure 3.1 were reduced in such a way that the radius of every cell was cut in half. In order to cover the entire service area with smaller cells, approximately four times as many cells would be required. This can be easily shown by considering a circle with radius R. The area covered by such a circle is four times as large as the area covered by a circle with radius $R/2$. The increased number of cells would increase the number of clusters over the coverage region, which in turn would increase the number of channels, and thus capacity, in the coverage area. Cell splitting allows a system to grow by replacing large cells with smaller cells, while not upsetting the channel allocation scheme required to maintain the minimum co-channel reuse ratio Q (see Equation (3.4)) between co-channel cells.

An example of cell splitting is shown in Figure 3.8. In Figure 3.8, the base stations are placed at corners of the cells, and the area served by base station A is assumed to be saturated with traffic (i.e., the blocking of base station A exceeds acceptable rates). New base stations are therefore needed in the region to increase the number of channels in the area and to reduce the area served by the single base station. Note in the figure that the original base station A has been surrounded by six new microcells. In the example shown in Figure 3.8, the smaller cells were added in such a way as to preserve the frequency reuse plan of the system. For example, the microcell base station labeled G was placed half way between two larger stations utilizing the same channel set G. This is also the case for the other microcells in the figure. As can be seen from Figure 3.8, cell splitting merely scales the geometry of the cluster. In this case, the radius of each new microcell is half that of the original cell.

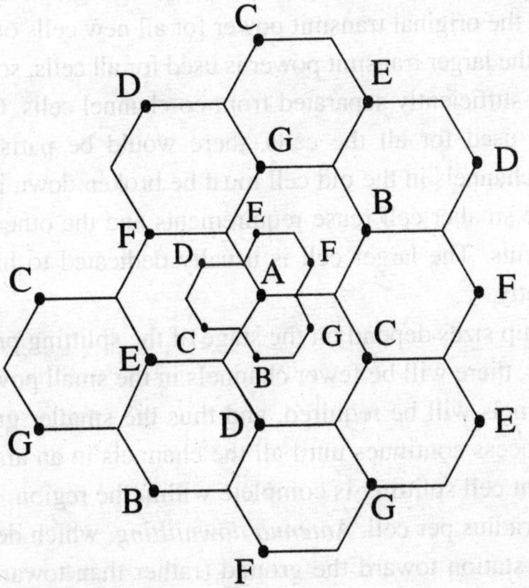

Figure 3.8 Illustration of cell splitting.

For the new cells to be smaller in size, the transmit power of these cells must be reduced. The transmit power of the new cells with radius half that of the original cells can be found by examining the received power P_r at the new and old cell boundaries and setting them equal to each other. This is necessary to ensure that the frequency reuse plan for the new microcells behaves exactly as for the original cells. For Figure 3.8

$$P_r[\text{at old cell boundary}] \propto P_{t1}R^{-n} \tag{3.20}$$

and

$$P_r[\text{at new cell boundary}] \propto P_{t2}(R/2)^{-n} \tag{3.21}$$

where P_{t1} and P_{t2} are the transmit powers of the larger and smaller cell base stations, respectively, and n is the path loss exponent. If we take $n = 4$ and set the received powers equal to each other, then

$$P_{t2} = \frac{P_{t1}}{16} \tag{3.22}$$

In other words, the transmit power must be reduced by 12 dB in order to fill in the original coverage area with microcells, while maintaining the S/I requirement.

In practice, not all cells are split at the same time. It is often difficult for service providers to find real estate that is perfectly situated for cell splitting. Therefore, different cell sizes will exist simultaneously. In such situations, special care needs to be taken to keep the distance between co-channel cells at the required minimum, and hence channel assignments become more complicated [Rap97]. Also, handoff issues must be addressed so that high speed and low speed traffic can be simultaneously accommodated (the umbrella cell approach of Section 3.4 is commonly used). When there are two cell sizes in the same region as shown in Figure 3.8, Equation (3.22) shows that one cannot simply use the original transmit power for all new cells or the new transmit power for all the original cells. If the larger transmit power is used for all cells, some channels used by the smaller cells would not be sufficiently separated from co-channel cells. On the other hand, if the smaller transmit power is used for all the cells, there would be parts of the larger cells left unserved. For this reason, channels in the old cell must be broken down into two channel groups, one that corresponds to the smaller cell reuse requirements and the other that corresponds to the larger cell reuse requirements. The larger cell is usually dedicated to high speed traffic so that handoffs occur less frequently.

The two channel group sizes depend on the stage of the splitting process. At the beginning of the cell splitting process, there will be fewer channels in the small power groups. However, as demand grows, more channels will be required, and thus the smaller groups will require more channels. This splitting process continues until all the channels in an area are used in the lower power group, at which point cell splitting is complete within the region, and the entire system is rescaled to have a smaller radius per cell. *Antenna downtilting*, which deliberately focuses radiated energy from the base station toward the ground (rather than toward the horizon), is often used to limit the radio coverage of newly formed microcells.

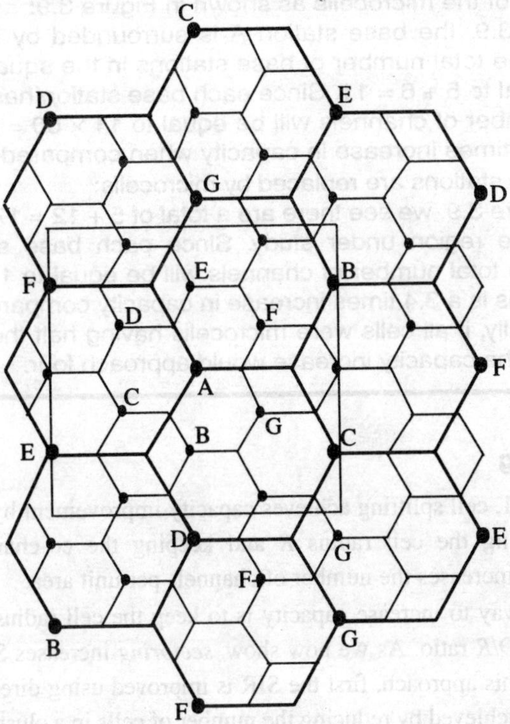

Figure 3.9 Illustration of cell splitting within a 3 km by 3 km square centered around base station A.

Example 3.8

Consider Figure 3.9. Assume each base station uses 60 channels, regardless of cell size. If each original cell has a radius of 1 km and each microcell has a radius of 0.5 km, find the number of channels contained in a 3 km by 3 km square centered around A under the following conditions: (a) without the use of microcells; (b) when the lettered microcells as shown in Figure 3.9 are used; and (c) if all the original base stations are replaced by microcells. Assume cells on the edge of the square to be contained within the square.

Solution

(a) without the use of microcells:

A cell radius of 1 km implies that the sides of the larger hexagons are also 1 km in length. To cover the 3 km by 3 km square centered around base station A, we need to cover 1.5 km (1.5 times the hexagon radius) toward the right, left, top, and bottom of base station A. This is shown in Figure 3.9. From Figure 3.9, we see that this area contains five base stations. Since each base station has 60 channels, the total number of channels without cell splitting is equal to $5 \times 60 = 300$ channels.

(b) with the use of the microcells as shown in Figure 3.9:
In Figure 3.9, the base station A is surrounded by six microcells. Therefore, the total number of base stations in the square area under study is equal to 5 + 6 = 11. Since each base station has 60 channels, the total number of channels will be equal to 11 × 60 = 660 channels. This is a 2.2 times increase in capacity when compared to case (a).

(c) if all the base stations are replaced by microcells:
From Figure 3.9, we see there are a total of 5 + 12 = 17 base stations in the square region under study. Since each base station has 60 channels, the total number of channels will be equal to 17 × 60 = 1020 channels. This is a 3.4 times increase in capacity compared to case (a).
Theoretically, if all cells were microcells having half the radius of the original cell, the capacity increase would approach four.

3.7.2 Sectoring

As shown in Section 3.7.1, cell splitting achieves capacity improvement by essentially rescaling the system. By decreasing the cell radius R and keeping the co-channel reuse ratio D/R unchanged, cell splitting increases the number of channels per unit area.

However, another way to increase capacity is to keep the cell radius unchanged and seek methods to decrease the D/R ratio. As we now show, *sectoring* increases SIR so that the cluster size may be reduced. In this approach, first the SIR is improved using directional antennas, then capacity improvement is achieved by reducing the number of cells in a cluster, thus increasing the frequency reuse. However, in order to do this successfully, it is necessary to reduce the relative interference without decreasing the transmit power.

The co-channel interference in a cellular system may be decreased by replacing a single omnidirectional antenna at the base station by several directional antennas, each radiating within a specified sector. By using directional antennas, a given cell will receive interference and transmit with only a fraction of the available co-channel cells. The technique for decreasing co-channel interference and thus increasing system performance by using directional antennas is called *sectoring*. The factor by which the co-channel interference is reduced depends on the amount of sectoring used. A cell is normally partitioned into three 120° sectors or six 60° sectors as shown in Figure 3.10(a) and (b).

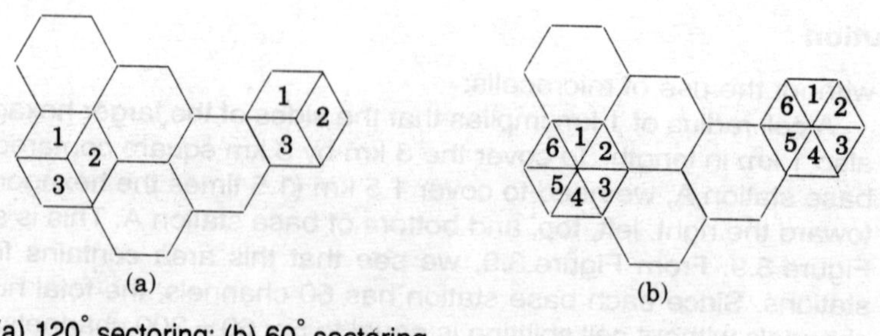

Figure 3.10 (a) 120° sectoring; (b) 60° sectoring.

When sectoring is employed, the channels used in a particular cell are broken down into sectored groups and are used only within a particular sector, as illustrated in Figure 3.10(a) and (b). Assuming seven-cell reuse, for the case of 120° sectors, the number of interferers in the first tier is reduced from six to two. This is because only two of the six co-channel cells receive interference with a particular sectored channel group. Referring to Figure 3.11, consider the interference experienced by a mobile located in the right-most sector in the center cell labeled "5". There are three co-channel cell sectors labeled "5" to the right of the center cell, and three to the left of the center cell. Out of these six co-channel cells, only two cells have sectors with antenna patterns which radiate into the center cell, and hence a mobile in the center cell will experience interference on the forward link from only these two sectors. The resulting S/I for this case can be found using Equation (3.8) to be 24.2 dB, which is a significant improvement over the omnidirectional case in Section 3.5, where the worst case S/I was shown to be 17 dB. This S/I improvement allows the wireless engineer to then decrease the cluster size N in order to improve the frequency reuse, and thus the system capacity (see Problem 3.28). In practical systems, further improvement in S/I is achieved by downtilting the sector antennas such that the radiation pattern in the vertical (elevation) plane has a notch at the nearest co-channel cell distance.

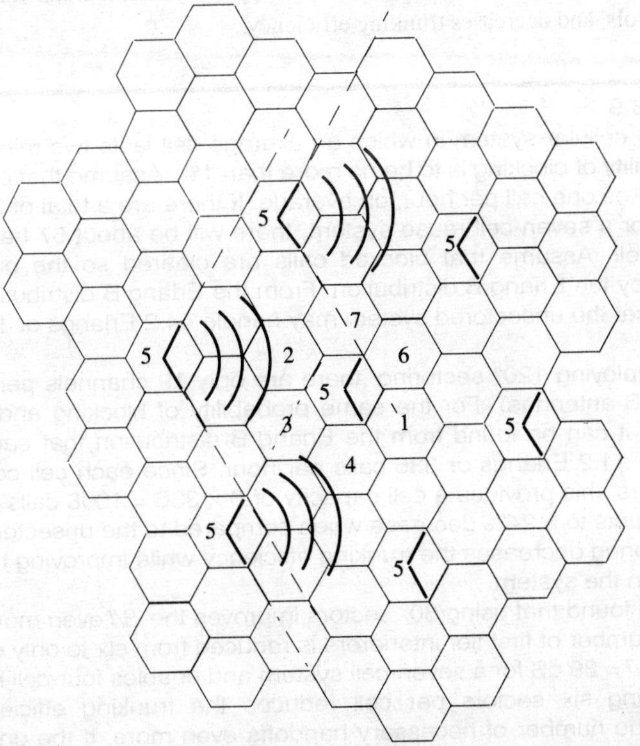

Figure 3.11 Illustration of how 120° sectoring reduces interference from co-channel cells. Out of the 6 co-channel cells in the first tier, only two of them interfere with the center cell. If omnidirectional antennas were used at each base station, all six co-channel cells would interfere with the center cell.

The improvement in S/I implies that with 120° sectoring, the minimum required S/I of 18 dB can be easily achieved with seven-cell reuse, as compared to 12-cell reuse for the worst possible situation in the unsectored case (see Section 3.5.1). Thus, sectoring reduces interference, which amounts to an increase in capacity by a factor of 12/7, or 1.714. In practice, the reduction in interference offered by sectoring enable planners to reduce the cluster size N, and provides an additional degree of freedom in assigning channels. The penalty for improved S/I and the resulting capacity improvement from the shrinking cluster size is an increased number of antennas at each base station, and a decrease in trunking efficiency due to channel sectoring at the base station. Since sectoring reduces the coverage area of a particular group of channels, the number of handoffs increases, as well. Fortunately, many modern base stations support sectorization and allow mobiles to be handed off from sector to sector within the same cell without intervention from the MSC, so the handoff problem is often not a major concern.

It is the loss of traffic due to decreased trunking efficiency that causes some operators to shy away from the sectoring approach, particularly in dense urban areas where the directional antenna patterns are somewhat ineffective in controlling radio propagation. Because sectoring uses more than one antenna per base station, the available channels in the cell must be subdivided and dedicated to a specific antenna. This breaks up the available trunked channel pool into several smaller pools, and decreases trunking efficiency.

Example 3.9

Consider a cellular system in which an average call lasts two minutes, and the probability of blocking is to be no more than 1%. Assume that every subscriber makes one call per hour, on average. If there are a total of 395 traffic channels for a seven-cell reuse system, there will be about 57 traffic channels per cell. Assume that blocked calls are cleared so the blocking is described by the Erlang B distribution. From the Erlang B distribution, it can be found that the unsectored system may handle 44.2 Erlangs or 1326 calls per hour.

Now employing 120° sectoring, there are only 19 channels per antenna sector (57/3 antennas). For the same probability of blocking and average call length, it can be found from the Erlang B distribution that each sector can handle 11.2 Erlangs or 336 calls per hour. Since each cell consists of three sectors, this provides a cell capacity of $3 \times 336 = 1008$ calls per hour, which amounts to a 24% decrease when compared to the unsectored case. Thus, sectoring decreases the trunking efficiency while improving the S/I for each user in the system.

It can be found that using 60° sectors improves the S/I even more. In this case, the number of first tier interferers is reduced from six to only one. This results in $S/I = 29$ dB for a seven-cell system and enables four-cell reuse. Of course, using six sectors per cell reduces the trunking efficiency and increases the number of necessary handoffs even more. If the unsectored system is compared to the six sector case, the degradation in trunking efficiency can be shown to be 44%. (The proof of this is left as an exercise.)

3.7.3 Repeaters for Range Extension

Often a wireless operator needs to provide dedicated coverage for hard-to-reach areas, such as within buildings, or in valleys or tunnels. Radio retransmitters, known as *repeaters*, are often used to provide such range extension capabilities. Repeaters are bidirectional in nature, and simultaneously send signals to and receive signals from a serving base station. Repeaters work using over-the-air signals, so they may be installed anywhere and are capable of repeating an entire cellular or PCS band. Upon receiving signals from a base station forward link, the repeater amplifies and reradiates the base station signals to the specific coverage region. Unfortunately, the received noise and interference is also reradiated by the repeater on both the forward and reverse link, so care must be taken to properly place the repeaters, and to adjust the various forward and reverse link amplifier levels and antenna patterns. Repeaters can be easily thought of as bidirectional "bent pipes" that retransmit what has been received. In practice, directional antennas or *distributed antenna systems (DAS)* are connected to the inputs or outputs of repeaters for localized spot coverage, particularly in tunnels or buildings.

By modifying the coverage of a serving cell, an operator is able to dedicate a certain amount of the base station's traffic for the areas covered by the repeater. However, the repeater does not add capacity to the system—it simply serves to reradiate the base station signal into specific locations. Repeaters are increasingly being used to provide coverage into and around buildings, where coverage has been traditionally weak [Rap96], [Mor00]. Many carriers have opted to provide in-building wireless penetration by installing microcells outside of large buildings, and then installing many repeaters with DAS networks within the buildings. This approach provides immediate coverage into targeted areas, but does not accommodate the increases in capacity that will arise due to increased outdoor and indoor user traffic. Eventually, dedicated base stations within buildings will be needed to accommodate the large number of in-building cellular users.

Determining the proper location for repeaters and distributed antenna systems within buildings requires careful planning, particularly due to the fact that interference levels are reradiated into the building from the base station and from the interior of the building back to the base station. Also, repeaters must be provisioned to match the available capacity from the serving base station. Fortunately, software products, such as *SitePlanner* [Wir01], allow engineers to rapidly determine the best placements for repeaters and the required DAS network while simultaneously computing the available traffic and associated cost of the installation. *SitePlanner* is protected by US Patent 6,317,599 and other patents. Using *SitePlanner*, engineers can very quickly determine the proper provisioning for a particular level of range extension (see Figure 3.12).

3.7.4 A Microcell Zone Concept

The increased number of handoffs required when sectoring is employed results in an increased load on the switching and control link elements of the mobile system. A solution to this problem was presented by Lee [Lee91b]. This proposal is based on a microcell concept for seven cell reuse, as illustrated in Figure 3.13. In this scheme, each of the three (or possibly more) zone sites

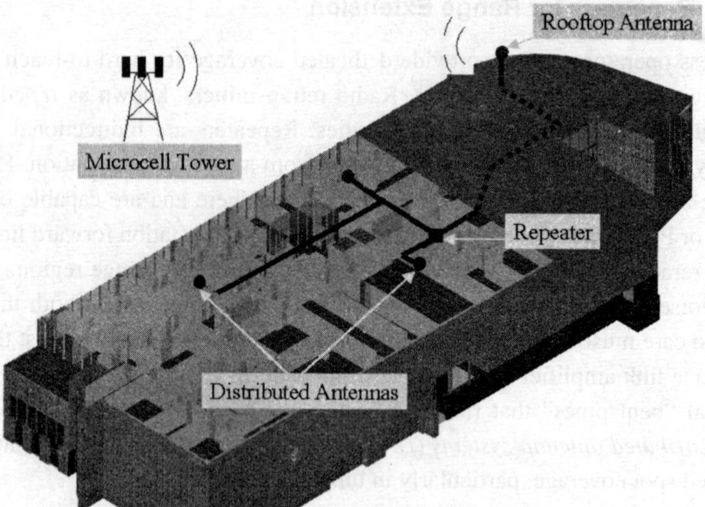

Figure 3.12 Illustration of how a distributed antenna system (DAS) may be used inside a building. Figure produced in SitePlanner®. (Courtesy of Wireless Valley Communications Inc.)

(represented as Tx/Rx in Figure 3.13) are connected to a single base station and share the same radio equipment. The zones are connected by coaxial cable, fiberoptic cable, or microwave link to the base station. Multiple zones and a single base station make up a cell. As a mobile travels within the cell, it is served by the zone with the strongest signal. This approach is superior to sectoring since antennas are placed at the outer edges of the cell, and any base station channel may be assigned to any zone by the base station.

As a mobile travels from one zone to another within the cell, it retains the same channel. Thus, unlike in sectoring, a handoff is not required at the MSC when the mobile travels between zones within the cell. The base station simply switches the channel to a different zone site. In this way, a given channel is active only in the particular zone in which the mobile is traveling, and hence the base station radiation is localized and interference is reduced. The channels are distributed in time and space by all three zones and are also reused in co-channel cells in the normal fashion. This technique is particularly useful along highways or along urban traffic corridors.

The advantage of the zone cell technique is that while the cell maintains a particular coverage radius, the co-channel interference in the cellular system is reduced since a large central base station is replaced by several lower powered transmitters (zone transmitters) on the edges of the cell. Decreased co-channel interference improves the signal quality and also leads to an increase in capacity without the degradation in trunking efficiency caused by sectoring. As mentioned earlier, an S/I of 18 dB is typically required for satisfactory system performance in narrowband FM. For a system with $N = 7$, a D/R of 4.6 was shown to achieve this. With respect to

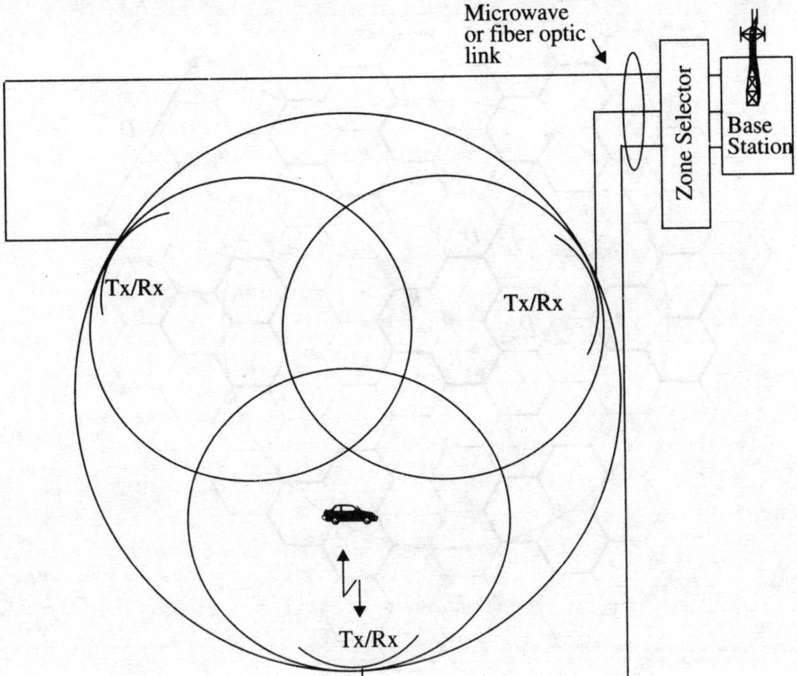

Figure 3.13 The microcell concept [adapted from [Lee91b] © IEEE].

the zone microcell system, since transmission at any instant is confined to a particular zone, this implies that a D_z/R_z of 4.6 (where D_z is the minimum distance between active co-channel zones and R_z is the zone radius) can achieve the required link performance. In Figure 3.14, let each individual hexagon represents a zone, while each group of three hexagons represents a cell. The zone radius R_z is approximately equal to one hexagon radius. Now, the capacity of the zone microcell system is directly related to the distance between co-channel cells, and not zones. This distance is represented as D in Figure 3.14. For a D_z/R_z value of 4.6, it can be seen from the geometry of Figure 3.14 that the value of co-channel reuse ratio, D/R, is equal to three, where R is the radius of the cell and is equal to twice the length of the hexagon radius. Using Equation (3.4), $D/R = 3$ corresponds to a cluster size of $N = 3$. This reduction in the cluster size from $N = 7$ to $N = 3$ amounts to a 2.33 times increase in capacity for a system completely based on the zone microcell concept. Hence for the same S/I requirement of 18 dB, this system provides a significant increase in capacity over conventional cellular planning.

By examining Figure 3.14 and using Equation (3.8) [Lee91b], the exact worst case S/I of the zone microcell system can be estimated to be 20 dB. Thus, in the worst case, the system provides a margin of 2 dB over the required signal-to-interference ratio while increasing the capacity by 2.33 times over a conventional seven-cell system using omnidirectional antennas.

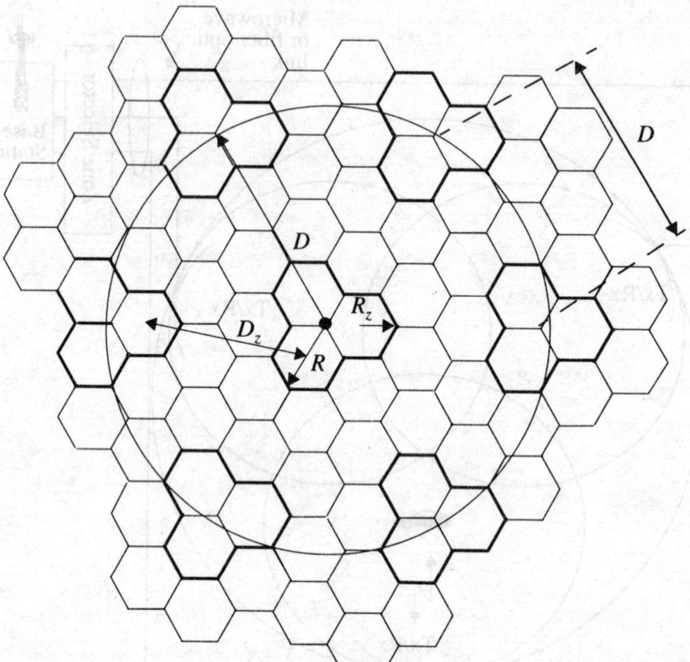

Figure 3.14 Define D, D_z, R, and R_z for a microcell architecture with $N = 7$. The smaller hexagons form zones and three hexagons (outlined in bold) together form a cell. Six nearest co-channel cells are shown.

No loss in trunking efficiency is experienced. Zone cell architectures are being adopted in many cellular and personal communication systems.

3.8 Summary

In this chapter, the fundamental concepts of handoff, frequency reuse, trunking efficiency, and frequency planning have been presented. Handoffs are required to pass mobile traffic from cell to cell, and there are various ways handoffs are implemented. The capacity of a cellular system is a function of many variables. The S/I in a wireless propagation channel, along with the specific performance of the air interface in an interference environment, limits the frequency reuse factor of a system, which limits the number of channels within the coverage area. The trunking efficiency limits the number of users that can access a trunked radio system. Trunking is affected by the number of available channels and how they are partitioned in a trunked cellular system. Trunking efficiency is quantified by the GOS. Finally, cell splitting, sectoring, and the zone microcell technique are all shown to improve capacity by increasing S/I in some fashion. The overriding objective in all of these methods is to increase the number of users within the system. The radio propagation characteristics influence the effectiveness of all of these methods in an actual system. Radio propagation is the subject of the following two chapters.

3.9 Problems

3.1 Prove that for a hexagonal geometry, the co-channel reuse ratio is given by $Q = \sqrt{3N}$, where $N = i^2 + ij + j^2$. Hint: Use the cosine law and the hexagonal cell geometry.

3.2 If two independent voltage signals, v1(t) and v2(t), are added together to provide a new resulting signal, prove that under certain conditions the resulting signal has the same power as the sum of the individual powers. What are these conditions? What special conditions must apply for this result to be valid when the signals are uncorrelated?

3.3 Show that the frequency reuse factor for a cellular system is given by k/S, where k is the average number of channels per cell and S is the total number of channels available to the cellular service provider.

3.4 If 20 MHz of total spectrum is allocated for a duplex wireless cellular system and each simplex channel has 25 kHz RF bandwidth, find:

(a) the number of duplex channels.

(b) the total number of channels per cell site, if $N = 4$ cell reuse is used.

3.5 A cellular service provider decides to use a digital TDMA scheme which can tolerate a signal-to-interference ratio of 15 dB in the worst case. Find the optimal value of N for (a) omnidirectional antennas, (b) 120° sectoring, and (c) 60° sectoring. Should sectoring be used? If so, which case (60° or 120°) should be used? (Assume a path loss exponent of $n = 4$ and consider trunking efficiency.)

3.6 You are asked to determine the signal-to-interference ratio (SIR or C/I) on the forward link of a cellular system, when the mobile is located on the fringe of its serving cell. Assume that all cells have equal radii, and that base stations have equal power and are located in the centers of each cell. Also assume that each cell transmits an independent signal, such that interfering signal powers may be added. Let us define a "tier" of cells as being the collection of co-channel cells that are more-or-less the same distance away from the mobile in the serving cell. This problem explores the impact of the cluster size (i.e., frequency reuse distance), the number of tiers used in the calculation of C/I and the effect of the propagation path loss exponent on C/I.

(a) What is the average distance (in terms of R) between the mobile on the fringe of the serving cell and the first tier of co-channel cells? (These cells are called the "nearest neighbors.") How many cells are located in the first tier? Solve for the case of $N = 1$, $N = 3$, $N = 4$, $N = 7$, and $N = 12$ cluster sizes. How does the average distance compare to the value of $D = QR$, where $Q = \sqrt{3N}$?

(b) What is the average distance (in terms of R) between the mobile on the fringe of the serving cell and the second and third tier of co-channel cells, and how many cells are in the second and third tier of co-channel cells for the cases of $N = 1$, $N = 3$, $N = 4$, $N = 7$, and $N = 12$ cluster sizes?

(c) Determine the forward link C/I for the following frequency reuse designs: $N = 1$, $N = 3$, $N = 4$, $N = 7$, and $N = 12$. Assume that the propagation path loss exponent is four, and evaluate the S/I contribution due to just the first tier and then due to additional outer tiers of co-channel cells. Indicate the number of tiers at which there is a diminishing contribution to the interference at the mobile.

(d) Repeat part (c), except now consider a line-of-sight path loss exponent of $n = 2$. Notice the huge impact that the propagation path loss exponent has on C/I. What can you say

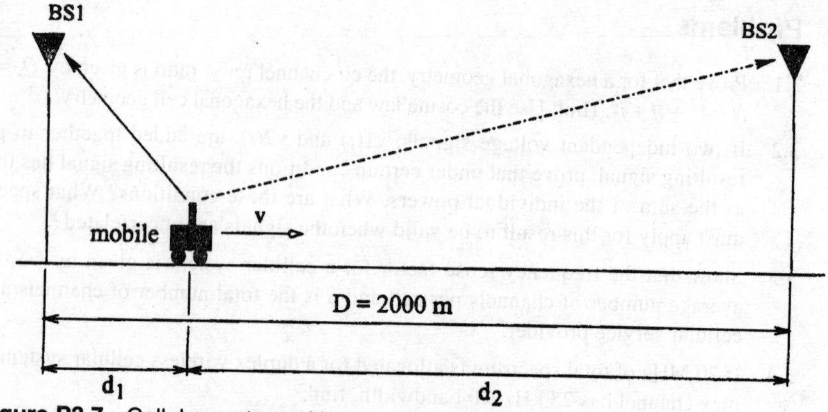

Figure P3.7 Cellular system with two base stations.

about the cluster size, path loss exponent, and the C/I values which result? How would this impact practical wireless system design?

3.7 Suppose that a mobile station is moving along a straight line between base stations BS_1 and BS_2, as shown in Figure P3.7. The distance between the base stations is $D = 2000$ m. For simplicity, assume small scale fading is neglected and the received power (in dBm) at base station i, from the mobile station, is modeled as a function of distance on the reverse link

$$P_{r,i}(d_i) = P_0 - 10n\log_{10}(d_i/d_0) \quad \text{(dBm)} \quad i = 1,2$$

where d_i is the distance between the mobile and the base station i, in meters. P_0 is the received power at distance d_0 from the mobile antenna. Assume that $P_0 = 0$ dBm and $d_0 = 1$ m. Let n denote the path loss which is assumed to be equal to 2.9.

Assume the minimum usable signal level for acceptable voice quality at the base station receiver is $P_{r,min} = -88$ dBm, and the threshold level used by the switch for handoff initiation is $P_{r,HO}$. Consider that the mobile is currently connected to BS_1 and is moving toward a handoff (time required to complete a handoff, once that received signal level reaches the handoff threshold $P_{r,HO}$ is $\Delta t = 4.5$ seconds).

(a) Determine the minimum required margin $\Delta = P_{r,HO} - P_{r,min}$ to assure that calls are not lost due to weak signal condition during handoff. Assume that the base station antenna heights are negligible compared to the distance between the mobile and the base stations.

(b) Describe the effects of the margin $\Delta = P_{r,HO} - P_{r,min}$ on the performance of cellular systems.

3.8 If an intensive propagation measurement campaign showed that the mobile radio channel provided a propagation path loss exponent of $n = 3$ instead of four, how would your design decisions in Problem 3.5 change? What is the optimal value of N for the case of $n = 3$?

3.9 Consider a cellular radio system with hexagonal cells and cluster size N. Since a hexagonal shape is assumed, the number of co-channel cells in the tth tier of co-channel cells is $6t$, regardless of the cluster size. Considering the forward link, the *total co-channel interference* power level I received at a particular mobile can be modeled as the sum $\sum_{i=1}^{M} I_i$, where I_i is the interference caused by the ith base station.

Let us suppose that only the base stations in the first three tiers produce significant interference. Interference signals from base stations in more distant tiers are assumed to be negligible.

(a) Assuming that a mobile is located at the boundary of the cell (worst case situation), compute the contribution of co-channel base stations in each tier to the total co-channel interference received at the mobile.

Also, compute the signal-to-interference ratio (*SIR*) at the mobile when only the first T tiers are considered, with $T = 1$, 2, and 3 (all tiers).

Assume that the power received at distance d from the transmitting antenna is given by

$$P_r = P_t\left(\frac{1}{d}\right)^n,$$

where P_t is the transmitted power and n is the path loss exponent. Also, assume that:

- the mobile and base stations are equipped with omnidirectional antennas,
- all base stations are located at the center of the cells and transmit the same power level, and
- all cells have the same radius (R).

Present the results for cluster size $N = 1$, 3, 4, and 7 and path loss exponents $n = 2$, 3, and 4.

(b) Suppose that you are asked to analyze co-channel interference on the forward link of a cellular system with the same characteristics as the system in part (a). In order to reduce the complexity of the analysis (or the computation time, if your analysis is based on simulation), you want to consider as few as possible tiers of co-channel base stations. On the other hand, you want to obtain accurate results from your analysis. Based on the results of part (a), determine the number of tiers that you would use in your co-channel interference analysis for cluster sizes $N = 1$, 3, 4, and 7, and path loss exponents $n = 2$, 3, and 4. Assume that you can tolerate an error of 0.5 dB in the computation of SIR with respect to the true value of *SIR*. Explain and justify your decision.

3.10 A total of 24 MHz of bandwidth is allocated to a particular FDD cellular telephone system that uses two 30 kHz simplex channels to provide full duplex voice and control channels. Assume each cell phone user generates 0.1 Erlangs of traffic. Assume Erlang B is used.

(a) Find the number of channels in each cell for a four-cell reuse system.

(b) If each cell is to offer capacity that is 90% of perfect scheduling, find the maximum number of users that can be supported per cell where omnidirectional antennas are used at each base station.

(c) What is the blocking probability of the system in (b) when the maximum number of users are available in the user pool?

(d) If each new cell now uses 120° sectoring instead of omnidirectional for each base station, what is the new total number of users that can be supported per cell for the same blocking probability as in (c)?

(e) If each cell covers five square kilometers, then how many subscribers could be supported in an urban market that is 50 km × 50 km for the case of omnidirectional base station antennas?

(f) If each cell covers five square kilometers, then how many subscribers could be supported in an urban market that is 50 km × 50 km for the case of 120° sectored antennas?

3.11 For a $N = 7$ system with a $Pr[Blocking] = 1\%$ and average call length of two minutes, find the traffic capacity loss due to trunking for 57 channels when going from omnidirectional antennas to 60° sectored antennas. (Assume that blocked calls are cleared and the average per user call rate is $\lambda = 1$ per hour.)

3.12 Assume that a cell named "Radio Knob" has 57 channels, each with an effective radiated power of 32 W and a cell radius of 10 km. The path loss is 40 dB per decade. The grade of service is established to be a probability of blocking of 5% (assuming blocked calls are cleared). Assume the average call length is two minutes, and each user averages two calls per hour. Further, assume the cell has just reached its maximum capacity and must be split into four new microcells to provide four times the capacity in the same area. (a) What is the current capacity of the "Radio Knob" cell? (b) What is the radius and transmit power of the new cells? (c) How many channels are needed in each of the new cells to maintain frequency reuse stability in the system? (d) If traffic is uniformly distributed, what is the new traffic carried by each new cell? Will the probability of blocking in these new cells be below 0.1% after the split? Assume 57 channels are used at the original base station and the split cells.

3.13 A certain area is covered by a cellular radio system with 84 cells and a cluster size N. 300 voice channels are available for the system. Users are uniformly distributed over the area covered by the cellular system, and the offered traffic per user is 0.04 Erlang. Assume that blocked calls are cleared and the designated blocking probability is $P_b = 1\%$.

(a) Determine the maximum carried traffic per cell if cluster size $N = 4$ is used. Repeat for cluster sizes $N = 7$ and 12.

(b) Determine the maximum number of users that can be served by the system for a blocking probability of 1% and cluster size $N = 4$. Repeat for cluster sizes $N = 7$ and 12.

3.14 The offered traffic in a cellular communication system can be specified by the average call duration H (also know as holding time) and call request rate λ. The quantities H and λ fairly represent the offered traffic in a particular cell if we assume that mobiles are not crossing cell boundaries. Quantitatively describe the effects of mobile stations that cross cell boundaries on both average call duration and call request rate.

3.15 Exercises in trunking (queueing) theory:

(a) What is the maximum system capacity (*total* and *per channel*) in Erlangs when providing a 2% blocking probability with four channels, with 20 channels, with 40 channels?

(b) How many users can be supported with 40 channels at 2% blocking? Assume $H = 105$ s, $\lambda = 1$ call/hour.

(c) Using the traffic intensity calculated in part (a), find the grade of service in a lost call delayed system for the case of delays being greater than 20 seconds. Assume that $H =$ 105 s, and determine the GOS for four channels, for 20 channels, for 40 channels.

(d) Comparing part (a) and part (c), does a lost call delayed system with a 20 second queue perform better than a system that clears blocked calls?

3.16 A receiver in an urban cellular radio system detects a 1 mW signal at $d = d_0 = 1$ meter from the transmitter. In order to mitigate co-channel interference effects, it is required that the signal received at any base station receiver from another base station transmitter which operates with the same channel must be below −100 dBm. A measurement team has determined that the average path loss exponent in the system is $n = 3$. Determine the major radius of each cell if a seven-cell reuse pattern is used. What is the major radius if a four-cell reuse pattern is used?

3.17 A cellular system using a cluster size of seven is described in Problem 3.16. It is operated with 660 channels, 30 of which are designated as setup (control) channels so that there are about 90 voice channels available per cell. If there is a potential user density of 9000 users/km^2 in the system, and each user makes an average of one call per hour and each call lasts 1 minute during peak hours, determine the probability that a user will experience a delay greater than 20 seconds if all calls are queued.

3.18 Show that if $n = 4$, a cell can be split into four smaller cells, each with half the radius and 1/16 of the transmitter power of the original cell. If extensive measurements show that the path loss exponent is three, how should the transmitter power be changed in order to split a cell into four smaller cells? What impact will this have on the cellular geometry? Explain your answer and provide drawings that show how the new cells would fit within the original macrocells. For simplicity use omnidirectional antennas.

3.19 Using the frequency assignment chart in Table 3.2, design a channelization scheme for a B-side carrier that uses four-cell reuse and three sectors per cell. Include an allocation scheme for the 21 control channels.

3.20 Repeat Problem 3.19 for the case of four-cell reuse and six sectors per cell.

3.21 In practical cellular radio systems, the MSC is programmed to allocate radio channels differently over time for the closest co-channel cells. This technique, called a *hunting sequence,* ensures that co-channel cells first use different channels from within the co-channel set before the same channels are assigned to calls in nearby cells. This minimizes co-channel interference when the cellular system is not fully loaded. Consider three adjoining clusters, and design an algorithm that may be used by the MSC to hunt for appropriate channels when requested from co-channel cells. Assume a seven-cell reuse pattern with three sectors per cell, and use the U.S. cellular channel allocation scheme for the A-side carrier.

3.22 Determine the noise floor (in dBm) for mobile receivers which implement the following standards: (a) AMPS, (b) GSM, (c) USDC, (d) DECT, (e) IS-95, and (f) CT2. Assume all receivers have a noise figure of 10 dB.

3.23 If a base station provides a signal level of –90 dBm at the cell fringe, find the SNR for each of the mobile receivers described in Problem 3.22.

3.24 From first principles, derive the expression for Erlang B given in this chapter.

3.25 Carefully analyze the tradeoff between sectoring and trunking efficiency for a four-cell cluster size. While sectoring improves capacity by improving SIR, there is a loss due to decreased trunking efficiency, since each sector must be trunked separately. Consider a wide range of total available channels per cell and consider the impact of using three sectors and six sectors per cell. Your analysis may involve computer simulation and should indicate the "break even" point when sectoring is not practical.

3.26 Assume each user of a single base station mobile radio system averages three calls per hour, each call lasting an average of 5 minutes.

(a) What is the traffic intensity for each user?

(b) Find the number of users that could use the system with 1% blocking if only one channel is available.

(c) Find the number of users that could use the system with 1% blocking if five trunked channels are available.

(d) If the number of users you found in (c) is suddenly doubled, what is the new blocking probability of the five channel trunked mobile radio system? Would this be acceptable performance? Justify why or why not.

3.27 The U.S. AMPS system is allocated 50 MHz of spectrum in the 800 MHz range and provides 832 channels. Forty-two of those channels are control channels. The forward channel frequency is exactly 45 MHz greater than the reverse channel frequency.

(a) Is the AMPS system simplex, half-duplex, or duplex? What is the bandwidth for each channel and how is it distributed between the base station and the subscriber?

(b) Assume a base station transmits control information on channel 352, operating at 880.560 MHz. What is the transmission frequency of a subscriber unit transmitting on channel 352?

(c) The A-side and B-side cellular carriers evenly split the AMPS channels. Find the number of voice channels and number of control channels for each carrier.

(d) Let's suppose you are chief engineer of a cellular carrier using seven-cell reuse. Propose a channel assignment strategy for a uniform distribution of users throughout your cellular system. Specifically, assume that each cell has three control channels (120° sectoring is employed) and specify the number of voice channels you would assign to each control channel in your system.

(e) For an ideal hexagonal cellular layout which has identical cell coverage, what is the distance between the centers of two nearest co-channel cells for seven-cell reuse? For four-cell reuse?

3.28 Suppose that you work with a cellular service provider and the cellular radio system your company deployed in a given service area just reached its maximum system capacity. Your boss then asks you to carry out a study to analyze the application of cluster size reduction technique combined with sectoring, aiming to increase the carried traffic of the system.

The current deployed system employs the AMPS system, with 300 voice channels, cluster size $N = 7$, and omnidirectional antennas at the base stations. Base stations are located at the center of the cells and transmit the same power on the forward link. The designed blocking probability is 2% and all voice channels have been used. The maximum carried traffic per cell is, therefore, 32.8 Erlangs. The minimum *SIR* (worst case) on the forward link can be computed using the expression

$$SIR = 10\log_{10}\left[\frac{(\sqrt{3N})^n}{i_0}\right] \quad \text{(in dB)},$$

where n is the path loss exponent, N is the cluster size, and i_0 is the number of interfering base stations in the first tier. For cluster size $N = 7$, omnidirectional base station antennas ($i_0 = 6$), and $n = 4$, we find that $SIR = 18.7$ dB.

When the cluster size is reduced, the maximum carried traffic per cell increases, at the expense of SIR degradation. Sectorized base station antennas can then be used in order to increase *SIR* and guarantee that the link quality is maintained. In other words, the minimum *SIR* achieved when cluster size is reduced and sectorized antennas are used must be equal to or exceed the minimum *SIR* achieved in the current deployed system ($SIR = 18.7$ dB).

In your analysis of cluster size reduction and sectoring, consider forward link only. Two sectorized antennas types are available: $BW = 60°$ for six sectors per cell, and $BW = 120°$ for three sectors per cell, as shown in Figure P3.28a. Assume that all cells have hexagonal shape, with radius R.

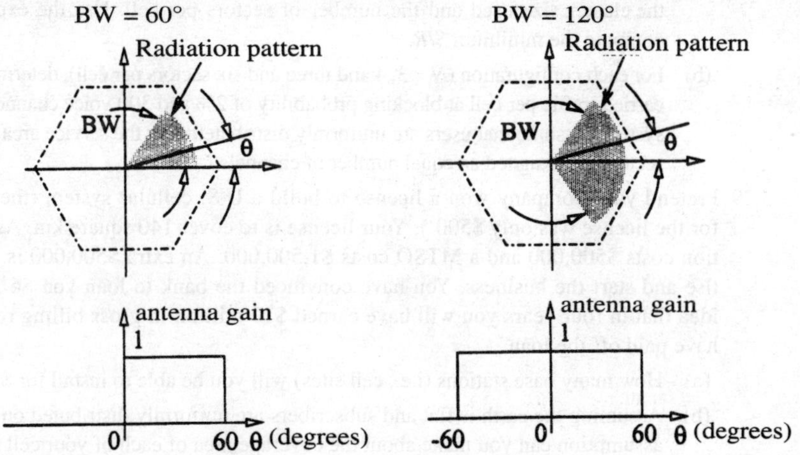

Figure P3.28a Radiation patterns for $BW = 60°$ and $BW = 120°$.

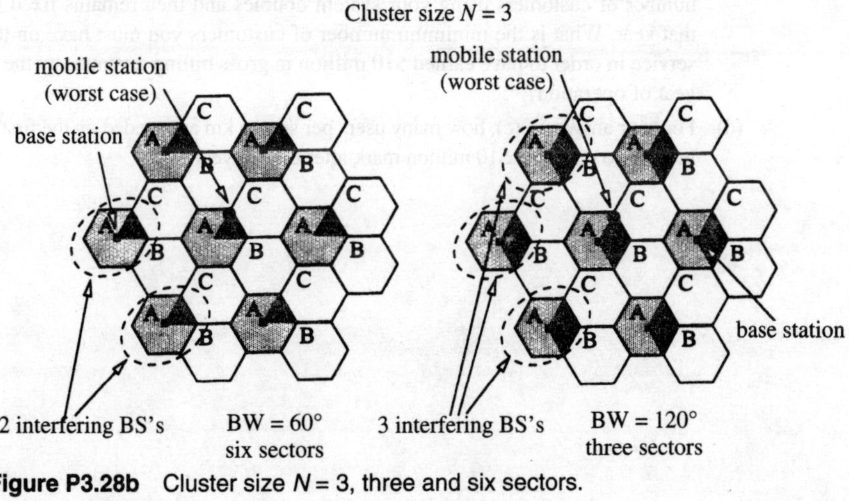

Figure P3.28b Cluster size $N = 3$, three and six sectors.

We want to determine the maximum carried traffic per cell when cluster size is reduced to $N = 3$ and $N = 4$, using three sectors ($BW = 60°$) and six sectors ($BW = 120°$) (four possible configurations). Assume that all sectorized antennas are installed at the same time. Consider the first tier of co-channel cells only.

(a) Determine the minimum *SIR* at the mobile (i.e., when the mobile is located at the cell boundary, as indicated in Figure P3.28b), for cluster sizes $N = 3$ and 4, with three and six sectors. Determine which configurations (cluster size N, number of sectors) are feasible regarding co-channel interference (i.e., configurations where the minimum *SIR* is equal to or exceeds 18.7 dB). Note that the number of interferers in the first tier depends on the cluster size used and the number of sectors per cell. Use the expression above to compute the minimum *SIR*.

(b) For each configuration ($N = 3, 4$ and three and six sectors per cell), determine the maximum carried traffic per cell at blocking probability of 2% and 300 voice channels available in the system. Assume that users are uniformly distributed over the service area and, therefore, all sectors are assigned an equal number of channels.

3.29 Pretend your company won a license to build a U.S. cellular system (the application cost for the license was only $500!). Your license is to cover 140 square km. Assume a base station costs $500,000 and a MTSO costs $1,500,000. An extra $500,000 is needed to advertise and start the business. You have convinced the bank to loan you $6 million, with the idea that in four years you will have earned $10 million in gross billing revenues, and will have paid off the loan.

(a) How many base stations (i.e., cell sites) will you be able to install for $6 million?

(b) Assuming the earth is flat and subscribers are uniformly distributed on the ground, what assumption can you make about the coverage area of each of your cell sites? What is the major radius of each of your cells, assuming a hexagonal mosaic?

(c) Assume that the average customer will pay $50 per month over a four year period. Assume that on the first day you turn your system on, you have a certain number of customers which remains fixed throughout the year. On the first day of each new year, the number of customers using your system doubles and then remains fixed for the rest of that year. What is the minimum number of customers you must have on the first day of service in order to have earned $10 million in gross billing revenues by the end of the 4th year of operation?

(d) For your answer in (c), how many users per square km are needed on the first day of service in order to reach the $10 million mark after the 4th year?

CHAPTER 4

Mobile Radio Propagation: Large-Scale Path Loss

The mobile radio channel places fundamental limitations on the performance of wireless communication systems. The transmission path between the transmitter and the receiver can vary from simple line-of-sight to one that is severely obstructed by buildings, mountains, and foliage. Unlike wired channels that are stationary and predictable, radio channels are extremely random and do not offer easy analysis. Even the speed of motion impacts how rapidly the signal level fades as a mobile terminal moves in space. Modeling the radio channel has historically been one of the most difficult parts of mobile radio system design, and is typically done in a statistical fashion, based on measurements made specifically for an intended communication system or spectrum allocation.

4.1 Introduction to Radio Wave Propagation

The mechanisms behind electromagnetic wave propagation are diverse, but can generally be attributed to reflection, diffraction, and scattering. Most cellular radio systems operate in urban areas where there is no direct line-of-sight path between the transmitter and the receiver, and where the presence of high-rise buildings causes severe diffraction loss. Due to multiple reflections from various objects, the electromagnetic waves travel along different paths of varying lengths. The interaction between these waves causes multipath fading at a specific location, and the strengths of the waves decrease as the distance between the transmitter and receiver increases.

Propagation models have traditionally focused on predicting the average received signal strength at a given distance from the transmitter, as well as the variability of the signal strength in close spatial proximity to a particular location. Propagation models that predict the mean signal strength for an arbitrary transmitter–receiver (T–R) separation distance are useful in estimating the radio coverage area of a transmitter and are called *large-scale* propagation models, since they characterize signal strength over large T–R separation distances (several hundreds or thousands of meters). On the other hand, propagation models that characterize the rapid fluctuations of the received signal strength over very short travel distances (a few wavelengths) or short time durations (on the order of seconds) are called *small-scale* or *fading* models.

As a mobile moves over very small distances, the instantaneous received signal strength may fluctuate rapidly giving rise to small-scale fading. The reason for this is that the received signal is a sum of many contributions coming from different directions, as described in Chapter 5. Since the phases are random, the sum of the contributions varies widely; for example, obeys a Rayleigh fading distribution. In small-scale fading, the received signal power may vary by as much as three or four orders of magnitude (30 or 40 dB) when the receiver is moved by only a fraction of a wavelength. As the mobile moves away from the transmitter over much larger distances, the local average received signal will gradually decrease, and it is this local average signal level that is predicted by large-scale propagation models. Typically, the local average received power is computed by averaging signal measurements over a measurement track of 5 λ to 40 λ. For cellular and PCS frequencies in the 1 GHz to 2 GHz band, this corresponds to measuring the local average received power over movements of 1 m to 10 m.

Figure 4.1 illustrates small-scale fading and the more gradual large-scale variations for an indoor radio communication system. Notice in the figure that the signal fades rapidly (small-scale fading) as the receiver moves, but the local average signal changes much more gradually with distance. This chapter covers large-scale propagation and presents a number of common methods used to predict received power in mobile communication systems. Chapter 5 treats small-scale fading models and describes methods to measure and model multipath in the mobile radio environment.

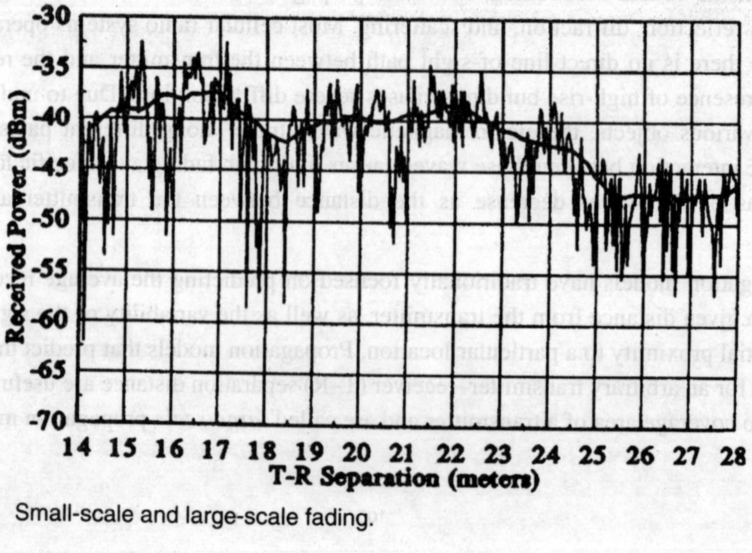

Figure 4.1 Small-scale and large-scale fading.

4.2 Free Space Propagation Model

The free space propagation model is used to predict received signal strength when the transmitter and receiver have a clear, unobstructed line-of-sight path between them. Satellite communication systems and microwave line-of-sight radio links typically undergo free space propagation. As with most large-scale radio wave propagation models, the free space model predicts that received power decays as a function of the T–R separation distance raised to some power (i.e. a power law function). The free space power received by a receiver antenna which is separated from a radiating transmitter antenna by a distance *d*, is given by the Friis free space equation,

$$P_r(d) = \frac{P_t G_t G_r \lambda^2}{(4\pi)^2 d^2 L} \tag{4.1}$$

where P_t is the transmitted power, $P_r(d)$ is the received power which is a function of the T–R separation, G_t is the transmitter antenna gain, G_r is the receiver antenna gain, d is the T–R separation distance in meters, L is the system loss factor not related to propagation ($L \geq 1$), and λ is the wavelength in meters. The gain of an antenna is related to its effective aperture, A_e, by

$$G = \frac{4\pi A_e}{\lambda^2} \tag{4.2}$$

The effective aperture A_e is related to the physical size of the antenna, and λ is related to the carrier frequency by

$$\lambda = \frac{c}{f} = \frac{2\pi c}{\omega_c} \tag{4.3}$$

where f is the carrier frequency in Hertz, ω_c is the carrier frequency in radians per second, and c is the speed of light given in meters/s. The values for P_t and P_r must be expressed in the same units, and G_t and G_r are dimensionless quantities. The miscellaneous losses L ($L \geq 1$) are usually due to transmission line attenuation, filter losses, and antenna losses in the communication system. A value of $L = 1$ indicates no loss in the system hardware.

The Friis free space equation of (4.1) shows that the received power falls off as the square of the T–R separation distance. This implies that the received power decays with distance at a rate of 20 dB/decade.

An *isotropic* radiator is an ideal antenna which radiates power with unit gain uniformly in all directions, and is often used to reference antenna gains in wireless systems. The *effective isotropic radiated power (EIRP)* is defined as

$$EIRP = P_t G_t \tag{4.4}$$

and represents the maximum radiated power available from a transmitter in the direction of maximum antenna gain, as compared to an isotropic radiator.

In practice, *effective radiated power (ERP)* is used instead of EIRP to denote the maximum radiated power as compared to a half-wave dipole antenna (instead of an isotropic antenna). Since a dipole antenna has a gain of 1.64 (2.15 dB above an isotrope), the ERP will be

2.15 dB smaller than the EIRP for the same transmission system. In practice, antenna gains are given in units of dBi (dB gain with respect to an isotropic antenna) or dBd (dB gain with respect to a half-wave dipole) [Stu81].

The *path loss*, which represents signal attenuation as a positive quantity measured in dB, is defined as the difference (in dB) between the effective transmitted power and the received power, and may or may not include the effect of the antenna gains. The path loss for the free space model when antenna gains are included is given by

$$PL(\text{dB}) = 10\log\frac{P_t}{P_r} = -10\log\left[\frac{G_t G_r \lambda^2}{(4\pi)^2 d^2}\right] \tag{4.5}$$

When antenna gains are excluded, the antennas are assumed to have unity gain, and path loss is given by

$$PL(\text{dB}) = 10\log\frac{P_t}{P_r} = -10\log\left[\frac{\lambda^2}{(4\pi)^2 d^2}\right] \tag{4.6}$$

The Friis free space model is only a valid predictor for P_r for values of d which are in the far-field of the transmitting antenna. The far-field, or *Fraunhofer region*, of a transmitting antenna is defined as the region beyond the far-field distance d_f, which is related to the largest linear dimension of the transmitter antenna aperture and the carrier wavelength. The Fraunhofer distance is given by

$$d_f = \frac{2D^2}{\lambda} \tag{4.7.a}$$

where D is the largest physical linear dimension of the antenna. Additionally, to be in the far-field region, d_f must satisfy

$$d_f \gg D \tag{4.7.b}$$

and

$$d_f \gg \lambda \tag{4.7.c}$$

Furthermore, it is clear that Equation (4.1) does not hold for $d = 0$. For this reason, large-scale propagation models use a close-in distance, d_0, as a known received power reference point. The received power, $P_r(d)$, at any distance $d > d_0$, may be related to P_r at d_0. The value $P_r(d_0)$ may be predicted from Equation (4.1), or may be measured in the radio environment by taking the average received power at many points located at a close-in radial distance d_0 from the transmitter. The reference distance must be chosen such that it lies in the far-field region, that is, $d_0 \geq d_f$, and d_0 is chosen to be smaller than any practical distance used in the mobile communication system. Thus, using Equation (4.1), the received power in free space at a distance greater than d_0 is given by

$$P_r(d) = P_r(d_0)\left(\frac{d_0}{d}\right)^2 \qquad d \geq d_0 \geq d_f \tag{4.8}$$

In mobile radio systems, it is not uncommon to find that P_r may change by many orders of magnitude over a typical coverage area of several square kilometers. Because of the large dynamic range of received power levels, often dBm or dBW units are used to express received power levels. Equation (4.8) may be expressed in units of dBm or dBW by simply taking the logarithm of both sides and multiplying by 10. For example, if P_r is in units of dBm, the received power is given by

$$P_r(d)\ \text{dBm} = 10\log\left[\frac{P_r(d_0)}{0.001\ \text{W}}\right] + 20\log\left(\frac{d_0}{d}\right) \qquad d \geq d_0 \geq d_f \tag{4.9}$$

where $P_r(d_0)$ is in units of watts.

The reference distance d_0 for practical systems using low-gain antennas in the 1–2 GHz region is typically chosen to be 1 m in indoor environments and 100 m or 1 km in outdoor environments, so that the numerator in Equations (4.8) and (4.9) is a multiple of 10. This makes path loss computations easy in dB units.

Example 4.1

Find the far-field distance for an antenna with maximum dimension of 1 m and operating frequency of 900 MHz.

Solution

Given:

Largest dimension of antenna, $D = 1$ m

Operating frequency $f = 900$ MHz, $\lambda = c/f = \dfrac{3 \times 10^8\ \text{m/s}}{900 \times 10^6\ \text{Hz}}$ m

Using Equation (4.7.a), far-field distance is obtained as

$$d_f = \frac{2(1)^2}{0.33} = 6\ \text{m}$$

Example 4.2

If a transmitter produces 50 W of power, express the transmit power in units of (a) dBm, and (b) dBW. If 50 W is applied to a unity gain antenna with a 900 MHz carrier frequency, find the received power in dBm at a free space distance of 100 m from the antenna. What is P_r(10 km)? Assume unity gain for the receiver antenna.

Solution

Given:

Transmitter power, $P_t = 50$ W

Carrier frequency, $f_c = 900$ MHz

Using Equation (4.9),

(a) Transmitter power,

$$P_t(\text{dBm}) = 10\log[P_t(\text{mW})/(1\text{ mW})]$$
$$= 10\log[50\times 10^3] = 47.0\text{ dBm}.$$

(b) Transmitter power,

$$P_t(\text{dBW}) = 10\log[P_t(\text{W})/(1\text{ W})]$$
$$= 10\log[50] = 17.0\text{ dBW}.$$

The received power can be determined using Equation (4.1)

$$P_r = \frac{P_t G_t G_r \lambda^2}{(4\pi)^2 d^2 L} = \frac{50(1)(1)(1/3)^2}{(4\pi)^2(100)^2(1)} = (3.5\times 10^{-6})\text{ W} = 3.5\times 10^{-3}\text{ mW}$$

$$P_r(\text{dBm}) = 10\log P_r(\text{mW}) = 10\log(3.5\times 10^{-3}\text{ mW}) = -24.5\text{ dBm}.$$

The received power at 10 km can be expressed in terms of dBm using Equation (4.9), where d_0 = 100 m and d = 10 km

$$P_r(10\text{ km}) = P_r(100) + 20\log\left[\frac{100}{10000}\right] = -24.5\text{ dBm} - 40\text{ dB}$$

$$= -64.5\text{ dBm}.$$

4.3 Relating Power to Electric Field

The free space path loss model of Section 4.2 is readily derived from first principles. It can be proven that any radiating structure produces electric and magnetic fields [Gri87], [Kra50]. Consider a small linear radiator of length L, that is placed coincident with the z-axis and has its center at the origin, as shown in Figure 4.2.

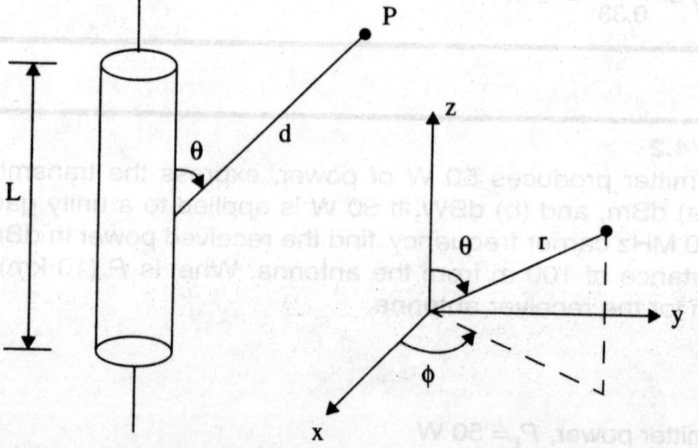

Figure 4.2 Illustration of a linear radiator of length $L (L \ll \lambda)$, carrying a current of amplitude i_0 and making an angle θ with a point, at distance d.

If a current flows through such an antenna, it launches electric and magnetic fields that can be expressed as

$$E_r = \frac{i_0 L\cos\theta}{2\pi\varepsilon_0 c}\left\{\frac{1}{d^2} + \frac{c}{j\omega_c d^3}\right\}e^{j\omega_c(t-d/c)} \tag{4.10}$$

$$E_\theta = \frac{i_0 L\sin\theta}{4\pi\varepsilon_0 c^2}\left\{\frac{j\omega_c}{d} + \frac{c}{d^2} + \frac{c^2}{j\omega_c d^3}\right\}e^{-j\omega_c(t-d/c)} \tag{4.11}$$

$$H_\phi = \frac{i_0 L\sin\theta}{4\pi c}\left\{\frac{j\omega_c}{d} + \frac{c}{d^2}\right\}e^{j\omega_c(t-d/c)} \tag{4.12}$$

with $E_\phi = H_r = H_\theta = 0$. In the above equations, all $1/d$ terms represent the radiation field component, all $1/d^2$ terms represent the induction field component, and all $1/d^3$ terms represent the electrostatic field component. As seen from Equations (4.10) to (4.12), the electrostatic and inductive fields decay much faster with distance than the radiation field. At regions far away from the transmitter (far-field region), the electrostatic and inductive fields become negligible and only the radiated field components of E_θ and H_ϕ need be considered.

In free space, the *power flux density* P_d (expressed in W/m^2) is given by

$$P_d = \frac{EIRP}{4\pi d^2} = \frac{P_t G_t}{4\pi d^2} = \frac{E^2}{R_{fs}} = \frac{E^2}{\eta}\ \text{W/m}^2 \tag{4.13}$$

where R_{fs} is the intrinsic impedance of free space given by $\eta = 120\,\pi\Omega$ (377 Ω). Thus, the power flux density is

$$P_d = \frac{|E|^2}{377\Omega}\ \text{W/m}^2 \tag{4.14}$$

where $|E|$ represents the magnitude of the radiating portion of the electric field in the far field. Figure 4.3a illustrates how the power flux density disperses in free space from an isotropic point source. P_d may be thought of as the *EIRP* divided by the surface area of a sphere with radius *d*. The power received at distance *d*, $P_r(d)$, is given by the power flux density times the effective aperture of the receiver antenna, and can be related to the electric field using Equations (4.1), (4.2), (4.13), and (4.14).

$$P_r(d) = P_d A_e = \frac{|E|^2}{120\pi}A_e = \frac{P_t G_t G_r \lambda^2}{(4\pi)^2 d^2} = \frac{|E|^2 G_r \lambda^2}{480\pi}\ \text{W} \tag{4.15}$$

Equation (4.15) relates electric field (with units of V/m) to received power (with units of watts), and is identical to Equation (4.1) with $L = 1$.

Often it is useful to relate the received power level to a receiver input voltage, as well as to an induced E-field at the receiver antenna. If the receiver antenna is modeled as a matched resistive load to the receiver, then the receiver antenna will induce an rms voltage into the receiver

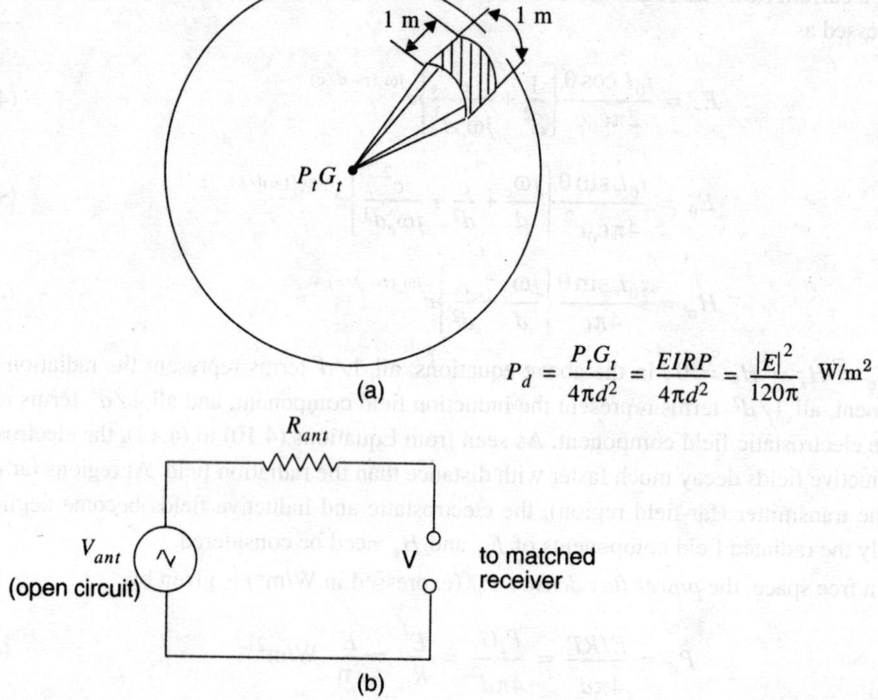

Figure 4.3 (a) Power flux density at a distance *d* from a point source; (b) model for voltage applied to the input of a receiver.

which is half of the open circuit voltage at the antenna. Thus, if V is the rms voltage at the input of a receiver (measured by a high impedance voltmeter), and R_{ant} is the resistance of the matched receiver, the received power is given by

$$P_r(d) = \frac{V^2}{R_{ant}} = \frac{[V_{ant}/2]^2}{R_{ant}} = \frac{V_{ant}^{\ 2}}{4R_{ant}} \tag{4.16}$$

Through Equations (4.14) to (4.16), it is possible to relate the received power to the received E-field or the open circuit rms voltage at the receiver antenna terminals. Figure 4.3b illustrates an equivalent circuit model. Note $V_{ant} = V$ when there is no load.

Example 4.3

Assume a receiver is located 10 km from a 50 W transmitter. The carrier frequency is 900 MHz, free space propagation is assumed, $G_t = 1$, and $G_r = 2$, find (a) the power at the receiver, (b) the magnitude of the E-field at the receiver antenna, (c) the rms voltage applied to the receiver input assuming that the receiver antenna has a purely real impedance of 50 Ω and is matched to the receiver.

Solution

Given:

Transmitter power, $P_t = 50$ W

Carrier frequency, $f_c = 900$ MHz

Transmitter antenna gain, $G_t = 1$

Receiver antenna gain, $G_r = 2$

Receiver antenna resistance = 50 Ω

(a) Using Equation (4.5), the power received at distance $d = 10$ km is

$$P_r(d) = 10\log\left(\frac{P_t G_t G_r \lambda^2}{(4\pi)^2 d^2}\right) = 10\log\left(\frac{50 \times 1 \times 2 \times (1/3)^2}{(4\pi)^2 10000^2}\right)$$

$$= -91.5 \text{ dBW} = -61.5 \text{ dBm}$$

(b) Using Equation (4.15), the magnitude of the received E-field is

$$|E| = \sqrt{\frac{P_r(d)120\pi}{A_e}} = \sqrt{\frac{P_r(d)120\pi}{G_r\lambda^2/4\pi}} = \sqrt{\frac{7 \times 10^{-10} \times 120\pi}{2 \times 0.33^2/(4\pi)}} = 0.0039 \text{ V/m}$$

(c) Using Equation (4.16), the applied rms voltage at the receiver input is

$$V_{ant} = \sqrt{P_r(d) \times R_{ant}} = \sqrt{7 \times 10^{-10} \times 50} = 0.187 \text{ mV}$$

4.4 The Three Basic Propagation Mechanisms

Reflection, diffraction, and scattering are the three basic propagation mechanisms which impact propagation in a mobile communication system. These mechanisms are briefly explained in this section, and propagation models which describe these mechanisms are discussed subsequently in this chapter. Received power (or its reciprocal, path loss) is generally the most important parameter predicted by large-scale propagation models based on the physics of reflection, scattering, and diffraction. Small-scale fading and multipath propagation (discussed in Chapter 5) may also be described by the physics of these three basic propagation mechanisms.

Reflection occurs when a propagating electromagnetic wave impinges upon an object which has very large dimensions when compared to the wavelength of the propagating wave. Reflections occur from the surface of the earth and from buildings and walls.

Diffraction occurs when the radio path between the transmitter and receiver is obstructed by a surface that has sharp irregularities (edges). The secondary waves resulting from the obstructing surface are present throughout the space and even behind the obstacle, giving rise to a bending of waves around the obstacle, even when a line-of-sight path does not exist between transmitter and receiver. At high frequencies, diffraction, like reflection, depends on the geometry of the object, as well as the amplitude, phase, and polarization of the incident wave at the point of diffraction.

Scattering occurs when the medium through which the wave travels consists of objects with dimensions that are small compared to the wavelength, and where the number of obstacles per unit volume is large. Scattered waves are produced by rough surfaces, small objects, or by other irregularities in the channel. In practice, foliage, street signs, and lamp posts induce scattering in a mobile communications system.

4.5 Reflection

When a radio wave propagating in one medium impinges upon another medium having different electrical properties, the wave is partially reflected and partially transmitted. If the plane wave is incident on a perfect dielectric, part of the energy is transmitted into the second medium and part of the energy is reflected back into the first medium, and there is no loss of energy in absorption. If the second medium is a perfect conductor, then *all* incident energy is reflected back into the first medium without loss of energy. The electric field intensity of the reflected and transmitted waves may be related to the incident wave in the medium of origin through the *Fresnel reflection coefficient* (Γ). The reflection coefficient is a function of the material properties, and generally depends on the wave polarization, angle of incidence, and the frequency of the propagating wave.

In general, electromagnetic waves are *polarized*, meaning they have instantaneous electric field components in orthogonal directions in space. A polarized wave may be mathematically represented as the sum of two spatially orthogonal components, such as vertical and horizontal, or left-hand or right-hand circularly polarized components. For an arbitrary polarization, superposition may be used to compute the reflected fields from a reflecting surface.

4.5.1 Reflection from Dielectrics

Figure 4.4 shows an electromagnetic wave incident at an angle θ_i with the plane of the boundary between two dielectric media. As shown in the figure, part of the energy is reflected back to the first media at an angle θ_r, and part of the energy is transmitted (refracted) into the second media at an angle θ_t. The nature of reflection varies with the direction of polarization of the E-field. The behavior for arbitrary directions of polarization can be studied by considering the two distinct cases shown in Figure 4.4. The *plane of incidence* is defined as the plane containing the incident, reflected, and transmitted rays [Ram65]. In Figure 4.4a, the E-field polarization is parallel with the plane of incidence (that is, the E-field has a vertical polarization, or normal component, with respect to the reflecting surface) and in Figure 4.4b, the E-field polarization is perpendicular to the plane of incidence (that is, the incident E-field is pointing out of the page toward the reader, and is perpendicular to the page and parallel to the reflecting surface).

In Figure 4.4, the subscripts *i, r, t* refer to the incident, reflected, and transmitted fields, respectively. Parameters $\varepsilon_1, \mu_1, \sigma_1$, and $\varepsilon_2, \mu_2, \sigma_2$ represent the permittivity, permeability, and conductance of the two media, respectively. Often, the dielectric constant of a perfect (lossless) dielectric is related to a relative value of permittivity, ε_r, such that $\varepsilon = \varepsilon_0\varepsilon_r$, where ε_0 is a

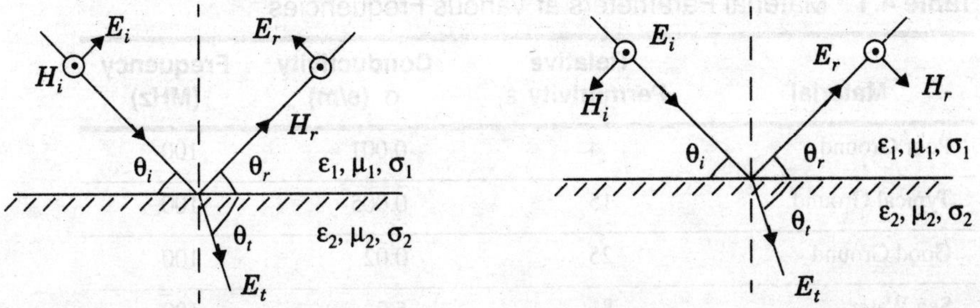

Figure 4.4 Geometry for calculating the reflection coefficients between two dielectrics.

constant given by 8.85×10^{-12} F/m. If a dielectric material is lossy, it will absorb power and may be described by a complex dielectric constant given by

$$\varepsilon = \varepsilon_0 \varepsilon_r - j\varepsilon' \tag{4.17}$$

where

$$\varepsilon' = \frac{\sigma}{2\pi f} \tag{4.18}$$

and σ is the conductivity of the material measured in Siemens/meter. The terms ε_r and σ are generally insensitive to operating frequency when the material is a good conductor ($f < \sigma/(\varepsilon_0 \varepsilon_r)$). For lossy dielectrics, ε_0 and ε_r are generally constant with frequency, but σ may be sensitive to the operating frequency, as shown in Table 4.1. Electrical properties of a wide range of materials were characterized over a large frequency range by Von Hipple [Von54].

Because of superposition, only two orthogonal polarizations need be considered to solve general reflection problems. The reflection coefficients for the two cases of parallel and perpendicular E-field polarization at the boundary of two dielectrics are given by

$$\Gamma_{\parallel} = \frac{E_r}{E_i} = \frac{\eta_2 \sin\theta_t - \eta_1 \sin\theta_i}{\eta_2 \sin\theta_t + \eta_1 \sin\theta_i} \quad \text{(E-field in plane of incidence)} \tag{4.19}$$

$$\Gamma_{\perp} = \frac{E_r}{E_i} = \frac{\eta_2 \sin\theta_i - \eta_1 \sin\theta_t}{\eta_2 \sin\theta_i + \eta_1 \sin\theta_t} \quad \text{(E-field normal to the plane of incidence)} \tag{4.20}$$

where η_i is the intrinsic impedance of the i th medium ($i = 1, 2$), and is given by $\sqrt{\mu_i/\varepsilon_i}$, the ratio of electric to magnetic field for a uniform plane wave in the particular medium. The velocity of an electromagnetic wave is given by $1/(\sqrt{\mu\varepsilon})$, and the boundary conditions at the surface of incidence obey Snell's Law which, referring to Figure 4.4, is given by

$$\sqrt{\mu_1 \varepsilon_1} \sin(90 - \theta_i) = \sqrt{\mu_2 \varepsilon_2} \sin(90 - \theta_t) \tag{4.21}$$

Table 4.1 Material Parameters at Various Frequencies

Material	Relative Permittivity ε_r	Conductivity σ (s/m)	Frequency (MHz)
Poor Ground	4	0.001	100
Typical Ground	15	0.005	100
Good Ground	25	0.02	100
Sea Water	81	5.0	100
Fresh Water	81	0.001	100
Brick	4.44	0.001	4000
Limestone	7.51	0.028	4000
Glass, Corning 707	4	0.00000018	1
Glass, Corning 707	4	0.000027	100
Glass, Corning 707	4	0.005	10000

The boundary conditions from Maxwell's equations are used to derive Equations (4.19) and (4.20) as well as Equations (4.22), (4.23.a), and (4.23.b).

$$\theta_i = \theta_r \tag{4.22}$$

and

$$E_r = \Gamma E_i \tag{4.23.a}$$

$$E_t = (1 + \Gamma) E_i \tag{4.23.b}$$

where Γ is either $\Gamma_{\|}$ or $\Gamma_{\perp}$, depending on whether the E-field is in (vertical) or normal (horizontal) to the plane of incidence.

For the case when the first medium is free space and $\mu_1 = \mu_2$, the reflection coefficients for the two cases of vertical and horizontal polarization can be simplified to

$$\Gamma_{\|} = \frac{-\varepsilon_r \sin\theta_i + \sqrt{\varepsilon_r - \cos^2\theta_i}}{\varepsilon_r \sin\theta_i + \sqrt{\varepsilon_r - \cos^2\theta_i}} \tag{4.24}$$

and

$$\Gamma_{\perp} = \frac{\sin\theta_i - \sqrt{\varepsilon_r - \cos^2\theta_i}}{\sin\theta_i + \sqrt{\varepsilon_r - \cos^2\theta_i}} \tag{4.25}$$

For the case of elliptical polarized waves, the wave may be broken down (depolarized) into its vertical and horizontal E-field components, and superposition may be applied to determine transmitted and reflected waves. In the general case of reflection or transmission, the horizontal and vertical

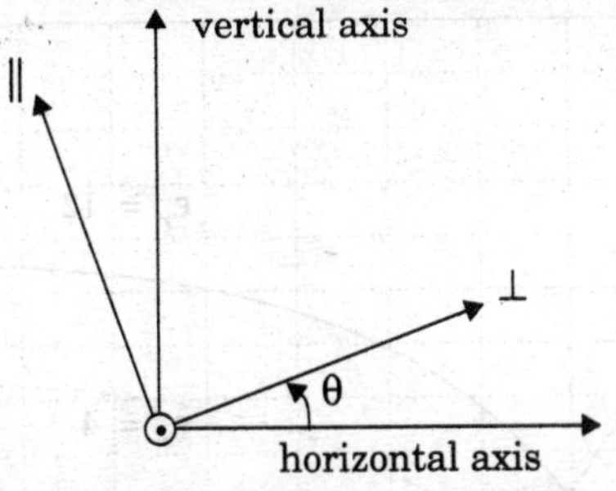

Figure 4.5 Axes for orthogonally polarized components. Parallel and perpendicular components are related to the horizontal and vertical spatial coordinates. Wave is shown propagating out of the page toward the reader.

axes of the spatial coordinates may not coincide with the perpendicular and parallel axes of the propagating waves. An angle θ measured counter-clockwise from the horizontal axis is defined as shown in Figure 4.5 for a propagating wave out of the page (toward the reader) [Stu93]. The vertical and horizontal field components at a dielectric boundary may be related by

$$\begin{bmatrix} E_H^d \\ E_V^d \end{bmatrix} = R^T D_C R \begin{bmatrix} E_H^i \\ E_V^i \end{bmatrix} \tag{4.26}$$

where E_H^d and E_V^d are the depolarized field components in the horizontal and vertical directions, respectively, E_H^i and E_V^i are the horizontally and vertically polarized components of the incident wave, respectively, and E_H^d, E_V^d, E_H^i, and E_V^i are time varying components of the E-field which may be represented as phasors. R is a transformation matrix which maps vertical and horizontal polarized components to components which are perpendicular and parallel to the plane of incidence. The matrix R is given by

$$R = \begin{bmatrix} \cos\theta & \sin\theta \\ -\sin\theta & \cos\theta \end{bmatrix}$$

where θ is the angle between the two sets of axes, as shown in Figure 4.5. The depolarization matrix D_C is given by

$$D_C = \begin{bmatrix} D_{\perp\perp} & 0 \\ 0 & D_{\parallel\parallel} \end{bmatrix}$$

where $D_{xx} = \Gamma_x$ for the case of reflection and $D_{xx} = T_x = 1 + \Gamma_x$ for the case of transmission [Stu93].

Figure 4.6 shows a plot of the reflection coefficient for both horizontal and vertical polarization as a function of the incident angle for the case when a wave propagates in free space ($\varepsilon_r = 1$) and the reflection surface has (a) $\varepsilon_r = 4$, and (b) $\varepsilon_r = 12$.

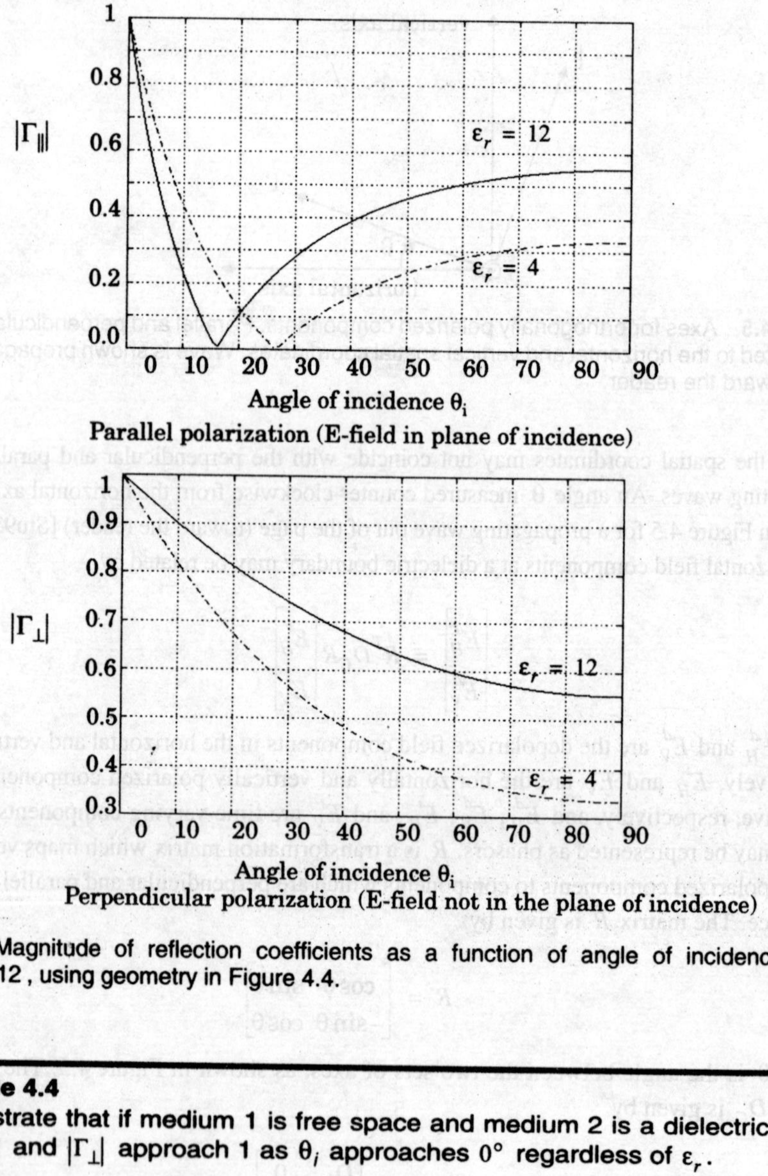

Figure 4.6 Magnitude of reflection coefficients as a function of angle of incidence for $\varepsilon_r = 4, \varepsilon_r = 12$, using geometry in Figure 4.4.

Example 4.4

Demonstrate that if medium 1 is free space and medium 2 is a dielectric, both $|\Gamma_{\parallel}|$ and $|\Gamma_{\perp}|$ approach 1 as θ_i approaches 0° regardless of ε_r.

Solution

Substituting $\theta_i = 0°$ in Equation (4.24)

$$\Gamma_{\parallel} = \frac{-\varepsilon_r \sin 0 + \sqrt{\varepsilon_r - \cos^2 0}}{\varepsilon_r \sin 0 + \sqrt{\varepsilon_r - \cos^2 0}}$$

$$|\Gamma_{\parallel}| = \frac{\sqrt{\varepsilon_r - 1}}{\sqrt{\varepsilon_r - 1}} = 1$$

Substituting $\theta_i = 0°$ in Equation (4.25)

$$\Gamma_\perp = \frac{\sin 0 - \sqrt{\varepsilon_r - \cos^2 0}}{\sin 0 + \sqrt{\varepsilon_r - \cos^2 0}}$$

$$\Gamma_\perp = \frac{-\sqrt{\varepsilon_r - 1}}{\sqrt{\varepsilon_r - 1}} = -1$$

This example illustrates that ground may be modeled as a perfect reflector with a reflection coefficient of unit magnitude when an incident wave grazes the earth, regardless of polarization or ground dielectric properties (some texts define the direction of E_r to be opposite to that shown in Figure 4.4a, resulting in $\Gamma = -1$ for both parallel and perpendicular polarization).

4.5.2 Brewster Angle

The *Brewster angle* is the angle at which no reflection occurs in the medium of origin. It occurs when the incident angle θ_B is such that the reflection coefficient $\Gamma_{\parallel}$ is equal to zero (see Figure 4.6). The Brewster angle is given by the value of θ_B which satisfies

$$\sin(\theta_B) = \sqrt{\frac{\varepsilon_1}{\varepsilon_1 + \varepsilon_2}} \tag{4.27}$$

For the case when the first medium is free space and the second medium has a relative permittivity ε_r, Equation (4.27) can be expressed as

$$\sin(\theta_B) = \frac{\sqrt{\varepsilon_r - 1}}{\sqrt{\varepsilon_r^2 - 1}} \tag{4.28}$$

Note that the Brewster angle occurs only for vertical (i.e. parallel) polarization.

Example 4.5

Calculate the Brewster angle for a wave impinging on ground having a permittivity of $\varepsilon_r = 4$.

Solution

The Brewster angle can be found by substituting the values for ε_r in Equation (4.28).

$$\sin(\theta_i) = \frac{\sqrt{(4) - 1}}{\sqrt{(4)^2 - 1}} = \sqrt{\frac{3}{15}} = \sqrt{\frac{1}{5}}$$

$$\theta_i = \sin^{-1}\sqrt{\frac{1}{5}} = 26.56°$$

Thus Brewster angle for $\varepsilon_r = 4$ is equal to 26.56°.

4.5.3 Reflection from Perfect Conductors

Since electromagnetic energy cannot pass through a perfect conductor a plane wave incident on a conductor has all of its energy reflected. As the electric field at the surface of the conductor must be equal to zero at all times in order to obey Maxwell's equations, the reflected wave must be equal in magnitude to the incident wave. For the case when E-field polarization is in the plane of incidence, the boundary conditions require that [Ram65]

$$\theta_i = \theta_r \tag{4.29}$$

and

$$E_i = E_r \quad \text{(E-field in plane of incidence)} \tag{4.30}$$

Similarly, for the case when the E-field is horizontally polarized, the boundary conditions require that

$$\theta_i = \theta_r \tag{4.31}$$

and

$$E_i = -E_r \quad \text{(E-field normal to plane of incidence)} \tag{4.32}$$

Referring to Equations (4.29) to (4.32), we see that for a perfect conductor, $\Gamma_{\parallel} = 1$, and $\Gamma_{\perp} = -1$, regardless of incident angle. Elliptical polarized waves may be analyzed by using superposition, as shown in Figure 4.5 and Equation (4.26).

4.6 Ground Reflection (Two-Ray) Model

In a mobile radio channel, a single direct path between the base station and a mobile is seldom the only physical means for propagation, and hence the free space propagation model of Equation (4.5) is in most cases inaccurate when used alone. The two-ray ground reflection model shown in Figure 4.7 is a useful propagation model that is based on geometric optics, and considers both the direct path and a ground reflected propagation path between transmitter and receiver. This model has been found to be reasonably accurate for predicting the large-scale signal strength over distances of several kilometers for mobile radio systems that use tall towers (heights which exceed 50 m), as well as for line-of-sight microcell channels in urban environments [Feu94].

In most mobile communication systems, the maximum T–R separation distance is at most only a few tens of kilometers, and the earth may be assumed to be flat. The total received E-field, E_{TOT}, is then a result of the direct line-of-sight component, E_{LOS}, and the ground reflected component, E_g.

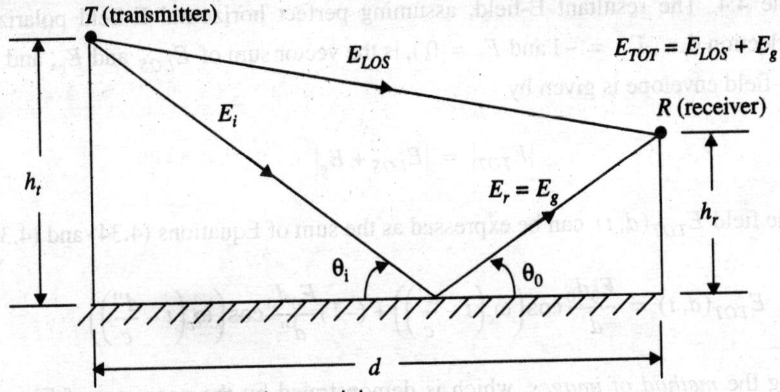

Figure 4.7 Two-ray ground reflection model.

Referring to Figure 4.7, h_t is the height of the transmitter and h_r is the height of the receiver. If E_0 is the free space E-field (in units of V/m) at a reference distance d_0 from the transmitter, then for $d > d_0$, the free space propagating E-field is given by

$$E(d, t) = \frac{E_0 d_0}{d} \cos\left(\omega_c\left(t - \frac{d}{c}\right)\right) \qquad (d > d_0) \tag{4.33}$$

where $|E(d, t)| = E_0 d_0 / d$ represents the envelope of the E-field at d meters from the transmitter.

Two propagating waves arrive at the receiver: the direct wave that travels a distance d'; and the reflected wave that travels a distance d''. The E-field due to the line-of-sight component at the receiver can be expressed as

$$E_{LOS}(d', t) = \frac{E_0 d_0}{d'} \cos\left(\omega_c\left(t - \frac{d'}{c}\right)\right) \tag{4.34}$$

and the E-field for the ground reflected wave, which has a propagation distance of d'', can be expressed as

$$E_g(d'', t) = \Gamma \frac{E_0 d_0}{d''} \cos\left(\omega_c\left(t - \frac{d''}{c}\right)\right) \tag{4.35}$$

According to laws of reflection in dielectrics given in Section 4.5.1

$$\theta_i = \theta_0 \tag{4.36}$$

and

$$E_g = \Gamma E_i \tag{4.37.a}$$

$$E_t = (1 + \Gamma) E_i \tag{4.37.b}$$

where Γ is the reflection coefficient for ground. For small values of θ_i (i.e., grazing incidence), the reflected wave is equal in magnitude and 180° out of phase with the incident wave, as shown in Example 4.4. The resultant E-field, assuming perfect horizontal E-field polarization and ground reflection (i.e., $\Gamma_{\perp} = -1$ and $E_t = 0$), is the vector sum of E_{LOS} and E_g, and the resultant total E-field envelope is given by

$$|E_{TOT}| = |E_{LOS} + E_g| \tag{4.38}$$

The electric field $E_{TOT}(d, t)$ can be expressed as the sum of Equations (4.34) and (4.35)

$$E_{TOT}(d, t) = \frac{E_0 d_0}{d'} \cos\left(\omega_c\left(t - \frac{d'}{c}\right)\right) + (-1)\frac{E_0 d_0}{d''} \cos\left(\omega_c\left(t - \frac{d''}{c}\right)\right) \tag{4.39}$$

Using the *method of images*, which is demonstrated by the geometry of Figure 4.8, the path difference, Δ, between the line-of-sight and the ground reflected paths can be expressed as

$$\Delta = d'' - d' = \sqrt{(h_t + h_r)^2 + d^2} - \sqrt{(h_t - h_r)^2 + d^2} \tag{4.40}$$

When the T–R separation distance d is very large compared to $h_t + h_r$, Equation (4.40) can be simplified using a Taylor series approximation

$$\Delta = d'' - d' \approx \frac{2h_t h_r}{d} \tag{4.41}$$

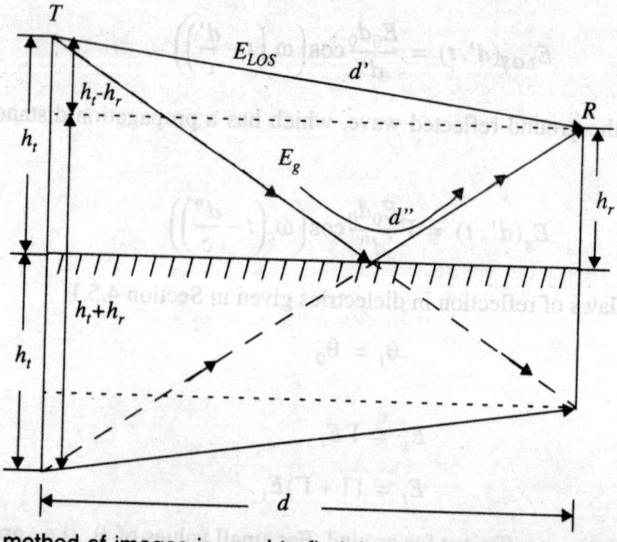

Figure 4.8 The method of images is used to find the path difference between the line-of-sight and the ground reflected paths.

Once the path difference is known, the phase difference θ_Δ between the two E-field components and the time delay τ_d between the arrival of the two components can be easily computed using the following relations

$$\theta_\Delta = \frac{2\pi\Delta}{\lambda} = \frac{\Delta\omega_c}{c} \tag{4.42}$$

and

$$\tau_d = \frac{\Delta}{c} = \frac{\theta_\Delta}{2\pi f_c} \tag{4.43}$$

It should be noted that as d becomes large, the difference between the distances d' and d'' becomes very small, and the amplitudes of E_{LOS} and E_g are virtually identical and differ only in phase. That is

$$\left|\frac{E_0 d_0}{d}\right| \approx \left|\frac{E_0 d_0}{d'}\right| \approx \left|\frac{E_0 d_0}{d''}\right| \tag{4.44}$$

If the received E-field is evaluated at some time, say at $t = d''/c$, Equation (4.39) can be expressed as a phasor sum

$$E_{TOT}\left(d, t = \frac{d''}{c}\right) = \frac{E_0 d_0}{d'}\cos\left(\omega_c\left(\frac{d'' - d'}{c}\right)\right) - \frac{E_0 d_0}{d''}\cos 0^\circ \tag{4.45}$$

$$= \frac{E_0 d_0}{d'}\angle\theta_\Delta - \frac{E_0 d_0}{d''}$$

$$\approx \frac{E_o d_0}{d}[\angle\theta_\Delta - 1]$$

where d is the distance over a flat earth between the bases of the transmitter and receiver antennas. Referring to the phasor diagram of Figure 4.9 which shows how the direct and ground reflected rays combine, the electric field (at the receiver) at a distance d from the transmitter can be written as

$$|E_{TOT}(d)| = \sqrt{\left(\frac{E_0 d_0}{d}\right)^2 (\cos\theta_\Delta - 1)^2 + \left(\frac{E_0 d_0}{d}\right)^2 \sin^2\theta_\Delta} \tag{4.46}$$

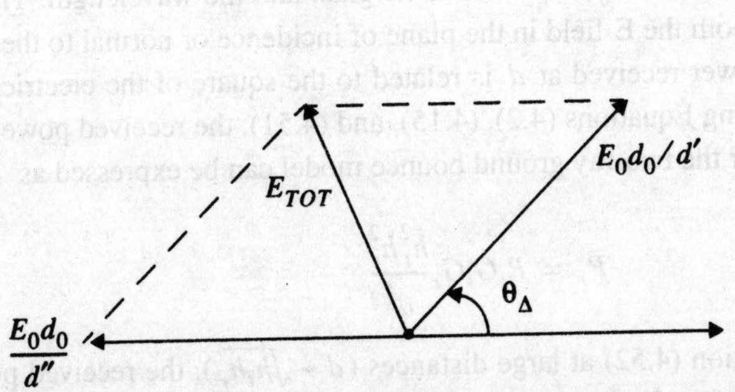

Figure 4.9 Phasor diagram showing the electric field components of the line-of-sight, ground reflected, and total received E-fields, derived from Equation (4.45).

or

$$|E_{TOT}(d)| = \frac{E_0 d_0}{d}\sqrt{2-2\cos\theta_\Delta} \tag{4.47}$$

Note that if the E-field is assumed to be in the plane of incidence (i.e., vertical polarization) then $\Gamma_{\|} = 1$ and Equation (4.47) would have a "+" instead of a "–".

Using trigonometric identities, Equation (4.47) can be expressed as

$$|E_{TOT}(d)| = 2\frac{E_0 d_0}{d}\sin\left(\frac{\theta_\Delta}{2}\right) \tag{4.48}$$

Equation (4.48) is an important expression, as it provides the exact received E-field for the two-ray ground reflection model. One notes that for increasing distance from the transmitter, $E_{TOT}(d)$ decays in an oscillatory fashion, with local maxima being 6 dB greater than the free space value and the local minima plummeting to $-\infty$ dB (the received E-field cancels out to zero volts at certain values of d, although in reality this never happens). Once the distance d is sufficiently large, θ_Δ becomes $\leq \pi$ and the received E-field, $E_{TOT}(d)$, then falls off asymtotically with increasing distance. Note that Equation (4.48) may be simplified whenever $\sin(\theta_\Delta/2) \approx \theta_\Delta/2$. This occurs when $\theta_\Delta/2$ is less than 0.3 radian. Using Equations (4.41) and (4.42)

$$\frac{\theta_\Delta}{2} \approx \frac{2\pi h_t h_r}{\lambda d} < 0.3 \text{ rad} \tag{4.49}$$

which implies that Equation (4.48) may be simplified whenever

$$d > \frac{20\pi h_t h_r}{3\lambda} \approx \frac{20 h_t h_r}{\lambda} \tag{4.50}$$

Thus, as long as d satisfies (4.50), the received E-field can be approximated as

$$E_{TOT}(d) \approx \frac{2E_0 d_0}{d}\frac{2\pi h_t h_r}{\lambda d} \approx \frac{k}{d^2} \text{ V/m} \tag{4.51}$$

where k is a constant related to E_0, the antenna heights, and the wavelength. This asymptotic behavior is identical for both the E-field in the plane of incidence or normal to the plane of incidence. The free space power received at d is related to the square of the electric field through Equation (4.15). Combining Equations (4.2), (4.15), and (4.51), the received power at a distance d from the transmitter for the two-ray ground bounce model can be expressed as

$$P_r = P_t G_t G_r \frac{h_t^2 h_r^2}{d^4} \tag{4.52}$$

As seen from Equation (4.52) at large distances ($d \gg \sqrt{h_t h_r}$), the received power falls off with distance raised to the fourth power, or at a rate of 40 dB/decade. This is a much more rapid path loss than is experienced in free space. Note also that at large values of d, the received power and path loss become independent of frequency. The path loss for the two-ray model (with antenna gains) can be expressed in dB as

$$PL(\text{dB}) = 40\log d - (10\log G_t + 10\log G_r + 20\log h_t + 20\log h_r) \tag{4.53}$$

At small T–R separation distances, Equation (4.39) must be used to compute the total E-field. When Equation (4.42) is evaluated for $\theta_\Delta = \pi$, then $d = (4h_t h_r)/\lambda$ is where the ground appears in the first *Fresnel zone* between the transmitter and receiver (Fresnel zones are treated in Section 4.7.1). The first Fresnel zone distance is a useful parameter in microcell path loss models [Feu94].

Example 4.6

A mobile is located 5 km away from a base station and uses a vertical $\lambda/4$ monopole antenna with a gain of 2.55 dB to receive cellular radio signals. The E-field at 1 km from the transmitter is measured to be 10^{-3} V/m. The carrier frequency used for this system is 900 MHz.

(a)Find the length and the effective aperture of the receiving antenna.

(b)Find the received power at the mobile using the two-ray ground reflection model assuming the height of the transmitting antenna is 50 m and the receiving antenna is 1.5 m above ground.

Solution

Given:

T–R separation distance = 5 km

E-field at a distance of 1 km = 10^{-3} V/m

Frequency of operation, f = 900 MHz

$$\lambda = \frac{c}{f} = \frac{3\times10^8}{900\times10^6} = 0.333\text{ m.}$$

(a)Length of the antenna, $L = \lambda/4 = 0.333/4 = 0.0833\text{ m} = 8.33\text{ cm}$.

Effective aperture of $\lambda/4$ monopole antenna can be obtained using Equation (4.2).

Effective aperture of antenna = 0.016 m^2.

(b)Since $d \gg \sqrt{h_t h_r}$, the electric field is given by

$$E_R(d) \approx \frac{2E_0 d_0}{d}\frac{2\pi h_t h_r}{\lambda d} \approx \frac{k}{d^2}\text{ V/m}$$

$$= \frac{2\times10^{-3}\times1\times10^3}{5\times10^3}\left[\frac{2\pi(50)(1.5)}{0.333(5\times10^3)}\right]$$

$$= 113.1\times10^{-6}\text{ V/m.}$$

The received power at a distance d can be obtained using Equation (4.15)

$$P_r(d) = \frac{(113.1\times10^{-6})^2}{377}\left[\frac{1.8(0.333)^2}{4\pi}\right]$$

$$P_r(d = 5\text{ km}) = 5.4\times10^{-13}\text{ W} = -122.68\text{ dBW or } -92.68\text{ dBm.}$$

4.7 Diffraction

Diffraction allows radio signals to propagate around the curved surface of the earth, beyond the horizon, and to propagate behind obstructions. Although the received field strength decreases rapidly as a receiver moves deeper into the obstructed (shadowed) region, the diffraction field still exists and often has sufficient strength to produce a useful signal.

The phenomenon of diffraction can be explained by Huygen's principle, which states that all points on a wavefront can be considered as point sources for the production of secondary wavelets, and that these wavelets combine to produce a new wavefront in the direction of propagation. Diffraction is caused by the propagation of secondary wavelets into a shadowed region. The field strength of a diffracted wave in the shadowed region is the vector sum of the electric field components of all the secondary wavelets in the space around the obstacle.

4.7.1 Fresnel Zone Geometry

Consider a transmitter and receiver separated in free space as shown in Figure 4.10a. Let an obstructing screen of effective height h with infinite width (going into and out of the paper) be placed between them at a distance d_1 from the transmitter and d_2 from the receiver. It is apparent that the wave propagating from the transmitter to the receiver via the top of the screen travels a longer distance than if a direct line-of-sight path (through the screen) existed. Assuming $h \ll d_1, d_2$ and $h \gg \lambda$, then the difference between the direct path and the diffracted path, called the *excess path length* (Δ), can be obtained from the geometry of Figure 4.10b as

$$\Delta \approx \frac{h^2}{2} \frac{(d_1 + d_2)}{d_1 d_2} \tag{4.54}$$

The corresponding phase difference is given by

$$\phi = \frac{2\pi\Delta}{\lambda} \approx \frac{2\pi}{\lambda} \frac{h^2}{2} \frac{(d_1 + d_2)}{d_1 d_2} \tag{4.55}$$

and when $\tan x \approx x$, then $\alpha = \beta + \gamma$ from Figure 4.10c and

$$\alpha \approx h\left(\frac{d_1 + d_2}{d_1 d_2}\right)$$

(a proof of Equations (4.54) and (4.55) is left as an exercise for the reader).

Equation (4.55) is often normalized using the dimensionless *Fresnel–Kirchoff* diffraction parameter v which is given by

$$v = h\sqrt{\frac{2(d_1 + d_2)}{\lambda d_1 d_2}} = \alpha\sqrt{\frac{2 d_1 d_2}{\lambda(d_1 + d_2)}} \tag{4.56}$$

where α has units of radians and is shown in Figure 4.10b and Figure 4.10c. The parameter v is convenient because it allows ϕ to be expressed in a convenient form.

$$\phi = \frac{\pi}{2}v^2 \tag{4.57}$$

From the above equations it is clear that the phase difference between a direct line-of-sight path and diffracted path is a function of height and position of the obstruction, as well as the transmitter and receiver location.

In practical diffraction problems, it is advantageous to reduce all heights by a constant, so that the geometry is simplified without changing the values of the angles. This procedure is shown in Figure 4.10c.

The concept of diffraction loss as a function of the path difference around an obstruction is explained by Fresnel zones. Fresnel zones represent successive regions where secondary waves have a path length from the transmitter to receiver which are $n\lambda/2$ greater than the total path length of a line-of-sight path. Figure 4.11 demonstrates a transparent plane located between a transmitter and receiver. The concentric circles on the plane represent the loci of the origins of secondary wavelets which propagate to the receiver such that the total path length increases by $\lambda/2$ for successive circles. These circles are called Fresnel zones. The successive Fresnel zones have the effect of alternately providing constructive and destructive interference to the total received signal. The radius of the nth Fresnel zone circle is denoted by r_n and can be expressed in terms of n, λ, d_1, and d_2 by

$$r_n = \sqrt{\frac{n\lambda d_1 d_2}{d_1 + d_2}} \tag{4.58}$$

This approximation is valid for $d_1, d_2 \gg r_n$.

The excess total path length traversed by a ray passing through each circle is $n\lambda/2$, where n is an integer. Thus, the path traveling through the smallest circle corresponding to $n = 1$ in Figure 4.11 will have an excess path length of $\lambda/2$ as compared to a line-of-sight path, and circles corresponding to $n = 2, 3,$ etc. will have an excess path length of λ, $3\lambda/2$, etc. The radii of the concentric circles depend on the location of the plane. The Fresnel zones of Figure 4.11 will have maximum radii if the plane is midway between the transmitter and receiver, and the radii become smaller when the plane is moved toward either the transmitter or the receiver. This effect illustrates how shadowing is sensitive to the frequency as well as the location of obstructions with relation to the transmitter or receiver.

In mobile communication systems, diffraction loss occurs from the blockage of secondary waves such that only a portion of the energy is diffracted around an obstacle. That is, an obstruction causes a blockage of energy from some of the Fresnel zones, thus allowing only some of the transmitted energy to reach the receiver. Depending on the geometry of the obstruction, the received energy will be a vector sum of the energy contributions from all unobstructed Fresnel zones.

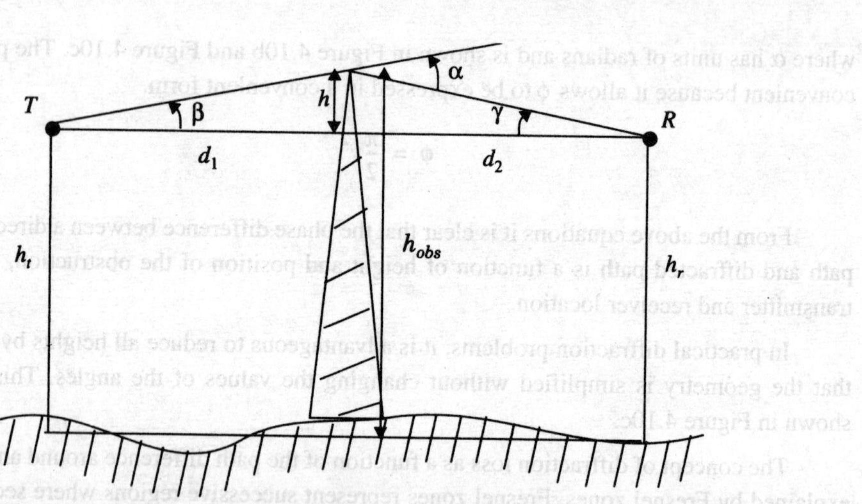

(a) Knife-edge diffraction geometry. The point *T* denotes the transmitter and *R* denotes the receiver, with an infinite knife-edge obstruction blocking the line-of-sight path.

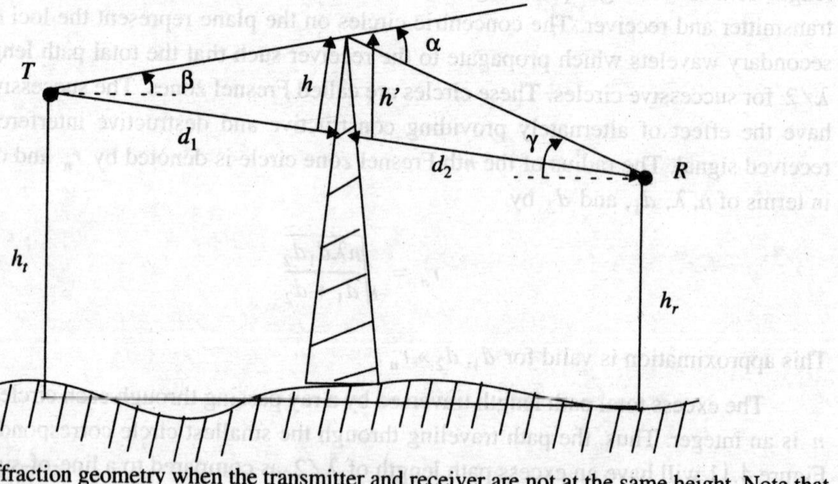

(b) Knife-edge diffraction geometry when the transmitter and receiver are not at the same height. Note that if α and β are small and $h \ll d_1$ and d_2, then *h* and *h'* are virtually identical and the geometry may be redrawn as shown in Figure 4.10c.

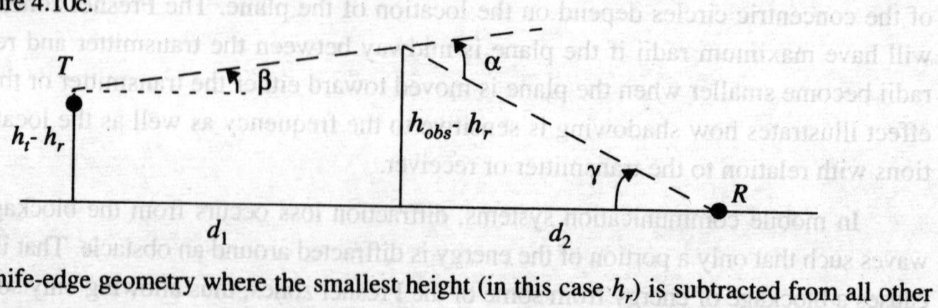

(c) Equivalent knife-edge geometry where the smallest height (in this case h_r) is subtracted from all other heights.

Figure 4.10 Diagrams of knife-edge geometry.

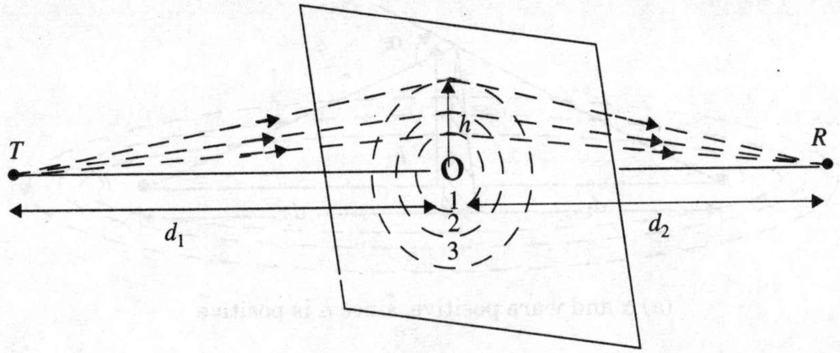

Figure 4.11 Concentric circles which define the boundaries of successive Fresnel zones.

As shown in Figure 4.12, an obstacle may block the transmission path, and a family of ellipsoids can be constructed between a transmitter and receiver by joining all the points for which the excess path delay is an integer multiple of half wavelengths. The ellipsoids represent Fresnel zones. Note that the Fresnel zones are elliptical in shape with the transmitter and receiver antenna at their foci. In Figure 4.12, different knife edge diffraction scenarios are shown. In general, if an obstruction does not block the volume contained within the first Fresnel zone, then the diffraction loss will be minimal, and diffraction effects may be neglected. In fact, a rule of thumb used for design of line-of-sight microwave links is that as long as 55% of the first Fresnel zone is kept clear, then further Fresnel zone clearance does not significantly alter the diffraction loss.

4.7.2 Knife-edge Diffraction Model

Estimating the signal attenuation caused by diffraction of radio waves over hills and buildings is essential in predicting the field strength in a given service area. Generally, it is impossible to make very precise estimates of the diffraction losses, and in practice prediction is a process of theoretical approximation modified by necessary empirical corrections. Though the calculation of diffraction losses over complex and irregular terrain is a mathematically difficult problem, expressions for diffraction losses for many simple cases have been derived. As a starting point, the limiting case of propagation over a knife-edge gives good insight into the order of magnitude of diffraction loss.

When shadowing is caused by a single object such as a hill or mountain, the attenuation caused by diffraction can be estimated by treating the obstruction as a diffracting knife edge. This is the simplest of diffraction models, and the diffraction loss in this case can be readily estimated using the classical Fresnel solution for the field behind a knife edge (also called a half-plane). Figure 4.13 illustrates this approach.

Consider a receiver at point R, located in the shadowed region (also called the *diffraction zone*). The field strength at point R in Figure 4.13 is a vector sum of the fields due to all of the

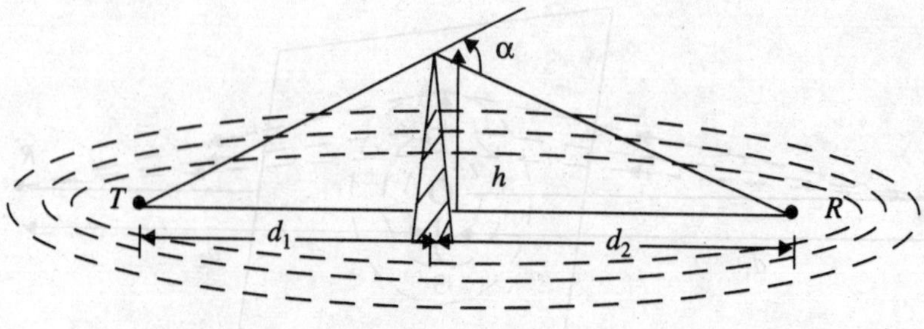

(a) α and ν are positive, since h is positive

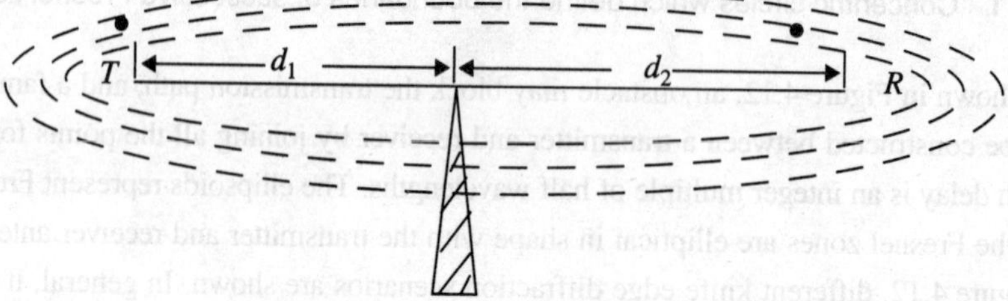

(b) α and ν are equal to zero, since h is equal to zero

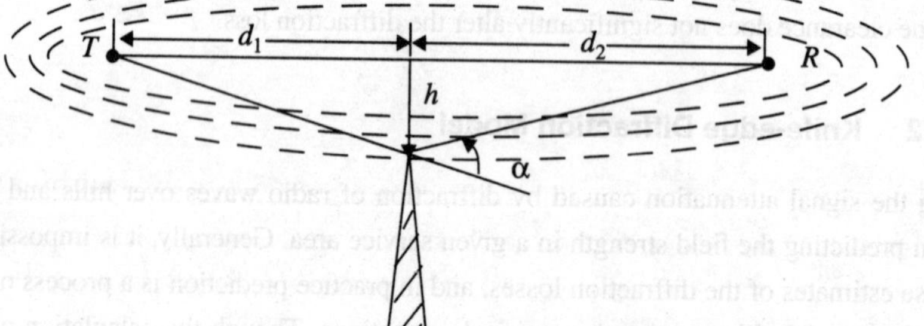

(c) α and ν are negative, since h is negative

Figure 4.12 Illustration of Fresnel zones for different knife-edge diffraction scenarios.

secondary Huygen's sources in the plane above the knife edge. The electric field strength, E_d, of a knife-edge diffracted wave is given by

$$\frac{E_d}{E_o} = F(v) = \frac{(1+j)}{2}\int_v^{\infty} \exp((-j\pi t^2)/2)\,dt \qquad (4.59)$$

where E_o is the free space field strength in the absence of both the ground and the knife edge, and $F(v)$ is the complex Fresnel integral. The Fresnel integral, $F(v)$, is a function of the

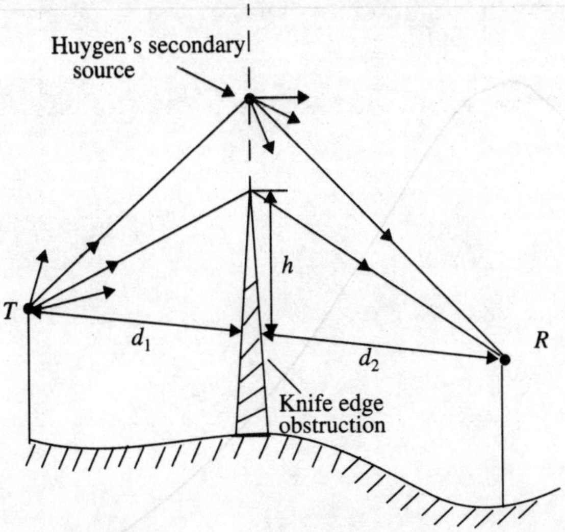

Figure 4.13 Illustration of knife-edge diffraction geometry. The receiver *R* is located in the shadow region.

Fresnel–Kirchoff diffraction parameter v, defined in Equation (4.56), and is commonly evaluated using tables or graphs for given values of v. The diffraction gain due to the presence of a knife edge, as compared to the free space E-field, is given by

$$G_d(\text{dB}) = 20\log|F(v)| \tag{4.60}$$

In practice, graphical or numerical solutions are relied upon to compute diffraction gain. A graphical representation of $G_d(\text{dB})$ as a function of v is given in Figure 4.14. An approximate solution for Equation (4.60) provided by Lee [Lee85] is

$$G_d(dB) = 0 \qquad v \le -1 \tag{4.61.a}$$

$$G_d(\text{dB}) = 20\log(0.5 - 0.62v) \qquad -1 \le v \le 0 \tag{4.61.b}$$

$$G_d(\text{dB}) = 20\log(0.5\exp(-0.95v)) \qquad 0 \le v \le 1 \tag{4.61.c}$$

$$G_d(\text{dB}) = 20\log(0.4 - \sqrt{0.1184 - (0.38 - 0.1v)^2}) \qquad 1 \le v \le 2.4 \tag{4.61.d}$$

$$G_d(\text{dB}) = 20\log\left(\frac{0.225}{v}\right) \qquad v > 2.4 \tag{4.61.e}$$

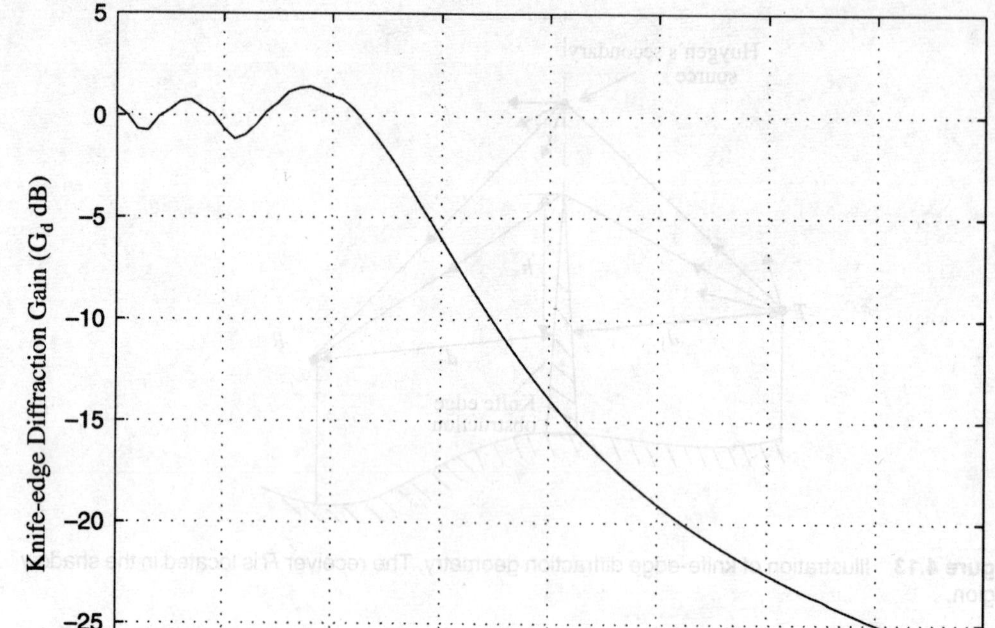

Example 4.7

Compute the diffraction loss for the three cases shown in Figure 4.12. Assume λ = 1/3 m, d_1 = 1km, d_2 = 1 km, and (a) h = 25 m, (b) h = 0, (c) h = −25 m. Compare your answers using values from Figure 4.14, as well as the approximate solution given by Equation (4.61.a)–(4.61.e). For each of these cases, identify the Fresnel zone within which the tip of the obstruction lies.

Given:

λ = 1/3 m

d_1 = 1 km

d_2 = 1 km

(a)h = 25 m

Using Equation (4.56), the Fresnel diffraction parameter is obtained as

$$v = h\sqrt{\frac{2(d_1+d_2)}{\lambda d_1 d_2}} = 25\sqrt{\frac{2(1000+1000)}{(1/3)\times 1000\times 1000}} = 2.74.$$

From Figure 4.14, the diffraction loss is obtained as 22 dB.

Using the numerical approximation in Equation (4.61.e), the diffraction loss is equal to 21.7 dB.

The path length difference between the direct and diffracted rays is given by Equation (4.54) as

$$\Delta \approx \frac{h^2}{2}\frac{(d_1+d_2)}{d_1 d_2} = \frac{25^2}{2}\frac{(1000+1000)}{1000\times1000} = 0.625 \text{ m.}$$

To find the Fresnel zone in which the tip of the obstruction lies, we need to compute n which satisfies the relation $\Delta = n\lambda/2$. For $\lambda = 1/3$ m, and $\Delta = 0/625$ m, we obtain

$$n = \frac{2\Delta}{\lambda} = \frac{2\times0.625}{0.3333} = 3.75.$$

Therefore, the tip of the obstruction completely blocks the first three Fresnel zones.

(b) $h = 0$ m

Therefore, the Fresnel diffraction parameter $v = 0$.

From Figure 4.14, the diffraction loss is obtained as 6 dB.

Using the numerical approximation in Equation (4.61.b), the diffraction loss is equal to 6 dB.

For this case, since $h = 0$, we have $\Delta = 0$, and the tip of the obstruction lies in the middle of the first Fresnel zone.

(c) $h = -25$ m

Using Equation (4.56), the Fresnel diffraction parameter is obtained as –2.74.

From Figure 4.14, the diffraction loss is approximately equal to 1 dB.

Using the numerical approximation in Equation (4.61.a), the diffraction loss is equal to 0 dB.

Since the absolute value of the height h is the same as part (a), the excess path length Δ and hence n will also be the same. It should be noted that although the tip of the obstruction completely blocks the first three Fresnel zones, the diffraction losses are negligible, since the obstruction is below the line-of-sight (h is negative).

Example 4.8

Given the following geometry, determine (a) the loss due to knife-edge diffraction, and (b) the height of the obstacle required to induce 6 dB diffraction loss. Assume $f = 900$ MHz.

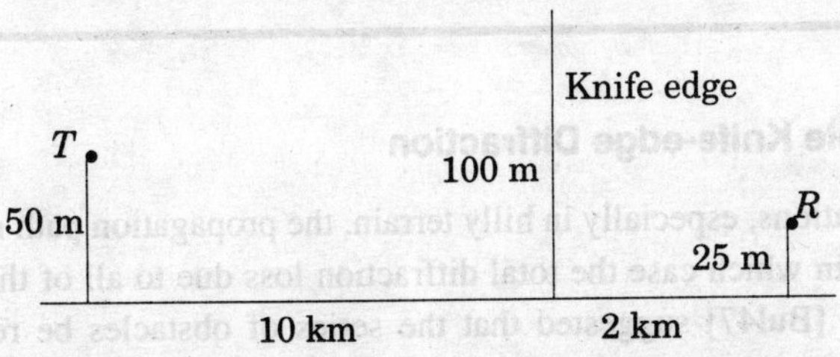

Solution

(a) The wavelength $\lambda = \frac{c}{f} = \frac{3 \times 10^8}{900 \times 10^6} = \frac{1}{3}$ m.

Redraw the geometry by subtracting the height of the smallest structure.

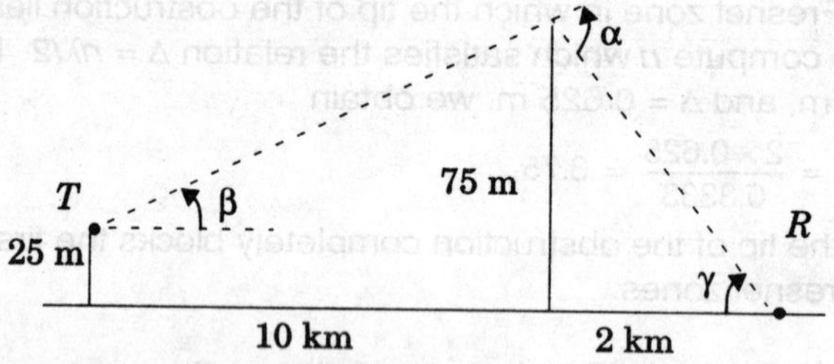

$$\beta = \tan^{-1}\left(\frac{75-25}{10000}\right) = 0.2865°$$

$$\gamma = \tan^{-1}\left(\frac{75}{2000}\right) = 2.15°$$

and

$$\alpha = \beta + \gamma = 2.434° = 0.0424 \text{ rad}$$

Then using Equation (4.56)

$$v = 0.0424\sqrt{\frac{2 \times 10000 \times 2000}{(1/3) \times (10000 + 2000)}} = 4.24.$$

From Figure 4.14 or (4.61.e), the diffraction loss is 25.5 dB.

(b) For 6 dB diffraction loss, $v = 0$. The obstruction height h may be found using similar triangles ($\beta = \gamma$), as shown below.

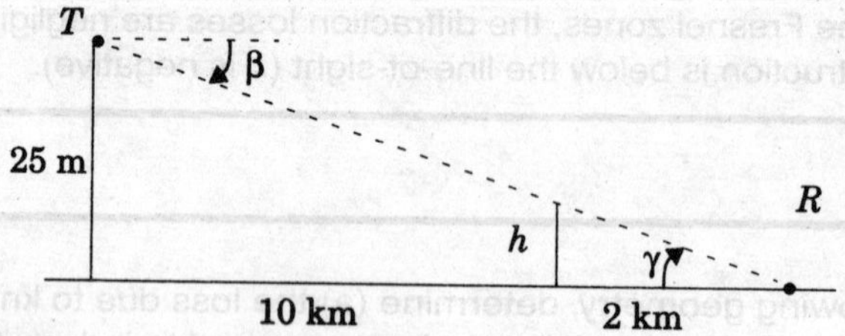

It follows that $\frac{h}{2000} = \frac{25}{12000}$, thus $h = 4.16$ m.

4.7.3 Multiple Knife-edge Diffraction

In many practical situations, especially in hilly terrain, the propagation path may consist of more than one obstruction, in which case the total diffraction loss due to all of the obstacles must be computed. Bullington [Bul47] suggested that the series of obstacles be replaced by a single

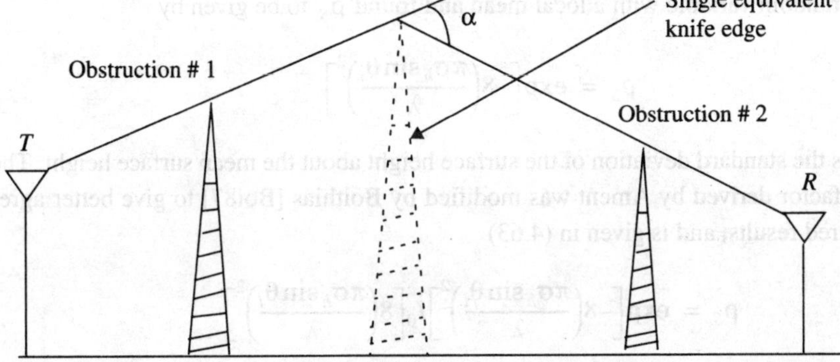

Figure 4.15 Bullington's construction of an equivalent knife edge [from [Bul47] © IEEE].

equivalent obstacle so that the path loss can be obtained using single knife-edge diffraction models. This method, illustrated in Figure 4.15, oversimplifies the calculations and often provides very optimistic estimates of the received signal strength. In a more rigorous treatment, Millington et al. [Mil62] gave a wave-theory solution for the field behind two knife edges in series. This solution is very useful and can be applied easily for predicting diffraction losses due to two knife edges. However, extending this to more than two knife edges becomes a formidable mathematical problem. Many models that are mathematically less complicated have been developed to estimate the diffraction losses due to multiple obstructions [Eps53], [Dey66].

4.8 Scattering

The actual received signal in a mobile radio environment is often stronger than what is predicted by reflection and diffraction models alone. This is because when a radio wave impinges on a rough surface, the reflected energy is spread out (diffused) in all directions due to scattering. Objects such as lamp posts and trees tend to scatter energy in all directions, thereby providing additional radio energy at a receiver.

Flat surfaces that have much larger dimension than a wavelength may be modeled as reflective surfaces. However, the roughness of such surfaces often induces propagation effects different from the specular reflection described earlier in this chapter. Surface roughness is often tested using the Rayleigh criterion which defines a critical height (h_c) of surface protuberances for a given angle of incidence θ_i, given by

$$h_c = \frac{\lambda}{8 \sin \theta_i} \tag{4.62}$$

A surface is considered smooth if its minimum to maximum protuberance h is less than h_c, and is considered rough if the protuberance is greater than h_c. For rough surfaces, the flat surface reflection coefficient needs to be multiplied by a scattering loss factor, ρ_S, to account for the diminished reflected field. Ament [Ame53] assumed that the surface height h is a Gaussian distributed random variable with a local mean and found ρ_S to be given by

$$\rho_S = \exp\left[-8\left(\frac{\pi\sigma_h \sin\theta_i}{\lambda}\right)^2\right] \tag{4.63}$$

where σ_h is the standard deviation of the surface height about the mean surface height. The scattering loss factor derived by Ament was modified by Boithias [Boi87] to give better agreement with measured results, and is given in (4.63)

$$\rho_S = \exp\left[-8\left(\frac{\pi\sigma_h \sin\theta_i}{\lambda}\right)^2\right] I_0\left[8\left(\frac{\pi\sigma_h \sin\theta_i}{\lambda}\right)^2\right] \tag{4.64}$$

where I_0 is the Bessel function of the first kind and zero order.

The reflected E-fields for $h > h_c$ can be solved for rough surfaces using a modified reflection coefficient given as

$$\Gamma_{rough} = \rho_S \Gamma \tag{4.65}$$

Figure 4.16a and Figure 4.16b illustrate experimental results found by Landron et al. [Lan96]. Measured reflection coefficient data is shown to agree well with the modified reflection coefficients of Equations (4.64) and (4.65) for large exterior walls made of rough limestone.

4.8.1 Radar Cross Section Model

In radio channels where large, distant objects induce scattering, knowledge of the physical location of such objects can be used to accurately predict scattered signal strengths. The *radar cross section* (RCS) of a scattering object is defined as the ratio of the power density of the signal scattered in the direction of the receiver to the power density of the radio wave incident upon the scattering object, and has units of square meters. Analysis based on the geometric theory of diffraction and physical optics may be used to determine the scattered field strength.

For urban mobile radio systems, models based on the *bistatic radar equation* may be used to compute the received power due to scattering in the far field. The bistatic radar equation describes the propagation of a wave traveling in free space which impinges on a distant scattering object, and is then reradiated in the direction of the receiver, given by

$$P_R(\text{dBm}) = P_T(\text{dBm}) + G_T(\text{dBi}) + 20\log(\lambda) + RCS[\text{dB m}^2] - 30\log(4\pi) - 20\log d_T - 20\log d_R \tag{4.66}$$

where d_T and d_R are the distance from the scattering object to the transmitter and receiver, respectively. In Equation (4.66), the scattering object is assumed to be in the far field (Fraunhofer region) of both the transmitter and receiver. The variable RCS is given in units of $\text{dB} \cdot \text{m}^2$, and can be approximated by the surface area (in square meters) of the scattering object, measured in dB with respect to a one square meter reference [Sei91]. Equation (4.66) may be applied to scatterers

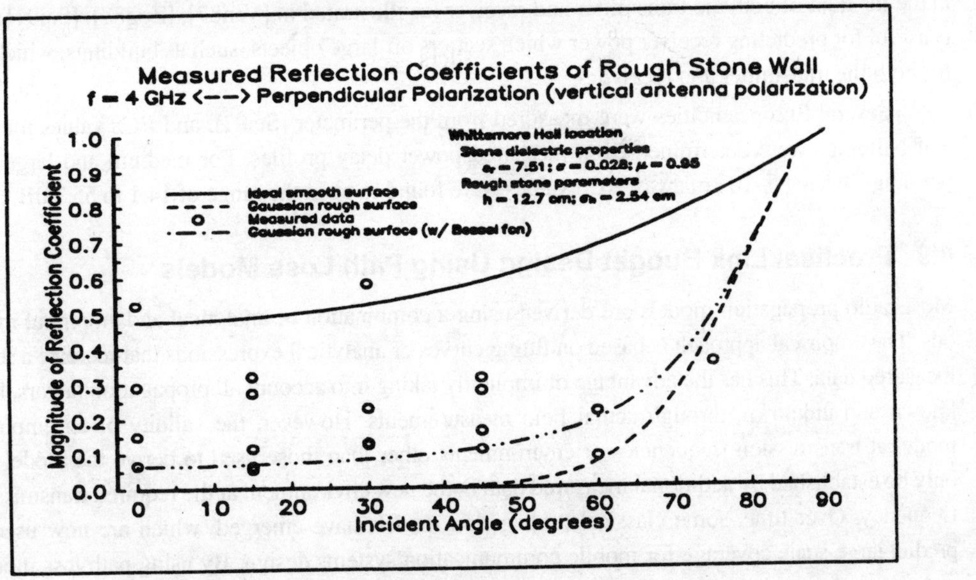

(a) E-field in the plane of incidence (parallel polarization).

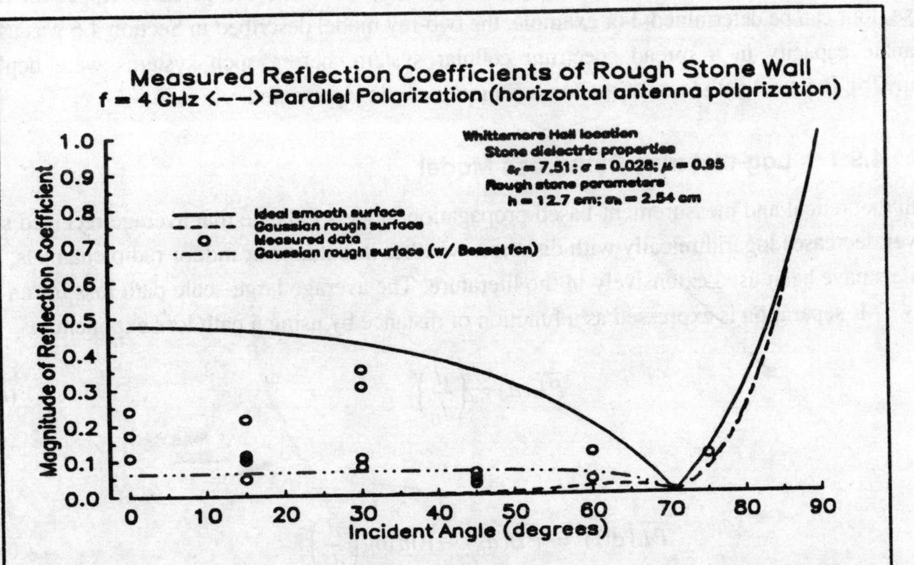

(b) E-field normal to plane of incidence (perpendicular polarization).

Figure 4.16 Measured reflection coefficients versus incident angle at a rough stone wall site. In these graphs, incident angle is measured with respect to the normal, instead of with respect to the surface boundary as defined in Figure 4.4. These graphs agree with Figure 4.6 [Lan96].

in the far-field of both the transmitter and receiver (as illustrated in [Van87], [Zog87], [Sei91]) and is useful for predicting receiver power which scatters off large objects, such as buildings, which are for both the transmitter and receiver.

Several European cities were measured from the perimeter [Sei91], and *RCS* values for several buildings were determined from measured power delay profiles. For medium and large size buildings located 5–10 km away, *RCS* values were found to be in the range of 14.1 to 55.7 dB · m^2.

4.9 Practical Link Budget Design Using Path Loss Models

Most radio propagation models are derived using a combination of analytical and empirical methods. The empirical approach is based on fitting curves or analytical expressions that recreate a set of measured data. This has the advantage of implicitly taking into account all propagation factors, both known and unknown, through actual field measurements. However, the validity of an empirical model at transmission frequencies or environments other than those used to derive the model can only be established by additional measured data in the new environment at the required transmission frequency. Over time, some classical propagation models have emerged, which are now used to predict large-scale coverage for mobile communication systems design. By using path loss models to estimate the received signal level as a function of distance, it becomes possible to predict the SNR for a mobile communication system. Using noise analysis techniques given in Appendix B, the noise floor can be determined. For example, the two-ray model described in Section 4.6 was used to estimate capacity in a spread spectrum cellular system, before such systems were deployed [Rap92b]. Practical path loss estimation techniques are now presented.

4.9.1 Log-distance Path Loss Model

Both theoretical and measurement-based propagation models indicate that average received signal power decreases logarithmically with distance, whether in outdoor or indoor radio channels. Such models have been used extensively in the literature. The average large-scale path loss for an arbitrary T–R separation is expressed as a function of distance by using a path loss exponent, n

$$\overline{PL}(d) \propto \left(\frac{d}{d_0}\right)^n \tag{4.67}$$

or

$$\overline{PL}(\text{dB}) = \overline{PL}(d_0) + 10n\log\left(\frac{d}{d_0}\right) \tag{4.68}$$

where n is the path loss exponent which indicates the rate at which the path loss increases with distance, d_0 is the close-in reference distance which is determined from measurements close to the transmitter, and d is the T–R separation distance. The bars in Equations (4.67) and (4.68) denote the ensemble average of all possible path loss values for a given value of d. When plotted on a log–log scale, the modeled path loss is a straight line with a slope equal to $10n$ dB per

Table 4.2 Path Loss Exponents for Different Environments

Environment	Path Loss Exponent, n
Free space	2
Urban area cellular radio	2.7 to 3.5
Shadowed urban cellular radio	3 to 5
In building line-of-sight	1.6 to 1.8
Obstructed in building	4 to 6
Obstructed in factories	2 to 3

decade. The value of n depends on the specific propagation environment. For example, in free space, n is equal to 2, and when obstructions are present, n will have a larger value.

It is important to select a free space reference distance that is appropriate for the propagation environment. In large coverage cellular systems, 1 km reference distances are commonly used [Lee85], whereas in microcellular systems, much smaller distances (such as 100 m or 1 m) are used. The reference distance should always be in the far field of the antenna so that near-field effects do not alter the reference path loss. The reference path loss is calculated using the free space path loss formula given by Equation (4.5) or through field measurements at distance d_0. Table 4.2 lists typical path loss exponents obtained in various mobile radio environments.

4.9.2 Log-normal Shadowing

The model in Equation (4.68) does not consider the fact that the surrounding environmental clutter may be vastly different at two different locations having the same T–R separation. This leads to measured signals which are vastly different than the *average* value predicted by Equation (4.68). Measurements have shown that at any value of d, the path loss $PL(d)$ at a particular location is random and distributed log-normally (normal in dB) about the mean distance-dependent value [Cox84], [Ber87]. That is

$$PL(d)[dB] = \overline{PL}(d) + X_\sigma = \overline{PL}(d_0) + 10n\log\left(\frac{d}{d_0}\right) + X_\sigma \tag{4.69.a}$$

and

$$P_r(d)[dBm] = P_t[dBm] - PL(d)[dB] \quad \text{(antenna gains included in } PL(d)\text{)} \tag{4.69.b}$$

where X_σ is a zero-mean Gaussian distributed random variable (in dB) with standard deviation σ (also in dB).

The log-normal distribution describes the random *shadowing* effects which occur over a large number of measurement locations which have the same T–R separation, but have different levels of clutter on the propagation path. This phenomenon is referred to as *log-normal shadowing*. Simply put, log-normal shadowing implies that measured signal levels at a specific T–R separation have a Gaussian (normal) distribution about the distance-dependent mean of (4.68), where the measured signal levels have values in dB units. The standard deviation of the Gaussian distribution that describes the shadowing also has units in dB. Thus, the random effects of shadowing are accounted for using the Gaussian distribution which lends itself readily to evaluation (see Appendix F).

The close-in reference distance d_0, the path loss exponent n, and the standard deviation σ, statistically describe the path loss model for an arbitrary location having a specific T–R separation, and this model may be used in computer simulation to provide received power levels for random locations in communication system design and analysis.

In practice, the values of n and σ are computed from measured data, using linear regression such that the difference between the measured and estimated path losses is minimized in a mean square error sense over a wide range of measurement locations and T–R separations. The value of $\overline{PL}(d_0)$ in (4.69.a) is based on either close-in measurements or on a free space assumption from the transmitter to d_0. An example of how the path loss exponent is determined from measured data follows. Figure 4.17 illustrates actual measured data in several cellular radio systems and demonstrates the random variations about the mean path loss (in dB) due to shadowing at specific T–R separations.

Since $PL(d)$ is a random variable with a normal distribution in dB about the distance-dependent mean, so is $P_r(d)$, and the Q-function or error function (*erf*) may be used to determine the probability that the received signal level will exceed (or fall below) a particular level. The Q-function is defined as

$$Q(z) = \frac{1}{\sqrt{2\pi}}\int_z^{\infty} \exp\left(-\frac{x^2}{2}\right)dx = \frac{1}{2}\left[1 - erf\left(\frac{z}{\sqrt{2}}\right)\right] \tag{4.70.a}$$

where

$$Q(z) = 1 - Q(-z) \tag{4.70.b}$$

The probability that the received signal level (in dB power units) will exceed a certain value γ can be calculated from the cumulative density function as

$$Pr[P_r(d) > \gamma] = Q\left(\frac{\gamma - \overline{P_r(d)}}{\sigma}\right) \tag{4.71}$$

Similarly, the probability that the received signal level will be below γ is given by

$$Pr[P_r(d) < \gamma] = Q\left(\frac{\overline{P_r(d)} - \gamma}{\sigma}\right) \tag{4.72}$$

Appendix F provides tables for evaluating the Q and *erf* functions.

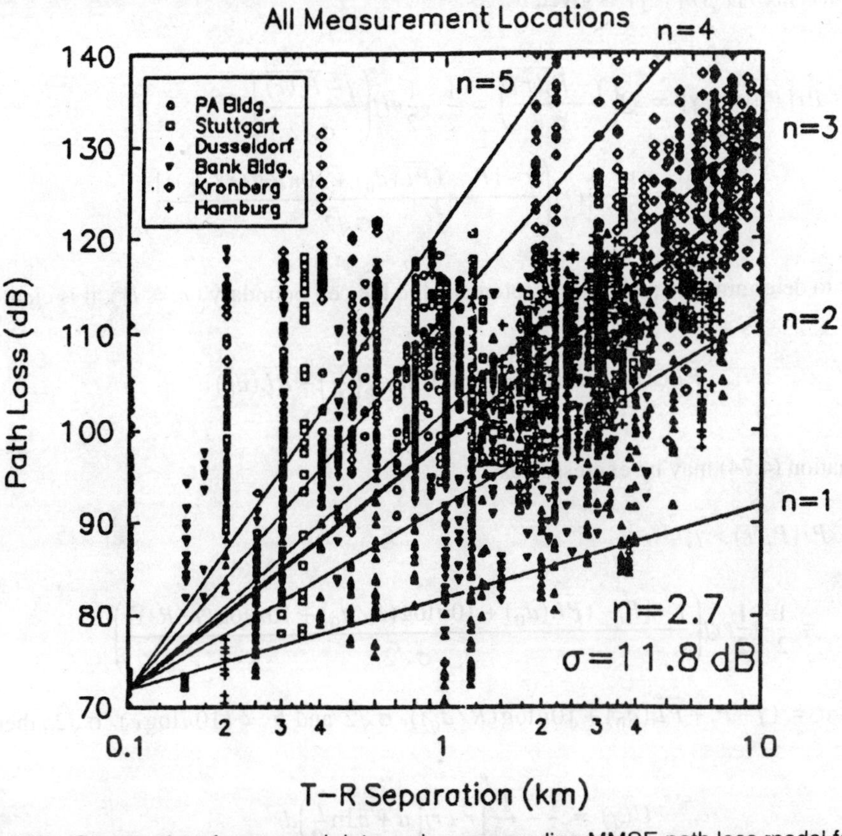

Figure 4.17 Scatter plot of measured data and corresponding MMSE path loss model for many cities in Germany. For this data, $n = 2.7$ and $\sigma = 11.8$ dB [from [Sei91] © IEEE].

4.9.3 Determination of Percentage of Coverage Area

It is clear that due to random effects of shadowing, some locations within a coverage area will be below a particular desired received signal threshold. It is often useful to compute how the boundary coverage relates to the percent of area covered within the boundary. For a circular coverage area having radius R from a base station, let there be some desired received signal threshold γ. We are interested in computing $U(\gamma)$, the percentage of useful service area (i.e. the percentage of area with a received signal that is equal or greater than γ), given a known likelihood of coverage at the cell boundary. Letting $d = r$ represent the radial distance from the transmitter, it can be shown that if $Pr[P_r(r) > \gamma]$ is the probability that the random received signal at $d = r$ exceeds the threshold γ within an incremental area dA, then $U(\gamma)$ can be found by [Jak74]

$$U(\gamma) = \frac{1}{\pi R^2}\int Pr[P_r(r) > \gamma]dA = \frac{1}{\pi R^2}\int_0^{2\pi}\int_0^R Pr[P_r(r) > \gamma]r\,dr\,d\theta \quad (4.73)$$

Using (4.71), $Pr[P_r(r) > \gamma]$ is given by

$$Pr[P_r(r) > \gamma] = Q\left(\frac{\gamma - \overline{P_r(r)}}{\sigma}\right) = \frac{1}{2} - \frac{1}{2}erf\left(\frac{\gamma - \overline{P_r(r)}}{\sigma\sqrt{2}}\right) \tag{4.74}$$

$$= \frac{1}{2} - \frac{1}{2}erf\left(\frac{\gamma - [P_t - (\overline{PL}(d_0) + 10n\log(r/d_0))]}{\sigma\sqrt{2}}\right)$$

In order to determine the path loss as referenced to the cell boundary ($r = R$), it is clear that

$$\overline{PL}(r) = 10n\log\left(\frac{R}{d_0}\right) + 10n\log\left(\frac{r}{R}\right) + \overline{PL}(d_0) \tag{4.75}$$

and Equation (4.74) may be expressed as

$$Pr[P_r(r) > \gamma] \tag{4.76}$$

$$= \frac{1}{2} - \frac{1}{2}erf\left(\frac{\gamma - [P_t - (\overline{PL}(d_0) + 10n\log(R/d_0) + 10n\log(r/R))]}{\sigma\sqrt{2}}\right)$$

If we let $a = (\gamma - P_t + \overline{PL}(d_0) + 10n\log(R/d_0))/\sigma\sqrt{2}$ and $b = (10n\log e)/\sigma\sqrt{2}$, then

$$U(\gamma) = \frac{1}{2} - \frac{1}{R^2}\int_0^R r\, erf\left(a + b\ln\frac{r}{R}\right)dr \tag{4.77}$$

By substituting $t = a + b\log(r/R)$ in Equation (4.77), it can be shown that

$$U(\gamma) = \frac{1}{2}\left(1 - erf(a) + \exp\left(\frac{1 - 2ab}{b^2}\right)\left[1 - erf\left(\frac{1 - ab}{b}\right)\right]\right) \tag{4.78}$$

By choosing the signal level such that $\overline{P_r}(R) = \gamma$ (i.e. $a = 0$), $U(\gamma)$ can be shown to be

$$U(\gamma) = \frac{1}{2}\left[1 + \exp\left(\frac{1}{b^2}\right)\left(1 - erf\left(\frac{1}{b}\right)\right)\right] \tag{4.79}$$

Equation (4.78) may be evaluated for a large number of values of σ and n, as shown in Figure 4.18 [Reu74]. For example, if $n = 4$ and $\sigma = 8$ dB, and if the boundary is to have 75% boundary coverage (75% of the time the signal is to exceed the threshold at the boundary), then the area coverage is equal to 90%. If $n = 2$ and $\sigma = 8$ dB, a 75% boundary coverage provides 86% area coverage. If $n = 3$ and $\sigma = 9$ dB, then 50% boundary coverage provides 71% area coverage.

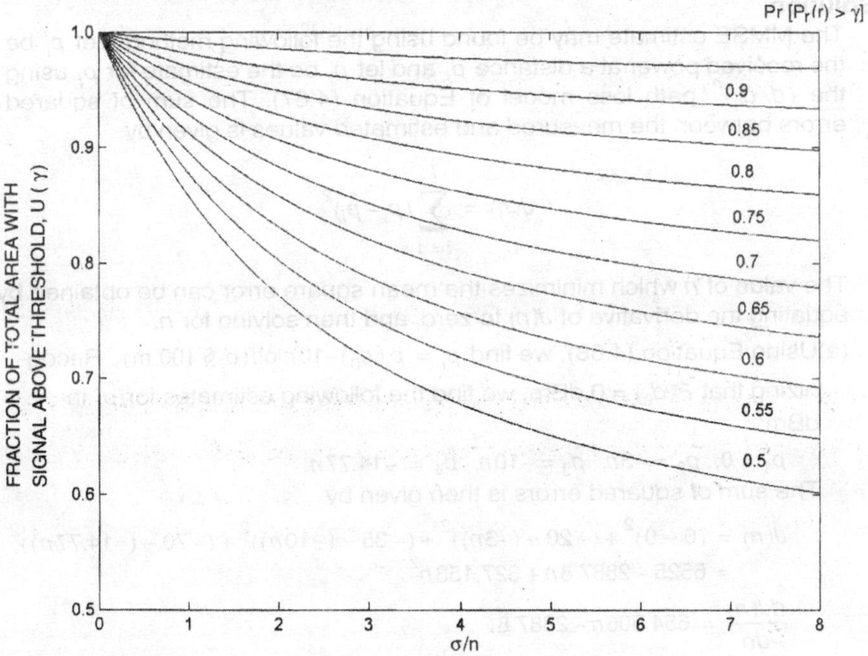

Figure 4.18 Family of curves relating fraction of total area with signal above threshold, $U(\gamma)$ as a function of probability of signal above threshold on the cell boundary.

Example 4.9

Four received power measurements were taken at distances of 100 m, 200 m, 1 km, and 3 km from a transmitter. These measured values are given in the following table. It is assumed that the path loss for these measurements follows the model in Equation (4.69.a), where d_0 = 100 m: (a) find the minimum mean square error (MMSE) estimate for the path loss exponent, n; (b) calculate the standard deviation about the mean value; (c) estimate the received power at d = 2 km using the resulting model; (d) predict the likelihood that the received signal level at 2 km will be greater than -60 dBm; and (e) predict the percentage of area within a 2 km radius cell that receives signals greater than −60 dBm, given the result in (d).

Distance from Transmitter	Received Power
100 m	0 dBm
200 m	−20 dBm
1000 m	−35 dBm
3000 m	−70 dBm

Solution

The MMSE estimate may be found using the following method. Let p_i be the received power at a distance d_i and let $\hat{p}_i$ be the estimate for p_i using the $(d/d_0)^n$ path loss model of Equation (4.67). The sum of squared errors between the measured and estimated values is given by

$$J(n) = \sum_{i=1}^{k} (p_i - \hat{p}_i)^2$$

The value of n which minimizes the mean square error can be obtained by equating the derivative of $J(n)$ to zero, and then solving for n.

(a)Using Equation (4.68), we find $\hat{p}_i = p_i(d_0) - 10n\log(d_i \S\ 100 \text{ m})$. Recognizing that $P(d_0) = 0$ dBm, we find the following estimates for $\hat{p}_i$ in dBm:

$\hat{p}_1 = 0,\ \hat{p}_2 = -3n,\ \hat{p}_3 = -10n,\ \hat{p}_4 = -14.77n.$

The sum of squared errors is then given by

$$J(n) = (0-0)^2 + (-20-(-3n))^2 + (-35-(-10n))^2 + (-70-(-14.77n))^2$$
$$= 6525 - 2887.8n + 327.153n^2$$

$$\frac{dJ(n)}{dn} = 654.306n - 2887.8.$$

Setting this equal to zero, the value of n is obtained as $n = 4.4$.

(b)The sample variance $\sigma^2 = J(n)/4$ at $n = 4.4$ can be obtained as follows.

$$J(n) = (0+0) + (-20+13.2)^2 + (-35+44)^2 + (-70+64.988)^2$$
$$= 152.36.$$

$$\sigma^2 = 152.36/4 = 38.09\,\text{dB}^2$$

therefore

$\sigma = 6.17$ dB, which is a biased estimate. In general, a greater number of measurements are needed to reduce σ^2.

(c)The estimate of the received power at $d = 2$ km is given by

$p(d = 2 \text{ km}) = 0 - 10(4.4)\log(2000/100) = -57.24$ dBm.

A Gaussian random variable having zero mean and $\sigma = 6.17$ dB could be added to this value to simulate random shadowing effects at $d = 2$ km.

(d)The probability that the received signal level will be greater than -60 dBm is given by

$$Pr[P_r(d) > -60 \text{ dBm}] = Q\left(\frac{\gamma - \overline{P_r(d)}}{\sigma}\right) = Q\left(\frac{-60+57.24}{6.17}\right) = 67.4\ \%.$$

(e)If 67.4% of the users on the boundary receive signals greater than -60 dBm, then Equation (4.78) or Figure 4.18 may be used to determine that 88% of the cell area receives coverage above -60 dBm.

4.10 Outdoor Propagation Models

Radio transmission in a mobile communications system often takes place over irregular terrain. The terrain profile of a particular area needs to be taken into account for estimating the path loss. The terrain profile may vary from a simple curved earth profile to a highly mountainous profile. The presence of trees, buildings, and other obstacles also must be taken into account. A number of propagation models are available to predict path loss over irregular terrain. While all these models aim to predict signal strength at a particular receiving point or in a specific local area (called a *sector*), the methods vary widely in their approach, complexity, and accuracy. Most of these models are based on a systematic interpretation of measurement data obtained in the service area. Some of the commonly used outdoor propagation models are now discussed.

4.10.1 Longley–Rice Model

The Longley–Rice model [Ric67], [Lon68] is applicable to point-to-point communication systems in the frequency range from 40 MHz to 100 GHz, over different kinds of terrain. The median transmission loss is predicted using the path geometry of the terrain profile and the refractivity of the troposphere. Geometric optics techniques (primarily the two-ray ground reflection model) are used to predict signal strengths within the radio horizon. Diffraction losses over isolated obstacles are estimated using the Fresnel–Kirchoff knife-edge models. Forward scatter theory is used to make troposcatter predictions over long distances, and far field diffraction losses in double horizon paths are predicted using a modified Van der Pol-Bremmer method. The Longley–Rice propagation prediction model is also referred to as the *ITS irregular terrain model*.

The Longley–Rice model is also available as a computer program [Lon78] to calculate large-scale median transmission loss relative to free space loss over irregular terrain for frequencies between 20 MHz and 10 GHz. For a given transmission path, the program takes as its input the transmission frequency, path length, polarization, antenna heights, surface refractivity, effective radius of earth, ground conductivity, ground dielectric constant, and climate. The program also operates on path-specific parameters such as horizon distance of the antennas, horizon elevation angle, angular trans-horizon distance, terrain irregularity, and other specific inputs.

The Longley–Rice method operates in two modes. When a detailed terrain path profile is available, the path-specific parameters can be easily determined and the prediction is called a *point-to-point mode* prediction. On the other hand, if the terrain path profile is not available, the Longley–Rice method provides techniques to estimate the path-specific parameters, and such a prediction is called an *area mode* prediction.

There have been many modifications and corrections to the Longley–Rice model since its original publication. One important modification [Lon78] deals with radio propagation in urban areas, and this is particularly relevant to mobile radio. This modification introduces an excess term as an allowance for the additional attenuation due to urban clutter near the receiving antenna. This extra term, called the *urban factor* (UF), has been derived by comparing the predictions by the original Longley–Rice model with those obtained by Okumura [Oku68].

One shortcoming of the Longley–Rice model is that it does not provide a way of determining corrections due to environmental factors in the immediate vicinity of the mobile receiver, or consider correction factors to account for the effects of buildings and foliage. Further, multipath is not considered.

4.10.2 Durkin's Model—A Case Study

A classical propagation prediction approach similar to that used by Longley–Rice is discussed by Edwards and Durkin [Edw69], as well as Dadson [Dad75]. These papers describe a computer simulator, for predicting field strength contours over irregular terrain, that was adopted by the Joint Radio Committee (JRC) in the U.K. for the estimation of effective mobile radio coverage areas. Although this simulator only predicts large-scale phenomena (i.e. path loss), it provides an interesting perspective into the nature of propagation over irregular terrain and the losses caused by obstacles in a radio path. An explanation of the Edwards and Durkin method is presented here in order to demonstrate how all of the concepts described in this chapter are used in a single model.

The execution of the Durkin path loss simulator consists of two parts. The first part accesses a topographic data base of a proposed service area and reconstructs the ground profile information along the radial joining the transmitter to the receiver. The assumption is that the receiving antenna receives all of its energy along that radial and, therefore, experiences no multipath propagation. In other words, the propagation phenomena that is modeled is simply LOS and diffraction from obstacles along the radial, and excludes reflections from other surrounding objects and local scatterers. The effect of this assumption is that the model is somewhat pessimistic in narrow valleys, although it identifies isolated weak reception areas rather well. The second part of the simulation algorithm calculates the expected path loss along that radial. After this is done, the simulated receiver location can be iteratively moved to different locations in the service area to deduce the signal strength contour.

The topographical data base can be thought of as a two-dimensional array. Each array element corresponds to a point on a service area map while the actual contents of each array element contain the elevation above sea level data as shown in Figure 4.19. These types of digital elevation models (DEM) are readily available from the United States Geological Survey (USGS). Using this quantized map of service area heights, the program reconstructs the ground profile along the radial that joins the transmitter and the receiver. Since the radial may not always pass through discrete data points, interpolation methods are used to determine the approximate heights that are observed when looking along that radial. Figure 4.20a shows the topographic grid with arbitrary transmitter and receiver locations, the radial between the transmitter and receiver, and the points with which to use diagonal linear interpolation. Figure 4.20b also shows what a typical reconstructed radial terrain profile might look like. In actuality, the values are not simply determined by one interpolation routine, but by a combination of three for increased accuracy. Therefore, each point of the reconstructed profile consists of an average of the heights obtained by diagonal, vertical (row), and horizontal (column) interpolation methods.

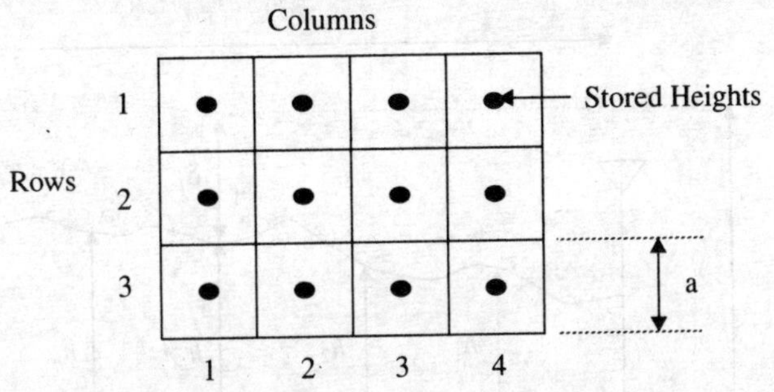

Figure 4.19 Illustration of a two-dimensional array of elevation information.

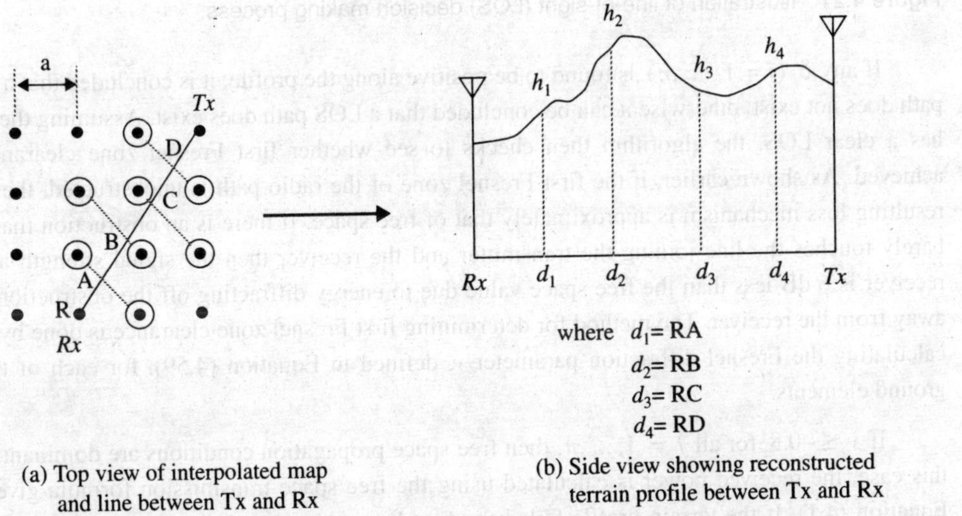

Figure 4.20 Illustration of terrain profile reconstruction using diagonal interpolation.

From these interpolation routines, a matrix of distances from the receiver and corresponding heights along the radial is generated. Now the problem is reduced to a one-dimensional point-to-point link calculation. These types of problems are well-established and procedures for calculating path loss using knife-edge diffraction techniques described previously are used.

At this point, the algorithm must make decisions as to what the expected transmission loss should be. The first step is to decide whether a line-of-sight (LOS) path exists between the transmitter and the receiver. To do this, the program computes the difference, δ_j, between the height of the line joining the transmitter and receiver antennas from the height of the ground profile for each point along the radial (see Figure 4.21).

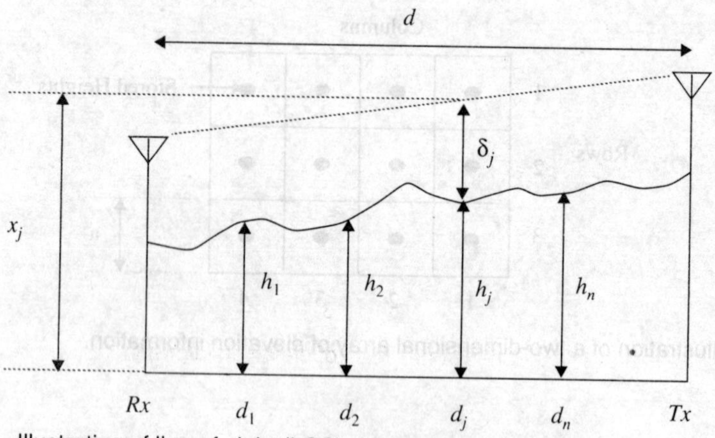

Figure 4.21 Illustration of line-of-sight (LOS) decision making process.

If any δ_j ($j = 1, ...,n$) is found to be positive along the profile, it is concluded that a LOS path does not exist, otherwise it can be concluded that a LOS path does exist. Assuming the path has a clear LOS, the algorithm then checks to see whether first Fresnel zone clearance is achieved. As shown earlier, if the first Fresnel zone of the radio path is unobstructed, then the resulting loss mechanism is approximately that of free space. If there is an obstruction that just barely touches the line joining the transmitter and the receiver then the signal strength at the receiver is 6 dB less than the free space value due to energy diffracting off the obstruction and away from the receiver. The method for determining first Fresnel zone clearance is done by first calculating the Fresnel diffraction parameter v, defined in Equation (4.59), for each of the j ground elements.

If $v_j \le -0.8$ for all $j = 1, ...,n$, then free space propagation conditions are dominant. For this case, the received power is calculated using the free space transmission formula given in Equation (4.1). If the terrain profile failed the first Fresnel zone test (i.e. any $v_j > -0.8$), then there are two possibilities:

a. Non-LOS

b. LOS, but with inadequate first Fresnel-zone clearance.

For both of these cases, the program calculates the free space power using Equation (4.1) and the received power using the plane earth propagation equation given by Equation (4.52). The algorithm then selects the smaller of the powers calculated with Equations (4.1) and (4.52) as the appropriate received power for the terrain profile. If the profile is LOS with inadequate first Fresnel zone clearance, the next step is to calculate the additional loss due to inadequate Fresnel zone clearance and add it (in dB) to the appropriate received power. This additional diffraction loss is calculated by Equation (4.60).

For the case of non-LOS, the system grades the problem into one of four categories:

a. Single diffraction edge

b. Two diffraction edges

c. Three diffraction edges

d. More than three diffraction edges

The method tests for each case sequentially until it finds the one that fits the given profile. A diffraction edge is detected by computing the angles between the line joining the transmitter and receiver antennas and the lines joining the receiver antenna to each point on the reconstructed terrain profile. The maximum of these angles is located and labeled by the profile point (d_i, h_i). Next, the algorithm steps through the reverse process of calculating the angles between the line joining the transmitter and receiver antennas and the lines joining the transmitter antenna to each point on the reconstructed terrain profile. The maximum of these angles is found, and it occurs at (d_j, h_j) on the terrain profile. If $d_i = d_j$, then the profile can be modeled as a single diffraction edge. The Fresnel parameter, v_j, associated with this edge can be determined from the length of the obstacle above the line joining the transmitter and receiver antennas. The loss can then be evaluated by calculating PL using the Equation (4.60). This extra loss caused by the obstacle is then added to either the free space or plane earth loss, whichever is greater.

If the condition for a single diffraction edge is not satisfied, then the check for two diffraction edges is executed. The test is similar to that for a single diffraction edge, with the exception that the computer looks for two edges in sight of each other (see Figure 4.22).

The Edwards and Durkin [Edw69] algorithm uses the Epstein and Peterson method [Eps53] to calculate the loss associated with two diffraction edges. In short, it is the sum of two attenuations. The first attenuation is the loss at the second diffraction edge caused by the first diffraction edge with the transmitter as the source. The second attenuation is the loss at the

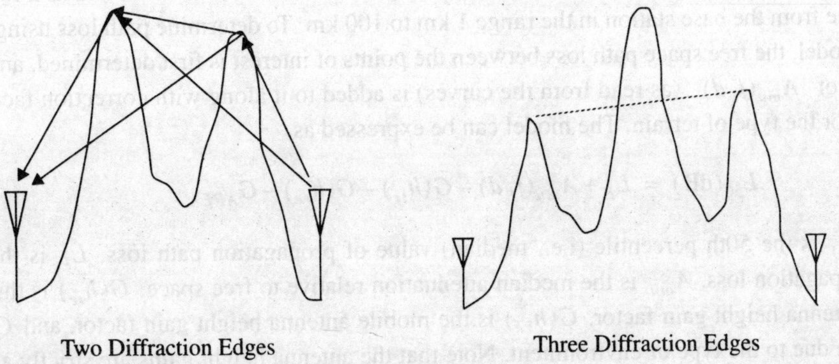

Figure 4.22 Illustration of multiple diffraction edges.

receiver caused by the second diffraction edge with the first diffraction edge as the source. The two attenuations sum to give the additional loss caused by the obstacles that is added to the free space loss or the plane earth loss, whichever is larger.

For three diffraction edges, the outer diffraction edges must contain a single diffraction edge in between. This is detected by calculating the line between the two outer diffraction edges. If an obstacle between the two outer edges passes through the line, then it is concluded that a third diffraction edge exists (see Figure 4.22). Again, the Epstein and Peterson method is used to calculate the shadow loss caused by the obstacles. For all other cases of more than three diffraction edges, the profile between the outer two obstacles is approximated by a single, virtual knife edge. After the approximation, the problem is that of a three edge calculation.

This method is very attractive because it can read in a digital elevation map and perform a site-specific propagation computation on the elevation data. It can produce a signal strength contour that has been reported to be good within a few dB. The disadvantages are that it cannot adequately predict propagation effects due to foliage, buildings, other man-made structures, and it does not account for multipath propagation other than ground reflection, so additional loss factors are often included. Propagation prediction algorithms which use terrain information are typically used for the design of modern wireless systems.

4.10.3 Okumura Model

Okumura's model is one of the most widely used models for signal prediction in urban areas. This model is applicable for frequencies in the range 150 MHz to 1920 MHz (although it is typically extrapolated up to 3000 MHz) and distances of 1 km to 100 km. It can be used for base station antenna heights ranging from 30 m to 1000 m.

Okumura developed a set of curves giving the median attenuation relative to free space (A_{mu}), in an urban area over a quasi-smooth terrain with a base station effective antenna height (h_{te}) of 200 m and a mobile antenna height (h_{re}) of 3 m. These curves were developed from extensive measurements using vertical omnidirectional antennas at both the base and mobile, and are plotted as a function of frequency in the range 100 MHz to 1920 MHz and as a function of distance from the base station in the range 1 km to 100 km. To determine path loss using Okumura's model, the free space path loss between the points of interest is first determined, and then the value of $A_{mu}(f, d)$ (as read from the curves) is added to it along with correction factors to account for the type of terrain. The model can be expressed as

$$L_{50}(\text{dB}) = L_F + A_{mu}(f, d) - G(h_{te}) - G(h_{re}) - G_{AREA} \tag{4.80}$$

where L_{50} is the 50th percentile (i.e., median) value of propagation path loss, L_F is the free space propagation loss, A_{mu} is the median attenuation relative to free space, $G(h_{te})$ is the base station antenna height gain factor, $G(h_{re})$ is the mobile antenna height gain factor, and G_{AREA} is the gain due to the type of environment. Note that the antenna height gains are strictly a function of height and have nothing to do with antenna patterns.

Plots of $A_{mu}(f, d)$ and G_{AREA} for a wide range of frequencies are shown in Figure 4.23 and Figure 4.24. Furthermore, Okumura found that $G(h_{te})$ varies at a rate of 20 dB/decade and $G(h_{re})$ varies at a rate of 10 dB/decade for heights less than 3 m

$$G(h_{te}) = 20\log\left(\frac{h_{te}}{200}\right) \qquad 1000\text{ m} > h_{te} > 30\text{ m} \tag{4.81.a}$$

$$G(h_{re}) = 10\log\left(\frac{h_{re}}{3}\right) \qquad h_{re} \le 3\text{ m} \tag{4.81.b}$$

$$G(h_{re}) = 20\log\left(\frac{h_{re}}{3}\right) \qquad 10\text{ m} > h_{re} > 3\text{ m} \tag{4.81.c}$$

Other corrections may also be applied to Okumura's model. Some of the important terrain related parameters are the terrain undulation height (Δh), isolated ridge height, average slope of the terrain and the mixed land–sea parameter. Once the terrain related parameters are calculated, the necessary correction factors can be added or subtracted as required. All these correction factors are also available as Okumura curves [Oku68].

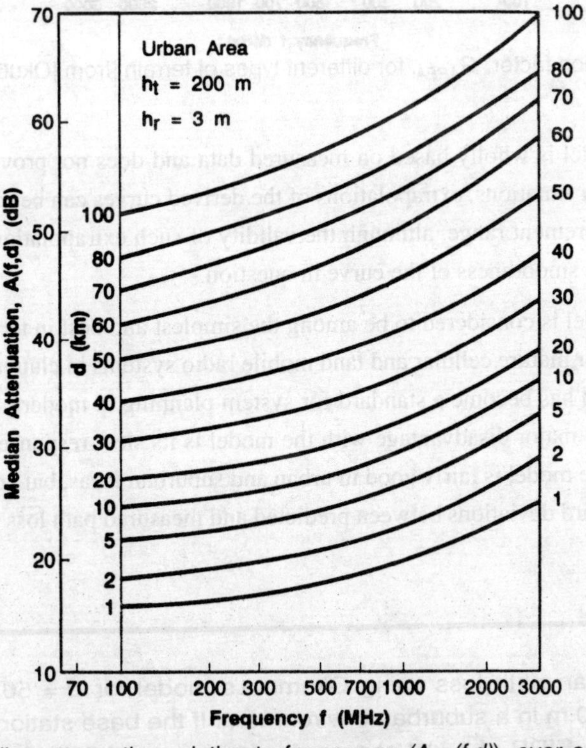

Figure 4.23 Median attenuation relative to free space ($A_{mu}(f,d)$), over a quasi-smooth terrain [from [Oku68] © IEEE].

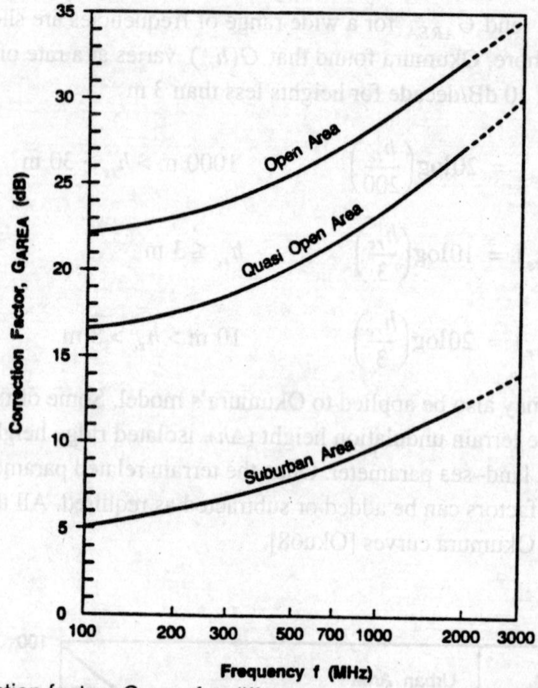

Figure 4.24 Correction factor, G_{AREA}, for different types of terrain [from [Oku68] © IEEE].

Okumura's model is wholly based on measured data and does not provide any analytical explanation. For many situations, extrapolations of the derived curves can be made to obtain values outside the measurement range, although the validity of such extrapolations depends on the circumstances and the smoothness of the curve in question.

Okumura's model is considered to be among the simplest and best in terms of accuracy in path loss prediction for mature cellular and land mobile radio systems in cluttered environments. It is very practical and has become a standard for system planning in modern land mobile radio systems in Japan. The major disadvantage with the model is its slow response to rapid changes in terrain, therefore the model is fairly good in urban and suburban areas, but not as good in rural areas. Common standard deviations between predicted and measured path loss values are around 10 dB to 14 dB.

Example 4.10

Find the median path loss using Okumura's model for d = 50 km, h_{te} = 100 m, h_{re} = 10 m in a suburban environment. If the base station transmitter radiates an EIRP of 1 kW at a carrier frequency of 900 MHz, find the power at the receiver (assume a unity gain receiving antenna).

Solution

The free space path loss L_F can be calculated using Equation (4.6) as

$$L_F = 10\log\left[\frac{\lambda^2}{(4\pi)^2 d^2}\right] = 10\log\left[\frac{(3\times 10^8/900\times 10^6)^2}{(4\pi)^2\times(50\times 10^3)^2}\right] = 125.5 \text{ dB.}$$

From the Okumura curves

$$A_{mu}(900 \text{ MHz}(50 \text{ km})) = 43 \text{ dB}$$

and

$$G_{AREA} = 9 \text{ dB.}$$

Using Equation (4.81.a) and (4.81.c), we have

$$G(h_{te}) = 20\log\left(\frac{h_{te}}{200}\right) = 20\log\left(\frac{100}{200}\right) = -6 \text{ dB.}$$

$$G(h_{re}) = 20\log\left(\frac{h_{re}}{3}\right) = 20\log\left(\frac{10}{3}\right) = 10.46 \text{ dB.}$$

Using Equation (4.80), the total mean path loss is

$$\begin{aligned} L_{50}(\text{dB}) &= L_F + A_{mu}(f, d) - G(h_{te}) - G(h_{re}) - G_{AREA} \\ &= 125.5 \text{ dB} + 43 \text{ dB} - (-6) \text{ dB} - 10.46 \text{ dB} - 9 \text{ dB} \\ &= 155.04 \text{ dB.} \end{aligned}$$

Therefore, the median received power is

$$\begin{aligned} P_r(d) &= EIRP(\text{dBm}) - L_{50}(\text{dB}) + G_r(\text{dB}) \\ &= 60 \text{ dBm} - 155.04 \text{ dB} + 0 \text{ dB} = -95.04 \text{ dBm.} \end{aligned}$$

4.10.4 Hata Model

The Hata model [Hat90] is an empirical formulation of the graphical path loss data provided by Okumura, and is valid from 150 MHz to 1500 MHz. Hata presented the urban area propagation loss as a standard formula and supplied correction Equations for application to other situations. The standard formula for median path loss in urban areas is given by

$$\begin{aligned} L_{50}(urban)(\text{dB}) &= 69.55 + 26.16\log f_c - 13.82\log h_{te} - a(h_{re}) \\ &\quad + (44.9 - 6.55\log h_{te})\log d \end{aligned} \quad (4.82)$$

where f_c is the frequency (in MHz) from 150 MHz to 1500 MHz, h_{te} is the effective transmitter (base station) antenna height (in meters) ranging from 30 m to 200 m, h_{re} is the effective receiver (mobile) antenna height (in meters) ranging from 1 m to 10 m, d is the T–R separation distance (in km), and $a(h_{re})$ is the correction factor for effective mobile antenna height which is a function of the size of the coverage area. For a small to medium sized city, the mobile antenna correction factor is given by

$$a(h_{re}) = (1.1\log f_c - 0.7)h_{re} - (1.56\log f_c - 0.8) \text{ dB} \quad (4.83)$$

and for a large city, it is given by

$$a(h_{re}) = 8.29(\log 1.54h_{re})^2 - 1.1 \text{ dB} \quad \text{for } f_c \leq 300 \text{ MHz} \tag{4.84.a}$$

$$a(h_{re}) = 3.2(\log 11.75h_{re})^2 - 4.97 \text{ dB} \quad \text{for } f_c \geq 300 \text{ MHz} \tag{4.84.b}$$

To obtain the path loss in a suburban area, the standard Hata formula in Equation (4.82) is modified as

$$L_{50}(\text{dB}) = L_{50}(urban) - 2[\log(f_c/28)]^2 - 5.4 \tag{4.85}$$

and for path loss in open rural areas, the formula is modified as

$$L_{50}(\text{dB}) = L_{50}(urban) - 4.78(\log f_c)^2 + 18.33\log f_c - 40.94 \tag{4.86}$$

Although Hata's model does not have any of the path-specific corrections which are available in Okumura's model, the above expressions have significant practical value. The predictions of the Hata model compare very closely with the original Okumura model, as long as d exceeds 1 km. This model is well suited for large cell mobile systems, but not personal communications systems (PCS) which have cells on the order of 1 km radius.

4.10.5 PCS Extension to Hata Model

The European Cooperative for Scientific and Technical research (EURO-COST) formed the COST-231 working committee to develop an extended version of the Hata model. COST-231 proposed the following formula to extend Hata's model to 2 GHz. The proposed model for path loss is [EUR91]

$$\begin{aligned} L_{50}(urban) = {} & 46.3 + 33.9\log f_c - 13.82\log h_{te} - a(h_{re}) \\ & + (44.9 - 6.55\log h_{te})\log d + C_M \end{aligned} \tag{4.87}$$

where $a(h_{re})$ is defined in Equations (4.83), (4.84.a), and (4.84.b) and

$$C_M = \begin{cases} 0 \text{ dB} & \text{for medium sized city and suburban areas} \\ 3 \text{ dB} & \text{for metropolitan centers} \end{cases} \tag{4.88}$$

The COST-231 extension of the Hata model is restricted to the following range of parameters:

f : 1500 MHz to 2000 MHz

h_{te} : 30 m to 200 m

h_{re} : 1 m to 10 m

d : 1 km to 20 km

4.10.6 Walfisch and Bertoni Model

A model developed by Walfisch and Bertoni [Wal88] considers the impact of rooftops and building height by using diffraction to predict average signal strength at street level. The model considers the path loss, S, to be a product of three factors.

$$S = P_0 Q^2 P_1 \tag{4.89}$$

where P_0 represents free space path loss between isotropic antennas given by

$$P_0 = \left(\frac{\lambda}{4\pi R}\right)^2 \tag{4.90}$$

The factor Q^2 gives the reduction in the rooftop signal due to the row of buildings which immediately shadow the receiver at street level. The P_1 term is based upon diffraction and determines the signal loss from the rooftop to the street.

In dB, the path loss is given by

$$S(\text{dB}) = L_0 + L_{rts} + L_{ms} \tag{4.91}$$

where L_0 represents free space loss, L_{rts} represents the "rooftop-to-street diffraction and scatter loss," and L_{ms} denotes multiscreen diffraction loss due to the rows of buildings [Xia92]. Figure 4.25 illustrates the geometry used in the Walfisch Bertoni model [Wal88], [Mac93]. This model is being considered for use by ITU-R in the IMT-2000 standards activities.

4.10.7 Wideband PCS Microcell Model

Work by Feuerstein et al. in 1991 used a 20 MHz pulsed transmitter at 1900 MHz to measure path loss, outage, and delay spread in typical microcellular systems in San Francisco and Oakland. Using base station antenna heights of 3.7 m, 8.5 m, and 13.3 m, and a mobile receiver with an antenna height of 1.7 m above ground, statistics for path loss, multipath, and coverage area

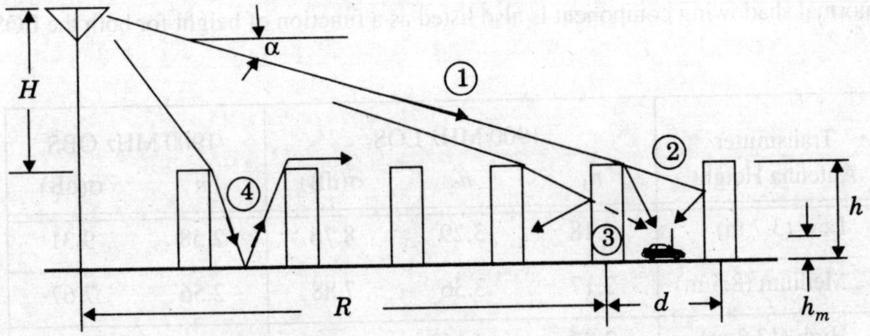

Figure 4.25 Propagation geometry for model proposed by Walfisch and Bertoni [from [Wal88] © IEEE].

were developed from extensive measurements in line-of-sight (LOS) and obstructed (OBS) environments [Feu94]. This work revealed that a two-ray ground reflection model (shown in Figure 4.7) is a good estimate for path loss in LOS microcells, and a simple log-distance path loss model holds well for OBS microcell environments.

For a flat earth ground reflection model, the distance d_f at which the first Fresnel zone just becomes obstructed by the ground (first Fresnel zone clearance) is given by

$$d_f = \frac{1}{\lambda}\sqrt{(\Sigma^2 - \Delta^2)^2 - 2(\Sigma^2 + \Delta^2)\left(\frac{\lambda}{2}\right)^2 + \left(\frac{\lambda}{2}\right)^4} \tag{4.92.a}$$

$$= \frac{1}{\lambda}\sqrt{16h_t^2h_r^2 - \lambda^2(h_t^2 + h_r^2) + \frac{\lambda^4}{16}}$$

For LOS cases, a double regression path loss model that uses a regression breakpoint at the first Fresnel zone clearance was shown to fit well to measurements. The model assumes omnidirectional vertical antennas and predicts average path loss as

$$\overline{PL}(d) = \begin{cases} 10n_1\log(d) + p_1 & \text{for } 1 < d < d_f \\ 10n_2\log(d/d_f) + 10n_1\log d_f + p_1 & \text{for } d > d_f \end{cases} \tag{4.92.b}$$

where p_1 is equal to $\overline{PL}(d_0)$ (the path loss in decibels at the reference distance of $d_0 = 1$ m), d is in meters and n_1, n_2 are path loss exponents which are a function of transmitter height, as given in Figure 4.8. It can easily be shown that at 1900 MHz, $p_1 = 38.0$ dB.

For the OBS case, the path loss was found to fit the standard log-distance path loss law of Equation (4.69.a)

$$PL(d)[dB] = 10n\log(d) + p_1 \tag{4.92.c}$$

where n is the OBS path loss exponent given in Figure 4.26 as a function of transmitter height. The standard deviation (in dB) of the log-normal shadowing component about the distance-dependent mean was found from measurements using the techniques described in Example 4.9. The log-normal shadowing component is also listed as a function of height for both the LOS and

Transmitter Antenna Height	1900 MHz LOS n_1	n_2	σ(dB)	1900 MHz OBS n	σ(dB)
Low (3.7 m)	2.18	3.29	8.76	2.58	9.31
Medium (8.5 m)	2.17	3.36	7.88	2.56	7.67
High (13.3 m)	2.07	4.16	8.77	2.69	7.94

Figure 4.26 Parameters for the wideband microcell model at 1900 MHz [from [Feu94] © IEEE].

OBS microcell environments. Figure 4.26 indicates that the log-normal shadowing component is between 7 and 9 dB regardless of antenna height. It can be seen that LOS environments provide slightly less path loss than the theoretical two-ray ground reflected model, which would predict $n_1 = 2$ and $n_2 = 4$.

4.11 Indoor Propagation Models

With the advent of Personal Communication Systems (PCS), there is a great deal of interest in characterizing radio propagation inside buildings. The indoor radio channel differs from the traditional mobile radio channel in two aspects—the distances covered are much smaller, and the variability of the environment is much greater for a much smaller range of T–R separation distances. It has been observed that propagation within buildings is strongly influenced by specific features such as the layout of the building, the construction materials, and the building type. This section outlines models for path loss within buildings.

Indoor radio propagation is dominated by the same mechanisms as outdoor: reflection, diffraction, and scattering. However, conditions are much more variable. For example, signal levels vary greatly depending on whether interior doors are open or closed inside a building. Where antennas are mounted also impacts large-scale propagation. Antennas mounted at desk level in a partitioned office receive vastly different signals than those mounted on the ceiling. Also, the smaller propagation distances make it more difficult to insure far-field radiation for all receiver locations and types of antennas.

The field of indoor radio propagation is relatively new, with the first wave of research occurring in the early 1980s. Cox [Cox83b] at AT&T Bell Laboratories and Alexander [Ale82] at British Telecom were the first to carefully study indoor path loss in and around a large number of homes and office buildings. Excellent literature surveys are available on the topic of indoor propagation [Mol91], [Has93].

In general, indoor channels may be classified either as line-of-sight (LOS) or obstructed (OBS), with varying degrees of clutter [Rap89]. Some of the key models which have recently emerged are now presented.

4.11.1 Partition Losses (same floor)

Buildings have a wide variety of partitions and obstacles which form the internal and external structure. Houses typically use a wood frame partition with plaster board to form internal walls and have wood or nonreinforced concrete between floors. Office buildings, on the other hand, often have large open areas (open plan) which are constructed by using moveable office partitions so that the space may be reconfigured easily, and use metal reinforced concrete between floors. Partitions that are formed as part of the building structure are called *hard partitions*, and partitions that may be moved and which do not span to the ceiling are called *soft partitions*. Partitions vary widely in their physical and electrical characteristics, making it difficult to apply general models to specific indoor installations. Nevertheless, researchers have formed extensive data bases of losses for a great number of partitions, as shown in Table 4.3.

Table 4.3 Average Signal Loss Measurements Reported by Various Researchers for Radio Paths Obstructed by Common Building Material

Material Type	Loss (dB)	Frequency	Reference
All metal	26	815 MHz	[Cox83b]
Aluminum siding	20.4	815 MHz	[Cox83b]
Foil insulation	3.9	815 MHz	[Cox83b]
Concrete block wall	13	1300 MHz	[Rap91c]
Loss from one floor	20-30	1300 MHz	[Rap91c]
Loss from one floor and one wall	40-50	1300 MHz	[Rap91c]
Fade observed when transmitter turned a right angle corner in a corridor	10-15	1300 MHz	[Rap91c]
Light textile inventory	3-5	1300 MHz	[Rap91c]
Chain-like fenced in area 20 ft high containing tools, inventory, and people	5-12	1300 MHz	[Rap91c]
Metal blanket — 12 sq ft	4-7	1300 MHz	[Rap91c]
Metallic hoppers which hold scrap metal for recycling — 10 sq ft	3-6	1300 MHz	[Rap91c]
Small metal pole — 6" diameter	3	1300 MHz	[Rap91c]
Metal pulley system used to hoist metal inventory — 4 sq ft	6	1300 MHz	[Rap91c]
Light machinery < 10 sq ft	1-4	1300 MHz	[Rap91c]
General machinery — 10 - 20 sq ft	5-10	1300 MHz	[Rap91c]
Heavy machinery > 20 sq ft	10-12	1300 MHz	[Rap91c]
Metal catwalk/stairs	5	1300 MHz	[Rap91c]
Light textile	3-5	1300 MHz	[Rap91c]
Heavy textile inventory	8-11	1300 MHz	[Rap91c]
Area where workers inspect metal finished products for defects	3-12	1300 MHz	[Rap91c]
Metallic inventory	4-7	1300 MHz	[Rap91c]
Large 1-beam — 16 - 20"	8-10	1300 MHz	[Rap91c]
Metallic inventory racks — 8 sq ft	4-9	1300 MHz	[Rap91c]
Empty cardboard inventory boxes	3-6	1300 MHz	[Rap91c]
Concrete block wall	13-20	1300 MHz	[Rap91c]
Ceiling duct	1-8	1300 MHz	[Rap91c]
2.5 m storage rack with small metal parts (loosely packed)	4-6	1300 MHz	[Rap91c]
4 m metal box storage	10-12	1300 MHz	[Rap91c]

Table 4.3 Average Signal Loss Measurements Reported by Various Researchers for Radio Paths Obstructed by Common Building Material (Continued)

Material Type	Loss (dB)	Frequency	Reference
5 m storage rack with paper products (loosely packed)	2-4	1300 MHz	[Rap91c]
5 m storage rack with large paper products (tightly packed)	6	1300 MHz	[Rap91c]
5 m storage rack with large metal parts (tightly packed)	20	1300 MHz	[Rap91c]
Typical N/C machine	8-10	1300 MHz	[Rap91c]
Semi-automated assembly line	5-7	1300 MHz	[Rap91c]
0.6 m square reinforced concrete pillar	12-14	1300 MHz	[Rap91c]
Stainless steel piping for cook-cool process	15	1300 MHz	[Rap91c]
Concrete wall	8-15	1300 MHz	[Rap91c]
Concrete floor	10	1300 MHz	[Rap91c]
Commercial absorber	38	9.6 GHz	[Vio88]
Commercial absorber	51	28.8 GHz	[Vio88]
Commercial absorber	59	57.6 GHz	[Vio88]
Sheetrock (3/8 in) — 2 sheets	2	9.6 GHz	[Vio88]
Sheetrock (3/8 in) — 2 sheets	2	28.8 GHz	[Vio88]
Sheetrock (3/8 in) — 2 sheets	5	57.6 GHz	[Vio88]
Dry plywood (3/4 in) — 1 sheet	1	9.6 GHz	[Vio88]
Dry plywood (3/4 in) — 1 sheet	4	28.8 GHz	[Vio88]
Dry plywood (3/4 in) — 1 sheet	8	57.6 GHz	[Vio88]
Dry plywood (3/4 in) — 2 sheets	4	9.6 GHz	[Vio88]
Dry plywood (3/4 in) — 2 sheets	6	28.8 GHz	[Vio88]
Dry plywood (3/4 in) — 2 sheets	14	57.6 GHz	[Vio88]
Wet plywood (3/4 in) — 1 sheet	19	9.6 GHz	[Vio88]
Wet plywood (3/4 in) — 1 sheet	32	28.8 GHz	[Vio88]
Wet plywood (3/4 in) — 1 sheet	59	57.6 GHz	[Vio88]
Wet plywood (3/4 in) — 2 sheets	39	9.6 GHz	[Vio88]
Wet plywood (3/4 in) — 2 sheets	46	28.8 GHz	[Vio88]
Wet plywood (3/4 in) — 2 sheets	57	57.6 GHz	[Vio88]
Aluminum (1/8 in) — 1 sheet	47	9.6 GHz	[Vio88]
Aluminum (1/8 in) — 1 sheet	46	28.8 GHz	[Vio88]
Aluminum (1/8 in) — 1 sheet	53	57.6 GHz	[Vio88]

Table 4.4 Total Floor Attenuation Factor and Standard Deviation σ (dB) for Three Buildings. Each Point Represents the Average Path Loss Over a 20λ Measurement Track [Sei92a]

Building	915 MHz FAF (dB)	σ (dB)	Number of locations	1900 MHz FAF (dB)	σ (dB)	Number of locations
Walnut Creek						
One Floor	33.6	3.2	25	31.3	4.6	110
Two Floors	44.0	4.8	39	38.5	4.0	29
SF PacBell						
One Floor	13.2	9.2	16	26.2	10.5	21
Two Floors	18.1	8.0	10	33.4	9.9	21
Three Floors	24.0	5.6	10	35.2	5.9	20
Four Floors	27.0	6.8	10	38.4	3.4	20
Five Floors	27.1	6.3	10	46.4	3.9	17
San Ramon						
One Floor	29.1	5.8	93	35.4	6.4	74
Two Floors	36.6	6.0	81	35.6	5.9	41
Three Floors	39.6	6.0	70	35.2	3.9	27

4.11.2 Partition Losses between Floors

The losses between floors of a building are determined by the external dimensions and materials of the building, as well as the type of construction used to create the floors and the external surroundings [Sei92a], [Sei92b]. Even the number of windows in a building and the presence of tinting (which attenuates radio energy) can impact the loss between floors. Table 4.4 illustrates values for *floor attenuation factors* (FAF) in three buildings in San Francisco [Sei92a]. It can be seen that for all three buildings, the attenuation between one floor of the building is greater than the incremental attenuation caused by each additional floor. Table 4.5 illustrates very similar tendencies. After about five or six floor separations, very little additional path loss is experienced.

Table 4.5 Average Floor Attenuation Factor in dB for One, Two, Three, and Four Floors in Two Office Buildings [Sei92b]

Building	FAF (dB)	σ (dB)	Number of locations
Office Building 1:			
Through One Floor	12.9	7.0	52
Through Two Floors	18.7	2.8	9
Through Three Floors	24.4	1.7	9
Through Four Floors	27.0	1.5	9
Office Building 2:			
Through One Floor	16.2	2.9	21
Through Two Floors	27.5	5.4	21
Through Three Floors	31.6	7.2	21

4.11.3 Log-distance Path Loss Model

Indoor path loss has been shown by many researchers to obey the distance power law in Equation (4.93)

$$PL(\text{dB}) = PL(d_0) + 10n\log\left(\frac{d}{d_0}\right) + X_\sigma \tag{4.93}$$

where the value of n depends on the surroundings and building type, and X_σ represents a normal random variable in dB having a standard deviation of σ dB. Notice that Equation (4.93) is identical in form to the log-normal shadowing model of Equation (4.69.a). Typical values for various buildings are provided in Table 4.6 [And94].

4.11.4 Ericsson Multiple Breakpoint Model

The Ericsson radio system model was obtained by measurements in a multiple floor office building [Ake88]. The model has four breakpoints and considers both an upper and lower bound on the path loss. The model also assumes that there is 30 dB attenuation at $d_0 = 1$ m, which can be shown to be accurate for $f = 900$ MHz and unity gain antennas. Rather than assuming a log-normal shadowing component, the Ericsson model provides a deterministic limit on the range of path loss at a particular distance. Bernhardt [Ber89] used a uniform distribution to generate path loss values within the maximum and minimum range as a function of distance for in-building simulation. Figure 4.27 shows a plot of in-building path loss based on the Ericsson model as a function of distance.

Table 4.6 Path Loss Exponent and Standard Deviation Measured in Different Buildings [And94]

Building	Frequency (MHz)	n	σ (dB)
Retail Stores	914	2.2	8.7
Grocery Store	914	1.8	5.2
Office, hard partition	1500	3.0	7.0
Office, soft partition	900	2.4	9.6
Office, soft partition	1900	2.6	14.1
Factory LOS			
Textile/Chemical	1300	2.0	3.0
Textile/Chemical	4000	2.1	7.0
Paper/Cereals	1300	1.8	6.0
Metalworking	1300	1.6	5.8
Suburban Home			
Indoor Street	900	3.0	7.0
Factory OBS			
Textile/Chemical	4000	2.1	9.7
Metalworking	1300	3.3	6.8

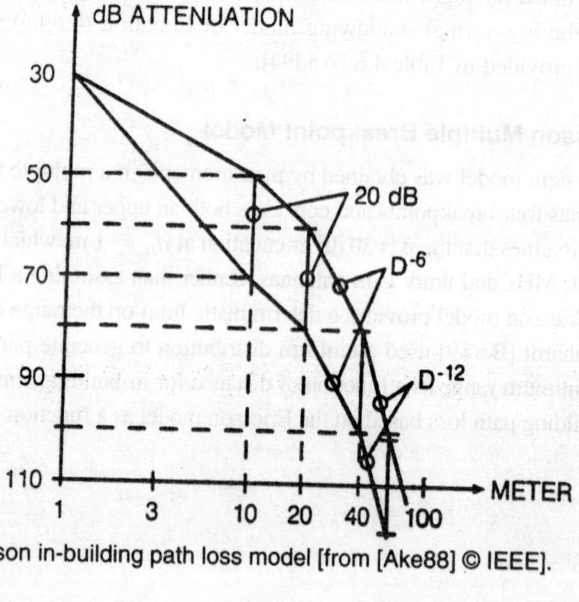

Figure 4.27 Ericsson in-building path loss model [from [Ake88] © IEEE].

4.11.5 Attenuation Factor Model

An in-building site-specific propagation model that includes the effect of building type as well as the variations caused by obstacles was described by Seidel [Sei92b] and has been used to accurately deploy indoor and campus networks [Mor00, Ski96]. This model provides flexibility and was shown to reduce the standard deviation between measured and predicted path loss to around 4 dB, as compared to 13 dB when only a log-distance model was used in two different buildings. The attenuation factor model is given by

$$\overline{PL}(d)[\text{dB}] = \overline{PL}(d_0)[\text{dB}] + 10n_{SF}\log\left(\frac{d}{d_0}\right) + FAF[\text{dB}] + \sum PAF[\text{dB}] \tag{4.94}$$

where n_{SF} represents the exponent value for the "same floor" measurement, FAF represents a floor attenuation factor for a specified number of building floors, and PAF represents the partition attenuation factor for a specific obstruction encountered by a ray drawn between the transmitter and receiver in 3-D. This technique of drawing a single ray between the transmitter and receiver is called *primary ray tracing*. Summing the cumulative partition losses along the primary ray has been shown to yield excellent accuracy while offering tremendous computational efficiency [Mor00, Ski96, Rap00]. Thus, if a good estimate for n exists (e.g., selected from Table 4.4 or Table 4.6) on the same floor, then the path loss on a different floor can be predicted by adding an appropriate value of FAF (e.g., selected from Table 4.5), and then summing the partition losses selected from Table 4.3. Alternatively, in Equation (4.94), FAF may be replaced by an exponent which already considers the effects of multiple floor separation

$$\overline{PL}(d)[\text{dB}] = \overline{PL}(d_0) + 10n_{MF}\log\left(\frac{d}{d_0}\right) + \sum PAF[\text{dB}] \tag{4.95}$$

where n_{MF} denotes a path loss exponent based on measurements through multiple floors.

Table 4.7 illustrates typical values of n for a wide range of locations in many buildings. This table also illustrates how the standard deviation decreases as the average region becomes smaller and more site specific. Scatter plots illustrating actual measured path loss in two multi-floored office buildings are shown in Figure 4.28 and Figure 4.29.

Devasirvatham et al. [Dev90b] found that in-building path loss obeys free space plus an additional loss factor which increases exponentially with distance, as shown in Table 4.8. Based on this work in multi-floor buildings, it would be possible to modify Equation (4.94) such that

$$\overline{PL}(d)[\text{dB}] = \overline{PL}(d_0)[\text{dB}] + 20\log\left(\frac{d}{d_0}\right) + \alpha d + FAF[\text{dB}] + \sum PAF[\text{dB}] \tag{4.96}$$

where α is the attenuation constant for the channel with units of dB per meter (dB/m). Table 4.8 provides typical values of α as a function of frequency as measured in [Dev90b].

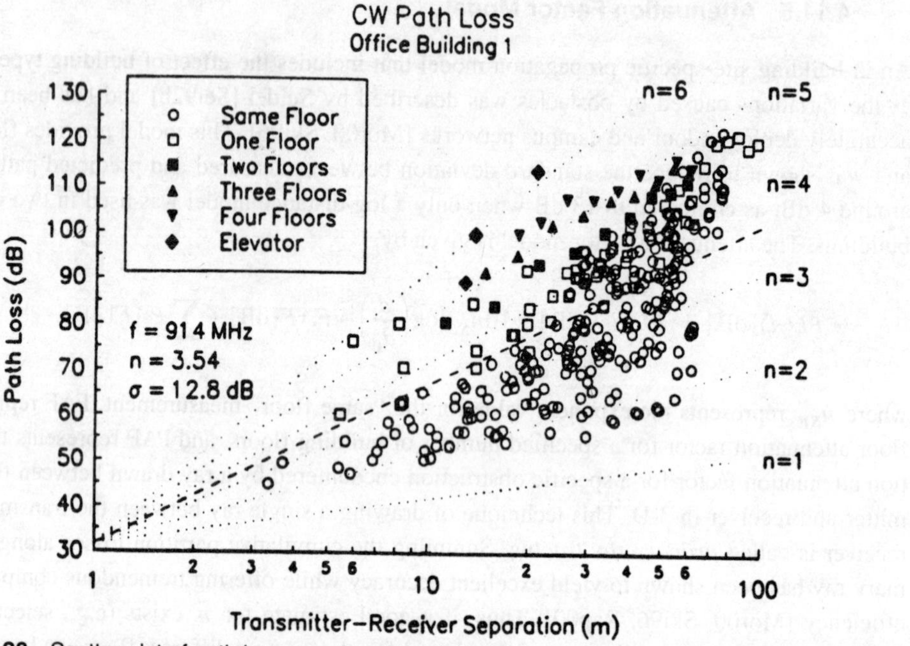

Figure 4.28 Scatter plot of path loss as a function of distance in Office Building 1 [from [Sei92b] © IEEE].

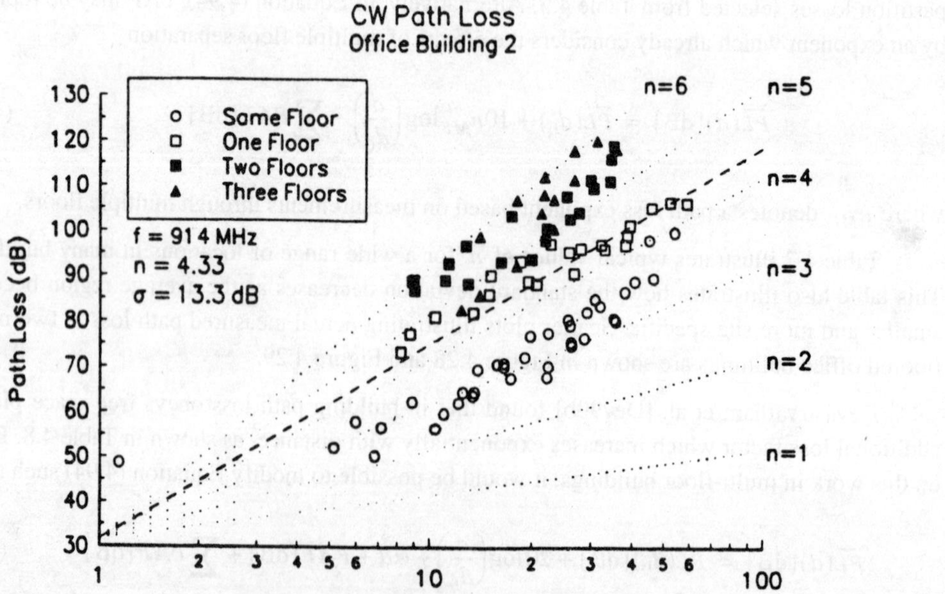

Figure 4.29 Scatter plot of path loss as a function of distance in Office Building 2 [from [Sei92b] © IEEE].

Table 4.7 Path Loss Exponent and Standard Deviation for Various Types of Buildings [Sei92b]

	n	σ (dB)	Number of locations
All Buildings:			
All locations	3.14	16.3	634
Same Floor	2.76	12.9	501
Through One Floor	4.19	5.1	73
Through Two Floors	5.04	6.5	30
Through Three Floors	5.22	6.7	30
Grocery Store	1.81	5.2	89
Retail Store	2.18	8.7	137
Office Building 1:			
Entire Building	3.54	12.8	320
Same Floor	3.27	11.2	238
West Wing 5th Floor	2.68	8.1	104
Central Wing 5th Floor	4.01	4.3	118
West Wing 4th Floor	3.18	4.4	120
Office Building 2:			
Entire Building	4.33	13.3	100
Same Floor	3.25	5.2	37

Table 4.8 Free Space Plus Linear Path Attenuation Model [Dev90b]

Location	Frequency	α–Attenuation (dB/m)
Building 1: 4 story	850 MHz	0.62
	1.7 GHz	0.57
	4.0 GHz	0.47
Building 2: 2 story	850 MHz	0.48
	1.7 GHz	0.35
	4.0 GHz	0.23

Example 4.11

This example demonstrates how to use Equations (4.94) and (4.95) to predict the mean path loss 30 m from the transmitter, through three floors of Office Building 1 (see Table 4.5). Assume that two concrete block walls are between the transmitter and receiver on the intermediate floors. From Tables 4.5 and 4.7, the mean path loss exponent for same-floor measurements in a building is $n = 3.27$, the mean path loss exponent for three-floor measurements is $n = 5.22$, and the average floor attenuation factor is FAF = 24.4 dB for three floors between the transmitter and receiver. Table 4.3 shows a concrete block wall has about 13 dB of attenuation. Let $d_0 = 1$ m.

Solution

The mean path loss using Equation (4.94) is

$$\overline{PL}(30\text{ m})[\text{dB}] = \overline{PL}(1\text{m})[\text{dB}] + 10 \times 3.27 \times \log(30) + 24.4 + 2 \times 13$$
$$= 130.2 \text{ dB}.$$

The mean path loss using Equation (4.95) is

$$\overline{PL}(30\text{ m})[\text{dB}] = \overline{PL}(1\text{ m})[\text{dB}] + 10 \times 5.22 \times \log(30) + 2 \times 13 = 108.6 \text{ dB}.$$

4.12 Signal Penetration into Buildings

The signal strength received inside of a building due to an external transmitter is important for wireless systems that share frequencies with neighboring buildings or with outdoor systems. As with propagation measurements between floors, it is difficult to determine exact models for penetration as only a limited number of experiments have been published, and they are sometimes difficult to compare. However, some generalizations can be made from the literature. In measurements reported to date, signal strength received inside a building increases with height. At the lower floors of a building, the urban clutter induces greater attenuation and reduces the level of penetration. At higher floors, a LOS path may exist, thus causing a stronger incident signal at the exterior wall of the building.

RF penetration has been found to be a function of frequency as well as height within the building. The antenna pattern in the elevation plane also plays an important role in how much signal penetrates a building from the outside. Most measurements have considered outdoor transmitters with antenna heights far less than the maximum height of the building under test. Measurements in Liverpool [Tur87] showed that penetration loss decreases with increasing frequency. Specifically, penetration attenuation values of 16.4 dB, 11.6 dB, and 7.6 dB were measured on the ground floor of a building at frequencies of 441 MHz, 896.5 MHz, and 1400 MHz, respectively. Measurements by Turkmani [Tur92] showed penetration loss of 14.2 dB, 13.4 dB, and 12.8 dB for 900 MHz, 1800 MHz, and 2300 MHz, respectively. Measurements made in front of windows indicated 6 dB less penetration loss on average than did measurements made in parts of the buildings without windows.

Walker [Wal92] measured radio signals into fourteen different buildings in Chicago from seven external cellular transmitters. Results showed that building penetration loss decreased at a rate of 1.9 dB per floor from the ground level up to the fifteenth floor and then began increasing above the fifteenth floor. The increase in penetration loss at higher floors was attributed to shadowing effects of adjacent buildings. Similarly, Turkmani [Tur87] reported penetration loss decreased at a rate of 2 dB per floor from the ground level up to the ninth floor and then increased above the ninth floor. Similar results were also reported by Durante [Dur73].

Measurements have shown that the percentage of windows, when compared with the building face surface area, impacts the level of RF penetration loss, as does the presence of tinted metal in the windows. Metallic tints can provide from 3 dB to 30 dB RF attenuation in a single pane of glass. The angle of incidence of the transmitted wave upon the face of the building also has a strong impact on the penetration loss, as was shown by Horikishi [Hor86].

4.13 Ray Tracing and Site Specific Modeling

In recent years, the computational and visualization capabilities of computers have accelerated rapidly. New methods for predicting radio signal coverage involve the use of Site Specific (SISP) propagation models and *graphical information system* (GIS) databases [Rus93]. SISP models support ray tracing as a means of deterministically modeling any indoor or outdoor propagation environment. Through the use of building databases, which may be drawn or digitized using standard graphical software packages, wireless system designers are able to include accurate representations of building and terrain features.

For outdoor propagation prediction, ray tracing techniques are used in conjunction with aerial photographs so that three-dimensional (3-D) representations of buildings may be integrated with software that carries out reflection, diffraction, and scattering models. Photogrammetric techniques are used to convert aerial or satellite photographs of cities into usable 3-D databases for the models [Sch92], [Ros93], [Wag94], [Rap00]. In indoor environments, architectural drawings provide a site specific representation for propagation models [Val93], [Sei94], [Kre94], [Ski96], [Mor00].

As building databases become prevalent, wireless systems will be developed using computer aided design tools that provide deterministic, rather than statistical, prediction models of small-scale and large-scale path loss in a wide range of operating environments. For example, in the SitePlanner® computer-aided design (CAD) environment, measurements and predictions of coverage and capacity may be simultaneously viewed, manipulated, optimized, and then archived for future use [Rap00]. SitePlanner® has become a popular research and teaching tool for students and engineers new to the wireless field. Some day such site specific modeling techniques may be downloadable into wireless phones and used to determine instantaneous air interface parameters.

4.14 Problems

4.1 If $P_t = 10$ W, $G_t = 0$ dB, $G_r = 0$ dB, and $f_c = 900$ MHz, find P_r in Watts at a free space distance of 1 km.

4.2 Assume a receiver is located 10 km from a 50 W transmitter. The carrier frequency is 6 GHz and free space propagation is assumed, $G_t = 1$ and $G_r = 1$.

(a) Find the power at the receiver.

(b) Find the magnitude of the E-field at the receiver antenna.

(c) Find the rms voltage applied to the receiver input, assuming that the receiver antenna has a purely real impedance of 50 Ω and is matched to the receiver.

4.3 *Fraunhofer distance*: Calculate the gain, half power beamwidth (HPBW), and Fraunhofer distance for a uniformly illuminated horn antenna at 60 GHz with dimensions of 4.6 cm × 3.5 cm. Hint: HPBW for the horn antenna can be estimated as HPBW = $51\lambda/a$, where a is the aperture width, as discussed in [Stu81].

4.4 *Free space propagation*: Assume the transmitter power is 1 W at 60 GHz fed into the transmitter antenna. Using the horn antenna from Problem 4.3 at both the transmitter and receiver:

(a) Calculate the free space path loss at 1 m, 100 m, and 1000 m.

(b) Calculate the received signal power at these distances.

(c) What is the rms voltage received at the antenna if the receiver antenna has purely real impedance of 50 Ω and is matched to the receiver?

4.5 *Reflection coefficients*: Find the reflection coefficients for typical ground, brick, limestone, glass, and water from data given in Table 4.1 at an incident angle of 30°. Assume lossless dielectrics. Present your final answers in a table.

4.6 *Surface roughness*: Explain the dependence of surface roughness on the frequency and angle of incidence.

4.7 Show that the Brewster angle (case where $\Gamma_{\parallel} = 0$) is given by θ_i where $\sin\theta_i = \sqrt{\dfrac{\varepsilon_r^2 - \varepsilon_r}{\varepsilon_r^2 - 1}}$.

4.8 (a) Explain the advantages and disadvantages of the two-ray ground reflection model in the analysis of path loss.

(b) In the following cases, tell whether the two-ray model could be applied, and explain why or why not:

$$h_t = 35 \text{ m}, h_r = 3 \text{ m}, d = 250 \text{ m}$$
$$h_t = 30 \text{ m}, h_r = 1.5 \text{ m}, d = 450 \text{ m}$$

(c) What insight does the two-ray model provide about large-scale path loss that was disregarded when cellular systems used very large cells?

4.9 Prove that in the two-ray ground reflected model, $\Delta = d'' - d' \approx 2h_t h_r / d$. Show when this holds as a good approximation. Hint: Use the geometry of Figure P4.9.

4.10 In a two-ray ground reflected model, assume that θ_Δ must be kept below 6.261 radians for phase cancellation reasons. Assuming a receiver height of 2 m, and given a requirement that θ_i be less than 5°, what are the minimum allowable values for the T–R separation distance and the height of the transmitter antenna? The carrier frequency is 900 MHz. Refer to Figure P4.9.

4.11 In the two-ray path loss model with $\Gamma_{\perp} = -1$, derive an appropriate expression for the location of the signal nulls at the receiver.

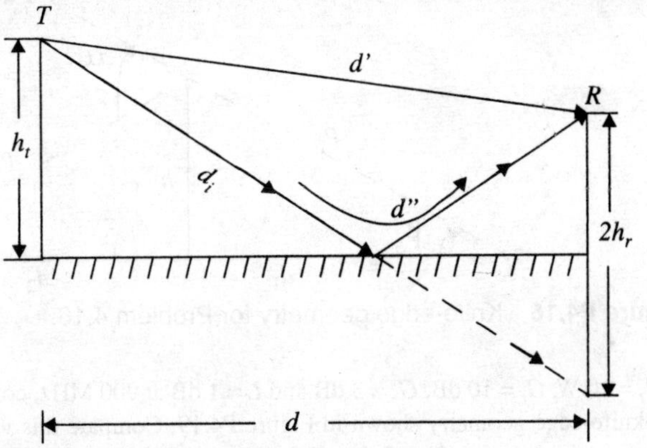

Figure P4.9 Illustration of two-ray ground reflection model.

4.12 Compare the received power for the exact (Equation (4.47)) and approximate (Equation (4.52)) expressions for the two-ray ground reflection model. Assume the height of the transmitter is 40 m and the height of the receiver is 3 m. The frequency is 1800 MHz, and unity gain antennas are used. Plot the received power for both models continuously over the range of 1 km to 20 km, assuming the ground reflection coefficient of –1 for horizontal polarization.

4.13 Redo Problem 4.12 for the case where the ground reflection coefficient is 1 (e.g., vertical polarization).

4.14 Assuming a receiver is located 10 km from a 50 W transmitter. The carrier frequency is 1900 MHz, free space propagation is assumed, $G_t = 1$, $G_r = 2$, find: (a) the power at the receiver; (b) the magnitude of the E-field at the receiver antenna; (c) the open-circuit rms voltage applied to the receiver input assuming that the receiver antenna has a purely real impedance of 50 Ω and is matched to the receiver; (d) find the received power at the mobile using the two-ray ground reflection model assuming the height of the transmitting antenna is 50 m, receiving antenna is 1.5 m above the ground, and the ground reflection is –1.

4.15 Referring to Figure P4.9, compute $d = d_f$, the first Fresnel zone distance between transmitter and receiver for a two-ray ground reflected propagation path, in terms of h_t, h_r, and λ. This is the distance at which path loss begins to transition from d^2 to d^4 behavior. Assume $\Gamma = -1$.

4.16 For the knife-edge geometry in Figure P4.16, show that

(a) $\phi = \frac{2\pi\Delta}{\lambda} = \frac{2\pi}{\lambda}\left[\frac{h^2}{2}\left(\frac{d_1+d_2}{d_1d_2}\right)\right]$ and

(b) $\upsilon = \alpha\sqrt{\frac{2d_1d_2}{\lambda(d_1+d_2)}}$ where $\frac{\upsilon^2\pi}{2} = \phi$, $d_1, d_2 \gg h$, $h \gg \lambda$, and $\Delta = p_1 + p_2 - (d_1 + d_2)$.

4.17 A general design rule for microwave links is 55% clearance of the first Fresnel zone. For a 1 km link at 2.5 GHz, what is the maximum first Fresnel zone radius? What clearance is required for this system?

4.18 *Diffraction*: From the knife-edge diffraction model, show how the diffracted power depends on frequency. Assume $d_1 = d_2 = 500$ m and $h = 10$ m in Figure P4.16. Hint: You may need to calculate Fresnel's integral or use Lee's approximation, Equations (4.59) and (4.61), respectively.

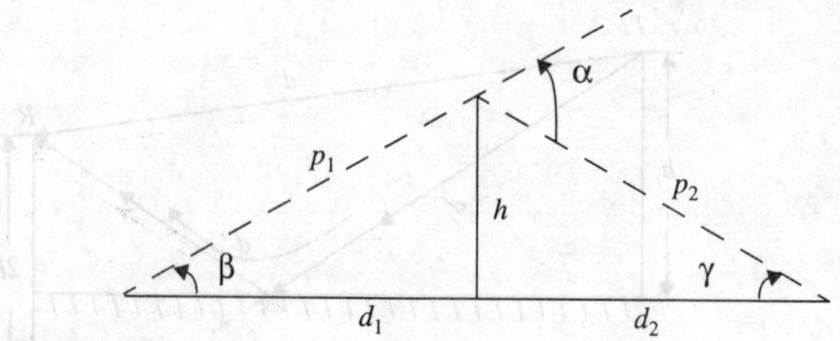

Figure P4.16 Knife-edge geometry for Problem 4.16.

4.19 If $P_t = 10$ W, $G_t = 10$ dB, $G_r = 3$ dB and $L = 1$ dB at 900 MHz, compute the received power for the knife-edge geometry shown in Figure P4.19. Compare this value with the theoretical free space received power if an obstruction did not exist. What is the path loss due to diffraction for this case?

4.20 If the geometry and all other system parameters remain exactly the same in Problem 4.19, but the frequency is changed, redo Problem 4.19 for the case of (a) $f = 50$ MHz and (b) $f = 1900$ MHz.

4.21 *Path loss model*: During the first month of work, you get an assignment to perform a measurement campaign to estimate the channel path loss exponent for a new wireless product. You performed field measurements and collected the following data:

Reference path loss: $PL_0(d_0)$
Path loss measurements: $PL_1(d_1)$, ... $PL_n(d_n)$ at distances: d_1 ... d_n

Using the path loss exponent model from Equation (4.69), find an expression for the optimum value of the path loss exponent n, which minimizes the mean square error between measurements and the model. Hint: The optimum value of n should minimize the mean square error (MSE) between your predicted path loss and measured path loss.

4.22 Assume that local average signal strength field measurements were made inside a building, and post processing revealed that the measured data fit a distant-dependent mean power law model having a log-normal distribution about the mean. Assume the mean power law was found to be $P_r(d) \propto d^{-3.5}$. If a signal of 1 mW was received at $d_0 = 1$ m from the transmitter, and at a distance of 10 m, 10% of the measurements were stronger than –25 dBm, define the standard deviation, σ, for the path loss model at $d = 10$ m.

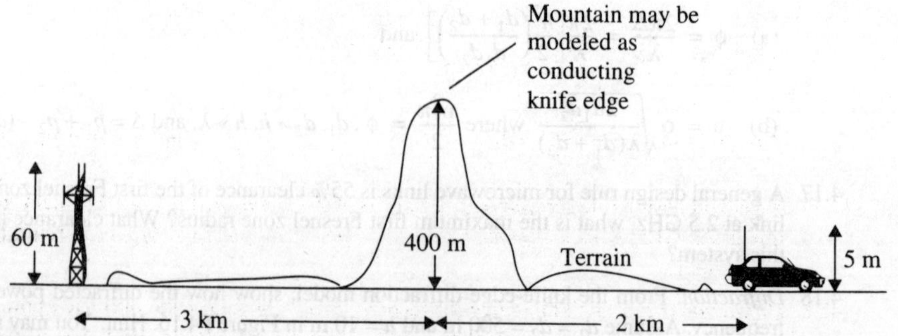

Figure P4.19 Knife-edge geometry for Problem 4.19.

4.23 If the received power at a reference distance $d_0 = 1$ km is equal to 1 microwatt, find the received powers at distances of 2 km, 5 km, 10 km, and 20 km from the same transmitter for the following path loss models: (a) Free space; (b) $n = 3$; (c) $n = 4$; (d) two-ray ground reflection using the exact expression; and (e) extended Hata model for a large city environment. Assume $f = 1800$ MHz, $h_t = 40$ m, $h_r = 3$ m, $G_t = G_r = 0$ dB. Plot each of these models on the same graph over the range of 1 km to 20 km. Comment on the differences between these five models.

4.24 Assume the received power at a reference distance $d_0 = 1$ km is equal to 1 microwatt, and $f = 1800$ MHz, $h_t = 40$ m, $h_r = 3$ m, $G_t = G_r = 0$ dB. Compute, compare, and plot the exact two-ray ground reflection model of (4.47) with the approximate expression given in Equation (4.52). At what T–R separations do the models agree and disagree? What are the ramifications of using the approximate expression instead of the exact expression in cellular system design?

4.25 Suppose that a mobile station is moving along a straight line between base stations BS1 and BS2, as shown in Figure P4.25. The distance between the base stations is $D = 1600$ m. The received power (in dBm) at base station i, from the mobile station, is modeled as (reverse link)

$$P_{r,i}(d) = P_0 - 10n\log_{10}(d_i/d_0) + \chi_i \quad \text{(dBm)} \quad i = 1,2$$

where d_i is the distance between the mobile and base station i, in meters, P_0 is the received power at distance d_0 from the mobile antenna, and n is the path loss exponent. The term $P_0 - 10n\log_{10}(d_i/d_0)$ is usually called *local area mean power*. The terms χ_i are zero-mean Gaussian random variables with standard deviation σ, in dB, that model the variation of the received signals due to shadowing. Assume that the random components χ_i of the signals received at different base stations are independent of each other. n is the path loss exponent.

The minimum usable signal for acceptable voice quality at the base station receiver is $P_{r,min}$, and the threshold level for handoff initiation is $P_{r,HO}$, both in dBm.

Assume that the mobile is currently connected to BS_1. A handoff occurs when the received signal at the base station BS_1, from the mobile, drops below threshold $P_{r,HO}$, and the signal received at candidate base station BS_2 is greater than the minimum acceptable level $P_{r,min}$.

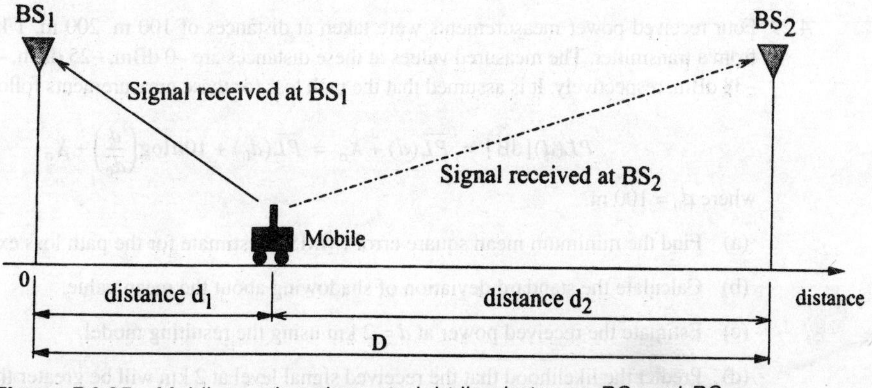

Figure P4.25 Mobile moving along straight line between BS_1 and BS_2.

Table P4.25 Parameters for Problem 4.25

Parameter	Value
n	4
σ	6 dB
P_0	0 dBm
d_0	1 m
$P_{r,min}$	−118 dBm
$P_{r,HO}$	−112 dBm

Using the parameters in Table P4.25, determine:

(a) The probability that a handoff occurs (Pr[handoff]), as a function of the distance between the mobile and its serving base station. Show your result in a plot Pr[handoff] vs. distance d_1.

(b) The distance d_{ho} between base station BS_1 and the mobile, such that the probability that a handoff occurs is equal to 80%.

4.26 Derive Equations (4.78) and (4.79) from first principles and reproduce some of the curves on Figure 4.18.

4.27 A transmitter provides 15 W to an antenna having 12 dB gain. The receiver antenna has a gain of 3 dB and the receiver bandwidth is 30 kHz. If the receiver system noise figure is 8 dB and the carrier frequency is 1800 MHz, find the maximum T–R separation that will ensure that a SNR of 20 dB is provided for 95% of the time. Assume $n = 4$, $\sigma = 8$ dB, and $d_0 = 1$ km.

4.28 Assume a SNR of 25 dB is desired at the receiver. If a 900 MHz cellular transmitter has an EIRP of 100 W, and the AMPS receiver uses a 0 dB gain antenna and has a 10 dB noise figure, find the percentage of time that the desired SNR is achieved at a distance of 10 km from the transmitter. Assume $n = 4$, $\sigma = 8$ dB, and $d_0 = 1$ km.

4.29 Four received power measurements were taken at distances of 100 m, 200 m, 1 km, and 2 km from a transmitter. The measured values at these distances are −0 dBm, −25 dBm, −35 dBm, and −38 dBm, respectively. It is assumed that the path loss for these measurements follows the model

$$PL(d)[\text{dB}] = \overline{PL}(d) + X_\sigma = \overline{PL}(d_0) + 10n\log\left(\frac{d}{d_0}\right) + X_\sigma$$

where $d_0 = 100$ m.

(a) Find the minimum mean square error (MMSE) estimate for the path loss exponent, n.

(b) Calculate the standard deviation of shadowing about the mean value.

(c) Estimate the received power at $d = 2$ km using the resulting model.

(d) Predict the likelihood that the received signal level at 2 km will be greater than −35 dBm. Express your answer as a Q-function.

4.30 Read "Path Loss, Delay Spread, and Outage Models as Functions of Antenna Height for Microcellular System Design," which appeared in the August 1994 issue of *IEEE Transactions on Vehicular Technology*, Vol. 43, No. 3. (This paper also appears on page 211 of *Cellular Radio and Personal Communications: Advanced Selected Readings* by the IEEE Press.)

(a) Derive Equation (10) in the paper from first principles and from the definition of Fresnel zone. After deriving this result, simplify your answer further.

(b) Using the models for mean path loss given in the paper, determine the received signal powers at T–R separation distances of 50 m, 100 m, and 1 km for a 1 W transmitter and unity gain antennas operating at 1900 MHz for:

(1) obstructed environments

(2) LOS environments

Assume an 8.5 m tall base station antenna and a 1.7 m tall mobile antenna are used.

(c) For your answers in (b), use a log-normal shadowing model to determine the likelihood that the received signal will be greater than or equal to –70 dBm at each of the three T–R separations, for obstructed and for LOS environments.

(d) Using the overbound model for rms delay spread given on pages 493 of the journal paper, estimate the rms delay spread at each of the three T–R separation distances, for obstructed and for LOS environments.

(e) Using your values in (d), determine the maximum unequalized symbol data rates that may be successfully transmitted by the base station at each of the three T–R separation distances in obstructed and in LOS environments. Assume an adaptive equalizer is not needed at the mobile receiver when the symbol duration is greater than 10 times the rms delay spread, and assume the noise figures of IS-136 and GSM mobile receivers are 6 dB. Would it be possible to receive IS-136 signals at these distances and environments without an equalizer? Would it be possible to transmit GSM signals at these distances without an equalizer? Hint: Consider both time delay spread and thermal noise-limited receiver power to provide answers. Assume IS-136 needs C/I = 15 dB and GSM needs C/I = 12 dB.

4.31 Design and create a computer program that produces an arbitrary number of samples of propagation path loss using a d^n path loss model with log normal shadowing. Your program is a radio propagation simulator, and should use, as inputs, the T–R separation, frequency, the path loss exponent, the standard deviation of the log-normal shadowing, the close-in-reference distance, and the number of desired predicted samples. Your program should provide a check that insures that the input T–R separation is equal to or exceeds the specified input close-in-reference distance, and should provide a graphical output of the produced samples as a function of path loss and distance (this is called a *scatter plot*).

Verify the accuracy of your computer program by running it for 50 samples at each of five different T–R separation distances (a total of 250 predicted path loss values), and determine the best fit path loss exponent and the standard deviation about the mean path loss exponent of the predicted data using the techniques described in Example 4.9. Draw the best fit mean path loss model on the scatter plot to illustrate the fit of the model to the predicted values. You will know your simulator is working if the best fit path loss model and the standard deviation for your simulated data is equal to the parameters you specified as inputs to your simulator.

4.32 Using the computer program developed in Problem 4.31, develop an interface that allows a user to specify inputs as described in Problem 4.31, as well as transmitter and receiver parameters such as transmit power, transmit antenna gain, receiver antenna gain, receiver bandwidth, and receiver noise figure. Using these additional input parameters, and using knowledge of the

Q-function and noise calculations (see Appendices), you may now statistically determine coverage levels for any specific mobile radio system. You may wish to implement table look-ups for Q and *erf* functions so that your simulator provides answers to the following wireless system design problems:

(a) If a user specifies all input parameters listed above, and specifies a desired received SNR and a specific value of T–R separation distance, what is the percentage of time that the SNR will be exceeded at the receiver?

(b) If a user specifies all input parameters listed above, and specifies a desired percentage of time that the SNR will be exceeded at the receiver, then what is the maximum value of T–R separation that will meet or exceed the specified percentage?

(c) If a user specifies a particular percentage that a given SNR is provided for a particular T–R separation d (assumed to be on the boundary of a cell), then what is the percentage of area that will be covered within the cell having the same radius d?

(d) Handle questions (a)-(c) above, except for the case where the user wishes to specify the received signal power level (in dBm) instead of specifying SNR.

Verify the functionality of your simulator by example.

4.33 A PCS licensee plans to build out a 30 MHz license in the new U.S. PCS band of 1850 MHz to 1880 MHz (reverse link) and 1930 MHz to 1960 MHz (forward link). They intend to use DCS 1900 radio equipment. DCS 1900 provides a GSM-like service and supports eight users per 200 kHz radio channel using TDMA. Because of GSM's digital techniques, GSM vendors have convinced the licensee that when the path loss exponent is equal to four, GSM can be deployed using four-cell reuse.

(a) How many GSM radio channels can be used by the licensee?

(b) If each DCS 1900 base station can support a maximum of 64 radio channels, how many users can be served by a base station during fully loaded operation?

(c) If the licensee wishes to cover a city having a circular shaped area of 2500 sq km, and the base stations use 20 W transmitter powers and 10 dB gain omnidirectional antennas, determine the number of cells required to provide forward link coverage to all parts of the city. Assume four-cell reuse, and let $n = 4$ and the standard deviation of 8 dB hold as the path loss model for each cell in the city. Also assume that a required signal level of –90 dBm must be provided for 90% of the coverage area in each cell, and that each mobile uses a 3 dBi gain antenna. Assume $d_o = 1$ km.

(d) For your answer in (c), define in exact detail a suitable channel reuse scheme for each cell in the city, and define the channels used by each cell. Your scheme should include details such as how many channels each base station should use, what the nearest reuse distance should be, and other issues which clearly define how to assign channels geographically throughout the city? You may assume that users are distributed uniformly throughout the city, that each cell is equidistant from its neighbors, and you may ignore the effect of control channels (that is, assume all radio channels carry only voice users).

(e) How many (i) cells (base stations), (ii) total radio channels, and (iii) total user channels (there are eight user channels per radio channel) are available throughout the entire city, based on your answer in (d)? The total number of user channels is equal to the maximum capacity of the system and is a hard limit on the number of users that can be simultaneously served at full capacity.

(f) If each base station costs $500,000, and each radio channel within the base station costs $50,000, what is the cost of the system in (e)? This is the initial cost of the system.

(g) If the system in (d) is designed for 5% blocking probability at start-up, what is the maximum number of subscribers that can be supported at start-up? This is the number of phones that may be initially subscribed at start-up. Assume that each user channel is trunked along with the other user channels on other radio channels within the base station.

(h) Using your answer in (g), what is the average cost per user needed to recoup 10% of the initial system buildout cost after one year if the number of subscribers is static during year 1?

4.34 Consider seven-cell frequency reuse. Cell B1 is the desired cell and B2 is a co-channel cell as shown in Figure P4.34(a). For a mobile located in cell B1, find the minimum cell radius R to give a forward link C/I ratio of at least 18 dB at least 99% of the time. Assume the following:

Co-channel interference is due to base B2 only.
Carrier frequency, $f_c = 890$ MHz.
Reference distance, $d_0 = 1$ km (assume free space propagation from the transmitter to d_0).
Assume omnidirectional antennas for both transmitter and receiver, where $G_{base} = 6$ dBi and $G_{mobile} = 3$ dBi.
Transmitter power, $P_t = 10$ W (assume equal power for all base stations).
PL(dB) between the mobile and base B1 is given as

$$\overline{PL}(\mathrm{dB}) = \overline{PL}(d_0) + 10(2.5)\log\left(\frac{d_1}{d_0}\right) - X_\sigma \qquad \sigma = 0 \text{ dB}.$$

PL(dB) between the mobile and base B2 is given as

$$\overline{PL}(\mathrm{dB}) = \overline{PL}(d_0) + 10(4.0)\log\left(\frac{d_2}{d_0}\right) - X_\sigma \qquad \sigma = 7 \text{ dB}.$$

Cell boundaries are shown in the Figure P4.34(b).

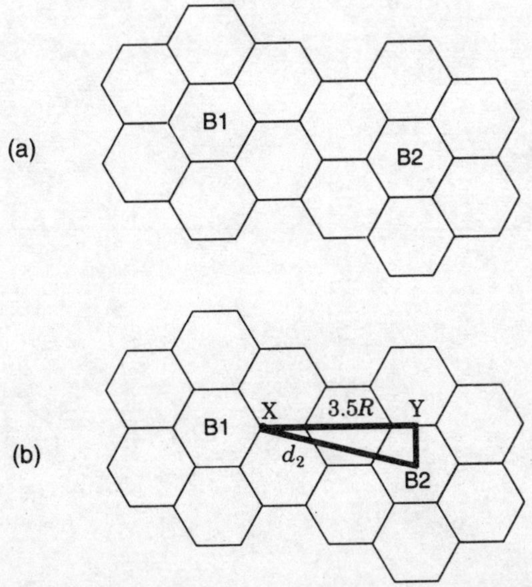

Figure P4.34 (a) Seven-cell reuse structure; (b) co-channel interference geometry between B1 and B2.

4.35 Given an indoor path loss model of the form:

$$\overline{PL(d)}\text{dB} = 40 + 20\log d + \Sigma FAF \quad d \geq 1 \text{ m}$$

where d is measured in meters, find the mean received power between three floors of a building if FAF is 15 dB per floor. Assume the transmitter radiates 20 dBm and unity gain antennas are used at both the transmitter and receiver, and that the straight-line path between the transmitter and receiver is 15 m through the floors.

CHAPTER 5

Mobile Radio Propagation: Small-Scale Fading and Multipath

Small-scale fading, or simply *fading*, is used to describe the rapid fluctuations of the amplitudes, phases, or multipath delays of a radio signal over a short period of time or travel distance, so that large-scale path loss effects may be ignored. Fading is caused by interference between two or more versions of the transmitted signal which arrive at the receiver at slightly different times. These waves, called *multipath waves*, combine at the receiver antenna to give a resultant signal which can vary widely in amplitude and phase, depending on the distribution of the intensity and relative propagation time of the waves and the bandwidth of the transmitted signal.

5.1 Small-Scale Multipath Propagation

Multipath in the radio channel creates small-scale fading effects. The three most important effects are:

- Rapid changes in signal strength over a small travel distance or time interval
- Random frequency modulation due to varying Doppler shifts on different multipath signals
- Time dispersion (echoes) caused by multipath propagation delays.

In built-up urban areas, fading occurs because the height of the mobile antennas are well below the height of surrounding structures, so there is no single line-of-sight path to the base station. Even when a line-of-sight exists, multipath still occurs due to reflections from the ground and surrounding structures. The incoming radio waves arrive from different directions with different propagation delays. The signal received by the mobile at any point in space may consist of a large number of plane waves having randomly distributed amplitudes, phases, and angles of arrival. These multipath components combine vectorially at the receiver antenna, and can cause the signal received by the mobile to distort or fade. Even when a mobile receiver is stationary, the received signal may fade due to movement of surrounding objects in the radio channel.

If objects in the radio channel are static, and motion is considered to be only due to that of the mobile, then fading is purely a spatial phenomenon. The spatial variations of the resulting signal are seen as temporal variations by the receiver as it moves through the multipath field. Due to the constructive and destructive effects of multipath waves summing at various points in space, a receiver moving at high speed can pass through several fades in a small period of time. In a more serious case, a receiver may stop at a particular location at which the received signal is in a deep fade. Maintaining good communications can then become very difficult, although passing vehicles or people walking in the vicinity of the mobile can often disturb the field pattern, thereby diminishing the likelihood of the received signal remaining in a deep null for a long period of time. Antenna space diversity can prevent deep fading nulls, as shown in Chapter 6. Figure 3.1 shows typical rapid variations in the received signal level due to small-scale fading as a receiver is moved over a distance of a few meters.

Due to the relative motion between the mobile and the base station, each multipath wave experiences an apparent shift in frequency. The shift in received signal frequency due to motion is called the Doppler shift, and is directly proportional to the velocity and direction of motion of the mobile with respect to the direction of arrival of the received multipath wave.

5.1.1 Factors Influencing Small-Scale Fading

Many physical factors in the radio propagation channel influence small-scale fading. These include the following:

- **Multipath propagation** — The presence of reflecting objects and scatterers in the channel creates a constantly changing environment that dissipates the signal energy in amplitude, phase, and time. These effects result in multiple versions of the transmitted signal that arrive at the receiving antenna, displaced with respect to one another in time and spatial orientation. The random phase and amplitudes of the different multipath components cause fluctuations in signal strength, thereby inducing small-scale fading, signal distortion, or both. Multipath propagation often lengthens the time required for the baseband portion of the signal to reach the receiver which can cause signal smearing due to intersymbol interference.
- **Speed of the mobile** — The relative motion between the base station and the mobile results in random frequency modulation due to different Doppler shifts on each of the multipath components. Doppler shift will be positive or negative depending on whether the mobile receiver is moving toward or away from the base station.
- **Speed of surrounding objects** — If objects in the radio channel are in motion, they induce a time varying Doppler shift on multipath components. If the surrounding objects move at a greater rate than the mobile, then this effect dominates the small-scale fading.

Otherwise, motion of surrounding objects may be ignored, and only the speed of the mobile need be considered. The *coherence time* defines the "staticness" of the channel, and is directly impacted by the Doppler shift.

- **The transmission bandwidth of the signal** — If the transmitted radio signal bandwidth is greater than the "bandwidth" of the multipath channel, the received signal will be distorted, but the received signal strength will not fade much over a local area (i.e., the small-scale signal fading will not be significant). As will be shown, the bandwidth of the channel can be quantified by the *coherence bandwidth* which is related to the specific multipath structure of the channel. The coherence bandwidth is a measure of the maximum frequency difference for which signals are still strongly correlated in amplitude. If the transmitted signal has a narrow bandwidth as compared to the channel, the amplitude of the signal will change rapidly, but the signal will not be distorted in time. Thus, the statistics of small-scale signal strength and the likelihood of signal smearing appearing over small-scale distances are very much related to the specific amplitudes and delays of the multipath channel, as well as the bandwidth of the transmitted signal.

5.1.2 Doppler Shift

Consider a mobile moving at a constant velocity v, along a path segment having length d between points X and Y, while it receives signals from a remote source S, as illustrated in Figure 5.1. The difference in path lengths traveled by the wave from source S to the mobile at points X and Y is $\Delta l = d\cos\theta = v\Delta t\cos\theta$, where Δt is the time required for the mobile to travel from X to Y, and θ is assumed to be the same at points X and Y since the source is assumed to be very far away. The phase change in the received signal due to the difference in path lengths is therefore

$$\Delta\phi = \frac{2\pi\Delta l}{\lambda} = \frac{2\pi v\Delta t}{\lambda}\cos\theta \tag{5.1}$$

and hence the apparent change in frequency, or Doppler shift, is given by f_d, where

$$f_d = \frac{1}{2\pi}\cdot\frac{\Delta\phi}{\Delta t} = \frac{v}{\lambda}\cdot\cos\theta \tag{5.2}$$

Equation (5.2) relates the Doppler shift to the mobile velocity and the spatial angle between the direction of motion of the mobile and the direction of arrival of the wave. It can be seen from Equation (5.2) that if the mobile is moving toward the direction of arrival of the wave, the Doppler shift is positive (i.e., the apparent received frequency is increased), and if the mobile is moving away from the direction of arrival of the wave, the Doppler shift is negative (i.e., the apparent received frequency is decreased). As shown in Section 5.7.1, multipath components from a CW signal that arrive from different directions contribute to Doppler spreading of the received signal, thus increasing the signal bandwidth.

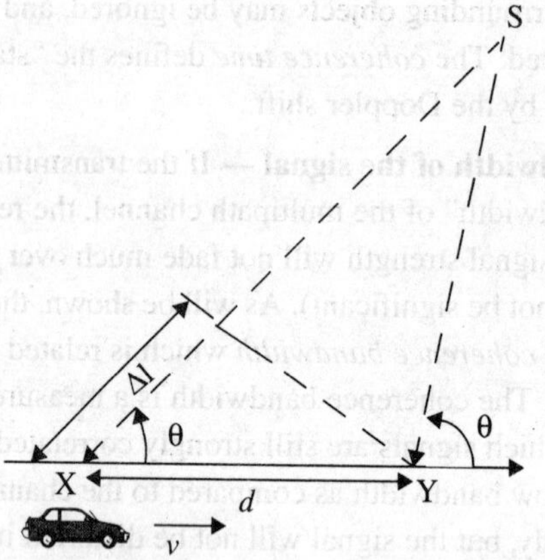

Figure 5.1 Illustration of Doppler effect.

Example 5.1

Consider a transmitter which radiates a sinusoidal carrier frequency of 1850 MHz. For a vehicle moving 60 mph, compute the received carrier frequency if the mobile is moving (a) directly toward the transmitter, (b) directly away from the transmitter, and (c) in a direction which is perpendicular to the direction of arrival of the transmitted signal.

Solution

Given:

Carrier frequency $f_c = 1850$ MHz

Therefore, wavelength $\lambda = c/f_c = \dfrac{3 \times 10^8}{1850 \times 10^6} = 0.162$ m

Vehicle speed $v = 60$ mph $= 26.82$ m/s

(a) The vehicle is moving directly toward the transmitter.

The Doppler shift in this case is positive and the received frequency is given by Equation (5.2)

$$f = f_c + f_d = 1850 \times 10^6 + \frac{26.82}{0.162} = 1850.00016 \text{ MHz}$$

(b) The vehicle is moving directly away from the transmitter.

The Doppler shift in this case is negative and hence the received frequency is given by

$$f = f_c - f_d = 1850 \times 10^6 - \frac{26.82}{0.162} = 1849.999834 \text{ MHz}$$

(c) The vehicle is moving perpendicular to the angle of arrival of the transmitted signal.

In this case, $\theta = 90°$, $\cos\theta = 0$, and there is no Doppler shift.

The received signal frequency is the same as the transmitted frequency of 1850 MHz.

5.2 Impulse Response Model of a Multipath Channel

The small-scale variations of a mobile radio signal can be directly related to the impulse response of the mobile radio channel. The impulse response is a wideband channel characterization and contains all information necessary to simulate or analyze any type of radio transmission through the channel. This stems from the fact that a mobile radio channel may be modeled as a linear filter with a time varying impulse response, where the time variation is due to receiver motion in space. The filtering nature of the channel is caused by the summation of amplitudes and delays of the multiple arriving waves at any instant of time. The impulse response is a useful characterization of the channel, since it may be used to predict and compare the performance of many different mobile communication systems and transmission bandwidths for a particular mobile channel condition.

To show that a mobile radio channel may be modeled as a linear filter with a time varying impulse response, consider the case where time variation is due strictly to receiver motion in space. This is shown in Figure 5.2.

In Figure 5.2, the receiver moves along the ground at some constant velocity v. For a fixed position d, the channel between the transmitter and the receiver can be modeled as a linear time invariant system. However, due to the different multipath waves which have propagation delays which vary over different spatial locations of the receiver, the impulse response of the linear time invariant channel should be a function of the position of the receiver. That is, the channel impulse response can be expressed as $h(d,t)$. Let $x(t)$ represent the transmitted signal, then the received signal $y(d,t)$ at position d can be expressed as a convolution of $x(t)$ with $h(d,t)$

$$y(d, t) = x(t) \otimes h(d, t) = \int_{-\infty}^{\infty} x(\tau)h(d, t-\tau)d\tau \tag{5.3}$$

For a causal system, $h(d, t) = 0$ for $t < 0$, thus Equation (5.3) reduces to

$$y(d, t) = \int_{-\infty}^{t} x(\tau)h(d, t-\tau)d\tau \tag{5.4}$$

Since the receiver moves along the ground at a constant velocity v, the position of the receiver can by expressed as

$$d = vt \tag{5.5}$$

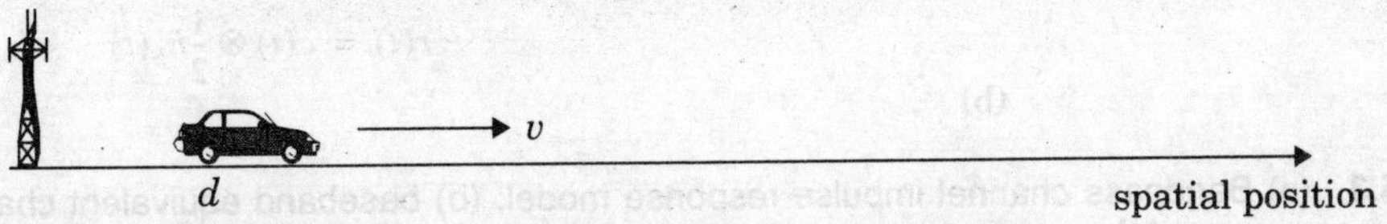

Figure 5.2 The mobile radio channel as a function of time and space.

Substituting (5.5) in (5.4), we obtain

$$y(vt, t) = \int_{-\infty}^{t} x(\tau)h(vt, t-\tau)d\tau \tag{5.6}$$

Since v is a constant, $y(vt, t)$ is just a function of t. Therefore, Equation (5.6) can be expressed as

$$y(t) = \int_{-\infty}^{t} x(\tau)h(vt, t-\tau)d\tau = x(t) \otimes h(vt, t) = x(t) \otimes h(d, t) \tag{5.7}$$

From Equation (5.7), it is clear that the mobile radio channel can be modeled as a linear time varying channel, where the channel changes with time and distance.

Since v may be assumed constant over a short time (or distance) interval, we may let $x(t)$ represent the transmitted bandpass waveform, $y(t)$ the received waveform, and $h(t, \tau)$ the impulse response of the time varying multipath radio channel. The impulse response $h(t, \tau)$ completely characterizes the channel and is a function of both t and τ. The variable t represents the time variations due to motion, whereas τ represents the channel multipath delay for a fixed value of t. One may think of τ as being a vernier adjustment of time. The received signal $y(t)$ can be expressed as a convolution of the transmitted signal $x(t)$ with the channel impulse response (see Figure 5.3a)

$$y(t) = \int_{-\infty}^{\infty} x(\tau)h(t, \tau)d\tau = x(t) \otimes h(t, \tau) \tag{5.8}$$

$x(t)$ ▶ $h(t, \tau) = Re\left\{h_b(t, \tau)e^{j\omega_c t}\right\}$ ▶ $y(t)$

$y(t) = Re\left\{r(t)e^{j\omega_c t}\right\}$

(a)

$y(t) = x(t) \otimes h(t)$

$c(t)$ ▶ $\frac{1}{2}h_b(t, \tau)$ ▶ $r(t)$

$r(t) = c(t) \otimes \frac{1}{2}h_b(t)$

(b)

Figure 5.3 (a) Bandpass channel impulse response model; (b) baseband equivalent channel impulse response model.

If the multipath channel is assumed to be a bandlimited bandpass channel, which is reasonable, then $h(t,\tau)$ may be equivalently described by a complex baseband impulse response $h_b(t, \tau)$ with the input and output being the complex envelope representations of the transmitted and received signals, respectively (see Figure 5.3b). That is,

$$r(t) = c(t) \otimes \frac{1}{2} h_b(t, \tau) \tag{5.9}$$

where $c(t)$ and $r(t)$ are the complex envelopes of $x(t)$ and $y(t)$, defined as

$$x(t) = Re\{c(t)\exp(j2\pi f_c t)\} \tag{5.10}$$

$$y(t) = Re\{r(t)\exp(j2\pi f_c t)\} \tag{5.11}$$

The factor of $1/2$ in Equation (5.9) is due to the properties of the complex envelope, in order to represent the passband radio system at baseband. The lowpass characterization removes the high frequency variations caused by the carrier, making the signal analytically easier to handle. It is shown by Couch [Cou93] that the average power of a bandpass signal $\overline{x^2(t)}$ is equal to $0.5\overline{|c(t)|^2}$, where the overbar denotes ensemble average for a stochastic signal, or time average for a deterministic or ergodic stochastic signal.

It is useful to discretize the multipath delay axis τ of the impulse response into equal time delay segments called *excess delay bins*, where each bin has a time delay width equal to $\tau_{i+1} - \tau_i$, where τ_0 is equal to 0, and represents the first arriving signal at the receiver. Letting $i = 0$, it is seen that $\tau_1 - \tau_0$ is equal to the time delay bin width given by $\Delta\tau$. For convention, $\tau_0 = 0$, $\tau_1 = \Delta\tau$, and $\tau_i = i\Delta\tau$, for $i = 0$ to $N-1$, where N represents the total number of possible equally-spaced multipath components, including the first arriving component. Any number of multipath signals received within the ith bin are represented by a single resolvable multipath component having delay τ_i. This technique of quantizing the delay bins determines the time delay resolution of the channel model, and the useful frequency span of the model can be shown to be $2/\Delta\tau$. That is, the model may be used to analyze transmitted RF signals having bandwidths which are less than $2/\Delta\tau$. Note that $\tau_0 = 0$ is the excess time delay of the first arriving multipath component, and neglects the propagation delay between the transmitter and receiver. *Excess delay* is the relative delay of the ith multipath component as compared to the first arriving component and is given by τ_i. The *maximum excess delay* of the channel is given by $N\Delta\tau$.

Since the received signal in a multipath channel consists of a series of attenuated, time-delayed, phase shifted replicas of the transmitted signal, the baseband impulse response of a multipath channel can be expressed as

$$h_b(t, \tau) = \sum_{i=0}^{N-1} a_i(t, \tau)\exp[j(2\pi f_c \tau_i(t) + \phi_i(t, \tau))]\delta(\tau - \tau_i(t)) \tag{5.12}$$

where $a_i(t, \tau)$ and $\tau_i(t)$ are the real amplitudes and excess delays, respectively, of ith multipath component at time t [Tur72]. The phase term $2\pi f_c \tau_i(t) + \phi_i(t, \tau)$ in (5.12) represents the phase shift due to free space propagation of the ith multipath component, plus any additional phase shifts which are encountered in the channel. In general, the phase term is simply represented by a single variable $\theta_i(t, \tau)$ which lumps together all the mechanisms for phase shifts of a single multipath component within the ith excess delay bin. Note that some excess delay bins may have no multipath at some time t and delay τ_i, since $a_i(t, \tau)$ may be zero. In Equation (5.12), N is the total possible number of multipath components (bins), and $\delta(\bullet)$ is the unit impulse function which determines the specific multipath bins that have components at time t and excess delays τ_i. Figure 5.4 illustrates an example of different snapshots of $h_b(t, \tau)$, where t varies into the page, and the time delay bins are quantized to widths of $\Delta\tau$. Modern wireless communication systems have recently used spatial filtering to increase capacity and coverage, and often it is useful to modify Equation (5.12) to include the effects of angle of arrival of each multipath component [Lib99], [Ert98], [Mol01].

It is important to note that depending on the choice of $\Delta\tau$ and the physical channel delay properties, there may be two or more multipath signals that arrive within an excess delay bin that are unresolvable and that vectorially combine to yield the instantaneous amplitude and phase of a single modeled multipath component. Such situations cause the multipath amplitude within an excess delay bin to fade over the local area. However, when only a single multipath component arrives within an excess delay bin, the amplitude over the local area for that particular time delay will generally not fade significantly.

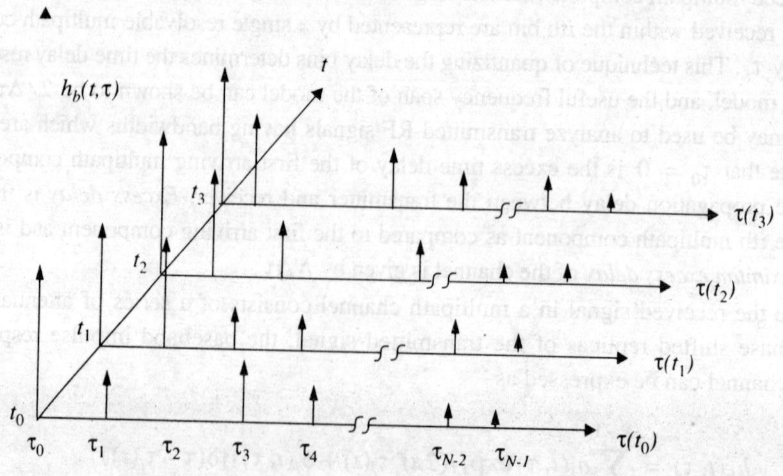

Figure 5.4 An example of the time varying discrete-time impulse response model for a multipath radio channel. Discrete models are useful in simulation where modulation data must be convolved with the channel impulse response [Tra02].

If the channel impulse response is assumed to be time invariant, or is at least wide sense stationary over a small-scale time or distance interval, then the channel impulse response may be simplified as

$$h_b(\tau) = \sum_{i=0}^{N-1} a_i \exp(j\theta_i)\delta(\tau - \tau_i) \tag{5.13}$$

The assumption of time invariance over a local area is valid when the time delay resolution of the channel impulse response model accurately and uniquely resolves every multipath component over the local area.

When measuring or predicting $h_b(\tau)$, a probing pulse $p(t)$ which approximates a delta function is used at the transmitter. That is,

$$p(t) \approx \delta(t - \tau) \tag{5.14}$$

is used to sound the channel to determine $h_b(\tau)$.

For small-scale channel modeling, the *power delay profile* of the channel is found by taking the spatial average of $|h_b(t;\tau)|^2$ over a local area. By making several local area measurements of $|h_b(t;\tau)|^2$ in different locations, it is possible to build an ensemble of power delay profiles, each one representing a possible small-scale multipath channel state [Rap91a].

Based on work by Cox [Cox72], [Cox75], if $p(t)$ has a time duration much smaller than the impulse response of the multipath channel, $p(t)$ does not need to be deconvolved from the received signal $r(t)$ in order to determine relative multipath signal strengths. The received power delay profile in a local area is given by

$$P(\tau) \approx k\overline{|h_b(t;\tau)|^2} \tag{5.15}$$

where the bar represents the average over the local area and many snapshots of $|h_b(t;\tau)|^2$ are typically averaged over a local (small-scale) area to provide a single time-invariant multipath power delay profile $P(\tau)$. The gain k in Equation (5.15) relates the transmitted power in the probing pulse $p(t)$ to the total power received in a multipath delay profile.

5.2.1 Relationship Between Bandwidth and Received Power

In actual wireless communication systems, the impulse response of a multipath channel is measured in the field using channel sounding techniques. We now consider two extreme channel sounding cases as a means of demonstrating how the small-scale fading behaves quite differently for two signals with different bandwidths in the identical multipath channel.

Consider a pulsed, transmitted RF signal of the form

$$x(t) = \text{Re}\{p(t)\exp(j2\pi f_c t)\}$$

where $p(t)$ is a repetitive baseband pulse train with very narrow pulse width T_{bb} and repetition period T_{REP} which is much greater than the maximum measured excess delay τ_{max} in the channel. Such a wideband pulse will produce an output that approximates $h_b(t, \tau)$. Now let

$$p(t) = 2\sqrt{\tau_{max}/T_{bb}} \quad \text{for } 0 \le t \le T_{bb}$$

and let $p(t)$ be zero elsewhere for all excess delays of interest. The low pass channel output $r(t)$ is found by convolving $p(t)$ with $h_b(t, \tau)$ and yields

$$r(t) = \frac{1}{2}\sum_{i=0}^{N-1} a_i(\exp(j\theta_i)) \cdot p(t-\tau_i) \tag{5.16}$$

$$= \sum_{i=0}^{N-1} a_i \exp(j\theta_i) \cdot \sqrt{\frac{\tau_{max}}{T_{bb}}}\ \text{rect}\left[t - \frac{T_{bb}}{2} - \tau_i\right]$$

To determine the received power at some time t_0, the power $|r(t_0)|^2$ is measured. The quantity $|r(t_0)|^2$ is found by summing up the multipath powers resolved in the *instantaneous multipath power delay profile* $|h_b(t_0;\tau)|^2$ of the channel, and is equal to the energy received over the time duration of the multipath delay divided by τ_{max}. That is, using Equation (5.16)

$$|r(t_0)|^2 = \frac{1}{\tau_{max}}\int_0^{\tau_{max}} r(t) \times r^*(t)dt \tag{5.17}$$

$$= \frac{1}{\tau_{max}}\int_0^{\tau_{max}} \frac{1}{4}\text{Re}\left\{\sum_{j=0}^{N-1}\sum_{i=0}^{N-1} a_j(t_0)a_i(t_0)p(t-\tau_j)p(t-\tau_i)\exp(j(\theta_j-\theta_i))\right\}dt$$

Note that if all the multipath components are resolved by the probe $p(t)$, then $|\tau_j - \tau_i| > T_{bb}$ for all $j \ne i$, and

$$|r(t_0)|^2 = \frac{1}{\tau_{max}}\int_0^{\tau_{max}} \frac{1}{4}\left(\sum_{k=0}^{N-1} a_k^2(t_0)p^2(t-\tau_k)\right)dt \tag{5.18}$$

$$= \frac{1}{\tau_{max}}\sum_{k=0}^{N-1} a_k^2(t_0)\int_0^{\tau_{max}} \left\{\sqrt{\frac{\tau_{max}}{T_{bb}}}\ \text{rect}\left[t - \frac{T_{bb}}{2} - \tau_k\right]\right\}^2 dt$$

$$= \sum_{k=0}^{N-1} a_k^2(t_0)$$

For a wideband probing signal $p(t)$, T_{bb} is smaller than the delays between multipath components in the channel, and Equation (5.18) shows that the total received power is simply related to the sum of the powers in the individual multipath components, and is scaled by the ratio of the probing pulse's width and amplitude, and the maximum observed excess delay of the channel. Assuming that the received power from the multipath components forms a random process where each component has a random amplitude and phase at any time t, the average small-scale received power for the wideband probe is found from Equation (5.17) as

$$E_{a,\theta}[P_{WB}] = E_{a,\theta}\left[\sum_{i=0}^{N-1} |a_i \exp(j\theta_i)|^2\right] \approx \sum_{i=0}^{N-1} \overline{a_i^2} \tag{5.19}$$

In Equation (5.19), $E_{a,\theta}[\bullet]$ denotes the ensemble average over all possible values of a_i and θ_i in a local area, and the overbar denotes sample average over a local measurement area which is generally measured using multipath measurement equipment. The striking result of Equations (5.18) and (5.19) is that if a transmitted signal is able to resolve the multipaths, then the *average small-scale received power is simply the sum of the average powers received in each multipath component*. In practice, the amplitudes of individual multipath components do not fluctuate widely in a local area. Thus, the received power of a wideband signal such as $p(t)$ does not fluctuate significantly when a receiver is moved about a local area [Rap89].

Now, instead of a pulse, consider a CW signal which is transmitted into the exact same channel, and let the complex envelope be given by $c(t) = 2$. Then, the instantaneous complex envelope of the received signal is given by the phasor sum

$$r(t) = \sum_{i=0}^{N-1} a_i \exp(j\theta_i(t, \tau)) \tag{5.20}$$

and the instantaneous power is given by

$$|r(t)|^2 = \left|\sum_{i=0}^{N-1} a_i \exp(j\theta_i(t, \tau))\right|^2 \tag{5.21}$$

As the receiver is moved over a local area, the channel induces changes on $r(t)$, and the received signal strength will vary at a rate governed by the fluctuations of a_i and θ_i. As mentioned earlier, a_i varies little over local areas, but θ_i will vary greatly due to changes in propagation distance over space, resulting in large fluctuations of $r(t)$ as the receiver is moved over small distances (on the order of a wavelength). That is, since $r(t)$ is the phasor sum of the individual multipath components, the instantaneous phases of the multipath components cause the large fluctuations which typifies small-scale fading for CW signals. The average received power over a local area is then given by

$$E_{a,\theta}[P_{CW}] = E_{a,\theta}\left[\left|\sum_{i=0}^{N-1} a_i \exp(j\theta_i)\right|^2\right] \tag{5.22}$$

$$E_{a,\theta}[P_{CW}] \approx \overline{[(a_0 e^{j\theta_0} + a_1 e^{j\theta_1} + \ldots + a_{N-1} e^{j\theta_{N-1}})} \times \overline{(a_0 e^{-j\theta_0} + a_1 e^{-j\theta_1} + \ldots + a_{N-1} e^{-j\theta_{N-1}})]} \tag{5.23}$$

$$E_{a,\theta}[P_{CW}] \approx \sum_{i=0}^{N-1} \overline{a_i^2} + 2\sum_{i=0}^{N-1} \sum_{i,j \neq i}^{N} r_{ij} \overline{\cos(\theta_i - \theta_j)} \tag{5.24}$$

where r_{ij} is the path amplitude correlation coefficient defined to be

$$r_{ij} = E_a[a_i a_j] \tag{5.25}$$

and the overbar denotes time average for CW measurements made by a mobile receiver over the local measurement area [Rap89]. Note that when $\overline{\cos(\theta_i - \theta_j)} = 0$ and/or $r_{ij} = 0$, then the *average power for a CW signal is equivalent to the average received power for a wideband signal in a small-scale region.* This is seen by comparing Equation (5.19) and Equation (5.24). This can occur when either the multipath phases are identically and independently distributed (i.i.d uniform) over $[0, 2\pi]$ or when the path amplitudes are uncorrelated. The i.i.d uniform distribution of θ is a valid assumption since multipath components traverse differential path lengths that measure hundreds of wavelengths and are likely to arrive with random phases. If for some reason it is believed that the phases are not independent, the average wideband power and average CW power will still be equal if the paths have uncorrelated amplitudes. However, if the phases of the paths are dependent upon each other, then the amplitudes are likely to be correlated, since the same mechanism which affects the path phases is likely to also affect the amplitudes. This situation is highly unlikely at transmission frequencies used in wireless mobile systems.

Thus it is seen that the *received local ensemble average power of wideband and narrowband signals are equivalent.* When the transmitted signal has a bandwidth much greater than the bandwidth of the channel, then the multipath structure is completely resolved by the received signal at any time, and the received power varies very little since the individual multipath amplitudes do not change rapidly over a local area. However, if the transmitted signal has a very narrow bandwidth (e.g., the baseband signal has a duration greater than the excess delay of the channel), then multipath is not resolved by the received signal, and large signal fluctuations (fading) occur at the receiver due to the phase shifts of the many unresolved multipath components.

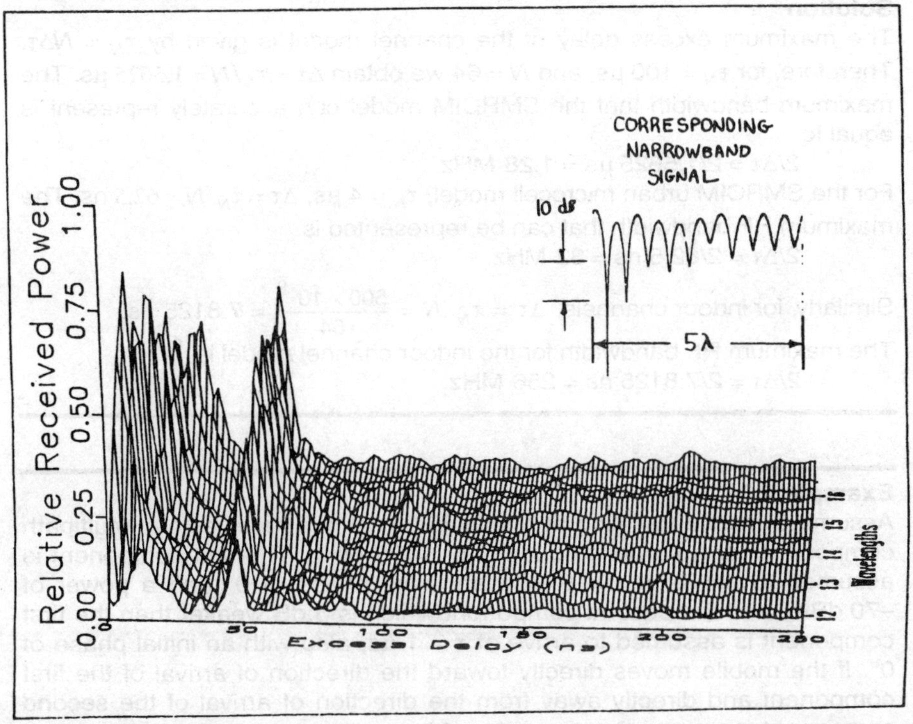

Figure 5.5 Measured wideband and narrowband received signals over a 5λ (0.375 m) measurement track inside a building. Carrier frequency is 4 GHz. Wideband power is computed using Equation (5.19), which can be thought of as the area under the power delay profile. The axis into the page is distance (wavelengths) instead of time.

Figure 5.5 illustrates actual indoor radio channel measurements made simultaneously with a wideband probing pulse having $T_{bb} = 10$ ns, and a CW transmitter. The carrier frequency was 4 GHz. It can be seen that the CW signal undergoes rapid fades, whereas the wideband measurements change little over the 5λ measurement track. However, the local average received powers of both signals were measured to be virtually identical [Haw91].

Example 5.2

Assume a discrete channel impulse response is used to model urban RF radio channels with excess delays as large as 100 μs and microcellular channels with excess delays no larger than 4 μs. If the number of multipath bins is fixed at 64, find (a) $\Delta\tau$, and (b) the maximum RF bandwidth which the two models can accurately represent. Repeat the exercise for an indoor channel model with excess delays as large as 500 ns. As described in section 5.7.6, SIRCIM and SMRCIM are statistical channel models based on Equation (5.12) that use parameters in this example.

Solution

The maximum excess delay of the channel model is given by $\tau_N = N\Delta\tau$. Therefore, for $\tau_N = 100\ \mu s$, and $N = 64$ we obtain $\Delta\tau = \tau_N/N = 1.5625\ \mu s$. The maximum bandwidth that the SMRCIM model can accurately represent is equal to

$$2/\Delta\tau = 2/1.5625\ \mu s = 1.28\ MHz.$$

For the SMRCIM urban microcell model, $\tau_N = 4\ \mu s$, $\Delta\tau = \tau_N/N = 62.5$ ns. The maximum RF bandwidth that can be represented is

$$2/\Delta\tau = 2/62.5\ ns = 32\ MHz.$$

Similarly, for indoor channels, $\Delta\tau = \tau_N/N = \dfrac{500 \times 10^{-9}}{64} = 7.8125$ ns.

The maximum RF bandwidth for the indoor channel model is

$$2/\Delta\tau = 2/7.8125\ ns = 256\ MHz.$$

Example 5.3

Assume a mobile traveling at a velocity of 10 m/s receives two multipath components at a carrier frequency of 1000 MHz. The first component is assumed to arrive at $\tau = 0$ with an initial phase of 0° and a power of −70 dBm, and the second component which is 3 dB weaker than the first component is assumed to arrive at $\tau = 1\ \mu s$, also with an initial phase of 0°. If the mobile moves directly toward the direction of arrival of the first component and directly away from the direction of arrival of the second component, compute the narrowband instantaneous power at time intervals of 0.1 s from 0 s to 0.5 s. Compute the average narrowband power received over this observation interval. Compare average narrowband and wideband received powers over the interval, assuming the amplitudes of the two multipath components do not fade over the local area.

Solution

Given $v = 10$ m/s, time intervals of 0.1 s correspond to spatial intervals of 1 m. The carrier frequency is given to be 1000 MHz, hence the wavelength of the signal is

$$\lambda = \frac{c}{f} = \frac{3 \times 10^8}{1000 \times 10^6} = 0.3\ m$$

The narrowband instantaneous power can be computed using Equation (5.21).

Note −70 dBm = 100 pW. At time $t = 0$, the phases of both multipath components are 0°, hence the narrowband instantaneous power is equal to

$$|r(t)|^2 = \left|\sum_{i=0}^{N-1} a_i \exp(j\theta_i(t, \tau))\right|^2$$

$$= \left|\sqrt{100\ pW} \times \exp(0) + \sqrt{50\ pW} \times \exp(0)\right|^2 = 291\ pW$$

Now, as the mobile moves, the phase of the two multipath components changes in opposite directions.

At $t = 0.1$ s, the phase of the first component is

$$\theta_i = \frac{2\pi d}{\lambda} = \frac{2\pi vt}{\lambda} = \frac{2\pi \times 10(\text{m/s}) \times 0.1\ \text{s}}{0.3\ \text{m}}$$

$$= 20.94\ \text{rad} = 2.09\ \text{rad} = 120°$$

Since the mobile moves toward the direction of arrival of the first component, and away from the direction of arrival of the second component, θ_1 is positive, and θ_2 is negative.

Therefore, at $t = 0.1$ s, $\theta_1 = 120°$, and $\theta_2 = -120°$, and the instantaneous power is equal to

$$|r(t)|^2 = \left|\sum_{i=0}^{N-1} a_i \exp(j\theta_i(t,\tau))\right|^2$$

$$= \left|\sqrt{100\ \text{pW}} \times \exp(j120°) + \sqrt{50\ \text{pW}} \times \exp(-j120°)\right|^2 = 79.3\ \text{pW}$$

Similarly, at $t = 0.2$ s, $\theta_1 = 240°$, and $\theta_2 = -240°$, and the instantaneous power is equal to

$$|r(t)|^2 = \left|\sum_{i=0}^{N-1} a_i \exp(j\theta_i(t,\tau))\right|^2$$

$$= \left|\sqrt{100\ \text{pW}} \times \exp(j240°) + \sqrt{50\ \text{pW}} \times \exp(-j240°)\right|^2 = 79.3\ \text{pW}$$

Similarly, at $t = 0.3$ s, $\theta_1 = 360° = 0°$, and $\theta_2 = -360° = 0°$, and the instantaneous power is equal to

$$|r(t)|^2 = \left|\sum_{i=0}^{N-1} a_i \exp(j\theta_i(t,\tau))\right|^2$$

$$= \left|\sqrt{100\ \text{pW}} \times \exp(j0°) + \sqrt{50\ \text{pW}} \times \exp(-j0°)\right|^2 = 291\ \text{pW}$$

It follows that at $t = 0.4$ s, $|r(t)|^2 = 79.3$pW, and at $t = 0.5$ s, $|r(t)|^2 = 79.3$ pW. The average narrowband received power is equal to

$$\frac{(2)(291) + (4)(79.3)}{6}\ \text{pW} = 149\ \text{pW}$$

Using Equation (5.19), the wideband power is given by

$$E_{a,\theta}[P_{W,B}] = E_{a,\theta}\left[\sum_{i=0}^{N-1} |a_i \exp(j\theta_i)|^2\right] \approx \sum_{i=0}^{N-1} \overline{a_i^2}$$

$$E_{a,\theta}[P_{W,B}] = 100\ \text{pW} + 50\ \text{pW} = 150\ \text{pW}$$

As can be seen, the narrowband and wideband received power are virtually identical when averaged over 0.5 s (or 5 m). While the CW signal fades over the observation interval, the wideband signal power remains constant over the same spatial interval.

5.3 Small-Scale Multipath Measurements

Because of the importance of the multipath structure in determining the small-scale fading effects, a number of wideband channel sounding techniques have been developed. These techniques may be classified as *direct pulse measurements*, *spread spectrum sliding correlator measurements*, and *swept frequency measurements*.

5.3.1 Direct RF Pulse System

A simple channel sounding approach is the direct RF pulse system (see Figure 5.6). This technique allows engineers to determine rapidly the power delay profile of any channel, as demonstrated by Rappaport and Seidel [Rap89], [Rap90]. Essentially a wideband pulsed bistatic radar, this system transmits a repetitive pulse of width T_{bb} s, and uses a receiver with a wide bandpass filter ($BW = 2/T_{bb}\text{Hz}$). The signal is then amplified, detected with an envelope detector, and displayed and stored on a high speed oscilloscope. This gives an immediate measurement of the square of the channel impulse response convolved with the probing pulse (see Equation (5.17)). If the oscilloscope is set on averaging mode, then this system can provide a local average power delay profile. Another attractive aspect of this system is the lack of complexity, since off-the-shelf equipment may be used.

The minimum resolvable delay between multipath components is equal to the probing pulse width T_{bb}. The main problem with this system is that it is subject to interference and noise, due to the wide passband filter required for multipath time resolution. Also, the pulse system relies on the ability to trigger the oscilloscope on the first arriving signal. If the first arriving signal is blocked or fades, severe fading occurs, and it is possible the system may not

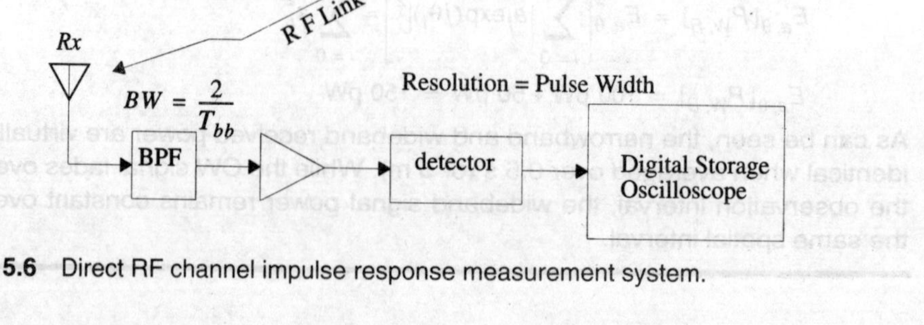

Figure 5.6 Direct RF channel impulse response measurement system.

trigger properly. Another disadvantage is that the phases of the individual multipath components are not received, due to the use of an envelope detector. However, use of a coherent detector permits measurement of the multipath phase using this technique.

5.3.2 Spread Spectrum Sliding Correlator Channel Sounding

The basic block diagram of a spread spectrum channel sounding system is shown in Figure 5.7. The advantage of a spread spectrum system is that, while the probing signal may be wideband, it is possible to detect the transmitted signal using a narrowband receiver preceded by a wideband mixer, thus improving the dynamic range of the system as compared to the direct RF pulse system.

In a spread spectrum channel sounder, a carrier signal is "spread" over a large bandwidth by mixing it with a binary pseudo-noise (PN) sequence having a chip duration T_c and a chip rate R_c equal to $1/T_c$ Hz. The power spectrum envelope of the transmitted spread spectrum signal is given by [Dix84] as

$$S(f) = \left[\frac{\sin\pi(f-f_c)T_c}{\pi(f-f_c)T_c}\right]^2 = \mathrm{Sa}^2(\pi(f-f_c)T_c) \tag{5.26}$$

and the null-to-null RF bandwidth is

$$BW = 2R_c \tag{5.27}$$

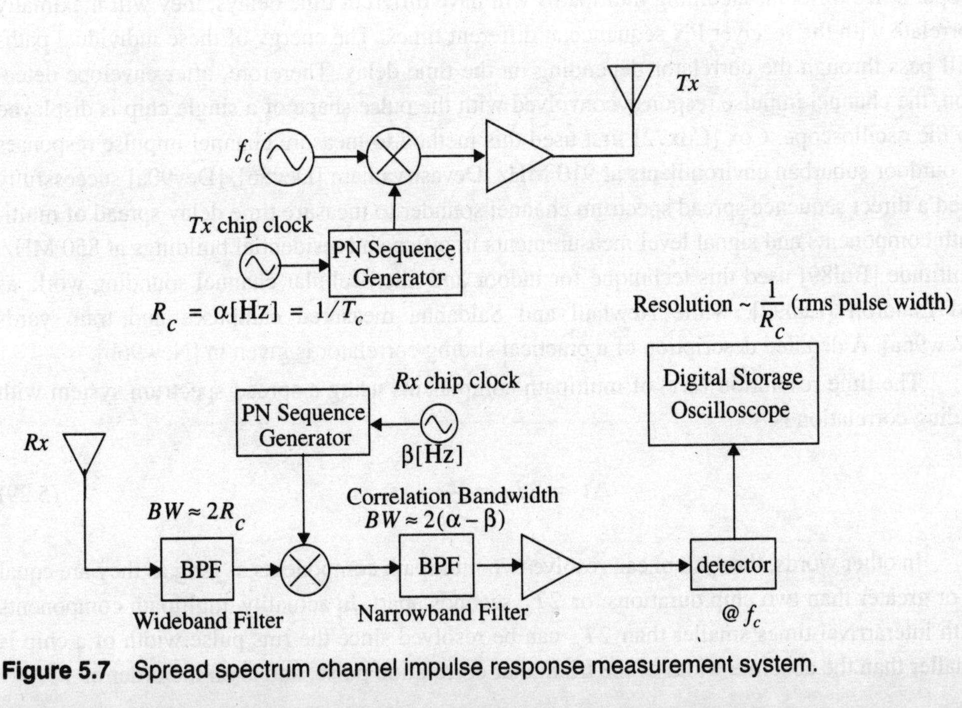

Figure 5.7 Spread spectrum channel impulse response measurement system.

The spread spectrum signal is then received, filtered, and *despread* using a PN sequence generator identical to that used at the transmitter. Although the two PN sequences are identical, the transmitter chip clock is run at a slightly faster rate than the receiver chip clock. Mixing the chip sequences in this fashion implements a *sliding correlator* [Dix84]. When the PN code of the faster chip clock catches up with the PN code of the slower chip clock, the two chip sequences will be virtually identically aligned, giving maximal correlation. When the two sequences are not maximally correlated, mixing the incoming spread spectrum signal with the unsynchronized receiver chip sequence will spread this signal into a bandwidth at least as large as the receiver's reference PN sequence. In this way, the narrowband filter that follows the correlator can reject almost all of the incoming signal power. This is how *processing gain* is realized in a spread spectrum receiver and how it can reject passband interference, unlike the direct RF pulse sounding system.

Processing gain (PG) is given as

$$PG = \frac{2R_c}{R_{bb}} = \frac{2T_{bb}}{T_c} = \frac{(S/N)_{out}}{(S/N)_{in}} \tag{5.28}$$

where $T_{bb} = 1/R_{bb}$, is the period of the baseband information. For the case of a sliding correlator channel sounder, the baseband information rate is equal to the frequency offset of the PN sequence clocks at the transmitter and receiver.

When the incoming signal is correlated with the receiver sequence, the signal is collapsed back to the original bandwidth (i.e., "despread"), envelope detected, and displayed on an oscilloscope. Since different incoming multipaths will have different time delays, they will maximally correlate with the receiver PN sequence at different times. The energy of these individual paths will pass through the correlator depending on the time delay. Therefore, after envelope detection, the channel impulse response convolved with the pulse shape of a single chip is displayed on the oscilloscope. Cox [Cox72] first used this method to measure channel impulse responses in outdoor suburban environments at 910 MHz. Devasirvatham [Dev86], [Dev90a] successfully used a direct sequence spread spectrum channel sounder to measure time delay spread of multipath components and signal level measurements in office and residential buildings at 850 MHz. Bultitude [Bul89] used this technique for indoor and microcellular channel sounding work, as did Landron [Lan92], while Newhall and Saldanha measured campuses and train yards [New96a]. A detailed description of a practical sliding correlator is given in [New96b].

The time resolution ($\Delta\tau$) of multipath components using a spread spectrum system with sliding correlation is

$$\Delta\tau = 2T_c = \frac{2}{R_c} \tag{5.29}$$

In other words, the system can resolve two multipath components as long as they are equal to or greater than two chip durations, or $2T_c$ seconds apart. In actuality, multipath components with interarrival times smaller than $2T_c$ can be resolved since the rms pulse width of a chip is smaller than the absolute width of the triangular correlation pulse, and is on the order of T_c.

The sliding correlation process gives *equivalent time* measurements that are updated every time the two sequences are maximally correlated. The time between maximal correlations (ΔT) can be calculated from Equation (5.30)

$$\Delta T = T_c \gamma l = \frac{\gamma l}{R_c} \tag{5.30}$$

where T_c = chip period (s)
R_c = chip rate (Hz)
γ = slide factor (dimensionless)
l = sequence length (chips)

The slide factor is defined as the ratio between the transmitter chip clock rate and the difference between the transmitter and receiver chip clock rates [Dev86]. Mathematically, this is expressed as

$$\gamma = \frac{\alpha}{\alpha - \beta} \tag{5.31}$$

where α = transmitter chip clock rate (Hz)
β = receiver chip clock rate (Hz)

For a maximal length PN sequence, the sequence length is

$$l = 2^n - 1 \tag{5.32}$$

where n is the number of shift registers in the sequence generator [Dix84].

Since the incoming spread spectrum signal is mixed with a receiver PN sequence that is slower than the transmitter sequence, the signal is essentially down-converted ("collapsed") to a low-frequency narrowband signal. In other words, the relative rate of the two codes slipping past each other is the rate of information transferred to the oscilloscope. This narrowband signal allows narrowband processing, eliminating much of the passband noise and interference. The processing gain of Equation (5.28) is then realized using a narrowband filter ($BW = 2(\alpha - \beta)$).

The equivalent time measurements refer to the relative times of multipath components as they are displayed on the oscilloscope. The observed time scale on the oscilloscope using a sliding correlator is related to the actual propagation time scale by

$$\text{Actual Propagation Time} = \frac{\text{Observed Time}}{\gamma} \tag{5.33}$$

This effect is due to the relative rate of information transfer in the sliding correlator. For example, ΔT of Equation (5.30) is an observed time measured on an oscilloscope and not actual propagation time. This effect, known as *time dilation*, occurs in the sliding correlator system because the propagation delays are actually expanded in time by the sliding correlator.

Caution must be taken to ensure that the sequence length has a period which is greater than the longest multipath propagation delay. The PN sequence period is

$$\tau_{PNseq} = T_c l \tag{5.34}$$

The sequence period gives an estimate of the maximum unambiguous range of incoming multipath signal components. This range is found by multiplying the speed of light with τ_{PNseq} in Equation (5.34).

There are several advantages to the spread spectrum channel sounding system. One of the key spread spectrum modulation characteristics is the ability to reject passband noise, thus improving the coverage range for a given transmitter power. Transmitter and receiver PN sequence synchronization is eliminated by the sliding correlator. Sensitivity is adjustable by changing the sliding factor and the post-correlator filter bandwidth. Also, required transmitter powers can be considerably lower than comparable direct pulse systems due to the inherent "processing gain" of spread spectrum systems.

A disadvantage of the spread spectrum system, as compared to the direct pulse system, is that measurements are not made in real time, but they are compiled as the PN codes slide past one another. Depending on system parameters and measurement objectives, the time required to make power delay profile measurements may be excessive. Another disadvantage of the system described here is that a noncoherent detector is used, so that phases of individual multipath components can not be measured. Even if coherent detection is used, the sweep time of a spread spectrum signal induces delay such that the phases of individual multipath components with different time delays would be measured at substantially different times, during which the channel might change.

5.3.3 Frequency Domain Channel Sounding

Because of the dual relationship between time domain and frequency domain techniques, it is possible to measure the channel impulse response in the frequency domain. Figure 5.8 shows a frequency domain channel sounder used for measuring channel impulse responses. A vector network analyzer controls a synthesized frequency sweeper, and an S-parameter test set is used to monitor the frequency response of the channel. The sweeper scans a particular frequency band (centered on the carrier) by stepping through discrete frequencies. The number and spacings of these frequency steps impact the time resolution of the impulse response measurement. For each frequency step, the S-parameter test set transmits a known signal level at port 1 and monitors the received signal level at port 2. These signal levels allow the analyzer to determine the complex response (i.e., transmissivity $S_{21}(\omega)$) of the channel over the measured frequency range. The transmissivity response is a frequency domain representation of the channel impulse response. This response is then converted to the time domain using inverse discrete Fourier transform (IDFT) processing, giving a band-limited version of the impulse response. In theory, this technique works well and indirectly provides amplitude and phase information in the time domain. However, the system requires careful calibration and hardwired synchronization between the transmitter and receiver, making it useful only for very close measurements (e.g., indoor channel sounding). Another limitation with this system is the non-real-time nature of the measurement. For time varying channels, the channel frequency response can change rapidly, giving an erroneous impulse response measurement. To mitigate this effect, fast sweep times are necessary to

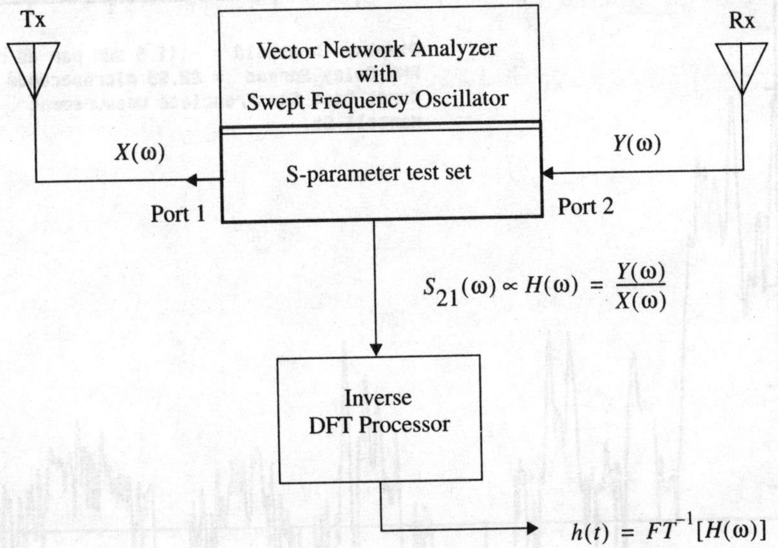

Figure 5.8 Frequency domain channel impulse response measurement system.

keep the total swept frequency response measurement interval as short as possible. A faster sweep time can be accomplished by reducing the number of frequency steps, but this sacrifices time resolution and excess delay range in the time domain. The swept frequency system has been used successfully for indoor propagation studies by Pahlavan [Pah95] and Zaghloul et al. [Zag91a], [Zag91b].

5.4 Parameters of Mobile Multipath Channels

Many multipath channel parameters are derived from the power delay profile, given by Equation (5.18). Power delay profiles are measured using the techniques discussed in Section 5.4 and are generally represented as plots of relative received power as a function of excess delay with respect to a fixed time delay reference. Power delay profiles are found by averaging instantaneous power delay profile measurements over a local area in order to determine an average small-scale power delay profile. Depending on the time resolution of the probing pulse and the type of multipath channels studied, researchers often choose to sample at spatial separations of a quarter of a wavelength and over receiver movements no greater than 6 m in outdoor channels and no greater than 2 m in indoor channels in the 450 MHz–6 GHz range. This small-scale sampling avoids large-scale averaging bias in the resulting small-scale statistics. Figure 5.9 shows typical power delay profile plots from outdoor and indoor channels, determined from a large number of closely sampled instantaneous profiles.

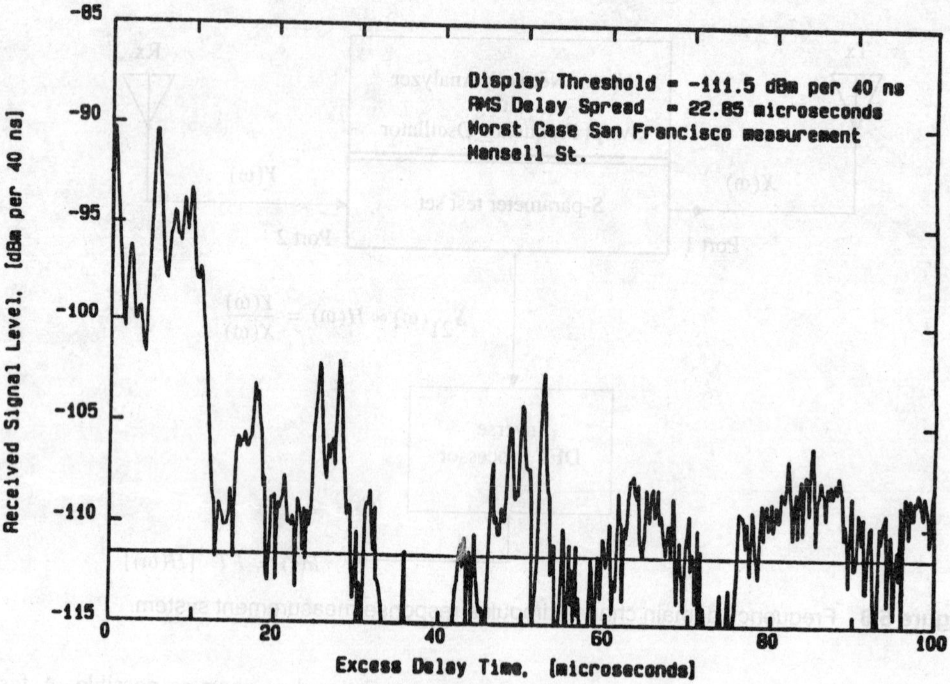

(a)

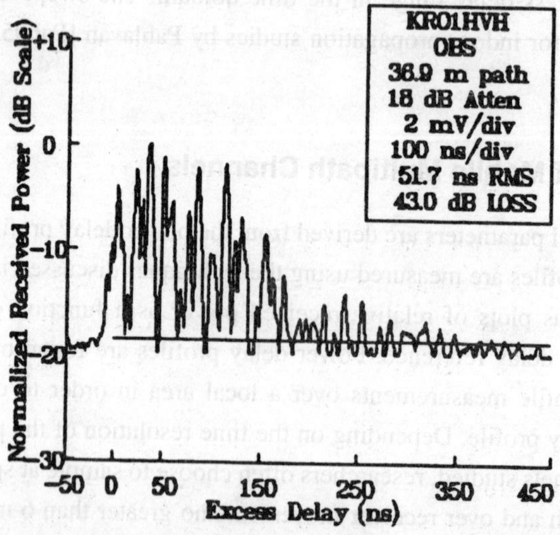

(b)

Figure 5.9 Measured multipath power delay profiles: a) From a 900 MHz cellular system in San Francisco [from [Rap90] © IEEE]; b) inside a grocery store at 4 GHz [from [Haw91] © IEEE].

5.4.1 Time Dispersion Parameters

In order to compare different multipath channels and to develop some general design guidelines for wireless systems, parameters which grossly quantify the multipath channel are used. The *mean excess delay, rms delay spread,* and *excess delay spread (X* dB*)* are multipath channel parameters that can be determined from a power delay profile. The time dispersive properties of wide band multipath channels are most commonly quantified by their mean excess delay ($\bar{\tau}$) and rms delay spread (σ_τ). The mean excess delay is the first moment of the power delay profile and is defined to be

$$\bar{\tau} = \frac{\sum_k a_k^2 \tau_k}{\sum_k a_k^2} = \frac{\sum_k P(\tau_k)\tau_k}{\sum_k P(\tau_k)} \tag{5.35}$$

The rms delay spread is the square root of the second central moment of the power delay profile and is defined to be

$$\sigma_\tau = \sqrt{\overline{\tau^2} - (\bar{\tau})^2} \tag{5.36}$$

where

$$\overline{\tau^2} = \frac{\sum_k a_k^2 \tau_k^2}{\sum_k a_k^2} = \frac{\sum_k P(\tau_k)\tau_k^2}{\sum_k P(\tau_k)} \tag{5.37}$$

These delays are measured relative to the first detectable signal arriving at the receiver at $\tau_0 = 0$. Equations (5.35)–(5.37) do not rely on the absolute power level of $P(\tau)$, but only the relative amplitudes of the multipath components within $P(\tau)$. Typical values of rms delay spread are on the order of microseconds in outdoor mobile radio channels and on the order of nanoseconds in indoor radio channels. Table 5.1 shows the typical measured values of rms delay spread.

It is important to note that the rms delay spread and mean excess delay are defined from a single power delay profile which is the temporal or spatial average of consecutive impulse response measurements collected and averaged over a local area. Typically, many measurements are made at many local areas in order to determine a statistical range of multipath channel parameters for a mobile communication system over a large-scale area [Rap90].

The *maximum excess delay (X* dB*)* of the power delay profile is defined to be the time delay during which multipath energy falls to *X* dB below the maximum. In other words, the maximum excess delay is defined as $\tau_X - \tau_0$, where τ_0 is the first arriving signal and τ_X is the maximum delay at which a multipath component is within *X* dB of the strongest arriving multipath signal (which does not necessarily arrive at τ_0). Figure 5.10 illustrates the computation of the maximum excess delay for multipath components within 10 dB of the maximum. The maximum excess delay (*X* dB) defines the temporal extent of the multipath that is above a particular threshold. The value of τ_X is sometimes called the *excess delay spread* of a power delay profile, but in all cases must be specified with a threshold that relates the multipath noise floor to the maximum received multipath component.

Table 5.1 Typical Measured Values of RMS Delay Spread

Environment	Frequency (MHz)	RMS Delay Spread (σ_τ)	Notes	Reference
Urban	910	1300 ns avg. 600 ns st. dev. 3500 ns max.	New York City	[Cox75]
Urban	892	10–25 μs	Worst case San Francisco	[Rap90]
Suburban	910	200–310 ns	Averaged typical case	[Cox72]
Suburban	910	1960–2110 ns	Averaged extreme case	[Cox72]
Indoor	1500	10–50 ns 25 ns median	Office building	[Sal87]
Indoor	850	270 ns max.	Office building	[Dev90a]
Indoor	1900	70–94 ns avg. 1470 ns max.	Three San Francisco buildings	[Sei92a]

Figure 5.10 Example of an indoor power delay profile; rms delay spread, mean excess delay, maximum excess delay (10 dB), and threshold level are shown.

In practice, values for $\bar{\tau}$, $\overline{\tau^2}$, and σ_τ depend on the choice of noise threshold used to process $P(\tau)$. The noise threshold is used to differentiate between received multipath components and thermal noise. If the noise threshold is set too low, then noise will be processed as multipath, thus giving rise to values of $\bar{\tau}$, $\overline{\tau^2}$, and σ_τ that are artificially high.

It should be noted that the power delay profile and the magnitude frequency response (the spectral response) of a mobile radio channel are related through the Fourier transform. It is therefore possible to obtain an equivalent description of the channel in the frequency domain using its frequency response characteristics. Analogous to the delay spread parameters in the time domain, *coherence bandwidth* is used to characterize the channel in the frequency domain. The rms delay spread and coherence bandwidth are inversely proportional to one another, although their exact relationship is a function of the exact multipath structure.

Example 5.4
Compute the RMS delay spread for the following power delay profile:

(a)

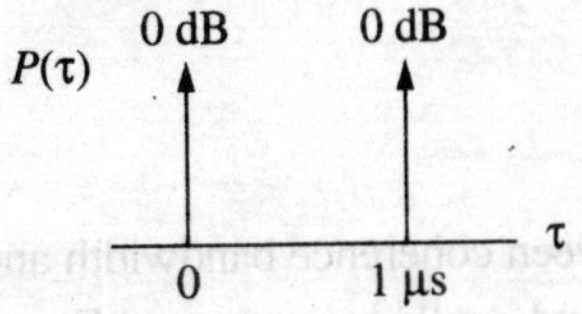

(b) If BPSK modulation is used, what is the maximum bit rate that can be sent through the channel without needing an equalizer?

Solution

(a) $\bar{\tau} = \dfrac{(1)(0)+(1)(1)}{1+1} = \dfrac{1}{2} = 0.5\mu s$

$$\overline{\tau^2} = \frac{(1)(0)^2+(1)(1)^2}{1+1} = \frac{1}{2} = 0.5\mu s^2$$

$$\sigma_\tau = \sqrt{\overline{\tau^2} - (\bar{\tau})^2} = \sqrt{0.5-(0.5)^2} = \sqrt{0.25} = 0.5\mu s$$

(b) $\dfrac{\sigma_\tau}{T_s} \le 0.1$

$$T_s \ge \frac{\sigma_\tau}{0.1}$$

$$T_s \ge \frac{0.5\mu s}{0.1}$$

$$T_s \ge 5\mu s$$

$$R_s = \frac{1}{T_s} = 0.2\times 10^6 \text{sps} = 200\text{ksps}$$

$$R_b = 200\text{kbps}$$

5.4.2 Coherence Bandwidth

While the delay spread is a natural phenomenon caused by reflected and scattered propagation paths in the radio channel, the coherence bandwidth, B_c, is a defined relation derived from the rms delay spread. Coherence bandwidth is a statistical measure of the range of frequencies over which the channel can be considered "flat" (i.e., a channel which passes all spectral components with approximately equal gain and linear phase). In other words, coherence bandwidth is the range of frequencies over which two frequency components have a strong potential for amplitude correlation. Two sinusoids with frequency separation greater than B_c are affected quite differently by the channel. If the coherence bandwidth is defined as the bandwidth over which the frequency correlation function is above 0.9, then the coherence bandwidth is approximately [Lee89b]

$$B_c \approx \frac{1}{50\sigma_\tau} \tag{5.38}$$

If the definition is relaxed so that the frequency correlation function is above 0.5, then the coherence bandwidth is approximately

$$B_c \approx \frac{1}{5\sigma_\tau} \tag{5.39}$$

It is important to note that an exact relationship between coherence bandwidth and rms delay spread is a funtion of specific channel impulse responses and applied signals, and Equations (5.38) and (5.39) are "ball park estimates." In general, spectral analysis techniques and simulation are required to determine the exact impact that time varying multipath has on a particular transmitted signal [Chu87], [Fun93], [Ste94]. For this reason, accurate multipath channel models must be used in the design of specific modems for wireless applications [Rap91a], [Woe94].

Example 5.5

Calculate the mean excess delay, rms delay spread, and the maximum excess delay (10 dB) for the multipath profile given in the figure below. Estimate the 50% coherence bandwidth of the channel. Would this channel be suitable for AMPS or GSM service without the use of an equalizer?

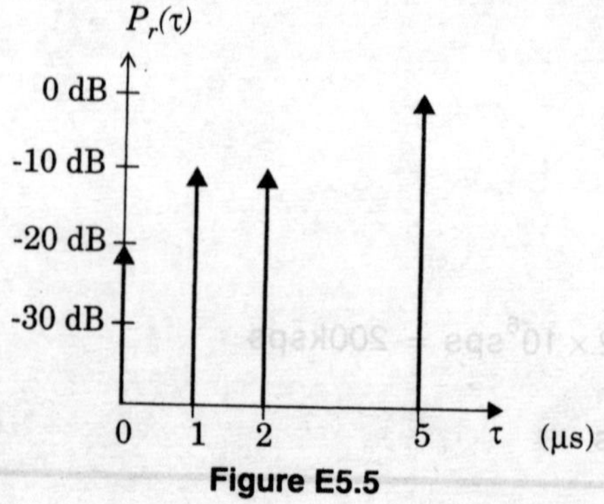

Figure E5.5

Solution

Using the definition of maximum excess delay (10 dB), it can be seen that $\tau_{10\,dB}$ is 5 μs. The rms delay spread for the given multipath profile can be obtained using Equations (5.35)–(5.37). The delays of each profile are measured relative to the first detectable signal. The mean excess delay for the given profile is

$$\bar{\tau} = \frac{(1)(5) + (0.1)(1) + (0.1)(2) + (0.01)(0)}{[0.01 + 0.1 + 0.1 + 1]} = 4.38\ \mu s$$

The second moment for the given power delay profile can be calculated as

$$\overline{\tau^2} = \frac{(1)(5)^2 + (0.1)(1)^2 + (0.1)(2)^2 + (0.01)(0)}{1.21} = 21.07\ \mu s^2$$

Therefore the rms delay spread is $\sigma_\tau = \sqrt{21.07 - (4.38)^2} = 1.37\ \mu s$

The coherence bandwidth is found from Equation (5.39) to be

$$B_C \approx \frac{1}{5\sigma_\tau} = \frac{1}{5(1.37\mu s)} = 146\ \text{kHz}$$

Since B_c is greater than 30 kHz, AMPS will work without an equalizer. However, GSM requires 200 kHz bandwidth which exceeds B_c, thus an equalizer would be needed for this channel.

5.4.3 Doppler Spread and Coherence Time

Delay spread and coherence bandwidth are parameters which describe the time dispersive nature of the channel in a local area. However, they do not offer information about the time varying nature of the channel caused by either relative motion between the mobile and base station, or by movement of objects in the channel. *Doppler spread* and *coherence time* are parameters which describe the time varying nature of the channel in a small-scale region.

Doppler spread B_D is a measure of the spectral broadening caused by the time rate of change of the mobile radio channel and is defined as the range of frequencies over which the received Doppler spectrum is essentially non-zero. When a pure sinusoidal tone of frequency f_c is transmitted, the received signal spectrum, called the Doppler spectrum, will have components in the range $f_c - f_d$ to $f_c + f_d$, where f_d is the Doppler shift. The amount of spectral broadening depends on f_d which is a function of the relative velocity of the mobile, and the angle θ between the direction of motion of the mobile and direction of arrival of the scattered waves. *If the baseband signal bandwidth is much greater than B_D, the effects of Doppler spread are negligible at the receiver.* This is a *slow* fading channel.

Coherence time T_c is the time domain dual of Doppler spread and is used to characterize the time varying nature of the frequency dispersiveness of the channel in the time domain. The Doppler spread and coherence time are inversely proportional to one another. That is,

$$T_C \approx \frac{1}{f_m} \tag{5.40.a}$$

Coherence time is actually a statistical measure of the time duration over which the chan-nel impulse response is essentially invariant, and quantifies the similarity of the channel response at different times. In other words, coherence time is the time duration over which two received signals have a strong potential for amplitude correlation. If the reciprocal bandwidth of the baseband signal is greater than the coherence time of the channel, then the channel will change during the transmission of the baseband message, thus causing distortion at the receiver. If the coherence time is defined as the time over which the time correlation function is above 0.5, then the coherence time is approximately [Ste94]

$$T_C \approx \frac{9}{16\pi f_m} \tag{5.40.b}$$

where f_m is the maximum Doppler shift given by $f_m = v/\lambda$. In practice, (5.40.a) suggests a time duration during which a Rayleigh fading signal may fluctuate wildly, and (5.40.b) is often too restrictive. A popular rule of thumb for modern digital communications is to define the coherence time as the geometric mean of Equations (5.40.a) and (5.40.b). That is,

$$T_C = \sqrt{\frac{9}{16\pi f_m^2}} = \frac{0.423}{f_m} \tag{5.40.c}$$

The definition of coherence time implies that two signals arriving with a time separation greater than T_C are affected differently by the channel. For example, for a vehicle traveling 60 mph using a 900 MHz carrier, a conservative value of T_C can be shown to be 2.22 ms from Equation (5.40.b). If a digital transmission system is used, then as long as the symbol rate is greater than $1/T_C$ = 454 bps, the channel will not cause distortion due to motion (however, distortion could result from multipath time delay spread, depending on the channel impulse response). Using the practical formula of (5.40.c), T_C = 6.77 ms and the symbol rate must exceed 150 bits/s in order to avoid distortion due to frequency dispersion.

Example 5.6

Determine the proper spatial sampling interval required to make small-scale propagation measurements which assume that consecutive samples are highly correlated in time. How many samples will be required over 10 m travel distance if f_c = 1900 MHz and v = 50 m/s. How long would it take to make these measurements, assuming they could be made in real time from a moving vehicle? What is the Doppler spread B_D for the channel?

Solution

For correlation, ensure that the time between samples is equal to $T_C/2$, and use the smallest value of T_C for conservative design.

Using Equation (5.40.b)

$$T_C \approx \frac{9}{16\pi f_m} = \frac{9\lambda}{16\pi v} = \frac{9c}{16\pi v f_c} = \frac{9 \times 3 \times 10^8}{16 \times 3.14 \times 50 \times 1900 \times 10^6}$$

$$T_C = 565 \mu s$$

Taking time samples at less than half T_C, at 282.5 μs corresponds to a spatial sampling interval of

$$\Delta x = \frac{vT_C}{2} = \frac{50 \times 565\ \mu s}{2} = 0.014125\ \text{m} = 1.41\ \text{cm}$$

Therefore, the number of samples required over a 10 m travel distance is

$$N_x = \frac{10}{\Delta x} = \frac{10}{0.014125} = 708\ \text{samples}$$

The time taken to make this measurement is equal to $\frac{10\ \text{m}}{50\ \text{m/s}} = 0.2\ \text{s}$

The Doppler spread is $B_D = f_m = \frac{vf_c}{c} = \frac{50 \times 1900 \times 10^6}{3 \times 10^8} = 316.66\ \text{Hz}$

5.5 Types of Small-Scale Fading

Section 5.3 demonstrated that the type of fading experienced by a signal propagating through a mobile radio channel depends on the nature of the transmitted signal with respect to the characteristics of the channel. Depending on the relation between the signal parameters (such as bandwidth, symbol period, etc.) and the channel parameters (such as rms delay spread and Doppler spread), different transmitted signals will undergo different types of fading. The time dispersion and frequency dispersion mechanisms in a mobile radio channel lead to four possible distinct effects, which are manifested depending on the nature of the transmitted signal, the channel, and the velocity. While multipath delay spread leads to *time dispersion* and *frequency selective fading*, Doppler spread leads to *frequency dispersion* and *time selective fading*. The two propagation mechanisms are independent of one another. Figure 5.11 shows a tree of the four different types of fading.

5.5.1 Fading Effects Due to Multipath Time Delay Spread

Time dispersion due to multipath causes the transmitted signal to undergo either flat or frequency selective fading.

5.5.1.1 Flat fading

If the mobile radio channel has a constant gain and linear phase response over a bandwidth which is greater than the bandwidth of the transmitted signal, then the received signal will undergo *flat fading*. This type of fading is historically the most common type of fading described in the technical literature. In flat fading, the multipath structure of the channel is such that the spectral characteristics of the transmitted signal are preserved at the receiver. However the strength of the received signal changes with time, due to fluctuations in the gain of the channel caused by multipath. The characteristics of a flat fading channel are illustrated in Figure 5.12.

It can be seen from Figure 5.12 that if the channel gain changes over time, a change of amplitude occurs in the received signal. Over time, the received signal $r(t)$ varies in gain, but the spectrum of the transmission is preserved. In a flat fading channel, the reciprocal bandwidth

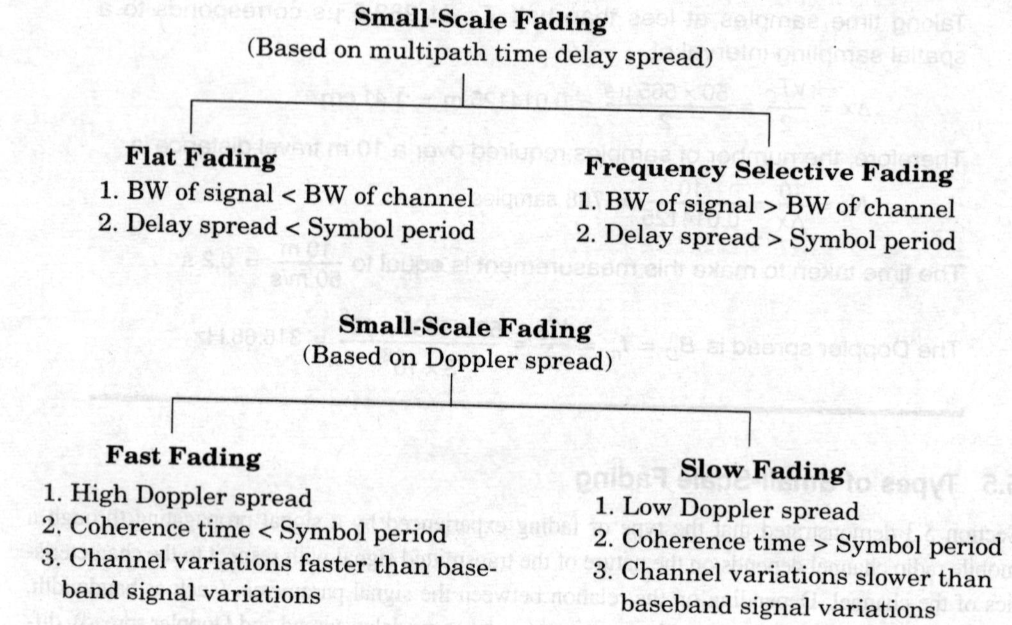

Figure 5.11 Types of small-scale fading.

of the transmitted signal is much larger than the multipath time delay spread of the channel, and $h_b(t, \tau)$ can be approximated as having no excess delay (i.e., a single delta function with $\tau = 0$). Flat fading channels are also known as *amplitude varying channels* and are sometimes referred to as *narrowband channels*, since the bandwidth of the applied signal is *narrow* as compared to the channel flat fading bandwidth. Typical flat fading channels cause deep fades, and thus may require 20 or 30 dB more transmitter power to achieve low bit error rates during times of deep fades as compared to systems operating over non-fading channels. The distribution of the instantaneous gain of flat fading channels is important for designing radio links, and the most common amplitude distribution is the Rayleigh distribution. The Rayleigh flat fading channel model assumes that the channel induces an amplitude which varies in time according to the Rayleigh distribution.

To summarize, a signal undergoes flat fading if

$$B_S \ll B_C \tag{5.41}$$

and

$$T_S \gg \sigma_\tau \tag{5.42}$$

where T_S is the reciprocal bandwidth (e.g., symbol period) and B_S is the bandwidth, respectively, of the transmitted modulation, and σ_τ and B_C are the rms delay spread and coherence bandwidth, respectively, of the channel.

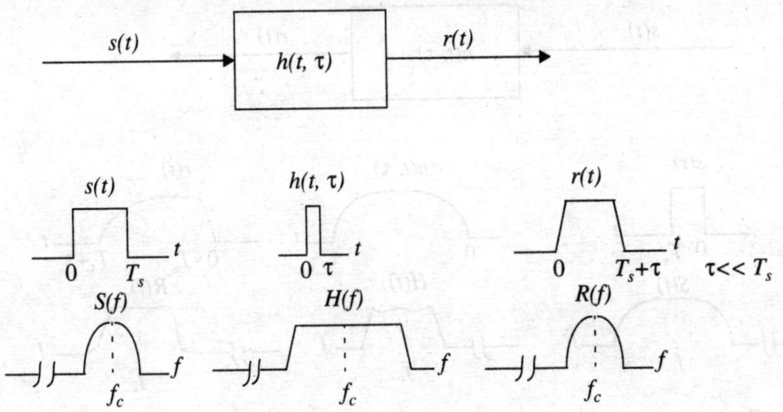

Figure 5.12 Flat fading channel characteristics.

5.5.1.2 Frequency Selective Fading

If the channel possesses a constant-gain and linear phase response over a bandwidth that is smaller than the bandwidth of transmitted signal, then the channel creates *frequency selective fading* on the received signal. Under such conditions, the channel impulse response has a multipath delay spread which is greater than the reciprocal bandwidth of the transmitted message waveform. When this occurs, the received signal includes multiple versions of the transmitted waveform which are attenuated (faded) and delayed in time, and hence the received signal is distorted. Frequency selective fading is due to time dispersion of the transmitted symbols within the channel. Thus the channel induces *intersymbol interference* (ISI). Viewed in the frequency domain, certain frequency components in the received signal spectrum have greater gains than others.

Frequency selective fading channels are much more difficult to model than flat fading channels since each multipath signal must be modeled and the channel must be considered to be a linear filter. It is for this reason that wideband multipath measurements are made, and models are developed from these measurements. When analyzing mobile communication systems, statistical impulse response models such as the two-ray Rayleigh fading model (which considers the impulse response to be made up of two delta functions which independently fade and have sufficient time delay between them to induce frequency selective fading upon the applied signal), or computer generated or measured impulse responses, are generally used for analyzing frequency selective small-scale fading. Figure 5.13 illustrates the characteristics of a frequency selective fading channel.

For frequency selective fading, the spectrum $S(f)$ of the transmitted signal has a bandwidth which is greater than the coherence bandwidth B_C of the channel. Viewed in the frequency domain, the channel becomes frequency selective, where the gain is different for different frequency components. Frequency selective fading is caused by multipath delays which

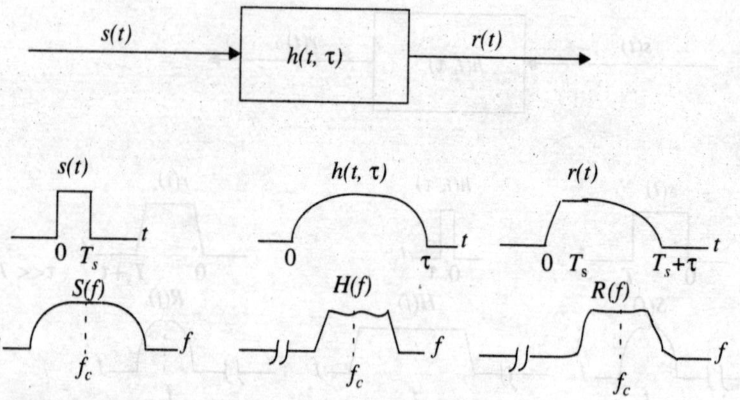

Figure 5.13 Frequency selective fading channel characteristics.

approach or exceed the symbol period of the transmitted symbol. Frequency selective fading channels are also known as *wideband channels* since the bandwidth of the signal $s(t)$ is wider than the bandwidth of the channel impulse response. As time varies, the channel varies in gain and phase across the spectrum of $s(t)$, resulting in time varying distortion in the received signal $r(t)$. To summarize, a signal undergoes frequency selective fading if

$$B_S > B_C \tag{5.43}$$

and

$$T_S < \sigma_\tau \tag{5.44}$$

A common rule of thumb is that a channel is flat fading if $T_s \geq 10\,\sigma_\tau$ and a channel is frequency selective if $T_s < 10\,\sigma_\tau$, although this is dependent on the specific type of modulation used. Chapter 6 presents simulation results which illustrate the impact of time delay spread on bit error rate (BER).

5.5.2 Fading Effects Due to Doppler Spread

5.5.2.1 Fast Fading

Depending on how rapidly the transmitted baseband signal changes as compared to the rate of change of the channel, a channel may be classified either as a *fast fading* or *slow fading* channel. In a *fast fading channel*, the channel impulse response changes rapidly within the symbol duration. That is, the coherence time of the channel is smaller than the symbol period of the transmitted signal. This causes frequency dispersion (also called time selective fading) due to Doppler spreading, which leads to signal distortion. Viewed in the frequency domain, signal distortion due to fast fading increases with increasing Doppler spread relative to the bandwidth of the transmitted signal. Therefore, a signal undergoes fast fading if

$$T_S > T_C \tag{5.45}$$

and

$$B_S < B_D \tag{5.46}$$

It should be noted that when a channel is specified as a fast or slow fading channel, it does not specify whether the channel is flat fading or frequency selective in nature. Fast fading only deals with the rate of change of the channel due to motion. In the case of the flat fading channel, we can approximate the impulse response to be simply a delta function (no time delay). Hence, a *flat fading, fast fading* channel is a channel in which the amplitude of the delta function varies faster than the rate of change of the transmitted baseband signal. In the case of a *frequency selective, fast fading* channel, the amplitudes, phases, and time delays of any one of the multipath components vary faster than the rate of change of the transmitted signal. In practice, fast fading only occurs for very low data rates.

5.5.2.2 Slow Fading

In a *slow fading channel*, the channel impulse response changes at a rate much slower than the transmitted baseband signal *s(t)*. In this case, the channel may be assumed to be static over one or several reciprocal bandwidth intervals. In the frequency domain, this implies that the Doppler spread of the channel is much less than the bandwidth of the baseband signal. Therefore, a signal undergoes slow fading if

$$T_S \ll T_C \tag{5.47}$$

and

$$B_S \gg B_D \tag{5.48}$$

It should be clear that the velocity of the mobile (or velocity of objects in the channel) and the baseband signaling determines whether a signal undergoes fast fading or slow fading.

The relation between the various multipath parameters and the type of fading experienced by the signal are summarized in Figure 5.14. Over the years, some authors have confused the terms fast and slow fading with the terms large-scale and small-scale fading. It should be emphasized that fast and slow fading deal with the relationship between the time rate of change in the channel and the transmitted signal, and not with propagation path loss models.

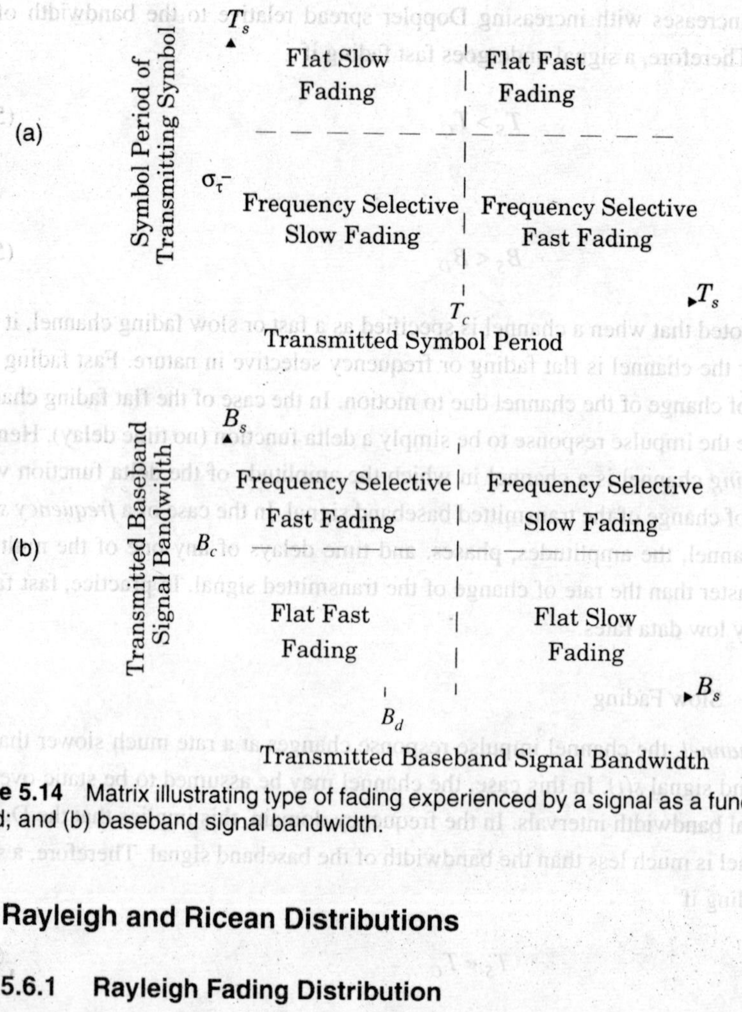

Figure 5.14 Matrix illustrating type of fading experienced by a signal as a function of: (a) symbol period; and (b) baseband signal bandwidth.

5.6 Rayleigh and Ricean Distributions

5.6.1 Rayleigh Fading Distribution

In mobile radio channels, the Rayleigh distribution is commonly used to describe the statistical time varying nature of the received envelope of a flat fading signal, or the envelope of an individual multipath component. It is well known that the envelope of the sum of two quadrature Gaussian noise signals obeys a Rayleigh distribution. Figure 5.15 shows a Rayleigh distributed signal envelope as a function of time. The Rayleigh distribution has a probability density function (pdf) given by

$$p(r) = \begin{cases} \dfrac{r}{\sigma^2}\exp\left(-\dfrac{r^2}{2\sigma^2}\right) & (0 \le r \le \infty) \\ 0 & (r < 0) \end{cases} \tag{5.49}$$

where σ is the rms value of the received voltage signal before *envelope detection*, and σ^2 is the time-average power of the received signal *before* envelope detection. The probability that the

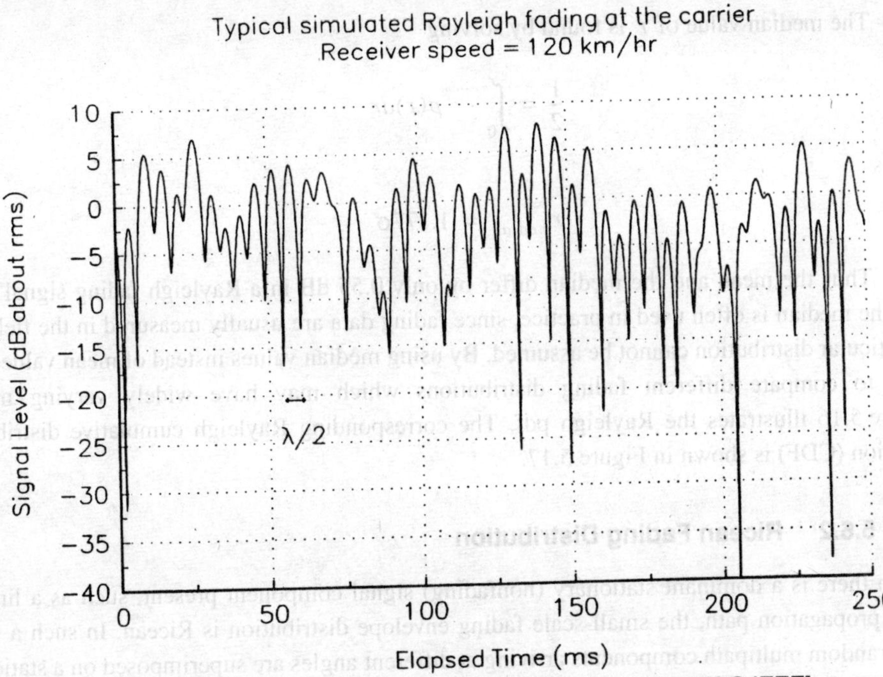

Figure 5.15 A typical Rayleigh fading envelope at 900 MHz [from [Fun93] © IEEE].

envelope of the received signal does not exceed a specified value R is given by the corresponding cumulative distribution function (CDF)

$$P(R) = Pr(r \le R) = \int_0^R p(r)dr = 1 - \exp\left(-\frac{R^2}{2\sigma^2}\right) \tag{5.50}$$

The mean value r_{mean} of the Rayleigh distribution is given by

$$r_{mean} = E[r] = \int_0^\infty rp(r)dr = \sigma\sqrt{\frac{\pi}{2}} = 1.2533\sigma \tag{5.51}$$

and the variance of the Rayleigh distribution is given by σ_r^2, which represents the ac power in the signal envelope

$$\sigma_r^2 = E[r^2] - E^2[r] = \int_0^\infty r^2 p(r)dr - \frac{\sigma^2\pi}{2} \tag{5.52}$$

$$= \sigma^2\left(2 - \frac{\pi}{2}\right) = 0.4292\sigma^2$$

The *rms value of the envelope* is the square root of the mean square, or $\sqrt{2}\sigma$, where σ is the standard deviation of the original complex Gaussian signal prior to envelope detection.

The median value of r is found by solving

$$\frac{1}{2} = \int_0^{r_{median}} p(r)dr \tag{5.53}$$

and is

$$r_{median} = 1.177\sigma \tag{5.54}$$

Thus the mean and the median differ by only 0.55 dB in a Rayleigh fading signal. Note that the median is often used in practice, since fading data are usually measured in the field and a particular distribution cannot be assumed. By using median values instead of mean values, it is easy to compare different fading distributions which may have widely varying means. Figure 5.16 illustrates the Rayleigh pdf. The corresponding Rayleigh cumulative distribution function (CDF) is shown in Figure 5.17.

5.6.2 Ricean Fading Distribution

When there is a dominant stationary (nonfading) signal component present, such as a line-of-sight propagation path, the small-scale fading envelope distribution is Ricean. In such a situation, random multipath components arriving at different angles are superimposed on a stationary dominant signal. At the output of an envelope detector, this has the effect of adding a dc component to the random multipath.

Just as for the case of detection of a sine wave in thermal noise [Ric48], the effect of a dominant signal arriving with many weaker multipath signals gives rise to the Ricean distribution. As the dominant signal becomes weaker, the composite signal resembles a noise signal which has an envelope that is Rayleigh. Thus, the Ricean distribution degenerates to a Rayleigh distribution when the dominant component fades away.

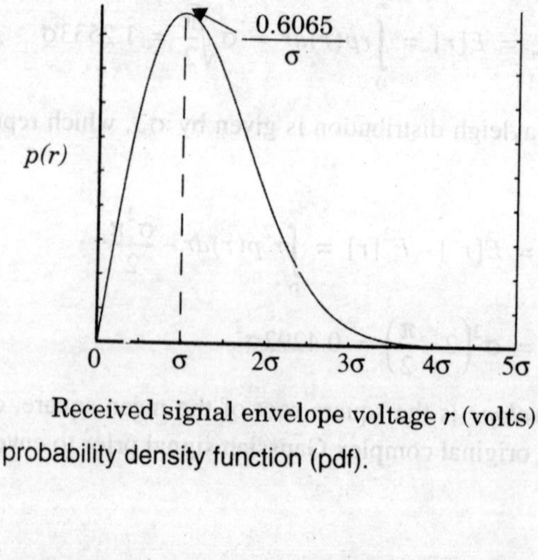

Figure 5.16 Rayleigh probability density function (pdf).

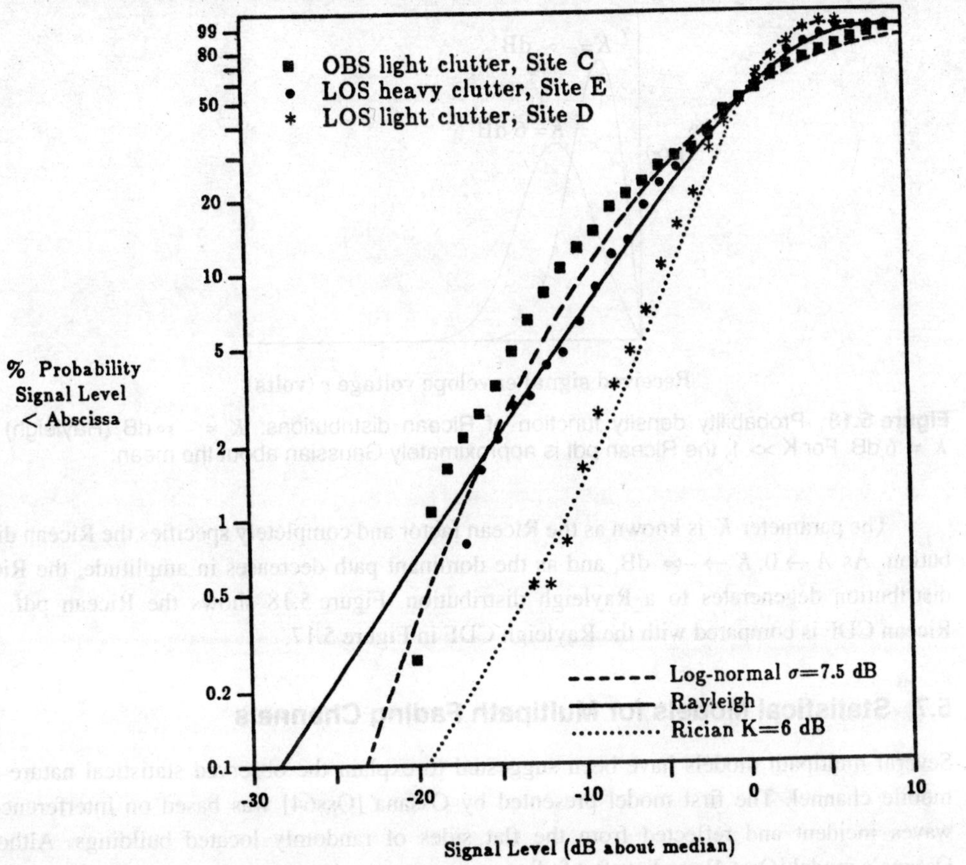

Figure 5.17 Cumulative distribution for three small-scale fading measurements and their fit to Rayleigh, Ricean, and log-normal distributions [from [Rap89] © IEEE].

The Ricean distribution is given by

$$p(r) = \begin{cases} \dfrac{r}{\sigma^2} e^{-\frac{(r^2 + A^2)}{2\sigma^2}} I_0\left(\dfrac{Ar}{\sigma^2}\right) & \text{for}(A \geq 0, r \geq 0) \\ 0 & \text{for}(r < 0) \end{cases} \tag{5.55}$$

The parameter A denotes the peak amplitude of the dominant signal and $I_0(\bullet)$ is the modified Bessel function of the first kind and zero-order. The Ricean distribution is often described in terms of a parameter K which is defined as the ratio between the deterministic signal power and the variance of the multipath. It is given by $K = A^2/(2\sigma^2)$ or, in terms of dB

$$K(\text{dB}) = 10\log\frac{A^2}{2\sigma^2} \text{ dB} \tag{5.56}$$

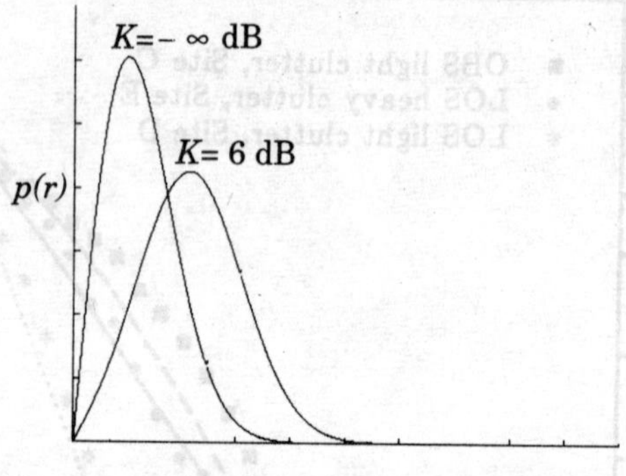

Figure 5.18 Probability density function of Ricean distributions: $K = -\infty$ dB (Rayleigh) and $K = 6$ dB. For K >> 1, the Ricean pdf is approximately Gaussian about the mean.

The parameter K is known as the Ricean factor and completely specifies the Ricean distribution. As $A \rightarrow 0$, $K \rightarrow -\infty$ dB, and as the dominant path decreases in amplitude, the Ricean distribution degenerates to a Rayleigh distribution. Figure 5.18 shows the Ricean pdf. The Ricean CDF is compared with the Rayleigh CDF in Figure 5.17.

5.7 Statistical Models for Multipath Fading Channels

Several multipath models have been suggested to explain the observed statistical nature of a mobile channel. The first model presented by Ossana [Oss64] was based on interference of waves incident and reflected from the flat sides of randomly located buildings. Although Ossana's model [Oss64] predicts flat fading power spectra that were in agreement with measurements in suburban areas, it assumes the existence of a direct path between the transmitter and receiver, and is limited to a restricted range of reflection angles. Ossana's model is therefore rather inflexible and inappropriate for urban areas where the direct path is almost always blocked by buildings or other obstacles. Clarke's model [Cla68] is based on scattering and is widely used.

5.7.1 Clarke's Model for Flat Fading

Clarke [Cla68] developed a model where the statistical characteristics of the electromagnetic fields of the received signal at the mobile are deduced from scattering. The model assumes a fixed transmitter with a vertically polarized antenna. The field incident on the mobile antenna is assumed to be comprised of N azimuthal plane waves with arbitrary carrier phases, arbitrary azimuthal angles of arrival, and each wave having equal average amplitude. It should be noted that the equal average amplitude assumption is based on the fact that in the absence of a direct line-of-sight path, the scattered components arriving at a receiver will experience similar attenuation over small-scale distances.

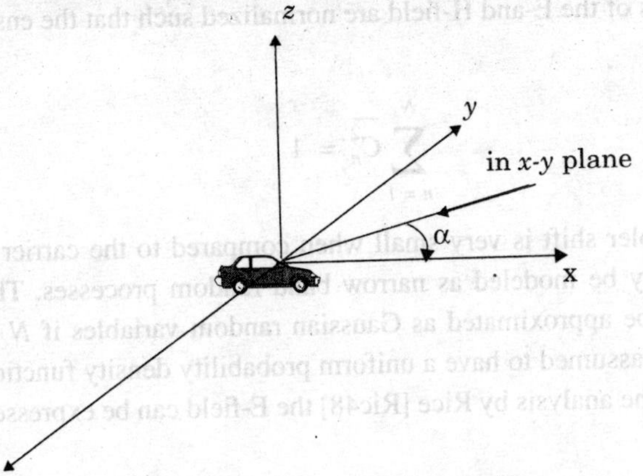

Figure 5.19 Illustrating plane waves arriving at random angles.

Figure 5.19 shows a diagram of plane waves incident on a mobile traveling at a velocity v, in the x-direction. The angle of arrival is measured in the x-y plane with respect to the direction of motion. Every wave that is incident on the mobile undergoes a Doppler shift due to the motion of the receiver and arrives at the receiver at the same time. That is, no excess delay due to multipath is assumed for any of the waves (flat fading assumption). For the nth wave arriving at an angle α_n to the x-axis, the Doppler shift in Hertz is given by

$$f_n = \frac{v}{\lambda}\cos\alpha_n \tag{5.57}$$

where λ is the wavelength of the incident wave.

The vertically polarized plane waves arriving at the mobile have E and H field components given by

$$E_z = E_o \sum_{n=1}^{N} C_n \cos(2\pi f_c t + \theta_n) \tag{5.58}$$

$$H_x = -\frac{E_o}{\eta} \sum_{n=1}^{N} C_n \sin\alpha_n \cos(2\pi f_c t + \theta_n) \tag{5.59}$$

$$H_y = -\frac{E_o}{\eta} \sum_{n=1}^{N} C_n \cos\alpha_n \cos(2\pi f_c t + \theta_n) \tag{5.60}$$

where E_0 is the real amplitude of local average E-field (assumed constant), C_n is a real random variable representing the amplitude of individual waves, η is the intrinsic impedance of free space (377Ω), and f_c is the carrier frequency. The random phase of the nth arriving component θ_n is given by

$$\theta_n = 2\pi f_n t + \phi_n \tag{5.61}$$

The amplitudes of the E-and H-field are normalized such that the ensemble average of the C_n's is given by

$$\sum_{n=1}^{N} \overline{C_n^2} = 1 \tag{5.62}$$

Since the Doppler shift is very small when compared to the carrier frequency, the three field components may be modeled as narrow band random processes. The three components E_z, H_x, and H_y can be approximated as Gaussian random variables if N is sufficiently large. The phase angles are assumed to have a uniform probability density function (pdf) on the interval $(0,2\pi]$. Based on the analysis by Rice [Ric48] the E-field can be expressed in an in-phase and quadrature form

$$E_z(t) = T_c(t)\cos(2\pi f_c t) - T_s(t)\sin(2\pi f_c t) \tag{5.63}$$

where

$$T_c(t) = E_0 \sum_{n=1}^{N} C_n \cos(2\pi f_n t + \phi_n) \tag{5.64}$$

and

$$T_s(t) = E_0 \sum_{n=1}^{N} C_n \sin(2\pi f_n t + \phi_n) \tag{5.65}$$

Both $T_c(t)$ and $T_s(t)$ are Gaussian random processes which are denoted as T_c and T_s, respectively, at any time t. T_c and T_s are uncorrelated zero-mean Gaussian random variables with an equal variance given by

$$\overline{T_c^2} = \overline{T_s^2} = \overline{|E_z|^2} = E_0^2/2 \tag{5.66}$$

where the overbar denotes the ensemble average.

The envelope of the received E-field, $E_z(t)$, is given by

$$|E_z(t)| = \sqrt{T_c^2(t) + T_s^2(t)} = r(t) \tag{5.67}$$

Since T_c and T_s are Gaussian random variables, it can be shown through a Jacobean transformation [Pap91] that the random received signal envelope r has a Rayleigh distribution given by

$$p(r) = \begin{cases} \dfrac{r}{\sigma^2}\exp\left(-\dfrac{r^2}{2\sigma^2}\right) & 0 \le r \le \infty \\ 0 & r < 0 \end{cases} \tag{5.68}$$

where $\sigma^2 = E_0^2/2$.

5.7.1.1 Spectral Shape Due to Doppler Spread in Clarke's Model

Gans [Gan72] developed a spectrum analysis for Clarke's model. Let $p(\alpha)d\alpha$ denote the fraction of the total incoming power within $d\alpha$ of the angle α, and let A denote the average received power with respect to an isotropic antenna. As $N \to \infty$, $p(\alpha)d\alpha$ approaches a continuous, rather than a discrete, distribution. If $G(\alpha)$ is the azimuthal gain pattern of the mobile antenna as a function of the angle of arrival, the total received power can be expressed as

$$P_r = \int_0^{2\pi} AG(\alpha)p(\alpha)d\alpha \tag{5.69}$$

where $AG(\alpha)p(\alpha)d\alpha$ is the differential variation of received power with angle. If the scattered signal is a CW signal of frequency f_c, then the instantaneous frequency of the received signal component arriving at an angle α is obtained using Equation (5.57)

$$f(\alpha) = f = \frac{v}{\lambda}\cos(\alpha) + f_c = f_m \cos\alpha + f_c \tag{5.70}$$

where f_m is the maximum Doppler shift. It should be noted that $f(\alpha)$ is an even function of α, (i.e., $f(\alpha) = f(-\alpha)$).

If $S(f)$ is the power spectrum of the received signal, the differential variation of received power with frequency is given by

$$S(f)|df| \tag{5.71}$$

Equating the differential variation of received power with frequency to the differential variation in received power with angle, we have

$$S(f)|df| = A[p(\alpha)G(\alpha) + p(-\alpha)G(-\alpha)]|d\alpha| \tag{5.72}$$

Differentiating Equation (5.70), and rearranging the terms, we have

$$|df| = |d\alpha||-\sin\alpha|f_m \tag{5.73}$$

Using Equation (5.70), α can be expressed as a function of f as

$$\alpha = \cos^{-1}\left[\frac{f - f_c}{f_m}\right] \tag{5.74}$$

This implies that

$$\sin\alpha = \sqrt{1 - \left(\frac{f - f_c}{f_m}\right)^2} \tag{5.75}$$

Substituting Equation (5.73) and (5.75) into both sides of (5.72), the power spectral density $S(f)$ can be expressed as

$$S(f) = \frac{A[p(\alpha)G(\alpha) + p(-\alpha)G(-\alpha)]}{f_m\sqrt{1-\left(\frac{f-f_c}{f_m}\right)^2}} \tag{5.76}$$

where

$$S(f) = 0, \quad |f-f_c| > f_m \tag{5.77}$$

The spectrum is centered on the carrier frequency and is zero outside the limits of $f_c \pm f_m$. Each of the arriving waves has its own carrier frequency (due to its direction of arrival) which is slightly offset from the center frequency. For the case of a vertical $\lambda/4$ antenna ($G(\alpha) = 1.5$), and a uniform distribution $p(\alpha) = 1/2\pi$ over 0 to 2π, the output spectrum is given by (5.76) as

$$S_{E_z}(f) = \frac{1.5}{\pi f_m\sqrt{1-\left(\frac{f-f_c}{f_m}\right)^2}} \tag{5.78}$$

In Equation (5.78), the power spectral density at $f = f_c \pm f_m$ is infinite, i.e., Doppler components arriving at exactly 0° and 180° have an infinite power spectral density. This is not a problem since α is continuously distributed and the probability of components arriving at exactly these angles is zero.

Figure 5.20 shows the power spectral density of the resulting RF signal due to Doppler fading. Smith [Smi75] demonstrated an easy way to simulate Clarke's model using a computer simulation as described Section 5.7.2.

After envelope detection of the Doppler-shifted signal, the resulting baseband spectrum has a maximum frequency of $2f_m$. It can be shown [Jak74] that the electric field produces a baseband power spectral density given by

$$S_{bbE_z}(f) = \frac{1}{8\pi f_m}K\left[\sqrt{1-\left(\frac{f}{2f_m}\right)^2}\right] \tag{5.79}$$

where $K[\bullet]$ is the complete elliptical integral of the first kind. Equation (5.79) is not intuitive and is a result of the temporal correlation of the received signal when passed through a nonlinear envelope detector. Figure 5.21 illustrates the baseband spectrum of the received signal after envelope detection.

The spectral shape of the Doppler spread determines the time domain fading waveform and dictates the temporal correlation and fade slope behaviors. Rayleigh fading simulators must use a fading spectrum such as Equation (5.78) in order to produce realistic fading waveforms that have proper time correlation.

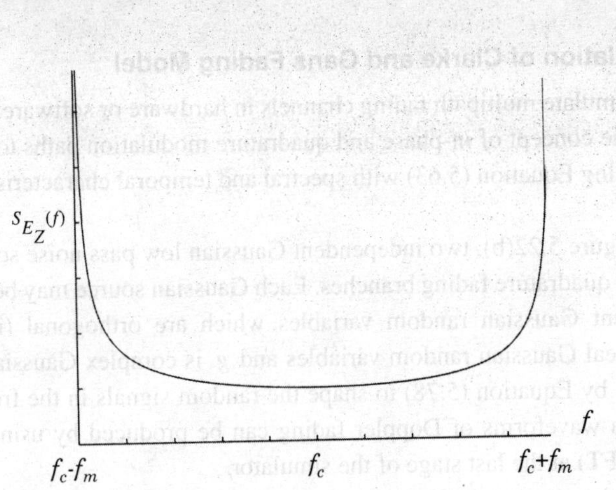

Figure 5.20 Doppler power spectrum for an unmodulated CW carrier [from [Gan72] © IEEE].

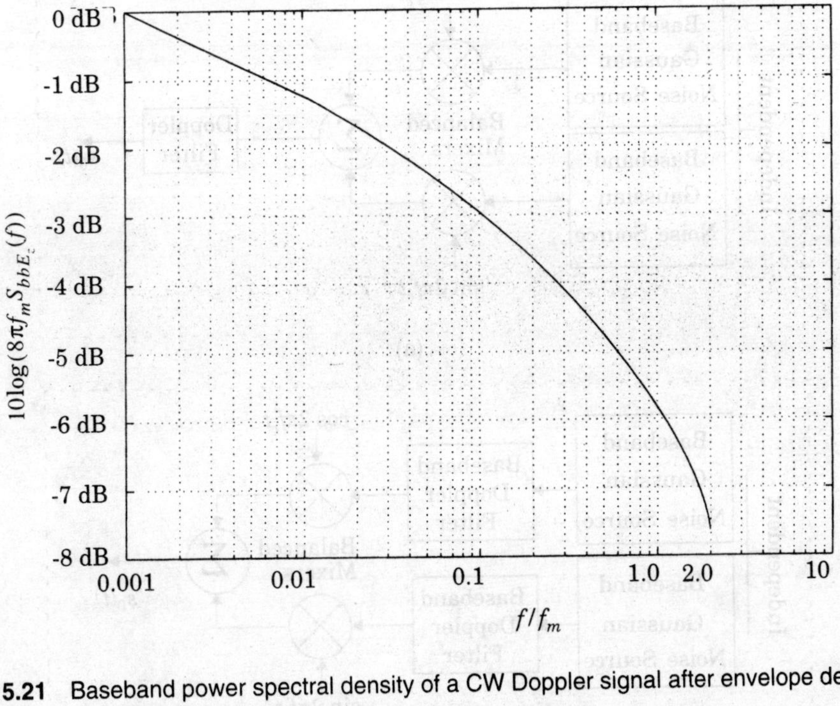

Figure 5.21 Baseband power spectral density of a CW Doppler signal after envelope detection.

5.7.2 Simulation of Clarke and Gans Fading Model

It is often useful to simulate multipath fading channels in hardware or software. A popular simulation method uses the concept of in-phase and quadrature modulation paths to produce a simulated signal representing Equation (5.63) with spectral and temporal characteristics very close to measured data.

As shown in Figure 5.22(b), two independent Gaussian low pass noise sources are used to produce in-phase and quadrature fading branches. Each Gaussian source may be formed by summing two independent Gaussian random variables which are orthogonal (i.e., $g = a + jb$, where a and b are real Gaussian random variables and g is complex Gaussian). By using the spectral filter defined by Equation (5.78) to shape the random signals in the frequency domain, accurate time domain waveforms of Doppler fading can be produced by using an inverse fast Fourier transform (IFFT) at the last stage of the simulator.

Smith [Smi75] demonstrated a simple computer program that implements Figure 5.22(b). His method uses a complex Gaussian random number generator (noise source) to produce a baseband line spectrum with complex weights in the positive frequency band. The maximum

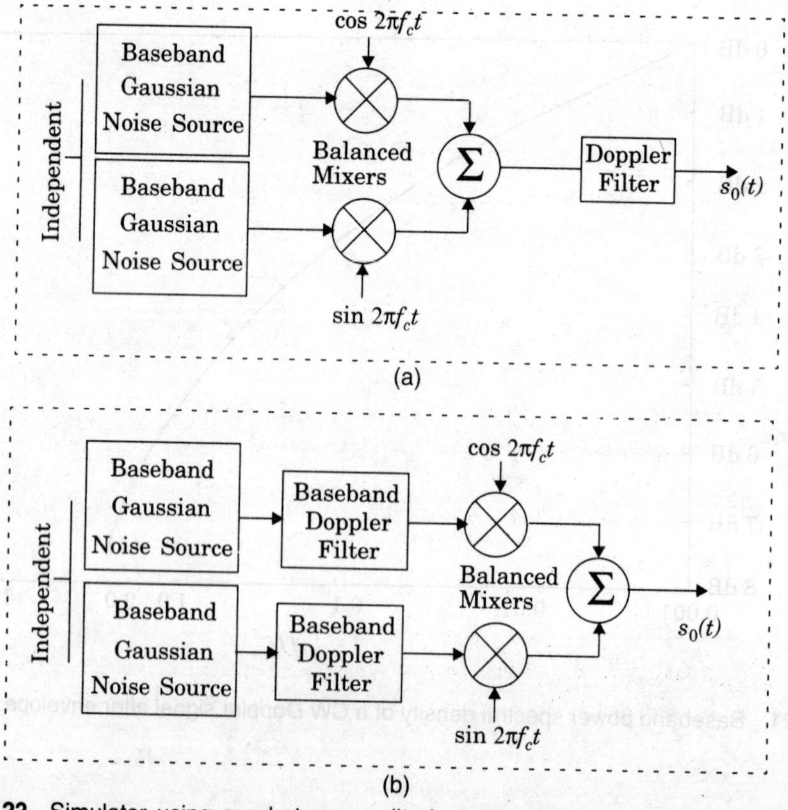

Figure 5.22 Simulator using quadrature amplitude modulation with (a) RF Doppler filter and (b) baseband Doppler filter.

frequency component of the line spectrum is f_m. Using the property of real signals, the negative frequency components are constructed by simply conjugating the complex Gaussian values obtained for the positive frequencies. Note that the IFFT of each complex Gaussian signal should be a purely real Gaussian random process in the time domain which is used in each of the quadrature arms shown in Figure 5.24. The random valued line spectrum is then multiplied with a discrete frequency representation of $\sqrt{S_{E_z}(f)}$ having the same number of points as the noise source. To handle the case where Equation (5.78) approaches infinity at the passband edge, Smith truncated the value of $S_{E_z}(f_m)$ by computing the slope of the function at the sample frequency just prior to the passband edge and increasing the slope to the passband edge. Simulations using the architecture in Figure 5.22 are usually implemented in the frequency domain using complex Gaussian line spectra to take advantage of easy implementation of Equation (5.78). This, in turn, implies that the low pass Gaussian noise components are actually a series of frequency components (line spectrum from $-f_m$ to f_m), which are equally spaced and each have a complex Gaussian weight. Smith's simulation methodology is shown in Figure 5.24.

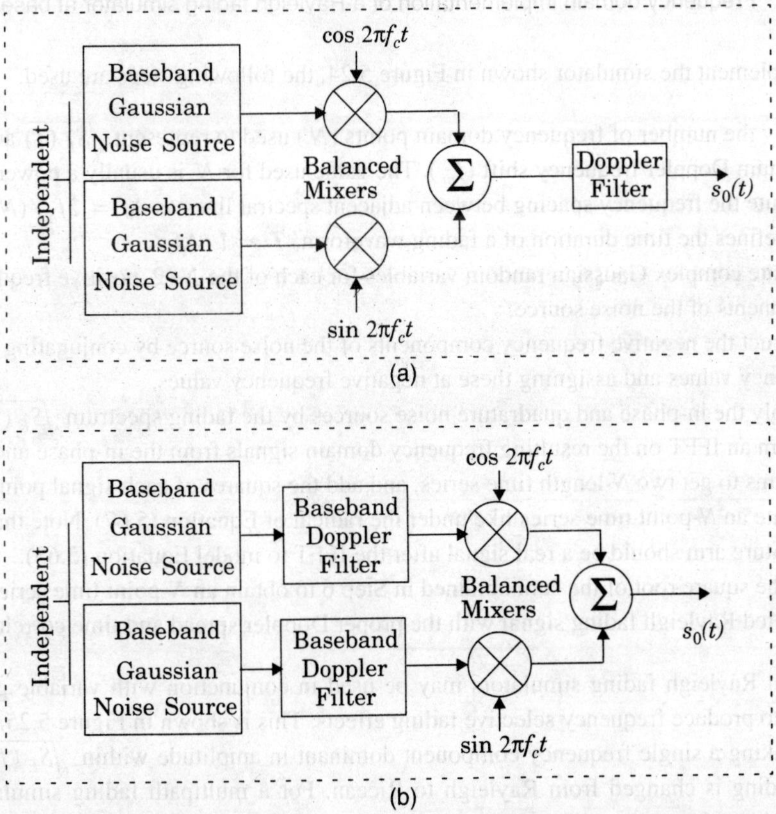

Figure 5.23 Simulator using quadrature amplitude modulation with (a) RF Doppler filter and (b) baseband Doppler filter.

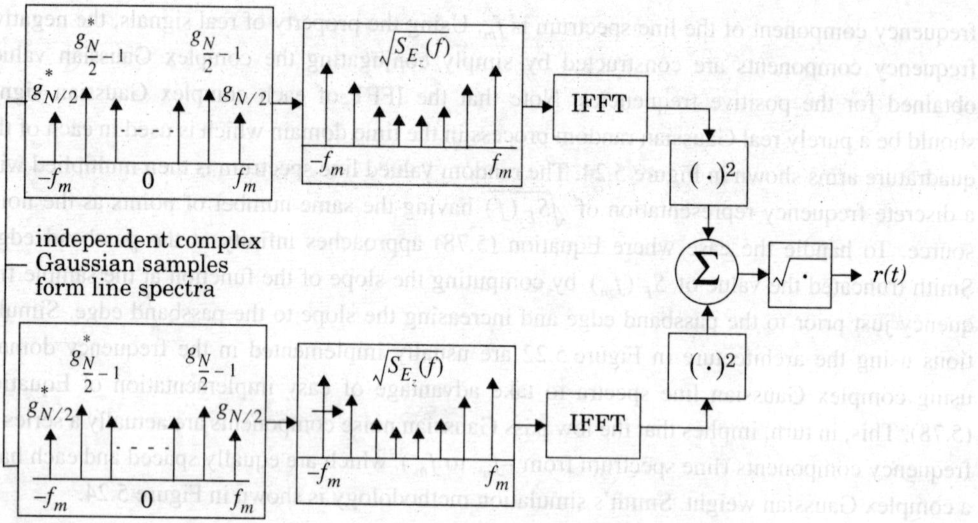

Figure 5.24 Frequency domain implementation of a Rayleigh fading simulator at baseband

To implement the simulator shown in Figure 5.24, the following steps are used:

1. Specify the number of frequency domain points (N) used to represent $\sqrt{S_{E_z}(f)}$ and the maximum Doppler frequency shift (f_m). The value used for N is usually a power of two.
2. Compute the frequency spacing between adjacent spectral lines as $\Delta f = 2f_m/(N-1)$. This defines the time duration of a fading waveform, $T = 1/\Delta f$.
3. Generate complex Gaussian random variables for each of the $N/2$ positive frequency components of the noise source.
4. Construct the negative frequency components of the noise source by conjugating positive frequency values and assigning these at negative frequency values.
5. Multiply the in-phase and quadrature noise sources by the fading spectrum $\sqrt{S_{E_z}(f)}$.
6. Perform an IFFT on the resulting frequency domain signals from the in-phase and quadrature arms to get two N-length time series, and add the squares of each signal point in time to create an N-point time series like under the radical of Equation (5.67). Note that each quadrature arm should be a real signal after the IFFT to model Equation (5.63).
7. Take the square root of the sum obtained in Step 6 to obtain an N-point time series of a simulated Rayleigh fading signal with the proper Doppler spread and time correlation.

Several Rayleigh fading simulators may be used in conjunction with variable gains and time delays to produce frequency selective fading effects. This is shown in Figure 5.25.

By making a single frequency component dominant in amplitude within $\sqrt{S_{E_z}(f)}$ and at $f = 0$, the fading is changed from Rayleigh to Ricean. For a multipath fading simulator with many resolvable components, this mtheod can be used to alter the probability distributions of the individual multipath components in the simulator of Figure 5.25. One must take care to properly

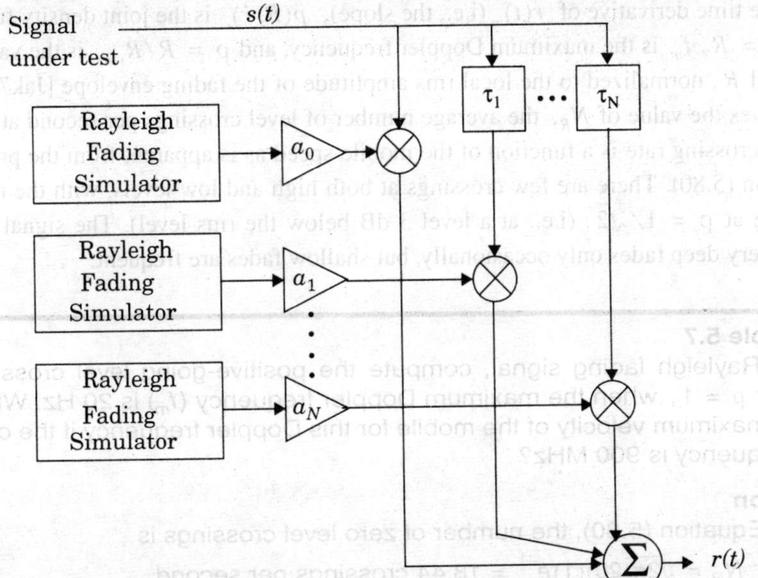

Figure 5.25 A signal may be applied to a Rayleigh fading simulator to determine performance in a wide range of channel conditions. Both flat and frequency selective fading conditions may be simulated, depending on gain and time delay settings.

implement the IFFT such that each arm of Figure 5.24 produces a real time domain signal as given by $T_c(t)$ and $T_s(t)$ in Equations (5.64) and (5.65).

To determine the impact of flat fading on an applied signal $s(t)$, one merely needs to multiply the applied signal by $r(t)$, the output of the fading simulator. To determine the impact of more than one multipath component, a convolution must be performed as shown in Figure 5.25.

5.7.3 Level Crossing and Fading Statistics

Rice computed joint statistics for a mathematical problem which is similar to Clarke's fading model [Cla68], and thereby provided simple expressions for computing the average number of level crossing and the duration of fades. The *level crossing rate* (LCR) and *average fade duration* of a Rayleigh fading signal are two important statistics which are useful for designing error control codes and diversity schemes to be used in mobile communication systems, since it becomes possible to relate the time rate of change of the received signal to the signal level and velocity of the mobile.

The *level crossing rate* (LCR) is defined as the expected rate at which the Rayleigh fading envelope, normalized to the local rms signal level, crosses a specified level in a positive-going direction. The number of level crossings per second is given by

$$N_R = \int_0^\infty \dot{r}\, p(R, \dot{r})d\dot{r} = \sqrt{2\pi} f_m \rho e^{-\rho^2} \tag{5.80}$$

where $\dot{r}$ is the time derivative of $r(t)$ (i.e., the slope), $p(R, \dot{r})$ is the joint density function of r and $\dot{r}$ at $r = R$, f_m is the maximum Doppler frequency, and $\rho = R/R_{rms}$ is the value of the specified level R, normalized to the local rms amplitude of the fading envelope [Jak74]. Equation (5.80) gives the value of N_R, the average number of level crossings per second at specified R. The level crossing rate is a function of the mobile speed as is apparent from the presence of f_m in Equation (5.80). There are few crossings at both high and low levels, with the maximum rate occurring at $\rho = 1/\sqrt{2}$, (i.e., at a level 3 dB below the rms level). The signal envelope experiences very deep fades only occasionally, but shallow fades are frequent.

Example 5.7

For a Rayleigh fading signal, compute the positive-going level crossing rate for $\rho = 1$, when the maximum Doppler frequency (f_m) is 20 Hz. What is the maximum velocity of the mobile for this Doppler frequency if the carrier frequency is 900 MHz?

Solution

Using Equation (5.80), the number of zero level crossings is

$$N_R = \sqrt{2\pi}(20)(1)e^{-1} = 18.44 \text{ crossings per second}$$

The maximum velocity of the mobile can be obtained using the Doppler relation, $f_{d,\,max} = v/\lambda$.

Therefore velocity of the mobile at $f_m = 20$ Hz is

$$v = f_d\lambda = 20 \text{ Hz}(1/3 \text{ m}) = 6.66 \text{ m/s} = 24 \text{ km/hr}$$

The *average fade duration* is defined as the average period of time for which the received signal is below a specified level R. For a Rayleigh fading signal, this is given by

$$\bar{\tau} = \frac{1}{N_R} Pr[r \le R] \tag{5.81}$$

where $Pr[r \le R]$ is the probability that the received signal r is less than R and is given by

$$Pr[r \le R] = \frac{1}{T}\sum_i \tau_i \tag{5.82}$$

where τ_i is the duration of the fade and T is the observation interval of the fading signal. The probability that the received signal r is less than the threshold R is found from the Rayleigh distribution as

$$P_r[r \le R] = \int_0^R p(r)dr = 1 - \exp(-\rho^2) \tag{5.83}$$

where $p(r)$ is the pdf of a Rayleigh distribution. Thus, using Equations (5.80), (5.81), and (5.83), the average fade duration as a function of ρ and f_m can be expressed as

$$\bar{\tau} = \frac{e^{\rho^2} - 1}{\rho f_m \sqrt{2\pi}} \tag{5.84}$$

The average duration of a signal fade helps determine the most likely number of signaling bits that may be lost during a fade. Average fade duration primarily depends upon the speed of the mobile, and decreases as the maximum Doppler frequency f_m becomes large. If there is a particular fade margin built into the mobile communication system, it is appropriate to evaluate the receiver performance by determining the rate at which the input signal falls below a given level R, and how long it remains below the level, on average. This is useful for relating SNR during a fade to the instantaneous BER which results.

Example 5.8
Find the average fade duration for threshold levels $\rho = 0.01$, $\rho = 0.1$, and $\rho = 1$, when the Doppler frequency is 200 Hz.

Solution
Average fade duration can be found by substituting the given values in Equation (5.84)

$$\text{For } \rho = 0.01,\ \bar{\tau} = \frac{e^{0.01^2} - 1}{(0.01)200\sqrt{2\pi}} = 19.9\ \mu s$$

$$\text{For } \rho = 0.1,\ \bar{\tau} = \frac{e^{0.1^2} - 1}{(0.1)200\sqrt{2\pi}} = 200\ \mu s$$

$$\text{For } \rho = 1,\ \bar{\tau} = \frac{e^{1^2} - 1}{(1)200\sqrt{2\pi}} = 3.43\text{ ms}$$

Example 5.9
Find the average fade duration for a threshold level of $\rho = 0.707$ when the Doppler frequency is 20 Hz. For a binary digital modulation with bit duration of 50 bps, is the Rayleigh fading slow or fast? What is the average number of bit errors per second for the given data rate. Assume that a bit error occurs whenever any portion of a bit encounters a fade for which $\rho < 0.1$.

Solution
The average fade duration can be obtained using Equation (5.84).

$$\bar{\tau} = \frac{e^{0.707^2} - 1}{(0.707)20\sqrt{2\pi}} = 18.3\text{ ms}$$

For a data rate of 50 bps, the bit period is 20 ms. Since the bit period is greater than the average fade duration, for the given data rate the signal undergoes fast Rayleigh fading. Using Equation (5.84), the average fade duration for $\rho = 0.1$ is equal to 0.002 s. This is less than the duration of one bit. Therefore, only one bit on average will be lost during a fade. Using Equation (5.80), the number of level crossings for $\rho = 0.1$ is $N_r = 4.96$ crossings per seconds. Since a bit error is assumed to occur whenever a portion of a bit encounters a fade, and since average fade duration spans only a fraction of a bit duration, the total number of bits in error is 5 per second, resulting in a BER = (5/50) = 0.1.

5.7.4 Two-ray Rayleigh Fading Model

Clarke's model and the statistics for Rayleigh fading are for flat fading conditions and do not consider multipath time delay. In modern mobile communication systems with high data rates, it has become necessary to model the effects of multipath delay spread as well as fading. A commonly used multipath model is an independent Rayleigh fading two-ray model (which is a specific implementation of the generic fading simulator shown in Figure 5.25). Figure 5.26 shows a block diagram of the two-ray independent Rayleigh fading channel model. The impulse response of the model is represented as

$$h_b(t) = \alpha_1 \exp(j\phi_1)\delta(t) + \alpha_2 \exp(j\phi_2)\delta(t-\tau) \tag{5.85}$$

where α_1 and α_2 are independent and Rayleigh distributed, ϕ_1 and ϕ_2 are independent and uniformly distributed over $[0, 2\pi]$, and τ is the time delay between the two rays. By setting α_2 equal to zero, the special case of a flat Rayleigh fading channel is obtained as

$$h_b(t) = \alpha_1 \exp(j\phi_1)\delta(t) \tag{5.86}$$

By varying τ, it is possible to create a wide range of frequency selective fading effects. The proper time correlation properties of the Rayleigh random variables α_1 and α_2 are guaranteed by generating two independent waveforms, each produced from the inverse Fourier transform of the spectrum described in Section 5.7.2.

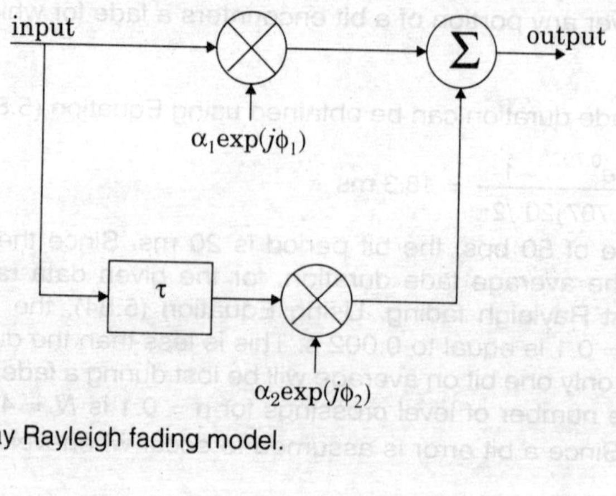

Figure 5.26 Two-ray Rayleigh fading model.

5.7.5 Saleh and Valenzuela Indoor Statistical Model

Saleh and Valenzuela [Sal87] reported the results of indoor propagation measurements between two vertically polarized omnidirectional antennas located on the same floor of a medium sized office building. Measurements were made using 10 ns, 1.5 GHz, radar-like pulses. The method involved averaging the square law detected pulse response while sweeping the frequency of the transmitted pulse. Using this method, multipath components within 5 ns were resolvable.

The results obtained by Saleh and Valenzuela show that: (a) the indoor channel is quasi-static or very slowly time varying, and (b) the statistics of the channel impulse response are independent of transmitting and receiving antenna polarization, if there is no line-of-sight path between them. They reported a maximum multipath delay spread of 100 ns to 200 ns within the rooms of a building, and 300 ns in hallways. The measured rms delay spread within rooms had a median of 25 ns and a maximum of 50 ns. The large-scale path loss with no line-of-sight path was found to vary over a 60 dB range and obey a log-distance power law (see Equation (4.68)) with an exponent between three and four.

Saleh and Valenzuela developed a simple multipath model for indoor channels based on measurement results. The model assumes that the multipath components arrive in clusters. The amplitudes of the received components are independent Rayleigh random variables with variances that decay exponentially with cluster delay as well as excess delay within a cluster. The corresponding phase angles are independent uniform random variables over $[0, 2\pi]$. The clusters and multipath components within a cluster form Poisson arrival processes with different rates. The clusters and multipath components within a cluster have exponentially distributed interarrival times. The formation of the clusters is related to the building structure, while the components within the cluster are formed by multiple reflections from objects in the vicinity of the transmitter and the receiver.

5.7.6 SIRCIM and SMRCIM Indoor and Outdoor Statistical Models

Rappaport and Seidel [Rap91a] reported measurements at 1300 MHz in five factory buildings and carried out subsequent measurements in other types of buildings. The authors developed an elaborate, empirically derived statistical model to generate measured channels based on the discrete impulse response channel model of Equation (5.12) and wrote a computer program called SIRCIM (Simulation of Indoor Radio Channel Impulse-response Models). SIRCIM generates realistic samples of small-scale indoor channel impulse response measurements [Rap91a]. Subsequent work by Huang produced SMRCIM (Simulation of Mobile Radio Channel Impulse-response Models), a similar program that generates small-scale urban cellular and microcellular channel impulse responses [Rap93a]. These programs are currently in use at over 100 institutions throughout the world, and have been updated to include angle of arrival information for microcell, indoor, and macrocell channels [Nuc99], [Lib99].

By recording power delay profile impulse responses at $\lambda/4$ intervals on a 1 m track at many indoor measurement locations, the authors were able to characterize local small-scale fading of individual multipath components, and the small-scale variation in the number and arrival times of multipath components within a local area. Thus, the resulting statistical models are functions of multipath time delay bin τ_i, the small-scale receiver spacing, X_l, within a 1 m local area, the topography S_m which is either line-of-sight (LOS) or obstructed, the large-scale T–R separation distance D_n, and the particular measurement location P_n. Therefore, each individual baseband power delay profile is expressed in a manner similar to Equation (5.12), except the random amplitudes and time delays are random variables which depend on the surrounding environment. Phases are synthesized using a pseudo-deterministic model which provides realistic results, so that a complete time varying complex baseband channel impulse response $h_b(t;\tau_i)$ may be obtained over a local area through simulation.

$$h_b(t, X_l, S_m, D_n, P_n) = \sum_i A_i(\tau_i, X_l, S_m, D_n, P_n) e^{j\theta_i(\tau_i, X_l, S_m, D_n, P_n)} \delta(t - \tau_i(X_l, S_m, D_n, P_n)) \tag{5.87}$$

In Equation (5.87), A_i^2 is the average multipath receiver power within a discrete excess delay interval of 7.8125 ns.

The measured multipath delays inside open-plan buildings ranged from 40 ns to 800 ns. Mean multipath delay and rms delay spread values ranged from 30 ns to 300 ns, with median values of 96 ns in LOS paths and 105 ns in obstructed paths. Delay spreads were found to be uncorrelated with T–R separation but were affected by factory inventory, building construction materials, building age, wall locations, and ceiling heights. Measurements in a food processing factory that manufactures dry-goods and has considerably less metal inventory than other factories had an rms delay spread that was half of those observed in factories producing metal products. Newer factories which incorporate steel beams and steel reinforced concrete in the building structure have stronger multipath signals and less attenuation than older factories which used wood and brick for perimeter walls. The data suggested that radio propagation in buildings may be described by a hybrid geometric/statistical model that accounts for both reflections from walls and ceilings and random scattering from inventory and equipment.

By analyzing the measurements from fifty local areas in many buildings, it was found that the number of multipath components, N_p, arriving at a certain location is a function of X, S_m, and P_n, and almost always has a Gaussian distribution. The average number of multipath components ranges between 9 and 36, and is generated based on an empirical fit to measurements. The probability that a multipath component will arrive at a receiver at a particular excess delay T_i in a particular environment S_m is denoted as $P_R(T_i, S_m)$. This was found from measurements by counting the total number of detected multipath components at a particular discrete excess delay time, and dividing by the total number of possible multipath components for each excess delay interval. The probabilities for multipath arriving at a particular excess delay values may be modeled as piecewise functions of excess delay, and are given by

$$\begin{array}{l} P_R(T_i, S_1) \\ \text{for LOS} \end{array} = \begin{cases} 1 - \dfrac{T_i}{367} & (T_i < 110 \text{ ns}) \\ 0.65 - \dfrac{(T_i - 110)}{360} & (110 \text{ ns} < T_i < 200 \text{ ns}) \\ 0.22 - \dfrac{(T_i - 200)}{1360} & (200 \text{ ns} < T_i < 500 \text{ ns}) \end{cases} \tag{5.88}$$

$$\begin{array}{l} P_R(T_i, S_2) \\ \text{for OBS} \end{array} = \begin{cases} 0.55 + \dfrac{T_i}{667} & (T_i < 100 \text{ ns}) \\ 0.08 + 0.62\exp\left(-\dfrac{(T_i - 100)}{75}\right) & (100 \text{ ns} < T_i < 500 \text{ ns}) \end{cases} \tag{5.89}$$

where S_1 corresponds to the LOS topography, and S_2 corresponds to obstructed topography. SIRCIM uses the probability of arrival distributions described by Equation (5.88) or (5.89) along with the probability distribution of the number of multipath components, $N_P(X, S_m, P_n)$, to simulate power delay profiles over small-scale distances. A recursive algorithm repeatedly compares Equation (5.88) or (5.89) with a uniformly distributed random variable until the proper N_P is generated for each profile [Hua91], [Rap91a].

Figure 5.27 shows an example of measured power delay profiles at 19 discrete receiver locations along a 1 m track, and illustrates accompanying narrowband information which SIRCIM computes based on synthesized phases for each multipath component [Rap91a]. Measurements reported in the literature provide excellent agreement with impulse responses predicted by SIRCIM.

Using similar statistical modeling techniques, urban cellular and microcellular multipath measurement data from [Rap90], [Sei91], [Sei92a] were used to develop SMRCIM. Both large cell and microcell models were developed. Figure 5.28 shows an example of SMRCIM output for an outdoor microcell environment [Rap93a].

5.8 Theory of Multipath Shape Factors for Small-Scale Fading Wireless Channels

A new method of analysis has been developed that characterizes the flat, small-scale fading experienced by a receiver in an arbitrary spatial-temporal channel [Dur00]. This method characterizes a multipath channel with arbitrary spatial complexity to three shape factors that have simple, intuitive geometrical interpretations. Furthermore, these shape factors describe the statistics of received

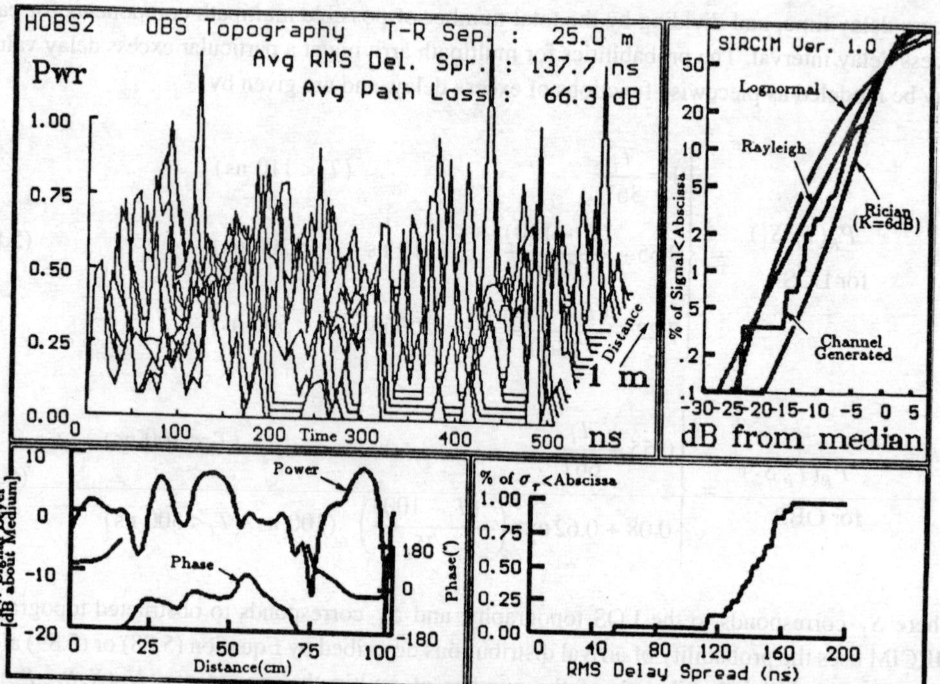

Figure 5.27 Indoor wideband impulse responses simulated by SIRCIM at 1.3 GHz. Also shown are the distributions of the rms delay spread and the narrowband signal power distribution. The channel is simulated as being obstructed in an open-plan building, T–R separation is 25 m. The rms delay spread is 137.7 ns. All multipath components and parameters are stored on disk [from [Rap93a] © IEEE].

signal fluctuations in a fading multipath channel. Analytical expressions for level-crossing rate, average fade duration, envelope autocovariance, and coherence distance are easily derived using the new shape factor theory, and match all of the classical results in [Jak74].

5.8.1 Introduction to Shape Factors

The term *small-scale fading* describes the rapid fluctuations of received power level due to small, sub-wavelength changes in receiver position. This effect is due to the constructive and destructive interference of the numerous multipath waves that impinge upon a wireless receiver [Jak74]. The resulting signal strength fluctuations affect, in some way, nearly every aspect of receiver design: dynamic range, equalization, diversity, modulation scheme, and channel and error-correction coding. These fluctuations are a function of direction of travel as related to the angle of arrival of multipath delay.

Numerous researchers have measured and analyzed the *first-order* statistics of these processes, which mostly involves the characterization of small-scale fading with a probability density function (PDF) discussed in Section 5.6 [Ric48], [Suz77], [Cou98]. The autocorrelation statistics of

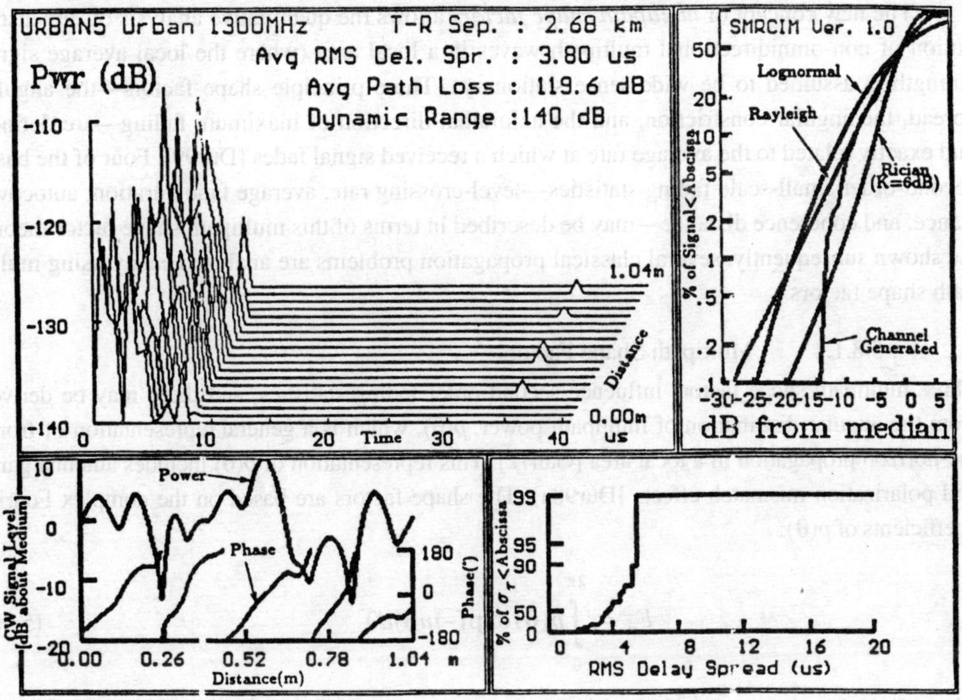

Figure 5.28 Urban wideband impulse responses simulated by SMRCIM at 1.3 GHz. Also shown are the distributions of the rms delay spread and the narrowband fading. T–R separation is 2.68 km. The rms delay spread is 3.8 µs. All multipath components and parameters are saved on disk. [from [Rap93a] © IEEE].

fading processes, or *second-order* statistics, include measures of a process such as power spectral density (PSD), level-crossing rate, and average fade duration, as discussed in Section 5.7

It turns out that second-order statistics are heavily dependent on the angles-of-arrival of received multipath, yet they have traditionally been studied using an omnidirectional, azimuthal propagation model as shown in Section 5.7 [Jak74]. That is, multipath waves usually are assumed to arrive at the receiver with equal power from the horizon in every possible direction. Truthfully, no realistic channel resembles this idealized model, but it is a reasonable multipath propagation model for receivers operating in heavily shadowed regions with a dense concentration of scatterers, and yields analytical results which resembled early field measurements [Cla68]. Clarke's model conveniently produces analytical statistics that are isotropic, unrealistically identical regardless of the direction traveled by the mobile receiver. Unfortunately, recent measurements and models have shown that the arriving multipath in a local area bears little resemblance to the omnidirectional propagation assumption and, in fact, the direction of travel relative to the arriving multipath is a key factor in producing the observed fading [Ros97], [Fuh97]. An approximately omnidirectional channel model does not accurately describe fading statistics if directional or smart antenna systems are employed at a receiver [Win98, Lib99, Mol01].

The new concept of *multipath shape factors* allows the quantitative analysis of *any* distribution of non-omnidirectional multipath waves in a local area (where the local average signal strength is assumed to be wide-sense stationary). Three principle shape factors—the angular spread, the angular constriction, and the azimuthal direction of maximum fading—are defined and exactly related to the average rate at which a received signal fades [Dur99]. Four of the basic second-order small-scale fading statistics—level-crossing rate, average fade duration, autocovariance, and coherence distance—may be described in terms of this multipath shape factor theory. As shown subsequently, several classical propagation problems are analyzed easily using multipath shape factors.

5.8.1.1 Multipath Shape Factors

Three multipath shape factors influence second-order fading statistics, and these may be derived from the angular distribution of multipath power, $p(\theta)$, which is a general representation of from-the-horizon propagation in a local area [Gan72]. This representation of $p(\theta)$ includes antenna gains and polarization mismatch effects [Dur98a]. The shape factors are based on the complex Fourier coefficients of $p(\theta)$:

$$F_n = \int_0^{2\pi} p(\theta)\exp(-jn\theta)d\theta \tag{5.90}$$

where F_n is the nth complex Fourier coefficient. The utility of these three shape factors becomes clear in Section 5.8.1.2.

Angular Spread, Λ

The shape factor *angular spread*, Λ, is a measure of how multipath concentrates about a single azimuthal direction of arrival. We define angular spread to be

$$\Lambda = \sqrt{1 - \frac{|F_1|^2}{F_0^2}} \tag{5.91}$$

where F_0 and F_1 are defined by Equation (5.90). There are several advantages to defining angular spread by Equation (5.91). First, since angular spread is normalized by F_0 (the total amount of local average received power), it is invariant under changes in transmitted power. Second, Λ is invariant under any series of rotational or reflective transformations of $p(\theta)$. Finally, this definition is intuitive; angular spread ranges from 0 to 1, whereby 0 denotes the extreme case of a single multipath component from a single direction and 1 denotes no clear bias in the angular distribution of received power (e.g., Clarke's model).

It should be noted that other definitions exist in the literature for angular spread. These definitions involve either beamwidth or the RMS θ calculations and are often ill-suited for general application to arbitrary channels or periodic functions such as $p(\theta)$ [Ebi91], [Nag96], [Ful98], [Jen98].

Angular Constriction, γ

The shape factor *angular constriction*, γ, is a measure of how multipath concentrates about *two* azimuthal directions. We define angular constriction to be

$$\gamma = \frac{|F_0 F_2 - F_1^2|}{F_0^2 - |F_1|^2} \tag{5.92}$$

where F_0, F_1, and F_2 are defined by Equation (5.90). Much like the definition of angular spread, the measure for angular constriction is invariant under changes in transmitted power or any series of rotational or reflective transformations of $p(\theta)$. The possible values of angular constriction, γ, range from 0 to 1, with 0 denoting no clear bias in two arrival directions and 1 denoting the extreme case of exactly two multipath components arriving from different directions.

Azimuthal Direction of Maximum Fading, θ_{max}

A third shape factor, which may be thought of as a directional, or orientation, parameter, is the *azimuthal direction of maximum fading*, $\theta_{\max}$. We define this parameter to be

$$\theta_{max} = \frac{1}{2}\arg\{F_0 F_2 - F_1^2\} \tag{5.93}$$

The $\theta_{\max}$ value corresponds to the direction in which a mobile user would move in order to experience the maximum fading rate in the local area.

5.8.1.2 Fading Rate Variance Relationships

Complex received voltage, received power, and received envelope are the three basic stochastic processes that are studied in small-scale fading. In order to understand how these stochastic processes evolve over space, it is useful to study the position derivatives or rate-of-changes of the three processes. Since the mean derivative of a stationary process is zero, the mean-squared derivative is the simplest statistic that measures the fading rate of a channel. In fact, a mean-squared derivative of a stationary process is actually the *variance* of the rate-of-change. This section, therefore, presents equations for describing the rate variance relationships of small-scale received complex voltage, power, and envelope fluctuations. All of these relationships are proven exactly in Appendix C.

Complex Received Voltage, $\tilde{V}(r)$

The complex received voltage, $\tilde{V}(r)$, is a baseband representation of the summation of numerous multipath waves that have impinged upon the receiver antenna and have excited a complex voltage component at the input of a receiver (see Section 5.2). Appendix C.1 derives the rate variance, $\sigma_{\tilde{V}'}^2$, for the complex voltage of a receiver traveling along the azimuthal direction θ:

$$\sigma_{\tilde{V}'}^2(\theta) = E\left\{\left|\frac{d\tilde{V}(r)}{dr}\right|^2\right\} = \frac{2\pi^2\Lambda^2 P_T}{\lambda^2}(1 + \gamma\cos[2(\theta - \theta_{\max})]) \tag{5.94}$$

where λ is the wavelength of the carrier frequency, P_T is the local average mean-squared received power (units of *volts-squared*). Note that the dependence on multipath angle-of-arrival in Equation (5.94) may be reduced to the three basic shape factors: angular spread, angular constriction, and the azimuthal direction of maximum fading. The physical significance of $\sigma_{\tilde{V}'}^2$ is that it describes the spatial selectivity of a channel in a local area and, by extension, the average *complex voltage fluctuations* for a mobile receiver as it moves over a local area.

Received Power, P(r)

Received power, P_r, is equal to the magnitude-squared of complex voltage, $\tilde{V}(r)$. Note that this definition of power yields units of *volts-squared* rather than *watts*, which would differ only by a constant of proportionality related to the input impedance of the receiver; the *volts-squared* definition is more general and independent of the receiver used.

The mathematical operation of taking the squared magnitude of a complex quantity is a nonlinear operation, so in order to derive a rate variance relationship for received power, we will assume that the channel is *Rayleigh fading*. This assumption, however, is unnecessary for the derivation of Equation (5.94). Appendix C.2 derives the rate variance, $\sigma_{P'}^2$, for the power of a receiver traveling along the azimuthal direction θ:

$$\sigma_{P'}^2(\theta) = E\left\{\left(\frac{dP(r)}{dr}\right)\right\} = \frac{4\pi^2\Lambda^2 P_T^2}{\lambda^2}(1+\gamma\cos[2(\theta-\theta_{max})]) \quad (5.95)$$

Once again, the dependence on multipath angle-of-arrival in Equation (5.95) may be reduced entirely to the three basic shape factors. The physical significance of $\sigma_{P'}^2$ is that it describes the average received *power fluctuations* in a local area where the signal envelope undergoes Rayleigh flat fading.

Received Envelope, R(r)

Received envelope, $R(r)$, is equal to the magnitude of complex voltage, $\tilde{V}(r)$. Once again, we assume that the channel is *Rayleigh fading* to calculate the mean-squared fading rate. Appendix C.3 shows how this assumption leads to the envelope rate variance,

$$\sigma_{R'}^2(\theta) = E\left\{\left(\frac{dR(r)}{dr}\right)^2\right\} = \frac{\pi^2\Lambda^2 P_T}{\lambda^2}(1+\gamma\cos[2(\theta-\theta_{max})]) \quad (5.96)$$

Again, Equation (5.96) depends on Λ, γ, and θ_{max}. The physical significance of $\sigma_{R'}^2$ is that it describes the average *envelope fluctuations* in a local area where the signal envelope undergoes Rayleigh flat fading.

5.8.1.3 Comparison to Omnidirectional Propagation

Applying the three shape factors, Λ, γ, and θ_{max}, to the classical omnidirectional propagation model of Section 5.7, we find that there is not a bias in either one or two directions of angle-of-arrival, leading to maximum angular spread ($\Lambda = 1$) and minimum angular constriction ($\gamma = 0$). The statistics of omnidirectional propagation are *isotropic*, exhibiting no dependence on the azimuthal direction of receiver travel, θ.

If the rate variance relationships of Equations (5.94)–(5.96) are normalized against their values for omnidirectional propagation, then they reduce to the following form:

$$\begin{aligned}\bar{\sigma}^2(\theta) &= \frac{\sigma^2_{\tilde{V}'}(\theta)}{\sigma^2_{\tilde{V}'(\text{omni})}} \\ &= \frac{\sigma^2_{P'}(\theta)}{\sigma^2_{P'(\text{omni})}} \\ &= \frac{\sigma^2_{R'}(\theta)}{\sigma^2_{R'(\text{omni})}} \\ &= \Lambda^2(1+\gamma\cos[2(\theta-\theta_{max})])\end{aligned} \tag{5.97}$$

where $\bar{\sigma}^2$ is a normalized fading rate variance. Equation (5.97) provides a convenient way to analyze the effects of the shape factors on the second-order statistics of small-scale fading.

First, notice that angular spread, Λ, describes the *average* fading rate within a local area. A convenient way of viewing this effect is to consider the fading rate variance taken along two perpendicular directions within the same local area. From Equation (5.97), the average of the two fading rate variances, regardless of the orientation of the measurement, is always given by averaging the variances observed over two perpendicular directions within the local area

$$\frac{1}{2}[\bar{\sigma}^2(\theta) + \bar{\sigma}^2(\theta + \pi/2)] = \Lambda^2 \tag{5.98}$$

Equation (5.98) clearly shows that the average fading rate within a local area decreases with respect to omnidirectional propagation as multipath power becomes more and more concentrated about a single azimuthal direction. A method for measuring multipath angular spread based on this relationship has been presented in [Pat99].

Second, notice that angular constriction, γ, does not affect the average fading rate within a local area, but describes the variability of fading rates taken along different azimuthal directions, θ. From Equation (5.97), fading rate variance $\bar{\sigma}^2$ will change as a function of direction of receiver travel θ, but will always fall within the following range:

$$\sqrt{1-\gamma} \le \frac{\bar{\sigma}(\theta)}{\Lambda} \le \sqrt{1+\gamma} \tag{5.99}$$

The upper limit of Equation (5.99) corresponds to a receiver traveling in the azimuthal direction of maximum fading ($\theta = \theta_{max}$) while the lower limit corresponds to travel in a perpendicular direction ($\theta = \theta_{max} + \pi/2$). Equation (5.99) clearly shows that the variability of fading rates within the same local area increases as the channel becomes more and more constricted.

It is interesting to note that the propagation mechanisms of a channel are not uniquely described by the three shape factors Λ, γ, and θ_{max}. An infinitum of propagation mechanisms exist which may have the same set of shape factors and, by extension, lead to channels which exhibit nearly the same end-to-end performance. In fact, Equation (5.97) provides rigorous mathematical criteria for a multipath channel that may be treated as "pseudo-omnidirectional":

$$|F_1|, |F_2| \ll F_0 \tag{5.100}$$

Under the condition of Equation (5.100), angular spread becomes approximately 1 and angular constriction becomes approximately 0. Thus, the second-order statistics of the channel behave nearly identical to the classical omnidirectional channel developed by Clarke and Gans.

5.8.2 Examples of Fading Behavior

This section presents four different analytical examples of non-omnidirectional propagation channels that provide insight into the shape factor definitions and how they describe fading rates.

Consider the simplest small-scale fading situation where two coherent, constant-amplitude multipath components, with individual powers defined by P_1 and P_2, arrive at a mobile receiver separated by an azimuthal angle α. We call this the *two-wave channel model*. Figure 5.29 illustrates this angular distribution of power, which is mathematically defined as

$$p(\theta) = P_1\delta(\theta-\theta_o) + P_2\delta(\theta-\theta_o-\alpha) \tag{5.101}$$

where θ_o is an arbitrary offset angle and $\delta(\cdot)$ is an impulse function. By applying Equations (5.91)–(5.93), the expressions for Λ, γ, and θ_{max} for this distribution are

$$\Lambda = \frac{2\sqrt{P_1P_2}}{P_1+P_2}\sin\frac{\alpha}{2}, \quad \gamma = 1, \quad \left(\theta_{max} = \theta_0 + \frac{\alpha+\pi}{2}\right) \tag{5.102}$$

The angular constriction, γ, is always 1 because the two-wave model represents perfect clustering about two directions. The limiting case of two multipath components arriving from the same direction ($\alpha = 0$) results in an angular spread, Λ, of 0. An angular spread of 1 results only when two multipath of identical powers ($P_1 = P_2$) are separated by $\alpha = 180°$. Figure 5.29 shows how the fading behavior changes as multipath separation angle, α, increases for the case of two equal-powered waves. Thus, increasing α changes a channel with low spatial selectivity into a channel with high spatial selectivity that exhibits a strong dependence on the azimuthal direction of receiver motion.

5.8.2.1 Sector Channel Model

Consider another theoretical situation where multipath power is arriving continuously and uniformly over a range of azimuth angles. This model has been used to describe propagation for directional receiver antennas with a distinct azimuthal beam [Gan72]. The function $p(\theta)$ will be defined by

$$p(\theta) = \begin{cases} \frac{P_T}{\alpha}: & \theta_o \le \theta \le \theta_o + \alpha \\ 0: & \text{elsewhere} \end{cases} \tag{5.103}$$

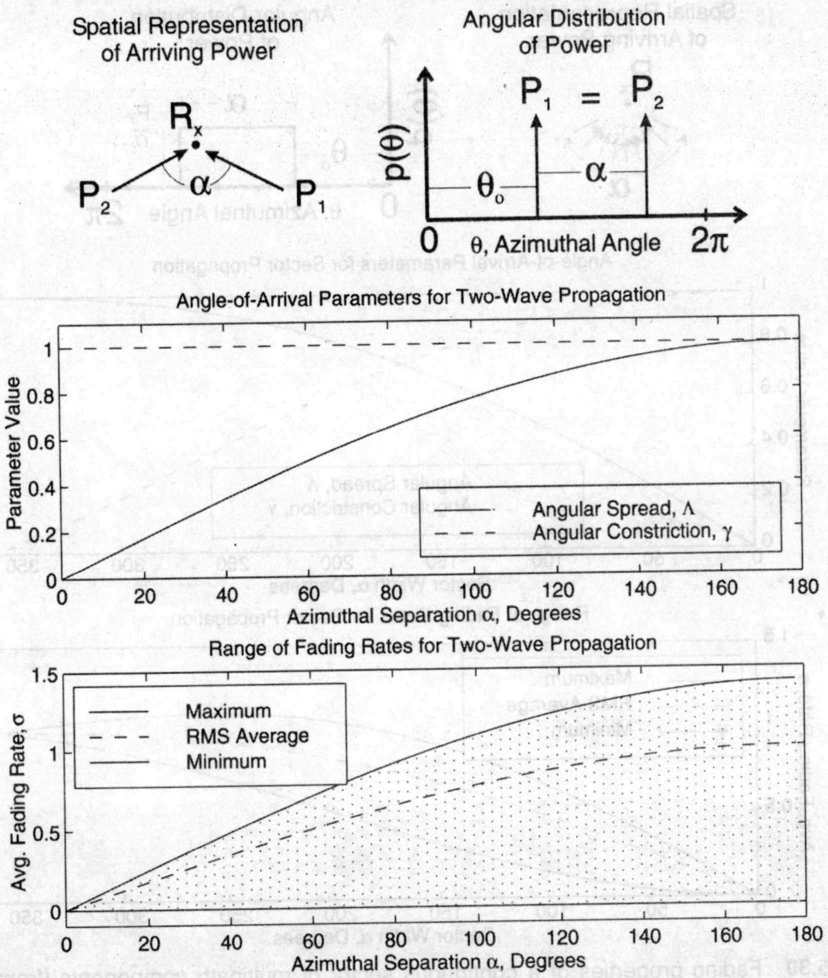

Figure 5.29 Fading properties of two multipath components of equal power [from [Dur00] ©IEEE].

The angle α indicates the width of the sector (in radians) of arriving multipath power and the angle θ_0 is an arbitrary offset angle, as illustrated by Figure 5.30. By applying Equations (5.91)–(5.93), the expressions for Λ, γ, and θ_{max} for this distribution are

$$\Lambda = \sqrt{1 - \frac{4\sin^2\frac{\alpha}{2}}{\alpha^2}} \qquad \gamma = \frac{4\sin^2\frac{\alpha}{2} - \alpha\sin\alpha}{\alpha^2 - 4\sin^2\frac{\alpha}{2}}, \qquad \theta_{max} = \theta_0 + \frac{\alpha + \pi}{2} \tag{5.104}$$

The limiting cases of these parameters and Equation (5.95) provide deeper understanding of angular spread and constriction.

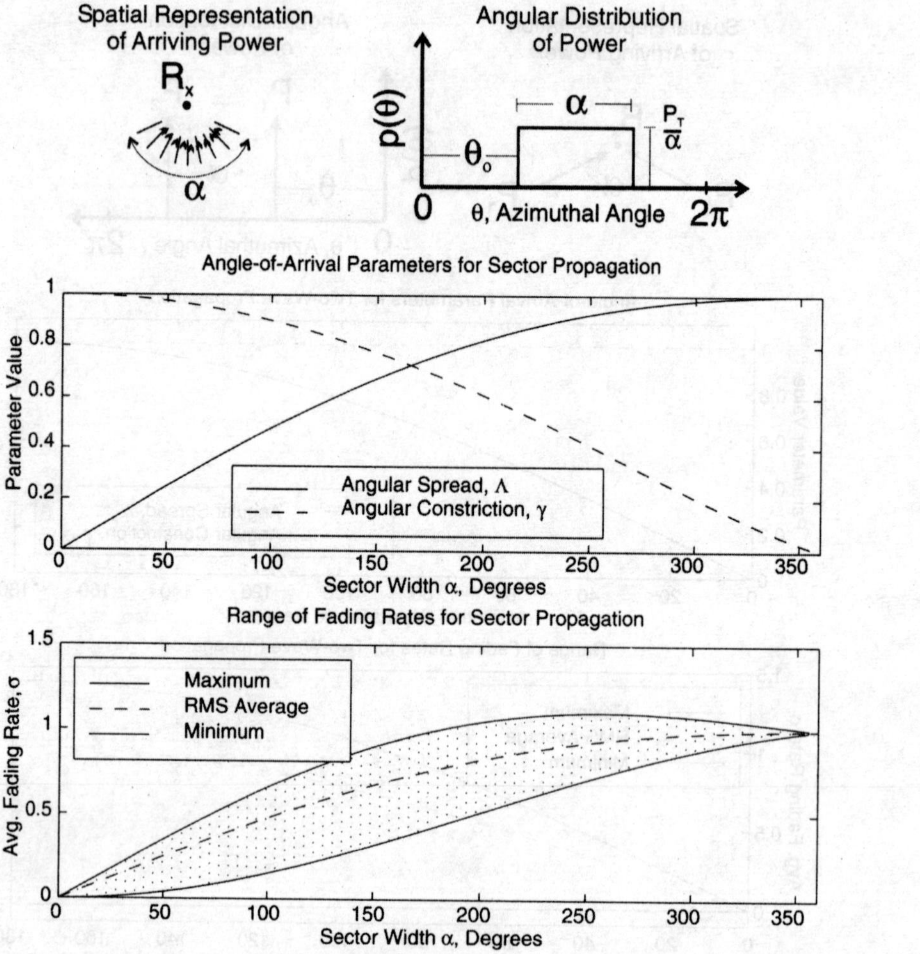

Figure 5.30 Fading properties of a continuous sector of multipath components [from [Dur00] ©IEEE].

Figure 5.30 graphs the spatial channel parameters, Λ and γ, as a function of sector width, α. The limiting case of a single multipath arriving from precisely one direction corresponds to $\alpha = 0$, which results in the minimum angular spread of $\Lambda = 0$. The other limiting case of uniform illumination in all directions corresponds to $\alpha = 360°$ (omnidirectional Clarke model), which results in the maximum angular spread of $\Lambda = 1$. The angular constriction, γ, follows an opposite trend. It is at a maximum ($\gamma = 1$) when $\alpha = 0$ and at a minimum ($\gamma = 0$) when $\alpha = 360°$. The graph in Figure 5.30 shows that as the multipath angles of arrival are condensed into a smaller and smaller sector, the directional dependence of fading rates within the same local area increases. Overall, however, fading rates decrease with decreasing sector size α.

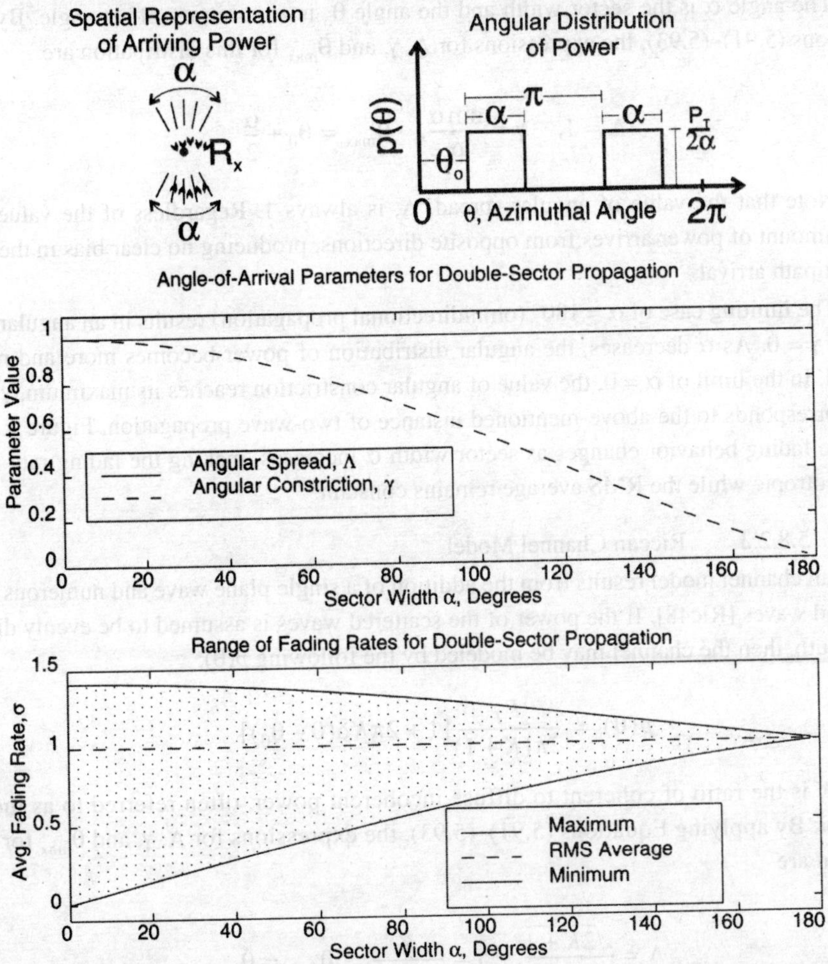

Figure 5.31 Fading properties of double-sectored multipath components [from [Dur00] ©IEEE].

5.8.2.2 Double Sector Channel Model

Another example of angular constriction may be studied using the Double Sector model of Figure 5.31. Diffuse multipath propagation over two equal and opposite sectors of azimuthal angles characterize the incoming power. The equation that describes this angular distribution of power is

$$p(\theta) = \begin{cases} \dfrac{P_T}{2\alpha}: \ \theta_o \le \theta \le \theta_o + \alpha, \quad \theta_o + \pi \le \theta \le \theta_o + \alpha + \pi \\ 0: \ \text{elsewhere} \end{cases} \tag{5.105}$$

The angle α is the sector width and the angle θ_o is an arbitrary offset angle. By applying Equations (5.91)–(5.93), the expressions for Λ, γ, and θ_{max} for this distribution are

$$\Lambda = 1, \quad \gamma = \frac{\sin\alpha}{\alpha}, \quad \theta_{max} = \theta_0 + \frac{\alpha}{2} \tag{5.106}$$

Note that the value of angular spread, Λ, is always 1. Regardless of the value of α, an equal amount of power arrives from opposite directions, producing no clear bias in the direction of multipath arrival.

The limiting case of $\alpha = 180°$ (omnidirectional propagation) results in an angular constriction of $\gamma = 0$. As α decreases, the angular distribution of power becomes more and more constricted. In the limit of $\alpha = 0$, the value of angular constriction reaches its maximum, $\gamma = 1$. This case corresponds to the above-mentioned instance of two-wave propagation. Figure 5.31 shows how the fading behavior changes as sector width α increases, making the fading rate more and more isotropic while the RMS average remains constant.

5.8.2.3 Ricean Channel Model

A Ricean channel model results from the addition of a single plane wave and numerous diffusely scattered waves [Ric48]. If the power of the scattered waves is assumed to be evenly distributed in azimuth, then the channel may be modeled by the following $p(\theta)$:

$$p(\theta) = \frac{P_T}{2\pi(K+1)}[1 + 2\pi K\delta(\theta - \theta_0)] \tag{5.107}$$

where K is the ratio of coherent to diffuse incoherent power, often referred to as the Ricean K-factor. By applying Equations (5.91)–(5.93), the expressions for Λ, γ, and θ_{max} for this distribution are

$$\Lambda = \frac{\sqrt{2K+1}}{K+1}, \quad \gamma = \frac{K}{2K+1}, \quad \theta_{max} = \theta_0 \tag{5.108}$$

Figure 5.32 depicts the spatial channel parameters, Λ and γ, as a function of K-factor. For very small K-factors, the channel appears to be omnidirectional ($\Lambda = 1$ and $\gamma = 0$). As the K-factor increases, the angular spread of the Ricean channel decreases and the angular constriction increases. This indicates that the overall fading rate in the Ricean channel decreases and that the differences between the minimum and maximum fading rate variances within the same local area but different directions increases.

5.8.3 Second-Order Statistics Using Shape Factors [Dur00]

With an understanding of how shape factors describe fading rate variances, it is possible to re-derive many of the basic second-order statistical measures of fading channels given in Section 5.7.3 in terms of the three shape factors. Level-crossing rates, average fade duration, spatial autocovariance,

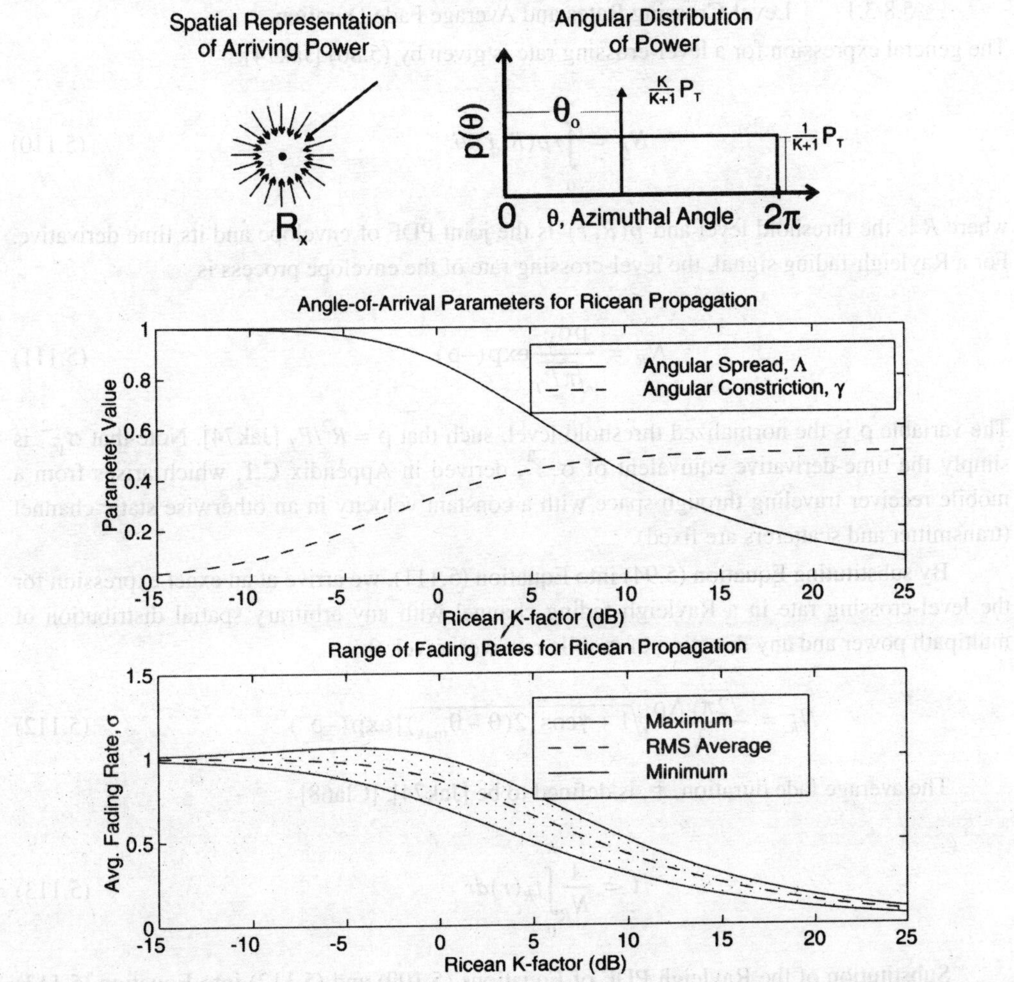

Figure 5.32 Fading properties of Ricean-model multipath components [from [Dur00] ©IEEE].

and coherence distance expressions that were originally derived under the assumption of omnidirectional multipath propagation will now be cast in terms of the angular spread, the angular constriction, and the azimuthal direction of maximum fading [Dur99], [Dur99a], [Dur99b].

The derivations focus on Rayleigh channels, since these types of channels are analytically tractable. A Rayleigh fading signal is one whose envelope, R, follows a Rayleigh PDF, $p_R(r)$, given by Equation (5.49) which can be expressed as

$$p_R(r) = r\sqrt{\frac{2}{P_T}}\exp\left(\frac{-r^2}{P_T}\right), \qquad r \geq 0 \tag{5.109}$$

where P_T is the average total power received in a local area (units of *volts-squared*).

5.8.3.1 Level-Crossing Rates and Average Fade Duration

The general expression for a level-crossing rate is given by (5.80) [Jak74]:

$$N_R = \int_0^{\infty} \dot{r} p(R, \dot{r}) d\dot{r} \tag{5.110}$$

where R is the threshold level and $p(R, \dot{r})$ is the joint PDF of envelope and its time derivative. For a Rayleigh-fading signal, the level-crossing rate of the envelope process is

$$N_R = \frac{\rho \sigma_{\dot{V}}}{\sqrt{\pi P_T}} \exp(-\rho) \tag{5.111}$$

The variable ρ is the normalized threshold level, such that $\rho = R^2/P_T$ [Jak74]. Note that $\sigma_{\dot{V}}^2$ is simply the time-derivative equivalent of $\sigma_{\dot{V}}{}'^2$, derived in Appendix C.1, which arises from a mobile receiver traveling through space with a constant velocity in an otherwise static channel (transmitter and scatterers are fixed).

By substituting Equation (5.94) into Equation (5.111), we arrive at an exact expression for the level-crossing rate in a Rayleigh fading channel with any arbitrary spatial distribution of multipath power and any direction of mobile receiver travel, θ:

$$N_R = \frac{\sqrt{2\pi} v \Lambda \rho}{\lambda} \sqrt{1 + \gamma \cos[2(\theta - \theta_{max})]} \exp(-\rho^2) \tag{5.112}$$

The average fade duration, $\bar{\tau}$, is defined to be [Jak74], [Cla68]

$$\bar{\tau} = \frac{1}{N_R} \int_0^R f_R(r) dr \tag{5.113}$$

Substitution of the Rayleigh PDF of Equations (5.109) and (5.112) into Equation (5.113) yields

$$\bar{\tau} = \frac{\lambda[\exp((\rho^2) - 1)]}{\sqrt{2\pi} v \Lambda \rho \sqrt{1 + \gamma \cos[2(\theta - \theta_{max})]}} \tag{5.114}$$

Equations (5.112) and (5.114) are useful tools for studying small-scale fading statistics in the presence of non-omnidirectional multipath, and yield identical results to those given in Section 5.7.3 when an omnidirectional channel is assumed.

5.8.3.2 Spatial Autocovariance

Another important second-order statistic is the spatial autocovariance of received voltage envelope. The autocovariance function determines the correlation of received voltage envelope as a function of change in receiver position and is useful for studies in spatial diversity [Jak74], [Vau93].

Appendix D develops an approximate expression for the spatial autocovariance function of envelope based on shape factors [Dur99a]. The approximation is given by

$$\rho(r, \theta) \approx \exp\left[-23\Lambda^2(1+\gamma\cos[2(\theta-\theta_{max})])\left(\frac{r}{\lambda}\right)^2\right] \quad (5.115)$$

Equation (5.115) allows us to estimate the envelope correlation between two points in space separated by a distance r along an azimuthal direction θ. The behavior of Equation (5.115) is benchmarked in Section 5.8.5 against several known analytical solutions presented in [Jak74].

5.8.3.3 Coherence Distance

Coherence distance, D_c, is the separation distance in space over which a fading channel appears to be unchanged. As shown in Chapter 7, coherence distance is important in the design of wireless receivers that employ spatial diversity to combat spatial selectivity. For mobile receivers, a similar parameter called *coherence time*, T_c, is the elapsed time over which a fading channel appears to be constant (see Equation (5.40.b)). For the case of a static channel, the coherence time of a mobile receiver may be calculated from the coherence distance ($T_c = D_c/v$, where v is the speed of the mobile).

Definitions for coherence distance may be based on the envelope autocovariance function. A convenient definition for the coherence distance, D_c, is the value that satisfies the equation $\rho(D_c) = 0.5$ [Ste94]. The classical value for coherence distance in an omnidirectional Rayleigh channel is given by

$$D_c \approx \frac{9\lambda}{16\pi} \quad (5.116)$$

Using the generalized autocovariance function of Equation (5.115) and evaluating $\rho(r, \theta)|_{r = D_c} = 0.5$ leads to a new definition of coherence distance:

$$D_c \approx \frac{\lambda\sqrt{\ln 2}}{\Lambda\sqrt{23(1-\gamma\cos[2(\theta-\theta_{max})])}} \quad (5.117)$$

For omnidirectional propagation, Equation (5.117) differs from Equation (5.116) by only −3.0%. Furthermore, Equation (5.117) captures the behavior of non-omnidirectional multipath. As angular spread, Λ, decreases, the coherence distance in a local area increases. As the angular constriction, γ, increases, the coherence distance develops a strong dependence on orientation, θ.

5.8.4 Applying Shape Factors to Wideband Channels

The theory presented in Section 5.8 was originally developed for a flat fading small scale assumption. By realizing that wideband channels may be modeled as discrete, resolvable multipath components in time delay, one can readily see how the theory may be applied to *each* resolvable time delay bin, as shown in Figure 5.4. The shape factor theory allows the fading statistics of individual multipath to be studied [Pat99].

5.8.5 Revisiting Classical Channel Models with Shape Factors

As a point of comparison, we now analyze three well-known cases of propagation that have analytical solutions as described in Sections 5.7.1–5.7.3 [Jak74]. The cases are analyzed using the shape factor approach as outlined in Section 5.7.4 for mobile receivers with speed v. This approach is shown to produce quick, comprehensive, and—most importantly—accurate solutions.

The first case corresponds to a narrowband receiver operating in a local area with multipath arriving from all directions, such that the angular distribution of power, $p(\theta)$, is a constant. The receiver antenna is assumed to be an omnidirectional whip, oriented perpendicular to the ground. Due to the vertical electric-field polarization of the whip antenna, this propagation scenario is referred to as the E_z-case [Cla68].

The second two cases correspond to the same narrowband receiver in the same omnidirectional multipath channel, but with a small loop antenna mounted atop the receiver such that the plane of the loop is perpendicular to the ground. The antenna pattern of the small loop antenna attenuates the arriving multipath such that the angular distribution of power becomes

$$p(\theta) = A\sin^2\theta \tag{5.118}$$

where A is some arbitrary gain constant. Unlike the omnidirectional E_z-case, the statistics of this propagation scenario will depend on the direction of travel by the receiver. The H_x-case will refer to a receiver traveling in a direction perpendicular to the main lobes of the loop antenna pattern ($\theta = 0$). The H_y-case will refer to a receiver traveling in a direction parallel to the main lobes ($\theta = \pi/2$). Figure 5.33 illustrates the E_z, H_x, and H_y cases for the modeled receiver antennas.

The first step is to calculate the three spatial parameters from the angular distribution of power, $p(\theta)$, using Equations (5.91)–(5.93). The spatial parameters for the E_z-case are Λ, γ, and $\theta_{max} = 0$. Since this case is omnidirectional, the angular spread is at a maximum ($\Lambda = 1$) and the angular constriction is at a minimum ($\gamma = 0$). For the H_x- and H_y-cases, the spatial parameters are

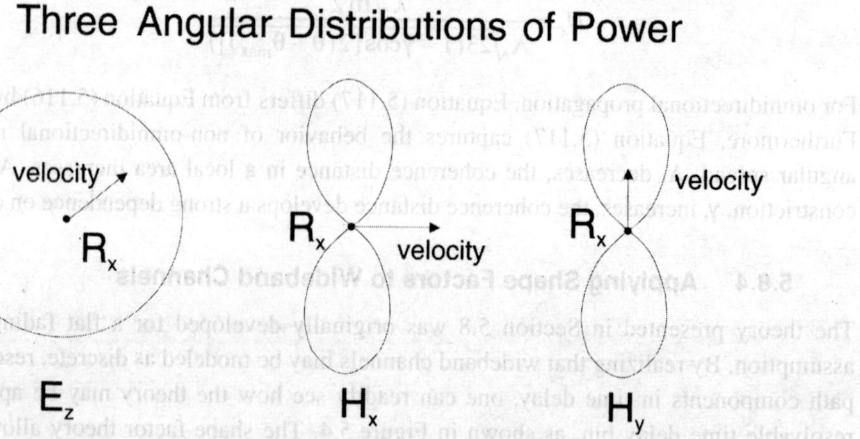

Figure 5.33 Three different multipath-induced mobile-fading scenarios [from [Dur00] ©IEEE].

$\Lambda = 1$, $\gamma = 1/2$, and $\theta_{max} = \pi/2$. Since the impinging multipath have no clear bias in *one* direction, the angular spread is at a maximum just like the E_z-case. However, there is clearly a bias in *two* directions, resulting in an increased angular constriction of $\gamma = 1/2$.

After substitution of these parameters into Equation (5.112) along with the appropriate direction of mobile travel, the level-crossing rates for the three cases become

$$E_z: \quad N_R = \frac{\sqrt{2\pi}\nu\rho}{\lambda}\exp(-\rho^2) \tag{5.119}$$

$$H_x: \quad N_R = \frac{\sqrt{\pi}\nu\rho}{\lambda}\exp(-\rho^2) \tag{5.120}$$

$$H_y: \quad N_R = \frac{\sqrt{3\pi}\nu\rho}{\lambda}\exp(-\rho^2) \tag{5.121}$$

The corresponding average fade durations are

$$E_z: \quad \bar{\tau} = \frac{\lambda}{\sqrt{2\pi}\nu\rho}[\exp(\rho^2) - 1] \tag{5.122}$$

$$H_x: \quad \bar{\tau} = \frac{\lambda}{\sqrt{\pi}\nu\rho}[\exp(\rho^2) - 1] \tag{5.123}$$

$$H_y: \quad \bar{\tau} = \frac{\lambda}{\sqrt{3\pi}\nu\rho}[\exp(\rho^2) - 1] \tag{5.124}$$

These expressions exactly match the original solutions presented by Clarke in [Cla68].

Now substitute the channel shape factors into the approximate spatial autocovariance functions in Equation (5.115). The results for the three cases are

$$E_z: \quad \rho(r) = \exp\left[-23\left(\frac{r}{\lambda}\right)^2\right] \tag{5.125}$$

$$H_x: \quad \rho(r) = \exp\left[-11.5\left(\frac{r}{\lambda}\right)^2\right] \tag{5.126}$$

$$H_y: \quad \rho(r) = \exp\left[-34.5\left(\frac{r}{\lambda}\right)^2\right] \tag{5.127}$$

These three functions are compared to their more rigorous analytical solutions in Figure 5.34 through Figure 5.36. Note that all three model the spatial autocovariance function consistent with the approximation made in the derivation of Equation (5.115). The behavior is nearly exact for values of r equal to or less than a correlation distance.

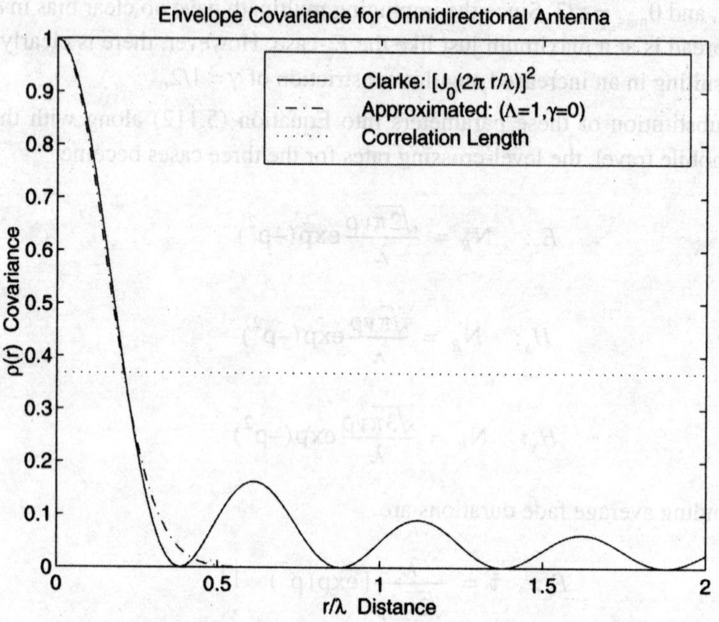

Figure 5.34 Comparison between Clarke theoretical and the shape theory approximation for envelope autocovariance functions for E_z-case [from [Dur00] ©IEEE].

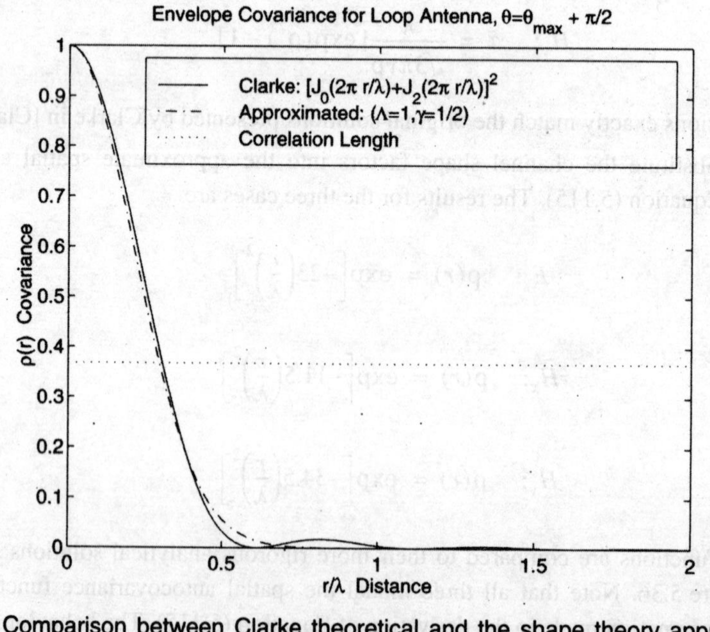

Figure 5.35 Comparison between Clarke theoretical and the shape theory approximation for envelope autocovariance functions for H_x-case [from [Dur00] ©IEEE].

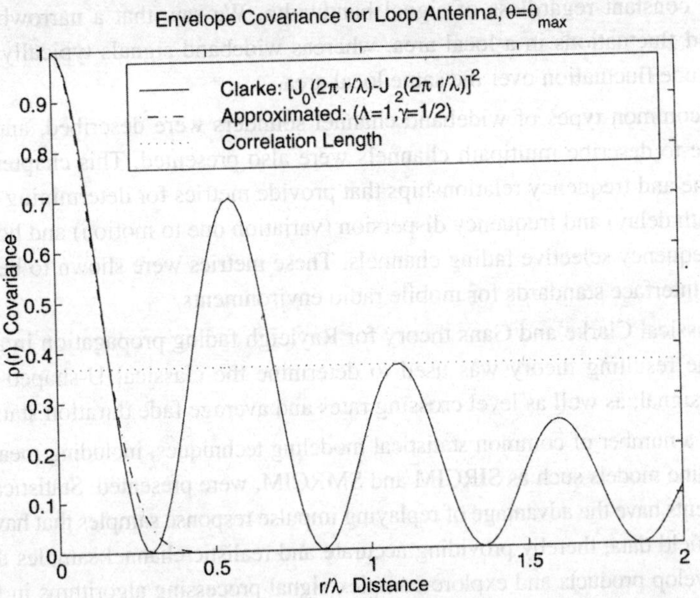

Figure 5.36 Comparison between Clarke theoretical and approximate envelope autocovariance functions for H_y-case [from [Dur00] ©IEEE].

The shape factor technique for finding fading statistics is an intuitive way to relate the physical channel characteristics to the fading behavior. In the previous examples, the spatial parameters may be calculated analytically or even estimated intuitively by simply looking at the distributions of multipath power in Figure 5.33. The use of spatial parameters to find level crossing rate, average fade duration, and spatial autocovariance is quite simple when compared to the full analytical solutions of the E_z, H_x, and H_y-cases presented in [Jak74]. The proposed solution is also more comprehensive. For example, once the shape factors have been found, Equations (5.112), (5.114), and (5.115) provide statistics for *all* directions of travel for the H_x- and H_y-cases, and not just specific directions such as $\theta = 0$ or $\theta = \pi/2$. Thus, specific fading behaviors for various directions of receiver motion are modeled easily.

The solution form of Equations (5.112), (5.114), and (5.115) reveals an interesting property about statistics in Rayleigh-fading channels. Since the three shape factors only depend on low-order Fourier coefficients, many of the second-order statistics of Rayleigh-fading channels are insensitive to the higher-order multipath structure. The general biases of angular spread and angular constriction truly dominate the space and time evolution of these fading processes.

5.9 Summary

Small-scale fading impacts the time delay and the dynamic fading range of signal levels within a small local area at a receiver antenna. This chapter demonstrated the important principle that local received power is not a function of bandwidth, but rather the average signal level within a local area is constant regardless of signal bandwidth. We saw that a narrowband signal may undergo rapid fluctuations in a local area, whereas wideband signals typically have very little signal amplitude fluctuation over the same local area.

Three common types of wideband channel sounders were described, and measurements that are made to describe multipath channels were also presented. This chapter also presented important time and frequency relationships that provide metrics for determining the time dispersion (multipath delay) and frequency dispersion (variation due to motion) and how they relate to flat versus frequency selective fading channels. These metrics were shown to be valuable in the design of air interface standards for mobile radio environments.

The classical Clarke and Gans theory for Rayleigh fading propagation in a local area was given, and the resulting theory was used to determine the classical U-shaped spectrum for a mobile radio signal, as well as level crossing rates and average fade duration statistics.

Finally, a number of common statistical modeling techniques, including measurement-based tapped delay line models such as SIRCIM and SMRCIM, were presented. Statistical models based on measurements have the advantage of replaying impulse response samples that have similar statistics to actual field data, thereby providing accurate and realistic channel samples that can be used reliably to develop products and explore complex signal processing algorithms in the lab, without the need of actual working hardware.

This chapter concluded by presenting a new and powerful theory that uses knowledge of the distribution of multipath energy arriving azimuthally at a receiver antenna. Multipath shape factor theory provides an easy, intuitive, and accurate method for analyzing small-scale fading channels with non-omnidirectional multipath propagation. The theory also has many implications for the measurement of wireless channels. For example, fading along specific but perpendicular directions may be measured in a local area with a simple, non-coherent receiver to calculate various multipath angle-of-arrival and fading rate characteristics. Conversely, angle-of-arrival characteristics may be measured with a directional antenna to calculate local area fading behavior.

All of the above small-scale channel modeling topics are critical in the design of a practical air interface, as they impact the selection of modulation data rates and modulation methods for time varying mobile channels. Modulation techniques are the subject of the next chapter.

5.10 Problems

5.1 Determine the maximum and minimum spectral frequencies received from a stationary GSM transmitter that has a center frequency of exactly 1950.000000 MHz, assuming that the receiver is traveling at speeds of: (a) 1 km/hr; (b) 5 km/hr; (c) 100 km/hr; and (d) 1000 km/hr.

5.2 Describe all the physical circumstances that relate to a stationary transmitter and a moving receiver such that the Doppler shift at the receiver is equal to: (a) 0 Hz; (b) $f_{d_{max}}$; (c) $-f_{d_{max}}$; and (d) $f_{d_{max/2}}$

5.3 Using first principles from linear system theory and the definition of the complex envelope, prove that Figure 5.3 is correct. That is, prove that for bandpass signals x(t) and y(t), Equation (5.9) is indeed valid. This is the key principle used in simulation and DSP.

5.4 Draw a block diagram of a binary spread spectrum sliding correlator multipath measurement system. Explain in words how it is used to measure power delay profiles.

(a) If the transmitter chip period is 10 ns, the PN sequence has length 1023, and a 6 GHz carrier is used at the transmitter, find the time between maximal correlation and the slide factor if the receiver uses a PN sequence clock that is 30 kHz slower than the transmitter.

(b) If an oscilloscope is used to display one complete cycle of the PN sequence (that is, if two successive maximal correlation peaks are to be displayed on the oscilloscope), and if 10 divisions are provided on the oscilloscope time axis, what is the most appropriate sweep setting (in seconds/division) to be used?

(c) What is the required IF passband bandwidth for this system? How is this much better than a direct pulse system with similar time resolution?

5.5 Given that the coherence bandwidth is approximated by Equation (5.39), show that a flat fading channel occurs when $T_s \geq 10\,\sigma_\tau$. Hint: Note that B_c is an RF bandwidth, and assume that T_s is the reciprocal of the baseband signal bandwidth.

5.6 If a particular modulation provides suitable BER performance whenever $\sigma_\tau / T_s \leq 0.1$ determine the smallest symbol period T_s (and thus the greatest symbol rate) that may be sent through RF channels shown in Figure P5.6, without using an equalizer.

5.7 If a baseband binary message with a bit rate $R_b = 100$ kbps is modulated by an RF carrier using BPSK, answer the following:

(a) Find the range of values required for the rms delay spread of the channel such that the received signal is a flat-fading signal.

(b) If the modulation carrier frequency is 5.8 GHz, what is the coherence time of the channel, assuming a vehicle speed of 30 miles per hour?

(c) For your answer in (b), is the channel "fast" or "slow" fading?

(d) Given your answer in (b), how many bits are sent while the channel appears "static"?

(e) A CDMA Rake receiver is able to exploit multipath when the channel is (circle all that apply)
(a) flat; (b) slow; (c) fast; (d) frequency selective

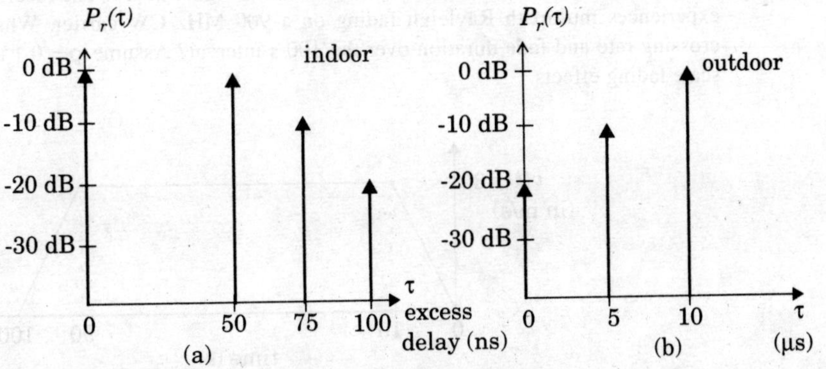

Figure P5.6 Two channel responses for Problem 5.6.

5.8 For the power delay profiles in Figure P5.6, estimate the 90% correlation and 50% correlation coherence bandwidths.

5.9 Approximately how large can the rms delay spread be in order for a binary modulated signal with a bit rate of 25 kbps to operate without an equalizer? What about an 8-PSK system with a bit rate of 75 kbps?

5.10 Given that a Rayleigh-faded mobile radio signal has a level crossing rate of $N_r = \sqrt{2\pi} f_m \rho e^{-\rho^2}$, find the value of ρ for which N_r is a maximum.

5.11 Given that the probability density function of a Rayleigh distributed envelope is given by $p(r) = \frac{r}{\sigma^2}\exp\left(\frac{-r^2}{2\sigma^2}\right)$, where σ^2 is the variance, show that the cumulative distribution function is given as $p(r<R) = 1 - \exp\left(\frac{-R^2}{2\sigma^2}\right)$. Find the percentage of time that a signal is 10 dB or more below the rms value for a Rayleigh fading signal.

5.12 The fading characteristics of a CW carrier in an urban area are to be measured. The following assumptions are made:

(1) The mobile receiver uses a simple vertical monopole.

(2) Large-scale fading due to path loss is ignored.

(3) The mobile has no line-of-sight path to the base station.

(4) The pdf of the received signal follows a Rayleigh distribution.

(a) Derive the ratio of the desired signal level to the rms signal level that maximizes the level crossing rate. Express your answer in dB.

(b) Assuming the maximum velocity of the mobile is 50 km/hr, and the carrier frequency is 900 MHz, determine the maximum number of times the signal envelope will fade below the level found in (a) during a 1 minute test.

(c) How long, on average, will each fade in (b) last?

5.13 A vehicle receives a 900 MHz transmission while traveling at a constant velocity for 10 s. The average fade duration for a signal level 10 dB below the rms level is 1 ms. How far does the vehicle travel during the 10 s interval? How many fades does the signal undergo at the rms threshold level during a 10 s interval? Assume that the local mean remains constant during travel.

5.14 An automobile moves with velocity $v(t)$ shown in Figure P5.14. The received mobile signal experiences multipath Rayleigh fading on a 900 MHz CW carrier. What is the average crossing rate and fade duration over the 100 s interval? Assume ρ = 0.1 and ignore large-scale fading effects.

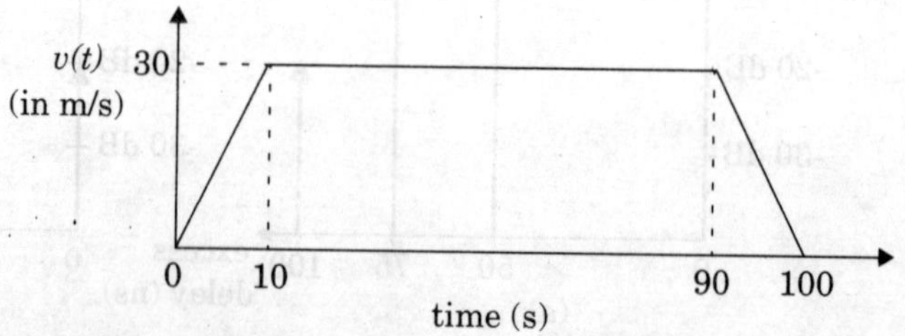

Figure P5.14 Graph of velocity of mobile.

5.15 For a mobile receiver operating at frequency of 860 MHz and moving at 100 km/hr

(a) sketch the Doppler spectrum if a CW signal is transmitted and indicate the maximum and minimum frequencies

(b) calculate the level crossing rate and average fade duration if $\rho = -20$ dB.

5.16 For the following digital wireless systems, estimate the maximum rms delay spread for which no equalizer is required at the receiver (neglect channel coding, antenna diversity, or use of extremely low power levels).

System	RF Data Rate	Modulation
USDC	48.6 kbps	$\pi/4$DQPSK
GSM	270.833 kbps	GMSK
DECT	1152 kbps	GMSK

5.17 In the Clarke and Gans model for small-scale fading, the E-field of the vertically polarized signal is given by

$$E_z(t) = E_0 \sum_{n=1}^{\infty} C_n \cos(2\pi f_c t + \theta_n)$$

where $\tau_n = 2\pi f_n t + \phi_n$ and

$$\sum_{n=1}^{N} C_n^2 = 1$$

and f_n is the Doppler shift of the nth plane wave, given by $f_n = v/\lambda \cos \alpha_n$.

(a) Write E_z in terms of narrowband in-phase and quadrature components $T_c(t)$ and $T_s(t)$ such that $E_z(t) = T_c(t) \cos 2\pi f_c t - T_s(t) \sin 2\pi f_c t$. Note that $T_c(t)$ and $T_s(t)$ are uncorrelated zero-mean Gaussian random variables at any instant of time.

(b) What is the distribution of ϕ_n?

(c) Are each of the C_n's a random variable or a random process?

(d) Prove that $\overline{|E_z(t)|^2} = (E_0^2)/2$.

(e) Let $|E_z(t)| = r$. Write the probability distribution of r. What is the name of this distribution?

(f) If the term A $\cos 2\pi f_c t$ is added to $E_z(t)$, where A is a constant, what type of fading will r undergo?

(g) Using your result in (f), find the K-factor, where $K = A^2/2\sigma^2$, for the case where $A = 5E_0$.

5.18 Derive the RF Doppler spectrum for a $5/8\lambda$ vertical monopole receiving a CW signal using the models by Clarke and Gans. Plot the RF Doppler spectrum and the corresponding base-band spectrum out of an envelope detector. Assume isotropic scattering and unit average received power.

5.19 Show that the magnitude (envelope) of the sum of two independent identically distributed complex (quadrature) Gaussian sources is Rayleigh distributed. Assume that the Gaussian sources are zero mean and have unit variance.

5.20 Design a Rayleigh fading simulator: Write a MATLAB program that simulates Rayleigh fading, using the frequency domain method described in Figure 5.24. Assume the maximum Doppler frequency is 200 Hz. Confirm that the level crossing rates and average fade durations of your simulated waveforms agree with Example 5.8. Explain any discrepancies you observed in your simulated outputs. Turn in printouts of your source code, waveform samples, and other pertinent results.

5.21 How would you convert your simulation of Problem 5.20 into a Ricean fading simulator? You do not need to actually do it, just comment on specifics.

5.22 Using the method described in Chapter 5, generate a time sequence of 8192 sample values of a Rayleigh fading signal for

(a) $f_d = 20$ Hz, and

(b) $f_d = 200$ Hz.

5.23 Generate 100 sample functions of fading data described in Problem 5.22, and compare the simulated and theoretical values of the resulting CDF of the data set. Using your data, find R_{RMS}, N_R, and $\bar{\tau}$ for $\rho = 1, 0.1$, and 0.01. Do your simulations agree with theory? They should!

5.24 Recreate the plots of the CDFs shown in Figure 5.17, starting with the pdfs for Rayleigh, Ricean, and log-normal distributions.

5.25 Plot the probability density function and the CDF for a Ricean distribution having (a) $K = 10$ dB and (b) $K = 3$ dB. The abscissa of the CDF plot should be labeled in dB relative to the median signal level for both plots. Note that the median value for a Ricean distribution changes as K changes.

5.26 Based on your answer in Problem 5.25, if the median RSSI is −70 dBm, what is the likelihood that a signal greater than −80 dBm will be received in a Ricean fading channel having (a) $K = 10$ dB, and (b) $K = 3$ dB?

5.27 The local average power delay profile in a particular environment is found to be

$$P(\tau) = \sum_{n=0}^{2} \frac{10^{-6}}{n^2+1}\delta(\tau - n10^{-6})$$

(a) Sketch the Power Delay Profile of the channel in dBm.

(b) What is the local average power in dBm?

(c) What is the rms delay spread of the channel?

(d) If 256 QAM modulation having a bit rate of 2 Megabits per second is applied to the channel, will the modulation undergo flat or frequency selective fading? Explain your answer.

(e) Over what bandwidth will the channel appear to have constant gain?

5.28 A local spatial average of a power delay profile measured at 900 MHz is shown in Figure P5.28.

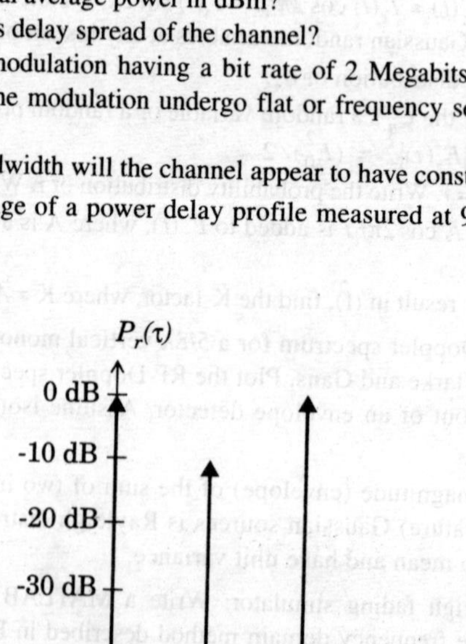

Figure P5.28 Power delay profile.

(a) Determine the rms delay spread and mean excess delay for the channel.

(b) Determine the maximum excess delay (20 dB).

(c) If the channel is to be used with a modulation that requires an equalizer whenever the symbol duration T is less than 10 σ_τ, determine the maximum RF symbol rate that can be supported without requiring an equalizer.

(d) If a mobile traveling at 30 km/hr receives a signal through the channel, determine the time over which the channel appears stationary (or at least highly correlated).

5.29 A flat Rayleigh fading signal at 6 GHz is received by a mobile traveling at 80 km/hr.

(a) Determine the number of positive-going zero crossings about the rms value that occur over a 5 s interval.

(b) Determine the average duration of a fade below the rms level.

(c) Determine the average duration of a fade at a level of 20 dB below the rms value.

5.30 For each of the three scenarios below, decide if the received signal is best described as undergoing fast fading, frequency selective fading, or flat fading.

(a) A binary modulation has a data rate of 500 kbps, $f_c = 1$ GHz and a typical urban radio channel is used.

(b) A binary modulation has a data rate of 5 kbps, $f_c = 1$ GHz and a typical urban radio channel is used to provide communications to cars moving on a highway.

(c) A binary modulation has a data rate of 10 bps, $f_c = 1$ GHz and a typical urban radio channel is used to provide communications to cars moving on a highway.

5.31 Using computer simulation, create a Rayleigh fading simulator that has three independent Rayleigh fading multipath components, each having variable multipath time delay and average power. Then convolve a random binary bit stream through your simulator and observe the time waveforms of the output stream. You may wish to use several samples for each bit (seven is a good number). Observe the effects of multipath spread as you vary the bit period and time delay of the channel.

5.32 Based on concepts taught in this chapter, propose methods that could be used by a base station to determine the vehicular speed of a mobile user. Such methods are useful for handoff algorithms.

5.33 From the shape factor theory described in Section 5.8, describe the physical significance of angular spread, Λ, and determine two examples of $p(\theta)$ that produce: (a) $\Lambda = 1$; (b) $\Lambda = 0$.

5.34 Using Equation (5.117), determine the coherence distance D_c for each of the four $p(\theta)$ examples you found in Problem 5.33. Note that you must assume a particular direction of travel. Assume $\lambda = 10$ cm. How does the direction of travel, relative to the arriving multipath, impact D_c? Explore by proposing four different directions of travel for each of the four $p(\theta)$ functions and determine D_c for each case.

CHAPTER 6

Modulation Techniques for Mobile Radio

M*odulation* is the process of encoding information from a message source in a manner suitable for transmission. It generally involves translating a baseband message signal (called the *source*) to a bandpass signal at frequencies that are very high when compared to the baseband frequency. The bandpass signal is called the *modulated* signal and the baseband message signal is called the *modulating* signal. Modulation may be done by varying the amplitude, phase, or frequency of a high frequency carrier in accordance with the amplitude of the message signal. *Demodulation* is the process of extracting the baseband message from the carrier so that it may be processed and interpreted by the intended receiver (also called the *sink*).

This chapter describes various modulation techniques that are used in mobile communication systems. Analog modulation schemes that are employed in first generation mobile radio systems, as well as digital modulation schemes proposed for use in present and future systems, are covered. Since digital modulation offers numerous benefits and is already being used to replace conventional analog systems, the primary emphasis of this chapter is on digital modulation schemes. However, since analog systems are in widespread use, and will continue to exist, they are treated first.

Modulation is a topic that is covered in great detail in various communications textbooks. Here, the coverage focuses on modulation and demodulation as it applies to mobile radio systems. A large variety of modulation techniques have been studied for use in mobile radio communications systems, and research is ongoing. Given the hostile fading and multipath conditions in the mobile radio channel, designing a modulation scheme that is resistant to mobile channel impairments is a challenging task. Since the ultimate goal of a modulation technique is to transport the message signal through a radio channel with the best possible quality while occupying the least amount of radio spectrum, new advances in digital signal processing continue to bring about new forms of modulation and demodulation. This chapter describes many practical modulation schemes, receiver architectures, design tradeoffs, and their performance under various types of channel impairments.

6.1 Frequency Modulation vs. Amplitude Modulation

Frequency modulation (FM) is the most popular analog modulation technique used in mobile radio systems. In FM, the amplitude of the modulated carrier signal is kept constant while its frequency is varied by the modulating message signal. Thus, FM signals have all their information in the *phase* or *frequency* of the carrier. As shown subsequently, this provides a nonlinear and very rapid improvement in reception quality once a certain minimum received signal level, called the FM threshold, is achieved. In amplitude modulation (AM) schemes, there is a linear relationship between the quality of the received signal and the power of the received signal since AM signals superimpose the exact relative amplitudes of the modulating signal onto the carrier. Thus, AM signals have all their information in the *amplitude* of the carrier. FM offers many advantages over amplitude modulation (AM), which makes it a better choice for many mobile radio applications.

Frequency modulation has better noise immunity when compared to amplitude modulation. Since signals are represented as frequency variations rather than amplitude variations, FM signals are less susceptible to atmospheric and impulse noise, which tend to cause rapid fluctuations in the amplitude of the received radio signal. Also, message amplitude variations do not carry information in FM, so burst noise does not affect FM system performance as much as AM systems, provided that the FM received signal is above the FM threshold. Chapter 5 illustrated how small-scale fading can cause rapid fluctuations in the received signal, thus FM offers superior qualitative performance in fading when compared to AM. Also, in an FM system, it is possible to tradeoff bandwidth occupancy for improved noise performance. Unlike AM, in an FM system, the *modulation index*, and hence bandwidth occupancy, can be varied to obtain greater signal-to-noise performance. It can be shown that, under certain conditions, the FM signal-to-noise ratio improves 6 dB for each doubling of bandwidth occupancy. This ability of an FM system to trade bandwidth for SNR is perhaps the most important reason for its superiority over AM. However, AM signals are able to occupy less bandwidth as compared to FM signals, since the transmission system is linear. In modern AM systems, susceptibility to fading has been dramatically improved through the use of in-band pilot tones which are transmitted along with the standard AM signal. The modern AM receiver is able to monitor the pilot tone and rapidly adjust the receiver gain to compensate for the amplitude fluctuations.

An FM signal is a *constant envelope* signal, due to the fact that the envelope of the carrier does not change with changes in the modulating signal. Hence the transmitted power of an FM signal is constant regardless of the amplitude of the message signal. The constant envelope of the transmitted signal allows efficient Class C power amplifiers to be used for RF power amplification of FM. In AM, however, it is critical to maintain linearity between the applied message and the amplitude of the transmitted signal, thus linear Class A or AB amplifiers, which are not as power efficient, must be used.

The issue of amplifier efficiency is extremely important when designing portable subscriber terminals since the battery life of the portable is tied to the power amplifier efficiency. Typical efficiencies for Class C amplifiers are 70%, meaning that 70% of the applied DC power to the final amplifier circuit is converted into radiated RF power. Class A or AB amplifiers have efficiencies on the order of 30-40%. This implies that for the same battery, constant envelope FM modulation may provide twice as much talk time as AM.

Frequency modulation exhibits a so-called *capture effect* characteristic. The capture effect is a direct result of the rapid nonlinear improvement in received quality for an increase in received power. If two signals in the same frequency band are available at an FM receiver, the one appearing at the higher received signal level is accepted and demodulated, while the weaker one is rejected. This inherent ability to pick up the strongest signal and reject the rest makes FM systems very resistant to co-channel interference and provides excellent subjective received quality. In AM systems, on the other hand, all of the interferers are received at once and must be discriminated after the demodulation process.

While FM systems have many advantages over AM systems, they also have certain disadvantages. FM systems require a wider frequency band in the transmitting media (generally several times as large as that needed for AM) in order to obtain the advantages of reduced noise and capture effect. FM transmitter and receiver equipment is also more complex than that used by amplitude modulation systems. Although frequency modulation systems are tolerant to certain types of signal and circuit nonlinearities, special attention must be given to phase characteristics. Both AM and FM may be demodulated using inexpensive noncoherent detectors. AM is easily demodulated using an envelope detector whereas FM is demodulated using a discriminator or slope detector. AM may be detected coherently with a product detector, and in such cases AM can outperform FM in weak signal conditions since FM must be received above threshold.

6.2 Amplitude Modulation

In amplitude modulation, the amplitude of a high frequency carrier signal is varied in accordance to the instantaneous amplitude of the modulating message signal. If $A_c \cos(2\pi f_c t)$ is the carrier signal and $m(t)$ is the modulating message signal, the AM signal can be represented as

$$s_{AM}(t) = A_c[1 + m(t)]\cos(2\pi f_c t) \tag{6.1}$$

The *modulation index k* of an AM signal is defined as the ratio of the peak message signal amplitude to the peak carrier amplitude. For a sinusoidal modulating signal $m(t) = (A_m / A_c)\cos(2\pi f_m t)$, the modulation index is given by

$$k = \frac{A_m}{A_c} \tag{6.2}$$

The modulation index is often expressed as a percentage, and is called *percentage modulation.* Figure 6.1 shows a sinusoidal modulating signal and the corresponding AM signal. For the case shown in Figure 6.1, $A_m = 0.5A_c$, and the signal is said to be 50% modulated. A percentage of

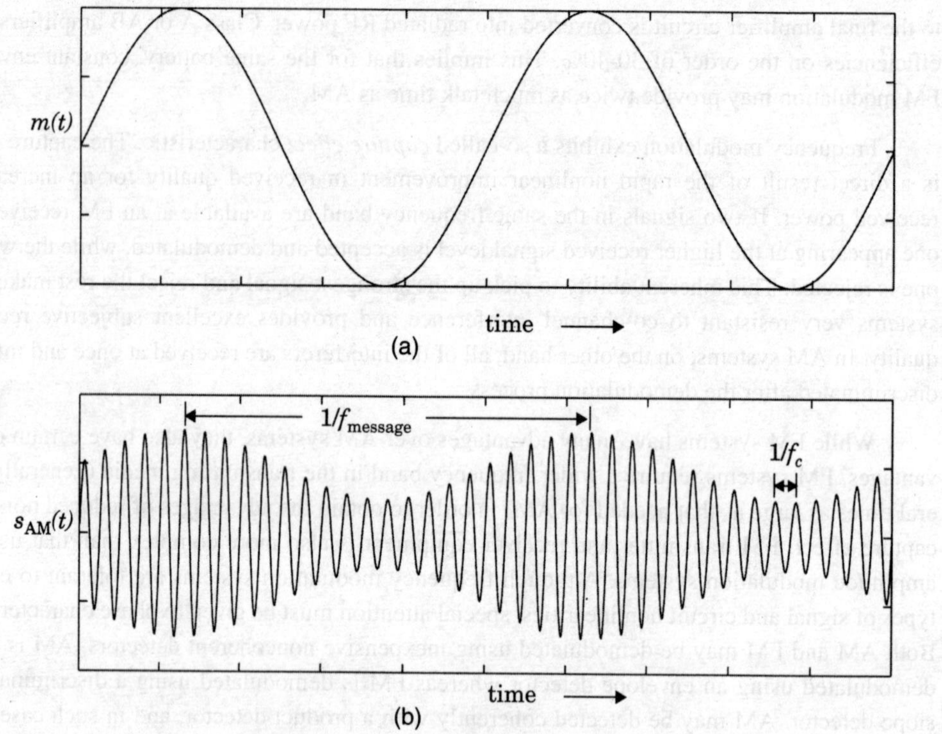

Figure 6.1 (a) A sinusoidal modulating signal and (b) the corresponding AM signal with modulation index 0.5.

modulation greater than 100% will distort the message signal if detected by an envelope detector. Equation (6.1) may be equivalently expressed as

$$s_{AM}(t) = Re\{g(t)\exp(j2\pi f_c t)\} \tag{6.3}$$

where $g(t)$ is the complex envelope of the AM signal given by

$$g(t) = A_c[1 + m(t)] \tag{6.4}$$

The spectrum of an AM signal can be shown to be

$$S_{AM}(f) = \frac{1}{2}A_c[\delta(f-f_c) + M(f-f_c) + \delta(f+f_c) + M(f+f_c)] \tag{6.5}$$

where $\delta(\bullet)$ is the unit impulse function, and $M(f)$ is the message signal spectrum. Figure 6.2 shows an AM spectrum for a message signal whose magnitude spectrum is a triangular function. As seen from Figure 6.2, the AM spectrum consists of an impulse at the carrier frequency, and two sidebands which replicate the message spectrum. The sidebands above and below the carrier frequency are called the *upper* and *lower* sidebands, respectively. The RF bandwidth of an AM signal is equal to

$$B_{AM} = 2f_m \tag{6.6}$$

where f_m is the maximum frequency contained in the modulating message signal. The total power in an AM signal can be shown to be

$$P_{AM} = \frac{1}{2}A_c^2[1 + 2\langle m(t)\rangle + \langle m^2(t)\rangle] \tag{6.7}$$

where $\langle \bullet \rangle$ represents the average value. If the modulating signal is $m(t) = k\cos(2\pi f_m t)$, Equation (6.7) may be simplified as

$$P_{AM} = \frac{1}{2}A_c^2[1 + P_m] = P_c\left[1 + \frac{k^2}{2}\right] \tag{6.8}$$

where $P_c = A_c^2/2$ is the power in the carrier signal, $P_m = \langle m^2(t)\rangle$ is the power in the modulating signal *m(t)*, and k is the modulation index.

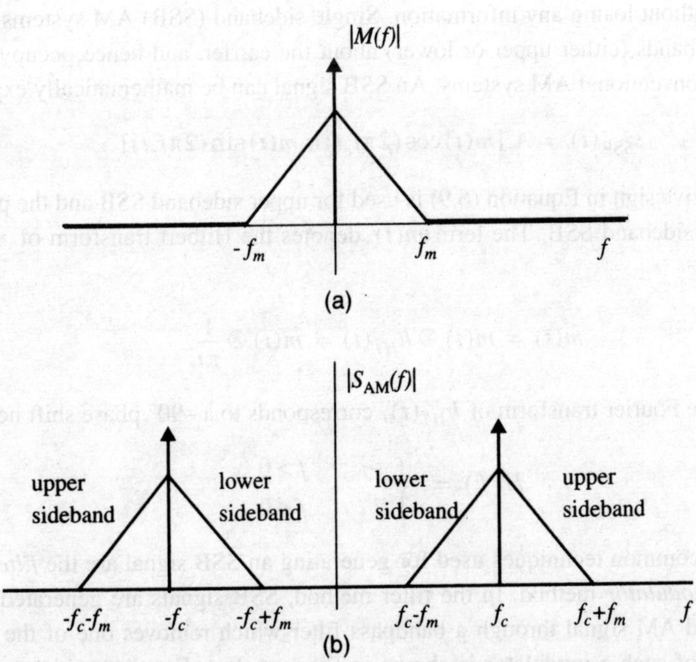

Figure 6.2 (a) Spectrum of a message signal; (b) spectrum of the corresponding AM signal.

Example 6.1

A zero mean sinusoidal message is applied to a transmitter that radiates an AM signal with 10 kW power. Compute the carrier power if the modulation index is 0.6. What percentage of the total power is in the carrier? Calculate the power in each sideband.

Solution

Using Equation (6.8), we have

$$P_c = \frac{P_{AM}}{1+k^2/2} = \frac{10}{1+0.6^2/2} = 8.47 \text{ kW}$$

Percentage power in the carrier is

$$\frac{P_c}{P_{AM}} \times 100 = \frac{8.47}{10} \times 100 = 84.7\,\%$$

Power in each sideband is given by

$$\frac{1}{2}(P_{AM} - P_c) = 0.5 \times (10 - 8.47) = 0.765 \text{ kW}$$

6.2.1 Single Sideband AM

Since both the sidebands of an AM signal carry the same information, it is possible to remove one of them without losing any information. Single sideband (SSB) AM systems transmit only one of the sidebands (either upper or lower) about the carrier, and hence occupy only half the bandwidth of conventional AM systems. An SSB signal can be mathematically expressed as

$$s_{SSB}(t) = A_c[m(t)\cos(2\pi f_c t) \mp \hat{m}(t)\sin(2\pi f_c t)] \tag{6.9}$$

where the negative sign in Equation (6.9) is used for upper sideband SSB and the positive sign is used for lower sideband SSB. The term $\hat{m}(t)$ denotes the Hilbert transform of $m(t)$ which is given by

$$\hat{m}(t) = m(t) \otimes h_{HT}(t) = m(t) \otimes \frac{1}{\pi t} \tag{6.10}$$

and $H_{HT}(f)$, the Fourier transform of $h_{HT}(t)$, corresponds to a –90° phase shift network

$$H(f) = \begin{cases} -j & f > 0 \\ j & f < 0 \end{cases} \tag{6.11}$$

The two common techniques used for generating an SSB signal are the *filter method* and the *balanced modulator* method. In the filter method, SSB signals are generated by passing a double sideband AM signal through a bandpass filter which removes one of the sidebands. A block diagram of such a modulator is shown in Figure 6.3(a). Excellent sideband suppression can be obtained using crystal filters at an intermediate frequency (IF).

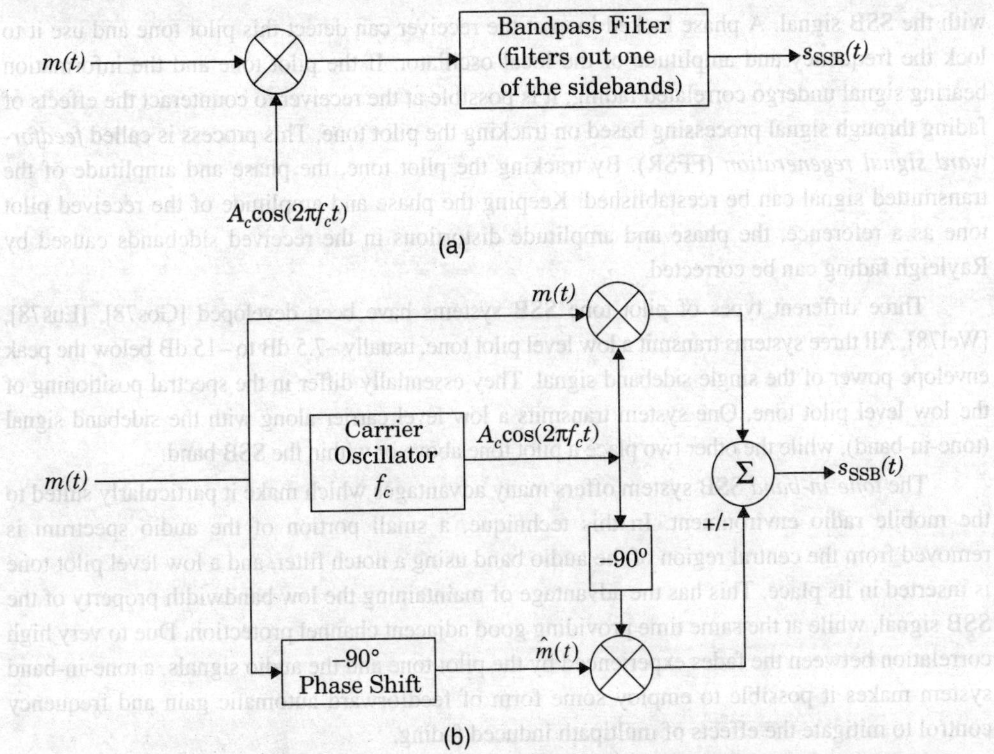

Figure 6.3 Generation of SSB using (a) a sideband filter and (b) a balanced modulator.

Figure 6.3(b) shows a block diagram of a balanced modulator which is a direct implementation of Equation (6.9). The modulating signal is split into two identical signals, one which modulates the in-phase carrier and the other which is passed through a –90° phase shifter before modulating a quadrature carrier. The sign used for the quadrature component determines whether USSB or LSSB is transmitted.

6.2.2 Pilot Tone SSB

While SSB systems have the advantage of being very bandwidth efficient, their performance in fading channels is very poor. For proper detection of SSB signals, the frequency of the oscillator at the product detector mixer in the receiver must be the same as that of the incoming carrier frequency. If these two frequencies are not identical, product detection will lead to shifting the demodulated spectrum by an amount equal to the difference in the frequencies between the incoming carrier and local oscillator. This leads to an increase or decrease in the pitch of the received audio signal. In conventional SSB receivers, it is difficult to electronically tune the local oscillator frequency to the identical frequency of the incoming carrier. Doppler spreading and Rayleigh fading can shift the signal spectrum causing pitch and amplitude variations in the received signal. These problems may be overcome by transmitting a low level pilot tone along with the SSB signal. A phase locked loop at the receiver can detect this pilot tone and use it to lock the frequency and amplitude of the local oscillator. If the pilot tone and the information bearing signal undergo correlated fading, it is possible at the receiver to counteract the effects of fading through signal processing based on tracking the pilot tone. This process is called *feedforward signal regeneration* (FFSR). By tracking the pilot tone, the phase and amplitude of the transmitted signal can be reestablished. Keeping the phase and amplitude of the received pilot tone as a reference, the phase and amplitude distortions in the received sidebands caused by Rayleigh fading can be corrected.

Three different types of pilot tone SSB systems have been developed [Gos78], [Lus78], [Wel78]. All three systems transmit a low level pilot tone, usually –7.5 dB to –15 dB below the peak envelope power of the single sideband signal. They essentially differ in the spectral positioning of the low level pilot tone. One system transmits a low level carrier along with the sideband signal (tone-in-band), while the other two place a pilot tone above or within the SSB band.

The *tone-in-band* SSB system offers many advantages which make it particularly suited to the mobile radio environment. In this technique, a small portion of the audio spectrum is removed from the central region of the audio band using a notch filter, and a low level pilot tone is inserted in its place. This has the advantage of maintaining the low bandwidth property of the SSB signal, while at the same time providing good adjacent channel protection. Due to very high correlation between the fades experienced by the pilot tone and the audio signals, a tone-in-band system makes it possible to employ some form of feedforward automatic gain and frequency control to mitigate the effects of multipath induced fading.

For proper operation of tone-in-band SSB, the tone must be transparent to data and be spaced across the band to avoid spectral overlap with audio frequencies. McGeehan and Bateman [McG84] proposed a *Transparent Tone-in-Band* (TTIB) system which satisfies these requirements. Figure 6.4 illustrates the proposed technique. The baseband signal spectrum is split into two approximately equal width segments. The upper frequency band is filtered out separately and upconverted by an amount equal to the required notch width. The low level pilot tone is added to the center of the resultant notch, and the composite signal is then transmitted. At the receiver, the pilot tone is removed for automatic gain and frequency control purposes, and complementary frequency translation operations are performed to regenerate the audio spectrum. The TTIB system directly trades system bandwidth for notch width. The selection of notch width depends on the maximum Doppler spread induced by the channel, as well as practical filter rolloff factors.

6.2.3 Demodulation of AM signals

AM demodulation techniques may be broadly divided into two categories: *coherent* and *noncoherent* demodulation. Coherent demodulation requires knowledge of the transmitted carrier frequency and phase at the receiver, whereas noncoherent detection requires no phase information. In practical AM receivers, the received signal is filtered and amplified at the carrier frequency and then converted to an intermediate frequency (IF) using a superheterodyne receiver. The IF signal retains the exact spectral shape as the RF signal.

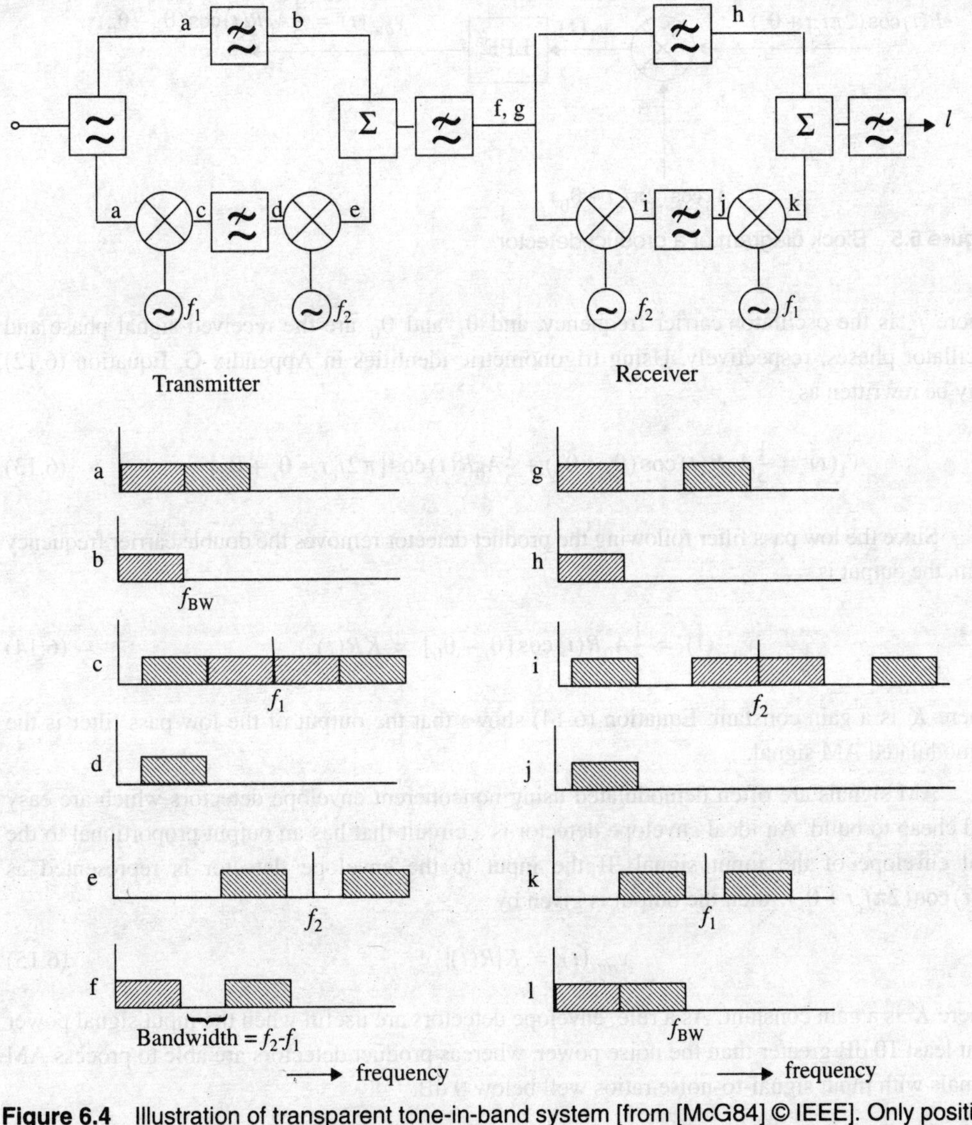

Figure 6.4 Illustration of transparent tone-in-band system [from [McG84] © IEEE]. Only positive frequencies are shown, and the two different cross-hatchings denote different spectral bands.

Figure 6.5 shows a block diagram of a *product detector* which forms a coherent demodulator for AM signals. A product detector (also called a phase detector) is a down converter circuit which converts the input bandpass signal to a baseband signal. If the input to the product detector is an AM signal of the form $R(t)\cos(2\pi f_c t + \theta_r)$, the output of the multiplier can be expressed as

$$v_1(t) = R(t)\cos(2\pi f_c t + \theta_r)A_0\cos(2\pi f_c t + \theta_0) \tag{6.12}$$

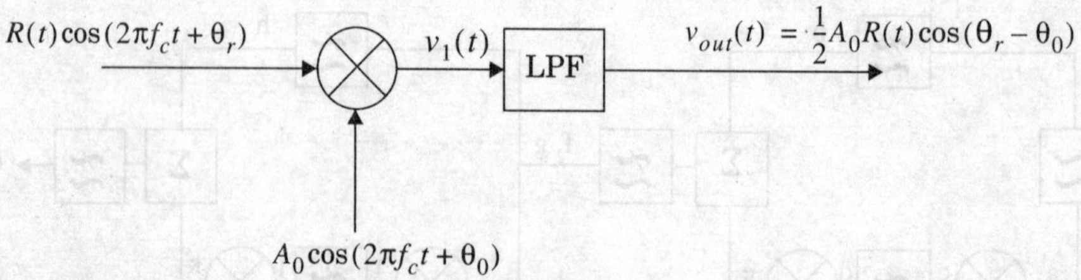

Figure 6.5 Block diagram of a product detector

where f_c is the oscillator carrier frequency, and θ_r and θ_0 are the received signal phase and oscillator phases, respectively. Using trigonometric identities in Appendix G, Equation (6.12) may be rewritten as

$$v_1(t) = \frac{1}{2}A_0R(t)\cos(\theta_r-\theta_0)+\frac{1}{2}A_0R(t)\cos[\pi 2f_c t+\theta_r+\theta_0] \tag{6.13}$$

Since the low pass filter following the product detector removes the double carrier frequency term, the output is

$$v_{out}(t) = \frac{1}{2}A_0R(t)\cos[\theta_r-\theta_0] = KR(t) \tag{6.14}$$

where K is a gain constant. Equation (6.14) shows that the output of the low pass filter is the demodulated AM signal.

AM signals are often demodulated using noncoherent envelope detectors which are easy and cheap to build. An ideal envelope detector is a circuit that has an output proportional to the real envelope of the input signal. If the input to the envelope detector is represented as $R(t)\cos(2\pi f_c t+\theta_r)$, then the output is given by

$$v_{out}(t) = K|R(t)| \tag{6.15}$$

where K is a gain constant. As a rule, envelope detectors are useful when the input signal power is at least 10 dB greater than the noise power, whereas product detectors are able to process AM signals with input signal-to-noise ratios well below 0 dB.

6.3 Angle Modulation

FM is part of a more general class of modulation known as *angle modulation*. Angle modulation varies a sinusoidal carrier signal in such a way that the angle of the carrier is varied according to the amplitude of the modulating baseband signal. In this method, the amplitude of the carrier wave is kept constant (this is why FM is called *constant envelope*). There are a number of ways in which the phase $\theta(t)$ of a carrier signal may be varied in accordance with the baseband signal; the two most important classes of angle modulation being *frequency modulation* and *phase modulation*.

Frequency modulation (FM) is a form of angle modulation in which the instantaneous frequency of the carrier signal is varied linearly with the baseband message signal $m(t)$, as shown in Equation (6.16)

$$s_{FM}(t) = A_c \cos[2\pi f_c t + \theta(t)] = A_c \cos\left[2\pi f_c t + 2\pi k_f \int_{-\infty}^{t} m(\eta)d\eta\right] \tag{6.16}$$

where A_c is the amplitude of the carrier, f_c is the carrier frequency, and k_f is the frequency deviation constant (measured in units of Hz/V). If the modulating signal is a sinusoid of amplitude A_m, and frequency f_m, then the FM signal may be expressed as

$$s_{FM}(t) = A_c \cos\left[2\pi f_c t + \frac{k_f A_m}{f_m} \sin(2\pi f_m t)\right] \tag{6.17}$$

Phase modulation (PM) is a form of angle modulation in which the angle $\theta(t)$ of the carrier signal is varied linearly with the baseband message signal $m(t)$, as shown in Equation (6.18)

$$s_{PM}(t) = A_c \cos[2\pi f_c t + k_\theta m(t)] \tag{6.18}$$

In Equation (6.18), k_θ is the phase deviation constant (measured in units of radians/volt).

From the above equations, it is clear that an FM signal can be regarded as a PM signal in which the modulating wave is integrated before modulation. This means that an FM signal can be generated by first integrating $m(t)$ and then using the result as an input to a phase modulator. Conversely, a PM wave can be generated by first differentiating $m(t)$ and then using the result as the input to a frequency modulator.

The frequency modulation index β_f defines the relationship between the message amplitude and the bandwidth of the transmitted signal, and is given by

$$\beta_f = \frac{k_f A_m}{W} = \frac{\Delta_f}{W} \tag{6.19}$$

where A_m is the peak value of the modulating signal, Δf is the peak frequency deviation of the transmitter, and W is the maximum bandwidth of the modulating signal. If the modulating signal is a low pass signal, as is usually the case, then W is equal to the highest frequency component f_{max} present in the modulating signal.

The phase modulation index β_p is given by

$$\beta_p = k_\theta A_m = \Delta\theta \tag{6.20}$$

where $\Delta\theta$ is the peak phase deviation of the transmitter.

Example 6.2

A sinusoidal modulating signal, $m(t) = 4\cos 2\pi 4 \times 10^3 t$, is applied to an FM modulator that has a frequency deviation constant gain of 10 kHz/V. Compute (a) the peak frequency deviation, and (b) the modulation index.

Solution

Given:

Frequency deviation constant $k_f = 10$ kHz/V

Modulating frequency, $f_m = 4$ kHz

a) The maximum frequency deviation will occur when the instantaneous value of the input signal is at its maximum. For the given *m*(*t*), the maximum value is 4 V, and hence the peak deviation is equal to

$$\Delta f = 4\text{V} \times 10\ \text{kHz/V} = 40\ \text{kHz}$$

b) The modulation index is given by

$$\beta_f = \frac{k_f A_m}{f_m} = \frac{\Delta f}{f_m} = \frac{40}{4} = 10$$

6.3.1 Spectra and Bandwidth of FM Signals

When a sinusoidal test tone is used such that $m(t) = A_m \cos 2\pi f_m t$, the spectrum of $S_{\text{FM}}(t)$ contains a carrier component and an infinite number of sidebands located on either side of the carrier frequency, spaced at integer multiples of the modulating frequency f_m. Since $S_{\text{FM}}(t)$ is a nonlinear function of *m*(*t*), the spectrum of an FM signal must be evaluated on a case-by-case basis for a particular modulating wave shape of interest. It can be shown that for a sinusoidal message, amplitudes of the spectral components are given by Bessel functions of the modulation index β_f.

An FM signal has 98% of the total transmitted power in a RF bandwidth B_T, given by

$$B_T = 2(\beta_f + 1)f_m \qquad \text{(Upper bound)} \tag{6.21}$$

$$B_T = 2\Delta f \qquad \text{(Lower bound)} \tag{6.22}$$

The above approximation of FM bandwidth is called Carson's rule. Carson's rule states that for small values of modulation index ($\beta_f < 1$), the spectrum of an FM wave is effectively limited to the carrier frequency f_c, and one pair of sideband frequencies at $f_c \pm f_m$, and that for large values of modulation index, the bandwidth approaches, and is only slightly greater than, $2\Delta f$.

As a practical example of quantifying the spectrum of an FM signal, the US AMPS cellular system uses a modulation index $\beta_f = 3$, and $f_m = 4$ kHz. Using Carson's rule, the AMPS channel bandwidth has an upper bound of 32 kHz and a lower bound of 24 kHz. However, in practice, the AMPS standard only specifies that the modulation products outside 20 kHz from the carrier shall not exceed 26 dB below the unmodulated carrier. It is further specified that the modulation products outside ±45 kHz from the carrier shall not exceed 45 dB below the unmodulated carrier [EIA90].

Example 6.3

An 880 MHz carrier signal is frequency modulated using a 100 kHz sinusoidal modulating waveform. The peak deviation of the FM signal is 500 kHz. If this FM signal is received by a superheterodyne receiver having an IF frequency of 5 MHz, determine the IF bandwidth necessary to pass the signal.

Solution

Given:

Modulating frequency, $f_m = 100$ kHz

Frequency deviation, $\Delta_f = 500$ kHz

Therefore modulation index $\beta_f = \Delta_f / f_m = 500/100 = 5$

Using Carson's rule, the bandwidth occupied by the FM signal is given by

$$B_T = 2(\beta_f + 1)f_m = 2(5+1)100 \text{ kHz} = 1200 \text{ kHz}$$

The IF filter at the receiver needs to pass all the components in this bandwidth, hence the IF filter should be designed for a bandwidth of 1200 kHz.

6.3.2 FM Modulation Methods

There are basically two methods of generating an FM signal: the *direct method* and the *indirect method*. In the direct method, the carrier frequency is directly varied in accordance with the input modulating signal. In the indirect method, a narrowband FM signal is generated using a balanced modulator, and frequency multiplication is used to increase both the frequency deviation and the carrier frequency to the required level.

Direct Method

In this method, voltage-controlled oscillators (VCOs) are used to vary the frequency of the carrier signal in accordance with the baseband signal amplitude variations. These oscillators use devices with reactance that can be varied by the application of a voltage, where the reactance causes the instantaneous frequency of the VCO to change proportionally. The most commonly used variable reactance device is the voltage-variable capacitor called a *varactor*. The voltage-variable capacitor may be obtained, for example, by using a reverse biased p-n junction diode. The larger the reverse voltage applied to such a diode, the smaller the transition capacitance will be of the diode. By incorporating such a device into a standard Hartley or Colpitts oscillator, FM signals can be generated. Figure 6.6 shows a simple reactance modulator. While VCOs offer a simple way to generate narrowband FM signals, the stability of the center frequency (carrier) of the VCO becomes a major issue when it is used for wideband FM generation. The stability of the VCO can be improved by incorporating a phase locked loop (PLL) which locks the center frequency to a stable crystal reference frequency.

Indirect Method

The indirect method of generating FM was first proposed by its inventor, Major Edwin Armstrong, in 1936. It is based on approximating a narrowband FM signal as the sum of a car-

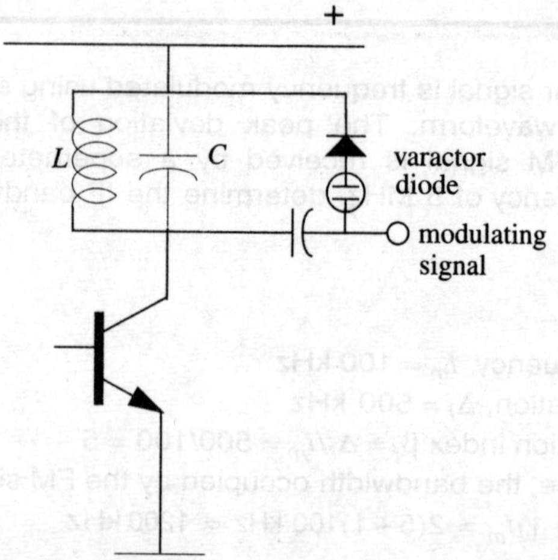

Figure 6.6 A simple reactance modulator in which the capacitance of a varactor diode is changed to vary the frequency of a simple oscillator. This circuit serves as a VCO.

rier signal and a single sideband (SSB) signal where the sideband is 90° out of phase with the carrier. Using a Taylor series for small values of $\theta(t)$, Equation (6.16) can be expressed as

$$s_{FM}(t) \cong A_c \cos 2\pi f_c t - A_c \theta(t) \sin 2\pi f_c t \tag{6.23}$$

where the first term represents the carrier and the second term represents the sideband.

A simple block diagram of the indirect FM transmitter is shown in Figure 6.7. A narrowband FM signal is generated using a balanced modulator which modulates a crystal controlled oscillator. Figure 6.7 is a direct implementation of Equation (6.23). The maximum frequency deviation is kept constant and small in order to maintain the validity of Equation (6.23), and hence the output is a narrowband FM signal. A wideband FM signal is then produced by multiplying in frequency the narrowband FM signal using frequency multipliers. A disadvantage of using the indirect method for wideband FM generation is that the phase noise in the system increases with the frequency multiplying factor N.

6.3.3 FM Detection Techniques

There are many ways to recover the original information from an FM signal. The objective of all FM demodulators is to produce a transfer characteristic that is the inverse of that of the frequency modulator. That is, a frequency demodulator should produce an output voltage with an instantaneous amplitude that is directly proportional to the instantaneous frequency of the input FM signal. Thus, a frequency-to-amplitude converter circuit is a frequency demodulator. Various techniques such as slope detection, zero-crossing detection, phase locked discrimination, and quadrature detection are used to demodulate FM. Devices which perform FM demodulation are

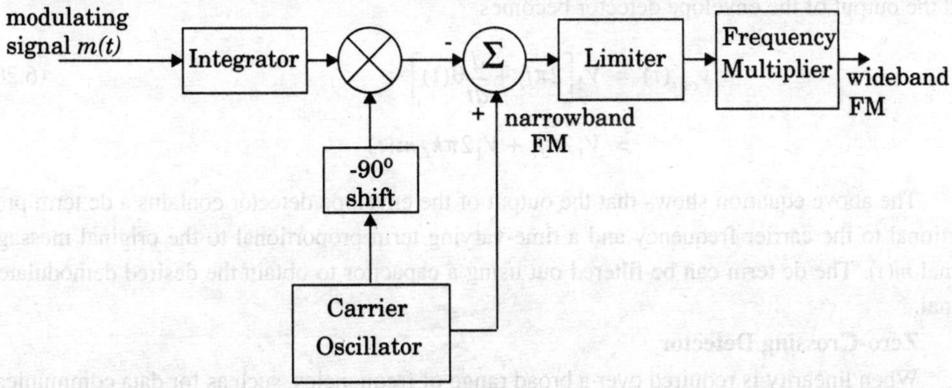

Figure 6.7 Indirect method for generating a wideband FM signal. A narrowband FM signal is generated using a balanced modulator and then frequency multiplied to generate a wideband FM signal.

often called *frequency discriminators*. In practical receivers, the RF signal is received, amplified, and filtered at the carrier, and then converted to an intermediate frequency (IF) which contains the same spectrum as the original received signal.

Slope Detector

It can be easily shown that FM demodulation can be performed by taking the time derivative (often called *slope detection*) of the FM signal, followed by envelope detection. A block diagram of such an FM demodulator is shown in Figure 6.8. The FM signal is first passed through an amplitude limiter which removes any amplitude perturbations which the signal might have undergone due to fading in the channel, and produces a constant envelope signal. Using Equation (6.16), the signal at the output of the limiter can be represented as

$$v_1(t) = V_1\cos[2\pi f_c t + \theta(t)] = V_1\cos\left[2\pi f_c t + 2\pi k_f \int_{-\infty}^{t} m(\eta)d\eta\right] \tag{6.24}$$

Equation (6.24) can be differentiated in practice by passing the signal through a filter with a transfer function that has gain that increases linearly with frequency. Such a filter is called a slope filter (which is where the term *slope detector* derives its name). The output of the differentiator then becomes

$$v_2(t) = -V_1\left[2\pi f_c t + \frac{d\theta}{dt}\right]\sin(2\pi f_c t + \theta(t)) \tag{6.25}$$

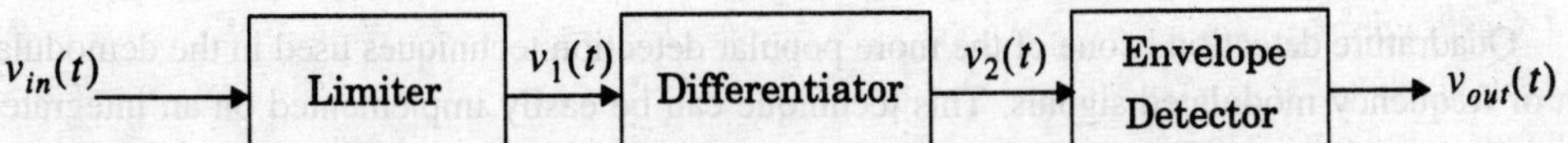

Figure 6.8 Block diagram of a slope detector type FM demodulator.

and the output of the envelope detector becomes

$$v_{out}(t) = V_1\left[2\pi f_c + \frac{d}{dt}\theta(t)\right] \tag{6.26}$$
$$= V_1 2\pi f_c + V_1 2\pi k_f m(t)$$

The above equation shows that the output of the envelope detector contains a dc term proportional to the carrier frequency and a time-varying term proportional to the original message signal $m(t)$. The dc term can be filtered out using a capacitor to obtain the desired demodulated signal.

Zero-Crossing Detector

When linearity is required over a broad range of frequencies, such as for data communications, a zero-crossing detector is used to perform frequency-to-amplitude conversion by directly counting the number of zero crossings in the input FM signal. The rationale behind this technique is to use the output of the zero-crossing detector to generate a pulse train with an average value that is proportional to the frequency of the input signal. This demodulator is sometimes referred to as a *pulse-averaging discriminator.* A block diagram of a pulse-averaging discriminator is shown in Figure 6.9. The input FM signal is first passed through a limiter circuit which converts the input signal to a frequency modulated pulse train. This pulse train $v_1(t)$ is then passed through a differentiator whose output is used to trigger a monostable multivibrator (also called a "one-shot"). The output of the one-shot consists of a train of pulses with average duration proportional to the desired message signal. A low pass filter is used to perform the averaging operation by extracting the slowly varying dc component of the signal at the output of the one-shot. The output of the low pass filter is the desired demodulated signal.

PLL for FM Detection

The phase locked loop (PLL) method is another popular technique to demodulate an FM signal. The PLL is a closed loop control system which can track the variations in the received signal phase and frequency. A block diagram of a PLL circuit is shown in Figure 6.10. It consists of a voltage controlled oscillator $H(s)$ with an output frequency which is varied in accordance with the demodulated output voltage level. The output of the voltage controlled oscillator is compared with the input signal using a phase comparator, which produces an output voltage proportional to the phase difference. The phase difference signal is then fed back to the VCO to control the output frequency. The feedback loop functions in a manner that facilitates locking of the VCO frequency to the input frequency. Once the VCO frequency is locked to the input frequency, the VCO continues to track the variations in the input frequency. Once this tracking is achieved, the control voltage to the VCO is simply the demodulated FM signal.

Quadrature Detection

Quadrature detection is one of the more popular detection techniques used in the demodulation of frequency modulated signals. This technique can be easily implemented on an integrated circuit at a very low cost. The detector consists of a network which shifts the phase of the incoming FM signal by an amount proportional to its instantaneous frequency, and uses a product detector

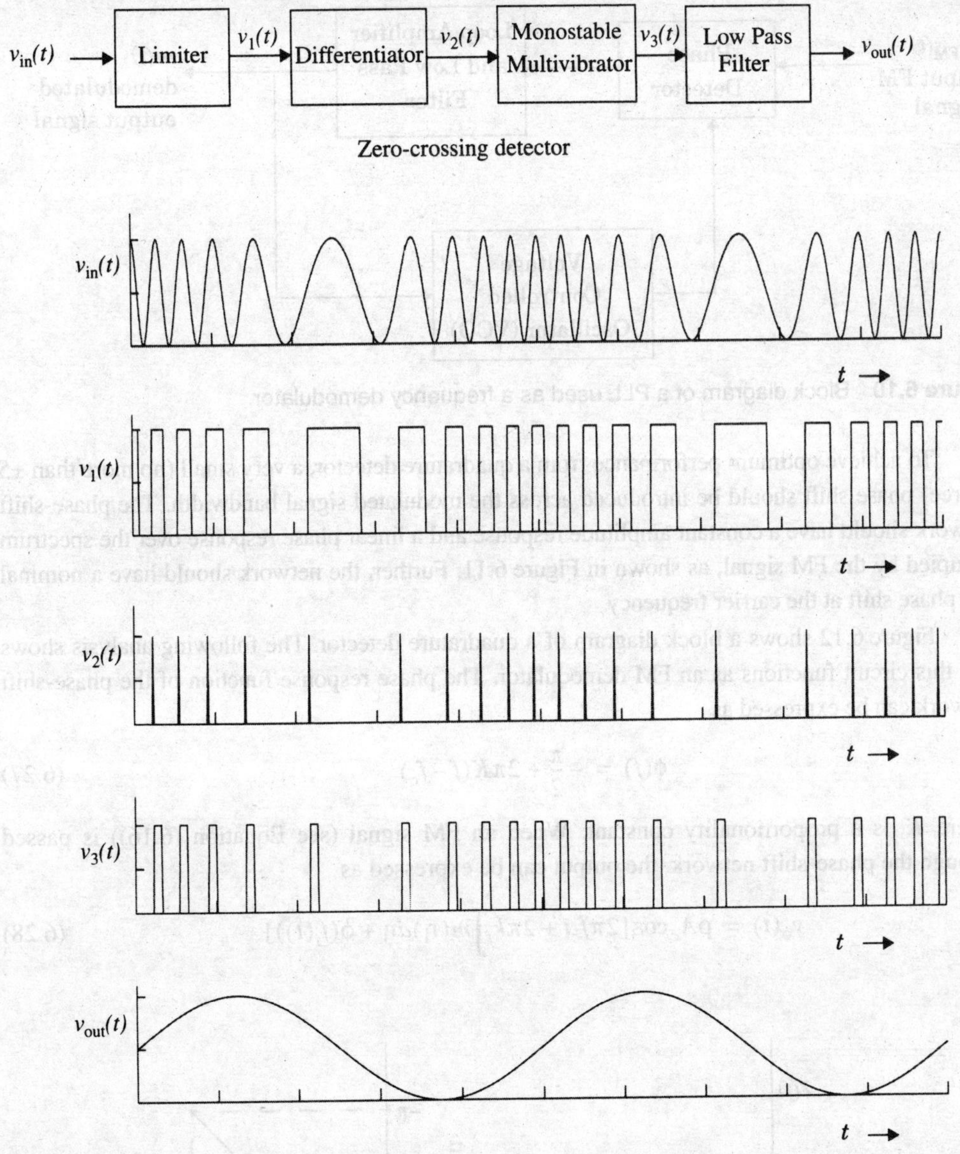

Figure 6.9 Block diagram of a zero-crossing detector and associated waveforms.

(phase detector) to detect the phase difference between the original FM signal and the signal at the output of the phase-shift network. Since the phase shift introduced by the phase-shift network is proportional to the instantaneous frequency of the FM signal, the output voltage of the phase detector will also be proportional to the instantaneous frequency of the input FM signal. In this manner, a frequency-to-amplitude conversion is achieved, and the FM signal is demodulated.

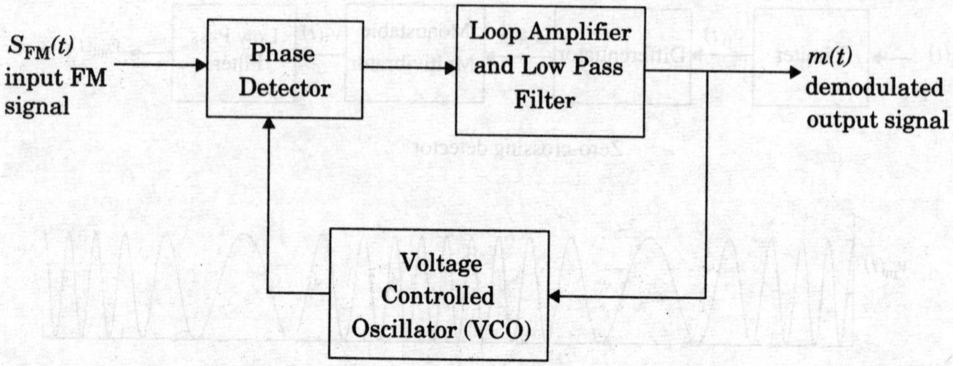

Figure 6.10 Block diagram of a PLL used as a frequency demodulator.

To achieve optimum performance from a quadrature detector, a very small (no more than ±5 degree) phase shift should be introduced across the modulated signal bandwidth. The phase-shift network should have a constant amplitude response and a linear phase response over the spectrum occupied by the FM signal, as shown in Figure 6.11. Further, the network should have a nominal 90° phase shift at the carrier frequency.

Figure 6.12 shows a block diagram of a quadrature detector. The following analysis shows that this circuit functions as an FM demodulator. The phase response function of the phase-shift network can be expressed as

$$\phi(f) = -\frac{\pi}{2} + 2\pi K(f - f_c) \tag{6.27}$$

where K is a proportionality constant. When an FM signal (see Equation (6.16)) is passed through the phase-shift network, the output can be expressed as

$$v_\phi(t) = \rho A_c \cos[2\pi f_c t + 2\pi k_f \int m(\eta) d\eta + \phi(f_i(t))] \tag{6.28}$$

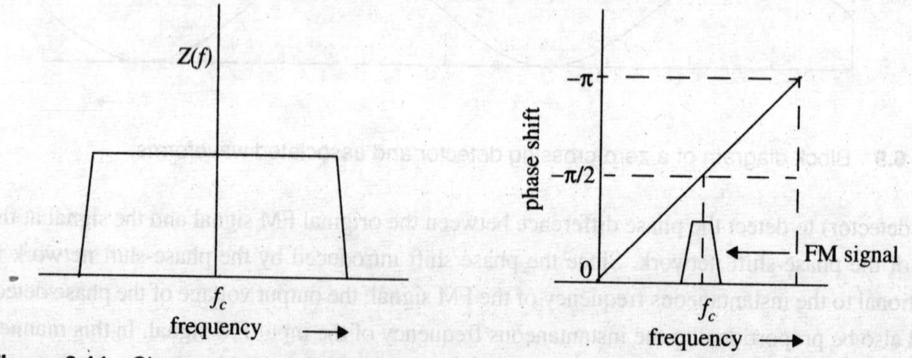

Figure 6.11 Characteristics of the phase-shift network with constant gain and linear phase.

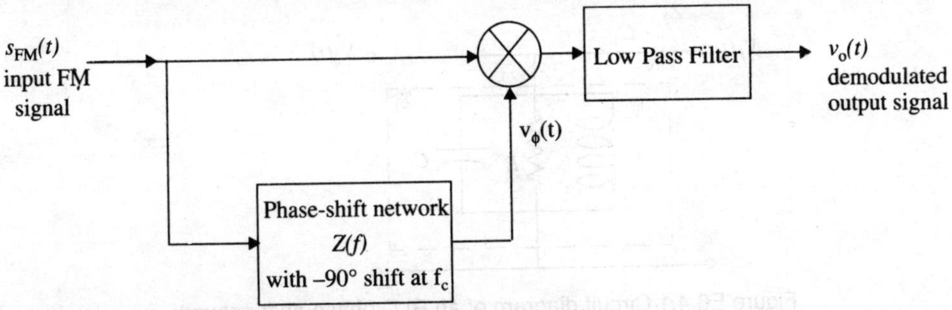

Figure 6.12 Block diagram of a quadrature detector.

where ρ is a constant, and $f_i(t)$ is the instantaneous frequency of the input FM signal, which is defined as

$$f_i(t) = f_c + k_f\, m(t) \tag{6.29}$$

The output of the product detector is proportional to the cosine of the phase difference between $v_\phi(t)$ and $s_{FM}(t)$ (see Figure 6.12), and is given by

$$\begin{aligned} v_0(t) &= \rho^2 A_c^2 \cos(\phi(f_i(t))) \\ &= \rho^2 A_c^2 \cos(-\pi/2 + 2\pi K[f_i(t) - f_c]) \\ &= \rho^2 A_c^2 \sin[2\pi K k_f\, m(t)] \end{aligned} \tag{6.30}$$

If the phase shift varies only over a small angle, the above expression simplifies to

$$v_0(t) = \rho^2 A_c^2 2\pi K k_f\, m(t) = Cm(t) \tag{6.31}$$

Hence, the output of the quadrature detector is the desired message signal multiplied by a constant.

In practice, the phase-shift network is realized using a quadrature tank circuit or a delay line. More often, a quadrature tank circuit is used, since it is cheap and easy to implement. Parallel RLC circuits tuned to the carrier or IF frequency can be used to build the quadrature tank circuit.

Example 6.4

Design an RLC network that implements an IF quadrature FM detector with f_c = 10.7 MHz, and a 500 kHz symmetrical bandpass spectrum. Also plot the transfer function of the designed network to verify that it will work.

Solution

A quadrature detector is represented by the block diagram in Figure 6.12, and the phase-shift network is implemented by the RLC circuit shown in Figure E6.4.1. Here the phase shift is 90° instead of –90° for $f = f_c$. With reference to Figure E6.4.1

$$\frac{V_q(\omega)}{V_f(\omega)} = \frac{Z_1(\omega)}{Z_1(\omega) + Z_2(w)} \tag{E6.4.1}$$

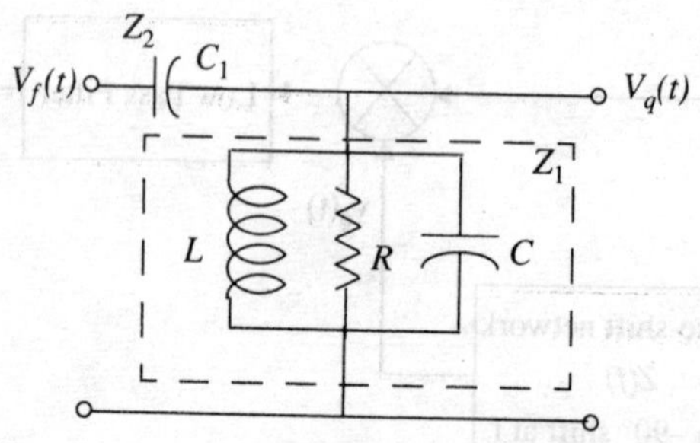

Figure E6.4.1 Circuit diagram of an RLC phase-shift network.

Multiplying and dividing by $1/(Z_1Z_2)$, we get

$$\frac{V_q(\omega)}{V_f(\omega)} = \frac{Y_2}{Y_1+Y_2} = \frac{j\omega C_1}{j\omega C + \frac{1}{R} + \frac{1}{j\omega L} + j\omega C_1} = \frac{j\omega RC_1}{1 + jR\left(\omega(C+C_1) - \frac{1}{\omega L}\right)} \quad \text{(E6.4.2)}$$

Let $\omega_c^2 = 1/(L(C_1+C))$ for the overall circuit. Then

$$Q = \frac{R}{\omega_c L} = R\omega_c(C_1+C) \quad \text{(E6.4.3)}$$

$$\frac{V_q}{V_f} = \frac{j\omega RC_1}{1 + jQ\left(\frac{\omega}{\omega_c} - \frac{\omega_c}{\omega}\right)}$$

So, for $\omega = \omega_c$:

$$\frac{V_q}{V_f} = j\omega_c RC_1$$

This provides the desired 90° phase shift at ω_c. At IF frequencies, the phase shift introduced by the network may be expressed as

$$\phi(\omega_i) = \frac{\pi}{2} + \tan^{-1}\left[Q\left(\frac{\omega_i}{\omega_c} - \frac{\omega_c}{\omega_i}\right)\right] = 90° + \eta$$

For a good system we need $-5° < \phi(\omega_i) < 5°$ (approximately). Therefore, for $f_c = 10.7$ MHz and $B = 500$ kHz, at the largest IF frequency $f_i = f_c + 250$ kHz. Thus, we require

$$Q\left(\frac{10.7\times10^6 + 250\times10^3}{10.7\times10^6} - \frac{10.7\times10^6}{10.7\times10^6 + 250\times10^3}\right) = \tan 5°$$

Therefore, $Q = 1.894$.

Using $Q = 1.894$, one may verify the phase shift at the smallest IF frequency $f_i = f_c - 250$ kHz,

$$\tan^{-1}\left[1.894\left(\frac{10.45}{10.7} - \frac{10.7}{10.45}\right)\right] = -5.12° \approx -5°$$

We have verified that a circuit with $Q = 1.894$ will satisfy the phase shift requirements.

Now, to compute the values of L, R, C, and C_1.

Choose $L = 10\ \mu H$. Using the first part of Equation (E6.4.3), the value of R can be computed as 1.273 kΩ.
Using the second part of Equation (E5.4.3)

$$C_1 + C = \frac{Q}{R\omega_c} = \frac{1.894}{(1.273 \times 10^3)2\pi(10.7 \times 10^6)} = 22.13\ \text{pF}.$$

Assuming $C_1 = 12.13$ pF $\cong$ 12 pF, we get $C = 10$ pF.
The magnitude transfer function of the designed phase shift network is given by

$$|H(f)| = \frac{2\pi f R C_1}{\sqrt{1 + Q^2\left(\frac{f}{f_c} - \frac{f_c}{f}\right)^2}} = \frac{97.02 \times 10^{-9} f}{\sqrt{1 + 3.587\left(\frac{f}{10.7 \times 10^6} - \frac{10.7 \times 10^6}{f}\right)^2}}$$

and the phase transfer function is given by

$$\angle H(f) = \frac{\pi}{2} + \tan^{-1}\left[Q\left(\frac{f}{f_c} - \frac{f_c}{f}\right)\right] = \frac{\pi}{2} + \tan\left[1.894\left(\frac{f}{10.7 \times 10^6} - \frac{10.7 \times 10^6}{f}\right)\right]$$

Both the magnitude and phase transfer functions are plotted in Figure E6.4.2. It is clearly seen from the plots that the transfer function satisfies the requirements of the phase-shift network, thus allowing detection of FM.

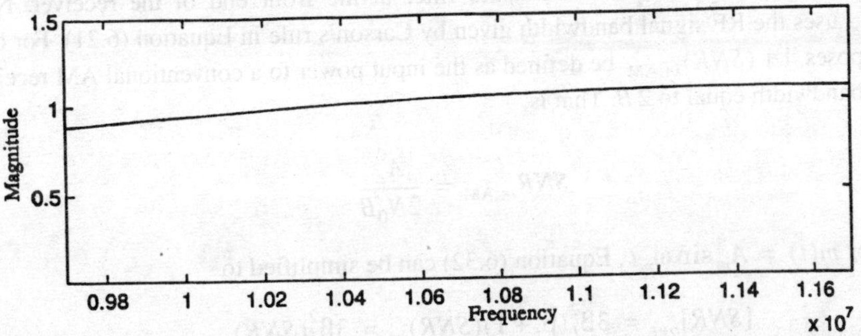

(a)

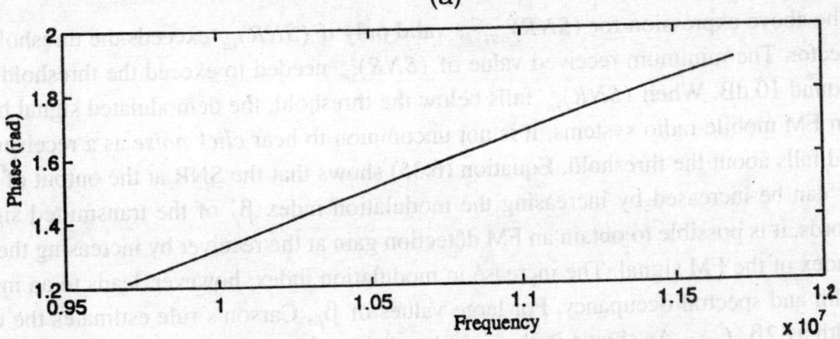

(b)

Figure E6.4.2 (a) Magnitude response of the designed phase-shift network; (b) phase response of the designed phase-shift network.

6.3.4 Tradeoff Between SNR and Bandwidth in an FM Signal

In angle modulation systems, the signal-to-noise ratio *before* detection is a function of the receiver IF filter bandwidth, received carrier power, and received interference. However, the signal-to-noise ratio *after* detection is a function of f_{max}, the maximum frequency of the message, β_f, the modulation index, and the given input signal-to-noise ratio $(SNR)_{in}$.

The SNR at the output of a properly designed FM receiver is dependent on the modulation index and is given by [Cou93]

$$(SNR)_{out} = 6(\beta_f + 1)\beta_f^2\overline{\left(\frac{m(t)}{V_p}\right)^2}(SNR)_{in} \tag{6.32}$$

where V_p is the peak-to-zero value of the modulating signal $m(t)$, and the input signal-to-noise ratio $(SNR)_{in}$ is given by

$$(SNR)_{in} = \frac{A_c^2/2}{2N_0(\beta_f + 1)B} \tag{6.33}$$

where A_c is the carrier amplitude, N_0 is the white noise RF power spectral density, and B is the equivalent RF bandwidth of the bandpass filter at the front end of the receiver. Note that $(SNR)_{in}$ uses the RF signal bandwidth given by Carson's rule in Equation (6.21). For comparison purposes, let $(SNR)_{in;\mathrm{AM}}$ be defined as the input power to a conventional AM receiver having RF bandwidth equal to $2B$. That is,

$$SNR_{in;\mathrm{AM}} = \frac{A_c^2}{2N_0B} \tag{6.34}$$

Then, for $m(t) = A_m \sin\omega_m t$, Equation (6.32) can be simplified to

$$[SNR]_{out} = 3\beta_f^2(\beta_f + 1)(SNR)_{in} = 3\beta_f^2(SNR)_{in;\mathrm{AM}} \tag{6.35}$$

The above expression for $(SNR)_{out}$ is valid only if $(SNR)_{in}$ exceeds the threshold of the FM detector. The minimum received value of $(SNR)_{in}$ needed to exceed the threshold is typically around 10 dB. When $(SNR)_{in}$ falls below the threshold, the demodulated signal becomes noisy. In FM mobile radio systems, it is not uncommon to hear *click noise* as a received signal rises and falls about the threshold. Equation (6.35) shows that the SNR at the output of the FM detector can be increased by increasing the modulation index β_f of the transmitted signal. In other words, it is possible to obtain an FM detection gain at the receiver by increasing the modulation index of the FM signal. The increase in modulation index, however, leads to an increased bandwidth and spectral occupancy. For large values of β_f, Carson's rule estimates the channel bandwidth as $2\beta_f f_{max}$. As shown in the right-hand side of Equation (6.35), the SNR at the output of an FM detector is $3\beta_f^2$ greater than the input SNR for an AM signal with the same RF bandwidth. Since AM detectors have a linear detection gain, it follows that $(SNR)_{out}$ for FM is much greater than $(SNR)_{out}$ for AM.

Equation (6.35) shows the SNR at the output of an FM detector increases as the cube of the bandwidth of the message. This clearly illustrates why FM offers excellent performance for fading signals. As long as $(SNR)_{in}$ remains above threshold, $(SNR)_{out}$ is much greater than $(SNR)_{in}$. A technique called *threshold extension* is used in FM demodulators to improve detection sensitivity to about $(SNR)_{in} = 6$ dB.

FM can improve receiver performance through adjustment of the modulation index at the transmitter, and not the transmitted power. This is not the case in AM, since linear modulation techniques do not trade bandwidth for SNR.

Example 6.5

How much bandwidth is required for an analog frequency modulated signal that has an audio bandwidth of 5 kHz and a modulation index of three? How much output SNR improvement would be obtained if the modulation index is increased to five? What is the tradeoff bandwidth for this improvement?

Solution

From Carson's rule, the bandwidth is

$$B_T = 2(\beta_f + 1)f_m = 2(3+1)5 \text{ kHz} = 40 \text{ kHz}$$

From Equation (6.35), the output SNR improvement factor is approximately

$$3\beta_f^3 + 3\beta_f^2 .$$

Therefore

for $\beta_f = 3$, the output SNR factor is $\approx 3(3)^3 + 3(3)^2 = 108 = 20.33$ dB

for $\beta_f = 5$, the output SNR factor is $\approx 3(5)^3 + 3(5)^2 = 450 = 26.53$ dB

The improvement in output SNR by increasing the modulation index from three to five is therefore $26.53 - 20.33 = 6.2$ dB.

This improvement is achieved at the expense of bandwidth. For $\beta_f = 3$, a bandwidth of 40 kHz is needed, while $\beta_f = 5$ requires a bandwidth of 60 kHz.

6.4 Digital Modulation—an Overview

Modern mobile communication systems use digital modulation techniques. Advancements in very large-scale integration (VLSI) and digital signal processing (DSP) technology have made digital modulation more cost effective than analog transmission systems. Digital modulation offers many advantages over analog modulation. Some advantages include greater noise immunity and robustness to channel impairments, easier multiplexing of various forms of information (e.g., voice, data, and video), and greater security. Furthermore, digital transmissions accommodate digital error-control codes which detect and/or correct transmission errors, and support complex signal conditioning and processing techniques such as source coding, encryption, and equalization to improve the performance of the overall communication link. New multipurpose programmable digital signal processors have made it possible to implement digital modulators and demodulators completely in software. Instead of having a particular modem design permanently frozen as hardware, embedded software implementations now allow alterations and improvements without having to redesign or replace the modem.

In digital wireless communication systems, the modulating signal (e.g., the message) may be represented as a time sequence of symbols or pulses, where each symbol has m finite states. Each symbol represents n bits of information, where $n = \log_2 m$ bits/symbol. Many digital modulation schemes are used in modern wireless communication systems, and many more are sure to be introduced. Some of these techniques have subtle differences between one another, and each technique belongs to a family of related modulation methods. For example, phase shift keying (PSK) may be either coherently or differentially detected; and may have two, four, eight or more possible levels (e.g., n = 1, 2, 3, or more bits) per symbol, depending on the manner in which information is transmitted within a single symbol.

6.4.1 Factors That Influence the Choice of Digital Modulation

Several factors influence the choice of a digital modulation scheme. A desirable modulation scheme provides low bit error rates at low received signal-to-noise ratios, performs well in multipath and fading conditions, occupies a minimum of bandwidth, and is easy and cost-effective to implement. Existing modulation schemes do not simultaneously satisfy all of these requirements. Some modulation schemes are better in terms of the bit error rate performance, while others are better in terms of bandwidth efficiency. Depending on the demands of the particular application, tradeoffs are made when selecting a digital modulation.

The performance of a modulation scheme is often measured in terms of its *power efficiency* and *bandwidth efficiency*. Power efficiency describes the ability of a modulation technique to preserve the fidelity of the digital message at low power levels. In a digital communication system, in order to increase noise immunity, it is necessary to increase the signal power. However, the amount by which the signal power should be increased to obtain a certain level of fidelity (i.e., an acceptable bit error probability) depends on the particular type of modulation employed. The *power efficiency*, η_p (sometimes called energy efficiency) of a digital modulation scheme is a measure of how favorably this tradeoff between fidelity and signal power is made, and is often expressed as the ratio of the *signal energy per bit* to *noise power spectral density* (E_b/N_0) required at the receiver input for a certain probability of error (say 10^{-5}).

Bandwidth efficiency describes the ability of a modulation scheme to accommodate data within a limited bandwidth. In general, increasing the data rate implies decreasing the pulse-width of a digital symbol, which increases the bandwidth of the signal. Thus, there is an unavoidable relationship between data rate and bandwidth occupancy. However, some modulation schemes perform better than the others in making this tradeoff. Bandwidth efficiency reflects how efficiently the allocated bandwidth is utilized and is defined as the ratio of the *throughput data rate per Hertz* in a given bandwidth. If R is the data rate in bits per second, and B is the bandwidth occupied by the modulated RF signal, then bandwidth efficiency η_B is expressed as

$$\eta_B = \frac{R}{B} \text{ bps/Hz} \tag{6.36}$$

The system capacity of a digital mobile communication system is directly related to the bandwidth efficiency of the modulation scheme, since a modulation with a greater value of η_B will transmit more data in a given spectrum allocation.

There is a fundamental upper bound on achievable bandwidth efficiency. Shannon's channel coding theorem states that for an arbitrarily small probability of error, the maximum possible bandwidth efficiency is limited by the noise in the channel, and is given by the channel capacity formula [Sha48]. Note that Shannon's bound applies for AWGN non-fading channels.

$$\eta_{Bmax} = \frac{C}{B} = \log_2\left(1 + \frac{S}{N}\right) \tag{6.37}$$

where C is the channel capacity (in bps), B is the RF bandwidth, and S/N is the signal-to-noise ratio.

In the design of a digital communication system, very often there is a tradeoff between bandwidth efficiency and power efficiency. For example, as shown in Chapter 7, adding error control coding to a message increases the bandwidth occupancy (and this, in turn, reduces the bandwidth efficiency), but at the same time reduces the required received power for a particular bit error rate, and hence trades bandwidth efficiency for power efficiency. On the other hand, higher level modulation schemes (M-ary keying) decrease bandwidth occupancy but increase the required received power, and hence trade power efficiency for bandwidth efficiency.

While power and bandwidth efficiency considerations are very important, other factors also affect the choice of a digital modulation scheme. For example, for all personal communication systems which serve a large user community, the cost and complexity of the subscriber receiver must be minimized, and a modulation which is simple to detect is most attractive. The performance of the modulation scheme under various types of channel impairments such as Rayleigh and Ricean fading and multipath time dispersion, given a particular demodulator implementation, is another key factor in selecting a modulation. In cellular systems where interference is a major issue, the performance of a modulation scheme in an interference environment is extremely important. Sensitivity to detection of timing jitter, caused by time-varying channels, is also an important consideration in choosing a particular modulation scheme. In general, the modulation, interference, and implementation of the time-varying effects of the channel as well as the performance of the specific demodulator are analyzed as a complete system using simulation to determine relative performance and ultimate selection.

Example 6.6

If the SNR of a wireless communication link is 20 dB and the RF bandwidth is 30 kHz, determine the maximum theoretical data rate that can be transmitted. Compare this rate to the US Digital Cellular Standard described in Chapter 1.

Solution

Given:

$S/N = 20\text{ dB} = 100$

RF Bandwidth $B = 30000$ Hz

Using Shannon's channel capacity formula (6.37), the maximum possible data rate

$$C = B\log_2\left(1 + \frac{S}{N}\right) = 30000\log_2(1 + 100) = 199.75\text{ kbps}$$

The USDC data rate is 48.6 kbps, which is only about one fourth the theoretical limit under 20 dB SNR conditions.

Example 6.7

What is the theoretical maximum data rate that can be supported in a 200 kHz channel for SNR = 10 dB, 30 dB. How does this compare to the GSM standard described in Chapter 1?

Solution

For $SNR = 10\text{ dB} = 10$, $B = 200$ kHz.

Using Shannon's channel capacity formula (6.37), the maximum possible data rate

$$C = B\log_2\left(1 + \frac{S}{N}\right) = 200000\log_2(1 + 10) = 691.886\ \text{ kbps}$$

The GSM data rate is 270.833 kbps, which is only about 40% of the theoretical limit for 10 dB SNR conditions.

For $SNR = 30\text{ dB} = 1000$, $B = 200$ kHz.

The maximum possible data rate

$$C = B\log_2\left(1 + \frac{S}{N}\right) = 200000\log_2(1 + 1000) = 1.99\text{ Mbps.}$$

6.4.2 Bandwidth and Power Spectral Density of Digital Signals

The definition of signal *bandwidth* varies with context, and there is no single definition which suits all applications [Amo80]. All definitions, however, are based on some measure on the *power spectral density* (PSD) of the signal. The power spectral density of a random signal $w(t)$ is defined as [Cou93]

$$P_w(f) = \lim_{T \to \infty}\left(\frac{\overline{|W_T(f)|^2}}{T}\right) \tag{6.38}$$

where the bar denotes an ensemble average, and $W_T(f)$ is the Fourier transform of $w_T(t)$, which is the truncated version of the signal $w(t)$, defined as

$$w_T(t) = \begin{cases} w(t) & -T/2 < t < T/2 \\ 0 & \text{elsewhere} \end{cases} \tag{6.39}$$

The power spectral density of a modulated (bandpass) signal is related to the power spectral density of its baseband complex envelope. If a bandpass signal $s(t)$ is represented as

$$s(t) = Re\{g(t)\exp(j2\pi f_c t)\} \tag{6.40}$$

where $g(t)$ is the complex baseband envelope, then the PSD of the bandpass signal is given by

$$P_s(f) = \frac{1}{4}[P_g(f-f_c) + P_g(-f-f_c)] \tag{6.41}$$

where $P_g(f)$ is the PSD of $g(t)$.

The *absolute bandwidth* of a signal is defined as the range of frequencies over which the signal has a non-zero power spectral density. For symbols represented as rectangular baseband pulses, the PSD has a $(\sin f)^2/f^2$ profile which extends over an infinite range of frequencies, and has an absolute bandwidth of infinity. A simpler and more widely accepted measure of bandwidth is the first *null-to-null bandwidth*. The null-to-null bandwidth is equal to the width of the main spectral lobe.

A very popular measure of bandwidth which measures the dispersion of the spectrum is the *half-power bandwidth*. The half-power bandwidth is defined as the interval between frequencies at which the PSD has dropped to half power, or 3 dB below the peak value. Half-power bandwidth is also called the *3 dB bandwidth*.

The definition adopted by the Federal Communications Commission (FCC) defines occupied bandwidth as the band which leaves exactly 0.5 percent of the signal above the upper band limit and exactly 0.5 percent of the signal power below the lower band limit. In other words, 99 percent of the signal power is contained within the occupied bandwidth.

Another commonly used method to specify bandwidth is to state that everywhere outside the specified band, the PSD is below a certain stated level. Typically, 45 dB to 60 dB attenuation is specified.

6.5 Line Coding

Digital baseband signals often use line codes to provide particular spectral characteristics of a pulse train. The most common codes for mobile communication are *return-to-zero* (RZ), *non-return-to-zero* (NRZ), and *Manchester* codes (see Figure 6.13 and Figure 6.14). All of these may either be unipolar (with voltage levels being either 0 or V) or bipolar (with voltage levels being either –V or V). RZ implies that the pulse returns to zero within every bit period. This leads to spectral widening, but improves timing synchronization. NRZ codes, on the other hand, do not return to zero during a bit period—the signal stays at constant levels throughout a bit period. NRZ codes are more spectrally efficient than RZ codes, but offer poorer synchronization capabilities. Because of the large dc component in some line codes, they are not useful for data that must be passed through dc blocking circuits such as audio amplifiers or phone switching equipment.

The Manchester code is a special type of NRZ line code that is ideally suited for signaling that must pass through phone lines and other dc blocking circuits, as it has no dc component and offers simple synchronization. Manchester codes use two pulses to represent each binary symbol, and thereby provide easy clock recovery since zero-crossings are guaranteed in every bit period. The power spectral density of these line codes are shown in Figure 6.13 and the time waveforms are given in Figure 6.14.

6.6 Pulse Shaping Techniques

When rectangular pulses are passed through a bandlimited channel, the pulses will spread in time, and the pulse for each symbol will smear into the time intervals of succeeding symbols. This causes *intersymbol interference* (ISI) and leads to an increased probability of the receiver making an error in detecting a symbol. One obvious way to minimize intersymbol interference is to increase the channel bandwidth. However, mobile communication systems operate with minimal bandwidth, and techniques that reduce the modulation bandwidth and suppress out-of-band radiation, while reducing intersymbol interference, are highly desirable. Out-of-band radiation in the adjacent channel in a mobile radio system should generally be 40 dB to 80 dB below that in the desired passband. Since it is difficult to directly manipulate the transmitter spectrum at RF frequencies, spectral shaping is done through baseband or IF processing. There are a number of well known pulse shaping techniques which are used to simultaneously reduce the intersymbol effects and the spectral width of a modulated digital signal.

6.6.1 Nyquist Criterion for ISI Cancellation

Nyquist was the first to solve the problem of overcoming intersymbol interference while keeping the transmission bandwidth low [Nyq28]. He observed that the effect of ISI could be completely nullified if the overall response of the communication system (including transmitter, channel, and receiver) is designed so that at every sampling instant at the receiver, the response due to all

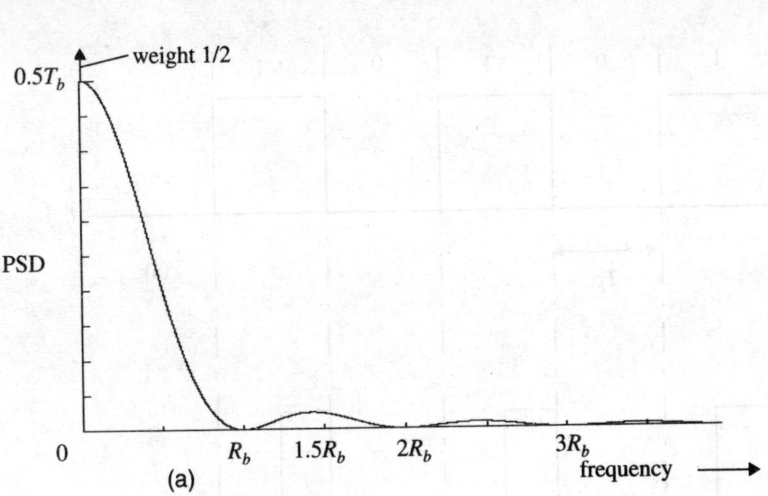

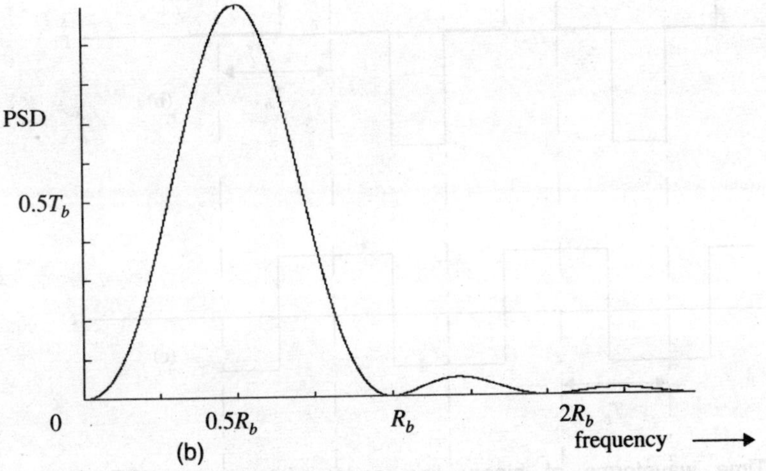

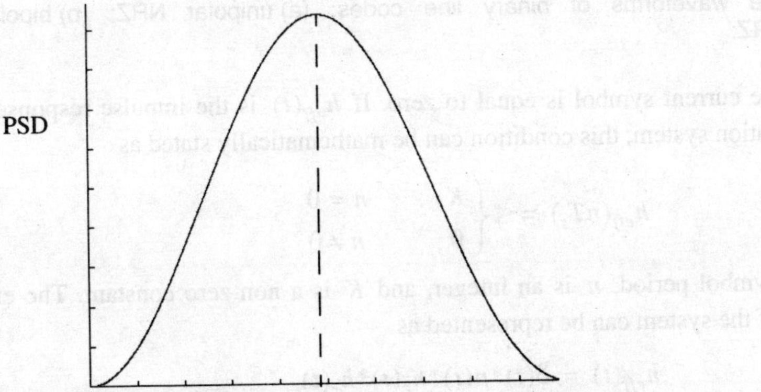

Figure 6.13 Power spectral density of (a) unipolar NRZ, (b) bipolar RZ, and (c) Manchester NRZ line codes.

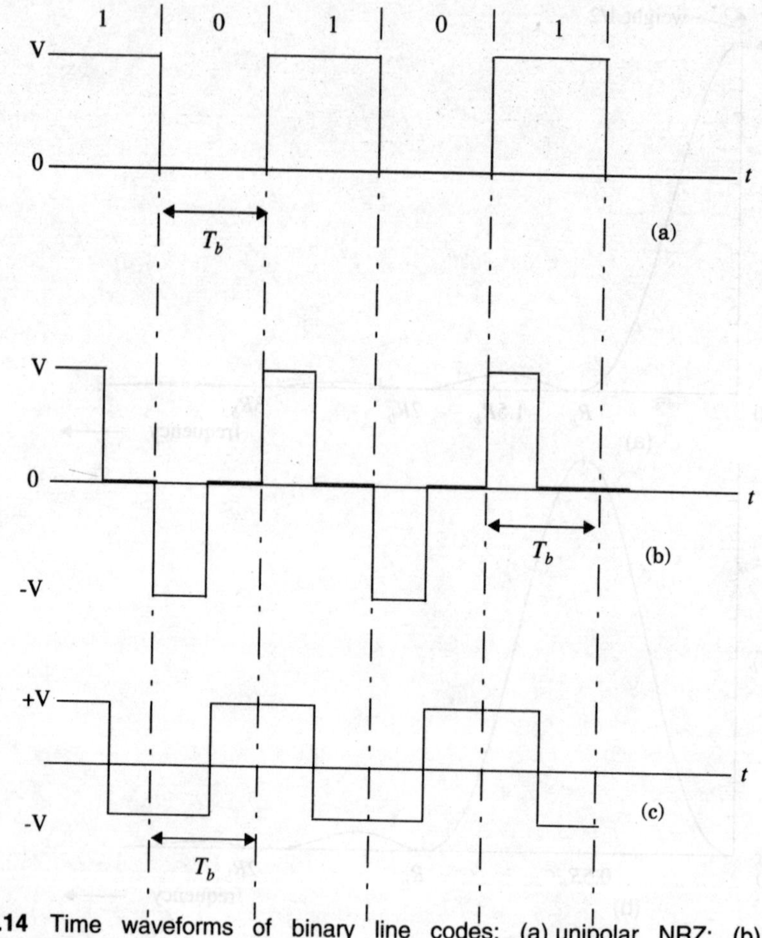

Figure 6.14 Time waveforms of binary line codes: (a) unipolar NRZ; (b) bipolar RZ; (c) Manchester NRZ.

symbols except the current symbol is equal to zero. If $h_{eff}(t)$ is the impulse response of the overall communication system, this condition can be mathematically stated as

$$h_{eff}(nT_s) = \begin{cases} K & n = 0 \\ 0 & n \neq 0 \end{cases} \tag{6.42}$$

where T_s is the symbol period, n is an integer, and K is a non-zero constant. The effective transfer function of the system can be represented as

$$h_{eff}(t) = \delta(t)*p(t)*h_c(t)*h_r(t) \tag{6.43}$$

where $p(t)$ is the pulse shape of a symbol, $h_c(t)$ is the channel impulse response, and $h_r(t)$ is the receiver impulse response. Nyquist derived transfer functions $H_{eff}(f)$ which satisfy the conditions of Equation (6.42) [Nyq28].

There are two important considerations in selecting a transfer function $H_{eff}(f)$ which satisfy Equation (6.42). First, $h_{eff}(t)$ should have a fast decay with a small magnitude near the sample values for $n \neq 0$. Second, if the channel is ideal ($h_c(t) = \delta(t)$), then it should be possible to realize or closely approximate shaping filters at both the transmitter and receiver to produce the desired $H_{eff}(f)$. Consider the impulse response in (6.44)

$$h_{eff}(t) = \frac{\sin(\pi t/T_s)}{(\pi t)/T_s} \tag{6.44}$$

Clearly, this impulse response satisfies the Nyquist condition for ISI cancellation given in Equation (6.42) (see Figure 6.15). Therefore, if the overall communication system can be modeled as a filter with the impulse response of Equation (6.44), it is possible to completely eliminate the effects of ISI. The transfer function of the filter can be obtained by taking the Fourier transform of the impulse response, and is given by

$$H_{eff}(f) = \frac{1}{f_s}\,\text{rect}\left(\frac{f}{f_s}\right) \tag{6.45}$$

This transfer function corresponds to a rectangular "brick-wall" filter with absolute bandwidth $f_s/2$, where f_s is the symbol rate. While this transfer function satisfies the zero ISI criterion with a minimum of bandwidth, there are practical difficulties in implementing it, since it corresponds to a noncausal system ($h_{eff}(t)$ exists for $t < 0$) and is thus difficult to approximate. Also, the $(\sin t)/t$ pulse has a waveform slope that is $1/t$ at each zero crossing, and is zero only at exact multiples of T_s, thus any error in the sampling time of zero-crossings will cause significant ISI due to overlapping from adjacent symbols. (A slope of $1/t^2$ or $1/t^3$ is more desirable to minimize the ISI due to timing jitter in adjacent samples.)

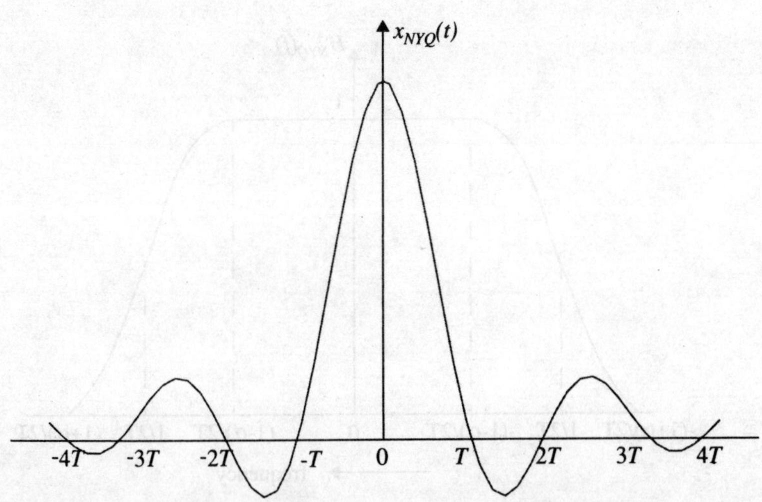

Figure 6.15 Nyquist ideal pulse shape for zero intersymbol interference.

Nyquist also proved that any filter with a transfer function having a rectangular filter of bandwidth $f_0 \geq 1/2T_s$, convolved with any arbitrary even function $Z(f)$ with zero magnitude outside the passband of the rectangular filter, satisfies the zero ISI condition. Mathematically, the transfer function of the filter which satisfies the zero ISI condition can be expressed as

$$H_{eff}(f) = \text{rect}\left(\frac{f}{f_0}\right) \otimes Z(f) \tag{6.46}$$

where $Z(f) = Z(-f)$, and $Z(f) = 0$ for $|f| \geq f_0 \geq 1/2T_s$. Expressed in terms of the impulse response, the Nyquist criterion states that any filter with an impulse response

$$h_{eff}(t) = \frac{\sin(\pi t/T_s)}{\pi t} z(t) \tag{6.47}$$

can achieve ISI cancellation. Filters which satisfy the Nyquist criterion are called Nyquist filters (Figure 6.16).

Assuming that the distortions introduced in the channel can be completely nullified by using an equalizer which has a transfer function that is equal to the inverse of the channel response, then the overall transfer function $H_{eff}(f)$ can be approximated as the product of the transfer functions of the transmitter and receiver filters. An effective end-to-end transfer function of $H_{eff}(f)$ is often achieved by using filters with transfer functions $\sqrt{H_{eff}(f)}$ at both the transmitter and receiver. This has the advantage of providing a matched filter response for the system, while at the same time minimizing the bandwidth and intersymbol interference.

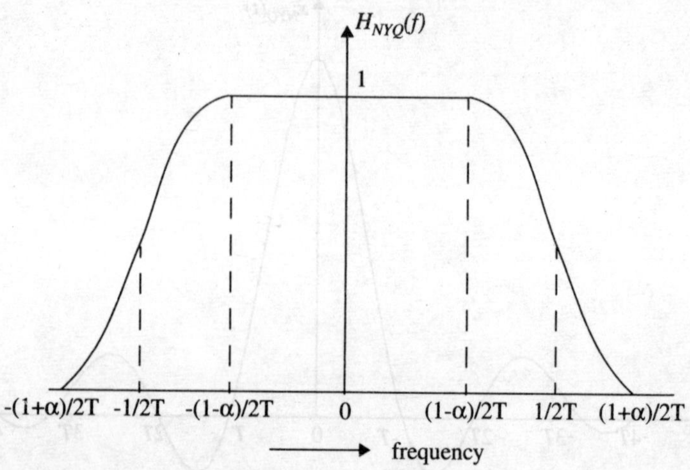

Figure 6.16 Transfer function of a Nyquist pulse-shaping filter at baseband.

6.6.2 Raised Cosine Rolloff Filter

The most popular pulse shaping filter used in mobile communications is the raised cosine filter. A raised cosine filter belongs to the class of filters which satisfy the Nyquist criterion. The transfer function of a raised cosine filter is given by

$$H_{RC}(f) = \begin{cases} 1 & 0 \le |f| \le \dfrac{(1-\alpha)}{2T_s} \\ \dfrac{1}{2}\left[1+\cos\left[\dfrac{\pi(|f|\cdot 2T_s - 1 + \alpha)}{2\alpha}\right]\right] & \dfrac{(1-\alpha)}{2T_s} \le |f| \le \dfrac{(1+\alpha)}{2T_s} \\ 0 & |f| > \dfrac{(1+\alpha)}{2T_s} \end{cases} \tag{6.48}$$

where α is the rolloff factor which ranges between 0 and 1. This transfer function is plotted in Figure 6.17 for various values of α. When $\alpha = 0$, the raised cosine rolloff filter corresponds to a rectangular filter of minimum bandwidth. The corresponding impulse response of the filter can be obtained by taking the inverse Fourier transform of the transfer function, and is given by

$$h_{RC}(t) = \frac{\sin\left(\dfrac{\pi t}{T_s}\right)}{\pi t} \cdot \frac{\cos\left(\dfrac{\pi \alpha t}{T_s}\right)}{1 - \left(\dfrac{4\alpha t}{2T_s}\right)^2} \tag{6.49}$$

The impulse response of the cosine rolloff filter at baseband is plotted in Figure 6.18 for various values of α. Notice that the impulse response decays much faster at the zero-crossings (approximately as $1/t^3$ for $t \gg T_s$) when compared to the "brick-wall" filter ($\alpha = 0$). The rapid time rolloff allows it to be truncated in time with little deviation in performance from theory. As seen from Figure 6.17, as the rolloff factor α increases, the bandwidth of the filter also increases, and the time sidelobe levels decrease in adjacent symbol slots. This implies that increasing α decreases the sensitivity to timing jitter, but increases the occupied bandwidth.

The symbol rate R_s that can be passed through a baseband raised cosine rolloff filter is given by

$$R_s = \frac{1}{T_s} = \frac{2B}{1+\alpha} \tag{6.50}$$

where B is the absolute filter bandwidth. For RF systems, the RF passband bandwidth doubles and

$$R_s = \frac{B}{1+\alpha} \tag{6.51}$$

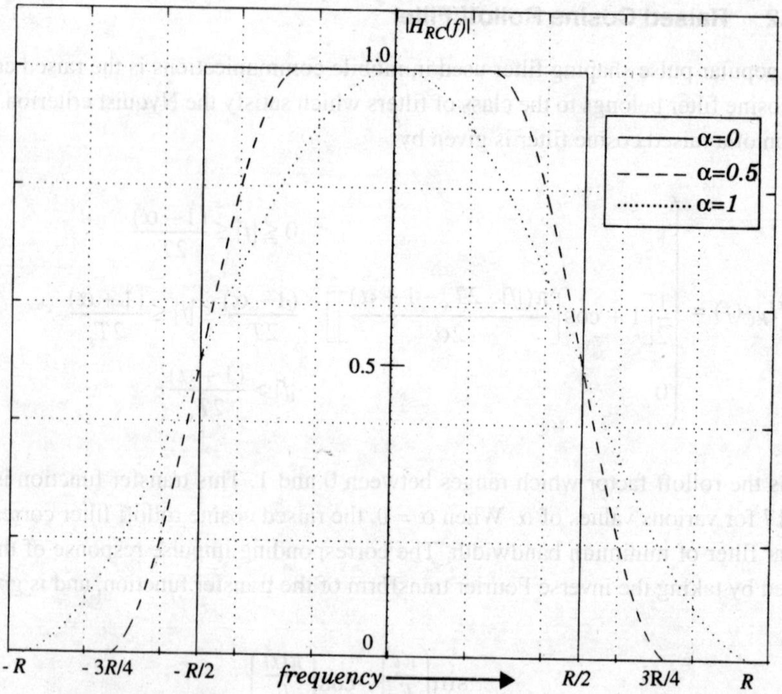

Figure 6.17 Magnitude transfer function of a raised cosine filter at baseband.

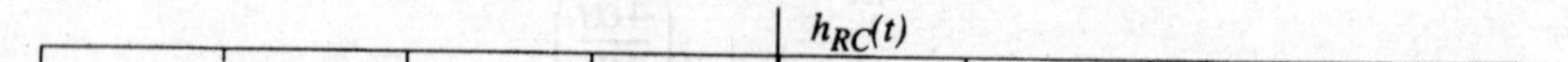

Figure 6.18 Impulse response of a raised cosine rolloff filter at baseband.

The cosine rolloff transfer function can be achieved by using identical $\sqrt{H_{RC}(f)}$ filters at the transmitter and receiver, while providing a matched filter for optimum performance in a flat-fading channel. To implement the filter responses, pulse shaping filters can be used either on the baseband data or at the output of the transmitter. As a rule, pulse shaping filters are implemented in DSP in baseband. Because $h_{RC}(t)$ is noncausal, it must be truncated, and pulse shaping filters are typically implemented for $\pm 6T_s$ about the $t = 0$ point for each symbol. For this reason, digital communication systems which use pulse shaping often store several symbols at a time inside the modulator, and then clock out a group of symbols by using a look-up table which represents a discrete-time waveform of the stored symbols. As an example, assume binary baseband pulses are to be transmitted using a raised cosine rolloff filter with $\alpha = 1/2$. If the modulator stores three bits at a time, then there are eight possible waveform states that may be produced at random for the group. If $\pm 6T_s$ is used to represent the timespan for each symbol (a symbol is the same as a bit in this case), then the timespan of the discrete-time waveform will be $14T_s$. Figure 6.19 illustrates the RF time waveform for the data sequence 1, 0, 1. The optimal bit decision points occur at $4T_s$, $5T_s$, and $6T_s$, and the time dispersive nature of pulse shaping can be seen.

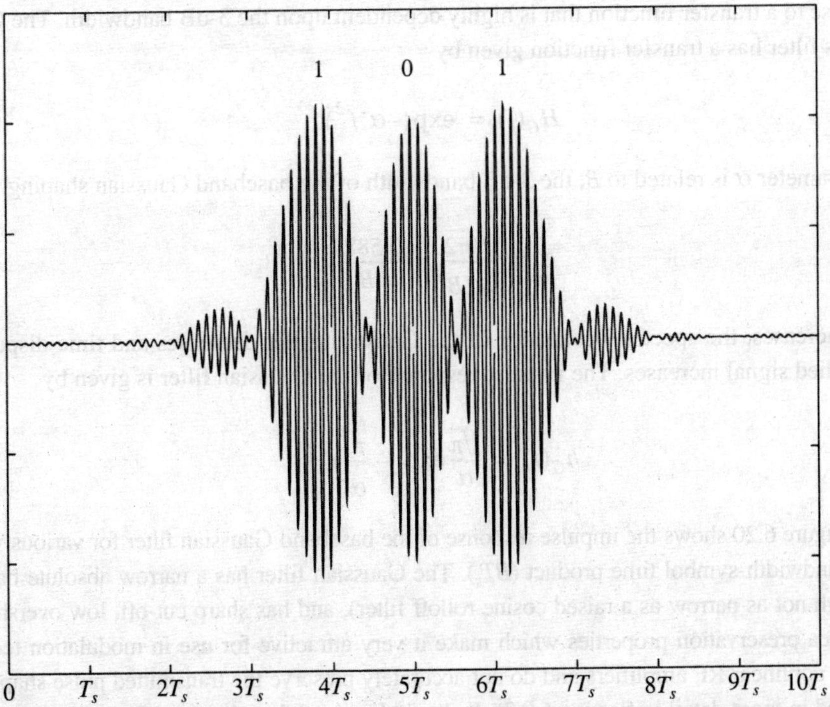

Figure 6.19 Raised cosine filtered ($\alpha = 0.5$) pulses corresponding to 1, 0, 1 data stream for a BPSK signal. Notice that the decision points (at $4T_s$, $5T_s$, $6T_s$) do not always correspond to the maximum values of the RF waveform.

The spectral efficiency offered by a raised cosine filter only occurs if the exact pulse shape is preserved at the carrier. This becomes difficult if nonlinear RF amplifiers are used. Small distortions in the baseband pulse shape can dramatically change the spectral occupancy of the transmitted signal. If not properly controlled, this can cause serious adjacent channel interference in mobile communication systems. A dilemma for mobile communication designers is that the reduced bandwidth offered by Nyquist pulse shaping requires linear amplifiers which are not power efficient. An obvious solution to this problem would be to develop linear amplifiers which use real-time feedback to offer more power efficiency, and this is currently an active research thrust for mobile communications.

6.6.3 Gaussian Pulse-Shaping Filter

It is also possible to use non-Nyquist techniques for pulse shaping. Prominent among such techniques is the use of a Gaussian pulse-shaping filter which is particularly effective when used in conjunction with Minimum Shift Keying (MSK) modulation, or other modulations which are well suited for power efficient nonlinear amplifiers. Unlike Nyquist filters which have zero-crossings at adjacent symbol peaks and a truncated transfer function, the Gaussian filter has a smooth transfer function with no zero-crossings. The impulse response of the Gaussian filter gives rise to a transfer function that is highly dependent upon the 3-dB bandwidth. The Gaussian lowpass filter has a transfer function given by

$$H_G(f) = \exp(-\alpha^2 f^2) \tag{6.52}$$

The parameter α is related to B, the 3-dB bandwidth of the baseband Gaussian shaping filter,

$$\alpha = \frac{\sqrt{ln2}}{\sqrt{2}B} = \frac{0.5887}{B} \tag{6.53}$$

As α increases, the spectral occupancy of the Gaussian filter decreases and time dispersion of the applied signal increases. The impulse response of the Gaussian filter is given by

$$h_G(t) = \frac{\sqrt{\pi}}{\alpha}\exp\left(-\frac{\pi^2}{\alpha^2}t^2\right) \tag{6.54}$$

Figure 6.20 shows the impulse response of the baseband Gaussian filter for various values of 3-dB bandwidth-symbol time product (BT_s). The Gaussian filter has a narrow absolute bandwidth (although not as narrow as a raised cosine rolloff filter), and has sharp cut-off, low overshoot, and pulse area preservation properties which make it very attractive for use in modulation techniques that use nonlinear RF amplifiers and do not accurately preserve the transmitted pulse shape (this is discussed in more detail in Section 6.9.3). It should be noted that since the Gaussian pulse-shaping filter *does not* satisfy the Nyquist criterion for ISI cancellation, reducing the spectral occupancy creates degradation in performance due to increased ISI. Thus, a tradeoff is made between the desired

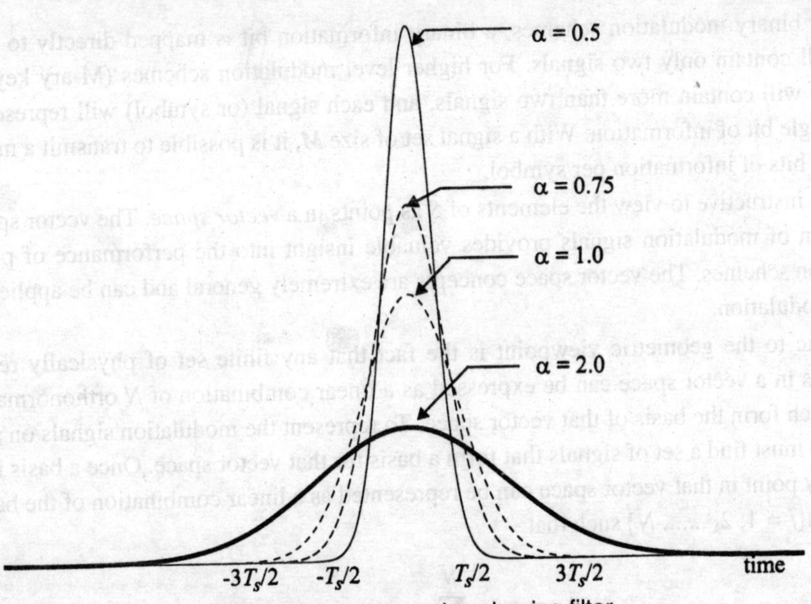

Figure 6.20 Impulse response of a Gaussian pulse-shaping filter.

RF bandwidth and the irreducible error due to ISI of adjacent symbols when Gaussian pulse shaping is used. Gaussian pulses are used when cost and power efficiency are major factors and the bit error rates due to ISI are deemed to be lower than what is nominally required.

Example 6.8

Find the first zero-crossing RF bandwidth of a rectangular pulse which has $T_s = 41.06\ \mu s$. Compare this to the bandwidth of a raised cosine filter pulse with $T_s = 41.06\ \mu s$ and $\alpha = 0.35$.

Solution

The first zero-crossing (null-to-null) bandwidth of a rectangular pulse is equal to

$$2/T_s = 2/(41.06\ \mu s) = 48.71\text{ kHz}$$

and that of a raised cosine filter with $\alpha = 0.35$ is

$$\frac{1}{T_s}(1+\alpha) = \frac{1}{41.06\ \mu s}(1+0.35) = 32.88\text{ kHz}$$

6.7 Geometric Representation of Modulation Signals

Digital modulation involves choosing a particular signal waveform $s_i(t)$, from a finite set of possible signal waveforms (or symbols) based on the information bits applied to the modulator. If there are a total of M possible signals, the modulation signal set S can be represented as

$$S = \{s_1(t), s_2(t), \ldots\ldots\ldots, s_M(t)\} \tag{6.55}$$

For binary modulation schemes, a binary information bit is mapped directly to a signal, and S will contain only two signals. For higher level modulation schemes (M-ary keying) the signal set will contain more than two signals, and each signal (or symbol) will represent more than a single bit of information. With a signal set of size M, it is possible to transmit a maximum of $\log_2 M$ bits of information per symbol.

It is instructive to view the elements of S as points in a *vector space*. The vector space representation of modulation signals provides valuable insight into the performance of particular modulation schemes. The vector space concepts are extremely general and can be applied to any type of modulation.

Basic to the geometric viewpoint is the fact that any finite set of physically realizable waveforms in a vector space can be expressed as a linear combination of N orthonormal waveforms which form the basis of that vector space. To represent the modulation signals on a vector space, one must find a set of signals that form a basis for that vector space. Once a basis is determined, any point in that vector space can be represented as a linear combination of the basis signals $\{\phi_j(t) | j = 1, 2, ..., N\}$ such that

$$s_i(t) = \sum_{j=1}^{N} s_{ij}\phi_j(t) \tag{6.56}$$

The basis signals are orthogonal to one another in time such that

$$\int_{-\infty}^{\infty} \phi_i(t)\phi_j(t)dt = 0 \qquad i \neq j \tag{6.57}$$

Each of the basis signals is normalized to have unit energy, i.e.,

$$E = \int_{-\infty}^{\infty} \phi_i^2(t)dt = 1 \tag{6.58}$$

The basis signals can be thought of as forming a coordinate system for the vector space. The Gram–Schmidt procedure provides a systematic way of obtaining the basis signals for a given set of signals [Zie92].

For example, consider the set of BPSK signals $s_1(t)$ and $s_2(t)$ given by

$$s_1(t) = \sqrt{\frac{2E_b}{T_b}}\cos(2\pi f_c t) \qquad 0 \le t \le T_b \tag{6.59.a}$$

and

$$s_2(t) = -\sqrt{\frac{2E_b}{T_b}}\cos(2\pi f_c t) \qquad 0 \le t \le T_b \tag{6.59.b}$$

where E_b is the energy per bit, T_b is the bit period, and a rectangular pulse shape $p(t) = \text{rect}((t-T_b/2)/T_b)$ is assumed. $\phi_i(t)$ for this signal set simply consists of a single waveform $\phi_1(t)$ where

$$\phi_1(t) = \sqrt{\frac{2}{T_b}}\cos(2\pi f_c t) \qquad 0 \le t \le T_b \tag{6.60}$$

Using this basis signal, the BPSK signal set can be represented as

$$S_{\text{BPSK}} = \left\{\sqrt{E_b}\phi_1(t), -\sqrt{E_b}\phi_1(t)\right\} \tag{6.61}$$

This signal set can be shown geometrically in Figure 6.21. Such a representation is called a *constellation diagram* which provides a graphical representation of the complex envelope of each possible symbol state. The x-axis of a constellation diagram represents the in-phase component of the complex envelope, and the y-axis represents the quadrature component of the complex envelope. The distance between signals on a constellation diagram relates to how different the modulation waveforms are, and how well a receiver can differentiate between all possible symbols when random noise is present.

It should be noted that the number of basis signals will always be less than or equal to the number of signals in the set. The number of basis signals required to represent the complete modulation signal set is called the *dimension* of the vector space. If there are as many basis signals as there are signals in the modulation signal set, then all the signals in the set are necessarily *orthogonal* to one another.

Some of the properties of a modulation scheme can be inferred from its constellation diagram. For example, the bandwidth occupied by the modulation signals decreases as the number of signal points/dimension increases. Therefore, if a modulation scheme has a constellation that is densely packed, it is more bandwidth efficient than a modulation scheme with a sparsely packed constellation. However, it should be noted that the bandwidth occupied by a modulated signal increases with the dimension N of the constellation.

The probability of bit error is proportional to the distance between the closest points in the constellation. This implies that a modulation scheme with a constellation that is densely packed is less energy efficient than a modulation scheme that has a sparse constellation.

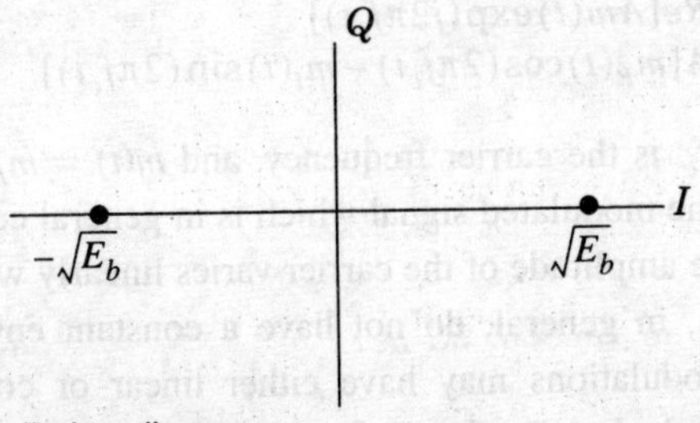

Figure 6.21 BPSK constellation diagram.

A simple upper bound for the probability of symbol error in an additive white Gaussian noise channel (AWGN) channel with a noise spectral density N_0 for an arbitrary constellation can be obtained using the union bound [Zie92]. The union bound provides a representative estimate for the average probability of error for a particular modulation signal, $P_s(\varepsilon|s_i)$

$$P_s(\varepsilon|s_i) \leq \sum_{\substack{j=1 \\ j \neq i}} Q\left(\frac{d_{ij}}{\sqrt{2N_0}}\right) \tag{6.62}$$

where d_{ij} is the Euclidean distance between the ith and jth signal point in the constellation, and $Q(x)$ is the Q-function defined in Appendix F

$$Q(x) = \int_x^{\infty} \frac{1}{\sqrt{2\pi}} \exp(-x^2/2)dx \tag{6.63}$$

If all of the M modulation waveforms are equally likely to be transmitted, then the average probability of error for a modulation can be estimated by

$$P_s(\varepsilon) = P_s(\varepsilon|s_i)P(s_i) = \frac{1}{M}\sum_{i=1}^{M} P_s(\varepsilon|s_i) \tag{6.64}$$

For symmetric constellations, the distance between all constellation points are equivalent, and the conditional error probability $P_s(\varepsilon|s_i)$ is the same for all i. Hence Equation (6.62) gives the average probability of symbol error for a particular constellation set.

6.8 Linear Modulation Techniques

Digital modulation techniques may be broadly classified as *linear* and *nonlinear*. In linear modulation techniques, the amplitude of the transmitted signal, $s(t)$, varies linearly with the modulating digital signal, $m(t)$. Linear modulation techniques are bandwidth efficient and hence are very attractive for use in wireless communication systems where there is an increasing demand to accommodate more and more users within a limited spectrum.

In a linear modulation scheme, the transmitted signal $s(t)$ can be expressed as [Zie92]

$$\begin{aligned} s(t) &= Re[Am(t)\exp(j2\pi f_c t)] \\ &= A[m_R(t)\cos(2\pi f_c t) - m_I(t)\sin(2\pi f_c t)] \end{aligned} \tag{6.65}$$

where A is the amplitude, f_c is the carrier frequency, and $m(t) = m_R(t) + jm_I(t)$ is a complex envelope representation of the modulated signal which is in general complex form. From Equation (6.65), it is clear that the amplitude of the carrier varies linearly with the modulating signal. Linear modulation schemes, in general, do not have a constant envelope. As shown subsequently, some nonlinear modulations may have either linear or constant carrier envelopes, depending on whether or not the baseband waveform is pulse shaped.

While linear modulation schemes have very good spectral efficiency, they must be transmitted using linear RF amplifiers which have poor power efficiency [You79]. Using power efficient nonlinear amplifiers leads to the regeneration of filtered sidelobes which can cause severe adjacent channel interference, and results in the loss of all the spectral efficiency gained by linear modulation. However, clever ways have been developed to get around these difficulties. The most popular linear modulation techniques include pulse-shaped QPSK, OQPSK, and $\pi/4$ QPSK, which are discussed subsequently.

6.8.1 Binary Phase Shift Keying (BPSK)

In binary phase shift keying (BPSK), the phase of a constant amplitude carrier signal is switched between two values according to the two possible signals m_1 and m_2 corresponding to binary 1 and 0, respectively. Normally, the two phases are separated by 180°. If the sinusoidal carrier has an amplitude A_c and energy per bit $E_b = \frac{1}{2}A_c^2 T_b$, then the transmitted BPSK signal is either

$$s_{\mathrm{BPSK}}(t) = \sqrt{\frac{2E_b}{T_b}}\cos(2\pi f_c t + \theta_c) \qquad 0 \le t \le T_b \text{ (binary 1)} \tag{6.66.a}$$

or

$$s_{\mathrm{BPSK}}(t) = \sqrt{\frac{2E_b}{T_b}}\cos(2\pi f_c t + \pi + \theta_c)$$

$$= -\sqrt{\frac{2E_b}{T_b}}\cos(2\pi f_c t + \theta_c) \quad 0 \le t \le T_b \text{ (binary 0)} \tag{6.66.b}$$

It is often convenient to generalize m_1 and m_2 as a binary data signal *m(t)*, which takes on one of two possible pulse shapes. Then the transmitted signal may be represented as

$$s_{\mathrm{BPSK}}(t) = m(t)\sqrt{\frac{2E_b}{T_b}}\cos(2\pi f_c t + \theta_c) \tag{6.67}$$

The BPSK signal is equivalent to a double sideband suppressed carrier amplitude modulated waveform, where $\cos(2\pi f_c t)$ is applied as the carrier, and the data signal $m(t)$ is applied as the modulating waveform. Hence a BPSK signal can be generated using a balanced modulator.

Spectrum and Bandwidth of BPSK

The BPSK signal using a polar baseband data waveform $m(t)$ can be expressed in complex envelope form as

$$s_{\mathrm{BPSK}}(t) = Re\{g_{\mathrm{BPSK}}(t)\exp(j2\pi f_c t)\} \tag{6.68}$$

where $g_{\mathrm{BPSK}}(t)$ is the complex envelope of the signal given by

$$g_{\mathrm{BPSK}}(t) = \sqrt{\frac{2E_b}{T_b}}m(t)e^{j\theta_c} \tag{6.69}$$

The power spectral density (PSD) of the complex envelope can be shown to be

$$P_{g_{BPSK}}(f) = 2E_b\left(\frac{\sin \pi f T_b}{\pi f T_b}\right)^2 \tag{6.70}$$

The PSD for the BPSK signal at RF can be evaluated by translating the baseband spectrum to the carrier frequency using the relation given in Equation (6.41).

Hence, the PSD of a BPSK signal at RF is given by

$$P_{BPSK}(f) = \frac{E_b}{2}\left[\left(\frac{\sin \pi(f-f_c)T_b}{\pi(f-f_c)T_b}\right)^2 + \left(\frac{\sin \pi(-f-f_c)T_b}{\pi(-f-f_c)T_b}\right)^2\right] \tag{6.71}$$

The PSD of the BPSK signal for both rectangular and raised cosine rolloff pulse shapes is plotted in Figure 6.22. The null-to-null bandwidth is found to be equal to twice the bit rate ($BW = 2R_b = 2/T_b$). From the plot, it can also be shown that 90% of the BPSK signal energy is contained within a bandwidth approximately equal to $1.6R_b$ for rectangular pulses, and all of the energy is within $1.5R_b$ for pulses with $\alpha = 0.5$ raised cosine filtering.

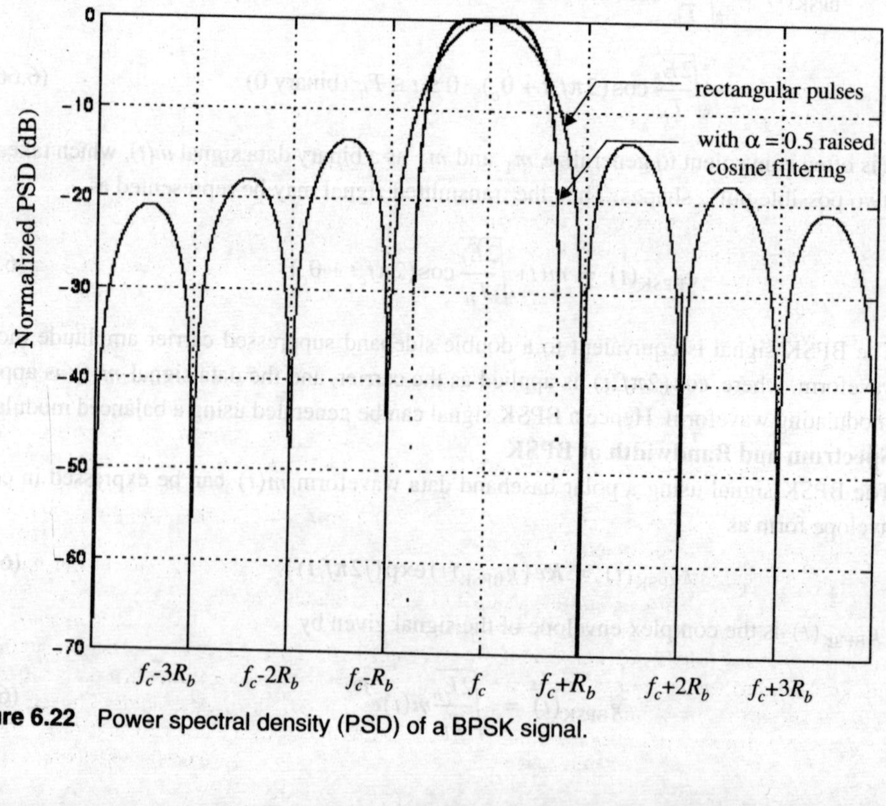

Figure 6.22 Power spectral density (PSD) of a BPSK signal.

BPSK Receiver

If no multipath impairments are induced by the channel, the received BPSK signal can be expressed as

$$\begin{aligned} s_{\text{BPSK}}(t) &= m(t)\sqrt{\frac{2E_b}{T_b}}\cos(2\pi f_c t + \theta_c + \theta_{ch}) \\ &= m(t)\sqrt{\frac{2E_b}{T_b}}\cos(2\pi f_c t + \theta) \end{aligned} \tag{6.72}$$

where θ_{ch} is the phase shift corresponding to the time delay in the channel. BPSK uses *coherent* or *synchronous* demodulation, which requires that information about the phase and frequency of the carrier be available at the receiver. If a low level pilot carrier signal is transmitted along with the BPSK signal, then the carrier phase and frequency may be recovered at the receiver using a phase locked loop (PLL). If no pilot carrier is transmitted, a Costas loop or squaring loop may be used to synthesize the carrier phase and frequency from the received BPSK signal. Figure 6.23 shows the block diagram of a BPSK receiver along with the carrier recovery circuits.

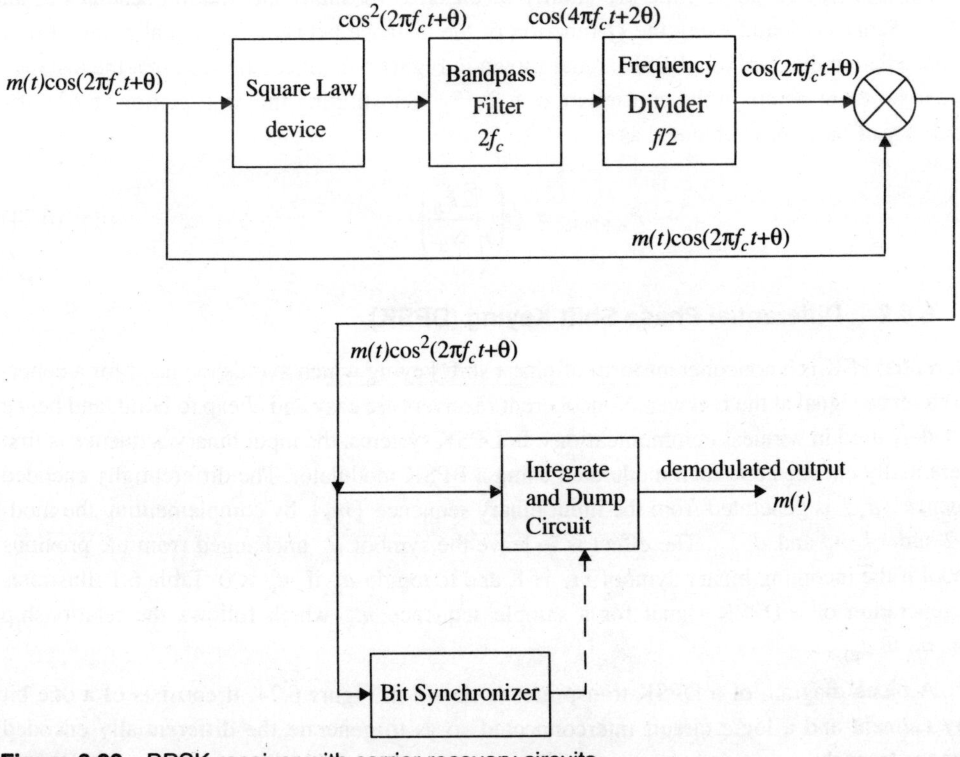

Figure 6.23 BPSK receiver with carrier recovery circuits.

The received signal $\cos(2\pi f_c t + \theta)$ is squared to generate a dc signal and an amplitude varying sinusoid at twice the carrier frequency. The dc signal is filtered out using a bandpass filter with center frequency tuned to $2f_c$. A frequency divider is then used to recreate the waveform $\cos(2\pi f_c t + \theta)$. The output of the multiplier after the frequency divider is given by

$$m(t)\sqrt{\frac{2E_b}{T_b}}\cos^2(2\pi f_c t + \theta) = m(t)\sqrt{\frac{2E_b}{T_b}}\left[\frac{1}{2} + \frac{1}{2}\cos 2(2\pi f_c t + \theta)\right] \quad (6.73)$$

This signal is applied to an integrate and dump circuit which forms the low pass filter segment of a BPSK detector. If the transmitter and receiver pulse shapes are matched, then the detection will be optimum. A bit synchronizer is used to facilitate sampling of the integrator output precisely at the end of each bit period. At the end of each bit period, the switch at the output of the integrator closes to dump the output signal to the decision circuit. Depending on whether the integrator output is above or below a certain threshold, the decision circuit decides that the received signal corresponds to a binary 1 or 0. The threshold is set at an optimum level such that the probability of error is minimized. If it is equally likely that a binary 1 or 0 is transmitted, then the voltage level corresponding to the midpoint between the detector output voltage levels of binary 1 and 0 is used as the optimum threshold.

As seen in Section 6.7, the probability of bit error for *many* modulation schemes in an AWGN channel is found using the Q-function of the distance between the signal points. From the constellation diagram of a BPSK signal shown in Figure 6.21, it can be seen that the distance between adjacent points in the constellation is $2\sqrt{E_b}$. Substituting this in Equation (6.62), the probability of bit error is obtained as

$$P_{e,\text{BPSK}} = Q\left(\sqrt{\frac{2E_b}{N_0}}\right) \quad (6.74)$$

6.8.2 Differential Phase Shift Keying (DPSK)

Differential PSK is a noncoherent form of phase shift keying which avoids the need for a coherent reference signal at the receiver. Noncoherent receivers are easy and cheap to build, and hence are widely used in wireless communications. In DPSK systems, the input binary sequence is first differentially encoded and then modulated using a BPSK modulator. The differentially encoded sequence $\{d_k\}$ is generated from the input binary sequence $\{m_k\}$ by complementing the modulo-2 sum of m_k and d_{k-1}. The effect is to leave the symbol d_k unchanged from the previous symbol if the incoming binary symbol m_k is 1, and to toggle d_k if m_k is 0. Table 6.1 illustrates the generation of a DPSK signal for a sample sequence m_k which follows the relationship $d_k = \overline{m_k \oplus d_{k-1}}$.

A block diagram of a DPSK transmitter is shown in Figure 6.24. It consists of a one bit delay element and a logic circuit interconnected so as to generate the differentially encoded sequence from the input binary sequence. The output is passed through a product modulator to

Table 6.1 Illustration of the Differential Encoding Process

$\{m_k\}$		1	0	0	1	0	1	1	0
$\{d_{k-1}\}$		1	1	0	1	1	0	0	0
$\{d_k\}$	1	1	0	1	1	0	0	0	1

obtain the DPSK signal. At the receiver, the original sequence is recovered from the demodulated differentially encoded signal through a complementary process, as shown in Figure 6.25.

While DPSK signaling has the advantage of reduced receiver complexity, its energy efficiency is inferior to that of coherent PSK by about 3 dB. The average probability of error for DPSK in additive white Gaussian noise is given by

$$P_{e,\,\mathrm{DPSK}} = \frac{1}{2}\exp\left(-\frac{E_b}{N_0}\right) \tag{6.75}$$

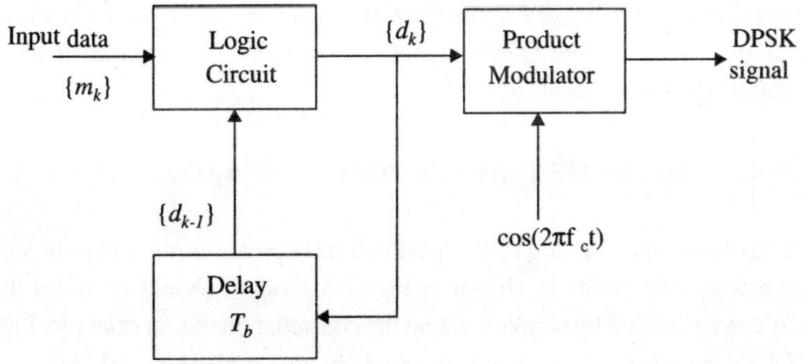

Figure 6.24 Block diagram of a DPSK transmitter.

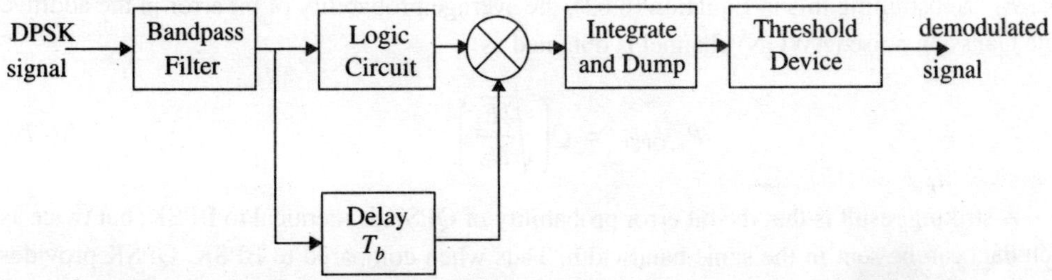

Figure 6.25 Block diagram of DPSK receiver.

6.8.3 Quadrature Phase Shift Keying (QPSK)

Quadrature phase shift keying (QPSK) has twice the bandwidth efficiency of BPSK, since two bits are transmitted in a single modulation symbol. The phase of the carrier takes on one of four equally spaced values, such as 0, $\pi/2$, π, and $3\pi/2$, where each value of phase corresponds to a unique pair of message bits. The QPSK signal for this set of symbol states may be defined as

$$s_{QPSK}(t) = \sqrt{\frac{2E_s}{T_s}}\cos\left[2\pi f_c t + (i-1)\frac{\pi}{2}\right] \qquad 0 \le t \le T_s \quad i = 1, 2, 3, 4 \tag{6.76}$$

where T_s is the symbol duration and is equal to twice the bit period.

Using trigonometric identities, the above equations can be rewritten for the interval $0 \le t \le T_s$ as

$$s_{QPSK}(t) = \sqrt{\frac{2E_s}{T_s}}\cos\left[(i-1)\frac{\pi}{2}\right]\cos(2\pi f_c t) - \sqrt{\frac{2E_s}{T_s}}\sin\left[(i-1)\frac{\pi}{2}\right]\sin(2\pi f_c t) \tag{6.77}$$

If basis functions $\phi_1(t) = \sqrt{2/T_s}\cos(2\pi f_c t)$, $\phi_2(t) = \sqrt{2/T_s}\sin(2\pi f_c t)$ are defined over the interval $0 \le t \le T_s$ for the QPSK signal set, then the four signals in the set can be expressed in terms of the basis signals as

$$s_{QPSK}(t) = \left\{\sqrt{E_s}\cos\left[(i-1)\frac{\pi}{2}\right]\phi_1(t) - \sqrt{E_s}\sin\left[(i-1)\frac{\pi}{2}\right]\phi_2(t)\right\} \qquad i = 1, 2, 3, 4 \tag{6.78}$$

Based on this representation, a QPSK signal can be depicted using a two-dimensional constellation diagram with four points as shown in Figure 6.26(a). It should be noted that different QPSK signal sets can be derived by simply rotating the constellation. As an example, Figure 6.26(b) shows another QPSK signal set where the phase values are $\pi/4$, $3\pi/4$, $3\pi/4$, and $7\pi/4$.

From the constellation diagram of a QPSK signal, it can be seen that the distance between adjacent points in the constellation is $\sqrt{2E_s}$. Since each symbol corresponds to two bits, then $E_s = 2E_b$, thus the distance between two neighboring points in the QPSK constellation is equal to $2\sqrt{E_b}$. Substituting this in Equation (6.62), the average probability of bit error in the additive white Gaussian noise (AWGN) channel is obtained as

$$P_{e,QPSK} = Q\left(\sqrt{\frac{2E_b}{N_0}}\right) \tag{6.79}$$

A striking result is that the bit error probability of QPSK is identical to BPSK, but twice as much data can be sent in the same bandwidth. Thus when compared to BPSK, QPSK provides twice the spectral efficiency with exactly the same energy efficiency.

Similar to BPSK, QPSK can also be differentially encoded to allow noncoherent detection.

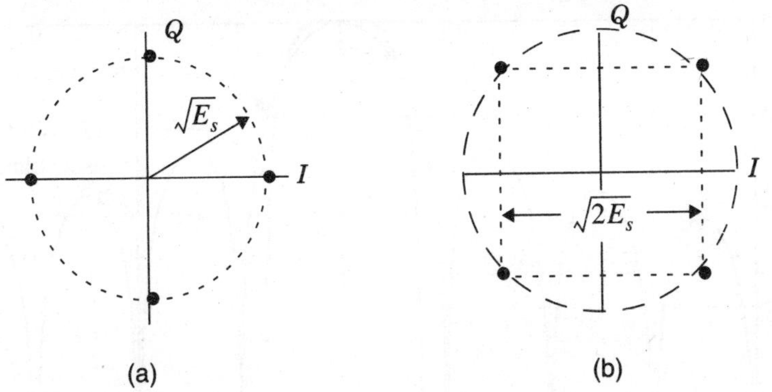

Figure 6.26 (a) QPSK constellation where the carrier phases are 0, π/2, π, 3π/2; (b) QPSK constellation where the carrier phases are π/4, 3π/4, 5π/4, 7π/4.

Spectrum and Bandwidth of QPSK Signals

The power spectral density of a QPSK signal can be obtained in a manner similar to that used for BPSK, with the bit periods T_b replaced by symbol periods T_s. Hence, the PSD of a QPSK signal using rectangular pulses can be expressed as

$$\begin{aligned} P_{\text{QPSK}}(f) &= \frac{E_s}{2}\left[\left(\frac{\sin\pi(f-f_c)T_s}{\pi(f-f_c)T_s}\right)^2 + \left(\frac{\sin\pi(-f-f_c)T_s}{\pi(-f-f_c)T_s}\right)^2\right] \\ &= E_b\left[\left(\frac{\sin 2\pi(f-f_c)T_b}{2\pi(f-f_c)T_b}\right)^2 + \left(\frac{\sin 2\pi(-f-f_c)T_b}{2\pi(-f-f_c)T_b}\right)^2\right] \end{aligned} \tag{6.80}$$

The PSD of a QPSK signal for rectangular and raised cosine filtered pulses is plotted in Figure 6.27. The null-to-null RF bandwidth is equal to the bit rate R_b, which is half that of a BPSK signal.

6.8.4 QPSK Transmission and Detection Techniques

Figure 6.28 shows a block diagram of a typical QPSK transmitter. The unipolar binary message stream has bit rate R_b and is first converted into a bipolar non-return-to-zero (NRZ) sequence using a unipolar to bipolar converter. The bit stream $m(t)$ is then split into two bit streams $m_I(t)$ and $m_Q(t)$ (in-phase and quadrature streams), each having a bit rate of $R_s = R_b/2$. The bit stream $m_I(t)$ is called the "even" stream and $m_Q(t)$ is called the "odd" stream. The two binary sequences are separately modulated by two carriers $\phi_1(t)$ and $\phi_2(t)$, which are in quadrature. The two modulated signals, each of which can be considered to be a BPSK signal, are summed to produce a QPSK signal. The filter at the output of the modulator confines the power spectrum of the QPSK signal within the allocated band. This prevents spill-over of signal energy into adjacent channels and also removes out-of-band spurious signals generated during the modulation process. In most implementations, pulse shaping is done at baseband to provide proper RF filtering at the transmitter output.

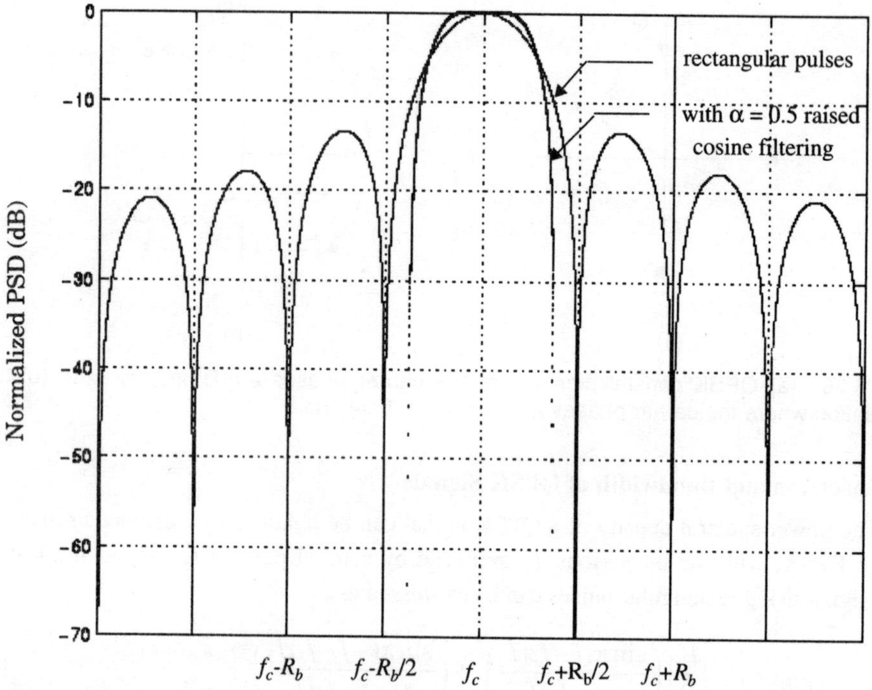

Figure 6.27 Power spectral density of a QPSK signal.

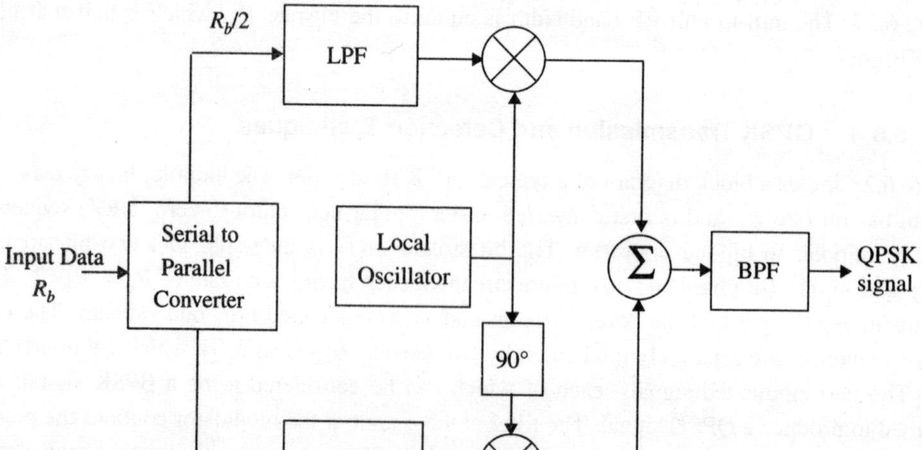

Figure 6.28 Block diagram of a QPSK transmitter.

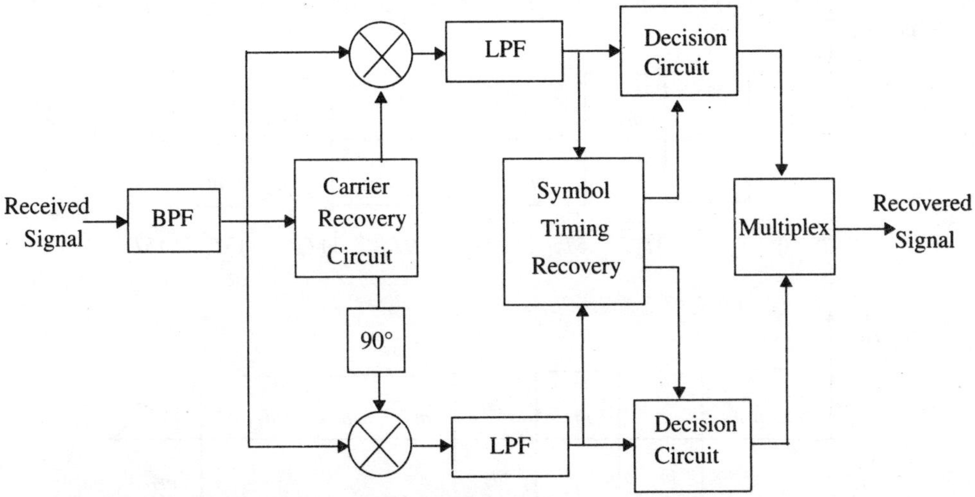

Figure 6.29 Block diagram of a QPSK receiver.

Figure 6.29 shows a block diagram of a coherent QPSK receiver. The frontend bandpass filter removes the out-of-band noise and adjacent channel interference. The filtered output is split into two parts, and each part is coherently demodulated using the in-phase and quadrature carriers. The coherent carriers used for demodulation are recovered from the received signal using carrier recovery circuits of the type described in Figure 6.23. The outputs of the demodulators are passed through decision circuits which generate the in-phase and quadrature binary streams. The two components are then multiplexed to reproduce the original binary sequence.

6.8.5 Offset QPSK

The amplitude of a QPSK signal is ideally constant. However, when QPSK signals are pulse shaped, they lose the constant envelope property. The occasional phase shift of π radians can cause the signal envelope to pass through zero for just an instant. Any kind of hardlimiting or nonlinear amplification of the zero-crossings brings back the filtered sidelobes since the fidelity of the signal at small voltage levels is lost in transmission. To prevent the regeneration of sidelobes and spectral widening, it is imperative that QPSK signals that use pulse shaping be amplified only using linear amplifiers, which are less efficient. A modified form of QPSK, called *offset* QPSK (OQPSK) or *staggered* QPSK is less susceptible to these deleterious effects [Pas79] and supports more efficient amplification. That is, OQPSK ensures there are fewer baseband signal transitions applied to the RF amplifier, which helps eliminate spectrum regrowth after amplification.

OQPSK signaling is similar to QPSK signaling, as represented by Equation (6.77), except for the time alignment of the even and odd bit streams. In QPSK signaling, the bit transitions of the even and odd bit streams occur at the same time instants, but in OQPSK signaling, the even and odd bit streams, $m_I(t)$ and $m_Q(t)$, are offset in their relative alignment by one bit period (half-symbol period). This is shown in the waveforms of Figure 6.30.

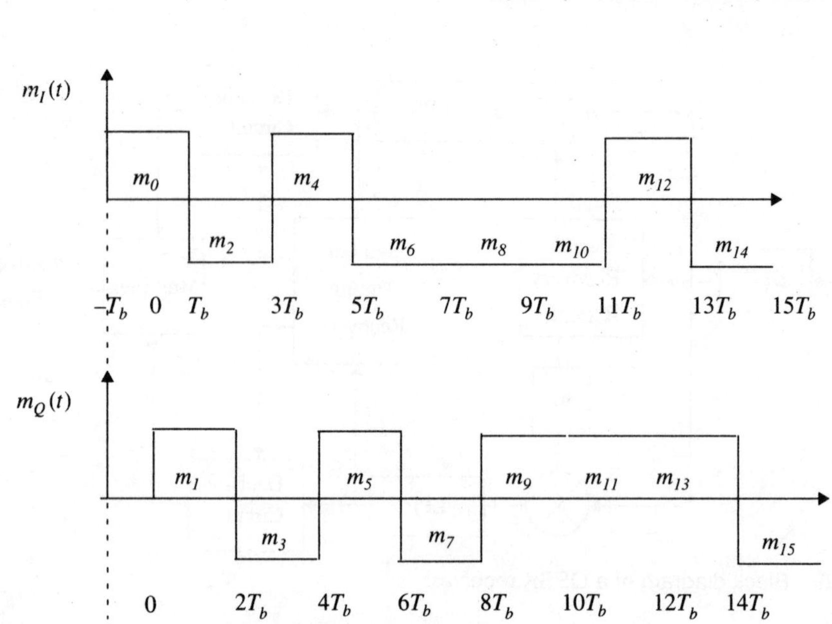

Figure 6.30 The time offset waveforms that are applied to the in-phase and quadrature arms of an OQPSK modulator. Notice that a half-symbol offset is used.

Due to the time alignment of $m_I(t)$ and $m_Q(t)$ in standard QPSK, phase transitions occur only once every $T_s = 2T_b$ s, and will be a maximum of 180° if there is a change in the value of both $m_I(t)$ and $m_Q(t)$. However, in OQPSK signaling, bit transitions (and, hence, phase transitions) occur every T_b s. Since the transition instants of $m_I(t)$ and $m_Q(t)$ are offset, at any given time only one of the two bit streams can change values. This implies that the maximum phase shift of the transmitted signal at any given time is limited to ±90°. Hence, by switching phases more frequently (i.e., every T_b s instead of $2T_b$ s) OQPSK signaling eliminates 180° phase transitions.

Since 180° phase transitions have been eliminated, bandlimiting of (i.e., pulse shaping) OQPSK signals does not cause the signal envelope to go to zero. Obviously, there will be some amount of ISI caused by the bandlimiting process, especially at the 90° phase transition points. But the envelope variations are considerably less, and hence hardlimiting or nonlinear amplification of OQPSK signals does not regenerate the high frequency sidelobes as much as in QPSK. Thus, spectral occupancy is significantly reduced, while permitting more efficient RF amplification.

The spectrum of an OQPSK signal is identical to that of a QPSK signal, hence both signals occupy the same bandwidth. The staggered alignment of the even and odd bit streams does not change the nature of the spectrum. OQPSK retains its bandlimited nature even after nonlinear amplification, and therefore is very attractive for mobile communication systems where bandwidth efficiency and efficient nonlinear amplifiers are critical for low power drain. Further, OQPSK signals also appear to perform better than QPSK in the presence of phase jitter due to noisy reference signals at the receiver [Chu87].

6.8.6 π/4 QPSK

The $\pi/4$ shifted QPSK modulation is a quadrature phase shift keying technique which offers a compromise between OQPSK and QPSK in terms of the allowed maximum phase transitions. It may be demodulated in a coherent or noncoherent fashion. In $\pi/4$ QPSK, the maximum phase change is limited to ±135°, as compared to 180° for QPSK and 90° for OQPSK. Hence, the bandlimited $\pi/4$ QPSK signal preserves the constant envelope property better than bandlimited QPSK, but is more susceptible to envelope variations than OQPSK. An extremely attractive feature of $\pi/4$ QPSK is that it can be noncoherently detected, which greatly simplifies receiver design. Further, it has been found that in the presence of multipath spread and fading, $\pi/4$ QPSK performs better than OQPSK [Liu89]. Very often, $\pi/4$ QPSK signals are differentially encoded to facilitate easier implementation of differential detection or coherent demodulation with phase ambiguity in the recovered carrier. When differentially encoded, $\pi/4$ QPSK is called $\pi/4$ DQPSK.

In a $\pi/4$ QPSK modulator, signaling points of the modulated signal are selected from two QPSK constellations which are shifted by $\pi/4$ with respect to each other. Figure 6.31 shows the two constellations along with the combined constellation where the links between two signal points indicate the possible phase transitions. Switching between two constellations, every successive bit ensures that there is at least a phase shift which is an integer multiple of $\pi/4$ radians between successive symbols. This ensures that there is a phase transition for every symbol, which enables a receiver to perform timing recovery and synchronization.

6.8.7 π/4 QPSK Transmission Techniques

A block diagram of a generic $\pi/4$ QPSK transmitter is shown in Figure 6.32. The input bit stream is partitioned by a serial-to-parallel (S/P) converter into two parallel data streams $m_{I,k}$ and $m_{Q,k}$, each with a symbol rate equal to half that of the incoming bit rate. The kth in-phase and quadrature pulses, I_k and Q_k, are produced at the output of the signal mapping circuit over time $kT \le t \le (k+1)T$ and are determined by their previous values, I_{k-1} and Q_{k-1}, as well as θ_k, which itself is a function of ϕ_k, which is a function of the current input symbols m_{Ik} and m_{Qk}. I_k and Q_k represent rectangular pulses over one symbol duration having amplitudes given by

$$I_k = \cos\theta_k = I_{k-1}\cos\phi_k - Q_{k-1}\sin\phi_k \tag{6.81}$$

$$Q_k = \sin\theta_k = I_{k-1}\sin\phi_k + Q_{k-1}\cos\phi_k \tag{6.82}$$

where

$$\theta_k = \theta_{k-1} + \phi_k \tag{6.83}$$

and θ_k and θ_{k-1} are phases of the kth and $k-1$st symbols. The phase shift ϕ_k is related to the input symbols m_{Ik} and m_{Qk} according to Table 6.2.

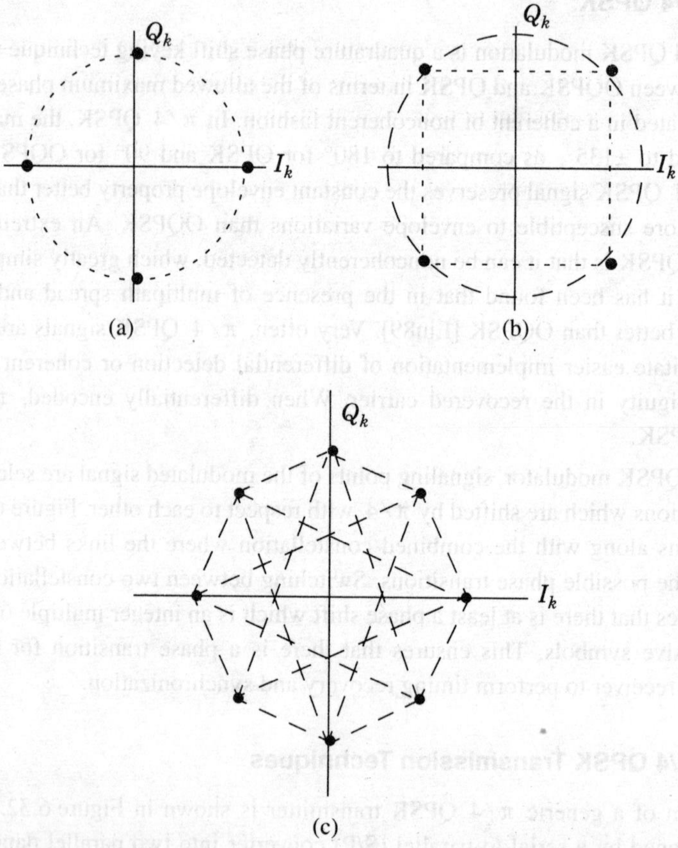

Figure 6.31 Constellation diagram of a π/4 QPSK signal: (a) possible states for θ_k when $\theta_{k-1} = n\pi/4$; (b) possible states when $\theta_{k-1} = n\pi/2$; (c) all possible states.

Table 6.2 Carrier Phase Shifts Corresponding to Various Input Bit Pairs [Feh91], [Rap91b]

Information bits m_{Ik}, m_{Qk}	Phase shift ϕ_k
1 1	$\pi/4$
0 1	$3\pi/4$
0 0	$-3\pi/4$
1 0	$-\pi/4$

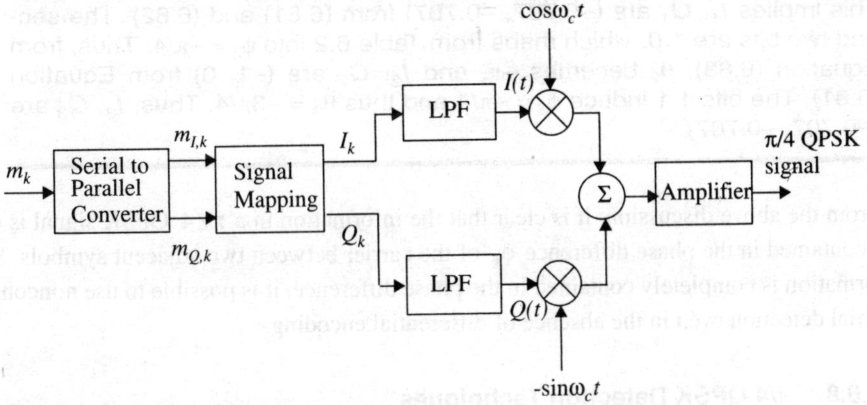

Figure 6.32 Generic π/4 QPSK transmitter.

Just as in a QPSK modulator, the in-phase and quadrature bit streams I_k and Q_k are then separately modulated by two carriers which are in quadrature with one another, to produce the $\pi/4$ QPSK waveform given by

$$s_{\pi/4\mathrm{QPSK}}(t) = I(t)\cos\omega_c t - Q(t)\sin\omega_c t \tag{6.84}$$

where

$$I(t) = \sum_{k=0}^{N-1} I_k p(t-kT_s-T_s/2) = \sum_{k=0}^{N-1} \cos\theta_k p(t-kT_s-T_s/2) \tag{6.85}$$

$$Q(t) = \sum_{k=0}^{N-1} Q_k p(t-kT_s-T_s/2) = \sum_{k=0}^{N-1} \sin\theta_k p(t-kT_s-T_s/2) \tag{6.86}$$

Both I_k and Q_k are usually passed through raised cosine rolloff pulse shaping filters before modulation, in order to reduce the bandwidth occupancy. The function $p(t)$ in Equations (6.85) and (6.86) corresponds to the pulse shape, and T_s is the symbol period. Pulse shaping also reduces the spectral restoration problem which may be significant in fully saturated, nonlinear amplified systems. It should be noted that the values of I_k and Q_k and the peak amplitude of the waveforms $I(t)$ and $Q(t)$ can take one of the five possible values, 0, +1, –1, $+1/\sqrt{2}$, $-1/\sqrt{2}$.

Example 6.9

Assume that $\theta_0 = 0°$. The bit stream 0 0 1 0 1 1 is to be sent using $\pi/4$ DQPSK. The leftmost bits are first applied to the transmitter. Determine the phase of θ_k, and the values of I_k, Q_k during transmission.

Solution

Given $\theta_0 = 0°$, the first two bits are 0 0, which implies that

$$\theta_1 = \theta_0 + \phi_1 = -3\pi/4 \text{ from Table 6.2.}$$

This implies I_1, Q_1 are (−0.707, −0.707) from (6.81) and (6.82). The second two bits are 1 0, which maps from Table 6.2 into $\phi_2 = -\pi/4$. Thus, from Equation (6.83), θ_2 becomes $-\pi$, and I_2, Q_2 are (−1, 0) from Equation (6.81). The bits 1 1 induce $\phi_3 = -\pi/4$ and thus $\theta_3 = -3\pi/4$. Thus, I_3, Q_3 are (−0.707, −0.707).

From the above discussion, it is clear that the information in a $\pi/4$ QPSK signal is completely contained in the phase difference ϕ_k of the carrier between two adjacent symbols. Since the information is completely contained in the phase difference, it is possible to use noncoherent differential detection even in the absence of differential encoding.

6.8.8 $\pi/4$ QPSK Detection Techniques

Due to ease of hardware implementation, differential detection is often employed to demodulate $\pi/4$ QPSK signals. In an AWGN channel, the BER performance of a differentially detected $\pi/4$ QPSK is about 3 dB inferior to QPSK, while coherently detected $\pi/4$ QPSK has the same error performance as QPSK. In low bit rate, fast Rayleigh fading channels, differential detection offers a lower error floor since it does not rely on phase synchronization [Feh91]. There are various types of detection techniques that are used for the detection of $\pi/4$ QPSK signals. They include *baseband differential detection*, IF *differential detection*, and FM *discriminator detection*. While both the baseband and IF differential detector determine the cosine and sine functions of the phase difference, and then decide on the phase difference accordingly, the FM discriminator detects the phase difference directly in a noncoherent manner. Interestingly, simulations have shown that all three receiver structures offer very similar bit error rate performances, although there are implementation issues which are specific to each technique [Anv91].

Baseband Differential Detection

Figure 6.33 shows a block diagram of a baseband differential detector. The incoming $\pi/4$ QPSK signal is quadrature demodulated using two local oscillator signals that have the same frequency as the unmodulated carrier at the transmitter, but not necessarily the same phase. If $\phi_k = \tan^{-1}(Q_k/I_k)$ is the phase of the carrier due to the kth data bit, the output w_k and z_k from the two low pass filters in the in-phase and quadrature arms of the demodulator can be expressed as

$$w_k = \cos(\phi_k - \gamma) \tag{6.87}$$

$$z_k = \sin(\phi_k - \gamma) \tag{6.88}$$

where γ is a phase shift due to noise, propagation, and interference. The phase γ is assumed to change much slower than ϕ_k, so it is essentially a constant. The two sequences w_k and z_k are passed through a differential decoder which operates on the following rule.

$$x_k = w_k w_{k-1} + z_k z_{k-1} \tag{6.89}$$

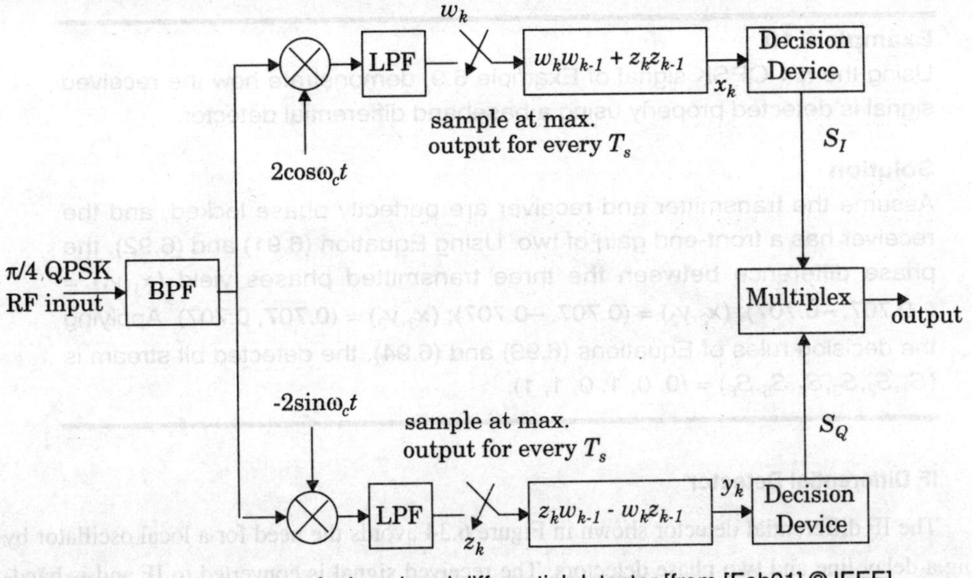

Figure 6.33 Block diagram of a baseband differential detector [from [Feh91] © IEEE].

$$y_k = z_k w_{k-1} - w_k z_{k-1} \tag{6.90}$$

The output of the differential decoder can be expressed as

$$\begin{aligned} x_k &= \cos(\phi_k - \gamma)\cos(\phi_{k-1} - \gamma) + \sin(\phi_k - \gamma)\sin(\phi_{k-1} - \gamma) \\ &= \cos(\phi_k - \phi_{k-1}) \end{aligned} \tag{6.91}$$

$$\begin{aligned} y_k &= \sin(\phi_k - \gamma)\cos(\phi_{k-1} - \gamma) + \cos(\phi_k - \gamma)\sin(\phi_{k-1} - \gamma) \\ &= \sin(\phi_k - \phi_{k-1}) \end{aligned} \tag{6.92}$$

The output of the differential decoder is applied to the decision circuit, which uses Table 6.2 to determine

$$S_I = 1,\ \text{if}\ x_k > 0 \quad \text{or} \quad S_I = 0,\ \text{if}\ x_k < 0 \tag{6.93}$$

$$S_Q = 1,\ \text{if}\ y_k > 0 \quad \text{or} \quad S_Q = 0,\ \text{if}\ y_k < 0 \tag{6.94}$$

where S_I and S_Q are the detected bits in the in-phase and quadrature arms, respectively.

It is important to ensure the local receiver oscillator frequency is the same as the transmitter carrier frequency, and that it does not drift. Any drift in the carrier frequency will cause a drift in the output phase which will lead to BER degradation.

Example 6.10

Using the $\pi/4$ QPSK signal of Example 6.9, demonstrate how the received signal is detected properly using a baseband differential detector.

Solution

Assume the transmitter and receiver are perfectly phase locked, and the receiver has a front-end gain of two. Using Equation (6.91) and (6.92), the phase difference between the three transmitted phases yield $(x_1, y_1) = (-0.707, -0.707)$; $(x_2, y_2) = (0.707, -0.707)$; $(x_3, y_3) = (0.707, 0.707)$. Applying the decision rules of Equations (6.93) and (6.94), the detected bit stream is $(S_1, S_2, S_3, S_4, S_5, S_6) = (0, 0, 1, 0, 1, 1)$.

IF Differential Detector

The IF differential detector shown in Figure 6.34 avoids the need for a local oscillator by using a delay line and two phase detectors. The received signal is converted to IF and is bandpass filtered. The bandpass filter is designed to match the transmitted pulse shape, so that the carrier phase is preserved and noise power is minimized. To minimize the effect of ISI and noise, the bandwidth of the filters are chosen to be $0.57/T_s$ [Liu91]. The received IF signal is differentially decoded using a delay line and two mixers. The bandwidth of the signal at the output of the differential detector is twice that of the baseband signal at the transmitter end.

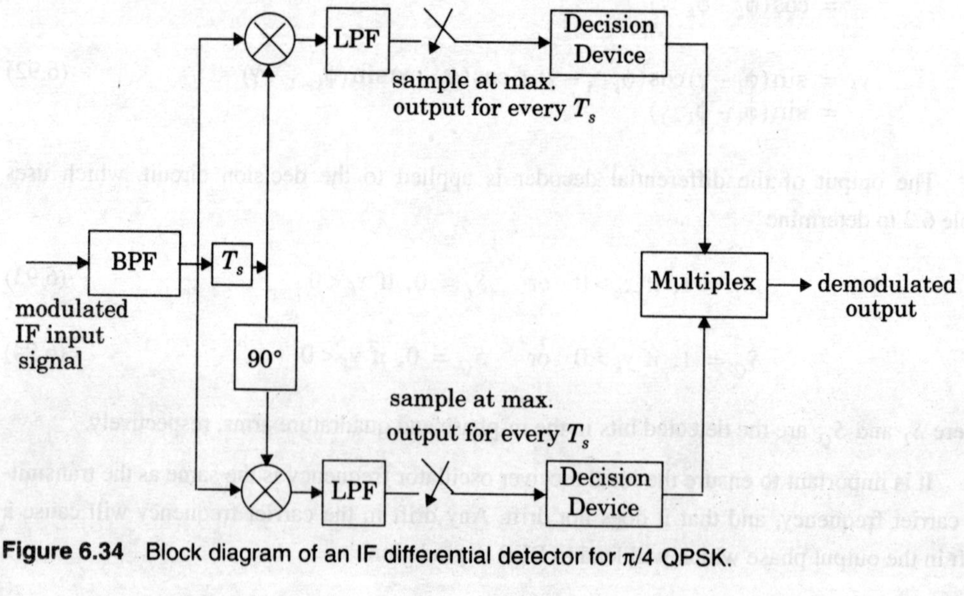

Figure 6.34 Block diagram of an IF differential detector for $\pi/4$ QPSK.

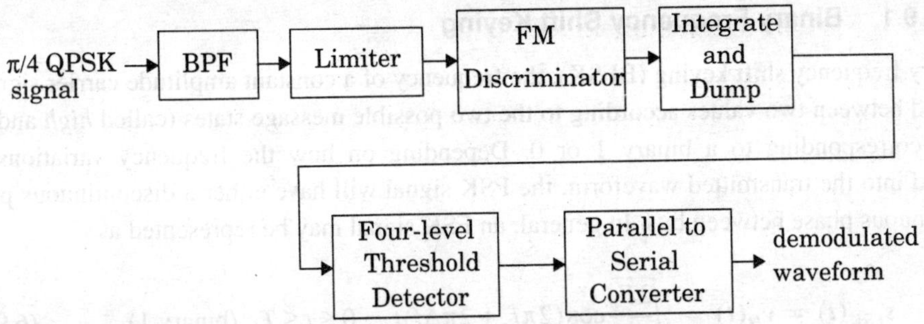

Figure 6.35 FM discriminator detector for $\pi/4$ DQPSK demodulation.

FM Discriminator

Figure 6.35 shows a block diagram of an FM discriminator detector for $\pi/4$ QPSK. The input signal is first filtered using a bandpass filter that is matched to the transmitted signal. The filtered signal is then hardlimited to remove any envelope fluctuations. Hardlimiting preserves the phase changes in the input signal and hence no information is lost. The FM discriminator extracts the instantaneous frequency deviation of the received signal which, when integrated over each symbol period gives the phase difference between two sampling instants. The phase difference is then detected by a four level threshold comparator to obtain the original signal. The phase difference can also be detected using a modulo-2π phase detector. The modulo-2π phase detector improves the BER performance and reduces the effect of click noise [Feh91].

6.9 Constant Envelope Modulation

Many practical mobile radio communications systems use nonlinear modulation methods, where the amplitude of the carrier is constant, regardless of the variation in the modulating signal. The constant envelope family of modulations has the advantage of satisfying a number of conditions [You79], some of which are:

- Power efficient Class C amplifiers can be used without introducing degradation in the spectrum occupancy of the transmitted signal.
- Low out-of-band radiation of the order of –60 dB to –70 dB can be achieved.
- Limiter-discriminator detection can be used, which simplifies receiver design and provides high immunity against random FM noise and signal fluctuations due to Rayleigh fading.

While constant envelope modulations have many advantages, they occupy a larger bandwidth than linear modulation schemes. In situations where bandwidth efficiency is more important than power efficiency, constant envelope modulation is not well-suited.

6.9.1 Binary Frequency Shift Keying

In binary frequency shift keying (BFSK), the frequency of a constant amplitude carrier signal is switched between two values according to the two possible message states (called *high* and *low* tones), corresponding to a binary 1 or 0. Depending on how the frequency variations are imparted into the transmitted waveform, the FSK signal will have either a discontinuous phase or continuous phase between bits. In general, an FSK signal may be represented as

$$s_{FSK}(t) = v_H(t) = \sqrt{\frac{2E_b}{T_b}}\cos(2\pi f_c + 2\pi\Delta f)t \qquad 0 \le t \le T_b \text{ (binary 1)} \qquad (6.95.a)$$

$$s_{FSK}(t) = v_L(t) = \sqrt{\frac{2E_b}{T_b}}\cos(2\pi f_c - 2\pi\Delta f)t \qquad 0 \le t \le T_b \text{ (binary 0)} \qquad (6.95.b)$$

where $2\pi\Delta f$ is a constant offset from the nominal carrier frequency.

One obvious way to generate an FSK signal is to switch between two independent oscillators according to whether the data bit is a 0 or a 1. Normally, this form of FSK generation results in a waveform that is discontinuous at the switching times, and for this reason this type of FSK is called *discontinuous* FSK. A discontinuous FSK signal is represented as

$$s_{FSK}(t) = v_H(t) = \sqrt{\frac{2E_b}{T_b}}\cos(2\pi f_H t + \theta_1) \qquad 0 \le t \le T_b \text{ (binary 1)} \qquad (6.96.a)$$

$$s_{FSK}(t) = v_L(t) = \sqrt{\frac{2E_b}{T_b}}\cos(2\pi f_L t + \theta_2) \qquad 0 \le t \le T_b \text{ (binary 0)} \qquad (6.96.b)$$

Since the phase discontinuities pose several problems, such as spectral spreading and spurious transmissions, this type of FSK is generally not used in highly regulated wireless systems.

The more common method for generating an FSK signal is to frequency modulate a single carrier oscillator using the message waveform. This type of modulation is similar to analog FM generation, except that the modulating signal $m(t)$ is a binary waveform. Therefore, FSK may be represented as

$$\begin{aligned} s_{FSK}(t) &= \sqrt{\frac{2E_b}{T_b}}\cos[2\pi f_c t + \theta(t)] \qquad (6.97) \\ &= \sqrt{\frac{2E_b}{T_b}}\cos\left[2\pi f_c t + 2\pi k_f \int_{-\infty}^{t} m(\eta)d\eta\right] \end{aligned}$$

It should be noted that even though the modulating waveform $m(t)$ is discontinuous at bit transitions, the phase function $\theta(t)$ is proportional to the integral of $m(t)$ and is continuous.

Spectrum and Bandwidth of BFSK signals

As the complex envelope of an FSK signal is a nonlinear function of the message signal $m(t)$, evaluation of the spectra of an FSK signal is, in general, quite involved, and is usually performed using actual time averaged measurements. The power spectral density of a binary FSK signal consists of discrete frequency components at f_c, $f_c + n\Delta f$, $f_c - n\Delta f$, where n is an integer. It can be shown that the PSD of a continuous phase FSK ultimately falls off as the inverse fourth power of the frequency offset from f_c. However, if phase discontinuities exist, the PSD falls off as the inverse square of the frequency offset from f_c [Cou93].

The transmission bandwidth B_T of an FSK signal is given by Carson's rule as

$$B_T = 2\Delta f + 2B \tag{6.98}$$

where B is the bandwidth of the digital baseband signal. Assuming that first null bandwidth is used, the bandwidth of rectangular pulses is $B = R$. Hence, the FSK transmission bandwidth becomes

$$B_T = 2(\Delta f + R) \tag{6.99}$$

If a raised cosine pulse-shaping filter is used, then the transmission bandwidth reduces to

$$B_T = 2\Delta f + (1 + \alpha)R \tag{6.100}$$

where α is the rolloff factor of the filter.

Coherent Detection of Binary FSK

A block diagram of a coherent detection scheme for demodulation of binary FSK signals is shown in Figure 6.36. The receiver shown is the optimum detector for coherent binary FSK in the presence of additive white Gaussian noise. It consists of two correlators which are supplied with locally generated coherent reference signals. The difference of the correlator outputs is then compared with a threshold comparator. If the difference signal has a value greater than the threshold, the receiver decides in favor of a 1, otherwise it decides in favor of a 0.

It can be shown that the probability of error for a coherent FSK receiver is given by

$$P_{e,\mathrm{FSK}} = Q\left(\sqrt{\frac{E_b}{N_0}}\right) \tag{6.101}$$

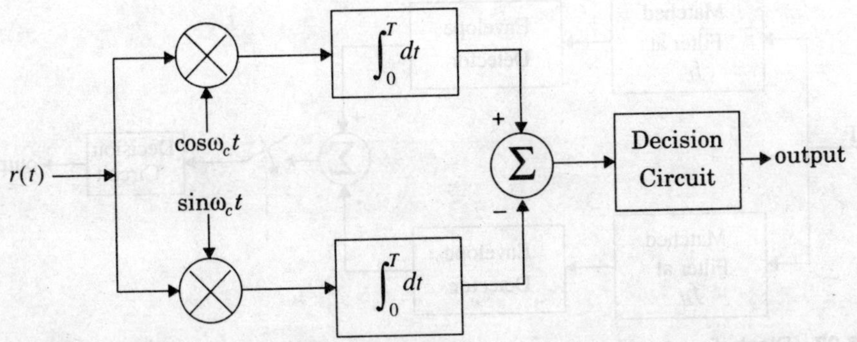

Figure 6.36 Coherent detection of FSK signals.

Noncoherent Detection of Binary FSK

Unlike phase-shift keying, it is possible to detect FSK signals in the presence of noise without using a coherent carrier reference. A block diagram of a noncoherent FSK receiver is shown in Figure 6.37. The receiver consists of a pair of matched filters followed by envelope detectors. The filter in the upper path is matched to the FSK signal of frequency f_H and the filter in the lower path is matched to the signal of frequency f_L. These matched filters function as bandpass filters centered at f_H and f_L, respectively. The outputs of the envelope detectors are sampled at every $t = kT_b$, where k is an integer, and their values compared. Depending on the magnitude of the envelope detector output, the comparator decides whether the data bit was a 1 or 0.

The average probability of error of an FSK system employing noncoherent detection is given by

$$P_{e,\,\mathrm{FSK,\,NC}} = \frac{1}{2}\exp\left(-\frac{E_b}{2N_0}\right) \tag{6.102}$$

6.9.2 Minimum Shift Keying (MSK)

Minimum shift keying (MSK) is a special type of *continuous phase-frequency shift keying* (CPFSK) wherein the peak frequency deviation is equal to $1/4$ the bit rate. In other words, MSK is continuous phase FSK with a modulation index of 0.5. The modulation index of an FSK signal is similar to the FM modulation index, and is defined as $k_{FSK} = (2\Delta F)/R_b$, where ΔF is the peak RF frequency deviation and R_b is the bit rate. A modulation index of 0.5 corresponds to the minimum frequency spacing that allows two FSK signals to be coherently orthogonal, and the name minimum shift keying implies the minimum frequency separation (i.e., bandwidth) that allows orthogonal detection. Two FSK signals $v_H(t)$ and $v_L(t)$ are said to be orthogonal if

$$\int_0^T v_H(t)v_L(t)dt = 0 \tag{6.103}$$

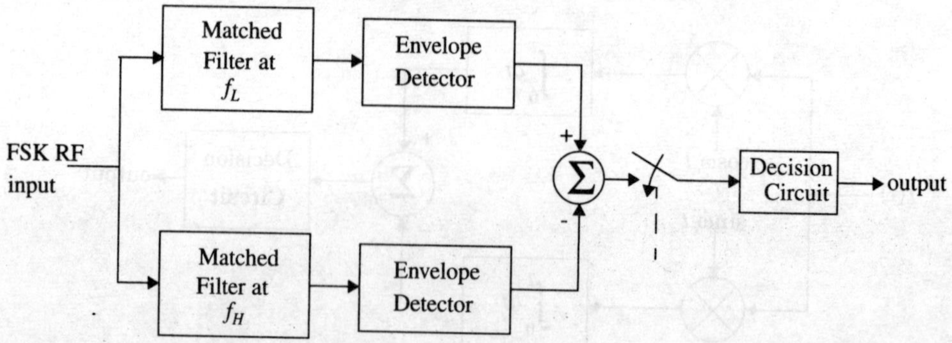

Figure 6.37 Block diagram of noncoherent FSK receiver.

MSK is sometimes referred to as *fast FSK*, as the frequency spacing used is only half as much as that used in conventional noncoherent FSK [Xio94].

MSK is a spectrally efficient modulation scheme and is particularly attractive for use in mobile radio communication systems. It possesses properties such as constant envelope, spectral efficiency, good BER performance, and self-synchronizing capability.

An MSK signal can be thought of as a special form of OQPSK where the baseband rectangular pulses are replaced with half-sinusoidal pulses [Pas79]. These pulses have shapes like the St. Louis arch during a period of $2T_b$. Consider the OQPSK signal with the bit streams offset as shown in Figure 6.30. If half-sinusoidal pulses are used instead of rectangular pulses, the modified signal can be defined as MSK and for an N-bit stream is given by

$$s_{MSK}(t) = \sum_{i=0}^{N-1} m_{I_i}(t)p(t-2iT_b)\cos 2\pi f_c t + \sum_{i=0}^{N-1} m_{Q_i}(t)p(t-2iT_b-T_b)\sin 2\pi f_c t \tag{6.104}$$

where

$$p(t) = \begin{cases} \cos\left(\frac{\pi t}{2T_b}\right) & 0 \le t \le 2T_b \\ 0 & \text{elsewhere} \end{cases} \tag{6.105}$$

and where $m_{I_i}(t)$ and $m_{Q_i}(t)$ are the "odd" and "even" bits of the bipolar serial data stream which have values of ±1 and which feed the in-phase and quadrature arms of the modulator at a rate of $R_b/2$. It should be noted that there are a number of variations of MSK that exist in the literature [Sun86]. For example, while one version of MSK uses only positive half-sinusoids as the basic pulse shape, another version uses alternating positive and negative half-sinusoids as the basic pulse shape. However, all variations of MSK are continuous phase FSK employing different techniques to achieve spectral efficiency [Sun86].

The MSK waveform can be seen as a special type of a continuous phase FSK if Equation (6.104) is rewritten using trigonometric identities as

$$s_{MSK}(t) = \sqrt{\frac{2E_b}{T_b}}\cos\left[2\pi f_c t - m_{I_i}(t)m_{Q_i}(t)\frac{\pi t}{2T_b} + \phi_k\right] \tag{6.106}$$

where ϕ_k is 0 or π depending on whether $m_I(t)$ is 1 or −1. From Equation (6.106), it can be deduced that MSK has a constant amplitude. Phase continuity at the bit transition periods is ensured by choosing the carrier frequency to be an integral multiple of one fourth the bit rate, $1/4T$. Comparing Equation (6.106) with Equation (6.97), it can be concluded that the MSK signal is an FSK signal with binary signaling frequencies of $f_c + 1/4T$ and $f_c - 1/4T$. It can further be seen from Equation (6.106) that the phase of the MSK signal varies linearly during the course of each bit period [Pro94, Chapter 10].

MSK Power Spectrum

From Equation (6.41), the RF power spectrum is obtained by frequency shifting the magnitude squared of the Fourier transform of the baseband pulse-shaping function. For MSK, the baseband pulse shaping function is given by

$$p(t) = \begin{cases} \cos\left(\dfrac{\pi t}{2T}\right) & |t| < T \\ 0 & \text{elsewhere} \end{cases} \quad (6.107)$$

Thus, the normalized power spectral density for MSK is given by [Pas79]

$$P_{\text{MSK}}(f) = \frac{16}{\pi^2}\left(\frac{\cos 2\pi(f+f_c)T}{1.16f^2T^2}\right)^2 + \frac{16}{\pi^2}\left(\frac{\cos 2\pi(f-f_c)T}{1.16f^2T^2}\right)^2 \quad (6.108)$$

Figure 6.38 shows the power spectral density of an MSK signal. The spectral density of QPSK and OQPSK are also drawn for comparison. From Figure 6.38, it is seen that the MSK spectrum has lower sidelobes than QPSK and OQPSK. Ninety-nine percent of the MSK power is contained within a bandwidth $B = 1.2/T$, while for QPSK and OQPSK, the 99 percent bandwidth B is equal to $8/T$. The faster rolloff of the MSK spectrum is due to the fact that smoother pulse functions are used. Figure 6.38 also shows that the main lobe of MSK is wider than that of QPSK and OQPSK, and hence when compared in terms of first null bandwidth, MSK is less spectrally efficient than the phase-shift keying techniques [Pas79].

Since there is no abrupt change in phase at bit transition periods, bandlimiting the MSK signal to meet required out-of-band specifications does not cause the envelope to go through zero. The envelope is kept more or less constant even after bandlimiting. Any small variations in the envelope level can be removed by hardlimiting at the receiver without raising the out-of-band radiation levels. Since the amplitude is kept constant, MSK signals can be amplified using efficient nonlinear amplifiers. The continuous phase property makes it highly desirable for highly reactive loads. In addition to these advantages, MSK has simple demodulation and synchronization circuits. It is for these reasons that MSK is a popular modulation scheme for mobile radio communications.

MSK Transmitter and Receiver

Figure 6.39 shows a typical MSK modulator. Multiplying a carrier signal with $\cos[\pi t/2T]$ produces two phase-coherent signals at $f_c + 1/4T$ and $f_c - 1/4T$. These two FSK signals are separated using two narrow bandpass filters and appropriately combined to form the in-phase and quadrature carrier components $x(t)$ and $y(t)$, respectively. These carriers are multiplied with the odd and even bit streams, $m_I(t)$ and $m_Q(t)$, to produce the MSK modulated signal $s_{\text{MSK}}(t)$.

The block diagram of an MSK receiver is shown in Figure 6.40. The received signal $s_{\text{MSK}}(t)$ (in the absence of noise and interference) is multiplied by the respective in-phase and quadrature carriers $x(t)$ and $y(t)$. The output of the multipliers are integrated over two bit periods and dumped to a decision circuit at the end of each two bit periods. Based on the level of the signal at the output of the integrator, the threshold detector decides whether the signal is a 0 or a 1. The output data streams correspond to $m_I(t)$ and $m_Q(t)$, which are offset combined to obtain the demodulated signal.

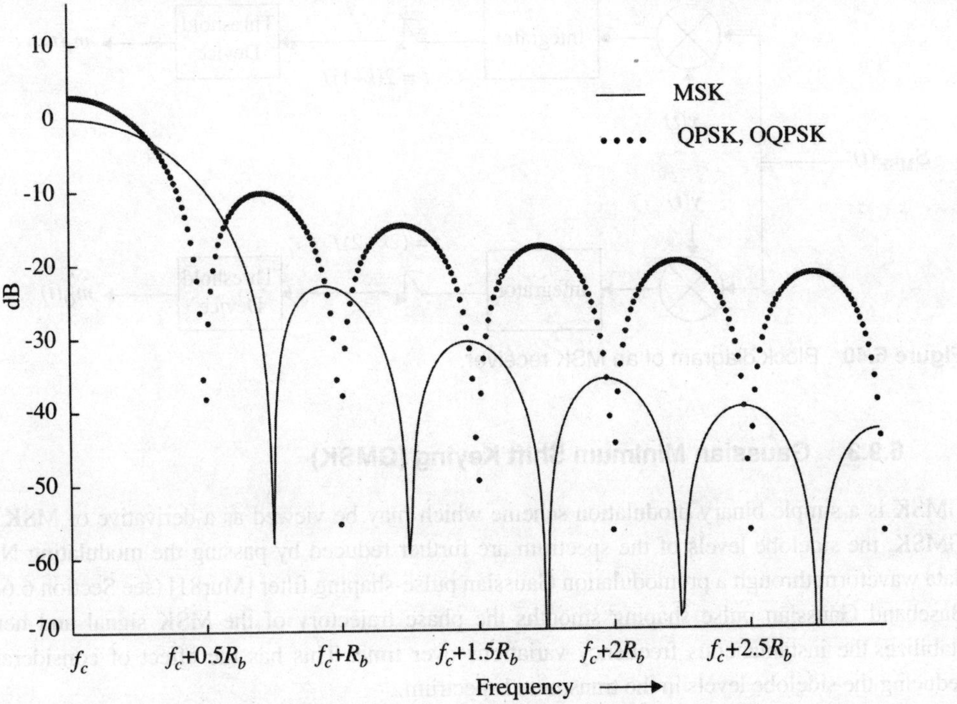

Figure 6.38 Power spectral density of MSK signals as compared to QPSK and OQPSK signals.

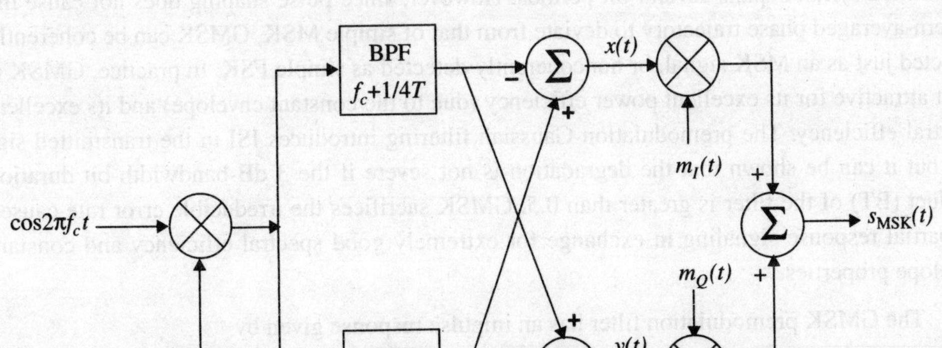

Figure 6.39 Block diagram of an MSK transmitter. Note that $m_I(t)$ and $m_Q(t)$ are offset by T_b.

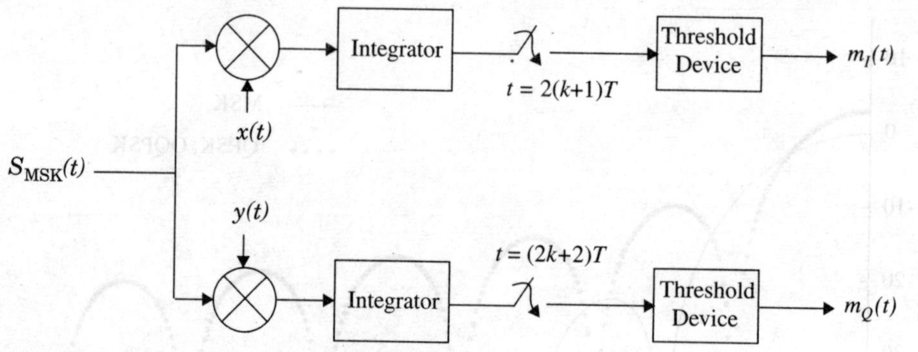

Figure 6.40 Block diagram of an MSK receiver.

6.9.3 Gaussian Minimum Shift Keying (GMSK)

GMSK is a simple binary modulation scheme which may be viewed as a derivative of MSK. In GMSK, the sidelobe levels of the spectrum are further reduced by passing the modulating NRZ data waveform through a premodulation Gaussian pulse-shaping filter [Mur81] (see Section 6.6.3). Baseband Gaussian pulse shaping smooths the phase trajectory of the MSK signal and hence stabilizes the instantaneous frequency variations over time. This has the effect of considerably reducing the sidelobe levels in the transmitted spectrum.

Premodulation Gaussian filtering converts the full response message signal (where each baseband symbol occupies a single bit period T) into a partial response scheme where each transmitted symbol spans several bit periods. However, since pulse shaping does not cause the pattern-averaged phase trajectory to deviate from that of simple MSK, GMSK can be coherently detected just as an MSK signal, or noncoherently detected as simple FSK. In practice, GMSK is most attractive for its excellent power efficiency (due to the constant envelope) and its excellent spectral efficiency. The premodulation Gaussian filtering introduces ISI in the transmitted signal, but it can be shown that the degradation is not severe if the 3 dB-bandwidth-bit duration product (BT) of the filter is greater than 0.5. GMSK sacrifices the irreducible error rate caused by partial response signaling in exchange for extremely good spectral efficiency and constant envelope properties.

The GMSK premodulation filter has an impulse response given by

$$h_G(t) = \frac{\sqrt{\pi}}{\alpha}\exp\left(-\frac{\pi^2}{\alpha^2}t^2\right) \tag{6.109}$$

and the transfer function given by

$$H_G(f) = \exp(-\alpha^2 f^2) \tag{6.110}$$

The parameter α is related to B, the 3 dB baseband bandwidth of $H_G(f)$, by

$$\alpha = \frac{\sqrt{ln2}}{\sqrt{2}B} = \frac{0.5887}{B} \tag{6.111}$$

and the GMSK filter may be completely defined from B and the baseband symbol duration T. It is therefore customary to define GMSK by its BT product.

Figure 6.41 shows the simulated RF power spectrum of the GMSK signal for various values of BT. The power spectrum of MSK, which is equivalent to GMSK with a BT product of infinity, is also shown for comparison purposes. It is clearly seen from the graph that as the BT product decreases, the sidelobe levels fall off very rapidly. For example, for a $BT = 0.5$, the peak of the second lobe is more than 30 dB below the main lobe, whereas for simple MSK, the second lobe is only 20 dB below the main lobe. However, reducing BT increases the irreducible error rate produced by the low pass filter due to ISI. As shown in Section 6.12, mobile radio channels induce an irreducible error rate due to mobile velocity, so *as long as the GMSK irreducible error rate is less than that produced by the mobile channel, there is no penalty in using GMSK.* Table 6.3 shows occupied bandwidth containing a given percentage of power in a GMSK signal as a function of the BT product [Mur81].

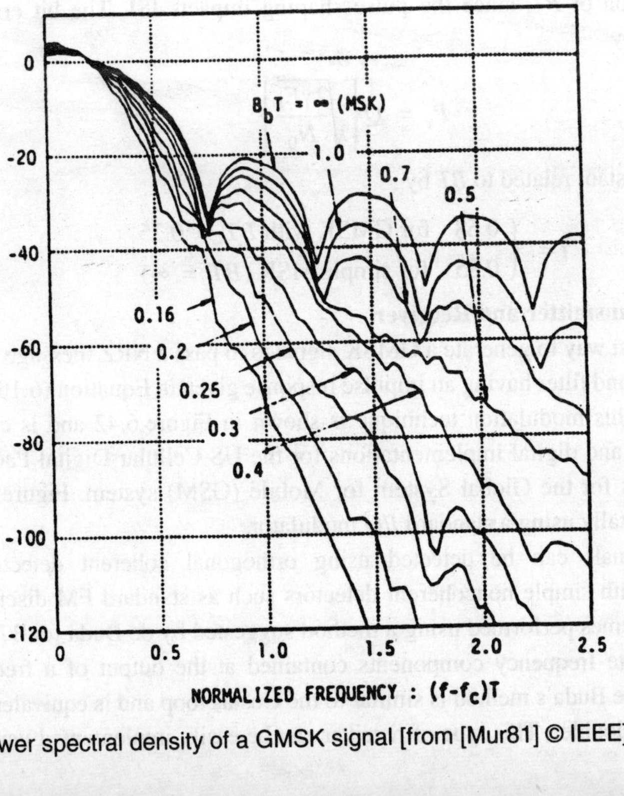

Figure 6.41 Power spectral density of a GMSK signal [from [Mur81] © IEEE].

Table 6.3 Occupied RF Bandwidth (for GMSK and MSK as a fraction of R_b) Containing a Given Percentage of Power [Mur81]. Notice that GMSK is Spectrally Tighter than MSK

BT	90%	99%	99.9%	99.99%
0.2 GMSK	0.52	0.79	0.99	1.22
0.25 GMSK	0.57	0.86	1.09	1.37
0.5 GMSK	0.69	1.04	1.33	2.08
MSK	0.78	1.20	2.76	6.00

While the GMSK spectrum becomes more and more compact with decreasing BT value, the degradation due to ISI increases. It was shown by Ishizuka [Ish80] that the BER degradation due to ISI caused by filtering is minimum for a BT value of 0.5887, where the degradation in the required E_b/N_0 is only 0.14 dB from the case of no ISI.

GMSK Bit Error Rate

The bit error rate for GMSK was first found in [Mur81] for AWGN channels, and was shown to offer performance within 1 dB of optimum MSK when $BT = 0.25$. The bit error probability is a function of BT, since the pulse shaping impacts ISI. The bit error probability for GMSK is given by

$$P_e = Q\left\{\sqrt{\frac{2\gamma E_b}{N_0}}\right\} \tag{6.112.a}$$

where γ is a constant related to BT by

$$\gamma \cong \begin{cases} 0.68 & \text{for GMSK with } BT = 0.25 \\ 0.85 & \text{for simple MSK } (BT = \infty) \end{cases} \tag{6.112.b}$$

GMSK Transmitter and Receiver

The simplest way to generate a GMSK signal is to pass a NRZ message bit stream through a Gaussian baseband filter having an impulse response given in Equation (6.109), followed by an FM modulator. This modulation technique is shown in Figure 6.42 and is currently used in a variety of analog and digital implementations for the US Cellular Digital Packet Data (CDPD) system as well as for the Global System for Mobile (GSM) system. Figure 6.42 may also be implemented digitally using a standard I/Q modulator.

GMSK signals can be detected using orthogonal coherent detectors as shown in Figure 6.43, or with simple noncoherent detectors such as standard FM discriminators. Carrier recovery is sometimes performed using a method suggested by de Buda [deB72], where the sum of the two discrete frequency components contained at the output of a frequency doubler is divided by four. De Buda's method is similar to the Costas loop and is equivalent to that of a PLL with a frequency doubler. This type of receiver can be easily implemented using digital logic as

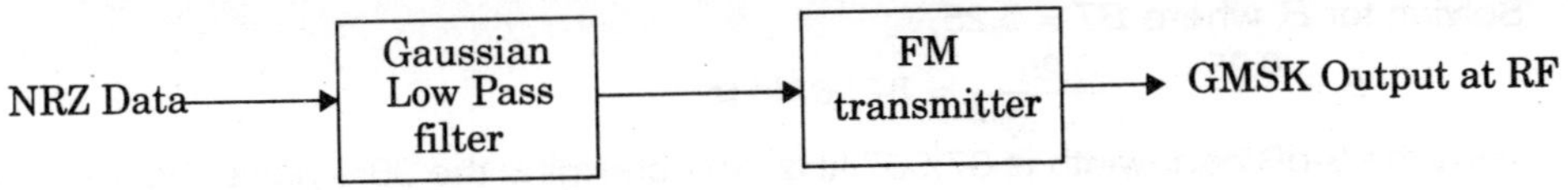

Figure 6.42 Block diagram of a GMSK transmitter using direct FM generation.

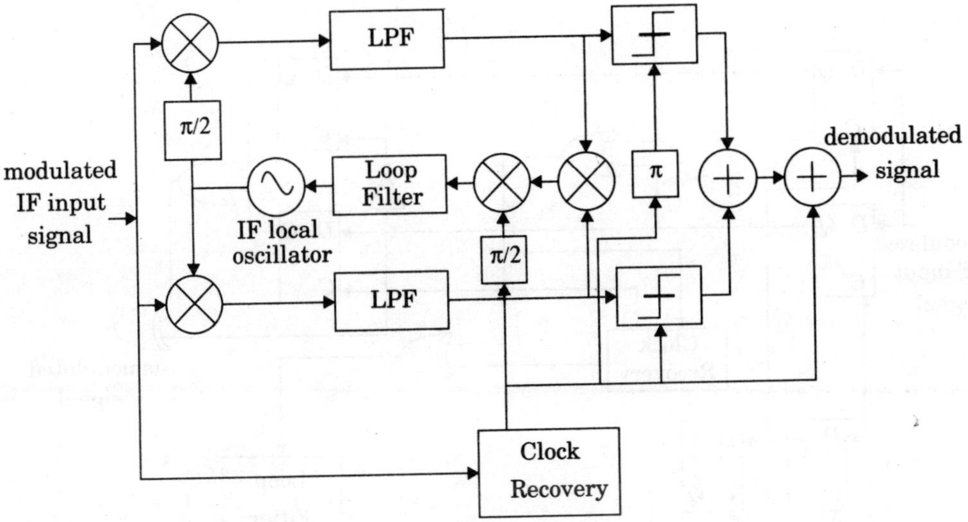

Figure 6.43 Block diagram of a GMSK receiver.

shown in Figure 6.44. The two *D* flip-flops act as a quadrature product demodulator and the XOR gates act as baseband multipliers. The mutually orthogonal reference carriers are generated using two *D* flip-flops, and the VCO center frequency is set equal to four times the carrier center frequency. A nonoptimum, but highly effective method of detecting GMSK signal is to simply sample the output of an FM demodulator.

Example 6.11

Find the 3-dB bandwidth for a Gaussian low pass filter used to produce 0.25 GMSK with a channel data rate of R_b = 270 kbps. What is the 90% power bandwidth in the RF channel? Specify the Gaussian filter parameter α.

Solution

From the problem statement

$$T = \frac{1}{R_b} = \frac{1}{270 \times 10^3} = 3.7\ \mu\text{s}$$

Solving for B, where $BT = 0.25$,

$$B = \frac{0.25}{T} = \frac{0.25}{3.7 \times 10^{-6}} = 67.567 \text{ kHz}$$

Thus the 3-dB bandwidth is 67.567 kHz. To determine the 90% power bandwidth, use Table 6.3 to find that $0.57R_b$ is the desired value. Thus, the occupied RF spectrum for a 90% power bandwidth is given by

$$\text{RF } BW = 0.57R_b = 0.57 \times 270 \times 10^3 = 153.9 \text{ kHz}$$

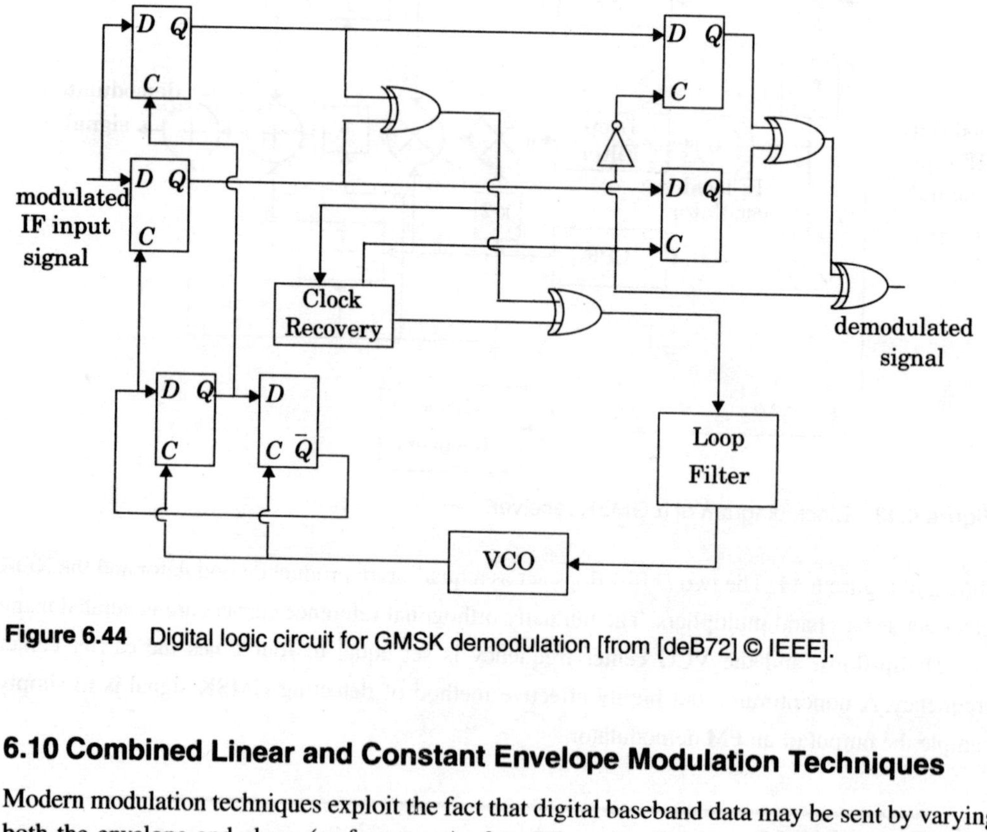

Figure 6.44 Digital logic circuit for GMSK demodulation [from [deB72] © IEEE].

6.10 Combined Linear and Constant Envelope Modulation Techniques

Modern modulation techniques exploit the fact that digital baseband data may be sent by varying both the envelope and phase (or frequency) of an RF carrier. Because the envelope and phase offer two degrees of freedom, such modulation techniques map baseband data into four or more possible RF carrier signals. Such modulation techniques are called M-ary modulation, since they can represent more signals than if just the amplitude or phase were varied alone.

In an M-ary signaling scheme, two or more bits are grouped together to form symbols and one of M possible signals, $s_1(t)$, $s_2(t)$, ..., $s_M(t)$ is transmitted during each symbol period of duration T_s. Usually, the number of possible signals is $M = 2^n$, where n is an integer. Depending on whether the amplitude, phase, or frequency of the carrier is varied, the modulation scheme is called M-ary ASK, M-ary PSK, or M-ary FSK. Modulations which alter both the amplitude and phase of the carrier are the subject of active research.

M-ary signaling is particularly attractive for use in bandlimited channels, but are limited in their applications due to sensitivity to timing jitter (i.e., timing errors increase when smaller distances between signals in the constellation diagram are used. This results in poorer error performance).

M-ary modulation schemes achieve better bandwidth efficiency at the expense of power efficiency. For example, an 8-PSK system requires a bandwidth that is $\log_2 8 = 3$ times smaller than a BPSK system, whereas its BER performance is significantly worse than BPSK since signals are packed more closely in the signal constellation.

6.10.1 M-ary Phase Shift Keying (MPSK)

In M-ary PSK, the carrier phase takes on one of M possible values, namely, $\theta_i = 2(i-1)\pi/M$, where $i = 1, 2, ..., M$. The modulated waveform can be expressed as

$$s_i(t) = \sqrt{\frac{2E_s}{T_s}}\cos\left(2\pi f_c t + \frac{2\pi}{M}(i-1)\right) \quad , 0 \le t \le T_s \quad i = 1, 2, ..., M \tag{6.113}$$

where $E_s = (\log_2 M)E_b$ is the energy per symbol and $T_s = (\log_2 M)\ T_b$ is the symbol period. The above equation can be rewritten in quadrature form as

$$\begin{aligned} s_i(t) = &\sqrt{\frac{2E_s}{T_s}}\cos\left[(i-1)\frac{2\pi}{M}\right]\cos(2\pi f_c t) \qquad i = 1, 2, ..., M \\ &- \sqrt{\frac{2E_s}{T_s}}\sin\left[(i-1)\frac{2\pi}{M}\right]\sin(2\pi f_c t) \end{aligned} \tag{6.114}$$

By choosing orthogonal basis signals $\phi_1(t) = \sqrt{\frac{2}{T_s}}\cos(2\pi f_c t)$, and $\phi_2(t) = \sqrt{\frac{2}{T_s}}\sin(2\pi f_c t)$ defined over the interval $0 \le t \le T_s$, the M-ary PSK signal set can be expressed as

$$s_{\text{M-PSK}}(t) = \left\{\sqrt{E_s}\cos\left[(i-1)\frac{\pi}{2}\right]\phi_1(t)\ ,-\sqrt{E_s}\sin\left[(i-1)\frac{\pi}{2}\right]\phi_2(t)\right\} \tag{6.115}$$

$$i = 1, 2, ..., M$$

Since there are only two basis signals, the constellation of M-ary PSK is two dimensional. The M-ary message points are equally spaced on a circle of radius $\sqrt{E_s}$ centered at the origin. The constellation diagram of an 8-ary PSK signal set is illustrated in Figure 6.45. It is clear from Figure 6.45 that MPSK is a constant envelope signal when no pulse shaping is used.

Equation (6.62), can be used to compute the probability of symbol error for MPSK systems in an AWGN channel. From the geometry of Figure 6.45, it is easily seen that the distance

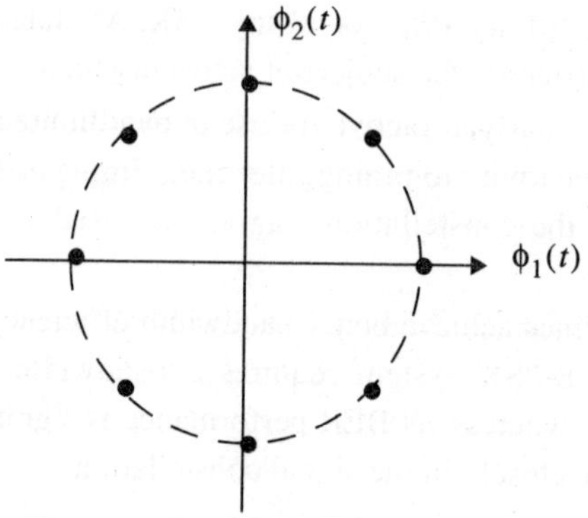

Figure 6.45 Constellation diagram of an M-ary PSK system ($M = 8$).

between adjacent symbols is equal to $2\sqrt{E_s}\sin\left(\frac{\pi}{M}\right)$. Hence, the average symbol error probability of an M-ary PSK system is given by

$$P_e \le 2Q\left(\sqrt{\frac{2E_b\log_2 M}{N_0}}\sin\left(\frac{\pi}{M}\right)\right) \tag{6.116}$$

Just as in BPSK and QPSK modulation, M-ary PSK modulation is either coherently detected or differentially encoded for noncoherent differential detection. The symbol error probability of a differential M-ary PSK system in AWGN channel for $M \ge 4$ is approximated by [Hay94]

$$P_e \approx 2Q\left(\sqrt{\frac{4E_s}{N_0}}\sin\left(\frac{\pi}{2M}\right)\right) \tag{6.117}$$

Power Spectra of M-ary PSK

The power spectral density (PSD) of an M-ary PSK signal can be obtained in a manner similar to that described for BPSK and QPSK signals. The symbol duration T_s of an M-ary PSK signal is related to the bit duration T_b by

$$T_s = T_b\log_2 M \tag{6.118}$$

The PSD of the M-ary PSK signal with rectangular pulses is given by

$$P_{\text{MPSK}} = \frac{E_s}{2}\left[\left(\frac{\sin\pi(f-f_c)T_s}{\pi(f-f_c)T_s}\right)^2 + \left(\frac{\sin\pi(-f-f_c)T_s}{\pi(-f-f_c)T_s}\right)^2\right] \tag{6.119}$$

$$P_{\text{MPSK}} = \frac{E_b\log_2 M}{2}\left[\left(\frac{\sin\pi(f-f_c)T_b\log_2 M}{\pi(f-f_c)T_b\log_2 M}\right)^2 + \left(\frac{\sin\pi(-f-f_c)T_b\log_2 M}{\pi(-f-f_c)T_b\log_2 M}\right)^2\right] \tag{6.120}$$

Table 6.4 Bandwidth and Power Efficiency of M-ary PSK Signals

M	2	4	8	16	32	64
$\eta_B = R_b/B^*$	0.5	1	1.5	2	2.5	3
E_b/N_o for BER=10^{-6}	10.5	10.5	14	18.5	23.4	28.5

* B: First null bandwidth of M-ary PSK signals

The PSD of M-ary PSK systems for $M = 8$ and $M = 16$ are shown in Figure 6.46. As clearly seen from Equation (6.120) and Figure 6.46, the first null bandwidth of M-ary PSK signals decrease as M increases while R_b is held constant. Therefore, as the value of M increases, the bandwidth efficiency also increases. That is, for fixed R_b, η_B increases and B decreases as M is increased. At the same time, increasing M implies that the constellation is more densely packed, and hence the power efficiency (noise tolerance) is decreased. The bandwidth and power efficiency of M-PSK systems using ideal Nyquist pulse shaping in AWGN for various values of M are listed in Table 6.4. These values assume no timing jitter or fading, which have a large negative effect on bit error rate as M increases. In general, simulation must be used to determine bit error values in actual wireless communication channels, since interference and multipath can alter the instantaneous phase of an MPSK signal, thereby creating errors at the detector. Also, the particular implementation of the receiver often impacts performance.

In practice, pilot symbols or equalization must be used to exploit MPSK in mobile channels, and this has not been a popular commercial practice.

6.10.2 M-ary Quadrature Amplitude Modulation (QAM)

In M-ary PSK modulation, the amplitude of the transmitted signal was constrained to remain constant, thereby yielding a circular constellation. By allowing the amplitude to also vary with the phase, a new modulation scheme called *quadrature amplitude modulation* (QAM) is obtained. Figure 6.47 shows the constellation diagram of 16-ary QAM. The constellation consists of a square lattice of signal points. The general form of an M-ary QAM signal can be defined as

$$s_i(t) = \sqrt{\frac{2E_{min}}{T_s}}a_i\cos(2\pi f_c t) + \sqrt{\frac{2E_{min}}{T_s}}b_i\sin(2\pi f_c t) \tag{6.121}$$

$$0 \le t \le T \qquad i = 1, 2, ..., M$$

where E_{min} is the energy of the signal with the lowest amplitude, and a_i and b_i are a pair of independent integers chosen according to the location of the particular signal point. Note that M-ary QAM does not have constant energy per symbol, nor does it have constant distance between possible symbol states. It reasons that particular values of $s_i(t)$ will be detected with higher probability than others.

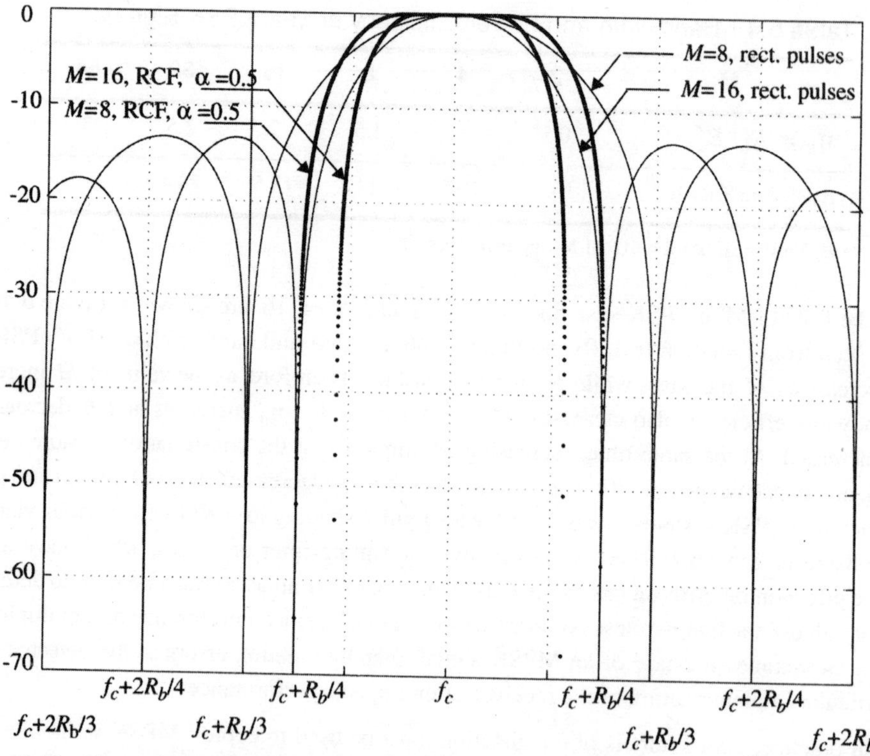

Figure 6.46 M-ary PSK power spectral density, for M = 8, 16 (PSD for both rectangular and raised cosine filtered pulses are shown for fixed R_b).

If rectangular pulse shapes are assumed, the signal $S_i(t)$ may be expanded in terms of a pair of basis functions defined as

$$\phi_1(t) = \sqrt{\frac{2}{T_s}}\cos(2\pi f_c t) \qquad 0 \le t \le T_s \tag{6.122}$$

$$\phi_2(t) = \sqrt{\frac{2}{T_s}}\sin(2\pi f_c t) \qquad 0 \le t \le T_s \tag{6.123}$$

The coordinates of the ith message point are $a_i\sqrt{E_{min}}$ and $b_i\sqrt{E_{min}}$, where (a_i, b_i) is an element of the L by L matrix given by

$$\{a_i, b_i\} = \begin{bmatrix} (-L+1, L-1) & (-L+3, L-1) & \ldots & (L-1, L-1) \\ (-L+1, L-3) & (-L+3, L-3) & \ldots & (L-1, L-3) \\ \cdot & \cdot & & \cdot \\ \cdot & \cdot & & \cdot \\ (-L+1, -L+1) & (-L+3, -L+1) & \ldots & (L-1, -L+1) \end{bmatrix} \tag{6.124}$$

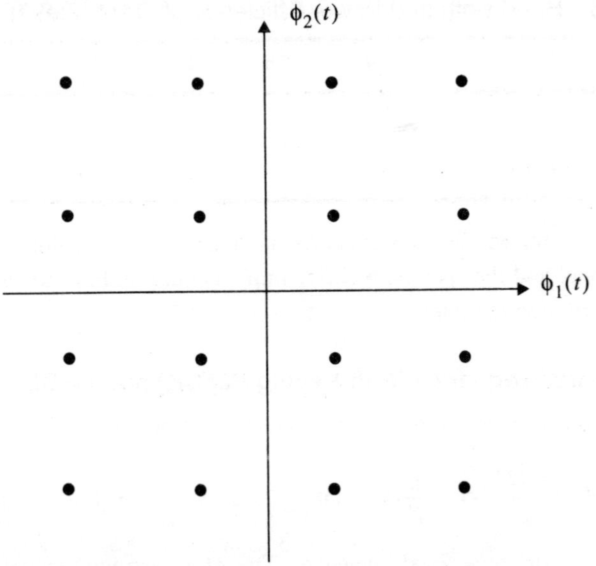

Figure 6.47 Constellation diagram of an M-ary QAM ($M = 16$) signal set.

where $L = \sqrt{M}$. For example, for a 16-QAM with signal constellation as shown in Figure 6.47, the L by L matrix is

$$\{a_i, b_i\} = \begin{bmatrix} (-3,3) & (-1,3) & (1,3) & (3,3) \\ (-3,1) & (-1,1) & (1,1) & (3,1) \\ (-3,-1) & (-1,-1) & (1,-1) & (3,-1) \\ (-3,-3) & (-1,-3) & (1,-3) & (3,-3) \end{bmatrix} \tag{6.125}$$

It can be shown that the average probability of error in an AWGN channel for M-ary QAM, using coherent detection, can be approximated by [Hay94]

$$P_e \cong 4\left(1 - \frac{1}{\sqrt{M}}\right) Q\left(\sqrt{\frac{2E_{min}}{N_0}}\right) \tag{6.126}$$

In terms of the average signal energy E_{av}, this can be expressed as [Zie92]

$$P_e \cong 4\left(1 - \frac{1}{\sqrt{M}}\right) Q\left(\sqrt{\frac{3E_{av}}{(M-1)N_0}}\right) \tag{6.127}$$

The power spectrum and bandwidth efficiency of QAM modulation is identical to M-ary PSK modulation. In terms of power efficiency, QAM is superior to M-ary PSK. Table 6.5 lists the bandwidth and power efficiencies of a QAM signal for various values of M, assuming optimum raised cosine rolloff filtering in AWGN. As with M-PSK, the table is optimistic, and actual

Table 6.5 Bandwidth and Power Efficiency of QAM [Zie92]

M	4	16	64	256	1024	4096
η_B	1	2	3	4	5	6
E_b/N_o for BER = 10^{-6}	10.5	15	18.5	24	28	33.5

bit error probabilities for wireless systems must be determined by simulating the various impairments of the channel and the specific receiver implementation. Pilot tones or equalization must be used for QAM in mobile systems.

6.10.3 M-ary Frequency Shift Keying (MFSK) and OFDM

In M-ary FSK modulation, the transmitted signals are defined by

$$s_i(t) = \sqrt{\frac{2E_s}{T_s}}\cos\left[\frac{\pi}{T_s}(n_c+i)t\right] \qquad 0 \le t \le T_s \quad i = 1, 2, \ldots.., M \tag{6.128}$$

where $f_c = n_c/2T_s$ for some fixed integer n_c. The M transmitted signals are of equal energy and equal duration, and the signal frequencies are separated by $1/2T_s$ Hz, making the signals orthogonal to one another.

For coherent M-ary FSK, the optimum receiver consists of a bank of M correlators, or matched filters, which are tuned to the M distinct carriers. The average probability of error based on the union bound is given by [Zie92]

$$P_e \le (M-1)Q\left(\sqrt{\frac{E_b \log_2 M}{N_0}}\right) \tag{6.129}$$

For noncoherent detection using matched filters followed by envelope detectors, the average probability of error is given by [Zie92]

$$P_e = \sum_{k=1}^{M-1}\left(\frac{(-1)^{k+1}}{k+1}\right)\binom{M-1}{k}\exp\left(\frac{-kE_s}{(k+1)N_0}\right) \tag{6.130}$$

Using only the leading terms of the binomial expansion, the probability of error can be bounded as

$$P_e \le \frac{M-1}{2}\exp\left(\frac{-E_s}{2N_0}\right) \tag{6.131}$$

The channel bandwidth of a coherent M-ary FSK signal may be defined as [Zie92]

$$B = \frac{R_b(M+3)}{2\log_2 M} \tag{6.132}$$

and that of a noncoherent MFSK may be defined as

$$B = \frac{R_b M}{2\log_2 M} \tag{6.133}$$

Table 6.6 Bandwidth and Power Efficiency of Coherent M-ary FSK [Zie92]

M	2	4	8	16	32	64
η_B	0.4	0.57	0.55	0.42	0.29	0.18
E_b/N_o for BER = 10^{-6}	13.5	10.8	9.3	8.2	7.5	6.9

This implies that the bandwidth efficiency of an M-ary FSK signal decreases with increasing M. Therefore, unlike M-PSK signals, M-FSK signals are bandwidth inefficient. However, since all the M signals are orthogonal, there is no crowding in the signal space, and hence the power efficiency increases with M. Furthermore, M-ary FSK can be amplified using nonlinear amplifiers with no performance degradation. Table 6.6 provides a listing of bandwidth and power efficiency of M-FSK signals for various values of M.

The orthogonality characteristic of MFSK has led researchers to explore Orthogonal Frequency Division Multiplexing (OFDM) as a means of providing power efficient signaling for a large number of users on the same channel. Each frequency in Equation (6.128) is modulated with binary data (on/off) to provide a number of parallel carriers each containing a portion of user data.

MFSK and OFDM modulation methods are being explored for high speed data connections as part of the IEEE 802.11a standards activities to provide 54 Mbps WLAN connections, as well as for high speed line-of-sight and non-line-of-sight microwave connections for MMDS operation.

6.11 Spread Spectrum Modulation Techniques

All of the modulation and demodulation techniques described so far strive to achieve greater power and/or bandwidth efficiency in a stationary additive white Gaussian noise channel. Since bandwidth is a limited resource, one of the primary design objectives of all the modulation schemes detailed thus far is to minimize the required transmission bandwidth. Spread spectrum techniques, on the other hand, employ a transmission bandwidth that is several orders of magnitude *greater* than the minimum required signal bandwidth. While this system is very bandwidth inefficient for a single user, the advantage of spread spectrum is that many users can simultaneously use the same bandwidth without significantly interfering with one another. In a multiple-user, *multiple access interference* (MAI) environment, spread spectrum systems become very bandwidth efficient.

Apart from occupying a very large bandwidth, spread spectrum signals are *pseudorandom* and have noise-like properties when compared with the digital information data. The spreading waveform is controlled by a *pseudo-noise (PN) sequence* or *pseudo-noise code*, which is a binary sequence that appears random but can be reproduced in a deterministic manner by intended receivers. Spread spectrum signals are demodulated at the receiver through cross-correlation with a locally-generated version of the pseudorandom carrier. Cross-correlation with the correct PN sequence *despreads* the spread spectrum signal and restores the modulated message in the same narrow band as the original data, whereas cross-correlating the signal from an undesired user results in a very small amount of wideband noise at the receiver output.

Spread spectrum modulation has many properties that make it particularly well-suited for use in the mobile radio environment. The most important advantage is its inherent interference rejection capability. Since each user is assigned a unique PN code which is approximately orthogonal to the codes of other users, the receiver can separate each user based on their codes, even though they occupy the same spectrum at all times. This implies that, up to a certain number of users, interference between spread spectrum signals using the same frequency is negligible. Not only can a particular spread spectrum signal be recovered from a number of other spread spectrum signals, it is also possible to completely recover a spread spectrum signal even when it is jammed by a narrowband interferer. Since narrowband interference effects only a small portion of the spread spectrum signal, it can easily be removed through notch filtering without much loss of information. Since all users are able to share the same spectrum, spread spectrum may eliminate frequency planning, since all cells can use the same channels.

Resistance to multipath fading is another fundamental reason for considering spread spectrum systems for wireless communications. Chapter 5 showed that wideband signals are frequency selective. Since spread spectrum signals have uniform energy over a very large bandwidth, at any given time only a small portion of the spectrum will undergo fading (recall the comparison between wideband and narrowband signal responses in multipath channels in Chapter 5). Viewed in the time domain, the multipath resistance properties are due to the fact that the delayed versions of the transmitted PN signal will have poor correlation with the original PN sequence, and will thus appear as another uncorrelated user which is ignored by the receiver. That is, as long as the multipath channel induces at least one chip of delay, the multipath signals will arrive at the receiver such that they are shifted in time by at least one chip from the intended signal. The correlation properties of PN sequences are such that this slight delay causes the multipath to appear uncorrelated with the intended signal, so that the multipath contributions appear invisible to the desired received signal. Spread spectrum systems are not only resistant to multipath fading, but they can also exploit the delayed multipath components to improve the performance of the system. This can be done using a RAKE receiver which anticipates multipath propagation delays of the transmitted spread spectrum signal and combines the information obtained from several resolvable multipath components to form a stronger version of the signal. A RAKE receiver consists of a bank of correlators, each of which correlate to a particular multipath component of the desired signal. The correlator outputs may be weighted according to their relative strengths and summed to obtain the final signal estimate [Pri58]. RAKE receivers are described in Chapter 7.

6.11.1 Pseudo-Noise (PN) Sequences

A pseudo-noise (PN) or pseudorandom sequence is a binary sequence with an autocorrelation that resembles, over a period, the autocorrelation of a random binary sequence. Its autocorrelation also roughly resembles the autocorrelation of bandlimited white noise. Although it is deter-

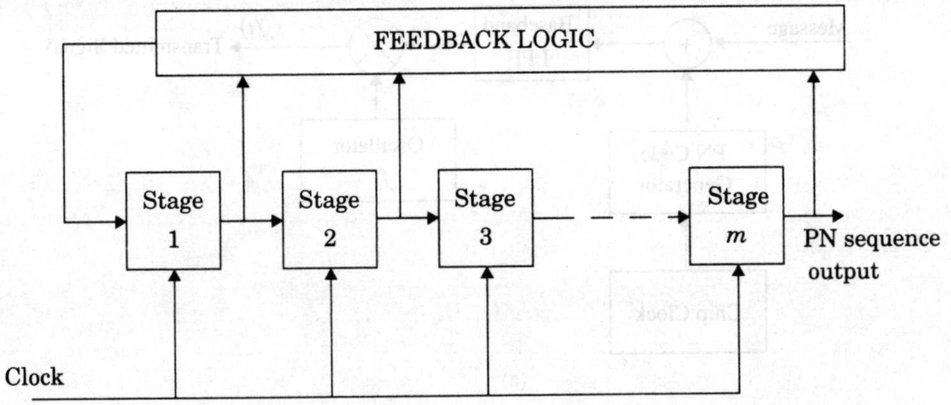

Figure 6.48 Block diagram of a generalized feedback shift register with m stages.

ministic, a pseudonoise sequence has many characteristics that are similar to those of random binary sequences, such as having a nearly equal number of 0s and 1s, very low correlation between shifted versions of the sequence, very low crosscorrelation between any two sequences, etc. The PN sequence is usually generated using sequential logic circuits. A feedback shift register, which is diagrammed in Figure 6.48, consists of consecutive stages of two state memory devices and feedback logic. Binary sequences are shifted through the shift registers in response to clock pulses, and the output of the various stages are logically combined and fed back as the input to the first stage. When the feedback logic consists of exclusive-OR gates, which is usually the case, the shift register is called a linear PN sequence generator.

The initial contents of the memory stages and the feedback logic circuit determine the successive contents of the memory. If a linear shift register reaches zero state at some time, it would always remain in the zero state, and the output would subsequently be all 0s. Since there are exactly $2^m - 1$ nonzero states for an m-stage feedback shift register, the period of a PN sequence produced by a linear m-stage shift register cannot exceed $2^m - 1$ symbols. A sequence of period $2^m - 1$ generated by a linear feedback register is called a *maximal length* (ML) sequence. An excellent treatment of PN codes is given in [Coo86b].

6.11.2 Direct Sequence Spread Spectrum (DS–SS)

A *direct sequence spread spectrum* (DS–SS) system spreads the baseband data by directly multiplying the baseband data pulses with a pseudo-noise sequence that is produced by a pseudo-noise code generator. A single pulse or symbol of the PN waveform is called a *chip*. Figure 6.49 shows a functional block diagram of a DS system with binary phase modulation. This system is one of the most widely used direct sequence implementations. Synchronized data symbols, which may be information bits or binary channel code symbols, are added in modulo-2 fashion to the chips before being phase modulated. A coherent or differentially coherent phase-shift keying (PSK) demodulation may be used in the receiver.

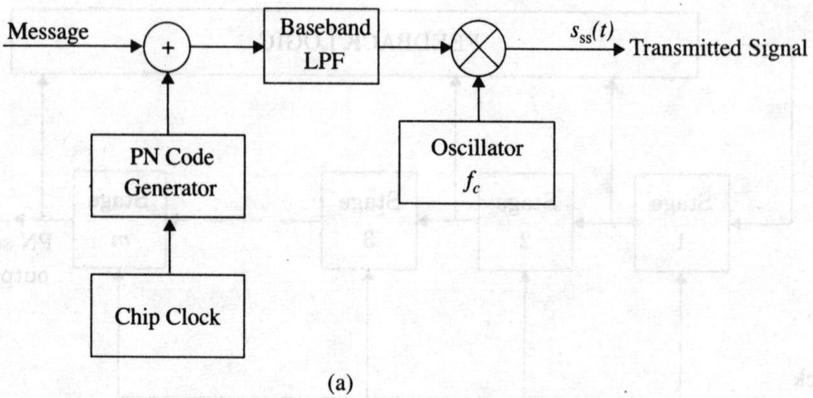

(a)

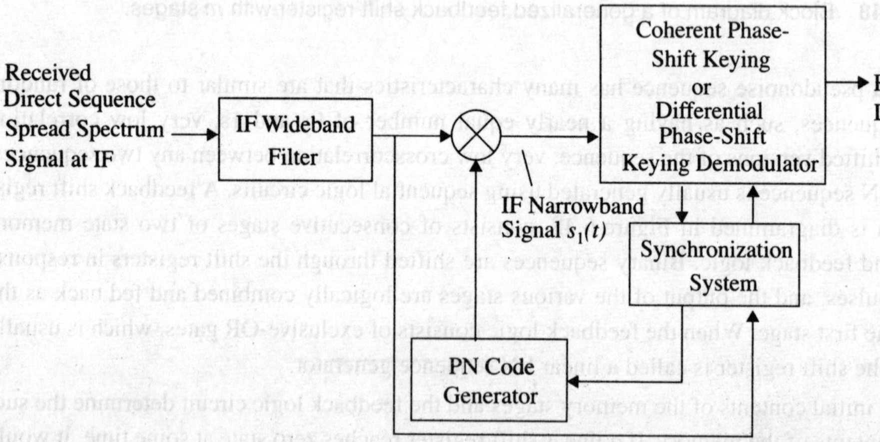

(b)

Figure 6.49 Block diagram of a DS–SS system with binary phase modulation: (a) transmitter; and (b) receiver.

The received spread spectrum signal for a single user can be represented as

$$s_{ss}(t) = \sqrt{\frac{2E_s}{T_s}}m(t)p(t)\cos(2\pi f_c t + \theta) \tag{6.134}$$

where $m(t)$ is the data sequence, $p(t)$ is the PN spreading sequence, f_c is the carrier frequency, and θ is the carrier phase angle at $t = 0$. The data waveform is a time sequence of nonoverlapping rectangular pulses, each of which has an amplitude equal to +1 or –1. Each symbol in $m(t)$ represents a data symbol and has duration T_s. Each pulse in $p(t)$ represents a chip, is usually rectangular with an amplitude equal to +1 or –1, and has a duration of T_c. The transitions of the data symbols and chips coincide such that the ratio T_s to T_c is an integer. If B_{ss} is the bandwidth of $s_{ss}(t)$ and B is the bandwidth of a conventionally modulated signal $m(t)\cos(2\pi f_c t)$, the spreading due to $p(t)$ gives $B_{ss} \gg B$.

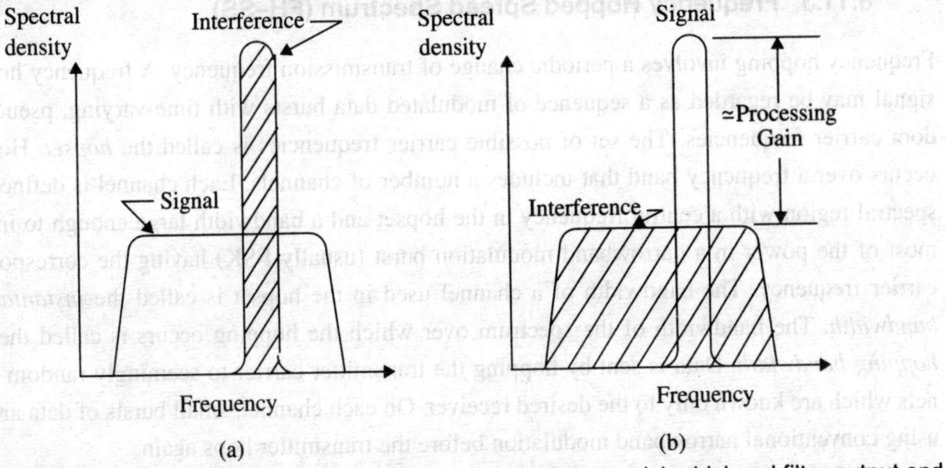

Figure 6.50 Spectra of desired received signal with interference: (a) wideband filter output and (b) correlator output after despreading.

Figure 6.49(b) illustrates a DS receiver. Assuming that code synchronization has been achieved at the receiver, the received signal passes through the wideband filter and is multiplied by a local replica of the PN code sequence $p(t)$. If $p(t) = \pm 1$, then $p^2(t) = 1$, and this multiplication yields the despread signal $s(t)$ given by

$$s_1(t) = \sqrt{\frac{2E_s}{T_s}} m(t) \cos(2\pi f_c t + \theta) \tag{6.135}$$

at the input of the demodulator. Because $s_1(t)$ has the form of a BPSK signal, the corresponding demodulation extracts $m(t)$.

Figure 6.50 shows the received spectra of the desired spread spectrum signal and the interference at the output of the receiver wideband filter. Multiplication by the spreading waveform produces the spectra of Figure 6.50(b) at the demodulator input. The signal bandwidth is reduced to B, while the interference energy is spread over an RF bandwidth exceeding B_{ss}. The filtering action of the demodulator removes most of the interference spectrum that does not overlap with the signal spectrum. Thus, most of the original interference energy is eliminated by spreading and minimally affects the desired receiver signal. An approximate measure of the interference rejection capability is given by the ratio B_{ss}/B, which is equal to the processing gain defined as

$$PG = \frac{T_s}{T_c} = \frac{R_c}{R_s} = \frac{B_{ss}}{2R_s} \tag{6.136}$$

The greater the processing gain of the system, the greater will be its ability to suppress in-band interference.

6.11.3 Frequency Hopped Spread Spectrum (FH–SS)

Frequency hopping involves a periodic change of transmission frequency. A frequency hopping signal may be regarded as a sequence of modulated data bursts with time-varying, pseudorandom carrier frequencies. The set of possible carrier frequencies is called the *hopset.* Hopping occurs over a frequency band that includes a number of channels. Each channel is defined as a spectral region with a central frequency in the hopset and a bandwidth large enough to include most of the power in a narrowband modulation burst (usually FSK) having the corresponding carrier frequency. The bandwidth of a channel used in the hopset is called the *instantaneous bandwidth.* The bandwidth of the spectrum over which the hopping occurs is called the *total hopping bandwidth.* Data is sent by hopping the transmitter carrier to seemingly random channels which are known only to the desired receiver. On each channel, small bursts of data are sent using conventional narrowband modulation before the transmitter hops again.

If only a single carrier frequency (single channel) is used on each hop, digital data modulation is called *single channel modulation.* Figure 6.51 shows a single channel FH–SS system. The time duration between hops is called the *hop duration* or the *hopping period* and is denoted by T_h. The total hopping bandwidth and the instantaneous bandwidth are denoted by B_{ss} and B, respectively. The processing gain = B_{ss}/B for FH systems.

After frequency hopping has been removed from the received signal, the resulting signal is said to be *dehopped.* If the frequency pattern produced by the receiver synthesizer in Figure 6.51(b) is synchronized with the frequency pattern of the received signal, then the mixer output is a dehopped signal at a fixed difference frequency. Before demodulation, the dehopped signal is applied to a conventional receiver. In FH, whenever an undesired signal occupies a particular hopping channel, the noise and interference in that channel are translated in frequency so that they enter the demodulator. Thus, it is possible to have collisions in an FH system where an undesired user transmits in the same channel at the same time as the desired user.

Frequency hopping may be classified as fast or slow. *Fast frequency hopping* occurs if there is more than one frequency hop during each transmitted symbol. Thus, fast frequency hopping implies that the hopping rate equals or exceeds the information symbol rate. *Slow frequency hopping* occurs if one or more symbols are transmitted in the time interval between frequency hops.

If binary frequency-shift keying (FSK) is used, the pair of possible instantaneous frequencies changes with each hop. The frequency channel occupied by a transmitted symbol is called the *transmission channel.* The channel that would be occupied if the alternative symbol were transmitted is called the *complementary channel.* The frequency hop rate of an FH–SS system is determined by the frequency agility of receiver synthesizers, the type of information being transmitted, the amount of redundancy used to code against collisions, and the distance to the nearest potential interferer.

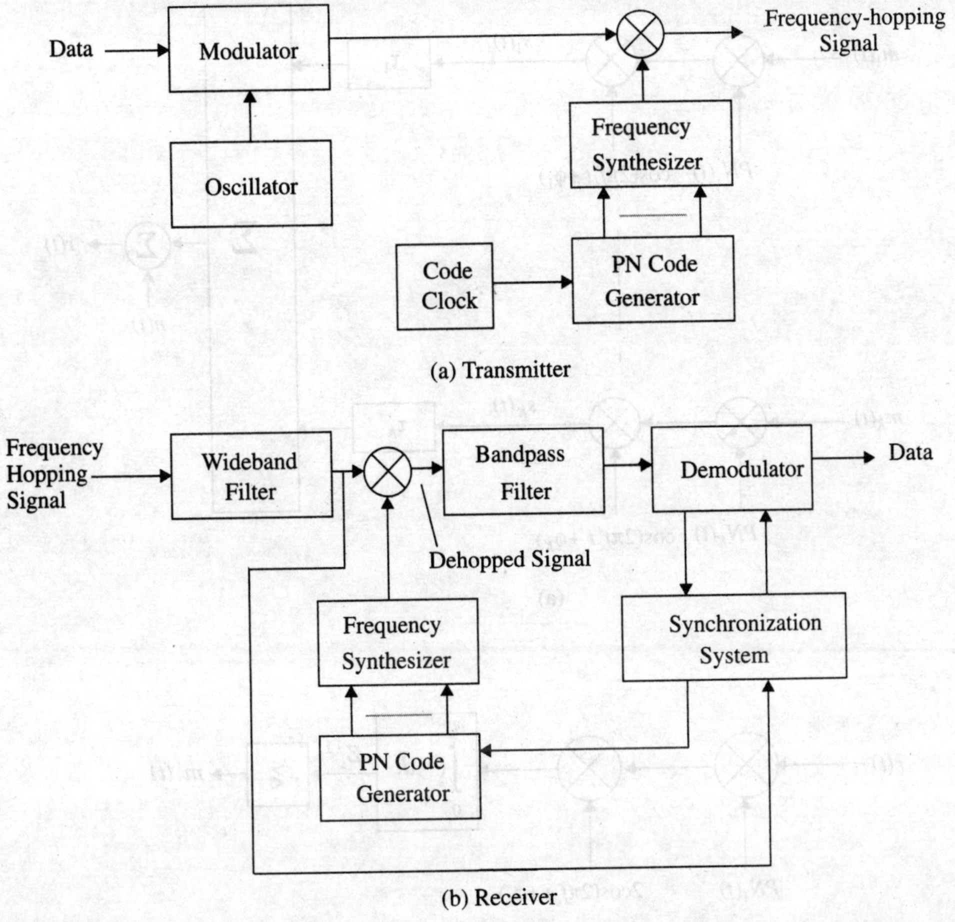

Figure 6.51 Block diagram of frequency hopping (FH) system with single channel modulation.

6.11.4 Performance of Direct Sequence Spread Spectrum

A direct sequence spread spectrum system with K multiple access users is shown in Figure 6.52. Assume each user has a PN sequence with N chips per message symbol period T such that $NT_c = T$.

The transmitted signal of the kth user can be expressed as

$$s_k(t) = \sqrt{\frac{2E_s}{T_s}} m_k(t) p_k(t) \cos(2\pi f_c t + \phi_k) \qquad (6.137)$$

where $p_k(t)$ is the PN code sequence of the kth user, and $m_k(t)$ is the data sequence of the kth user. The received signal will consist of the sum of K different transmitted signals (one desired

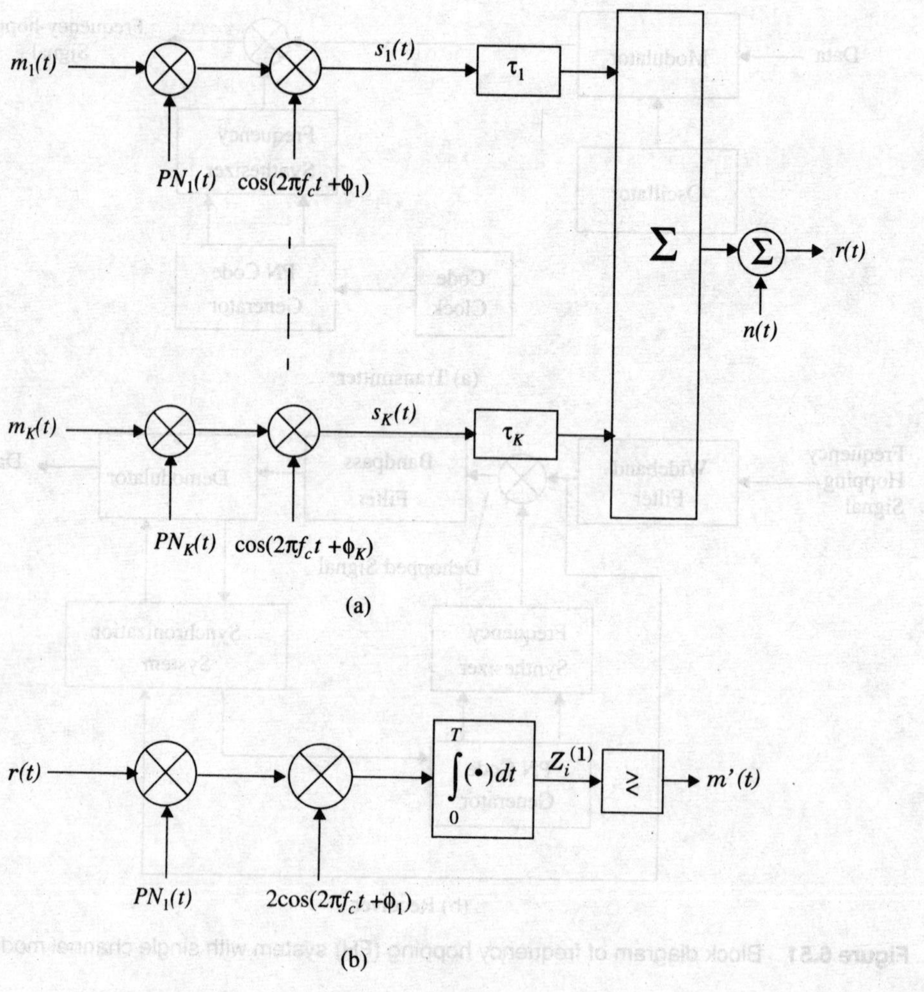

Figure 6.52 A simplified diagram of a DS–SS system with K users. (a) Model of K users in a CDMA spread spectrum system; (b) receiver structure for User 1.

user and $K-1$ undesired users) plus additive noise. Reception is accomplished by correlating the received signal with the appropriate signature sequence to produce a decision variable. The decision variable for the ith transmitted bit of User 1 is

$$Z_i^{(1)} = \int_{(i-1)T+\tau_1}^{iT+\tau_1} r(t)p_1(t-\tau_1)\cos[2\pi f_c(t-\tau_1)+\phi_1]dt \tag{6.138}$$

If $m_{1,i} = -1$, then the bit will be received in error if $Z_i^{(1)} > 0$. The probability of error can now be calculated as $Pr[Z_i^{(1)} > 0 | m_{1,i} = -1]$. Since the received signal $r(t)$ is a linear combination of signals plus additive noise, Equation (6.138) can be rewritten as

$$Z_i^{(1)} = I_1 + \sum_{k=2}^{K} I_k + \xi \tag{6.139}$$

where

$$I_1 = \int_0^T s_1(t) p_1(t) \cos(2\pi f_c t) dt = \sqrt{\frac{E_s T}{2}} \tag{6.140}$$

is the response of the receiver to the desired signal from User 1,

$$\xi = \int_0^T n(t) p_1(t) \cos(2\pi f_c t) dt \tag{6.141}$$

is a Gaussian random variable representing noise with mean zero and variance

$$E[\xi^2] = \frac{N_0 T}{4}, \tag{6.142}$$

and

$$I_k = \int_0^T s_k(t - \tau_k) p_1(t) \cos(2\pi f_c t) dt \tag{6.143}$$

represents the multiple access interference from User k. Assuming that I_k is composed of the cumulative effects of N random chips from the kth interferer over the integration period T of one bit, the central limit theorem implies that the sum of these effects will tend toward a Gaussian distribution (see Appendix E). Since there are $K - 1$ users which serve as identically distributed interferers, the total multiple access interference $I = \sum_{k=2}^{K} I_k$ may be approximated by a Gaussian random variable. As shown in Appendix E, the Gaussian approximation assumes that each I_k is independent, but in actuality they are not. The Gaussian approximation yields a convenient expression for the average probability of bit error given by

$$P_e = Q\left(\frac{1}{\sqrt{\frac{K-1}{3N} + \frac{N_0}{2E_b}}}\right) \tag{6.144}$$

For a single user, $K = 1$, this expression reduces to the BER expression for BPSK modulation. For the interference limited case where thermal noise is not a factor, E_b/N_0 tends to infinity, and the BER expression has a value equal to

$$P_e = Q\left(\sqrt{\frac{3N}{K-1}}\right) \tag{6.145}$$

This is the irreducible error floor due to multiple access interference and assumes that all interferers provide equal power, the same as the desired user, at the DS–SS receiver. In practice, the *near–far problem* presents difficulty for DS–SS systems. Without careful power control of each mobile user, one close-in user may dominate the received signal energy at a base station, making the Gaussian assumption inaccurate [Pic91]. For a large number of users, the bit error rate is limited more by the multiple access interference than by thermal noise [Lib99]. Appendix E provides a detailed analysis of how to compute the BER for DS–SS systems. Chapter 9 illustrates how capacity of a DS–SS system changes with propagation and with multiple access interference.

6.11.5 Performance of Frequency Hopping Spread Spectrum

In FH–SS systems, several users independently hop their carrier frequencies while using BFSK modulation. If two users are not simultaneously utilizing the same frequency band, the probability of error for BFSK can be given by

$$P_e = \frac{1}{2}\exp\left(-\frac{E_b}{2N_0}\right) \tag{6.146}$$

However, if two users transmit simultaneously in the same frequency band, a collision, or "hit", occurs. In this case, it is reasonable to assume that the probability of error is 0.5. Thus, the overall probability of bit error can be modeled as

$$P_e = \frac{1}{2}\exp\left(-\frac{E_b}{2N_0}\right)(1-p_h) + \frac{1}{2}p_h \tag{6.147}$$

where p_h is the probability of a hit, which must be determined. If there are M possible hopping channels (called slots), there is a $1/M$ probability that a given interferer will be present in the desired user's slot. If there are $K-1$ interfering users, the probability that at least one is present in the desired frequency slot is equal to one mm vs. the probability of no hits, given as

$$p_h = 1 - \left(1 - \frac{1}{M}\right)^{K-1} \approx \frac{K-1}{M} \tag{6.148}$$

assuming M is large. Substituting this in Equation (6.147) gives

$$P_e = \frac{1}{2}\exp\left(-\frac{E_b}{2N_0}\right)\left(1 - \frac{K-1}{M}\right) + \frac{1}{2}\left[\frac{K-1}{M}\right] \tag{6.149}$$

Now consider the following special cases. If $K = 1$, the probability of error reduces to Equation (6.146), the standard probability of error for BFSK. Also, if E_b/N_0 approaches infinity,

$$\lim_{\frac{E_b}{N_0} \to \infty} (P_e) = \frac{1}{2}\left[\frac{K-1}{M}\right] \tag{6.150}$$

which illustrates the irreducible error rate due to multiple access interference.

The previous analysis assumes that all users hop their carrier frequencies synchronously. This is called *slotted frequency hopping*. This may not be a realistic scenario for many FH–SS systems. Even when synchronization can be achieved between individual user clocks, radio signals will not arrive synchronously to each user due to the various propagation delays. As described by Geraniotis [Ger82], the probability of a hit in the asynchronous case is

$$p_h = 1 - \left\{1 - \frac{1}{M}\left(1 + \frac{1}{N_b}\right)\right\}^{K-1} \tag{6.151}$$

where N_b is the number of bits per hop. Comparing Equation (6.151) to (6.148), we see that for the asynchronous case, the probability of a hit is increased (this would be expected). Using Equation (6.151) in Equation (6.147), the probability of error for the asynchronous FH–SS case is

$$P_e = \frac{1}{2}\exp\left(-\frac{E_b}{N_0}\right)\left\{1 - \frac{1}{M}\left(1 + \frac{1}{N_b}\right)\right\}^{K-1} + \frac{1}{2}\left[1 - \left\{1 - \frac{1}{M}\left(1 + \frac{1}{N_b}\right)\right\}^{K-1}\right] \tag{6.152}$$

FH–SS has an advantage over DS–SS in that it is not as susceptible to the near–far problem. Because signals are generally not utilizing the same frequency simultaneously, the relative power levels of signals are not as critical as in DS–SS. The near–far problem is not totally avoided, however, since there will be some interference caused by stronger signals bleeding into weaker signals due to imperfect filtering of adjacent channels. To combat the occasional hits, error-correction coding is required on all transmissions. By applying strong Reed–Solomon or other burst error correcting codes, performance can be increased dramatically, even with an occasional collision.

6.12 Modulation Performance in Fading and Multipath Channels

As discussed in Chapter 4 and 5, the mobile radio channel is characterized by various impairments such as fading, multipath, and Doppler spread. In order to study the effectiveness of any modulation scheme in a mobile radio environment, it is required to evaluate the performance of the modulation scheme over such channel conditions. Although bit error rate (BER) evaluation gives a good indication of the performance of a particular modulation scheme, it does not provide information about the type of errors. For example, it does not give incidents of bursty errors. In a fading mobile radio channel, it is likely that a transmitted signal will suffer deep fades which can lead to outage or a complete loss of the signal.

Evaluating the *probability of outage* is another means to judge the effectiveness of the signaling scheme in a mobile radio channel. An outage event is specified by a specific number of bit errors occurring in a given transmission. Bit error rates and probability of outage for various modulation schemes under various types of channel impairments can be evaluated either through analytical techniques or through simulations. While simple analytical techniques for computing bit error rates in slow flat-fading channels exist, performance evaluation in frequency selective channels and computation of outage probabilities are often made through computer simulations. Computer simulations are based on convolving the input bit stream with a suitable channel impulse response model and counting the bit errors at the output of the receiver decision circuit [Rap91b], [Fun93].

Before a study of the performance of various modulation schemes in multipath and fading channels is made, it is imperative that a thorough understanding of the channel characteristics be obtained. The channel models described in Chapter 5 may be used in the evaluation of various modulation schemes.

6.12.1 Performance of Digital Modulation in Slow Flat-Fading Channels

As discussed in Chapter 5, flat-fading channels cause a multiplicative (gain) variation in the transmitted signal $s(t)$. Since slow flat-fading channels change much slower than the applied modulation, it can be assumed that the attenuation and phase shift of the signal is constant over at least one symbol interval. Therefore, the received signal $r(t)$ may be expressed as

$$r(t) = \alpha(t)\exp(-j\theta(t))s(t) + n(t) \qquad 0 \le t \le T \tag{6.153}$$

where $\alpha(t)$ is the gain of the channel, $\theta(t)$ is the phase shift of the channel, and $n(t)$ is additive Gaussian noise.

Depending on whether it is possible to make an accurate estimate of the phase $\theta(t)$, coherent or noncoherent matched filter detection may be employed at the receiver.

To evaluate the probability of error of any digital modulation scheme in a slow flat-fading channel, one must average the probability of error of the particular modulation in AWGN channels over the possible ranges of signal strength due to fading. In other words, the probability of error in AWGN channels is viewed as a conditional error probability, where the condition is that α is fixed. Hence, the probability of error in slow flat-fading channels can be obtained by averaging the error in AWGN channels over the fading probability density function. In doing so, the probability of error in a slow flat-fading channel can be evaluated as

$$P_e = \int_0^{\infty} P_e(X)p(X)dX \tag{6.154}$$

where $P_e(X)$ is the probability of error for an arbitrary modulation at a specific value of signal-to-noise ratio X, $X = \alpha^2 E_b/N_0$, and $p(X)$ is the probability density function of X due to the fading channel. E_b and N_0 are constants that represent the *average* energy per bit and noise power density in a non-fading AWGN channel, and the random variable α^2 is used to represent instantaneous power values of the fading channel, with respect to the non-fading E_b/N_0. It is convenient to assume $\overline{\alpha^2}$ is one, for a unity gain fading channel. Then, $p(X)$ can simply be viewed as the distribution of the instantaneous value of E_b/N_0 in a fading channel, and $P_e(X)$ can be seen to be the conditional probability of bit errors for a given value of the random E_b/N_0 due to fading.

For Rayleigh fading channels, the fading amplitude α has a Rayleigh distribution, so the fading power α^2 and consequently X have a chi-square distribution with two degrees of freedom. Therefore,

$$p(X) = \frac{1}{\Gamma}\exp\left(-\frac{X}{\Gamma}\right) \qquad X \geq 0 \tag{6.155}$$

where $\Gamma = \frac{E_b}{N_0}\overline{\alpha^2}$ is the average value of the signal-to-noise ratio. For $\overline{\alpha^2} = 1$, note that Γ corresponds to the average E_b/N_0 for the fading channel.

By using Equation (6.155) and the probability of error of a particular modulation scheme in AWGN, the probability of error in a slow flat-fading channel can be evaluated. It can be shown that for coherent binary PSK and coherent binary FSK, Equation (6.154) evaluates to [Ste87]

$$P_{e,\,\mathrm{PSK}} = \frac{1}{2}\left[1 - \sqrt{\frac{\Gamma}{1+\Gamma}}\right] \qquad \text{(coherent binary PSK)} \tag{6.156}$$

$$P_{e,\,\mathrm{FSK}} = \frac{1}{2}\left[1 - \sqrt{\frac{\Gamma}{2+\Gamma}}\right] \qquad \text{(coherent binary FSK)} \tag{6.157}$$

It can also be shown that the average error probability of DPSK and orthogonal noncoherent FSK in a slow, flat, Rayleigh fading channel are given by

$$P_{e,\,\mathrm{DPSK}} = \frac{1}{2(1+\Gamma)} \qquad \text{(differential binary PSK)} \tag{6.158}$$

$$P_{e,\,\mathrm{NCFSK}} = \frac{1}{2+\Gamma} \qquad \text{(noncoherent orthogonal binary FSK)} \tag{6.159}$$

Figure 6.53 illustrates how the BER for various modulations changes as a function of E_b/N_0 in a Rayleigh flat-fading environment. The figure was produced using simulation instead of analysis, but agrees closely with Equations (6.156) to (6.159) [Rap91b].

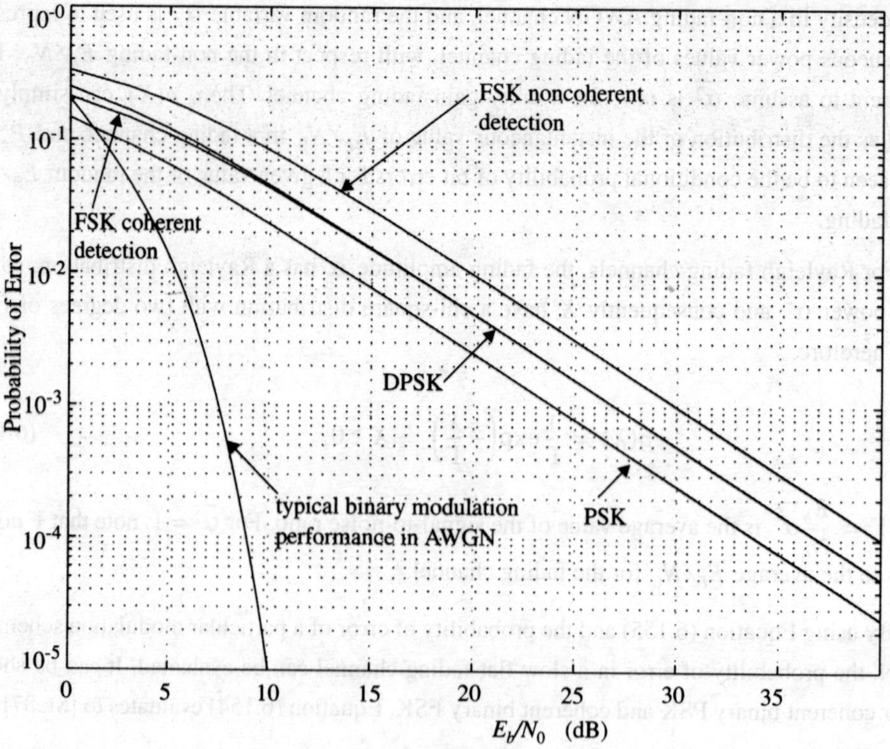

Figure 6.53 Bit error rate performance of binary modulation schemes in a Rayleigh flat-fading channel as compared to a typical performance curve in AWGN.

For large values of E_b/N_0 (i.e., large values of X), the error probability Equations may be simplified as

$$P_{e,\,\mathrm{PSK}} = \frac{1}{4\Gamma} \quad \text{(coherent binary PSK)} \tag{6.160}$$

$$P_{e,\,\mathrm{FSK}} = \frac{1}{2\Gamma} \quad \text{(coherent FSK)} \tag{6.161}$$

$$P_{e,\,\mathrm{DPSK}} = \frac{1}{2\Gamma} \quad \text{(differential PSK)} \tag{6.162}$$

$$P_{e,\,\mathrm{NCFSK}} = \frac{1}{\Gamma} \quad \text{(noncoherent orthogonal binary FSK)} \tag{6.163}$$

For GMSK, the expression for BER in the AWGN channel is given in Equation (6.112.a) which when evaluated in Equation (6.154) yields a Rayleigh fading BER of

$$P_{e,\mathrm{GMSK}} = \frac{1}{2}\left(1 - \sqrt{\frac{\delta\Gamma}{\delta\Gamma + 1}}\right) \cong \frac{1}{4\delta\Gamma} \quad \text{(coherent GMSK)} \tag{6.164}$$

where

$$\delta \cong \begin{cases} 0.68 & \text{for } BT = 0.25 \\ 0.85 & \text{for } BT = \infty \end{cases} \tag{6.165}$$

As seen from Equations (6.160) to (6.164), for lower error rates all five modulation techniques exhibit an inverse algebraic relation between error rate and mean SNR. This is in contrast with the exponential relationship between error rate and SNR in an AWGN channel. According to these results, it is seen that operating at BERs of 10^{-3} to 10^{-6} requires roughly a 30 dB to 60 dB mean SNR. This is significantly larger than that required when operating over a nonfading Gaussian noise channel (20 dB to 50 dB more link is required). However, it can easily be shown that the poor error performance is due to the non-zero probability of very deep fades, when the instantaneous BER can become as low as 0.5. Significant improvement in BER can be achieved by using efficient techniques such as diversity or error control coding to totally avoid the probability of deep fades, as shown in Chapter 7.

Work by Yao [Yao92] demonstrates how the analytical technique of Equation (6.154) may be applied to desired signals as well as interfering signals which undergo Rayleigh, Ricean, or log-normal fading.

Example 6.12

Using the methods described in this section, derive the probability of error expressions for DPSK and noncoherent orthogonal binary FSK in a slow flat-fading channel, where the received signal envelope has a Ricean probability distribution [Rob94].

Solution

The Ricean probability density function is given by

$$p(r) = \frac{r}{\sigma^2}\exp\left(\frac{-(r^2 + A^2)}{2\sigma^2}\right) I_0\left(\frac{Ar}{\sigma^2}\right) \quad \text{for } A \geq 0,\ r \geq 0 \tag{E6.12.1}$$

where r is the Ricean amplitude and A is the specular amplitude. By suitable transformation, the Ricean distribution can be expressed in terms of X as

$$p(X) = \frac{1+K}{\Gamma}\exp\left(-\frac{X(1+K) + K\Gamma}{\Gamma}\right) I_0\left(\sqrt{\frac{4(1+K)KX}{\Gamma}}\right) \tag{E6.12.2}$$

where $K = A^2/2\sigma^2$ is the specular-to-random ratio of the Ricean distribution. The probability of error of DPSK and noncoherent orthogonal FSK in an AWGN channel can be expressed as

$$P_e(X, k_1, k_2) = k_1 \exp(-k_2 X) \tag{E6.12.3}$$

where $k_1 = k_2 = 1/2$, for FSK and $k_1 = 1/2$, $k_2 = 1$ for DPSK.

To obtain the probability of error in a slow flat-fading channel we need to evaluate the expression

$$P_e = \int_0^{\infty} P_e(X)p(X)dX \qquad \text{(E6.12.4)}$$

Substituting Equations (E6.12.2) and (E6.12.3) in Equation (E6.12.4) and solving the integration we get the probability of error in a Ricean, slow flat-fading channel as

$$P_e = \frac{k_1(1+K)}{(k_2\Gamma+1+K)}\exp\left(\frac{-k_2K\Gamma}{k_2\Gamma+1+K}\right)$$

Substituting $k_1 = k_2 = 1/2$, for FSK, the probability of error is given by

$$P_{e,\,\text{NCFSK}} = \frac{(1+K)}{(\Gamma+2+2K)}\exp\left(\frac{-K\Gamma}{\Gamma+2+2K}\right)$$

Similarly, for DPSK, substituting $k_1 = 1/2, k_2 = 1$, we get

$$P_{e,\,\text{DPSK}} = \frac{(1+K)}{2(\Gamma+1+K)}\exp\left(\frac{-K\Gamma}{\Gamma+1+K}\right)$$

6.12.2 Digital Modulation in Frequency Selective Mobile Channels

Frequency selective fading caused by multipath time delay spread causes intersymbol interference, which results in an irreducible BER floor for mobile systems. However, even if a mobile channel is not frequency selective, the time-varying Doppler spread due to motion creates an irreducible BER floor due to the random spectral spreading. These factors impose bounds on the data rate and BER that can be transmitted reliably over a frequency selective channel. Simulation is the major tool used for analyzing frequency selective fading effects. Chuang [Chu87] studied the performance of various modulation schemes in frequency selective fading channels through simulations. Both filtered and unfiltered BPSK, QPSK, OQPSK, and MSK modulation schemes were studied, and their BER curves were simulated as a function of the normalized rms delay spread ($d = \sigma_\tau/T_s$).

The irreducible error floor in a frequency selective channel is primarily caused by the errors due to the intersymbol interference, which interferes with the signal component at the receiver sampling instants. This occurs when (a) the main (undelayed) signal component is removed through multipath cancellation, (b) a non-zero value of d causes ISI, or (c) the sampling time of a receiver is shifted as a result of delay spread. Chuang observed that errors in a frequency selective channel tend to be bursty. Based on the results of simulations, it is known that for small delay spreads (relative to the symbol duration), the resulting flat fading is the dominant cause of error bursts. For large delay spread, timing errors and ISI are the dominant error mechanisms.

Figure 6.54 shows the average irreducible BER as a function of d for different unfiltered modulation schemes using coherent detection. From the figure, it is seen that the BER performance of BPSK is the best among all the modulation schemes compared. This is because symbol offset interference (called *cross-rail* interference due to the fact that the eye diagram has multiple rails) does not exist in BPSK. Both OQPSK and MSK have a $T/2$ timing offset between two bit sequences, hence the cross-rail ISI is more severe, and their performances are similar to QPSK. Figure 6.55 shows the BER as a function of rms delay spread normalized to the bit period ($d' = \sigma_\tau / T_b$) rather than the symbol period as used in Figure 6.54. By comparing on a bit, rather than symbol basis, it becomes easier to compare different modulations. This is done in Figure 6.55, where it is clear that 4-level modulations (QPSK, OQPSK, and MSK) are more resistant to delay spread than BPSK for constant information throughput. Interestingly, 8-ary keying has been found to be less resistant than 4-ary keying, and this has led to the choice of 4-ary keying for many 2G and 3G wireless standards as described in Chapters 2 and 11.

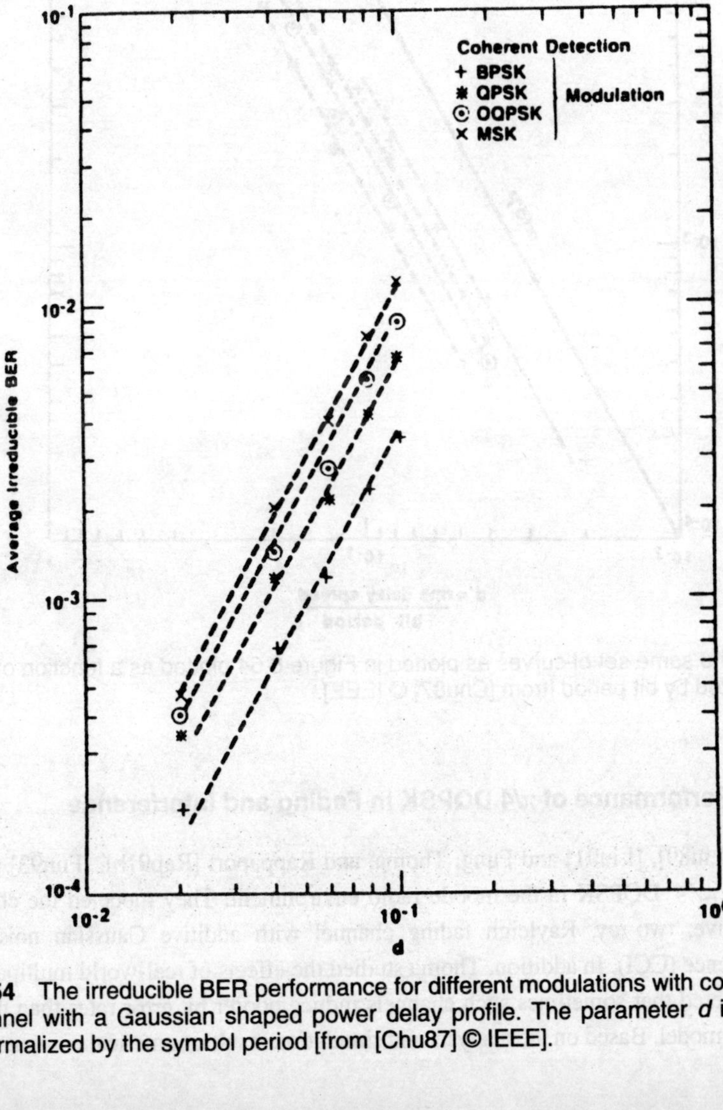

Figure 6.54 The irreducible BER performance for different modulations with coherent detection for a channel with a Gaussian shaped power delay profile. The parameter d is the rms delay spread normalized by the symbol period [from [Chu87] © IEEE].

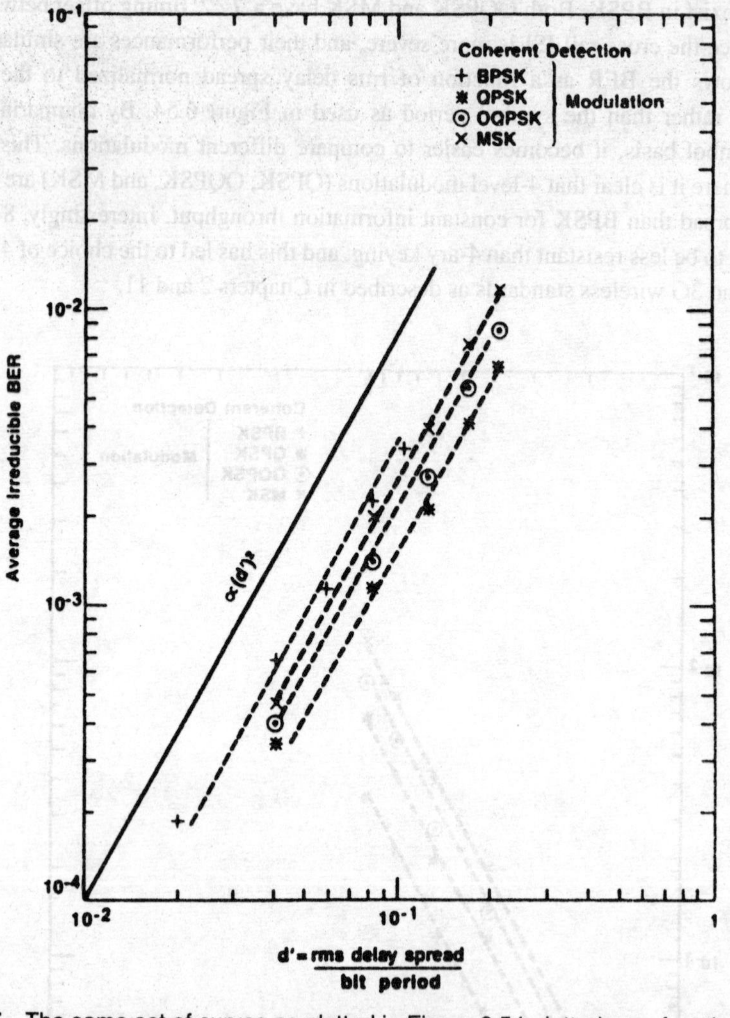

Figure 6.55 The same set of curves as plotted in Figure 6.54 plotted as a function of rms delay spread normalized by bit period [from [Chu87] © IEEE].

6.12.3 Performance of $\pi/4$ DQPSK in Fading and Interference

Liu and Feher [Liu89], [Liu91] and Fung, Thoma, and Rappaport [Rap91b], [Fun93] studied the performance of $\pi/4$ DQPSK in the mobile radio environment. They modeled the channel as a frequency selective, two-ray, Rayleigh fading channel with additive Gaussian noise and co-channel interference (CCI). In addition, Thoma studied the effects of real-world multipath channel data, and discovered that sometimes such channels induce poorer bit error rates than the two-ray Rayleigh fading model. Based on the analysis and simulation results, numerical computations were

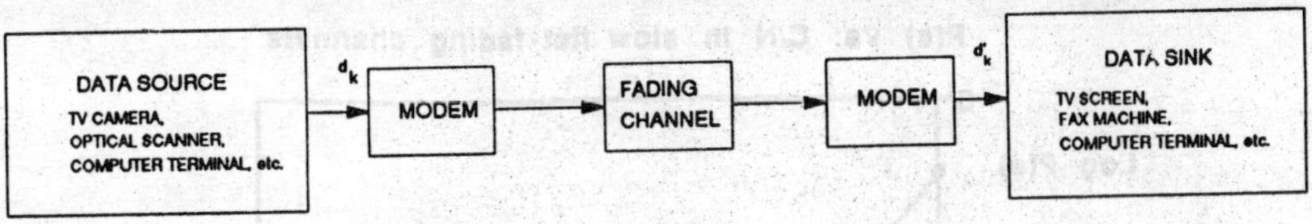

(a)

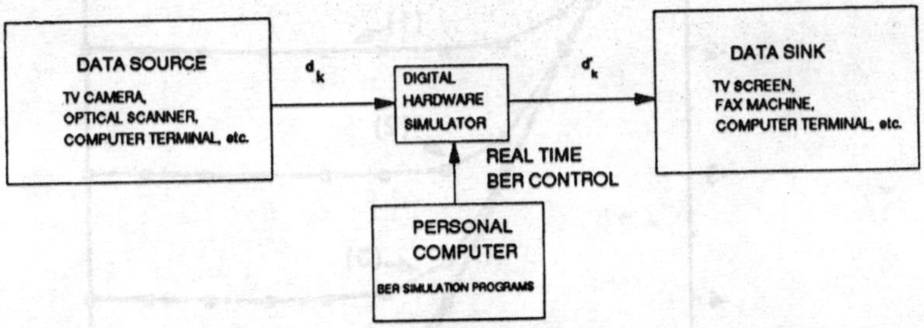

(b)

Figure 6.56 The BERSIM concept: (a) Block diagram of actual digital communication system; (b) block diagram of BERSIM using a baseband digital hardware simulator with software simulation as a driver for real-time BER control (US Patent 5,233,628).

carried out to evaluate the bit error rates at different multipath delays between the two rays, at different vehicle speeds (i.e., different Doppler shifts), and various co-channel interference levels. BER was calculated and analyzed as a function of the following parameters:

- The Doppler spread normalized to the symbol rate: $B_D T_s$ or B_D / R_s
- Delay of the second multipath τ, normalized to the symbol duration: τ / T
- Ratio of average carrier energy to noise power spectral density in decibels: E_b / N_0 dB
- Average carrier to interference power ratio in decibels: C/I dB
- Average main-path to delayed-path power ratio: C/D dB

Fung, Thoma, and Rappaport [Fun93] [Rap91b] developed a computer simulator called BERSIM (Bit Error Rate SIMulator) that confirmed the analysis by Liu and Feher [Liu91]. The BERSIM concept, covered under US Patent No. 5,233,628, is shown in Figure 6.56.

Figure 6.57 shows a plot of the average probability of error of a US digital cellular $\pi/4$ DQPSK system as a function of carrier-to-noise ratio (C/N) for different co-channel interference levels in a slow Rayleigh flat-fading channel. In a slow flat-fading channel, the multipath time dispersion and Doppler spread are negligible, and errors are caused mainly by fades and co-channel interference. It is clearly seen that for $C/I > 20$ dB, the errors are primarily due to fading, and interference has little effect. However, as C/I drops to below 20 dB, interference dominates the link performance. This is why high-capacity mobile systems are interference limited, not noise limited.

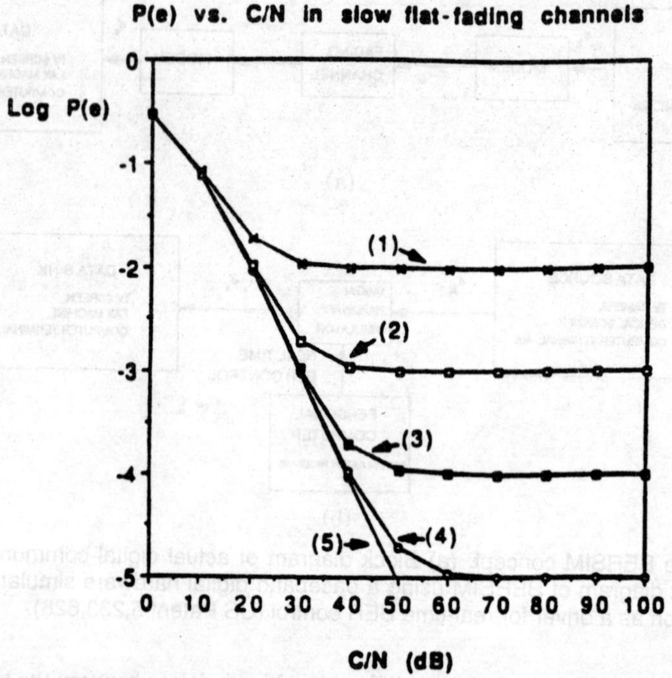

Figure 6.57 BER performance of $\pi/4$ DQPSK in a slow flat-fading channel corrupted by CCI and AWGN. f_c = 850 MHz, f_s = 24 ksps raised cosine roll-off factor = 0.2, C/I = (1) 20 dB, (2) 30 dB, (3) 40 dB, (4) 50 dB, (5) infinity [from [Liu91] © IEEE].

In mobile systems, even if there is no time dispersion and if C/N is infinitely large, the BER does not decrease below a certain irreducible floor. This irreducible error floor is due to the random FM caused by the Doppler spread, and was first shown to exist by Bello and Nelin [Bel62]. Figure 6.58 clearly illustrates the effects of Doppler-induced fading for $\pi/4$ DQPSK. As velocity increases, the irreducible error floor increases, despite an increase in E_b/N_0. Thus, once a certain E_b/N_0 is achieved, there can be no further improvement in link performance due to motion.

Figure 6.59 shows the BER of the US digital cellular $\pi/4$-DQPSK system in a two-ray Rayleigh fading channel for vehicle speeds of 40 km/hr and 120 km/hr, and with extremely large SNR (E_b/N_0 = 100 dB). The curves are plotted for C/D = 0 and 10 dB, and for various values of τ/T_s. When the delay between the two multipath rays approaches 20% of the symbol period (i.e., $\tau/T = 0.2$), the bit error rate due to multipath rises above 10^{-2} and makes the link unusable, even when the delayed ray has an average signal 10 dB below the main ray. The average bit error rate in the channel is important for speech coders. As a general rule, 10^{-2} channel bit error rate is needed for modem speech coders to work properly. Notice also that at $\tau/T = 0.1$, the probability of error is well below 10^{-2}, even when the second multipath component is equal in power to the first. Figure 6.59 shows how the delay and amplitude of the second ray have strong impact on the average BER.

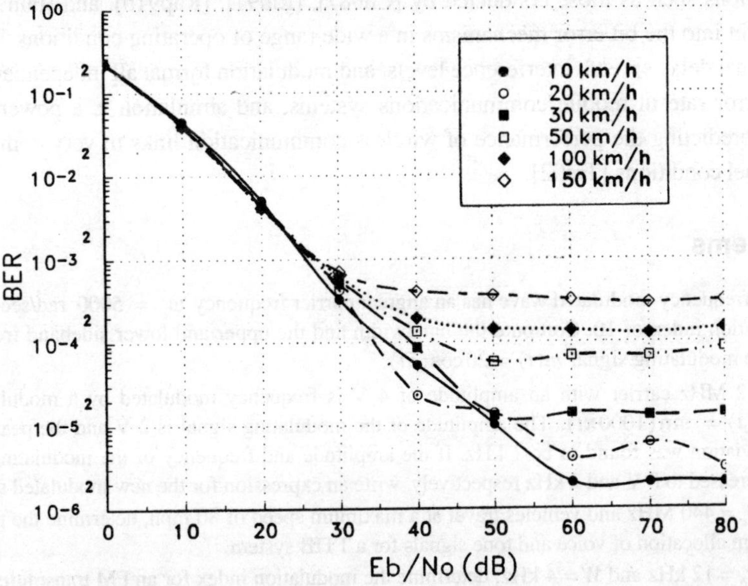

Figure 6.58 BER performance versus E_b/N_0 for π/4 DQPSK in a Raleigh flat-fading channel for various mobile speeds: f_c = 850 MHz, f_s = 24 ksps, raised cosine rolloff factor is 0.2, C/I = 100 dB. Generated by BERSIM [from [Fun93] © IEEE].

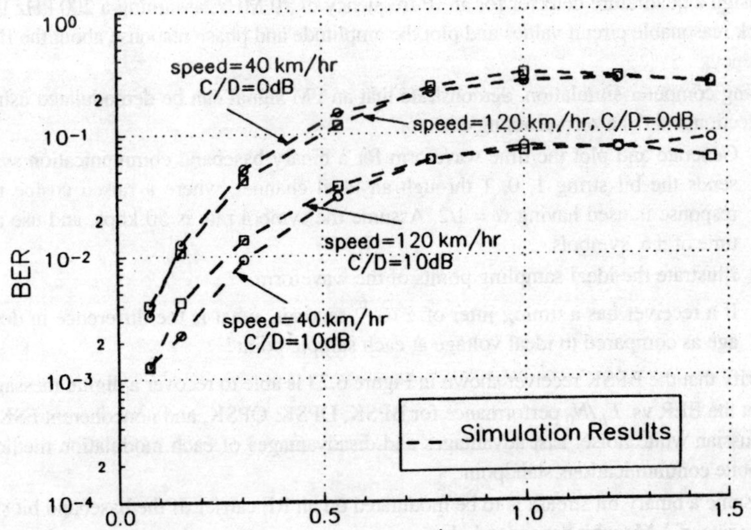

Figure 6.59 BER performance of π/4 DQPSK in a two-ray Rayleigh fading channel, where the time delay τ, and the power ratio C/D between the first and second ray are varied. f_c = 850 MHz, f_s = 24 ksps, raised cosine rolloff rate is 0.2, v = 40 km/hr, 120 km/hr E_b/N_0 = 100 dB. Produced by BERSIM [from [Fun93] © IEEE].

Simulations such as those conducted by [Chu87], [Liu91], [Rap91b], and [Fun93] provide valuable insight into the bit error mechanisms in a wide range of operating conditions. The mobile velocity, channel delay spread, interference levels, and modulation format all independently impact the raw bit error rate in mobile communications systems, and simulation is a powerful way of designing or predicting the performance of wireless communication links in very complex, time-varying channel conditions [Tra02].

6.13 Problems

6.1 A frequency modulated wave has an angular carrier frequency $\omega_c = 5000$ rad/sec and a modulation index of 10. Compute the bandwidth and the upper and lower sideband frequencies if the modulating signal $m(t) = 20\cos(5t)$.

6.2 A 2 MHz carrier with an amplitude of 4 V is frequency modulated by a modulating signal $m(t) = \sin(1000\pi t)$. The amplitude of the modulating signal is 2 V and the peak frequency deviation was found to be 1 kHz. If the amplitude and frequency of the modulating signal are increased to 8 V and 2 kHz respectively, write an expression for the new modulated signal.

6.3 If $f_c = 440$ MHz and vehicles travel at a maximum speed of 80 mph, determine the proper spectrum allocation of voice and tone signals for a TTIB system.

6.4 If $f_d = 12$ kHz and $W = 4$ kHz, determine the modulation index for an FM transmitter. These are parameters for the AMPS standard.

6.5 For AMPS FM transmissions, if the $SNR_{in} = 10$ dB, determine the SNR_{out} of the FM detector. If SNR_{in} is increased by 10 dB, what is the corresponding increase in SNR out of the detector?

6.6 Prove that for an FM signal, a quadrature detector is able to detect the message properly.

6.7 Design a quadrature detector for an IF frequency of 70 MHz, assuming a 200 kHz IF passband. Pick reasonable circuit values and plot the amplitude and phase response about the IF center frequency.

6.8 Using computer simulation, demonstrate that an FM signal can be demodulated using (a) slope detection and (b) a zero-crossing detector.

6.9 (a) Generate and plot the time waveform for a binary baseband communication system which sends the bit string 1, 0, 1 through an ideal channel, where a raised cosine rolloff filter response is used having $\alpha = 1/2$. Assume the symbol rate is 50 kbps, and use a truncation time of ± 6 symbols.

(b) Illustrate the ideal sampling points of the waveform.

(c) If a receiver has a timing jitter of $\pm 10^{-6}$ seconds, what is the difference in detected voltage as compared to ideal voltage at each sample point?

6.10 Verify that the BPSK receiver shown in Figure 6.23 is able to recover a digital message *m(t)*.

6.11 Plot the BER vs. E_b/N_0 performance for BPSK, DPSK, QPSK, and noncoherent FSK in additive Gaussian white noise. List advantages and disadvantages of each modulation method from the mobile communications standpoint.

6.12 Assume a binary bit stream is to be modulated on an RF carrier. If the baseband bit stream has a data rate of 1 Megabit per second, then:

(a) What is the first-zero crossing bandwidth of the RF spectrum if simple rectangular pulses are used, assuming BPSK is used?

(b) What is the absolute bandwidth of the RF spectrum if raised cosine rolloff pulses are used, for $\alpha = 1$? Assume BPSK is used.

(c) What is the absolute bandwidth of the RF spectrum if raised cosine rolloff pulses are used, for $\alpha = 1/3$? Assume BPSK is used.

(d) If a timing jitter of 10^{-6} seconds exists at the receiver and raised cosine rolloff pulses are used, will the detector experience intersymbol interference from the adjacent symbols? Explain.

(e) If GMSK modulation is to be generated as shown and a 3 dB bandwidth of 500 kHz is used for the Gaussian low pass filter, what is the proper choice for the FM peak frequency deviation, ΔF?

(f) For GMSK modulation using $BT \leq 0.5$, how many spectral sidelobes occur?

6.13 If a mobile radio link operates with 30 dB SNR and uses a 200 kHz channel, find the theoretic maximum data capacity possible. How does your answer compare to what is offered by the GSM standard, which operates at a channel rate of 270.8333 kbps?

6.14 Compare the channel spectral efficiencies of IS-54, GSM, PDC, and IS-95. What are the theoretical spectral efficiencies for each of these standards if they operate at 20 dB SNR?

6.15 Design a raised cosine rolloff filter for $T_s = 1/24300$ s and $\alpha = 0.35$. Write expressions for, and plot, the impulse response and the frequency response of the filter. If this filter were used for 30 kHz RF channels, what percentage of the total radiated energy would fall out-of-band? Computer simulation or numerical analysis may be used to determine results.

6.16 Design a Gaussian pulse-shaping filter with $BT = 0.5$ for a symbol rate of 19.2 kbps. Write expressions for, and plot, the impulse response and frequency response of the filter. If this filter were used to produce GMSK in 30 kHz RF channels, what percentage of the total radiated energy would fall out-of-band? Repeat for the case of $BT = 0.2$, and $BT = 0.75$. Computer simulation or numerical analysis may be used to determine results.

6.17 GMSK Computer Simulation: Recreate Table 6.3 and Figure 6.41 using computer simulation. Simply apply a random NRZ binary waveform through a Gaussian pulseshaped filter and then FM modulate, as in Figure 6.42. Be sure to include all documented source code, and clearly label all axes and document and display the PSD and spectral occupancy in relation to R_b for varying values of BT.

6.18 Derive Equation (6.106) for an MSK signal.

6.19 Generate the binary message 01100101 through MSK transmitter and receiver shown in Figure 6.39 and Figure 6.40. Sketch the waveshapes at the inputs, outputs, and through the system. Also plot the PSD of the output. Computer simulation may be used.

6.20 If 63 users share a CDMA system, and each user has a processing gain of 511, determine the average probability of error for each user. What assumptions have you made in determining your result?

6.21 For Problem 6.20, determine the percentage increase in the number of users if the probability of error is allowed to increase by an order of magnitude.

6.22 In IS-95 CDMA, assume $K = 20$ users share the same 1.25 MHz channel. The chip rate for each user is 1.2288 Mcps and each user has a baseband data rate of 13 kbps. If a maximum E_b/N_0 of 7.8 dB is provided for each user and the PN code lengths are 32,678 chips (2^{15}), find the bit error probability for a user. What is the processing gain of IS-95?

6.23 Assume that a synchronous frequency hopping multiple access system is used. Binary frequency shift keying having a bit error probability of

$$P_e = \frac{1}{2}e^{-\frac{E_b}{2N_0}}$$

is used by each user. Prove that if there are M possible hopping channels and K total users, that the irreducible error rate due to multiple access interference is given by

$$\lim_{\frac{E_b}{N_0} \to \infty} P_e = \frac{1}{2}\left[\frac{K-1}{M}\right]$$

6.24 (a) In a DS–SS multiple user system, how many simultaneous users may be supported such that an average bit error rate of less than 10–3 is maintained for each user? Assume all users employ power control such that the received powers of each user are maintained at an average $E_b/N_0 = 10$ dB, and assume each user has a PN code that is produced from an 11-bit shift register.

(b) Using your answer in (a), what is the resulting average Probability of Error for a user if one more simultaneous user is added? Would this be noticeable to all the other users? Why or why not?

6.25 A FH–SS system uses 50 kHz channels over a continuous 20 MHz spectrum. Fast frequency hopping is used, where two hops occur for each bit. If binary FSK is the modulation method used in this system, determine (a) the number of hops per second if each user transmits at 25 kbps; (b) the probability of error for a single user operating at an $E_b/N_0 = 20$ dB; (c) the probability of error for a user operating at $E_b/N_0 = 20$ dB with 20 other FH–SS users which are independently frequency hopped; (d) the probability of error for a user operating at $E_b/N_0 = 20$ dB with 200 other FH–SS users which are independently frequency hopped.

6.26 A frequency hopping WLAN system is proposed for Bluetooth, using binary FSK. Assume fifty 1-MHz channels are available, and K devices are to be connected in the same room. If an E_b/N_0 of 20 dB can be supplied to each user, plot the average probability of errors as a function of the number of devices, where K ranges from 1 to 100. What would you deem to be the maximum acceptable number of devices?

6.27 Simulate a GMSK signal and verify that the Gaussian filter bandwidth has a major impact on the spectral shape of the signal. Plot spectral shapes for (a) $BT = 0.2$, (b) $BT = 0.5$, and (c) $BT = 1$.

6.28 Compare the BER and RF bandwidth of a GMSK signal operating in additive white Gaussian noise (AWGN) for the following BT values: (a) 0.25, (b) 0.5, (c) 1, (d) 5. Discuss the practical advantages and disadvantages of these cases.

6.29 Demonstrate mathematically that a $\pi/4$ QPSK data stream may be detected using an FM receiver (Hint: consider how an FM receiver responds to phase changes.)

6.30 Using Equation (6.153), determine the probability of error, as a function of E_b/N_0, for 4-ary QAM, 16-ary QAM, and 64-ary QAM. Plot E_b/N_0 vs. BER for 4 QAM, 16 QAM, and 64 QAM on the same plot, and compare your results with BPSK and non-coherent orthogonal FSK on the plot.

6.31 (a) Given that binary DPSK modulation has a bit error probability of

$$P_e = \frac{1}{2}e^{-\frac{E_b}{2N_0}}$$

in AWGN, find the probability of error for DPSK in a Rayleigh flat-fading channel.

(b) If the average SNR for a Rayleigh faded DPSK signal is 30 dB, what is the probability of error ar the receiver?

6.32 Binary FSK (noncoherent) has a probability of error in AWGN given by

$$P_e = \frac{1}{2}\exp\left(-\frac{E_b}{N_0}\right)$$

(a) Derive the probability of error over a local area for binary FSK in a Rayleigh flat-fading channel.

(b) To achieve a BER of 10^{-3}, how much additional signal power is required in a Rayleigh fading environment as compared to the AWGN channel? Give your answer in dB.

6.33 Demonstrate mathematically that a $\pi/4$ QPSK signal can be detected using the IF and baseband differential detection circuits described in Chapter 6.

6.34 Using the expression for probability of error in a flat-fading channel, find the average probability of error for DPSK if a channel has an exponential SNR probability density of $p(x) = e^{-x}$ for $x > 0$.

6.35 Determine the necessary E_b/N_0 in order to detect DPSK with an average BER of 10^{-3} for a (a) Rayleigh fading channel, (b) Ricean fading channel, with $K = 6$ dB, 7 dB.

6.36 Determine the necessary E_b/N_0 in order to detect BPSK with an average BER of 10^{-5} for a (a) Rayleigh fading channel, (b) Ricean fading channel, with $K = 6$ dB, 7 dB.

6.37 Show that Equation (6.155) is correct. That is, prove that if α is Rayleigh distributed, then the pdf of α^2 is given by $p(\alpha^2) = \frac{1}{\overline{\alpha^2}}e^{-\alpha^2/\overline{\alpha^2}}$. This is the Chi-square pdf with two degrees of freedom.

6.38 Prove that the expression for the BER of GMSK as given in Equation (6.164) is correct, using the techniques described in Section 6.12.1 and the P_e expression for GMSK in an additive white Gaussian noise channel.

6.39 Prove that a Rayleigh fading signal has an exponential pdf for the power of the signal.

CHAPTER 7

Equalization, Diversity, and Channel Coding

Wireless communication systems require signal processing techniques that improve the link performance in hostile mobile radio environments. As seen in Chapters 4 and 5, the mobile radio channel is particularly dynamic due to multipath propagation and Doppler spread, and as shown in the latter part of Chapter 6, these effects have a strong negative impact on the bit error rate of any modulation technique. Mobile radio channel impairments cause the signal at the receiver to distort or fade significantly as compared to AWGN channels.

7.1 Introduction

Equalization, diversity, and channel coding are three techniques which can be used independently or in tandem to improve received signal quality and link performance over small-scale times and distances.

Equalization compensates for *intersymbol interference* (ISI) created by multipath within time dispersive channels. As shown in Chapters 5 and 6, if the modulation bandwidth exceeds the coherence bandwidth of the radio channel, ISI occurs and modulation pulses are spread in time into adjacent symbols. An equalizer within a receiver compensates for the average range of expected channel amplitude and delay characteristics. Equalizers must be adaptive since the channel is generally unknown and time varying.

Diversity is another technique used to compensate for fading channel impairments, and is usually implemented by using two or more receiving antennas. The evolving 3G common air interfaces also use transmit diversity, where base stations may transmit multiple replicas of the signal on spatially separated antennas or frequencies. As with an equalizer, diversity improves the quality of a wireless communications link without altering the common air interface, and without increasing the transmitted power or bandwidth. However, while equalization is used to counter the effects of time dispersion (ISI), diversity is usually employed to reduce the depth and duration of the fades experienced by a receiver in a local area which are due to motion. Diversity techniques are often employed at both base station and mobile receivers. The most common diversity technique is called *spatial diversity,* whereby multiple antennas are strategically spaced and connected to a common receiving system. While one antenna sees a signal null, one of the other antennas may see a signal peak, and the receiver is able to select the antenna with the best signal at any time. It can be seen in Figure 5.34, for example, that only 0.4λ spacing is needed to obtain uncorrelated fading between two antennas when they receive energy from all directions. Other diversity techniques include *antenna polarization diversity, frequency diversity,* and *time diversity.* CDMA systems make use of a RAKE receiver, which provides link improvement through time diversity.

Channel coding improves the small-scale link performance by adding redundant data bits in the transmitted message so that if an instantaneous fade occurs in the channel, the data may still be recovered at the receiver. At the baseband portion of the transmitter, a channel coder maps the user's digital message sequence into another specific code sequence containing a greater number of bits than originally contained in the message. The coded message is then modulated for transmission in the wireless channel.

Channel coding is used by the receiver to detect or correct some (or all) of the errors introduced by the channel in a particular sequence of message bits. Because decoding is performed after the demodulation portion of the receiver, coding can be considered to be a *post detection* technique. The added coding bits lower the raw data transmission rate through the channel (that is, coding expands the occupied bandwidth for a particular message data rate). There are three general types of channel codes: *block codes*, *convolutional codes*, and *turbo codes.* Channel coding is generally treated independently from the type of modulation used, although this has changed recently with the use of trellis coded modulation schemes, OFDM, and new space-time processing that combines coding, antenna diversity, and modulation to achieve large coding gains without any bandwidth expansion.

The three general techniques of equalization, diversity, and channel coding are used to improve radio link performance (i.e., to minimize the instantaneous bit error rate), but the approach, cost, complexity, and effectiveness of each technique varies widely in practical wireless communication systems.

7.2 Fundamentals of Equalization

Intersymbol interference (ISI) caused by multipath in bandlimited (frequency selective) time dispersive channels distorts the transmitted signal, causing bit errors at the receiver. ISI has been recognized as the major obstacle to high speed data transmission over wireless channels. Equalization is a technique used to combat intersymbol interference.

In a broad sense, the term *equalization* can be used to describe any signal processing operation that minimizes ISI [Qur85]. In radio channels, a variety of adaptive equalizers can be used to cancel interference while providing diversity [Bra70], [Mon84]. Since the mobile fading channel is random and time varying, equalizers must track the time varying characteristics of the mobile channel, and thus are called *adaptive equalizers*.

The general operating modes of an adaptive equalizer include *training* and *tracking*. First, a known, fixed-length training sequence is sent by the transmitter so that the receiver's equalizer may adapt to a proper setting for minimum bit error rate (BER) detection. The training sequence is typically a pseudorandom binary signal or a fixed, prescribed bit pattern. Immediately following this training sequence, the user data (which may or may not include coding bits) is sent, and the adaptive equalizer at the receiver utilizes a recursive algorithm to evaluate the channel and estimate filter coefficients to compensate for the distortion created by multipath in the channel. The training sequence is designed to permit an equalizer at the receiver to acquire the proper filter coefficients in the worst possible channel conditions (e.g., fastest velocity, longest time delay spread, deepest fades, etc.) so that when the training sequence is finished, the filter coefficients are near the optimal values for reception of user data. As user data are received, the adaptive algorithm of the equalizer tracks the changing channel [Hay86]. As a consequence, the adaptive equalizer is continually changing its filter characteristics over time. When an equalizer has been properly trained, it is said to have converged.

The timespan over which an equalizer converges is a function of the equalizer algorithm, the equalizer structure, and the time rate of change of the multipath radio channel. Equalizers require periodic retraining in order to maintain effective ISI cancellation, and are commonly used in digital communication systems where user data is segmented into short time blocks or time slots. Time division multiple access (TDMA) wireless systems are particularly well suited for equalizers. As discussed in Chapter 9, TDMA systems send data in fixed-length time blocks, and the training sequence is usually sent at the beginning of a block. Each time a new data block is received, the equalizer is retrained using the same training sequence [EIA90], [Gar99], [Mol01].

An equalizer is usually implemented at baseband or at IF in a receiver. Since the baseband complex envelope expression can be used to represent bandpass waveforms [Cou93], the channel response, demodulated signal, and adaptive equalizer algorithms are usually simulated and implemented at baseband [Lo90], [Cro89], [Mol01], [Tra02].

Figure 7.1 shows a block diagram of a communication system with an adaptive equalizer in the receiver. If $x(t)$ is the original information signal, and $f(t)$ is the combined complex baseband impulse response of the transmitter, channel, and the RF/IF sections of the receiver, the signal received by the equalizer may be expressed as

$$y(t) = x(t) \otimes f^*(t) + n_b(t) \tag{7.1}$$

where $f^*(t)$ denotes the complex conjugate of $f(t)$, $n_b(t)$ is the baseband noise at the input of the equalizer, and $\otimes$ denotes the convolution operation. If the impulse response of the equalizer is $h_{eq}(t)$, then the output of the equalizer is

$$\begin{aligned}\hat{d}(t) &= x(t) \otimes f^*(t) \otimes h_{eq}(t) + n_b(t) \otimes h_{eq}(t) \\ &= x(t) \otimes g(t) + n_b(t) \otimes h_{eq}(t)\end{aligned} \tag{7.2}$$

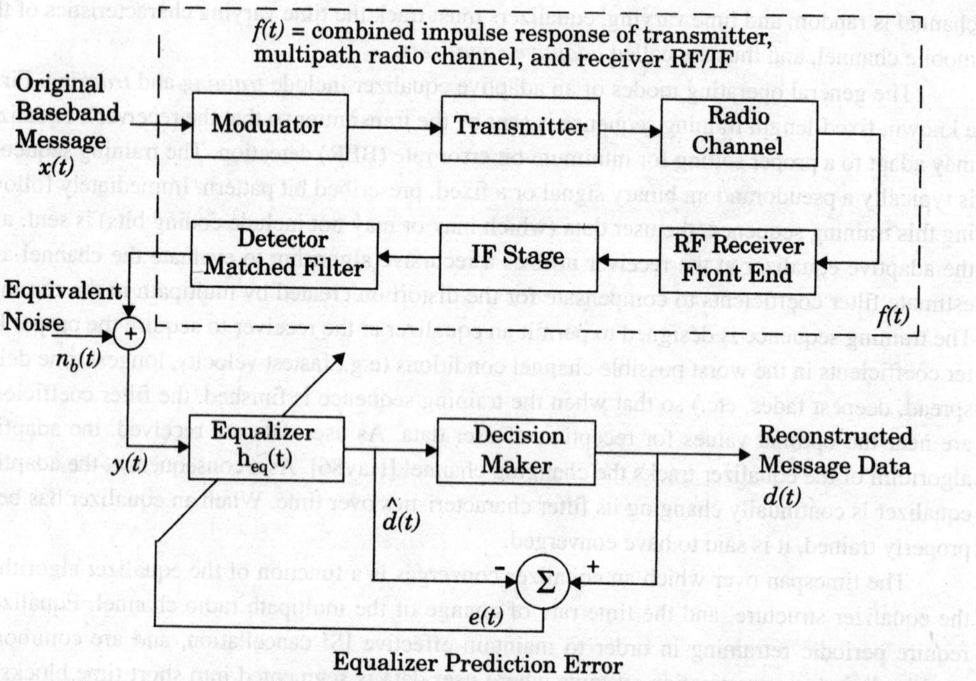

Figure 7.1 Block diagram of a simplified communications system using an adaptive equalizer at the receiver.

where $g(t)$ is the combined impulse response of the transmitter, channel, RF/IF sections of the receiver, and the equalizer at the receiver. The complex baseband impulse response of a transversal filter equalizer is given by

$$h_{eq}(t) = \sum_{n} c_n \delta(t - nT) \tag{7.3}$$

where c_n are the complex filter coefficients of the equalizer. The desired output of the equalizer is $x(t)$, the original source data. Assume that $n_b(t) = 0$. Then, in order to force $\hat{d}(t) = x(t)$ in Equation (7.2), $g(t)$ must be equal to

$$g(t) = f^*(t) \otimes h_{eq}(t) = \delta(t) \tag{7.4}$$

The goal of equalization is to satisfy Equation (7.4) so that the combination of the transmitter, channel, and receiver appear to be an all-pass channel. In the frequency domain, Equation (7.4) can be expressed as

$$H_{eq}(f)F^*(-f) = 1 \tag{7.5}$$

where $H_{eq}(f)$ and $F(f)$ are Fourier transforms of $h_{eq}(t)$ and $f(t)$, respectively.

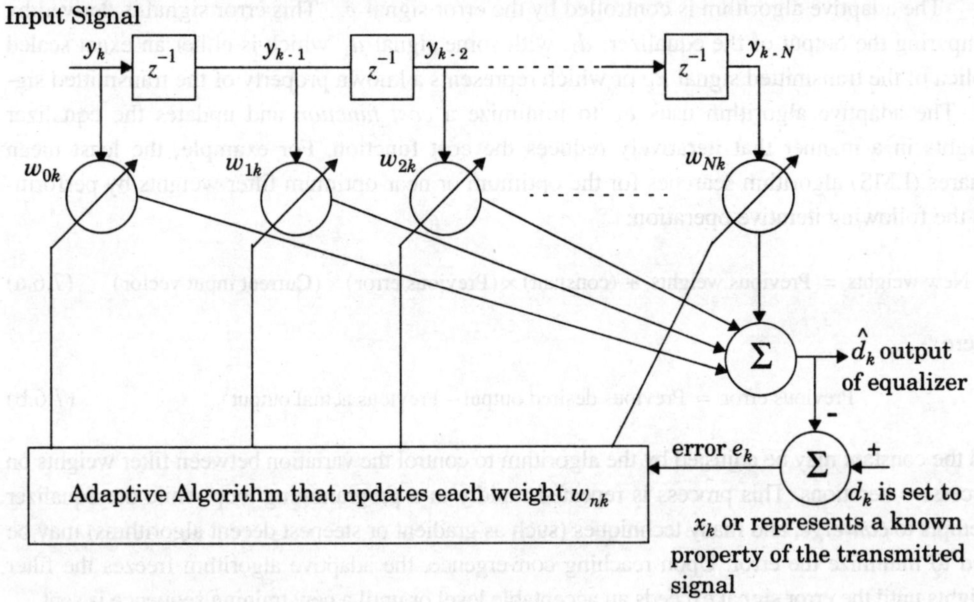

Figure 7.2 A basic linear equalizer during training.

Equation (7.5) indicates that an equalizer is actually an inverse filter of the channel. If the channel is frequency selective, the equalizer enhances the frequency components with small amplitudes and attenuates the strong frequencies in the received frequency spectrum in order to provide a flat, composite, received frequency response and linear phase response. For a time-varying channel, an adaptive equalizer is designed to track the channel variations so that Equation (7.5) is approximately satisfied.

7.3 Training A Generic Adaptive Equalizer

An adaptive equalizer is a time-varying filter which must constantly be retuned. The basic structure of an adaptive equalizer is shown in Figure 7.2, where the subscript k is used to denote a discrete time index (in Section 7.4, another notation is introduced to represent discrete time events—both notations have exactly the same meaning).

Notice in Figure 7.2 that there is a single input y_k into the equalizer at any time instant. The value of y_k depends upon the instantaneous state of the radio channel and the specific value of the noise (see Figure 7.1). As such, y_k is a random process. The adaptive equalizer structure shown above is called a *transversal filter*, and in this case has N delay elements, $N+1$ taps, and $N+1$ tunable complex multipliers, called *weights*. The weights of the filter are described by their physical location in the delay line structure, and have a second subscript, k, to explicitly show they vary with time. These weights are updated continuously by the adaptive algorithm, either on a sample by sample basis (i.e., whenever k is incremented by one) or on a block by block basis (i.e., whenever a specified number of samples have been clocked into the equalizer).

The adaptive algorithm is controlled by the error signal e_k. This error signal is derived by comparing the output of the equalizer, $\hat{d}_k$, with some signal d_k which is either an exact scaled replica of the transmitted signal x_k or which represents a known property of the transmitted signal. The adaptive algorithm uses e_k to minimize a *cost function* and updates the equalizer weights in a manner that iteratively reduces the cost function. For example, the least mean squares (LMS) algorithm searches for the optimum or near-optimum filter weights by performing the following iterative operation:

$$\text{New weights} = \text{Previous weights} + (\text{constant}) \times (\text{Previous error}) \times (\text{Current input vector}) \quad (7.6.a)$$

where

$$\text{Previous error} = \text{Previous desired output} - \text{Previous actual output} \quad (7.6.b)$$

and the constant may be adjusted by the algorithm to control the variation between filter weights on successive iterations. This process is repeated rapidly in a programming loop while the equalizer attempts to *converge*, and many techniques (such as gradient or steepest decent algorithms) may be used to minimize the error. Upon reaching convergence, the adaptive algorithm freezes the filter weights until the error signal exceeds an acceptable level or until a new training sequence is sent.

Based on classical equalization theory [Wid85], [Qur85], the most common cost function is the mean square error (MSE) between the desired signal and the output of the equalizer. The MSE is denoted by $E[e(k)e^*(k)]$, and a known *training sequence* must be periodically transmitted when a replica of the transmitted signal is required at the output of the equalizer (i.e., when d_k is set equal to x_k and is known *a priori*). By detecting the training sequence, the adaptive algorithm in the receiver is able to compute and minimize the cost function by driving the tap weights until the next training sequence is sent.

A more recent class of adaptive algorithms are able to exploit characteristics of the transmitted signal and do not require training sequences. These modern algorithms are able to acquire equalization through property restoral techniques of the transmitted signal, and are called *blind algorithms* because they provide equalizer convergence without burdening the transmitter with training overhead. These techniques include algorithms such as the *constant modulus algorithm* (CMA) and the *spectral coherence restoral algorithm* (SCORE). CMA is used for constant envelope modulation, and forces the equalizer weights to maintain a constant envelope on the received signal [Tre83], whereas SCORE exploits spectral redundancy or cyclostationarity in the transmitted signal [Gar91]. Blind algorithms are not described in this text, but are becoming important for wireless applications.

To study the adaptive equalizer of Figure 7.2, it is helpful to use vector and matrix algebra. Define the input signal to the equalizer as a vector $\mathbf{y}_k$ where

$$\mathbf{y}_k = \begin{bmatrix} y_k & y_{k-1} & y_{k-2} & \dots & y_{k-N} \end{bmatrix}^T \quad (7.7)$$

It should be clear that the output of the adaptive equalizer is a scalar given by

$$\hat{d}_k = \sum_{n=0}^{N} w_{nk} y_{k-n} \tag{7.8}$$

and following Equation (7.7) a weight vector can be written as

$$\boldsymbol{w}_k = \begin{bmatrix} w_{0k} & w_{1k} & w_{2k} & \dots & w_{Nk} \end{bmatrix}^T \tag{7.9}$$

Using Equations (7.7) and (7.9), Equation (7.8) may be written in vector notation as

$$\hat{d}_k = \boldsymbol{y}_k^T \boldsymbol{w}_k = \boldsymbol{w}_k^T \boldsymbol{y}_k \tag{7.10}$$

It follows that when the desired equalizer output is known (i.e., $d_k = x_k$), the error signal e_k is given by

$$e_k = d_k - \hat{d}_k = x_k - \hat{d}_k \tag{7.11}$$

and from Equation (7.10)

$$e_k = x_k - \boldsymbol{y}_k^T \boldsymbol{w}_k = x_k - \boldsymbol{w}_k^T \boldsymbol{y}_k \tag{7.12}$$

To compute the mean square error $|e_k|^2$ at time instant k, Equation (7.12) is squared to obtain

$$|e_k|^2 = x_k^2 + \boldsymbol{w}_k^T \boldsymbol{y}_k \boldsymbol{y}_k^T \boldsymbol{w}_k - 2 x_k \boldsymbol{y}_k^T \boldsymbol{w}_k \tag{7.13}$$

Taking the expected value of $|e_k|^2$ over k (which in practice amounts to computing a time average) yields

$$E[|e_k|^2] = E[x_k^2] + \boldsymbol{w}_k^T E[\boldsymbol{y}_k \boldsymbol{y}_k^T] \boldsymbol{w}_k - 2E[x_k \boldsymbol{y}_k^T] \boldsymbol{w}_k \tag{7.14}$$

Notice that the filter weights $\boldsymbol{w}_k$ are not included in the time average since, for convenience, it is assumed that they have converged to the optimum value and are not varying with time.

Equation (7.14) would be trivial to simplify if x_k and y_k were independent. However, this is not true in general since the input vector should be correlated with the desired output of the equalizer (otherwise, the equalizer would be unable to successfully extract the desired signal). Instead, the cross correlation vector $\boldsymbol{p}$ between the desired response $\hat{d}_k = x_k$ and the input signal $\boldsymbol{y}_k$ is defined as

$$\boldsymbol{p} = E[x_k \boldsymbol{y}_k] = E\begin{bmatrix} x_k y_k & x_k y_{k-1} & x_k y_{k-2} & \dots & x_k y_{k-N} \end{bmatrix}^T \tag{7.15}$$

and the *input correlation matrix* is defined as the $(N+1) \times (N+1)$ square matrix $\boldsymbol{R}$, where

$$\boldsymbol{R} = E[\boldsymbol{y}_k \boldsymbol{y}_k^*] = E\begin{bmatrix} y_k^2 & y_k y_{k-1} & y_k y_{k-2} & \cdots & y_k y_{k-N} \\ y_{k-1} y_k & y_{k-1}^2 & y_{k-1} y_{k-2} & \cdots & y_{k-1} y_{k-N} \\ \cdots & \cdots & \cdots & \cdots & \cdots \\ y_{k-N} y_k & y_{k-N} y_{k-1} & y_{k-N} y_{k-2} & \cdots & y_{k-N}^2 \end{bmatrix} \tag{7.16}$$

The matrix $\boldsymbol{R}$ is sometimes called the *input covariance matrix*. The major diagonal of $\boldsymbol{R}$ contains the mean square values of each input sample, and the cross terms specify the autocorrelation terms resulting from delayed samples of the input signal.

If x_k and $\boldsymbol{y}_k$ are stationary, then the elements in $\boldsymbol{R}$ and $\boldsymbol{p}$ are second order statistics which do not vary with time. Using Equations (7.15) and (7.16), Equation (7.14) may be rewritten as

$$\text{Mean Square Error} \equiv \xi = E[x_k^2] + \boldsymbol{w}^T \boldsymbol{R} \boldsymbol{w} - 2\boldsymbol{p}^T \boldsymbol{w} \tag{7.17}$$

By minimizing Equation (7.17) in terms of the weight vector $\boldsymbol{w}_k$, it becomes possible to adaptively tune the equalizer to provide a flat spectral response (minimal ISI) in the received signal. This is due to the fact that when the input signal $\boldsymbol{y}_k$ and the desired response $\hat{d}_k = x_k$ are stationary, the mean square error (MSE) is quadratic on $\boldsymbol{w}_k$, and minimizing the MSE leads to optimal solutions for $\boldsymbol{w}_k$.

Example 7.1

The MSE of Equation (7.17) is a multidimensional function. When two tap weights are used in an equalizer, then the MSE function is a bowl-shaped paraboloid where MSE is plotted on the vertical axis and weights w_0 and w_1 are plotted on the horizontal axes. If more than two tap-weights are used in the equalizer, then the error function is a hyperparaboloid. In all cases, the error function is concave upward, which implies that a minimum may be found [Wid85].

To determine the minimum MSE (MMSE), the gradient of Equation (7.17) can be used. As long as $\boldsymbol{R}$ is nonsingular (has an inverse), the MMSE occurs when $\boldsymbol{w}_k$ are such that the gradient is zero. The gradient of ξ is defined as

$$\nabla \equiv \frac{\partial \xi}{\partial \boldsymbol{w}} = \begin{bmatrix} \frac{\partial \xi}{\partial w_0} & \frac{\partial \xi}{\partial w_1} & \cdots & \frac{\partial \xi}{\partial w_N} \end{bmatrix}^T \tag{E7.1.1}$$

By expanding Equation (7.17) and differentiating with respect to each signal in the weight vector, it can be shown that Equation (E7.1.1) yields

$$\nabla = 2\boldsymbol{R}\boldsymbol{w} - 2\boldsymbol{p} \tag{E7.1.2}$$

Setting $\nabla = 0$ in Equation (E7.1.2), the optimum weight vector $\hat{\boldsymbol{w}}$ for MMSE is given by

$$\hat{\boldsymbol{w}} = \boldsymbol{R}^{-1}\boldsymbol{p} \tag{E7.1.3}$$

Example 7.2

Four matrix algebra rules are useful in the study of adaptive equalizers [Wid85]:

1. Differentiation of $w^T R w$ can be differentiated as the product $(w^T)(Rw)$.
2. For any square matrix, $AA^{-1} = I$.
3. For any matrix product, $(AB)^T = B^T A^T$.
4. For any symmetric matrix, $A^T = A$ and $(A^{-1})^T = A^{-1}$.

Using Equation (E7.1.3) to substitute $\hat{w}$ for w in Equation (7.17), and using the above rules, ξ_{min} is found to be

$$\xi_{min} = \text{MMSE} = E[x_k^2] - p^T R^{-1} p = E[x_k^2] - p^T \hat{w} \quad \text{(E7.2.1)}$$

Equation (E7.2.1) solves the MMSE for optimum weights.

7.4 Equalizers in a Communications Receiver

The previous section demonstrated how a generic adaptive equalizer works during training and defined common notation for algorithm design and analysis. This section describes how the equalizer fits into the wireless communications link.

Figure 7.1 shows that the received signal includes channel noise. Because the noise $n_b(t)$ is present, an equalizer is unable to achieve perfect performance. Thus there is always some residual ISI and some small tracking error. Noise makes Equation (7.4) hard to realize in practice. Therefore, the instantaneous combined frequency response will not always be flat, resulting in some finite *prediction error*. The prediction error of the equalizer is defined in Equation (7.19).

Because adaptive equalizers are implemented using digital logic, it is most convenient to represent all time signals in discrete form. Let T represent some increment of time between successive observations of signal states. Letting $t = t_n$, where n is an integer that represents time $t_n = nT$, time waveforms may be equivalently expressed as a sequence on n in the discrete domain. Using this notation, Equation (7.2) may be expressed as

$$\hat{d}(n) = x(n) \otimes g(n) + n_b(n) \otimes h_{eq}(n) \quad (7.18)$$

The prediction error is

$$e(n) = d(n) - \hat{d}(n) = d(n) - [x(n) \otimes g(n) + n_b(n) \otimes h_{eq}(n)] \quad (7.19)$$

The *mean squared error* $E[|e(n)|^2]$ is one of the most important measures of how well an equalizer works. $E[|e(n)|^2]$ is the expected value (ensemble average) of the squared prediction error $|e(n)|^2$, but time averaging can be used if $e(n)$ is ergodic. In practice, ergodicity is impossible to prove, and algorithms are developed and implemented using time averages instead of ensemble averages. This proves to be highly effective, and in general, better equalizers provide smaller values of $E[|e(n)|^2]$.

Minimizing the mean square error tends to reduce the bit error rate. This can be understood with a simple intuitive explanation. Suppose $e(n)$ is Gaussian distributed with zero mean. Then $E[|e(n)|^2]$ is the variance (or the power) of the error signal. If the variance is minimized, then there is less chance of perturbing the output signal $d(n)$. Thus, the decision device is likely to detect $d(n)$ as the transmitted signal $x(n)$ (see Figure 7.1). Consequently, there is a smaller probability of error when $E[|e(n)|^2]$ is minimized. For wireless communication links, it would be best to minimize the instantaneous probability of error (P_e) instead of the mean squared error, but minimizing P_e generally results in nonlinear equations, which are much more difficult to solve in real-time than the linear Equations (7.1)–(7.19) [Pro89].

7.5 Survey of Equalization Techniques

Equalization techniques can be subdivided into two general categories—linear and nonlinear equalization. These categories are determined from how the output of an adaptive equalizer is used for subsequent control (feedback) of the equalizer. In general, the analog signal $\hat{d}(t)$ is processed by the decision making device in the receiver. The decision maker determines the value of the digital data bit being received and applies a slicing or thresholding operation (a nonlinear operation) in order to determine the value of $d(t)$ (see Figure 7.1). If $d(t)$ is not used in the feedback path to adapt the equalizer, the equalization is *linear.* On the other hand, if $d(t)$ is fed back to change the subsequent outputs of the equalizer, the equalization is *nonlinear.* Many filter structures are used to implement linear and nonlinear equalizers. Further, for each structure, there are numerous algorithms used to adapt the equalizer. Figure 7.3 provides a general categorization of the equalization techniques according to the types, structures, and algorithms used.

The most common equalizer structure is a *linear transversal equalizer* (LTE). A linear transversal filter is made up of tapped delay lines, with the tappings spaced a symbol period (T_s) apart, as shown in Figure 7.4. Assuming that the delay elements have unity gain and delay T_s, the transfer function of a linear transversal equalizer can be written as a function of the delay operator $\exp(-j\omega T_s)$ or z^{-1}. The simplest LTE uses only feed forward taps, and the transfer function of the equalizer filter is a polynomial in z^{-1}. This filter has many zeroes but poles only at $z = 0$, and is called a *finite impulse response* (FIR) filter, or simply a transversal filter. If the equalizer has both feed forward and feedback taps, its transfer function is a rational function of z^{-1}, and is called an *infinite impulse response* (IIR) filter with poles and zeros. Figure 7.5 shows a tapped delay line filter with both feed forward and feedback taps. Since IIR filters tend to be unstable when used in channels where the strongest pulse arrives after an echo pulse (i.e., leading echoes), they are rarely used.

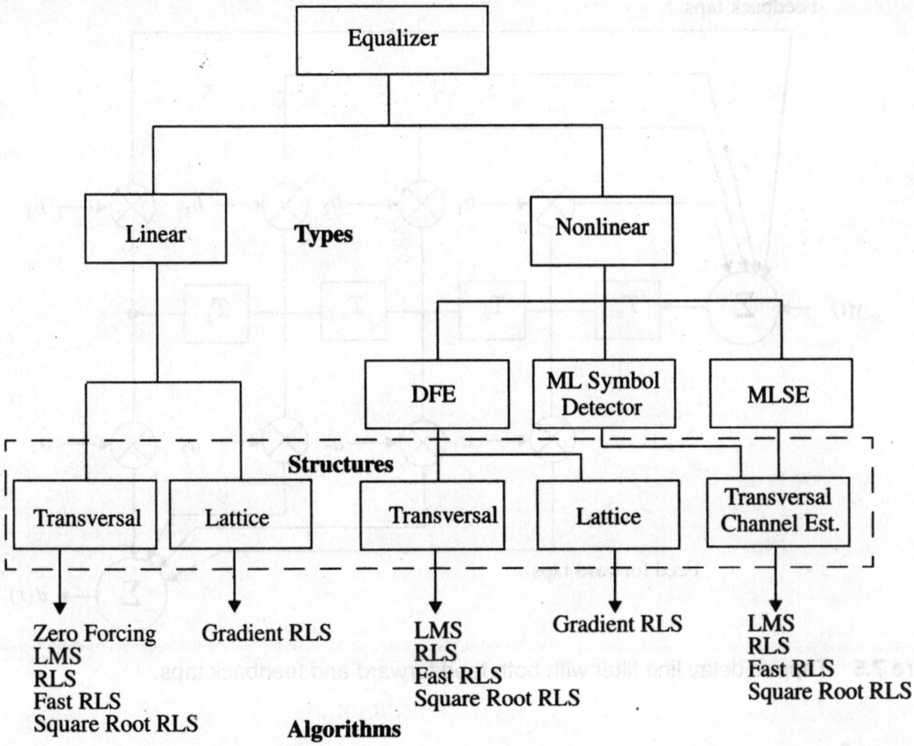

Figure 7.3 Classification of equalizers.

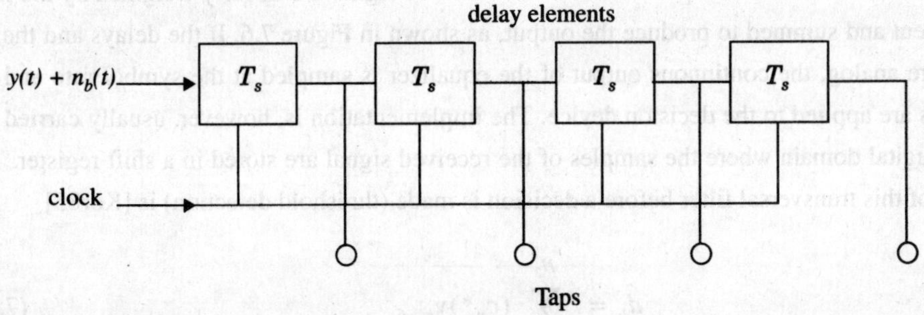

Figure 7.4 Basic linear transversal equalizer structure.

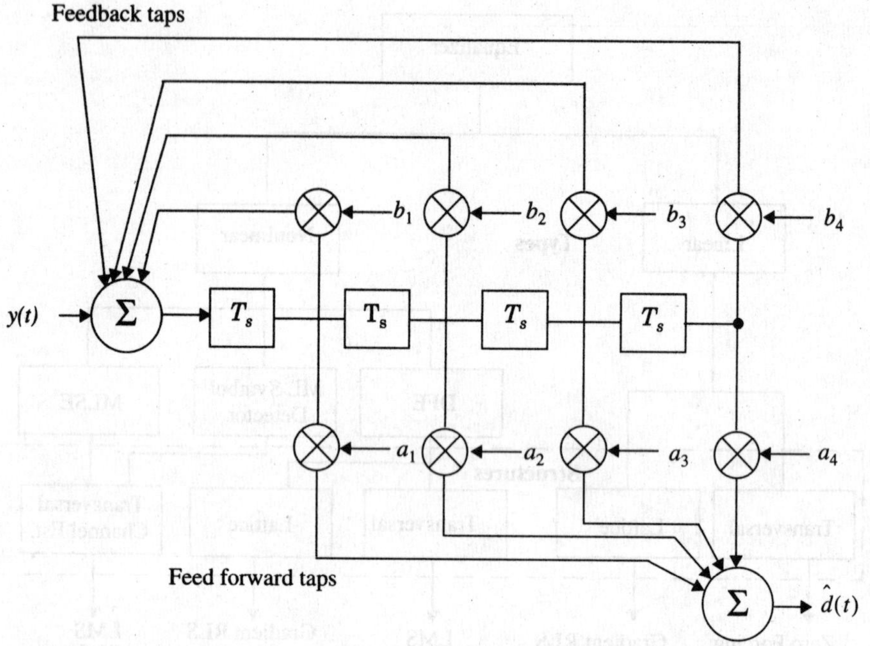

Figure 7.5 Tapped delay line filter with both feed forward and feedback taps.

7.6 Linear Equalizers

As mentioned in Section 7.5, a linear equalizer can be implemented as an FIR filter, otherwise known as the *transversal filter*. This type of equalizer is the simplest type available. In such an equalizer, the current and past values of the received signal are linearly weighted by the filter coefficient and summed to produce the output, as shown in Figure 7.6. If the delays and the tap gains are analog, the continuous output of the equalizer is sampled at the symbol rate and the samples are applied to the decision device. The implementation is, however, usually carried out in the digital domain where the samples of the received signal are stored in a shift register. The output of this transversal filter before a decision is made (threshold detection) is [Kor85]

$$\hat{d}_k = \sum_{n=-N_1}^{N_2} (c_n^*) y_{k-n} \tag{7.20}$$

where c_n^* represents the complex filter coefficients or tap weights, $\hat{d}_k$ is the output at time index k, y_i is the input received signal at time $t_0 + iT$, t_0 is the equalizer starting time, and $N = N_1 + N_2 + 1$ is the number of taps. The values N_1 and N_2 denote the number of taps used

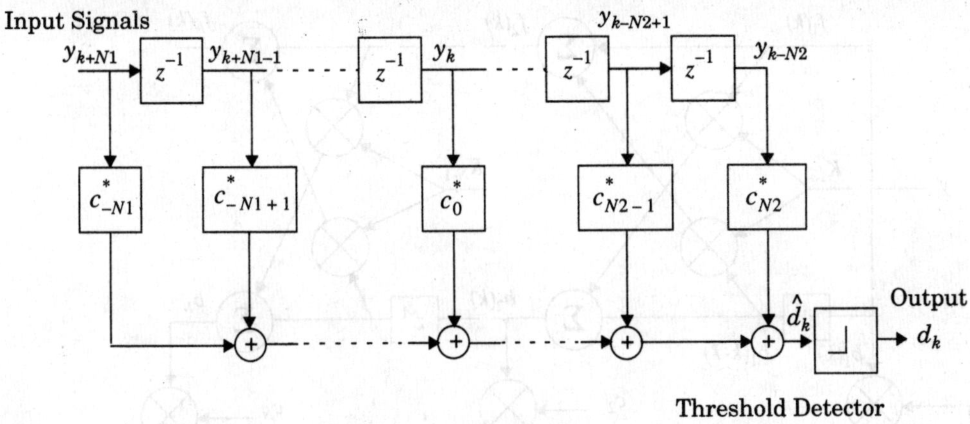

Figure 7.6 Structure of a linear transversal equalizer.

in the forward and reverse portions of the equalizer, respectively. The minimum mean squared error $E[|e(n)|^2]$ that a linear transversal equalizer can achieve is [Pro89]

$$E[|e(n)|^2] = \frac{T}{2\pi}\int_{-\pi/T}^{\pi/T}\frac{N_0}{|F(e^{j\omega T})|^2 + N_0}d\omega \tag{7.21}$$

where $F(e^{j\omega T})$ is the frequency response of the channel, and N_0 is the noise power spectral density.

The linear equalizer can also be implemented as a *lattice filter*, whose structure is shown in Figure 7.7. In a lattice filter, the input signal y_k is transformed into a set of N intermediate forward and backward error signals, $f_n(k)$ and $b_n(k)$ respectively, which are used as inputs to the tap multipliers and are used to calculate the updated coefficients. Each stage of the lattice is then characterized by the following recursive equations [Bin88]:

$$f_1(k) = b_1(k) = y(k) \tag{7.22}$$

$$f_n(k) = y(k) - \sum_{i=1}^{n} K_i y(k-i) = f_{n-1}(k) + K_{n-1}(k) b_{n-1}(k-1) \tag{7.23}$$

$$b_n(k) = y(k-n) - \sum_{i=1}^{n} K_i y(k-n+i) \tag{7.24}$$

$$= b_{n-1}(k-1) + K_{n-1}(k) f_{n-1}(k)$$

where $K_n(k)$ is the reflection coefficient for the nth stage of the lattice. The backward error signals, b_n, are then used as inputs to the tap weights, and the output of the equalizer is given by

$$\hat{d}_k = \sum_{n=1}^{N} c_n(k) b_n(k) \tag{7.25}$$

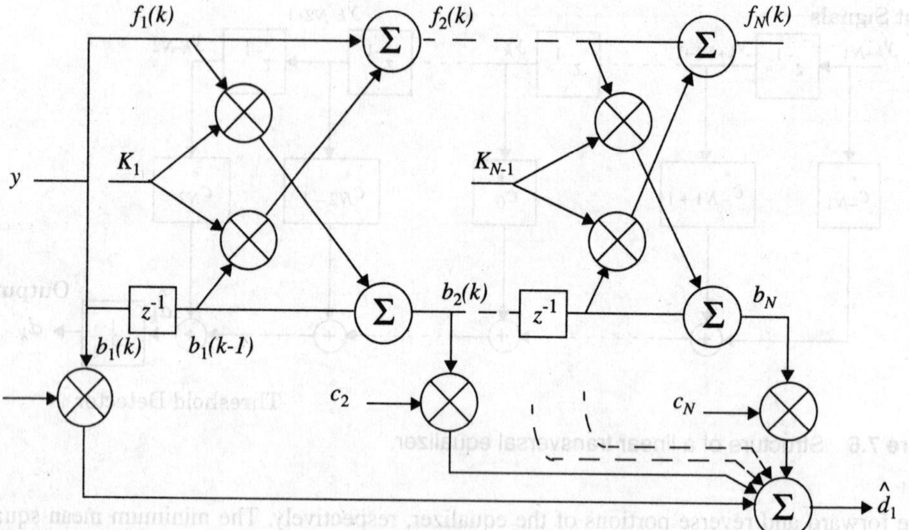

Figure 7.7 The structure of a lattice equalizer [from [Pro91] © IEEE].

Two main advantages of the lattice equalizer is its numerical stability and faster convergence. Also, the unique structure of the lattice filter allows the dynamic assignment of the most effective length of the lattice equalizer. Hence, if the channel is not very time dispersive, only a fraction of the stages are used. When the channel becomes more time dispersive, the length of the equalizer can be increased by the algorithm without stopping the operation of the equalizer. The structure of a lattice equalizer, however, is more complicated than a linear transversal equalizer.

7.7 Nonlinear Equalization

Nonlinear equalizers are used in applications where the channel distortion is too severe for a linear equalizer to handle, and are commonplace in practical wireless systems. Linear equalizers do not perform well on channels which have deep spectral nulls in the passband. In an attempt to compensate for the distortion, the linear equalizer places too much gain in the vicinity of the spectral null, thereby enhancing the noise present in those frequencies.

Three very effective nonlinear methods have been developed which offer improvements over linear equalization techniques and are used in most 2G and 3G systems. These are [Pro91]:

1. Decision Feedback Equalization (DFE)
2. Maximum Likelihood Symbol Detection
3. Maximum Likelihood Sequence Estimation (MLSE)

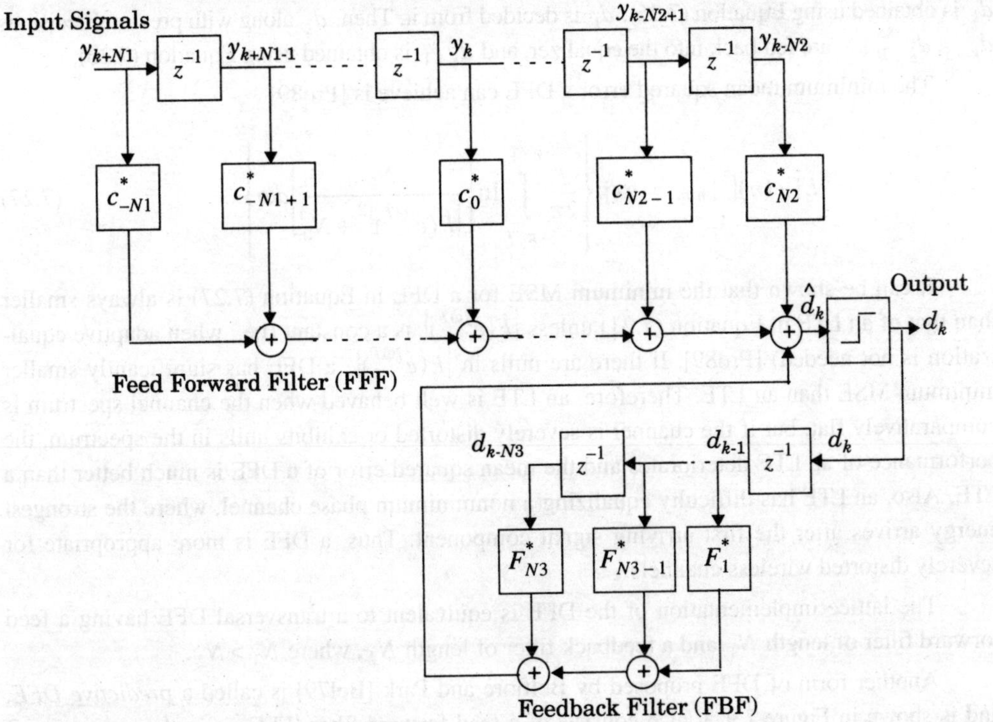

Figure 7.8 Decision feedback equalizer (DFE).

7.7.1 Decision Feedback Equalization (DFE)

The basic idea behind decision feedback equalization is that once an information symbol has been detected and decided upon, the ISI that it induces on future symbols can be estimated and subtracted out before detection of subsequent symbols [Pro89]. The DFE can be realized in either the direct transversal form or as a lattice filter. The direct form is shown in Figure 7.8. It consists of a feed forward filter (FFF) and a feedback filter (FBF). The FBF is driven by decisions on the output of the detector, and its coefficients can be adjusted to cancel the ISI on the current symbol from past detected symbols. The equalizer has $N_1 + N_2 + 1$ taps in the feed forward filter and N_3 taps in the feedback filter, and its output can be expressed as:

$$\hat{d}_k = \sum_{n=-N_1}^{N_2} c_n^* y_{k-n} + \sum_{i=1}^{N_3} F_i d_{k-i} \tag{7.26}$$

where c_n^* and y_n are tap gains and the inputs, respectively, to the forward filter, F_i^* are tap gains for the feedback filter, and $d_i (i < k)$ is the previous decision made on the detected signal. That is, once

$\hat{d}_k$ is obtained using Equation (7.26), d_k is decided from it. Then, d_k along with previous decisions $d_{k-1}, d_{k-2}, \ldots$ are fed back into the equalizer, and $\hat{d}_{k+1}$ is obtained using Equation (7.26).

The minimum mean squared error a DFE can achieve is [Pro89]

$$E[|e(n)|^2]_{min} = \exp\left\{\frac{T}{2\pi}\int_{-\pi/T}^{\pi/T} \ln\left[\frac{N_0}{|F(e^{j\omega T})|^2 + N_0}\right] d\omega\right\} \tag{7.27}$$

It can be shown that the minimum MSE for a DFE in Equation (7.27) is always smaller than that of an LTE in Equation (7.21) unless $|F(e^{j\omega T})|$ is a constant (i.e., when adaptive equalization is not needed) [Pro89]. If there are nulls in $|F(e^{j\omega T})|$, a DFE has significantly smaller minimum MSE than an LTE. Therefore, an LTE is well behaved when the channel spectrum is comparatively flat, but if the channel is severely distorted or exhibits nulls in the spectrum, the performance of an LTE deteriorates and the mean squared error of a DFE is much better than a LTE. Also, an LTE has difficulty equalizing a nonminimum phase channel, where the strongest energy arrives after the first arriving signal component. Thus, a DFE is more appropriate for severely distorted wireless channels.

The lattice implementation of the DFE is equivalent to a transversal DFE having a feed forward filter of length N_1 and a feedback filter of length N_2, where $N_1 > N_2$.

Another form of DFE proposed by Belfiore and Park [Bel79] is called a *predictive DFE*, and is shown in Figure 7.9. It also consists of a feed forward filter (FFF) as in the conventional DFE. However, the feedback filter (FBF) is driven by an input sequence formed by the difference of the output of the detector and the output of the feed forward filter. Hence, the FBF here is called a *noise predictor* because it predicts the noise and the residual ISI contained in the signal at the FFF output and subtracts from it the detector output after some feedback delay. The predictive DFE performs as well as the conventional DFE as the limit in the number of taps in the FFF and the FBF approach infinity. The FBF in the predictive DFE can also be realized as a lattice structure [Zho90]. The RLS lattice algorithm (discussed in Section 7.8) can be used in this case to yield fast convergence.

7.7.2 Maximum Likelihood Sequence Estimation (MLSE) Equalizer

The MSE-based linear equalizers described previously are optimum with respect to the criterion of minimum probability of symbol error when the channel does not introduce any amplitude distortion. Yet this is precisely the condition in which an equalizer is needed for a mobile communications link. This limitation on MSE-based equalizers led researchers to investigate optimum or nearly optimum nonlinear structures. These equalizers use various forms of the classical maximum likelihood receiver structure. Using a channel impulse response simulator within the algorithm, the MLSE tests all possible data sequences (rather than decoding each received symbol by itself), and chooses the data sequence with the maximum probability as the output. An MLSE usually has a large computational requirement, especially when the delay spread of the channel is large. Using the MLSE as an

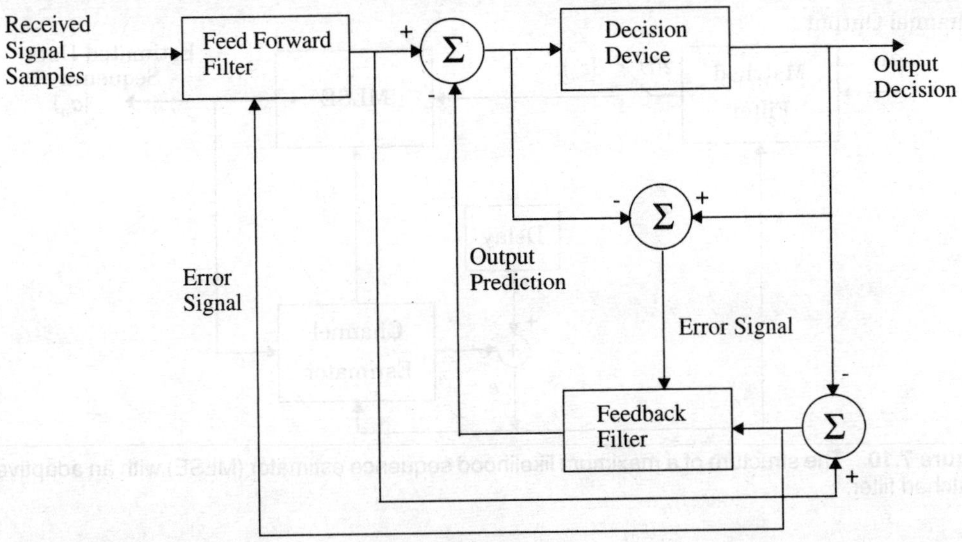

Figure 7.9 Predictive decision feedback equalizer.

equalizer was first proposed by Forney [For78] in which he set up a basic MLSE estimator structure and implemented it with the Viterbi algorithm. This algorithm, described in Section 7.15, was recognized to be a maximum likelihood sequence estimator (MLSE) of the state sequences of a finite state Markov process observed in memoryless noise. It has recently been implemented successfully for equalizers in mobile radio channels.

The MLSE can be viewed as a problem in estimating the state of a discrete-time finite state machine, which in this case happens to be the radio channel with coefficients f_k, and with a channel state which at any instant of time is estimated by the receiver based on the L most recent input samples. Thus, the channel has M^L states, where M is the size of the symbol alphabet of the modulation. That is, an M^L trellis is used by the receiver to model the channel over time. The Viterbi algorithm then tracks the state of the channel by the paths through the trellis and gives at stage k a rank ordering of the M^L most probable sequences terminating in the most recent L symbols.

The block diagram of a MLSE receiver based on the DFE is shown in Figure 7.10. The MLSE is optimal in the sense that it minimizes the probability of a sequence error. The MLSE requires knowledge of the channel characteristics in order to compute the metrics for making decisions. The MLSE also requires knowledge of the statistical distribution of the noise corrupting the signal. Thus, the probability distribution of the noise determines the form of the metric for optimum demodulation of the received signal. Notice that the matched filter operates on the continuous time signal, whereas the MLSE and channel estimator rely on discretized (nonlinear) samples.

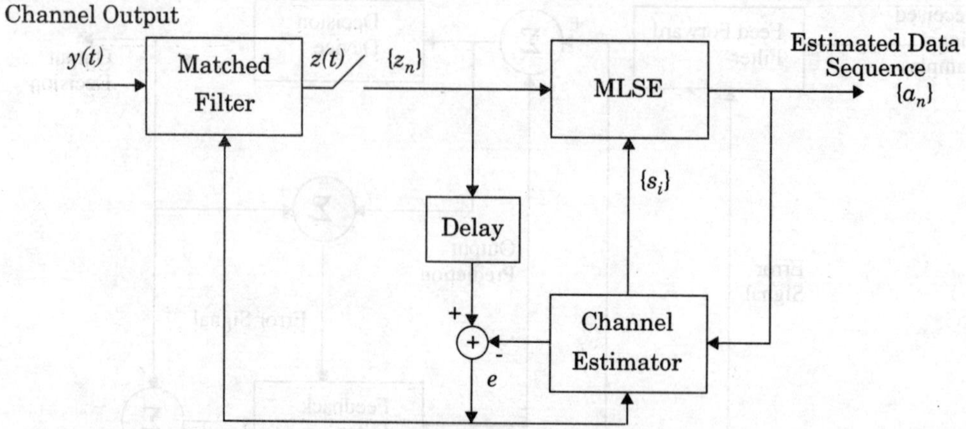

Figure 7.10 The structure of a maximum likelihood sequence estimator (MLSE) with an adaptive matched filter.

7.8 Algorithms for Adaptive Equalization

Since an adaptive equalizer compensates for an unknown and time-varying channel, it requires a specific algorithm to update the equalizer coefficients and track the channel variations. A wide range of algorithms exist to adapt the filter coefficients. The development of adaptive algorithms is a complex undertaking, and it is beyond the scope of this text to delve into great detail on how this is done. Excellent references exist which treat algorithm development [Wid85], [Hay86], [Pro91]. This section describes some practical issues regarding equalizer algorithm design, and outlines three of the basic algorithms for adaptive equalization. Though the algorithms detailed in this section are derived for the linear, transversal equalizer, they can be extended to other equalizer structures, including nonlinear equalizers.

The performance of an algorithm is determined by various factors which include:

- **Rate of convergence** — This is defined as the number of iterations required for the algorithm, in response to stationary inputs, to converge close enough to the optimum solution. A fast rate of convergence allows the algorithm to adapt rapidly to a stationary environment of unknown statistics. Furthermore, it enables the algorithm to track statistical variations when operating in a nonstationary environment.
- **Misadjustment** — For an algorithm of interest, this parameter provides a quantitative measure of the amount by which the final value of the mean square error, averaged over an ensemble of adaptive filters, deviates from the optimal minimum mean square error.
- **Computational complexity** — This is the number of operations required to make one complete iteration of the algorithm.
- **Numerical properties** — When an algorithm is implemented numerically, inaccuracies are produced due to round-off noise and representation errors in the computer. These kinds of errors influence the stability of the algorithm.

In practice, the cost of the computing platform, the power budget, and the radio propagation characteristics dominate the choice of an equalizer structure and its algorithm. In portable radio applications, battery drain at the subscriber unit is a paramount consideration, as customer talk time needs to be maximized. Equalizers are implemented only if they can provide sufficient link improvement to justify the cost and power burden.

The radio channel characteristics and intended use of the subscriber equipment is also key. The speed of the mobile unit determines the channel fading rate and the Doppler spread, which is directly related to the coherence time of the channel (see Chapter 5). The choice of algorithm, and its corresponding rate of convergence, depends on the channel data rate and coherence time.

The maximum expected time delay spread of the channel dictates the number of taps used in the equalizer design. An equalizer can only equalize over delay intervals less than or equal to the maximum delay within the filter structure. For example, if each delay element in an equalizer (such as the ones shown in Figures 7.2–7.8) offers a 10 microsecond delay, and four delay elements are used to provide a five tap equalizer, then the maximum delay spread that could be successfully equalized is $4 \times 10\ \mu s = 40\ \mu s$. Transmissions with multipath delay spread in excess of 40 μs could not be equalized. Since the circuit complexity and processing time increases with the number of taps and delay elements, it is important to know the maximum number of delay elements before selecting an equalizer structure and its algorithm. The effects of channel fading are discussed by Proakis [Pro91], with regard to the design of the US Digital Cellular equalizer. A study which considered a number of equalizers for a wide range of channel conditions was conducted by Rappaport, et al. [Rap93a].

Three classic equalizer algorithms are discussed below. These include the zero forcing (ZF) algorithm, the least mean squares (LMS) algorithm, and the recursive least squares (RLS) algorithm. While these algorithms are primitive for most of today's wireless standards, they offer fundamental insight into algorithm design and operation.

Example 7.3

Consider the design of the US Digital Cellular equalizer [Pro91]. If f = 900 MHz and the mobile velocity v = 80 km/hr, determine the following:

(a) the maximum Doppler shift
(b) the coherence time of the channel
(c) the maximum number of symbols that could be transmitted without updating the equalizer, assuming that the symbol rate is 24.3 ksymbols/sec

Solution

(a) From Equation (5.2), the maximum Doppler shift is given by

$$f_d = \frac{v}{\lambda} = \frac{(80{,}000/3600)\text{m/s}}{(1/3)\text{m}} = 66.67 \text{ Hz}$$

(b) From Equation (5.40.c), the coherence time is approximately

$$T_C = \sqrt{\frac{9}{16\pi f_d^2}} = \frac{0.423}{66.67} = 6.34 \text{ msec}$$

Note that if Equations (5.40.a) or (5.40.b) were used, T_C would increase or decrease by a factor of 2–3.

(c) To ensure coherence over a TDMA time slot, data must be sent during a 6.34 ms interval. For R_s = 24.3 ksymbols/sec, the number of bits that can be sent is

$$N_b = R_s T_C = 24{,}300 \times 0.00634 = 154 \text{ symbols}$$

As shown in Chapter 11, each time slot in the US digital cellular standard has a 6.67 ms duration and 162 symbols per time slot, which are very close to values in this example.

7.8.1 Zero Forcing Algorithm

In a zero forcing equalizer, the equalizer coefficients c_n are chosen to force the samples of the combined channel and equalizer impulse response to zero at all but one of the NT spaced sample points in the tapped delay line filter. By letting the number of coefficients increase without bound, an infinite length equalizer with zero ISI at the output can be obtained. When each of the delay elements provide a time delay equal to the symbol duration T, the frequency response $H_{eq}(f)$ of the equalizer is periodic with a period equal to the symbol rate $1/T$. The combined response of the channel with the equalizer must satisfy Nyquist's first criterion (see Chapter 6)

$$H_{ch}(f)H_{eq}(f) = 1, \; |f| < 1/2T \tag{7.28}$$

where $H_{ch}(f)$ is the folded frequency response of the channel. Thus, an infinite length, zero, ISI equalizer is simply an inverse filter which inverts the folded frequency response of the channel. This infinite length equalizer is usually implemented by a truncated length version.

The zero forcing algorithm was developed by Lucky [Luc65] for wireline communication. The zero forcing equalizer has the disadvantage that the inverse filter may excessively amplify noise at frequencies where the folded channel spectrum has high attenuation. The ZF equalizer thus neglects the effect of noise altogether, and is not often used for wireless links. However, it performs well for static channels with high SNR, such as local wired telephone lines.

7.8.2 Least Mean Square Algorithm

A more robust equalizer is the LMS equalizer where the criterion used is the minimization of the mean square error (MSE) between the desired equalizer output and the actual equalizer output. Using the notation developed in Section 7.3, the LMS algorithm can be readily understood.

Referring to Figure 7.2, the prediction error is given by

$$e_k = d_k - \hat{d}_k = x_k - \hat{d}_k \tag{7.29}$$

and from Equation (7.10)

$$e_k = x_k - \mathbf{y}_k^T \mathbf{w}_k = x_k - \mathbf{w}_k^T \mathbf{y}_k \tag{7.30}$$

To compute the mean square error $|e_k|^2$ at time instant k, Equation (7.12) is squared to obtain

$$\xi = E[e_k^* e_k] \tag{7.31}$$

The LMS algorithm seeks to minimize the mean square error given in Equation (7.31).

For a specific channel condition, the prediction error e_k is dependent on the tap gain vector $\boldsymbol{w}_N$, so the MSE of an equalizer is a function of $\boldsymbol{w}_N$. Let the cost function $J(\boldsymbol{w}_N)$ denote the mean squared error as a function of tap gain vector $\boldsymbol{w}_N$. Following the derivation in Section 7.3, in order to minimize the MSE, it is required to set the derivative of Equation (7.32) to zero

$$\frac{\partial}{\partial \boldsymbol{w}_N} J(\boldsymbol{w}_N) = -2\boldsymbol{p}_N + 2\boldsymbol{R}_{NN}\boldsymbol{w}_N = 0 \tag{7.32}$$

Simplifying Equation (7.32) (see Examples 7.1 and 7.2),

$$\boldsymbol{R}_{NN}\hat{\boldsymbol{w}}_N = \boldsymbol{p}_N \tag{7.33}$$

Equation (7.33) is a classic result, and is called the *normal equation*, since the error is minimized and is made orthogonal (normal) to the projection related to the desired signal x_k. When Equation (7.33) is satisfied, the MMSE of the equalizer is

$$J_{opt} = J(\hat{\boldsymbol{w}}_N) = E[x_k x_k^*] - \boldsymbol{p}_N^T \hat{\boldsymbol{w}}_N \tag{7.34}$$

To obtain the optimal tap gain vector $\hat{\boldsymbol{w}}_N$, the normal equation in (7.33) must be solved iteratively as the equalizer converges to an acceptably small value of J_{opt}. There are several ways to do this, and many variants of the LMS algorithm have been built upon the solution of Equation (7.34). One obvious technique is to calculate

$$\hat{\boldsymbol{w}} = \boldsymbol{R}_{NN}^{-1}\boldsymbol{p}_N \tag{7.35}$$

However, inverting a matrix requires $O(N^3)$ arithmetic operations [Joh82]. Other methods such as Gaussian elimination [Joh82] and Cholesky factorization [Bie77] require $O(N^2)$ operations per iteration. The advantage of these methods which directly solve Equation (7.35) is that only N symbol inputs are required to solve the normal equation. Consequently, a long training sequence is not necessary.

In practice, the minimization of the MSE is carried out recursively, and may be performed by use of the *stochastic gradient algorithm* introduced by Widrow [Wid66]. This is more commonly called the *least mean square* (LMS) *algorithm*. The LMS algorithm is the simplest equalization algorithm and requires only $2N+1$ operations per iteration. The filter weights are updated by the update equations given below [Ale86]. Letting the variable n denote the sequence of iterations, LMS is computed iteratively by

$$\hat{d}_k(n) = \mathbf{w}_N^T(n)\mathbf{y}_N(n) \tag{7.36.a}$$

$$e_k(n) = x_k(n) - \hat{d}_k(n) \tag{7.36.b}$$

$$\mathbf{w}_N(n+1) = \mathbf{w}_N(n) - \alpha e_k^*(n)\mathbf{y}_N(n) \tag{7.36.c}$$

where the subscript N denotes the number of delay stages in the equalizer, and α is the step size which controls the convergence rate and stability of the algorithm.

The LMS equalizer maximizes the signal to distortion ratio at its output within the constraints of the equalizer filter length. If an input signal has a time dispersion characteristic that is greater than the propagation delay through the equalizer, then the equalizer will be unable to reduce distortion. The convergence rate of the LMS algorithm is slow due to the fact that there is only one parameter, the step size α, that controls the adaptation rate. To prevent the adaptation from becoming unstable, the value of α is chosen from

$$0 < \alpha < 2/\sum_{i=1}^{N} \lambda_i \tag{7.37}$$

where λ_i is the ith eigenvalue of the covariance matrix $\mathbf{R}_{NN}$. Since $\sum_{i=1}^{N} \lambda_i = \mathbf{y}_N^T(n)\mathbf{y}_N(n)$, the step size α can be controlled by the total input power in order to avoid instability in the equalizer [Hay86].

7.8.3 Recursive Least Squares Algorithm

The convergence rate of the gradient-based LMS algorithm is very slow, especially when the eigenvalues of the input covariance matrix $\mathbf{R}_{NN}$ have a very large spread, i.e., $\lambda_{max}/\lambda_{min} \gg 1$. In order to achieve faster convergence, complex algorithms which involve additional parameters are used. Faster converging algorithms are based on a least squares approach, as opposed to the statistical approach used in the LMS algorithm. That is, rapid convergence relies on error measures expressed in terms of a time average of the actual received signal instead of a statistical average. This leads to the family of powerful, albeit complex, adaptive signal processing techniques known as *recursive least squares* (RLS), which significantly improves the convergence of adaptive equalizers.

The least square error based on the time average is defined as [Hay86], [Pro91]

$$J(n) = \sum_{i=1}^{n} \lambda^{n-i} e^*(i, n)e(i, n) \tag{7.38}$$

where λ is the weighting factor close to 1, but smaller than 1, $e^*(i, n)$ is the complex conjugate of $e(i, n)$, and the error $e(i, n)$ is

$$e(i, n) = x(i) - \boldsymbol{y}_N^T(i)\boldsymbol{w}_N(n) \qquad 0 \le i \le n \tag{7.39}$$

and

$$\boldsymbol{y}_N(i) = [y(i), y(i-1), \ldots.., y(i-N+1)]^T \tag{7.40}$$

where $\boldsymbol{y}_N(i)$ is the data input vector at time i, and $\boldsymbol{w}_N(n)$ is the new tap gain vector at time n. Therefore, $e(i, n)$ is the error using the new tap gain at time n to test the old data at time i, and $J(n)$ is the cumulative squared error of the new tap gains on all the old data.

The RLS solution requires finding the tap gain vector of the equalizer $\boldsymbol{w}_N(n)$ such that the cumulative squared error $J(n)$ is minimized. It uses all the previous data to test the new tap gains. The parameter λ is a data weighting factor that weights recent data more heavily in the computations, so that $J(n)$ tends to forget the old data in a nonstationary environment. If the channel is stationary, λ may be set to one [Pro89].

To obtain the minimum of least square error $J(n)$, the gradient of $J(n)$ in Equation (7.38) is set to zero,

$$\frac{\partial}{\partial \boldsymbol{w}_N} J(n) = 0 \tag{7.41}$$

Using Equations (7.39)–(7.41), it can be shown that [Pro89]

$$\boldsymbol{R}_{NN}(n)\hat{\boldsymbol{w}}_N(n) = \boldsymbol{p}_N(n) \tag{7.42}$$

where $\hat{\boldsymbol{w}}_N$ is the optimal tap gain vector of the RLS equalizer,

$$\boldsymbol{R}_{NN}(n) = \sum_{i=1}^{n} \lambda^{n-i} \boldsymbol{y}_N^*(i)\boldsymbol{y}_N^T(i) \tag{7.43}$$

$$\boldsymbol{p}_N(n) = \sum_{i=1}^{n} \lambda^{n-i} x^*(i)\boldsymbol{y}_N(i) \tag{7.44}$$

The matrix $\boldsymbol{R}_{NN}(n)$ in Equation (7.43) is the deterministic correlation matrix of input data of the equalizer $\boldsymbol{y}_N(i)$, and $\boldsymbol{p}_N(i)$ in Equation (7.44) is the deterministic cross-correlation vector between inputs of the equalizer $\boldsymbol{y}_N(i)$ and the desired output $d(i)$, where $d(i) = x(i)$. To compute the equalizer weight vector $\hat{\boldsymbol{w}}_N$ using Equation (7.42), it is required to compute $\boldsymbol{R}_{NN}^{-1}(n)$.

From the definition of $\boldsymbol{R}_{NN}(n)$ in Equation (7.43), it is possible to obtain a recursive equation expressing $\boldsymbol{R}_{NN}(n)$ in terms of $\boldsymbol{R}_{NN}(n-1)$

$$\boldsymbol{R}_{NN}(n) = \lambda \boldsymbol{R}_{NN}(n-1) + \boldsymbol{y}_N(n)\boldsymbol{y}_N^T(n) \tag{7.45}$$

Since the three terms in Equation (7.45) are all N by N matrices, a matrix inverse lemma [Bie77] can be used to derive a recursive update for R_{NN}^{-1} in terms of the previous inverse, $R_{NN}^{-1}(n-1)$

$$R_{NN}^{-1}(n) = \frac{1}{\lambda}\left[R_{NN}^{-1}(n-1) - \frac{R_{NN}^{-1}(n-1)y_N(n)y_N^T(n)R_{NN}^{-1}(n-1)}{\lambda+\mu(n)}\right] \quad (7.46)$$

where

$$\mu(n) = y_N^T(n)R_{NN}^{-1}(n-1)y_N(n) \quad (7.47)$$

Based on these recursive equations, the RLS minimization leads to the following weight update equations:

$$w_N(n) = w_N(n-1) + k_N(n)e^*(n, n-1) \quad (7.48)$$

where

$$k_N(n) = \frac{R_{NN}^{-1}(n-1)y_N(n)}{\lambda+\mu(n)} \quad (7.49)$$

The RLS algorithm may be summarized as follows:

1. Initialize $w(0) = k(0) = x(0) = 0$, $R^{-1}(0) = \delta I_{NN}$, where I_{NN} is an $N \times N$ identity matrix, and δ is a large positive constant.
2. Recursively compute the following:

$$\hat{d}(n) = w^T(n-1)y(n) \quad (7.50)$$

$$e(n) = x(n) - \hat{d}(n) \quad (7.51)$$

$$k(n) = \frac{R^{-1}(n-1)y(n)}{\lambda + y^T(n)R^{-1}(n-1)y(n)} \quad (7.52)$$

$$R^{-1}(n) = \frac{1}{\lambda}[R^{-1}(n-1) - k(n)y^T(n)R^{-1}(n-1)] \quad (7.53)$$

$$w(n) = w(n-1) + k(n)e^*(n) \quad (7.54)$$

In Equation (7.53), λ is the weighting coefficient that can change the performance of the equalizer. If a channel is time-invariant, λ can be set to one. Usually $0.8 < \lambda < 1$ is used. The value of λ has no influence on the rate of convergence, but does determines the tracking ability of the RLS equalizers. The smaller the λ, the better the tracking ability of the equalizer. However, if λ is too small, the equalizer will be unstable [Lin84]. The RLS algorithm described above, called the *Kalman RLS* algorithm, uses $2.5N^2 + 4.5N$ arithmetic operations per iteration.

7.8.4 Summary of Algorithms

There are number of variations of the LMS and RLS algorithms that exist for adapting an equalizer. Table 7.1 shows the computational requirements of different algorithms, and lists some advantages and disadvantages of each algorithm. Note that the RLS algorithms have similar convergence and tracking performances, which are much better than the LMS algorithm. However, these RLS algorithms usually have high computational requirement and complex program structures. Also, some RLS algorithms tend to be unstable. The fast transversal filter (FTF) algorithm requires the least computation among the RLS algorithms, and it can use a rescue variable to avoid instability. However, rescue techniques tend to be a bit tricky for widely varying mobile radio channels, and the FTF is not widely used.

Table 7.1 Comparison of Various Algorithms for Adaptive Equalization [Pro91]

Algorithm	Number of Multiply Operations	Advantages	Disadvantages
LMS Gradient DFE	$2N + 1$	Low computational complexity, simple program	Slow convergence, poor tracking
Kalman RLS	$2.5N^2 + 4.5N$	Fast convergence, good tracking ability	High computational complexity
FTF	$7N + 14$	Fast convergence, good tracking, low computational complexity	Complex programming, unstable (but can use rescue method)
Gradient Lattice	$13N - 8$	Stable, low computational complexity, flexible structure	Performance not as good as other RLS, complex programming
Gradient Lattice DFE	$13N_1 + 33N_2 - 36$	Low computational complexity	Complex programming
Fast Kalman DFE	$20N + 5$	Can be used for DFE, fast convergence and good tracking	Complex programming, computation not low, unstable
Square Root RLS DFE	$1.5N^2 + 6.5N$	Better numerical properties	High computational complexity

7.9 Fractionally Spaced Equalizers

The equalizers discussed so far have tap spacings at the symbol rate. It is well known that the optimum receiver for a communication signal corrupted by Gaussian noise consists of a matched filter sampled periodically at the symbol rate of the message. In the presence of channel distortion, the matched filter prior to the equalizer must be matched to the channel and the corrupted signal. In practice, the channel response is unknown, and hence the optimum matched filter must be adaptively estimated. A suboptimal solution in which the matched filter is matched to the transmitted signal pulse may result in a significant degradation in performance. In addition, such a suboptimal filter is extremely sensitive to any timing error in the sampling of its output [Qur77]. A *fractionally spaced equalizer* (FSE) is based on sampling the incoming signal at least as fast as the Nyquist rate [Pro91]. The FSE compensates for the channel distortion before aliasing effects occur due to the symbol rate sampling. In addition, the equalizer can compensate for any timing delay for any arbitrary timing phase. In effect, the FSE incorporates the functions of a matched filter and equalizer into a single filter structure. Simulation results demonstrating the effectiveness of the FSE over a symbol rate equalizer have been given in the papers by Qureshi and Forney [Qur77], and Gitlin and Weinstein [Git81].

Nonlinear equalizers based on MLSE techniques appear to be gaining popularity in modern wireless systems (these were described in Section 7.7.2). The interested reader may find Chapter 6 of [Ste94] useful for further work in this area.

7.10 Diversity Techniques

Diversity is a powerful communication receiver technique that provides wireless link improvement at relatively low cost. Unlike equalization, diversity requires no training overhead since a training sequence is not required by the transmitter. Furthermore, there are a wide range of diversity implementations, many which are very practical and provide significant link improvement with little added cost.

Diversity exploits the random nature of radio propagation by finding independent (or at least highly uncorrelated) signal paths for communication. In virtually all applications, diversity decisions are made by the receiver, and are unknown to the transmitter.

The diversity concept can be explained simply. If one radio path undergoes a deep fade, another independent path may have a strong signal. By having more than one path to select from, both the instantaneous and average SNRs at the receiver may be improved, often by as much as 20 dB to 30 dB.

As shown in Chapters 4 and 5, there are two types of fading—small-scale and large-scale fading. Small-scale fades are characterized by deep and rapid amplitude fluctuations which occur as the mobile moves over distances of just a few wavelengths. These fades are caused by multiple reflections from the surroundings in the vicinity of the mobile. For narrowband signals, small-scale fading typically results in a Rayleigh fading distribution of signal strength over small distances. In order to prevent deep fades from occurring, *microscopic diversity techniques* can exploit the rapidly changing signal. For example, the small-scale fading shown in Figure 4.1 reveals that if two antennas are separated by a fraction of a meter, one may receive a null while the other receives a strong signal. By selecting the best signal at all times, a receiver can mitigate small-scale fading effects (this is called *antenna diversity* or *space diversity*).

Large-scale fading is caused by shadowing due to variations in both the terrain profile and the nature of the surroundings. In deeply shadowed conditions, the received signal strength at a mobile can drop well below that of free space. In Chapter 4, large-scale fading was shown to be log-normally distributed with a standard deviation of about 10 dB in urban environments. By selecting a base station which is not shadowed when others are, the mobile can improve substantially the average signal-to-noise ratio on the forward link. This is called *macroscopic diversity*, since the mobile is taking advantage of large separations (the macro-system differences) between the serving base stations.

Macroscopic diversity is also useful at the base station receiver. By using base station antennas that are sufficiently separated in space, the base station is able to improve the reverse link by selecting the antenna with the strongest signal from the mobile.

7.10.1 Derivation of Selection Diversity Improvement

Before discussing the many diversity techniques that are used, it is worthwhile to quantitatively determine the advantage that can be achieved using diversity. Consider M independent Rayleigh fading channels available at a receiver. Each channel is called a diversity *branch*. Further, assume that each branch has the same average *SNR* given by

$$SNR = \Gamma = \frac{E_b}{N_0}\overline{\alpha^2} \tag{7.55}$$

where we assume $\overline{\alpha^2} = 1$.

If each branch has an instantaneous $SNR = \gamma_i$, then from Equation (6.155), the pdf of γ_i is

$$p(\gamma_i) = \frac{1}{\Gamma}e^{\frac{-\gamma_i}{\Gamma}} \qquad \gamma_i \geq 0 \tag{7.56}$$

where Γ is the mean *SNR* of each branch. The probability that a single branch has an instantaneous *SNR* less than some threshold γ is

$$Pr[\gamma_i \leq \gamma] = \int_0^{\gamma} p(\gamma_i)d\gamma_i = \int_0^{\gamma}\frac{1}{\Gamma}e^{\frac{-\gamma_i}{\Gamma}}d\gamma_i = 1 - e^{\frac{-\gamma}{\Gamma}} \tag{7.57}$$

Now, the probability that all M independent diversity branches receive signals which are *simultaneously* less than some specific *SNR* threshold γ is

$$Pr[\gamma_1, ..., \gamma_M \leq \gamma] = (1 - e^{-\gamma/\Gamma})^M = P_M(\gamma) \tag{7.58}$$

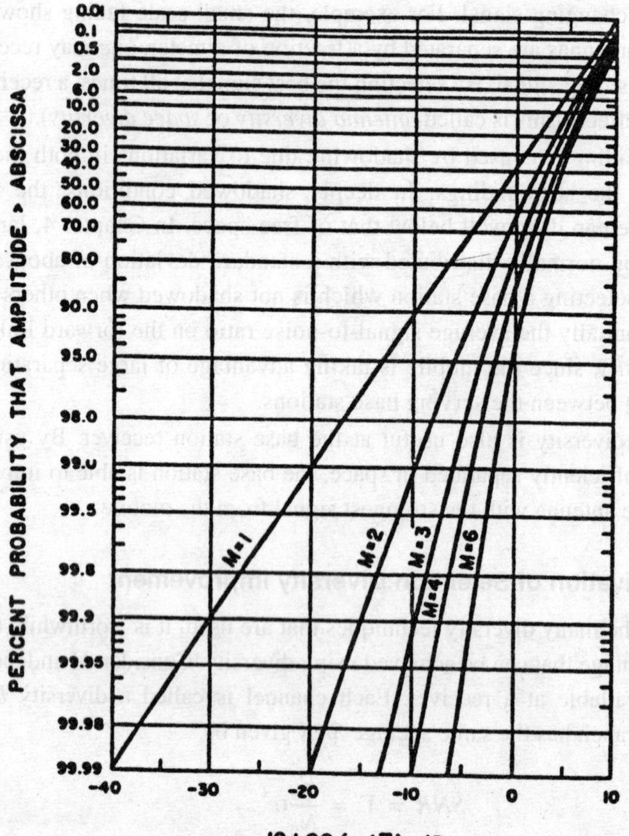

Figure 7.11 Graph of probability distributions of *SNR* = γ threshold for *M* branch selection diversity. The term Γ represents the mean *SNR* on each branch [from [Jak71] © IEEE].

$P_M(\gamma)$ in Equation (7.58) is the probability of all branches failing to achieve an instantaneous $SNR = \gamma$. If a single branch achieves $SNR > \gamma$, then the probability that $SNR > \gamma$ for one or more branches is given by

$$Pr[\gamma_i > \gamma] = 1 - P_M(\gamma) = 1 - (1 - e^{-\gamma/\Gamma})^M \tag{7.59}$$

Equation (7.59) is an expression for the probability of exceeding a threshold when *selection diversity* is used [Jak71], and is plotted in Figure 7.11.

To determine the average signal-to-noise ratio of the received signal when diversity is used, it is first necessary to find the pdf of the fading signal. For selection diversity, the average SNR is found by first computing the derivative of the CDF $P_M(\gamma)$ in order to find the pdf of γ, the instantaneous SNR when *M* branches are used. Proceeding along these lines,

$$p_M(\gamma) = \frac{d}{d\gamma}P_M(\gamma) = \frac{M}{\Gamma}(1 - e^{-\gamma/\Gamma})^{M-1} e^{-\gamma/\Gamma} \tag{7.60}$$

Then, the mean *SNR*, $\bar{\gamma}$, may be expressed as

$$\bar{\gamma} = \int_0^{\infty} \gamma p_M(\gamma) d\gamma = \Gamma \int_0^{\infty} Mx(1-e^{-x})^{M-1} e^{-x} dx \tag{7.61}$$

where $x = \gamma/\Gamma$. Note that Γ is the average SNR for a single branch (when no diversity is used). Equation (7.61) is evaluated to yield the average SNR improvement offered by selection diversity

$$\frac{\bar{\gamma}}{\Gamma} = \sum_{k=1}^{M} \frac{1}{k} \tag{7.62}$$

The following example illustrates the advantage that diversity provides.

Example 7.4

Assume four branch diversity is used, where each branch receives an independent Rayleigh fading signal. If the average *SNR* is 20 dB, determine the probability that the *SNR* will drop below 10 dB. Compare this with the case of a single receiver without diversity.

Solution

For this example, the specified threshold γ = 10 dB, Γ = 20 dB, and there are four branches. Thus γ/Γ = 0.1 and using Equation (7.58),

$$P_4(10\text{ dB}) = (1-e^{-0.1})^4 = 0.000082$$

When diversity is not used, Equation (7.58) may be evaluated using $M = 1$

$$P_1(10\text{ dB}) = (1-e^{-0.1})^1 = 0.095$$

Notice that without diversity, the *SNR* drops below the specified threshold with a probability that is three orders of magnitude greater than if four branch diversity is used!

From Equation (7.62), it can be seen that the average SNR in the branch which is selected using selection diversity naturally increases, since it is always guaranteed to be above the specified threshold. Thus, selection diversity offers an average improvement in the link margin without requiring additional transmitter power or sophisticated receiver circuitry. The diversity improvement can be directly related to the average bit error rate for various modulations by using the principles discussed in Section 6.12.1.

Selection diversity is easy to implement because all that is needed is a side monitoring station and an antenna switch at the receiver. However, it is not an optimal diversity technique because it does not use all of the possible branches simultaneously. *Maximal ratio combining* uses each of the M branches in a co-phased and weighted manner such that the highest achievable SNR is available at the receiver at all times.

7.10.2 Derivation of Maximal Ratio Combining Improvement

In maximal ratio combining, the voltage signals r_i from each of the M diversity branches are co-phased to provide coherent voltage addition and are individually weighted to provide optimal SNR. If each branch has gain G_i, then the resulting signal envelope applied to the detector is

$$r_M = \sum_{i=1}^{M} G_i r_i \tag{7.63}$$

Assuming that each branch has the same average noise power N, the total noise power N_T applied to the detector is simply the weighted sum of the noise in each branch. Thus,

$$N_T = N \sum_{i=1}^{M} G_i^2 \tag{7.64}$$

which results in an SNR applied to the detector, γ_M, given by

$$\gamma_M = \frac{r_M^2}{2N_T} \tag{7.65}$$

Using Chebychev's inequality [Cou93], γ_M is maximized when $G_i = r_i/N$, which leads to

$$\gamma_M = \frac{1}{2} \frac{\left(\sum (r_i^2/N)\right)^2}{N \sum (r_i^2/N^2)} = \frac{1}{2} \sum_{i=1}^{M} \frac{r_i^2}{N} = \sum_{i=1}^{M} \gamma_i \tag{7.66}$$

Thus, the SNR out of the diversity combiner (see in Figure 7.14) is simply the sum of the SNRs in each branch.

The value for γ_i is $r_i^2/2N$, where r_i is equal to $r(t)$ as defined in Equation (6.67). As shown in Chapter 5, the received signal envelope for a fading mobile radio signal can be modeled from two independent Gaussian random variables T_c and T_s, each having zero mean and equal variance σ^2. That is,

$$\gamma_i = \frac{1}{2N} r_i^2 = \frac{1}{2N}(T_c^2 + T_s^2) \tag{7.67}$$

Hence γ_M is a Chi-square distribution of $2M$ Gaussian random variables with variance $\sigma^2/(2N) = \Gamma/2$, where Γ is defined in Equation (7.55). The resulting pdf for γ_M can be shown to be

$$p(\gamma_M) = \frac{\gamma_M^{M-1} e^{-\gamma_M/\Gamma}}{\Gamma^M (M-1)!} \quad \text{for } \gamma_M \ge 0 \tag{7.68}$$

The probability that γ_M is less than some SNR threshold γ is

$$Pr\{\gamma_M \le \gamma\} = \int_0^{\gamma} p(\gamma_M)d\gamma_M = 1 - e^{-\gamma/\Gamma}\sum_{k=1}^{M}\frac{(\gamma/\Gamma)^{k-1}}{(k-1)!} \tag{7.69}$$

Equation (7.69) is the probability distribution for maximal ratio combining [Jak71]. It follows directly from Equation (7.66) that the average SNR, $\overline{\gamma_M}$, is simply the sum of the individual $\overline{\gamma_i}$ from each branch. In other words,

$$\overline{\gamma_M} = \sum_{i=1}^{M}\overline{\gamma_i} = \sum_{i=1}^{M}\Gamma = M\Gamma \tag{7.70}$$

The control algorithms for setting the gains and phases for maximal ratio combining receivers are similar to those required in equalizers and RAKE receivers. Figure 7.14 and Figure 7.16 illustrate maximal ratio combining structures. Maximal ratio combining is discussed in Section 7.10.3.3, and can be applied to virtually any diversity application, although often at much greater cost and complexity than other diversity techniques.

7.10.3 Practical Space Diversity Considerations

Space diversity, also known as antenna diversity, is one of the most popular forms of diversity used in wireless systems. Conventional wireless systems consist of an elevated base station antenna and a mobile antenna close to the ground. The existence of a direct path between the transmitter and the receiver is not guaranteed and the possibility of a number of scatterers in the vicinity of the mobile suggests a Rayleigh fading signal. From this model [Jak70], Jakes deduced that the signals received from spatially separated antennas on the mobile would have essentially uncorrelated envelopes for antenna separations of one half wavelength or more.

The concept of antenna space diversity is also used in base station design. At each cell site, multiple base station receiving antennas are used to provide diversity reception. However, since the important scatterers are generally on the ground in the vicinity of the mobile, the base station antennas must be spaced considerably far apart to achieve decorrelation. Separations on the order of several tens of wavelengths are required at the base station. Space diversity can thus be used at either the mobile or base station, or both. Figure 7.12 shows a general block diagram of a space diversity scheme [Cox83a].

Space diversity reception methods can be classified into four categories [Jak71]:

1. Selection diversity
2. Feedback diversity
3. Maximal ratio combining
4. Equal gain diversity

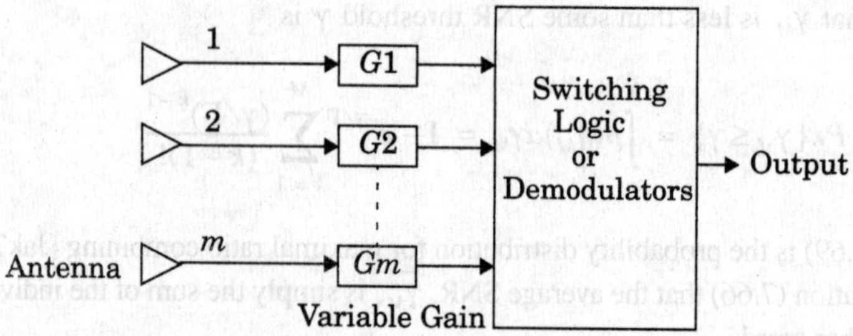

Figure 7.12 Generalized block diagram for space diversity.

7.10.3.1 Selection Diversity

Selection diversity is the simplest diversity technique analyzed in Section 7.10.1. A block diagram of this method is similar to that shown in Figure 7.12, where m demodulators are used to provide m diversity branches whose gains are adjusted to provide the same average SNR for each branch. As derived in Section 7.10.1, the receiver branch having the highest instantaneous SNR is connected to the demodulator. The antenna signals themselves could be sampled and the best one sent to a single demodulator. In practice, the branch with the largest $(S+N)/N$ is used, since it is difficult to measure SNR alone. A practical selection diversity system cannot function on a truly instantaneous basis, but must be designed so that the internal time constants of the selection circuitry are shorter than the reciprocal of the signal fading rate.

7.10.3.2 Feedback or Scanning Diversity

Scanning diversity is very similar to selection diversity except that instead of always using the best of M signals, the M signals are scanned in a fixed sequence until one is found to be above a predetermined threshold. This signal is then received until it falls below threshold and the scanning process is again initiated. The resulting fading statistics are somewhat inferior to those obtained by the other methods, but the advantage with this method is that it is very simple to implement—only one receiver is required. A block diagram of this method is shown in Figure 7.13.

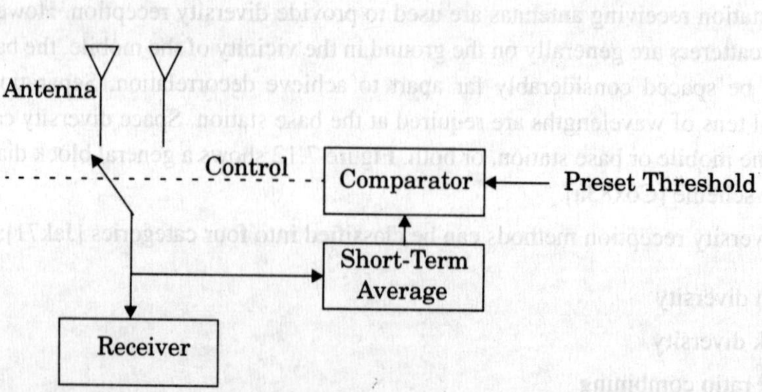

Figure 7.13 Basic form of scanning diversity.

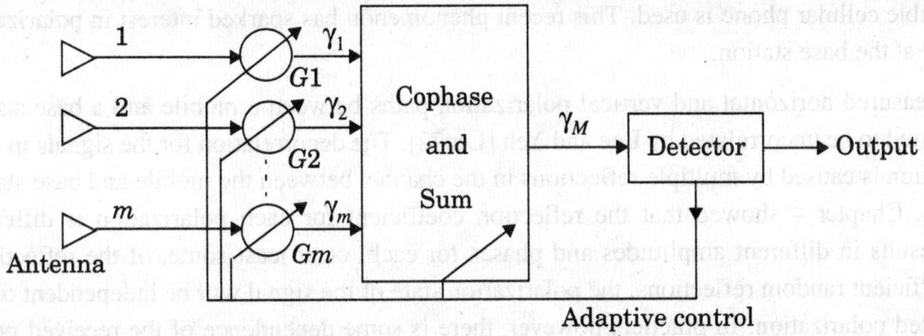

Figure 7.14 Maximal ratio combiner.

7.10.3.3 Maximal Ratio Combining

In this method first proposed by Kahn [Kah54], the signals from all of the M branches are weighted according to their individual signal voltage to noise power ratios and then summed. Figure 7.14 shows a block diagram of the technique. Here, the individual signals must be co-phased before being summed (unlike selection diversity) which generally requires an individual receiver and phasing circuit for each antenna element. Maximal ratio combining produces an output SNR equal to the sum of the individual SNRs, as explained in Section 7.10.2. Thus, it has the advantage of producing an output *with an acceptable SNR even when none of the individual signals are themselves acceptable*. This technique gives the best statistical reduction of fading of any known linear diversity combiner. Modern DSP techniques and digital receivers are now making this optimal form of diversity practical.

7.10.3.4 Equal Gain Combining

In certain cases, it is not convenient to provide for the variable weighting capability required for true maximal ratio combining. In such cases, the branch weights are all set to unity, but the signals from each branch are co-phased to provide *equal gain combining* diversity. This allows the receiver to exploit signals that are simultaneously received on each branch. The possibility of producing an acceptable signal from a number of unacceptable inputs is still retained, and performance is only marginally inferior to maximal ratio combining and superior to selection diversity.

7.10.4 Polarization Diversity

At the base station, space diversity is considerably less practical than at the mobile because the narrow angle of incident fields requires large antenna spacings [Vau90]. The comparatively high cost of using space diversity at the base station prompts the consideration of using orthogonal polarization to exploit polarization diversity. While this only provides two diversity branches, it does allow the antenna elements to be co-located.

In the early days of cellular radio, all subscriber units were mounted in vehicles and used vertical whip antennas. Today, however, over half of the subscriber units are portable. This means that most subscribers are no longer using vertical polarization due to hand-tilting when the portable cellular phone is used. This recent phenomenon has sparked interest in polarization diversity at the base station.

Measured horizontal and vertical polarization paths between a mobile and a base station are reported to be uncorrelated by Lee and Yeh [Lee72]. The decorrelation for the signals in each polarization is caused by multiple reflections in the channel between the mobile and base station antennas. Chapter 4 showed that the reflection coefficient for each polarization is different, which results in different amplitudes and phases for each, or at least some, of the reflections. After sufficient random reflections, the polarization state of the signal will be independent of the transmitted polarization. In practice, however, there is some dependence of the received polarization on the transmitted polarization.

Circular and linear polarized antennas have been used to characterize multipath inside buildings [Haw91], [Rap92a], [Ho94]. When the path was obstructed, polarization diversity was found to dramatically reduce the multipath delay spread without significantly decreasing the received power.

While polarization diversity has been studied in the past, it has primarily been used for fixed radio links which vary slowly in time. Line-of-sight microwave links, for example, typically use polarization diversity to support two simultaneous users on the same radio channel. Since the channel does not change much in such a link, there is little likelihood of cross polarization interference. As portable users proliferate, polarization diversity is likely to become more important for improving link margin and capacity. An outline of a theoretical model for the base station *polarization diversity reception* as suggested by Kozono [Koz85] is given below.

Theoretical Model for Polarization Diversity

It is assumed that the signal is transmitted from a mobile with vertical (or horizontal) polarization. It is received at the base station by a polarization diversity antenna with two branches. Figure 7.15 shows the theoretical model and the system coordinates. As seen in the figure, a polarization diversity antenna is composed of two antenna elements V_1 and V_2, which make a $\pm\alpha$ angle (polarization angle) with the Y axis. A mobile station is located in the direction of offset angle β from the main beam direction of the diversity antenna as seen in Figure 7.15(b).

Some of the vertically polarized signals transmitted are converted to the horizontal polarized signal because of multipath propagation. The signal arriving at the base station can be expressed as

$$x = r_1 \cos(\omega t + \phi_1) \tag{7.71.a}$$

$$y = r_2 \cos(\omega t + \phi_2) \tag{7.71.b}$$

where x and y are signal levels which are received when $\beta = 0$. It is assumed that r_1 and r_2 have independent Rayleigh distributions, and ϕ_1 and ϕ_2 have independent uniform distributions.

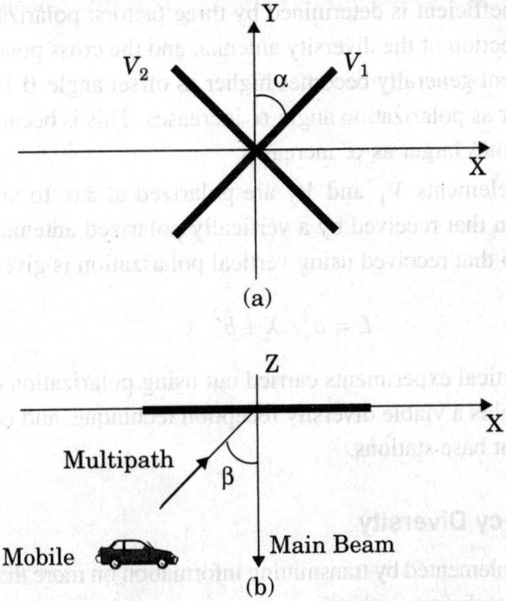

Figure 7.15 Theoretical model for base station polarization diversity based on [Koz85]: (a) x–y plane; (b) x–z plane.

The received signal values at elements V_1 and V_2 can be written as:

$$V_1 = (ar_1\cos\phi_1 + r_2 b\cos\phi_2)\cos\omega t - (ar_1\sin\phi_1 + r_2 b\sin\phi_2)\sin\omega t \tag{7.72}$$

$$V_2 = (-ar_1\cos\phi_1 + r_2 b\cos\phi_2)\cos\omega t - (-ar_1\sin\phi_1 + r_2 b\sin\phi_2)\sin\omega t \tag{7.73}$$

where $a = \sin\alpha\cos\beta$ and $b = \cos\alpha$.

The correlation coefficient ρ can be written as

$$\rho = \left(\frac{\tan^2(\alpha)\cos^2(\beta) - \Gamma}{\tan^2(\alpha)\cos^2(\beta) + \Gamma}\right)^2 \tag{7.74}$$

where

$$X = \frac{\langle R_2^2\rangle}{\langle R_1^2\rangle} \tag{7.75}$$

and

$$R_1 = \sqrt{r_1^2 a^2 + r_2^2 b^2 + 2r_1 r_2 ab\cos(\phi_1 + \phi_2)} \tag{7.76}$$

$$R_2 = \sqrt{r_1^2 a^2 + r_2^2 b^2 - 2r_1 r_2 ab\cos(\phi_1 + \phi_2)} \tag{7.77}$$

Here, X is the cross polarization discrimination of the propagation path between a mobile and a base station.

The correlation coefficient is determined by three factors: polarization angle, offset angle from the main beam direction of the diversity antenna, and the cross polarization discrimination. The correlation coefficient generally becomes higher as offset angle β becomes larger. Also, ρ generally becomes lower as polarization angle α increases. This is because the horizontal polarization component becomes larger as α increases.

Because antenna elements V_1 and V_2 are polarized at $\pm\alpha$ to the vertical, the received signal level is lower than that received by a vertically polarized antenna. The average value of signal loss L, relative to that received using vertical polarization is given by

$$L = a^2 / X + b^2 \tag{7.78}$$

The results of practical experiments carried out using polarization diversity [Koz85] show that polarization diversity is a viable diversity reception technique, and is exploited within wireless handsets as well as at base stations.

7.10.5 Frequency Diversity

Frequency diversity is implemented by transmitting information on more than one carrier frequency. The rationale behind this technique is that frequencies separated by more than the coherence bandwidth of the channel will be uncorrelated and will thus not experience the same fades [Lem91]. Theoretically, if the channels are uncorrelated, the probability of simultaneous fading will be the product of the individual fading probabilities (see Equation (7.58)).

Frequency diversity is often employed in microwave line-of-sight links which carry several channels in a frequency division multiplex mode (FDM). Due to tropospheric propagation and resulting refraction, deep fading sometimes occurs. In practice, *1:N protection switching* is provided by a radio licensee, wherein one frequency is nominally idle but is available on a stand-by basis to provide frequency diversity switching for any one of the N other carriers (frequencies) being used on the same link, each carrying independent traffic. When diversity is needed, the appropriate traffic is simply switched to the backup frequency. This technique has the disadvantage that it not only requires spare bandwidth but also requires that there be as many receivers as there are channels used for the frequency diversity. However, for critical traffic, the expense may be justified.

New OFDM modulation and access techniques exploit frequency diversity by providing simultaneous modulation signals with error control coding across a large bandwidth, so that if a particular frequency undergoes a fade, the composite signal will still be demodulated.

7.10.6 Time Diversity

Time diversity repeatedly transmits information at time spacings that exceed the coherence time of the channel, so that multiple repetitions of the signal will be received with independent fading conditions, thereby providing for diversity. One modern implementation of time diversity involves the use of the RAKE receiver for spread spectrum CDMA, where the multipath channel provides redundancy in the transmitted message. By demodulating several replicas of the transmitted

CDMA signal, where each replica experiences a particular multipath delay, the RAKE receiver is able to align the replicas in time so that a better estimate of the original signal may be formed at the receiver.

7.11 RAKE Receiver

In CDMA spread spectrum systems (see Chapter 6), the chip rate is typically much greater than the flat-fading bandwidth of the channel. Whereas conventional modulation techniques require an equalizer to undo the intersymbol interference between adjacent symbols, CDMA spreading codes are designed to provide very low correlation between successive chips. Thus, propagation delay spread in the radio channel merely provides multiple versions of the transmitted signal at the receiver. If these multipath components are delayed in time by more than a chip duration, they appear like uncorrelated noise at a CDMA receiver, and equalization is not required. The spread spectrum processing gain makes uncorrelated noise negligible after despreading.

However, since there is useful information in the multipath components, CDMA receivers may combine the time delayed versions of the original signal transmission in order to improve the signal-to-noise ratio at the receiver. A RAKE receiver does just this—it attempts to collect the time-shifted versions of the original signal by providing a separate correlation receiver for each of the multipath signals. Each correlation receiver may be adjusted in time delay, so that a microprocessor controller can cause different correlation receivers to search in different time windows for significant multipath. The range of time delays that a particular correlator can search is called a *search window.* The RAKE receiver, shown in Figure 7.16, is essentially a diversity receiver designed specifically for CDMA, where the diversity is provided by the fact that the multipath components are practically uncorrelated from one another when their relative propagation delays exceed a chip period.

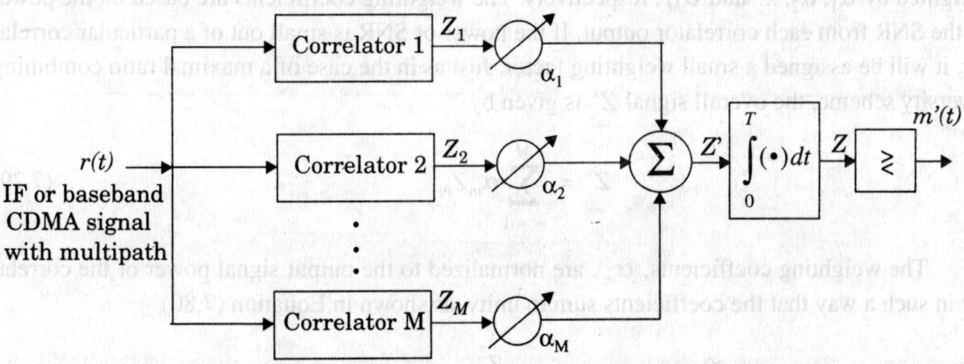

Figure 7.16 An *M*-branch (*M*-finger) RAKE receiver implementation. Each correlator detects a time shifted version of the original CDMA transmission, and each finger of the RAKE correlates to a portion of the signal which is delayed by at least one chip in time from the other fingers.

A RAKE receiver utilizes multiple correlators to separately detect the M strongest multipath components. The outputs of each correlator are then weighted to provide a better estimate of the transmitted signal than is provided by a single component. Demodulation and bit decisions are then based on the weighted outputs of the M correlators.

The basic idea of a RAKE receiver was first proposed by Price and Green [Pri58]. In outdoor environments, the delay between multipath components is usually large and, if the chip rate is properly selected, the low autocorrelation properties of a CDMA spreading sequence can assure that multipath components will appear nearly uncorrelated with each other. However, the RAKE receiver in IS-95 CDMA has been found to perform poorly in indoor environments, which is to be expected since the multipath delay spreads in indoor channels ($\approx$100 ns) are much smaller than an IS-95 chip duration ($\approx$800 ns). In such cases, a RAKE will not work since multipath is unresolveable, and Rayleigh flat-fading typically occurs within a single chip period.

To explore the performance of a RAKE receiver, assume M correlators are used in a CDMA receiver to capture the M strongest multipath components. A weighting network is used to provide a linear combination of the correlator output for bit detection. Correlator 1 is synchronized to the strongest multipath m_1. Multipath component m_2 arrives τ_1 later than component m_1 where $\tau_2 - \tau_1$ is assumed to be greater than a chip duration. The second correlator is synchronized to m_2. It correlates strongly with m_2, but has low correlation with m_1. Note that if only a single correlator is used in the receiver (see Figure 6.52), once the output of the single correlator is corrupted by fading, the receiver cannot correct the value. Bit decisions based on only a single correlation may produce a large bit error rate. In a RAKE receiver, if the output from one correlator is corrupted by fading, the others may not be, and the corrupted signal may be discounted through the weighting process. Decisions based on the combination of the M separate decision statistics offered by the RAKE provide a form of diversity which can overcome fading and thereby improve CDMA reception.

The M decision statistics are weighted to form an overall decision statistic as shown in Figure 7.16. The outputs of the M correlators are denoted as $Z_1, Z_2, \ldots$ and Z_M. They are weighted by α_1, α_2, ... and α_M, respectively. The weighting coefficients are based on the power or the SNR from each correlator output. If the power or SNR is small out of a particular correlator, it will be assigned a small weighting factor. Just as in the case of a maximal ratio combining diversity scheme, the overall signal Z' is given by

$$Z' = \sum_{m=1}^{M} \alpha_m Z_m \tag{7.79}$$

The weighting coefficients, α_m, are normalized to the output signal power of the correlator in such a way that the coefficients sum to unity, as shown in Equation (7.80)

$$\alpha_m = \frac{Z_m^2}{\sum_{m=1}^{M} Z_m^2} \tag{7.80}$$

As in the case of adaptive equalizers and diversity combining, there are many ways to generate the weighting coefficients. However, due to multiple access interference, RAKE fingers with strong multipath amplitudes will not necessarily provide strong output after correlation. Choosing weighting coefficients based on the actual outputs of the correlators yields better RAKE performance.

7.12 Interleaving

Interleaving is used to obtain time diversity in a digital communications system without adding any overhead. Interleaving has become an extremely useful technique in all second and third generation wireless systems, due to the rapid proliferation of digital speech coders which transform analog voices into efficient digital messages that are transmitted over wireless links (speech coders are presented in Chapter 8).

Because speech coders attempt to represent a wide range of voices in a uniform and efficient digital format, the encoded data bits (called *source bits*) carry a great deal of information, and as explained in Chapters 8 and 11, some source bits are more important than others and must be protected from errors. It is typical for many speech coders to produce several "important" bits in succession, and it is the function of the interleaver to spread these bits out in time so that if there is a deep fade or noise burst, the important bits from a block of source data are not corrupted at the same time. By spreading the source bits over time, it becomes possible to make use of error control coding (called *channel coding*) which protects the source data from corruption by the channel. Since error control codes are designed to protect against channel errors that may occur randomly or in a bursty manner, interleavers scramble the time order of source bits before they are channel coded.

An interleaver can be one of two forms—a block structure or a convolutional structure. A block interleaver formats the encoded data into a rectangular array of m rows and n columns, and interleaves nm bits at a time. Usually, each row contains a word of source data having n bits. An interleaver of degree m (or depth m) consists of m rows. The structure of a block interleaver is shown in Figure 7.17. As seen, source bits are placed into the interleaver by sequentially increasing the row number for each successive bit, and filling the columns. The interleaved source data is then read out row-wise and transmitted over the channel. This has the effect of separating the original source bits by m bit periods.

At the receiver, the de-interleaver stores the received data by sequentially increasing the row number of each successive bit, and then clocks out the data row-wise, one word (row) at a time.

Convolutional interleavers can be used in place of block interleavers in much the same fashion. Convolutional interleavers are ideally suited for use with convolutional codes.

There is an inherent delay associated with an interleaver since the received message block cannot be fully decoded until all of the nm bits arrive at the receiver and are de-interleaved. In practice, human speech is tolerable to listen to until delays of greater than 40 ms occur. It is for this reason that all of the wireless data interleavers have delays which do not exceed 40 ms. The interleaver word size and depth are closely related to the type of speech coder used, the source coding rate, and the maximum tolerable delay.

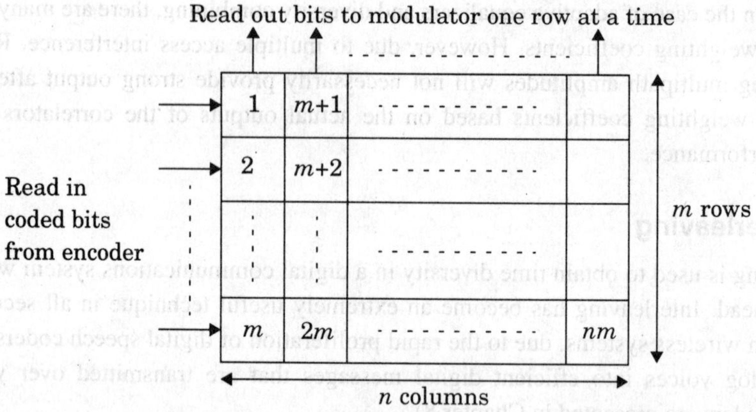

Figure 7.17 Block interleaver where source bits are read into columns and read out as *n*-bit rows.

7.13 Fundamentals of Channel Coding

Channel coding protects digital data from errors by selectively introducing redundancies in the transmitted data. Channel codes that are used to detect errors are called *error detection codes,* while codes that can detect and correct errors are called *error correction codes.*

In 1948, Shannon demonstrated that by proper encoding of the information, errors induced by a noisy channel can be reduced to any desired level without sacrificing the rate of information transfer [Sha48]. Shannon's channel capacity formula is applicable to the AWGN channel and is given by

$$C = B\log_2\left(1 + \frac{P}{N_0 B}\right) = B\log_2\left(1 + \frac{S}{N}\right) \tag{7.81}$$

where C is the channel capacity (bits per second), B is the transmission bandwidth (Hz), P is the received signal power (W), and N_0 is the single-sided noise power density (W/Hz). The received power at a receiver is given as

$$P = E_b R_b \tag{7.82}$$

where E_b is the average bit energy, and R_b is the transmission bit rate. Equation (7.81) can be normalized by the transmission bandwidth and is given by

$$\frac{C}{B} = \log_2\left(1 + \frac{E_b R_b}{N_0 B}\right) \tag{7.83}$$

where C/B denotes *bandwidth efficiency.*

The basic purpose of error detection and error correction techniques is to introduce redundancies in the data to improve wireless link performance. The introduction of redundant bits increases the raw data rate used in the link, and, hence, it increases the bandwidth requirement for a fixed source data rate. This reduces the bandwidth efficiency of the link in high SNR conditions, but provides excellent BER performance at low SNR values.

It is well known that the use of orthogonal signaling allows the probability of error to become arbitrarily small by expanding the signal set, i.e., by making the number of waveforms $M \to \infty$, provided that the SNR per bit exceeds the Shannon limit of $SNR_b \geq -1.6$ dB [Vit79]. In the limit, Shannon's result indicates that extremely wideband signals could be used to achieve error free communications, as long as sufficient SNR exists, and this is partly why wideband CDMA is being adopted for 3G. Error control coding waveforms, on the other hand, have bandwidth expansion factors that grow only linearly with the code block length. Error correction coding thus offers advantages in bandwidth limited applications, and also provides link protection in power limited applications.

A channel coder operates on digital message (source) data by encoding the source information into a code sequence for transmission through the channel. There are three basic types of error correction and detection codes: *block codes*, *convolutional codes*, and *turbo codes*.

7.14 Block Codes and Finite Fields

Block codes are *forward error correction* (FEC) codes that enable a limited number of errors to be detected and corrected without retransmission. Block codes can be used to improve the performance of a communications system when other means of improvement (such as increasing transmitter power or using a more sophisticated demodulator) are impractical.

In block codes, parity bits are added to blocks of message bits to make *codewords* or *code blocks*. In a block encoder, k information bits are encoded into n code bits. A total of $n-k$ redundant bits are added to the k information bits for the purpose of detecting and correcting errors [Lin83]. The block code is referred to as an (n, k) code, and the rate of the code is defined as $R_c = k/n$ and is equal to the rate of information divided by the raw channel rate.

The ability of a block code to correct errors is a function of the *code distance*. Many families of codes exist that provide varying degrees of error protection [Cou93], [Hay94], [Lin83], [Skl93], and [Vit79].

Example 7.5

Interleavers and block codes are typically combined for wireless speech transmission. Consider an interleaver with m rows and n-bit words. Assume each word of the interleaver is actually made up of k source bits and $(n-k)$ bits from a block code. The resulting interleaver/coder combination will break up a burst of channel errors of length $l = mb$ into m bursts of length b.

Thus, an (n,k) code that can handle burst errors of length $b < (n-k)/2$ can be combined with an interleaver of degree m to create an interleaved (mn,mk) block code that can handle bursts of length mb. As long as mb or fewer bits are corrupted during the transmission of the coded speech signal from the interleaver, the received data will be error free.

Besides the code rate, other important parameters are the code distance and the weight of particular codewords. These are defined below.

Distance of a Code — The distance between two codewords is the number of elements in which two codewords C_i and C_j differ

$$d(C_i, C_j) = \sum_{l=1}^{N} C_{i,l} \oplus C_{j,l} \,(modulo\ q) \tag{7.84}$$

where d is the distance between the codewords and q is the total number of possible values of C_i and C_j. The length of each codeword is N elements or characters. If the code used is binary, the distance is known as the *Hamming distance*. The minimum distance d_{min} is the smallest distance for the given codeword set and is given as

$$d_{min} = Min\{d(C_i, C_j)\} \tag{7.85}$$

Weight of a Code — The weight of a codeword of length N is given by the number of nonzero elements in the codeword. For a binary code, the weight is basically the number of 1s in the codeword and is given as

$$w(C_i) = \sum_{l=1}^{N} C_{i,l} \tag{7.86}$$

Properties of Block Codes

Linearity — Suppose C_i and C_j are two codewords in an (n, k) block code. Let α_1 and α_2 be any two elements selected from the alphabet. Then the code is said to be linear if and only if $\alpha_1 C_1 + \alpha_2 C_2$ is also a code word. A linear code must contain the all-zero code word. Consequently, a constant-weight code is nonlinear.

Systematic — A systematic code is one in which the parity bits are appended to the end of the information bits. For an (n, k) code, the first k bits are identical to the information bits, and the remaining $n - k$ bits of each code word are linear combinations of the k information bits.

Cyclic — Cyclic codes are a subset of the class of linear codes, which satisfy the following cyclic shift property: If $C = [c_{n-1}, c_{n-2}, \ldots, c_0]$ is a codeword of a cyclic code, then $[c_{n-2}, c_{n-3}, \ldots, c_0, c_{n-1}]$, obtained by a cyclic shift of the elements of C, is also a code word [Pro89]. In other words, all cyclic shifts of C are code words. From the cyclic property, the codes possess a great deal of structure which is exploited to greatly simplify the encoding and decoding operations.

Encoding and decoding techniques make use of the mathematical constructs know as *finite fields*. Finite fields are algebraic systems that contain a finite set of elements. Addition, subtraction, multiplication, and division of finite field elements are accomplished without leaving the set (i.e., the sum/product of two field elements is a field element). Addition and multiplication must satisfy the commutative, associative, and distributive laws. A formal definition of a finite field is given below:

> Let F be a finite set of elements on which two binary operations—addition and multiplication—are defined. The set F together with the two binary operations is a field if the following conditions are satisfied:
>
> - F is a commutative group under addition. The identity element with respect to addition is called the *zero* element and is denoted by 0.
> - The set of nonzero elements in F is a commutative group under multiplication. The identity element with respect to multiplication is called the *unit* element and is denoted by 1.
> - Multiplication is distributive over addition; that is, for any three elements *a, b,* and *c* in *F*:
>
> $$a \cdot (b + c) = a \cdot b + a \cdot c$$

The *additive inverse* of a field element *a*, denoted by *-a*, is the field element which produces the sum 0 when added to a [so that $a + (-a) = 0$]. The multiplicative inverse of a, denoted by a^{-1}, is the field element which produces the product 1 when multiplied by a [so that $a \cdot a^{-1} = 1$].

Four basic properties of fields can be derived from the definition of a field. They are as follows:

Property I: $a \cdot 0 = 0 = 0 \cdot a$

Property II: For nonzero field elements a and b, $a \cdot b \neq 0$

Property III: $a \cdot b = 0$ and $a \neq 0$ imply $b = 0$

Property IV: $-(a \cdot b) = (-a) \cdot b = a \cdot (-b)$

For any prime number p, there exists a finite field which contains p elements. This prime field is denoted as $GF(p)$ because finite fields are also called *Galois fields*, in honor of their discoverer [Lin83]. It is also possible to extend the prime field $GF(p)$ to a field of p^m elements which is called an *extension field* of $GF(p)$ and is denoted by $GF(p^m)$, where m is a positive integer. Codes with symbols from the binary field $GF(2)$ or its extension field $GF(2^m)$ are most commonly used in digital data transmission and storage systems, since information in these systems is always encoded in binary form in practice.

In binary arithmetic, modulo-2 addition and multiplication are used. This arithmetic is actually equivalent to ordinary arithmetic except that two is considered equal to 0 $(1 + 1 = 2 = 0)$. Note that since 1 + 1 = 0, it follows that 1= –1, and hence for the arithmetic used to generate error control codes, addition is equivalent to subtraction.

Reed–Solomon codes make use of nonbinary fields $GF(2^m)$. These fields have more than two elements and are extensions of the binary field $GF(2) = \{0, 1\}$. The additional elements in the extension field $GF(2^m)$ cannot be 0 or 1, since all of the elements must be unique, so a new symbol α is used to represent the other elements in the field. Each nonzero element can be represented by a power of α.

The multiplication operation "·" for the extension field must be defined so that the remaining elements of the field can be represented as sequence of powers of α. The multiplication operation can be used to produce the *infinite* set of elements F shown below

$$F = \{0, 1, \alpha, \alpha^2, ..., \alpha^j, ...\} = \{0, \alpha^0, \alpha^1, \alpha^2, ..., \alpha^j, ...\} \quad (7.87)$$

To obtain the *finite* set of elements of $GF(2^m)$ from F, a condition must be imposed on F so that it may contain only 2^m elements and is a closed set under multiplication (i.e., multiplication of two field elements is performed without leaving the set). The condition which closes the set of field elements under multiplication is known as the *irreducible polynomial*, and it typically takes the following form [Rhe89]:

$$\alpha^{(2^m - 1)} + 1 = 0 \text{ or equivalently } \alpha^{(2^m - 1)} = 1 = \alpha^0 \quad (7.88)$$

Using the irreducible polynomial of Equation (7.88), any element which has a power greater than $2^m - 2$ can be reduced to an element with a power less than $2^m - 2$ as follows:

$$\alpha^{(2^m + n)} = \alpha^{(2^m - 1)} \cdot \alpha^{n+1} = \alpha^{n+1} \quad (7.89)$$

The sequence of elements F thus becomes the following sequence F^*, whose nonzero terms are closed under multiplication:

$$F^* = \left\{0, 1, \alpha, \alpha^2, ..., \alpha^{2^m - 2}, \alpha^{2^m - 1}, \alpha^{2^m}, ...\right\} \quad (7.90)$$

$$= \left\{0, \alpha^0, \alpha^1, \alpha^2, ..., \alpha^{2^m - 2}, \alpha^0, \alpha, \alpha^2, ...\right\}$$

Take the first 2^m terms of F^* and you have the elements of the finite field $GF(2^m)$ in their *power representation*

$$GF(2^m) = \left\{0, 1, \alpha, \alpha^2, ..., \alpha^{2^m - 2}\right\} = \left\{0, \alpha^0, \alpha, \alpha^2, ..., \alpha^{2^m - 2}\right\} \quad (7.91)$$

It can be shown that each of the 2^m elements of the finite field can be represented as a distinct polynomial of degree $m - 1$ or less (the element 0 is represented by the *zero polynomial*, a polynomial with no nonzero terms) [Rhe89]. Each of the nonzero elements of $GF(2^m)$, can be denoted as a polynomial $a_i(x)$, where at least one of the m coefficients is nonzero

$$\alpha^i = a_i(x) = a_{i,0} + a_{i,1}x + a_{i,2}x^2 + ... + a_{i,m-1}x^{m-1} \quad (7.92)$$

Addition of two elements of the finite field is then defined as the modulo-2 addition of each of the polynomial coefficients of like powers, as shown below

$$\alpha^i + \alpha^j = (a_{i,0} + a_{j,0}) + (a_{i,1} + a_{j,1})x + \dots + (a_{i,m-1} + a_{j,m-1})x^{m-1} \quad (7.93)$$

Thus, $GF(2^m)$ may be constructed, and using Equations (7.92) and (7.93) the polynomial representation for the 2^m elements of the field may be obtained.

7.14.1 Examples of Block Codes

Hamming Codes

Hamming codes were among the first of the nontrivial error correction codes [Ham50]. These codes and their variations have been used for error control in digital communication systems. There are both binary and nonbinary Hamming codes. A binary Hamming code has the property that

$$(n, k) = (2^m - 1, 2^m - 1 - m) \quad (7.94)$$

where k is the number of information bits used to form a n bit codeword, and m is any positive integer. The number of parity symbols are $n - k = m$.

Hadamard Codes

Hadamard codes are obtained by selecting as codewords the rows of a Hadamard matrix. A Hadamard matrix A is a $N \times N$ matrix of 1s and 0s, such that each row differs from any other row in exactly $N/2$ locations. One row contains all zeros with the remainder containing $N/2$ zeros and $N/2$ ones. The minimum distance for these codes is $N/2$.

For $N = 2$, the Hadamard matrix A is

$$A = \begin{bmatrix} 0 & 0 \\ 0 & 1 \end{bmatrix} \quad (7.95)$$

In addition to the special case considered above when $N = 2^m$ (m being a positive integer), Hadamard codes of other block lengths are possible, but the codes are not linear.

Golay Codes

Golay codes are linear binary (23,12) codes with a minimum distance of seven and a error correction capability of three bits [Gol49]. This is a special, one of a kind code in that this is the only nontrivial example of a perfect code. (Hamming codes and some repetition codes are also perfect.) Every codeword lies within distance three of any codeword, thus making maximum likelihood decoding possible.

Cyclic Codes

Cyclic codes are a subset of the class of linear codes which satisfy the cyclic property as discussed before. As a result of this property, these codes possess a considerable amount of structure which can be exploited.

A cyclic code can be generated by using a generator polynomial $g(p)$ of degree $(n-k)$. The generator polynomial of an (n, k) cyclic code is a factor of $p^n + 1$ and has the general form

$$g(p) = p^{n-k} + g_{n-k-1}p^{n-k-1} + \ldots + g_1 p + 1 \tag{7.96}$$

A message polynomial $x(p)$ can also be defined as

$$x(p) = x_{k-1}p^{k-1} + \ldots + x_1 p + x_0 \tag{7.97}$$

where $(x_{k-1}, \ldots, x_0)$ represents the k information bits. The resultant codeword $c(p)$ can be written as

$$c(p) = x(p)g(p) \tag{7.98}$$

where $c(p)$ is a polynomial of degree less than n.

Encoding for a cyclic code is usually performed by a linear feedback shift register based on either the generator or parity polynomial.

BCH Codes

BCH cyclic codes are among the most important block codes, since they exist for a wide range of rates, achieve significant coding gains, and can be implemented even at high speeds [Bos60]. The block length of the codes is $n = 2^m - 1$ for $m \geq 3$, and the number of errors that they can correct is bounded by $t < (2^m - 1)/2$. The binary BCH codes can be generalized to create classes of nonbinary codes which use m bits per code symbol. The most important and common class of nonbinary BCH codes is the family of codes known as Reed–Solomon codes. The (63,47) Reed–Solomon code in US *Cellular Digital Packet Data* (CDPD) uses $m = 6$ bits per code symbol.

Reed–Solomon Codes

Reed–Solomon (RS) are nonbinary codes which are capable of correcting errors which appear in bursts and are commonly used in concatenated coding systems [Ree60]. The block length of these codes is $n = 2^m - 1$. These can be extended to 2^m or $2^m + 1$. The number of parity symbols that must be used to correct e errors is $n - k = 2e$. The minimum distance $d_{min} = 2e + 1$. RS codes achieve the largest possible d_{min} of any linear code.

7.14.2 Case Study: Reed–Solomon Codes for CDPD

For the purpose of explanation, the field choice will be $GF(64)$, since this is the same field used in CDPD systems. CDPD uses $m = 6$, so each of the 64 field elements is represented by a 6 bit symbol. CDPD packets have 282 user bits in a 378 bit block, and eight six-bit symbols (48 bits) may be corrected per block.

A finite field entity $p(X)$ is introduced in order to map the 64 distinct 6-bit symbols to the elements of the field. An irreducible polynomial $p(X)$ of degree m is said to be *primitive* if the smallest integer n for which $p(X)$ divides $X^n + 1$ is $n = 2^m - 1$. This primitive polynomial $p(X)$ is vital for all coding operations as it defines the field and is typically of the form

$$p(X) = 1 + X + X^m \tag{7.99}$$

In the case of the Reed–Solomon code used for CDPD, Equation (7.99) is indeed the form of $p(X)$. Primitive polynomials have been tabulated for a wide range of field sizes, so $p(X)$ is a known quantity and is part of the definition of any code. CDPD's primitive polynomial is

$$p_{CDPD}(X) = 1 + X + X^6 \tag{7.100}$$

In order to map symbols to field elements, set the primitive polynomial $p(\alpha) = 0$. This yields the following result, which closes the set of field elements:

$$\alpha^6 + \alpha + 1 = 0 \tag{7.101}$$

Table 7.2 shows the proper mapping of 6-bit symbols to field elements and this mapping is used to govern all computations. The field elements of Table 7.2 were generated by first starting with the element $1(\alpha^0)$ and then by multiplying by α to obtain the next field element. Any element which contains an α^5 term will yield an α^6 term in the next element, but α^6 is not in $GF(64)$. The primitive polynomial rule is used to convert α^6 to $\alpha + 1$. Also note that $\alpha^{62} \cdot \alpha = \alpha^{63} = \alpha^0 = 1$. This simple result is critical when implementing finite field multiplication in software. Multiplication can be accomplished quickly and efficiently by using modulo $2^m - 1$ addition of the powers of the elemental operands. For the (63, 47) Reed–Solomon code used in CDPD systems, multiplication of two field elements corresponds to adding the powers of the two operands modulo-63 to arrive at the power of the product.

Addition in $GF(2^m)$ corresponds to modulo-2 adding the coefficients of the polynomial representation of the elements. Since the coefficients are either 1s or 0s (because the field is an extension of the binary field $GF(2)$), this can simply be implemented with the bit-wise exclusive-OR of the 6-bit symbol representation of the elemental operands. Some examples of finite field addition in $GF(64)$ are shown below:

$$\alpha^{27} + \alpha^5 = (001110)_2 XOR(100000)_2 = (101110)_2 = \alpha^{55} \tag{7.102.a}$$

$$\alpha^{19} + \alpha^{62} = (011110)_2 XOR(100001)_2 = (111111)_2 = \alpha^{58} \tag{7.102.b}$$

7.14.2.1 Reed–Solomon Encoding

In the discussion of a Reed–Solomon encoder, the following polynomials are used frequently:

$d(x)$: raw information polynomial

$p(x)$: parity polynomial

$c(x)$: codeword polynomial

$g(x)$: generator polynomial

$q(x)$: quotient polynomial

$r(x)$: remainder polynomial

Table 7.2 Three Representations of the Elements of GF(64) for CDPD

Power Representation	Polynomial Representation						6-Bit Symbol Representation					
$0=\alpha^{63}$						0	0	0	0	0	0	0
$1=\alpha^{0}$						1	0	0	0	0	0	1
α					x^1		0	0	0	0	1	0
α^2				x^2			0	0	0	1	0	0
α^3			x^3				0	0	1	0	0	0
α^4		x^4					0	1	0	0	0	0
α^5	x^5						1	0	0	0	0	0
α^6					x^1	1	0	0	0	0	1	1
α^7				x^2	x^1		0	0	0	1	1	0
α^8			x^3	x^2			0	0	1	1	0	0
α^9		x^4	x^3				0	1	1	0	0	0
α^{10}	x^5	x^4					1	1	0	0	0	0
α^{11}	x^5				x^1	1	1	0	0	0	1	1
α^{12}				x^2		1	0	0	0	1	0	1
α^{13}			x^3		x^1		0	0	1	0	1	0
α^{14}		x^4		x^2			0	1	0	1	0	0
α^{15}	x^5		x^3				1	0	1	0	0	0
α^{16}		x^4			x^1	1	0	1	0	0	1	1
α^{17}	x^5			x^2	x^1		1	0	0	1	1	0
α^{18}			x^3	x^2	x^1	1	0	0	1	1	1	1
α^{19}		x^4	x^3	x^2	x^1		0	1	1	1	1	0
α^{20}	x^5	x^4	x^3	x^2			1	1	1	1	0	0
α^{21}	x^5	x^4	x^3		x^1	1	1	1	1	0	1	1
α^{22}	x^5	x^4		x^2		1	1	1	0	1	0	1
α^{23}	x^5		x^3			1	1	0	1	0	0	1
α^{24}		x^4				1	0	1	0	0	0	1
α^{25}	x^5				x^1		1	0	0	0	1	0
α^{26}				x^2	x^1	1	0	0	0	1	1	1
α^{27}			x^3	x^2	x^1		0	0	1	1	1	0
α^{28}		x^4	x^3	x^2			0	1	1	1	0	0
α^{29}	x^5	x^4	x^3				1	1	1	0	0	0
α^{30}	x^5	x^4			x^1	1	1	1	0	0	1	1
α^{31}	x^5			x^2		1	1	0	0	1	0	1
α^{32}			x^3			1	0	0	1	0	0	1
α^{33}		x^4			x^1		0	1	0	0	1	0
α^{34}	x^5			x^2			1	0	0	1	0	0
α^{35}			x^3		x^1	1	0	0	1	0	1	1
α^{36}		x^4		x^2	x^1		0	1	0	1	1	0
α^{37}	x^5		x^3	x^2			1	0	1	1	0	0
α^{38}		x^4	x^3		x^1	1	0	1	1	0	1	1
α^{39}	x^5	x^4		x^2	x^1		1	1	0	1	1	0
α^{40}	x^5		x^3	x^2	x^1	1	1	0	1	1	1	1
α^{41}		x^4	x^3	x^2		1	0	1	1	1	0	1
α^{42}	x^5	x^4	x^3		x^1		1	1	1	0	1	0
α^{43}	x^5	x^4		x^2	x^1	1	1	1	0	1	1	1
α^{44}	x^5		x^3	x^2		1	1	0	1	1	0	1
α^{45}		x^4	x^3			1	0	1	1	0	0	1
α^{46}	x^5	x^4			x^1		1	1	0	0	1	0
α^{47}	x^5			x^2	x^1	1	1	0	0	1	1	1
α^{48}			x^3	x^2		1	0	0	1	1	0	1
α^{49}		x^4	x^3		x^1		0	1	1	0	1	0
α^{50}	x^5	x^4		x^2			1	1	0	1	0	0
α^{51}	x^5		x^3		x^1	1	1	0	1	0	1	1
α^{52}		x^4		x^2		1	0	1	0	1	0	1
α^{53}	x^5		x^3		x^1		1	0	1	0	1	0
α^{54}		x^4		x^2	x^1	1	0	1	0	1	1	1
α^{55}	x^5		x^3	x^2	x^1		1	0	1	1	1	0
α^{56}		x^4	x^3	x^2	x^1	1	0	1	1	1	1	1
α^{57}	x^5	x^4	x^3	x^2	x^1		1	1	1	1	1	0
α^{58}	x^5	x^4	x^3	x^2	x^1	1	1	1	1	1	1	1
α^{59}	x^5	x^4	x^3	x^2		1	1	1	1	1	0	1
α^{60}	x^5	x^4	x^3			1	1	1	1	0	0	1
α^{61}	x^5	x^4				1	1	1	0	0	0	1
α^{62}	x^5					1	1	0	0	0	0	1

Let

$$d(x) = c_{n-1}x^{n-1} + c_{n-2}x^{n-2} + ... + c_{2t+1}x^{2t+1} + c_{2t}x^{2t} \quad (7.103)$$

be the information polynomial which is received before decoding and represents the user data, and let

$$p(x) = c_0 + c_1x + ... + c_{2t-1}x^{2t-1} \quad (7.104)$$

be the parity polynomial (c_i are all elements of *GF(64)*). The encoded RS polynomial can thus be expressed as

$$c(x) = d(x) + p(x) = \sum_{i=0}^{n-1} c_i x^i \quad (7.105)$$

A vector of n field elements $(c_0, c_1, ..., c_{n-1})$ is a codeword if and only if it is a multiple of the generator polynomial *g*(*x*). The generator polynomial for a t-error, correcting, Reed–Solomon code has the form

$$g(x) = (x + \alpha)(x + \alpha^2).....(x + \alpha^{2t}) = \sum_{i=0}^{2t} g_i x^i \quad (7.106)$$

A common method for encoding a cyclic code like an RS code is to derive $p(x)$ by dividing $d(x)$ by *g*(*x*). This yields an irrelevant quotient polynomial $q(x)$ and an important polynomial $r(x)$ as follows:

$$d(x) = g(x)q(x) + r(x) \quad (7.107)$$

Thus, using Equation (7.105), the codeword polynomial can be expressed as

$$c(x) = p(x) + g(x)q(x) + r(x) \quad (7.108)$$

If the parity polynomial is defined as being equal to the negatives of the coefficients of $r(x)$, then it follows that

$$c(x) = g(x)q(x) \quad (7.109)$$

Thus, by ensuring that the codeword polynomial is a multiple of the generator polynomial, a Reed–Solomon encoder can be constructed by using Equation (7.108) to obtain *p*(*X*). The key to encoding and decoding is to find $r(x)$, the remainder polynomial, which maps to the transmitted data. A straightforward method of obtaining the remainder from the division process by using the monic polynomial $g(x)$ is to connect a shift register according to $g(x)$ as shown in Figure 7.18. Each "+" represents an exclusive-OR of two *m*-bit numbers, each *X* represents a multiplication of two *m*-bit numbers under $GF(2^m)$, where each *m*-bit register contains an *m*-bit number denoted by b_i.

Initially, all registers are set to 0, and the switch is set to the data position. Code symbols c_{n-1} through c_{n-k} are sequentially shifted into the circuit and simultaneously transmitted to the output line. As soon as code symbol c_{n-k} enters the circuit, the switch is flipped to the parity

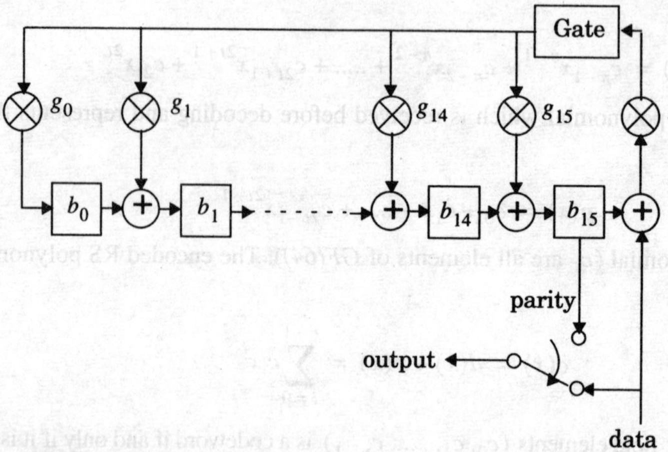

Figure 7.18 Reed–Solomon encoding circuit.

position, and the gate to the feedback network is opened so that no further feedback is provided. At that same instant, the registers b_0 through b_{2t-1} contain the parity symbols p_0 through p_{2t-1}, which correspond directly to the coefficients of the parity polynomial. They can be sequentially shifted to the output to complete the Reed–Solomon encoding process.

7.14.2.2 Reed–Solomon Decoding

Suppose that a codeword

$$c(x) = v_0 + v_1 x + \dots + v_{n-1} x^{n-1} \tag{7.110}$$

is transmitted and that channel errors result in the received codeword

$$r(x) = r_0 + r_1 x + \dots + r_{n-1} x^{n-1} \tag{7.111}$$

The error pattern $e(x)$ is the difference between $c(x)$ and $r(x)$. Using Equations (7.110) and (7.111),

$$e(x) = r(x) - c(x) = e_0 + e_1 x + \dots + e_{n-1} x^{n-1} \tag{7.112}$$

Let the $2t$ *partial syndromes* S_i, $1 < i \le 2t$, be defined as $S_i = r(\alpha^i)$. Since $\alpha^1, \alpha^2, \dots, \alpha^{2t}$ are roots of each transmitted codeword $c(x)$ (because each codeword is a multiple of the generator polynomial $g(x)$), it follows that $c(\alpha^i) = 0$ and $S_i = c(\alpha^i) + e(\alpha^i) = e(\alpha^i)$. Thus, it is clear that the $2t$ partial syndromes S_i depend only on the error pattern $e(x)$ and not on the specific received codeword $r(x)$.

Suppose the error pattern contains k errors ($k \le t$) at locations $x^{j_1}, x^{j_2}, \ldots, x^{j_k}$, where $0 \le j_1 < j_2 < \ldots < j_k < n-1$. Let the error magnitude at each location x^{j_i} be denoted as e_{j_i}. Then $e(x)$ has the form

$$e(x) = e_{j_1}x^{j_1} + e_{j_2}x^{j_2} + \ldots + e_{j_k}x^{j_k} \tag{7.113}$$

Define the set of error locator numbers $\beta_i = \alpha^{j_i}$, $i = 1, 2, \ldots, k$. Then the set of $2t$ partial syndromes yields the following system of equations:

$$S_1 = e_{j_1}\beta_1 + e_{j_2}\beta_2 + \ldots + e_{j_k}\beta_k \tag{7.114.a}$$

$$S_2 = e_{j_1}\beta_1^2 + e_{j_2}\beta_2^2 + \ldots + e_{j_k}\beta_k^2 \tag{7.114.b}$$

$$\ldots\ldots\ldots$$

$$S_{2t} = e_{j_1}\beta_1^{2t} + e_{j_2}\beta_2^{2t} + \ldots + e_{j_k}\beta_k^{2t} \tag{7.114.c}$$

Any algorithm which solves this system of equations is a Reed–Solomon decoding algorithm. The error magnitudes e_{j_i} are found directly, and the error locations x^{j_i} can be determined from β_i.

Reed–Solomon decoders can be implemented in hardware, software, or a mix of hardware and software. Hardware implementations are typically very fast, but they cannot be used for a wide variety of Reed–Solomon code sizes. For example, there are several single-chip, Reed–Solomon decoders available which decode codes commonly used in satellite communications, digital video applications, and compact disk technology. Hardware decoders can operate at speeds in excess of 50 Mbits per second, but specific hardware solutions operate with specific symbol definitions, such as 8-bit or 9-bit symbols from $GF(255)$, whereas the (63, 47) Reed–Solomon code used in CDPD systems operates with a 6-bit symbol. Since CDPD operates at a slow data rate of 19.2 kbps, a real-time software implementation of a $(63, 47)$ Reed–Solomon decoder can be achieved. A software approach may be more attractive to a modem developer, because it will have a shorter development time, lower development cost, and greater flexibility.

A typical Reed–Solomon decoder uses five distinct algorithms. The first algorithm calculates the $2t$ partial syndromes S_i. The second step in the RS decoding process is the Berlekamp–Massey algorithm, which calculates the error locator polynomial $\sigma(x)$. This polynomial is a function of the error locations in the received codeword $r(x)$, but it does not directly indicate which symbols of the received codeword are in error. A Chien search algorithm is then used to calculate these specific error locations from the error locator polynomial. The fourth step in the decoding process is the calculation of the magnitude of the error at each location. Finally, knowing both the error locations in the received codeword and the magnitude of the error at each location, an error correction algorithm may be implemented to correct up to t errors successfully [Rhe89].

Syndrome Calculation

The syndrome of a cyclic code is typically defined as the remainder obtained by dividing the received codeword $r(x)$ by the generator polynomial $g(x)$. However, for Reed–Solomon codes, $2t$ *partial syndromes* are computed. Each partial syndrome S_i is defined as the remainder obtained when dividing the received codeword $r(x)$ by $x + \alpha^i$

$$S_i = rem\left[\frac{r(x)}{x+\alpha^i}\right], \ i = 1, 2, ..., 2t \tag{7.115}$$

The division of two polynomials results in a quotient polynomial $q(x)$ and a remainder polynomial $rem(x)$. The degree of the remainder $rem(x)$ must be less than the degree of the dividing polynomial $p(x)$. Thus, if $p(x)$ has degree 1 (i.e., $p(x) = x + \alpha^i$), $rem(x)$ must have degree 0. In other words, $rem(x)$ is simply a field element and can be denoted as rem. Thus, the determination of the $2t$ partial syndromes begins with the calculation

$$\frac{r(x)}{x+\alpha^i} = q(x) + \frac{rem}{x+\alpha^i} \tag{7.116}$$

Rearranging the above equation yields

$$r(x) = q(x)\cdot(x+\alpha^i) + rem \tag{7.117}$$

Letting $x = \alpha^i$,

$$\begin{aligned} r(\alpha^i) &= q(\alpha^i)\cdot(\alpha^i+\alpha^i) + rem \\ &= rem = S_i \end{aligned} \tag{7.118}$$

Thus, the calculation of the $2t$ partial syndromes S_i can be simplified from a full-blown polynomial division (which is computationally intense) to merely evaluating the received polynomial $r(x)$ at $x = \alpha^i$ [Rhe89]:

$$S_i = r(\alpha^i), \ i = 1, 2, ..., 2t \tag{7.119}$$

where

$$r(x) = r_0 + r_1 x + ... + r_{n-1}x^{n-1} \tag{7.120}$$

Thus, $r(\alpha^i)$ has the form

$$r(\alpha^i) = r_0 + r_1\alpha^i + r_2\alpha^{2i} + ... + r_{n-1}\alpha^{(n-1)i} \tag{7.121}$$

The evaluation of $r(\alpha^i)$ can be implemented very efficiently in software by arranging the function so that it has the following form

$$r(\alpha^i) = (.....((r_{n-1}\alpha^i + r_{n-2})\alpha^i + r_{n-3})\alpha^i + ...)\alpha^i + r_0 \tag{7.122}$$

Error Locator Polynomial Calculation

The Reed–Solomon decoding process is simply any implementation which solves Equations (7.114.a) through (7.114.c). These $2t$ equations are symmetric function in $\beta_1, \beta_2, \ldots, \beta_k$, known as *power-sum symmetric functions*. We now define the polynomial

$$\sigma(x) = (1+\beta_1 x)(1+\beta_2 x)\ldots(1+\beta_k x) = \sigma_0 + \sigma_1 x + \ldots + \sigma_k x^k \tag{7.123}$$

The roots of $\sigma(x)$ are $\beta_1^{-1}, \beta_2^{-1}, \ldots, \beta_k^{-1}$, which are the inverses of the error location numbers β_i. Thus, $\sigma(x)$ is called the *error locator polynomial* because it indirectly contains the exact locations of each of the errors in $r(x)$. Note that $\sigma(x)$ is an unknown polynomial whose coefficients must also be determined during the Reed–Solomon decoding process.

The coefficients of $\sigma(x)$ and the error-location numbers β_i are related by the following equations

$$\sigma_0 = 1 \tag{7.124.a}$$

$$\sigma_1 = \beta_1 + \beta_2 + \ldots + \beta_k \tag{7.124.b}$$

$$\sigma_2 = \beta_1\beta_2 + \beta_2\beta_3 + \ldots + \beta_{k-1}\beta_k \tag{7.124.c}$$

$$\ldots\ldots$$

$$\sigma_k = \beta_1\beta_2\beta_3\ldots\beta_k \tag{7.124.d}$$

The unknown quantities σ_i and β_i can be related to the known partial syndromes S_j by the following set of equations known as *Newton's Identities*.

$$S_1 + \sigma_1 = 0 \tag{7.125.a}$$

$$S_2 + \sigma_1 S_1 + 2\sigma_2 = 0 \tag{7.125.b}$$

$$S_3 + \sigma_2 S_2 + \sigma_1 S_1 + 3\sigma_3 = 0 \tag{7.125.c}$$

$$S_k + \sigma_1 S_{k-1} + \ldots + \sigma_{k-1} S_1 + k\sigma_k = 0 \tag{7.125.d}$$

The most common method for determining $\sigma(x)$ is the Berlekamp–Massey algorithm [Lin83].

7.15 Convolutional Codes

Convolutional codes are fundamentally different from block codes in that information sequences are not grouped into distinct blocks and encoded [Vit79]. Instead a continuous sequence of information bits is mapped into a continuous sequence of encoder output bits. This mapping is highly structured, enabling a decoding method considerably different from that of block codes to be employed. It can be argued that convolutional coding can achieve a larger coding gain than can be achieved using a block coding with the same complexity.

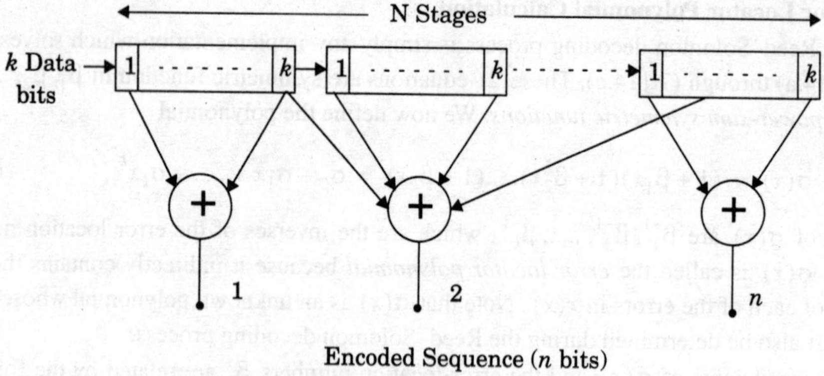

Figure 7.19 General block diagram of convolutional encoder.

A convolutional code is generated by passing the information sequence through a finite state shift register. In general, the shift register contains N k-bit stages and m linear algebraic function generators based on the generator polynomials as shown in Figure 7.19. The input data is shifted into and along the shift register, k bits at a time. The number of output bits for each k bit user input data sequence is n bits. The code rate $R_c = k/n$. The parameter N is called the *constraint length* and indicates the number of input data bits that the current output is dependent upon. The constraint length determines how powerful and complex the code is. Following is an outline of the various ways of representing convolutional codes.

Generator Matrix — The generator matrix for a convolutional code can define the code and is semi-infinite since the input is semi-infinite in length. Hence, this is not a convenient way of representing a convolutional code.

Generator Polynomials — For convolutional codes, we specify a set of n vectors, one for each of the n modulo-2 adders used. Each vector of dimension $2k$ indicates the connection of the encoder to that modulo-2 adder. A 1 in the ith position of the vector indicates that the corresponding shift register stage is connected and a 0 indicates no connection.

Logic Table — A logic table or lookup table can be built showing the outputs of the convolutional encoder and the state of the encoder for all of the specific input sequences present in the shift register.

State Diagram — Since the output of the encoder is determined by the input and the current state of the encoder, a state diagram can be used to represent the encoding process. The state diagram is simply a graph of the possible states of the encoder and the possible transitions from one state to another.

Tree Diagram — The tree diagram shows the structure of the encoder in the form of a tree with the branches representing the various states and the outputs of the coder.

Trellis Diagram — Close observation of the tree reveals that the structure repeats itself once the number of stages is greater than the constraint length. It is observed that all branches emanating from two nodes having the same state are identical in the sense that they generate identical output sequences. This means that the two nodes having the same label can be merged. By doing this throughout the tree diagram, we can obtain another diagram called a *trellis diagram* which is a more compact representation.

7.15.1 Decoding of Convolutional Codes

The function of the decoder is to estimate the encoded input information using a rule or method that results in the minimum possible number of errors. There is a one-to-one correspondence between the information sequence and the code sequence. Further, any information and code sequence pair is uniquely associated with a path through the trellis. Thus, the job of the convolutional decoder is to estimate the path through the trellis that was followed by the encoder.

There are a number of techniques for decoding convolutional codes. The most important of these methods is the Viterbi algorithm which performs *maximum likelihood decoding* of convolutional codes. The algorithm was first described by A. J. Viterbi [Vit67], [For78]. Both *hard* and *soft decision* decoding can be implemented for *convolutional codes*. Soft decision decoding is superior by about 2–3 dB.

7.15.1.1 The Viterbi Algorithm

The Viterbi algorithm can be described as follows:

Let the trellis node corresponding to state S_j at time i be denoted $S_{j,i}$. Each node in the trellis is to be assigned a value $V(S_{j,i})$ based on a metric. The node values are computed in the following manner.

1. Set $V(S_{0,0}) = 0$ and $i = 1$.
2. At time i, compute the partial path metrics for all paths entering each node.
3. Set $V(S_{j,i})$ equal to the smallest partial path metric entering the node corresponding to state S_j at time i. Ties can be broken by previous node choosing a path randomly. The nonsurviving branches are deleted from the trellis. In this manner, a group of minimum paths is created from $S_{0,0}$.
4. If $i < L + m$, where L is the number of input code segments (k bits for each segment) and m is the length of the longest shift register in the encoder, let $i = i + 1$ and go back to step 2.

Once all node values have been computed, start at state S_0, time $i = L + m$, and follow the surviving branches backward through the trellis. The path thus defined is unique and corresponds to the decoded output. When hard decision decoding is performed, the metric used is the Hamming distance, while the Euclidean distance is used for soft decision decoding.

7.15.1.2 Other Decoding Algorithms for Convolutional Codes

Fano's Sequential Decoding

Fano's algorithm searches for the most probable path through the trellis by examining one path at a time [Fan63]. The increment added to the metric along each branch is proportional to the probability of the received signal for that branch, as in Viterbi decoding, with the exception that an additional negative constant is added to each branch metric. The value of this constant is selected such that the metric for the correct path will increase on the average while the metric for any incorrect path will decrease on the average. By comparing the metric of a candidate path with an increasing threshold, the algorithm detects and discards incorrect paths. The error rate performance of the Fano algorithm is comparable to that of Viterbi decoding. However, in comparison to Viterbi decoding, sequential decoding has a significantly larger delay. Its advantage over Viterbi decoding is that it requires less storage, and thus codes with larger constraint lengths can be employed.

The Stack Algorithm

In contrast to the Viterbi algorithm which keeps track of $2^{(N-1)k}$ paths and their corresponding metrics, the *stack algorithm* deals with fewer paths and their corresponding metrics. In a stack algorithm, the more probable paths are ordered according to their metrics, with the path at the top of the stack having the largest metric. At each step of the algorithm, only the path at the top of the stack is extended by one branch. This yields 2^k successors and their metrics. These 2^k successors along with the other paths are then reordered according to the values of the metrics, and all paths with metrics that fall below some preselected amount from the metric of the top path may be discarded. Then the process of extending the path with the largest metric is repeated. In comparison with Viterbi decoding, the stack algorithm requires fewer metric calculations, but this computational savings is offset to a large extent by the computations involved in reordering the stack after every iteration. In comparison with the *Fano algorithm*, the stack algorithm is computationally simpler since there is no retracing over the same path, but on the other hand, the stack algorithm requires more storage than the Fano algorithm.

Feedback Decoding

Here, the decoder makes a hard decision on the information bit at stage j based on the metrics computed from stage j to stage $j+m$, where m is a preselected positive integer. Thus, the decision on whether the information bit was a 1 or a 0 depends on whether the minimum *Hamming distance* path which begins at stage j and ends at stage $j+m$ contains a 0 or 1 in the branch emanating from stage j. Once a decision is made, only that part of the tree which stems from the bit selected at stage j is kept and the remainder is discarded. This is the feedback feature of the decoder. The next step is to extend the part of the tree that has survived to stage $j+1+m$ and to consider the paths from stage $j+1$ to $j+1+m$ in deciding on the bit at stage $j+1$. This procedure is repeated at every stage. The parameter m is simply the number of stages in the tree that the decoder looks ahead before making a hard decision. Instead of computing the metrics, the feedback decoder can be implemented by computing the syndrome from the received sequence and using a table look up method to correct errors. For some convolutional codes, the feedback decoder can be simplified to a majority logic decoder or a threshold decoder.

7.16 Coding Gain

The advantage of error control codes, whether they be block codes or convolutional codes, is that they provide a *coding gain* for the communications link. The coding gain describes how much better the user's decoded message performs as compared to the raw bit error performance of the coded transmission within the channel. Coding gain is what allows a channel error rate of 10^{-2} to support decoded user data rates which are 10^{-5} or better.

Each error control code has a particular coding gain, which depends on the particular code, the decoder implementation, and the channel BER probability, P_c. It can be shown that a good approximation for the decoded message error probability, P_B is given by

$$P_B \cong \frac{1}{n} \sum_{i=t+1}^{n} i \binom{n}{i} P_c^i (1-P_c)^{n-i} \qquad (7.126)$$

where t denotes the number of errors that can be corrected in an (n,k) block code. Thus, given a known channel BER, it is possible to determine the user's decoded message error rate easily. The coding gain measures the amount of additional SNR that would be required to provide the same BER performance for an uncoded message signal in the same channel conditions.

Example 7.6

Equalization

The IS-136 USDC standard specifies the use of decision feedback equalizers (DFEs).

Diversity

1. The US AMPS system makes use of spatial selection diversity.
2. The PACS standard specifies the use of antenna diversity for base stations and portable units.

Channel Coding

1. The IS-95 standard as proposed makes use of a rate 1/3, constraint length $L = 9$ convolutional code with block interleaving. The interleaver used is a 32*18 block interleaver.
2. The AMPS system makes use of a (40,28) BCH code for the forward control channel and a (48,30) BCH code for the reverse control channel.

Equalization, diversity, and channel coding, as discussed, have the same goal of improving the reliability and quality of the communication service over small-scale channel changes. Each technique has its own advantages and disadvantages. The tradeoffs to be considered are those of complexity/power/cost versus system performance. Each technique is capable of improving system performance significantly.

7.17 Trellis Coded Modulation

Trellis coded modulation (TCM) is a technique which combines both coding and modulation to achieve significant coding gains without compromising bandwidth efficiency [Ung87]. TCM schemes employ redundant nonbinary modulation in combination with a finite state encoder which decides the selection of modulation signals to generate coded signal sequences. TCM uses signal set expansion to provide redundancy for coding and to design coding and signal mapping functions jointly so as to maximize directly the free distance (minimum Euclidean distance) between the coded signals. In the receiver, the signals are decoded by a soft decision maximum likelihood sequence decoder. Coding gains as large as 6 dB can be obtained without any bandwidth expansion or reduction in the effective information rate.

7.18 Turbo Codes

An exciting new family of codes, called turbo codes, have been found recently and are being incorporated in 3G wireless standards. Turbo codes combine the capabilities of convolutional codes with channel estimation theory, and can be thought of as nested or parallel convolutional codes. When implemented properly, turbo codes allow coding gains which are far superior to all previous error correcting codes and allow a wireless communications link to come amazingly close to realizing the Shannon capacity bound. However, this level of performance requires a receiver that can determine the instantaneous SNR of the link. Turbo codes are beyond the scope of this text, but many books and papers have been written about them since their discovery in 1993. The original concepts of turbo codes were first presented in [Ber93].

7.19 Problems

7.1 Use identical notation described in Section 7.3, except now let $d_k = \sum_{n=0}^{N} w_{nk} y_{nk}$, and verify that the MSE is identical for the multiple input linear filter shown in Figure P7.1 (this structure is used for maximal ratio combining diversity, RAKE receivers, and adaptive antennas).

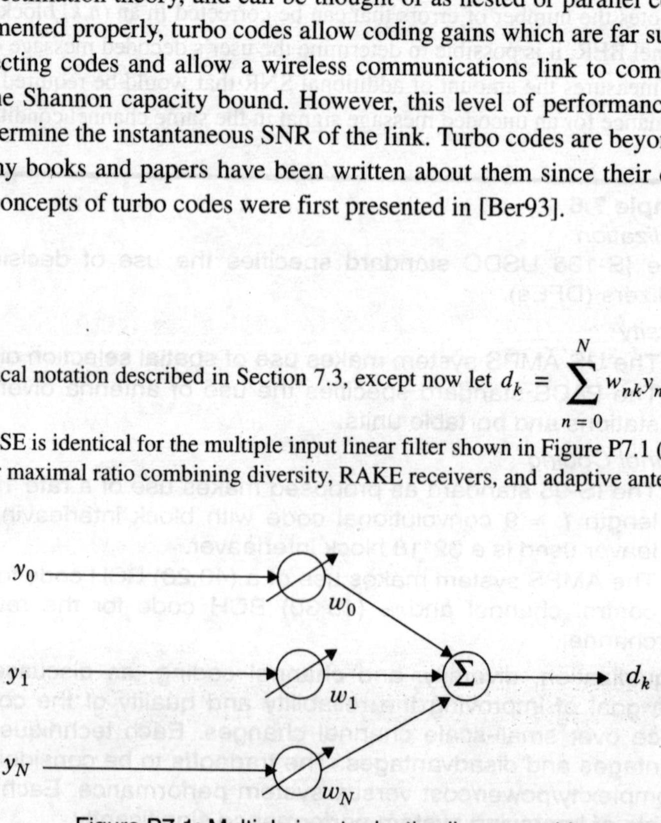

Figure P7.1: Multiple input adaptive linear combiner.

7.2 Consider the two-tap adaptive equalizer shown in Figure P7.2.

(a) Find an expression for MSE in terms of w_0, w_1, and N.

(b) If $N > 2$, find the minimum MSE.

(c) If $w_0 = 0$, $w_1 = -2$, and $N = 4$ samples/cycle, what is the MSE?

(d) For parameters in (c), what is the MSE if $d_k = 2\sin(2\pi k/N)$?

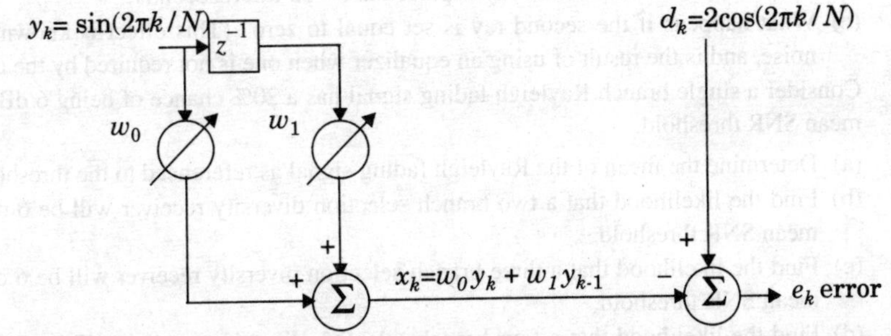

Figure P7.2: A two-tap adaptive linear equalizer.

7.3 For the equalizer in Figure P7.2, what weight values will produce a rms value of $\varepsilon_k = 2$? Assume $N = 5$, and express your answer in terms of w_0 and w_1.

7.4 If a digital signal processing chip can perform one million multiplications per second, determine the time required between each iteration for the following adaptive equalizer algorithms.

(a) LMS

(b) Kalman RLS

(c) Square root RLS DFE

(d) Gradient lattice DFE

7.5 Suppose a quick rule of thumb is that an RLS algorithm requires 50 iterations to converge, whereas the LMS algorithm requires 1000 iterations. For a DSP chip that performs 25 million multiplications per second, determine the maximum symbol rate and maximum time interval before retraining if a five tap equalizer requires 10% transmission overhead, and the following Doppler spreads are found in a 1900 MHz channel. In cases where 25 million multiplications per second is not fast enough, determine the minimum DSP multiplications per second required for each equalizer implementation and compare maximum symbol rates for a fixed number of multiplications per second.

(a) 100 Hz

(b) 1000 Hz

(c) 10,000 Hz

(Hint: Consider the coherence time and its impact on equalizer training.)

7.6 Use computer simulation to implement a two stage (three tap) LMS equalizer based on the circuit shown in Figure 7.2. Assume each delay element offers 10 microseconds of delay, and the transmitted baseband signal $x(t)$ is a rectangular binary pulse train of alternating 1s and 0s, where each pulse has a duration of 10 microseconds. Assume that $x(t)$ passes through a time dispersive channel before being applied to the equalizer. If the channel is a stationary two-ray channel, with equal amplitude impulses at $t = 0$ and $t = 15$ microseconds, use Equations (7.35)–(7.37) to verify that the original $x(t)$ can be recreated by the equalizer. Use pulses with raised cosine rolloff with $\alpha = 1$.

(a) Provide graphical data illustrating the equalizer converges.
(b) Plot the MMSE as a function of the number of iterations.
(c) How many iterations are required to obtain convergence?
(d) What happens if the second ray is placed at $t = 25$ microseconds?
(e) What happens if the second ray is set equal to zero? (This effect is known as equalizer noise, and is the result of using an equalizer when one is not required by the channel.)

7.7 Consider a single branch Rayleigh fading signal has a 20% chance of being 6 dB below some mean SNR threshold.

(a) Determine the mean of the Rayleigh fading signal as referenced to the threshold.
(b) Find the likelihood that a two branch selection diversity receiver will be 6 dB below the mean SNR threshold.
(c) Find the likelihood that a three branch selection diversity receiver will be 6 dB below the mean SNR threshold.
(d) Find the likelihood that a four branch selection diversity receiver will be 6 dB below the mean SNR threshold.
(e) Based on your answers above, is there a law of diminishing returns when diversity is used?

7.8 Using computer simulation, reconstruct Figure 7.11 which illustrates the improvements offered by selection diversity.

7.9 Prove that the maximal ratio combining results in Equations (7.66)–(7.69) are accurate, and plot the probability distributions of $SNR = \gamma_M$ as a function of γ/Γ for one-, two-, three-, and four-branch diversity.

7.10 Compare $\bar{\gamma}/\Gamma$ (selection diversity) with γ_M/Γ (maximal ratio combining) for one to six branches. Specifically, compare how the average SNR increases for each diversity scheme as a new branch is added. Does this make sense? What is the average SNR improvement offered by six-branch maximal ratio combining as compared to six-branch selection diversity? If $\gamma/\Gamma = 0.01$, determine the probability that the received signal will be below this threshold for maximal ratio combining and selection diversity (assume six branches are used). How does this compare with a single Rayleigh fading channel with the same threshold?

7.11 Extending the diversity concepts in this chapter and using the flat fading BER analysis of Chapter 6, it is possible to determine the BER for a wide range of modulation techniques when selection diversity is applied.
Define γ_0 as the required E_b/N_0 to achieve a specific BER = y in a Rayleigh flat-fading channel, and let γ denote the random SNR due to fading. Furthermore let $P(\gamma)$ denote a function that describes the BER for a particular modulation when the $SNR = \gamma$. It follows:

$$y = Pr[P(\gamma) > x] = Pr[\gamma < P^{-1}(x)] = 1 - e^{(-P^{-1}(x))/\gamma_0}$$

(a) Find an expression that solves γ_0 in terms of $P^{-1}(x)$ and y.
(b) When M uncorrelated fading branches are used for diversity selection, write a new expression for y.
(c) Determine the required average E_b/N_0 for BPSK in order to sustain a 10^{-3} BER in a Rayleigh fading channel.
(d) When four branch diversity is used, determine the required average E_b/N_0 for BPSK in order to sustain a 10^{-3} BER in a Rayleigh fading channel.

CHAPTER 8

Speech Coding

Speech coders have assumed considerable importance in communication systems as their performance, to a large extent, determines the quality of the recovered speech and the capacity of the system. In wireless communication systems, bandwidth is a precious commodity, and service providers are continuously met with the challenge of accommodating more users within a limited allocated bandwidth. Low bit-rate speech coding offers a way to meet this challenge. The lower the bit rate at which the coder can deliver toll-quality speech, the more speech channels can be compressed within a given bandwidth. For this reason, manufacturers and service providers are continuously in search of speech coders that will provide toll quality speech at lower bit rates. All 2G wireless standards, in fact, were designed so that their common air interfaces instantly support twice the number of users on a single radio channel as soon as speech coders allow toll-quality speech using half the rate of the original specification.

8.1 Introduction

In mobile communication systems, the design and subjective test of speech coders has been extremely difficult. Without low data rate speech coding, digital modulation schemes offer little in the way of spectral efficiency for voice traffic. To make speech coding practical, implementations must consume little power and provide tolerable, if not excellent, speech quality.

The goal of all speech coding systems is to transmit speech with the highest possible quality using the least possible channel capacity. This has to be accomplished while maintaining certain required levels of complexity of implementation and communication delay. In general, there is a positive correlation between coder bit-rate efficiency and the algorithmic complexity required to achieve it. The more complex an algorithm is, the more its processing delay and cost

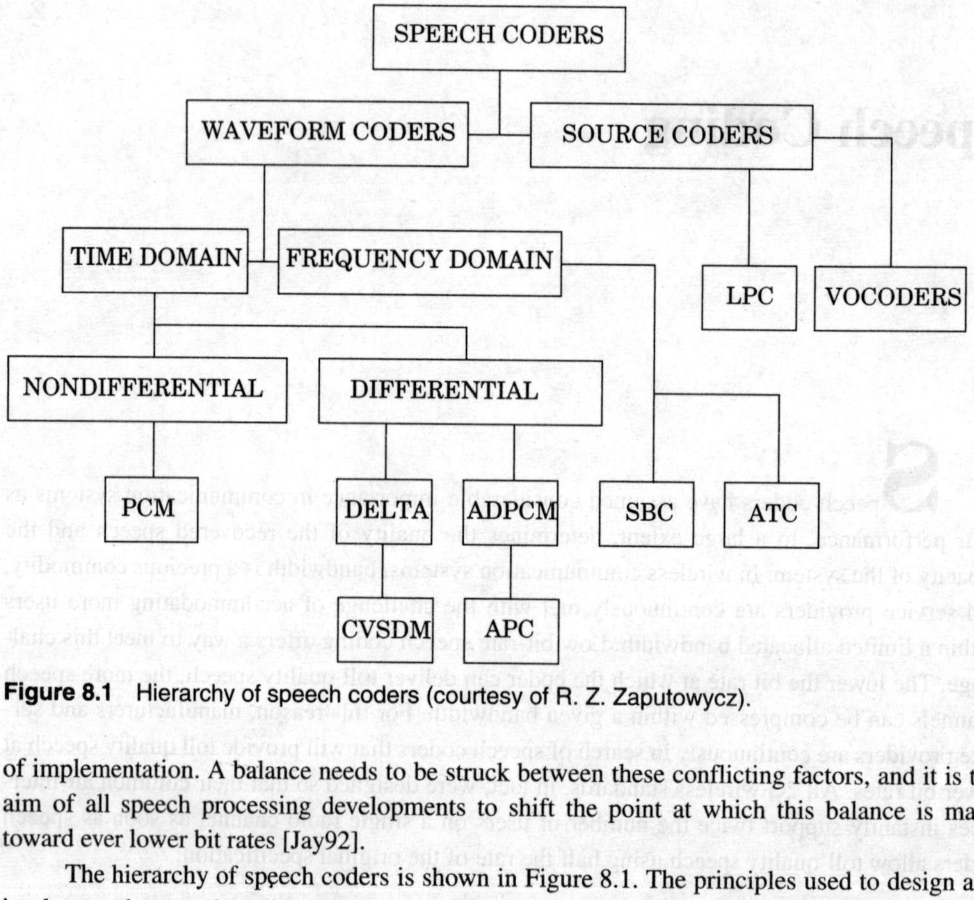

Figure 8.1 Hierarchy of speech coders (courtesy of R. Z. Zaputowycz).

of implementation. A balance needs to be struck between these conflicting factors, and it is the aim of all speech processing developments to shift the point at which this balance is made toward ever lower bit rates [Jay92].

The hierarchy of speech coders is shown in Figure 8.1. The principles used to design and implement the speech coding techniques in Figure 8.1 are described throughout this chapter.

Speech coders differ widely in their approaches to achieving signal compression. Based on the means by which they achieve compression, speech coders are broadly classified into two categories: *waveform coders* and *vocoders.* Waveform coders essentially strive to reproduce the time waveform of the speech signal as closely as possible. They are, in principle, designed to be source independent and can hence code equally well a variety of signals. They have the advantage of being robust for a wide range of speech characteristics and for noisy environments. All these advantages are preserved with minimal complexity, and in general this class of coders achieves only moderate economy in transmission bit rate. Examples of waveform coders include *pulse code modulation* (PCM), *differential pulse code modulation* (DPCM), *adaptive differential pulse code modulation* (ADPCM), *delta modulation* (DM), *continuously variable slope delta modulation* (CVSDM), and *adaptive predictive coding* (APC) [Del93]. Vocoders on the other hand achieve very high economy in transmission bit rate and are in general more complex. They are based on using *a priori* knowledge about the signal to be coded, and for this reason, they are, in general, signal specific.

8.2 Characteristics of Speech Signals

Speech waveforms have a number of useful properties that can be exploited when designing efficient coders [Fla79]. Some of the properties that are most often utilized in coder design include the nonuniform probability distribution of speech amplitude, the nonzero autocorrelation between successive speech samples, the nonflat nature of the speech spectra, the existence of voiced and unvoiced segments in speech, and the quasiperiodicity of voiced speech signals. The most basic property of speech waveforms that is exploited by all speech coders is that they are bandlimited. A finite bandwidth means that it can be time-discretized (sampled) at a finite rate and reconstructed completely from its samples, provided that the sampling frequency is greater than twice the highest frequency component in the low pass signal. While the band limited property of speech signals makes sampling possible, the aforementioned properties allow quantization, the other most important process in speech coding, to be performed with greater efficiency.

probability density function (pdf) — The nonuniform probability density function of speech amplitudes is perhaps the next most exploited property of speech. The pdf of a speech signal is in general characterized by a very high probability of near-zero amplitudes, a significant probability of very high amplitudes, and a monotonically decreasing function of amplitudes between these extremes. The exact distribution, however, depends on the input bandwidth and recording conditions. The two-sided exponential (Laplacian) function given in Equation (8.1) provides a good approximation to the long-term pdf of telephone quality speech signals [Jay84]

$$p(x) = \frac{1}{\sqrt{2}\sigma_x}\exp(-\sqrt{2}|x|/\sigma_x) \tag{8.1}$$

Note that this pdf shows a distinct peak at zero, which is due to the existence of frequent pauses and low level speech segments. Short-time pdfs of speech segments are also single-peaked functions and are usually approximated as a Gaussian distribution.

Nonuniform quantizers, including the vector quantizers, attempt to match the distribution of quantization levels to that of the pdf of the input speech signal by allocating more quantization levels in regions of high probability and fewer levels in regions where the probability is low.

Autocorrelation Function (ACF) — Another very useful property of speech signals is that there exists much correlation between adjacent samples of a segment of speech. This implies that in every sample of speech, there is a large component that is easily predicted from the value of the previous samples with a small random error. All differential and predictive coding schemes are based on exploiting this property.

The autocorrelation function (ACF) gives a quantitative measure of the closeness or similarity between samples of a speech signal as a function of their time separation. This function is mathematically defined as [Jay84]

$$C(k) = \frac{1}{N}\sum_{n=0}^{N-|k|-1} x(n)x(n+|k|) \tag{8.2}$$

where $x(k)$ represents the kth speech sample. The autocorrelation function is often normalized to the variance of the speech signal and hence is constrained to have values in the range $\{-1,1\}$ with $C(0) = 1$. Typical signals have an adjacent sample correlation, $C(1)$, as high as 0.85 to 0.9.

Power Spectral Density function (PSD) — The nonflat characteristic of the power spectral density of speech makes it possible to obtain significant compression by coding speech in the frequency domain. The nonflat nature of the PSD is basically a frequency domain manifestation of the nonzero autocorrelation property. Typical long-term averaged PSDs of speech show that high frequency components contribute very little to the total speech energy. This indicates that coding speech separately in different frequency bands can lead to significant coding gain. However, it should be noted that the high frequency components, though insignificant in energy are very important carriers of speech information and hence need to be adequately represented in the coding system.

A qualitative measure of the theoretical maximum coding gain that can be obtained by exploiting the nonflat characteristics of the speech spectra is given by the *spectral flatness measure* (SFM). The SFM is defined as the ratio of the arithmetic to geometric mean of the samples of the PSD taken at uniform intervals in frequency. Mathematically,

$$SFM = \frac{\left[\frac{1}{N}\sum_{k=1}^{N} S_k^2\right]}{\left[\prod_{k=1}^{N} S_k^2\right]^{\frac{1}{N}}} \tag{8.3}$$

where, S_k is the kth frequency sample of the PSD of the speech signal. Typically, speech signals have a long-term SFM value of 8 and a short-time SFM value varying widely between 2 and 500.

8.3 Quantization Techniques

8.3.1 Uniform Quantization

Quantization is the process of mapping a continuous range of amplitudes of a signal into a finite set of discrete amplitudes. Quantizers can be thought of as devices that remove the irrelevancies in the signal, and their operation is irreversible. Unlike sampling, quantization introduces distortion. Amplitude quantization is an important step in any speech coding process, and it determines to a great extent the overall distortion as well as the bit rate necessary to represent the speech waveform. A quantizer that uses n bits can have $M = 2^n$ discrete amplitude levels. The distortion introduced by any quantization operation is directly proportional to the square of the step size, which in turn is inversely proportional to the number of levels for a given amplitude range. One of the most frequently used measures of distortion is the *mean square error distortion* which is defined as:

$$MSE = E[(x - f_Q(x))^2] = \frac{1}{T}\int_0^T [f_Q(x) - x(t)]^2 dt \tag{8.4}$$

where $x(t)$ represents the original speech signal and $f_Q(t)$ represents the quantized speech signal. The distortion introduced by a quantizer is often modeled as additive quantization noise, and the performance of a quantizer is measured as the output *signal-to-quantization noise ratio* (SQNR). A pulse code modulation (PCM) coder is basically a quantizer of sampled speech amplitudes. PCM coding, using 8 bits per sample at a sampling frequency of 8 kHz, was the first digital coding standard adopted for commercial telephony. The SQNR of a PCM encoder is related to the number of bits used for encoding through the following relation:

$$(SQNR)_{dB} = 6.02n + \alpha \tag{8.5}$$

where $\alpha = 4.77$ dB for peak SQNR and $\alpha = 0$ dB for the average SQNR. The above equation indicates that with every additional bit used for encoding, the output SQNR improves by 6 dB.

8.3.2 Nonuniform Quantization

The performance of a quantizer can be improved by distributing the quantization levels in a more efficient manner. Nonuniform quantizers distribute the quantization levels in accordance with the pdf of the input waveform. For an input signal with a pdf $p(x)$, the mean square distortion is given by

$$D = E[(x - f_Q(x))^2] = \int_{-\infty}^{\infty} [x - f_Q(x)]^2 p(x) dx \tag{8.6}$$

where $f_Q(x)$ is the output of the quantizer. From the above equation, it is clear that the total distortion can be reduced by decreasing the quantization noise, $[x - f_Q(x)]^2$, where the pdf, $p(x)$, is large. This means that quantization levels need to be concentrated in amplitude regions of high probability.

To design an optimal nonuniform quantizer, we need to determine the quantization levels which will minimize the distortion of a signal with a given pdf. The Lloyd–Max algorithm [Max60] provides a method to determine the optimum quantization levels by iteratively changing the quantization levels in a manner that minimizes the mean square distortion.

A simple and robust implementation of a nonuniform quantizer used in commercial telephony is the logarithmic quantizer. This quantizer uses fine quantization steps for the frequently occurring low amplitudes in speech and uses much coarser steps for the less frequent, large amplitude excursions. Different companding techniques known as μ-*law* and *A-law* companding are used in the US and Europe, respectively.

Nonuniform quantization is obtained by first passing the analog speech signal through a compression (logarithmic) amplifier, and then passing the compressed speech into a standard uniform quantizer. In US μ-law companding, weak speech signals are amplified where strong speech signals are compressed. Let the speech voltage level into the compander be $w(t)$ and the speech output voltage be $v_o(t)$. Following [Smi57],

$$|v_o(t)| = \frac{\ln(1+\mu|w(t)|)}{\ln(1+\mu)} \tag{8.7}$$

where μ is a positive constant and has a value typically between 50 and 300. The peak value of $w(t)$ is normalized to 1.

In Europe, A-law companding is used [Cat69], and is defined by

$$v_o(t) = \begin{cases} \dfrac{A|w(t)|}{1+\ln A} & 0 \le |w(t)| \le \dfrac{1}{A} \\ \dfrac{1+\ln(A|w(t)|)}{1+\ln A} & \dfrac{1}{A} \le |w(t)| \le 1 \end{cases} \tag{8.8}$$

Example 8.1

Let the input signal to a quantizer have a probability density function (pdf) as shown in Figure E8.1. Assume the quantization levels to be {1, 3, 5, 7}. Compute the mean square error distortion at the quantizer output and the output signal-to-distortion ratio. How would you change the distribution of quantization levels to decrease the distortion? For what input pdf would this quantizer be optimal?

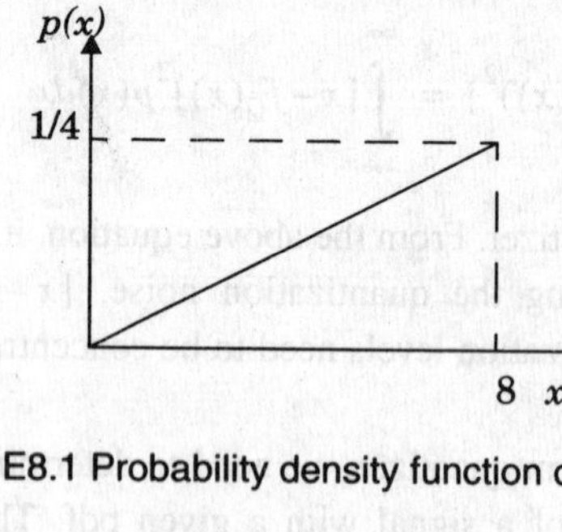

Figure E8.1 Probability density function of the input signal.

Solution

From Figure E8.1, the pdf of the input signal can be recognized as:

$$p(x) = \frac{x}{32} \qquad 0 \le x \le 8$$

$$p(x) = 0 \qquad \text{elsewhere}$$

Given the quantization levels to be {1, 3, 5, 7}, we can define the quantization boundaries as {0, 2, 4, 6, 8}.

$$\text{Mean square error distortion} = D = \int_{-\infty}^{\infty} (x - f_Q(x))^2 p(x)dx$$

$$D = \int_0^2 (x-1)^2 p(x)dx + \int_2^4 (x-3)^2 p(x)dx + \int_4^6 (x-5)^2 p(x)dx + \int_6^8 (x-7)^2 p(x)dx$$

This expression evaluates to 0.333.

$$\text{Signal Power} = E[x^2] = \int_0^8 p(x)x^2 dx = \int_0^8 \frac{1}{32}(x \cdot x^2)dx = 32$$

$$\text{Signal to distortion ratio} = 10\log[E[x^2]/D] = 10\log(32/0.333) = 19.82 \text{ dB}$$

To minimize the distortion, we need to concentrate the quantization levels in regions of higher probability. Since the input signal has a greater probability of higher amplitude levels than lower amplitudes, we need to place the quantization levels closer (i.e., more quantization levels) at amplitudes close to eight and farther (i.e., less quantization levels) at amplitudes close to zero.

Since this quantizer has quantization levels uniformly distributed, this would be optimal for an input signal with a uniform pdf.

8.3.3 Adaptive Quantization

As noted earlier, there is a distinction between the long term and short term pdf of speech waveforms. This fact is a result of the nonstationarity of speech signals. The time-varying or nonstationary nature of speech signals results in a dynamic range of 40 dB or more. An efficient way to accommodate such a huge dynamic range is to adopt a time varying quantization technique. An adaptive quantizer varies its step size in accordance to the input speech signal power. Its characteristics shrink and expand in time like an accordion. The idea is illustrated in Figure 8.2 through two snapshots of the quantizer characteristics at two different times. The input power level of the speech signal varies slowly enough that simple adaptation algorithms can be easily designed and implemented. One simple adaptation strategy would be to make the step size, Δ_k, of the quantizer at any given sampling instant, proportional to the quantizer output f_Q at the preceding sampling instant as shown below.

Since the adaptation follows the quantizer output rather than the input, step size information need not be explicitly transmitted, but can be recreated at the receiver.

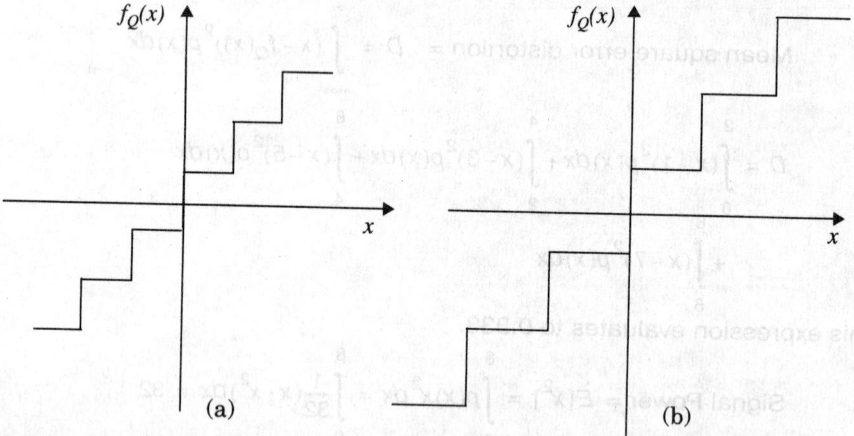

Figure 8.2 Adaptive quantizer characteristics (a) when the input signal has a low amplitude swing and (b) when the input signal has a large amplitude swing.

8.3.4 Vector Quantization

Shannon's *Rate-Distortion Theorem* [Sha48] states that there exists a mapping from a source waveform to output code words such that for a given distortion D, $R(D)$ bits per sample are sufficient to reconstruct the waveform with an average distortion arbitrarily close to D. Therefore, the actual rate R has to be greater than $R(D)$. The function $R(D)$, called the rate-distortion function, represents a fundamental limit on the achievable rate for a given distortion. Scalar quantizers do not achieve performance close to this information theoretical limit. Shannon predicted that better performance can be achieved by coding many samples at a time instead of one sample at a time.

Vector quantization (VQ) [Gra84] is a delayed-decision coding technique which maps a group of input samples (typically a speech frame), called a vector, to a *code book index*. A code book is set up consisting of a finite set of vectors covering the entire anticipated range of values. In each quantizing interval, the code-book is searched and the index of the entry that gives the best match to the input signal frame is selected. Vector quantizers can yield better performance even when the samples are independent of one another. Performance is greatly enhanced if there is strong correlation between samples in the group.

The number of samples in a block (vector) is called the dimension L of the vector quantizer. The rate R of the vector quantizer is defined as:

$$R = \frac{\log_2 n}{L} \text{ bits/sample} \tag{8.9}$$

where n is the size of the VQ code book. R may take fractional values also. All the quantization principles used in scalar quantization apply to vector quantization as a straightforward extension. Instead of quantization levels, we have quantization vectors, and distortion is measured as the squared Euclidean distance between the quantization vector and the input vector.

Vector quantization is known to be most efficient at very low bit rates ($R = 0.5$ bits/sample or less). This is because when R is small, one can afford to use a large vector dimension L, and yet have a reasonable size, 2^{RL}, of the VQ code book. Use of larger dimensions tends to bring out the inherent capability of VQ to exploit the redundancies in the components of the vector being quantized. Vector quantization is a computationally intensive operation and, for this reason, is not often used to code speech signals directly. However, it is used in many speech coding systems to quantize the speech analysis parameters like the linear prediction coefficients, spectral coefficients, filter bank energies, etc. These systems use improved versions of VQ algorithms which are more computationally efficient such as the multistage VQ, tree-structured VQ, and shape-gain VQ.

8.4 Adaptive Differential Pulse Code Modulation (ADPCM)

Pulse code modulation systems do not attempt to remove the redundancies in the speech signal. Adaptive differential pulse code modulation (ADPCM) [Jay84] is a more efficient coding scheme which exploits the redundancies present in the speech signal. As mentioned earlier, adjacent samples of a speech waveform are often highly correlated. This means that the variance of the difference between adjacent speech amplitudes is much smaller than the variance of the speech signal itself. ADPCM allows speech to be encoded at a bit rate of 32 kbps, which is half the standard 64 kbps PCM rate, while retaining the same voice quality. Efficient algorithms for ADPCM have been developed and standardized. The CCITT standard G.721 ADPCM algorithm for 32 kbps speech coding is used in cordless telephone systems like CT2 and DECT.

In a differential PCM scheme, the encoder quantizes a succession of adjacent sample differences, and the decoder recovers an approximation to the original speech signal by essentially integrating quantized adjacent sample differences. Since the quantization error variance for a given number of bits/sample R, is directly proportional to the input variance, the reduction obtained in the quantizer input variance leads directly to a reduction of reconstruction error variance for a given value of R.

In practice, ADPCM encoders are implemented using signal prediction techniques. Instead of encoding the difference between adjacent samples, a linear predictor is used to predict the current sample. The difference between the predicted and actual sample called the prediction error is then encoded for transmission. Prediction is based on the knowledge of the autocorrelation properties of speech.

Figure 8.3 shows a simplified block diagram of an ADPCM encoder used in the CT2 cordless telephone system [Det89]. This encoder consists of a quantizer that maps the input signal sample onto a four-bit output sample. The ADPCM encoder makes best use of the available dynamic range of four bits by varying its step size in an adaptive manner. The step size of the quantizer depends on the dynamic range of the input, which is speaker dependent and varies with time. The adaptation is, in practice, achieved by normalizing the input signals via a scaling factor derived from a prediction of the dynamic range of the current input. This prediction is obtained from two components: a *fast* component for signals with rapid amplitude fluctuations and a *slow* component for signals that vary more slowly. The two components are weighted to give a single quantization scaling factor. It should

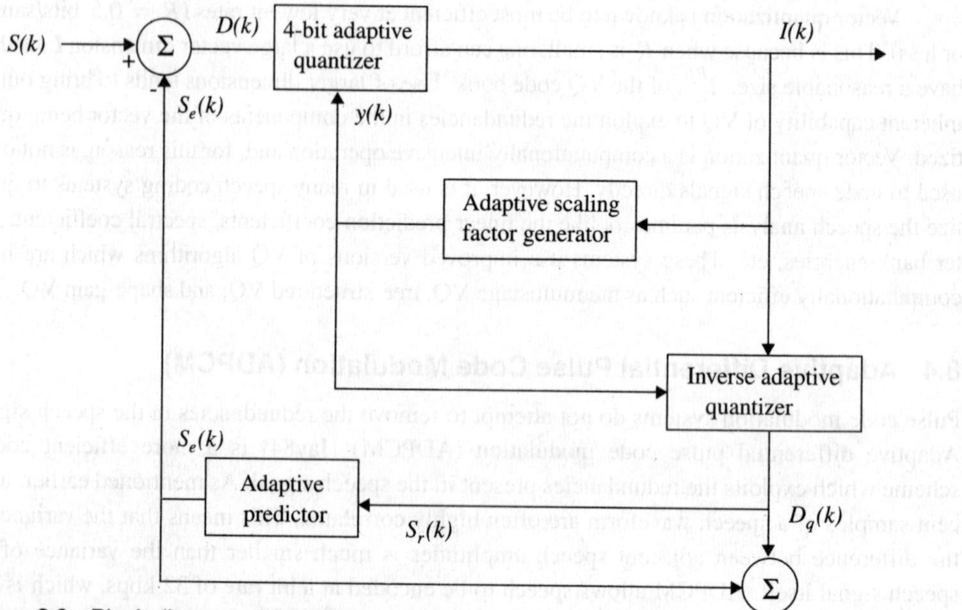

Figure 8.3 Block diagram of ADPCM encoder.

be noted that the two feedback signals that drive the algorithm—$s_e(k)$, the estimate of the input signal and $y(k)$, the quantization scaling factor—are ultimately derived solely from $I(k)$, the transmitted 4-bit ADPCM signal. The ADPCM encoder at the transmitter and the ADPCM decoder, at the receiver, are thus driven by the same control signals, with decoding simply the reverse of encoding.

Example 8.2

In an adaptive PCM system for speech coding, the input speech signal is sampled at 8 kHz, and each sample is represented by 8 bits. The quantizer step size is recomputed every 10 ms, and it is encoded for transmission using 5 bits. Compute the transmission bit rate of such a speech coder. What would be the average and peak SQNR of this system?

Solution

Given:

Sampling frequency = f_s = 8 kHz

Number of bits per sample = n = 8 bits

Number of information bits per second = 8000 × 8 = 64000 bits

Since the quantization step size is recomputed every 10 ms, we have 100 step size samples to be transmitted every second.

Therefore, the number of overhead bits = 100 × 5 = 500 bits/s

Therefore, the effective transmission bit rate = 64000 + 500 = 64.5 kbps.

The signal-to-quantization noise ratio depends only on the number of bits used to quantize the samples.
Peak signal to quantization noise ratio in dB
$= 6.02n + 4.77 = (6.02 \times 8) + 4.77 = 52.93$ dB.
Average signal-to-noise ratio in dB $= 6.02n = 48.16$ dB.

8.5 Frequency Domain Coding of Speech

Frequency domain coders [Tri79] are a class of speech coders which take advantage of speech perception and generation models without making the algorithm totally dependent on the models used. In this class of coders, the speech signal is divided into a set of frequency components which are quantized and encoded separately. In this way, different frequency bands can be preferentially encoded according to some perceptual criteria for each band, and hence the quantization noise can be contained within bands and prevented from creating harmonic distortions outside the band. These schemes have the advantage that the number of bits used to encode each frequency component can be dynamically varied and shared among the different bands.

Many frequency domain coding algorithms, ranging from simple to complex are available. The most common types of frequency domain coding include *sub-band coding* (SBC) and *block transform coding*. While a sub-band coder divides the speech signal into many smaller sub-bands and encodes each sub-band separately according to some perceptual criterion, a transform coder codes the short-time transform of a windowed sequence of samples and encodes them with number of bits proportional to its perceptual significance.

8.5.1 Sub-band Coding

Sub-band coding can be thought of as a method of controlling and distributing quantization noise across the signal spectrum. Quantization is a nonlinear operation which produces distortion products that are typically broad in spectrum. The human ear does not detect the quantization distortion at all frequencies equally well. It is therefore possible to achieve substantial improvement in quality by coding the signal in narrower bands. In a sub-band coder, speech is typically divided into four or eight sub-bands by a bank of filters, and each sub-band is sampled at a bandpass Nyquist rate (which is lower than the original sampling rate) and encoded with different accuracy in accordance to a perceptual criteria. Band-splitting can be done in many ways. One approach could be to divide the entire speech band into unequal sub-bands that contribute equally to the articulation index. One partitioning of the speech band according to this method as suggested by Crochiere et al. [Cro76] is given below.

Sub-band Number	Frequency Range
1	200–700 Hz
2	700–1310 Hz
3	1310–2020 Hz
4	2020–3200 Hz

Another way to split the speech band would be to divide it into equal width sub-bands and assign to each sub-band number of bits proportional to perceptual significance while encoding them. Instead of partitioning into equal width bands, octave band splitting is often employed. As the human ear has an exponentially decreasing sensitivity to frequency, this kind of splitting is more in tune with the perception process.

There are various methods for processing the sub-band signals. One obvious way is to make a low pass translation of the sub-band signal to zero frequency by a modulation process equivalent to single sideband modulation. This kind of translation facilitates sampling rate reduction and possesses other benefits that accrue from coding low-pass signals. Figure 8.4 shows a simple means of achieving this low pass translation. The input signal is filtered with a bandpass filter of width w_n for the n th band. w_{1n} is the lower edge of the band and w_{2n} is the upper edge of the band. The resulting signal $s_n(t)$ is modulated by a cosine wave $\cos(w_{1n}t)$, and filtered using a low pass filter $h_n(t)$ with bandwidth $(0 - w_n)$. The resulting signal $r_n(t)$ corresponds to the low pass translated version of $s_n(t)$ and can be expressed as

$$r_n(t) = [s_n(t)\cos(w_{1n}t)] \otimes h_n(t) \tag{8.10}$$

where $\otimes$ denotes a convolution operation. The signal $r_n(t)$ is sampled at a rate $2w_n$. This signal is then digitally encoded and multiplexed with encoded signals from other channels as shown in Figure 8.4. At the receiver, the data is demultiplexed into separate channels, decoded, and band-pass translated to give the estimate of $r_n(t)$ for the nth channel.

The low pass translation technique is straightforward and takes advantage of a bank of nonoverlapping bandpass filters. Unfortunately, unless we use sophisticated bandpass filters, this approach will lead to perceptible aliasing effects. Estaban and Galand proposed [Est77] a scheme which avoids this inconvenience even with quasiperfect, sub-band splitting. Filter banks known as quadrature mirror filters (QMFs) are used to achieve this. By designing a set of mirror filters which satisfy certain symmetry conditions, it is possible to obtain perfect alias cancellation. This facilitates the implementation of sub-band coding without the use of very high order filters. This is particularly attractive for real time implementation as a reduced filter order means a reduced computational load and also a reduced latency.

Sub-band coding can be used for coding speech at bit rates in the range 9.6 kbps to 32 kbps. In this range, speech quality is roughly equivalent to that of ADPCM at an equivalent bit rate. In addition, its complexity and relative speech quality at low bit rates make it particularly advantageous for coding below about 16 kbps. However, the increased complexity of sub-band coding when compared to other higher bit rate techniques does not warrant its use at bit rates greater than about 20 kbps. The CD-900 cellular telephone system uses sub-band coding for speech compression.

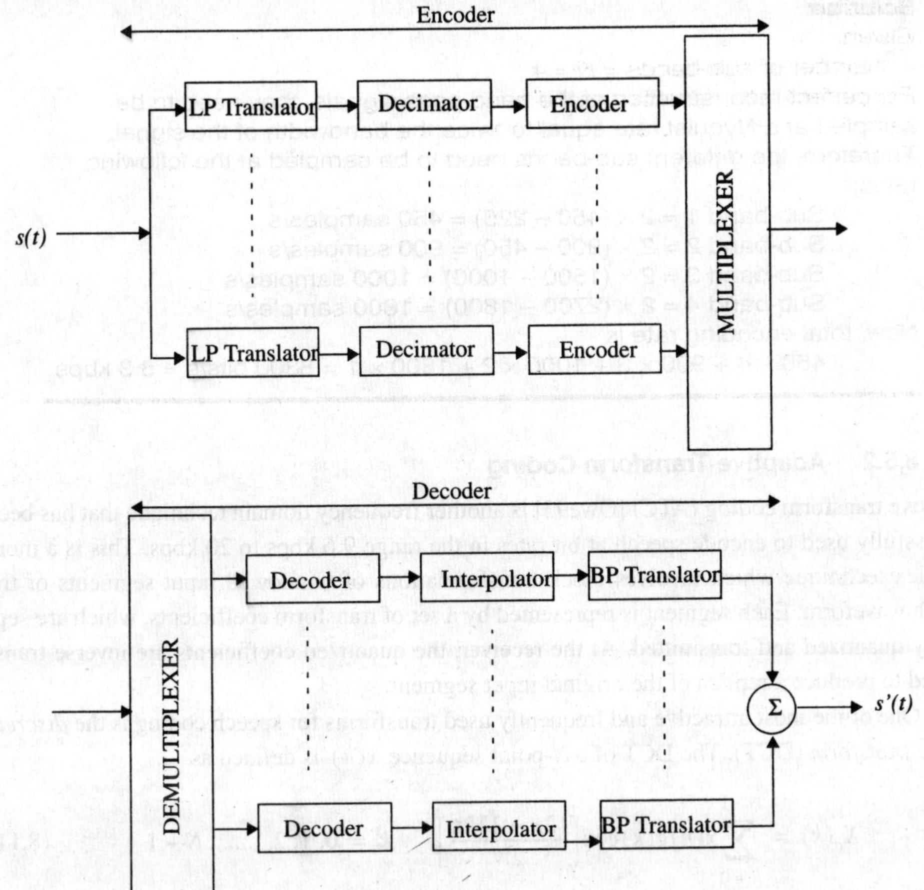

Figure 8.4 Block diagram of a sub-band coder and decoder.

Example 8.3

Consider a sub-band coding scheme where the speech bandwidth is partitioned into four bands. The Table below gives the corner frequencies of each band along with the number of bits used to encode each band. Assuming that no side information need be transmitted, compute the minimum encoding rate of this SBC coder.

Sub-band Number	Frequency Band (Hz)	# of Encoding Bits
1	225–450	4
2	450–900	3
3	1000–1500	2
4	1800–2700	1

Solution

Given:

Number of sub-bands = $N = 4$

For perfect reconstruction of the band-pass signals, they need to be sampled at a Nyquist rate equal to twice the bandwidth of the signal. Therefore, the different sub-bands need to be sampled at the following rates:

Sub-band 1 = 2 × (450 – 225) = 450 samples/s
Sub-band 2 = 2 × (900 – 450) = 900 samples/s
Sub-band 3 = 2 × (1500 – 1000) = 1000 samples/s
Sub-band 4 = 2 × (2700 – 1800) = 1800 samples/s

Now, total encoding rate is

450 × 4 + 900 × 3 + 1000 × 2 + 1800 × 1 = 8300 bits/s = 8.3 kbps

8.5.2 Adaptive Transform Coding

Adaptive transform coding (ATC) [Owe93] is another frequency domain technique that has been successfully used to encode speech at bit rates in the range 9.6 kbps to 20 kbps. This is a more complex technique which involves block transformations of windowed input segments of the speech waveform. Each segment is represented by a set of transform coefficients, which are separately quantized and transmitted. At the receiver, the quantized coefficients are inverse transformed to produce a replica of the original input segment.

One of the most attractive and frequently used transforms for speech coding is the *discrete cosine transform* (DCT). The DCT of a N-point sequence $x(n)$ is defined as

$$X_c(k) = \sum_{n=0}^{N-1} x(n)g(k)\cos\left[\frac{(2n+1)k\pi}{2N}\right] \qquad k = 0, 1, 2, \ldots\ldots, N-1 \tag{8.11}$$

where $g(0) = 1$ and $g(k) = \sqrt{2}$, $k = 1, 2, \ldots\ldots, N-1$. The inverse DCT is defined as:

$$x(n) = \frac{1}{N}\sum_{k=0}^{N-1} X_c(k)g(k)\cos\left[\frac{(2n+1)k\pi}{2N}\right] \qquad n = 0, 1, 2, \ldots\ldots, N-1 \tag{8.12}$$

In practical situations the DCT and IDCT are not evaluated directly using the above equations. Fast algorithms developed for computing the DCT in a computationally efficient manner are used.

Most of the practical transform coding schemes vary the bit allocation among different coefficients adaptively from frame to frame while keeping the total number of bits constant. This dynamic bit allocation is controlled by time-varying statistics which have to be transmitted as side information. This constitutes an overhead of about 2 kbps. The frame of N samples to be transformed or inverse-transformed is accumulated in the buffer in the transmitter and receiver respectively. The side information is also used to determine the step size of the various coefficient quantizers. In a practical system, the side information transmitted is a coarse representation of the log-energy spectrum. This typically consists of L frequency points, where L is in the range 15–20, which are computed by averaging sets of N/L adjacent squared values of the transform coefficients $X(k)$. At the receiver, an N-point spectrum is reconstructed from the L-point spectrum by geometric interpolation in the log-domain. The number of bits assigned to each transform coefficient is proportional to its corresponding spectral energy value.

8.6 Vocoders

Vocoders are a class of speech coding systems that analyze the voice signal at the transmitter, transmit parameters derived from the analysis, and then synthesize the voice at the receiver using those parameters. All vocoder systems attempt to model the speech generation process as a dynamic system and try to quantify certain physical constraints of the system. These physical constraints are used to provide a parsimonious description of the speech signal. Vocoders are, in general, much more complex than the waveform coders and achieve very high economy in transmission bit rate. However, they are less robust, and their performance tends to be talker dependent. The most popular among the vocoding systems is the *linear predictive coder* (LPC). The other vocoding schemes include the channel vocoder, formant vocoder, cepstrum vocoder and voice excited vocoder.

Figure 8.5 shows the traditional speech generation model that is the basis of all vocoding systems [Fla79]. The sound generating mechanism forms the *source* and is linearly separated from the intelligence modulating vocal tract filter which forms the *system*. The speech signal is assumed to be of two types: *voiced* and *unvoiced*. Voiced sound (*"m"*, *"n"*, *"v"* pronunciations) are a result of quasiperiodic vibrations of the vocal chord and unvoiced sounds (*"f"*, *"s"*, *"sh"* pronunciations) are fricatives produced by turbulent air flow through a constriction. The parameters associated with this model are the voice pitch, the pole frequencies of the modulating filter, and the corresponding amplitude parameters. The pitch frequency for most speakers is below 300 Hz, and extracting this information from the signal is very difficult. The pole frequencies correspond to the resonant frequencies of the vocal tract and are often called the formants of the speech signal. For adult speakers, the formants are centered around 500 Hz, 1500 Hz, 2500 Hz, and 3500 Hz. By meticulously adjusting the parameters of the speech generation model, good quality speech can be synthesized.

8.6.1 Channel Vocoders

The channel vocoder was the first among the analysis–synthesis systems of speech demonstrated practically. Channel vocoders are frequency domain vocoders that determine the envelope of the speech signal for a number of frequency bands and then sample, encode, and multiplex these samples with the encoded outputs of the other filters. The sampling is done synchronously every 10 ms to 30 ms. Along with the energy information about each band, the voiced/unvoiced decision, and the pitch frequency for voiced speech are also transmitted.

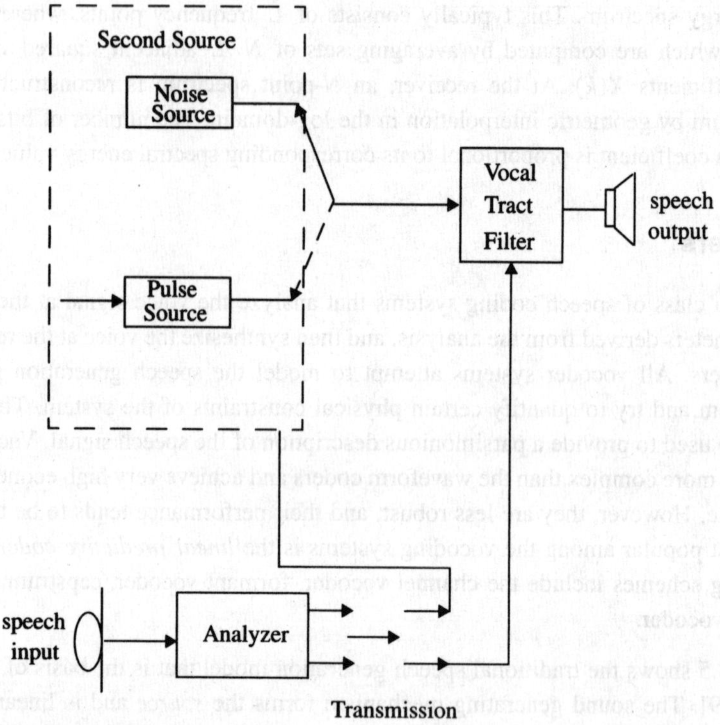

Figure 8.5 Speech generation model.

8.6.2 Formant Vocoders

The formant vocoder [Bay73] is similar in concept to the channel vocoder. Theoretically, the formant vocoder can operate at lower bit rates than the channel vocoder because it uses fewer control signals. Instead of sending samples of the power spectrum envelope, the formant vocoder attempts to transmit the positions of the peaks (formants) of the spectral envelope. Typically, a formant vocoder must be able to identify at least three formants for representing the speech sounds, and it must also control the intensities of the formants.

Formant vocoders can reproduce speech at bit rates lower than 1200 bits/s. However, due to difficulties in accurately computing the location of formants and formant transitions from human speech, they have not been very successful.

8.6.3 Cepstrum Vocoders

The Cepstrum vocoder separates the excitation and vocal tract spectrum by inverse Fourier transforming of the log magnitude spectrum to produce the cepstrum of the signal. The low frequency coefficients in the cepstrum correspond to the vocal tract spectral envelope, with the high frequency excitation coefficients forming a periodic pulse train at multiples of the sampling period. Linear filtering is performed to separate the vocal tract cepstral coefficients from the excitation coefficients. In the receiver, the vocal tract cepstral coefficients are Fourier transformed to produce the vocal tract impulse response. By convolving this impulse response with a synthetic excitation signal (random noise or periodic pulse train), the original speech is reconstructed.

8.6.4 Voice-Excited Vocoder

Voice-excited vocoders eliminate the need for pitch extraction and voicing detection operations. This system uses a hybrid combination of PCM transmission for the low frequency band of speech, combined with channel vocoding of higher frequency bands. A pitch signal is generated at the synthesizer by rectifying, bandpass filtering, and clipping the baseband signal, thus creating a spectrally flat signal with energy at pitch harmonics. Voice excited vocoders have been designed for operation at 7200 bits/s to 9600 bits/s, and their quality is typically superior to that obtained by the traditional pitch excited vocoders.

8.7 Linear Predictive Coders

8.7.1 LPC Vocoders

Linear predictive coders (LPCs) [Sch85a] belong to the time domain class of vocoders. This class of vocoders attempts to extract the significant features of speech from the time waveform. Though LPC coders are computationally intensive, they are by far the most popular among the class of low bit rate vocoders. With LPC, it is possible to transmit good quality voice at 4.8 kbps and poorer quality voice at even lower rates.

The linear predictive coding system models the vocal tract as an all pole linear filter with a transfer function described by

$$H(z) = \frac{G}{1 + \sum_{k=1}^{M} b_k z^{-k}} \tag{8.13}$$

where G is a gain of the filter and z^{-1} represents a unit delay operation. The excitation to this filter is either a pulse at the pitch frequency or random white noise depending on whether the speech segment is voiced or unvoiced. The coefficients of the all pole filter are obtained in the time domain using linear prediction techniques [Mak75]. The prediction principles used are similar to those in ADPCM coders. However, instead of transmitting quantized values of the error signal representing the difference between the predicted and actual waveform, the LPC system transmits only selected characteristics of the error signal. The parameters include the gain factor, pitch information, and the voiced/unvoiced decision information, which allow approximation of the correct error signal. At the receiver, the received information about the error signal is used to determine the appropriate excitation for the synthesis filter. That is, the error signal is the excitation to the decoder. The synthesis filter is designed at the receiver using the received predictor coefficients. In practice, many LPC coders transmit the filter coefficients which already represent the error signal and can be directly synthesized by the receiver. Figure 8.6 shows a block diagram of an LPC system [Jay86].

Determination of Predictor Coefficients — The linear predictive coder uses a weighted sum of p past samples to estimate the present sample, where p is typically in the range of 10–15. Using this technique, the current sample s_n can be written as a linear sum of the immediately preceding samples s_{n-k}

$$s_n = \sum_{k=1}^{p} a_k s_{n-k} + e_n \tag{8.14}$$

where e_n is the prediction error (residual). The predictor coefficients are calculated to minimize the average energy E in the error signal that represents the difference between the predicted and actual speech amplitude

$$E = \sum_{n=1}^{N} e_n^2 = \sum_{n=1}^{N}\left(\sum_{k=0}^{p} a_k s_{n-k}\right)^2 \tag{8.15}$$

where $a_0 = -1$. Typically, the error is computed for a time window of 10 ms, which corresponds to a value of $N = 80$. To minimize E with respect to a_m, it is required to set the partial derivatives equal to zero

$$\frac{\partial E}{\partial a_m} = \sum_{n=1}^{N} 2s_{n-m} \sum_{k=0}^{p} a_k s_{n-k} = 0 \tag{8.16}$$

$$= \sum_{k=0}^{p} \sum_{n=1}^{N} s_{n-m} s_{n-k} a_k = 0 \tag{8.17}$$

The inner summation can be recognized as the correlation coefficient C_{rm} and hence the above equation can be rewritten as

$$\sum_{k=0}^{p} C_{mk} a_k = 0 \tag{8.18}$$

After determining the correlation coefficients C_{rm}, Equation (8.18) can be used to determine the predictor coefficients. Equation (8.18) is often expressed in matrix notation and the predictor coefficients calculated using matrix inversion. A number of algorithms have been developed to speed up the calculation of predictor coefficients. Normally, the predictor coefficients are not coded directly, as they would require 8 bits to 10 bits per coefficient for accurate representation [Del93]. The accuracy requirements are lessened by transmitting the reflection coefficients (a closely related parameter), which have a smaller dynamic range. These reflection coefficients can

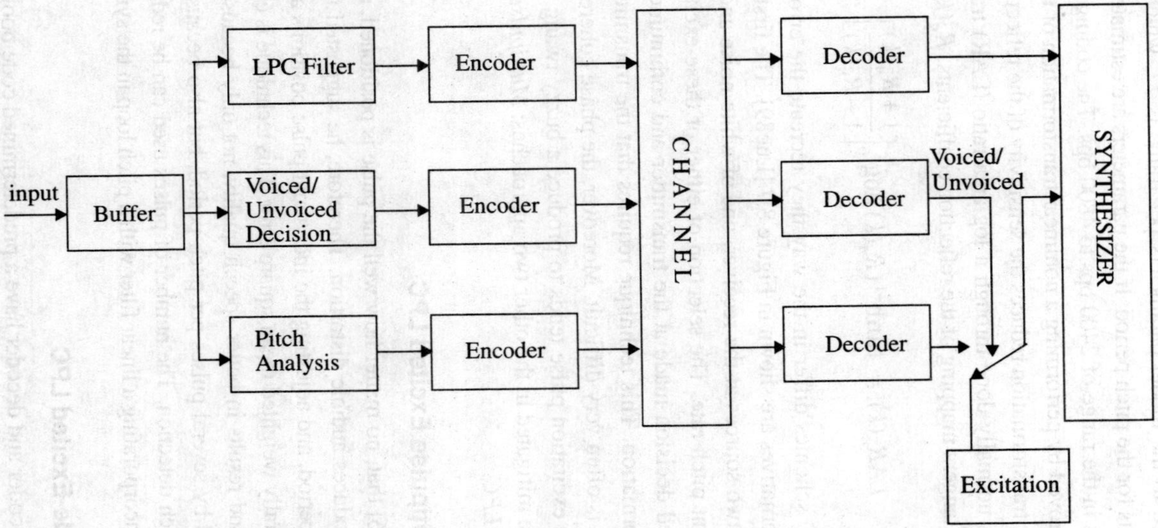

Figure 8.6 Block diagram of a LPC coding system.

be adequately represented by 6 bits per coefficient. Thus, for a 10th order predictor, the total number of bits assigned to the model parameters per frame is 72, which includes 5 bits for a gain parameter and 6 bits for the pitch period. If the parameters are estimated every 15 ms to 30 ms, the resulting bit rate is in the range of 2400 bps to 4800 bps. The coding of the reflection coefficient can be further improved by performing a nonlinear transformation of the coefficients prior to coding. This nonlinear transformation reduces the sensitivity of the reflection coefficients to quantization errors. This is normally done through a log-area ratio (LAR) transform which performs an inverse hyperbolic tangent mapping of the reflection coefficients, $R_n(k)$

$$LAR_n(k) = \tanh^{-1}(R_n(k))\log_{10}\left[\frac{1+R_n(k)}{1-R_n(k)}\right] \tag{8.19}$$

Various LPC schemes differ in the way they recreate the error signal (excitation) at the receiver. Three alternatives are shown in Figure 8.7 [Luc89]. The first one shows the most popular means. It uses two sources at the receiver, one of white noise and the other with a series of pulses at the current pitch rate. The selection of either of these excitation methods is based on the voiced/unvoiced decision made at the transmitter and communicated to the receiver along with the other information. This technique requires that the transmitter extract pitch frequency information which is often very difficult. Moreover, the phase coherence between the harmonic components of the excitation pulse tends to produce a buzzy twang in the synthesized speech. These problems are mitigated in the other two approaches: *Multipulse excited LPC* and *stochastic or code excited LPC.*

8.7.2 Multipulse Excited LPC

Atal showed [Ata86] that, no matter how well the pulse is positioned, excitation by a single pulse per pitch period produces audible distortion. Therefore, he suggested using more than one pulse, typically eight per period, and adjusting the individual pulse positions and amplitudes sequentially to minimize a spectrally weighted mean square error. This technique is called the multipulse excited LPC (MPE-LPC) and results in better speech quality, not only because the prediction residual is better approximated by several pulses per pitch period, but also because the multipulse algorithm does not require pitch detection. The number of pulses used can be reduced, in particular for high pitched voices, by incorporating a linear filter with a pitch loop in the synthesizer.

8.7.3 Code-Excited LPC

In this method, the coder and decoder have a predetermined code book of stochastic (zero-mean white Gaussian) excitation signals [Sch85b]. For each speech signal, the transmitter searches through its code book of stochastic signals for the one that gives the best perceptual match to the sound when used as an excitation to the LPC filter. The index of the code book where the best match was found is then transmitted. The receiver uses this index to pick the correct excitation signal for its synthesizer filter. The code excited LPC (CELP) coders are extremely complex and can require more than 500 million multiply and add operations per second. They can provide high quality even when the excitation is coded at only 0.25 bits per sample. These coders can achieve transmission bit rates as low as 4.8 kbps.

Figure 8.8 illustrates the procedure for selecting the optimum excitation signal. The procedure is best illustrated through an example. Consider the coding of a short 5 ms block of speech signal. At a sampling frequency of 8 kHz, each block consists of 40 speech samples. A bit rate of 1/4 bit per sample corresponds to 10 bits per block. Therefore, there are $2^{10} = 1024$ possible sequences of length 40 for each block. Each member of the code book provides 40 samples of the excitation signal with a scaling factor that is changed every 5 ms block. The scaled samples are passed sequentially through two recursive filters, which introduce voice periodicity and adjust the spectral envelope. The regenerated speech samples at the output of the second filter are compared with samples of the original speech signal to form a difference signal. The difference signal represents the objective error in the regenerated speech signal. This is further processed through a linear filter which amplifies the perceptually more important frequencies and attenuates the perceptually less important frequencies.

Though computationally intensive, advances in DSP and VLSI technology have made real-time implementation of CELP codecs possible. The CDMA digital cellular standard (IS-95) proposed by QUALCOMM uses a variable rate CELP codec at 1.2 to 14.4 kbps. In 1995, QUALCOMM introduced QCELP13, a 13.4 kbps CELP coder that operates on a 14.4 kbps channel.

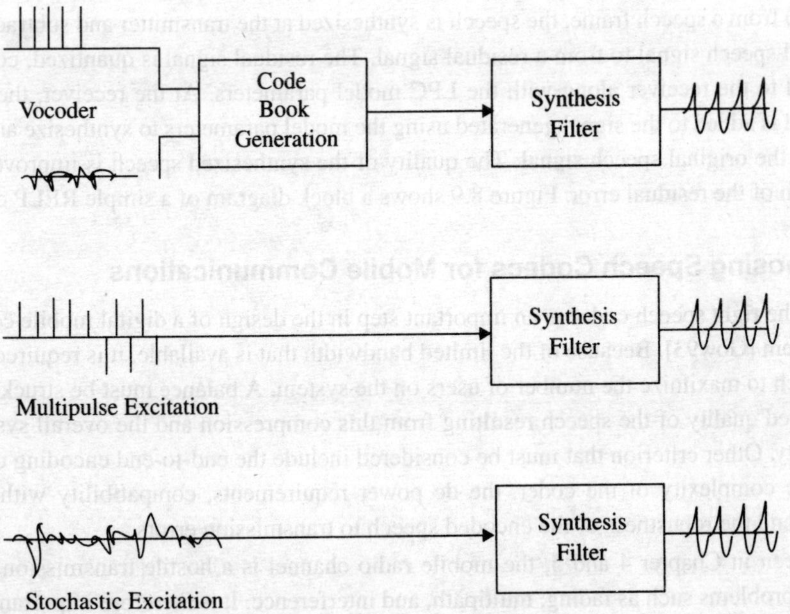

Figure 8.7 LPC excitation methods.

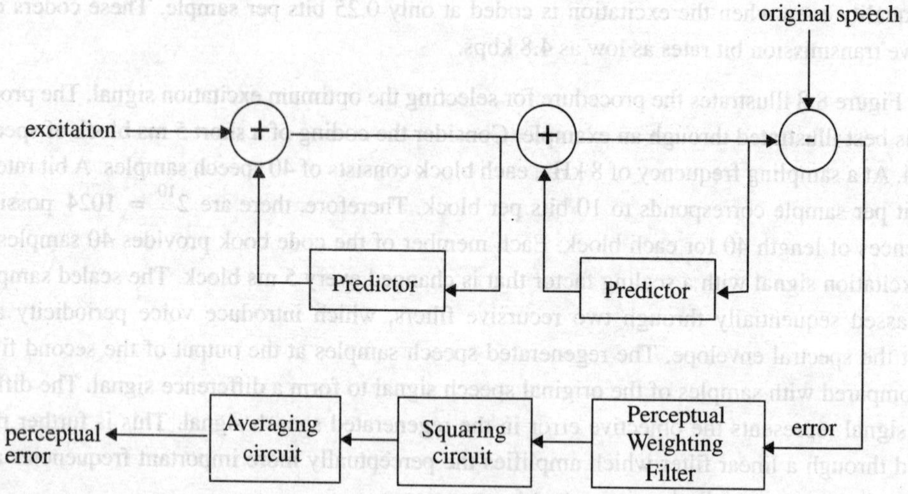

Figure 8.8 Block diagram illustrating the CELP code book search.

8.7.4 Residual Excited LPC

The rationale behind the residual excited LPC (RELP) is related to that of the DPCM technique in waveform coding [Del93]. In this class of LPC coders, after estimating the model parameters (LP coefficients or related parameters) and excitation parameters (voiced/unvoiced decision, pitch, gain) from a speech frame, the speech is synthesized at the transmitter and subtracted from the original speech signal to from a residual signal. The residual signal is quantized, coded, and transmitted to the receiver along with the LPC model parameters. At the receiver, the residual error signal is added to the signal generated using the model parameters to synthesize an approximation of the original speech signal. The quality of the synthesized speech is improved due to the addition of the residual error. Figure 8.9 shows a block diagram of a simple RELP codec.

8.8 Choosing Speech Codecs for Mobile Communications

Choosing the right speech codec is an important step in the design of a digital mobile communication system [Gow93]. Because of the limited bandwidth that is available, it is required to compress speech to maximize the number of users on the system. A balance must be struck between the perceived quality of the speech resulting from this compression and the overall system cost and capacity. Other criterion that must be considered include the end-to-end encoding delay, the algorithmic complexity of the coder, the dc power requirements, compatibility with existing standards, and the robustness of the encoded speech to transmission errors.

As seen in Chapter 4 and 5, the mobile radio channel is a hostile transmission medium beset with problems such as fading, multipath, and interference. It is therefore important that the speech codec be robust to transmission errors. Depending on the technique used, different

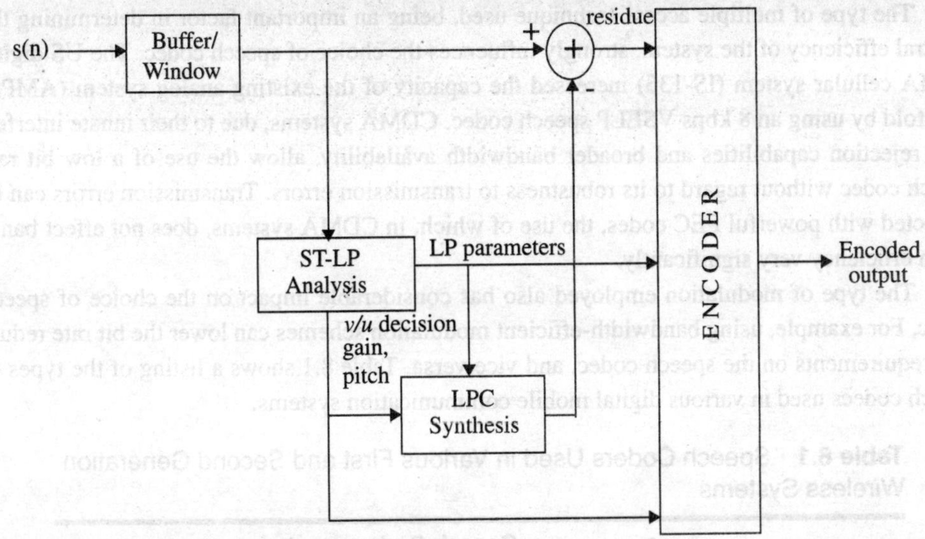

Figure 8.9 Block diagram of a RELP encoder.

speech coders show varying degree of immunity to transmission errors. For example, under same bit error rate conditions, 40 kbps adaptive delta modulation (ADM) sounds much better than 56 kbps log-PCM [Ste93]. This does *not* mean that decreasing bit rate enhances the coder robustness to transmission errors. On the contrary, as speech signals are represented by fewer and fewer bits, the information content per bit increases and hence need to be more safely preserved. Low bit rate vocoder type codecs, which do parametric modeling of the vocal tract and auditory mechanisms, have some bits carrying critical information which if corrupted would lead to unacceptable distortion. While transmitting low bit rate encoded speech, it is imperative to determine the perceptual importance of each bit and group them according to their sensitivity to errors. Depending on their perceptual significance, bits in each group are provided with different levels of error protection through the use of different forward error correction (FEC) codes.

The choice of the speech coder will also depend on the cell size used. When the cell size is sufficiently small such that high spectral efficiency is achieved through frequency reuse, it may be sufficient to use a simple high rate speech codec. In the cordless telephone systems like CT2 and DECT, which use very small cells (microcells), 32 kbps ADPCM coders are used to achieve acceptable performance even without channel coding and equalization. Cellular systems operating with much larger cells and poorer channel conditions need to use error correction coding, thereby requiring the speech codecs to operate at lower bit rates. In mobile satellite communications, the cell sizes are very large and the available bandwidth is very small. In order to accommodate realistic number of users the speech rate must be of the order of 3 kbps, requiring the use of vocoder techniques [Ste93].

The type of multiple access technique used, being an important factor in determining the spectral efficiency of the system, strongly influences the choice of speech codec. The US digital TDMA cellular system (IS-136) increased the capacity of the existing analog system (AMPS) threefold by using an 8 kbps VSELP speech codec. CDMA systems, due to their innate interference rejection capabilities and broader bandwidth availability, allow the use of a low bit rate speech codec without regard to its robustness to transmission errors. Transmission errors can be corrected with powerful FEC codes, the use of which, in CDMA systems, does not effect bandwidth efficiency very significantly.

The type of modulation employed also has considerable impact on the choice of speech codec. For example, using bandwidth-efficient modulation schemes can lower the bit rate reduction requirements on the speech codec, and vice versa. Table 8.1 shows a listing of the types of speech codecs used in various digital mobile communication systems.

Table 8.1 Speech Coders Used in Various First and Second Generation Wireless Systems

Standard	Service Type	Speech Coder Type Used	Bit Rate (kbps)
GSM	Cellular	RPE-LTP	9.6, 13
CD-900	Cellular	SBC	16
USDC (IS-136)	Cellular	VSELP	8
IS-95	Cellular	CELP	1.2, 2.4, 4.8, 9.6, 13.4, 14.4
IS-95 PCS	PCS	CELP	13.4, 14.4
PDC	Cellular	VSELP	4.5, 6.7, 11.2
CT2	Cordless	ADPCM	32
DECT	Cordless	ADPCM	32
PHS	Cordless	ADPCM	32
DCS-1800	PCS	RPE-LTP	13
PACS	PCS	ADPCM	32

Example 8.4

A digital mobile communication system has a forward channel frequency band ranging between 810 MHz to 826 MHz and a reverse channel band between 940 MHz to 956 MHz. Assume that 90 percent of the bandwidth is used by traffic channels. It is required to support at least 1150 simultaneous calls using FDMA. The modulation scheme employed has a spectral efficiency of 1.68 bps/Hz. Assuming that the channel impairments necessitate the use of rate 1/2 FEC codes, find the upper bound on the transmission bit rate that a speech coder used in this system should provide?

Solution

Total Bandwidth available for traffic channels = $0.9 \times (810 - 826) = 14.4$ MHz.

Number of simultaneous users = 1150.

Therefore, maximum channel bandwidth = 14.4 /1150 MHz = 12.5 kHz.

Spectral Efficiency = 1.68 bps/Hz.

Therefore, maximum channel data rate = 1.68×12500 bps = 21 kbps.

FEC coder rate = 0.5.

Therefore, maximum net data rate = 21×0.5 kbps = 10.5 kbps.

Therefore, we need to design a speech coder with a data rate less than or equal to 10.5 kbps.

Example 8.5

The output of a speech coder has bits which contribute to signal quality with varying degree of importance. Encoding is done on blocks of samples of 20 ms duration (260 bits of coder output). The first 50 of the encoded speech bits (say type 1) in each block are considered to be the most significant and hence to protect them from channel errors are appended with 10 CRC bits and convolutionally encoded with a rate 1/2 FEC coder. The next 132 bits (say type 2) are appended with 5 CRC bits and the last 78 bits (say type 3) are not error protected. Compute the gross channel data rate achievable.

Solution

Number of type 1 channel bits to be transmitted every 20 ms

$(50 + 10) \times 2 = 120$ bits

Number of type 2 channel bits to be transmitted every 20 ms

$132 + 5 = 137$ bits

Number of type 3 channel bits to be encoded = 78 bits

Total number of channel bits to be transmitted every 20 ms

$120 + 137 + 78$ bits = 335 bits

Therefore, gross channel bit rate = $335/(20 \times 10^{-3})$ = 16.75 kbps.

8.9 The GSM Codec

The original speech coder used in the pan-European digital cellular standard GSM goes by a rather grandiose name of *regular pulse excited long-term prediction* (RPE-LTP) codec. This codec has a net bit rate of 13 kbps and was chosen after conducting exhaustive subjective tests [Col89] on various competing codecs. More recent GSM upgrades have improved upon the original codec specification.

The RPE-LTP codec [Var88] combines the advantages of the earlier French proposed baseband RELP codec with those of the multipulse excited long-term prediction (MPE-LTP) codec proposed by Germany. The advantage of the baseband RELP codec is that it provides good quality speech at low complexity. The speech quality of a RELP codec is, however, limited due to the tonal noise introduced by the process of high frequency regeneration and by the bit errors introduced during transmission. The MPE-LTP technique, on the other hand, produces excellent speech quality at high complexity and is not much affected by bit errors in the channel. By modifying the RELP codec to incorporate certain features of the MPE-LTP codec, the net bit rate was reduced from 14.77 kbps to 13.0 kbps without loss of quality. The most important modification was the addition of a long-term prediction loop.

The GSM codec is relatively complex and power hungry. Figure 8.10 shows a block diagram of the speech encoder [Ste94]. The encoder is comprised of four major processing blocks. The speech sequence is first pre-emphasized, ordered into segments of 20 ms duration, and then Hamming-windowed. This is followed by short-term prediction (STP) filtering analysis where the logarithmic area ratios (LARs) of the reflection coefficients $r_n(k)$ (eight in number) are computed. The eight LAR parameters have different dynamic ranges and probability distribution functions, and hence all of them are not encoded with the same number of bits for transmission. The LAR parameters are also decoded by the LPC inverse filter so as to minimize the error e_n.

LTP analysis which involves finding the pitch period p_n and gain factor g_n is then carried out such that the LTP residual r_n is minimized. To minimize r_n, pitch extraction is done by the LTP by determining that value of delay, D, which maximizes the cross-correlation between the current STP error sample, e_n, and a previous error sample e_{n-D}. The extracted pitch p_n and gain g_n are transmitted and encoded at a rate of 3.6 kbps. The LTP residual, r_n, is weighted and decomposed into three candidate excitation sequences. The energies of these sequences are identified, and the one with the highest energy is selected to represent the LTP residual. The pulses in the excitation sequence are normalized to the highest amplitude, quantized, and transmitted at a rate of 9.6 kbps.

Figure 8.11 shows a block diagram of the GSM speech decoder [Ste94]. It consists of four blocks which perform operations complementary to those of the encoder. The received excitation parameters are RPE decoded and passed to the LTP synthesis filter which uses the pitch and gain parameter to synthesize the long-term signal. Short-term synthesis is carried out using the received reflection coefficients to recreate the original speech signal.

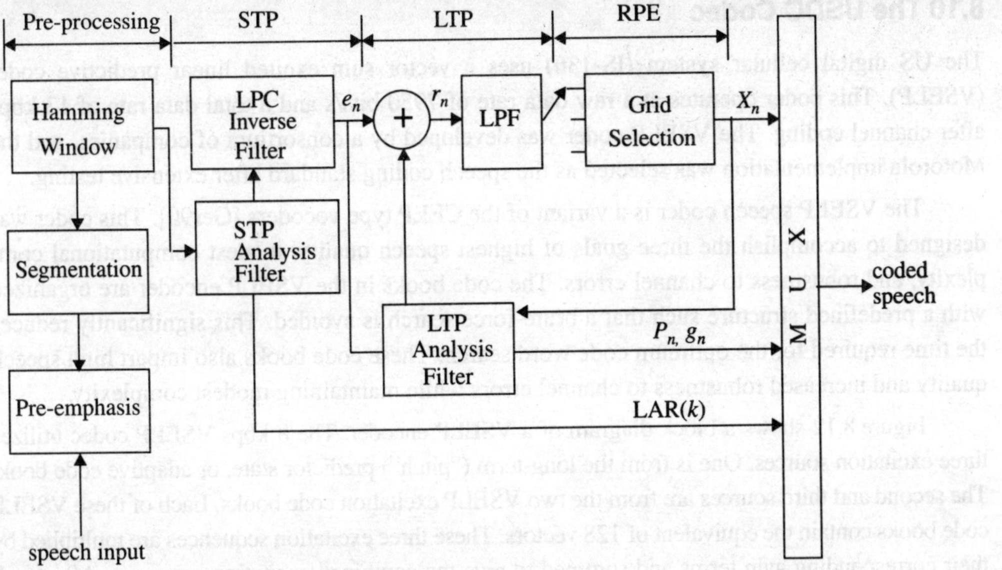

Figure 8.10 Block diagram of GSM speech encoder.

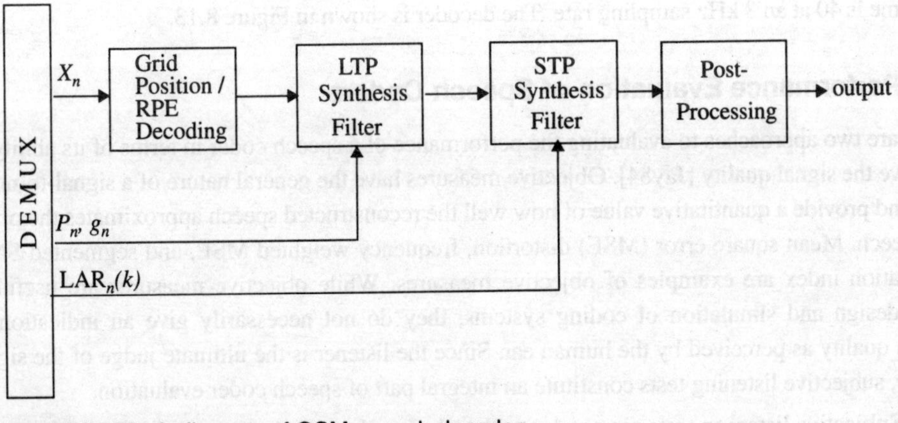

Figure 8.11 Block diagram of GSM speech decoder.

Every 260 bits of the coder output (i.e., 20 ms blocks of speech) are ordered, depending on their importance, into groups of 50, 132, and 78 bits each. The bits in the first group are very important bits called type *Ia* bits. The next 132 bits are important bits called *Ib* bits, and the last 78 bits are called type *II* bits. Since type *Ia* bits are the ones which effect speech quality the most, they have error detection CRC bits added. Both *Ia* and *Ib* bits are convolutionally encoded for forward error correction. The least significant type *II* bits have no error correction or detection.

8.10 The USDC Codec

The US digital cellular system (IS-136) uses a vector sum excited linear predictive coder (VSELP). This coder operates at a raw data rate of 7950 bits/s and a total data rate of 13 kbps after channel coding. The VSELP coder was developed by a consortium of companies, and the Motorola implementation was selected as the speech coding standard after extensive testing.

The VSELP speech coder is a variant of the CELP type vocoders [Ger90]. This coder was designed to accomplish the three goals of highest speech quality, modest computational complexity, and robustness to channel errors. The code books in the VSELP encoder are organized with a predefined structure such that a brute-force search is avoided. This significantly reduces the time required for the optimum code word search. These code books also impart high speech quality and increased robustness to channel errors while maintaining modest complexity.

Figure 8.12 shows a block diagram of a VSELP encoder. The 8 kbps VSELP codec utilizes three excitation sources. One is from the long-term ("pitch") predictor state, or adaptive code book. The second and third sources are from the two VSELP excitation code books. Each of these VSELP code books contain the equivalent of 128 vectors. These three excitation sequences are multiplied by their corresponding gain terms and summed to give the combined excitation sequence. After each subframe, the combined excitation sequence is used to update the long-term filter state (adaptive code book). The synthesis filter is a direct form 10th order LPC all pole-filter. The LPC coefficients are coded once per 20 ms frame and updated in each 5 ms subframe. The number of samples in a subframe is 40 at an 8 kHz sampling rate. The decoder is shown in Figure 8.13.

8.11 Performance Evaluation of Speech Coders

There are two approaches to evaluating the performance of a speech coder in terms of its ability to preserve the signal quality [Jay84]. Objective measures have the general nature of a signal-to-noise ratio and provide a quantitative value of how well the reconstructed speech approximates the original speech. Mean square error (MSE) distortion, frequency weighted MSE, and segmented SNR, articulation index are examples of objective measures. While objective measures are useful in initial design and simulation of coding systems, they do not necessarily give an indication of speech quality as perceived by the human ear. Since the listener is the ultimate judge of the signal quality, subjective listening tests constitute an integral part of speech coder evaluation.

Subjective listening tests are conducted by playing the sample to a number of listeners and asking them to judge the quality of the speech. Speech coders are highly speaker dependent in that the quality varies with the age and gender of the speaker, the speed at which the speaker speaks, and other factors. The subjective tests are carried out in different environments to simulate real life conditions such as noisy, multiple speakers, etc. These tests provide results in terms of overall quality, listening effort, intelligibility, and naturalness. The intelligibility tests measure the listeners ability to identify the spoken word. The diagnostic rhyme test (DRT) is the most popular and widely used intelligibility test. In this test, a word from a pair of rhymed words such as "those-dose" is presented to the listener and the listener is asked to identify which word was

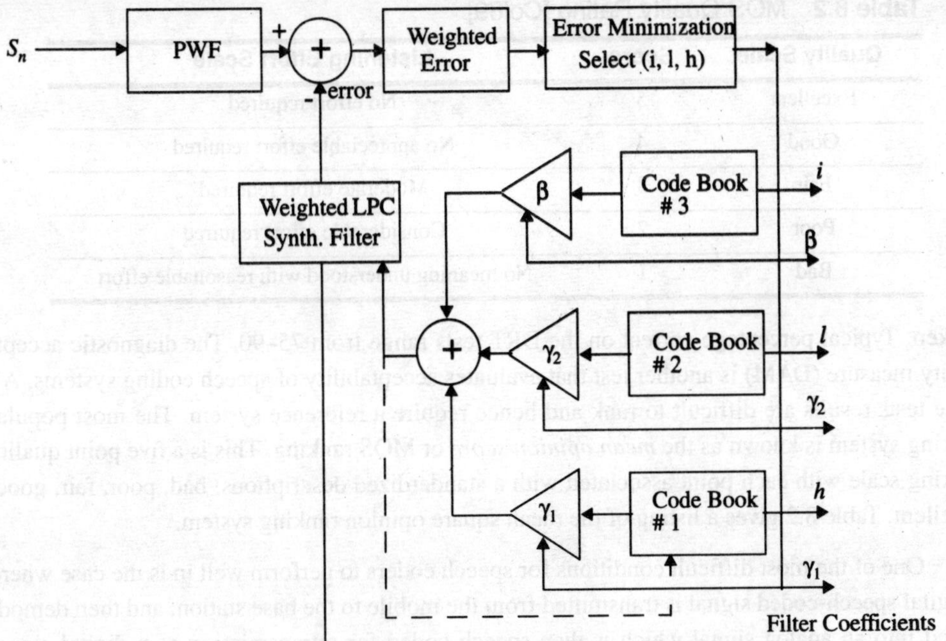

Figure 8.12 Block diagram of the USDC speech encoder.

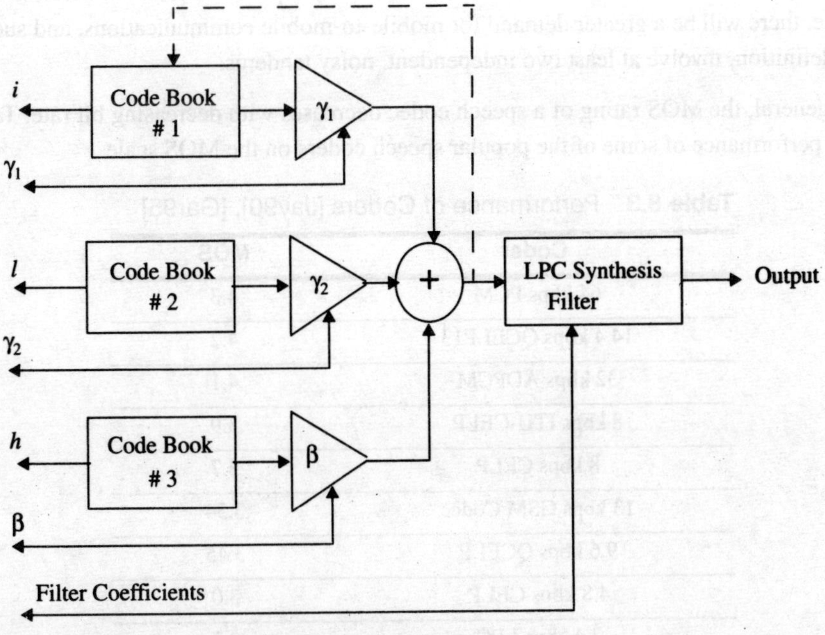

Figure 8.13 Diagram of the USDC speech decoder.

Table 8.2 MOS Quality Rating [Col89]

Quality Scale	Score	Listening Effort Scale
Excellent	5	No effort required
Good	4	No appreciable effort required
Fair	3	Moderate effort required
Poor	2	Considerable effort required
Bad	1	No meaning understood with reasonable effort

spoken. Typical percentage correct on the DRT tests range from 75–90. The diagnostic acceptability measure (DAM) is another test that evaluates acceptability of speech coding systems. All these tests results are difficult to rank and hence require a reference system. The most popular ranking system is known as the *mean opinion score* or MOS ranking. This is a five point quality ranking scale with each point associated with a standardized descriptions: bad, poor, fair, good, excellent. Table 8.2 gives a listing of the mean square opinion ranking system.

One of the most difficult conditions for speech coders to perform well in is the case where a digital speech-coded signal is transmitted from the mobile to the base station, and then demodulated into an analog signal which is then speech coded for retransmission as a digital signal over a landline or wireless link. This situation, called *tandem* signaling, tends to exaggerate the bit errors originally received at the base station. Tandem signaling is difficult to protect against, but is an important evaluation criterion in the evaluation of speech coders. As wireless systems proliferate, there will be a greater demand for mobile-to-mobile communications, and such links will, by definition, involve at least two independent, noisy tandems.

In general, the MOS rating of a speech codec decreases with decreasing bit rate. Table 8.3 gives the performance of some of the popular speech coders on the MOS scale.

Table 8.3 Performance of Coders [Jay90], [Gar95]

Coder	MOS
64 kbps PCM	4.3
14.4 kbps QCELP13	4.2
32 kbps ADPCM	4.1
8 kbps ITU-CELP	3.9
8 kbps CELP	3.7
13 kbps GSM Codec	3.54
9.6 kbps QCELP	3.45
4.8 kbps CELP	3.0
2.4 kbps LPC	2.5

8.12 Problems

8.1 For an 8 bit uniform quantizer that spans the range (–1 V, 1 V), determine the step size of the quantizer. Compute the SNR due to quantization if the signal is a sinusoid that spans the entire range of the quantizer.

8.2 Derive a general expression that relates the signal-to-noise ratio due to quantization as a function of the number of bits.

8.3 For a μ-law compander with $\mu = 255$, plot the magnitude of the output voltage as a function of the magnitude of the input voltage. If an input voltage of 0.1 V is applied to the compander, what is the resulting output voltage? If an input voltage of 0.01 V is applied to the input, determine the resulting output voltage. Assume the compander has a maximum input of 1 V.

8.4 For an A-law compander with $A = 90$, plot the magnitude of the output voltage as a function of the magnitude of the input voltage. If an input voltage of 0.1 V is applied to the compander, what is the resulting output voltage? If an input voltage of 0.01 V is applied to the input, determine the resulting output voltage. Assume the compander has a maximum input of 1 V.

8.5 A compander relies on speech *compression* and speech *expansion* (decompression) at the receiver in order to restore signals to their correct relative values. The *expander* has an inverse characteristic when compared to the *compressor*. Determine the proper compressor characteristics for the speech compressors in Problems 8.3 and 8.4.

8.6 A speech signal has an amplitude pdf that can be characterized as a zero-mean Gaussian process with a standard deviation of 0.5 V. For such a speech signal, determine the mean square error distortion at the output of a 4 bit quantizer if quantization levels are uniformly spaced by 0.25 V. Design a nonuniform quantizer that would minimize the mean square error distortion, and determine the level of distortion.

8.7 Consider a sub-band speech coder that allocates 5 bits for the audio spectrum between 225 Hz and 500 Hz, 3 bits for 500 Hz to 1200 Hz, and 2 bits for frequencies between 1300 Hz and 3 kHz. Assume that the sub-band coder output is then applied to a rate 3/4 convolutional coder. Determine the data rate out of the channel coder.

8.8 List four significant factors which influence the choice of speech coders in mobile communication systems. Elaborate on the tradeoffs which are caused by each factor. Rank order the factors based on your personal view point, and defend your position.

8.9 Professors Deller, Proakis, and Hansen co-authored an extensive text entitled "Discrete-Time Processing of Speech Signals" [Del93]. As part of this work, they have created an Internet "ftp" site which contains numerous speech files. Browse the site and download several files which demonstrate several speech coders. Report your findings and indicate which files you found to be most useful.

The files are available via ftp at archive.egr.msu.edu in the directory pub/jojo/DPHTEXT. The file README.DPH includes instructions and file descriptions. These files are in ASCII, one signed integer decimal sample per line, and are easily read by MATLAB.

8.10 *Scalar quantization computer program*: Consider a data sequence of random variables $\{X_i\}$, where each $X_i \sim N(0, 1)$ has a Gaussian distribution with mean zero and variance 1. Construct a scalar quantizer which quantizes each sample at a rate of 3 bits/sample (so there will be eight quantizer levels). Use the generalized Lloyd algorithm to determine your quantization levels. Train your quantizer on a sequence of 250 samples. Your solution should include:

A listing of your eight quantization levels

The mean squared error distortion of your quantizer, computed by running your quantizer on a sequence of 10,000 samples

A calculation of the theoretical lower bound on mean-squared error distortion for a rate three scalar quantizer

8.11 *Vector quantization computer program*: Consider data sequence of random variables $\{X_i\}$, where each $X_i \sim N(0, 1)$ has a Gaussian distribution with mean zero and variance 1. Now construct a two-dimensional vector quantizer which quantizes each sample at a rate of 3 bits/sample (so there will be $8 \times 8 = 64$ quantization vectors). Use the generalized Lloyd algorithm to determine your quantization vectors. Train your quantizer using a sequence of 1200 vectors (2400 samples). Your solution should include:

A listing of your 64 quantization vectors

The mean squared error distortion of your quantizer, computed by running your quantizer on a sequence of 10,000 vectors (20,000 samples)

A calculation of the theoretical lower bound on mean-squared error distortion for a rate 3 quantizer of large dimension

8.12 *Vector quantization with correlated samples*: Consider a sequence of random variables $\{Y_i\}$ and $\{X_i\}$, where $X_i \sim N(0, 1)$, $Y_1 \sim N(0, 1)$, and

$$Y_{i+1} = \frac{1}{\sqrt{2}}Y_i + \frac{1}{\sqrt{2}}X_i$$

As a result, each Y_i in the sequence $\{Y_i\}$ will have a Gaussian distribution with mean zero and variance 1, but the samples will be correlated (this is a simple example of what is called a Gauss–Markov Source). Now construct a two-dimensional vector quantizer which quantizes each sample at a rate of 3 bits/sample. Use the generalized Lloyd algorithm to determine your quantization vectors. Train your quantizer on a sequence of 1200 vectors (2400 samples). Your solution should include:

A listing of your 64 quantization vectors

The mean squared error distortion of your quantizer, computed by running your quantizer on a sequence of 10,000 (20,000 samples)

What happens as the length of the training sequence varies, as the relative correlation values between Y_i change, or as dimensions of your vector quantizer varies

CHAPTER 9

Multiple Access Techniques for Wireless Communications

Multiple access schemes are used to allow many mobile users to share simultaneously a finite amount of radio spectrum. The sharing of spectrum is required to achieve high capacity by simultaneously allocating the available bandwidth (or the available amount of channels) to multiple users. For high quality communications, this must be done without severe degradation in the performance of the system.

9.1 Introduction

In wireless communications systems, it is often desirable to allow the subscriber to send simultaneously information to the base station while receiving information from the base station. For example, in conventional telephone systems, it is possible to talk and listen simultaneously, and this effect, called *duplexing*, is generally required in wireless telephone systems.

Duplexing may be done using frequency or time domain techniques. *Frequency division duplexing* (FDD) provides two distinct bands of frequencies for every user. The *forward band* provides traffic from the base station to the mobile, and the *reverse band* provides traffic from the mobile to the base station. In FDD, any *duplex channel* actually consists of two simplex channels (a forward and reverse), and a device called a *duplexer* is used inside each subscriber unit and base station to allow simultaneous bidirectional radio transmission and reception for both the subscriber unit and the base station on the duplex channel pair. The frequency separation between each forward and reverse channel is constant throughout the system, regardless of the particular channel being used.

Time division duplexing (TDD) uses time instead of frequency to provide both a forward and reverse link. In TDD, multiple users share a single radio channel by taking turns in the time domain. Individual users are allowed to access the channel in assigned *time slots*, and each

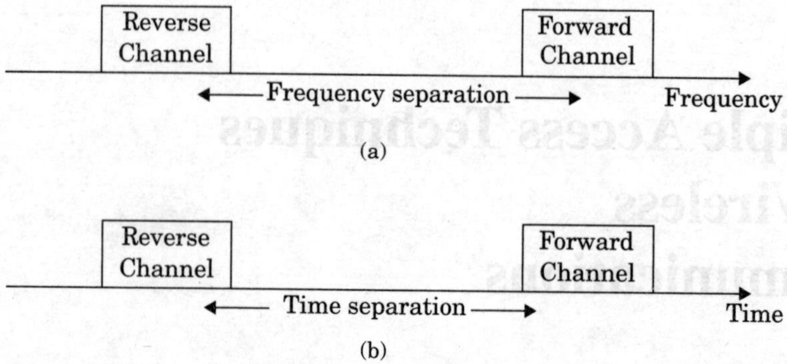

Figure 9.1 (a) FDD provides two simplex channels at the same time; (b) TDD provides two simplex time slots on the same frequency.

duplex channel has both a forward time slot and a reverse time slot to facilitate bidirectional communication. If the time separation between the forward and reverse time slot is small, then the transmission and reception of data appears simultaneous to the users at both the subscriber unit and on the base station side. Figure 9.1 illustrates FDD and TDD techniques. TDD allows communication on a single channel (as opposed to requiring two separate simplex or dedicated channels) and simplifies the subscriber equipment since a duplexer is not required.

There are several tradeoffs between FDD and TDD approaches. FDD is geared toward radio communications systems that allocate individual radio frequencies for each user. Because each transceiver simultaneously transmits and receives radio signals which can vary by more than 100 dB, the frequency allocation used for the forward and reverse channels must be carefully coordinated within its own system and with out-of-band users that occupy spectrum between these two bands. Furthermore, the frequency separation must be coordinated to permit the use of inexpensive RF and oscillator technology. TDD enables each transceiver to operate as either a transmitter or receiver on the same frequency, and eliminates the need for separate forward and reverse frequency bands. However, there is a time latency created by TDD due to the fact that communications is not full duplex in the truest sense, and this latency creates inherent sensitivities to propagation delays of individual users. Because of the rigid timing required for time slotting, TDD generally is limited to cordless phone or short range portable access. TDD is effective for fixed wireless access when all users are stationary so that propagation delays do not vary in time among the users.

9.1.1 Introduction to Multiple Access

Frequency division multiple access (FDMA), *time division multiple access* (TDMA), and *code division multiple access* (CDMA) are the three major access techniques used to share the available bandwidth in a wireless communication system. These techniques can be grouped as *narrowband* and *wideband* systems, depending upon how the available bandwidth is allocated to the users. The duplexing technique of a multiple access system is usually described along with the particular multiple access scheme, as shown in the examples that follow.

Narrowband Systems — The term *narrowband* is used to relate the bandwidth of a single channel to the expected coherence bandwidth of the channel. In a narrowband multiple access system, the available radio spectrum is divided into a large number of narrowband channels. The channels are usually operated using FDD. To minimize interference between forward and reverse links on each channel, the frequency separation is made as great as possible within the frequency spectrum, while still allowing inexpensive duplexers and a common transceiver antenna to be used in each subscriber unit. In narrowband FDMA, a user is assigned a particular channel which is not shared by other users in the vicinity, and if FDD is used (that is, each duplex channel has a forward and reverse simplex channel), then the system is called FDMA/FDD. Narrowband TDMA, on the other hand, allows users to share the same radio channel but allocates a unique time slot to each user in a cyclical fashion on the channel, thus separating a small number of users in time on a single channel. For narrowband TDMA systems, there generally are a large number of radio channels allocated using either FDD or TDD, and each channel is shared using TDMA. Such systems are called TDMA/FDD or TDMA/TDD access systems.

Wideband systems — In wideband systems, the transmission bandwidth of a single channel is much larger than the coherence bandwidth of the channel. Thus, multipath fading does not greatly vary the received signal power within a wideband channel, and frequency selective fades occur in only a small fraction of the signal bandwidth at any instance of time. In wideband multiple access systems a large number of transmitters are allowed to transmit on the same channel. TDMA allocates time slots to the many transmitters on the same channel and allows only one transmitter to access the channel at any instant of time, whereas spread spectrum CDMA allows all of the transmitters to access the channel at the same time. TDMA and CDMA systems may use either FDD or TDD multiplexing techniques.

In addition to FDMA, TDMA, and CDMA, two other multiple access schemes will soon be used for wireless communications. These are *packet radio* (PR) and *space division multiple access* (SDMA). In this chapter, the above mentioned multiple access techniques, their performance, and their capacity in digital wireless systems are discussed. Table 9.1 shows the different multiple access techniques being used in various wireless communications systems.

9.2 Frequency Division Multiple Access (FDMA)

Frequency division multiple access (FDMA) assigns individual channels to individual users. It can be seen from Figure 9.2 that each user is allocated a unique frequency band or channel. These channels are assigned on demand to users who request service. During the period of the call, no other user can share the same channel. In FDD systems, the users are assigned a channel as a pair of frequencies; one frequency is used for the forward channel, while the other frequency is used for the reverse channel. The features of FDMA are as follows:

- The FDMA channel carries only one phone circuit at a time.
- If an FDMA channel is not in use, then it sits idle and cannot be used by other users to increase or share capacity. It is essentially a wasted resource.

Table 9.1 Multiple Access Techniques Used in Different Wireless Communication Systems

Cellular System	Multiple Access Technique
Advanced Mobile Phone System (AMPS)	FDMA/FDD
Global System for Mobile (GSM)	TDMA/FDD
US Digital Cellular (USDC)	TDMA/FDD
Pacific Digital Cellular (PDC)	TDMA/FDD
CT2 (Cordless Telephone)	FDMA/TDD
Digital European Cordless Telephone (DECT)	FDMA/TDD
US Narrowband Spread Spectrum (IS-95)	CDMA/FDD
W-CDMA (3GPP)	CDMA/FDD CDMA/TDD
cdma2000 (3GPP2)	CDMA/FDD CDMA/TDD

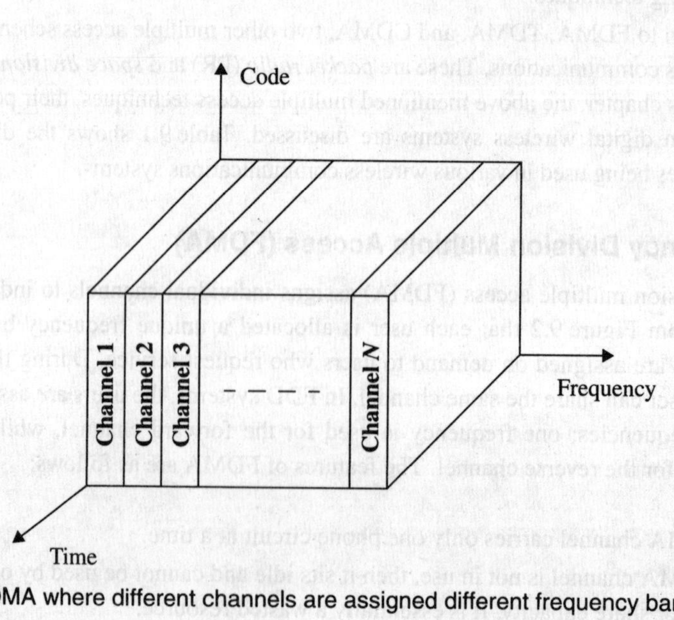

Figure 9.2 FDMA where different channels are assigned different frequency bands.

- After the assignment of a voice channel, the base station and the mobile transmit simultaneously and continuously.
- The bandwidths of FDMA channels are relatively narrow (30 kHz in AMPS) as each channel supports only one circuit per carrier. That is, FDMA is usually implemented in narrowband systems.
- The symbol time of a narrowband signal is large as compared to the average delay spread. This implies that the amount of intersymbol interference is low and, thus, little or no equalization is required in FDMA narrowband systems.
- The complexity of FDMA mobile systems is lower when compared to TDMA systems, though this is changing as digital signal processing methods improve for TDMA.
- Since FDMA is a continuous transmission scheme, fewer bits are needed for overhead purposes (such as synchronization and framing bits) as compared to TDMA.
- FDMA systems have higher cell site system costs as compared to TDMA systems, because of the single channel per carrier design, and the need to use costly bandpass filters to eliminate spurious radiation at the base station.
- The FDMA mobile unit uses duplexers since both the transmitter and receiver operate at the same time. This results in an increase in the cost of FDMA subscriber units and base stations.
- FDMA requires tight RF filtering to minimize adjacent channel interference.

Nonlinear Effects in FDMA — In a FDMA system, many channels share the same antenna at the base station. The power amplifiers or the power combiners, when operated at or near saturation for maximum power efficiency, are nonlinear. The nonlinearities cause signal spreading in the frequency domain and generate *intermodulation* (IM) frequencies. IM is undesired RF radiation which can interfere with other channels in the FDMA systems. Spreading of the spectrum results in adjacent-channel interference. Intermodulation is the generation of undesirable harmonics. Harmonics generated outside the mobile radio band cause interference to adjacent services, while those present inside the band cause interference to other users in the wireless system [Yac93].

Example 9.1

Find the intermodulation frequencies generated if a base station transmits two carrier frequencies at 1930 MHz and 1932 MHz that are amplified by a saturated clipping amplifier. If the mobile radio band is allocated from 1920 MHz to 1940 MHz, designate the IM frequencies that lie inside and outside the band.

Solution

Intermodulation distortion products occur at frequencies $mf_1 + nf_2$ for all integer values of m and n, i.e., $-\infty < m,n < \infty$. Some of the possible intermodulation frequencies that are produced by a nonlinear device are

$$(2n+1)f_1 - 2nf_2,\ (2n+2)f_1 - (2n+1)f_2,\ (2n+1)f_1 - 2nf_2,$$
$$(2n+2)f_2 - (2n+1)f_1, \text{ etc.} \qquad \text{for } n = 0, 1, 2, \ldots\ldots$$

Table E8.1 lists several intermodulation product terms.

Table E8.1 Intermodulation Products

$n = 0$	$n = 1$	$n = 2$	$n = 3$
1930	1926	1922	1918
1928	1924	1920	1916
1932	1936	1940	1944*
1934	1938	1942*	1946*

The frequencies in the table marked with an asterisk (*) are the frequencies that lie outside the allocated mobile radio band.

The first US analog cellular system, the *Advanced Mobile Phone System* (AMPS), is based on FDMA/FDD. A single user occupies a single channel while the call is in progress, and the single channel is actually two simplex channels which are frequency duplexed with a 45 MHz split. When a call is completed, or when a handoff occurs, the channel is vacated so that another mobile subscriber may use it. Multiple or simultaneous users are accommodated in AMPS by giving each user a unique channel. Voice signals are sent on the forward channel from the base station to mobile unit, and on the reverse channel from the mobile unit to the base station. In AMPS, analog narrowband frequency modulation (NBFM) is used to modulate the carrier. The number of channels that can be simultaneously supported in a FDMA system is given by

$$N = \frac{B_t - 2B_{guard}}{B_c} \qquad (9.1)$$

where B_t is the total spectrum allocation, B_{guard} is the guard band allocated at the edge of the allocated spectrum band, and B_c is the channel bandwidth. Note that B_t and B_c may be specified in terms of simplex bandwidths where it is understood that there are symmetric frequency allocations for the forward band and reverse band.

Example 9.2

If a US AMPS cellular operator is allocated 12.5 MHz for each simplex band, and if B_t is 12.5 MHz, B_{guard} is 10 kHz, and B_c is 30 kHz, find the number of channels available in an FDMA system.

Solution

The number of channels available in the FDMA system is given as

$$N = \frac{12.5 \times 10^6 - 2(10 \times 10^3)}{30 \times 10^3} = 416$$

In the US, each cellular carrier is allocated 416 channels.

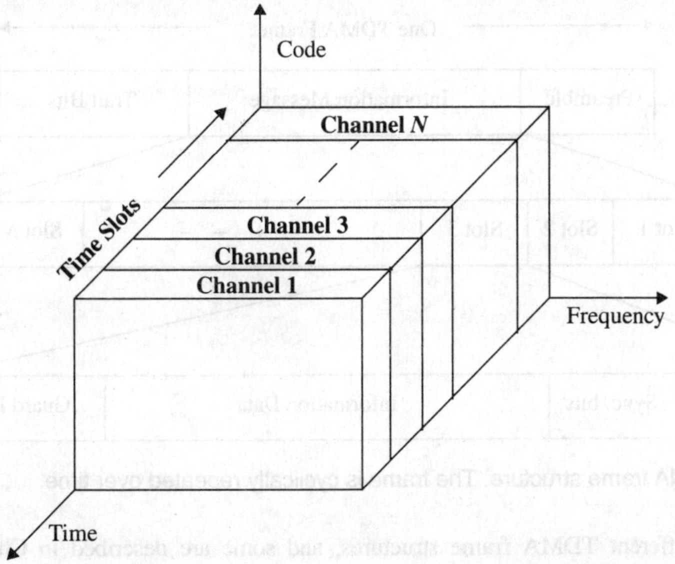

Figure 9.3 TDMA scheme where each channel occupies a cyclically repeating time slot.

9.3 Time Division Multiple Access (TDMA)

Time division multiple access (TDMA) systems divide the radio spectrum into time slots, and in each slot only one user is allowed to either transmit or receive. It can be seen from Figure 9.3 that each user occupies a cyclically repeating time slot, so a channel may be thought of as a particular time slot that reoccurs every frame, where N time slots comprise a frame. TDMA systems transmit data in a *buffer-and-burst* method, thus the transmission for any user is noncontinuous. This implies that, unlike in FDMA systems which accommodate analog FM, digital data and digital modulation must be used with TDMA. The transmission from various users is interlaced into a repeating frame structure as shown in Figure 9.4. It can be seen that a frame consists of a number of slots. Each frame is made up of a preamble, an information message, and tail bits. In TDMA/TDD, half of the time slots in the frame information message would be used for the forward link channels and half would be used for reverse link channels. In TDMA/FDD systems, an identical or similar frame structure would be used solely for either forward or reverse transmission, but the carrier frequencies would be different for the forward and reverse links. In general, TDMA/FDD systems intentionally induce several time slots of delay between the forward and reverse time slots for a particular user, so that duplexers are not required in the subscriber unit.

In a TDMA frame, the preamble contains the address and synchronization information that both the base station and the subscribers use to identify each other. Guard times are utilized to allow synchronization of the receivers between different slots and frames. Different TDMA wireless

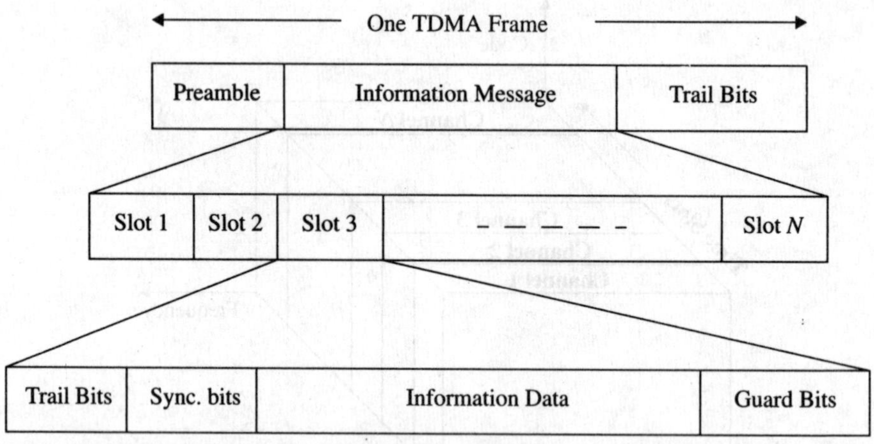

Figure 9.4 TDMA frame structure. The frame is cyclically repeated over time.

standards have different TDMA frame structures, and some are described in Chapter 11. The features of TDMA include the following:

- TDMA shares a single carrier frequency with several users, where each user makes use of nonoverlapping time slots. The number of time slots per frame depends on several factors, such as modulation technique, available bandwidth, etc.
- Data transmission for users of a TDMA system is not continuous, but occurs in bursts. This results in low battery consumption, since the subscriber transmitter can be turned off when not in use (which is most of the time).
- Because of discontinuous transmissions in TDMA, the handoff process is much simpler for a subscriber unit, since it is able to listen for other base stations during idle time slots. An enhanced link control, such as that provided by *mobile assisted handoff* (MAHO) can be carried out by a subscriber by listening on an idle slot in the TDMA frame.
- TDMA uses different time slots for transmission and reception, thus duplexers are not required. Even if FDD is used, a switch rather than a duplexer inside the subscriber unit is all that is required to switch between transmitter and receiver using TDMA.
- Adaptive equalization is usually necessary in TDMA systems, since the transmission rates are generally very high as compared to FDMA channels.
- In TDMA, the guard time should be minimized. If the transmitted signal at the edges of a time slot are suppressed sharply in order to shorten the guard time, the transmitted spectrum will expand and cause interference to adjacent channels.
- High synchronization overhead is required in TDMA systems because of burst transmissions. TDMA transmissions are slotted, and this requires the receivers to be synchronized for each data burst. In addition, guard slots are necessary to separate users, and this results in the TDMA systems having larger overheads as compared to FDMA.

- TDMA has an advantage in that it is possible to allocate different numbers of time slots per frame to different users. Thus, bandwidth can be supplied on demand to different users by concatenating or reassigning time slots based on priority.

Efficiency of TDMA — The efficiency of a TDMA system is a measure of the percentage of transmitted data that contains information as opposed to providing overhead for the access scheme. The frame efficiency, η_f, is the percentage of bits per frame which contain transmitted data. Note that the transmitted data may include source and channel coding bits, so the raw end-user efficiency of a system is generally less than η_f. The frame efficiency can be found as follows.

The number of overhead bits per frame is [Zie92],

$$b_{OH} = N_r b_r + N_t b_p + N_t b_g + N_r b_g \tag{9.2}$$

where N_r is the number of reference bursts per frame, N_t is the number of traffic bursts per frame, b_r is the number of overhead bits per reference burst, b_p is the number of overhead bits per preamble in each slot, and b_g is the number of equivalent bits in each guard time interval. The total number of bits per frame, b_T, is

$$b_T = T_f R \tag{9.3}$$

where T_f is the frame duration, and R is the channel bit rate. The frame efficiency η_f is thus given as

$$\eta_f = \left(1 - \frac{b_{OH}}{b_T}\right) \times 100\% \tag{9.4}$$

Number of channels in TDMA system — The number of TDMA channel slots that can be provided in a TDMA system is found by multiplying the number of TDMA slots per channel by the number of channels available and is given by

$$N = \frac{m(B_{tot} - 2B_{guard})}{B_c} \tag{9.5}$$

where m is the maximum number of TDMA users supported on each radio channel. Note that two guard bands, one at the low end of the allocated frequency band and one at the high end, are required to ensure that users at the edge of the band do not "bleed over" into an adjacent radio service.

Example 9.3

Consider Global System for Mobile, which is a TDMA/FDD system that uses 25 MHz for the forward link, which is broken into radio channels of 200 kHz. If 8 speech channels are supported on a single radio channel, and if no guard band is assumed, find the number of simultaneous users that can be accommodated in GSM.

Solution

The number of simultaneous users that can be accommodated in GSM is given as

$$N = \frac{25 \text{ MHz}}{(200 \text{ kHz})/8} = 1000$$

Thus, GSM can accommodate 1000 simultaneous users.

Example 9.4

If GSM uses a frame structure where each frame consists of eight time slots, and each time slot contains 156.25 bits, and data is transmitted at 270.833 kbps in the channel, find (a) the time duration of a bit, (b) the time duration of a slot, (c) the time duration of a frame, and (d) how long must a user occupying a single time slot wait between two successive transmissions.

Solution

(a) The time duration of a bit, $T_b = \dfrac{1}{270.833 \text{ kbps}} = 3.692\ \mu\text{s}$.

(b) The time duration of a slot, $T_{slot} = 156.25 \times T_b = 0.577$ ms.

(c) The time duration of a frame, $T_f = 8 \times T_{slot} = 4.615$ ms.

(d) A user has to wait 4.615 ms, the arrival time of a new frame, for its next transmission.

Example 9.5

If a normal GSM time slot consists of six trailing bits, 8.25 guard bits, 26 training bits, and two traffic bursts of 58 bits of data, find the frame efficiency.

Solution

A time slot has 6 + 8.25 + 26 + 2(58) = 156.25 bits.

A frame has 8 × 156.25 = 1250 bits/frame.

The number of overhead bits per frame is given by

$$b_{OH} = 8(6) + 8(8.25) + 8(26) = 322 \text{ bits}$$

Thus, the frame efficiency

$$\eta_f = \left[1 - \frac{322}{1250}\right] \times 100 = 74.24\%.$$

9.4 Spread Spectrum Multiple Access

Spread spectrum multiple access (SSMA) uses signals which have a transmission bandwidth that is several orders of magnitude greater than the minimum required RF bandwidth. A pseudo-noise (PN) sequence (discussed in Chapter 6) converts a narrowband signal to a wideband noise-like signal before transmission. SSMA also provides immunity to multipath interference and robust multiple access capability. SSMA is not very bandwidth efficient when used by a single user. However, since many users can share the same spread spectrum bandwidth without interfering with one another, spread spectrum systems become bandwidth efficient in a multiple user environment. It is exactly this situation that is of interest to wireless system designers. There are two main types of spread spectrum multiple access techniques; *frequency hopped multiple access* (FH) and *direct sequence multiple access* (DS). Direct sequence multiple access is also called *code division multiple access* (CDMA).

9.4.1 Frequency Hopped Multiple Access (FHMA)

Frequency hopped multiple access (FHMA) is a digital multiple access system in which the carrier frequencies of the individual users are varied in a pseudorandom fashion within a wideband channel. Figure 9.5 illustrates how FHMA allows multiple users to simultaneously occupy the same spectrum at the same time, where each user dwells at a specific narrowband channel at a particular instance of time, based on the particular PN code of the user. The digital data of each user is broken into uniform sized bursts which are transmitted on different channels within the allocated spectrum band. The instantaneous bandwidth of any one transmission burst is much smaller than the total spread bandwidth. The pseudorandom change of the channel frequencies of the user randomizes the occupancy of a specific channel at any given time, thereby allowing for multiple access over a wide range of frequencies. In the FH receiver, a locally generated PN code is used to synchronize the receiver's instantaneous frequency with that of the transmitter. At any given point in time, a frequency hopped signal only occupies a single, relatively narrow channel since narrowband FM or FSK is used. The difference between FHMA and a traditional FDMA system is that the frequency hopped signal changes channels at rapid intervals. If the rate of change of the carrier frequency is greater than the symbol rate, then the system is referred to as a *fast frequency hopping system*. If the channel changes at a rate less than or equal to the symbol rate, it is called *slow frequency hopping*. A fast frequency hopper may thus be thought of as an FDMA system which employs frequency diversity. FHMA systems often employ energy efficient constant envelope modulation. Inexpensive receivers may be built to provide noncoherent detection of FHMA. This implies that linearity is not an issue, and the power of multiple users at the receiver does not degrade FHMA performance.

A frequency hopped system provides a level of security, especially when a large number of channels are used, since an unintended (or an intercepting) receiver that does not know the pseudorandom sequence of frequency slots must retune rapidly to search for the signal it wishes to intercept. In addition, the FH signal is somewhat immune to fading, since error control coding and interleaving can be used to protect the frequency hopped signal against deep fades which may occasionally occur during the hopping sequence. Error control coding and interleaving can also be combined to guard against *erasures* which can occur when two or more users transmit on the same channel at the same time. Bluetooth and HomeRF wireless technologies have adopted FHMA for power efficiency and low cost implementation.

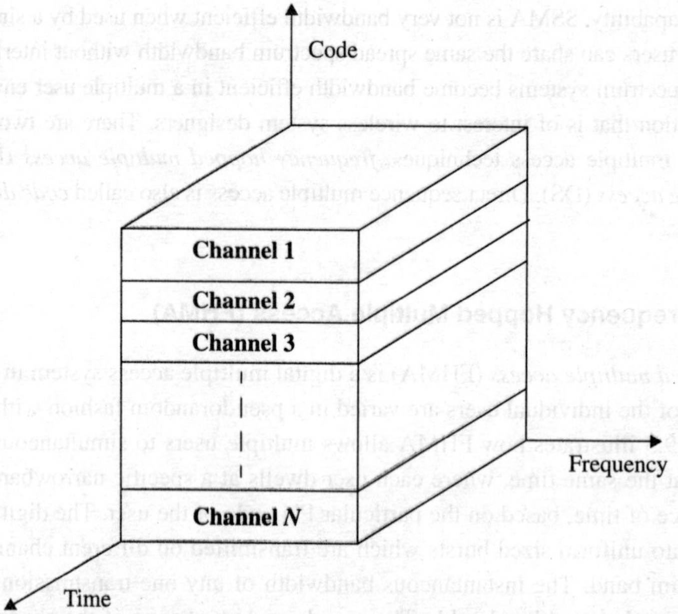

Figure 9.5 Spread spectrum multiple access in which each channel is assigned a unique PN code which is orthogonal or approximately orthogonal to PN codes used by other users.

9.4.2 Code Division Multiple Access (CDMA)

In *code division multiple access* (CDMA) systems, the narrowband message signal is multiplied by a very large bandwidth signal called the *spreading signal*. The spreading signal is a pseudonoise code sequence that has a chip rate which is orders of magnitudes greater than the data rate of the message. All users in a CDMA system, as seen from Figure 9.5, use the same carrier frequency and may transmit simultaneously. Each user has its own pseudorandom codeword which is approximately orthogonal to all other codewords. The receiver performs a time correlation operation to detect only the specific desired codeword. All other codewords appear as noise due to decorrelation. For detection of the message signal, the receiver needs to know the codeword used by the transmitter. Each user operates independently with no knowledge of the other users.

In CDMA, the power of multiple users at a receiver determines the noise floor after decorrelation. If the power of each user within a cell is not controlled such that they do not appear equal at the base station receiver, then the *near–far problem* occurs.

The near–far problem occurs when many mobile users share the same channel. In general, the strongest received mobile signal will *capture* the demodulator at a base station. In CDMA, stronger received signal levels raise the noise floor at the base station demodulators for the weaker signals, thereby decreasing the probability that weaker signals will be received. To combat the near–far problem, *power control* is used in most CDMA implementations. Power control is provided by each base station in a cellular system and assures that each mobile within the base station coverage area provides the same signal level to the base station receiver. This solves the problem of a nearby subscriber overpowering the base station receiver and drowning out the signals of far away subscribers. Power control is implemented at the base station by rapidly sampling the radio signal strength indicator (RSSI) levels of each mobile and then sending a power change command over the forward radio link. Despite the use of power control within each cell, out-of-cell mobiles provide interference which is not under the control of the receiving base station. The features of CDMA including the following:

- Many users of a CDMA system share the same frequency. Either TDD or FDD may be used.
- Unlike TDMA or FDMA, CDMA has a soft capacity limit. Increasing the number of users in a CDMA system raises the noise floor in a linear manner. Thus, there is no absolute limit on the number of users in CDMA. Rather, the system performance gradually degrades for all users as the number of users is increased, and improves as the number of users is decreased.
- Multipath fading may be substantially reduced because the signal is spread over a large spectrum. If the spread spectrum bandwidth is greater than the coherence bandwidth of the channel, the inherent frequency diversity will mitigate the effects of small-scale fading.
- Channel data rates are very high in CDMA systems. Consequently, the symbol (chip) duration is very short and usually much less than the channel delay spread. Since PN sequences have low autocorrelation, multipath which is delayed by more than a chip will appear as noise. A RAKE receiver can be used to improve reception by collecting time delayed versions of the required signal.
- Since CDMA uses co-channel cells, it can use macroscopic spatial diversity to provide soft handoff. Soft handoff is performed by the MSC, which can simultaneously monitor a particular user from two or more base stations. The MSC may chose the best version of the signal at any time without switching frequencies.
- Self-jamming is a problem in CDMA system. Self-jamming arises from the fact that the spreading sequences of different users are not exactly orthogonal, hence in the despreading of a particular PN code, non-zero contributions to the receiver decision statistic for a desired user arise from the transmissions of other users in the system.
- The near–far problem occurs at a CDMA receiver if an undesired user has a high detected power as compared to the desired user.

9.4.3 Hybrid Spread Spectrum Techniques

In addition to the frequency hopped and direct sequence, spread spectrum multiple access techniques, there are certain other hybrid combinations that provide certain advantages. These hybrid techniques are described below.

Hybrid FDMA/CDMA (FCDMA) — This technique can be used as an alternative to the DS-CDMA techniques discussed above. Figure 9.6 shows the spectrum of this hybrid scheme. The available wideband spectrum is divided into a number of subspectras with smaller bandwidths.

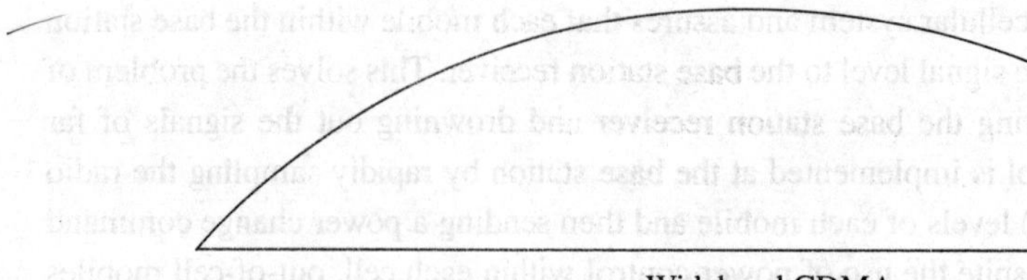

Figure 9.6 Spectrum of wideband CDMA compared to the spectrum of a hybrid, frequency division, direct sequence multiple access.

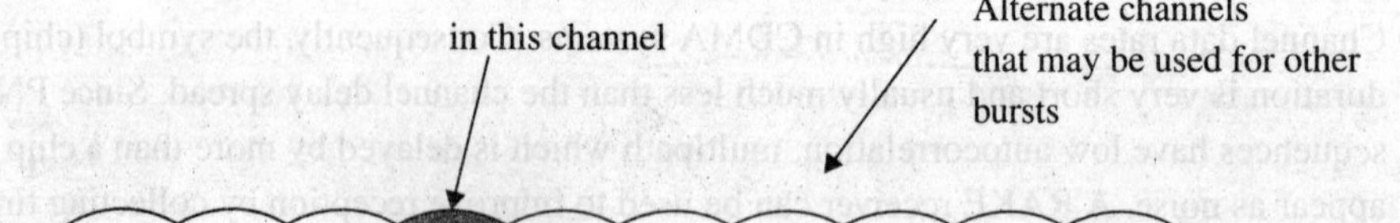

Figure 9.7 Frequency spectrum of a hybrid FH/DS system.

Each of these smaller subchannels becomes a narrowband CDMA system having processing gain lower than the original CDMA system. This hybrid system has an advantage in that the required bandwidth need not be contiguous and different users can be allotted different subspectrum bandwidths depending on their requirements. The capacity of this FDMA/CDMA technique is calculated as the sum of the capacities of a system operating in the subspectra [Eng93].

Hybrid Direct Sequence/Frequency Hopped Multiple Access (DS/FHMA) — This technique consists of a direct sequence modulated signal whose center frequency is made to hop periodically in a pseudorandom fashion. Figure 9.7 shows the frequency spectrum of such a signal [Dix94]. Direct sequence, frequency hopped systems have an advantage in that they avoid the near–far effect. However, frequency hopped CDMA systems are not adaptable to the soft handoff process since it is difficult to synchronize the frequency hopped base station receiver to the multiple hopped signals.

Time Division CDMA (TCDMA) — In a TCDMA (also called TDMA/CDMA) system, different spreading codes are assigned to different cells. Within each cell, only one user per cell is allotted a particular time slot. Thus at any time, only one CDMA user is transmitting in each cell.

When a handoff takes place, the spreading code of the user is changed to that of the new cell. Using TCDMA has an advantage in that it avoids the near–far effect since only one user transmits at a time within a cell.

Time Division Frequency Hopping (TDFH) — This multiple access technique has an advantage in severe multipath or when severe co-channel interference occurs. The subscriber can hop to a new frequency at the start of a new TDMA frame, thus avoiding a severe fade or erasure event on a particular channel. This technique has been adopted for the GSM standard, where the hopping sequence is predefined and the subscriber is allowed to hop only on certain frequencies which are assigned to a cell. This scheme also avoids co-channel interference problems between neighboring cells if two interfering base station transmitters are made to transmit on different frequencies at different times. The use of TDFH can increase the capacity of GSM by several fold [Gud92]. Chapter 11 describes the GSM standard in more detail.

9.5 Space Division Multiple Access (SDMA)

Space division multiple access (SDMA) controls the radiated energy for each user in space. It can be seen from Figure 9.8 that SDMA serves different users by using spot beam antennas. These different areas covered by the antenna beam may be served by the same frequency (in a TDMA or CDMA system) or different frequencies (in an FDMA system). Sectorized antennas may be thought of as a primitive application of SDMA. In the future, adaptive antennas will likely be used to simultaneously steer energy in the direction of many users at once and appear to be best suited for TDMA and CDMA base station architectures.

The reverse link presents the most difficulty in cellular systems for several reasons [Lib94b]. First, the base station has complete control over the power of all the transmitted signals on the forward link. However, because of different radio propagation paths between each

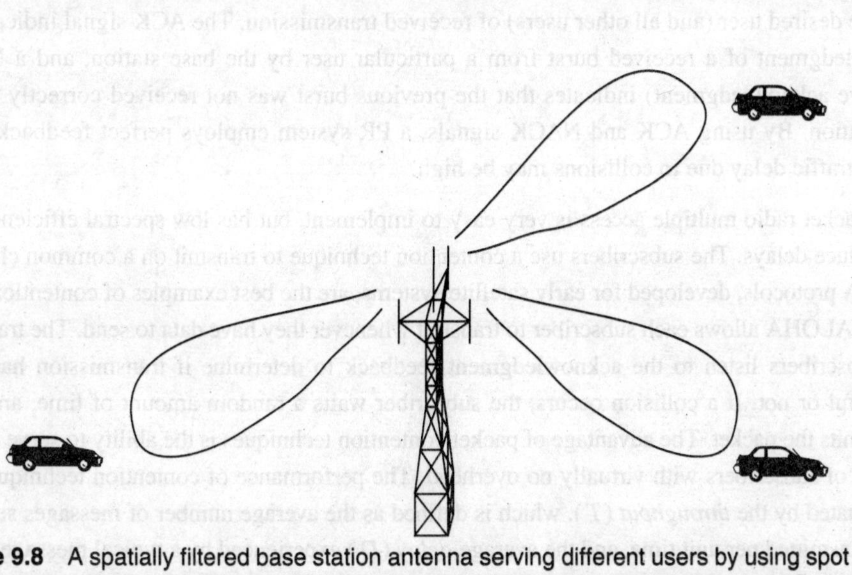

Figure 9.8 A spatially filtered base station antenna serving different users by using spot beams.

user and the base station, the transmitted power from each subscriber unit must be dynamically controlled to prevent any single user from driving up the interference level for all other users. Second, transmit power is limited by battery consumption at the subscriber unit, therefore there are limits on the degree to which power may be controlled on the reverse link. If the base station antenna is made to spatially filter each desired user so that more energy is detected from each subscriber, then the reverse link for each user is improved and less power is required.

Adaptive antennas used at the base station (and eventually at the subscriber units) promise to mitigate some of the problems on the reverse link. In the limiting case of infinitesimal beamwidth and infinitely fast tracking ability, adaptive antennas implement optimal SDMA, thereby providing a unique channel that is free from the interference of all other users in the cell. With SDMA, all users within the system would be able to communicate at the same time using the same channel. In addition, a perfect adaptive antenna system would be able to track individual multipath components for each user and combine them in an optimal manner to collect all of the available signal energy from each user. The perfect adaptive antenna system is not feasible since it requires infinitely large antennas. However, Section 9.7.2 illustrates what gains might be achieved using reasonably sized arrays with moderate directivities.

9.6 Packet Radio

In *packet radio* (PR) access techniques, many subscribers attempt to access a single channel in an uncoordinated (or minimally coordinated) manner. Transmission is done by using bursts of data. Collisions from the simultaneous transmissions of multiple transmitters are detected at the base station receiver, in which case an *ACK* or *NACK* signal is broadcast by the base station to alert the desired user (and all other users) of received transmission. The ACK signal indicates an acknowledgment of a received burst from a particular user by the base station, and a NACK (negative acknowledgment) indicates that the previous burst was not received correctly by the base station. By using ACK and NACK signals, a PR system employs perfect feedback, even though traffic delay due to collisions may be high.

Packet radio multiple access is very easy to implement, but has low spectral efficiency and may induce delays. The subscribers use a contention technique to transmit on a common channel. ALOHA protocols, developed for early satellite systems, are the best examples of contention techniques. ALOHA allows each subscriber to transmit whenever they have data to send. The transmitting subscribers listen to the acknowledgment feedback to determine if transmission has been successful or not. If a collision occurs, the subscriber waits a random amount of time, and then retransmits the packet. The advantage of packet contention techniques is the ability to serve a large number of subscribers with virtually no overhead. The performance of contention techniques can be evaluated by the *throughput* (T), which is defined as the average number of messages successfully transmitted per unit time, and the average *delay* (D) experienced by a typical message burst.

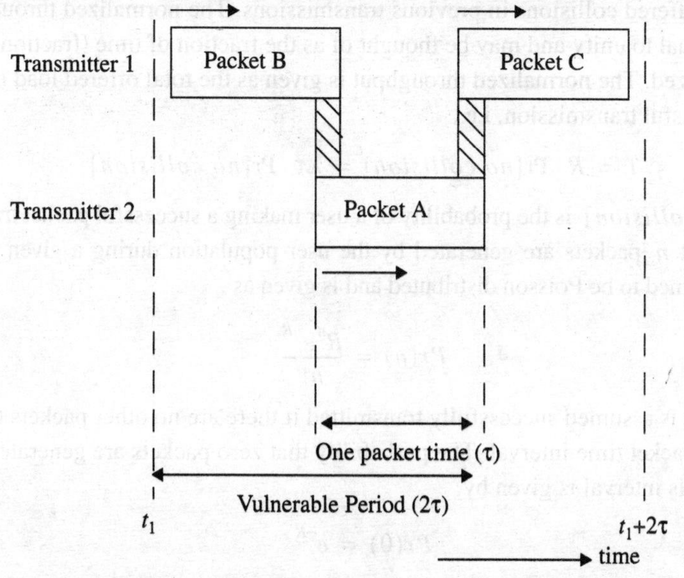

Packet A will collide with packets B and C because of overlap in transmission time.

Figure 9.9 Vulnerable period for a packet using the ALOHA protocol.

9.6.1 Packet Radio Protocols

In order to determine the throughput, it is important to determine the *vulnerable period,* V_p, which is defined as the time interval during which the packets are susceptible to collisions with transmissions from other users. Figure 9.9 shows the vulnerable period for a packet using ALOHA [Tan81]. The Packet A will suffer a collision if other terminals transmit packets during the period t_1 to $t_1 + 2\tau$. Even if only a small portion of packet A sustains a collision, the interference may render the message useless.

To study packet radio protocols, it is assumed that all packets sent by all users have a constant packet length and fixed, channel data rate, and all other users may generate new packets at random time intervals. Furthermore, it is assumed that packet transmissions occur with a Poisson distribution having a mean arrival rate of λ packets per second. If τ is the packet duration in seconds, then the *traffic occupancy* or *throughput* R of a packet radio network is given by

$$R = \lambda\tau \tag{9.6}$$

In Equation (9.6), R is the normalized channel traffic (measured in Erlangs) due to arriving and buffered packets, and is a relative measure of the channel utilization. If $R > 1$, then the packets generated by the users exceed the maximum transmission rate of the channel [Tan81]. Thus, to obtain a reasonable throughput, the rate at which new packets are generated must lie within $0 < R < 1$. Under conditions of normal loading, the throughput T is the same as the total offered load, L. The load L is the sum of the newly generated packets and the retransmitted packets that suffered collisions in previous transmissions. The normalized throughput is always less than or equal to unity and may be thought of as the fraction of time (fraction of an Erlang) a channel is utilized. The normalized throughput is given as the total offered load times the probability of successful transmission, i.e.,

$$T = R \cdot \Pr[no\ collision] = \lambda\tau \cdot \Pr[no\ collision] \tag{9.7}$$

where $\Pr[no\ collision]$ is the probability of a user making a successful packet transmission. The probability that n packets are generated by the user population during a given packet duration interval is assumed to be Poisson distributed and is given as

$$Pr(n) = \frac{R^n e^{-R}}{n!} \tag{9.8}$$

A packet is assumed successfully transmitted if there are no other packets transmitted during the given packet time interval. The probability that zero packets are generated (i.e., no collision) during this interval is given by

$$Pr(0) = e^{-R} \tag{9.9}$$

Based on the type of access, contention protocols are categorized as *random access*, *scheduled access*, and *hybrid access*. In random access, there is no coordination among the users and the messages are transmitted from the users as they arrive at the transmitter. Scheduled access is based on a coordinated access of users on the channel, and the users transmit messages within allotted slots or time intervals. Hybrid access is a combination of random access and scheduled access.

9.6.1.1 Pure ALOHA

The pure ALOHA protocol is a random access protocol used for data transfer. A user accesses a channel as soon as a message is ready to be transmitted. After a transmission, the user waits for an acknowledgment on either the same channel or a separate feedback channel. In case of collisions, (i.e., when a NACK is received), the terminal waits for a random period of time and retransmits the message. As the number of users increase, a greater delay occurs because the probability of collision increases.

For the ALOHA protocol, the vulnerable period is double the packet duration (see Figure 9.9). Thus, the probability of no collision during the interval of 2τ is found by evaluating $Pr(n)$ given as

$$Pr(n) = \frac{(2R)^n e^{-2R}}{n!} \quad \text{at } n = 0 \tag{9.10}$$

One may evaluate the mean of Equation (9.10) to determine the average number of packets sent during 2τ. (This is useful in determining the average offered traffic.) The probability of collision is $Pr(0) = e^{-2R}$. The throughput of the ALOHA protocol is found by using Equation (9.7) as

$$T = Re^{-2R} \tag{9.11}$$

9.6.1.2 Slotted ALOHA

In slotted ALOHA, time is divided into equal time slots of length greater than the packet duration τ. The subscribers each have synchronized clocks and transmit a message only at the beginning of a new time slot, thus resulting in a discrete distribution of packets. This prevents partial collisions, where one packet collides with a portion of another. As the number of users increase, a greater delay will occur due to complete collisions and the resulting repeated transmissions of those packets originally lost. The number of slots which a transmitter waits prior to retransmitting also determines the delay characteristics of the traffic. The vulnerable period for slotted ALOHA is only one packet duration, since partial collisions are prevented through synchronization. The probability that no other packets will be generated during the vulnerable period is e^{-R}. The throughput for the case of slotted ALOHA is thus given by

$$T = Re^{-R} \tag{9.12}$$

Figure 9.10 illustrates how ALOHA and slotted ALOHA systems tradeoff throughput for delay.

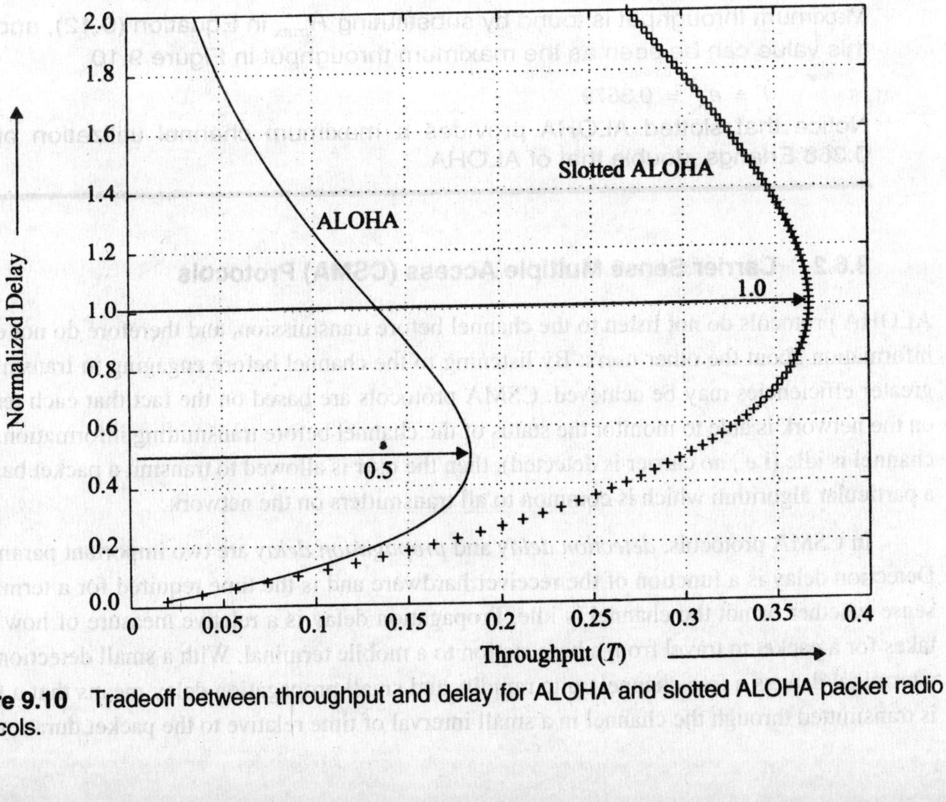

Figure 9.10 Tradeoff between throughput and delay for ALOHA and slotted ALOHA packet radio protocols.

Example 9.6

Determine the maximum throughput that can be achieved using ALOHA and slotted ALOHA protocols.

Solution The rate of arrival which maximizes the throughput for ALOHA is found by taking the derivative of Equation (9.11) and equating it to zero

$$\frac{dT}{dR} = e^{-2R} - 2Re^{-2R} = 0$$

$$R_{max} = 1/2$$

Maximum throughput achieved by using the ALOHA protocol is found by substituting R_{max} in Equation (9.11), and this value can be seen as the maximum throughput in Figure 9.10

$$T = \frac{1}{2}e^{-1} = 0.1839$$

Thus the best traffic utilization one can hope for using ALOHA is 0.184 Erlangs.

The maximum throughput for slotted ALOHA is found by taking the derivative of Equation (9.12) and equating it to zero

$$\frac{dT}{dR} = e^{-R} - Re^{-R} = 0$$

$$R_{max} = 1$$

Maximum throughput is found by substituting R_{max} in Equation (9.12), and this value can be seen as the maximum throughput in Figure 9.10

$$T = e^{-1} = 0.3679$$

Notice that slotted ALOHA provides a maximum channel utilization of 0.368 Erlangs, double that of ALOHA.

9.6.2 Carrier Sense Multiple Access (CSMA) Protocols

ALOHA protocols do not listen to the channel before transmission, and therefore do not exploit information about the other users. By listening to the channel before engaging in transmission, greater efficiencies may be achieved. CSMA protocols are based on the fact that each terminal on the network is able to monitor the status of the channel before transmitting information. If the channel is idle (i.e., no carrier is detected), then the user is allowed to transmit a packet based on a particular algorithm which is common to all transmitters on the network.

In CSMA protocols, *detection delay* and *propagation delay* are two important parameters. Detection delay is a function of the receiver hardware and is the time required for a terminal to sense whether or not the channel is idle. Propagation delay is a relative measure of how fast it takes for a packet to travel from a base station to a mobile terminal. With a small detection time, a terminal detects a free channel quite rapidly, and small propagation delay means that a packet is transmitted through the channel in a small interval of time relative to the packet duration.

Propagation delay is important, since just after a user begins sending a packet, another user may be ready to send and may be sensing the channel at the same time. If the transmitting packet has not reached the user who is poised to send, the latter user will sense an idle channel and will also send its packet, resulting in a collision between the two packets. Propagation delay impacts the performance of CSMA protocols. If t_p is the propagation time in seconds, R_b is the channel bit rate, and m is the expected number of bits in a data packet [Tan81], [Ber92], then the propagation delay t_d (in packet transmission units) can be expressed as

$$t_d = \frac{t_p R_b}{m} \tag{9.13}$$

There exist several variations of the CSMA strategy [Kle75], [Tob75]:

- ***1-persistent CSMA*** — The terminal listens to the channel and waits for transmission until it finds the channel idle. As soon as the channel is idle, the terminal transmits its message with probability one.
- ***non-persistent CSMA*** — In this type of CSMA strategy, after receiving a negative acknowledgment the terminal waits a random time before retransmission of the packet. This is popular for wireless LAN applications, where the packet transmission interval is much greater than the propagation delay to the farthermost user.
- ***p-persistent CSMA*** — *p*-persistent CSMA is applied to slotted channels. When a channel is found to be idle, the packet is transmitted in the first available slot with probability *p* or in the next slot with probability 1-*p*.
- ***CSMA/CD*** — In CSMA with collision detection (CD), a user monitors its transmission for collisions. If two or more terminals start a transmission at the same time, collision is detected, and the transmission is immediately aborted in midstream. This is handled by a user having both a transmitter and receiver which is able to support *listen-while-talk* operation. For a single radio channel, this is done by interrupting the transmission in order to sense the channel. For duplex systems, a full duplex transceiver is used [Lam80].
- ***Data sense multiple access*** (DSMA) — DSMA is a special type of CSMA that relies on successfully demodulating a forward control channel before broadcasting data back on a reverse channel. Each user attempts to detect a *busy-idle* message which is interspersed on the forward control channel. When the busy-idle message indicates that no users are transmitting on the reverse channel, a user is free to send a packet. This technique is used in the cellular digital packet data (CDPD) cellular network described in Chapter 10.

9.6.3 Reservation Protocols

9.6.3.1 Reservation ALOHA

Reservation ALOHA is a packet access scheme based on time division multiplexing. In this protocol, certain packet slots are assigned with priority, and it is possible for users to reserve slots for the transmission of packets. Slots can be permanently reserved or can be reserved on request.

For high traffic conditions, reservations on request offers better throughput. In one type of reservation ALOHA, the terminal making a successful transmission reserves a slot permanently until its transmission is complete, although very large duration transmissions may be interrupted. Another scheme allows a user to transmit a request on a subslot which is reserved in each frame. If the transmission is successful (i.e., no collisions are detected), the terminal is allocated the next regular slot in the frame for data transmission [Tan81].

9.6.3.2 Packet Reservation Multiple Access (PRMA)

PRMA uses a discrete packet time technique similar to reservation ALOHA and combines the cyclical frame structure of TDMA in a manner that allows each TDMA time slot to carry either voice or data, where voice is given priority. PRMA was proposed in [Goo89] as a means of integrating bursty data and human speech. PRMA defines a frame structure, much like is used in TDMA systems. Within each frame, there are a fixed number of time slots which may be designated as either "reserved" or "available", depending on the traffic as determined by the controlling base station. PRMA is discussed in Chapter 10.

9.6.4 Capture Effect in Packet Radio

Packet radio multiple access techniques are based on contention within a channel. When used with FM or spread spectrum modulation, it is possible for the strongest user to successfully *capture* the intended receiver, even when many other users are also transmitting. Often, the closest transmitter is able to capture a receiver because of the small propagation path loss. This is called the *near–far effect*. The capture effect offers both advantages and disadvantages in practical systems. Because a particular transmitter may capture an intended receiver, many packets may survive despite collision on the channel. However, a strong transmitter may make it impossible for the receiver to detect a much weaker transmitter which is attempting to communicate to the same receiver. This problem is known as the *hidden transmitter* problem.

A useful parameter in analyzing the capture effects in packet radio protocols is the minimum power ratio of an arriving packet, relative to the other colliding packets, such that it is received. This ratio is called the *capture ratio*, and is dependent upon the receiver and the modulation used.

In summary, packet radio techniques support mobile transmitters sending bursty traffic in the form of data packets using random access. Ideal channel throughput can be increased if terminals synchronize their packet transmissions into common time slots, such that the risk of partial packet overlap is avoided. With high traffic loads, both unslotted and slotted ALOHA protocols become inefficient, since the contention between all transmitted packets exposes most of the offered traffic to collisions, and thus results in multiple retransmissions and increased delays. To reduce this situation, CSMA can be used where the transmitter first listens either to the common radio channel or to a separate dedicated acknowledgment control channel from the base station. In a real world mobile system, the CSMA protocols may fail to detect ongoing radio transmissions of packets subject to deep fading on the reverse channel path. Utilization of an ALOHA channel can be improved by

Table 9.2 Multiple Access Techniques for Different Traffic Types

Type of Traffic	Multiple Access Technique
Bursty, short messages	Contention protocols
Bursty, long messages, large number of users	Reservation protocols
Bursty, long messages, small number of users	Reservation protocols with fixed TDMA reservation channel
Stream or deterministic (voice)	FDMA, TDMA, CDMA

deliberately introducing differences between the transmit powers of multiple users competing for the base station receiver. Table 9.2 shows the multiple access techniques which should be used for different types of traffic conditions.

9.7 Capacity of Cellular Systems

Channel capacity for a radio system can be defined as the maximum number of channels or users that can be provided in a fixed frequency band. Radio capacity is a parameter which measures spectrum efficiency of a wireless system. This parameter is determined by the required carrier-to-interference ratio (C/I) and the channel bandwidth B_c.

In a cellular system, the interference at a base station receiver will come from the subscriber units in the surrounding cells. This is called *reverse channel interference*. For a particular subscriber unit, the desired base station will provide the desired forward channel while the surrounding co-channel base stations will provide the *forward channel interference*. Considering the forward channel interference problem, let D be the distance between two co-channel cells and R be the cell radius. Then the minimum ratio of D/R that is required to provide a tolerable level of co-channel interference is called the co-channel reuse ratio and is given by [Lee89a]

$$Q = \frac{D}{R} \tag{9.14}$$

The radio propagation characteristics determine the *carrier-to-interference ratio (C/I)* at a given location, and models presented in Chapter 4 and Appendix B are used to find sensible C/I values. As shown in Figure 9.11, the M closest co-channel cells may be considered as first order interference, in which case C/I is given by

$$\frac{C}{I} = \frac{D_0^{-n_o}}{\sum_{k=1}^{M} D_k^{-n_k}} \tag{9.15}$$

where n_0 is the path loss exponent in the desired cell, D_0 is the distance from the desired base station to the mobile, D_k is the distance of the kth cell from the mobile, and n_k is the path loss

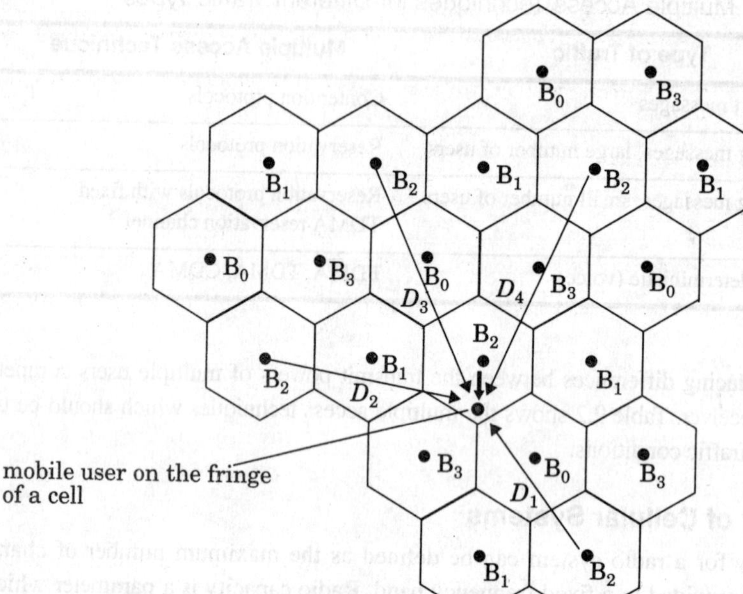

Figure 9.11 Illustration of forward channel interference for a cluster size of $N = 4$. Shown here are four co-channel base stations which interfere with the serving base station. The distance from the serving base station to the user is D_0, and interferers are a distance D_k from the user.

exponent to the kth interfering base station. If only the six closest interfering cells are considered, and all are approximately at the same distance D and have similar path loss exponents equal to that in the desired cell, then C/I is given by

$$\frac{C}{I} = \frac{D_0^{-n}}{6D^{-n}} \tag{9.16}$$

Now, if it is assumed that maximum interference occurs when the mobile is at the cell edge $D_0 = R$, and if the C/I for each user is required to be greater than some minimum $(C/I)_{min}$, which is the minimum carrier-to-interference ratio that still provides acceptable signal quality at the receiver, then the following equation must hold for acceptable performance:

$$\frac{1}{6}\left(\frac{R}{D}\right)^{-n} \geq \left(\frac{C}{I}\right)_{min} \tag{9.17}$$

Thus, from Equation (9.14), the co-channel reuse factor is

$$Q = \left(6\left(\frac{C}{I}\right)_{min}\right)^{1/n} \tag{9.18}$$

The radio capacity of a cellular system is defined as

$$m = \frac{B_t}{B_c N} \text{ radio channels/cell} \tag{9.19}$$

where m is the radio capacity metric, B_t is the total allocated spectrum for the system, B_c is the channel bandwidth, and N is the number of cells in a complete frequency reuse cluster. As shown in Chapter 3, N is related to the co-channel reuse factor Q by

$$Q = \sqrt{3N} \tag{9.20}$$

From Equations (9.18), (9.19), and (9.20), the radio capacity is given as

$$m = \frac{B_t}{B_c \frac{Q^2}{3}} = \frac{B_t}{B_c \left(\frac{6}{3^{n/2}} \left(\frac{C}{I} \right)_{min} \right)^{2/n}} \tag{9.21}$$

As shown by Lee [Lee89a], when $n = 4$, the radio capacity is given by

$$m = \frac{B_t}{B_c \sqrt{\frac{2}{3} \left(\frac{C}{I} \right)_{min}}} \text{ radio channels/cell} \tag{9.22}$$

In order to provide the same voice quality, $(C/I)_{min}$ may be lower in a digital systems when compared to an analog system. Typically, the minimum required C/I is about 12 dB for narrowband digital systems and 18 dB for narrowband analog FM systems, although exact values are determined by subjective listening tests in real-world propagation conditions. Each digital wireless standard has a different $(C/I)_{min}$, and in order to compare different systems, an equivalent C/I must be used. Lower $(C/I)_{min}$ values imply more capacity. If B_t and m are kept constant in Equation (9.22), then it is clear that B_c and $(C/I)_{min}$ are related by

$$\left(\frac{C}{I} \right)_{eq} = \left(\frac{C}{I} \right)_{min} \left(\frac{B_c}{B_c'} \right)^2 \tag{9.23}$$

where B_c is the bandwidth of a particular system, $(C/I)_{min}$ is the tolerable value for the same system, B_c' is the channel bandwidth for a different system, and $(C/I)_{eq}$ is the minimum C/I value for the different system when compared to the $(C/I)_{min}$ for a particular system. Notice that for a constant number of users per radio channel, the same voice quality will be maintained in a different system if $(C/I)_{min}$ increases by a factor of four when the bandwidth is halved. Equation (9.22) indicates that maximum radio capacity occurs when $(C/I)_{min}$ and B_c are minimized, yet Equation (9.23) shows that $(C/I)_{min}$ and B_c are inversely related.

Example 9.7

Evaluate four different cellular radio standards, and choose the one with the maximum radio capacity. Assume $n = 4$ propagation path loss.

System A: B_c = 30 kHz, $(C/I)_{min}$ = 18 dB
System B: B_c = 25 kHz, $(C/I)_{min}$ = 14 dB
System C: B_c = 12.5 kHz, $(C/I)_{min}$ = 2 dB
System D: B_c = 6.25 kHz, $(C/I)_{min}$ = 9 dB

Solution

Consider each system for 6.25 kHz bandwidth, and use Equation (9.23)

System A; B_c = 6.25 kHz, $(C/I)_{eq}$ = 18 – 20 log (6.25/30) = 31.680 dB
System B; B_c = 6.25 kHz, $(C/I)_{eq}$ = 14 – 20 log (6.25/25) = 26.00 dB
System C; B_c = 6.25 kHz, $(C/I)_{eq}$ = 2 – 20 log (6.25/12.5) = –4 dB
System D; B_c = 6.25 kHz, $(C/I)_{eq}$ = 9 – 20 log (6.25/6.25) = 9 dB

Based on comparison, the smallest value of $(C/I)_{eq}$ should be selected for maximum capacity in Equation (9.22). System C offers the best capacity.

In a digital cellular system, C/I can be expressed as

$$\frac{C}{I} = \frac{E_b R_b}{I} = \frac{E_c R_c}{I} \tag{9.24}$$

where R_b is channel bit rate, E_b is the energy per bit, R_c is the rate of the channel code, and E_c is the energy per code symbol. From Equations (9.23) and (9.24) $n = 4$, the ratio of C/I to $(C/I)_{eq}$ of a different system is given as

$$\frac{\left(\frac{C}{I}\right)}{\left(\frac{C}{I}\right)_{eq}} = \frac{\frac{E_c R_c}{I}}{\frac{E_c' R_c'}{I'}} = \left(\frac{B_c'}{B_c}\right)^2 \tag{9.25}$$

The relationship between R_c and B_c is always linear, and if the interference level I is the same in the mobile environment for two different digital systems, then Equation (9.25) can be rewritten as

$$\frac{E_c}{E_c'} = \left(\frac{B_c'}{B_c}\right)^3 \tag{9.26}$$

Equation (9.26) shows that if B_c is reduced by half, then the energy code symbol increases eight times. This gives the relationship between E_b/N_0 and B_c in a digital cellular system.

A comparison can now be made between the spectrum efficiency for FDMA and TDMA. In FDMA, B_t is divided into M channels, each with bandwidth B_c. Therefore, the radio capacity for FDMA in $n = 4$ propagation path loss conditions is given by

$$m = \frac{B_t}{\frac{B_t}{M}\sqrt{\frac{2}{3}\left(\frac{C}{I}\right)}} \tag{9.27}$$

Consider the case where a multichannel FDMA system occupies the same spectrum as a single channel TDMA system with multiple time slots. The carrier and interference terms for the first access technique (in this case FDMA) can be written as, $C = E_bR_b$, $I = I_0B_c$, whereas the second access technique (in this case TDMA) has carrier and interference terms represented by $C' = E_bR_b'$, $I' = I_0B_c'$, where R_b and R_b' are the radio transmission rates of two digital systems, E_b is the energy per bit, and I_0 represents the interference power per Hertz. The terms C' and I' are the parameters for the TDMA channels, and the terms C and I apply to the FDMA channels.

Example 9.8

Consider an FDMA system with three channels, each having a bandwidth of 10 kHz and a transmission rate of 10 kbps. A TDMA system has three time slots, channel bandwidth of 30 kHz, and a transmission rate of 30 kbps.

For the TDMA scheme, the received carrier-to-interference ratio for a single user is measured for 1/3 of the time the channel is in use. For example, C'/I' can be measured in 333.3 ms in one second. Thus, C'/I' is given by

$$C' = E_bR_b' = \frac{E_b10^4 \text{ bits}}{0.333 \text{ s}} = 3R_bE_b = 3C \tag{E.8.8.1}$$

$$I' = I_0B_c' = I_030 \text{ kHz} = 3I$$

It can be seen that the received carrier-to-interference ratio for a user in this TDMA system C'/I' is the same as C/I for a user in the FDMA system. Therefore, for this example, FDMA and TDMA have the same radio capacity and consequently the same spectrum efficiency. However, the required peak power for TDMA is $10\log k$ higher than FDMA, where k is the number of time slots in a TDMA system of equal bandwidth.

Capacity of Digital Cellular TDMA — In practice, TDMA systems improve capacity by a factor of three to six times as compared to analog cellular radio systems. Powerful error control and speech coding enable better link performance in high interference environments. By exploiting speech activity, some TDMA systems are able to better utilize each radio channel. Mobile assisted handoff (MAHO) allows subscribers to monitor the neighboring base stations, and the best base station choice may be made by each subscriber. MAHO allows the deployment of densely packed microcells, thus giving substantial capacity gains in a system. TDMA also makes it possible to introduce *adaptive channel allocation* (ACA). ACA eliminates system planning since it is not

Table 9.3 Comparison of AMPS with Digital TDMA Based Cellular Systems [Rai91]

Parameter	AMPS	GSM	USDC	PDC
Bandwidth (MHz)	25	25	25	25
Voice Channels	833	1000	2500	3000
Frequency Reuse (Cluster sizes)	7	4 or 3	7 or 4	7 or 4
Channels/Site	119	250 or 333	357 or 625	429 or 750
Traffic (Erlangs/sq. km)	11.9	27.7 or 40	41 or 74.8	50 or 90.8
Capacity Gain	1.0	2.3 or 3.4	3.5 or 6.3	4.2 or 7.6

required to plan frequencies for cells. Various proposed standards such as the GSM, US digital cellular (USDC), and Pacific Digital Cellular (PDC) have adopted digital TDMA for high capacity. Table 9.3 compares analog FM based AMPS to other digital TDMA based cellular systems.

9.7.1 Capacity of Cellular CDMA

The capacity of CDMA systems is interference limited, while it is bandwidth limited in FDMA and TDMA. Therefore, any reduction in the interference will cause a linear increase in the capacity of CDMA. Put another way, in a CDMA system, the link performance for each user increases as the number of users decreases. A straightforward way to reduce interference is to use multisectorized antennas, which results in spatial isolation of users. The directional antennas receive signals from only a fraction of the current users, thus leading to the reduction of interference. Another way of increasing CDMA capacity is to operate in a *discontinuous transmission mode* (DTX), where advantage is taken of the intermittent nature of speech. In DTX, the transmitter is turned off during the periods of silence in speech. It has been observed that voice signals have a duty factor of about 3/8 in landline networks [Bra68], and 1/2 for mobile systems, where background noise and vibration can trigger voice activity detectors. Thus, the average capacity of a CDMA system can be increased by a factor inversely proportional to the duty factor. While TDMA and FDMA reuse frequencies depending on the isolation between cells provided by the path loss in terrestrial radio propagation, CDMA can reuse the entire spectrum for all cells, and this results in an increase of capacity by a large percentage over the normal frequency reuse factor. A number of recent texts provide details on CDMA capacity and system design [Lib99], [Kim00], [Gar00}, [Mol01].

For evaluating the capacity of a CDMA system, first consider a single cell system [Gil91]. The cellular network consists of a large number of mobile users communicating with a base station. (In a multiple cell system, all the base stations are interconnected by the mobile switching center.) The cell-site transmitter consists of a linear combiner which adds the spread signals of the individual users and also uses a weighting factor for each signal for forward link power control purposes. For a single cell system under consideration, these weighting factors can be assumed to be equal. A pilot signal is also included in the cell-site transmitter and is used by each mobile to set its own power control for the reverse link. For a single-cell system with power control, all the signals on the reverse channel are received at the same power level at the base station.

Let the number of users be N. Then, each demodulator at the cell site receives a composite waveform containing the desired signal of power S and $(N-1)$ interfering users, each of which has power, S. Thus, the signal-to-noise ratio is [Gil91],

$$SNR = \frac{S}{(N-1)S} = \frac{1}{(N-1)} \tag{9.28}$$

In addition to SNR, bit energy-to-noise ratio is an important parameter in communication systems. It is obtained by dividing the signal power by the baseband information bit rate, R, and the interference power by the total RF bandwidth, W. The SNR at the base station receiver can be represented in terms of E_b/N_0 given by

$$\frac{E_b}{N_0} = \frac{S/R}{(N-1)(S/W)} = \frac{W/R}{N-1} \tag{9.29}$$

Equation (9.29) does not take into account the background thermal noise, η, in the spread bandwidth. To take this noise into consideration, E_b/N_0 can be represented as

$$\frac{E_b}{N_0} = \frac{W/R}{(N-1)+(\eta/S)} \tag{9.30}$$

The number of users that can access the system is thus given as

$$N = 1 + \frac{W/R}{E_b/N_0} - (\eta/S) \tag{9.31}$$

where W/R is called the processing gain. The background noise determines the cell radius for a given transmitter power.

In order to achieve an increase in capacity, the interference due to other users should be reduced. This can be done by decreasing the denominator of Equations (9.28) or (9.29). The first technique for reducing interference is antenna sectorization. As an example, a cell site with three antennas, each having a beam width of 120°, has interference N_0' which is one-third of the interference received by an omnidirectional antenna. This increases the capacity by a factor of three, since three times as many users may now be served within a sector while matching the performance of the omnidirectional antenna system. Looking at it another way, the same number of users in an omnidirectional cell may now be served in 1/3rd the area. The second technique involves the monitoring of voice activity such that each transmitter is switched off during periods of no *voice activity*. Voice activity is denoted by a factor α, and the interference term in

Equation (9.29) becomes $(N_s - 1)\alpha$, where N_s is the number of users per sector. With the use of these two techniques, the new average value of E_b/N_0' *within a sector* is given as

$$\frac{E_b}{N_0'} = \frac{W/R}{(N_s - 1)\alpha + (\eta/S)} \tag{9.32}$$

When the number of users is large and the system is interference limited rather than noise limited, the number of users can be shown to be

$$N_s = 1 + \frac{1}{\alpha}\left[\frac{W/R}{\frac{E_b}{N_0'}}\right] \tag{9.33}$$

If the voice activity factor is assumed to have a value of 3/8, and three sectors per cell site are used, Equation (9.33) demonstrates that the SNR increases by a factor of eight, which leads to an eight-fold increase in the number of users compared to an omnidirectional antenna system with no voice activity detection.

CDMA Power Control — In CDMA, the system capacity is maximized if each mobile transmitter power level is controlled so that its signal arrives at the cell site with the minimum required signal-to-interference ratio [Sal91]. If the signal powers of all mobile transmitters within an area covered by a cell site are controlled, then the total signal power received at the cell site from all mobiles will be equal to the average received power times the number of mobiles operating in the region of coverage. A tradeoff must be made if a mobile signal arrives at the cell site with a signal that is too weak, and often the weak user will be dropped. If the received power from a mobile user is too great, the performance of this mobile unit will be acceptable, but it will add undesired interference to all other users in the cell.

Example 9.9

If W = 1.25 MHz, R = 9600 bps, and a minimum acceptable E_b/N_0 is found to be 10 dB, determine the maximum number of users that can be supported in a single-cell CDMA system using (a) omnidirectional base station antennas and no voice activity detection, and (b) three-sectors at the base station and activity detection with α = 3/8. Assume the system is interference limited.

Solution

(a) Using Equation (9.31)

$$N = 1 + \frac{1.25 \times 10^6/9600}{10} = 1 + 13.02 = 14$$

(b) Using Equation (9.33) for each sector, we can find N_s.

$$N_s = 1 + \frac{1}{0.375}\left[\frac{1.25 \times 10^6/9600}{10}\right] = 35.7$$

The total number of users is given by $3N_s$, since three sectors exist within a cell; therefore $N = 3 \times 35.7 = 107$ users/ cell.

9.7.2 Capacity of CDMA with Multiple Cells

In actual CDMA cellular systems that employ separate forward and reverse links, neighboring cells share the same frequency, and each base station controls the transmit power of each of its own in-cell users. However, a particular base station is unable to control the power of users in neighboring cells, and these users add to the noise floor and decrease capacity on the reverse link of the particular cell of interest. Figure 9.12 illustrates an example of how users in adjacent cells may be distributed over the coverage area. The transmit powers of each out-of-cell user will add to the in-cell interference (where users are under power control) at the base station receiver. The amount of out-of-cell interference determines the *frequency reuse factor*, f, of a CDMA cellular system. Ideally, each cell shares the same frequency and the maximum possible value of f ($f = 1$) is achieved. In practice, however, the out-of-cell interference reduces f significantly. In contrast to CDMA systems which use the same frequency for each cell, narrowband FDMA/FDD systems typically reuse channels every seven cells, in which case f is simply 1/7 (see Chapter 3).

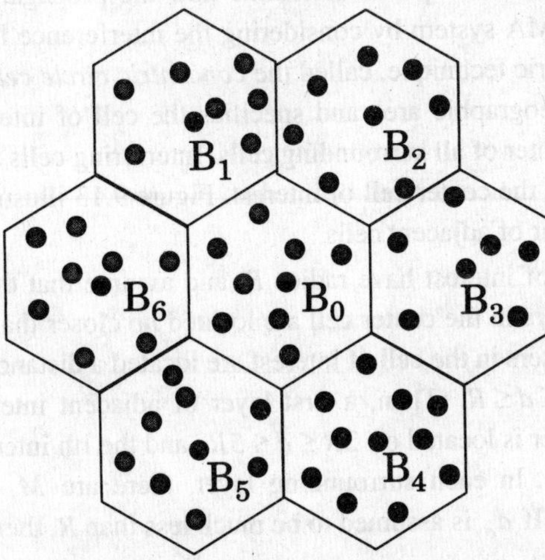

Figure 9.12 Illustration of users within a CDMA cellular radio system. Each base station reuses the same frequency. The small circles represent users within the system, which have their transmit power controlled by their own base station.

The frequency reuse factor for a CDMA system on the reverse link can be defined as [Rap92b]

$$f = \frac{N_0}{N_0 + \sum_i U_i N_{ai}} \tag{9.34}$$

and the frequency reuse efficiency, F, is defined as

$$F = f \times 100\ \% \tag{9.35}$$

In Equation (9.34), N_0 is the total interference power received from the $N-1$ in-cell users, U_i is the number of users in the ith adjacent cell, and N_{ai} is the average interference power for a user located in the ith adjacent cell. Within the cell of interest, the desired user will have the same received power as the $N-1$ undesired in-cell users when power control is employed, and the average received power from users in an adjacent cell can be found by

$$N_{ai} = \sum_j N_{ij}/U_i \tag{9.36}$$

where N_{ij} is the power received at the base station of interest from the jth user in the ith cell. Each adjacent cell may have a different number of users, and each out-of-cell user will offer a different level of interference depending on its exact transmitted power and location relative to the base station of interest. The variance of N_{ai} can be computed using standard statistical techniques for a particular cell.

An analysis described by Liberti and Rappaport and Milstein [Lib94b] [Rap92b] [Lib99] uses a recursive geometric technique to determine how the propagation path loss impacts the frequency reuse of a CDMA system by considering the interference from both in-cell and out-of-cell users. The geometric technique, called the *concentric circle cellular geometry*, considers all cells to have equal geographic area and specifies the cell of interest to be a circular cell, which is located in the center of all surrounding cells. Interfering cells are wedge-shaped and are arranged in layers around the center cell of interest. Figure 9.13 illustrates the concentric circle geometry for a single layer of adjacent cells.

Let the center cell of interest have radius R, and assume that there is some close-in distance d_o such that all users in the center cell are located no closer than d_o meters to the center base station and that all users in the cell of interest are located a distance d from the base station of interest such that $d_o \le d \le R$. Then, a first layer of adjacent interfering cells is found on $R \le d \le 3R$, a second layer is located on $3R \le d \le 5R$, and the ith interfering layer is located on $(2i-1)R \le d \le (2i+1)R$. In each surrounding layer, there are M_i adjacent cells, where i denotes the layer number. If d_o is assumed to be much less than R, then the area A of the center cell of interest is

$$A = \pi R^2 - \pi d_0^2 \approx \pi R^2 \tag{9.37}$$

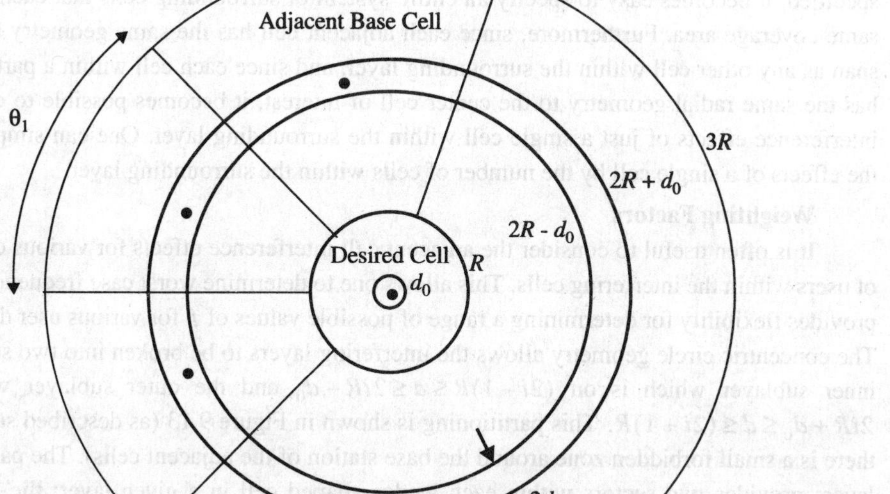

Figure 9.13 The concentric circle cellular geometry proposed by Rappaport and Milstein [Rap92b]. Notice that the center cell is circular, and that the surrounding cells are wedge-shaped. Each cell, however, covers the same area.

Within the first surrounding layer of cells, let A_1 denote the entire area of the region. If each cell in the first surrounding layer is to have the same area A, then there should be M_1 wedge-shaped cells that each span a particular angle θ_1. Neglecting d_o, it is clear that for the first surrounding layer

$$A_1 = \pi(3R)^2 - \pi R^2 = M_1 A \tag{9.38}$$

$$\theta_1 = 2\pi / M_1 \tag{9.39}$$

Solving Equations (9.38) and (9.39), $M_1 = 8$ and $\theta_1 = 45°$. In other words, there are eight wedge-shaped cells in the first surrounding layer, each cell covering a span of 45°. By recursion, it can be shown that for the second, and all subsequent surrounding layers, the area of the ith surrounding layer is related to the number of cells within the layer by

$$A_i = M_i A = i M_1 A = i8A \quad i \geq 1 \tag{9.40}$$

$$\theta_i = \theta_1 / i = \pi / 4i \tag{9.41}$$

The concentric circle geometry is appealing because, once the area of a cell of interest is specified, it becomes easy to specify an entire system of surrounding cells that each occupy the same coverage area. Furthermore, since each adjacent cell has the same geometry and angular span as any other cell within the surrounding layer, and since each cell within a particular layer has the same radial geometry to the center cell of interest, it becomes possible to consider the interference effects of just a single cell within the surrounding layer. One can simply multiply the effects of a single cell by the number of cells within the surrounding layer.

Weighting Factors

It is often useful to consider the adjacent cell interference effects for various distributions of users within the interfering cells. This allows one to determine worst case frequency reuse and provides flexibility for determining a range of possible values of f for various user distributions. The concentric circle geometry allows the interfering layers to be broken into two sublayers, an inner sublayer which is on $(2i-1)R \le d \le 2iR - d_0$, and the outer sublayer which is on $2iR + d_0 \le d \le (2i+1)R$. This partitioning is shown in Figure 9.13 (as described subsequently, there is a small forbidden zone around the base station of the adjacent cells). The partitioning of layers provides two sectors within each wedge-shaped cell in a given layer: the inner sector (which contains a smaller fraction of the area of the cell) and the outer sector (which contains a greater fraction of the area of the cell). Since each cell contains the same area as the center cell, it is clear that for a uniform distribution of users over an adjacent cell, the inner sector will contain fewer users than the outer sector, and this will certainly impact the interference power received at the center cell base station. To account for a wide range of user distributions in the interfering layers, weighting factors are used to redistribute users in the inner and outer sectors of an adjacent cell.

If K is the user density (i.e., the number of users per unit area), then the total number of users within the center cell is given by $U = KA$. If it is assumed that all cells have the same number of users, then in the first surrounding layer there will also be KA users. Weighting factors can be used to break up the distribution of adjacent cell users between the inner and outer sectors. In the first surrounding layer, the inner and outer sectors of each cell have areas given by

$$A_{1in}/M_1 = (\pi(2R)^2 - \pi R^2)/8 = 3A/8 \tag{9.42}$$

and

$$A_{1out}/M_1 = (\pi(3R)^2 - \pi(2R)^2)/8 = 5A/8 \tag{9.43}$$

For each first layer cell to possess $U = KA$ users, weighting factors for the user density within the inner (W_{1in}) and outer (W_{1out}) sectors may be applied such that

$$U = KA = (KW_{1in}A_{1in})/M_1 + (KW_{1out}\, A_{1out})/M_1 \tag{9.44}$$

and

$$U = KA = KA[3/8W_{1in} + 5/8W_{1out}] \tag{9.45}$$

Using Equation (9.45), it can be seen that if $W_{1in} = 1$ and $W_{1out} = 1$, then 3/8 of the users will be in the inner sector and 5/8 of the users will be in the outer sector. This can be thought of as an optimistic condition (or upper bound) for frequency reuse, since not even half of the interferers are less than $2R$ away from the base station, and 5/8 of the users are farther than $2R$ away and will offer smaller levels of interference to the center cell. However, if $W_{1in} = 4/3$ and $W_{1out} = 4/5$, then half of the users in the first layer cells will be closer than $2R$ and half will be farther than $2R$ from the center base station (this corresponds to the case of hexagonal cells, where half of the users would be closer to the base station of interest, and half would be farther away from the base station of interest). For a worst case interference scenario, all of the U users in each of the first layer cells would be located in the inner sector (thereby providing more interference to the center cell due to smaller distance and smaller path loss). The weighting factors account for this worst case by setting $W_{1in} = 8/3$ and $W_{1out} = 0$. It is left as an exercise to determine appropriate weighting factors for the second and subsequent layer cells.

The area of the center and wedge-shaped cells in the concentric circle geometry exceeds the area of a traditional hexagonal cell described in Chapter 3. Whereas a hexagonal cell occupies an area of $A_{hex} = (3\sqrt{3}R^2)/2 = 2.598R^2$, the cells in the concentric circle geometry each possess and area of πR^2. Thus, the center cell occupies an area which is 1.21 times as large as a traditional hexagonal cell and the first layer of eight wedge-shaped cells shown in Figure 9.13 occupies the area of 9.666 hexagonal cells. Since frequency reuse is based on the relative amount of interference from neighboring cells, as long as the number of users and the coverage area can be accurately represented and scaled, the particular geometry does not dramatically impact capacity predictions [Lib99], [Lib94b], [Rap92b]. Thus, the concentric circle geometry offers analytical advantages for analyzing the effects of co-channel cells.

Using Concentric Circle Geometry to Find CDMA Capacity

To find the capacity of a multicell CDMA system, the concentric circle geometry can be used in conjunction with a propagation path loss model to determine interference from adjacent cell users. Then, using Equation (9.34), the frequency reuse factor can be found. Note that the in-cell interference power N_0 is simply given by

$$N_0 = P_0(U-1) \approx P_0 U = P_0 KA \tag{9.46}$$

where P_0 is the power received from any one of the U users in the center cell (since all users are assumed to be under power control and thus provide the same received power at the base station receiver). In general, it is practical to assume that any adjacent cells will also contain U users and will receive power P_0 from each of its own in-cell users. In the adjacent cells, each subscriber is under power control within its own cell, and is a distance d' from its own base station. Since propagation path loss laws are based on all distances greater than d_0, a small forbidden zone having width $2d_0$ is assumed to exist in all surrounding rings (see Figure 9.14). The forbidden zone is a small annulus in each layer which is assumed not to contain users, so that any propagation path loss model may be used in analysis without having $d' < d_0$. It is easy to show that when $d_0 < R$, the small forbidden zone occupies negligible area and provides virtually the same interference results as for the case when the forbidden zone is a circle of radius d_0 around each adjacent cell.

A slight approximation for d' is made when computing the power of the adjacent cell user to its own base station. Figure 9.14 illustrates how the distances are computed for inner and outer sector users within a first layer interfering cell. Using the law of cosines, it can be shown that within any cell in the ith layer

$$d' = \sqrt{d^2\sin^2\theta + (2Ri - d_0 - d\cos\theta)^2} \quad \text{for} \quad (2i-1)R \le d \le (2i)R - d_0 \tag{9.47}$$

$$d' = \sqrt{d^2\sin^2\theta + (d\cos\theta - 2Ri - d_0)^2} \quad \text{for} \quad (2i)R + d_0 \le d \le (2i+1)R \tag{9.48}$$

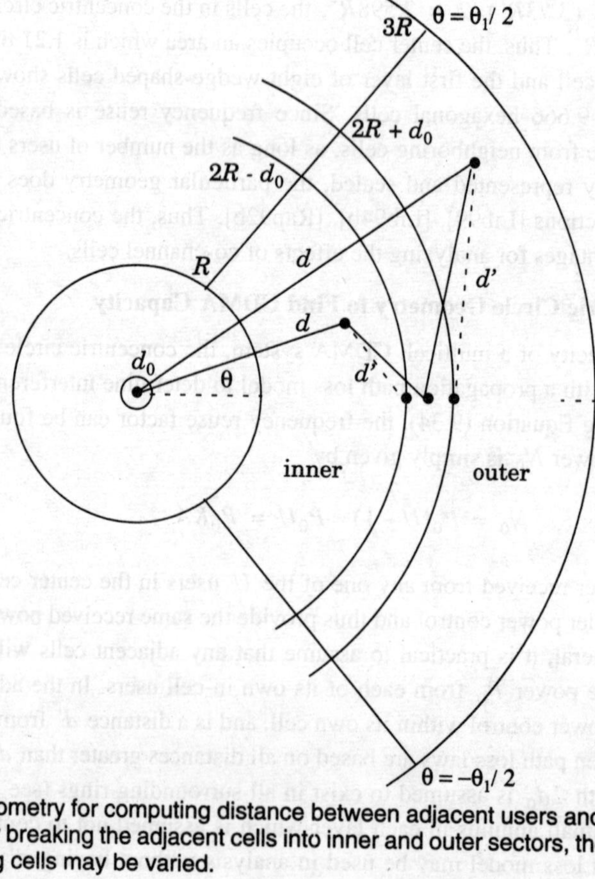

Figure 9.14 Geometry for computing distance between adjacent users and the center base station of interest. By breaking the adjacent cells into inner and outer sectors, the distribution of users within neighboring cells may be varied.

Then, using d' and d, the interference power $P_{0,i,j}$ at the center cell from the jth user in the ith interfering cell can be given by

$$P_{0,i,j}(r, \theta, d_0) = N_{i,j} = P_0(d'/d_0)^n (d_0/d)^n \tag{9.49}$$

where n is the propagation path loss exponent described in Chapters 3 and 4, and d' is a function of θ as given by Equations (9.47) and (9.48). The two factors on the right side of Equation (9.49) represent the actual transmitter power radiated by the jth subscriber in the ith cell, multiplied by the propagation path loss from that subscriber to the center base station receiver. By evaluating Equation (9.49) for each user in an adjacent cell, it is possible to compute N_{ai} using Equation (9.36) and then apply Equation (9.34) to determine f.

Simulations which considered various user weighting factors, as well as path loss exponents of $n = 2$, 3, and 4, and varying cell sizes were carried out by Rappaport and Milstein [Rap92b]. Table 9.4 indicates typical results, which show that f can range between 0.316 and 0.707, depending on the path loss exponent and the distribution of users. Thus, while a single cell CDMA system offers ideal frequency reuse ($f = 1$), the actual frequency reuse is a strong function of user distribution and path loss.

Table 9.4 Frequency Reuse Factor for Reverse Channel of CDMA Cellular System, as a Function of n for Two System Implementations [from [Rap92b] © IEEE]

		Frequency reuse efficiency		
d (km)	***n***	**lower bound** $W_1 = 3.0$ $W_2 = 0.0$	**hex** $W_1 = 1.38$ $W_2 = 0.78$	**upper bound** $W_1 = 1.0$ $W_2 = 1.0$
2	2	0.316	0.425	0.462
2	3	0.408	0.558	0.613
2	4	0.479	0.646	0.707
10	2	0.308	0.419	0.455
10	3	0.396	0.550	0.603
10	4	0.462	0.634	0.695

9.7.3 Capacity of Space Division Multiple Access

For interference limited CDMA operating in an AWGN channel, with perfect power control with no interference from adjacent cells and with omnidirectional antennas used at the base stations, the average bit error rate, P_b, for a user can be found from the Gaussian approximation in Chapter 6 and Appendix E as

$$P_b = Q\left(\sqrt{\frac{3N}{K-1}}\right) \tag{9.50}$$

where K is the number of users in a cell and N is the spreading factor. $Q(x)$ is the standard Q-function. Equation (9.35) assumes that the signature sequences are random and that K is sufficiently large to allow the Gaussian approximation to be valid.

To illustrate how directive antennas can improve the reverse link in a single-cell CDMA system, consider Figure 9.15, which illustrates three possible base station antenna configurations. The omnidirectional receiver antenna will detect signals from all users in the system, and thus will receive the greatest amount of noise. The sectored antenna will divide the received noise into a smaller value and will increase the number of users in the CDMA system (as illustrated in Example 9.9). The adaptive antenna shown in Figure 9.15(c) provides a spot beam for each user, and it is this implementation which is the most powerful form of SDMA. An ideal adaptive antenna is able to form a beam for each user in the cell of interest, and the base station tracks each user in the cell as it moves. Assume that a beam pattern, $G(\phi)$, is formed such that the pattern has maximum gain in the direction of the desired user. Such a directive pattern can be formed at the base station using an N-element adaptive array antenna. Assume that a beam pattern, $G(\phi)$, with no variation in the elevation plane, such as shown in Figure 9.16, can be formed by an array. The pattern, $G(\phi)$, can be steered through 360° in the horizontal (ϕ) plane such that the desired user is always in the main beam of the pattern. It is assumed that K users in the single-cell CDMA system are uniformly distributed throughout a two-dimensional cell (in the horizontal plane, $\theta = \pi/2$), and the base station antenna is capable of simultaneously providing such a pattern for all users in the cell. On the reverse link, the power received from the desired mobile signals is $P_{r;0}$. The powers of the signal incident at the base station antenna from $K-1$ interfering users are given by $P_{r;i}$ for $i = 1, \ldots .k-1$. The average total interference power, I, seen by a single desired user, (measured in the received signal at the array port of the base station antenna array, which is steered to the User 0), is given by

$$I = E\left\{\sum_{i=1}^{K-1} G(\phi_i)P_{r;i}\right\} \tag{9.51}$$

where ϕ_i is the direction of the ith user in the horizontal plane, measured in the x-axis, and E is the expectation operator. No interference from adjacent cells contributes to total received inter-

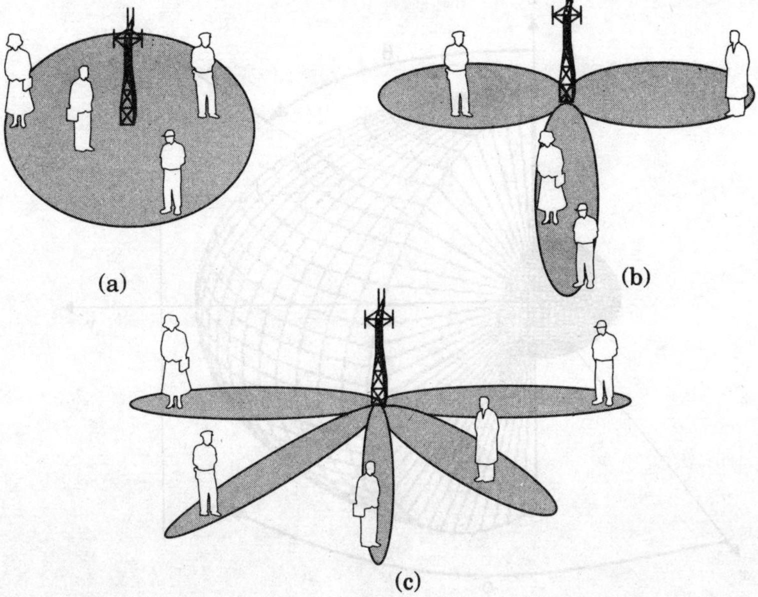

Figure 9.15 Illustration showing different antenna patterns. (a) An omni-directional base station antenna pattern; (b) sectorized base station antenna pattern; (c) adaptive antenna pattern which provides individual spot beams for each user in the cell.

ference in Equation (9.51). If perfect power control is applied such that the power incident at the base station antenna from each user is the same, then $P_{r;i} = P_c$ for each of the K users, and the average interference power seen by User 0 is given by

$$I = P_c E\left\{\sum_{i=1}^{K-1} G(\phi_i)\right\} \tag{9.52}$$

Assuming that users are independently and identically distributed throughout the cell, the average total interference seen by a user in the central cell is given by

$$I = \frac{P_c(K-1)}{D} \tag{9.53}$$

where D is the directivity of the antenna, given by $max(G(\phi))$. In typical cellular installations, D ranges between 3 dB to 10 dB. As the antenna beam pattern is made more narrow, D increases,

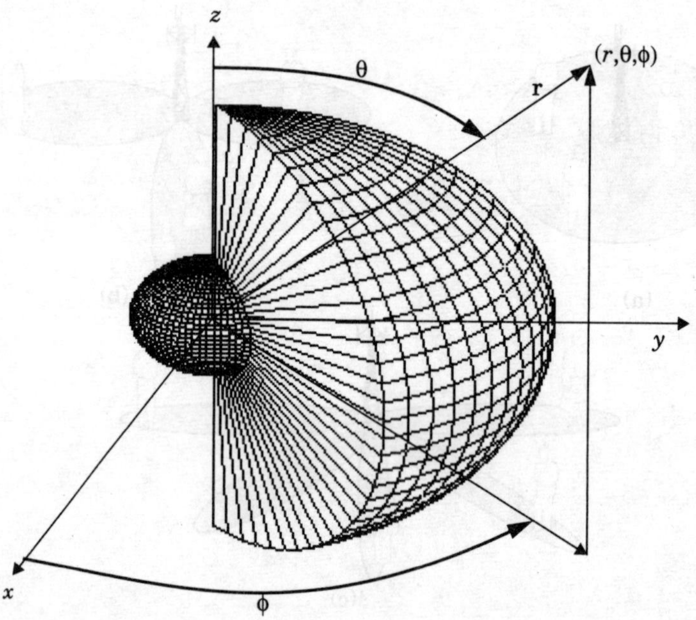

Figure 9.16 An idealized flat-topped pattern with a 60 degree beamwidth and a –6dB sidelobe level. The pattern has no variation in the elevation axis to account for users which are close to, and far from, the base station [from [Lib94b] © IEEE].

and the received interference I decreases proportionally. The average bit error rate for User 0 can thus be given by

$$P_b = Q\left(\sqrt{\frac{3DN}{K-1}}\right) \tag{9.54}$$

Thus, it can be seen that the probability of bit error is dependent on the beam pattern of a receiver, and there is considerable improvement that is achieved using high gain adaptive antennas at the base station.

Using the fact that the additional interference from adjacent cells simply adds to the interference level, the average probability of error for a particular user using directive antennas in a multiple-cell environment is given by

$$P_b = Q\left(\sqrt{\frac{3fDN}{K-1}}\right) \tag{9.55}$$

where f is the frequency reuse factor described by Equation (9.34) and Table 9.4. Figure 9.17 illustrates the average probability of error for different propagation path loss exponents, where two different types of base station antennas are compared using simulations which considered a single layer of interfering cells using the geometry described in Section 9.7.2 [Lib94b]. In the

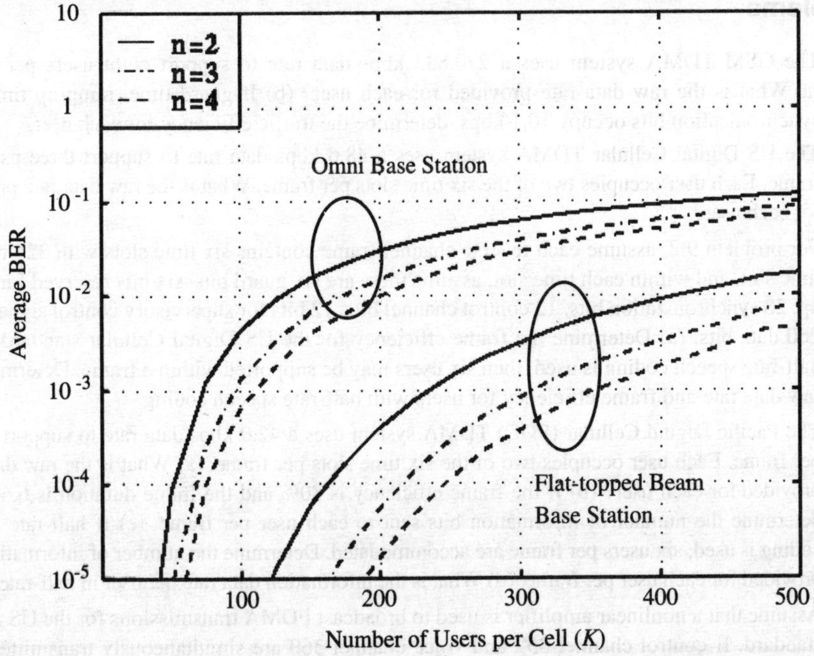

Figure 9.17 Average probability of error for a user in a CDMA system with one interfering layer of co-channel cells. Base station of interest using (a) an omnidirectional base station antenna and (b) SDMA with a flat top beam having $D = 5.1$ dB and pointed at each of the K users within the cell of interest. Notice that SDMA offers significant capacity gains for a given average probability of error.

figure, one set of average probability of error curves is found for a standard omnidirectional base station antenna, and another set of curves is found for a flat top beam (a beam with constant gain over a specific angular region) having a directivity of about 5.1 dB. The flat top beam is assumed to have a constant maximum gain lobe spanning an azimuth of 30 degrees, and a constant side lobe level which is 6 dB down from the maximum gain. Furthermore, it is assumed that K separate flat top beams can be formed by the base station and pointed at each of the K users within the cell of interest. Notice that for an average probability of error of 0.001 in a propagation path loss environment of $n = 4$, the flat top beam system will support 350 users, whereas the omni-directional antenna will support only 100 users [Lib94b]. This increase in the number of users is roughly equal to the directivity offered by the flat top beam system, and illustrates the promise SDMA offers for improving capacity in wireless systems. Note that multipath is not considered. The impact of scattering and diffuse multipath on the performance of SDMA is currently a topic of research and is certain to impact performance and implementation strategies for emerging SDMA techniques.

9.8 Problems

9.1 The GSM TDMA system uses a 270.833 kbps data rate to support eight users per frame. (a) What is the raw data rate provided for each user? (b) If guard time, ramp-up time, and synchronization bits occupy 10.1 kbps, determine the traffic efficiency for each user.

9.2 The US Digital Cellular TDMA system uses a 48.6 kbps data rate to support three users per frame. Each user occupies two of the six time slots per frame. What is the raw data rate provided for each user?

9.3 For problem 9.2, assume each reverse channel frame contains six time slots with 324 bits per time slot, and within each time slot, assume there are six guard bits, six bits reserved for ramp-up, 28 synchronization bits, 12 control channel bits, 12 bits for supervisory control signals, and 260 data bits. (a) Determine the frame efficiency for the US Digital Cellular standard. (b) If half-rate speech coding is used, then six users may be supported within a frame. Determine the raw data rate and frame efficiency for users with half-rate speech coding.

9.4 The Pacific Digital Cellular (PDC) TDMA system uses a 42.0 kbps data rate to support 3 uses per frame. Each user occupies two of the six time slots per frame. (a) What is the raw data rate provided for each user? (b) If the frame efficiency is 80% and the frame duration is 6.667 ms, determine the number of information bits sent to each user per frame. (c) If half-rate speech coding is used, six users per frame are accommodated. Determine the number of information bits provided for each user per frame. (d) What is the information data rate per user in half-rate PDC?

9.5 Assume that a nonlinear amplifier is used to broadcast FDMA transmissions for the US AMPS standard. If control channel 352 and voice channel 360 are simultaneously transmitted by a base station, determine all cellular channels on the forward link that might carry interference due to intermodulation.

9.6 If a paging system transmits at 931.9375 MHz, and a cellular base station broadcasts on AMPS control channel 318, and both antennas are co-located on the same broadcast tower, determine the cellular channels (if any) that may contain intermodulation interference, if detected by a receiver with a nonlinear amplifier. In what practical situations might intermodulation of this type be produced?

9.7 In an unslotted ALOHA system the packet arrival times form a Poisson process having a rate of 10^3 packets/sec. If the bit rate is 10 Mbps and there are 1000 bits/packet, find (a) the normalized throughput of the system, and (b) the number of bits per packet that will maximize the throughput.

9.8 Repeat problem 9.7 for a slotted ALOHA system.

9.9 Determine the propagation delay in packet transmission units if a 19.2 kbps channel data rate is used and each packet contains 256 bits. Assume a line-of-sight radio path exists for a user 10 km away from the transmitter. If slotted ALOHA is to be used, what is the best choice for the number of bits/packet for this system (assuming that 10 km is the maximum distance between the transmitter and receiver)?

9.10 Determine the number of analog channels per cell for the case of $n = 3$ propagation path loss, where the minimum acceptable $C/I = 14$ dB. What is the appropriate cluster size for the system? Assume the channel bandwidth is 30 kHz and the total spectrum allocation is 20 MHz.

9.11 Repeat problem 9.10 for the cases where $n = 2$ and $n = 4$.

9.12 In an omnidirectional (single-cell, single-sector) CDMA cellular system, $E_b/N_0 = 20$ dB is required for each user. If 100 users, each with a baseband data rate of 13 kbps, are to be accommodated, determine the minimum channel bit rate of the spread spectrum chip sequence. Ignore voice activity considerations.

9.13 Repeat problem 9.12 for the case where voice activity is considered and is equal to 40%.

9.14 Repeat problem 9.12 for the case of a tri-sectored CDMA system. Include the effects of voice activity, where it is assumed that each user is active 40% of the time.

9.15 Using the geometry shown in Section 9.7.2, verify Equations (9.47) and (9.48).

9.16 Using simulation which assumes 1000 users are uniformly distributed throughout the inner and outer sectors of the first ring cell of Figure 9.14, verify the values given in Table 9.4 for $R = 2$ km and $d_0 = 100$ m for $n = 2$, 3, and 4.

9.17 In a single-cell CDMA system using spatial division multiple access (SDMA), determine the number of simultaneous users that can be supported at an average probability of error of 10^{-3} when a processing gain of $R_c/R_b = 511$ is used. Assume 10 dB gain beam patterns may be formed and that perfect power control is used. Neglect voice activity.

9.18 Repeat problem 9.17 for the case where voice activity of 40% is considered.

9.19 A CDMA cellular system uses SDMA, and multiple cells are used, where each cell shares the same radio channel. Consider propagation path loss exponents of $n = 2$, 3, and 4, and determine the number of simultaneous users that can be supported at an average probability of error of 10^{-2}. Assume $K = 511$ and 6 dB of directionality is provided by the base station for each user.

9.20 Using the concentric cellular geometry, determine recursive expressions for the two weighting factors for the equivalent hexagonal geometry for the second layer and all subsequent layer cells.

9.21 Simulate reverse channel interference in a one-cell reuse CDMA system. To do this, consider seven hexagonal cells and assume each one has equal area of 10 km^2. Randomly place 30 users in each cell, and assume that $d_0 = 1$ m is the close-in reference distance for propagation and $n = 4$ is the path loss exponent. If power control is used for the 30 in-cell users, find

(a) the received in-cell interference power

(b) the received out-of-cell interference power

(c) the frequency reuse factor

9.22 Repeat the simulation of problem 9.21 using $n = 3$, and find new answers for (a), (b), and (c).

CHAPTER 10

Wireless Networking

10.1 Introduction to Wireless Networks

The demand for ubiquitous personal communications is driving the development of new networking techniques that accommodate mobile voice and data users who move throughout buildings, cities, or countries. Consider the cellular telephone system shown in Figure 10.1. The cellular telephone system is responsible for providing coverage throughout a particular territory, called a *coverage region* or *market*. The interconnection of many such systems defines a wireless network capable of providing service to mobile users throughout a country or continent.

To provide wireless communications within a particular geographic region (a city, for example), an integrated network of base stations must be deployed to provide sufficient radio coverage to all mobile users. The base stations, in turn, must be connected to a central hub called the mobile switching center (MSC). The MSC provides connectivity between the public switched telephone network (PSTN) and the numerous base stations, and ultimately between all of the wireless subscribers in a system. The PSTN forms the global telecommunications grid which connects conventional (landline) telephone switching centers (called central offices) with MSCs throughout the world.

Figure 10.1 illustrates a typical cellular system of the early 1990s, but there is currently a major thrust to develop new transport architectures for the wireless end-users. For example, PCS may be distributed over the existing cable television plant to neighborhoods or city blocks, where microcells are used to provide local wireless coverage. Fiber optic transport architectures are also being used to connect radio ports, base stations, and MSCs.

To connect mobile subscribers to the base stations, radio links are established using a carefully defined communication protocol called *common air interface* (CAI) which in essence is a precisely defined *handshake* communication protocol. The common air interface specifies

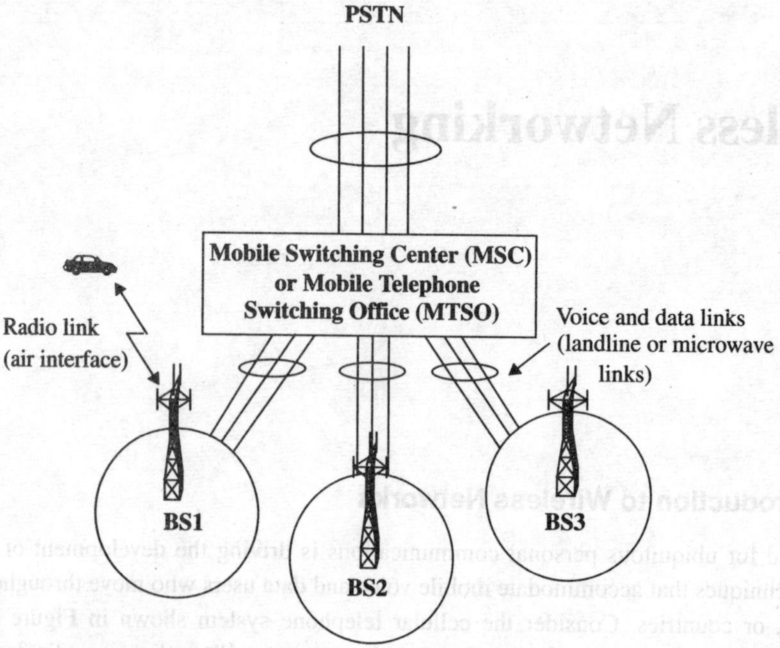

Figure 10.1 Block diagram of a cellular system.

exactly how mobile subscribers and base stations communicate over radio frequencies and also defines the control channel signaling methods. The CAI must provide a great deal of channel reliability to ensure that data is properly sent and received between the mobile and the base station, and as such specifies speech and channel coding.

At the base station, the air interface portion (i.e., signaling and synchronization data) of the mobile transmission is discarded, and the remaining voice traffic is passed along to the MSC on fixed networks. While each base station may handle on the order of 50 simultaneous calls, a typical MSC is responsible for connecting as many as 100 base stations to the PSTN (as many as 5,000 calls at one time), so the connection between the MSC and the PSTN requires substantial capacity at any instant of time. It becomes clear that networking strategies and standards may vary widely depending on whether a single voice circuit or an entire metropolitan population is served.

Unfortunately, the term *network* may be used to describe a wide range of voice or data connections, from the case of a single mobile user to the base station, to the connection of a large MSC to the PSTN. This broad network definition presents a challenge in describing the large number of strategies and standards used in networking, and it is not feasible to cover all aspects of wireless networking in this chapter. However, the basic concepts and standards used in today's wireless networks are covered in a manner which first addresses the mobile-to-base link, followed by the connection of the base station to the MSC, the connection of the MSC to the PSTN, and the interconnection of MSCs throughout the world.

10.2 Differences Between Wireless and Fixed Telephone Networks

Transfer of information in the public switched telephone network (PSTN) takes place over landline trunked lines (called *trunks*) comprised of fiber optic cables, copper cables, microwave links, and satellite links. The network configurations in the PSTN are virtually static, since the network connections may only be changed when a subscriber changes residence and requires reprogramming at the local *central office* (CO) of the subscriber. Wireless networks, on the other hand, are highly dynamic, with the network configuration being rearranged every time a subscriber moves into the coverage region of a different base station or a new market. While fixed networks are difficult to change, wireless networks must reconfigure themselves for users within small intervals of time (on the order of seconds) to provide roaming and imperceptible handoffs between calls as a mobile moves about. The available channel bandwidth for fixed networks can be increased by installing high capacity cables (fiberoptic or coaxial cable), whereas wireless networks are constrained by the meager RF cellular bandwidth provided for each user.

10.2.1 The Public Switched Telephone Network (PSTN)

The PSTN is a highly integrated communications network that connects over 70% of the world's inhabitants. In early 2001, the International Telecommunications Union estimated that there were 1 billion public landline telephone numbers, as compared to 600 million cellular telephone numbers. While landline telephones are being added at a 3% rate, wireless subscriptions are growing at greater than a 40% rate. Every telephone in the world is given calling access over the PSTN.

Each country is responsible for the regulation of the PSTN within its borders. Over time, some government telephone systems have become privatized by corporations which provide local and long distance service for profit.

In the PSTN, each city or a geographic grouping of towns is called a *local access and transport area* (LATA). Surrounding LATAs are connected by a company called a *local exchange carrier* (LEC). A LEC is a company that provides intralata telephone service, and may be a local telephone company, or may be a telephone company that is regional in scope.

A long distance telephone company collects toll fees to provide connections between different LATAs over its long distance network. These companies are referred to as *interexchange carriers* (IXCs), and own and operate large fiber optic and microwave radio networks which are connected to LECs throughout a country or continent.

In the United States, the 1984 divestiture decree (called the *modified final judgement* or MFJ) resulted in the break-up of AT&T (once the main local and long distance company in the US) into seven major Bell Operating Companies (BOCs), each with its own service region. By US Government mandate, AT&T is forbidden to provide local service within each BOC region (see Figure 10.2), although it is allowed to provide long distance service between LATAs within a BOC region and interexchange service between each region. BOCs are forbidden to provide interLATA calling within their own region and are also forbidden to provide the long distance

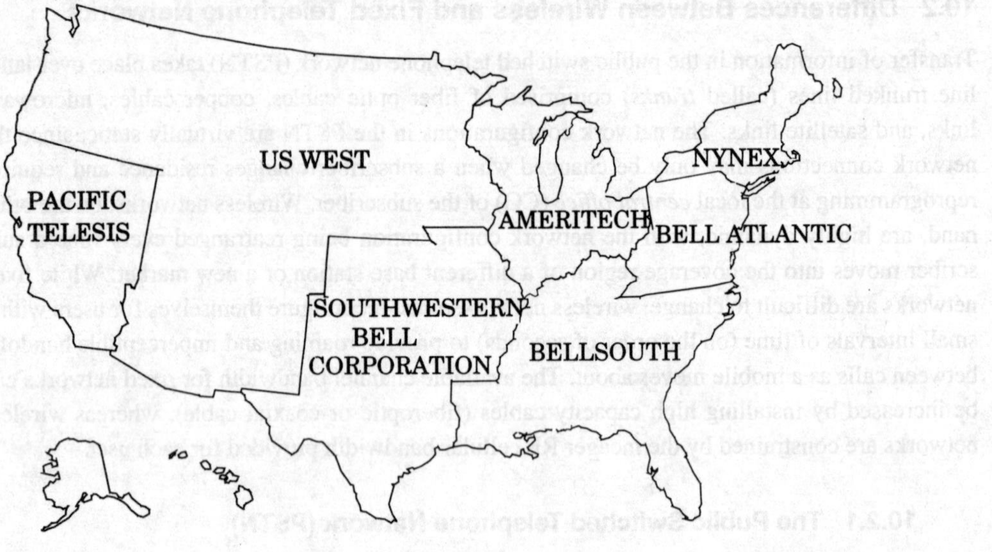

Figure 10.2 Service areas of US regional Bell Operating Companies.

interexchange service. In the US, there are about 2000 telephone companies, although the Bell Operating Companies (BOCs) are the most widely known (see Figure 10.2).

Figure 10.3 is a simplified illustration of a local telephone network, called a *local exchange*. Each local exchange consists of a central office (CO) which provides PSTN connection to the *customer premises equipment* (CPE) which may be an individual phone at a residence or a *private branch exchange* (PBX) at a place of business. The CO may handle as many as a million telephone connections. The CO is connected to a *tandem* switch which in turn connects the local exchange to the PSTN. The tandem switch physically connects the local telephone network to the *point of presence* (POP) of trunked long distance lines provided by one or more IXCs [Pec92]. Sometimes IXCs connect directly to the CO switch to avoid local transport charges levied by the LEC.

Figure 10.3 also shows how a PBX may be used to provide telephone connections throughout a building or campus. A PBX allows an organization or entity to provide internal calling and other in-building services (which do not involve the LEC), as well as private networking between other organizational sites (through leased lines from LEC and IXC providers), in addition to conventional local and long distance services which pass through the CO. Telephone connections within a PBX are maintained by the private owner, whereas connection of the PBX to the CO is provided and maintained by the LEC.

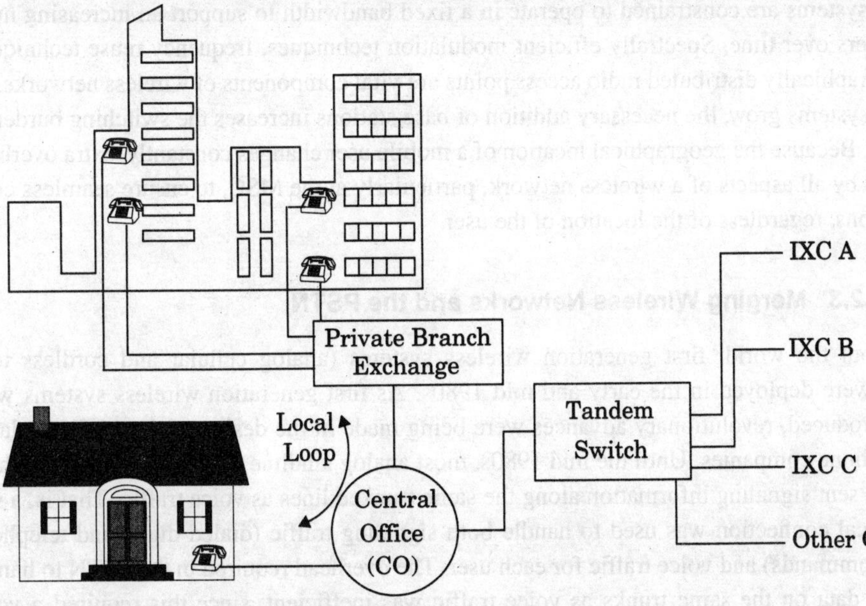

Figure 10.3 Local landline telephone network.

10.2.2 Limitations in Wireless Networking

As compared with the local, fixed telephone network, where all end-users are static, a wireless communications system is extremely complex. First, the wireless network requires an air interface between base stations and subscribers to provide telephone grade communications under a wide range of propagation conditions and for any possible user location. To assure adequate area coverage, the deployment of many (sometimes hundreds) of base stations throughout a market is necessary, and each of these base stations must be connected to the MSC. Furthermore, the MSC must eventually provide connection for each of the mobile users to the PSTN. This requires simultaneous connections to the LEC, one or more IXCs, and to other MSCs via a separate cellular signaling network.

Historically, the demand for wireless communications has consistently exceeded the capacity of available technology, and this is most evident in the design of MSCs. While a central office (CO) telephone switch may handle up to a million landline subscribers simultaneously, the most sophisticated MSCs of the mid 1990s are only able to handle 100,000 to 200,000 simultaneous cellular telephone subscribers.

A problem unique to wireless networks is the extremely hostile and random nature of the radio channel, and since users may request service from any physical location while traveling over a wide range of velocities, the MSC is forced to switch calls imperceptibly between base stations throughout the system. The radio spectrum available for this purpose is limited, thus wireless systems are constrained to operate in a fixed bandwidth to support an increasing number of users over time. Spectrally efficient modulation techniques, frequency reuse techniques, and geographically distributed radio access points are vital components of wireless networks. As wireless systems grow, the necessary addition of base stations increases the switching burden of the MSC. Because the geographical location of a mobile user changes constantly, extra overhead is needed by all aspects of a wireless network, particularly at the MSC, to ensure seamless communications, regardless of the location of the user.

10.2.3 Merging Wireless Networks and the PSTN

Throughout the world, first generation wireless systems (analog cellular and cordless telephones) were deployed in the early and mid 1980s. As first generation wireless systems were being introduced, revolutionary advances were being made in the design of the PSTN by landline telephone companies. Until the mid 1980s, most analog landline telephone links throughout the world sent signaling information along the same trunked lines as voice traffic. That is, a single physical connection was used to handle both signaling traffic (dialed digits and telephone ringing commands) and voice traffic for each user. The overhead required in the PSTN to handle signaling data on the same trunks as voice traffic was inefficient, since this required a voice trunk to be dedicated during periods of time when no voice traffic was actually being carried. Put simply, valuable LEC and long distance voice trunks were being used to provide low, data rate signaling information that a parallel signaling channel could have provided with much less bandwidth.

The advantage of a separate but parallel signaling channel allows the voice trunks to be used strictly for revenue-generating voice traffic, and supports many more users on each trunked line. Thus, during the mid 1980s, the PSTN was transformed into two parallel networks—one dedicated to user traffic, and one dedicated to call signaling traffic. This technique is called *common channel signaling*.

Common channel signaling is used in all modern telephone networks. Most recently, dedicated signaling channels have been used by cellular MSCs to provide global signaling interconnection, thereby enabling MSCs throughout the world to pass subscriber information. In many of today's cellular telephone systems, voice traffic is carried on the PSTN while signaling information for each call is carried on a separate signaling channel. Access to the signaling network is usually provided by IXCs for a negotiated fee. In North America, the cellular telephone signaling network uses No. 7 Signaling System (SS7), and each MSC uses the IS-41 protocol to communicate with other MSCs on the continent [Rap95].

In first generation cellular systems, common signaling channels were not used, and signaling data was sent on the same trunked channel as the voice user. In second generation wireless systems, however, the air interfaces have been designed to provide parallel user and signaling channels for each mobile, so that each mobile receives the same features and services as fixed wireline telephones in the PSTN.

10.3 Development of Wireless Networks

10.3.1 First Generation Wireless Networks

First generation cellular and cordless telephone networks are based on analog technology. All first generation cellular systems use FM modulation, and cordless telephones use a single base station to communicate with a single portable terminal. A typical example of a first generation cellular telephone system is the *Advanced Mobile Phone Services* (AMPS) system used in the United States (see Chapter 11). Basically, all first generation systems use the transport architecture shown in Figure 10.4.

Figure 10.5 shows a diagram of a first generation cellular radio network, which includes the mobile terminals, the base stations, and MSCs. In first generation cellular networks, the system control for each market resides in the MSC, which maintains all mobile related information and controls each mobile handoff. The MSC also performs all of the network management functions, such as call handling and processing, billing, and fraud detection within the market. The MSC is interconnected with the PSTN via landline trunked lines (trunks) and a tandem switch. MSCs also are connected with other MSCs via dedicated signaling channels (see Figure 10.6) for exchange of location, validation, and call signaling information.

Notice that in Figure 10.6, the PSTN is a *separate* network from the SS7 signaling network. In modern cellular telephone systems, long distance voice traffic is carried on the PSTN, but the signaling information used to provide call set-up and to inform MSCs about a particular user is carried on the SS7 network.

First generation wireless systems provide analog speech and inefficient, low-rate, data transmission between the base station and the mobile user. However, the speech signals are usually digitized using a standard, time division multiplex format for transmission between the base station and the MSC and are always digitized for distribution from the MSC to the PSTN.

The global cellular network is required to keep track of all mobile users that are registered in all markets throughout the network, so that it is possible to forward incoming calls to roaming users at any location throughout the world. When a mobile user's phone is activated but is not

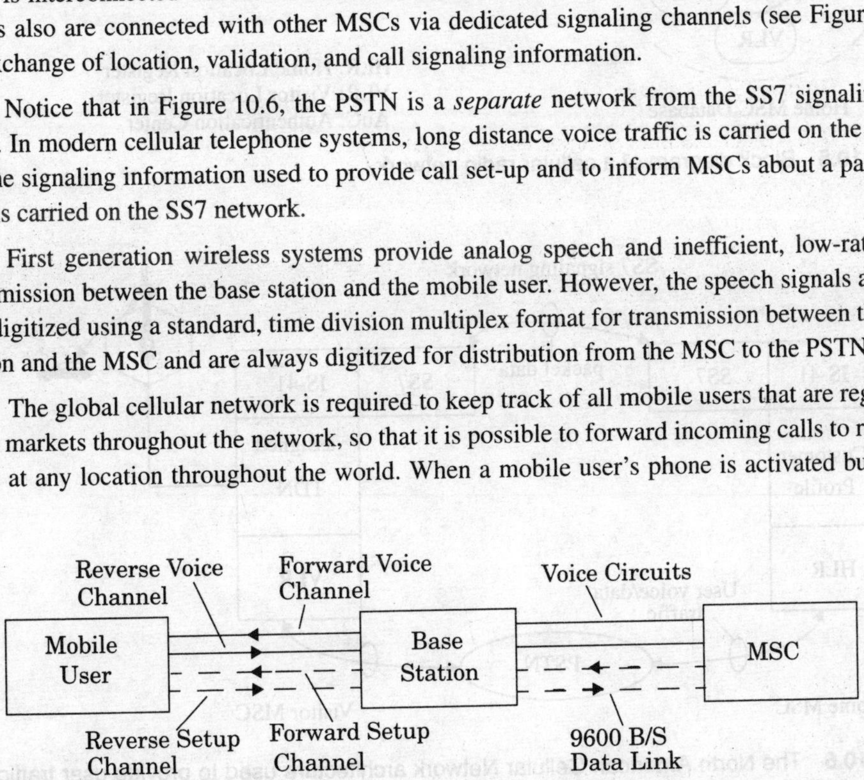

Figure 10.4 Communication signaling between mobile, base station, and MSC in first generation wireless networks.

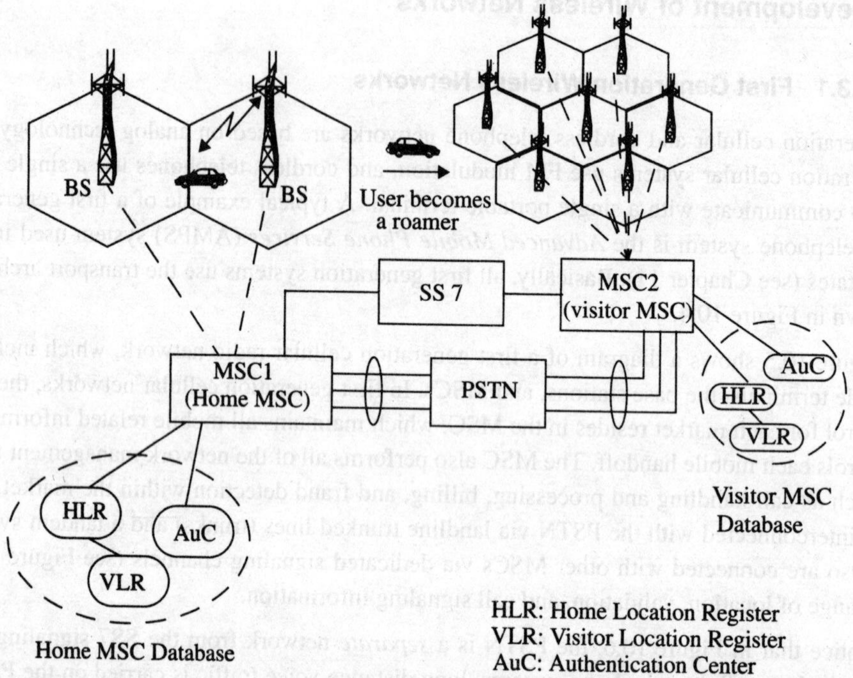

Figure 10.5 Block diagram of a cellular radio network.

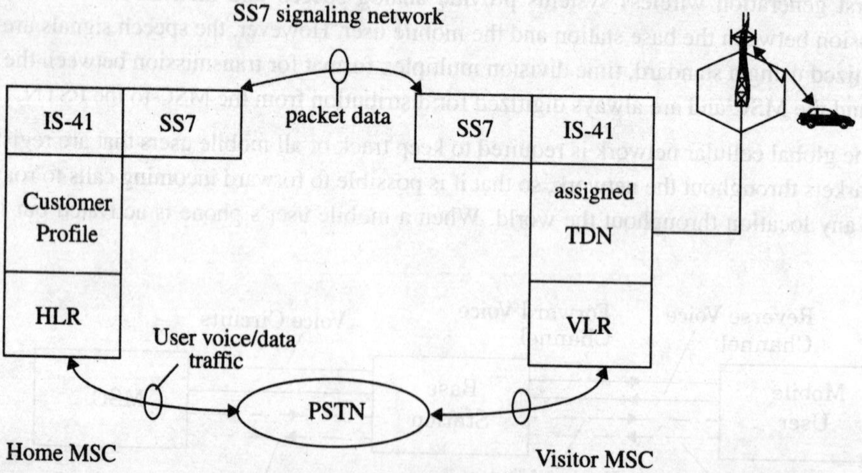

Figure 10.6 The North American Cellular Network architecture used to provide user traffic and signaling traffic between MSCs [from [NAC94] © IEEE]. The components of the SS7 network and their applications are described later in this chapter.

involved in a call, it monitors the strongest control channel in the vicinity. When the user roams into a new market covered by a different service provider, the wireless network must register the user in the new area and cancel its registration with the previous service provider so that calls may be routed to the roamer as it moves through the coverage areas of different MSCs.

Until the early 1990s, US cellular customers that roamed between different cellular systems had to register manually each time they entered a new market during long distance travel. This required the user to call an operator to request registration. In the early 1990s, US cellular carriers implemented the network protocol standard IS-41 to allow different cellular systems to automatically accommodate subscribers who roam into their coverage region. This is called *interoperator roaming*. IS-41 allows MSCs of different service providers to pass information about their subscribers to other MSCs on demand.

IS-41 relies on a feature of AMPS called *autonomous registration*. Autonomous registration is a process by which a mobile notifies a serving MSC of its presence and location. The mobile accomplishes this by periodically keying up and transmitting its identity information, which allows the MSC to constantly update its customer list. The registration command is sent in the overhead message of each control channel at five or ten minute intervals, and includes a timer value which each mobile uses to determine the precise time at which it should respond to the serving base station with a registration transmission. Each mobile reports its MIN and ESN during the brief registration transmission so that the MSC can validate and update the customer list within the market. The MSC is able to distinguish home users from roaming users based on the MIN of each active user, and maintains a real-time user list in the home location register (HLR) and visitor location register (VLR) as shown in Figure 10.5. IS-41 allows the MSCs of neighboring systems to automatically handle the registration and location validation of roamers so that users no longer need to manually register as they travel. The visited system creates a VLR record for each new roamer and notifies the home system via IS-41 so it can update its own HLR.

10.3.2 Second Generation Wireless Networks

Second generation wireless systems employ digital modulation and advanced call processing capabilities. Examples of second generation wireless systems include the *Global System for Mobile* (GSM), the TDMA and CDMA US digital standards (the Telecommunications Industry Association IS-136 and IS-95 standards), *Second Generation Cordless Telephone* (CT2), the British standard for cordless telephony, the *Personal Access Communications System* (PACS) local loop standard, and *Digital European Cordless Telephone* (DECT), which is the European standard for cordless and office telephony. There are many other second generation systems, as described in Chapter 11.

Second generation wireless networks have introduced new network architectures that have reduced the computational burden of the MSC. As shown in Chapter 11, GSM introduced the concept of a *base station controller* (BSC), which is inserted between several base stations and the MSC. In PACS/WACS, the BSC is called a *radio port control unit*. This architectural change has allowed the data interface between the base station controller and the MSC to be standardized, thereby allowing carriers to use different manufacturers for MSC and BSC components. This trend in standardization and interoperability is new to second generation wireless networks. Eventually, wireless network components, such as the MSC and BSC, will be available as off-the-shelf components, much like their wireline telephone counterparts.

All second generation systems use digital voice coding and digital modulation. The systems employ dedicated control channels (common channel signaling—see Section 10.7) within the air interface for simultaneously exchanging voice and control information between the subscriber, the base station, and the MSC while a call is in progress. Second generation systems also provide dedicated voice and signaling trunks between MSCs, and between each MSC and the PSTN.

In contrast to first generation systems, which were designed primarily for voice, second generation wireless networks have been specifically designed to provide paging, and other data services such as facsimile and high-data rate network access. The network controlling structure is more distributed in second generation wireless systems, since mobile stations assume greater control functions. In second generation wireless networks, the handoff process is mobile-controlled and is known as *mobile assisted handoff* (MAHO—explained in Chapter 3). The mobile units in these networks perform several other functions not performed by first generation subscriber units, such as received power reporting, adjacent base station scanning, data encoding, and encryption.

DECT is an example of a second generation cordless telephone standard which allows each cordless phone to communicate with any of a number of base stations, by automatically selecting the base station with the greatest signal level. In DECT, the base stations have greater control in terms of switching, signaling, and controlling handoffs. In general, second generation systems have been designed to reduce the computational and switching burden at the base station or MSC, while providing more flexibility in the channel allocation scheme so that systems may be deployed rapidly and in a less coordinated manner.

10.3.3 Third Generation Wireless Networks

As discussed in Chapter 2, third generation wireless systems will evolve from mature second generation systems. The aim of third generation wireless networks is to provide a single set of standards that can meet a wide range of wireless applications and provide universal access throughout the world. In third generation wireless systems, the distinctions between cordless telephones and cellular telephones will disappear, and a universal personal communicator (a personal handset) will provide access to a variety of voice, data, and video communication services.

Third generation systems will use the *Broadband Integrated Services Digital Network* (B-ISDN) (described in Section 10.8) to provide access to information networks, such as the Internet and other public and private databases. Third generation networks will carry many types of information (voice, data, and video), will operate in varied regions (dense or sparsely populated regions), and will serve both stationary users and vehicular users traveling at high speeds. Packet radio communications will likely be used to distribute network control while providing a reliable information transfer [Goo90].

The terms *3G Personal Communication System* (PCS) and *3G Personal Communication Network* (PCN) are used to imply emerging third generation wireless systems for hand-held devices. Other names for PCS include *Future Public Land Mobile Telecommunication Systems* (FPLMTS) for worldwide use which has more recently been called *International Mobile Telecommunication* (IMT-2000), and *Universal Mobile Telecommunication System* (UMTS) for advanced mobile personal services in Europe.

10.4 Fixed Network Transmission Hierarchy

Wireless networks rely heavily on landline connections. For example, the MSC connects to the PSTN and SS7 networks using fiberoptic or copper cable or microwave links. Base stations within a cellular system are connected to the MSC using line-of-sight (LOS) microwave links, or copper or fiber optic cables. These connections require high data rate serial transmission schemes in order to reduce the number of physical circuits between two points of connection.

Several standard digital signaling (DS) formats form a transmission hierarchy that allows high data rate digital networks which carry a large number of voice channels to be interconnected throughout the world. These DS formats use time division multiplexing (TDM). The most basic DS format in the US is called DS-0, which represents one duplex voice channel which is digitized into a 64 kbps binary PCM format. The next DS format is DS-1, which represents twenty-four full duplex DS-0 voice channels that are time division multiplexed into a 1.544 Mbps data stream (8 kbps is used for control purposes). Related to digital transmission hierarchy is the T(N) designation, which is used to denote transmission line *compatibility* for a particular DS format. DS-1 signaling is used for a T1 trunk, which is a popular point-to-point network signaling format used to connect base stations to the MSC. T1 trunks digitize and distribute the twenty-four voice channels onto a simple four-wire full duplex circuit. In Europe, CEPT (Conference Européene des Administration des Postes et des Télécommunications/European Conference of Postal and Telecommunications Administrations) has defined a similar digital hierarchy. Level 0 represents a duplex 64 kbps voice channel, whereas level 1 concentrates thirty channels into a 2.048 Mbps TDM data stream. Most of the world's PTTs have adopted the European hierarchy. Table 10.1 illustrates the digital hierarchy for North America and Europe [Pec92].

Typically, coaxial or fiber optic cable or wideband microwave links are used to transmit data rates in excess of 10 Mbps, whereas inexpensive wire (twisted pair) or coaxial cable may be used for slower data transfer. When connecting base stations to a MSC, or distributing trunked voice channels throughout a wireless network, T1 (DS1) or level 1 links are most commonly used and utilize common-twisted pair wiring. DS-3 and higher rate circuits are used to connect MSCs and COs to the PSTN.

Table 10.1 Digital Transmission Hierarchy

Signal Level	Digital Bit Rate	Equivalent Voice Circuits	Carrier System
North America and Japan			
DS-0	64.0 kbps	1	
DS-1	1.544 Mbps	24	T-1
DS-1C	3.152 Mbps	48	T-1C
DS-2	6.312 Mbps	96	T-2
DS-3	44.736 Mbps	672	T-3
DS-4	274.176 Mbps	4032	T-4
CEPT (Europe and most other PTTs)			
0	64.0 kbps	1	
1	2.048 Mbps	30	E-1
2	8.448 Mbps	120	E-1C
3	34.368 Mbps	480	E-2
4	139.264 Mbps	1920	E-3
5	565.148 Mbps	7680	E-4

10.5 Traffic Routing in Wireless Networks

The amount of traffic capacity required in a wireless network is highly dependent upon the type of traffic carried. For example, a subscriber's telephone call (voice traffic) requires dedicated network access to provide real-time communications, whereas control and signaling traffic may be bursty in nature and may be able to share network resources with other bursty users. Alternatively, some traffic may have an urgent delivery schedule while some may have no need to be sent in real-time. The type of traffic carried by a network determines the routing services, protocols, and call handling techniques which must be employed.

Two general routing services are provided by networks. These are *connection-oriented services* (virtual circuit routing), and *connectionless services* (datagram services). In connection-oriented routing, the communications path between the message source and destination is fixed for the entire duration of the message, and a call set-up procedure is required to dedicate network resources to both the called and calling parties. Since the path through the network is fixed, the traffic in connection-oriented routing arrives at the receiver in the exact order it was transmitted. A connection-oriented service relies heavily on error control coding to provide data protection in case the network connection becomes noisy. If coding is not sufficient to protect the traffic, the call is broken, and the entire message must be retransmitted from the beginning.

Connectionless routing, on the other hand, does not establish a firm connection for the traffic, and instead relies on packet-based transmissions. Several packets form a message, and each individual packet in a connectionless service is routed separately. Successive packets within the same message might travel completely different routes and encounter widely varying delays throughout the network. Packets sent using connectionless routing do not necessarily arrive in the order of transmission and must to be reordered at the receiver. Because packets take different routes in a connectionless service, some packets may be lost due to network or link failure, however others may get through with sufficient redundancy to enable the entire message to be recreated at the receiver. Thus, connectionless routing often avoids having to retransmit an entire message, but requires more overhead information for each packet. Typical packet overhead information includes the packet source address, the destination address, the routing information, and information needed to properly order packets at the receiver. In a connectionless service, a call set-up procedure is not required at the beginning of a call, and each message burst is treated independently by the network.

10.5.1 Circuit Switching

First generation cellular systems provide connection-oriented services for each voice user. Voice channels are dedicated for users at a serving base station, and network resources are dedicated to the voice traffic upon initiation of a call. That is, the MSC dedicates a voice channel connection between the base station and the PSTN for the duration of a cellular telephone call. Furthermore, a call initiation sequence is required to connect the called and calling parties on a cellular system. When used in conjunction with radio channels, connection-oriented services are provided by a technique called *circuit switching*, since a physical radio channel is dedicated ("switched in to use") for two-way traffic between the mobile user and the MSC, and the PSTN dedicates a voice circuit between the MSC and the end-user. As calls are initiated and completed, different radio circuits and dedicated PSTN voice circuits are switched in and out to handle the traffic.

Circuit switching establishes a dedicated connection (a radio channel between the base and mobile, and a dedicated phone line between the MSC and the PSTN) for the entire duration of a call. Despite the fact that a mobile user may hand off to different base stations, there is always a dedicated radio channel to provide service to the user, and the MSC dedicates a fixed, full duplex phone connection to the PSTN.

Wireless data networks are not well supported by circuit switching, due to their short, bursty transmissions which are often followed by periods of inactivity. Often, the time required to establish a circuit exceeds the duration of the data transmission. Circuit switching is best suited for dedicated voice-only traffic, or for instances where data is continuously sent over long periods of time.

10.5.2 Packet Switching

Connectionless services exploit the fact that dedicated resources are not required for message transmission. Packet switching (also called *virtual switching*) is the most common technique used to implement connectionless services and allows a large number of data users to remain virtually connected to the same physical channel in the network. Since all users may access the network randomly and at will, call set-up procedures are not needed to dedicate specific circuits when a particular user needs to send data. Packet switching breaks each message into smaller units for transmission and recovery [Ber92], [DeR94]. When a message is broken into packets, a certain amount of control information is added to each packet to provide source and destination identification, as well as error recovery provisions.

Figure 10.7 illustrates the sequential format of a packet transmission. The packet consists of header information, the user data, and a trailer. The header specifies the beginning of a new packet and contains the source address, destination address, packet sequence number, and other routing and billing information. The user data contains information which is generally protected with error control coding. The trailer contains a cyclic redundancy checksum which is used for error detection at the receiver.

Figure 10.8 shows the structure of a transmitted packet, which typically consists of five fields: the flag bits, the address field, the control field, the information field, and the frame check sequence field. The flag bits are specific (or reserved) bit sequences that indicate the beginning and end of each packet. The address field contains the source and the destination address for transmitting messages and for receiving acknowledgments. The control field defines functions such as transfer of acknowledgments, automatic repeat requests (ARQs), and packet sequencing. The information field contains the user data and may have variable length. The final field is the frame check sequence field or the CRC (Cyclic Redundancy Check) that is used for error detection.

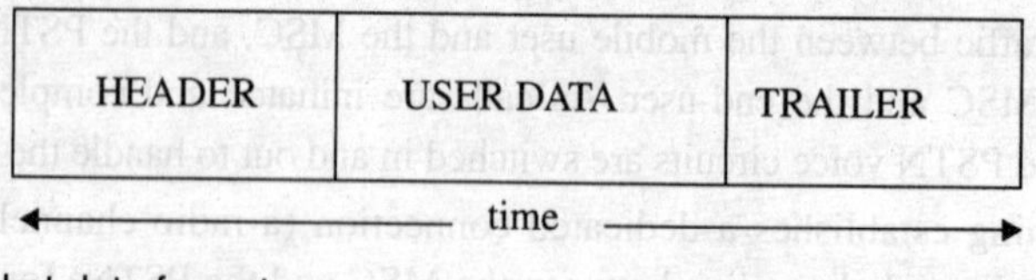

Figure 10.7 Packet data format.

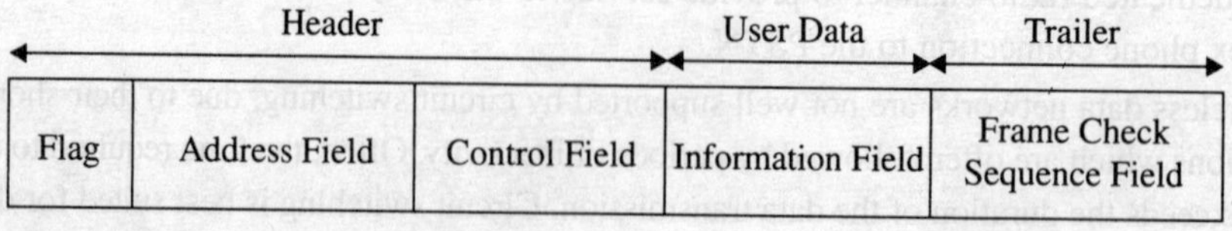

Figure 10.8 Fields in a typical packet of data.

In contrast to circuit switching, packet switching (also called packet radio when used over a wireless link) provides excellent channel efficiency for bursty data transmissions of short length. An advantage of packet-switched data is that the channel is utilized only when sending or receiving bursts of information. This benefit is valuable for the case of mobile services where the available bandwidth is limited. The packet radio approach supports intelligent protocols for data flow control and retransmission, which can provide highly reliable transfer in degraded channel conditions. X.25 is a widely used packet radio protocol that defines a data interface for packet switching [Ber92], [Tan81].

10.5.3 The X.25 Protocol

X.25 was developed by CCITT (now ITU-T) to provide standard connectionless network access (packet switching) protocols for the three lowest layers (layers 1, 2, and 3) of the *open systems interconnection* (OSI) model (see Figure 10.14 for the OSI layer hierarchy). The X.25 protocols provide a standard network interface between originating and terminating subscriber equipment (called *data terminal equipment* or DTE), the base stations (called *data circuit-terminating equipment* or DCE), and the MSC (called the *data switching exchange* or DSE). The X.25 protocols are used in many packet radio air-interfaces, as well as in fixed networks [Ber92], [Tan81].

Figure 10.9 shows the hierarchy of X.25 protocols in the OSI model. The Layer 1 protocol deals with the electrical, mechanical, procedural, and functional interface between the subscriber (DTE), and the base station (DCE). The Layer 2 protocol defines the data link on the common air-interface between the subscriber and the base station. Layer 3 provides connection between the base station and the MSC, and is called the *packet layer protocol*. A packet assembler disassembler (PAD) is used at Layer 3 to connect networks using the X.25 interface with devices that are not equipped with a standard X.25 interface.

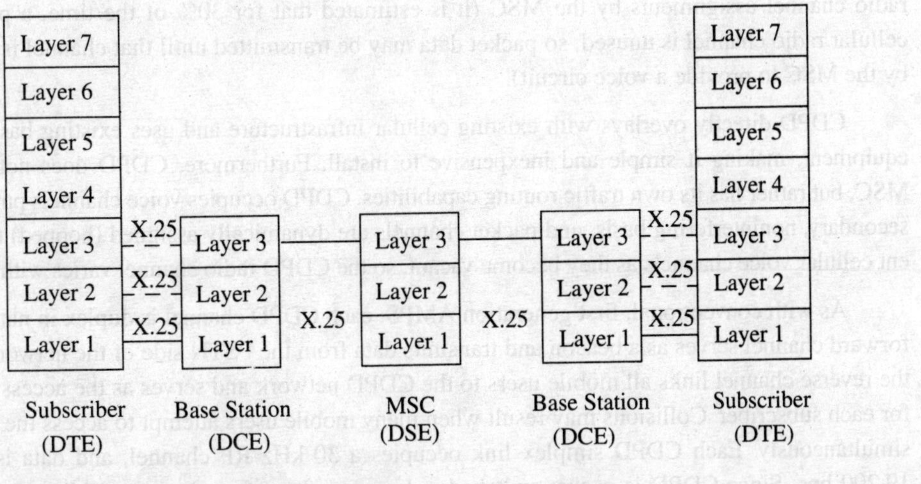

Figure 10.9 Hierarchy of X.25 in OSI model.

The X.25 protocol does not specify particular data rates or how packet-switched networks are implemented. Rather, X.25 provides a series of standard functions and formats which give structure to the design of software that is used to provide packet data on a generic connectionless network.

10.6 Wireless Data Services

As discussed in Section 10.5, circuit switching is inefficient for dedicated mobile data services such as facsimile (fax), electronic mail (e-mail), and short messaging. First generation cellular systems that provide data communications using circuit switching have difficulty passing modem signals through the audio filters of receivers designed for analog, FM, common air-interfaces. Inevitably, voice filtering must be deactivated when data is transmitted over first generation cellular networks, and a dedicated data link must be established over the common air-interface. The demand for packet data services has, until recently, been significantly less than the demand for voice services, and first generation subscriber equipment design has focused almost solely on voice-only cellular communications. However, in 1993, the US cellular industry developed the *cellular digital packet data* (CDPD) standard to coexist with the conventional voice-only cellular system. In the 1980s, two other data-only mobile services called ARDIS and RAM Mobile Data (RMD) were developed to provide packet radio connectivity throughout a network.

10.6.1 Cellular Digital Packet Data (CDPD)

CDPD is a data service for first and second generation US cellular systems and uses a full 30 kHz AMPS channel on a shared basis [CTI93], [DeR94]. CDPD provides mobile packet data connectivity to existing data networks and other cellular systems without any additional bandwidth requirements. It also capitalizes on the unused air time which occurs between successive radio channel assignments by the MSC (it is estimated that for 30% of the time, a particular cellular radio channel is unused, so packet data may be transmitted until that channel is selected by the MSC to provide a voice circuit).

CDPD directly overlays with existing cellular infrastructure and uses existing base station equipment, making it simple and inexpensive to install. Furthermore, CDPD does not use the MSC, but rather has its own traffic routing capabilities. CDPD occupies voice channels purely on a secondary, noninterfering basis, and packet channels are dynamically assigned (hopped) to different cellular voice channels as they become vacant, so the CDPD radio channel varies with time.

As with conventional, first generation AMPS, each CDPD channel is duplex in nature. The forward channel serves as a beacon and transmits data from the PSTN side of the network, while the reverse channel links all mobile users to the CDPD network and serves as the access channel for each subscriber. Collisions may result when many mobile users attempt to access the network simultaneously. Each CDPD simplex link occupies a 30 kHz RF channel, and data is sent at 19,200 bps. Since CDPD is packet-switched, a large number of modems are able to access the same channel on an as needed, packet-by-packet basis. CDPD supports broadcast, dispatch, electronic mail, and field monitoring applications. GMSK $BT = 0.5$ modulation is used so that existing analog FM cellular receivers can easily detect the CDPD format without redesign.

CDPD transmissions are carried out using fixed-length blocks. User data is protected using a Reed–Solomon (63,47) block code with 6-bit symbols. For each packet, 282 user bits are coded into 378 bit blocks, which provide correction for up to eight symbols.

Two lower layer protocols are used in CDPD. The *mobile data link protocol* (MDLP) is used to convey information between data link layer entities (layer 2 devices) across the CDPD air interface. The MDLP provides logical data link connections on a radio channel by using an address contained in each packet frame. The MDLP also provides sequence control to maintain the sequential order of frames across a data link connection, as well as error detection and flow control. The *radio resource management protocol* (RRMP) is a higher, layer 3 protocol used to manage the radio channel resources of the CDPD system and enables an M-ES to find and utilize a duplex radio channel without interfering with standard voice services. The RRMP handles base-station identification and configuration messages for all M-ES stations, and provides information that the M-ES can use to determine usable CDPD channels without knowledge of the history of channel usage. The RRMP also handles channel hopping commands, cell handoffs, and M-ES change of power commands. CDPD version 1.0 uses the X.25 *wide area network* (WAN) subprofile and frame relay capabilities for internal subnetworks.

Table 10.2 lists the link layer characteristics for CDPD. Figure 10.10 illustrates a typical CDPD network. Note that the subscribers (the *mobile end system*, or M-ES) are able to connect through the *mobile data base stations* (MDBS) to the Internet via *intermediate systems* (MD-IS), which act as servers and routers for the subscribers. In this way, mobile users are able to connect to the Internet or the PSTN. Through the I-interface, CDPD can carry either Internet protocol (IP) or OSI connectionless protocol (CLNP) traffic.

Table 10.2 Link Layer Characteristics for CDPD

Protocols	MDLP, RRMP, X.25
Channel Data Rate (bps)	19,200
Channel Bandwidth (kHz)	30
Spectrum Efficiency (b/Hz)	0.64
Random Error Strategy	cover with burst protect
Burst Error Strategy	RS 63,47 (6 bits per symbol)
Fading Performance	withstands 2.2 ms fade
Channel Access	slotted DSMA/CD

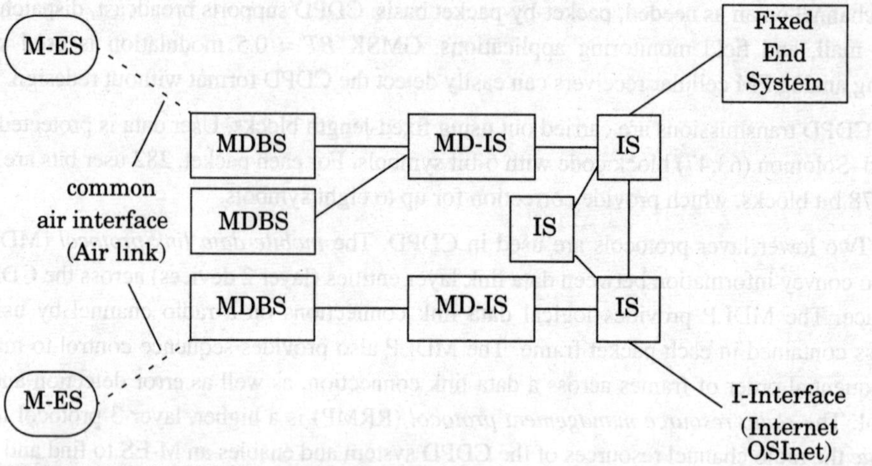

M-ES : Mobile End Station
MDBS : Mobile Data Base Station
MD-IS : Intermediate Server for CDPD traffic

Figure 10.10 The CDPD network.

10.6.2 Advanced Radio Data Information Systems (ARDIS)

Advance Radio Data Information Systems (ARDIS) is a private network service provided by Motorola and IBM and is based on MDC 4800 and RD-LAP (Radio Data Link Access Procedure) protocols developed at Motorola [DeR94]. ARDIS provides 800 MHz two-way mobile data communications for short-length radio messages in urban and in-building environments, and for users traveling at low speeds. Short ARDIS messages have low retry rates but high packet overhead, while long messages spread the overhead over the length of the packet but have a higher retry rate. ARDIS has been deployed to provide excellent in-building penetration, and large-scale spatial antenna diversity is used to receive messages from mobile users. When a mobile sends a packet, many base stations which are tuned to the transmission frequency attempt to detect and decode the transmission, in order to provide diversity reception for the case when multiple mobiles contend for the reverse link. In this manner, ARDIS base stations are able to insure detection of simultaneous transmissions, as long as the users are sufficiently separated in space. Table 10.3 lists some characteristics for ARDIS.

10.6.3 RAM Mobile Data (RMD)

RAM Mobile Data (RMD) is a public, two-way data service based upon the Mobitex protocol developed by Ericsson. RAM provides street level coverage for short and long messages for users moving in an urban environment. RAM has capability for voice and data transmission, but has been designed primarily for data and facsimile. Fax messages are transmitted as normal

Table 10.3 Channel Characteristics for ARDIS

Protocol	MDC 4800	RD-LAP
Speed (bps)	4800	19,200
Channel Bandwidth (kHz)	25	25
Spectrum Efficiency (b/Hz)	0.19	0.77
Random Error Strategy	convolutional 1/2, k = 7	trellis coded modulation, rate = 3/4
Burst Error Strategy	interleave 16 bits	interleave 32 bits
Fading Performance	withstands 3.3 ms fade	withstands 1.7 ms fade
Channel Access	CSMA nonpersistent	slot CSMA

Table 10.4 Channel Characteristics for RAM Mobile Data

Protocol	Mobitex
Speed (bps)	8000
Channel Bandwidth (kHz)	12.5
Spectrum Efficiency (b/Hz)	0.64
Random Error Strategy	12, 8 Hamming code
Burst Error Strategy	interleave 21 bits
Fading Performance	withstands 2.6 ms fade
Channel Access	slotted CSMA

text to a gateway processor, which then converts the radio message to an appropriate format by merging it with a background page. Thus, the packet-switched wireless transmission consists of a normal length message instead of a much larger fax image, even though the end-user receives what appears to be a standard fax [DeR94]. Table 10.4 lists some characteristics of the RAM mobile data service.

10.7 Common Channel Signaling (CCS)

Common channel signaling (CCS) is a digital communications technique that provides simultaneous transmission of user data, signaling data, and other related traffic throughout a network. This is accomplished by using *out-of-band* signaling channels which logically separate the network data from the user information (voice or data) on the same channel. For second generation wireless communications systems, CCS is used to pass user data and control/supervisory signals between the subscriber and the base station, between the base station and the MSC, and between MSCs. Even though the concept of CCS implies dedicated, parallel channels, it is implemented in a TDM format for serial data transmissions.

Before the introduction of CCS in the 1980s, signaling traffic between the MSC and a subscriber was carried in the same band as the end-user's audio. The network control data passed between MSCs in the PSTN was also carried in-band, requiring that network information be carried within the same channel as the subscriber's voice traffic throughout the PSTN. This technique, called *in-band signaling*, reduced the capacity of the PSTN, since the network signaling data rates were greatly constrained by the limitations of the carried voice channels, and the PSTN was forced to sequentially (not simultaneously) handle signaling and user data for each call.

CCS is an out-of-band signaling technique which allows much faster communications between two nodes within the PSTN. Instead of being constrained to signaling data rates which are on the order of audio frequencies, CCS supports signaling data rates from 56 kbps to many megabits per second. Thus, network signaling data is carried in a seemingly parallel, out-of-band, signaling channel while only user data is carried on the PSTN. CCS provides a substantial increase in the number of users which are served by trunked PSTN lines, but requires that a dedicated portion of the trunk time be used to provide a signaling channel used for network traffic. In first generation cellular systems, the SS7 family of protocols, as defined by the Integrated System Digital Network (ISDN) are used to provide CCS.

Since network signaling traffic is bursty and of short duration, the signaling channel may be operated in a connectionless fashion where packet data transfer techniques are efficiently used. CCS generally uses variable length packet sizes and a layered protocol structure. The expense of a parallel signaling channel is minor compared to the capacity improvement offered by CCS throughout the PSTN, and often the same physical network connection (i.e., a fiber optic cable) carries both the user traffic and the network signaling data.

10.7.1 The Distributed Central Switching Office for CCS

As more users subscribe to wireless services, backbone networks that link MSCs together will rely more heavily on network signaling to preserve message integrity, to provide end-to-end connectivity for each mobile user, and to maintain a robust network that can recover from failures. CCS forms the foundation of network control and management functions in second and third generation networks. Out-of-band signaling networks which connect MSCs throughout the world enable the entire wireless network to update and keep track of specific mobile users, wherever they happen to be. Figure 10.6 illustrates how an MSC is connected to both the PSTN and the signaling network.

As shown in Figure 10.11, the CCS network architecture is composed of geographically distributed central switching offices, each with embedded *switching end points* (SEPs), *signaling transfer points* (STPs), a *service management system* (SMS), and a *database service management system* (DBAS) [Mod92], [Boy90], [Mar90].

The MSC provides subscriber access to the PSTN via the SEP. The SEP implements a stored-program-control switching system known as the *service control point* (SCP) that uses CCS to set up calls and to access a network database. The SCP instructs the SEP to create billing records based on the call information recorded by the SCP.

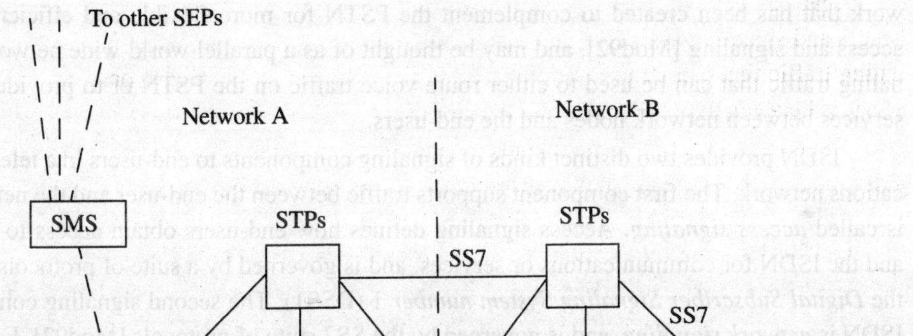

SEPs: Switching End Points
STPs: Signaling Transfer Points
SMS: Service Management System
SS7: Signaling System No. 7

Figure 10.11 Common channel signaling (CCS) network architecture showing STPs, SEPs, and SMS embedded within a central switching office, based on SS7.

The STP controls the switching of messages between nodes in the CCS network. For higher reliability of transmission (redundancy), SEPs are required to be connected to the SS7 network (described in Section 10.8) via at least two STPs. This combination of two STPs in parallel is known as a *mated pair*, and provides connectivity to the network in the event one STP fails.

The SMS contains all subscriber records, and also houses toll-free databases which may be accessed by the subscribers. The DBAS is the administrative database that maintains service records and investigates fraud throughout the network. The SMS and DBAS work in tandem to provide a wide range of customer and network provider services, based on SS7.

10.8 Integrated Services Digital Network (ISDN)

Integrated Services Digital Network (ISDN) is a complete network framework designed around the concept of common channel signaling. While telephone users throughout the world rely on the PSTN to carry conventional voice traffic, new end-user data and signaling services can be provided with a parallel, dedicated signaling network. ISDN defines the dedicated signaling network that has been created to complement the PSTN for more flexible and efficient network access and signaling [Mod92], and may be thought of as a parallel world-wide network for signaling traffic that can be used to either route voice traffic on the PSTN or to provide new data services between network nodes and the end-users.

ISDN provides two distinct kinds of signaling components to end-users in a telecommunications network. The first component supports traffic between the end-user and the network, and is called *access signaling*. Access signaling defines how end-users obtain access to the PSTN and the ISDN for communications or services, and is governed by a suite of protocols known as the *Digital Subscriber Signaling System number* 1 (DSS1). The second signaling component of ISDN is *network signaling*, and is governed by the SS7 suite of protocols [Mod92]. For wireless communications systems, the SS7 protocols within ISDN are critical to providing backbone network connectivity between MSCs throughout the world, as they provide network interfaces for common channel signaling traffic.

ISDN provides a complete digital interface between end-users over twisted pair telephone lines. The ISDN interface is divided into three different types of channels. Information bearing channels called *bearer channels* (B channels) are used exclusively for end-user traffic (voice, data, video). Out-of-band signaling channels, called *data channels* (D channels), are used to send signaling and control information across the interface to end-users. As shown in Figure 10.12, ISDN provides integrated end-user access to both *circuit-switched* and *packet-switched networks* with digital end-to-end connectivity.

ISDN end-users may select between two different interfaces, the *basic rate interface* (BRI) or the *primary rate interface* (PRI). The BRI is intended to serve small capacity terminals (such as single line telephones) while the PRI is intended for large capacity terminals (such as PBXs). The B channels support 64 kbps data for both the primary rate and the basic rate interfaces. The D channel supports 64 kbps for the primary rate and 16 kbps for the basic rate. The

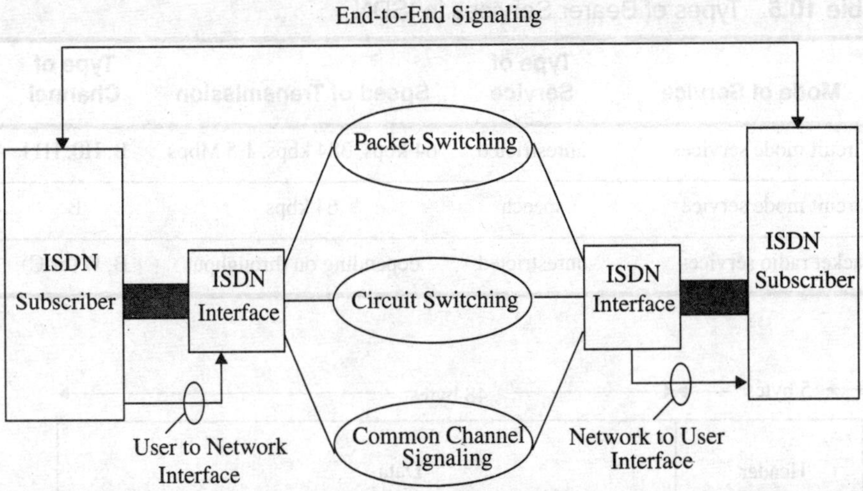

Figure 10.12 Block diagram of an Integrated Services Digital Network. Even though the diagram illustrates parallel channels, the TDM-based serial data structure uses a single twisted pair.

BRI provides two 64 kbps bearer channels and one 16 kbps signaling channel (2B+D), whereas the PRI provides twenty-three 64 kbps bearer channels and one 64 kbps signaling channel (23B+D) for North America and Japan. In Europe, the primary rate interface provides thirty basic information channels and one 64 kbps signaling channel (30B+D). The PRI service is designed to be carried by DS-1 or CEPT level 1 links (see Section 10.4).

For wireless service subscribers, an ISDN basic rate interface is provided in exactly the same manner as for a fixed terminal. To differentiate between wireless and fixed subscribers, the mobile BRI defines signaling data (D channels in the fixed network) as control channels (C channels in the mobile network), so that a wireless subscriber has 2B+C service.

Much like the digital signaling hierarchy described in Section 10.2, several ISDN circuits may be concatenated into high speed information channels (H channels). H channels are used by the ISDN backbone to provide efficient data transport of many users on a single physical connection, and may also be used by PRI end-users to allocate higher transmission rates on demand. ISDN defines H0 channels (384 kbps), H11 (1536 kbps), and H12 channels (1920 kbps) as shown in Table 10.5

10.8.1 Broadband ISDN and ATM

With the proliferation of computer systems and video imaging, end-user applications are requiring much greater bandwidths than the standard 64 kbps B channel provided by ISDN. Recent work has defined ISDN interface standards that increase the end-user transmission bandwidth to several Mb/s. This emerging networking technique is known as *broadband ISDN* (B-ISDN) and is based on *asynchronous transfer mode* (ATM) technology which allows packet switching rates up to 2.4 Gbps and total switching capacities as high as 100 Gbps.

Table 10.5 Types of Bearer Services in ISDN

Mode of Service	Type of Service	Speed of Transmission	Type of Channel
Circuit mode services	unrestricted	64 kbps, 384 kbps, 1.5 Mbps	B, H0, H11
Circuit mode service	speech	64 kbps	B
Packet radio services	unrestricted	depending on throughput	B, D (or C)

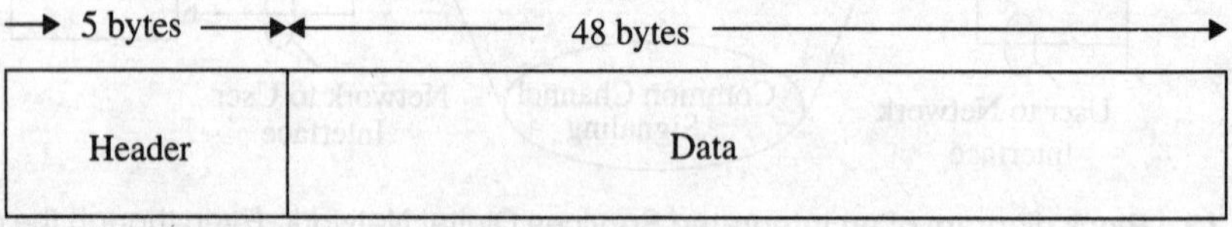

Figure 10.13 Cell format of Asynchronous Transfer Mode (ATM).

ATM is a packet switching and multiplexing technique which has been specifically designed to handle both voice users and packet data users in a single physical channel. ATM data rates vary from low traffic rates (64 kbps) over twisted pair to over 100 Mbps over fiberoptic cables for high traffic rates between network nodes. ATM supports bidirectional transfer of data packets of fixed length between two end points, while preserving the order of transmission. ATM data units, called *cells*, are routed based on header information in each unit (called a *label*) that identifies the cell as belonging to a specific ATM virtual connection. The label is determined upon virtual connection of a user, and remains the same throughout the transmission for a particular connection. The ATM header also includes data for congestion control, priority information for queuing of packets, and a priority which indicates which ATM packets can be dropped in case of congestion in the network.

Figure 10.13 shows the cell format of ATM. ATM cells (packets) have a fixed length of 53 bytes, consisting of 48 bytes of data and 5 bytes of header information. Fixed length packets result in simple implementation of fast packet switches, since packets arrive synchronously at the switch [Ber92]. A compromise was made in selecting the length of ATM cells to accommodate both voice and data users.

10.9 Signaling System No. 7 (SS7)

The SS7 signaling protocol is widely used for common channel signaling between interconnected networks (see Figure 10.11, for example). SS7 is used to interconnect most of the cellular MSCs throughout the US, and is the key factor in enabling autonomous registration and automated roaming in first generation cellular systems. The structure of SS7 signaling is discussed in greater detail in the text by Modarressi and Skoog [Mod92].

SS7 is an outgrowth of the out-of band signaling first developed by the CCITT under *common channel signaling standard, CCS No. 6*. Further work caused SS7 to evolve along the lines of the ISO-OSI seven layer network definition, where a highly layered structure (transparent from layer to layer) is used to provide network communications. Peer layers in the ISO model communicate with each other through a virtual (packet data) interface, and a hierarchical interface structure is established. A comparison of the OSI-7 network model and the SS7 protocol standard is given in Figure 10.14. The lowest three layers of the OSI model are handled in SS7 by the *network service part* (NSP) of the protocol, which in turn is made up of three *message transfer parts* (MTPs) and the *signaling connection control part* (SCCP) of the SS7 protocol.

10.9.1 Network Services Part (NSP) of SS7

The NSP provides ISDN nodes with a highly reliable and efficient means of exchanging signaling traffic using connectionless services. The SCCP in SS7 actually supports packet data network interconnections as well as connection-oriented networking to virtual circuit networks. The NSP allows network nodes to communicate throughout the world without concern for the application or context of the signaling traffic.

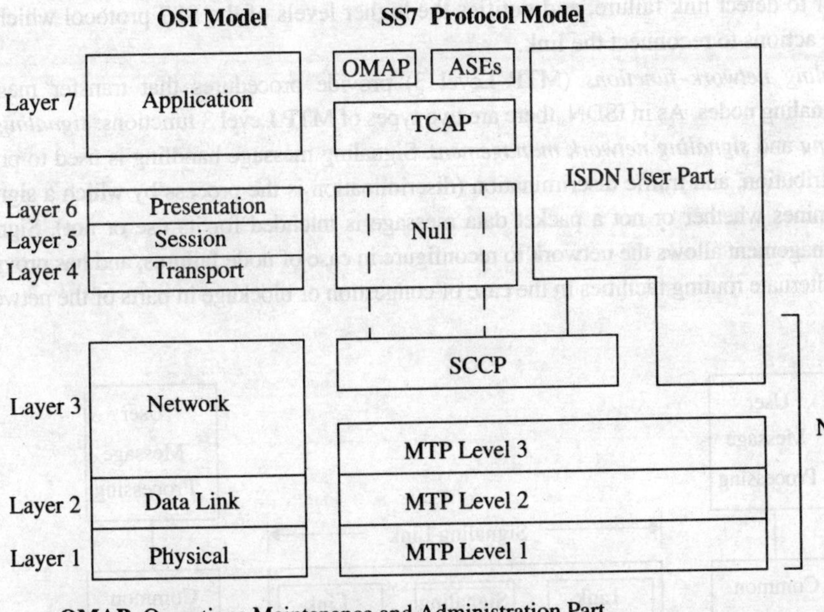

OMAP: Operations Maintenance and Administration Part
ASE: Application Service Element
TCAP: Transaction Capabilities Application Part
SCCP: Signaling Connection Control Part
MTP: Message Transfer Part
NSP: Network Service Part

Figure 10.14 SS7 protocol architecture [from [Mod92] © IEEE].

10.9.1.1 Message Transfer Part (MTP) of SS7

The function of the MTP is to ensure that signaling traffic can be transferred and delivered reliably between the end-users and the network. MTP is provided at three levels. Figure 10.15 shows the functionality of the various MTP levels that will be described.

Signaling data link functions (MTP Level 1) provide an interface to the actual physical channel over which communication takes place. Physical channels may include copper wire, twisted pair, fiber, mobile radio, or satellite links, and are transparent to the higher layers. CCITT recommends that MTP Level 1 use 64 kbps transmissions, whereas ANSI recommends 56 kbps. The minimum data rate provided for telephony control operations is 4.8 kbps [Mod92].

Signaling link functions (MTP Level 2) correspond to the second layer in the OSI reference model and provide a reliable link for the transfer of traffic between two directly connected signaling points. Variable length packet messages, called *message signal units* (MSUs), are defined in MTP Level 2. A single MSU cannot have a packet length which exceeds 272 octets, and a standard 16 bit cyclic redundancy check (CRC) checksum is included in each MSU for error detection. A wide range of error detection and correction features are provided in MTP Level 2.

MTP Level 2 also provides flow control data between two signaling points as a means of sensing link failure. If the receiving device does not respond to data transmissions, MTP Level 2 uses a timer to detect link failure, and notifies the higher levels of the SS7 protocol which take appropriate actions to reconnect the link.

Signaling network functions (MTP Level 3) provide procedures that transfer messages between signaling nodes. As in ISDN, there are two types of MTP Level 3 functions: *signaling message handling* and *signaling network management*. Signaling message handling is used to provide routing, distribution, and traffic discrimination (discrimination is the process by which a signaling point determines whether or not a packet data message is intended for its use or not). Signaling network management allows the network to reconfigure in case of node failures, and has provisions to allocate alternate routing facilities in the case of congestion or blockage in parts of the network.

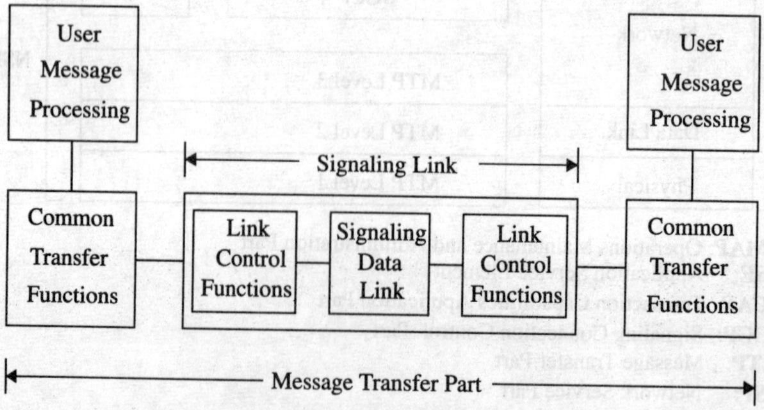

Figure 10.15 Functional diagram of message transfer part.

Table 10.6 Different Classes of Service Provided by SCCP

Class of Service	Type of Service
Class 0	Basic connection class
Class 1	Sequenced (MTP) connectionless class
Class 2	Basic connection-oriented class
Class 3	Flow control connection-oriented class

10.9.1.2 Signaling Connection Control Part (SCCP) of SS7

The *signaling connection control part* (SCCP) provides enhancement to the addressing capabilities provided by the MTP. While the addressing capabilities of MTP are limited in nature, SCCP uses local addressing based on subsystem numbers (SSNs) to identify users at a signaling node. SCCP also provides the ability to address global title messages, such as 800 numbers or nonbilled numbers. SCCP provides four classes of service: two are connectionless and two are connection-oriented, as shown in Table 10.6.

SCCP consists of four functional blocks. The SCCP connection-oriented control block provides data transfer on signaling connections. The SCCP management block provides functions to handle congestion and failure conditions that cannot be handled at the MTP. The SCCP routing block routes forwards messages received from MTP or other functional blocks.

10.9.2 The SS7 User Part

As shown in Figure 10.14, the SS7 user part provides call control and management functions and call set-up capabilities to the network. These are the higher layers in the SS7 reference model, and utilize the transport facilities provided by the MTP and the SCCP. The SS7 user part includes the *ISDN user part* (ISUP), the *transaction capabilities application part* (TCAP) and the *operations maintenance and administration part* (OMAP). The *telephone user part* (TUP) and the *data user part* (DUP) are included in the ISUP.

10.9.2.1 Integrated Services Digital Network User Part (ISUP)

The ISUP provides the signaling functions for carrier and supplementary services for voice, data, and video in an ISDN environment. In the past, telephony requirements were lumped in the TUP, but this is now a subset of ISUP. ISUP uses the MTP for transfer of messages between different exchanges. ISUP message includes a routing label that indicates the source and destination of the message, a circuit identification code (CIC), and a message code that serves to define the format and function of each message. They have variable lengths with a maximum of 272 octets that includes MTP level headers. In addition to the basic bearer services in an ISDN environment, the facilities of user-to-user signaling, closed user groups, calling line identification, and call forwarding are provided.

10.9.2.2 Transaction Capabilities Application Part (TCAP)

The transaction capabilities application part in SS7 refers to the application layer which invokes the services of the SCCP and the MTP in a hierarchical format. One application at a node is thus able to execute an application at another node and use these results. Thus, TCAP is concerned with remote operations. TCAP messages are used by IS-41.

10.9.2.3 Operation Maintenance and Administration Part (OMAP)

The OMAP functions include monitoring, coordination, and control functions to ensure that trouble free communications are possible. OMAP supports diagnostics are known throughout the global network to determine loading and specific subnetwork behaviors.

10.9.3 Signaling Traffic in SS7

Call set-ups, inter-MSC Handoffs, and location updates are the main activities that generate the maximum signaling traffic in a network, and which are all handled under SS7. Setting up of a call requires exchange of information about the location of the calling subscriber (call origination, calling-party procedures) and information about the location of the called subscriber. Either or both, of the calling and the called subscribers can be mobile, and whenever any of the mobile subscribers switches MSCs under a handoff condition, it adds to the amount of information exchanged. Table 10.7 shows the amount of signaling traffic that is generated for call set-up in GSM [Mei93]. Location update records are updated in the network whenever a subscriber moves to a new location. The traffic required by the location update process as a subscriber moves within and between VLR areas is shown in Table 10.8.

Table 10.7 Signaling Load for Call Setup and Handoffs in GSM

Call originating from a Mobile	Load
Information on the originating MSC and the terminating switch	120 bytes
Information on the originating MSC and the associated VLR	550 bytes
Call terminating at a Mobile	
Information on the switch and terminating MSC	120 bytes
Information on the terminating MSC and associated VLR	612 bytes
Information on the originating switch and HLR	126 bytes
InterMSC handoffs	
Information on the new MSC and associated VLR	148 bytes
Information on the new MSC and old MSC	383 bytes

Table 10.8 Signaling Load for Location Updating in GSM

Location Updating	Load
Information on the current MSC and associated VLR	406 bytes
Information on the current VLR and HLR	55 bytes
Information on new VLR and old VLR	406 bytes
Information on the new VLR and old VLR	213 bytes
Information on the old VLR and HLR	95 bytes
Information on the new VLR and HLR	182 bytes

10.9.4 SS7 Services

There are three main type of services offered by the SS7 network [Boy90]: the Touchstar, 800 services, and alternate billing services. These services are briefly explained below.

Touchstar — This kind of service is also known as CLASS and is a group of switch-controlled services that provide its users with certain call management capabilities. Services such as call return, call forwarding, repeat dialing, call block, call tracing, and caller ID are provided.

800 services — These services were introduced by Bell System to provide toll-free access to the calling party to the services and database which is offered by the private parties. The costs associated with the processing of calls is paid by the service subscriber. The service is offered under two plans known as the 800-NXX plan, and the 800 Database plan. In the 800-NXX plan the first six digits of an 800 call are used to select the *interexchange carrier* (IXC). In the 800 Database plan, the call is looked up in a database to determine the appropriate carrier and routing information.

Alternate Billing Service and Line Information Database (ADB/LIDB) — These services use the CCS network to enable the calling party to bill a call to a personal number (third party number, calling card, or collect etc.) from any number.

10.9.5 Performance of SS7

The performance of the signaling network is studied by connection set-up time (response time) or the end-to-end signaling information transfer time. The delays in the signaling point (SP) and the STP depend on the specific hardware configuration and switching software implementation. The maximum limits for these delay times have been specified in the CCITT recommendations Q.706, Q.716, and Q.766.

Congestion Control in SS7 networks — With an increasing number of subscribers, it becomes important to avoid congestion in the signaling network under heavy traffic conditions [Mod92], [Man93]. SS7 networking protocols provide several congestion control schemes, allowing traffic to avoid failed links and nodes.

Advantages of Common Channel Signaling over Conventional Signaling [Mar90] — CCS has several advantages over conventional signaling which have been outlined below:

- *Faster Call Set-up* — In CCS, high speed signaling networks are used for transferring the call set-up messages resulting in smaller delay times when compared to conventional signaling methods, such as multifrequency.
- *Greater trunking (or Queueing) Efficiency* — CCS has shorter call set-up and tear down times that result in less call-holding time, subsequently reducing the traffic on the network. In heavy traffic conditions, high trunking efficiency is obtained.
- *Information Transfer* — CCS allows the transfer of additional information along with the signaling traffic providing facilities such as caller identification and voice or data identification.

10.10 An Example of SS7 — Global Cellular Network Interoperability

Cellular radio networks provide connectivity for all mobile stations in a particular market and provide efficient means for *call set-up*, *call transfer* and *handoff*. Figure 10.5 shows a simplified block diagram of a cellular radio network. The base station is the basic building block in a cellular network which serves as the central point of network access for a subscriber in a particular geographical region (cell). The base stations are connected by either a radio or landline link to a MSC. The MSC controls the switching and billing functions and interacts with the PSTN to transfer traffic between the global grid and its own cluster of base stations. The MSC uses the SS7 signaling network for location validation and call delivery for its users which are roaming, and relies on several information databases. These database are the *home location register* (HLR), the *visitor location register* (VLR), and the *authentication center* (AuC), which are used to update location and registration records for all subscribers in the network at any time. These databases may be co-located at the MSC or may be remotely accessed.

To perform call set-up, call transfer, and call handoff, the roaming, registration, and routing functions are very important. Roaming is a fundamental requirement of wireless networks [Boy90], [Roc89], [NAC94]. A mobile subscriber becomes a roaming subscriber when it leaves the coverage area of the MSC to which it was originally subscribed (the *home MSC*). Existing wireline approaches are not optimized to meet the requirements of call delivery in a wireless network where the users are allowed to roam from switch to switch. To ensure that the PSTN is able to provide voice access to all mobile subscribers, the roaming subscriber (even if not engaged in a call) is required to *register* with the MSC in which it presently resides (the *visitor MSC*). Registration is a process in which each roaming subscriber notifies the serving MSC of its presence and location. This registration is then transferred to the home MSC where the HLR is updated. When a call is made to the mobile user, the network selects the path through which the call must be routed in order to obtain a connection between the calling party and the called subscriber. The selection of a path in the network is known as *routing*. The called subscriber is alerted of the presence of an incoming call, and a pickup procedure is then initiated by the called subscriber (as described in Chapter 3) to accept the call.

The home location register, as shown in Figure 10.5, contains a list of all users (along with their MIN and ESN) who originally subscribed to the cellular network in the covered geographic region. A home subscriber is billed at a different (less expensive) rate than a roaming subscriber, so the MSC must identify every call as being made by either a home or roaming user. The visitor location register is a time-varying list of users who have roamed into the coverage area of the network. The MSC updates the VLR by first determining which users are roamers (visitors) and by requesting VLR information for each roamer over the SS7 network. Remote MSCs which serve as the home switches for the roamers are able to supply the required VLR information. The authentication center matches the MIN and ESN of every active cellular phone in the system with the data stored in the home location register. If a phone does not match the data in the home database, the authentication center instructs the MSC to disable the offending phone, thereby preventing fraudulent phones access to the network.

Each subscriber unit is able to identify if it is roaming by comparing the received station ID (SID) on the control channel with the home SID programmed in its phone. If roaming, the subscriber unit periodically sends a small burst of data on the reverse control channel, notifying the visited MSC of its MIN and ESN. The SID identifies the geographic location of each MSC, so that every base station connected to the MSC transmits the same SID in the control channel message (see Chapter 11 for additional details on the operation of control channels for AMPS).

Each MSC has a unique identification number, called the MSCID. The MSCID is typically the same as the SID, except for large markets where a service provider may use multiple switches within a single market. When more than one switch exists within the same market, the MSCID is simply the SID appended with the switch number within the market.

Registration

By comparing the MIN of a roaming subscriber with the MINs contained in its HLR database, the visited MSC is able to quickly identify those users who are not from the home system. Once a roamer is identified, the visited MSC sends a *registration request* over the landline signaling network (see Figure 10.5) to the subscriber's home MSC. The home MSC updates the HLR for the particular subscriber by storing the MSCID of the visited MSC (thereby providing location information for the roaming user at the home MSC). The home MSC also validates that the roamer's MIN and ESN are correct, and using the signaling network, returns a *customer profile* to the visited MSC which indicates the availability of features for the subscriber. Typical features might include call waiting, call forwarding, three-way calling, and international dialing access. The visited MSC, upon receiving the profile of the roamer from the home MSC, updates its own VLR so that the MSC may mimic the features provided by the roamer's home network. The roamer is then said to be *registered* in the visited MSC. The home MSC may store additional antifraud information within its HLR, and this data is passed along in the profile to prevent illegal access by roamers in a visited MSC. Note that the PSTN is not involved with passing registration data (it is only used for user/voice traffic). The entire registration process requires less than four seconds throughout the world and accommodates MSCs made by many different manufacturers.

Call Delivery

Once a roamer is registered in a visited network, calls are transparently routed to it from the home MSC. If a call is made to a roaming subscriber from any telephone in the world, the phone call is routed directly to the home MSC. The home MSC checks the HLR to determine the location of the subscriber. Roaming subscribers have their current visited MSCID stored in the HLR, so the home MSC is able to route the incoming call to the visited network immediately.

The home MSC is responsible for notifying the visited MSC of the incoming call and delivering that call to the roamer. The home MSC first sends a *route* request to the visited MSC using the signaling network. The visited MSC returns a *temporary directory number* (TDN) to the home MSC, also via the signaling network. The TDN is a dynamically assigned temporary telephone number which the home MSC uses to forward the call via the PSTN. The incoming call is passed directly to the visited MSC over the PSTN, through the home MSC. If the roamer does not answer the call, or has certain call forwarding features in the customer profile, the visited MSC will return a *redirection* to the home MSC. The redirection command instructs the home MSC to reroute the incoming call (perhaps to voice mail or another telephone number).

Intersystem Handoffs

Intersystem handoffs are used to seamlessly connect roamers between MSCs. A standard interface is used over the signaling network to allow different MSCs to pass typical signal measurement (handoff) data, as well as HLR and VLR information, while the subscriber moves between different wireless networks. In this manner, it is possible for subscribers to maintain calls while in transit between different markets.

10.11 Personal Communication Services/Networks (PCS/PCNs)

The objective of *personal communication systems* (PCS) or *personal communication networks* (PCNs) is to provide ubiquitous wireless communications coverage, enabling users to access the telephone network and the Internet for different types of communication needs, without regard for the location of the user or the location of the information being accessed.

The concept of PCS/PCN is based on an *advanced intelligent network* (AIN). The mobile and fixed networks will be integrated to provide universal access to the network and its databases. AIN will also allow its users to have a single telephone number to be used for both wireless and wireline services. An architecture suggested by Ashity, Sheikh, and Murthy [Ash93] consists of three levels: the intelligent level, the transport level, and the access level. The intelligent level contains databases for the storage of information about the network users, the transport level handles the transmission of information, and the access level provides ubiquitous access to every user in the network and contains databases that update the location of each user in the network. Personal communication systems will be characterized by high user densities that will require enhanced network requirements. A large amount of signaling will be required for efficient working of these networks. Common channel signaling and efficient signaling protocols will play an

Table 10.9 Potential Data Loads for Wireless Networks

Application	Avg. data rates (kbps)	Peak data rate (kbps)	Maximum delay (sec)	Maximum packet loss rate
e-mail, paging	0.01–0.1	1–10	< 10–100	$< 10^{-9}$
computer data	0.1–1	10–100	< 1–10	$< 10^{-9}$
telephony	10–100	10–100	< 0.1–1	$< 10^{-4}$
digital audio	100–1000	100–1000	< 0.01–0.1	$< 10^{-5}$
video-conference	100–1000	1000–10000	0.001– 0.01	$< 10^{-5}$

important role in PCS/PCN. The intelligent networks that will be put to use for PCN will employ SS7 signaling. Table 10.9 gives approximate data requirements that PCS/PCN networks will be expected to carry.

10.11.1 Packet vs. Circuit Switching for PCN

Packet switching technology will have more advantages for PCS/PCN than circuit switching. The factors that influence the use of packet switching include the following:

- PCN will be required to serve a wide range of services including voice, data, e-mail, and digital video. Commercial grade Voice over IP will catapult packet switched PCNs.
- PCN will support large populations of infrequent users, so that economic viability will depend on the ability to effectively share the bandwidth and infrastructural equipment.
- The relatively unreliable channel is more suited for packet switching than for circuit switching. In addition, packet switching does not need a dedicated link at very low bit error rates and has the ability to compensate for lost or corrupt data through ARQ based transmission strategies.
- PCN will require a high-capacity switching infrastructure for routing of traffic between cells.

10.11.2 Cellular Packet-Switched Architecture

The *cellular packet-switched architecture* distributes network control among interference units and thus provides the capability to support highly dense user environments. Figure 10.16 indicates the conceptual block diagram of such an architecture for a *metropolitan area network* (MAN) [Goo90]. Information travels at several gigabits per second over the MAN, which is constructed of fiber optic cable and serves as the backbone for the entire wireless network in a particular geographical region. Data enters and leaves the various MAN interface units that are connected

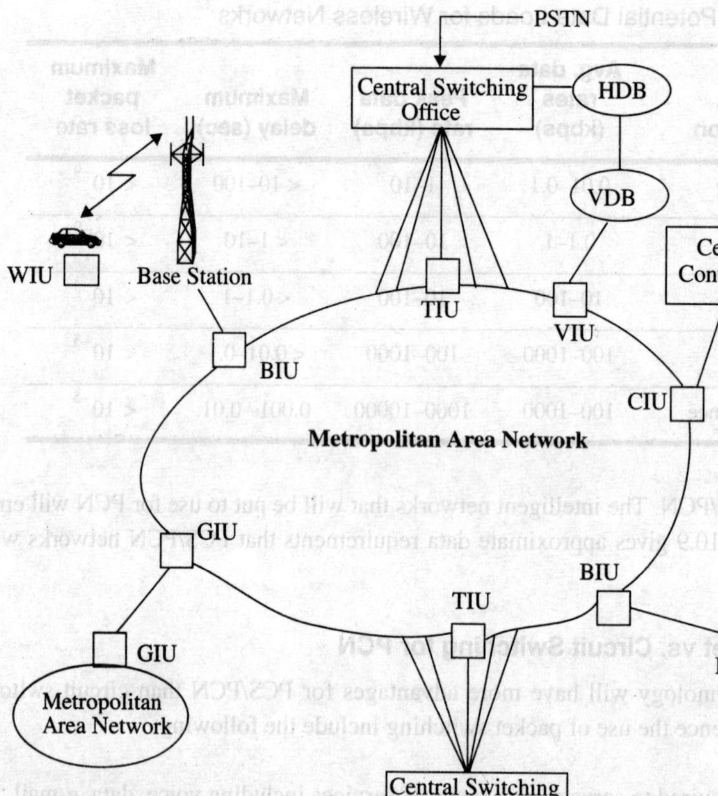

BIU - Base Station Interface Unit
TIU - Trunk Interface Unit
GIU - Gateway Interface Unit
CIU - Cellular Controller Interface Unit
VIU - Visitor Database Interface Unit
WIU - Wireless Interface Unit
HDB - Home Database
VDB - Visitor Database

Figure 10.16 Cellular packet switched architecture for a metropolitan area network [from [Goo90] © IEEE].

to base stations and the public network switches (including ISDN switches). Key elements in the network that facilitate transfer of information are the *base station interface unit* (BIU), *cellular controller interface unit* (CIU), *trunk interface unit* (TIU), and each subscriber's *wireless interface unit* (WIU). The BIUs are connected to the TIUs which are connected to the PSTN. The CIU connects to the cellular control unit. Different MANs are interconnected via *gateway interface units* (GIUs). *Visitor interface units* (VIUs) access the *visitor database* (VDB) and the home databases (HDBs) for registration and location updates. Packet switching techniques are used for transmission of packets in the *cellular-switched architecture*. Packet switching is attractive for wireless networks because the addresses and other information in packet headers make it possible for dispersed network elements to respond to a mobile user without the intervention of central controllers. In a packet switch, the addresses carried in each packet comprise a logical link between network elements.

The Trunk Interface Unit (TIU)

The function of the TIU is to accept information from the PSTN. Figure 10.17 shows how the TIU, acting as the physical layer, transforms the standard format of the PSTN into the wireless access physical layer. TIUs use transcoders and channel encoders to convert the format of the packets transmitted across the interface to the fixed network or the wireless access format. TIUs also contain a *packet assembler* and *disassembler* (PAD) that combines user information with a packet header. Information available in the packet header contains flags, error checksums, packet control information, and address fields. The TIU address is added to all the packets that are transmitted through this unit. The address can be a *permanent terminal identifier* (PTI) or *virtual circuit identifier* (VCI). The PTI is the address of the TIU from where the call has originated, and the VCI is the information contained in the packet header identifying the route through which the transmission will take place. The packet generation by the PAD is controlled by a speech activity detector so that resources are not wasted in idle time. Packets from the TIU are routed to a base station over the MAN by looking up the address from the TIU routing tables. The PAD reads the destination address of all packets arriving at the MAN, and matches it to the PTI (during call set-up) and the VCI (during a call). If a match is found, the PAD processes the packets or else the packet is ignored. Addresses of base stations engaged in traffic are maintained in the base station identification register for appropriate routing of the information.

The Wireless Terminal Interface Unit (WIU)

The WIU is directly connected to the source of the information, as is seen in Figure 10.18, and differs from the TIU in the sense that it does not interface to the PSTN or the ISDN. The addressing process remains the same for WIU as in the TIU. The PAD removes signaling overhead from all incoming data packets and provides the information stream (64 kbps) to the terminal. A channel quality monitor is accessed by the WIU for determining handoff conditions. The WIU reads the *base station identifier*, and a handoff takes place whenever there is a base station available with a higher signal level or smaller error performance.

Base Station Interface Unit (BIU)

The BIU provides information exchange between the TIUs and the WIUs. The BIU also broadcasts packets for providing feedback to the PRMA protocol. The BIU is addressed by its permanent address in the packet header. The major function of the BIU is to relay packets to either the WIU or the TIU using the virtual circuit identifiers of the incoming packets, or if no virtual circuit identifier exists, they are related to the WIU based on the permanent address of the WIU.

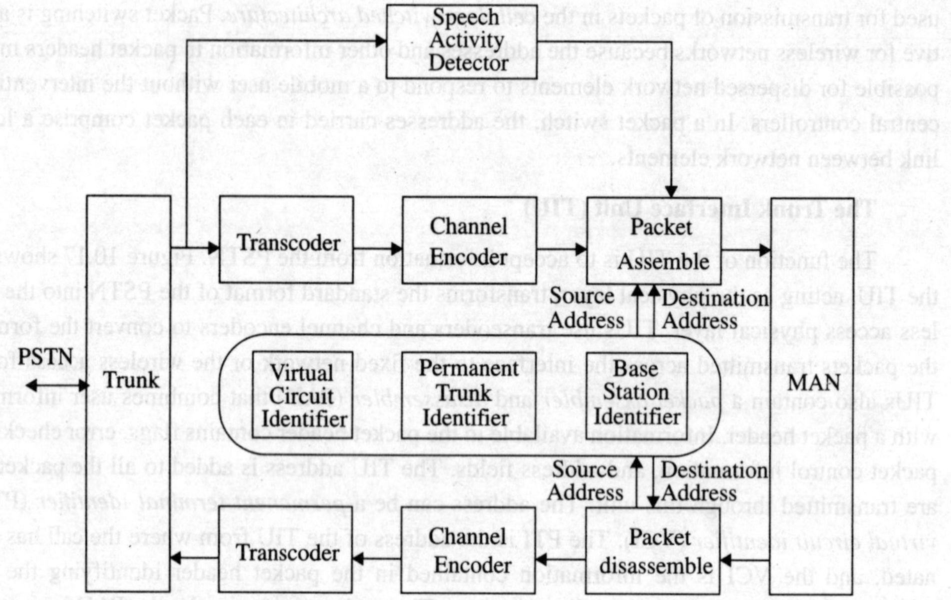

Figure 10.17 Cellular trunk interface unit [from [Goo90] © IEEE].

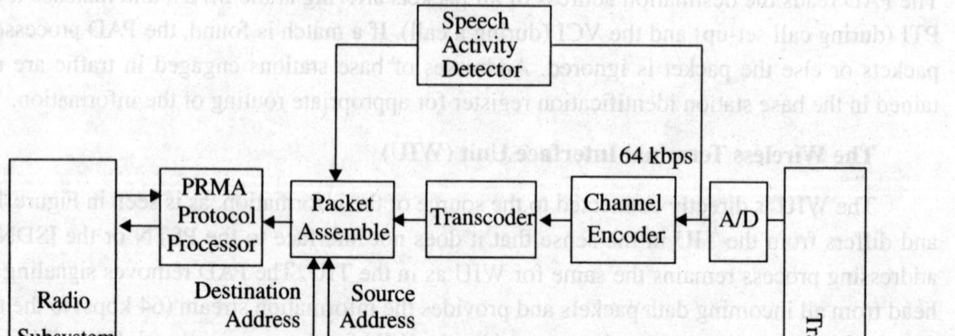

Figure 10.18 Cellular wireless interface unit [from [Goo90] © IEEE].

Cellular Controller Interface Unit (CIU)

The function of the cellular controller is to receive, process, and generate information packets for network control. Each of the various nodes may be addressed by use of appropriate signaling formats to enable centralized control of the network, even though the intelligence is distributed among the various nodes of the network.

10.11.2.1 Network Functionality in Cellular Packet-Switched Architecture

The control functions of a wireless network can be divided into three categories: call processing, mobility management, and radio resource management [Mei92]. Call processing is a function of the central switching office, while mobility management and radio resource management are functions of the metropolitan area network. The three operations of call set-up (initiated by the mobile), speech transmission, and handoff serve to illustrate the functionality of the system. Before a call is set up, the subscriber terminals and the trunks are addressed by their permanent addresses, but during call set up for speech, a virtual circuit is set up. The corresponding virtual addresses are updated in the TIU and the WIU. However, the base stations and the controller retain the permanent addresses.

Transmission of speech — Packets move between the subscriber terminal, the base station, and the central switching office in both directions over the MAN. Packets are sent on a first-in/first-out (FIFO) basis, since speech is involved and reordering of the packets is not allowed. A virtual circuit is assigned at the beginning of the call for transmission of speech in packets. Packets may be lost in the conversation, but this does not significantly affect speech quality as long as not too many packets are lost.

Handoff — The cellular packet switched handoff algorithms distributes the processing among different interface units [Mei92]. The WIU determines the channel quality, and when it becomes apparent that a call can be better handled by another base station, the call handoff procedure is initiated. A new base station is identified on the basis of the base station identifier read from the channel quality monitor, and the call is rerouted to the new base station. The TIU is informed of the handoff, and the routing table in the TIU is updated to reflect this information. The cellular controller is transparent to the handoff process. The WIU keeps the TIU informed of the location of the mobile when there are gaps in speech. As a result of the handoff, no packets are lost, and any packets sent during the duration of the handoff process can be retransmitted to the new base station from the TIU.

The cellular packet-switched architecture has not yet been implemented. Indications are, however, that such an architecture will be required as wireless systems continue to grow.

10.12 Protocols for Network Access

As discussed in Chapter 9, a packet radio contention technique may be used to transmit on a common channel. ALOHA protocols are the best example of a contention technique where the users transmit whenever they have data. The users listen to the acknowledgment feedback to determine if a transmission has been successful or not. In case of a collision, the subscriber units wait a random amount of time and retransmit the packet. The advantage of packet contention techniques is the ability to serve a large number of terminals with extremely low overhead.

Mobile transmitters sending bursty traffic in the form of data packets to a common base-station receiver can use random access. As shown in Chapter 9, ideal channel throughput can be doubled if active terminals are prepared to synchronize their packet transmissions into common time slots, such that the risk of partial packet overlap is avoided. With high traffic loads, both unslotted and slotted ALOHA protocols become inefficient, since the free competition between all transmitters exposes most of the offered data traffic to collisions, and thus results in multiple retransmissions and increased delays. To reduce this kind of situation, carrier sense multiple access (CSMA) can be used where the transmitter first listens either to the common radio channel or to a dedicated acknowledgment return channel from the base station.

10.12.1 Packet Reservation Multiple Access (PRMA)

Packet reservation multiple access (PRMA) is a transmission protocol proposed by Goodman et al, for packet voice terminals in a cellular system [Goo89]. PRMA is a time division multiplex (TDM) based multiple access protocol that allows a group of spatially dispersed terminals to transmit packet voice and low, bit rate data over a common channel. The key feature of this protocol is the utilization of user transmission to gain access to the radio resources. Once the radio resource has been acquired, it is up to the transmitter to release the reservation. PRMA is a derivative of reservation ALOHA, which is a combination of TDMA and slotted ALOHA. A reservation protocol like PRMA has an advantage in that it can utilize the discontinuous nature of speech with the help of a voice activity detector (VAD) to increase capacity of the radio channel.

The input to a voice terminal follows a pattern of talk spurt and silent gaps. The terminals begin contending and transmitting speech packets as soon as the first packet is generated. Both digital packet data and speech data are simultaneously supported with PRMA. The raw channel bit stream is divided into time slots with each slot designed for a single packet of information. The time slots are grouped as frames, which are repeated cyclically over the channel. In a frame, the individual slots are accessed by the mobile for communication with the base. A successful call setup ensures that the particular mobile is given a reservation in a slot which is at the same position in succeeding frames. Selection of the frame duration is based on the fact that a speech terminal can generate exactly one packet per frame. The allotted time slot is fixed within the frame until the conversation is over. When the speech terminal has completed its communications it halts transmission, the base station receives a null packet, and the time slot in the frame is unreserved once again and becomes available for use by other mobiles. The problem of contention is taken care of by designing the system using a probabilistic model based on trunking theory to predict the availability of time slots. The availability of time slots depends on the usage of the network, and if there are too many users, call set-up will be prolonged.

If congestion at a base station is encountered from many mobile users, data packets are dropped, and speech packets are given priority, since speech requires that the packets be delivered in order. A feedback signal from the base station to the mobiles concerning the previous transmitted packet is multiplexed along the stream of data from the base station. Based on ARQ error correction, the packets are retransmitted if a mobile receives a negative acknowledgment.

10.13 Network Databases

In first generation wireless networks, the network control was limited to the MSC, and MSCs of neighboring systems were not able to communicate easily with each other. This made graceful intersystem roaming impossible. Second and third generation wireless networks, however, distribute network control among several processors. For example, second generation networks access several databases for authentication of mobiles, location updates, billing, etc. The visitor location database, home location database, and the authentication center are the major databases that are accessed by various processing elements in the network. A distributed database has been proposed for interconnection of MSCs throughout a wireless network.

10.13.1 Distributed Database for Mobility Management

The distributed hierarchical database architecture has been proposed to facilitate the tracking and location update of the mobile subscriber [Mal92]. Figure 10.19 shows the interconnections in a distributed hierarchical database. The database partition at each access MAN node lists subscribers in the associated BSC control area. Each of the BSCs is able to receive the MAN broadcast and updates its database if the mobile is in its region. Higher level databases at the backbone MAN level enable subscriber tracking within these areas. The access MAN databases indicate the mobile's BSC area location, and the backbone MAN databases indicate the MAN access location. In a similar hierarchical manner, a mobile in a region can be tracked, and its location can be updated. The method of partitioning is an efficient technique for it reduces the time required to locate any mobile and hence minimizes the traffic congestion resulting from heavy broadcast traffic required to locate a roaming mobile. Each subscriber to the cellular service has an associated home access MAN, backbone MAN, and a MAN database. Home and visitor databases are logically distinctive, but physically integrated, in a single database. A mobile subscriber is enlisted in a visitor database when it enters a foreign area and remains in the new database until it leaves that area. Whenever a subscriber leaves its home area, the databases are updated so that the home access MAN database will contain the new location of the roaming subscriber. The CCITT recommendations E.164 suggest a network address that is based on a hierarchical distribution, such that the address indicates the access MAN node, backbone MAN, and MAN associated with a BSC. Based on this type of format a roaming subscriber can be identified with its home base, so that the new BSC can update its database for the visiting subscriber.

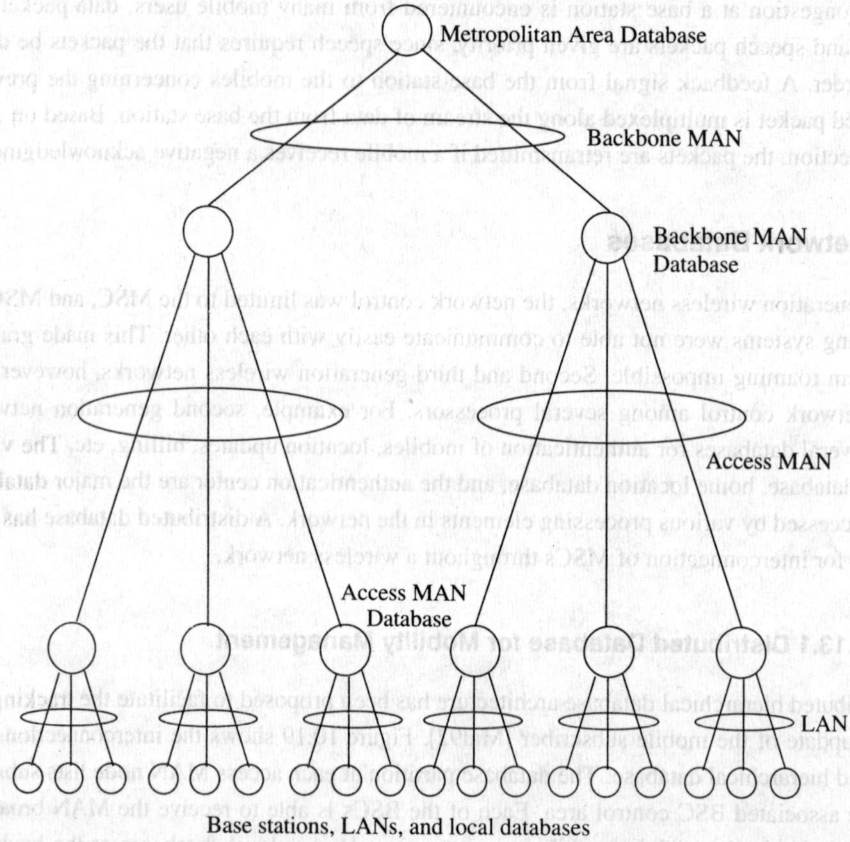

Figure 10.19 Illustration of a hierarchical distributed database.

10.14 Universal Mobile Telecommunication System (UMTS)

The *Universal Mobile Telecommunication System* (UMTS) is a system that is capable of providing a variety of mobile services to a wide range of global mobile communication standards. UMTS is being developed by RACE (R&D in advanced communications technologies in Europe) as the third generation wireless system. To handle a mixed range of traffic, a mixed cell layout (shown in the Figure 10.20), that would consist of macrocells overlaid on micro and picocells is one of the architecture plans being considered [Van92]. This type of network distributes the traffic with the local traffic operating on the micro and pico cells, while the highly mobile traffic is operated on the macrocells, thus reducing the number of handoffs required for the fast moving traffic. It is easily observed from Figure 10.20 that the macrocells cover the spots not covered by other cells and also provide redundancy in certain areas. Thus, macrocells will also be able to avoid the failures of the overlapped cells. However the major disadvantage

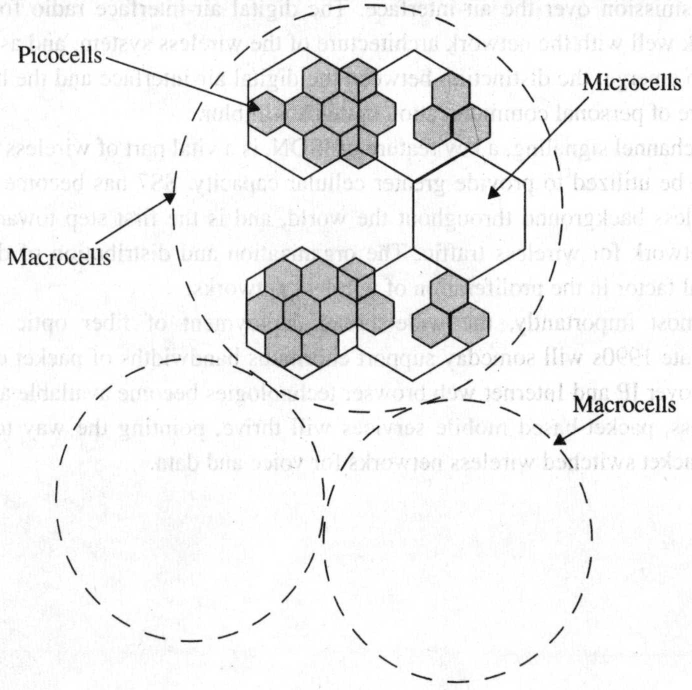

Figure 10.20 Network architecture for UMTS.

of the overlaid architecture is the reduced spectrum efficiency. The UMTS architecture will provide radio coverage with a network of base stations interconnected to each other and to a fixed network exchange. A metropolitan area network (MAN) is one of the possible choices for the network interconnection.

Network Reachability — The network maintains a constant location information on each of the terminals. The location will be updated by a terminal whenever it changes a *location area* (location area will consist of a cluster of cells), which is determined whenever the mobile terminal starts receiving a different broadcast message. The network will also take advantage of a distributed network database, for routing of calls once the exact location of the mobile has been accessed.

10.15 Summary

Modern cellular networks are based on digital radio and digital network technologies to maximize capacity and quality of service. Digital radio techniques such as equalization, channel coding, interleaving, and speech coding provide superior air-interface performance and spectral efficiency when compared with older analog systems in a constantly varying radio channel. For data applications, new wireless systems store a wide range of signals and organize them into packets for transmission over the air-interface. The digital air-interface radio format is often designed to work well with the network architecture of the wireless system, and as wireless systems continue to emerge, the distinction between the digital air-interface and the backbone network architecture of personal communication systems will blur.

Common channel signaling, a key feature of ISDN, is a vital part of wireless networks and will continue to be utilized to provide greater cellular capacity. SS7 has become an important part of the wireless background throughout the world, and is the first step toward a universal packet-based network for wireless traffic. The organization and distribution of databases will become a critical factor in the proliferation of wireless networks.

Perhaps most importantly, the wide-spread deployment of fiber optic infrastructure throughout the late 1990s will someday support enormous bandwidths of packet data transmissions. As Voice over IP and Internet web browser technologies become available and affordable for mobile access, packet-based mobile services will thrive, pointing the way toward the 4th generation all-packet switched wireless networks for voice and data.

CHAPTER 11

Wireless Systems and Standards

This chapter describes many of the original first and second generation cellular radio, cordless telephone, and personal communications standards in use throughout the world. Chapter 2 provides an overview of 2.5G and 3G air interface standards. First, the original analog cellular standards in the United States and Europe are described. Then, a description of second generation digital cellular and PCS standards is presented. A convenient summary of world-wide standards and a discussion about the US PCS, MMDS, WLAN, and wireless cable frequencies are provided at the end of the chapter.

11.1 AMPS and ETACS

In the late 1970s, AT&T Bell Laboratories developed the first US cellular telephone system called the Advance Mobile Phone Service (AMPS) [You79]. AMPS was first deployed in late 1983 in the urban and suburban areas of Chicago by Ameritech. In 1983, a total of 40 MHz of spectrum in the 800 MHz band was allocated by the Federal Communications Commission for the Advanced Mobile Phone Service. In 1989, as the demand for cellular telephone services increased, the Federal Communications Commission allocated an additional 10 MHz (called the extended spectrum) for cellular telecommunications. The first AMPS cellular system used large cells and omnidirectional base station antennas to minimize initial equipment needs, and the system was deployed in Chicago to cover approximately 2100 square miles.

The AMPS system uses a seven-cell reuse pattern with provisions for sectoring and cell splitting to increase capacity when needed. After extensive subjective tests, it was found that the AMPS 30 kHz channel requires a signal-to-interference ratio (SIR) of 18 dB for satisfactory system performance. The smallest reuse factor which satisfies this requirement using 120 degree directional antennas is $N = 7$ (see Chapter 3), and hence a seven-cell reuse pattern has been adopted.

AMPS was deployed throughout the world and is still popular in rural parts of the US, South America, Australia, and China. While the US system was originally designed for a duopoly market (e.g., two competing carriers per market), many countries initiated AMPS service with just a single provider. Thus, while US AMPS restricts the A and B side carriers to a subset of 416 channels each, other implementations of AMPS allow all possible channels to be used. Furthermore, the exact frequency allocations for AMPS differ from country to country. Nevertheless, the air interface standard remains identical throughout the world.

The European Total Access Communication System (ETACS) was developed in the mid-1980s, and is virtually identical to AMPS, except it is scaled to fit in 25 kHz (as opposed to 30 kHz) channels used throughout Europe. Another difference between ETACS and AMPS is how the telephone number of each subscriber (called the *mobile identification number* or MIN) is formatted, due to the need to accommodate different country codes throughout Europe as opposed to area codes in the US.

11.1.1 AMPS and ETACS System Overview

Like all other first generation, analog, cellular systems, AMPS and ETACS use frequency modulation (FM) and frequency division duplex (FDD) for radio transmission. In the United States, transmissions from mobiles to base stations (reverse link) use frequencies between 824 MHz and 849 MHz, while base stations transmit to mobiles (forward link) using frequencies between 869 MHz and 894 MHz. ETACS uses 890 MHz to 915 MHz for the reverse link and 935 MHz to 960 MHz for the forward link. Every radio channel actually consists of a pair of simplex channels separated by 45 MHz. A separation of 45 MHz between the forward and reverse channels was chosen to make use of inexpensive but highly selective duplexers in the subscriber units. For AMPS, the maximum deviation of the FM modulator is ±12 kHz (±10 kHz for ETACS). The control channel transmissions and blank-and-burst data streams are transmitted at 10 kbps for AMPS, and at 8 kbps for ETACS. These wideband data streams have a maximum frequency deviation of ±8 kHz and ±6.4 kHz for AMPS and ETACS, respectively.

AMPS and ETACS cellular radio systems were launched by using base stations with tall towers which support several receiving antennas and have transmitting antennas which typically radiate a few hundred watts of effective radiated power. Each base station typically has one control channel transmitter (that broadcasts on the forward control channel), one control channel receiver (that listens on the reverse control channel for any cellular phone switching to set-up a call), and eight or more FM duplex voice channels. Commercial base stations support as many as fifty-seven voice channels. Forward voice channels (FVCs) carry the portion of the telephone conversation originating from the landline telephone network caller and going to the cellular subscriber. Reverse voice channels (RVCs) carry the portion of the telephone conversation originating from the cellular subscriber and going to the landline telephone network caller. The actual number of control and voice channels used at a particular base station varies widely in different system installations depending on traffic, maturity of the system, and locations of other base stations. The number of base stations in a service area varies widely, as well, from as few as one cellular tower in a rural area to several hundred or more base stations in a large city. Chapters 3 and 4 discuss technical issues associated with *cell planning*.

Each base station in the AMPS or ETACS system continuously transmits digital FSK data on the forward control channel (FCC) at all times so that idle cellular subscriber units can lock onto the strongest FCC wherever they are. All subscribers must be locked, or "camped" onto a FCC in order to originate or receive calls. The base station reverse control channel (RCC) receiver constantly monitors transmissions from cellular subscribers that are locked onto the matching FCC. In the US AMPS system, there are twenty-one control channels for each of the two service providers in each market, and these control channels are standardized throughout the country. ETACS supports forty-two control channels for a single provider. Thus, any cellular telephone in the system only needs to scan a limited number of control channels to find the best serving base station. It is up to the service provider to ensure that neighboring base stations within a system are assigned forward control channels that do not cause adjacent channel interference to subscribers which monitor different control channels in nearby base stations.

In each US cellular market, the nonwireline service provider (the "A" provider") is assigned an odd *system identification number* (SID) and the wireline service provider (the "B" provider) is assigned an even SID. The SID is transmitted once every 0.8 seconds on each FCC, along with other overhead data which reports the status of the cellular system. Transmitted data might include information such as whether roamers are automatically registered, how power control is handled, and whether other standards, such as USDC or narrowband AMPS, can be handled by the cellular system. In the US, subscriber units generally access channels exclusively on the A or B side, although cellular phones are capable of allowing the user to access channels on both sides. For ETACS, *area identification numbers* (AIDs) are used instead of SID, and ETACS subscriber units are able to access any control or voice channel in the standard.

11.1.2 Call Handling in AMPS and ETACS

When a call to a cellular subscriber originates from a conventional telephone in the public-switched telephone network (PSTN) and arrives at the mobile switching center (MSC), a paging message is sent out with the subscriber's mobile identification number (MIN) simultaneously on every base station forward control channel in the system. If the intended subscriber unit successfully receives its page on a forward control channel, it will respond with an acknowledgment transmission on the reverse control channel. Upon receiving the subscriber's acknowledgment, the MSC directs the base station to assign a *forward voice channel* (FVC) and *reverse voice channel* (RVC) pair to the subscriber unit so that the new call can take place on a dedicated voice channel. The base station also assigns the subscriber unit a supervisory audio tone (SAT tone) and a voice mobile attenuation code (VMAC) as it moves the call to the voice channel. The subscriber unit automatically changes its frequency to the assigned voice channel pair.

The SAT, as described subsequently, has one of three different frequencies which allows the base and mobile to distinguish each other from co-channel users located in different cells. The SAT is transmitted continuously on both the forward and reverse voice channels during a call at frequencies above the audio band. The VMAC instructs the subscriber unit to transmit at a specific power level. Once on the voice channel, wideband FSK data is used by the base station and subscriber unit in a *blank-and-burst* mode to initiate handoffs, change the subscriber transmit power as needed, and provide other system data. Blank-and-burst signaling allows the MSC to send bursty data on the voice channel by temporarily omitting the speech and SAT, and replacing them with data. This is barely noticed by the voice users.

When a mobile user places a call, the subscriber unit transmits an origination message on the reverse control channel (RCC). The subscriber unit transmits its MIN, electronic serial number ESN), station class mark (SCM), and the destination telephone number. If received correctly by the base station, this information is sent to the MSC which checks to see if the subscriber is properly registered, connects the subscriber to the PSTN, assigns the call to a forward and reverse voice channel pair with a specific SAT and VMAC, and commences the conversation.

During a typical call, the MSC issues numerous blank-and-burst commands which switch subscribers between different voice channels on different base stations, depending on where the subscriber is travelling in the service area. In AMPS and ETACS, handoff decisions are made by the MSC when the signal strength on the reverse voice channel (RVC) of the serving base station drops below a preset threshold, or when the SAT tone experiences a certain level of interference. Thresholds are adjusted at the MSC by the service provider, are subject to continuous measurement, and must be changed periodically to accommodate customer growth, system expansion, and changing traffic patterns. The MSC uses scanning receivers called "locate receivers" in nearby base stations to determine the signal level of a particular subscriber which appears to be in need of a handoff. In doing so, the MSC is able to find the best neighboring base station which can accept the handoff.

When a new call request arrives from the PSTN or a subscriber, and all of the voice channels in a particular base station are occupied, the MSC will hold the PSTN line open while instructing the current base station to issue a *directed retry* to the subscriber on the FCC. A directed retry forces the subscriber unit to switch to a different control channel (i.e., different base station) for voice channel assignment. Depending on radio propagation effects, the specific location of the subscriber, and the current traffic on the base station to which the subscriber is directed, a directed retry may or may not result in a successful call.

Several factors may contribute to degraded cellular service or dropped or blocked calls. Factors such as the performance of the MSC, the current traffic demand in a geographic area, the specific channel reuse plan, the number of base stations relative to the subscriber population density, the specific propagation conditions between users of the system, and the signal threshold settings for handoffs play major roles in system performance. Maintaining perfect service and call quality in a heavily populated cellular system is practically impossible due to the tremendous system complexity and lack of control in determining radio coverage and customer usage patterns. System operators strive to forecast system growth and do their best to provide suitable coverage and sufficient capacity to avoid co-channel interference within a market, but inevitably some calls will be dropped or blocked. In a large metropolitan market, it is not unusual to have 3–5 percent dropped calls and in excess of 10 percent blocking during extremely heavy traffic conditions.

11.1.3 AMPS and ETACS Air Interface

AMPS and ETACS Channels: AMPS and ETACS use different physical rate channels for transmission of voice and control information. A *control channel* (also called *setup* or *paging channel*) is used by each base station in the system to simultaneously page subscriber units to alert them of incoming calls and to move connected calls to a voice channel. The FCC constantly transmits data at 10 kbps (8 kbps for ETACS) using binary FSK. FCC transmissions contain either *overhead messages*, mobile station *control messages,* or *control file messages*. The FVC and RVC are used for voice transmissions on the forward and reverse link, respectively. Some of the air interface specifications for AMPS and ETACS are listed in Table 11.1.

Table 11.1 AMPS and ETACS Radio Interface Specifications

Parameter	AMPS Specification	ETACS Specification
Multiple Access	FDMA	FDMA
Duplexing	FDD	FDD
Channel Bandwidth	30 kHz	25 kHz
Traffic Channel per RF Channel	1	1
Reverse Channel Frequency	824–849 MHz	890–915 MHz
Forward Channel Frequency	869–894 MHz	935–960 MHz
Voice Modulation	FM	FM
Peak Deviation: Voice Channels Control/Wideband Data	±12 kHz ±8 kHz	±10 kHz ±6.4 kHz
Channel Coding for Data Transmission	BCH(40,28) on FC BCH(48,36) on RC	BCH(40,28) on FC BCH(48,36) on RC
Data Rate on Control/Wideband Channel	10 kbps	8 kbps
Spectral Efficiency	0.33 bps/Hz	0.33 bps/Hz
Number of Channels	832	1000

While voice channels are in use, three additional signaling techniques are used to maintain supervision between the base station and subscriber unit. The supervisory signals are the *supervisory audio tone (SAT)* and the *signaling tone (ST)*, which will be described. In addition, *wideband data* signaling may be used on a voice channel to provide brief data messages that allow the subscriber and the base station to adjust subscriber power or initiate a handoff. The wideband data is provided by using a blank-and-burst technique, where the voice channel audio is muted and replaced with a brief *burst* of wide band signaling data sent at 10 kbps using FSK (8 kbps for ETACS). Typical blank-and-burst events last for less than 100 ms, so they are virtually imperceptible to the voice channel users.

Voice Modulation and Demodulation

Prior to frequency modulation, voice signals are processed using a compander, pre-emphasis filter, deviation limiter, and a postdeviation limiter filter. Figure 11.1 shows a block diagram of the AMPS modulation subsystem. At the receiver, these operations are reversed after demodulation.

Compander — In order to accommodate a large speech dynamic range, the input signals need to be compressed in amplitude range before modulation. The companding is done by a 2:1 compander which produces a 1 dB increase in output level for every 2 dB increase in input level. The characteristics are specified such that a nominal 1 kHz reference input tone at a nominal volume should produce a ±2.9 kHz peak frequency deviation of the transmitted carrier. Companding confines the energy to the 30 kHz channel bandwidth and generates a quieting effect during a speech burst. At the receiver, the inverse of compression is performed, thus assuring the restoral of the input voice level with a minimum of distortion.

Pre-emphasis — The output of the compressor is passed through a pre-emphasis filter which has a nominal 6 dB/octave highpass response between 300 Hz and 3 kHz.

Deviation Limiter — The deviation limiter ensures that the maximum frequency deviation at the mobile station is limited to ±12 kHz (±10 kHz for ETACS). The supervisory signals and wideband data signals are excluded from this restriction.

Postdeviation Limiter Filter — The output of the deviation limiter is filtered using a postdeviation limiter filter. This is a low pass filter specified to have an attenuation (relative to the response at 1 kHz) which is greater than or equal to $40\log_{10}(f(Hz)/3000)$ dB in the frequency ranges between 3 kHz to 5.9 kHz and 6.1 kHz to 15 kHz. For frequencies between 5.9 and 6.1 kHz, the attenuation (relative to the value at 1 kHz) must be greater than 35 dB, and

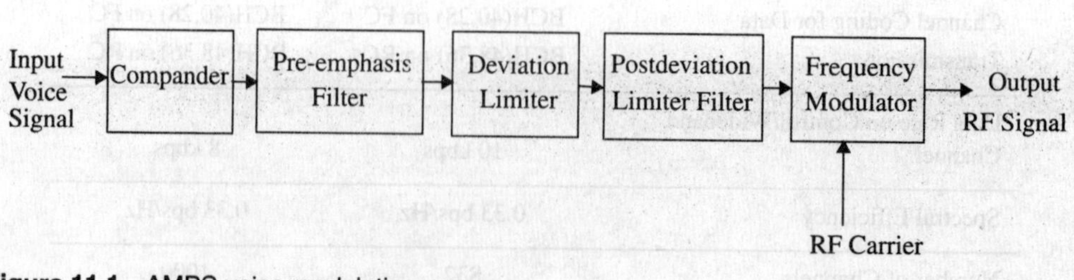

Figure 11.1 AMPS voice modulation process.

for 15 kHz and above, the attenuation must be greater than 28 dB (above that at 1 kHz). The postdeviation limiter filter ensures that the specifications on limitations of emission outside the specified band are met, and it ensures that the 6 kHz SAT tones, which are always present during a call, do not interfere with the transmitted speech signal.

Supervisory Signals (SAT and ST tones)

The AMPS and ETACS systems provide supervisory signals during voice channel transmissions which allow each base station and its subscribers to confirm they are properly connected during a call. The SAT always exists during the use of any voice channel.

The AMPS and ETACS systems use three SAT signals which are tones at frequencies of either 5970 Hz, 6000 Hz, or 6030 Hz. A given base station will constantly transmit one of the three SAT tones on each voice channel while it is in use. The SAT is superimposed on the voice signal on both the forward and reverse links and is barely audible to a user. The particular frequency of the SAT denotes the particular base station location for a given channel and is assigned by the MSC for each call. Since a highly built up cellular system might have as many as three co-channel base stations in a small geographic region, the SAT enables the subscriber unit and the base station to know which of the three co-channel base stations is handling the call.

When a call is set up and a voice channel assignment is issued, the FVC at the base station immediately begins transmission of the SAT. As the subscriber unit begins monitoring the FVC, it must detect, filter, and demodulate the SAT coming from the base station and then reproduce the same tone for continuous transmission back to the base station on the RVC. This "handshake" is required by AMPS and ETACS to dedicate a voice channel. If the SAT is not present or improperly detected within a one second interval, both the base station and subscriber unit cease transmission, and the MSC uses the vacated channel for new calls. Transmission of SAT by the mobile station is briefly suspended during blank-and-burst data transmissions on the reverse channel. The detection and rebroadcast of SAT must be performed at least every 250 ms at the subscriber unit. Dropped or prematurely terminated cellular calls can often be traced to interference or incorrect detection of the SAT at the subscriber unit or base station.

The *signaling tone* (ST) is a 10 kbps data burst which signals call termination by the subscriber. It is a special "*end-of-call*" message consisting of alternating 1s and 0s, which is sent on the RVC by the subscriber unit for 200 ms. Unlike blank-and-burst messages which briefly suspend the SAT transmission, the ST tone must be sent simultaneously with the SAT. The ST signal alerts the base station that the subscriber has ended the call. When a user terminates a call or turns the cellular phone off during a call, an ST tone is automatically sent by the subscriber unit. This allows the base station and the MSC to know that the call was terminated deliberately by the user, as opposed to being dropped by the system.

Wideband Blank-and-Burst Encoding

The AMPS voice channels carry wideband (10 kbps) data streams for blank-and-burst signaling. ETACS uses 8 kbps blank-and-burst transmissions. The wideband data stream is encoded such that each NRZ binary one is represented by a zero-to-one transition, and each NRZ binary zero is represented by a one-to-zero transition. This type of coding is called Manchester (or biphase) coding. The advantage of using a Manchester code in a voice channel is that the energy of the Manchester coded signal is concentrated at the transmission rate frequency of 10 kHz (see Chapter 6), and little energy leaks into the audio band below 4 kHz. Therefore, a burst of data transmitted over a voice channel can be easily detected within a 30 kHz RF channel, is barely audible to a user, and can be passed over phone lines that have dc blocking circuits. The Manchester code is applied to both control channel and voice channel blank-and-burst transmissions.

The Manchester coded wideband data stream is filtered and channel coded using BCH block codes. Wideband data bursts on the voice channels occur in short blasts of repetitive blocks having the same length as the error correction code. The (40, 28) BCH codes are used on forward voice channel blank-and-burst transmissions and are able to correct five errors, whereas (48, 36) BCH block codes are used on the reverse voice channel blank-and-burst transmissions. The encoded data are used to modulate the transmitter carrier using direct frequency-shift keying. Binary ones correspond to a frequency deviation of +8 kHz and binary zeros correspond to a deviation of –8 kHz (±6.4 kHz for ETACS).

A wide array of commands may be sent to and from subscriber units using blank-and-burst signaling. These are defined in the AMPS and ETACS air interface specifications.

11.1.4 N-AMPS

To increase capacity in large AMPS markets, Motorola developed an AMPS-like system called N-AMPS (narrowband AMPS) in 1991 [EIA91]. N-AMPS did not become widespread, as 2G digital technologies displaced many of the original analog FM systems (see Chapter 2). However, N-AMPS was a useful transition technology before 2G equipment became available. N-AMPS provided three users in a 30 kHz AMPS channel by using FDMA and 10 kHz channels, and provided three times the capacity of AMPS. By replacing AMPS channels with three N-AMPS channels at one time, service providers were able to provide more trunked radio channels (and thus a much better grade of service) at base stations in heavily populated areas. N-AMPS used the SAT and ST signaling and blank-and-burst functions in exactly the same manner as AMPS, except the signaling was done by using subaudible data streams.

Since 10 kHz channels are used, the FM deviation is decreased in N-AMPS. This, in turn, reduces the $S/(N+I)$ which degrades the audio quality with respect to AMPS. To counteract this, N-AMPS uses voice companding to provide a "synthetic" voice channel quieting.

N-AMPS specifies a 300 Hz high pass audio filter for each voice channel so that supervisory and signaling data may be sent without blanking the voice. The SAT and ST signaling is sent using a continuous 200 bps NRZ data stream that is FSK modulated. SAT and ST are called DSAT and DST in N-AMPS because they are sent digitally and repetitiously in small, predefined code blocks. There are seven different 24 bit DSAT codewords which may be selected by the MSC, and the DSAT codeword is constantly repeated by both the base station and mobile during a call. The DST signal is simply the binary inverse of the DSAT. The seven possible DSATs and DSTs are specially designed to provide a sufficient number of alternating 0s and 1s so that dc blocking may be conveniently implemented by receivers.

The voice channel signaling is done with 100 bps Manchester encoded FSK data and is sent in place of DSAT when traffic must be passed on the voice channel. As with AMPS wideband signaling, there are many messages that may be passed between the base station and subscriber unit, and these are transmitted in N-AMPS using the same BCH codes as in AMPS with a predefined format of 40 bit blocks on the FVC and 48 bit blocks on the RVC.

11.2 United States Digital Cellular (IS-54 and IS-136)

The first generation analog AMPS system was not designed to support the current demand for capacity in large cities. Cellular systems which use digital modulation techniques (called digital cellular) offer large improvements in capacity and system performance [Rai91]. After extensive research and comparison by major cellular manufacturers in the late 1980s, the United States Digital Cellular System (USDC) was developed to support more users in a fixed spectrum allocation. USDC is a time division multiple access (TDMA) system which supports three full-rate users or six half-rate users on each AMPS channel. Thus, USDC offers as much as six times the capacity of AMPS. The USDC standard uses the same 45 MHz FDD scheme as AMPS. The dual mode USDC/AMPS system was standardized as Interim Standard 54 (IS-54) by the Electronic Industries Association and Telecommunication Industry Association (EIA/TIA) in 1990 [EIA90] and later was upgraded to IS-136. USDC is also known as *North American Digital Cellular* (NADC), as it has been installed in Canada and Mexico.

The USDC system was designed to share the same frequencies, frequency reuse plan, and base stations as AMPS, so that base stations and subscriber units could be equipped with both AMPS and USDC channels within the same piece of equipment. By supporting both AMPS and USDC, cellular carriers were able to provide new customers with USDC phones and have gradually replaced AMPS base stations with USDC base stations, channel by channel, over time. Because USDC maintains compatibility with AMPS in a number of ways, USDC is also known as Digital AMPS (D-AMPS).

In rural areas where immature analog cellular systems are in use, only 666 of the 832 AMPS channels are activated (that is, some rural cellular operators are not yet using the extended spectrum allocated to them in 1989). In these markets, USDC channels may be installed in the extended spectrum to support USDC phones which roam into the system from metropolitan markets. In urban markets where every cellular channel is already in use, selected frequency banks in high traffic base stations are converted to the USDC digital standard. In larger cities, this gradual changeover results in a temporary increase in interference and dropped calls on the analog AMPS system, since each time a base station is changed over to digital, the number of analog channels in a geographic area is decreased. Thus, the changeover rate from analog to digital must carefully match the subscriber equipment transition in the market.

The smooth transition from analog to digital in the same radio band was a key force in the development of the USDC standard. In practice, only cities with capacity shortages (such as New York and Los Angeles) have aggressively changed out AMPS to USDC, while smaller cities are waiting until more subscribers are equipped with USDC phones. The introduction of N-AMPS and the competing and successful CDMA digital spread spectrum standard (IS-95, described later in this chapter) delayed the widespread deployment of USDC throughout the US and has led many carriers to declare that they will no longer rely on USDC past 2003, but instead will adopt GPRS and wideband CDMA (see Chapter 2).

To maintain compatibility with AMPS phones, USDC forward and reverse control channels use exactly the same signaling techniques as AMPS. Thus, while USDC voice channels use 4-ary $\pi/4$ DQPSK modulation with a channel rate of 48.6 kbps, the early implementations used forward and reverse control channels that were no different than AMPS, which used the same 10 kbps FSK signaling scheme and the same standardized control channels. The final version of the standard, IS-136 (formerly IS-54 Rev.C) also included $\pi/4$ DQPSK modulation for the USDC control channels [Pad95]. IS-54 Rev. C was introduced to provide 4-ary keying instead of FSK on dedicated USDC control channels in order to increase control channel data rate, and to provide specialized services such as paging and short messaging between private subscriber user groups.

11.2.1 USDC Radio Interface

In order to ensure a smooth transition from AMPS to USDC, the IS-136 system is specified to operate using both AMPS and USDC standards (dual mode) which makes roaming between the two systems possible with a single phone. The IS-136 system uses the same frequency band and channel spacing as AMPS and supports multiple USDC users on each AMPS channel. The USDC scheme uses TDMA which, as described in Chapter 9, has the flexibility of incorporating even more users within a single radio channel as lower bit rate speech coders become available. Table 11.2 summarizes the air interface for USDC.

Table 11.2 USDC Radio Interface Specifications Summary

Parameter	USDC IS-54 Specification
Multiple Access	TDMA/FDD
Modulation	$\pi/4$ DQPSK
Channel Bandwidth	30 kHz
Reverse Channel Frequency Band	824–849 MHz
Forward Channel Frequency Band	869–894 MHz
Forward and Reverse Channel Data Rate	48.6 kbps
Spectrum Efficiency	1.62 bps/Hz
Equalizer	Unspecified
Channel Coding	7 bit CRC and rate 1/2 convolutional coding of constraint length 6
Interleaving	2 slot interleaver
Users per Channel	3 (full-rate speech coder of 7.95 kbps/user) 6 (with half-rate speech coder of 3.975 kbps/user)

USDC Channels — The USDC control channels are identical to the analog AMPS control channels. In addition to the forty-two primary AMPS control channels, USDC specifies forty-two additional control channels called the *secondary control channels*. Thus, USDC has twice as many control channels as AMPS, so that double the amount of control channel traffic can be paged throughout a market. The secondary control channels conveniently allow carriers to dedicate them for USDC-only use, since AMPS phones do not monitor or decode the secondary control channels. When converting an AMPS system to USDC/AMPS, a carrier may decide to program the MSC to send pages for USDC mobiles over the secondary control channels only, while having existing AMPS traffic sent only on the AMPS control channels. For such a system, USDC subscriber units would be programmed to automatically monitor only the secondary forward control channels when operating in the USDC mode. Over time, as USDC users began to populate the system to the point that additional control channels were required, USDC pages were eventually sent simultaneously over both the primary and secondary control channels.

A USDC voice channel occupies 30 kHz of bandwidth in each of the forward and reverse links, and supports a maximum of three users (as compared to a single AMPS user). Each voice channel supports a TDMA scheme that provides six time slots. For full rate speech, three users utilize the six time slots in an equally spaced fashion. For example, User 1 occupies time slots 1 and 4, User 2 occupies time slots 2 and 5, and User 3 occupies time slots 3 and 6. For half-rate speech, each user occupies one time slot per frame.

On each USDC voice channel, there are actually four data channels which are provided simultaneously. The most important data channel, as far as the end user is concerned, is the *digital traffic channel* (DTC) which carries user information (i.e., speech or user data), and the other three channels carry supervisory information within the cellular system. The reverse DTC (RDTC) carries speech data from the subscriber to the base station, and the forward DTC (FDTC) carries user data from the base station to the subscriber. The three supervisory channels include the *Coded Digital Verification Color Code* (CDVCC), the *Slow Associated Control Channel* (SACCH), and the *Fast Associated Control Channel* (FACCH).

The CDVCC is a 12 bit message sent in every time slot, and is similar in functionality to the SAT used in AMPS. The CDVCC is an 8 bit number ranging between 1 and 255, which is protected with four additional channel coding bits from a shortened (12,8) Hamming code. The base station transmits a CDVCC value on the forward voice channel and each subscriber using the TDMA channel must receive, decode, and retransmit the same CDVCC value to the base station on the reverse voice channel. If the CDVCC "handshake" is not properly completed, then the time slot will be relinquished for other users and the subscriber transmitter will be turned off automatically.

The SACCH is sent in every time slot, and provides a signaling channel in parallel with the digital speech. The SACCH carries various control and supervisory messages between the subscriber unit and the base station. SACCH provides single messages over many consecutive time slots and is used to communicate power level changes or handoff requests. The SACCH is also used by the mobile unit to report the results of signal strength measurements of neighboring base stations so that the base station may implement *mobile assisted handoff* (MAHO).

The FACCH is another signaling channel which is used to send important control or specialized traffic data between the base station and mobile units. The FACCH data, when transmitted, takes the place of user information data (such as speech) within a frame. FACCH may be thought of as a blank-and-burst transmission in USDC. FACCH supports the transmission of dual tone multiple frequency (DTMF) information from touch tone keypads, call release instructions, flash hook instructions, and MAHO or subscriber status requests. FACCH also provides tremendous flexibility in that it allows carriers to handle traffic internal to the cellular network if the DTC is idle during some of the TDMA time slots. As discussed subsequently, FACCH data is treated similarly to speech data in the way it is packaged and interleaved to fit in a time slot. However, unlike the speech data which protects only certain bits with channel coding in the USDC time slot, FACCH data uses a 1/4 rate convolutional channel code to protect all bits that are transmitted in a time slot.

Frame Structure for USDC Traffic Channels — As shown in Figure 11.2, a TDMA frame in the USDC system consists of six timeslots that support three full-rate traffic channels or six half-rate traffic channels. The TDMA frame length is 40 milliseconds. Since USDC uses FDD, there are forward and reverse channel time slots operating simultaneously. Each time slot is designed to carry interleaved speech data from two adjacent frames of the speech coder. (The frame length for the speech coder is 20 ms, half the duration of a TDMA frame.) The USDC standard requires that data from two adjacent speech coder frames be sent in a particular time slot. The USDC speech coder, discussed in more detail below, produces 159 bits of raw, speech coded data in a frame lasting 20 ms, but channel coding brings each coded speech frame up to 260 bits for the same 20 ms period. If FACCH is sent instead of speech data, then one frame of speech coding data is replaced with a block of FACCH data, and the FACCH data within a time slot is actually made up of FACCH data from two adjacent FACCH data blocks.

In the reverse voice channel, each time slot consists of two bursts of 122 bits and one burst of 16 bits (for a total of 260 bits per time slot) from two interleaved speech frames (or FACCH data blocks). In addition, 28 sync bits, 12 bits of SACCH data, 12 bits of Coded Digital Verification Color Code (CDVCC), and 12 bits of guard and ramp-up time are sent in a reverse channel time slot.

On the forward voice channel, each time slot consists of two 130 bit bursts of data from two consecutive, interleaved speech frames (or FACCH data if speech is not sent), 28 sync bits, 12 bits of SACCH data, 12 bits of CDVCC, and 12 reserved bits. There are a total of 324 bits per time slot on both the forward and reverse channels, and each time slot lasts for 6.667 ms.

The time slots in the forward and reverse channels are staggered in time so that time slot 1 of the *N*th frame in the forward channel starts exactly one time slot plus 44 symbols (i.e., 206 symbols = 412 bits) after the beginning of time slot 1 of the *N*th frame on the reverse channel. As discussed in Chapter 9, this allows each mobile to simply use a transmit/receive switch, rather than a duplexer, for full duplex operation with the forward and reverse links.

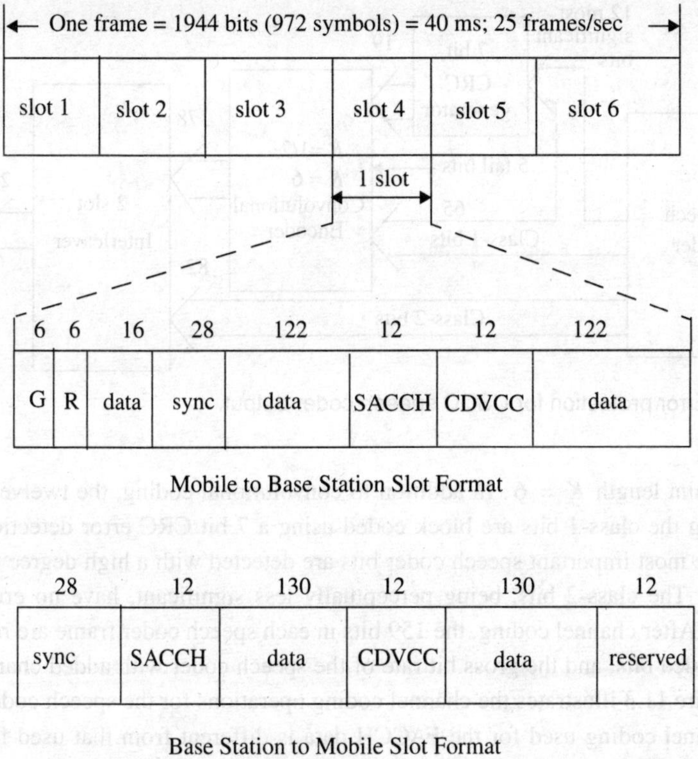

Figure 11.2 The USDC slot and frame structure on the forward and reverse link.

USDC provides the ability to adjust the time stagger between forward and reverse channel time slots in integer increments of half of a time slot so that the system may synchronize new subscribers that are assigned a time slot.

Speech Coding — The USDC speech coder is called the *Vector Sum Excited Linear Predictive coder* (VSELP). This belongs to the class of Code Excited Linear Predictive coders (CELP) or *Stochastically Excited Linear Predictive coders* (SELP). As discussed in Chapter 8, these coders are based upon codebooks which determine how to quantize the residual excitation signal. The VSELP algorithm uses a code book that has a predefined structure such that the number of computations required for the codebook search process is significantly reduced. The VSELP algorithm was developed by a consortium of companies and the Motorola implementation was chosen for the IS-54 standard. The VSELP coder has an output bit rate of 7950 bps and produces a speech frame every 20 ms. In one second, fifty speech frames, each containing 159 bits of speech, are produced by the coder for a particular user.

Channel Coding — The 159 bits within a speech coder frame are divided into two classes according to their perceptual significance. There are 77 class-1 bits and 82 class-2 bits. The class-1 bits, being the most significant bits, are error protected using a rate 1/2 convolutional

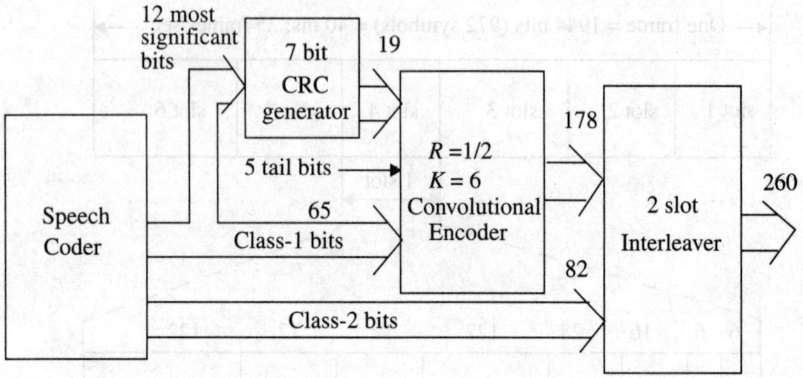

Figure 11.3 Error protection for USDC speech coder output.

code of constraint length $K = 6$. In addition to convolutional coding, the twelve most significant bits among the class-1 bits are block coded using a 7 bit CRC error detection code. This ensures that the most important speech coder bits are detected with a high degree of probability at the receiver. The class-2 bits, being perceptually less significant, have no error protection added to them. After channel coding, the 159 bits in each speech coder frame are represented by 260 channel coded bits, and the gross bit rate of the speech coder with added channel coding is 13.0 kbps. Figure 11.3 illustrates the channel coding operations for the speech coded data.

The channel coding used for the FACCH data is different from that used for the speech coded data. A FACCH data block contains forty-nine bits of data per each 20 ms frame. A 16 bit CRC codeword is appended to each FACCH data block, providing a coded FACCH word of sixty-five bits. The 65 bit word is then passed through a rate 1/4 convolutional coder of constraint length six in order to yield 260 bits of FACCH data per each 20 ms frame. A FACCH data block occupies the same amount of bandwidth as a single frame of coded speech, and in this manner speech data on the DTC can be replaced with coded FACCH data. Interleaving of DTC and FACCH data is handled identically in USDC.

The SACCH data word consists of 6 bits during each 20 ms speech frame. Each raw SACCH data word is passed through a rate 1/2 convolutional coder of constraint length five to produce twelve coded bits during every 20 ms interval, or twenty-four bits during each USDC frame.

Interleaving — Before transmission, the encoded speech data is interleaved over two time slots with the speech data from adjacent speech frames. In other words, each time slot contains exactly half of the data from each of two sequential speech coder frames. The speech data are placed into a rectangular 26×10 interleaver as shown in Figure 11.4. The data is entered into the columns of the interleaving array, and the two consecutive speech frames are referred to as x and y, where x is the previous speech frame and y is the present or most recent speech frame. It can be seen from Figure 11.4 that only 130 of the necessary 260 bits are provided for frames x and y. The encoded speech data for the two adjacent frames are placed into the interleaver in

$$\begin{bmatrix} 0x & 26x & 52x & 78x & 104x & 130x & 156x & 182x & 208x & 234x \\ 1y & 27y & 53y & 79y & 105y & 131y & 157y & 183y & 209y & 235y \\ 2x & 28x & 54x & 80x & 106x & 132x & 158x & 184x & 210x & 236x \\ \cdot & \cdot & \cdot & \cdot & \cdot & \cdot & \cdot & \cdot & \cdot & \cdot \\ \cdot & \cdot & \cdot & \cdot & \cdot & \cdot & \cdot & \cdot & \cdot & \cdot \\ 12x & 38x & 64x & 90x & 116x & 142x & 168x & 194x & 220x & 246x \\ 13y & 39y & 65y & 91y & 117y & 143y & 169y & 195y & 221y & 247y \\ \cdot & \cdot & \cdot & \cdot & \cdot & \cdot & \cdot & \cdot & \cdot & \cdot \\ \cdot & \cdot & \cdot & \cdot & \cdot & \cdot & \cdot & \cdot & \cdot & \cdot \\ \cdot & \cdot & \cdot & \cdot & \cdot & \cdot & \cdot & \cdot & \cdot & \cdot \\ 24x & 50x & 76x & 102x & 128x & 154x & 180x & 206x & 232x & 258x \\ 25y & 51y & 77y & 103y & 129y & 155y & 181y & 207y & 233y & 259y \end{bmatrix}$$

Figure 11.4 Interleaving for two adjacent speech coder frames in USDC.

such a manner that intermixes the class-2 bits and the class-1 bits. The speech data is then transmitted row-wise out of the interleaver. The interleaving approach for coded FACCH blocks is identical to that used for speech data. A 6 bit SACCH message word, on the other hand, is coded using a rate 1/2 convolutional code and uses an incremental interleaver that spans over twelve consecutive time slots [EIA90].

Modulation — To be compatible with AMPS, USDC uses 30 kHz channels. On control (paging) channels, USDC and AMPS use identical 10 kbps binary FSK with Manchester coding. On voice channels, the FM modulation is replaced with digital modulation having a gross bit rate of 48.6 kbps. In order to achieve this bit rate in a 30 kHz channel, the modulation requires a spectral efficiency of 1.62 bps/Hz. Also, to limit *adjacent channel interference* (ACI), spectral shaping on the digital channel must be used.

The spectral efficiency requirements are satisfied by conventional pulse-shaped, four-phase, modulation schemes such as QPSK and OQPSK. However, as discussed in Chapter 6, symmetric differential phase-shift keying, commonly known as $\pi/4$-DQPSK, has several advantages when used in a mobile radio environment and is the modulation used for USDC. The channel symbol rate is 24.3 ksps, and the symbol duration is $41.1523\mu s$.

Pulse shaping is used to reduce the transmission bandwidth while limiting the intersymbol interference (ISI). At the transmitter, the signal is filtered using a square root raised cosine filter with a rolloff factor equal to 0.35. The receiver may also employ a corresponding square root raised cosine filter. Once pulse-shaping is performed on phase-shift keying, it becomes a linear modulation technique, which requires linear amplification in order to preserve the pulse shape. Nonlinear amplification results in destruction of the pulse shape and expansion of the signal bandwidth. The use of pulse shaping with $\pi/4$-DQPSK supports the transmission of three (and eventually six) speech signals in a 30 kHz channel bandwidth with adjacent-channel protection of 50 dB.

Demodulation— The type of demodulation and decoding used at the receiver is left up to the manufacturer. As shown in Chapter 5, differential detection may be performed at IF or baseband. The latter implementation may be done conveniently using a simple discriminator or digital signal processor (DSP). This not only reduces the cost of the demodulator, but also simplifies the RF circuitry. DSPs also support the implementation of the USDC equalizer as well as dual mode functionality.

Equalization — Measurements conducted in 900 MHz mobile channels revealed that the rms delay spreads are less than 15 μs at 99% of all locations in four US cities and are less than 5 μs for nearly 80% of all locations [Rap90]. For a system employing DQPSK modulation at a symbol rate of 24.3 ksps, if the bit error rate due to intersymbol interference becomes intolerable for a σ/T value of 0.1 (where σ is the rms delay spread and T is the symbol duration), then the maximum value of rms delay spread that can be tolerated is 4.12 μs. If the rms delay spreads exceeds this, it is necessary to use equalization in order to reduce the BER. Work by Rappaport, Seidel, and Singh [Rap90] showed that the rms delays spread exceeds 4 μs at about 25% of the locations in four cities, so an equalizer was specified for USDC, although the specific implementation is not specified in the IS-54 standard.

One equalizer proposed for USDC is a Decision Feedback Equalizer (DFE) [Nar90] consisting of four feedforward taps and one feedback tap, where the feedforward taps have a 1/2 symbol spacing. This type of fractional spacing makes the equalizer robust against sample timing jitter. The coefficients of the adaptive filter are updated using the recursive least squares (RLS) algorithm described in Chapter 7. Many proprietary implementations for the USDC equalizer have been developed by equipment manufacturers.

11.2.2 United States Digital Cellular Derivatives (IS-94 and IS-136)

The added networking features provided in IS-136 led to new types of wireless services and transport topologies. Because TDMA provides MAHO capability, mobiles are able to sense channel conditions and report these to the base station. This, in turn, allows greater flexibility in cellular deployment. For example, MAHO is used to support dynamic channel allocation which can be carried out by the base station. This allows an MSC to use a larger number of base stations placed in strategic locations throughout a service area and provides each base station with greater control of its coverage characteristics.

The IS-94 standard exploited capabilities provided by the original IS-54 standard, and enabled cellular phones to interface directly with private branch exchanges (PBXs). By moving the intelligence of an MSC closer to the base station, it becomes possible to provide wireless PBX services in a building or on a campus, while using small base stations (microcells) that can be placed in closets throughout a building. IS-94 specifies a technique to provide private, or closed, cellular systems that use nonstandard control channels. IS-94 systems were introduced in 1994, and were proliferating throughout office buildings and hotels until 2001.

The IS-54 Rev.C standard provided 48.6 kbps control channel signaling on the USDC-only control channels and 10 kbps FSK control channels on the original AMPS channels. However, closed network capabilities are not fully developed under IS-54 Rev.C. The final USDC standard, IS-136, was developed to provide a host of new features and services that allowed USDC to be competitive with IS-95 and GSM 2G standards. IS-136 specifies short messaging capabilities and private, user group features, making it well-suited for wireless PBX applications and paging applications. Furthermore, IS-136 specifies a "sleep mode" that instructs compatible cellular phones to conserve battery power. IS-136 subscriber terminals are not compatible with those produced for IS-54, since IS-136 uses 48.6 kbps control channels exclusively on all control channels (the 10 kbps FSK is not supported). This allows IS-136 modems to be more cost effective, since only the 48.6 kbps modem is needed in each portable unit.

11.3 Global System for Mobile (GSM)

Global System for Mobile (GSM) is a second generation cellular system standard that was developed to solve the fragmentation problems of the first cellular systems in Europe. GSM was the world's first cellular system to specify digital modulation and network level architectures and services, and is the world's most popular 2G technology. Before GSM, European countries used different cellular standards throughout the continent, and it was not possible for a customer to use a single subscriber unit throughout Europe. GSM was originally developed to serve as the pan-European cellular service and promised a wide range of network services through the use of ISDN. GSM's success has exceeded the expectations of virtually everyone, and it is now the world's most popular standard for new cellular radio and personal communications equipment throughout the world. As of 2001, there were over 350 million GSM subscriers worldwide.

The task of specifying a common mobile communication system for Europe in the 900 MHz band was taken up in the mid-1980s by the GSM (Groupe spécial mobile) committee which was a working group of the CEPT. In 1992, GSM changed its name to the *Global System for Mobile Communications* for marketing reasons [Mou92]. The setting of standards for GSM is under the aegis of the European Technical Standards Institute (ETSI).

GSM was first introduced into the European market in 1991. By the end of 1993, several non-European countries in South America, Asia, and Australia had adopted GSM and the technically equivalent offshoot, DCS 1800, which supports Personal Communication Services (PCS) in the 1.8 GHz to 2.0 GHz radio bands recently created by governments throughout the world.

11.3.1 GSM Services and Features

GSM services follow ISDN guidelines and are classified as either *teleservices* or *data services*. Teleservices include standard mobile telephony and mobile-originated or base-originated traffic. Data services include computer-to-computer communication and packet-switched traffic. User services may be divided into three major categories:

- **Telephone services**, including emergency calling and facsimile. GSM also supports Videotex and Teletex, though they are not integral parts of the GSM standard.
- **Bearer services** or **data services** which are limited to layers 1, 2, and 3 of the open system interconnection (OSI) reference model (see Chapter 10). Supported services include packet switched protocols and data rates from 300 bps to 9.6 kbps. Data may be transmitted using either a transparent mode (where GSM provides standard channel coding for the user data) or nontransparent mode (where GSM offers special coding efficiencies based on the particular data interface).
- **Supplementary ISDN services**, are digital in nature, and include call diversion, closed user groups, and caller identification, and are not available in analog mobile networks. Supplementary services also include the *short messaging service* (SMS) which allows GSM subscribers and base stations to transmit alphanumeric pages of limited length (160 7 bit ASCII characters) while simultaneously carrying normal voice traffic. SMS also provides *cell broadcast*, which allows GSM base stations to repetitively transmit ASCII messages with as many as fifteen 93-character strings in concatenated fashion. SMS may be used for safety and advisory applications, such as the broadcast of highway or weather information to all GSM subscribers within reception range.

From the user's point of view, one of the most remarkable features of GSM is the *Subscriber Identity Module* (SIM), which is a memory device that stores information such as the subscriber's identification number, the networks and countries where the subscriber is entitled to service, privacy keys, and other user-specific information. A subscriber uses the SIM with a four-digit personal ID number to activate service from any GSM phone. SIMs are available as smart cards (credit card sized cards that may be inserted into any GSM phone) or plug-in modules, which are less convenient than the SIM cards but are nonetheless removable and portable. Without a SIM installed, all GSM mobiles are identical and nonoperational. It is the SIM that gives GSM subscriber units their identity. Subscribers may plug their SIM into any suitable terminal—such as a hotel phone, public phone, or any portable or mobile phone—and are then able to have all incoming GSM calls routed to that terminal and have all outgoing calls billed to their home phone, no matter where they are in the world.

A second remarkable feature of GSM is the on-the-air privacy which is provided by the system. Unlike analog FM cellular phone systems which can be readily monitored, it is virtually impossible to eavesdrop on a GSM radio transmission. The privacy is made possible by encrypting the digital bit stream sent by a GSM transmitter, according to a specific secret cryptographic key that is known only to the cellular carrier. This key changes with time for each user. Every carrier and GSM equipment manufacturer must sign the Memorandum of Understanding (MoU) before developing GSM equipment or deploying a GSM system. The MoU is an international agreement which allows the sharing of cryptographic algorithms and other proprietary information between countries and carriers.

11.3.2 GSM System Architecture

The GSM system architecture consists of three major interconnected subsystems that interact between themselves and with the users through certain network interfaces. The subsystems are the *Base Station Subsystem* (BSS), *Network and Switching Subsystem* (NSS), and the *Operation Support Subsystem* (OSS). The *Mobile Station* (MS) is also a subsystem, but is usually considered to be part of the BSS for architecture purposes. Equipment and services are designed within GSM to support one or more of these specific subsystems.

The BSS, also known as the *radio subsystem*, provides and manages radio transmission paths between the mobile stations and the Mobile Switching Center (MSC). The BSS also manages the radio interface between the mobile stations and all other subsystems of GSM. Each BSS consists of many Base Station Controllers (BSCs) which connect the MS to the NSS via the MSCs. The NSS manages the switching functions of the system and allows the MSCs to communicate with other networks such as the PSTN and ISDN. The OSS supports the operation and maintenance of GSM and allows system engineers to monitor, diagnose, and troubleshoot all aspects of the GSM system. This subsystem interacts with the other GSM subsystems, and is provided solely for the staff of the GSM operating company which provides service facilities for the network.

Figure 11.5 shows the block diagram of the GSM system architecture. The Mobile Stations (MSs) communicate with the Base Station Subsystem (BSS) over the radio air interface. The BSS consists of many BSCs which connect to a single MSC, and each BSC typically controls up to several hundred *Base Transceiver Stations* (BTSs). Some of the BTSs may be co-located at the BSC, and others may be remotely distributed and physically connected to the BSC by microwave link or dedicated leased lines. Mobile handoffs (called *handovers*, or HO, in the GSM specification) between two BTSs under the control of the same BSC are handled by the BSC, and not the MSC. This greatly reduces the switching burden of the MSC.

As shown in Figure 11.6, the interface which connects a BTS to a BSC is called the *Abis interface.* The Abis interface carries traffic and maintenance data, and is specified by GSM to be standardized for all manufacturers. In practice, however, the Abis for each GSM base station manufacturer has subtle differences, thereby forcing service providers to use the same manufacturer for the BTS and BSC equipment.

The BSCs are physically connected via dedicated/leased lines or microwave link to the MSC. The interface between a BSC and a MSC is called the *A interface*, which is standardized within GSM. The A interface uses an SS7 protocol called the *Signaling Correction Control Part*

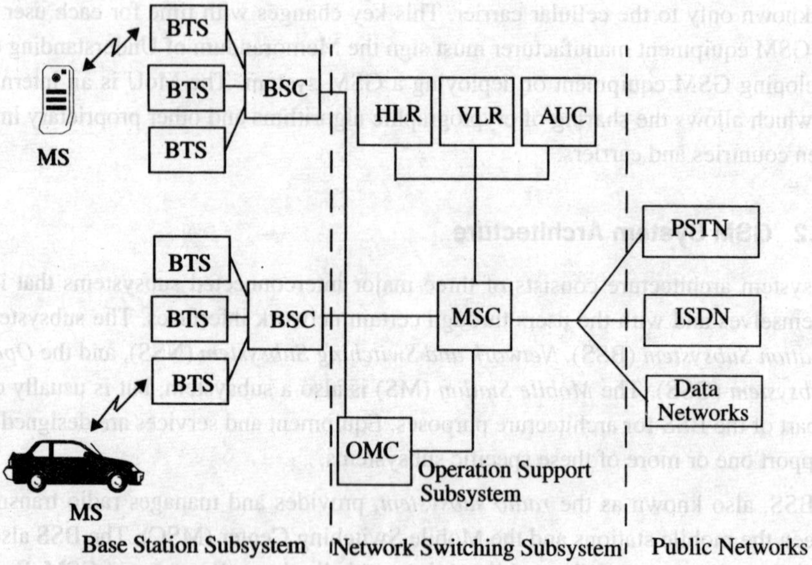

Figure 11.5 GSM system architecture.

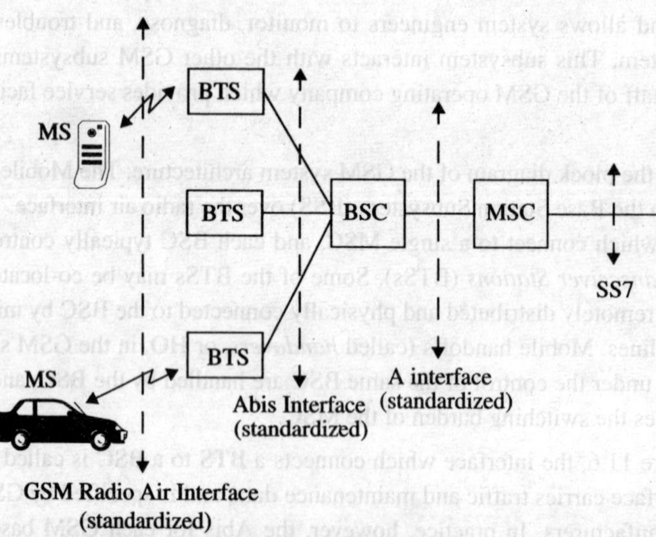

Figure 11.6 The various interfaces used in GSM.

(SCCP) which supports communication between the MSC and the BSS, as well as network messages between the individual subscribers and the MSC. The A interface allows a service provider to use base stations and switching equipment made by different manufacturers.

The NSS handles the switching of GSM calls between external networks and the BSCs in the radio subsystem and is also responsible for managing and providing external access to several customer databases. The MSC is the central unit in the NSS and controls the traffic among all of the BSCs. In the NSS, there are three different databases called the *Home Location Register* (HLR), *Visitor Location Register* (VLR), and the *Authentication Center* (AUC). The HLR is a database which contains subscriber information and location information for each user who resides in the same city as the MSC. Each subscriber in a particular GSM market is assigned a unique *International Mobile Subscriber Identity* (IMSI), and this number is used to identify each home user. The VLR is a database which temporarily stores the IMSI and customer information for each roaming subscriber who is visiting the coverage area of a particular MSC. The VLR is linked between several adjoining MSCs in a particular market or geographic region and contains subscription information of every visiting user in the area. Once a roaming mobile is logged in the VLR, the MSC sends the necessary information to the visiting subscriber's HLR so that calls to the roaming mobile can be appropriately routed over the PSTN by the roaming user's HLR. The Authentication Center is a strongly protected database which handles the authentication and encryption keys for every single subscriber in the HLR and VLR. The Authentication Center contains a register called the *Equipment Identity Register* (EIR) which identifies stolen or fraudulently altered phones that transmit identity data that does not match with information contained in either the HLR or VLR.

The OSS supports one or several *Operation Maintenance Centers* (OMC) which are used to monitor and maintain the performance of each MS, BS, BSC, and MSC within a GSM system. The OSS has three main functions, which are 1) to maintain all telecommunications hardware and network operations with a particular market, 2) manage all charging and billing procedures, and 3) manage all mobile equipment in the system. Within each GSM system, an OMC is dedicated to each of these tasks and has provisions for adjusting all base station parameters and billing procedures, as well as for providing system operators with the ability to determine the performance and integrity of each piece of subscriber equipment in the system.

11.3.3 GSM Radio Subsystem

GSM originally used two 25 MHz cellular bands set aside for all member countries, but now it is used globally in many bands. The 890–915 MHz band was for subscriber-to-base transmissions (reverse link), and the 935–960 MHz band was for base-to-subscriber transmissions (forward link). GSM uses FDD and a combination of TDMA and FHMA schemes to provide multiple access to mobile users. The available forward and reverse frequency bands are divided into 200 kHz wide channels called ARFCNs (Absolute Radio Frequency Channel Numbers). The ARFCN denotes a forward and reverse channel pair which is separated in frequency by 45 MHz and each channel is time shared between as many as eight subscribers using TDMA.

Each of the eight subscribers uses the same ARFCN and occupies a unique timeslot (TS) per frame. Radio transmissions on both the forward and reverse link are made at a channel data rate of 270.833 kbps (1625.0/6.0 kbps) using binary $BT = 0.3$ GMSK modulation. Thus, the signaling bit duration is 3.692 μs, and the effective channel transmission rate per user is 33.854 kbps (270.833 kpbs/8 users). With GSM overhead (described subsequently), user data is actually sent at a maximum rate of 24.7 kbps. Each TS has an equivalent time allocation of 156.25 channel bits, but of this, 8.25 bits of guard time and six total start and stop bits are provided to prevent overlap with adjacent time slots. Each TS has a time duration of 576.92 μs as shown in Figure 11.7, and a single GSM TDMA frame spans 4.615 ms. The total number of available channels within a 25 MHz bandwidth is 125 (assuming no guard band). Since each radio channel consists of eight time slots, there are thus a total of 1000 traffic channels within GSM. In practical implementations, a guard band of 100 kHz is provided at the upper and lower end of the GSM spectrum, and only 124 channels are implemented. Table 11.3 summarizes the GSM air interface.

The combination of a TS number and an ARFCN constitutes a *physical channel* for both the forward and reverse link. Each physical channel in a GSM system can be mapped into different *logical channels* at different times. That is, each specific time slot or frame may be dedicated to either handling traffic data (user data such as speech, facsimile, or teletext data), signaling data (required by the internal workings of the GSM system), or control channel data (from the MSC, base station, or mobile user). The GSM specification defines a wide variety of logical channels which can be used to link the physical layer with the data link layer of the GSM network. These logical channels efficiently transmit user data while simultaneously providing control of the network on each ARFCN. GSM provides explicit assignments of time slots and frames for specific logical channels, as described below.

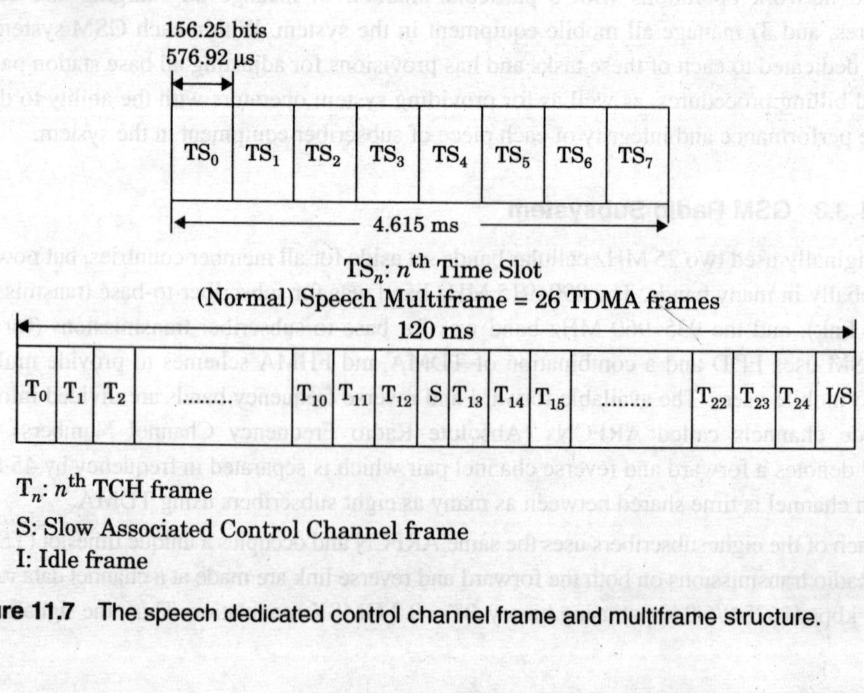

Figure 11.7 The speech dedicated control channel frame and multiframe structure.

Table 11.3 GSM Air Interface Specifications Summary

Parameter	Specifications
Reverse Channel Frequency	890–915 MHz
Forward Channel Frequency	935–960 MHz
ARFCN Number	0 to 124 and 975 to 1023
Tx/Rx Frequency Spacing	45 MHz
Tx/Rx Time Slot Spacing	3 Time slots
Modulation Data Rate	270.833333 kbps
Frame Period	4.615 ms
Users per Frame (Full Rate)	8
Time Slot Period	576.9 μs
Bit Period	3.692 μs
Modulation	0.3 GMSK
ARFCN Channel Spacing	200 kHz
Interleaving (max. delay)	40 ms
Voice Coder Bit Rate	13.4 kbps

11.3.4 GSM Channel Types

There are two types of GSM logical channels, called *traffic channels* (TCHs) and *control channels* (CCHs) [Hod90]. Traffic channels carry digitally encoded user speech or user data and have identical functions and formats on both the forward and reverse link. Control channels carry signaling and synchronizing commands between the base station and the mobile station. Certain types of control channels are defined for just the forward or reverse link. There are six different types of TCHs provided for in GSM, and an even larger number of CCHs, both of which are now described.

11.3.4.1 GSM Traffic Channels (TCHs)

GSM traffic channels may be either full-rate or half-rate and may carry either digitized speech or user data. When transmitted as full-rate, user data is contained within one TS per frame. When transmitted as half-rate, user data is mapped onto the same time slot, but is sent in alternate frames. That is, two half-rate channel users would share the same time slot, but would alternately transmit during every other frame.

In the GSM standard, TCH data may not be sent in TS 0 within a TDMA frame on certain ARFCNs which serve as the broadcast station for each cell (since this time slot is reserved for control channel bursts in most every frame, as described subsequently). Furthermore, frames of TCH data are broken up every thirteenth frame by either slow associated control channel data (SACCH) or idle frames. Figure 11.7 illustrates how the TCH data is transmitted in consecutive frames. Each group of twenty-six consecutive TDMA frames is called a *multiframe* (or *speech multiframe*, to distinguish it from the control channel multiframe described below). For every twenty-six frames, the thirteenth and twenty-sixth frames consist of Slow Associated Control Channel (SACCH) data, or the idle frame, respectively. The twenty-sixth frame contains idle bits for the case when full-rate TCHs are used, and contains SACCH data when half-rate TCHs are used.

Full-Rate TCH

The following full rate speech and data channels are supported:

- **Full-Rate Speech Channel (TCH/FS)** — The full-rate speech channel carries user speech which is digitized at a raw data rate of 13 kbps. With GSM channel coding added to the digitized speech, the full-rate speech channel carries 22.8 kbps.
- **Full-Rate Data Channel for 9600 bps (TCH/F9.6)** — The full-rate traffic data channel carries raw user data which is sent at 9600 bps. With additional forward error correction coding applied by the GSM standard, the 9600 bps data is sent at 22.8 kbps.
- **Full-Rate Data Channel for 4800 bps (TCH/F4.8)** — The full-rate traffic data channel carries raw user data which is sent at 4800 bps. With additional forward error correction coding applied by the GSM standard, the 4800 bps is sent at 22.8 kbps.
- **Full-Rate Data Channel for 2400 bps (TCH/F2.4)** — The full-rate traffic data channel carries raw user data which is sent at 2400 bps. With additional forward error correction coding applied by the GSM standard, the 2400 bps is sent at 22.8 kbps.

Half-Rate TCH

The following half-rate speech and data channels are supported:

- **Half-Rate Speech Channel (TCH/HS)** — The half-rate speech channel has been designed to carry digitized speech which is sampled at a rate half that of the full-rate channel. GSM anticipates the availability of speech coders which can digitize speech at about 6.5 kbps. With GSM channel coding added to the digitized speech, the half-rate speech channel will carry 11.4 kbps.
- **Half-Rate Data Channel for 4800 bps (TCH/H4.8)** — The half-rate traffic data channel carries raw user data which is sent at 4800 bps. With additional forward error correction coding applied by the GSM standard, the 4800 bps data is sent at 11.4 kbps.
- **Half-Rate Data Channel for 2400 bps (TCH/H2.4)** — The half-rate traffic data channel carries raw user data which is sent at 2400 bps. With additional forward error correction coding applied by the GSM standard, the 2400 bps data is sent at 11.4 kbps.

11.3.4.2 GSM Control Channels (CCH)

There are three main control channels in the GSM system. These are the *broadcast channel* (BCH), the *common control channel* (CCCH), and the *dedicated control channel* (DCCH). Each control channel consists of several logical channels which are distributed in time to provide the necessary GSM control functions.

The BCH and CCCH forward control channels in GSM are implemented only on certain ARFCN channels and are allocated timeslots in a very specific manner. Specifically, the BCH and CCCH forward control channels are allocated only TS 0 and are broadcast only during certain frames within a repetitive fifty-one frame sequence (called the *control channel multiframe*) on those ARFCNs which are designated as broadcast channels. TS1 through TS7 carry regular TCH traffic, so that ARFCNs which are designated as control channels are still able to carry full-rate users on seven of the eight time slots.

The GSM specification defines thirty-four ARFCNs as standard broadcast channels. For each broadcast channel, frame 51 does not contain any BCH/CCCH forward channel data and is considered to be an idle frame. However, the reverse channel CCCH is able to receive subscriber transmissions during TS 0 of any frame (even the idle frame). On the other hand, DCCH data may be sent during any time slot and any frame, and entire frames are specifically dedicated to certain DCCH transmissions. GSM control channels are now described in detail.

- **Broadcast Channels (BCHs)**— The broadcast channel operates on the forward link of a specific ARFCN within each cell, and transmits data only in the first time slot (TS 0) of certain GSM frames. Unlike TCHs which are duplex, BCHs only use the forward link. Just as the forward control channel (FCC) in AMPS is used as a beacon for all nearby mobiles to camp on to, the BCH serves as a TDMA beacon channel for any nearby mobile to identify and lock on to. The BCH provides synchronization for all mobiles within the cell and is occasionally monitored by mobiles in neighboring cells so that received power and MAHO decisions may be made by out-of-cell users. Although BCH data is transmitted in TS 0, the other seven timeslots in a GSM frame for that same ARFCN are available for TCH data, DCCH data, or are filled with dummy bursts. Furthermore, all eight timeslots on all other ARFCNs within the cell are available for TCH or DCCH data.

  The BCH is defined by three separate channels which are given access to TS 0 during various frames of the 51 frame sequence. Figure 11.8 illustrates how the BCH is allocated frames. The three types of BCH are now described.

  a) *Broadcast Control Channel (BCCH)* — The BCCH is a forward control channel that is used to broadcast information such as cell and network identity, and operating characteristics of the cell (current control channel structure, channel availability, and congestion). The BCCH also broadcasts a list of channels that are currently in use within the cell. Frame 2 through frame 5 in a control multiframe (4 out of every 51 frames) contain

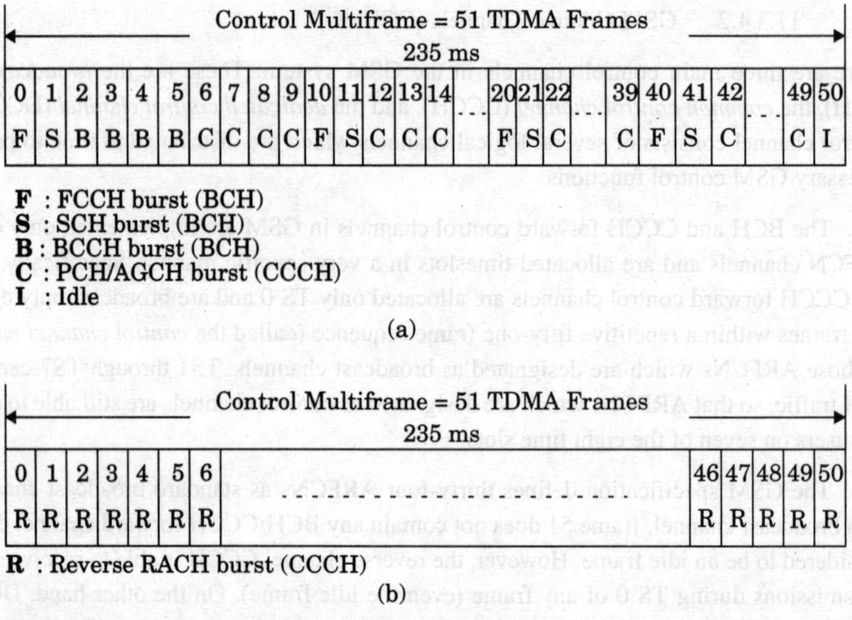

Figure 11.8 (a) The Control Channel Multiframe (forward link for TS0); (b) The Control Channel Multiframe (reverse link for TS0).

BCCH data. It should be noted from Figure 11.8 that TS 0 contains BCCH data during specific frames, and contains other BCH channels (FCCH and SCH), common control channels (CCCHs), or an idle frame (sent every 51st frame) during other specific frames.

b) *Frequency Correction Channel (FCCH)* — The FCCH is a special data burst which occupies TS 0 for the very first GSM frame (frame 0) and is repeated every ten frames within a control channel multiframe. The FCCH allows each subscriber unit to synchronize its internal frequency standard (local oscillator) to the exact frequency of the base station.

c) *Synchronization Channel (SCH)* — SCH is broadcast in TS 0 of the frame immediately following the FCCH frame and is used to identify the serving base station while allowing each mobile to frame synchronize with the base station. The *frame number* (FN), which ranges from 0 to 2,715,647, is sent with the *base station identity code* (BSIC) during the SCH burst. The BSIC is uniquely assigned to each BST in a GSM system. Since a mobile may be as far as 30 km away from a serving base station, it is often necessary to adjust the timing of a particular mobile user such that the received signal at the base station is synchronized with the base station clock. The BS issues coarse *timing advancement* commands to the mobile stations over the SCH, as well. The SCH is transmitted once every ten frames within the control channel multiframe, as shown in Figure 11.8.

- **Common Control Channels (CCCHs)** — On the broadcast (BCH) ARFCN, the common control channels occupy TS 0 of every GSM frame that is not otherwise used by the BCH or the Idle frame. CCCH consists of three different channels: the paging channel (PCH), which is a forward link channel, the random access channel (RACH) which is a reverse link channel, and the access grant channel (AGCH), which is a forward link channel. As seen in Figure 11.8, CCCHs are the most commonly used control channels and are used to page specific subscribers, assign signaling channels to specific users, and receive mobile requests for service. These channels are described below.

  a) *Paging Channel (PCH)* — The PCH provides paging signals from the base station to all mobiles in the cell, and notifies a specific mobile of an incoming call which originates from the PSTN. The PCH transmits the IMSI of the target subscriber, along with a request for acknowledgment from the mobile unit on the RACH. Alternatively, the PCH may be used to provide *cell broadcast* ASCII text messages to all subscribers, as part of the SMS feature of GSM.

  b) *Random Access Channel (RACH)* — The RACH is a reverse link channel used by a subscriber unit to acknowledge a page from the PCH, and is also used by mobiles to originate a call. The RACH uses a slotted ALOHA access scheme. All mobiles must request access or respond to a PCH alert within TS 0 of a GSM frame. At the BTS, every frame (even the idle frame) will accept RACH transmissions from mobiles during TS 0. In establishing service, the GSM base station must respond to the RACH transmission by allocating a channel and assigning a stand-alone dedicated control channel (SDCCH) for signaling during a call. This connection is confirmed by the base station over the AGCH.

  c) *Access Grant Channel (AGCH)* — The AGCH is used by the base station to provide forward link communication to the mobile, and carries data which instructs the mobile to operate in a particular physical channel (time slot and ARFCN) with a particular dedicated control channel. The AGCH is the final CCCH message sent by the base station before a subscriber is moved off the control channel. The AGCH is used by the base station to respond to a RACH sent by a mobile station in a previous CCCH frame.

- **Dedicated Control Channels (DCCHs)** — There are three types of dedicated control channels in GSM, and, like traffic channels (see Figure 11.7), they are bidirectional and have the same format and function on both the forward and reverse links. Like TCHs, DCCHs may exist in any time slot and on any ARFCN *except TS0* of the BCH ARFCN. The stand-alone dedicated control channels (SDCCHs) are used for providing signaling services required by the users. The Slow- and Fast-Associated Control Channels (SACCHs and FACCHs) are used for supervisory data transmissions between the mobile station and the base station during a call.

  a) *Stand-alone Dedicated Control Channels (SDCCHs)* — The SDCCH carries signaling data following the connection of the mobile with the base station, and just before a TCH assignment is issued by the base station. The SDCCH ensures that the mobile station and the base station remain connected while the base station and MSC verify the subscriber unit and allocate resources for the mobile. The SDCCH can be thought of as an intermediate and temporary channel which accepts a newly completed call from the BCH and holds the traffic while waiting for the base station to allocate a TCH channel. The SDCCH is used to send authentication and alert messages (but not speech) as the mobile synchronizes itself with the frame structure and waits for a TCH. SDCCHs may be assigned their own physical channel or may occupy TS0 of the BCH if there is low demand for BCH or CCCH traffic.

b) *Slow Associated Control Channel (SACCH)* — The SACCH is always associated with a traffic channel or a SDCCH and maps onto the same physical channel. Thus, each ARFCN systematically carries SACCH data for all of its current users. As in the USDC standard, the SACCH carries general information between the MS and BTS. On the forward link, the SACCH is used to send slow but regularly changing control information to the mobile, such as transmit power level instructions and specific timing advance instructions for each user on the ARFCN. The reverse SACCH carries information about the received signal strength and quality of the TCH, as well as BCH measurement results from neighboring cells. The SACCH is transmitted during the thirteenth frame (and the twenty-sixth frame when half-rate traffic is used) of every speech/dedicated control channel multiframe (Figure 11.7), and within this frame, the eight timeslots are dedicated to providing SACCH data to each of the eight full-rate (or sixteen half-rate) users on the ARFCN.

c) *Fast Associated Control Channels (FACCHs)* — FACCH carries urgent messages, and contains essentially the same type of information as the SDCCH. A FACCH is assigned whenever a SDCCH has not been dedicated for a particular user and there is an urgent message (such as a handoff request). The FACCH gains access to a time slot by "stealing" frames from the traffic channel to which it is assigned. This is done by setting two special bits, called stealing bits, in a TCH forward channel burst. If the stealing bits are set, the time slot is known to contain FACCH data, not a TCH, for that frame.

11.3.5 Example of a GSM Call

To understand how the various traffic and control channels are used, consider the case of a mobile call origination in GSM. First, the subscriber unit must be synchronized to a nearby base station as it monitors the BCH. By receiving the FCCH, SCH, and BCCH messages, the subscriber would be locked on to the system and the appropriate BCH. To originate a call, the user first dials the intended digit combination and presses the "send" button on the GSM phone. The mobile transmits a burst of RACH data, using the same ARFCN as the base station to which it is locked. The base station then responds with an AGCH message on the CCCH which assigns the mobile unit to a new channel for SDCCH connection. The subscriber unit, which is monitoring TS 0 of the BCH, would receive its ARFCN and TS assignment from the AGCH and would immediately tune to the new ARFCN and TS. This new ARFCN and TS assignment is physically the SDCCH (not the TCH). Once tuned to the SDCCH, the subscriber unit first waits for the SACCH frame to be transmitted (the wait would last, at most, 26 frames or 120 ms, as shown in Figure 11.7), which informs the mobile of any required timing advance and transmitter power command. The base station is able to determine the proper timing advance and signal level from the mobile's earlier RACH transmission and sends the proper value over the SACCH for the mobile to process. Upon receiving and processing the timing advance information in the SACCH, the subscriber is now able to transmit normal burst messages as required for speech traffic. The SDCCH sends messages between the mobile unit and the base station, taking care of authentication and user validation, while the PSTN connects the dialed party to the MSC, and the MSC switches the speech path to the serving base station. After a few seconds, the mobile unit is commanded by the base station via the SDCCH to retune to a new ARFCN and new TS for the TCH assignment. Once retuned to the TCH, speech data is transferred on both the forward and reverse links, the call is successfully underway, and the SDCCH is vacated.

When calls are originated from the PSTN, the process is quite similar. The base station broadcasts a PCH message during TS 0 within an appropriate frame on the BCH. The mobile station, locked on to that same ARFCN, detects its page and replies with an RACH message acknowledging receipt of the page. The base station then uses the AGCH on the CCCH to assign the mobile unit to a new physical channel for connection to the SDCCH and SACCH while the network and the serving base station are connected. Once the subscriber establishes timing advance and authentication on the SDCCH, the base station issues a new physical channel assignment over the SDCCH, and the TCH assignment is made.

11.3.6 Frame Structure for GSM

Each user transmits a burst of data during the time slot assigned to it. These data bursts may have one of five specific formats, as defined in GSM [Hod90]. Figure 11.9 illustrates the five types of data bursts used for various control and traffic bursts. Normal bursts are used for TCH and DCCH transmissions on both the forward and reverse link. FCCH and SCH bursts are used in TS 0 of specific frames (shown in Figure 11.8(a)) to broadcast the frequency and time synchronization control messages on the forward link. The RACH burst is used by all mobiles to access service from any base station, and the dummy burst is used as filler information for unused time slots on the forward link.

Figure 11.10 illustrates the data structure within a normal burst. It consists of 148 bits which are transmitted at a rate of 270.833333 kbps (an unused guard time of 8.25 bits is provided at the end of each burst). Out of the total 148 bits per TS, 114 are information-bearing bits which are transmitted as two 57 bit sequences close to the beginning and end of the burst. The midamble consists of a 26 bit training sequence which allows the adaptive equalizer in the mobile or base station receiver to analyze the radio channel characteristics before decoding the user data. On either side of the midamble, there are control bits called stealing flags. These two flags are used to distinguish whether the TS contains voice (TCH) or control (FACCH) data,

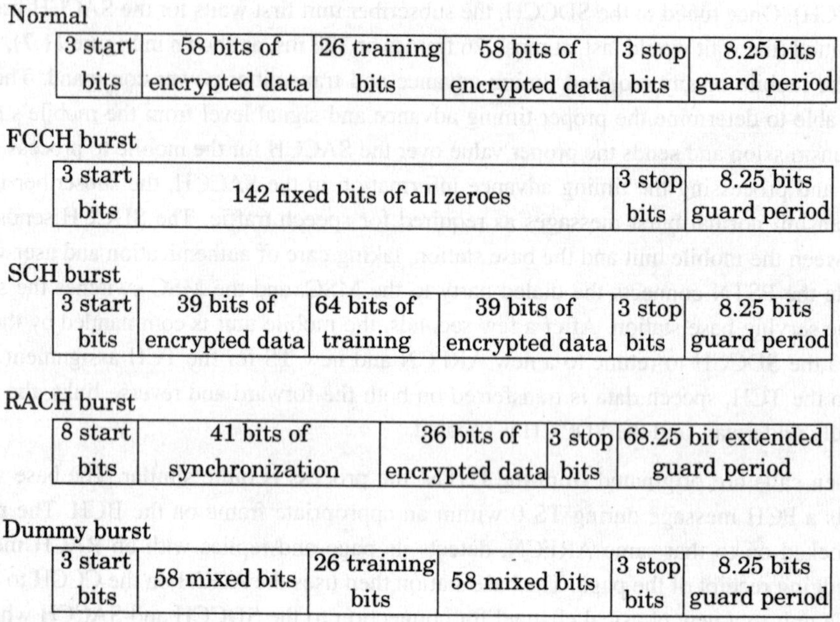

Figure 11.9 Time slot data bursts in GSM.

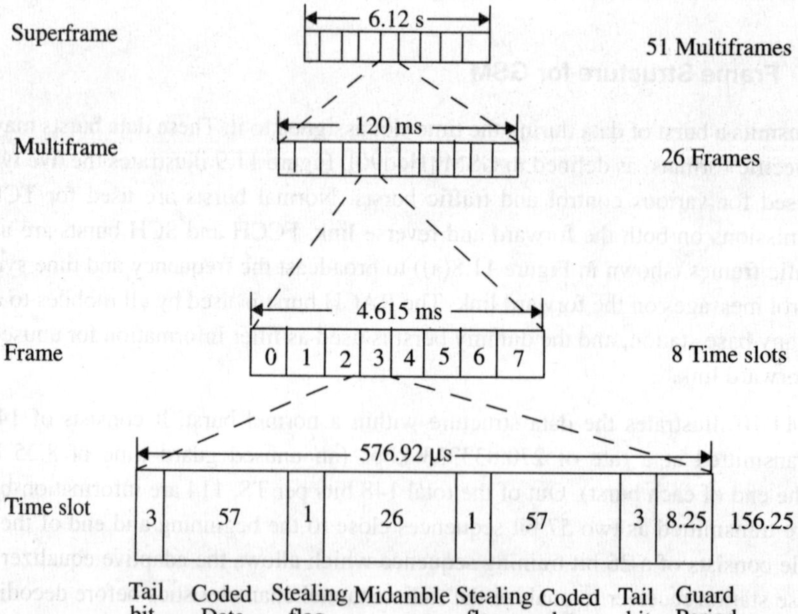

Figure 11.10 GSM frame structure.

both which share the same physical channel. During a frame, a GSM subscriber unit uses one TS to transmit, one TS to receive, and may use the six spare time slots to measure signal strength on five adjacent base stations as well as its own base station.

As shown in Figure 11.10, there are eight timeslots per TDMA frame, and the frame period is 4.615 ms. A frame contains $8 \times 156.25 = 1250$ bits, although some bit periods are not used. The frame rate is 270.833 kbps/1250 bits/frame, or 216.66 frames per second. The 13th or 26th frame are not used for traffic, but for control purposes. Each of the normal speech frames are grouped into larger structures called *multiframes* which in turn are grouped into *superframes* and *hyperframes* (hyperframes are not shown in Figure 11.10). One multiframe contains 26 TDMA frames, and one superframe contains 51 multiframes, or 1326 TDMA frames. A hyperframe contains 2048 superframes, or 2,715,648 TDMA frames. A complete hyperframe is sent about every 3 hours, 28 minutes, and 54 seconds, and is important to GSM since the encryption algorithms rely on the particular frame number, and sufficient security can only be obtained by using a large number of frames as provided by the hyperframe.

Figure 11.8 shows that the control multiframes span 51 frames (235.365 ms), as opposed to 26 frames (120 ms) used by the traffic/dedicated control channel multiframes. This is done intentionally to ensure that any GSM subscriber (whether in the serving or adjacent cell) will be certain to receive the SCH and FCCH transmissions from the BCH, no matter what particular frame or time slot they are using.

11.3.7 Signal Processing in GSM

Figure 11.11 illustrates all of the GSM operations from transmitter to receiver.

Speech Coding — The GSM speech coder is based on the Residually Excited Linear Predictive Coder (RELP), which is enhanced by including a Long-Term Predictor (LTP) [Hel89]. The coder provides 260 bits for each 20 ms blocks of speech, which yields a bit rate of 13 kbps. This speech coder was selected after extensive subjective evaluation of various candidate coders available in the late 1980s. Provisions for incorporating half-rate coders are included in the specifications.

The GSM speech coder takes advantage of the fact that in a normal conversation, each person speaks on average for less than 40% of the time. By incorporating a voice activity detector (VAD) in the speech coder, GSM systems operate in a *discontinuous transmission mode* (DTX) which provides a longer subscriber battery life and reduces instantaneous radio interference since the GSM transmitter is not active during silent periods. A comfort noise subsystem (CNS) at the receiving end introduces a background acoustic noise to compensate for the annoying switched muting which occurs due to DTX.

TCH/FS, SACCH, and FACCH Channel Coding — The output bits of the speech coder are ordered into groups for error protection, based upon their significance in contributing to speech quality. Out of the total 260 bits in a frame, the most important 50 bits, called type Ia bits, have 3 parity check (CRC) bits added to them. This facilitates the detection of non-correctable errors at the receiver. The next 132 bits along with the first 53 (50 type Ia bits + 3 parity bits) are

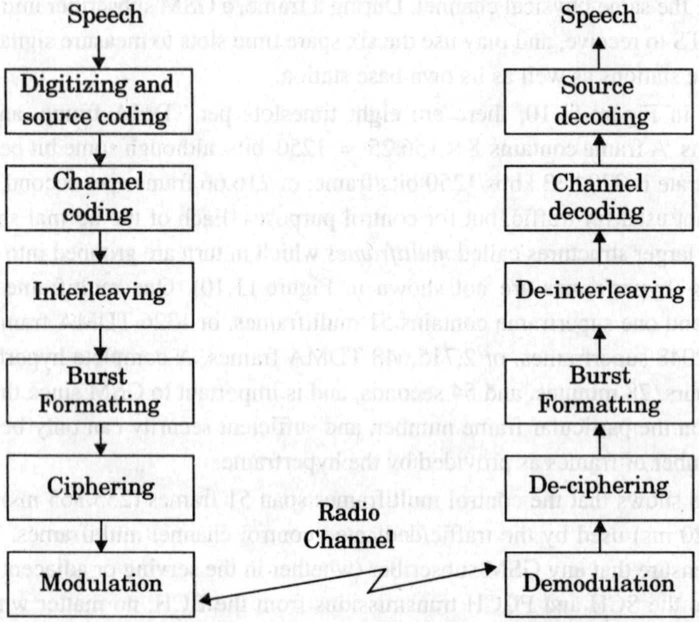

Figure 11.11 GSM operations from speech input to speech output.

reordered and appended by four trailing zero bits, thus providing a data block of 189 bits. This block is then encoded for error protection using a rate 1/2 convolutional encoder with constraint length $K = 5$, thus providing a sequence of 378 bits. The least important 78 bits do not have any error protection and are concatenated to the existing sequence to form a block of 456 bits in a 20 ms frame. The error protection coding scheme increases the gross data rate of the GSM speech signal, with channel coding, to 22.8 kbps. This error protection scheme as described is illustrated in Figure 11.12.

Channel Coding for Data Channels — The coding provided for GSM full rate data channels (TCH/F9.6) is based on handling 60 bits of user data at 5 ms intervals, in accordance with the modified CCITT V.110 modem standard. As described by Steele [Ste94]), 240 bits of user data are applied with four tailing bits to a half-rate punctured convolutional coder with constraint length $K = 5$. The resulting 488 coded bits are reduced to 456 encoded data bits through puncturing (32 bits are not transmitted), and the data is separated into four 114 bit data bursts that are applied in an interleaved fashion to consecutive time slots.

Channel Coding for Control Channels — GSM control channel messages are defined to be 184 bits long, and are encoded using a shortened binary cyclic fire code, followed by a half-rate convolutional coder.

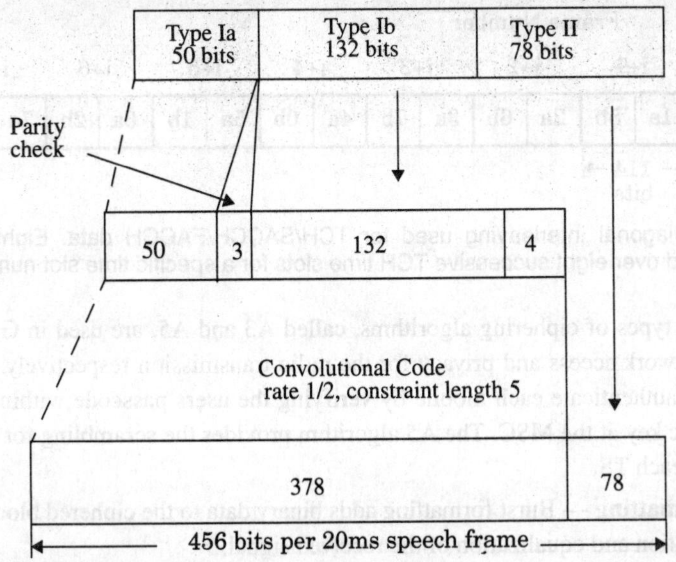

Figure 11.12 Error protection for speech signals in GSM.

The fire code uses the generator polynomial

$$G_5(x) = (x^{23}+1)(x^{17}+x^3+1) = x^{40}+x^{26}+x^{23}+x^{17}+x^3+1$$

which produces 184 message bits, followed by 40 parity bits. Four tail bits are added to clear the convolutional coder which follows, yielding a 228 bit data block. This block is applied to a half-rate $K = 5$ convolutional code (CC(2,1,5)) using the generator polynomials $G_0(x) = 1+x^3+x^4$ and $G_1(x) = 1+x+x^3+x^4$ (which are the same polynomials used to code TCH type Ia data bits). The resulting 456 encoded bits are interleaved onto eight consecutive frames in the same manner as TCH speech data.

Interleaving — In order to minimize the effect of sudden fades on the received data, the total of 456 encoded bits within each 20 ms speech frame or control message frame are broken into eight 57 bit sub-blocks. These eight sub-blocks which make up a single speech frame are spread over eight consecutive TCH time slots. (i.e., eight consecutive frames for a specific TS). If a burst is lost due to interference or fading, channel coding ensures that enough bits will still be received correctly to allow the error correction to work. Each TCH time slot carries two 57 bit blocks of data from two different 20 ms (456 bit) speech (or control) segments. Figure 11.13 illustrates exactly how the speech frames are diagonally interleaved within the time slots. Note that TS 0 contains 57 bits of data from the 0th sub-block of the nth speech coder frame (denoted as "a" in the figure) and 57 bits of data from the 4th sub-block of the (n - 1)st speech coder frame (denoted as "b" in the figure).

Ciphering — Ciphering modifies the contents of the eight interleaved blocks through the use of encryption techniques known only to the particular mobile station and base transceiver station. Security is further enhanced by the fact that the encryption algorithm is changed from

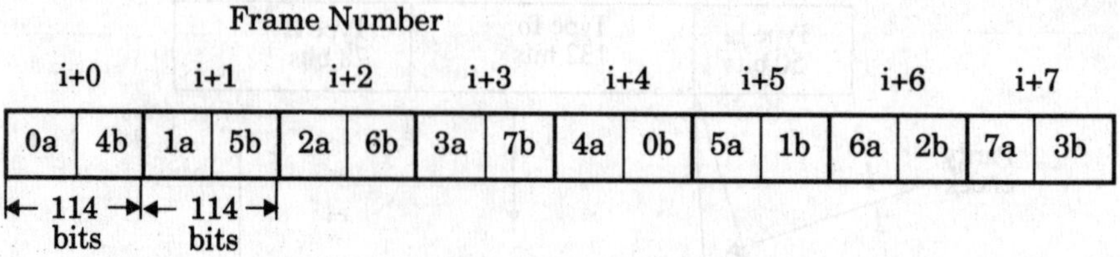

Figure 11.13 Diagonal interleaving used for TCH/SACCH/FACCH data. Eight speech sub-blocks are spread over eight successive TCH time slots for a specific time slot number.

call to call. Two types of ciphering algorithms, called A3 and A5, are used in GSM to prevent unauthorized network access and privacy for the radio transmission respectively. The A3 algorithm is used to authenticate each mobile by verifying the users passcode within the SIM with the cryptographic key at the MSC. The A5 algorithm provides the scrambling for the 114 coded data bits sent in each TS.

Burst Formatting — Burst formatting adds binary data to the ciphered blocks, in order to help synchronization and equalization of the received signal.

Modulation — The modulation scheme used by GSM is 0.3 GMSK, where 0.3 describes the 3 dB bandwidth of the Gaussian pulse shaping filter with relation to the bit rate (e.g., $BT = 0.3$). As described in Chapter 6, GMSK is a special type of digital FM modulation. Binary ones and zeros are represented in GSM by shifting the RF carrier by ±67.708 kHz. The channel data rate of GSM is 270.833333 kbps, which is exactly four times the RF frequency shift. This minimizes the bandwidth occupied by the modulation spectrum and hence improves channel capacity. The MSK modulated signal is passed through a Gaussian filter to smooth the rapid frequency transitions which would otherwise spread energy into adjacent channels.

Frequency Hopping — Under normal conditions, each data burst belonging to a particular physical channel is transmitted using the same carrier frequency. However, if users in a particular cell have severe multipath problems, the cell may be defined as a *hopping cell* by the network operator, in which case *slow frequency hopping* may be implemented to combat the multipath or interference effects in that cell. Frequency hopping is carried out on a frame-by-frame basis, thus hopping occurs at a maximum rate of 217.6 hops per second. As many as 64 different channels may be used before a hopping sequence is repeated. Frequency hopping is completely specified by the service provider.

Equalization — Equalization is performed at the receiver with the help of the training sequences transmitted in the midamble of every time slot. The type of equalizer for GSM is not specified and is left up to the manufacturer.

Demodulation — The portion of the transmitted forward channel signal which is of interest to a particular user is determined by the assigned TS and ARFCN. The appropriate TS is demodulated with the aid of synchronization data provided by the burst formatting. After demodulation, the binary information is deciphered, de-interleaved, channel decoded, and speech decoded.

11.4 CDMA Digital Cellular Standard (IS-95)

As discussed in Chapter 9, Code Division Multiple Access (CDMA) offers many advantages over TDMA and FDMA. A US digital cellular system based on CDMA which promised increased capacity [Gil91] was standardized as Interim Standard 95 (IS-95) by the US Telecommunications Industry Association (TIA) [TIA93]. Like IS-136, the IS-95 system was designed to be compatible with the existing US analog cellular system (AMPS) frequency band, hence mobiles and base stations can be economically produced for dual mode operation. Pilot production, CDMA/AMPS, dual mode phones were made available by Qualcomm in 1994, and as of 2001, there are over 80 million CDMA subscribers worldwide.

IS-95 allows each user within a cell to use the same radio channel, and users in adjacent cells also use the same radio channel, since this is a direct sequence spread spectrum CDMA system. CDMA completely eliminates the need for frequency planning within a market. To facilitate graceful transition from AMPS to CDMA, each IS-95 channel occupies 1.25 MHz of spectrum on each one-way link, or 10% of the available cellular spectrum for a US cellular provider (recall, the US cellular system is allocated 25 MHz and each service provider receives half the spectrum or 12.5 MHz). In practice, AMPS carriers must provide a 270 kHz guard band (typically 9 AMPS channels) on each side of the spectrum dedicated for IS-95. IS-95 is fully compatible with the IS-41 networking standard described in Chapter 10.

Unlike other cellular standards, the user data rate (but not the channel chip rate) changes in real-time, depending on the voice activity and requirements in the network. Also, IS-95 uses a different modulation and spreading technique for the forward and reverse links. On the forward link, the base station simultaneously transmits the user data for all mobiles in the cell by using a different spreading sequence for each mobile. A pilot code is also transmitted simultaneously and at a higher power level, thereby allowing all mobiles to use coherent carrier detection while estimating the channel conditions. On the reverse link, all mobiles respond in an asynchronous fashion and have ideally a constant signal level due to power control applied by the base station.

The speech coder used in the IS-95 system is the Qualcomm 9600 bps Code Excited Linear Predictive (QCELP) coder. The original implementation of this vocoder detects voice activity, and reduces the data rate to 1200 bps during silent periods. Intermediate user data rates of 2400, 4800, and 9600 bps are also used for special purposes. As discussed in Chapter 8 and Section 11.4.4, a 14,400 bps coder which uses 13.4 kbps of speech data (QCELP13) was introduced by Qualcomm in 1995.

11.4.1 Frequency and Channel Specifications

IS-95 is specified for reverse link operation in the 824–849 MHz band and 869–894 MHz for the forward link. A PCS version of IS-95 has also been designed for international use in the 1800–2000 MHz bands. A forward and reverse channel pair is separated by 45 MHz for cellular band operation. Many users share a common channel for transmission. The maximum user data rate is 9.6 kb/s. User data in IS-95 is spread to a channel chip rate of 1.2288 Mchip/s (a total spreading factor of 128) using a combination of techniques. The spreading process is different for the forward and reverse links in the original CDMA specification. On the forward link, the user data stream is encoded using a rate 1/2 convolutional code, interleaved, and spread by one of sixty-four orthogonal spreading sequences (Walsh functions). Each mobile in a given cell is assigned a different spreading sequence, providing perfect separation among the signals from different users, at least for the case where multipath does not exist. To reduce interference between mobiles that use the same spreading sequence in different cells, and to provide the desired wide-band spectral characteristics (not all of the Walsh functions yield a wideband power spectrum), all signals in a particular cell are scrambled using a pseudorandom sequence of length 2^{15} chips.

Orthogonality among all forward channel users within a cell is preserved because their signals are scrambled synchronously. A pilot channel (code) is provided on the forward link so that each subscriber within the cell can determine and react to the channel characteristics while employing coherent detection. The pilot channel is transmitted at higher power than the user channels.

On the reverse link, a different spreading strategy is used since each received signal arrives at the base station via a different propagation path. The reverse channel user data stream is first convolutionally encoded with a rate 1/3 code. After interleaving, each block of six encoded symbols is mapped to one of the 64 orthogonal Walsh functions, providing sixty-four-ary orthogonal signaling. A final fourfold spreading, giving a rate of 1.2288 Mchip/s, is achieved by spreading the resulting 307.2 kchip/s stream by user-specific and base-station specific codes having periods of $2^{42} - 1$ chips and 2^{15} chips, respectively. The rate 1/3 coding and the mapping onto Walsh functions result in a greater tolerance for interference than would be realized from traditional repetition spreading codes. This added robustness is important on the reverse link, due to the noncoherent detection and the in-cell interference received at the base station.

Another essential element of the reverse link is tight control of each subscriber's transmitter power, to avoid the "near–far" problem that arises from varying received powers of the users. A combination of open-loop and fast, closed-loop power control is used to adjust the transmit power of each in-cell subscriber so that the base station receives each user with the same received power. The commands for the closed-loop power control are sent at a rate of 800 b/s, and these bits are stolen from the speech frames. Without fast power control, the rapid power changes due to fading would degrade the performance of all users in the system.

At both the base station and the subscriber, RAKE receivers are used to resolve and combine multipath components, thereby reducing the degree of fading. As described in Chapter 7, a RAKE receiver exploits the multipath time delays in a channel and combines the delayed replicas of the transmitted signal in order to improve link quality. In IS-95, a three finger RAKE is used at the base station. The IS-95 architecture also provides base station diversity during "soft" handoffs, whereby a mobile making the transition between cells maintains links with both base stations during the transition. The mobile receiver combines the signals from the two base stations in the same manner as it would combine signals associated with different multipath components.

Table 11.4 IS-95 Forward Traffic Channel Modulation Parameters Summary (does not reflect new 13.4 kbps coder)

Parameter	Data Rate (bps)			
User data rate	**9600**	**4800**	**2400**	**1200**
Coding Rate	1/2	1/2	1/2	1/2
User Data Repetition Period	1	2	4	8
Baseband Coded Data Rate	19,200	19,200	19,200	19,200
PN Chips/Coded Data Bit	64	64	64	64
PN Chip Rate (Mcps)	1.2288	1.2288	1.2288	1.2288
PN Chips/Bit	128	256	512	1024

11.4.2 Forward CDMA Channel

The forward CDMA channel consists of a pilot channel, a synchronization channel, up to seven paging channels, and up to sixty-three forward traffic channels [Li93]. The pilot channel allows a mobile station to acquire timing for the Forward CDMA channel, provides a phase reference for coherent demodulation, and provides each mobile with a means for signal strength comparisons between base stations for determining when to handoff. The synchronization channel broadcasts synchronization messages to the mobile stations and operates at 1200 bps. The paging channel is used to send control information and paging messages from the base station to the mobiles and operates at 9600, 4800, and 2400 bps. The forward traffic channel (FTC) supports variable user data rates at 9600, 4800, 2400, or 1200 bps.

The forward traffic channel modulation process is described in Figure 11.14 [EIA90]. Data on the forward traffic channel is grouped into 20 ms frames. The user data is first convolutionally coded and then formatted and interleaved to adjust for the actual user data rate, which may vary. Then the signal is spread with a Walsh code and a long PN sequence at a rate of 1.2288 Mcps. Table 11.4 lists the coding and repetition parameters for the forward traffic channel.

The speech data rate applied to the transmitter is variable over the range of 1200 bps to 9600 bps.

11.4.2.1 Convolutional Encoder and Repetition Circuit

Speech coded voice or user data are encoded using a half-rate convolutional encoder with constraint length 9. The encoding process is described by generator vectors G_0 and G_1 which are 753 (octal) and 561 (octal), respectively.

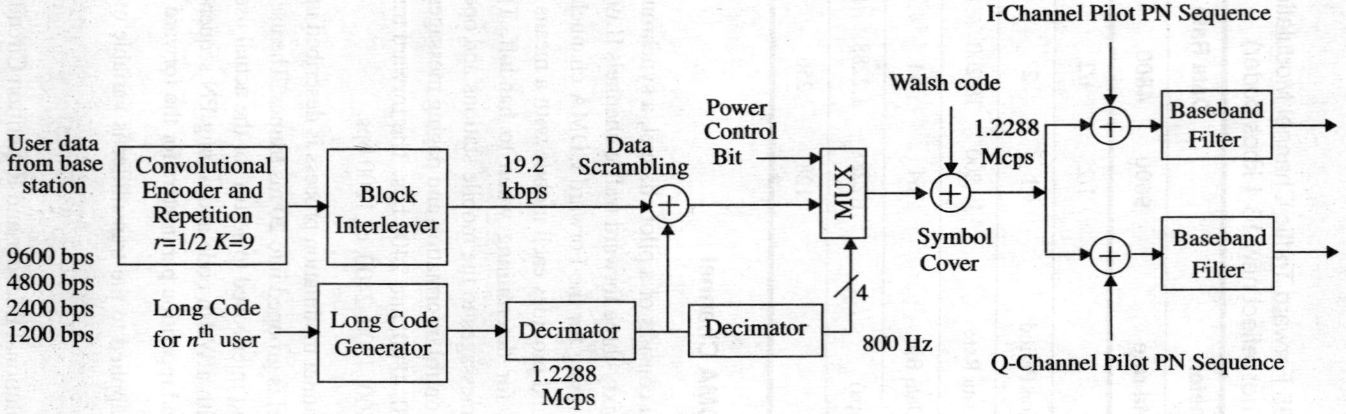

Figure 11.14 Forward CDMA channel modulation process.

The speech encoder exploits pauses and gaps in speech, and reduces its output from 9600 bps to 1200 bps during silent periods. In order to keep a constant baseband symbol rate of 19.2 kbps, whenever the user rate is less than 9600 bps, each symbol from the convolution encoder is repeated before block interleaving. If the information rate is 4800 bps, each code symbol is repeated one time. If the information rate is 2400 bps or 1200 bps, each code symbol is repeated three or seven times, respectively. The repetition results in a constant coded rate of 19,200 symbols per second for all possible information data rates.

11.4.2.2 Block Interleaver

After convolution coding and repetition, symbols are sent to a 20 ms block interleaver, which is a 24 by 16 array.

11.4.2.3 Long PN Sequence

In the forward channel, direct sequence is used for data scrambling. The long PN sequence is uniquely assigned to each user is a periodic long code with period 2^{42}-1 chips. (This corresponds to repeating approximately once per century.) The long code is specified by the following characteristic polynomial [TIA93]

$$p(x) = x^{42} + x^{35} + x^{33} + x^{31} + x^{27} + x^{26} + x^{25} + x^{22} + x^{21} + x^{19} + x^{18} + x^{17} + x^{16} + x^{10} + x^{7} + x^{6} + x^{5} + x^{3} + x^{2} + x^{1} + 1$$

Each PN chip of the long code is generated by the modulo-2 inner product of a 42 bit mask and the 42 bit state vector of the sequence generator. The initial state of the generator is defined to be when the output of the generator becomes '1' after following 41 consecutive '0' outputs, with the binary mask consisting of '1' in the most significant bit (MSB) followed by 41 '0's.

Two types of masks are used in the long code generator: a public mask for the mobile station's electronic serial number (ESN) and a private mask for the mobile station identification number (MIN). All CDMA calls are initiated using the public mask. Transition to the private mask is carried out after authentication is performed. The public long code is specified as follows: M_{41} through M_{32} is set to 1100011000, and M_{31} through M_0 is set to a permutation of the mobile station's ESN bits. The permutation is specified as follows [TIA93]:

ESN = $(E_{31}, E_{30}, E_{29}, E_{28}, E_{27}, \ldots\ldots\ldots E_3, E_2, E_1, E_0)$

Permuted ESN = $(E_0, E_{31}, E_{22}, E_{13}, E_4, E_{26}, E_{17}, E_8, E_{30}, E_{21}, E_{12}, E_3,$
$E_{25}, E_{16}, E_7, E_{29}, E_{20}, E_{11}, E_2, E_{24}, E_{15}, E_6, E_{28}, E_{19},$
$E_{10}, E_1, E_{23}, E_{14}, E_5, E_{27}, E_{18}, E_9)$

The private long code mask is specified so M_{41} and M_{40} are set to '01', and M_{39} through M_0 are set by a private procedure. Figure 11.15 illustrates the long code mask format.

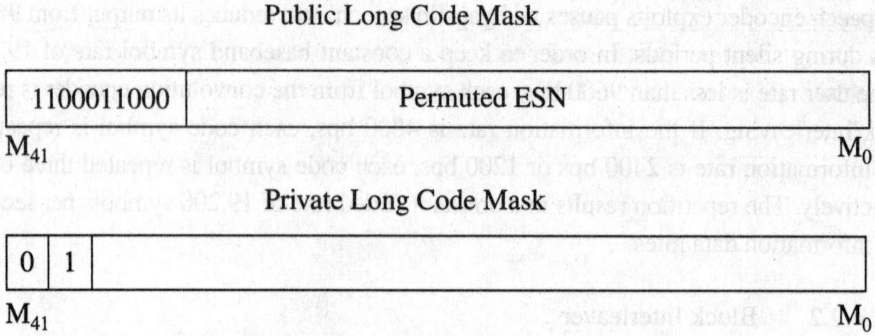

Figure 11.15 Long code mask format for IS-95.

11.4.2.4 Data Scrambler

Data scrambling is performed after the block interleaver. The 1.2288 MHz PN sequence is applied to a decimator, which keeps only the first chip out of every sixty-four consecutive PN chips. The symbol rate from the decimator is 19.2 ksps. The data scrambling is performed by modulo-2 addition of the interleaver output with the decimator output symbol as shown in Figure 11.14.

11.4.2.5 Power Control Subchannel

To minimize the average BER for each user, IS-95 strives to force each user to provide the same power level at the base station receiver. The base station reverse traffic channel receiver estimates and responds to the signal strength (actually, the signal strength and the interference) for a particular mobile station. Since both the signal and interference are continually varying, power control updates are sent by the base station every 1.25 ms. Power control commands are sent to each subscriber unit on the forward control subchannel which instruct the mobile to raise or lower its transmitted power in 1 dB steps. If the received signal is low, a '0' is transmitted over the power control subchannel, thereby instructing the mobile station to increase its mean output power level. If the mobile's power is high, a '1' is transmitted to indicate that the mobile station should decrease its power level. The power control bit corresponds to two modulation symbols on the forward traffic channel. Power control bits are inserted after data scrambling as shown in Figure 11.16.

Power control bits are transmitted by using puncturing techniques [TIA93]. During a 1.25 ms period, twenty-four data symbols are transmitted, and IS-95 specifies sixteen possible power control group positions for the power control bit. Each position corresponds to one of the first sixteen modulation symbols. Twenty-four bits from the long code decimator are used for data scrambling in a period of 1.25 ms. Only the last 4 bits of the 24 bits are used to determine the position of the power control bit. In the example shown in Figure 11.16, the last 4 bits (23, 22, 21, and 20) are '1011' (11 decimal), and the power control bit consequently starts in position eleven.

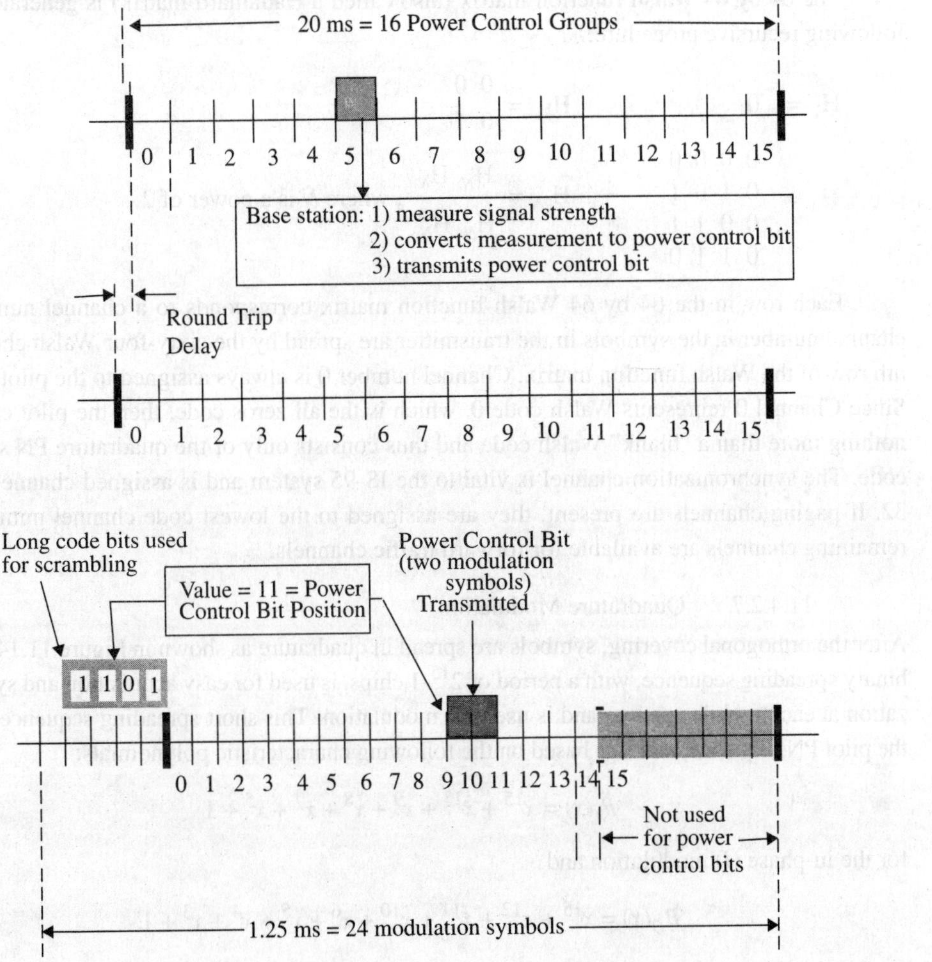

Figure 11.16 Randomization of power control bit positions in a IS-95 forward traffic channel.

11.4.2.6 Orthogonal Covering

Orthogonal covering is performed following the data scrambling on the forward link. Each traffic channel transmitted on the forward CDMA channel is spread with a Walsh function at a fixed chip rate of 1.2288 Mcps. The Walsh functions comprise of sixty-four binary sequences, each of length 64, which are completely orthogonal to each other and provide orthogonal channelization for all users on the forward link. A user that is spread using Walsh function n is assigned channel number n (n = 0 to 63). The Walsh sequence repeats every 52.083 μs, which is equal to one coded data symbol. In other words, each data symbol is spread by 64 Walsh chips.

The 64 by 64 Walsh function matrix (also called a Hadamard matrix) is generated by the following recursive procedure:

$$H_1 = 0 \qquad H_2 = \begin{matrix} 0 & 0 \\ 0 & 1 \end{matrix}$$

$$H_4 = \begin{matrix} 0 & 0 & 0 & 0 \\ 0 & 1 & 0 & 1 \\ 0 & 0 & 1 & 1 \\ 0 & 1 & 1 & 0 \end{matrix} \qquad H_{2N} = \begin{matrix} H_N & H_N \\ H_N & \overline{H_N} \end{matrix}, \text{ where } N \text{ is a power of 2.}$$

Each row in the 64 by 64 Walsh function matrix corresponds to a channel number. For channel number n, the symbols in the transmitter are spread by the sixty-four Walsh chips in the nth row of the Walsh function matrix. Channel number 0 is always assigned to the pilot channel. Since Channel 0 represents Walsh code 0, which is the all zeros code, then the pilot channel is nothing more than a "blank" Walsh code and thus consists only of the quadrature PN spreading code. The synchronization channel is vital to the IS-95 system and is assigned channel number 32. If paging channels are present, they are assigned to the lowest code channel numbers. All remaining channels are available for forward traffic channels.

11.4.2.7 Quadrature Modulation

After the orthogonal covering, symbols are spread in quadrature as shown in Figure 11.14. A short binary spreading sequence, with a period of 2^{15}-1 chips, is used for easy acquisition and synchronization at each mobile receiver and is used for modulation. This short spreading sequence is called the pilot PN sequence, and it is based on the following characteristic polynomials:

$$P_I(x) = x^{15} + x^{13} + x^9 + x^8 + x^7 + x^5 + 1$$

for the in-phase (I) modulation and

$$P_Q(x) = x^{15} + x^{12} + x^{11} + x^{10} + x^6 + x^5 + x^4 + x^3 + 1$$

for the quadrature (Q) modulation.

Based on the characteristic polynomials, the pilot PN sequences $i(n)$ and $q(n)$ are generated by the following linear recursions:

$$i(n) = i(n\text{-}15) \oplus i(n\text{-}10) \oplus i(n\text{-}8) \oplus i(n\text{-}7) \oplus i(n\text{-}6) \oplus i(n\text{-}2)$$

$$q(n) = q(n\text{-}15) \oplus q(n\text{-}13) \oplus q(n\text{-}11) \oplus q(n\text{-}10) \oplus q(n\text{-}9) \oplus q(n\text{-}5) \oplus q(n\text{-}4) \oplus q(n\text{-}3)$$

where the in-phase and quadrature PN codes are used respectively, and $\oplus$ represents modulo-2 addition. A '0' is inserted in each sequence after the contiguous succession of fourteen '0's to generate pilot PN sequences of length 2^{15}. The initial state of both I and Q pilot PN sequences is defined as the state in which the output of the pilot PN sequence generator is the first '1' output

Table 11.5 Forward CDMA Channel I and Q Mapping

I	Q	Phase
0	0	$\pi/4$
1	0	$3\pi/4$
1	1	$-3\pi/4$
0	1	$-\pi/4$

following fifteen consecutive '0' outputs. The chip rates for the pilot PN sequences are 1.2288 Mcps. The binary I and Q outputs of the quadrature spreading are mapped into phase according to Table 11.5.

11.4.3 Reverse CDMA Channel

The reverse traffic channel modulation process is shown in Figure 11.17. User data on the reverse channel are grouped into 20 ms frames. All data transmitted on the reverse channel are convolutionally encoded, block interleaved, modulated by a 64-ary orthogonal modulation, and spread prior to transmission. Table 11.6 shows the modulation parameters for the reverse traffic channel [EIA92]. The speech or user data rate in the reverse channel may be sent at 9600, 4800, 2400, or 1200 bps.

Table 11.6 Reverse Traffic Channel Modulation Parameters Summary (does not reflect recent 13.4 kbps coder)

Parameter	Data Rate (bps)			
User data rate	**9600**	**4800**	**2400**	**1200**
Code Rate	1/3	1/3	1/3	1/3
TX Duty Cycle (%)	100.0	50.0	25.0	12.5
Coded Data Rate (sps)	28,800	28,800	28,800	28,800
Bits per Walsh Symbol	6	6	6	6
Walsh Symbol Rate	4800	4800	4800	4800
Walsh Chip Rate (kcps)	307.2	307.2	307.2	307.2
Walsh Symbol Duration (μs)	208.33	208.33	208.33	208.33
PN Chips/Code Symbol	42.67	42.67	42.67	42.67
PN Chips/Walsh Symbol	256	256	256	256
PN Chips/Walsh Chip	4	4	4	4
PN Chip Rate (Mcps)	1.2288	1.2288	1.2288	1.2288

The reverse CDMA channels are made up of access channels (ACs) and reverse traffic channels (RTCs). Both share the same frequency assignment, and each Traffic/Access channel is identified by a distinct user long code. The access channel is used by the mobile to initiate communication with the base station and to respond to paging channel messages. The access channel is a random access channel with each channel user uniquely identified by their long codes. The Reverse CDMA channel may contain a maximum of 32 ACs per supported paging channel. While the RTC operates on a variable data rate, the AC works at a fixed data rate of 4800 bps.

11.4.3.1 Convolutional Encoder and Symbol Repetition

The convolutional coder used in the reverse traffic channel is rate 1/3 and constraint length 9. The three generator vectors g_0, g_1, and g_2 are 557 (octal), 663 (octal), and 771 (octal), respectively.

Coded bits after the convolutional encoder are repeated before interleaving when the data rate is less than 9600 bps. This is identical to the method used on the forward channel. After repetition, the symbol rate out of the coder is fixed at 28,800 bps.

11.4.3.2 Block Interleaver

Block interleaving is performed following convolutional encoding and repetition. The block interleaver spans 20 ms, and is an array with 32 rows and 18 columns. Code symbols are written into the matrix by columns and read out by rows.

11.4.3.3 Orthogonal Modulation

A 64-ary orthogonal modulation is used for the reverse CDMA channel. One of sixty-four possible Walsh functions is transmitted for each group of six coded bits. Within a Walsh function, sixty-four Walsh chips are transmitted. The particular Walsh function is selected according to the following formula:

$$\text{Walsh function number} = c_0 + 2c_1 + 4c_2 + 8c_3 + 16c_4 + 32c_5,$$

where c_5 represents the last coded bit and c_0 represents the first coded bit of each group of six coded symbols that are used to select a Walsh function. Walsh chips are transmitted at a rate of 307.2 kcps as shown in Equation (11.1)

$$28.8 \text{ kbps} \times (64 \text{ Walsh chips})/(6 \text{ coded bits}) = 307.2 \text{ kbps} \tag{11.1}$$

Note that Walsh functions are used for different purposes on the forward and reverse channels. On the forward channel, Walsh functions are used for spreading to denote a particular user channel, while on the reverse channel, Walsh functions are used for data modulation.

11.4.3.4 Variable Data Rate Transmission

Variable rate data are sent on the reverse CDMA channel. Code symbol repetition introduces redundancy when the data rate is less than 9600 bps. A data randomizer is used to transmit certain bits while turning the transmitter off at other times. When the data rate is 9600 bps, all interleaver output bits are transmitted. When the data rate is 4800 bps, half of the interleaver output bits are transmitted, and the mobile unit does not transmit 50% of the time, and so forth (see Table 11.6). Figure 11.18 illustrates the process under different data rates [EIA92]. Data in each

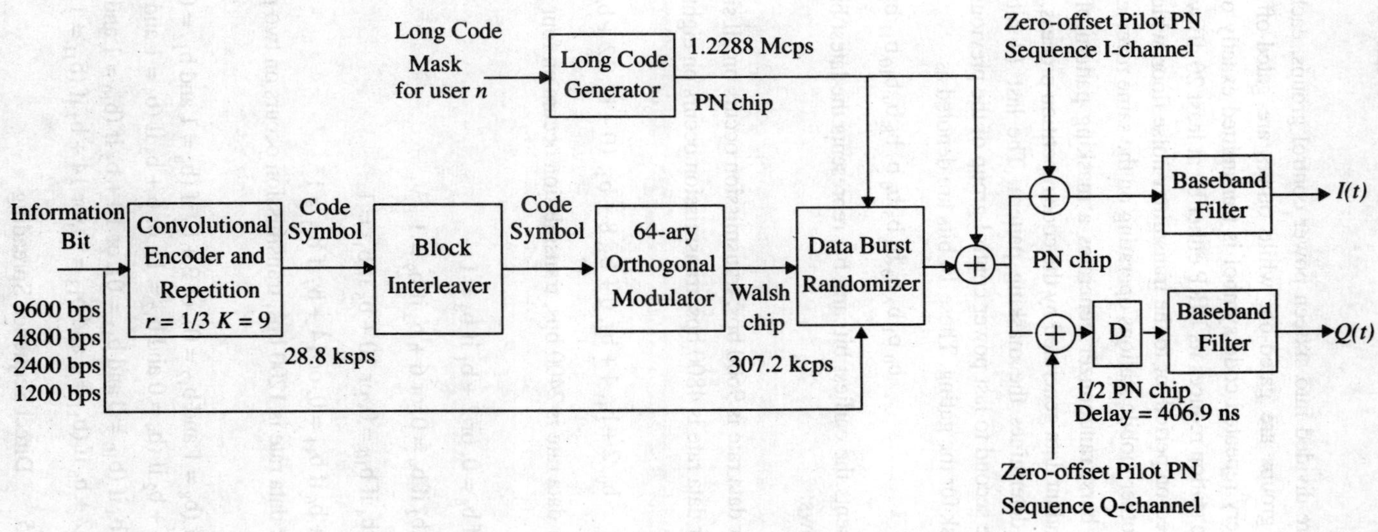

Figure 11.17 Reverse IS-95 channel modulation process for a single user.

20 ms frame are divided into sixteen power control groups, each with period 1.25 ms. Some power control groups are gated-on, while others are gated-off. The data burst randomizer ensures that every repeated code symbol is transmitted exactly once. During the gate-off process, the mobile station reduces its EIRP either by at least 20 dB with respect to the power of the most recent gated-on period, or to the transmitter noise floor, whichever is greater. This reduces interference to other mobile stations operating on the same reverse CDMA channel.

The data burst randomizer generates a masking pattern of '0's and '1's that randomly masks the redundant data generated by the code repetition process. A block of 14 bits taken from the long code determines the masking pattern. The last 14 bits of the long code used for spreading in the second to last power control group of the previous frame are used to determine the random mask for the gating. These 14 bits are denoted as

$$b_0\ b_1\ b_2\ b_3\ b_4\ b_5\ b_6\ b_7\ b_8\ b_9\ b_{10}\ b_{11}\ b_{12}\ b_{13}$$

where b_0 represents the earliest bit, and b_{13} represents the latest bit. The data randomizer algorithm is as follows:

- If the user data rate is 9600 bps, transmission occurs on all sixteen power control groups.
- If the user data rate is 4800 bps, transmission occurs on eight power control groups given as

$$b_0,\ 2 + b_1,\ 4 + b_2,\ 6 + b_3,\ 8 + b_4,\ 10 + b_5,\ 12 + b_6,\ 14 + b_7$$

- If the user data rate is 2400 bps, transmission occurs on four power control groups numbered.

  1) b_0 if $b_8 = 0$, or $2 + b_1$ if $b_8 = 1$
  2) $4 + b_2$ if $b_9 = 0$, or $6 + b_3$ if $b_9 = 1$
  3) $8 + b_4$ if $b_{10} = 0$, or $10 + b_5$ if $b_{10} = 1$
  4) $12 + b_6$ if $b_{11} = 0$, or $14 + b_7$ if $b_{11} = 1$

- If the user data rate is 1200 bps, transmission occurs on two power control groups numbered:

  1) b_0 if ($b_8 = 1$ and $b_{12} = 0$), or $2 + b_1$ if ($b_8 = 1$ and $b_{12} = 0$), or $4 + b_2$ if ($b_9 = 0$ and $b_{12} = 1$), or $6 + b_3$ if ($b_9 = 1$ and $b_{12} = 1$);
  2) $8 + b_4$ if ($b_{10} = 0$ and $b_{13} = 0$), or $10 + b_5$ if ($b_{10} = 1$ and $b_{13} = 0$), or $12 + b_6$ if ($b_{11} = 0$ and $b_{13} = 1$), or $14 + b_7$ if ($b_{11} = 1$ and $b_{13} = 1$).

11.4.3.5 Direct Sequence Spreading

The reverse traffic channel is spread by the long code PN sequence which operates at a rate of 1.2288 Mcps. The long code is generated as described in Section 11.4.2.3 for the forward channel. Each Walsh chip is spread by four long code PN chips.

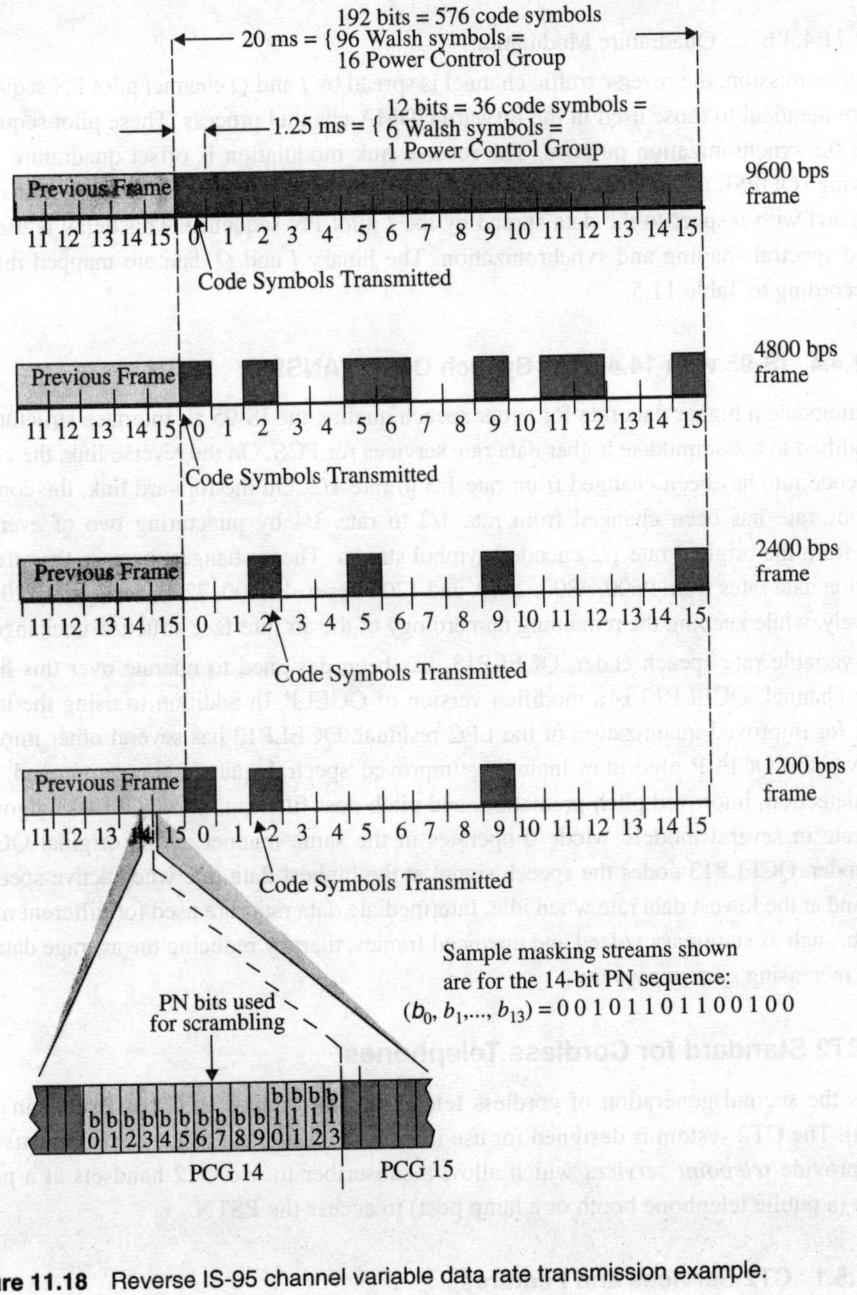

Figure 11.18 Reverse IS-95 channel variable data rate transmission example.

11.4.3.6 Quadrature Modulation

Prior to transmission, the reverse traffic channel is spread by *I* and *Q* channel pilot PN sequences which are identical to those used in the forward CDMA channel process. These pilot sequences are used for synchronization purpose. The reverse link modulation is offset quadrature phase shift keying (OQPSK). The data spread by the *Q* pilot PN sequence is delayed by half a chip (406.901 ns) with respect to the data spread by the *I* pilot PN sequence. This delay is used for improved spectral shaping and synchronization. The binary *I* and *Q* data are mapped into the phase according to Table 11.5.

11.4.4 IS-95 with 14.4 kbps Speech Coder [ANS95]

To accommodate a higher data rate for better speech quality, the IS-95 air interface structure has been modified to accommodate higher data rate services for PCS. On the reverse link, the convolutional code rate has been changed from rate 1/3 to rate 1/2. On the forward link, the convolutional code rate has been changed from rate 1/2 to rate 3/4 by puncturing two of every six symbols from the original rate 1/2 encoded symbol stream. These changes increase the effective information data rates from 9600, 4800, 2400, and 1200 bps to 14,400, 7200, 3600, and 1800 bps respectively, while keeping the remaining numerology of the air interface structure unchanged.

A variable rate speech coder, QCELP13, has been designed to operate over this higher data rate channel. QCELP13 is a modified version of QCELP. In addition to using the higher data rate for improved quantization of the LPC residual, QCELP13 has several other improvements over the QCELP algorithm including improved spectral quantization, improved voice activity detection, improved pitch prediction, and pitch post-filtering. The QCELP13 algorithm can operate in several models. Mode 0 operates in the same manner as the original QCELP speech coder. QCELP13 codes the speech signal at the highest data rate when active speech is present and at the lowest data rate when idle. Intermediate data rates are used for different modes of speech, such as stationary voiced and unvoiced frames, thereby reducing the average data rate and thus increasing system capacity.

11.5 CT2 Standard for Cordless Telephones

CT2 was the second generation of cordless telephones introduced in Great Britain in 1989 [Mor89a]. The CT2 system is designed for use in both domestic and office environments. It is used to provide *telepoint services* which allow a subscriber to use CT2 handsets at a public telepoint (a public telephone booth or a lamp post) to access the PSTN.

11.5.1 CT2 Services and Features

CT2 is a digital version of the first generation, analog, cordless telephones. When compared with analog cordless phones, CT2 offers good speech quality, is more resistant to interference, noise, and fading, and like other personal telephones, uses a compact handset with built-in antenna. The digital transmission provides better security. Calls may be made only after entering a PIN, thereby rendering handsets useless to unauthorized users. The battery in a CT2 subscriber unit typically has a talk-time of three hours and a standby-time of 40 hours. The CT2 system uses dynamic channel allocation which minimizes system planning and organization within a crowded office or urban environment.

11.5.2 The CT2 Standard

The CT2 standard defines how the Cordless Fixed Part (CFP) and the Cordless Portable Part (CPP) communicate through a radio link. The CFP corresponds to a base station and the CPP corresponds to a subscriber unit. The frequencies allocated to CT2 in Europe and Hong Kong are in the 864.10 MHz to 868.10 MHz band. Within this frequency range, forty TDD channels have been assigned, each with 100 kHz bandwidth.

The CT2 standard defines three air interface signaling layers and the speech coding techniques. Layer 1 defines the TDD technique, data multiplexing and link initiation, and handshaking. Layer 2 defines data acknowledgment and error detection as well as link maintenance. Layer 3 defines the protocols used to connect CT2 to the PSTN. Table 11.7 summarizes the CT2 air interface specification.

Table 11.7 CT2 Radio Specifications Summary

Parameter	Specification
Frequency	864.15–868.05 MHz
Multiple Access	FDMA
Duplexing	TDD
Number of Channels	40
Channel Spacing	100 kHz
Number of Channels/Carrier	1
Modulation Type	2 level GMSK ($BT = 0.3$)
Peak Frequency Deviation Range	14.4–25.2 kHz
Channel Data Rate	72 Kbps
Spectral Efficiency	50 Erlangs/km^2/MHz
Bandwidth Efficiency	0.72 bps/Hz
Speech Coding	32 kbps ADPCM (G.721)
Control Channel Rate (net)	1000/2000 bps
Max. Effective Radiated Power	10 mW
Power Control	Yes
Dynamic Channel Allocation	Yes
Receiver Sensitivity	40 dB V/m or better @ BER of 0.001
Frame Duration	2 ms
Channel Coding	(63,48) cyclic block code

Modulation — All channels use Gaussian filtered binary frequency-shift keying (GFSK) with bit transitions constrained to be phase continuous. The most commonly used filter has a bandwidth-bit period product $BT = 0.3$, and the peak frequency deviation is a maximum of 25.2 kHz under all possible data patterns. The channel transmission rate is 72 kbps.

Speech Coding — Speech waveforms are coded using ADPCM with a bit rate of 32 kbps [Det89]. The algorithm used is compliant with CCITT standard G.721.

Duplexing — Two-way full duplex conversation is achieved using time division duplex (TDD). A CT2 frame has a 2 ms duration and is divided equally between the forward and reverse link. The 32 kbps digitized speech is transmitted at a 64 kbps rate. Each 2 ms of user speech is transmitted in a 1 ms, with the 1ms gap used for the speech return path. This eliminates the need for paired frequencies or a duplex filter in the subscriber unit. Since each CT2 channel supports 72 kbps of data, the remaining 8 kbps is used for control data (the D subchannel) and burst synchronization (the SYN subchannel). Depending on CT2 situations, the channel bandwidth may be allocated to one or more of the subchannels. The different possible subchannel combinations are called *multiplexes*, and three different multiplexes may be used in CT2 (additional details may be found in [Ste90], [Pad95]).

11.6 Digital European Cordless Telephone (DECT)

The Digital European Cordless Telephone (DECT) is a universal cordless telephone standard developed by the European Telecommunications Standards Institute (ETSI) [Och89], [Mul91]. It is the first pan-European standard for cordless telephones and was finalized in July 1992.

11.6.1 Features and Characteristics

DECT provides a cordless communications framework for high traffic density, short range telecommunications, and covers a broad range of applications and environments. DECT offers excellent quality and services for voice and data applications [Owe91]. The main function of DECT is to provide local mobility to portable users in an in-building Private Branch Exchange (PBX). The DECT standard supports telepoint services, as well. DECT is configured around an open standard (OSI) which makes it possible to interconnect wide area fixed or mobile networks, such as ISDN or GSM, to a portable subscriber population. DECT provides low power radio access between portable parts and fixed base stations at ranges of up to a few hundred meters.

11.6.2 DECT Architecture

The DECT system is based on OSI (Open System Interconnection) principles in a manner similar to ISDN. A control plane (C-plane) and a user plane (U-plane) use the services provided by the lower layers (i.e., the physical layer and the medium access control (MAC) layer). DECT is able to page up to 6000 subscribers without the need to know in which cell they reside (no registration required), and unlike other cellular standards such as AMPS or GSM, DECT is not a total system concept. It is designed for radio local loop or metropolitan area access, but may be used in conjunction with wide area wireless systems such as GSM [Mul91]. DECT uses dynamic channel allocation based on signals received by the portable user and is specifically designed to only support handoffs at pedestrian speeds.

Physical Layer — DECT uses a FDMA/TDMA/TDD radio transmission method. Within a TDMA time slot, a dynamic selection of one out of ten carrier frequencies is used. The physical layer specification requires that the channels have a bandwidth which is 1.5 times the channel data rate of 1152 kbps, resulting in a channel bandwidth of 1.728 MHz. DECT has twenty-four time slots per frame, and twelve slots are used for communications from the fixed part to the portable (base to handset) and twelve time slots for portable to fixed (handset to base) communications. These twenty-four time slots make up a DECT frame which has a 10 ms duration. In each time slot, 480 bits are allocated for 32 synchronization bits, 388 data bits, and 60 bits of guard time. The DECT TDMA time slot and frame structures are shown in Figure 11.19.

Medium Access Control (MAC) Layer — The MAC layer consists of a paging channel and a control channel for the transfer of signaling information to the C-plane. The U-plane is served with channels for the transfer of user information (for ISDN services and frame-relay or frame-switching services). The normal bit rate of the user information channel is 32 kbps. DECT, however, also supports other bit rates. For example, 64 kbps and other multiples of 32 kbps for ISDN and LAN-type applications. The MAC layer also supports handover of calls and a broadcast "beacon" service that enables all idle portable units to find the best fixed radio port to lock onto.

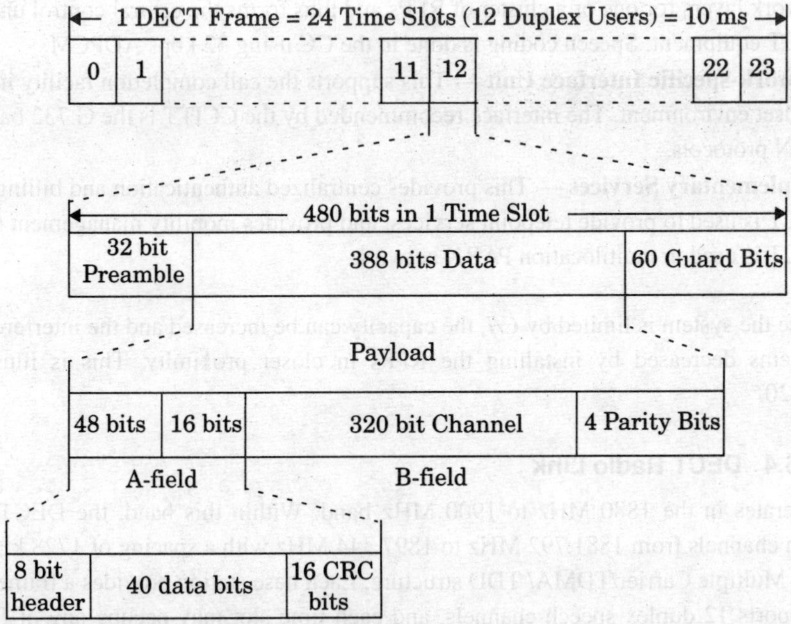

Figure 11.19 DECT TDMA frame structure.

Data Link Control (DLC) Layer — The DLC layer is responsible for providing reliable data links to the network layer and divides up the logical and physical channels into time slots for each user. The DLC provides formatting and error protection/correction for each time slot.

Network Layer — The network layer is the main signaling layer of DECT and is based on ISDN (layer 3) and GSM protocols. The DECT network layer provides call control and circuit-switched services selected from one of the DLC services, as well as connection-oriented message services and mobility management.

11.6.3 DECT Functional Concept

The DECT subsystem is a microcellular or picocellular cordless telephone system that may be integrated with or connected to a Private Automatic Branch Exchange (PABX) or to the Public Switched Telephone Network (PSTN). A DECT system always consists of the following five functional entities as shown in Figure 11.20:

- **Portable Handset (PH)** — This is the mobile handset or the terminal. In addition, cordless terminal adapters (CTAs) may be used to provide fax or video communications.
- **Radio Fixed Part (RFP)** — This supports the physical layer of the DECT common air interface. Every RFP covers one cell in the microcellular system. The radio transmission between RFP and the portable unit uses multi carrier TDMA. A full duplex operation is achieved using time division duplexing (TDD).
- **Cordless Controller (CC or Cluster Controller)** — This handles the MAC, DLC, and network layers for one or a cluster of RFPs and thus forms the central control unit for the DECT equipment. Speech coding is done in the CC using 32 kbps ADPCM.
- **Network-specific Interface Unit** — This supports the call completion facility in a multi-handset environment. The interface recommended by the CCITT is the G.732 based on ISDN protocols.
- **Supplementary Services** — This provides centralized authentication and billing when DECT is used to provide telepoint services, and provides mobility management when DECT is used in multilocation PABX network.

Since the system is limited by *C/I*, the capacity can be increased and the interference from other systems decreased by installing the RFPs in closer proximity. This is illustrated in Figure 11.20.

11.6.4 DECT Radio Link

DECT operates in the 1880 MHz to 1900 MHz band. Within this band, the DECT standard defines ten channels from 1881.792 MHz to 1897.344 MHz with a spacing of 1728 kHz. DECT supports a Multiple Carrier/TDMA/ TDD structure. Each base station provides a frame structure which supports 12 duplex speech channels, and each time slot may occupy any of the DECT channels. Thus, DECT base stations support FHMA on top of the TDMA/TDD structure. If the

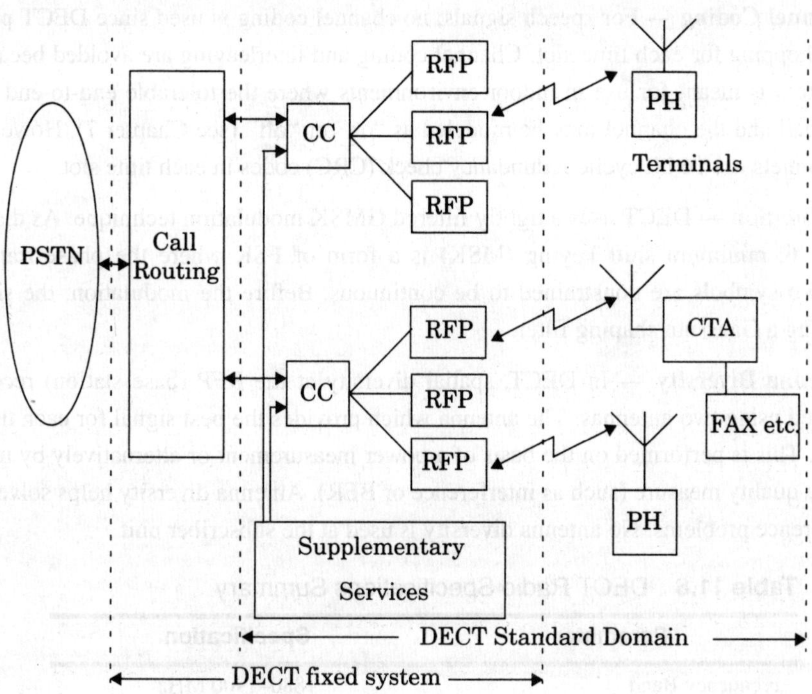

Figure 11.20 DECT functional concept.

frequency hopping option is disabled for each DECT base station, a total of 120 channels within the DECT spectrum are provided before frequency reuse is required. Each time slot may be assigned to a different channel in order to exploit advantages provided by frequency hopping, and to avoid interference from other users in an asynchronous fashion.

Channel Types — DECT user data is provided in each B-field time slot (see Figure 11.19). Three hundred twenty user bits are provided during each time slot yielding a 32 kbps data stream per user. No error correction is provided although 4 parity bits are used for crude error detection.

DECT control information is carried by 64 bits in every time slot of an established call (see Figure 11.19). These bits are assigned to one of the four logical channels depending on the nature of the control information. Thus, the gross control channel data rate is 6.4 kbps per user. DECT relies on error detection and retransmission for accurate delivery of control information. Each 64 bit control word contains 16 cyclic redundancy check (CRC) bits, in addition to the 48 control data bits. The maximum information throughput of the DECT control channel is 4.8 kbps.

Speech Coding — Analog speech is digitized into PCM using a 8 kHz sampling rate. The digital speech samples are ADPCM encoded at 32 kbps following CCITT G.721 recommendations.

Channel Coding — For speech signals, no channel coding is used since DECT provides frequency hopping for each time slot. Channel coding and interleaving are avoided because the DECT system is meant for use in indoor environments where the tolerable end-to-end system delay is small and the channel may be modeled as "on" or "off" (see Chapter 7). However, the control channels use 16 bit cyclic redundancy check (CRC) codes in each time slot.

Modulation — DECT uses a tightly filtered GMSK modulation technique. As discussed in Chapter 6, minimum shift keying (MSK) is a form of FSK where the phase transitions between two symbols are constrained to be continuous. Before the modulation, the signal is filtered using a Gaussian shaping filter.

Antenna Diversity — In DECT, spatial diversity at the RFP (base station) receiver is implemented using two antennas. The antenna which provides the best signal for each time slot is selected. This is performed on the basis of a power measurement or alternatively by using an appropriate quality measure (such as interference or BER). Antenna diversity helps solve fading and interference problems. No antenna diversity is used at the subscriber unit.

Table 11.8 DECT Radio Specifications Summary

Parameter	Specification
Frequency Band	1880–1900 MHz
Number of Carriers	10
RF Channel Bandwidth	1.728 MHz
Multiplexing	FDMA/TDMA 24 slots per frame
Duplex	TDD
Spectral Efficiency	500 Erlangs/km^2/MHz
Speech Coder	32 kbps ADPCM
Average Transmitted Power	10 mW
Frame Length	10 ms
Channel Bit Rate	1152 kbps
Data Rate	32 kbps Traffic Channel 6.2 kbps Control Channel
Channel Coding	CRC 16
Dynamic Channel Allocation	Yes
Modulation	GFSK ($BT = 0.3$)
Speech Channel/RF Channel	12

11.7 PACS — Personal Access Communication Systems

PACS is a third generation Personal Communications System originally developed and proposed by Bellcore in 1992 [Cox87], [Cox92]. PACS is able to support voice, data, and video images for indoor and microcell use. PACS is designed to provide coverage within a 500 meter range. The main objective of PACS is to integrate all forms of wireless local loop communications into one system with full telephone features, in order to provide wireless connectivity for local exchange carriers (LECs). Bellcore developed PACS concept with LECs in mind and named it *Wireless Access Communication System* (WACS), but when the Federal Communications Commission introduced an unlicensed PCS band (see Section 11.10), the WACS standard was modified to produce PACS. In the original WACS proposal, ten TDMA/FDM time slots were specified in a 2 ms frame, and a 500 kbps channel data rate was proposed for a channel bandwidth of 350 kHz using QPSK modulation. In PACS, the channel bandwidth, the data rate, the number of slots per frame, and the frame duration were altered slightly, and $\pi/4$ QPSK was chosen over QPSK.

11.7.1 PACS System Architecture

PACS was developed as a universal wireless access system for widespread applications in private and public telephone systems which operate in either licensed or unlicensed PCS bands. PACS may be connected to a PBX or Centrex, and may be served by a Central Office in residential applications [JTC95].

The PACS architecture consists of four main components: the *subscriber unit* (SU) which may be fixed or portable, the *radio ports* (RPs) which are connected to the *radio port control unit* (RPCU), and the *access manager* (AM), as shown in Figure 11.21. Interface A, the air interface, provides a connection between the SU and RP. Interface P provides the protocols required to connect the SUs through the RPs to the RPCU, and also connects the RPCU with its RPs by using an Embedded Operations Channel (EOC) provided within the interface.

The PACS PCS standard contains a fixed distribution network and network intelligence. Only the last 500 m of the distribution network is designed to be wireless.

11.7.2 PACS Radio Interface

The PACS system is designed for operation in the US PCS band (see Table 11.9). A large number of RF channels may be frequency division multiplexed with 80 MHz separation, or time division multiplexed. PACS and WACS channel bandwidth is 300 kHz [JTC95].

WACS originally used TDMA with frequency division duplexing (FDD), with eight time slots provided in a 2.0 ms frame on each radio channel. When used with FDD, the reverse link time slot is offset from its paired forward link time slot by exactly one time slot plus 62.5 μs. The forward link covers 1850 MHz to 1910 MHz and the reverse covers 1930 MHz to 1990 MHz.

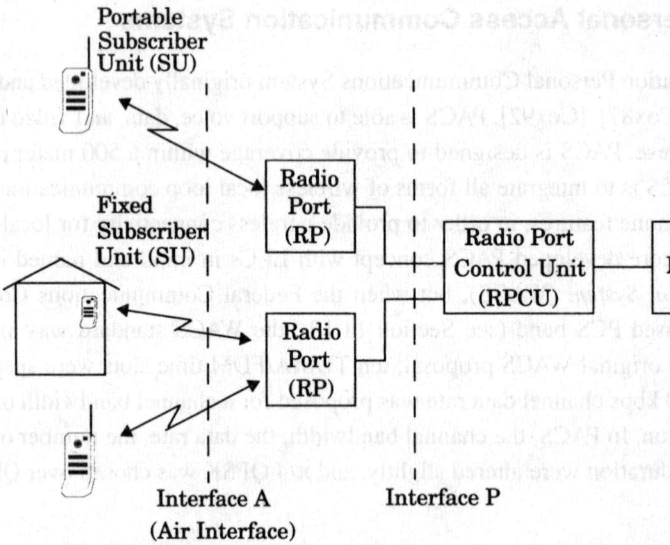

Figure 11.21 PACS system architecture.

Table 11.9 PACS Radio Specifications (FDD or TDD implementation)

Parameter	Specification
Multiple Access	TDMA
Duplexing	FDD or TDD
Frequency Band	1–3 GHz
Modulation	$\pi/4$ DQPSK
Channel Spacing	300 kHz
Portable Transmitter Average Power	200 mW
Base Station Average Power	800 mW
Probability of Coverage Within Service Area	greater than 90%
Channel coding	CRC
Speech coding	16 bit ADPCM
Time Slots per Frame	8
Frame Duration	2.5 ms
Users per Frame	8 (FDD) or 4 (TDD)
Channel Bit Rate	384 kbps
Speech Rate	32 kbps
Bit Error	Less than 10^{-2}
Voice Delay	less than 50 ms

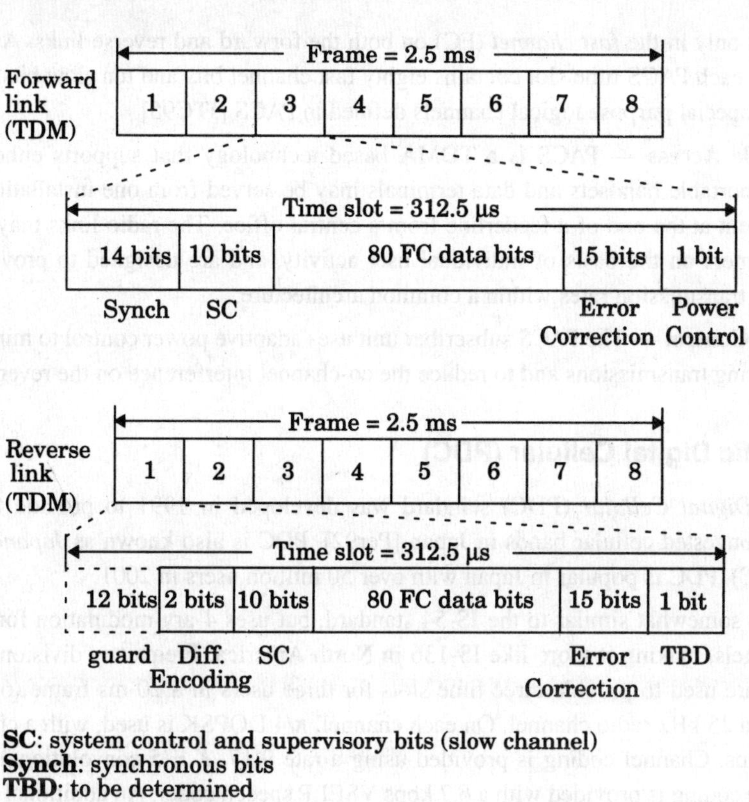

Figure 11.22 PACS frame structure.

The version of PACS developed for the unlicensed US PCS band (PACS-UB) between 1920 and 1930 MHz uses TDD instead of FDD [JTC95]. The PACS time slot and frame structure are shown in Figure 11.22.

Modulation — PACS uses $\pi/4$-DQPSK modulation. The RF signal is shaped using a raised cosine rolloff shaping filter (rolloff factor of 0.5) such that 99% of the transmitted signal power is contained within a channel bandwidth of 288 kHz. Eight time slots, each containing 120 bits, are sent in a 2.5 ms frame. When used with TDD, the time offset between the forward and reverse time slot for each user is exactly two time slots (625 μs) apart.

Speech Coding — WACS uses 32 kbps ADPCM for digital speech encoding. ADPCM provides low complexity, minimum cost, and radio link privacy.

PACS Channels — PACS provides *system broadcasting channels* (SBCs) which are used primarily on the forward link to broadcast paging messages. A 32 kbps SBC provides alerting and system information for up to 80,000 users. A *synchronization channel* (SYN) and the *slow channel* (SC) are used on the forward link to synchronize each subscriber unit. User information is transmitted only in the *fast channel* (FC) on both the forward and reverse links. As shown in Figure 11.22, each PACS time slot contains eighty fast channel bits and ten slow bits. There are several other special purpose logical channels defined in PACS [JTC95].

Multiple Access — PACS is a TDMA based technology that supports either FDD or TDD. Many portable handsets and data terminals may be served from one installation of fixed radio equipment at the end of a feederline from a central office. The radio links may be shared among customers on the basis of individual user activity, and are designed to provide a wide range of user transmission rates within a common architecture.

Power Control — The PACS subscriber unit uses adaptive power control to minimize battery drain during transmissions and to reduce the co-channel interference on the reverse path.

11.8 Pacific Digital Cellular (PDC)

The *Pacific Digital Cellular* (PDC) standard was developed in 1991 to provide for needed capacity in congested cellular bands in Japan [Per92]. PDC is also known as *Japanese Digital Cellular* (JDC). PDC is popular in Japan with over 50 million users in 2001.

PDC is somewhat similar to the IS-54 standard, but uses 4-ary modulation for voice and control channels, making it more like IS-136 in North America. Frequency division duplexing and TDMA are used to provide three time slots for three users in a 20 ms frame (6.67 ms per user slot) on a 25 kHz radio channel. On each channel, $\pi/4$ DQPSK is used, with a channel data rate of 42 kbps. Channel coding is provided using a rate 9/17, $K = 5$ convolutional code with CRC. Speech coding is provided with a 6.7 kbps VSELP speech coder. An additional 4.5 kbps is provided by the channel coding, thereby proving 11.2 kbps of combined speech and channel coding per user. A new half-rate speech and channel coding standard will support six users per 20 ms frame.

PDC is allocated 80 MHz in Japan. The low PDC band uses 130 MHz forward/reverse channel splits. The forward band uses 940 MHz to 956 MHz and the reverse band 810 MHz to 826 MHz. The high PDC band uses 48 MHz channel splits and operates in 1477 MHz to 1501 MHz for the forward link and 1429 MHz to 1453 MHz for the reverse link. PDC uses mobile assisted handoff (MAHO) and is able to support four-cell reuse.

11.9 Personal Handyphone System (PHS)

The Personal Handyphone System (PHS) is a Japanese air interface standard developed by the Research and Development Center for Radio Systems (RCR). The PHS network interface was specified by the Telecommunications Technical Committee of Japan [Per93].

The PHS standard, like DECT and PACS-UB, uses TDMA and TDD. Four duplex data channels are provided on each radio channel. $\pi/4$ DQPSK modulation at a channel rate of 384 kbps is used on both forward and reverse links. Each TDMA frame is 5 ms in duration, and 32 kbps ADPCM is used in conjunction with CRC error detection (without correction).

PHS supports seventy-seven radio channels, each 300 kHz wide, in the 1895 MHz to 1918.1 MHz band. Forty channels in the 1906.1 MHz to 1918.1 MHz are designated for public systems, and the other thirty-seven channels are used for home or office use in the 1895 MHz to 1906.1 MHz band.

PHS uses dynamic channel assignment, so base stations are able to allocate channels based on the RF (interference) signal strength seen at both the base and portable. PHS uses dedicated control channels (unlike DECT) which all subscribers lock to while idle. Handoffs are supported only at walking speeds, as PHS is designed for microcell/indoor PCS use [Oga94].

11.10 US PCS and ISM Bands

In the mid 1980s, the Federal Communications Commission provided unlicensed radio spectrum in the Industrial, Scientific and Medical (ISM) bands of 902 MHz to 928 MHz, 2400 MHz to 2483.5 MHz, and 5725 MHz to 5850 MHz. As long as radio transmitters use spread spectrum modulation and power levels below 1W, they may share ISM spectrum on a secondary basis. Part 15 of the FCC rules govern the use of unlicensed transmitters in the ISM band.

In 1993, the FCC allocated 140 MHz of spectrum for PCS. Figure 11.23 shows the frequencies between 1850 MHz and 1990 MHz which were licensed in 1994 and 1995. The 30 MHz A and B blocks are designated for large cities, called major trading areas (MTAs), while blocks C through F are licensed for large rural BTAs (basic trading areas). There are 51 MTAs and 492 BTAs in the US. In addition to the 120 MHz of licensed spectrum, a total of 20 MHz is allocated for unlicensed applications. Of this, 10 MHz is designated for "isochronous" (circuit switched) applications such as voice, and 10 MHz for "asynchronous" applications such as wireless packet data. Equipment operating in the PCS unlicensed band must comply with a "spectral etiquette" technique incorporated into Part 15 of the Federal Communications Commission rules. This etiquette was developed by the WINForum industrial body and promotes harmonious coexistence of diverse systems in the unlicensed band while giving designers flexibility with respect to system architecture (modulation, coding, signaling protocols, frame structure, etc.). Two of the essential ingredients in the etiquette are (1) a "listen before talk" (LBT) requirement, which prevents a transmitter from interrupting communications already in progress on a frequency; and (2) a transmit power limit that varies as the square root of the signal bandwidth. This is intended to make wideband and narrowband systems comparatively similar on an interference basis.

The winner of each US PCS license was free to use any desired air interface and system architecture, provided that it complied with FCC rules. There are no predetermined standards for systems that operate in the 2 GHz PCS spectrum. This led the TIA and Committee T1 of the Alliance for Telecommunications Industry Solutions to form a Joint Technical Committee (JTC) to review potential PCS standards and to make recommendations. The JTC recognized that PCS standards fall naturally into two categories: "higher tier," which support macrocells and high speed mobility, and "low tier" systems which are optimized for lower power, low complexity and low speed mobility. The JTC considered seven major standards, of which five are variations of existing air interfaces: GSM, IS-136, and IS-95 (high tier) as well as DECT and PACS (low

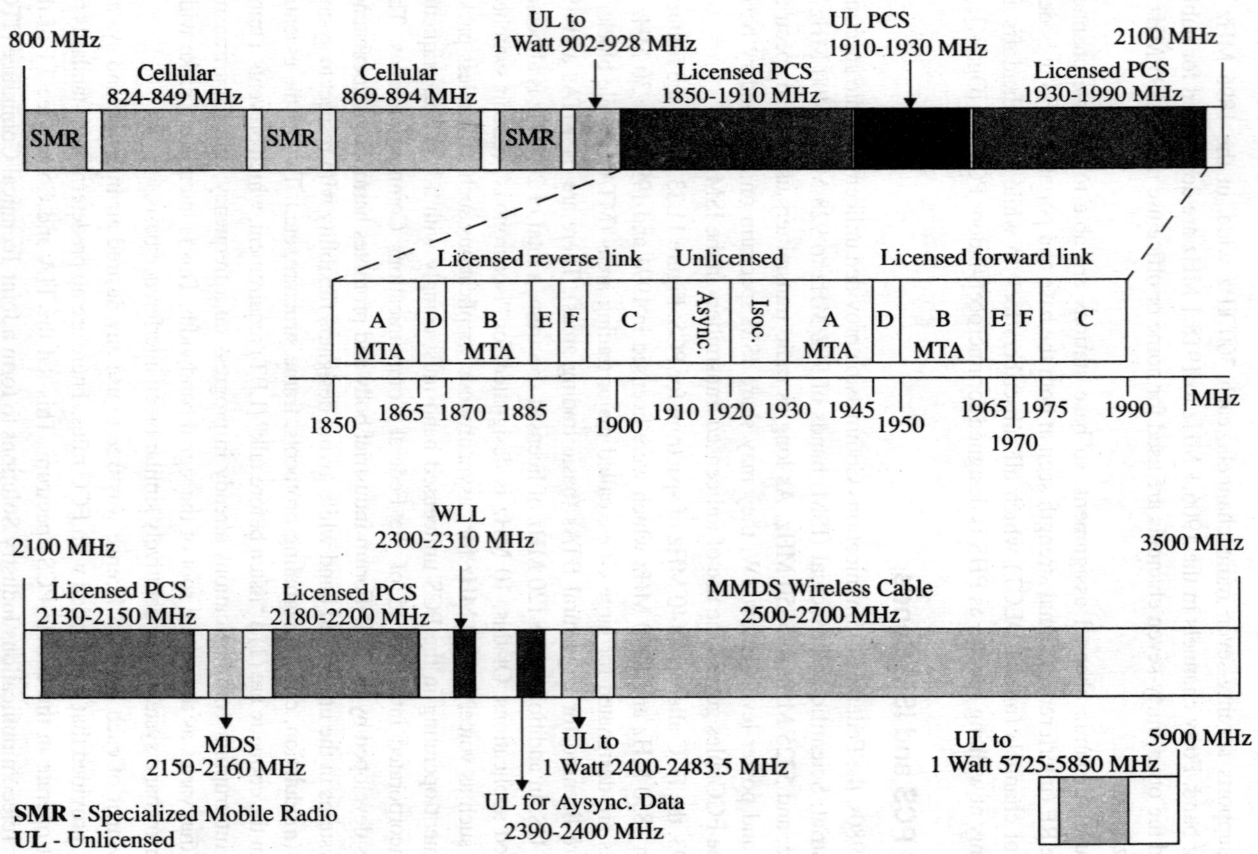

Figure 11.23 US radio spectrum for mobile applications.

tier). The other two are based on a hybrid TDMA/CDMA approach proposed by Omnipoint and a wideband CDMA (W-CDMA) approach offered by Interdigital. In addition, the TIA initiated activity under its TR41 technical committee to develop standards for wireless user premises equipment (WUPE) operating in the unlicensed PCS band [Pad95], if they comply with Part 15 of the FCC Regulations. All types of modulations are considered, including direct sequence and frequency hopped spread spectrum.

The US 2 GHz PCS spectrum currently is occupied by active point-to-point microwave radio systems. For the most part, these incumbent stations have been relocated to other frequencies (e.g., 6 GHz) or converted to optical fiber facilities before PCS systems were deployed. The PCS licensee was required to compensate the incumbent for the cost of relocating. For the unlicensed band, financing the cost of relocating the incumbents in less straightforward, since an equitable mechanism must be developed for sharing the cost of relocation among the purveyors of unlicensed equipment. In addition, during the transition period, the usage of specific frequencies in specific areas must be limited to those that have been cleared. The industry forum called UTAM Inc. was formed to deal with these issues [Pad95].

11.11 US Wireless Cable Television

US wireless cable systems use microwave radio frequencies in the 2150 MHz to 2160 MHz and 2500 MHz to 2700 MHz bands to provide multiple channel television programming similar to that offered by traditional hard wire ("wireline") cable systems. The microwave signals are transmitted over the air from a transmission tower to an antenna at each subscriber's home, thus eliminating the need for the large networks of cable and amplifiers required by wireline cable operators. A typical wireless system consists of head-end equipment (satellite signal reception equipment, radio transmitter, other broadcast equipment, and transmission antenna) and reception equipment at each subscriber location (antenna, frequency conversion device, and set-top device). Currently, wireless cable systems are licensed by the Federal Communications Commission to deliver up to thirty-three channels of programming and typically deliver programming on twenty to thirty-five channels, including local "off-air" broadcast channels that are received directly by the customer's antenna rather than retransmitted by the wireless cable operator.

The Federal Communications Commission has granted licenses for wireless cable service as a series of channel groups, consisting of certain channel groups specifically allocated for wireless cable (Multipoint Distribution Service, or MDS, and Multichannel Multipoint Distribution Service, or MMDS) and other channels originally authorized for educational purposes (Instructional Television Fixed Service, or ITFS). Excess capacity on the ITFS channels may be leased by commercial wireless cable providers. Currently, up to thirty-three total channels are potentially available for licensing, lease, or purchase by wireless cable companies in each market. The Federal Communications Commission imposes certain conditions and restrictions on the use and operation of channels.

The Federal Communications Commission imposed a freeze on the filing of new applications for MDS/MMDS licenses in 1992 and for ITFS licenses in 1993. The freezes were intended to allow the Federal Communications Commission time to update its wireless cable database and to review the rules for these services. New MDS/MMDS applications are subject to selection by auction, just as PCS licenses were auctioned. ITFS licenses will continue to be awarded on a comparative basis according to the Federal Communications Commission specified criteria. These frequencies may soon be reallocated to 3G wireless services.

Although the principal regulatory provisions of the 1992 Cable Act do not apply to wireless cable systems, such systems are affected by it. The US Congress stated that its intent in passing the 1992 Cable Act was in part to establish and support existing and new multichannel video services, such as wireless cable, to provide competition to the existing franchise cable television monopoly. A significant provision of the 1992 Cable Act guarantees access by new multichannel video providers to traditional cable television programming on nondiscriminatory terms.

11.12 Summary of Standards Throughout the World

The following tables summarize the major cellular, cordless, and personal communication standards throughout the world. In addition, the US mobile radio frequency spectrum allocation is shown in Figure 11.23.

First generation analog cellular radio systems throughout the world are compared in Table 11.10. Digital cordless standards are compared in Table 11.11. The three most popular second generation cellular radio standards are listed in Table 11.12. Table 11.13 lists three major second generation cordless/PCS standards.

Table 11.10 Analog Cellular Systems Overview

Standard	Mobile Tx/Base Tx (MHz)	Channel spacing (kHz)	Number of Channels	Region
AMPS	824–849/869–894	30	832	The Americas
TACS	890–915/935–960	25	1000	Europe
ETACS	872–905/917–950	25	1240	United Kingdom
NMT 450	453–457.5/463–467.5	25	180	Europe
NMT 900	890–915/935–960	12.5	1999	Europe
C-450	450–455.74/460–465.74	10	573	Germany, Portugal

Table 11.10 Analog Cellular Systems Overview (Continued)

Standard	Mobile Tx/Base Tx (MHz)	Channel spacing (kHz)	Number of Channels	Region
RTMS	450–455/460–465	25	200	Italy
Radiocom 2000	192.5–199.5/200.5–207.5		560	
	215.5–233.5/207.5–215.5		640	
	165.2–168.4/169.8–173		256	
	414.8–418/424.8–428	12.5	256	France
NTT	925–940/870–885	25/6.25	600/2400	
	915–918.5/860–863.5	6.25	560	
	922–925/867–870	6.25	480	Japan
JTACS/NTACS	915–925/860–870	25/12.5	400/800	
	898–901/843–846	25/12.5	120/240	
	918.5–922/863.5–867	12.5	280	Japan

Table 11.11 Digital Cordless Air Interface Parameters Summary

	CT2	CT2+	DECT	PHS	PACS
Region	Europe	Canada	Europe	Japan	US
Duplexing	TDD		TDD	TDD	FDD or TDD
Frequency band (MHz)	864–868	944–948	1880–1900	1895–1918	1850–1910/ 1930–1990 or 1920–1930
Carrier spacing (kHz)	100		1728	300	300/300
Number of carriers	40		10	77	400 or 32
Channels/carrier	1		12	4	8 or 4
Channel bit rate kbps	72		1152	384	384
Modulation	GFSK		GFSK	π/4 DQPSK	π/4 QPSK
Speech Coding	32 kb/s		32 kb/s	32 kb/s	32 kb/s
Average handset TX power (mW)	5		10	10	25
Peak handset TX power (mW)	10		250	80	100
Frame duration (ms)	2		10	5	2.5 or 2.0

Table 11.12 Second Generation Digital Cellular Standards Summary

	GSM	IS-136	PDC
Year of Introduction	1990	1991	1993
Frequencies	890–915 MHz (R) 935–960 MHz (F)	824–849 MHz (R) 869–894 MHz (F)	810–830 & 1429–1453 MHz (R) 940–960 & 1477–1501 MHz (F)
Multiple Access	TDMA/FDMA/FDD	TDMA/FDMA/FDD	TDMA/FDMA/FDD
Modulation	GMSK ($BT = 0.3$)	$\pi/4$ DQPSK	$\pi/4$ DQPSK
Carrier Separation	200 kHz	30 kHz	25 kHz
Channel Data Rate	270.833 kbps	48.6 kbps	42 kbps
Number of Voice Channels	1000	2500	3000
Spectrum Efficiency	1.35 bps/Hz	1.62 bps/Hz	1.68 bps/Hz
Speech Coding	RELP-LTP @ 13 kbps	VSELP @7.95 kbps	VSELP @ 6.7 kbps
Channel Coding	CRC with $r = 1/2$; $L = 5$ Conv.	7 bit CRC with $r = 1/2$; $L = 6$ Conv.	CRC with Conv.
Equalizers	Adaptive	Adaptive	Adaptive
Portable Tx. Power Max./Avg.	1 W/125 mW	600 mW/200 mW	

Table 11.13 Unlicensed/Short Range PCS Standards Overview

	PACS-UB	DCS 1800	PHS
Year of Introduction	1992	1993	1993
Frequencies	1920–1930 MHz	1710–1785 MHz (R) 1805–1880 MHz (F)	1895–1907 MHz
Multiple Access	TDMA/FDMA/TDD	TDMA/FDM/FDD	TDMA/FDMA/TDD
Modulation	$\pi/4$ QPSK	GMSK	$\pi/4$ QPSK
Carrier Separation	300 kHz	200 kHz	300 kHz
Data Rate	384 kbps	270.833 kbps	384 kbps
Voice Ch./RF. Ch.	4	8	4
Speech Coding	ADPCM @ 32 kbps	RELP-LTP @ 13 kbps	ADPCM @32 kbps
Channel Coding	CRC	Conv. $r = 1/2$	CRC
Receiver	Coherent	Coherent	Coherent
Portable Tx. Power Max./Avg.	200 mW/20 mW	1 W/125 mW	80 mW/10 mW

11.13 Problems

11.1 Of the following air interface standards, identify all that are digital, analog, TDMA, and CDMA: GSM, AMPS, ETACS, IS-95, IS-136, DECT.

11.2 Which of the following is NOT true of GSM? Check all that apply.

(a) The uplink and downlink channels are separated by 45 MHz.

(b) There are eight half-rate users in one timeslot.

(c) The peak frequency deviation of the GSM modulator is an integer multiple of the GSM data rate.

(d) GSM uses a constant envelope modulation.

11.3 List all the cellular systems that do not support Mobile Assisted Handoff.

11.4 What is the cut-off frequency of the baseband, Gaussian, pulse-shaping filter used in the GSM system?

11.5 The FCC allocated an additional 10 MHz spectrum for cellular services in 1989. How many additional channels can be accommodated in this bandwidth for each of the cellular standards?

11.6 The IS-95 system uses a rate 1/2 convolutional encoding in the forward channel and a rate 1/3 convolutional coding in the reverse channel. What were the reasons for doing so?

11.7 Which of the following is NOT true of the IS-95 system?

(a) No hard limits on capacity.

(b) Soft handoff possible.

(c) Uses slow frequency hopping.

(d) The number of channels that can be accommodated in the forward and reverse links are different.

11.8 How are different channels within the forward link in an IS-95 system identified?

11.9 What is the spectral efficiency of the GMSK modulation scheme used in GSM?

11.10 Which of the following systems is solely based on Frequency Division Multiple Access (FDMA)?

(a) DECT (b) CT2 (c) USDC (d) GSM

11.11 Which cellular system uses the most bandwidth efficient modulation?

11.12 Which cellular systems do not use a constant envelope modulation scheme?

11.13 What were the reasons for choosing $\pi/4$ DQPSK modulation scheme for USDC against DQPSK?

11.14 How many full-rate physical channels per cell can a GSM system accommodate?

11.15 Which of the following is a blank-and-burst channel in the AMPS system?

(a) Paging Channel (PC)

(b) Reverse Voice Channel (RVC)

(c) Slow Associated Control Channel (SACCH)

(d) Fast Associated Control Channel (FACCH)

11.16 Compute the modulation index of the FM modulator used in the AMPS system.

11.17 Digital cellular systems use convolutional coding for error protection as opposed to block coding. The primary reason for doing so is

(a) Convolutional coding performs better under Rayleigh fading conditions.

(b) Convolutional coders are more robust to burst errors.

(c) Convolutional coding is less complex when compared to block coding.

(d) Real time soft-decision decoding algorithms which improve performance are available for decoding convolutional codes.

11.18 Which of the following systems is based on a microcell architecture?

(a) GSM (b) DECT (c) USDC (d) IS-95

11.19 What is the maximum data rate at which a user can transmit data on a DECT system?

11.20 How many full-rate users can a USDC system accommodate in a single AMPS channel?

11.21 What is the maximum fade slope (in dB/s) which can be compensated for by the reverse power control subchannel in the IS-95 CDMA system?

11.22 In the normal GSM time slot of Figure 11.9, why would the 26 equalizer training bits be placed in the middle of the frame rather than at the beginning? What is the reason for having an 8.25 bit guard period after the data bursts?

11.23 Compare the number of omnidirectional cells required to cover a 1000 sq. km area using GSM at 800 MHz and DCS-1900 at 1900 MHz. Assume the sensitivity of both the GSM and the DCS-1900 receivers equal –104 dBm. Assume equal transmitter power and antenna gains for the two systems.

11.24 Compare the number of omnidirectional cells required to cover a 1000 sq. km area using DCS-1900 and IS-95. Assume equal transmitter powers and antenna gains.

11.25 How would the cell coverage radius be affected by the system loading for each of the following technologies: AMPS, IS-95 CDMA, and IS-54 TDMA?

11.26 What mechanisms would cause breakdown in the reverse link of an IS-95 CDMA systems as the number of users in a sector approaches the theoretical limit?

11.27 For what reasons would the PACS version for the unlicensed PCS band use TDD instead of FDD?

11.28 What is likely to happen to a DECT system if it is deployed outdoors in an environment where significant multipath could occur? Explain your answer and provide a qualitative analysis.

11.29 Draw the allocation of bits in a USDC half-rate time slot. Then answer the following:

(a) What is the channel data rate for the USDC air interface?

(b) How many user bits are there in each USDC time slot?

(c) What is the time duration for each USDC frame?

(d) Using the definition of frame efficiency in the text determine the frame efficiency for USDC.

11.30 Consider an AMPS or ETACS system.

(a) List the possible SAT tones in AMPS.

(b) Why would the ST tone be useful to a service provider?

(c) List at least five ways a cellular phone call may be terminated. How could a carrier distinguish between these?

11.31 For a full-rate USDC system, consider how the data is allocated between channels.

(a) What is the gross RF data rate?

(b) What is the gross RF data rate for the SACCH?

(c) What is the gross RF data rate for the CDDVC?

(d) What is the gross data rate for synchronization, ramp-up, and guard time?

(e) Verify that your answers in (b)–(d) add up to your answer in (a).

(f) What is the end-user data rate provided in full-rate USDC?

11.32 Prove that the GSM system allocates gross RF data rate of 33.854 kbps/user. Show this by summing up the individual user data rates for

(a) the speech coder

(b) speech error protection

(c) SACCH

(d) guard time, ramp-up, and synchronization

11.33 Compute the longest time over which a mobile station would have to wait in order to determine the frame number being transmitted by a GSM base station.

APPENDIX A

Trunking Theory

Two major classes of trunked radio systems are the Lost Call Cleared (LCC) systems and Lost Call Delayed (LCD) systems [Sta90].

In *Lost Call Cleared systems*, queueing is not provided for call requests. When a user requests service, there is minimal call set-up time and the user is given immediate access to a channel if one is available. If all channels are already in use and no new channels are available, the call is blocked without access to the system. The user does not receive service, but is free to try the call again later. Calls are assumed to arrive with a Poisson distribution, and it is further assumed that there are a nearly infinite number of users. The Erlang B formula describes the grade of service (GOS) as the probability that an arbitrary user will experience a blocked call in a Lost Call Cleared system. It is assumed that all blocked calls are instantly returned to an infinite user pool, and may be retried at any time in the future. The time between successive calls by a blocked user is a random process and is assumed to be Poisson distributed. This model is accurate for a large system with many channels and many users with similar calling patterns.

In *Lost Call Delayed systems*, queues are used to hold call requests that are initially blocked. When a user attempts a call and a channel is not immediately available, the call request may be delayed until a channel becomes available. For LCD systems, it is first necessary to find the likelihood that all channels are already in use. Then, given that no channel is available initially, it is necessary to know the probability of how long the call must be delayed before a channel is available for use. The likelihood of a call not having immediate access to a channel in a LCD system is determined by the Erlang C formula. For LCD systems, the GOS is measured by the probability that calls will have delays greater than t seconds. The knowledge of the Erlang C formula and the service distribution is used to analyze the GOS. It is assumed that a nearly infinite number of users are present in the system, and that all calls in the queue are eventually serviced. The Erlang C model also assumes a large number of channels and a large number of users with similar calling patterns. Typically five or more channels are considered to be a sufficiently large number of channels.

A.1 Erlang B

The Erlang B formula determines the probability that a call is blocked, and is a measure of the GOS for a trunked system that provides no queuing for blocked calls (an LCC system). The Erlang B model is based upon the following basic assumptions:

- Call requests are memoryless, implying that all users, including blocked users, may request a channel at any time.
- All free channels are fully available for servicing calls until all channels are occupied.
- The probability of a user occupying a channel (called the *service time*) is exponentially distributed. Longer calls are less likely to happen as described by an exponential distribution.
- There are a finite number of channels available in the trunking pool.
- Traffic requests are described by a Poisson distribution which implies exponentially distributed call interarrival times.
- Interarrival times of call requests are independent of each other.
- The number of busy channels is equal to the number of busy users, and the probability of blocking is given as

$$Pr[Blocking] = \frac{\left(\frac{A^C}{C!}\right)}{\sum_{k=0}^{C} \frac{A^k}{k!}} \tag{A.1}$$

where C is the number of trunked channels, and A is the total offered load to the trunked system.

A.1.1 Derivation of Erlang B

Consider a system with C channels and U users. Let λ be the total mean call arrival rate per unit time for the entire trunked system (average number of call requests per unit time over all channels and all users), and let H be the average call holding time (average duration of a call). If A is the offered load for the trunked system, then $A = \lambda H$.

The probability that a call requested by a user will be blocked is given by

$$Pr[Blocking] = Pr[None\ of\ the\ C\ channels\ are\ free] \tag{A.2}$$

It is assumed that calls arrive according to the Poisson distribution, such that

$$Pr = \{a(t+\tau) - a(t) = n\} = \frac{e^{-\lambda\tau}}{n!}(\lambda\tau)^n \quad \text{for } n = 0,1,2..... \tag{A.3}$$

where $a(t)$ is the number of call requests (arrivals) that have occurred since $t = 0$ and τ is the call interarrival time (the time between successive call requests). The term λ denotes the average number of call requests per unit time over the user population, and is called the *arrival rate*.

The Poisson process implies that the time of the nth call arrival and the interarrival times between successive call requests are mutually independent. The interarrival times between call requests are exponential and mutually independent, and the probability that the interarrival time will be less than some time s is given by $Pr(\tau_n \le s) = 1 - e^{-\lambda s}$, $s \ge 0$ where τ_n is the interarrival time of the nth arrival, and $\tau_n = t_{n+1} - t_n$, where t_n is the time at which the nth call request arrived. In other words, the probability density function for τ_n is [Ber92]

$$p(\tau_n) = \lambda e^{-\lambda\tau_n}, \quad \tau_n \ge 0 \tag{A.4}$$

For every $t \ge 0, \delta \ge 0$,

$$Pr\{a(t+\delta) - a(t) = 0\} = 1 - \lambda\delta + O(\delta) \tag{A.5}$$

$$Pr\{a(t+\delta) - a(t) = 1\} = \lambda\delta + O(\delta) \tag{A.6}$$

$$Pr\{a(t+\delta) - a(t) \ge 2\} = O(\delta) \tag{A.7}$$

where $O(\delta)$ is the probability of more than one call request arriving over the time interval δ and is a function of δ such that $\lim_{\delta \to 0}\left\{\frac{O(\delta)}{\delta}\right\} = 0$.

The probability of n arrivals in δ seconds is found from Equation (A.3)

$$Pr = \{a(t+\delta) - a(t) = n\} = \frac{e^{-\lambda\delta}}{n!}(\lambda\delta)^n \tag{A.8}$$

The *user service time* is the duration of a particular call that has successfully accessed the trunked system and has been allocated a channel for a call. Service times are assumed to be exponential with mean call duration H, where $\mu = 1/H$ is the mean service rate (average number of serviced calls per unit time). H is also called the *average holding time*. The probability that the service time of the nth serviced call will be less than some call duration s is given by

$$P_r\{s_n < s\} = 1 - e^{-\mu s} \quad s > 0 \tag{A.9}$$

and the probability density function of the service time is

$$p(s_n) = \mu e^{-\mu s_n} \tag{A.10}$$

where s_n is the service time of the nth call.

This trunking system (represented by the Erlang B formula) is called an *M/M/C/C* queueing system. The first *M* denotes a memoryless Poisson process for call arrivals, the second *M* denotes an exponential service time for the users, the first *C* denotes the number of trunked channels available, and the last *C* indicates a hard limit on the number of simultaneous users that are served.

The property of Markov chains can be used to derive the Erlang B formula. Consider a discrete time stochastic process $\{X_n | n = 0, 1, 2, ...\}$ that takes values from the set of nonnegative integers, so that the possible states of the process are $i = 0, 1, ...$. The process is said to be a *Markov chain* if its transition from the present state i to the next state $i+1$ depends solely on the state i and not on previous states. Discrete time Markov chains enable the traffic to be observed at discrete observation points for specific traffic conditions. The operation of a practical trunked system is continuous in time, but may be analyzed in small time intervals δ, where δ is a small positive number. If N_k is the number of calls (occupied channels) in the system at time $k\delta$, then N_k may be represented as

$$N_k = N(k\delta) \tag{A.11}$$

where N is a discrete random process representing the number of occupied channels at discrete times. N_k is a discrete time Markov chain with steady state occupancy probabilities which are identical to the continuous Markov chain, and can have values ranging on 0,1,2,....*C*.

The transition probability $P_{i,j}$ describes the probability of channel occupancies over a small observation interval, and is given by

$$P_{i,j} = Pr\{N_{k+1} = j | N_k = i\} \tag{A.12}$$

Using Equations (A.5) through (A.7), and letting $\delta \to 0$, we obtain

$$P_{oo} = 1 - \lambda\delta + O(\delta) \tag{A.13}$$

$$P_{ii} = 1 - \lambda\delta - \mu\delta + O(\delta) \quad i \geq 1 \tag{A.14}$$

$$P_{i,i+1} = \lambda\delta + O(\delta) \quad i \geq 0 \tag{A.15}$$

$$P_{i,i-1} = \mu\delta + O(\delta) \quad i \geq 1 \tag{A.16}$$

$$P_{i,j} = O(\delta) \quad j \neq i,\ j \neq i+1,\ j \neq i-1 \tag{A.17}$$

The transition state diagram for the Markov chain is shown in Figure A.1

Figure A.1 is a Markov chain representation of a trunked system with *C* channels. To understand the Markov chain state diagram, assume that there are 0 channels being used by the system, i.e., there are no users. Over a small interval of time, the likelihood that the system will continue to use 0 channels is $(1 - \lambda\delta)$. The probability that there will be a change from 0 channels to 1 channel in use is given by $\lambda\delta$. On the other hand, if one channel is in use, the probability

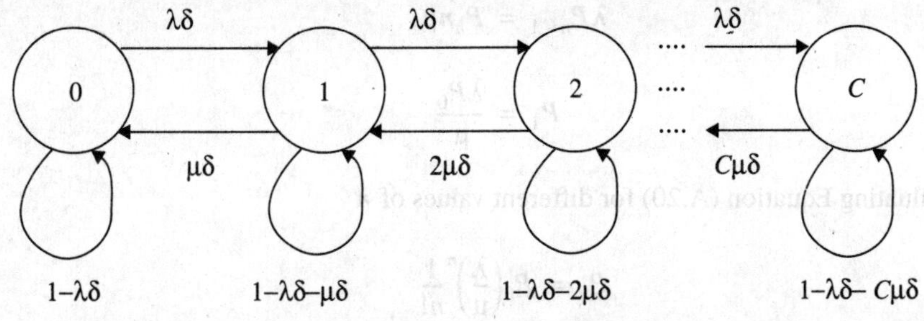

Figure A.1 The transition probabilities represented as a Markov chain state diagram for Erlang B.

that the system will transition to 0 used channels is given by $\mu\delta$. Similarly, the likelihood that the system will continue to use 1 channel is given by $1 - \lambda\delta - \mu\delta$. All of the outgoing probabilities from a certain state sum to 1.

Over a long period of time, the system reaches steady state and has n channels in use. Figure A.2 represents the steady state response of an LCC system.

At steady state, the probability of having n channels in use is equivalent to the probability of having $(n-1)$ channels in use, times the transition probability $\lambda\delta$.

Hence, under steady state conditions,

$$\lambda\delta P_{n-1} = n\mu\delta P_n,\ n \le C \tag{A.18}$$

Equation (A.18) is known as the *Global Balance Equation*. Furthermore,

$$\sum_{n=0}^{C} P_n = 1 \tag{A.19}$$

Using the Global Balance equation for different values of n, it is seen that

$$\lambda\delta P_{n-1} = P_n n\mu\delta \text{ ,n=1, 2, 3...., C} \tag{A.20}$$

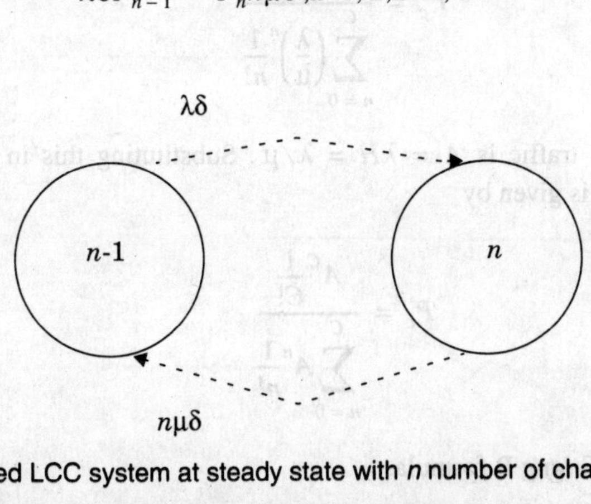

Figure A.2 A trunked LCC system at steady state with *n* number of channels in use.

$$\lambda P_{n-1} = P_n n\mu \tag{A.21}$$

$$P_1 = \frac{\lambda P_0}{\mu} \tag{A.22}$$

Evaluating Equation (A.20) for different values of n

$$P_n = P_0\left(\frac{\lambda}{\mu}\right)^n \frac{1}{n!} \tag{A.23}$$

and

$$P_0 = \left(\frac{\mu}{\lambda}\right)^n P_n n! = 1 - \sum_{i=1}^{C} P_i \tag{A.24}$$

Substituting Equation (A.23) in Equation (A.24)

$$P_0 = \frac{1}{\sum_{n=0}^{C}\left(\frac{\lambda}{\mu}\right)^n \frac{1}{n!}} \tag{A.25}$$

From Equation (A.23), the probability of blocking for C trunked channels is

$$P_c = P_0\left(\frac{\lambda}{\mu}\right)^C \frac{1}{C!} \tag{A.26}$$

Substituting Equation (A.25) in Equation (A.26),

$$P_c = \frac{\left(\frac{\lambda}{\mu}\right)^C \frac{1}{C!}}{\sum_{n=0}^{C}\left(\frac{\lambda}{\mu}\right)^n \frac{1}{n!}} \tag{A.27}$$

The total offered traffic is $A = \lambda H = \lambda/\mu$. Substituting this in Equation (A.27), the probability of blocking is given by

$$P_c = \frac{A^C \frac{1}{C!}}{\sum_{n=0}^{C} A^n \frac{1}{n!}} \tag{A.28}$$

Equation (A.28) is the Erlang B formula.

A.2 Erlang C

The Erlang C formula is derived from the assumption that a queue is used to hold all requested calls which cannot be immediately assigned a channel. The Erlang C formula is given by

$$Pr[call\ delayed] = \frac{A^C}{A^C + C!\left(1 - \frac{A}{C}\right)\sum_{k=0}^{C-1}\frac{A^k}{k!}} \tag{A.29}$$

If no channels are immediately available, the call is delayed and held in a queue, and the probability that the delayed call is forced to wait for more than t seconds in the queue is given by

$$Pr[wait > t \mid call\ delayed] = e^{-\frac{(C-A)}{H}t} \tag{A.30}$$

where C is the total number of available channels, t is the delay time of interest, and H is the average duration of a call. The probability that any caller is delayed in the queue for a wait time greater than t seconds is given by

$$\begin{aligned} Pr[wait > t] &= Pr[call\ delayed]Pr[wait > t \mid call\ delayed] \\ &= Pr[call\ delayed]e^{-\frac{(C-A)}{H}t} \end{aligned} \tag{A.31}$$

The average delay D for all calls in a queued system is given by

$$D = \int_0^{\infty} Pr[call\ delayed]e^{-\frac{(C-A)}{H}t}\, dt \tag{A.32}$$

$$D = Pr[call\ delayed]\frac{H}{(C-A)} \tag{A.33}$$

whereas the average delay for those calls which are queued is given by $H/(C-A)$.

A.2.1 Derivation of Erlang C

Consider a system where C is the number of trunked channels. The assumptions used to derive the Erlang C formula are similar to those used to derive Erlang B, except for the additional stipulation that if an offered call cannot be assigned a channel, it is placed in a queue which has an infinite length. Each call is then serviced in the order of its arrival, the arrival process obeying a Poisson distribution given by

$$Pr\{a(t+\Delta t) - a(t) = n\} = \frac{e^{-\lambda t}(\lambda \Delta t)}{n!} \quad , n = 0, 1, 2, ... \tag{A.34}$$

where a is the number of call arrivals which are waiting for service.

Just as the Erlang B formula was derived using the assumption that all call interarrival times are exponential and independent, the time between successive call arrivals is $\tau_n = t_{n+1} - t_n$ and the distribution of the interarrival times is such that

$$Pr\{\tau_n \le s\} = 1 - e^{-\lambda s} \quad , s \ge 0 \tag{A.35}$$

As was the case for Erlang B, the service time for each user already on the trunked system is assumed to be exponential and is given by

$$Pr\{s_n \le s\} = 1 - e^{-\mu s} \quad , s \ge 0 \tag{A.36}$$

Using discrete time Markov chains with transition probabilities given in Equations (A.12) to (A.17), the Erlang C formula is easily derived. Let $P_{i,j}$ denote the transition probability of going from state i to state j. The state diagram for the system is shown in Figure A.3.

The Erlang C formula is derived by assuming that the trunked system is a *M/M/C/D* queue, where C denotes the maximum number of simultaneous users and D is the maximum number of calls that may be held in the queue for service. If D is assumed to be infinite, then the system is an M/M/C/∞ queue, commonly referred to as simply M/M/C queue. If D is infinite, then P_k may denote the steady state probability of finding k calls in the system (both served and queued calls). That is,

$$P_k = \lim_{k \to \infty} Pr\{N_t = k\} \tag{A.37}$$

where N_t is the total number of calls either using or waiting for the system at time t. In steady state, the probability that the system is in state k and makes a transition to state $k-1$ in the next transition interval is the same as the probability that the system is in state $k-1$ and makes a transition to state k. Thus, from the state diagram shown in Figure A.3,

$$\lambda\delta P_{k-1} = k\mu\delta P_k \text{ for } k \le C \tag{A.38}$$

hence

$$P_k = \left(\frac{\lambda}{\mu}\right)\frac{1}{k}P_{k-1} \text{ for } k \le C \tag{A.39}$$

and

$$\lambda\delta P_{k-1} = C\mu\delta P_k \text{ for } k \ge C \tag{A.40}$$

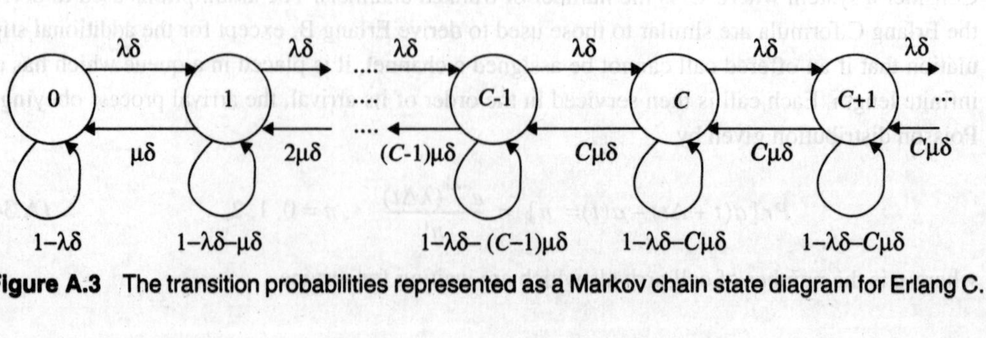

Figure A.3 The transition probabilities represented as a Markov chain state diagram for Erlang C.

hence

$$P_k = \left(\frac{\lambda}{\mu}\right)\frac{1}{C}P_{k-1} \text{ for } k \geq C \tag{A.41}$$

and it follows that

$$P_k = \begin{cases} \left(\frac{\lambda}{\mu}\right)^k \frac{1}{k!}P_0 & k \leq C \\ \frac{1}{C!}\left(\frac{\lambda}{\mu}\right)^k \frac{1}{C^{k-C}}P_0 & k \geq C \end{cases} \tag{A.42}$$

Since $\sum_{k=0}^{\infty} P_k = 1$, we have

$$P_0\left[1 + \left(\frac{\lambda}{\mu}\right) + \ldots + \frac{1}{C!}\left(\frac{\lambda}{\mu}\right)^{C+1} \frac{1}{C^{(C+1)-C}} + \ldots\right] = 1 \tag{A.43}$$

$$P_0\left[1 + \sum_{k=1}^{C-1}\left(\frac{\lambda}{\mu}\right)^k \frac{1}{k!} + \sum_{k=C}^{\infty}\frac{1}{C!}\left(\frac{\lambda}{\mu}\right)^k \frac{1}{C^{k-C}}\right] = 1 \tag{A.44}$$

$$\text{i.e., } P_0 = \frac{1}{\sum_{k=1}^{C-1}\left(\frac{\lambda}{\mu}\right)^k \frac{1}{k!} + \frac{1}{k!}\left(\frac{\lambda}{\mu}\right)^C \frac{1}{\left(1 - \frac{\lambda}{\mu C}\right)}} \tag{A.45}$$

The probability that an arriving call occurs when all C channels are busy and thus has to wait can be determined using Equation (A.42).

$$Pr[\text{C channels are busy}] = \sum_{k=C}^{\infty} P_k = \sum_{k=C}^{\infty}\frac{1}{C!}\left(\frac{\lambda}{\mu}\right)^k \frac{1}{C^{k-C}}P_0 \tag{A.46}$$

$$= P_0\frac{1}{C!}\left(\frac{\lambda}{\mu}\right)^C \sum_{k=C}^{\infty}\left(\frac{\lambda}{\mu}\right)^{k-C} \frac{1}{C^{k-C}}$$

$$= P_0\frac{1}{C!}\left(\frac{\lambda}{\mu}\right)^C \frac{1}{\left(1 - \frac{\lambda}{\mu C}\right)}$$

The above equation is valid for $\frac{\lambda}{\mu C} < 1$. Substituting for P_o from Equation (A.45)

$$Pr[\text{C channels are busy}] = \frac{\frac{1}{C!}\left(\frac{\lambda}{\mu}\right)^C}{\left(1-\frac{\lambda}{\mu C}\right)} \frac{1}{\left[\sum_{k=0}^{C-1}\left(\frac{\lambda}{\mu}\right)^k \frac{1}{k!} + \frac{1}{k!}\left(\frac{\lambda}{\mu}\right)^C \frac{1}{\left(1-\frac{\lambda}{\mu C}\right)}\right]} \tag{A.47}$$

$$= \frac{(\lambda/\mu)^C}{\left[(\lambda/\mu)^C + C!\left(1-\frac{\lambda}{\mu C}\right)\sum_{k=0}^{C-1}\left(\frac{\lambda}{\mu}\right)^k\left(\frac{1}{k!}\right)\right]}$$

But, $A = \lambda/\mu = \lambda H$. Substituting this in Equation (A.47)

$$Pr[\text{C channels are busy}] = \frac{A^C}{A^C + C!\left(1-\frac{A}{C}\right)\sum_{k=0}^{C-1}\frac{A^k}{k!}} \tag{A.48}$$

Equation (A.48) is the expression for Erlang C.

APPENDIX B

Noise Figure Calculations for Link Budgets

Computing receiver noise and SNR at a receiver is important for determining coverage and quality of service in a wireless communication system.

As shown in Chapters 3, 6, and 7, SNR determines the link quality and impacts the probability of error in a wireless communication system. Thus, the ability to estimate SNR is important for determining suitable transmitter powers or received signal levels in various propagation conditions.

The signal level at a receiver antenna may be computed based on path loss equations given in Chapters 3 and 4. To compute the noise level of a receiver, it is necessary to know the gains (or losses) of each receiver stage, as well as the ambient noise temperature at the receiver antenna. However, the *noise figure* of a receiver is a convenient metric that allows a designer to factor in the additional noise induced by the receiver without having to know about the specific components that make up the receiver stages.

All electronic components generate thermal noise, and hence contribute to the noise level seen at the detector output of a receiver. In order to refer the noise at the output of a receiver to an equivalent level at the receiver input terminals (where the signal is applied), the concept of *noise figure* is used [Cou93]. By referring noise levels to the receiver input, one merely needs to add the noise figure of the receiver to the ambient thermal noise level in order to model the total noise power at the receiver input terminals.

Noise figure, denoted by F, is defined as

$$F = \frac{\text{Measured noise power out of device at room temperature}}{\text{Power out of device if device were noiseless}} \tag{B.1}$$

F is always greater than 1 and assumes that a matched load operating at room temperature is connected to the input terminals of the device. A noise figure of 1 implies a noiseless device.

Noise figure may be related to the *effective noise temperature*, T_e, of a device by

$$T_e = (F-1)T_0 \tag{B.2}$$

where T_0 is ambient room temperature (typically taken as 290 K to 300 K, which corresponds to 63°F to 75°F, or 17°C to 27°C). Noise temperatures are measured in Kelvin, where 0 K is absolute zero, or –273°C. A noiseless device has $T_e = 0$ K.

Note that T_e does not necessarily correspond to the physical temperature of a device. For example, directional satellite dish antennas which beam toward space typically have effective antenna temperatures on the order of 50 K (this is because space appears cold and produces little in the way of thermal noise), whereas a 10 dB attenuator has an effective temperature of about 2700 K (this follows from Equations (B.2) and (B.4)). Antennas which beam toward earth generally have effective noise temperatures which correspond to the physical temperature of the earth, which is about 290 K.

A simple passive load (such as a resistor) at room temperature transfers a noise power of

$$P_n = kT_0B \tag{B.3}$$

into a matched load, where k is *Boltzmann's constant* given by 1.38×10^{-23} Joules/Kelvin and B is the equivalent bandwidth of the measuring device. For passive devices such as transmission lines or attenuators operating at room temperature, the device loss (L in dB) is equal to the noise figure of the device. That is,

$$F\text{ (dB)} = L\text{ (dB)} \tag{B.4}$$

For the purposes of noise calculations, antennas which are built with passive elements (such as wire) are considered to have unity gain, even if their radiation pattern has a measured gain.

The concepts of noise figure and noise temperature are useful in communications analysis, since the gains of the receiver stages are not needed in order to quantify the overall noise amplification of the receiver. If a resistive load operating at room temperature is connected to the input terminals of a receiver having noise figure F, then the noise power at the output of the receiver, referred to the input, is simply F times the input noise power, or

$$P_{out/\text{Ref.in}} = FkT_0B = \left(1 + \frac{T_e}{T_0}\right)kT_0B \tag{B.5}$$

and the actual noise power out of the receiver is

$$P_{out} = G_{sys}FkT_0B = G_{sys}kT_0B\left(1 + \frac{T_e}{T_0}\right) \tag{B.6}$$

where G_{sys} is the overall receiver gain due to cascaded stages.

For a cascaded system, the noise figure of the overall system may be computed from the noise figures and gains of the individual components. That is,

$$F_{sys} = F_1 + \frac{F_2 - 1}{G_1} + \frac{F_3 - 1}{G_1 G_2} + ... \tag{B.7}$$

or equivalently

$$T_{esys} = T_1 + \frac{T_2}{G_1} + \frac{T_3}{G_1 G_2} + ... \tag{B.8}$$

where gains are in absolute (not dB) values. The following examples illustrate how to compute the noise figure of a mobile receiver station, and consequently the average receiver noise floor that is used in a link budget.

Example B.1

If a wireless link provides an SNR of 20 dB to the receiver antenna input terminals, and the receiver is specified to have a noise figure of 6 dB, what is the SNR at the detector stage of the receiver?

Solution

Using the concept of noise figure, it is easy to compute the SNR going into the detector stage from Equation (B.5).

Since the receiver amplifies the signal and the noise by the same factor, and the noise out is F times the noise in, then

$$\text{SNR}_{\text{OUT}} = \frac{\text{SNR}_{\text{IN}}}{F}$$

or, in dB values, $\text{SNR}_{\text{OUT}} = \text{SNR}_{\text{IN}} - F$.

Thus, for this example,

$$\text{SNR}_{\text{OUT(dB)}} = 20 - 6$$

$$\text{SNR}_{\text{OUT(dB)}} = 14 \text{ dB}$$

The output SNR (SNR just prior to demodulation) is equal to 14 dB, even though the receiver input SNR is 20 dB.

Example B.2

Consider an AMPS cellular phone with a 30 kHz RF equivalent bandwidth. The phone is connected to a mobile antenna as shown in Figure B.2. If the noise figure of the phone is 6 dB, the coaxial cable loss is 3 dB, and the antenna has an effective temperature of 290 K, compute the noise figure of the mobile receiver system as referred to the input of the antenna terminals.

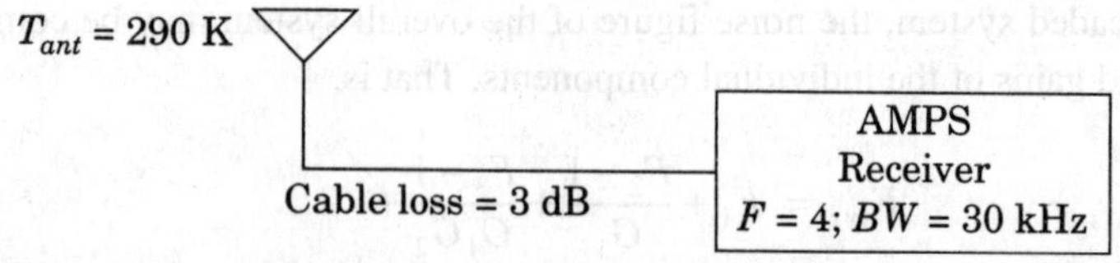

Figure B.2 A mobile receiver system with cable losses.

Solution

To find the noise figure of tne receiver system, it is necessary to first find the equivalent noise figure due to the cable and AMPS receiver. Note that 3 dB loss is equal to a loss factor of 2.0. Using Equation (B.4), which indicates that the cable has a noise figure equal to the loss, and keeping all values in absolute (rather than dB) units, the receiver system has a noise figure given by Equation (B.7)

$$F_{sys} = 2.0 + \frac{(4-1)}{0.5} = 8 = 9\text{ dB}.$$

Example B.3

For the receiver in Figure B.2, determine the a\ erage output thermal noise power, as referred to the input of the antenna terminals. Assume $T_o = 300$ K.

Solution

From Example B.2, the cable/receiver system has a noise figure of 9 dB. Using Equation (B.2), the effective noise temperature of the system is

$$T_e = (8-1)300 = 2100\text{ K}$$

Using Equation (B.8), the overall system noise temperature due to the antenna is given by

$$T_{total} = T_{ant} + T_{sys} = (290 + 2100)\text{K} = 2390\text{ K}$$

Now using the right-hand side of Equation (B.5), the average output thermal noise power referred to the antenna terminals is given by

$$P_n = \left(1 + \frac{2390}{300}\right)(1.38 \times 10^{-23})(300\text{ K})(30,000\text{ Hz})$$

$$= 1.1 \times 10^{-15}\text{ W} = -119.5\text{ dBm}$$

Example B.4

For the receiver in Figure B.2, determine the required average signal strength at the antenna terminals to provide a SNR of 30 dB at the receiver output.

Solution

From Example B.3, the average noise level is –119.5 dBm. Therefore, the signal power must be 30 dB greater than the noise

$$P_s(\text{dBm}) = SNR + (-119.5) = 30 + (-119.5) = -89.5\text{ dBm}.$$

APPENDIX C

Rate Variance Relationships for Shape Factor Theory

This Appendix derives the three rate variance relationships presented in Chapter 5.

C.1 Rate Variance for Complex Voltage

The power spectral density (PSD) of a baseband complex received voltage signal is related to the angular distribution of multipath power [Gan72]:

$$S_{\tilde{V}}(k) = \frac{p\left(\theta + \cos^{-1}\frac{k}{k_{\max}}\right) + p\left(\theta - \cos^{-1}\frac{k}{k_{\max}}\right)}{\sqrt{k_{\max}^2 - k^2}}, \text{ for } |k| \le k_{\max} \quad \text{(C.1)}$$

where θ is the azimuthal direction of travel and $p(\cdot)$ is the angular distribution of impinging multipath power. The value $k_{\max}$ is the maximum wavenumber, which is equal to $2\pi/\lambda$. Note that the PSD is a function of wavenumber, k, instead of frequency, ω, since multipath angles-of-arrival directly relate to *spatial* selectivity. By extension, the PSD is identical to the *Doppler Spectrum*, $S_{\tilde{V}}(\omega)$, of a mobile receiver if the receiver moves in a static channel.

The second moment of the fading process is given by the following integration [Jak74]:

$$\sigma_{\tilde{V}'}^2 = \frac{1}{2\pi} \int_{-k_{\max}}^{k_{\max}} (k - k_c)^2 S_{\tilde{V}}(k)\, dk \quad \text{(C.2)}$$

where k_c is the centroid of the PSD:

$$k_c = \frac{1}{2\pi F_0}\int_{-k_{max}}^{k_{max}} kS_{\tilde{V}}(k)dk \tag{C.3}$$

F_0 is defined by Equation (5.90)—this is really just the average power of the process.

Now insert Equation (C.3) into Equation (C.2), making the change of variable $\theta_x = \theta \pm \cos^{-1}(k/k_{max})$, where the + and – signs correspond to the left and right terms of p(·), respectively, of Equation (C.1). After rearranging the limits of integration, the equation for $\sigma^2_{\tilde{V}'}$, becomes

$$\sigma^2_{\tilde{V}'} = \frac{F_0 k^2_{max}}{2} - \frac{k^2_{max}}{(2\pi)^2 F_0}\left[\int_0^{2\pi} p(\theta_x)\cos(\theta-\theta_x)d\theta_x\right]^2 + \frac{k^2_{max}}{2\pi}\left[\int_0^{2\pi} p(\theta_x)\cos[2(\theta-\theta_x)]d\theta_x\right] \tag{C.4}$$

Consider a complex Fourier expansion of $\sigma^2_{\tilde{V}'}$ with respect to θ:

$$\sigma^2_{\tilde{V}'} = \frac{1}{2\pi}\text{Real}\left\{\sum_{n=0}^{\infty} A_n \exp(jn\theta)\right\} = \frac{A_0}{2\pi} + \frac{1}{2\pi}\text{Real}\{A_2\exp(j2\theta)\} \tag{C.5}$$

All of the A_n are zero for odd n. This is because $\sigma_{\tilde{V}'}(\theta) = \sigma_{\tilde{V}'}(\theta + \pi)$; that is, a 180° change in the direction of mobile travel should produce identical statistics. Furthermore, Equation (C.4) has no harmonic content with respect to θ for $n > 2$. Solving for the only two remaining complex coefficients produces

$$A_0 = \int_0^{2\pi}\sigma^2_{\tilde{V}'}d\theta = \pi k^2_{max}\left[F_0 - \frac{|F_1|^2}{F_0}\right] = \pi k^2_{max}\Lambda^2 E\{|\tilde{V}|^2\} \tag{C.6}$$

$$A_2 = \int_0^{2\pi}\sigma^2_{\tilde{V}'}\exp(-j2\theta)\,d\theta = \pi k^2_{max}\left[F_2 - \frac{F_1^2}{F_0}\right] = A_0\gamma\exp(-j2\theta_{max}) \tag{C.7}$$

where Λ, γ, and θ_{max}, are the three basic spatial channel parameters defined in Equations (5.91)–(5.93). If these two coefficients are placed back into Equation (C.5), the end result is the relationship for $\sigma^2_{\tilde{V}'}$ in Equation (5.94).

For a mobile receiver, it is often convenient to measure the fading rate variance in terms of change per unit time instead of distance. If the mobile receiver operates in an otherwise static channel, then the mean-squared time rate-of-change, $\sigma^2_{\dot{\tilde{V}}}$, is equal to $\sigma^2_{\tilde{V}'}$ multiplied by the squared velocity of the receiver.

C.2 Rate Variance for Power

The stochastic process of power is defined as P(r) = $\tilde{V}^*(r)\tilde{V}(r)$. Thus, the PSD of power for $k \neq 0$ is the convolution of two complex voltage PSDs: $S_P(k) = (1/2\pi)S_{\tilde{V}}(k) \otimes S_{\tilde{V}}(-k)$, provided the complex voltage, $\tilde{V}(r)$, is a Gaussian process (the condition for Rayleigh fading) [Pap91]. The rate variance relationship for power may then be written as

$$\sigma_{P'}^2 = \frac{1}{2\pi}\int_{-\infty}^{\infty} k^2 S_P(k)dk \tag{C.8}$$

$$= \frac{1}{2\pi}\int_{-\infty}^{\infty} k^2\left[\frac{1}{2\pi}\int_{-\infty}^{\infty} S_{\tilde{V}}(\lambda)S_{\tilde{V}}(\lambda - k)d\lambda\right]dk \tag{C.9}$$

Making the substitution $k = \lambda - k'$ leads to

$$\sigma_{P'}^2 = \int_{-\infty}^{\infty}\int_{-\infty}^{\infty}(\lambda - k')^2 S_{\tilde{V}}(\lambda)S_{\tilde{V}}(k')dk'd\lambda \tag{C.10}$$

which may be regrouped and re-expressed in terms of the spectral centroid, k_c:

$$\sigma_{P'}^2 = 2\underbrace{\left[\frac{1}{2\pi}\int_{-\infty}^{\infty} S_{\tilde{V}}(k)dk\right]}_{P_T}\underbrace{\left[\frac{1}{2\pi}\int_{-\infty}^{\infty}(k - k_c)^2 S_{\tilde{V}}(k)dk\right]}_{\sigma_{\tilde{V}'}^2} \tag{C.11}$$

Now simply substitute Equation (5.94) for $\sigma_{\tilde{V}'}^2$, to obtain Equation (5.95).

C.3 Rate Variance for Envelope

Based on the power relationship $P(r) = R^2(r)$, it is possible to write the following:

$$E\left\{\left(\frac{dP}{dr}\right)^2\right\} = 4E\{P(r)\}E\left\{\left(\frac{dR}{dr}\right)^2\right\} \tag{C.12}$$

which is valid for a Rayleigh fading process since R and its derivative are independent [Ric48]. Setting the left-hand side of Equation (C.12) equal to the rate variance relationship for power in Equation (5.95) produces the mean-squared fading rate result for a Rayleigh-fading voltage envelope in Equation (5.96).

Approximate Spatial Autocovariance Function for Shape Factor Theory

This Appendix derives the approximate spatial autocovariance function for small-scale Rayleigh fading signals.

The spatial autocovariance function for received envelope is defined as follows [Jak74], [Tur95]:

$$\rho(r) = \frac{E\{R(\vec{r}_o)R(\vec{r}_o + r\hat{r})\} - (E\{R\})^2}{E\{R^2\} - (E\{R\})^2} \tag{D.1}$$

where $\vec{r}_o$ is a position in the plane of the horizon (arbitrary if the fading process is considered to be wide-sense stationary) and $\hat{r}$ is a unit vector pointing in the direction of receiver travel, θ. To develop an approximate expression for the autocovariance of multipath fields, first expand the function, $\rho(r)$, into a Maclaurin series:

$$\rho(r) = \sum_{n=0}^{\infty} \frac{r^{2n}}{(2n)!} \left. \frac{d^{2n}\rho(r')}{dr'^{2n}} \right|_{r'=0} \tag{D.2}$$

Equation (D.2) contains only even powers of r, since any real autocovariance function is an even function. The differentiation of an autocovariance function satisfies the following relationship [Pap91]:

$$\left. \frac{d^{2n}}{dr^{2n}} E\{R(\vec{r}_o)R(\vec{r}_o + r\hat{r})\} \right|_{r'=0} = (-1)^n E\left\{\left(\frac{d^n R}{dr^n}\right)^2\right\} \tag{D.3}$$

and is useful for re-expressing the Maclaurin series:

$$\rho(r) = 1 + \frac{\sum_{n=1}^{\infty} \frac{(-1)^n r^{2n}}{(2n)!} E\left\{\left(\frac{d^n R}{dr^n}\right)^2\right\}}{E\{R^2\} - (E\{R\})^2} \tag{D.4}$$

$$= 1 - \frac{E\left\{\left(\frac{dR}{dr}\right)^2\right\}}{2[E\{R^2\} - (E\{R\})^2]} r^2 + \cdots$$

$$= 1 - \frac{\frac{\pi^2}{\lambda^2}\Lambda^2(1 + \gamma\cos[2(\theta - \theta_{\max})])P_T}{2\left(1 - \frac{\pi}{4}\right)P_T} r^2 + \cdots$$

Now consider $\rho(r)$ as being approximated by an arbitrary Gaussian function represented by a Maclaurin expansion:

$$\rho(r) \approx \exp\left[-a\left(\frac{r}{\lambda}\right)^2\right] \tag{D.5}$$

$$\approx \sum_{n=0}^{\infty} \frac{(-1)^n a^n}{n!}\left(\frac{r}{\lambda}\right)^{2n}$$

$$\approx 1 - a\left(\frac{r}{\lambda}\right)^2 + \cdots$$

A Gaussian function is chosen as a generic approximation to the true autocovariance, since it is a convenient and well-behaved correlation function. The appropriate constant a is chosen by setting equal the second terms of Equations (D.4) and (D.5), ensuring that the behavior of both autocovariance functions is identical for small r:

$$a = \underbrace{\left[\frac{2\pi^2}{4 - \pi}\right]}_{\approx 23.00} \Lambda^2(1 + \gamma\cos[2(\theta - \theta_{\max})]) \tag{D.6}$$

Therefore, using Equations (D.5) and (D.6), the approximate spatial autocovariance depends only on the three multipath shape factors, as shown in Equation (5.115).

Gaussian Approximations for Spread Spectrum CDMA

This Appendix contains detailed mathematical analysis which provides expressions for determining the average bit error rate for users in a single channel, CDMA, mobile radio system. Using the expressions provided in this appendix, it is possible to analyze CDMA systems for a wide range of interference conditions. These expressions may be used to reduce or eliminate the need for time intensive simulations of CDMA systems in some instances.

In a spread spectrum, Code Division Multiple Access (CDMA) system using binary signaling, the radio signal received at a base station from the kth mobile user (assuming no fading or multipath) is given by [Pur77]

$$s_k(t-\tau_k) = \sqrt{2P_k}a_k(t-\tau_k)b_k(t-\tau_k)\cos(\omega_c t+\varphi_k) \tag{E.1}$$

where $b_k(t)$ is the data sequence for user k, $a_k(t)$ is the spreading (or chip) sequence for user k, τ_k is the delay of user k relative to some reference user 0, P_k is the received power of user k, and φ_k is the carrier phase offset of user k relative to a reference user 0. Since τ_k and φ_k are relative terms, we can define $\tau_0 = 0$ and $\varphi_0 = 0$.

Both $a_k(t)$ and $b_k(t)$ are binary sequences with values –1 and +1. The cyclical pseudo noise (PN) chip sequence $a_k(t)$ is of the form

$$a_k(t) = \sum_{j=-\infty}^{\infty}\sum_{i=0}^{M-1} a_{k,i}\Pi\left(\frac{t-(i+jM)T_c}{T_c}\right) \qquad a_{k,i}\in\{-1, 1\} \tag{E.2}$$

where M is the number of chips sent before the PN sequence repeats itself, T_c is the chip period, MT_c is the repetition period of the PN sequence, $\Pi(t)$ represents the unit pulse function, and i is an index to denote the particular chip within a PN chip cycle.

$$\Pi(t) = \begin{cases} 1 & 0 \le t < 1 \\ 0 & \text{otherwise} \end{cases} \tag{E.3}$$

For the user data sequence, $b_k(t)$, T_b is the bit period. It is assumed that the bit period is an integer multiple of the chip period such that $T_b = NT_c$. Note that M and N are not necessarily equal. In the case where they are equal, the PN sequence is repeated for every bit period. The user data sequence $b_k(t)$ is given by

$$b_k(t) = \sum_{j=-\infty}^{\infty} b_{k,j}\Pi\left(\frac{t-jT_b}{T_b}\right) \qquad b_{k,j} \in \{-1, 1\} \tag{E.4}$$

In a mobile radio, spread spectrum, CDMA system, the signals from many users arrive at the input of the receiver. A correlation receiver is typically used to "filter" the desired user from all other users which share the same channel.

At the receiver, illustrated in Figure E.1, the signal available at the input to the correlator is given by

$$r(t) = \sum_{k=0}^{K-1} s_k(t-\tau_k) + n(t) \tag{E.5}$$

where $n(t)$ is additive Gaussian noise with two-sided power spectral density $N_0/2$. It is assumed in Equation (E.5) that there is no multipath in the channel with the possible exception of multipath that leads to purely flat, slow fading.

The received signal contains both the desired user and $(k-1)$ undesired users and is mixed down to baseband, multiplied by the PN sequence of the desired user (user 0, for example), and integrated over one bit period. Thus, assuming that the receiver is delay and phase synchronized with user 0, the decision statistic for user 0 is given by:

$$Z_0 = \int_{jT_b}^{(j+1)T_b} r(t)a_0(t)\cos(\omega_c t)dt \tag{E.6}$$

For convenience and simplicity of notation, the remainder of this analysis considers bit 0 ($j = 0$ in (E.6)).

Substituting Equations (E.1) and (E.5) into Equation (E.6), the decision statistic of the receiver is found to be

$$Z_0 = \int_{t=0}^{T_b} \left[\left(\sum_{k=0}^{K-1} \sqrt{2P_k}a_k(t-\tau_k)b_k(t-\tau_k)\cos(\omega_c t+\phi_k)\right) + n(t)\right] a_0(t)\cos(\omega_c t)dt \tag{E.7}$$

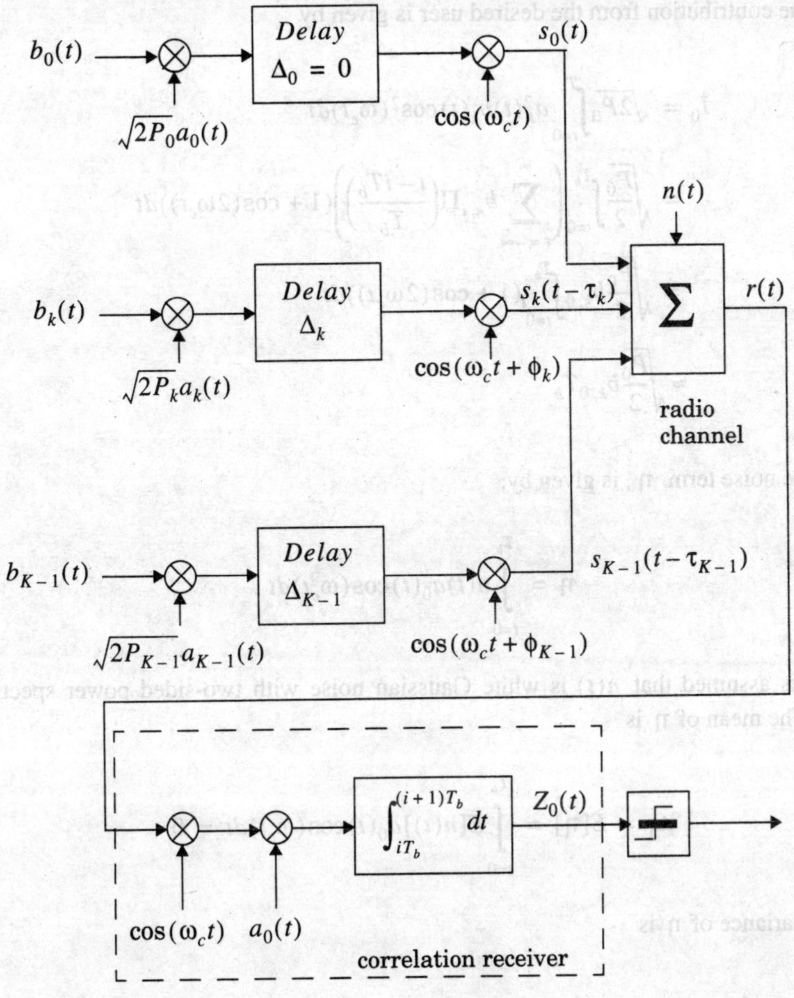

Figure E.1 Model for CDMA multiple access interference.

which may be expressed as

$$Z_0 = I_0 + \eta + \zeta \tag{E.8}$$

where I_0 is the desired contribution to the decision statistic from the desired user ($k = 0$), ζ is the multiple access interference from all co-channel users (which may be in the same cell or in a different cell), and η is the thermal noise contribution.

The contribution from the desired user is given by

$$I_0 = \sqrt{2P_0}\int_{t=0}^{T_b} a_k^2(t)b_k(t)\cos^2(\omega_c t)dt \tag{E.9}$$

$$= \sqrt{\frac{P_0}{2}}\int_{t=0}^{T_b}\left(\sum_{i=-\infty}^{\infty} b_{k,i}\Pi\left(\frac{t-iT_b}{T_b}\right)\right)(1+\cos(2\omega_c t))dt$$

$$= \sqrt{\frac{P_0}{2}}b_{k,0}\int_{t=0}^{T_b}(1+\cos(2\omega_c t))dt$$

$$\approx \sqrt{\frac{P_0}{2}}b_{k,0}T_b$$

The noise term, η, is given by:

$$\eta = \int_{t=0}^{T_b} n(t)a_0(t)\cos(\omega_c t)dt \tag{E.10}$$

It is assumed that $n(t)$ is white Gaussian noise with two-sided power spectral density $N_0/2$. The mean of η is

$$\mu_\eta = E[\eta] = \int_{t=0}^{T_b} E[n(t)]a_0(t)\cos(\omega_c t)dt = 0 \tag{E.11}$$

and the variance of η is

$$\sigma_\eta^2 = E[(\eta-\mu_\eta)^2] = E[\eta^2] \tag{E.12}$$

$$= E\left[\int_{\lambda=0}^{T_b}\int_{t=0}^{T_b} n(t)n(\lambda)a_0(t)a_0(\lambda)\cos(\omega_c t)\cos(\omega_c\lambda)dtd\lambda\right]$$

$$= \int_{\lambda=0}^{T_b}\int_{t=0}^{T_b} E[n(t)n(\lambda)]a_0(t)a_0(\lambda)\cos(\omega_c t)\cos(\omega_c\lambda)dtd\lambda$$

$$= \int_{\lambda=0}^{T_b}\int_{t=0}^{T_b}\frac{N_0}{2}\delta(t-\lambda)a_0(t)a_0(\lambda)\cos(\omega_c t)\cos(\omega_c\lambda)dtd\lambda$$

$$= \frac{N_0}{2}\int_{t=0}^{T_b} a_0^2(t)\cos^2(\omega_c t)dt = \frac{N_0}{4}\int_{t=0}^{T_b}(1+\cos(2\omega_c t))dt$$

$$= \frac{N_0}{4}\left(T_b + \frac{1}{2\omega_c}\sin(2\omega_c T_b)\right) \approx \frac{N_0 T_b}{4} \qquad \text{for } \omega_c \gg \frac{2}{T_b}$$

The third component in Equation (E.8), ζ, represents the contribution of multiple access interference to the decision statistic. ζ is the summation of $K-1$ terms, I_k,

$$\zeta = \sum_{k=1}^{K-1} I_k \tag{E.13}$$

each of which is given by

$$I_k = \int_{t=0}^{T_b} \sqrt{2P_k}\, b_k(t-\tau_k)\, a_k(t-\tau_k)\, a_0(t) \cos(\omega_c t + \phi_k) \cos(\omega_c t)\, dt \tag{E.14}$$

It is useful to simplify Equation (E.14) in order to examine the effects of multiple access interference on the average bit error probability for a single user (i.e., user 0 for simplicity). The relationship between $b_k(t-\tau_k)$, $a_k(t-\tau_k)$, and $a_0(t)$ is illustrated in Figure E.2.

The quantities γ_k and Δ_k in Figure E.2 are defined from the delay of user k relative to user 0, τ_k, such that [Pur77]

$$\tau_k = \gamma_k T_c + \Delta_k \qquad 0 \le \Delta_k < T_c \tag{E.15}$$

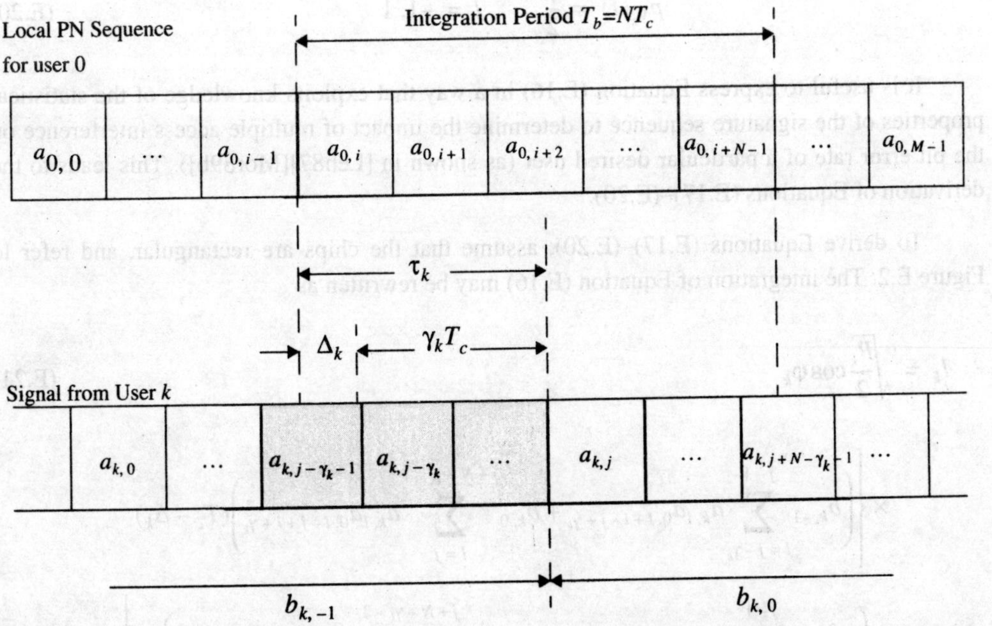

Figure E.2 Timing of the local PN sequence for user 0, $a_0(t)$, and the received signal from user k, $s_k(t-\tau_k)$.

The contribution from kth, interfering user, to the decision statistic is given by [Pur77], [Mor89b]

$$I_k = T_c\sqrt{\frac{P_k}{2}}\cos\varphi_k\left\{\left(X_k + \left(1-\frac{2\Delta_k}{T_c}\right)Y_k\right) + \left(1-\frac{\Delta_k}{T_c}\right)U_k + \left(\frac{\Delta_k}{T_c}\right)V_k\right\} \tag{E.16}$$

where X_k, Y_k, U_k, and V_k have distributions, conditioned on A and B, which are given by:

$$p_{X_k}(l) = \binom{A}{\frac{l+A}{2}}2^{-A} \qquad l = -A, -A+2, \ldots, A-2, A \tag{E.17}$$

$$p_{Y_k}(l) = \binom{B}{\frac{l+B}{2}}2^{-B} \qquad l = -B, -B+2, \ldots, B-2, B \tag{E.18}$$

$$p_{U_k}(l) = \frac{1}{2} \qquad l = -1, 1 \tag{E.19}$$

$$p_{V_k}(l) = \frac{1}{2} \qquad l = -1, 1 \tag{E.20}$$

It is useful to express Equation (E.16) in a way that exploits knowledge of the statistical properties of the signature sequence to determine the impact of multiple access interference on the bit error rate of a particular desired user (as shown in [Leh87][Mor89b]). This leads to the derivation of Equations (E.17)–(E.20).

To derive Equations (E.17)–(E.20), assume that the chips are rectangular, and refer to Figure E.2. The integration of Equation (E.16) may be rewritten as

$$I_k = \sqrt{\frac{P_k}{2}}\cos\varphi_k \tag{E.21}$$

$$\times\left\{\left(b_{k,-1}\sum_{l=j-\gamma_k}^{j-1} a_{k,l}a_{0,l+i-j+\gamma_k} + b_{k,0}\sum_{l=j}^{j+N-\gamma_k-1} a_{k,l}a_{0,l-j+i+\gamma_k}\right)(T_c-\Delta_k)\right.$$

$$\left.+\left(b_{k,-1}\sum_{l=j-\gamma_k-1}^{j-1} a_{k,l}a_{0,l+i-j+\gamma_k+1} + b_{k,0}\sum_{l=j}^{j+N-\gamma_k-2} a_{k,l}a_{0,l-j+i+\gamma_k+1}\right)\Delta_k\right\}$$

It is convenient to rewrite this as

$$I_k = T_c\sqrt{\frac{P_k}{2}}\cos\varphi_k \tag{E.22}$$

$$\times\left\{\left(b_{k,-1}\sum_{l=0}^{\gamma_k-1} a_{k,l+j-\gamma_k}a_{0,l+i} + b_{k,0}\sum_{l=\gamma_k}^{N-1} a_{k,l+j-\gamma_k}a_{0,l+i}\right)\left(1-\frac{\Delta_k}{T_c}\right)\right.$$

$$\left.+\left(b_{k,-1}\sum_{l=-1}^{\gamma_k-1} a_{k,l+j-\gamma_k}a_{0,l+i+1} + b_{k,0}\sum_{l=\gamma_k}^{N-2} a_{k,l+j-\gamma_k}a_{0,l+i+1}\right)\left(\frac{\Delta_k}{T_c}\right)\right\}$$

This may be rearranged to give [Leh87]

$$I_k = T_c\sqrt{\frac{P_k}{2}}\cos\varphi_k \tag{E.23}$$

$$\times\left\{\left(\sum_{l=0}^{\gamma_k-1} b_{k,-1}a_{k,l+j-\gamma_k}a_{l+i} +\right.\right.$$

$$\left.\sum_{l=\gamma_k}^{N-2} b_{k,0}a_{k,l+j-\gamma_k}a_{0,l+i} + b_0 a_{k,N-1+j-\gamma_k}a_{0,N-1+i}\right)\left(1-\frac{\Delta_k}{T_c}\right)$$

$$+\left(\sum_{l=0}^{\gamma_k-1} b_{k,-1}a_{k,l+j-\gamma_k}a_{0,l+i+1} +\right.$$

$$\left.\left.\sum_{l=\gamma_k}^{N-2} b_{k,0}a_{k,l+j-\gamma_k}a_{0,l+i+1} + b_{-1}a_{k,j-\gamma_k-1}a_{0,i}\right)\left(\frac{\Delta_k}{T_c}\right)\right\}$$

Lehnert defined random variables $Z_{k,l}$ as [Leh87]

$$Z_{k,l} = \begin{cases} b_{k,-1}a_{k,l+j-\gamma_k}a_{0,l+i} & l = 0, \gamma_k - 1 \\ b_{k,0}a_{k,l+j-\gamma_k}a_{0,l+i} & l = \gamma_k, N-2 \\ b_{k,0}a_{k,N-1+j-\gamma_k}a_{0,N-1+i} & l = N-1 \\ b_{k,-1}a_{k,j-\gamma_k-1}a_{0,i} & l = N \end{cases} \tag{E.24}$$

where each of the $Z_{k,j}$ are independent Bernoulli trials, equally distributed on $\{-1, 1\}$.

Then, using Equation (E.24) and the fact that $a_{0,l}a_{0,l} = 1$, Equation (E.23) may be expressed as

$$I_k = T_c\sqrt{\frac{P_k}{2}}\cos\varphi_k \times \left\{\left(\sum_{l=0}^{N-2} Z_{k,l}\left(\left(1-\frac{\Delta_k}{T_c}\right)+a_{0,l+i}a_{0,l+i+1}\left(\frac{\Delta_k}{T_c}\right)\right)\right)\right. \tag{E.25}$$
$$\left. + Z_{k,N-1}\left(1-\frac{\Delta_k}{T_c}\right)+Z_{k,N}\left(\frac{\Delta_k}{T_c}\right)\right\}$$

Let $\mathcal{A}$ be the set of all integers in $[0, N-2]$ for which $a_{0,l+i}a_{0,l+i+1} = 1$. Similarly, let $\mathcal{B}$ be defined as the set of all integers in $[0, N-2]$ for which $a_{0,l+i}a_{0,l+i+1} = -1$. Then, Equation (E.25) may be expressed as

$$I_k = T_c\sqrt{\frac{P_k}{2}}\cos\varphi_k\left\{\left(\sum_{l\in\mathcal{A}} Z_{k,l} + (1-2\Delta_k/T_c)\sum_{l\in\mathcal{B}} Z_{k,l}\right)\right. \tag{E.26}$$
$$\left. + Z_{k,N-1}\left(1-\frac{\Delta_k}{T_c}\right)+Z_{k,N}\left(\frac{\Delta_k}{T_c}\right)\right\}$$

Now define

$$X_k = \sum_{l\in\mathcal{A}} Z_{k,l} \tag{E.27}$$

$$Y_k = \sum_{l\in\mathcal{B}} Z_{k,l} \tag{E.28}$$

$$U_k = Z_{k,N-1} \tag{E.29}$$

$$V_k = Z_{k,N} \tag{E.30}$$

Note that $\{Z_{k,l}\}$ is a set of independent Bernoulli trials [Coo86], each with each outcome identically distributed on $\{-1,+1\}$. If we let A denote the number of elements in the set $\mathcal{A}$ and let B denote the number of elements in the set $\mathcal{B}$, then the probability density functions for X_k and Y_k are given by

$$p_{X_k}(l) = \begin{pmatrix} A \\ \frac{l+A}{2} \end{pmatrix} 2^{-A} \qquad l = -A, -A+2, \ldots, A-2, A \tag{E.31}$$

$$p_{Y_k}(l) = \begin{pmatrix} B \\ \frac{l+B}{2} \end{pmatrix} 2^{-B} \qquad l = -B, -B+2, \ldots, B-2, B \tag{E.32}$$

and the quantities U_k and V_k are each distributed as

$$p_{U_k}(l) = \frac{1}{2} \qquad l = -1, 1 \tag{E.33}$$

$$p_{V_k}(l) = \frac{1}{2} \qquad l = -1, 1 \tag{E.34}$$

Thus, the interference contributed to the decision statistic by a particular multiple access interferer is entirely defined by the quantities P_k, φ_k, Δ_k, A, and B as given in Equations (E.16)–(E.20). Note that A and B are solely dependent on the sequence of user 0. Furthermore, $A + B = N - 1$, since sets $\mathcal{A}$ and $\mathcal{B}$ are disjoint and span the set of total possible signature sequences of length N in which there are a total of $N - 1$ possible chip level transitions.

E.1 The Gaussian Approximation

The use of the Gaussian Approximation to determine the bit error rate in binary, CDMA, multiple access, communication systems is based on the argument that the decision statistic, Z_0, given by Equation (E.8), may be modeled as a Gaussian random variable [Pur77], [Mor89b]. The first component in Equation (E.8), I_0, is deterministic, and its value is given by Equation (E.9). The other two components of Z_0 (i.e., ζ and η), are assumed to be zero-mean Gaussian random variables. Assuming that the additive receiver noise, $n(t)$, is bandpass Gaussian noise, then η, which is given by Equation (E.10), is a zero-mean Gaussian random variable. This section derives an expression for the bit error rate based on the assumption that the multiple access interference term, ζ, may be approximated by a Gaussian random variable.

First define a combined noise and interference term ξ, given by

$$\xi = \zeta + \eta \tag{E.35}$$

such that the decision statistic, Z_0, is given by

$$Z_0 = I_0 + \xi \tag{E.36}$$

where Z_0 is a Gaussian random variable with mean I_0 and a variance which is equal to the variance, σ_ξ^2, of ξ.

The probability of error in determining the value of a received bit is equal to the probability that $\xi < -I_0$ when I_0 is positive and $\xi > I_0$ when I_0 is negative. Due to its structure, ξ is symmetrically distributed such that these two conditions occur with equal probability, therefore we may say that the probability of error is equal to the probability that $\xi > |I_0|$. If ξ is a zero-mean Gaussian random variable with variance, σ_ξ^2, the probability of a bit error is given by

$$P_e = \int_{|I_0|}^{\infty} p_\xi(x)dx \tag{E.37}$$

$$= \int_{|I_0|}^{\infty} \frac{1}{\sqrt{2\pi}\sigma_\xi} \exp\left(\frac{-x^2}{2\sigma_\xi^2}\right)dx$$

$$= \frac{1}{\sqrt{2\pi}} \int_{|I_0|/\sigma_\xi}^{\infty} \exp\left(\frac{-u^2}{2}\right)du$$

$$= Q\left(\frac{|I_0|}{\sigma_\xi}\right)$$

where the Q function is defined in Appendix F. Using Equation (E.9), this may be rewritten as:

$$P_e = Q\left(\sqrt{\frac{P_0 T_b^2}{2\sigma_\xi^2}}\right) \tag{E.38}$$

Assuming that the multiple access interference contribution to the decision statistic, ζ, can be modelled as a zero-mean Gaussian random variable with variance σ_ζ^2, and that the noise contribution to the decision statistic, η, may be modelled as a zero-mean Gaussian noise process with variance $\sigma_\eta^2 = N_o T_b/4$, then it follows that since the noise and the multiple access interference are independent, the variance of ξ is given simply by

$$\sigma_\xi^2 = \sigma_\zeta^2 + \sigma_\eta^2 \tag{E.39}$$

All that remains is to justify the Gaussian approximation for ζ, and to determine the value of σ_ζ^2.

Using Equations (E.13) and (E.16), the total multiple access interference contribution to the decision statistic for user 0, is given by

$$\zeta = \sum_{k=1}^{K-1} T_c \sqrt{\frac{P_k}{2}} \cos\varphi_k \left\{ X_k + \left(1 - \frac{2\Delta_k}{T_c}\right)Y_k + \left(1 - \frac{\Delta_k}{T_c}\right)U_k + \left(\frac{\Delta_k}{T_c}\right)V_k \right\} \tag{E.40}$$

which may be expressed as

$$\zeta = \sum_{k=1}^{K-1} W_k T_c \sqrt{\frac{P_k}{2}} \cos\varphi_k \tag{E.41}$$

where

$$W_k = X_k + \left(1 - \frac{2\Delta_k}{T_c}\right)Y_k + \left(1 - \frac{\Delta_k}{T_c}\right)U_k + \left(\frac{\Delta_k}{T_c}\right)V_k \tag{E.42}$$

The exact distributions for X_k and Y_k are given by Equations (E.17) and (E.18) and the distributions of U_k and V_k are given in Equations (E.19) and (E.20). Note that W_k may only take on discrete values (a maximum of $(N-1)B - B^2 + 6$ values) for a given Δ_k.

The Central Limit Theorem (CLT) [Sta86], [Coo86] is used to justify the approximation of ζ as a Gaussian random variable. The CLT considers the normalized sum of a large number of identically distributed random variables x_i, where y is the normalized random variable given by

$$y = \frac{1}{\sqrt{M}} \sum_{i=0}^{M-1} (x_i - \mu) \tag{E.43}$$

and each x_i has mean μ and variance σ^2. The random variable y is approximately normally distributed (a Gaussian distribution with zero mean and unit variance) as M becomes large. To justify the Gaussian approximation when the interferer power levels are not equal or not constant, a more general definition of the CLT is required as given by Stark and Woods [Sta86].

This more general statement of the CLT [Sta86], requires that the sum

$$y = \sum_{i=0}^{M-1} x_i \tag{E.44}$$

of M random variables, x_i (which are not necessarily identically distributed but are independent), each with mean μ_{x_i} and variance $\sigma^2_{x_i}$, approaches a Gaussian random variable as M gets large, provided that

$$\sigma^2_{x_j} \ll \sigma^2_y = \sum_{i=0}^{M-1} \sigma^2_{x_i} \qquad j = 0 \ldots M-1 \tag{E.45}$$

Furthermore, the mean and variance of the sum, y, are given by

$$\mu_y = \sum_{i=0}^{M-1} \mu_{x_i} \tag{E.46}$$

$$\sigma^2_y = \sum_{i=0}^{M-1} \sigma^2_{x_i} \tag{E.47}$$

The condition for Equation (E.45) to hold is equivalent to specifying that no single user dominates the total multiple access interference.

Consider the statistics of ζ conditioned on a specific set of operating conditions, namely, the set of $K-1$ delays $\{\Delta_k\}$, $K-1$ phase shifts $\{\phi_k\}$, $K-1$ received power levels $\{P_k\}$, and the number of chip transitions during on complete cycle of the PN sequence for user 0.

It can be shown that each of the multiple access interferers are uncorrelated given a particular set of operating conditions [Leh87]:

$$var(\zeta|\{\Delta_k\},\{\varphi_k\},\{P_k\},B) = E\left[\left(\sum_{k=1}^{K-1} I_k\right)^2 \middle| \{\Delta_k\},\{\varphi_k\},\{P_k\},B\right] \tag{E.48}$$

$$= \sum_{k=1}^{K-1} E[I_k^2|\Delta_k,\varphi_k,P_k,B]$$

$$= \sum_{k=1}^{K-1} \frac{T_c^2 P_k}{2}\cos^2\varphi_k E[W_k^2|\Delta_k,B]$$

The terms X_k, Y_k U_k, and V_k in Equation (E.42) are uncorrelated, so that

$$E[W_k^2|\Delta_k,B] = E[X_k^2|B] + \left(1-\frac{2\Delta_k}{T_c}\right)^2 E[Y_k^2|B] + \left(1-\frac{\Delta_k}{T_c}\right)^2 E[U_k^2] + \left(\frac{\Delta_k}{T_c}\right)^2 E[V_k^2] \tag{E.49}$$

Noting that the random variables U_k and V_k take on values of $\{-1,+1\}$ with equal probability, therefore $E[U_k^2] = 1$ and $E[V_k^2] = 1$, and it follows that

$$E[W_k^2|\Delta_k,B] = E[X_k^2|B] + \left(1-\frac{4\Delta_k}{T_c}+\frac{4\Delta_k^2}{T_c^2}\right)E[Y_k^2|B] + 1-\frac{2\Delta_k}{T_c}+\frac{2\Delta_k^2}{T_c^2} \tag{E.50}$$

where X_k is the summation of A independent and identically distributed Bernoulli trials, x_i, each with equally likely outcomes from $\{-1,+1\}$. In Equation (E.31), A is the number of possible values of l such that the bit patterns $a_{0,l+i}a_{0,l+i+1} = 1$ for $l \in [0, N-2]$ and i is the offset of first chip of the detected bit relative to the start of the PN sequence. Now, solving for $E[X_k|B]$

$$E[X_k^2|B] = E\left[\left(\sum_{i=0}^{A-1} x_i\right)^2\right] = \sum_{i=0}^{A-1} E[x_i^2] = A = N-B-1 \tag{E.51}$$

where B is the number of bit transitions, i.e., the values of l such that the bit patterns $a_{0,l+i}a_{0,l+i+1} = -1$. Similarly for Y_k,

$$E[Y_k^2|B] = E\left[\left(\sum_{i=0}^{B-1} b_i\right)^2\right] = \sum_{i=0}^{B-1} E[b_i^2] = B \tag{E.52}$$

Therefore, Equation (E.50) may be rewritten

$$E[W_k^2|\Delta_k, B] = N - B - 1 + \left(1 - \frac{4\Delta_k}{T_c} + \frac{4\Delta_k^2}{T_c^2}\right)B + \left(1 - \frac{2\Delta_k}{T_c} + \frac{\Delta_k^2}{T_c^2}\right) + \frac{\Delta_k^2}{T_c^2} \tag{E.53}$$
$$= N + 2(2B+1)\left(\left(\frac{\Delta_k}{T_c}\right)^2 - \frac{\Delta_k}{T_c}\right)$$

Using Equation (E.48)

$$E[I_k^2|\Delta_k, \varphi_k, P_k, B] = T_c^2 P_k \cos^2\varphi_k\left(\frac{N}{2} + (2B+1)\left(\left(\frac{\Delta_k}{T_c}\right)^2 - \frac{\Delta_k}{T_c}\right)\right) \tag{E.54}$$

Taking the expected value of Equation (E.54) over Δ_k and φ_k on a chip interval yields

$$E[I_k^2|P_k, B] = \frac{T_c^2 P_k}{2}\left(\frac{N}{2} + (2B+1)\left(-\frac{1}{6}\right)\right) \tag{E.55}$$

Finally, assuming random signature sequences for each user, and averaging Equation (E.55) over B with $E[B] = (N-1)/2$, the variance of the total multiple access interference conditioned on the received power level, P_k is found to be

$$E[I_k^2|P_k] = \frac{NT_c^2 P_k}{6} \tag{E.56}$$

If the set of power levels for the $K-1$ interfering users are constant, then

$$\sigma_{I_k}^2 = \frac{NT_c^2 P_k}{6} \tag{E.57}$$

If the $K-1$ values of $\sigma_{I_k}^2$ satisfy Equation (E.45), then ζ, will be a zero-mean Gaussian random variable as $K-1$ gets large. The variance of ζ is given by

$$\sigma_\zeta^2 = \frac{NT_c^2}{6}\sum_{k=1}^{K-1} P_k \tag{E.58}$$

Therefore the decision statistic Z_0 of Equation (E.36) may be modeled as a Gaussian random variable with mean given by Equation (E.9) and variance given by Equation (E.39)

$$\sigma_\xi^2 = \sigma_\zeta^2 + \sigma_\eta^2 \tag{E.59}$$
$$= \frac{NT_c^2}{6}\sum_{k=1}^{K-1} P_k + \frac{N_0 T_b}{4}$$

Therefore, from Equation (E.38), the average bit error probability is given by

$$P_e = Q\left(\frac{\sqrt{\frac{P_0}{2}}T_b}{\sqrt{\frac{NT_c^2}{6}\sum_{k=1}^{K-1}P_k + \frac{N_0T_b}{4}}}\right) \tag{E.60}$$

$$= Q\left(\sqrt{\frac{1}{\frac{1}{3N}\sum_{k=1}^{K-1}\frac{P_k}{P_0} + \frac{N_0}{2T_bP_0}}}\right)$$

In typical mobile radio environments, communication links are interference-limited and not noise-limited. For the interference-limited case, $\frac{N_0}{2T_b} \ll \frac{1}{3N}\sum_{k=1}^{K-1}P_k$, and the average bit error probability is given by

$$P_e = Q\left(\sqrt{\frac{3N}{\sum_{k=1}^{K-1}P_k/P_0}}\right) \tag{E.61}$$

In the noninterference limited case, for perfect power control where $P_k = P_0$ for all $k = 1\ldots K-1$,

$$P_e = Q\left(\sqrt{\frac{1}{\frac{K-1}{3N} + \frac{N_0}{2T_bP_0}}}\right) \tag{E.62}$$

Finally, in the interference limited case with perfect power control, Equation (E.62) may be approximated by

$$P_e = Q\left(\sqrt{\frac{3N}{K-1}}\right) \tag{E.63}$$

Note that in Equation (E.60), the bit error rate is evaluated assuming that variance of the multiple access interference assumes its average value. In Section E.2, an alternative expression for the bit error rate is presented in which the bit error rate expression is averaged over the possible operating conditions, rather than evaluated at the average operating condition.

E.2 The Improved Gaussian Approximation (IGA)

The expressions in Section E.1 are only valid when the number of users, K, is large. Furthermore, depending on the distribution of the power levels for the $K-1$ interfering users, even when K is large, if Equation (E.45) is not satisfied, ζ will not be accurately modelled as a Gaussian random variable.

In situations where the Gaussian Approximation of Section E.1 is not appropriate, a more in-depth analysis must be applied. This analysis defines the interference terms I_k, conditioned on the particular operating condition of each user. When this is done, each I_k becomes Gaussian for large K. Define ψ as the variance of the multiple access interference for a specific operating condition:

$$\psi = var(\zeta|(\{\varphi_k\}, \{\Delta_k\}, \{P_k\}, B)) \tag{E.64}$$

First note that the conditional variance of the multiple access interference, ψ, is itself a random variable which is conditioned on the operating conditions $\{\varphi_k\}$, $\{\Delta_k\}$, $\{P_k\}$, and B. In Equation (E.60), the bit error rate is evaluated assuming that the variance of the multiple access interference takes on its average value. Rather that evaluating Equation (E.37) for the average value of ψ, if the distribution of ψ is known, the bit error rate may be found by averaging overall possible values of ψ. This is given by

$$P_e = E\left[Q\left(\sqrt{\frac{P_0 T_b^2}{2\psi}}\right)\right] = \int_0^{\infty} Q\left(\sqrt{\frac{P_0 T_b^2}{2\psi}}\right) f_{\psi}(\psi) d\psi \tag{E.65}$$

From Equations (E.48) and (E.54)

$$\psi = \sum_{k=1}^{K-1} T_c^2 P_k \cos^2\varphi_k \left(\frac{N}{2} + (2B+1)\left(\left(\frac{\Delta_k}{T_c}\right)^2 - \frac{\Delta_k}{T_c}\right)\right) = \sum_{k=1}^{K-1} Z_k \tag{E.66}$$

where

$$Z_k = \frac{T_c^2}{2} P_k U_k V_k \tag{E.67}$$

and where

$$U_k = 1 + \cos(2\varphi_k) \tag{E.68}$$

$$V_k = \frac{N}{2} + (2B+1)\left(\left(\frac{\Delta_k}{T_c}\right)^2 - \frac{\Delta_k}{T_c}\right) \tag{E.69}$$

Since the U_k and V_k are identically distributed for all k, it is convenient to drop the subscripts to obtain

$$Z_k = \frac{T_c^2}{2} P_k UV = \frac{T_c^2}{2} P_k Z' \tag{E.70}$$

$$U = 1 + \cos(2\varphi) \tag{E.71}$$

$$V = \frac{N}{2} + (2B+1)\left(\left(\frac{\Delta}{T_c}\right)^2 - \frac{\Delta}{T_c}\right) \tag{E.72}$$

and it is easily shown that $E[Z'] = E[UV] = E[U]E[V] = N/3$.

The distribution of U is given as [Mor00]

$$f_U(u) = \frac{1}{\pi\sqrt{u(1-u)}} \qquad 0 < u < 2 \tag{E.73}$$

and the distribution of V is given by [Mor00] as

$$f_{V|B}(v) = \frac{1}{\sqrt{\tilde{B}(2v + \tilde{B} - N)}} \qquad \frac{N - \tilde{B}}{2} < v < \frac{N}{2} \tag{E.74}$$

where $\tilde{B} = B + \frac{1}{2}$.

The distribution of the product of U and V, denoted by Z', is given by [Mor89b]

$$f_{Z'|B}(z) = \frac{1}{2\pi\sqrt{\tilde{B}z}}\ln\left(\frac{\sqrt{N-z}+\sqrt{\tilde{B}}}{\sqrt{N-z}-\sqrt{\tilde{B}}}\right) \qquad 0 < z \le N,\ z \ne N - \tilde{B} \tag{E.75}$$

The distribution of Z_k, conditioned on the received power P_k of the kth user is

$$f_{Z_k|B,P_k}(z) = \frac{2}{T_c^2 P_k} f_{Z'|B}\left(\frac{2z}{T_c^2 P_k}\right) \tag{E.76}$$

Letting $\hat{B}_k = (T_c^2 P_k/2)(B + 1/2)$ and $\hat{N}_k = NT_c^2 P_k/2$ in Equation (E.75)

$$f_{Z|B,P_k}(z) = \frac{1}{2\pi\sqrt{\hat{B}_k z}}\ln\left(\frac{\sqrt{\hat{N}_k - z}+\sqrt{\hat{B}_k}}{\sqrt{\hat{N}_k - z}-\sqrt{\hat{B}_k}}\right) \qquad 0 < z \le \hat{N}_k,\ z \ne \hat{N}_k - \hat{B}_k \tag{E.77}$$

Since ψ is the summation of the $K-1$ Z_k terms, the probability density function for ψ is then given by the convolution

$$f_{\psi|B,\{P_k\}} = f_{Z|B,P_1}(z) * f_{Z|B,P_2}(z) * \ldots * f_{Z|B,P_{K-1}}(z) \tag{E.78}$$

If the set of received powers, $\{P_k\}$, is fixed and nonrandom, then Equation (E.78) may be computed numerically by evaluating Equation (E.77) for each value of P_k. If the received power is a random variable, then an expression may be found for $f_\Psi(\psi)$ based on the distribution of power levels for the interfering users. Making the reasonable assumption that the power level for each user is identically and randomly distributed, then the distributions of the Z_k terms are identical, such that $f_{Z_k|B}(z) = f_{Z|B}(z)$. Then assuming that the distribution of the received interfering powers is known and given by some distribution $f_P(p)$ [Lib95]

$$f_{Z|B}(z) = \int_0^\infty \frac{2}{T_c^2 p} f_{Z'|B,P}\left(\frac{2z}{T_c^2 p}\right) f_P(p)dp \tag{E.79}$$

in which case, Equation (E.78) reduces to

$$f_{\psi|B}(\psi) = f_{Z|B}(z) * f_{Z|B}(z) * \ldots * f_{Z|B}(z) \tag{E.80}$$

and the probability density function for the variance of the multiple access interference is given by

$$f_\psi(\psi) = E_B[f_{\psi|B}(\psi)] = 2^{1-N} \sum_{j=0}^{N-1} \binom{N-1}{j} f_{\psi|j}(\psi) \tag{E.81}$$

Equation (E.81) may be used in Equation (E.65) to determine the average bit error probability. This technique has been shown [Mor89b] to be accurate for a very small number of interfering users for the case of perfect power control.

Equation (E.65) assumes the interference-limited case. In general, when the noise term is significant

$$P_e = E\left[Q\left(\sqrt{\frac{P_0 T_b^2}{2\left(\psi + \frac{N_0 T_b}{4}\right)}}\right)\right] = \int_0^\infty Q\left(\sqrt{\frac{P_0 T_b^2}{2\left(\psi + \frac{N_0 T_b}{4}\right)}}\right) f_\psi(\psi)d\psi \tag{E.82}$$

Thus, using Equations (E.76) and (E.79), the results of Morrow and Lehnert [Mor00] may be extended to include the case in which the power levels of the interfering users are constant but unequal and the case in which the power levels of the interfering users are independent and identically distributed random variables [Lib94a], [Lib95].

E.3 A Simplified Expression for the Improved Gaussian Approximation (SEIGA) [Lib95]

The expressions presented in Section E.2 are complicated and require significant computational time to evaluate. Holtzman [Hol92] presents a technique is for evaluating Equation (E.65) with (E.81) for the case of perfect power control. In addition, his results have been extended by Liberti [Lib94a] [Lib99] to treat the power levels of the $K-1$ interfering users as independent and identically distributed random variables. This section also presents results for the case where the received power levels for the interfering users are constant but not identical (which is representative for very wideband CDMA systems).

The simplified bit error probability expressions are based on the fact that a continuous function $f(x)$, may be expressed as

$$f(x) = f(\mu) + (x-\mu)f'(\mu) + \frac{1}{2}(x-\mu)^2 f''(\mu) + \dots \tag{E.83}$$

If x is a random variable and μ is the mean of x, then [Coo86]

$$E[f(x)] = f(x) + \frac{1}{2}\sigma^2 f''(x) + \dots \tag{E.84}$$

where σ^2 is the variance of x.

Further computational savings can be obtained by expanding in differences rather than derivatives, so that

$$f(x) = f(\mu) + (x-\mu)\left(\frac{f(\mu+h)-f(\mu-h)}{2h}\right) + \frac{1}{2}(x-\mu)^2\left(\frac{f(\mu+h)-f(\mu)+f(\mu-h)}{h^2}\right) + \dots \tag{E.85}$$

which gives the approximation

$$E[f(x)] \approx f(\mu) + \frac{\sigma^2}{2}\left(\frac{f(\mu+h)-2f(\mu)+f(\mu-h)}{h^2}\right) \tag{E.86}$$

In [Hol92], it is suggested that an appropriate choice for h is $\sqrt{3}\sigma$ which yields

$$E[f(x)] \approx \frac{2}{3}f(\mu) + \frac{1}{6}f(\mu+\sqrt{3}\sigma) + \frac{1}{6}f(\mu-\sqrt{3}\sigma) \tag{E.87}$$

Using this approximation to evaluate Equation (E.65), the expression derived [Hol92] is found to be

$$P_e = E\left[Q\left(\sqrt{\frac{P_0 T_b^2}{2\psi}}\right)\right] \tag{E.88}$$

$$\approx \frac{2}{3}Q\left(\sqrt{\frac{P_0 T_b^2}{2\mu_\psi}}\right) + \frac{1}{6}Q\left(\sqrt{\frac{P_0 T_b^2}{2(\mu_\psi+\sqrt{3}\sigma_\psi)}}\right) + \frac{1}{6}Q\left(\sqrt{\frac{P_0 T_b^2}{2(\mu_\psi-\sqrt{3}\sigma_\psi)}}\right)$$

where μ_ψ is the mean of the variance of the multiple access interference, ψ, conditioned on a specific set of operating conditions, and σ_ψ^2 is the variance of ψ. The conditional variance of the multiple access interference is given by Equation (E.66). If the received power levels from the $K-1$ interfering users are identically distributed with mean μ_P and variance σ_P^2, then using the relationships in Equations (E.70)–(E.72), the mean and variance of ψ are given by

$$\mu_\psi = \sum_{k=1}^{K-1} E[Z_k] = \frac{T_c^2 E[UV]}{2} \sum_{k=1}^{K-1} E[P_k] = \frac{T_c^2 N}{6}(K-1)\mu_P \tag{E.89}$$

Using Equation (E.89), the variance of ψ is given by

$$\sigma_\psi^2 = E\left[\left(\sum_{k=1}^{K-1} Z_k\right)^2\right] - \mu_\psi^2 \tag{E.90}$$

$$= (K-1)E[Z_k^2] + (K-1)(K-2)E[Z_k Z_j] - \mu_\psi^2$$

$$= (K-1)\frac{T_c^4 E[P_k^2]}{160}(7N^2+2N-2) + (K-1)(K-2)\frac{T_c^4 E[P_k P_j]}{144}(4N^2+N-1) - \mu_\psi^2$$

$$= (K-1)\left(\frac{T_c^4}{4}\right)\left[\left(\frac{63N^2+18N-18}{360}\right)(\sigma_P^2+\mu_P^2) + \left(\frac{10(K-2)(N-1)-40N^2}{360}\right)\mu_P^2\right]$$

$$= (K-1)\left(\frac{T_c^4}{4}\right)\left[\frac{7N^2+2N-2}{40}\sigma_P^2 + \left(\frac{23N^2}{360} + N\left(\frac{1}{20}+\frac{K-2}{36}\right) - \frac{1}{20} - \frac{K-2}{36}\right)\mu_P^2\right]$$

where μ_P is the mean of the received power for each interfering user, and σ_P^2 is the variance of the received power.

The expressions in Equations (E.89) and (E.90) were developed by Liberti [Lib94a] and are more general than the results originally given by Holtzman [Hol92], because they allow for the case in which the power levels of the interfering users are independent and identically distributed random variables.

Note that Equation (E.88) is only valid for $\mu_\psi > \sqrt{3}\sigma_\psi$ to ensure that the denominator of the third term is positive. This leads to the following requirement

$$\frac{\sigma_P^2}{\mu_P^2} < \frac{10K(4N^2-3N+3) - (109N^2-6N+6)}{27(7N^2+2N-2)} \tag{E.91}$$

Note that, in addition to limiting the ratio σ_P^2/μ_P^2, Equation (E.91) bounds the lowest number of users K for which Equation (E.88) may be evaluated, since both σ_P^2 and μ_P^2 are positive. Examination of Equation (E.91) reveals that regardless of the values of σ_P and μ_P, for $N \geq 7$, K must be greater than 2 to use Equation (E.88). For $N < 7$, K must be greater than 3. For most practical systems $N \geq 7$ therefore a reasonable limitation is that Equation (E.88) may not be evaluated for the case of a single interfering user. Note that this is for the case of infinite signal-to-noise ratio. Later in this section, it is shown that for finite E_b/N_0, the simplified expression for the Improved Gaussian Approximation may be used for $K = 2$ under certain conditions. Therefore, the Improved Gaussian Approximation (IGA) of Section E.2 should be used if the bit error probability is required for the case of $K = 2$, and for random powers, Equation (E.91) should be used to determine the minimum value of K which is allowed.

In cases for which Equation (E.91) is not satisfied, a value of h smaller than $\sqrt{3}\sigma$ may be used in Equation (E.86). However, as h decreases, the simplified expression for the Improved Gaussian Approximation approaches the Gaussian Approximation of Equation (E.60) and, accordingly, it will become inaccurate for small numbers of users.

For the special case of perfect power control such that all users have identical power levels and these power levels are not random, Equation (E.90) may be used with $\sigma_p^2 = 0$. In particular, for $\mu_p = 2$ and $\sigma_p^2 = 0$ with the chip period normalized to $T_c = 1$, Equations (E.89) and (E.90) yield the results presented by Holtzman [Hol92]:

$$\mu_\psi = \frac{N}{3}(K-1) \tag{E.92}$$

$$\sigma_\psi^2 = (K-1)\left[\frac{23N^2}{360} + N\left(\frac{1}{20} + \frac{K-2}{36}\right) - \frac{1}{20} - \frac{K-2}{36}\right] \tag{E.93}$$

For the case where the $K-1$ interfering users have constant but unequal power levels, the mean and variance of ψ are given by

$$\mu_P = \frac{NT_c^2}{6}\sum_{k=1}^{K-1} P_k \tag{E.94}$$

$$\sigma_\psi^2 = \frac{T_c^4}{4}\left[\left(\frac{23N^2+18N-18}{360}\sum_{k=1}^{K-1} P_k^2\right) + \left(\frac{N-1}{36}\sum_{k=1}^{K-1}\sum_{\substack{j=1\\ j\neq k}}^{K-1} P_k P_j\right)\right] \tag{E.95}$$

For the case of perfect power control with $P_k = 2$ for all $k = 1\ldots K-1$ and normalized $T_c = 1$, Equations (E.94) and (E.95) reduce to Equations (E.92) and (E.93), respectively. Finally, in the most general case, in which the received power from each user is a random variable with mean $\mu_{p;k}$ and variance $\sigma_{p;k}^2$, the mean and variance of ψ are given by

$$\mu_\psi = \frac{NT_c^2}{6}\sum_{k=1}^{K-1}\mu_{p;k} \tag{E.96}$$

$$\sigma_\psi^2 = \frac{T_c^4}{4}\left[\left(\frac{23N^2+18N-18}{360}\sum_{k=1}^{K-1}\mu_{p;k}^2\right) + \left(\frac{N-1}{36}\sum_{k=1}^{K-1}\sum_{\substack{j=1\\ j\neq k}}^{K-1}\mu_{p;k}\mu_{p;j}\right) + \left(\frac{7N^2+2N-2}{40}\right)\sum_{k=1}^{K-1}\sigma_{p;k}^2\right] \tag{E.97}$$

The expressions given in Equations (E.94) through (E.97) generalize the results of Holtzman [Hol92] to the case in which the power levels of the interfering users are unequal and constant and to the case in which the power levels of the interfering users are independent and not identically distributed. Note that Equations (E.89) and (E.90), as well as Equations (E.96) and (E.97), hold for *any* power level distribution provided that the mean and variance exist for that power level.

In cases where the noise term is significant, Equation (E.88) should be rewritten as [Hol92]

$$P_e = E\left[Q\left(\sqrt{\frac{P_0T_b^2}{2\left(\psi + \frac{N_0T_b}{4}\right)}}\right)\right] \tag{E.98}$$

$$\approx \frac{2}{3}Q\left(\sqrt{\frac{P_0T_b^2}{2\left(\mu_\psi + \frac{N_oT_b}{4}\right)}}\right)$$

$$+\frac{1}{6}Q\left(\sqrt{\frac{P_0T_b^2}{2\left(\mu_\psi + \sqrt{3}\sigma_\psi + \frac{N_oT_b}{4}\right)}}\right) + \frac{1}{6}Q\left(\sqrt{\frac{P_0T_b^2}{2\left(\mu_\psi - \sqrt{3}\sigma_\psi + \frac{N_oT_b}{4}\right)}}\right)$$

As noted earlier, the conditions required on K to evaluate Equation (E.98) are somewhat relaxed compared with Equation (E.88). In particular, the condition required for σ_P, given μ_P is

$$\sigma_P^2 < \left([10K(4N^2 - 3N + 3) - (109N^2 - 6N + 6)]\mu_P^2 + \frac{120\mu_P N^2 N_0}{T_c^2}\right. \tag{E.99}$$

$$\left.+\frac{90N_0^2N^2}{(K-1)T_c^4}\right) \div (27(7N^2 + 2N - 2))$$

Examining Equation (E.99) for several values of E_b/N_0, we find the values given in Table E.1. Note that N_{min} may be approximated by $0.24(E_b/N_0)$ with E_b/N_0 in linear units. Note that when N is greater than N_{min} in Table E.1, Equation (E.99) must still be satisfied by appropriate values μ_p and σ_p in order to obtain a solution using Equation (E.98).

This technique extends the work of Holtzman [Hol92] to include cases other than those of perfect power control. Figure E.3 and Figure E.4 illustrate the average bit error rates for single-cell CDMA systems using the different analytical methods described in this appendix. For the results shown, the processing gain, N, is 31 chips per bit.

Table E.1 Minimum Values of N Required for a Given E_b/N_0 Such That Equation (E.98) May be Evaluated for the Case of a Single Interfering User

E_b/N_0 (dB)	N_{min}	E_b/N_0 (dB)	N_{min}
0.0	1	17.0	12
3.0	1	20.0	23
7.0	2	23.0	44
10.0	3	27.0	106
13.0	6	30.0	211

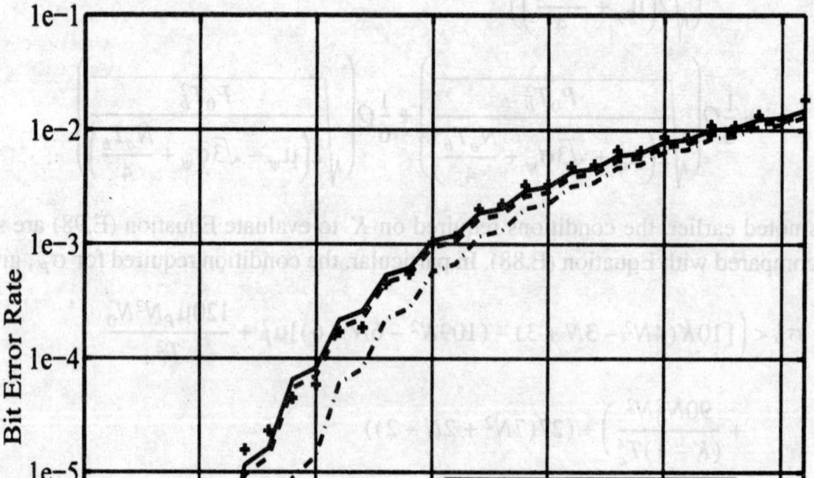

Figure E.3 Comparison of the calculated average bit error rates for a desired user as a function of the total number of system users ($N = 31$). It is assumed that the power levels for all K users are fixed. $K_2 = [K/2]$ users have a power level of $P_0/4$. The remaining $K_1 = K - 1 - K_2$ users each have power levels equal to that of the desired user, P_0. Note that the SEIGA provides a very close match to the IGA. The step-like appearance of the curves is due to the fact that as users are added, they alternate between low and high power levels.

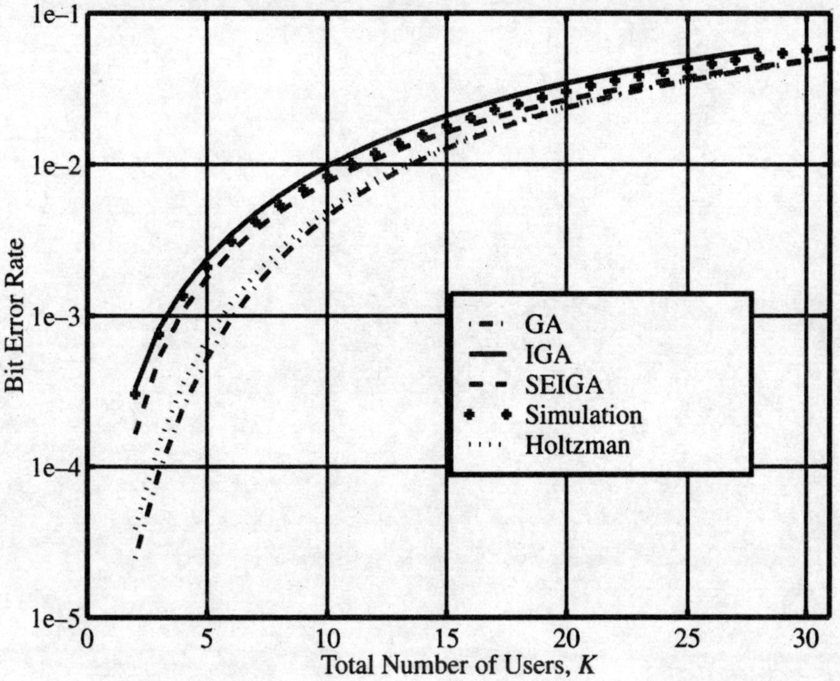

Figure E.4 Comparison of GA, IGA, and SEIGA for the case when interfering users have random, but identically distributed power levels. The interferer power levels obey a log-normal distribution with a standard deviation of 5 dB. The power level of the desired user is constant and equal to the mean value of the power level of each individual interfering user. The curve designated "Holtzman" represents the computation described in [Hol92] which is given by Equation (E.88). Note that the SEIGA, the generalization of Holtzman's results derived by [Lib94a], matches the IGA more closely.

APPENDIX F

Q, *erf* & *erfc* Functions

F.1 The Q-Function

Computation of probabilities that involve a Gaussian process require finding the area under the tail of the Gaussian (normal) probability density function as shown in Figure F.1.

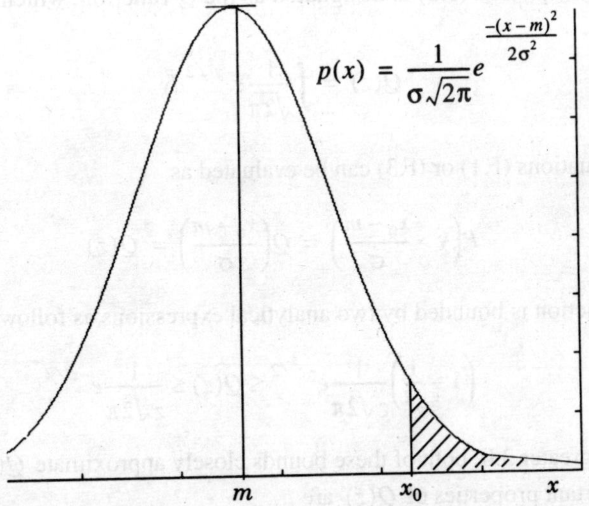

Figure F.1 Gaussian probability density function. Shaded area is $Pr(x \geq x_0)$ for a Gaussian random variable.

Figure F.1 illustrates the probability that a Gaussian random variable x exceeds x_0, $Pr(x \geq x_0)$, which is evaluated as

$$Pr(x \geq x_0) = \int_{x_0}^{\infty} \frac{1}{\sigma\sqrt{2\pi}} e^{-(x-m)^2/(2\sigma^2)} dx \qquad (F.1)$$

The Gaussian probability density function in Equation (F.1) cannot be integrated in closed form.

Any Gaussian probability density function may be rewritten through use of the substitution

$$y = \frac{x-m}{\sigma} \qquad (F.2)$$

to yield

$$Pr\left(y > \frac{x_0 - m}{\sigma}\right) = \int_{\left(\frac{x_0-m}{\sigma}\right)}^{\infty} \frac{1}{\sqrt{2\pi}} e^{-y^2/2} dy \qquad (F.3)$$

where the kernel of the integral on the right-hand side of Equation (F.3) is the normalized Gaussian probability density function with mean of 0 and standard deviation of 1. Evaluation of the integral in Equation (F.3) is designated as the Q-function, which is defined as

$$Q(z) = \int_{z}^{\infty} \frac{1}{\sqrt{2\pi}} e^{-y^2/2} dy \qquad (F.4)$$

Hence Equations (F.1) or (F.3) can be evaluated as

$$P\left(y > \frac{x_0 - m}{\sigma}\right) = Q\left(\frac{x_0 - m}{\sigma}\right) = Q(z) \qquad (F.5)$$

The Q-function is bounded by two analytical expressions as follows:

$$\left(1 - \frac{1}{z^2}\right)\frac{1}{z\sqrt{2\pi}} e^{-z^2/2} \leq Q(z) \leq \frac{1}{z\sqrt{2\pi}} e^{-z^2/2}$$

For values of z greater 3.0, both of these bounds closely approximate $Q(z)$.

Two important properties of $Q(z)$ are

$$Q(-z) = 1 - Q(z) \qquad (F.6)$$

$$Q(0) = \frac{1}{2} \qquad (F.7)$$

A graph of $Q(z)$ versus z is given in Figure F.2.

A tabulation of the Q-function for various values of z is given in Table F.1.

Table F.1 Tabulation of the *Q*-function

z	*Q*(*z*)	*z*	*Q*(*z*)
0.0	0.50000	2.0	0.02275
0.1	0.46017	2.1	0.01786
0.2	0.42074	2.2	0.01390
0.3	0.38209	2.3	0.01072
0.4	0.34458	2.4	0.00820
0.5	0.30854	2.5	0.00621
0.6	0.27425	2.6	0.00466
0.7	0.24196	2.7	0.00347
0.8	0.21186	2.8	0.00256
0.9	0.18406	2.9	0.00187
1.0	0.15866	3.0	0.00135
1.1	0.13567	3.1	0.00097
1.2	0.11507	3.2	0.00069
1.3	0.09680	3.3	0.00048
1.4	0.08076	3.4	0.00034
1.5	0.06681	3.5	0.00023
1.6	0.05480	3.6	0.00016
1.7	0.04457	3.7	0.00011
1.8	0.03593	3.8	0.00007
1.9	0.02872	3.9	0.00005

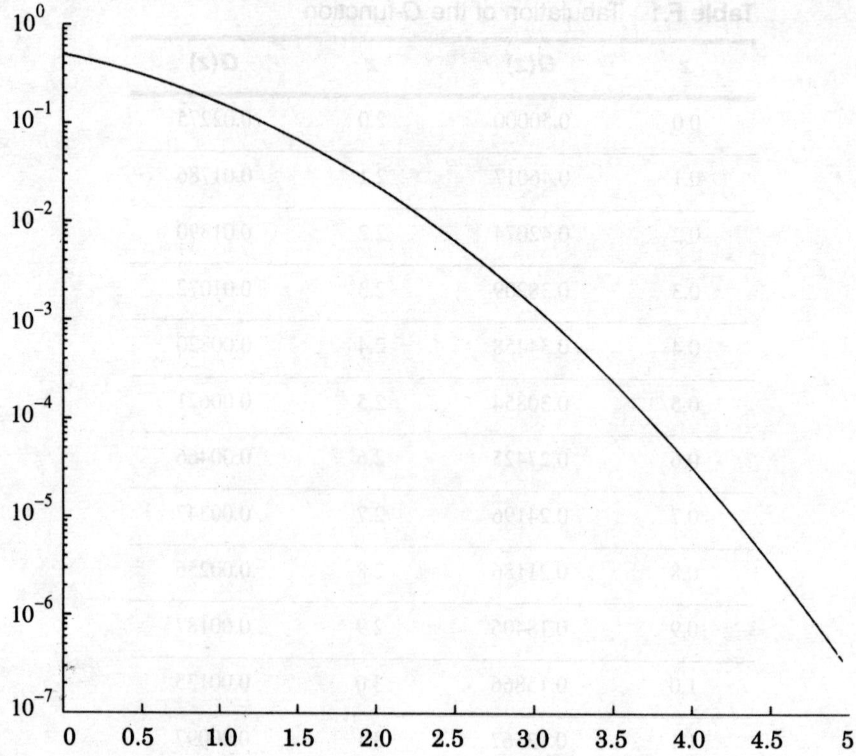

Figure F.2 Plot of the *Q*-function.

F.2 The *erf* and *erfc* Functions

The error function (*erf*) is defined as

$$erf(z) = \frac{2}{\sqrt{\pi}}\int_0^z e^{-x^2}\,dx \tag{F.8}$$

and the complementary error function (*erfc*) is defined as

$$erfc(z) = \frac{2}{\sqrt{\pi}}\int_z^\infty e^{-x^2}\,dx \tag{F.9}$$

The *erfc* function is related to the *erf* function by

$$erfc(z) = 1 - erf(z) \tag{F.10}$$

The Q-function is related to the *erf* and *erfc* functions by

$$Q(z) = \frac{1}{2}\left[1 - erf\left(\frac{z}{\sqrt{2}}\right)\right] = \frac{1}{2}erfc\left(\frac{z}{\sqrt{2}}\right) \tag{F.11}$$

$$erfc(z) = 2Q(\sqrt{2}z) \tag{F.12}$$

$$erf(z) = 1 - 2Q(\sqrt{2}z) \tag{F.13}$$

The relationships in Equations (F.11)–(F.13) are widely used in error probability computations. Table F.2 displays values for the *erf* function.

Table F.2 Tabulation of the Error Function *erf(z)*

z	*erf*(*z*)	*z*	*erf*(*z*)
0.1	0.11246	1.6	0.97635
0.2	0.22270	1.7	0.98379
0.3	0.32863	1.8	0.98909
0.4	0.42839	1.9	0.99279
0.5	0.52049	2.0	0.99532
0.6	0.60385	2.1	0.99702
0.7	0.67780	2.2	0.99814
0.8	0.74210	2.3	0.99885
0.9	0.79691	2.4	0.99931
1.0	0.84270	2.5	0.99959
1.1	0.88021	2.6	0.99976
1.2	0.91031	2.7	0.99987
1.3	0.93401	2.8	0.99993
1.4	0.95228	2.9	0.99996
1.5	0.96611	3.0	0.99998

Mathematical Tables, Functions, and Transforms

Table G.1 Trigonometric Identities

$\sin(A \pm B) = \sin A \cos B \pm \cos A \sin B$
$\cos(A \pm B) = \cos A \cos B \mp \sin A \sin B$
$\cos A \cos B = (1/2)[\cos(A+B) + \cos(A-B)]$
$\sin A \sin B = (1/2)[\cos(A-B) - \cos(A+B)]$
$\sin A \cos B = (1/2)[\sin(A+B) + \sin(A-B)]$
$\sin A + \sin B = 2\sin\left(\frac{A+B}{2}\right)\cos\left(\frac{A-B}{2}\right)$
$\sin A - \sin B = 2\sin\left(\frac{A-B}{2}\right)\cos\left(\frac{A+B}{2}\right)$
$\cos A + \cos B = 2\cos\left(\frac{A+B}{2}\right)\cos\left(\frac{A-B}{2}\right)$
$\cos A - \cos B = -2\sin\left(\frac{A+B}{2}\right)\sin\left(\frac{A-B}{2}\right)$
$\sin 2A = 2\sin A \cos A$
$\cos 2A = 2\cos^2 A - 1 = 1 - 2\sin^2 A = \cos^2 A - \sin^2 A$
$\sin A/2 = \sqrt{(1-\cos A)/2}$ $\quad$ $\cos A/2 = \sqrt{(1+\cos A)/2}$

Table G.1 Trigonometric Identities (Continued)

$$\sin^2 A = (1 - \cos 2A)/2 \qquad \cos^2 A = (1 + \cos 2A)/2$$

$$\sin x = \frac{e^{jx} - e^{-jx}}{2j} \qquad \cos x = \frac{e^{jx} + e^{-jx}}{2} \qquad e^{jx} = \cos x + j\sin x$$

$$A\cos(\omega t + \phi_1) + B\cos(\omega t + \phi_2) = C\cos(\omega t + \phi_3)$$

where

$$C = \sqrt{A^2 + B^2 - 2AB\cos(\phi_2 - \phi_1)}$$

and

$$\phi_3 = \tan^{-1}\left[\frac{A\sin\phi_1 + B\sin\phi_2}{A\cos\phi_1 + B\cos\phi_2}\right]$$

$$\sin(\omega t + \phi) = \cos(\omega t + \phi - 90°)$$

$$\cos(\omega t + \phi) = \sin(\omega t + \phi + 90°)$$

Table G.2 Approximations

Taylor's series	$f(x) = f(a) + \dot{f}(a)\frac{(x-a)}{1!} + \ddot{f}(a)\frac{(x-a)^2}{2!} + ...$
Maclaurin's series	$f(0) = f(0) + \dot{f}(0)\frac{x}{1!} + \ddot{f}(0)\frac{x^2}{2!} + ...$
For small values of x ($x \ll 1$)	$\frac{1}{1+x} \cong 1 - x$
	$(1+x)^n \cong 1 + nx \quad n \geq 1$
	$e^x \cong 1 + x$
	$\ln(1+x) \cong x$
	$\sin(x) \cong x$
	$\cos(x) \cong 1 - \frac{x^2}{2}$
	$\tan(x) \cong x$

Table G.3 Indefinite Integrals

$$\int \sin(ax)dx = -(1/a)\cos ax \qquad \int \cos(ax)dx = (1/a)\sin ax$$

$$\int \sin^2(ax)dx = \frac{x}{2} - \frac{\sin 2ax}{4a}$$

$$\int x\sin(ax)dx = (1/a^2)(\sin ax - ax\cos ax)$$

$$\int x^2\sin(ax)dx = (1/a^3)(2ax\cos ax + 2\cos ax - a^2x^2\cos ax)$$

$$\int \sin(ax)\sin(bx) = \frac{\sin(a-b)x}{2(a-b)} - \frac{\sin(a+b)x}{2(a+b)} \qquad (a^2 \neq b^2)$$

$$\int \sin(ax)\cos(bx) = -\left[\frac{\cos(a-b)x}{2(a-b)} + \frac{\cos(a+b)x}{2(a+b)}\right] \qquad (a^2 \neq b^2)$$

$$\int \cos(ax)\cos(bx) = \frac{\sin(a-b)x}{2(a-b)} + \frac{\sin(a+b)x}{2(a+b)} \qquad (a^2 \neq b^2)$$

$$\int e^{ax}dx = \frac{e^{ax}}{a}$$

$$\int xe^{ax}dx = \frac{e^{ax}}{a^2}(ax-1)$$

$$\int x^2e^{ax}dx = \frac{e^{ax}}{a^3}(a^2x^2 - 2ax + 2)$$

$$\int e^{ax}\sin(bx)dx = \frac{e^{ax}}{a^2+b^2}(a\sin(bx) - b\cos(bx))$$

$$\int e^{ax}\cos(bx)dx = \frac{e^{ax}}{a^2+b^2}(a\cos(bx) + b\sin(bx))$$

$$\int \cos^2 ax dx = \frac{x}{2} + \frac{\sin 2ax}{4a}$$

$$\int x\cos(ax)dx = (1/a^2)(\cos(ax) + ax\sin(ax))$$

$$\int x^2\cos(ax)dx = (1/a^3)(2ax\cos ax - 2\sin ax + a^2x^2\sin ax)$$

Table G.4 Definite Integrals

$$\int_0^\infty x^n e^{-ax} dx = \frac{n!}{a^{n+1}}$$

$$\int_0^\infty e^{-r^2x^2} dx = \frac{\sqrt{\pi}}{2r}$$

$$\int_0^\infty x e^{-r^2x^2} dx = \frac{1}{2r^2}$$

$$\int_0^\infty x^2 e^{-r^2x^2} dx = \frac{\sqrt{\pi}}{4r^3}$$

$$\int_0^\infty x^n e^{-r^2x^2} dx = \frac{\Gamma[(n+1)/2]}{2r^{n+1}}$$

$\Gamma(k) = (k-1)!$ for integers $k \geq 1$

$$\int_0^\infty \frac{\sin ax}{x} dx = \frac{\pi}{2}, 0, -\frac{\pi}{2} \qquad \text{for } a > 0,\ a = 0,\ a < 0$$

$$\int_0^\infty \frac{\sin^2 x}{x} dx = \frac{\pi}{2}$$

$$\int_0^\infty \frac{\sin^2 x}{x^2} dx = \frac{\pi}{2}$$

$$\int_0^\infty \frac{\sin^2 ax}{x^2} dx = |a|\frac{\pi}{2}$$

For m and n integers

$$\int_0^\pi \sin^2(mx)dx = \int_0^\pi \sin^2(x)dx = \int_0^\pi \cos^2(mx)dx = \int_0^\pi \cos^2(x)dx = \frac{\pi}{2}$$

$$\int_0^\pi \sin(mx)\cos(nx)dx = \begin{cases} \dfrac{(2m)}{(m^2-n^2)} & \text{if } (m+n) \text{ odd} \\ 0 & \text{if } (m+n) \text{ even} \end{cases}$$

Table G.5 Functions

Rectangular	$rect\left(\frac{t}{T}\right) = \begin{cases} 1 & \lvert t\rvert \le T/2 \\ 0 & \lvert t\rvert > T/2 \end{cases}$
Triangular	$\Lambda\left(\frac{t}{T}\right) = \begin{cases} 1 - \frac{\lvert t\rvert}{T} & \lvert t\rvert \le T \\ 0 & \lvert t\rvert > T \end{cases}$
Sinc	$Sa(x) = \frac{\sin x}{x}$
Unit Step	$u(t) = \begin{cases} 1 & t > 0 \\ 0 & t < 0 \end{cases}$
Signum	$\text{sgn}(t) = \begin{cases} 1 & t > 0 \\ -1 & t < 0 \end{cases}$
Impulse	$\delta(t) = \begin{cases} 1 & t = 0 \\ 0 & t \neq 0 \end{cases}$
Bessel	$J_n(\beta) = \frac{1}{2\pi}\int_{-\pi}^{\pi} e^{j(\beta \sin\theta - n\theta)} d\theta$
nth moment of a random variable X	$E[X^n] = \int_{-\infty}^{\infty} x^n p_X(x) dx$ where $n = 0,1,2,...$ and $p_X(x)$ is the *pdf* of X
nth central moment of X	$E[(X-\mu)^n] = \int_{-\infty}^{\infty} (x-\mu)^n p_X(x) dx$ where $\mu = E[X]$
Variance of X	$\sigma^2 = \int_{-\infty}^{\infty} (x-\mu)^2 p_X(x) dx$ where $\mu = E[X]$

Table G.6 Probability Functions

Discrete distribution

Binomial

$$Pr(k) = \binom{n}{k} p^k q^{n-k} \qquad k = 0, 1, 2, \ldots\ldots n$$
$$= 0 \qquad \text{otherwise}$$

$0 < p < 1, \quad q = 1 - p$

$$p(x) = \sum_{k=0}^{n} \binom{n}{k} p^k q^{n-k} \delta(x-k)$$

$\bar{x} = np$

$\sigma_x^2 = npq$

Poisson

$$Pr(k) = \frac{\lambda^k e^{-\lambda}}{k!} \qquad k = 0, 1, 2, \ldots\ldots$$

$$p(x) = \sum_{k=0}^{n} \frac{\lambda^k e^{-\lambda}}{k!} \delta(x-k)$$

$\bar{x} = \lambda$

$\sigma_x^2 = \lambda$

Continuous distribution

Exponential

$$p(x) = ae^{-ax} \qquad x > 0$$
$$= 0 \qquad \text{otherwise}$$

$\bar{x} = a^{-1}$

$\sigma_x^2 = a^{-2}$

Gaussian (normal)

$$p(x) = \frac{1}{\sigma_x\sqrt{2\pi}} \exp\left[-\frac{(x-\bar{x})^2}{2\sigma_x^2}\right] \qquad -\infty \le x \le \infty$$

$E\{x\} = \bar{x}$

$E\{(x-\bar{x})^2\} = \sigma_x^2$

Table G.6 Probability Functions (Continued)

Bivariate Gaussian (normal)

$$p(x, y) = \frac{1}{2\pi\sigma_x\sigma_y\sqrt{1-\rho^2}}\exp\left\{-\frac{1}{2(1-\rho^2)}\left[\left(\frac{x-\bar{x}}{\sigma_x}\right)^2 + \left(\frac{y-\bar{y}}{\sigma_y}\right)^2 - \frac{2\rho}{\sigma_x\sigma_y}(x-\bar{x})(y-\bar{y})\right]\right\}$$

$$E\{x\} = \bar{x}$$

$$E\{y\} = \bar{y}$$

$$E\{(x-\bar{x})^2\} = \sigma_x^2$$

$$E\{(y-\bar{y})^2\} = \sigma_y^2$$

$\rho = \dfrac{E[xy] - \mu_x\mu_y}{\sigma_x\sigma_y}$ is the correlation coefficient

$$E\{(x-\bar{x})(y-\bar{y})\} = \sigma_x\sigma_y\rho$$

Rayleigh

The *pdf* of the envelope of Gaussian random noise having zero mean and variance σ_n^2

$$p(r) = \frac{r}{\sigma_n^2}\exp[-r^2/2\sigma_n^2] \qquad r \geq 0$$

$$E\{r\} = \bar{r} = \sigma_n\sqrt{\pi/2}$$

$$E\{(r-\bar{r})^2\} = \sigma_r^2 = \left(2-\frac{\pi}{2}\right)\sigma_n^2$$

Ricean

The *pdf* of the envelope of a sinusoid with amplitude A plus zero mean Gaussian noise with variance σ^2

$$p(r) = \frac{r}{\sigma^2}\exp\left[-\frac{(r^2+A^2)}{2\sigma^2}\right]I_0\left(\frac{Ar}{\sigma^2}\right) \qquad r \geq 0$$

For $A/\sigma \gg 1$, this is closely approximated by the following Gaussian PDF:

$$p(r) \cong \frac{1}{\sigma\sqrt{2\pi}}\exp\left[-\frac{(r-A)^2}{2\sigma^2}\right]$$

Table G.6 Probability Functions (Continued)

Uniform

$$p(x) = \begin{cases} \dfrac{1}{b-a} & a < x < b \\ 0 & \text{elsewhere} \end{cases}$$

$$\bar{x} = \frac{a+b}{2}$$

$$\sigma_x^2 = \frac{(b-a)^2}{12}$$

Table G.7 Selected Fourier Transform Theorems

Operation	Function	Fourier Transform
Linearity	$a_1 w_1(t) + a_2 w_2(t)$	$a_1 W_1(f) + a_2 W_2(f)$
Time Delay	$w(t - T_d)$	$W(f)e^{-j\omega T_d}$
Scale Change	$w(at)$	$\frac{1}{\lvert a \rvert} W\left(\frac{f}{a}\right)$
Conjugation	$w^*(t)$	$W^*(-f)$
Duality	$W(t)$	$w(-f)$
Real Signal Frequency Translation [$w(t)$ is real]	$w(t)\cos(\omega_c t + \theta)$	$\frac{1}{2}[e^{j\theta} W(f - f_c) + e^{-j\theta} W(f + f_c)]$
Complex Signal Frequency Translation	$w(t)e^{j\omega_c t}$	$W(f - f_c)$
Bandpass Signal	$\text{Re}\{g(t)e^{j\omega_c t}\}$	$\frac{1}{2}[G(f - f_c) + G^*(-f - f_c)]$
Differentiation	$\frac{d^n w(t)}{dt^n}$	$(j2\pi f)^n W(f)$
Integration	$\int_{-\infty}^{t} w(\lambda) d\lambda$	$(j2\pi f)^{-1} W(f) + \frac{1}{2} W(0)\delta(f)$
Convolution	$w_1(t) * w_2(t) = \int_{-\infty}^{\infty} w_1(\lambda) \cdot w_2(t - \lambda) d\lambda$	$W_1(f) W_2(f)$
Multiplication	$w_1(t) w_2(t)$	$W_1(f) * W_2(f) = \int_{-\infty}^{\infty} W_1(\lambda) \cdot W_2(f - \lambda) d\lambda$
Multiplication by t^n	$t^n w(t)$	$(-j2\pi)^{-1} \frac{d^n W(f)}{df^n}$

Table G.8 Selected Fourier Transform Pairs

Function	Time Waveform $w(t)$	Spectrum $W(f)$
Rectangular	$\mathrm{rect}\left(\frac{t}{T}\right)$	$T[\mathrm{Sa}(\pi f T)]$
Triangular	$\Lambda\left(\frac{t}{T}\right)$	$T[\mathrm{Sa}(\pi f T)]^2$
Unit Step	$u(t) \triangleq \begin{cases} +1, & t>0 \\ -1, & t<0 \end{cases}$	$\frac{1}{2}\delta(f) + \frac{1}{j2\pi f}$
Signum	$\mathrm{sgn}(t) \triangleq \begin{cases} +1, & t>0 \\ -1, & t<0 \end{cases}$	$\frac{1}{j\pi f}$
Constant	1	$\delta(f)$
Impulse at $t = t_0$	$\delta(t - t_0)$	$e^{-j2\pi f t_0}$
Sinc	$\mathrm{Sa}(2\pi W t)$	$\frac{1}{2W}\mathrm{rect}\left(\frac{f}{2W}\right)$
Phasor	$e^{j(\omega_0 t + \phi)}$	$e^{j\phi}\delta(f - f_0)$
Sinusoid	$\cos(\omega_c t + \phi)$	$\frac{1}{2}e^{j\phi}\delta(f - f_c) + \frac{1}{2}e^{-j\phi}\delta(f + f_c)$
Gaussian	$e^{-\pi(t/t_0)^2}$	$t_0 e^{-\pi(f t_0)^2}$
Exponential, One-sided	$\begin{cases} e^{-t/T}, & t \geq 0 \\ 0, & t<0 \end{cases}$	$\frac{T}{1 + j2\pi f T}$
Exponential, Two-sided	$e^{-\lvert t\rvert/T}$	$\frac{2T}{1 + (2\pi f T)^2}$
Impulse Train	$\sum_{k=-\infty}^{k=\infty} \delta(t - kT)$	$f_0 \sum_{n=-\infty}^{n=\infty} \delta(f - n f_0)$, where $f_0 = 1/T$

Appendix H

Abbreviations and Acronyms

Numerics

1xDV 3G extension of IS-95B: shared data and voice
1xDO 3G extension of IS-95B: data only
1xEV 3G extension of IS-95B: data with circuit-switched voice
1xRTT 3G extension of IS-95B: one RF channel
2G Second Generation wireless technology
3G Third Generation wireless technology
3GPP 3G Partnership Project for Wideband CDMA standards base on backward compatability with GSM and IS-136/PDC
3GPP2 3G Partnership Project for cdma2000 standards base on backward compatability with IS-95
3xRTT 3G extension of IS-95B: three RF channels

A

AC Access Channel
ACA Adaptive Channel Allocation
ACF Autocorrelation function
ACI Adjacent Channel interference
ACK Acknowledge
ADB/LIDB Alternate Billing Service and Line Information Database
ADM Adaptive Delta Modulation
ADPCM Adaptive Digital Pulse Code Modulation

ADSL	Asynchronous Digital Subscriber Line
AGCH	Access Grant Channel
AIN	Advanced Intelligent Network
AM	Amplitude Modulation
AMPS	Advanced Mobile Phone System
ANSI	American National Standards Institute
APC	Adaptive Predictive Coding
ARDIS	Advance Radio Data Information Systems
ARFCN	Absolute Radio Frequency Channel Numbers
ARPU	Average Revenue Per User
ARQ	Automatic Repeat Request
ATC	Adaptive Transform Coding
ATM	Asynchronous Transfer Mode
AUC	Authentication Center
AWGN	Additive White Gaussian Noise

B

BER	Bit Error Rate
BERSIM	Bit Error Rate Simulator
BCH	Bose–Chaudhuri–Hocquenghem, *also* Broadcast Channel
BCCH	Broadcast Control Channel
BFSK	Binary Frequency Shift Keying
BISDN	Broadband Integrated Services Digital Network
BIU	Base Station Interface Unit
BOC	Bell Operating Company
BPSK	Binary Phase Shift Keying
BRAN	Broadband Radio Access Networks
BRI	Basic Rate Interface
BSC	Base Station Controller
BSIC	Base Station Identity Code
BSS	Base Station Subsystem
BT	3 dB bandwidth-bit-duration product for GMSK
BTA	Basic Trading Area
BTS	Base Transceiver Station

C

CAD	Computer-Aided Design
CAI	Common Air Interface

CATT China Academy of Telecommunication Technology
CB Citizens Band
CCCH Common Control Channel
CCH Control Channel
CCI Co-channel Interference
CCIR Consultative Committee for International Radiocommunications
CCITT International Telgraph and Telephone Consultative Committee
CCS Common Channel Signaling
CD Collision Detection
CDF Cumulative Distribution Function
CDMA Code Division Multiple Access
CDPD Cellular Digital Packet Data
CDVCC Coded Digital Verification Color Code
CELP Code Excited Linear Predictor
CFP Cordless Fixed Part
C/I Carrier-to-Interference Ratio
CIC Circuit Identification Code
CIR Carrier-to-Interference Ratio
CIU Cellular Controller Interface Unit
CLNP Connectionless Protocol (Open System Interconnect)
CMA Constant modulus algorithm
CNR Carrier-to-Noise Ratio
CNS Comfort Noise Subsystem
CO Central Office
codec Coder/decoder
COST Cooperative for Scientific and Technical Research
CPE Customer Premises Equipment
CPFSK Continuous Phase Frequency Shift Keying
CPP Cordless Portable Part
CRC Cyclic Redundancy Code
CSMA Carrier Sense Multiple Access
CT2 Cordless Telephone -2
CVSDM Continuously Variable Slope Delta Modulation
CW Continuous Wave

D

DAM Diagnostic Acceptability Measure
DAS Distributed Antenna System
DBAS Database Service Mangement System
dBi dB gain with respect to an isotropic antenna

dBd	dB gain with respect to a half-wave dipole
DCA	Dynamic Channel Allocation
DCCH	Dedicated Control Channel
DCE	Data Circuit Terminating Equipment
DCS	Digital Communication System
DCS1800	Digital Communication System—1800
DCT	Discrete Cosine Transform
DECT	Digital European Cordless Telephone
DEM	Digital Elevation Model
DFE	Decision Feedback Equalization
DFT	Discrete Fourier Transform
DLC	Data Link Control
DM	Delta Modulation
DPCM	Differential Pulse Code Modulation
DQPSK	Differential Quadrature Phase Shift Keying
DRT	Diagnostic Rhyme Test
DS	Direct Sequence
DSAT	Digital Supervisory Audio Tone
DSE	Data Switching Exchange
DS/FHMA	Hybrid Direct Sequence/Frequency Hopped Multiple Access
DSL	Digital Subscriber Line
DSP	Digital Signal Processing
DS-SS	Direct Sequence Spread Spectrum
DST	Digital Signaling Tone
DTC	Digital Traffic Channel
DTE	Data Terminal Equipment
DTMF	Dual Tone Multiple Frequency
DTX	Discontinuous Transmission Mode
DUP	Data User Part

E

EDGE	Enhanced Data Rates for GSM Evolution
EIA	Electronic Industry Association
EIR	Equipment Identity Register
EIRP	Effective Isotropic Radiated Power
E_b/N_0	Bit Energy-to-noise Density
EOC	Embedded Operations Channel
erf	Error Function
erfc	Complementary Error Function
ERMES	European Radio Message System

ERP Effective Radiated Power
E-SMR Extended — Specialized Mobile Radio
ESN Electronic Serial Number
ETACS Extended Total Access Communication System
also European Total Access Cellular System
ETSI European Telecommunications Standard Institute

F

FACCH Fast Associated Control Channel
FAF Floor Attenuation Factor
FBF Feedback Filter
FC Fast Channel
FCC Federal Communications Commission, Inc.,
also Forward Control Channel
FCCH Frequency Correction Channel
FCDMA Hybrid FDMA/CDMA
FDD Frequency Division Duplex
FDMA Frequency Division Multiple Access
FDTC Forward Data Traffic Channel
FEC Forward Error Correction
FFF Feed Forward Filter
FFSR Feed Forward Signal Regeneration
FH Frequency Hopping
FHMA Frequency Hopped Multiple Access
FH–SS Frequency Hopped Spread Spectrum
also Frequency Hopping Spread Spectrum
FLEX 4-level FSK-based paging standard developed by Motorola
FM Frequency Modulation
FN Frame Number
FPLMTS Future Public Land Mobile Telephone System
FSE Fractionally Spaced Equalizer
FSK Frequency Shift Keying
FTF Fast Transversal Filter
FVC Forward Voice Channel

G

GIS Graphical Information System
GIU Gateway Interface Unit
GMSK Gaussian Minimum Shift Keying

GOS Grade of Service
GPRS General Packet Radio Service
GSC Golay Sequential Coding (a 600 bps paging standard)
GSM Global System for Mobile Communication
also Global System Mobile

H

HAAT Height Above Average Terrain
HSCSD High Speed Circuit Switched Data
HDB Home Database
HDR High Data Rate
HIPERLAN High Performance Radio Local Area Network
HLR Home Location Register

I

IDCT Inverse Discrete Cosine Transform
iDen Integrated Digital Enhanced Network
IDFT Inverse Discrete Fourier Transform
IEEE Institute of Electrical and Electronics Engineers
IF Intermediate Frequency
IFFT Inverse Fast Fourier Transform
IGA Improved Gaussian Approximation
IIR Infinite Impulse Response
IM Intermodulation
IMSI International Mobile Subscriber Identity
IMT-2000 International Mobile Telecommuncation 2000
IMTS Improved Mobile Telephone Service
IP Internet Protocol
IS-54 EIA Interim Standard for U.S. Digital Cellular with Analog Control Channels
IS-95 EIA Interim Standard for U.S. Code Division Multiple Access
IS-136 EIA Interim Standard 136 — USDC with Digital Control Channels
ISDN Integrated Services Digital Network
ISI Intersymbol Interference
ISM Industrial, Scientific, and Medical
ISUP ISDN User Part
ITFS Instructional Television Fixed Service
ITU International Telecommunications Union
ITU-R ITU's Radiocommunications Secto
IXC Interexchange Carrier

J

JDC	Japanese Digital Cellular (later called Pacific Digital Cellular)
JRC	Joint Radio Committee
JTACS	Japanese Total Access Communication System
JTC	Joint Technical Committee

L

LAN	Local Area Network
LAR	Log-area Ratio
LATA	Local Access and Transport Area
LBT	Listen-before-talk
LCC	Lost Call Cleared
LCD	Lost Call Delayed
LCR	Level Crossing Rate
LEC	Local Exchange Carrier
LEO	Low Earth Orbit
LMDS	Local Multipoint Distribution Systems
LMS	Least Mean Square
LOS	Line-of-sight
LPC	Linear Predictive Coding
LSSB	Lower Single Side Band
LTE	Linear Transversal Equalizer
LTP	Long Term Prediction

M

MAC	Medium Access Control
MAHO	Mobile Assisted Handoff
MAI	Multiple Access Interference
MAN	Metropolitan Area Network
M-ary	Multiple Level Modulation
MC	Multicarrier
MCS	Multiple Modulation and Coding Schemes
MDBS	Mobile Database Stations
MDLP	Mobile Data Link Protocol
MDS	Multipoint Distribution Service
MDR	Medium Data Rate
MFJ	Modified Final Judgement
MFSK	Minimum Frequency Shift Keying

MIN	Mobile Identification Number
MIRS	Motorola Integrated Radio System (for SMR use)
ML	Maximal Length
MLSE	Maximum Likelihood Sequence Estimation
MMAC	Multimedia Mobile Access Communication System
MMDS	Multichannel Multipoint Distribution Service
MMSE	Minimum Mean Square Error
MOS	Mean Opinion Score
MoU	Memorandum of Understanding
MPE	Multipulse Excited
MPSK	Minimum Phase Shift Keying
MS	Mobile Station
MSB	Most Significant Bit
MSC	Mobile Switching Center
MSCID	MSC Identification
MSE	Mean Square Error
MSK	Minimum Shift Keying
MSU	Message Signal Unit
MTA	Major Trading Area
MTP	Message Transfer Part
MTSO	Mobile Telephone Switching Office
MUX	Multiplexer

N

NACK	Negative Acknowledge
NADC	North American Digital Cellular
NAMPS	Narrowband Advanced Mobile Phone System
NBFM	Narrowband Frequency Modulation
NEC	National
N-ISDN	Narrowband Integrated Service Digital Network
NMT-450	Nordic Mobile Telephone—450
NRZ	Non-return to Zero
NSP	Network Service Part
NSS	Network and Switching Subsystem
NTACS	Narrowband Total Access Communication System
NTT	Nippon Telephone and Telegraph

O

OBS	Obstructed
OFDM	Orthogonal Frequency Division Multiplexing
OMAP	Operations Maintenance and Administration Part
OMC	Operation Maintenance Center
OQPSK	Offset Quadrature Phase Shift Keying
OSI	Open System Interconnect
OSS	Operation Support Subsystem

P

PABX	Private Automatic Branch Exchange
PACS	Personal Access Communication System
PAD	Packet Assembler Disassembler
PAF	Partition Attenuation Factor
PAN	Personal Area Network
PBX	Private Branch Exchange
PCH	Paging Channel
PCM	Pulse Code Modulation
PCN	Personal Communication Network
PCS	Personal Communication System
PDC	Pacific Digital Cellular
pdf	probability density function
PG	Processing Gain
PH	Portable Handset
PHP	Personal Handyphone
PHS	Personal Handyphone System
PL	Path Loss
PLL	Phase Locked Loop
PLMR	Public Land Mobile Radio
PN	Pseudo-noise
POCSAG	Post Office Code Standard Advisory Group
POTS	Plain Old Telephone Service
PR	Packet Radio
PRI	Primary Rate Interface
PRMA	Packet Reservation Multiple Access
PSD	Power Spectral Density
PSK	Phase Shift Keying
PSTN	Public Switched Telephone Network
PTI	Permanent Terminal Identifier

Q

QAM	Quadrature Amplitude Modulation
QCELP	Qualcomm Code Excited Linear Predictive Coder
QMF	Quadrature Mirror Filter
QPSK	Quadrature Phase Shift Keying

R

RACE	Research on Advanced Communications in Europe
RACH	Random Access Channel
RCC	Reverse Control Channel
RCS	Radar Cross Section
RD-LAP	Radio Data Link Access Protocol
RDTC	Reverse Data Traffic Channel
RELP	Residual Excited Linear Predictor
RF	Radio Frequency
RFP	Radio Fixed Part
RLC	Resistor Inductor Capacitor
RLS	Recursive Least Square
RMD	RAM Mobile Data
RPCU	Radio Port Control Unit
RPE-LTP	Regular Pulse Excited Long-Term Prediction
RRMS	Radio Resource Management Protocol
RS	Reed–Solomon
RSSI	Received Signal Strength Indication
RTT	Radio Transmission Technology
RVC	Reverse Voice Channel
Rx	Receiver
RZ	Return to Zero

S

SACCH	Slow Associated Control Channel
SAT	Supervisory Audio Tone
SBC	System Broadcasting Channel *also* Sub-band Coding; Southwestern Bell Corporation
SC	Slow Channel
SCCP	Signaling Connection Control Part
SCH	Synchronization Channel
SCM	Station Class Mark

SCORE	Spectral Coherence Restoral Algorithm
SCP	Service Control Point
SDCCH	Stand-alone Dedicated Control Channel
SDMA	Space Division Multiple Access
SEIGA	Simplified Expression for the Improved Gaussian Approximation
SELP	Stochastically Excited Linear Predictive Coder
SEP	Switching End Points
SFM	Spectral Flatness Measure
S/I	*see* SIR
SID	Station Identity
SIM	Subscriber Identity Module
SIR	Signal-to-Interference Ratio
SIRCIM	Simulation of Indoor Radio Channel Impulse Response Models
SISP	Site Specific Propagation
SMR	Specialized Mobile Radio
SMRCIM	Simulation of Mobile Radio Channel Impulse Response Models
SMS	Short Messaging Service *also* Service Management System
S/N	*see* SNR
SNR	Signal-to-Noise Ratio
SOHO	Small Office/Home Office
SONET	Synchronous Optical Network
SP	Signaling Point
SQNR	Signal-to-Quantization Noise Ratio
SS	Spread Spectrum
SSB	Single Side Band
SSMA	Spread Spectrum Multiple Access
SS7	Signaling System No. 7
ST	Signaling Tone
STP	Short Term Prediction, *also* Signaling Transfer Point
SYN	Synchronization channel

T

TACS	Total Access Communications System
TCAP	Transaction Capabilities Application Part
TCDMA	Time Division CDMA
TCH	Traffic Channel
TCM	Trellis Coded Modulation
TDD	Time Division Duplex

TDFH Time Division Frequency Hopping
TDMA Time Division Multiple
TDN Temporary Directory Number
TD-SCDMA Time Division-Synchronous Code Division Multiple Access
TIA Telecommunications Industry Association
TIU Trunk Interface Unit
TTIB Transparent Tone-in-Band
TUP Telephone User Part
Tx Transmitter

U

UF Urban Factor
UMTS Universal Mobile Telecommunications System
UNII Unlicensed National Information Infrastructure
US United States of America
USDC United States Digital Cellular, *see* IS-136 and NADC
USGS United States Geological Survey
USSB Upper Single Side Band
UTRA UMTS Terrestrial Radio Access

V

VAD Voice Activity Detector
VCI Virtual Circuit Identifier
VCO Voltage Controlled Oscillator
VDB Visitor Database
VHE Virtual Home Entertainment
VIU Visitor Interface Unit
VLR Visitor Location Register
VLSI Very Large-Scale Integration
VMAC Voice Mobile Attenuation Code
VoIP Voice over Internet Protocol
VQ Vector Quantization
VSELP Vector Sum Excited Linear Predictor

W

WACS Wireless Access Communication System (later called PACS)
WAN Wide Area Network
WAP Wireless Applications Protocol
WARC World Administrative Radio Conference

W-CDMA	Wideband CDMA
WECA	Wireless Ethernet Compatability Alliance
WIN	Wireless Information Network
WIU	Wireless Interface Unit
WLAN	Wireless Local Area Network
WLL	Wireless Local Loop
WRC-2000	ITU World Radio Conference
WUPE	Wireless User Premises Equipment

Z

ZF	Zero Forcing

APPENDIX I

References

[Abe70] Abend, K. and Fritchman, B. D., "Statistical Detection for Communication Channels with Intersymbol Interference," *Proceedings of IEEE*, pp. 779–785, May 1970.

[Ald00] Aldridge, I., Analysis of Existing Wireless Communication Protocols, COMS E6998-5 Course Project taught by Prof. M. Lerner, Summer 2000, Columbia University, NY, USA, *http://www.columbia.edu/~ir94/wireless.html.*

[Aka87] Akaiwa, Y., and Nagata, Y., "Highly Efficient Digital Mobile Communications with a Linear Modulation Method," *IEEE Journal on Selected Areas in Communications*, Vol. SAC-5, No. 5, pp. 890–895, June 1987.

[Ake88] Akerberg, D., "Properties of a TDMA Picocellular Office Communication System," *IEEE Globecom*, pp. 1343–1349, December 1988.

[Ale82] Alexander, S. E., "Radio Propagation Within Buildings at 900 MHz," *Electronics Letters*, Vol. 18, No. 21, pp. 913–914, 1982.

[Ale86] Alexander, S. T., *Adaptive Signal Processing,* Springer-Verlag, 1986.

[Ame53] Ament, W. S., "Toward a Theory of Reflection by a Rough Surface," *Proceedings of the IRE*, Vol. 41, No. 1, pp. 142–146, January 1953.

[Amo80] Amoroso, F., "The Bandwidth of Digital Data Signals," *IEEE Communications Magazine*, pp. 13–24, November 1980.

[And94] Anderson, J. B., Rappaport, T. S., and Yoshida, S., "Propagation Measurements and Models for Wireless Communications Channels," *IEEE Communications Magazine*, November 1994.

[And98] Andrisano, O., Tralli, V., and Verdone, R., "Millimeter Waves for Short-range Multimedia Communication Systems," *Proceedings IEEE*, Vol. 86, pp. 1383–1401, July 1998.

[Anv91] Anvari, K., and Woo, D., "Susceptibility of p/4 DQPSK TDMA Channel to Receiver Impairments," *RF Design*, pp. 49–55, February 1991.

[ANS95] ANSI J-STD-008 - Personal Station-Base Compatibility Requirements for 1.8-2.0 GHz Code Division Multiple Access (CDMA) Personal Communication Systems, March 1995.

[Are01] Arensman, R., "Cutting the Cord," *Electronics Business Magazine*, pp 51–60, June 2001.

[Ash93] Ashitey, D., Sheikh, A., and Murthy, K. M. S., "Intelligent Personal Communication System," *43rd IEEE Vehicular Technology Conference*, pp. 696–699, 1993.

[Ata86] Atal, B. S., "High Quality Speech at Low Bit Rates: Multi-pulse and Stochastically Excited Linear Predictive Coders," *Proceedings of ICASSP*, pp. 1681–1684, 1986.

[Bay73] Bayless, J.W., et al., "Voice Signals: Bit-by-bit," *IEEE Spectrum*, pp. 28–34, October 1973.

[Bel62] Bello, P. A., and Nelin, B. D., "The Influence of Fading Spectrum on the Binary Error Probabilities of Incoherent and Differentially Coherent Matched Filter Receivers," *IRE Transactions on Communication Systems*, Vol. CS-10, pp. 160–168, June 1962.

[Bel79] Belfiori, C. A., and Park, J. H., "Decision Feedback Equalization," *Proceedings of IEEE*, Vol. 67, pp. 1143–1156, August 1979.

[Ber87] Bernhardt, R. C., "Macroscopic Diversity in Frequency Reuse Systems," *IEEE Journal on Selected Areas in Communications*, Vol-SAC 5, pp. 862–878, June 1987.

[Ber89] Bernhardt, R. C., "The Effect of Path Loss Models on the Simulated Performance of Portable Radio Systems," *IEEE Globecom*, pp. 1356–1360, 1989.

[Ber92] Bertsekas, D., and Gallager R., *Data Networks*, 2nd edition, Prentice Hall, Englewood Cliffs, NJ, 1992.

[Ber93] Berrou, C., Glavieux, A., and Thitimajshima, P., "Near Shannon Limit Error-Correcting Coding and Decoding: Turbo Codes," *IEEE International Communication Conference (ICC)*, Geneva, May 1993, pp. 1064–1070.

[Bie77] Bierman, G. J., *Factorization Method for Discrete Sequential Estimation*, Academic Press, New York, 1977.

[Bin88] Bingham, J. A. C., *The Theory and Practice of Modem Design*, John Wiley & Sons, New York, 1988.

[Boi87] Boithias, L., *Radio Wave Propagation*, McGraw-Hill Inc., New York, 1987.

[Bos60] Bose, R. C., and Ray-Chaudhuri, D. K., "On a Class of Error Correcting Binary Group Codes," *Information and Control*, Vol. 3, pp. 68–70, March 1960.

[Bou88] Boucher, J. R., *Voice Teletraffic Systems Engineering*, Artech House, c. 1988.

[Bou91] Boucher, N., *Cellular Radio Handbook*, Quantum Publishing, c. 1991.

[Boy90] Boyles, S. M., Corn, R. L., and Moseley, L. R., "Common Channel Signaling: The Nexus of an Advanced Communications Network," *IEEE Communications Magazine*, pp. 57–63, July 1990.

[Bra68] Brady, P. T., "A Statistical Analysis of On-Off Patterns in 16 Conversations," *Bell System Technical Journal*, Vol. 47, pp. 73–91, 1968.

[Bra70] Brady, D. M., "An Adaptive Coherent Diversity Receiver for Data Transmission through Dispersive Media," *Proceedings of IEEE International Conference on Communications*, pp. 21–35, June 1970.

[Bra00] Braley, R. C., Gifford, I. C., and Heile, R. F., "Wireless Personal Area Networks: An Overview of the IEEE P802.15 Working Group," *ACM Mobile Computing and Communications Review*, Vol. 4, No. 1, p. 20–27, Feb. 2000.

[Buc00] Buckley, S., "3G Wireless: Mobility Scales new Heights," Telecommunications Magazine, November 2000.

[Bul47] Bullington, K., "Radio Propagation at Frequencies above 30 Megacycles," *Proceedings of the IEEE*, 35, pp. 1122–1136, 1947.

[Bul89] Bultitude, R. J. C., and Bedal, G. K., "Propagation Characteristics on Microcellular Urban Mobile Radio Channels at 910 MHz," *IEEE Journal on Selected Areas in Communications*, Vol. 7, pp. 31–39, January 1989.

[Cal88] Calhoun, G., *Digital Cellular Radio,* Artech House Inc., 1988.

[Cat69] Cattermole, K. W., *Principles of Pulse-Code Modulation*, Elsevier, New York, 1969.

[CCI86] Radio Paging Code No. 1, *The Book of the CCIR*, RCSG, 1986.

[Chu87] Chuang, J., "The Effects of Time Delay Spread on Portable Communications Channels with Digital Modulation," *IEEE Journal on Selected Areas in Communications*, Vol. SAC-5, No. 5, pp. 879–889, June 1987.

[Cla68] Clarke, R. H., "A Statistical Theory of Mobile-Radio Reception," *Bell Systems Technical Journal,* Vol. 47, pp. 957–1000, 1968.

[Col89] Coleman, A., et al., "Subjective Performance Evaluation of the REP-LTP Codec for the Pan-European Cellular Digital Mobile Radio System," *Proceedings of ICASSP*, pp. 1075–1079, 1989.

[Coo86a] Cooper, G. R., and McGillem, C. D., *Probabilistic Methods of Signal and System Analysis*, Holt, Rinehart, and Winston, New York, 1986.

[Coo86b] Cooper, G. R., and McGillem, C. D., *Modern Communications and Spread Spectrum*, McGraw Hill, New York, 1986.

[Cor97] Correia, L., and Prasad, R., "An Overview of Wireless Broadband Communications," *IEEE Communications Magazine*, pp. 28–33, January 1997.

[Cou93] Couch, L. W., *Digital and Analog Communication Systems*, 4th edition, Macmillan, New York, 1993.

[Cou98] Coulson, A. J., Williamson, A. G., and Vaughan, R. G., "A Statistical Basis for Log-Normal Shadowing Effects in Multipath Fading Channels," *IEEE Transactions on Communications*, Vol 46, pp. 494–502, April 1998.

[Cox72] Cox, D. C., "Delay Doppler Characteristics of Multipath Delay Spread and Average Excess Delay for 910 MHz Urban Mobile Radio Paths," *IEEE Transactions on Antennas and Propagation*, Vol. AP-20, No. 5, pp. 625–635, September 1972.

[Cox75] Cox, D. C., and Leck, R. P., "Distributions of Multipath Delay Spread and Average Excess Delay for 910 MHz Urban Mobile Radio Paths," *IEEE Transactions on Antennas and Propagation*, Vol. AP-23, No.5, pp. 206–213, March 1975.

[Cox83a] Cox, D. C., "Antenna Diversity Performance in Mitigating the Effects of Portable Radiotelephone Orientation and Multipath Propagation," *IEEE Transactions on Communications*, Vol. COM-31, No. 5, pp. 620–628, May 1983.

[Cox83b] Cox, D. C., Murray, R. R., and Norris, A. W., "Measurements of 800 MHz Radio Transmission into Buildings with Metallic Walls," *Bell Systems Technical Journal,* Vol. 62, No. 9, pp. 2695–2717, November 1983.

[Cox84] Cox, D. C., Murray, R., and Norris, A., "800 MHz Attenuation Measured in and around Suburban Houses," *AT&T Bell Laboratory Technical Journal*, Vol. 673, No. 6, July–August 1984.

[Cox87] Cox, D. C., Arnold, W., and Porter, P. T., "Universal Digital Portable Communications: A System Perspective," *IEEE Journal on Selected Areas of Communications,* Vol. SAC-5, No. 5, pp. 764, 1987.

[Cox89] Cox, D. C., "Portable Digital Radio Communication—An Approach to Tetherless Access," *IEEE Communication Magazine,* pp. 30–40, July 1989.

[Cox92] Cox D. C., "Wireless Network Access for Personal Communications," *IEEE Communications Magazine*, pp. 96–114, December 1992.

[Cro76] Crochiere R. E., et al., "Digital Coding of Speech in Sub-bands," *Bell Systems Technical Journal*, Vol. 55, No. 8, pp. 1069–1085, October 1976.

[Cro89] Crozier, S. N., Falconer, D. D., and Mahmoud, S., "Short Block Equalization Techniques Employing Channel Estimation for Fading, Time Dispersive Channels," *IEEE Vehicular Technology Conference*, San Francisco, pp. 142–146, 1989.

[CTI93] Cellular Telphone Industry Association, *Cellular Digital Packet Data System Specification*, Release 1.0, July 1993.

[Dad75] Dadson, C. E., Durkin, J., and Martin, E., "Computer Prediction of Field Strength in the Planning of Radio Systems," *IEEE Transactions on Vehicular Technology*, Vol. VT-24, No. 1, pp. 1–7, February 1975.

[deB72] deBuda, R., "Coherent Demodulation of Frequency Shift Keying with Low Deviation Ratio," *IEEE Transactions on Communications*, Vol. COM-20, pp. 466–470, June 1972.

[Dec93] Dechaux, C., and Scheller, R., "What are GSM and DECT?" *Electrical Communication*, pp. 118–127, 2nd quarter, 1993.

[Del93] Deller, J. R., Proakis, J. G., and Hansen, J. H. L., *Discrete-time Processing of Speech Signals*, Macmillan Publishing Company, New York, 1993.

[DeR94] DeRose, J. F., *The Wireless Data Handbook*, Quantum Publishing, Inc., 1994.

[Det89] Dettmer, R., "Parts of a Speech transcoder for CT2," *IEE Review*, September 1989.

[Dev86] Devasirvatham, D. M. J., "Time Delay Spread and Signal Level Measurements of 850 MHz Radio Waves in Building Environments," *IEEE Transactions on Antennas and Propagation*, Vol. AP-34, No. 2, pp. 1300–1305, November 1986.

[Dev90a] Devasirvatham, D. J., Krain, M. J., and Rappaport, D. A., "Radio Propagation Measurements at 850 MHz, 1.7 GHz, and 4.0 GHz Inside Two Dissimilar Office Buildings," *Electronics Letters*, Vol. 26, No. 7, pp. 445–447, 1990.

[Dev90b] Devasirvatham, D. M. J., Banerjee, C., Krain, M. J., and Rappaport, D. A., "Multi-Frequency Radiowave Propagation Measurements in the Portable Radio Environment," *IEEE International Conference on Communications*, pp. 1334–1340, 1990.

[Dey66] Deygout J., "Multiple Knife-edge Diffraction of Microwaves," *IEEE Transactions on Antennas and Propagation*, Vol. AP-14, No. 4, pp. 480–489, 1966.

[Dix84] Dixon, R. C., *Spread Spectrum Systems*, 2nd Edition, John Wiley and Sons, New York, 1984.

[Dix94] Dixon, R. C., *Spread Spectrum Systems with Commercial Applications*, 3rd Edition, John Wiley & Sons Inc., New York, 1994.

[Don93] Donaldson, R. W., "Internetworking of Wireless Communication Networks," *Proceedings of the IEEE*, pp. 96–103, 1993.

[Dur73] Durante, J. M., "Building Penetration Loss at 900 MHz," *IEEE Vehicular Technology Conference*, 1973.

[Dur98] Durgin, G. D., Rappaport, T. S., and Xu, H., "Measurements and Models for Radio Path Loss and Penetration Loss in and Around Homes and Trees at 5.8 GHz," *IEEE Transactions on Communication*, Vol. 46, No. 11, pp. 1484–1496, November 1998.

[Dur98a] Durgin, G. D., and Rappaport, T. S., "A Basic Relationship Between Multipath Angular Spread and Narrow-Band Fading in a Wireless Channel," *IEE Electronics Letters*, Vol. 34, pp. 2431–2432, December 1998.

[Dur98b] Durgin, G. D., Rappaport, T. S., and Xu, H., "Radio Path Loss and Penetration Loss Measurements in and around Homes and Trees at 5.85 GHz," 1998 AP-S International Symposium, Atlanta, GA, pp. 618–634, June 21–26, 1998.

[Dur99] Durgin, G. D., and Rappaport, T. S., "Three Parameters for Relating Small-Scale Temporal Fading to Multipath Angles-of-Arrival," *PIMRC'99*, Osaka, Japan, September 1999, pp. 1077–1081.

[Dur99a] Durgin, G. D., and Rappaport, T. S., "Effects of Multipath Angular Spread on the Spatial Cross-Correlation of Received Volatage Envelopes," *IEEE Vehicular Technology Conference*, Houston, TX, May 1999, Vol. 2, pp. 996–1000.

[Dur99b] Durgin, G. D., and Rappaport, T. S., " Level Crossing Rates and Average Fade Duration of Wireless Channels with Spatially Complicated Multipath," Globecom'99, Brazil, December 1999, pp. 427–431.

[Dur00] Durgin, G. D., and Rappaport, T. S., "Theory of Multipath Shape Factors for Small-Scale Fading Wireless Channels," *IEEE Transactions on Antennas and Propagation*, Vol. 48, No. 5, pp. 682–693, May 2000.

[Ebi91] Ebine, Y., Takahashi, T., and Yamada, Y., "A Study of Vertical Space Diversity for a Land Mobile Radio," *Electronics Communication Japan*, Vol. 74, No. 10, pp. 68–76, 1991.

[Edw69] Edwards, R., and Durkin, J., "Computer Prediction of Service Area for VHF Mobile Radio Networks," *Proceedings of the IEE*, Vol. 116, No. 9, pp. 1493–1500, 1969.

[EIA90] EIA/TIA Interim Standard, "Cellular System Dual Mode Mobile Station—Land Station Compatibility Specifications," IS-54, *Electronic Industries Association*, May 1990.

[EIA91] EIA/TIA Interim Standard, "Cellular System Mobile Station—Land Station Compatibility Specification IS-88," Rev. A, November 1991.

[EIA92] "TR 45: Mobile Station - Base Station Compatibility Standard for Dual-mode Wideband Spread Spectrum Cellular System," PN-3118, *Electronics Industry Association*, December 1992.

[Eng93] Eng, T., and Milstein, L. B., "Capacities of Hybrid FDMA/CDMA Systems in Multipath Fading," *IEEE MILCOM Conference Records*, pp. 753–757, 1993.

[Eps53] Epstein, J., and Peterson, D. W., "An Experimental Study of Wave Propagation at 840 M/C," *Proceedings of the IRE*, 41, No. 5, pp. 595–611, 1953.

[Ert98] Ertel, R., Cardieri, P., Sowerby, K. W., Rappaport, T. S., and Reed, J. H., "Overview of Spatial Channel Models for Antenna Array Communication Systems," *Special Issue: IEEE Personal Communications*, Vol. 5, No. 1, pp.10–22, February 1998.

[Est77] Estaban, D., and Galand, C., "Application of Quadrature Mirror Filters to Split Band Voice Coding Schemes," *Proceedings of ICASSP*, pp. 191–195, May 1977.

[EUR91] European Cooperation in the Field of Scientific and Technical Research EURO-COST 231, "Urban Transmission Loss Models for Mobile Radio in the 900 and 1800 MHz Bands," Revision 2, The Hague, September 1991.

[Fan63] Fano, R. M., "A Heuristic Discussion of Probabilistic Coding," *IEEE Transactions on Information Theory*, Vol. IT-9, pp. 64–74, April 1963.

[FCC91] *FCC Notice of Inquiry for Refarming Spectrum below 470 MHz*, PLMR docket 91–170, November 1991.

[Feh91] Feher, K., "Modems for Emerging Digital Cellular Mobile Radio Systems," *IEEE Transactions on Vehicular Technology*, Vol. 40, No. 2, pp. 355–365, May 1991.

[Feu94] Feuerstein, M. J., Blackard, K. L., Rappaport, T. S., Seidel, S. Y., and Xia, H. H., "Path Loss, Delay Spread, and Outage Models as Functions of Antenna Height for Microcellular System Design," *IEEE Transactions on Vehicular Technology*, Vol. 43, No. 3, pp. 487–498, August 1994.

[Fil95] Filiey, G. B., and Poulsen, P. B., "MIRS Technology: On the Fast Track to Making the Virtual Office a Reality," *Communications*, pp. 34–39, January 1995.

[Fla79] Flanagan, J. L., et al., "Speech Coding," *IEEE Transactions on Communications*, Vol. COM-27, No. 4, pp. 710–735, April 1979.

[For78] Forney, G. D., "The Viterbi Algorithm," *Proceedings of the IEEE*, Vol. 61, No. 3, pp. 268–278, March 1973.

[Fuh97] Fuhl, J., Rossi, J.-P., and Bonek, E., "High-Resolution 3-D Direction-of-Arrival Determination for Urban mobile Radio," *IEEE Transactions on Antennas and Propagation*, Vol. 45, pp. 672–682, April 1997.

[Ful98] Fulghum, T. and Molnar, K., "The Jakes Fading Model Incorporating Angular Spread for a Disk of Scatterers," *IEEE Vehicular Technology Conference*, Ottawa, Canada, May 1998, pp. 489–493.

[Fun93] Fung, V., Rappaport, T. S., and Thoma, B., "Bit Error Simulation for π/4 DQPSK Mobile Radio Communication Using Two-ray and Measurement-based Impulse Response Models," *IEEE Journal on Selected Areas in Communication,* Vol. 11, No. 3, pp. 393–405, April 1993.

[Gan72] Gans, M. J., "A Power Spectral Theory of Propagation in the Mobile Radio Environment," *IEEE Transactions on Vehicular Technology,* Vol. VT-21, pp. 27–38, February 1972.

[Gar91] Gardner, W. A., "Exploitation of Spectral Redundancy in Cyclostationary Signals," *IEEE Signal Processing Magazine*, pp. 14–36, April 1991.

[Gar95] Gardner, W., QUALCOMM Inc., personal correspondence, June 1995.

[Gar99] Garg, V. K. and Wilkes, J. E., *Principles & Applications of GSM*, Prentice Hall, Upper Saddle River NJ, 1999.

[Gar00] Garg, V. K., *IS-95 CDMA and cdma2000*, Prentice Hall, Upper Saddle River, NJ, 2000.

[Ger82] Geraniotis, E. A., and Pursley, M. B., "Error Probabilities for Slow Frequency-Hopped Spread Spectrum Multiple-Access Communications Over Fading Channels," *IEEE Transactions on Communications,* Vol. COM-30, No. 5, pp. 996–1009, May 1982.

[Ger90] Gerson, I. A., and Jasiuk, M. A., "Vector Sum Excited Linear Prediction (VSELP): Speech Coding at 8 kbps," *Proceedings of ICASSP*, pp. 461–464, 1990.

[Gil91] Gilhousen, et al., "On the Capacity of Cellular CDMA System," *IEEE Transactions on Vehicular Technology,* Vol. 40, No. 2, pp. 303–311, May 1991.

[Git81] Gitlin, R. D., and Weinstein, S. B., "Fractionally Spaced Equalization: An Improved Digital Transversal Filter," *Bell Systems Technical Journal*, Vol. 60, pp. 275–296, February 1981.

[Gol49] Golay, M. J. E., "Notes on Digital Coding," *Proceedings of the IRE*, Vol. 37, p. 657, June 1949.

[Goo89] Goodman, D. J., Valenzula, R.A., Gayliard, K.T., and Ramamurthi, B., "Packet Reservation Multiple Access for Local Wireless Communication," *IEEE Transactions on Communications*, Vol. 37, No. 8, pp. 885–890, August 1989.

[Goo90] Goodman, D. J., "Cellular Packet Communications," *IEEE Transactions on Communications*, Vol. 38, No. 8, pp. 1272–1280, August 1990.

[Goo91] Goodman, D. J., "Trends in Cellular and Cordless Communications," *IEEE Communications Magazine*, pp. 31–39, June 1991.

[Gos78] Gosling, W., McGeehan, J. P., and Holland, P. G., "Receivers for the Wolfson SSB/VHF Land Mobile Radio System," *Proceedings of IERE Conference on Radio Receivers and Associated Systems*, Southampton, England, pp. 169–178, July 1978.

[Gow93] Gowd, K., et al., "Robust Speech Coding for Indoor Wireless Channel," *AT&T Technical Journal*, Vol. 72, No. 4, pp. 64–73, July/August 1993.

[Gra84] Gray, R. M., "Vector Quantization," *IEEE ASSP Magazine*, pp. 4–29, April 1984.

[Gri87] Griffiths, J., *Radio Wave Propagation and Antennas*, Prentice Hall International, 1987.

[Gud92] Gudmundson, B., Skold, J., and Ugland, J. K, "A Comparison of CDMA and TDMA systems," *Proceedings of the 42nd IEEE Vehicular Technology Conference*, Vol. 2, pp. 732–735, 1992.

[Ham50] Hamming, R. W., "Error Detecting and Error Correcting Codes," *Bell System Technical Journal*, April 1950.

[Has93] Hashemi, H., "The Indoor Radio Propagation Channel," *Proceedings of the IEEE,* Vol. 81, No. 7, pp. 943–968, July 1993.

[Hat90] Hata, Masaharu, "Empirical Formula for Propagation Loss in Land Mobile Radio Services," *IEEE Transactions on Vehicular Technology,* Vol. VT-29, No. 3, pp. 317–325, August 1980.

[Haw91] Hawbaker, D. A., *Indoor Wideband Radio Wave Propagation Measurements and Models at 1.3 GHz and 4.0 GHz*, Masters Thesis, Virginia Tech, Blacksburg, VA, May 1991.

[Hay86] Haykin, S., *Adaptive Filter Theory*, Prentice Hall, Englewood Cliffs, NJ, 1986.

[Hay94] Haykin, S., *Communication Systems*, John Wiley and Sons, New York, 1994.

[Hel89] Hellwig, K., Vary P., Massaloux, D., Petit, J. P., Galand, C., and Rasso, M., "Speech Codec for the European Mobile Radio Systems," *IEEE Global Telecommunication Conference & Exhibition,* Vol. 2, pp. 1065–1069, 1989.

[Hen01] Henty, B., "Throughput Measurements and Empirical Prediction Models for IEEE 802.11b Wireless LAN (WLAN) Installations," Masters Thesis, Virginia Tech, Blacksburg, VA, August 2001

[Ho94] Ho, P., Rappaport, T. S., and Koushik, M. P., "Antenna Effects on Indoor Obstructed Wireless Channels and a Deterministic Image-Based Wide-Band Propagation Model for In-Building Personal Communication Systems," *International Journal of Wireless Information Networks*, Vol. 1, No. 1, pp. 61–75, January 1994.

[Hod90] Hodges, M. R. L., "The GSM Radio Interface," *British Telecom Technological Journal,* Vol. 8, No. 1, pp. 31–43, January 1990.

[Hol92] Holtzman, J. M., "A Simple, Accurate Method to Calculate Spread-Spectrum Multiple-Access Error Probabilities," *IEEE Transactions on Communications*, Vol. 40, No. 3, March 1992.

[Hor86] Horikishi, J., et al., "1.2 GHz Band Wave Propagation Measurements in Concrete Buildings for Indoor Radio Communications," *IEEE Transactions on Vehicular Technology*, Vol. VT-35, No. 4, 1986.

[Hua91] Huang, W., "*Simulation of Adaptive Equalization in Two-Ray, SIRCIM and SMRCIM Mobile Radio Channels,*" Masters Thesis in Electrical Engineering, Virginia Tech, December 1991.

[IEE91] "Special Issue on Satellite Communications Systems and Services for Travelers," *IEEE Communications Magazine*, November 1991.

[Ish80] Ishizuka, M., and Hirade, K., "Optimum Gaussian filter and Deviated-Frequency-Locking Scheme for Coherent Detection of MSK," *IEEE Transactions on Communications*, Vol. COM-28, No.6, pp. 850–857, June 1980.

[ITU93] *ITU World Telecommunications Report*, December 1993.

[ITU94] *ITU Documents of TG8/1 (FPLMTS),* International Telecommunications Union, Radiocommunications Sector, Geneva, 1994.

[Jac94] Jacobsmeyer, J., "Improving Throughput and Availability of Cellular Digital Packet Data (CDPD)," *Proc. Virginia Tech 4th Symposium on Wireless Personal Communications*, pp. 18.1–18.12, June 1994.

[Jak70] Jakes, W. C., "New Techniques for Mobile Radio," *Bell Laboratory Rec.*, pp. 326–330, December 1970.

[Jak71] Jakes, W. C., "A Comparison of Specific Space Diversity Techniques for Reduction of Fast Fading in UHF Mobile Radio Systems," *IEEE Transactions on Vehicular Technology*, Vol. VT-20, No. 4, pp. 81–93, November 1971.

[Jak74] Jakes, W. C. Jr., *Microwave Mobile Communications*, Wiley-Interscience, 1974.

[Jay84] Jayant, N. S., Noll, P., *Digital Coding of Waveforms*, Prentice Hall, Englewood Cliffs, NJ, 1984.

[Jay86] Jayant, N. S., "Coding Speech at Low Bit Rates," *IEEE Spectrum*, pp. 58–63, August 1986.

[Jay90] Jayant, N. S., "High Quality Coding of Telephone Speech and Wideband Audio," *IEEE Communications Magazine*, pp. 10–19, January 1990.

[Jay92] Jayant, N. S., "Signal Compression: Technology, Targets, and Research Directions," *IEEE Journal on Selected Areas of Communications*, Vol. 10, No. 5, pp. 796–815, June 1992.

[Jen98] Jeng, S.-S., Xu, G., Lin, H.-P., and Vogel, W., J., "Experimental Studies of Spatial Signature Variation at 900 MHz for Smart Antenna Systems," *IEEE Transactions on Antennas and Propagation*, Vol. 46, pp. 953–962, July 1998.

[Joh82] Johnson, L. W., and Riess, R. D., *Numerical Analysis*, Addison-Wesley, 1982.

[JTC95] JTC Standards Project 066: "Baseline Text for TAG #3 PACS - UB," Motorola Inc., February 1995.

[Kah54] Kahn, L., "Ratio Squarer," *Proceedings of IRE (Correspondence)*, Vol. 42, pp. 1074, November 1954.

[Kim00] Kim, K. I., Ed., *Handbook of CDMA System Design, Engineering, and Optimization*, Prentice Hall, Upper Saddle River, NJ, 2000.

[Kle75] Kleinrock, L., and Tobagi, F. A., "Packet Switching in Radio Channels, Part 1: Carrier Sense Multiple-Access Models and Their Throughput-Delay Characteristics," *IEEE Transactions on Communications*, Vol. 23, No. 5, pp. 1400–1416, 1975.

[Kor85] Korn, I., *Digital Communications*, Van Nostrand Reinhold, 1985.

[Koz85] Kozono, S., et al., "Base Station Polarization Diversity Reception for Mobile Radio," *IEEE Transactions on Vehicular Technology*, Vol. VT-33, No. 4, pp. 301–306, November 1985.

[Kra50] Krauss, J. D., *Antennas*, McGraw-Hill, New York, 1950.

[Kre94] Kreuzgruber, P., et al., "Prediction of Indoor Radio Propagation with the Ray Splitting Model Including Edge Diffraction and Rough Surfaces," *1994 IEEE Vehicular Technology Conference*, Stockholm, Sweden, pp. 878–882, June 1994.

[Kuc91] Kucar, A. D., "Mobile Radio—An Overview," *IEEE Communications Magazine*, pp. 72–85, November 1991.

[Lam80] Lam, S. S., "A Carrier Sense Multiple Access Protocol for Local Networks," *Computer Networks*, Vol. 4, pp. 21–32, 1980.

[Lan96] Landron, O., Feuerstein, M. J., and Rappaport, T. S., "A Comparison of Theoretical and Empirical Reflection Coefficients for Typical Exterior Wall Surfaces in a Mobile Radio Environment," *IEEE Transactions on Antennas and Propagation*, Vol. 44, No. 3, pp. 341–351, March 1996.

[Lee72] Lee, W. C. Y., and Yeh, S. Y., "Polarization Diversity System for Mobile Radio," *IEEE Transactions on Communications*, Vol. 20, pp. 912–922, October 1972.

[Lee85] Lee, W. C. Y., *Mobile Communications Engineering*, McGraw Hill Publications, New York, 1985.

[Lee86] Lee, W. C. Y., "Elements of Cellular Mobile Radio systems," *IEEE Transactions on Vehicular Technology*, Vol. VT-35, No. 2, pp. 48–56, May 1986.

[Lee89a] Lee, W. C. Y., "Spectrum Efficiency in Cellular," *IEEE Transactions on Vehicular Technology*, Vol. 38, No. 2, pp. 69–75, May 1989.

[Lee89b] Lee, W. C. Y., *Mobile Cellular Telecommunications Systems*, McGraw Hill Publications, New York, 1989.

[Lee91a] Lee, W. C. Y., "Overview of Cellular CDMA," *IEEE Transactions on Vehicular Technology*, Vol. 40, No. 2, May 1991.

[Lee91b] Lee, W. C. Y., "Smaller Cells for Greater Performance," *IEEE Communications Magazine*, pp. 19–23, November 1991.

[Leh87] Lehnert, J. S., and Pursley, M. B., "Error Probabilities for Binary Direct-Sequence Spread-Spectrum Communications with Random Signature Sequences," *IEEE Transactions on Communications,* Vol. COM-35, No. 1, January 1987.

[Lem91] Lemieux, J. F., Tanany, M., and Hafez, H. M., "Experimental Evaluation of Space/Frequency/Polarization Diversity in the Indoor Wireless Channel," *IEEE Transactions on Vehicular Technology*, Vol. 40, No. 3, pp. 569–574, August 1991.

[Li93] Li, Y., *Bit Error Rate Simulation of a CDMA System for Personal Communications*, Masters Thesis in Electrical Engineering, Virginia Tech, 1993.

[LiC93] I., C.-L., Greenstein L. J., and Gitlin R.D., "A Microcell/Macrocell Cellular Architecture for Low- and High Mobility Wireless Users," *IEEE Vehicular Technology Transactions,* pp. 885–891, August 1993.

[Lib94a] Liberti, J. C., Jr., "CDMA Cellular Communication Systems Employing Adaptive Antennas," *Preliminary Draft of Research Including Literature Review and Summary of Work-in-Progress*, Virginia Tech, March 1994.

[Lib94b] Liberti, J. C. Jr., and Rappaport, T. S., "Analytical Results for Capacity Improvements in CDMA," *IEEE Transactions on Vehicular Technology,* Vol. 43, No. 3, pp. 680–690, August 1994.

[Lib95] Liberti, J. C. Jr., *Analysis of Code Division Multiple Access Mobile Radio Systems with Adapative Antennas,* Ph.D. Dissertation, Virginia Tech, Blacksburg, August, 1995.

[Lib99] Liberti, J. C. and Rappaport, T. S., *Smart Antennas for Wireless Communications: IS-95 and Third Generation Applications*, Prentice Hall, Upper Saddle River, NJ, 1999.

[Lin83] Lin, S., and Costello, D. J. Jr., *Error Control Coding: Fundamentals and Applications*, Prentice Hall, Englewood Cliffs, NJ, 1983.

[Lin84] Ling, F., and Proakis, J. G., "Nonstationary Learning Characteristics of Least Squares Adaptive Estimation Algorithms," *Proceedings ICASSP84*, San Diego, California, pp. 3.7.1–3.7.4, 1984.

[Liu89] Liu, C. L., and Feher, K., "Noncoherent Detection of p/4-Shifted Systems in a CCI-AWGN Combined Interference Environment," *Proceedings of the IEEE 40th Vehicular Technology Conference*, San Fransisco, 1989.

[Liu91] Liu, C., and Feher, K., "Bit Error Rate Performance of p/4 DQPSK in a Frequency Selective Fast Rayleigh Fading Channel," *IEEE Transactions on Vehicular Technology*, Vol. 40, No. 3, pp. 558–568, August 1991.

[Lo90] Lo, N. K. W., Falconer, D. D., and Sheikh, A. U. H., "Adaptive Equalization and Diversity Combining for a Mobile Radio Channel," *IEEE Globecom*, San Diego, December 1990.

[Lon68] Longley, A G., and Rice, P. L., "Prediction of Tropospheric Radio Transmission Loss Over Irregular Terrain; A Computer Method," *ESSA Technical Rep*ort, ERL 79-ITS 67, 1968.

[Lon78] Longley, A. G., "Radio Propagation in Urban Areas," *OT Report*, pp. 78-144, April 1978.

[Luc65] Lucky, R. W., "Automatic Equalization for Digital Communication," *Bell System Technical Journal*, Vol. 44, pp. 547–588, 1965.

[Luc89] Lucky, R. W., *Silicon Dreams: Information, Man and Machine*, St. Martin Press, New York, 1989.

[Lus78] Lusignan, B. B., "Single-sideband Transmission for Land Mobile Radio," *IEEE Spectrum*, pp. 33–37, July 1978.

[Mac79] MacDonald, V. H., "The Cellular Concept," *The Bell Systems Technical Journal*, Vol. 58, No. 1, pp. 15–43, January 1979.

[Mac93] Maciel, L. R., Bertoni, H. L., and Xia, H. H., "Unified Approach to Prediction of Propagation Over Buildings for all Ranges of Base Station Antenna Height," *IEEE Transactions on Vehicular Technology*, Vol. 42, No. 1, pp. 41–45, February 1993.

[Mak75] Makhoul, J., "Linear Prediction: A Tutorial Review," *Proceedings of IEEE*, Vol. 63, pp. 561–580, April 1975.

[Mal89] Maloberti, A., "Radio Transmission Interface of the Digital Pan European Mobile System," *IEEE Vehicular Technology Conference*, Orlando, FL, pp. 712–717, May 1989.

[Mal92] Malyan, A. D., Ng, L. J., Leung, V. C. M., and Donaldson, R. W., "A Microcellular Interconnection Architecture for Personal Communication Networks," *Proceedings of IEEE Vehicular Technology Conference*, pp. 502–505, May 1992.

[Man93] Mansfield, D. R., Millsteed, G., and Zukerman, M., "Congestion Controls in SS7 Signaling Networks," *IEEE Communications Magazine*, pp. 50–57, June 1993.

[Mar90] Marr, F. K., "Signaling System No.7 in Corporate Networks," *IEEE Communications Magazine*, pp. 72–77, July 1990.

[Max60] Max, J., "Quantizing for Minimizing Distortion," *IRE Transactions on Information Theory*, March 1960.

[McG84] McGeehan, J. P., and Bateman, A. J., "Phase Locked Transparent Tone-in-band (TTIB): A New Spectrum Configuration Particularly Suited to the Transmission of Data over SSB Mobile Radio Networks," *IEEE Transactions on Communications*, Vol. COM-32, No. 1, pp. 81–87, January 1984.

[Mei92] Meier-Hellstern, K. S., Pollini, G. P., and Goodman, D., "Network Protocols for the Cellular Packet Switch," *Proceedings of IEEE Vehicular Technology Conference*, Vol. 2, No. 2, pp. 705–710, 1992.

[Mei93] Meier-Hellstern, K. S., et al., "The Use of SS7 and GSM to Support High Density Personal Communications," *Wireless Communications: Future Directions*, Kluwer Academic Publishing, 1993.

[Mil62] Millington, G., Hewitt, R., and Immirzi, F. S., "Double Knife-edge Diffraction in Field Strength Predictions," *Proceedings of the IEE*, 109C, pp. 419–429, 1962.

[Mod92] Modarressi, A. R., and Skoog, R. A., "An Overview of Signal System No.7," *Proceedings of the IEEE*, Vol. 80, No. 4, pp. 590–606, April 1992.

[Mol91] Molkdar, D., "Review on Radio Propagation into and Within Buildings," *IEE Proceedings*, Vol. 138, No. 1, pp. 61–73, February 1991.

[Mol01] Molisch, A. F., Ed., *Wideband Wireless Digital Communications*, Prentice-Hall, Upper Saddle River, NJ, 2001.

[Mon84] Monsen, P., "MMSE Equalization of Interference on Fading Diversity Channels," *IEEE Transactions on Communications*, Vol. COM-32, pp. 5–12, January 1984.

[Mor89a] Moralee, D., "CT2 a New Generation of Cordless Phones," *IEE Review*, pp. 177–180, May 1989.

[Mor89b] Morrow, R. K., Jr., and Lehnert, J. S., "Bit-to-bit Error Deprndence in Slotted DS/SSMA Packet Systems with Random signature Sequences," IEEE Transactions on Communications, Vol. 37, No. 10, October 1989.

[Mor00] Morrow, R. K., and Rappaport, T. S. "Getting In," *Wireless Review*, pp. 42–44, March 1, 2000, *http://www.wirelessreview.com/issues/2000/00301/feat24.htm*

[Mou92] Mouly, M., and Pautet, M. B., *The GSM System for Mobile Communication*, ISBN: 2-9507190-0-7, 1992.

[Mul91] Mulder, R. J., "DECT—A Universal Cordless Access System," *Philips Telecommunications Review*, Vol. 49, No. 3, pp. 68–73, September 1991.

[Mur81] Murota, K., and Hirade, K., "GMSK Modulation for Digital Mobile Radio Telephony," *IEEE Transactions on Communications*, Vol. COM-29, No. 7, pp. 1044–1050, July 1981.

[NAC94] North American Cellular Network, *"An NACN Standard,"* Rev. 2.0, December 1994.

[Nag96] Naguib, A. F., and Paulraj, A., "Performance of Wireless CDMA with M-ary Orthogonal Modulation and Cell Site Arrays," *IEEE Journal on Selected Areas of Communications*, Vol. 14, pp. 1770–1783, December 1996.

[Nar90] Narasimhan, A., Chennakeshu, S., and Anderson, J. B., "An Adaptive Lattice Decision Equalizer for Digital Cellular Radio," *IEEE 40th Vehicular Technology Conference*, pp. 662–667, May 1990.

[New96a] Newhall, W. G., Saldanha, K., and Rappaport, T. S., "Propagation Time Delay Spread Measurements at 915 MHz in a Large Train Yard," *IEEE Vehicular Technology Conference*, Atlanta, GA, April 29–May 1, 1996, pp. 864–868.

[New96b] Newhall, W. G., Rappaport, T. S., and Sweeney, D. G., "A Spread Spectrum Sliding Correlator System for Propagation Measurements," *RF Design*, pp. 40–54, April 1996.

[Nob62] Noble, D., "The History of Land-Mobile Radio Communications," *IEEE Vehicular Technology Transactions*, pp. 1406–1416, May 1962.

[Nuc99] Nucols, E., "Implementation of Geometrically Based Single-Bounce Models for Simulation of Angle-of-Arrival of Multipath Delay Components in the Wireless Channel Simulation Tools, SMRCIM and SIRCIM," Masters Thesis, Virginia Tech, Blacksburg, VA, December 1999.

[Noe01] Noel, Frederic, "Higher Data Rates in GSM/Edge with Multicarrier," Masters Thesis, Chalmers University of Technology, April 2001, Technical Report EX024/2001.

[Nyq28] Nyquist, H., "Certain Topics in Telegraph Transmission Theory," *Transactions of the AIEE*, Vol. 47, pp. 617–644, Febuary 1928.

[Och89] Ochsner, H., "DECT — Digital European Cordless Telecommunications," *IEEE Vehicular Technology 39th Conference*, pp. 718–721, 1989.

[Oet83] Oeting, J., "Cellular Mobile Radio—An Emerging Technology," *IEEE Communications Magazine*, pp. 10–15, November 1983.

[Oga94] Ogawa, K., et al., "Toward the Personal Communication Era - the Radio Access Concept from Japan," *International Journal on Wireless Information Networks,* Vol. 1, No. 1, pp. 17–27, January 1994.

[Oku68] Okumura, T., Ohmori, E., and Fukuda, K., "Field Strength and Its Variability in VHF and UHF Land Mobile Service," *Review Electrical Communication Laboratory*, Vol. 16, No. 9–10, pp. 825–873, September–October 1968.

[Oss64] Ossana, J. Jr., "A Model for Mobile Radio Fading due to Building Reflections: Theoretical and Experimental Fading Waveform Power Spectra," *Bell Systems Technical Journal*, Vol. 43, No. 6, pp. 2935–2971, November 1964.

[Owe91] Owen, F. C. and Pudney, C., "DECT: Integrated Services for Cordless Telecommunications," *IEE Conference Publications*, No. 315, pp. 152–156, 1991.

[Owe93] Owens, F. J., *Signal Processing of Speech*, McGraw Hill, New York, 1993.

[Pad94] Padovani, R., "Reverse Link Performance of IS-95 Based Cellular Systems," *IEEE Personal Communications*, pp. 28–34, 3rd quarter, 1994.

[Pad95] Padyett, J., Gunther, E., and Hattari, T., "Overview of Wireless Personal Communications," *IEEE Communications Magazine*, January 1995.

[Pah95] Pahlavan, K., and Levesque, A. H., *Wireless Information Networks*, Chapter 5, John Wiley & Sons, New York, 1995.

[Pap91] Papoulis, A., *Probability, Random Variables, and Stochastic Processes*, 3rd Edition, McGraw Hill, New York, 1991.

[Par76] Parsons, J. D., et al., "Diversity Techniques for Mobile Radio Reception," *IEEE Transactions on Vehicular Technology*, Vol. VT-25, No. 3, pp. 75–84, August 1976.

[Pas79] Pasupathy, S., "Minimum Shift Keying: A Spectrally Efficient Modulation," *IEEE Communications Magazine*, pp. 14–22, July 1979.

[Pat99] Patwari, N., Durgin, G. D., Rappaport, T. S., and Boyle, R. J., "Peer-to-Peer Low Antenna Outdoor Radio Wave Propagation at 1.8 GHz," *IEEE Vehicular Technology Conference*, Houston, TX, May 1999, Vol. 1, pp. 371–375.

[Pec92] Pecar, J. A., O'Conner, R. J., and Garbin, D. A., *Telecommunications Factbook*, McGraw Hill, New York, 1992.

[Per92] Personal Digital Cellular, Japanese Telecommunication System Standard, RCR STD 27.B, 1992.

[Per93] Personal Handy Phone System, Japanese Telecommunication System Standard, RCR-STD 28, December 1993.

[Pic91] Pickholtz, R. L., Milstein, L. B., and Schilling, D., "Spread Spectrum for Mobile Communications," *IEEE Transactions on Vehicular Technology*, Vol. 40, No. 2, pp. 313–322, May 1991.

[Pri58] Price, R., and Green, P. E., "A Communication Technique for Multipath Channel," *Proceedings of the IRE*, pp. 555–570, March 1958.

[Pro89] Proakis, J. G., *Digital Communications*, McGraw-Hill, New York, 1989.

[Pro91] Proakis, J., "Adaptive Equalization for TDMA Digital Mobile Radio," *IEEE Transactions on Vehicular Technology*,Vol. 40, No. 2, pp 333–341, May 1991.

[Pro94] Proakis, J. G., and Salehi, M., *Communication Systems Engineering*, Prentice Hall, 1994.

[Pur77] Pursley, M. B., Sarwate, D. V., and Stark, W. E., "Performance Evaluation for Phase-Coded Spread-Spectrum Multiple-Access Communication—Part II: Code Sequence Analysis," *IEEE Transactions on Communications*, Vol. COM-25, No. 8, August 1987.

[Qur77] Qureshi, S. U. H., and Forney, G. D., "Performance Properties of a T/2 Equalizer," *IEEE Globecom*, pp. 11.1.1–11.1.14, Los Angeles, CA, December 1977.

[Qur85] Qureshi, S. U. H., "Adaptive Equalization," *Proceeding of IEEE*, Vol. 37, No. 9, pp. 1340–1387, September, 1985.

[Rai91] Raith, K., and Uddenfeldt, J., "Capacity of Digital Cellular TDMA Systems," *IEEE Transactions on Vehicular Technology*, Vol. 40, No. 2, pp. 323–331, May 1991.

[Ram65] Ramo, S., Whinnery, J. R., and Van Duzer, T., *Fields and Waves in Communication Electronics*, John Wiley & Sons, New York, 1965.

[Rap89] Rappaport, T. S., "Characterization of UHF Multipath Radio Channels in Factory Buildings," *IEEE Transactions on Antennas and Propagation*, Vol. 37, No. 8, pp. 1058–1069, August 1989.

[Rap90] Rappaport, T. S., Seidel, S.Y., and Singh, R., "900 MHz Multipath Propagation Measurements for U.S. Digital Cellular Radiotelephone," *IEEE Transactions on Vehicular Technology*, pp. 132–139, May 1990.

[Rap91a] Rappaport, T. S., et al., "Statistical Channel Impulse Response Models for Factory and Open Plan Building Radio Communication System Design," *IEEE Transactions on Communications*, Vol. COM-39, No. 5, pp. 794–806, May 1991.

[Rap91b] Rappaport, T. S., and Fung, V., "Simulation of Bit Error Performance of FSK, BPSK, and $\pi/4$ DQPSK in Flat Fading Indoor Radio Channels Using a Measurement-based Channel Model," *IEEE Transactions on Vehicular Technology*, Vol. 40, No. 4, pp. 731–739, November 1991.

[Rap91c] Rappaport, T. S., "The Wireless Revolution," *IEEE Communications Magazine*, pp. 52–71, November 1991.

[Rap92a] Rappaport, T. S., and Hawbaker, D. A., "Wide-band Microwave Propagation Parameters Using Circular and Linear Polarized Antennas for Indoor Wireless Channels," *IEEE Transactions on Communications*, Vol. 40, No. 2, pp. 240–245, February 1992.

[Rap92b] Rappaport, T. S., and Milstein, L. B., "Effects of Radio Propagation Path Loss on DS-CDMA Cellular Frequency Reuse Efficiency for the Reverse Channel," *IEEE Transactions on Vehicular Technology*, Vol. 41, No. 3, pp. 231–242, August 1992.

[Rap93a] Rappaport, T. S., Huang, W., and Feuerstein, M. J., "Performance of Decision Feedback Equalizers in Simulated Urban and Indoor Radio Channels," Special issue on land mobile/portable propagation, *IEICE Transactions on Communications*, Vol. E76-B, No. 2, February 1993.

[Rap93b] Rappaport, S. S., "Blocking, Hand-off and Traffic Performance for Cellular Communication Systems with Mixed Platforms," *IEE Proceedings*, Vol. 140, No. 5, pp. 389–401, October 1993.

[Rap95] *Cellular Radio & Personal Communications: Selected Readings*, edited by Rappaport, T. S., IEEE Press, New York, ISBN: 0-7803-2283-5, 1995.

[Rap96] Rappaport, T. S., "Coverage and Capacity," *Cellular Business*, pp. 90–96, February 1996.

[Rap97] Rappaport, T. S., and Brickhouse, R. A., "A Simulation Study of Urban In-Building Frequency Reuse," *IEEE Personal Communications Magazine*, pp. 19–23, February 1997.

[Rap00] Rappaport, T. S., "Isolating Interference," *Wireless Review*, pp. 33–35, May 1, 2000. *http://www.wirelessreview.com/issues/2000/00501/feat23.htm*.

[Ree60] Reed, I. S., and Solomon, G., "Polynomial Codes over Certain Finite Fields," *Journal of the Society for Industrial and Applied Mathematics*, June 1960.

[Reu74] Reudink, D. O., "Properties of Mobile Radio Propagation Above 400 MHz," *IEEE Transactions on Vehicular Technology*, Vol. 23, No. 2, pp. 1–20, November 1974.

[Rhe89] Rhee, M. Y., *Error Correcting Coding Theory*, McGraw-Hill, New York, 1989.

[Ric44] Rice, S. O., "Mathematical Analysis of Random Noise," *Bell Systems Technical Journal*, Vol. 23, pp. 282-332, July 1944; Vol. 24, pp. 46–156, January 1945;

[Ric48] Rice, S. O., "Statistical Properties of a Sine Wave Plus Random Noise," *Bell Systems Technical Journal*, Vol. 27, pp. 109–157, January 1948.

[Ric67] Rice, P. L., Longley, A. G., Norton, K. A., and Barsis, A. P., "Transmission Loss Predictions for Tropospheric Communication Circuits," *NBS Tech Note 101*; two volumes; issued May 7, 1965; revised May 1, 1966; revised January 1967.

[Rob01] Robert, M., "Bluetooth: A Short Tutorial," *Wireless Personal Communications: Bluetooth Tutorial and Other Technologies*, Tranter, W. H. et al., Eds. Kluwer Academic Publishers, 2001, pp. 249–270.

[Rob94] Roberts, J. A., and Bargallo, J. M., "DPSK Performance for Indoor Wireless Ricean Fading Channels," *IEEE Transactions on Communications*, pp. 592–596, April 1994.

[Roc89] Roca, R. T., "ISDN Architecture," *AT&T Technical Journal*, pp. 5–17, October 1989.

[Ros93] Rossi, J.-P. and Levi, A. J., "A Ray Model for Decimetric Radiowave Propagation in an Urban Area," *Radio Science*, Vol. 27, No. 6, pp. 971–979, 1993.

[Ros97] Rossi, J.-P., Barbot, J.-P., and Levy, A., J., "Theory and Measurement of the Angle of Arrival and Time Delay of UHF Radiowaves Using a Ring Array," *IEEE Transactions on Antennas and Propagation*, Vol. 45, pp. 876–884, May 1997.

[Rus93] Russel, T. A., Bostian, C. W., and Rappaport, T. S., "A Deterministic Approach to Predicting Microwave Diffraction by Buildings for Microcellular Systems," *IEEE Transactions on Antennas and Propagation*, Vol. 41, No. 12, pp. 1640–1649, December 1993.

[Sal87] Saleh, A. A. M., and Valenzeula, R. A., "A Statistical Model for Indoor Multipath Propagation," *IEEE Journal on Selected Areas in Communication*, Vol. JSAC-5, No. 2, pp. 128–137, Febuary 1987.

[Sal91] Salmasi, A., and Gilhousen, K. S., "On the System Design Aspects of Code Division Multiple Access (CDMA) Applied to Digital Cellular and Personal Communications Networks," *IEEE Vehicular Technology Conference*, pp. 57–62, 1991.

[San82] Sandvos, J. L., "A Comparison of Binary Paging Codes," *IEEE Vehicular Technology Conference*, pp. 392–402, 1982.

[Sch85a] Schroeder, M. R., "Linear Predictive Coding of Speech: Review and Current Directions," *IEEE Communications Magazine*, Vol. 23, No. 8, pp. 54–61, August 1985.

[Sch85b] Schroeder, M. R., and Atal, B. S., "Code-excited Linear Prediction (CELP): High Quality Speech at Very Low Bit Rates," *Proceedings of ICASSP*, pp. 937–940, 1985.

[Sch92] Schaubach, K. R., Davis, N. J. IV, and Rappaport, T. S., "A Ray Tracing Method for Predicting Path Loss and Delay Spread in Microcellular Environments," in *42nd IEEE Vehicular Technology Conference*, Denver, pp. 932–935, May 1992.

[Sei91] Seidel, S.Y., Rappaport, T. S., Jain, S., Lord, M., and Singh, R., "Path Loss, Scattering and Multipath Delay Statistics in Four European Cities for Digital Cellular and Microcellular Radiotelephone," *IEEE Transactions on Vehicular Technology*, Vol. 40, No. 4, pp. 721–730, November 1991.

[Sei92a] Seidel, S. Y., et al., "The Impact of Surrounding Buildings on Propagation for Wireless In-building Personal Communications System Design," *1992 IEEE Vehicular Technology Conference*, Denver, pp. 814–818, May 1992.

[Sei92b] Seidel, S. Y., and Rappaport, T. S., "914 MHz Path Loss Prediction Models for Indoor Wireless Communications in Multifloored Buildings," *IEEE Transactions on Antennas and Propagation*, Vol. 40, No. 2, pp. 207–217, Febuary 1992.

[Sei94] Seidel, S. Y., and Rappaport, T. S., "Site-Specific Propagation Prediction for Wireless In-Building Personal Communication System Design," *IEEE Transactions on Vehicular Technology*, Vol. 43, No. 4, November 1994.

[Sha48] Shannon, C. E., "A Mathematical Theory of Communications," *Bell Systems Technical Journal*, Vol. 27, pp. 379–423 and 623–656, 1948.

[Skl93] Sklar, B., "Defining, Designing, and Evaluating Digital Communication Systems," *IEEE Communications Magazine*, pp. 92–101, November 1993.

[Skl01] Sklar, B., *Digital Communications*, 2nd Edition, Prentice-Hall, Upper Saddle River, NJ, 2001.

[Ski96] Skidmore, R., Rappaport, T. S., and Abbott, A. L., "Interactive Coverage Region and System Design Simulation for Wireless Communication Systems in Multifloored Environments: SMT Plus," *IEEE International Conference on Universal Personal Communications*, Cambridge, MA, September 29–October 2, 1996, pp. 646–650.

[Smi57] Smith, B., "Instantaneous Companding of Quantized Signals," *Bell System Technical Journal*, Vol. 36, pp. 653–709, May 1957.

[Smi75] Smith, J. I., "A Computer Generated Multipath Fading Simulation for Mobile Radio," *IEEE Transactions on Vehicular Technology*, Vol. VT-24, No. 3, pp. 39–40, August 1975.

[Sta86] Stark, H., and Woods, J. W., *Probability, Random Variables, and Estimation Theory for Engineers*, Prentice Hall, Englewood Cliffs, NJ, 1986.

[Sta90] Stallings W., *Local Networks*, Macmillan Publishing Company, New York, 1990.

[Sta99] Starr, T., Cioffi, J. M., and Silverman, P. J., *Understanding Digital Subscriber Line Technology*, Prentice-Hall, Upper Saddle River, NJ, 1999.

[Ste87] Stein, S., "Fading Channel Issues in System Engineering," *IEEE Journal on Selected Areas in Communications*, Vol. SAC-5, No.2, February 1987.

[Ste90] Steedman, R., "The Common Air Interface MPT 1375," in *Cordless Telecommunications in Europe*, W. H. W. Tuttlebee, editor, Springer-Verlag, 1990.

[Ste93] Steele, R., "Speech codecs for Personal Communications," *IEEE Communications Magazine*, pp. 76–83, November 1993.

[Ste94] Steele, R. ed., *Mobile Radio Communications*, IEEE Press, 1994.

[Stu81] Stutzman, W. L., and Thiele, G. A., *Antenna Theory and Design*, John Wiley & Sons, New York, 1981.

[Stu93] Stutzman, W. L., *Polarization in Electromagnetic Systems*, Artech House, Boston, 1993.

[Sun86] Sundberg, C., "Continuous Phase Modulation," *IEEE Communications Magazine*, Vol. 24, No.4, pp. 25–38, April 1986.

[Sun94] Sung, C. W., and Wong, W. S., "User Speed Estimation and Dynamic Channel Allocation in Hierarchical Cellular System," *Proceedings of IEEE 1994 Vehicular Technology Conference*, Stockholm, Sweden, pp. 91–95, 1994.

[Suz77] Suzuki, H., "A Statistical Model for Urban Radio Propagation," *IEEE Transactions on Communications*, Vol. 25, pp. 673–680, July 1977.

[Tan81] Tanenbaum, A. S., *Computer Networks*, Prentice Hall Inc., 1981.

[TD-SCDMA Forum] TD-SCDMA Forum, *www.tdscdma-forum.org*.

[Tek91] Tekinay, S., and Jabbari, B., "Handover and Channel Assignment in Mobile Cellular Networks," *IEEE Communications Magazine*, pp. 42–46, November 1991.

[Tel01] Telecommunications News, Special Wireless Issue, Agilent Technologies, Issue 22, June 10, 2001

[TIA93] TIA/EIA Interim Standard-95, "Mobile Station—Base Station Compatibility Standard for Dual-Mode Wideband Spread Spectrum Cellular System," July 1993.

[Tie01] Tiedemann, E. G., "CDMA2000-1X: New Capabilities for CDMA Networks," *IEEE Vehicular Technology Society Newsletter*, Vol. 48, No. 4, November 2001.

[Tob75] Tobagi, F. A., and Kleinrock, L., "Packet Switching in Radio Channels, Part II: The Hidden-Terminal Problem in Carrier Sense Multiple Access and the Busy-Tone Solution," *IEEE Transactions on Communication*, Vol. 23, No. 5, pp. 1417–1433, 1975.

[Tra01] Tranter, W. H., Woerner, B. D., Reed, J. H., Rappaport, T. S., and Robert, M., Eds., *Wireless Personal Communications: Bluetooth Tutorial and Other Technologies*, Kluwer Academic Publishers, 2001.

[Tra02] Tranter, W. H., Shanmugan, K., Kosbar, K., and Rappaport, T. S., *Simulation of Modern Communication Systems with Wireless Applications*, Prentice Hall, Upper Saddle River, NJ, 2002.

[Tre83] Treichler, J. R., and Agee, B. G., "A New Approach to Multipath Correction of Constant Modulus Signals," *IEEE Transactions on Acoustics, Speech, and Signal Processing*, Vol. ASSP-31, pp. 459–471, 1983.

[Tri79] Tribolet, J. M., and Crochiere, R. E., "Frequency Domain Coding of Speech," *IEEE Transactions on Acoustics, Speech, and Signal Processing*, Vol. ASSP-27, pp. 512–530, October 1979.

[Tuc93] Tuch, B., "Development of WaveLAN, and ISM Band Wireless LAN," *AT&T Technical Journal*, pp. 27–37, July/August 1993.

[Tur72] Turin, G. L. et al., "A Statistical Model of Urban Multipath Propagation," *IEEE Transactions on Vehicular Technology*, Vol. VT-21, pp. 1–9, February 1972.

[Tur87] Turkmani, A. M. D., Parson, J. D., and Lewis, D. G., "Radio Propagation into Buildings at 441, 900, and 1400 MHz," *Proceedings of the 4th International Conference on Land Mobile Radio*, December 1987.

[Tur92] Turkmani, A. M. D., and Toledo, A. F., "Propagation into and within Buildings at 900, 1800, and 2300 MHz," *IEEE Vehicular Technology Conference*, 1992.

[Ung87] Ungerboeck, G., "Trellis Coded Modulation with Redundant Signal Sets Part 1: Introduction," *IEEE Communication Magazine*, Vol. 25, No. 2, pp. 5–21, February 1987.

[Val93] Valenzuela, R. A., "A Ray Tracing Approach to Predicting Indoor Wireless Transmission," *IEEE Vehicular Technology Conference Proceedings*, pp. 214–218, 1993.

[Van92] Van Nielen, M. J. J., "UMTS: A Third Generation Mobile System," *IEEE Third International Symposium on Personal, Indoor & Mobile Radio Communications*, pp. 17–21, 1992.

[Van87] Van Rees, J., "Measurements of the Wideband Radio Channel Characteristics for Rural, Residential and Suburban Areas," *IEEE Transactions on Vehicular Technology*, Vol. VT-36, pp.1–6, February 1987.

[Var88] Vary, P., et al., "Speech Codec for the Pan-European Mobile Radio System," *Proceedings of ICASSP*, pp. 227-230, 1988.

[Vau90] Vaughan, R. G., "Polarization Diversity in Mobile Communications," *IEEE Transactions on Vehicular Technology*, Vol. 39, No. 3, pp. 177–186, August 1990.

[Vau93] Vaughan, R. G., and Scott, N. L., "Closely Spaced Monopoles for Mobile Communications," *Radio Science*, Vol. 28, No. 6, pp. 1259–1266, November/December 1993.

[Vio88] Violette, E. J., Espeland, R. H., and Allen, K. C., "Millimeter-Wave Propagation Characteristics and Channel Performance for Urban-Suburban Environments," *National Telecommunications and Information Administration*, NTIA Report 88–239, December 1988.

[Vit67] Viterbi, A. J., "Error Bounds for Convolutional Codes and an Asymptotically Optimum Decoding Algorithm," *IEEE Transactions on Information Theory*, Vol. IT-13, pp. 260–269, April 1967.

[Vit79] Viterbi, A. J., and Omura, J. K., *Principles of Digital Communication and Coding*, McGraw Hill, New York, 1979.

[Von54] Von Hipple, A.R., *Dielectric Materials and Applications*, Publication of MIT Press, MA, 1954.

[Wag94] Wagen, J., and Rizk, K., "Ray Tracing Based Prediction of Impulse Responses in Urban Microcells," *1994 IEEE Vehicular Technology Conference*, Stockholm, Sweden, pp. 210–214, June 1994.

[Wal88] Walfisch, J., and Bertoni, H. L., "A Theoretical Model of UHF Propagation in Urban Environments," *IEEE Transactions on Antennas and Propagation*, Vol. AP-36, pp. 1788–1796, October 1988.

[Wal92] Walker, E. H., "Penetration of Radio Signals into Buildings in Cellular Radio Environments," *IEEE Vehicular Technology Conference*, 1992.

[Wel78] Wells, R., "SSB for VHF Mobile Radio at 5 kHz Channel Spacing," *Proceedings of IERE Conference on Radio Receivers and Associated Systems*, Southampton, England, pp. 29–36, July 1978.

[Wid66] Widrow, B., "Adaptive Filter, 1: Fundamentals," *Stanford Electronics Laboratory*, Stanford University, Stanford, CA, Tech. Rep. 6764–6, December 1966.

[Wid85] Widrow, B., and Stearns, S. D., *Adaptive Signal Processing*, Prentice Hall, 1985.

[Win98] Winters, J. H., "Smart Antennas for Wireless Systems," *IEEE Personal Communications*, Vol. 1, pp. 23–27, February 1998.

[Wir01] Wireless Valley Communications, Inc, *SitePlanner 2001 Product Manual*, Blacksburg, Virginia, c. 2001, www.wirelessvalley.com

[Woe94] Woerner, B. D., Reed, J. H., and Rappaport, T. S., "Simulation Issues for Future Wireless Modems," *IEEE Communications Magazine,* pp. 19–35, July 1994.

[Xia92] Xia, H., and Bertoni, H. L., "Diffraction of Cylindrical and Plane Waves by an Array of Absorbing Half Screens," *IEEE Transactions on Antennas and Propagation*, Vol. 40, No. 2, pp. 170–177, February 1992.

[Xia93] Xia, H., et al., "Radio Propagation Characteristics for Line-of-Sight Microcellular and Personal Communications," *EEE Transactions on Antennas and Propagation*, Vol. 41, No. 10, pp. 1439–1447, October 1993.

[Xio94] Xiong, F., "Modem Techniques in Satellite Communications," *IEEE Communications Magazine*, pp. 84–97, August 1994.

[Xu00] Xu, H., Boyle, R. J., Rappaport, T. S., and Schaffner, J. H., "Measurements and Models for 38 GHz Point-to-Multipoint Radiowave Propagation," *IEEE Journal on Selected Areas in Communications: Wireless Communications Series*, Vol. 18, No. 3, pp. 310–321, March 2000.

[Yac93] Yacoub, M. D., *Foundations of Mobile Radio Engineering*, CRC Press, 1993.

[Yao92] Yao, Y. D., and Sheikh, A. U. H., "Bit Error Probabilities of NCFSK and DPSK Signals in Microcellular Mobile Radio Systems," *Electronics Letters*, Vol. 28, No. 4, pp. 363–364, February 1992.

[You79] Young, W. R., "Advanced Mobile Phone Service: Introduction, Background, and Objectives," *Bell Systems Technical Journal*, Vol. 58, pp. 1–14, January 1979.

[Zag91a] Zaghloul, H., Morrison, G., and Fattouche, M., "Frequency Response and Path Loss Measurements of Indoor Channels," *Electronics Letters*, Vol. 27, No. 12, pp. 1021–1022, June 1991.

[Zag91b] Zaghloul, H., Morrison, G., and Fattouche, M., "Comparison of Indoor Propagation Channel Characteristics at Different Frequencies," *Electronics Letters*, Vol. 27, No. 22, pp. 2077–2079, October 1991.

[Zho90] Zhou, K., Proakis, J. G., and Ling, F., "Decision Feedback Equalization of Time Dispersive Channels with Coded Modulation," *IEEE Transactions on Communications*, Vol. 38, pp. 18–24, January 1990.

[Zie90] Ziemer, R. E., and Peterson, R. L., *Digital Communications*, Prentice Hall, Englewood Cliffs, NJ, 1990.

[Zie92] Ziemer, R. E., and Peterson, R. L., *Introduction to Digital Communications*, Macmillan Publishing Company, 1992.

[Zog87] Zogg, A., "Multipath Delay Spread in a Hilly Region at 210 MHz," *IEEE Transactions on Vehicular Technology*, Vol. VT-36, pp. 184–187, November 1987.

INDEX

Numerics

A

D

J

K

L

M

Q

R

T

X

Z